CASES AND MATERIALS ON EMPLOYMENT DISCRIMINATION

ASPEN CASEBOOK SERIES

CASES AND MATERIALS ON EMPLOYMENT DISCRIMINATION

Ninth Edition

CHARLES A. SULLIVAN
Professor of Law and Senior Associate Dean for Finance & Faculty
Seton Hall University

MICHAEL J. ZIMMER
Late Professor of Law
Loyola University of Chicago School of Law

Wolters Kluwer

Published by Wolters Kluwer in New York.

Wolters Kluwer Legal & Regulatory U.S. serves customers worldwide with CCH, Aspen Publishers, and Kluwer Law International products. (www.WKLegaledu.com)

To contact Customer Service, e-mail customer.service@wolterskluwer.com, call 1-800-234-1660, fax 1-800-901-9075, or mail correspondence to:

Wolters Kluwer
Attn: Order Department
PO Box 990
Frederick, MD 21705

Printed in the United States of America.

1 2 3 4 5 6 7 8 9 0

ISBN 978-1-4548-9219-9

Library of Congress Cataloging-in-Publication Data

Names: Zimmer, Michael J., 1942-2015 author. | Sullivan, Charles A., author.
Title: Cases and materials on employment discrimination / Michael J. Zimmer, Late Professor of Law, Loyola University of Chicago School of Law; Charles A. Sullivan, Professor of Law and Senior Associate Dean for Finance & Faculty, Seton Hall University.
Description: Ninth edition. | New York : Wolters Kluwer Legal & Regulatory US/Aspen Publishers, [2017] | Series: Aspen casebook series | Includes bibliographical references and index.
Identifiers: LCCN 2017022081 | ISBN 9781454892199
Subjects: LCSH: Discrimination in employment—Law and legislation—United States. | LCGFT: Casebooks
Classification: LCC KF3464 .Z56 2017 | DDC 344.7301/133—dc23
LC record available at https://lccn.loc.gov/2017022081

About Wolters Kluwer Legal & Regulatory U.S.

Wolters Kluwer Legal & Regulatory U.S. delivers expert content and solutions in the areas of law, corporate compliance, health compliance, reimbursement, and legal education. Its practical solutions help customers successfully navigate the demands of a changing environment to drive their daily activities, enhance decision quality and inspire confident outcomes.

Serving customers worldwide, its legal and regulatory portfolio includes products under the Aspen Publishers, CCH Incorporated, Kluwer Law International, ftwilliam.com and MediRegs names. They are regarded as exceptional and trusted resources for general legal and practice-specific knowledge, compliance and risk management, dynamic workflow solutions, and expert commentary.

To Leila, Meghan, Moira, the Marks,
and especially Jessica Leigh
C.A.S.

To Margaret, Michael, and Lanier
M.J.Z.

SUMMARY OF CONTENTS

CONTENTS

Chapter 2

Systemic Disparate Treatment Discrimination — 93

Chapter 3

Systemic Disparate Impact Discrimination — 167

Chapter 4

The Interrelation of the Three Theories of Discrimination 229

Chapter 6

Retaliation

Chapter 7

Disability Discrimination   441

Chapter 8

Procedures for Enforcing Antidiscrimination Laws   523

Chapter 9

Judicial Relief 561

Chapter 10

PREFACE

This Ninth Edition marks a poignant milestone for this project with the death of Mike Zimmer, a driving force since the First Edition in 1982, and the retirement of Rebecca White, an invaluable co-author since the Sixth Edition in 2003. Mike's name remains as an author to help perpetuate his memory; Rebecca, with her usual humility, chose not to continue to be listed. But it would be unforgiveable of me not to acknowledge that both their contributions (as well as those of prior co-authors Deborah Calloway and Dick Richards) pervade the current edition. They are much missed, personally and professionally. Mike was indescribable as a human and a scholar, and I continue to be thankful that Rebecca was able to pour so much intellect and energy into this project while guiding the University of Georgia Law School to even greater heights as Dean.

As for the subject matter of this book, it continues to evolve in the courts, albeit perhaps at a slower pace than in the past. But there are still eye-opening developments, such as the en banc Seventh Circuit's recognition in *Hively v. Ivy Tech Community College* that sex orientation discrimination is within Title VII's ban on sex discrimination. And as this is written, the Federal Arbitration Act is heading for an epic collision at the Supreme Court with the National Labor Relations and Norris LaGuardia Acts, an encounter that will decide whether employment agreements foreclosing class or collective suits will remain viable. Beyond the courts, the casebook, as has always been true, attempts to keep its adopters abreast of the literature, much of which brings important new insights from a new crop of discrimination scholars.

A new edition is always an occasion for reflecting not just on what's happening in the area but how it should be taught. While veteran adopters will find the structure of this book largely the same, they will notice many changes. Most visibly, it has shrunk substantially. The current edition is about 100 pages slimmer than its predecessor, despite the addition of several intervening Supreme Court cases (including *Young v. UPS, Vance v. Ball State University, EEOC v. Abercrombie and Fitch*, and *University of Texas Southwestern Medical Center v. Nassar*) and extensive exploration of *Hively*. Hopefully, that will enable a more efficient treatment of the material. This reduction was achieved in a variety of ways, including elimination of some principal cases from earlier edition, now discussed in the text.

As before, the casebook begins with the three chapters analyzing each of the three basic theories of discrimination—individual disparate treatment, systemic disparate treatment, and disparate impact (Chapters 1, 2, and 3), followed by a chapter on the interrelation of those theories (Chapter 4). It then moves to "special problems" of discrimination law (Chapter 5), treating coverage, sex discrimination, religion, national origin discrimination, and age. Chapter 6 then follows dealing with retaliation. These chapters continue the prior editions' merger of the treatment of the Age Discrimination in Employment Act and the Reconstruction Civil Rights Acts, primarily 42

U.S.C.A. §1981, into the Title VII discussion. Pedagogically, the casebook reflects the statutory and common law unification of discrimination analysis under all three statutes although the significant differences among these laws are noted in the relevant chapters or collected in Chapter 5 on "special problems."

Those who used the Seventh Edition will find significant changes in these core chapters. Most notably, the disparate impact discussion now demotes the ADEA variation on the Title VII theme to a breakout Note rather than two principal cases, saving space while avoiding what seemed like a digression. That chapters also flags what may be a revival of the alternative employment practice surrebuttal of disparate impact analysis in the First Circuit's decision in *Jones v. City of Boston*. The biggest changes, however, come in Chapter 5, Special Problems. In addition to reproducing *Hively* as a principal case, that Chapter adds *Young v. UPS*, *Vance v. Ball State University*, and *EEOC v. Abercrombie and Fitch*, resulting in a very different analyses for both Sex and Religion. Chapter 6, Retaliation, adds *University of Texas Southwestern Medical Center v. Nassar*.

Chapter 7, dealing with Disabilities, continues to evolve faster than the rest of the book but is beginning to mature in the wake of the substantial changes wrought by the 2008 Americans with Disabilities Act Amendments Act. Adopters will find less a historical development than in prior editions and more a focus on the law as it presently is. The remaining three chapters—Chapter 8, Procedures, Chapter 9, Remedies, and Chapter 10, Risk Management, try to concisely treat issues that, though critical for how employment discrimination is practiced "on the ground," often seem to be afterthoughts in many courses. To help cope with the problem of length, these chapters remain shorter and more didactic.

Some professors who use this book have asked about coverage. In a three-credit course, it is easily possible to teach Chapters 1 through 7. The choice of the remaining material is a matter of individual instructor preference but in an environment that seems to prefer more "practice ready" graduates, these three chapters are all candidates for inclusion although teaching all three may exhaust both professor and students.

As prior users know, a website supports the teaching mission of the casebook. Visit it at http://www.shulawconferences.com/discrimination. Within normal limits of scholarly procrastination, it is updated to reflect recent developments at least twice a semester. It does not attempt to track every judicial, legislative, or administrative change as there are services that do that far better; rather, the goal is to identify the more important developments and key them to the casebook. The webpage also suggest teaching ideas and provide links to a variety of other resources. Please visit it at http://law.shu.edu/discrimination. The site contains a "contact" button, but I can also be reached at:

Charles A. Sullivan: sullivch@shu.edu

A final word about the editing of excerpted material: All omissions are indicated by ellipses or brackets, except that citations (including parentheticals), footnotes, and internal cross-references are deleted with no indication. Footnotes in extract retain their original numbers, while those added by the author are indicated by asterisks and daggers.

Charles A. Sullivan

June 2017

ACKNOWLEDGMENTS

I acknowledge the insights of the many teachers who have used the earlier editions of this work and have shared their thoughts with us. As noted in the Preface, my deepest debts are to former co-authors, Michael J. Zimmer, Rebecca Hanner White, Deborah A. Calloway, and Richard F. Richards.

Our colleagues over the years have also provided numerous useful insights. A deep debt of gratitude to Steve Willborn for niggling (and not so niggling) corrections every time he uses the book. And I thank Jake Barnes and Calvin Sharpe for reviewing portions of earlier editions of this book and steering us closer to the correct path. Our students have also been essential to keeping this work grounded and accessible even as the field of employment discrimination becomes increasingly complex and sophisticated. We owe a special debt to Carol McGeehan (who copyedited the first edition) and who has gently nudged us through many subsequent editions.

Our research assistants have kept us honest and this book accurate, not to mention making the professors' lives easier in innumerable other ways. We thank the following (all of Seton Hall unless otherwise identified):

- Samira Paydar, '17;
- John G. Dumnich & Angela Raleigh, '16;
- Justine Abrams, '14; Nicole Zito, Columbia '14;
- Ezra Alter, Jinkal Pujara, Liana Nobile, & Kaitlyn Stone, '13;
- Mark Heftler, Temi Kolarova, Renee Levine, & Caitlin Petry, '12, Hillary Miller, '12 Georgia;
- Mariel Belanger, Anthony Marroney Noto, & Daniel McGrady, '11; Rachel Hinckley, Georgia '11;
- Elizabeth Losey, '10; Amy Smith, Georgia '10;
- Nathan Brown, Kaitlin Kennedy, Katherine Planer, & Tara Touloumis, '09;
- Christina Bae, Joseph Fanning, & Angela Kopolovich, '08;
- Lauren DeWitt, '07; Wright Frank, Georgetown '07; Merritt McAlister, Georgia '07; Lindsay Leonard, Fordham '07;
- M. J. Blakely, Georgia, '06;
- Lauren Walter, '05, Kira Fonteneau, Georgia, '05; Brendan Krasinzki, Georgia, '05;
- Stefania DiTrolio, Sonia Middlebrooks, Mara Timourian & Dawn Woodruff, '04; Caroline Castle, Georgia, '04;
- Jenny Kramer & Amanda Dowd, '01;
- Jonathan Green, Richard Kielbania, Chantal Kopp, & Shannon Philpott, '00;
- Tara Schillari, '99;
- Kim Essaf, Jessica Lerner, Michael MacManus, Jason Marx & Colleen Walsh, '98;

- Victoria Melillo, '97;
- Jessica Stein & Thomas Crino, '96;
- Dena Epstein, Wendy Whitbeck, Claudine Leone, & Thomas Sarno, '95;
- Susan Farrell, '89;
- Rosanne Maraziti, Linda Biancardi, Nancy Johnson, & Julie Murray, '88;
- Laurie Fierro & Lorrie Van de Castle, '83.

To these must be added the dedicated support staff at Seton Hall, especially Teresa Rizzo, Latisha Porter-Vaughn, Jo Ann Maldonado, Gwen Davis, and Silvia Cardoso. Ana Santos, Seton Hall's Web Coordinator, deserves special mention for her work in creating and updating the webpage supporting this casebook. Finally, we thank Moira Sullivan for dedicated proofreading.

NOTE TO STUDENTS

A. What You'll Be Studying

This book is devoted to employment discrimination, one of the most important areas of legal regulation of the rights and responsibilities of employers and employees. This course is concerned with the question of "discrimination" in employment and is, therefore, limited to legal doctrines that fall within the definition of that term. Indeed, much of this book is devoted to the twin questions of how "discrimination" should be defined and how it is proven in the litigation context. As you will see, employment discrimination, on both the social and the legal levels, is a complex and controversial problem, affecting the rights of all workers in one way or another.

But however important the topic of employment discrimination is, it is only a subset of the more general problem of legal regulation of the employment relationship. As you will learn, "employment discrimination" is usually limited to discrimination against employees on the basis of statutorily-defined characteristics. These characteristics may be immutable—such as race, gender, age, or national origin—or subject to change—such as religion, alienage, or marital status—or of either kind—such as disability discrimination, which includes mental and physical disabilities without regard to their causes.

While these categories are the traditional domain of the law of employment discrimination, employers routinely "discriminate" (perhaps we should use the word "differentiate") among employees or applicants in ways that have nothing to do with race, gender, age, or any of the other reasons prohibited by discrimination statutes. Further, employers may base their actions on rational reasons (hiring the best-qualified applicant); questionable reasons (promoting the daughter of an important customer over a better worker who lacks such "connections"); reasons that are eccentric but not necessarily legally wrong (choosing employees on the basis of astrological sign); or socially and morally unacceptable reasons (firing a "whistleblower" whose conduct had saved human lives).

The ultimate question, of course, is what, if any, limitations the law should place on the employer's power to deal with employees. The antidiscrimination laws reflect one societal answer, but the broader question is taken up in courses titled "Employment Law" or "Individual Employment Rights." *See generally* TIMOTHY P. GLYNN, CHARLES A. SULLIVAN, & RACHEL ARNOW-RICHMAN EMPLOYMENT LAW: PRIVATE ORDERING AND ITS LIMITATIONS (3d ed. 2015). It is also treated, albeit somewhat obliquely, in labor law.

As a discipline, employment law is a sprawling area that begins with a core commitment to private ordering through contracts. In employment, as in other areas of contract law, policing the fairness of bargains is the exception, rather than the rule. Contract law purported to implement this approach to employment by adopting a general rule that prevailed in the United States for nearly a century: absent an express written contract for a specified term, the relationship between an employer and its employees was "at will." One court explained the rule and its rationale: "Generally speaking, a contract for permanent employment, for life employment, or for other terms purporting permanent employment, where the employee furnishes no consideration additional to the services incident to the employment, amounts to an indefinite general hiring terminable at the will of either party, and a discharge without cause does not constitute a breach of such contract justifying recovery of damages." *Forrer v. Sears, Roebuck & Co.*, 153 N.W.2d 587, 589 (Wis. 1967). While framed neutrally, in the sense that either party can terminate the relationship without liability to the other, the at-will doctrine in practice meant that the employer could discharge an employee "for good reason, bad reason, or no reason at all."

Because contract law provided few rights for most workers, numerous legislative interventions were designed to address deficiencies, or perceived deficiencies, of the at-will regime. The antidiscrimination statutes are a prime example, but employment law treats a huge variety of other interventions of greater or lesser legal and practical significance. On the federal level, these include:

- Leave policies: the Family and Medical Leave Act (FMLA)
- Wage and hour laws: the Fair Labor Standards Act (FLSA), 29 U.S.C. §§201 et seq.
- Workplace safety: the Occupational Safety and Health Act (OSHA), 29 U.S.C. §651 et seq.
- Pension and fringe benefits: the Employee Retirement Income Security Act (ERISA), 29 U.S.C. §§1002 et seq.
- Privacy protection: the Employee Polygraph Protection Act (EPPA), 29 U.S.C. §2002, and the Genetic Information Nondiscrimination Act, 42 U.S.C. §2000ffet seq.
- Layoff: the Workers Adjustment and Retraining Notification Act (WARN), 29 U.S.C. §2101 et seq.
- Whistleblower protection: Sarbanes-Oxley, 18 U.S.C.S. § 1514A

These statutes vary greatly in terms of their protection and coverage. For example, EPPA covers essentially all private-sector employers in the United States, but WARN reaches only larger employers conducting "mass layoffs." Most federal statutes have state analogs, some of which provide substantially more employee rights than do their federal counterparts. Further, some areas of employment law, such as workers' compensation, are primarily state regimes, and, of course, state tort law provides limited but important protections, most notably the "public policy tort," which has been reinforced by broad "whistleblowing" statutes in a few states. *E.g.*, N.J. Conscientious Employee Protection Act, N.J. Stat. Ann. §§34:191 et seq. Finally, some groups of employees have their own sources of protection—public-sector workers have constitutional rights, and civil servants and public school and college and university teachers have tenure systems.

A third group of workers with special protection consists of unionized workers under collective bargaining agreements. This regime is studied as Labor Law, which deals with unionization and collective bargaining. The core notion is that employees gain countervailing power vis-à-vis their employers by organizing and then bargaining collectively with their employers. While the origins of the union movement reach back well before the nineteenth century, unions did not become legal, and respectable, for many years. During the Great Depression, the federal government adopted what is now known as the National Labor Relations Act (NLRA), 29 U.S.C.S. §§151 et seq. (2018), which encourages unions by declaring it an unfair labor practice for employers to discriminate against workers seeking to unionize and by requiring the employer to bargain with unions that succeed in organizing that employer's workforce. *See generally* THE DEVELOPING LABOR LAW: THE BOARD, THE COURTS, AND THE NATIONAL LABOR RELATIONS ACT (6th ed. 2012) (John E. Higgins, et al. eds.), While wages and hours are a prime area of concern, most unions also ensure job security for workers through seniority systems and requiring just cause for discharge. This legal regime, however, scarcely proved a panacea. While many unions succeeded in raising wages, improving working conditions, and providing increased job security for those they represented, large segments of the American workforce remained unorganized. The proportion of the organized workforce has shrunk to less than that when the NLRA was passed, reaching less than 7 percent of the private workforce in 2016 according to the Bureau of Labor Statistics. https://www.bls.gov/opub/ted/2017/union-membership-rate-10-point-7-percent-in-2016.htm. Unions are, however, stronger in the public sector.

One of the ironies of employment law and employment discrimination is that the very definition of employer and employee draws on doctrines invented for a different purpose altogether—whether an employer was liable for the torts committed by its employees (or, as it would have more typically been phrased, whether a master was liable for the torts of his servants). The answer to this question at common law was found in the law of agency and depended on whether the tortfeasor was a servant (or employee) as opposed to an "independent contractor." If the principal had sufficient "control" over the work of the agent, it was liable for the agent's torts. The principal was then called a master or an employer, and the agent became a servant or an employee. If the degree of control was insufficient, the agent was labeled an "independent contractor," and the principal was not liable for his torts.

B. The Organization of This Book

Antidiscrimination statutes have spawned complex legal theories defining discrimination and the methods used to prove it. Although the basic prohibitions enjoy broad support, the development of theories of proof and the enactment of statutory reforms expanding employer duties have generated considerable social controversy. Affirmative action, sexual harassment, discrimination on the basis of sexual orientation, and disparate impact liability are just a few of the issues that have tested the limits of discrimination theory.

This casebook undertakes a complete consideration of the federal antidiscrimination laws.

The enactment of Title VII as part of the Civil Rights Act of 1964 marked a legal watershed. Although the statute had state and federal precursors, they had proved insufficient to deal with the problem of employment discrimination. Title VII marked the first comprehensive national attack on the problem of employment discrimination.

In the wake of Title VII, a number of developments expanded the federal courts' involvement with employment problems. First, Congress passed additional statutes, most notably the Age Discrimination in Employment Act of 1967 (ADEA), prohibiting discrimination against older workers, and the Americans with Disabilities Act of 1990 (ADA), barring discrimination against individuals with disabilities. Second, the Supreme Court resuscitated civil rights statutes passed during the Reconstruction era following the Civil War. Sections 1981 and 1983 of Title 42 of the United States

Code were among the laws passed to protect the newly freed slaves in the South by implementing the Thirteenth, Fourteenth, and Fifteenth Amendments. Although these statutes had been eviscerated by the Supreme Court in the years shortly after their enactment, the Warren Court revived the early statutes, creating a wide range of statutory tools to deal with employment discrimination. While the Supreme Court thereafter restricted both the modern civil rights laws and their Reconstruction era predecessors, Congress has reacted strongly on a number of occasions to restore the effectiveness of the antidiscrimination statutes. Most notably, the Pregnancy Discrimination Act in 1978 defined pregnancy discrimination as sex discrimination after the Supreme Court had held to the contrary, and the Civil Rights Act of 1991 reversed or substantially modified a number of Supreme Court decisions limiting the effectiveness of Title VII and §1981. And more recently, Congress acted to overturn restrictive judicial interpretations in both the Americans with Disabilities Act Amendments Act of 2008 and the Lilly Ledbetter Fair Pay Act, passed in 2009.

This book considers all of these legislative and judicial efforts to address discrimination in employment, and it approaches the question through the lens of the three theories of liability the courts have developed—individual disparate treatment, systemic disparate treatment, and disparate impact. Some have questioned whether these understandings of discrimination adequately capture the underlying phenomenon, but they are obviously the place to start. To complicate matters, they apply somewhat differently across the four major statutes we will study—Title VII, the ADEA, 42 U.S.C. §1981, and the ADA.

Chapter 1 takes up the most basic concept, intentional discrimination against particular applicants or employees—individual disparate treatment discrimination. Chapter 2 then extends the intentional discrimination concept to broader patterns of such practices—systemic disparate treatment. Chapter 3 considers an alternative test of discrimination, disparate impact. Then Chapter 4 attempts to synthesize the approaches previously developed into a coherent theory of discrimination. Chapter 5 takes up special problems that arise when antidiscrimination law is applied to such issues as pregnancy, sexual harassment, sexual orientation, religion, national origin, and age. Chapter 6 then considers an issue that can arise in connection with all of the antidiscrimination statutes—retaliation for opposing discrimination or participating in proceedings under the various laws.

In Chapter 7, the casebook turns to a statute that approaches the question of discrimination somewhat differently. The Americans with Disabilities Act borrows discrimination concepts from the earlier statutes but applies them in unique ways to a form of discrimination that is itself very different from those studied previously. The ADA has recently been reinvigorated with the passage of the Americans with Disabilities Act Amendments Act of 2008.

Chapters 8 and 9 then turn to important but second-order questions that have arisen under the antidiscrimination statutes. Thus, Chapter 8 considers procedures focusing primarily on Title VII, which is the procedural paradigm for both the ADEA and the ADA. Chapter 9 then analyzes the remedies available to redress violations of all the statutes addressed in this book.

The remaining chapter takes a somewhat different tack. The centrality of the antidiscrimination statutes to employment in the United States has led to a number of "risk management" strategies by employers, and Chapter 10 undertakes a study of two of the most important of these—the use of arbitration as an alternative to litigation to resolve discrimination disputes and the settlement and release of potential claims.

CASES AND MATERIALS ON EMPLOYMENT DISCRIMINATION

Chapter 1

Individual Disparate Treatment Discrimination

A. INTRODUCTION

In order to address the pervasive problems of employment discrimination, Congress enacted a series of statutes that deal with various aspects of the phenomenon. These laws include Title VII of the Civil Rights Act of 1964; the Civil War Reconstruction statutes, especially 42 U.S.C. §1981; the Age Discrimination in Employment Act of 1967 (ADEA); and the Americans with Disabilities Act of 1990 (ADA).

The avenues of relief under the statutes differ from each other in important respects, but all are concerned with discrimination in employment. It is "discrimination" that provides the unifying theme for this casebook. That concept, however, has been developed by the courts in ways that are not always intuitively obvious. Indeed, "discrimination" is now a term of art that embraces several different theories, each with its own distinctive application.

In broad terms, three statutes adopt a unitary definition of what has been called "disparate treatment" discrimination. The term originated in cases decided under Title VII and has been applied in both ADEA cases and suits brought under §1981. Disparate treatment, however, has developed in two distinct ways. Individual disparate treatment is the focus of this chapter, while systemic disparate treatment is taken up in Chapter 2. In addition, Title VII jurisprudence developed the theory of disparate impact discrimination, which is available only in a considerably diluted form under the ADEA and not at all under §1981. Disparate impact is considered in Chapter 3. The Americans with Disabilities Act prohibits individual and systemic discrimination and also bars practices with a disparate impact; however, as developed in Chapter 7, the ADA is distinctive in many ways from the other antidiscrimination statutes.

1

B. PROVING DISCRIMINATION

Discrimination has two quite distinct meanings. One is the "recognition and under-standing of the differences between one thing and another." The second, the one this book focuses on, is "the unjust or prejudicial treatment of different categories of people . . . esp. on the grounds of race, age, or sex [disability, sexual orientation, etc.]." THE NEW OXFORD AMERICAN DICTIONARY 488 (2001). In *Teamsters v. United States*, 431 U.S. 324, 335, n.15 (1977), the Court provided a definition of disparate treatment discrimination and distinguished it from disparate impact:

> "Disparate treatment" . . . is the most easily understood type of discrimination. The employer simply treats some people less favorably than others because of their race, religion, sex, or national origin. Proof of discriminatory motive is critical, although it can in most situations be inferred from the mere fact of differences in treatment. . . . Undoubtedly disparate treatment was the most obvious evil Congress had in mind when it enacted Title VII. . . . Claims of disparate treatment may be distinguished from claims that stress "disparate impact." The latter involve employment practices that are facially neutral in their treatment of different groups but that in fact fall more harshly on one group than another and cannot be justified by business necessity. Proof of discriminatory motive . . . is not required under a disparate-impact theory. . . . Either theory may, of course, be applied to a particular set of facts.

This definition leaves much unexplored, particularly what it means to treat someone differently "because of" a prohibited trait, a question that has vexed the courts over the years. And, of course, this passage doesn't tell us what "discriminatory motive" means, which is a core question for all the antidiscrimination statutes. We will see that there is a live issue as to whether the motive must be conscious or whether "unconscious" discriminatory impulses suffice.

1. *What Is Discrimination, How Can It Be Proved?*

SLACK v. HAVENS
7 FEP 885 (S.D. Cal. 1973), *aff'd as modified,* **522 F.2d 1091 (9th Cir. 1975)**

THOMPSON, J.: This action is brought by the plaintiffs, four black women, who allege they were discriminatorily discharged, due to their race, in violation of the Civil Rights Act of 1964, specifically 42 U.S.C. §2000e-2(a)(1). . . .

4. On January 31, 1968, plaintiffs Berrel Matthews, Emily Hampton and Isabell Slack were working in the bonding and coating department of defendant Industries' plant, engaged in preparing and assembling certain tubing components for defen-dant's product. A white co-worker, Sharon Murphy, was also assigned to the bonding and coating department on that day and was performing the same general work as the three plaintiffs mentioned above. The fourth plaintiff, Kathleen Hale, was working in another department on January 31st.

Near the end of the working day, plaintiffs Matthews, Hampton and Slack were called together by their immediate supervisor, Ray Pohasky, and informed that the following morning, upon reporting to work, they would suspend regular production and engage in a general cleanup of the bonding and coating department. The cleanup was to consist of washing walls and windows whose sills were approximately 12 to 15 feet above the floor, cleaning light fixtures, and scraping the floor which was caked with deposits of hardened resin. Plaintiffs Matthews, Hampton and Slack protested the assigned work, arguing that it was not within their job description, which included only light cleanup in their immediate work areas, and that it was too hard and dangerous. Mr. Pohasky agreed that it was hard work and said that he would check to see if they had to do it.

5. On the following work day, February 1, 1968, plaintiffs Matthews, Hampton, and Slack reported to the bonding and coating department along with Sharon Murphy, their white co-worker. However, Mr. Pohasky excused Sharon Murphy to another department for the day, calling in plaintiff Kathleen Hale from the winding department where she had been on loan from the bonding and coating department for about a week. Mr. Pohasky then repeated his announcement that the heavy cleaning would have to be done. The four plaintiffs joined in protest against the heavy cleanup work. They pointed out that they had not been hired to do janitorial type work, and one of the plaintiffs inquired as to why Sharon Murphy had been excused from the cleanup detail even though she had very little seniority among the ladies in the bonding and coating department. In reply, they were told by Mr. Pohasky that they would do the work, "or else." There was uncontradicted testimony that at sometime during their conversation Pohasky injected the statement that "Colored people should stay in their places," or words to that effect. Some further discussion took place between plaintiffs and Pohasky and then with Gary Helming, plaintiffs' general supervisor, but eventually each of the plaintiffs was taken to the office of Mr. Helming where she was given her final paycheck and fired. Plaintiff Matthews testified without contradiction that on the way to Mr. Helming's office Mr. Pohasky made the comment that "Colored folks are hired to clean because they clean better."

6. The general cleanup work was later performed by newly-hired male employees. Sharon Murphy was never asked to participate in this cleanup before or after the plaintiffs' termination. . . .

B. Having concluded that defendant Industries is an "employer" under Title VII of the Civil Rights Act for the purposes of this action, we must next consider whether plaintiffs' termination amounted to unlawful discrimination against them because of their race. Defendants deny that the facts support such a conclusion, contending that plaintiffs' case amounts to nothing more than a dispute as to their job classification.

Admittedly, the majority of the discussion between plaintiffs and Industries' management on January 31 and February 1, 1968, centered around the nature of the duties which plaintiffs were ordered to perform. Plaintiffs pointed out that they had not been hired with the understanding that they would be expected to perform more than light cleanup work immediately adjacent to their work stations. They were met with an ultimatum that they do the work — or else. Additionally, no explanation was offered as to why Sharon Murphy, a white co-worker, had been transferred out of the bonding and coating department the morning that the heavy cleaning was to begin there, while plaintiff Hale was called back from the winding department, where she had been working, to the bonding and coating area, specifically for participation in the general cleanup. It is not disputed that Sharon Murphy had less seniority than all of the plaintiffs except plaintiff Hale (having been hired 8 days prior to plaintiff Hale) and no evidence of a bona fide business reason was ever educed by defendants as to why Sharon Murphy was excused from assisting the plaintiffs in the proposed cleaning project.

The only evidence that did surface at the trial regarding the motives for the decisions of the management of defendant Industries consisted of certain statements by supervisor Pohasky, who commented to plaintiff Matthews that "colored folks were hired to clean because they clean better," and "colored folks should stay in their place," or words to that effect. Defendants attempt to disown these statements with the argument that Pohasky's state of mind and arguably discriminatory conduct was immaterial and not causative of the plaintiffs' discharge.

But defendants cannot be allowed to divorce Mr. Pohasky's conduct from that of Industries so easily. First of all, 42 U.S.C. §2000e(b) expressly includes "any agent" of an employer within the definition of "employer." Secondly, there was a definite causal relation between Pohasky's apparently discriminatory conduct and the firings. Had Pohasky not discriminated against the plaintiffs by demanding they perform work he would not require of a white female employee, they would not have been faced with the unreasonable choice of having to choose between obeying his discriminatory work order and the loss of their employment. Finally, by backing up Pohasky's ultimatum the top level management of Industries ratified his discriminatory conduct and must be held liable for the consequences thereof. . . .

From all the evidence before it, this Court is compelled to find that defendant Industries, through its managers and supervisor, Mr. Pohasky, meant to require the plaintiffs to perform the admittedly heavy and possibly dangerous work of cleaning the bonding and coating department, when they would not require the same work from plaintiffs' white fellow employee. Furthermore, it meant to enforce that decision by firing the plaintiffs when they refused to perform that work. The consequence of the above was racial discrimination whatever the motivation of the management of defendant Industries may have been. Therefore, the totality of Industries' conduct amounted, in the Court's opinion, to an unlawful employment practice prohibited by the Civil Rights Act, specifically, 42 U.S.C. §2000e-2(a)(1).

Held: racial discrim [margin note]

NOTES

1. *At-Will Rule Modified.* In the United States, "at will" is the default rule for employment, RESTATEMENT OF EMPLOYMENT LAW §2.01 (Am. Law Inst. 2015), which means that employers can terminate employees at any time for good reason, bad reason, or no reason at all. An exception to the at-will rule is when the reason is an illegal one, such as conduct that violates an antidiscrimination statute or the public policy tort. RESTATEMENT §5.02.

2. *The Statutory Language.* The core prohibitions of Title VII are found in §703(a), which declares it an "unlawful employment practice" for an employer —

> (1) to fail or refuse to hire or to discharge any individual, or otherwise to discriminate against any individual with respect to his compensation, terms, conditions, or privileges of employment, because of such individual's race, color, religion, sex, or national origin; or
>
> (2) to limit, segregate, or classify his employees or applicants for employment in any way which would deprive or tend to deprive any individual of employment opportunities or otherwise adversely affect his status as an employee, because of such individual's race, color, religion, sex, or national origin.

42 U.S.C. §2000e-2(a) (2018). Succeeding sections have similar prohibitions for labor unions and employment agencies.

3. *Antiretaliation and Labor Law Protection*. In addition to this core prohibition on discrimination, Title VII also has an important ancillary provision that prohibits retaliation against employees who oppose discrimination. §704(a), 42 U.S.C. §2000e-3(a). Suppose Slack and her co-workers contended they were fired because they opposed what they reasonably and in good faith believed to be a discriminatory job assignment. Would they have won on that theory? Retaliation is discussed in Chapter 6.

For students of labor law, would the protest of the black workers against being assigned the cleaning work be "concerted activity for mutual aid or protection" that is safeguarded by the National Labor Relations Act, even if there is no union? *See* ROBERT A. GORDON & MATTHEW W. FINKIN, BASIC TEXT ON LABOR LAW: UNIONIZATION AND COLLECTIVE BARGAINING 402-05 (2d ed. 2004). And a union would have provided even more protection. But their insubordination by refusing to follow Pohasky's orders might have been "good cause" to discharge them even under a standard collective bargaining agreement. The general rule is that workers must work now, grieve later, even if the boss's order violates the collective bargaining agreement. *See* ELKOURI & ELKOURI, HOW ARBITRATION WORKS 262-67 (Alan Miles Ruben ed., 7th ed. 2012).

4. *Unequal Treatment Not Enough*. The four African American plaintiffs in *Slack* were treated differently than Sharon Murphy, a white worker. But unequal treatment, in and of itself, is not a statutory violation unless it is "because of" the plaintiffs' race. While unequal treatment is some evidence that the assignment was made *because of* race, is it enough evidence? Would there be sufficient evidence in the case without the statements of Pohasky to support a factfinding that the cleaning assignment was given to plaintiffs because they were African Americans? Suppose you represented the defendant in *Slack*. What information would you look for with respect to Sharon Murphy?

5. *Pohasky's Statements*. Many of us probably intuit that discrimination involves animus by the discriminator. Thus, this case would be easy if Pohasky said, "I hate African Americans and so I assign them to the worst jobs." While Pohasky may have harbored such emotions, animus isn't actually required for a violation. Pohasky's admission of assigning plaintiffs to the cleaning work because they were "colored" would seem to suffice. Even though he suggested that African Americans make better cleaners, the obvious negative implication is that they can only do menial jobs like cleaning. Given the history of assigning racial minorities to such jobs, Pohasky's views can be seen as part of a sad history of racial subordination. But does it matter whether he thought blacks inferior or superior in their ability to clean? So long as he was treating individuals unequally because of race, there would be a violation of §703(a). In short, Title VII generally considers acting with the motive of treating individuals differently on racial grounds as impermissible, regardless of whether the motive is malign, benign, or neutral.

6. *Admissions*. From an evidentiary standpoint, Pohasky was an agent of the employer acting within the scope of his agency in assigning the workers to their tasks. For that reason, Havens Industry was liable for his discrimination, even if the company was otherwise not discriminating. But Pohasky's agency has another effect: he was not only acting within the scope of his agency in assigning the plaintiffs but he was also speaking within the scope of his agency in explaining the reason for the assignment. Such statements as "colored folks are hired to clean because they clean better," therefore, could be introduced into evidence against the employer, despite the hearsay rule and regardless of their "truth." As a practical matter, statements as

unambiguous as this will almost always establish the key element in a discrimination case — that Pohasky assigned the cleaning to the plaintiffs because of their race. As we will see, such admissions-against-interest testimony related to the at-issue employment decision is sometimes described as "direct evidence" of discrimination and is very powerful. See Note 5, p. 74. But we will also see. that even such statements, if not linked to the decision or made by non-decisionmakers, may have so little probative value that a reasonable jury could not find for plaintiff.

7. *Acting on Stereotypes.* Pohasky's statements reflect the phenomenon of stereotyping individual members of a group because of the characteristics (or the perceived characteristics) of the group as a whole. Obviously, stereotyping is a key problem in the employment area because much discrimination stems from employer perceptions about the abilities of various groups (racial, ethnic, or gender) in society. Stereotypes are, in a sense, just generalizations, and generalizations can be accurate or inaccurate. To the extent that an employer acts against an individual on a generalization regarding race or gender, without pausing to consider whether that generalization is true of the individual in question, there is likely to be a violation of Title VII.

But stereotypes differ from other kinds of generalizations in that they may operate below the level of cognition; that is, the individual decisionmaker may be acting without being aware that bias is influencing her actions. Professor Linda Hamilton Krieger, in *The Content of Our Categories: A Cognitive Bias Approach to Discrimination and Equal Employment Opportunity*, 47 STAN. L. REV. 1161 (1995), used the insights from cognitive psychology to conclude that stereotyping by race and gender is an "unintended consequence" of the necessity for humans to categorize their sensory perceptions in order to make any sense of the world:

> [The] central premise of social cognition theory [is] that cognitive structures and processes involved in categorization and information processing can in and of themselves result in stereotyping and other forms of biased intergroup judgment previously attributed to motivational processes. The social cognition approach to discrimination comprises three claims. . . . The first is that stereotyping . . . is nothing special. It is simply a form of categorization [of our sensory perceptions], similar in structure and function to the categorization of natural objects. According to this view, stereotypes, like other categorical structures, are cognitive mechanisms that all people, not just "prejudiced" ones, use to simplify the task of perceiving, processing, and retaining information about people in memory. They are central, and indeed essential to normal cognitive functioning.
>
> The second claim posited in social cognition theory is that, once in place, stereotypes bias intergroup judgment and decisionmaking. . . . [T]hey function as implicit theories, biasing in predictable ways the perception, interpretation, encoding, retention, and recall of information about other people. These biases are cognitive rather than motivational. They operate absent intent to favor or disfavor members of a particular social group. And, perhaps most significant for present purposes, they bias a decisionmaker's judgment long before the "moment of decision" [when the employment decision in question is made], as a decisionmaker attends to relevant data and interprets, encodes, stores, and retrieves it from memory. These biases "sneak up on" the decisionmaker, distorting bit by bit the data upon which his decision is eventually based.
>
> The third claim follows from the second. Stereotypes, when they function as implicit prototypes or schemas [by which we evaluate each other], operate beyond the reach of decisionmaker self-awareness. Empirical evidence indicates that people's access to their own cognitive processes is in fact poor. Accordingly, cognitive bias may well be both unintentional and unconscious.

Id. at 1187-88. The phenomenon that Professor Krieger identified has a number of labels, including "unconscious discrimination," "implicit attitudes," "cognitive bias," and others. Whatever the label, if Professor Krieger is right, one would anticipate that discrimination is very common in the workplace (and elsewhere). And we will see that there is strong reason to believe that discrimination occurs far more often than we would like to believe. But, even assuming that is correct, Krieger's analysis raises two critical questions for employment discrimination law: first, to what extent is unequal treatment in the workplace the result of cognitive bias (as opposed, for example, to old-fashioned animus or what has been called "rational discrimination"), and, second, does a law often described in terms of "intentional" discrimination reach unconscious actions?

A complete answer to these questions will have to be deferred until later in the course, but you'll learn that the inference of discriminatory intent is often drawn mainly from the circumstances of a particular adverse employment decision, which means that the factfinder will rarely consider whether a particular decision was consciously discriminatory or simply the result of cognitive bias.

NOTE ON THE EXTENT OF WORKPLACE DISCRIMINATION

Despite the reluctance of many to appreciate the extent of the problem, *see* Katie R. Eyer, *That's Not Discrimination: American Beliefs and the Limits of Anti-Discrimination Law*, 96 MINN. L. REV. 1275 (2012), social science research suggests pervasive bias exists. Perhaps most cogent but least numerous are "field experiments" or "audit studies" in which researchers try to directly test the operation of bias by having matched pairs of applicants — each pair as similar as possible except for the variable of interest (race or sex) — apply for real-world positions. If one group is more successful than the other, there is reason both to believe that bias exists and that it affects actual decisionmaking. A significant study in the employment context sent otherwise identical resumes to employers; those using names that did not "sound" African American received more favorable treatment. Marianne Bertrand & Sendhil Mullainathan, *Are Emily and Greg More Employable than Lakisha and Jamal? A Field Experiment on Labor Market Discrimination*, 94 AM. ECON. REV. 991, 991-92 (2004). *See also* David Neumark, *Sex Discrimination in Restaurant Hiring: An Audit Study*, 111 Q.J. ECON. 915, 917-18 (1996). An earlier instance was a study by the Urban Institute that sent matched pairs of black and white testers into the job market, with African Americans faring substantially worse. MARGERY A. TURNER, MICHAEL FIX & RAYMOND J. STRUYK, OPPORTUNITIES DENIED, OPPORTUNITIES DIMINISHED: RACIAL DISCRIMINATION IN HIRING 37-66 (1991). *But see* RICHARD A. EPSTEIN, FORBIDDEN GROUNDS: THE CASE AGAINST EMPLOYMENT DISCRIMINATION LAWS 55-58 (1992).

A second approach to the question of the pervasiveness of bias is statistical and uses retrospective data to seek to hold constant a large number of variables in order to determine whether racial bias exists. A dramatic example (albeit not in the employment context) is research showing that the NBA referees were more likely to call fouls on players of a different race than themselves. *See* Joseph Price & Justin Wolfers, *Racial Discrimination Among NBA Referees*, 125 Q.J. ECON. 1859, 1859-60 (2010) (finding statistically significant evidence of own-race bias among NBA referees). More attuned to the employment setting, another study found that store managers were more likely to hire members of their own race than members of another race. Laura Guliano, David Levine & Jonathan Leonard, *Manager Race and the Race of New Hires*, 27 J. LAB. ECON. 589 (2008).

A third approach to appreciating the extent of discrimination is the most controversial and returns us to the question of cognitive bias.

NOTE ON COGNITIVE BIAS

No one seems to doubt that cognitive bias exists, but there is substantial debate about how pervasive it is and the extent to which it affects real-world decisionmaking. There are a host of studies bearing on the question, but the social science research that has perhaps received the most attention is the Implicit Association Test, which purports to measure "attitudes" at variance with the subjects' expressed views. Hosted at Harvard and available on the Internet, Project Implicit, https://implicit.harvard. edu/implicit, is open to anyone with an Internet connection. It measures biases (or "implicit attitudes") by comparing how quickly a test taker equates positive and negative words with images of members of different races (and other categories of interest). These results are then compared with the subject's self-reported views on race. The IAT has generated a substantial social science literature analyzing the results of literally hundreds of thousands of visits. *E.g.,* Jerry Kang et al., in *Implicit Bias in the Courtroom,* 59 UCLA L. REV. 1124 (2012), offer a straightforward review of much of the literature followed by a discussion of how implicit bias enters the courtroom, including in employment discrimination cases, and propose a number of steps to "debias" decisionmaking.

Perhaps needless to say, the IAT has generated harsh criticism in the legal academy. The critics have argued that measuring attitudes by millisecond responses to stimuli is inherently flawed and that, even if the test does in some sense identify attitudes, there is no evidence that they affect real-world decisionmaking. *See* Amy L. Wax, *Supply Side or Discrimination? Assessing The Role of Unconscious Bias,* 83 TEMP. L. REV. 877, 883-902 (2011); Gregory Mitchell, *Second Thoughts,* 40 McGEORGE L. REV. 687, 687 (2009); Gregory Mitchell & Philip E. Tetlock, *Facts Do Matter: A Reply to Bagenstos,* 37 HOFSTRA L. REV. 737, 738 (2009); Amy L. Wax, *The Discriminating Mind: Define It, Prove It,* 40 CONN. L. REV. 979, 984-85 (2008); Gregory Mitchell & Philip E. Tetlock, *Antidiscrimination Law and the Perils of Mindreading,* 67 OHIO ST. L.J. 1023, 1023 (2006). But the IAT has also garnered enthusiastic support. *See* Samuel R. Bagenstos, *Implicit Bias, "Science," and Antidiscrimination Law,* 1 HARV. L. & POL'Y REV. 477, 482 (2007). *See also* Jerry Kang & Mahzarin R. Banaji, *Fair Measures: A Behavioral Realist Revision of "Affirmative Action,"* 94 CAL. L. REV. 1063 (2006); Linda Hamilton Krieger & Susan T. Fiske, *Behavioral Realism in Employment Discrimination Law: Implicit Bias and Disparate Treatment,* 94 CAL. L. REV. 997 (2006); Jerry Kang, *Trojan Horses of Race,* 118 HARV. L. REV. 1489 (2005).

The intensity of the debate sometimes causes the participants to lose sight of the fact that, even accepting the IAT's results on its own terms, it does not follow that any divergence between expressed attitudes and implicit attitudes reflects cognitive bias; it might instead reveal conscious mental operations that the actor is unwilling to admit, even in the context of an anonymous test. Any discrimination may or may not be unconscious. *See* Ralph Richard Banks & Richard Thompson Ford, *(How) Does Unconscious Bias Matter?: Law, Politics, and Racial Inequality,* 58 EMORY L.J. 1053, 1058 (2009). Indeed, perhaps the conscious/unconscious division suggests a false dichotomy — that is, biases may often lie somewhere between those the subject is fully aware of (whether or not willing to admit to them) and those buried deep in the unconscious. *See* Leora F. Eisenstadt & Jeffrey R. Boles, *Intent and Liability in Employment Discrimination,* 53 AM. BUS. L.J. 607 (2016). Indeed, this mistake is apparent in Justice Ginsburg's dissent in *Wal-Mart Stores, Inc. v. Dukes,* 564 U.S. 338 (2011). Citing one well-known study revealing bias in the real world, she wrote:

An example vividly illustrates how subjective decisionmaking can be a vehicle for discrimination. Performing in symphony orchestras was long a male preserve. In the 1970's orchestras began hiring musicians through auditions open to all comers. Reviewers were to judge applicants solely on their musical abilities, yet *subconscious bias led some reviewers to disfavor women.* Orchestras that permitted reviewers to see the applicants hired far fewer female musicians than orchestras that conducted blind auditions, in which candidates played behind opaque screens.

Id. at 373 n.6 (emphasis added) (internal citations omitted) (citing Claudia Goldin & Cecilia Rouse, *Orchestrating Impartiality: The Impact of "Blind" Auditions on Female Musicians,* 90 AM. ECON. REV. 715, 715-16 (2000)). The Justice did not notice that the third sentence does not necessarily follow from the first. That is, subjective decisionmaking could facilitate discrimination of either the conscious or subconscious variety. In short, even if the IAT is correct in discerning a difference, it does not necessarily establish that the subject is unaware of his biases, as opposed to being reluctant to honestly report them. And some have urged that there is still plenty of old-fashioned bias around. *See* Michael Selmi, *Sex Discrimination in the Nineties, Seventies Style: Case Studies in the Preservation of Male Workplace Norms,* 9 EMP. RTS. & EMP. POL'Y J. 1 (2005).

But suppose the IAT is correct and reveals unconscious biases that operate in the workplace. Is that illegal? Some believe that "unconscious discrimination" is an oxymoron. Although the Supreme Court has said that acting on the basis of stereotypes can violate Title VII, *Price Waterhouse v. Hopkins,* 490 U.S. 228, 251 (1989) ("we are beyond the day when an employer could evaluate employees by assuming or insisting that they matched the stereotype associated with their group"); *Hazen Paper Co. v. Biggins,* 507 U.S. 604 (1993) (acting on the basis of the stereotype that "productivity and competence decline with old age" is "the very essence of age discrimination"), it is not clear that it was referring to unconscious mental operations. Recently, however, the Court explicitly invoked that concept in justifying the disparate impact theory under the Fair Housing Act. *Tex. Dep't of Hous. & Cmty. Affairs v. Inclusive Cmtys. Project, Inc.,* 135 S. Ct. 2507, 2511-12 (2014) ("Recognition of disparate-impact liability under the FHA plays an important role in uncovering discriminatory intent: it permits plaintiffs to counteract unconscious prejudices and disguised animus that escape easy classification as disparate treatment.").

Consistent with that view, many scholars, not least of all Professor Krieger, argue that causation is all that is required; that is, if cognitive bias results in an adverse employment action, liability follows. 47 STAN. L. REV. at 1170. *Accord* Amy L. Wax, *The Discriminating Mind: Define It, Prove It,* 40 CONN. L. REV. 979, 982-83 (2008); Katharine T. Bartlett, *Making Good on Good Intentions: The Critical Role of Motivation in Reducing Implicit Workplace Discrimination,* 95 VA. L. REV. 1893, 1900 (2009); Michael Selmi, *Proving Intentional Discrimination: The Reality of Supreme Court Rhetoric,* 86 GEO. L.J. 279, 294 (1997). Nevertheless, the normative question remains important for some of these and other scholars: *should* the statute be read to impose liability on those not consciously motivated to discriminate? Patrick S. Shin, *Liability for Unconscious Discrimination? A Thought Experiment in the Theory of Employment Discrimination Law,* 62 HASTINGS L.J. 67, 89-90 (2010); Amy Wax, *Discrimination as Accident,* 74 IND. L.J. 1129 (1999).

Yet a third group of scholars view the legitimacy question as turning not on whether the employer has a conscious motivation to discriminate but rather whether the employer is taking steps to minimize the operation of bias in its workplace or even inciting it. Tristin K. Green, DISCRIMINATION LAUNDERING: THE RISE OF ORGANIZATIONAL

INNOCENCE AND THE CRISIS OF EQUAL OPPORTUNITY LAW (2016). Kevin Woodson, *Derivative Racial Discrimination*, 12 STAN. J. C.R. & C.L. 335 (2016); Tristin K. Green, *A Structural Approach as Antidiscrimination Mandate: Locating Employer Wrong*, 60 VAND. L. REV. 849 (2007); Tristin K. Green, *Discrimination in Workplace Dynamics: Toward a Structural Account of Disparate Treatment Theory*, 38 HARV. C.R.-C.L. L. REV. 91, 128 (2002); Tristin K. Green, *Work Culture and Discrimination*, 93 CAL. L. REV. 623 (2005); Tristin K. Green & Alexandra Kalev, *Discrimination-Reducing Measures at the Relational Level*, 59 HASTINGS L.J. 1435, 1435 (2008); Susan Sturm, *Second Generation Employment Discrimination: A Structural Approach*, 101 COLUM. L. REV. 458, 485-90 (2001); Benjamin Oppenheimer, *Negligent Discrimination*, 141 U. PA. L. REV. 899 (1993). *But see* Samuel R. Bagenstos, *The Structural Turn and the Limits of Antidiscrimination Law*, 94 CAL. L. REV. 1, 2-3 (2006). There is, in fact, a line of scholarship dealing with "debiasing" efforts. *See* Christine Jolls & Cass R. Sunstein, *Debiasing Through Law*, 35 J. LEGAL STUD. 199 (2006).

HAZEN PAPER CO. v. BIGGINS
507 U.S. 604 (1993)

Justice O'CONNOR delivered the opinion of the Court.

[Hazen Paper Company manufactures coated, laminated, and printed paper and paperboard. It is owned and operated by two cousins, petitioners Robert Hazen and Thomas N. Hazen. Walter F. Biggins was hired as technical director in 1977. He was fired in 1986, when he was 62 years old. Biggins sued, claiming to have been discharged in violation of both the Age Discrimination in Employment Act and the Employee Retirement Income Security Act of 1974 (ERISA), 29 U.S.C. §1140. The company claimed that he had been fired for doing business with competitors. The case was tried to a jury, which rendered a verdict for Biggins on his ADEA claim and also found a violation of ERISA. The district court denied defendant's motion for a judgment as a matter of law and the court of appeals affirmed.]

In affirming the judgments of liability, the Court of Appeals relied heavily on the evidence that petitioners had fired respondent in order to prevent his pension benefits from vesting. That evidence, as construed most favorably to respondent by the court, showed that the Hazen Paper pension plan had a 10-year vesting period and that respondent would have reached the 10-year mark had he worked "a few more weeks" after being fired. There was also testimony that petitioners had offered to retain respondent as a consultant to Hazen Paper, in which capacity he would not have been entitled to receive pension benefits. The Court of Appeals found this evidence of pension interference to be sufficient for ERISA liability, and also gave it considerable emphasis in upholding ADEA liability.

. . . The courts of appeals repeatedly have faced the question whether an employer violates the ADEA by acting on the basis of a factor, such as an employee's pension status or seniority, that is empirically correlated with age. We now clarify that there is no disparate treatment under the ADEA when the factor motivating the employer is some feature other than the employee's age. . . .

. . . In a disparate treatment case, liability depends on whether the protected trait (under the ADEA, age) actually motivated the employer's decision. The employer may have relied upon a formal, facially discriminatory policy requiring adverse treatment of employees with that trait. Or the employer may have been motivated by the protected trait on an ad hoc, informal basis. Whatever the employer's decisionmaking process, a disparate treatment claim cannot succeed unless the employee's protected trait actually played a role in that process and had a determinative influence on the outcome.

Disparate treatment, thus defined, captures the essence of what Congress sought to prohibit in the ADEA. It is the very essence of age discrimination for an older employee to be fired because the employer believes that productivity and competence decline with old age. As we explained in *EEOC v. Wyoming*, 460 U.S. 226 (1983), Congress' promulgation of the ADEA was prompted by its concern that older workers were being deprived of employment on the basis of inaccurate and stigmatizing stereotypes.

> Although age discrimination rarely was based on the sort of animus motivating some other forms of discrimination, it was based in large part on stereotypes unsupported by objective fact. . . . Moreover, the available empirical evidence demonstrated that arbitrary age lines were in fact generally unfounded and that, as an overall matter, the performance of older workers was at least as good as that of younger workers.

Thus the ADEA commands that "employers are to evaluate [older] employees . . . on their merits and not their age." *Western Air Lines, Inc. v. Criswell*, 472 U.S. 400 (1985). The employer cannot rely on age as a proxy for an employee's remaining characteristics, such as productivity, but must instead focus on those factors directly.

When the employer's decision is wholly motivated by factors other than age, the problem of inaccurate and stigmatizing stereotypes disappears. This is true even if the motivating factor is correlated with age, as pension status typically is. Pension plans typically provide that an employee's accrued benefits will become nonforfeitable, or "vested," once the employee completes a certain number of years of service with the employer. On average, an older employee has had more years in the work force than a younger employee and thus may well have accumulated more years of service with a particular employer. Yet an employee's age is analytically distinct from his years of service. An employee who is younger than 40, and therefore outside the class of older workers as defined by the ADEA, may have worked for a particular employer his entire career, while an older worker may have been newly hired. Because age and years of service are analytically distinct, an employer can take account of one while ignoring the other, and thus it is incorrect to say that a decision based on years of service is necessarily "age-based."

The instant case is illustrative. Under the Hazen Paper pension plan, as construed by the Court of Appeals, an employee's pension benefits vest after the employee completes 10 years of service with the company. Perhaps it is true that older employees of Hazen Paper are more likely to be "close to vesting" than younger employees. Yet a decision by the company to fire an older employee solely because he has nine-plus years of service and therefore is "close to vesting" would not constitute discriminatory treatment on the basis of age. The prohibited stereotype ("Older employees are likely to be ____") would not have figured in this decision, and the attendant stigma would not ensue. The decision would not be the result of an inaccurate and denigrating generalization about age, but would rather represent an accurate judgment about the employee — that he indeed is "close to vesting."

We do not mean to suggest that an employer lawfully could fire an employee in order to prevent his pension benefits from vesting. Such conduct is actionable under §510 of ERISA, as the Court of Appeals rightly found in affirming judgment for respondent under that statute. But it would not, without more, violate the ADEA.

That law requires the employer to ignore an employee's age (absent a statutory exemption or defense); it does not specify further characteristics that an employer must also ignore. Although some language in our prior decisions might be read to mean that an employer violates the ADEA whenever its reason for firing an employee is improper in any respect, see *McDonnell Douglas Corp. v. Green* (creating proof framework applicable to ADEA; employer must have "legitimate, nondiscriminatory reason" for action against employee), this reading is obviously incorrect. For example, it cannot be true that an employer who fires an older black worker because the worker is black thereby violates the ADEA. The employee's race is an improper reason, but it is improper under Title VII, not the ADEA.

We do not preclude the possibility that an employer who targets employees with a particular pension status on the assumption that these employees are likely to be older thereby engages in age discrimination. Pension status may be a proxy for age, not in the sense that the ADEA makes the two factors equivalent, *cf. Metz [v. Transit Mix Co.*, 828 F.2d 1202, 1208 (7th Cir. 1987)] (using "proxy" to mean statutory equivalence), but in the sense that the employer may suppose a correlation between the two factors and act accordingly. Nor do we rule out the possibility of dual liability under ERISA and the ADEA where the decision to fire the employee was motivated both by the employee's age and by his pension status. Finally, we do not consider the special case where an employee is about to vest in pension benefits as a result of his age, rather than years of service, and the employer fires the employee in order to prevent vesting. That case is not presented here. Our holding is simply that an employer does not violate the ADEA just by interfering with an older employee's pension benefits that would have vested by virtue of the employee's years of service.

Besides the evidence of pension interference, the Court of Appeals cited some additional evidentiary support for ADEA liability. Although there was no "direct evidence" of petitioners' motivation, except for two isolated comments by the Hazens, the Court of Appeals did note the following indirect evidence: Respondent was asked to sign a confidentiality agreement, even though no other employee had been required to do so, and his replacement was a younger man who was given a less onerous agreement. In the ordinary ADEA case, indirect evidence of this kind may well suffice to support liability if the plaintiff also shows that the employer's explanation for its decision — here, that respondent had been disloyal to Hazen Paper by doing business with its competitors — is "'unworthy of credence.'" But inferring age-motivation from the implausibility of the employer's explanation may be problematic in cases where other unsavory motives, such as pension interference, were present. . . . We therefore remand the case for the Court of Appeals to reconsider whether the jury had sufficient evidence to find an ADEA violation. . . .

NOTES

1. *Mixed Motives and Causation.* When a decision is "wholly motivated" by pension discrimination, age discrimination cannot be a determinative factor, or even a motivating factor. One reason Biggins was discharged was to prevent his pension from vesting. That reason is illegal under ERISA but nevertheless would be a nondiscriminatory reason under the ADEA. (If you're wondering why the defendant took the ADEA claim to the Supreme Court, it probably was due to the "liquidated damage" provision of the ADEA, absent from ERISA, which would double a part of his recovery. See Chapter 9, p. 592.)

However, pension discrimination might not be the only cause of the discharge. The Court recognized that both age bias and pension discrimination might coexist. Further, it necessarily recognized that either or both could be a "but for" cause in the sense that the same decision would have resulted from one had the other been absent. Otherwise, with a verdict finding pension discrimination, the Court would not have remanded for a trial on the age claim. In short, if either age or vesting would have caused the discharge, both would be but-for causes. In the language of tort law, causation in this situation can be "overdetermined," that is, when either of two negligent acts would have independently produced the harm, liability is appropriate for both. We'll explore this later in more depth, see p. 60.

Despite this logical possibility, the existence of two motives makes it harder for a jury to find that either actually caused the discharge when "but for" causation is the operative standard. Recall that the placement of the burden of persuasion on plaintiff means that he bears the risk of jury equipoise. If the jury finds each to be a 50 percent cause, plaintiff loses. If the jury cannot choose which of the two causes is determinative, it must find for the defendant on both counts. How often a plaintiff's case fails because of this possibility is unclear. In *Biggins* itself, plaintiff won on one ground, but the success of his ERISA claim may have doomed his ADEA claim. On remand, the second jury found for the defendants on the ADEA claim. 11 F.3d 205, 208 (1st Cir. 1997).

In the more typical case, of course, the nondiscriminatory reason will not be independently illegal. So a scenario in which the employer was motivated by *both*, say, race and *any other legal consideration* raises the mixed motive question at its starkest: if race is determinative, employer loses. If it is not, employer wins. But the analysis doesn't change: the factfinder must find by a preponderance of the evidence that the prohibited consideration was a determinative factor, a but-for cause of the adverse employment action. It must, in other words, be at least the straw that broke the camel's back. *See Burrage v. United States*, 134 S. Ct. 881, 888 (2014) ("[I]f poison is administered to a man debilitated by multiple diseases, it is a but-for cause of his death even if those diseases played a part in his demise, so long as, without the incremental effect of the poison, he would have lived."). Other considerations may or may not be present but it is the plaintiff's burden to prove but-for causation.

2. *Getting Inside the Employer's Mind to Prove Age Discrimination.* The Hazens made several "stray comments" about Biggins's age, *i.e.*, comments showing that his age was on their minds, but these were not made at the moment of his discharge. Does that support finding that age may have played a role in his discharge but not sufficiently to show that, but for his age, he would not have been fired? Suppose an employer asks an older worker about her plans for retirement. Courts have been very reluctant to see bias in such comments. *See, e.g., Fleishman v. Cont'l Cas. Co.*, 698 F.3d 598, 605-06 (7th Cir. 2012). In contrast, in *Sharp v. Aker Plant Servs. Group, Inc.*, 726 F.3d 789, 799 (6th Cir. 2013), an employee tape-recorded a conversation regarding his layoff, which provided "a window into the mind of an employment decision maker." The recorded comments were that the employer's "succession plan was to hire or retain younger workers at the expense of older workers because it was more likely that the former would stay with the company longer than the latter." The statements "disclose[d] no analytical step between computing an employee's potential longevity with the company and his age." *Id.* at 801. *See also Hilde v. City of Eveleth*, 777 F.3d 998, 1006 (8th Cir. 2015) (to assume that a candidate "was uncommitted to a position because his age made him retirement-eligible is age-stereotyping that the ADEA prohibits").

3. *Age Discrimination as Acting on Stereotypes.* Whether the jury properly found age discrimination depends on what it was supposed to have been looking for. The

Court found the answer easy: "[i]t is the very essence of age discrimination for an older employee to be fired because the employer believes that productivity and competence decline with old age." Another stereotype is that older workers are "set in their ways," unwilling or unable to adapt to new technologies and techniques. *See EEOC v. Board of Regents of the University of Wisconsin*, 288 F.3d 296, 303 (7th Cir. 2002) (references to plaintiff as having "skills suited to the 'pre-electronic'" and having "to be brought 'up to speed' on 'new trends of advertising with electronic means'" could be found to be code words for age stereotypes).

To find age discrimination in *Biggins*, must the jury believe that the Hazens fired Biggins because his increasing age led them to (incorrectly) conclude that his competence was declining? How likely is that? Aren't employers more likely to act on "inaccurate and stigmatizing stereotypes" regarding competence in refusing to hire older workers than in firing them? In this case, the Hazens had the opportunity to watch plaintiff perform over almost a decade. If they fired him because they believed his competence was diminishing, how could that be the result of a stereotype? Or does the implicit bias literature explain this? *See* Michael Winerip, *Three Men, Three Ages. Which Do You Like?*, N.Y. TIMES, July 27, 2013, at B-1 (reporting a study in which versions of the same person at three different ages were treated differently by a test group of Princeton undergraduates; the "assertive" version of the character was viewed more negatively than the younger versions even when saying the same thing). *See also* Ina Jaffe, *Older Workers Find Age Discrimination Built Right into Some Job Websites* (report about websites with resume-building applications that excluded older workers through their use of drop-down menus with limited ages), http://www.npr.org/2017/03/28/521771515/older-workers-find-age-discrimination-built-right-into-some-job-sites. To prevail, would Biggins have had to show (a) that the Hazens incorrectly evaluated his competence and (b) that they attributed his perceived loss of competence to his age? What if they correctly believed Biggins's competence was dropping but also attributed it to his age as a result of implicit bias? An employer can discharge a worker for becoming less competent but not if a worker younger than Biggins with a similar level of competence would have been retained.

4. *What If Stereotypes Are True?* Don't productivity and competence, in fact, decline with increasing age, at least in many jobs and at some age? This may be a stereotype that can be "true." In such situations, there is little need for cognitive bias as an explanation. Ironically, the more accurate the stereotype, that is, the greater the degree to which it conforms to reality, the less need there is for implicit bias, animus, or subordination as an explanation. If the law did not intervene, a "rational" employer might exclude older workers if, say, their health insurance costs were substantially higher than younger workers or, say, women, if pregnancy or childcare responsibilities made them, on average, less productive workers. *See* David A. Strauss, *The Law and Economics of Racial Discrimination in Employment: The Case for Numerical Standards*, 79 GEO. L.J. 1619, 1622 (1991). The point is not that such "statistical discrimination" is legal if it's rational: it is almost always not, even if the employer is correct in its perceptions (and often it isn't). Rather, the point is that discrimination is a more plausible explanation when the employer's self-interest is furthered by it.

McDONNELL DOUGLAS CORP. v. GREEN
411 U.S. 792 (1973)

Justice POWELL delivered the opinion of the Court.

. . . Petitioner, McDonnell Douglas Corp., is an aerospace and aircraft manufacturer headquartered in St. Louis, Missouri, where it employs over 30,000 people.

Respondent, a black citizen of St. Louis, worked for petitioner as a mechanic and laboratory technician from 1956 until August 28, 1964, when he was laid off in the course of a general reduction in petitioner's work force.

Respondent, a long-time activist in the civil rights movement, protested vigorously that his discharge and the general hiring practices of petitioner were racially motivated. As part of this protest, respondent and other members of the Congress on Racial Equality illegally stalled their cars on the main roads leading to petitioner's plant for the purpose of blocking access to it at the time of the morning shift change. The District Judge described the plan for, and respondent's participation in, the "stall-in" as follows:

> [F]ive teams, each consisting of four cars would "tie up" five main access roads into McDonnell at the time of the morning rush hour. The drivers of the cars were instructed to line up next to each other completely blocking the intersections or roads. The drivers were also instructed to stop their cars, turn off the engines, pull the emergency brake, raise all windows, lock the doors, and remain in their cars until the police arrived. The plan was to have the cars remain in position for one hour.
>
> Acting under the "stall in" plan, plaintiff [respondent in the present action] drove his car onto Brown Road, a McDonnell access road, at approximately 7:00 A.M., at the start of the morning rush hour. Plaintiff was aware of the traffic problem that would result. He stopped his car with the intent to block traffic. The police arrived shortly and requested plaintiff to move his car. He refused to move his car voluntarily. Plaintiff's car was towed away by the police, and he was arrested for obstructing traffic. Plaintiff pleaded guilty to the charge of obstructing traffic and was fined.

[O]n July 25, 1965, petitioner publicly advertised for qualified mechanics, respondent's trade, and respondent promptly applied for re-employment. Petitioner turned down respondent, basing its rejection on respondent's participation in the "stall-in." . . .

The District Court . . . found that petitioner's refusal to rehire respondent was based solely on his participation in the illegal demonstrations and not on his legitimate civil rights activities. The court concluded that nothing in Title VII or §704 [the antiretaliation provision] protected "such activity as employed by the plaintiff in the 'stall-in' and 'lock in' demonstrations."

On appeal, the Eighth Circuit affirmed that unlawful protests were not protected activities under §704(a), but reversed the dismissal of respondent's §703(a)(1) claim relating to racially discriminatory hiring practices. . . .

Procedural

II

The critical issue before us concerns the order and allocation of proof in a private, non-class action challenging employment discrimination. The language of Title VII makes plain the purpose of Congress to assure equality of employment opportunities and to eliminate those discriminatory practices and devices which have fostered racially stratified job environments to the disadvantage of minority citizens. *Griggs v. Duke Power Co.* [reproduced at p. 167]. As noted in *Griggs*, "Congress did not intend by Title VII, however, to guarantee a job to every person regardless of qualifications. In short, the Act does not command that any person be hired simply because he was formerly the subject of discrimination, or because he is a member of a minority group. Discriminatory preference for any group, minority or majority, is precisely and only what Congress has proscribed. . . .

There are societal as well as personal interests on both sides of this equation. The broad, overriding interest, shared by employer, employee, and consumer, is efficient and trustworthy workmanship assured through fair and racially neutral employment and personnel decisions. In the implementation of such decisions, it is abundantly clear that Title VII tolerates no racial discrimination, subtle or otherwise. In this case, respondent, the complainant below, charges that he was denied employment "because of his involvement in civil rights activities" and "because of his race and color." Petitioner denied discrimination of any kind, asserting that its failure to re-employ respondent was based upon and justified by his participation in the unlawful conduct against it. Thus, the issue at the trial on remand is framed by those opposing factual contentions. . . .

just an approach - not a set of elements - light burden ✳

The complainant in a Title VII trial must carry the initial burden under the statute of establishing a prima facie case of racial discrimination. This may be done by showing (i) that he belongs to a racial minority; (ii) that he applied and was qualified for a job for which the employer was seeking applicants; (iii) that, despite his qualifications, he was rejected; and (iv) that, after his rejection, the position remained open and the employer continued to seek applicants from persons of complainant's qualifications.[13] In the instant case, we agree with the Court of Appeals that respondent proved a prima facie case. Petitioner sought mechanics, respondent's trade, and continued to do so after respondent's rejection. Petitioner, moreover, does not dispute respondent's qualifications[14] and acknowledges that his past work performance in petitioner's employ was "satisfactory."

The burden then must shift to the employer to articulate some legitimate, nondiscriminatory reason for the employee's rejection. We need not attempt in the instant case to detail every matter which fairly could be recognized as a reasonable basis for a refusal to hire. Here petitioner has assigned respondent's participation in unlawful conduct against it as the cause for his rejection. We think that this suffices to discharge petitioner's burden of proof at this stage and to meet respondent's prima facie case of discrimination.

The Court of Appeals intimated, however, that petitioner's stated reason for refusing to rehire respondent was a "subjective" rather than objective criterion which "carr[ies] little weight in rebutting charges of discrimination." This was among the statements which caused the dissenting judge to read the opinion as taking "the position that such unlawful acts as Green committed against McDonnell would not legally entitle McDonnell to refuse to hire him, even though no racial motivation was involved . . . ." Regardless of whether this was the intended import of the opinion, we think the court below seriously underestimated the rebuttal weight to which petitioner's reasons were entitled. Respondent admittedly had taken part in a carefully planned "stall-in," designed to tie up access to and egress from petitioner's plant at a peak traffic hour. Nothing in Title VII compels an employer to absolve and rehire one who has engaged in such deliberate, unlawful activity against it.[17] In upholding, under the National Labor Relations Act, the discharge of employees who had seized

---

13. The facts necessarily will vary in Title VII cases, and the specification above of the prima facie proof required from respondent is not necessarily applicable in every respect to differing factual situations.

14. We note that the issue of what may properly be used to test qualifications for employment is not present in this case. Where employers have instituted employment tests and qualifications with an exclusionary effect on minority applicants, such requirements must be "shown to bear a demonstrable relationship to successful performance of the jobs" for which they were used, *Griggs v. Duke Power Co.*

17. The unlawful activity in this case was directed specifically against petitioner. We need not consider or decide here whether, or under what circumstances, unlawful activity not directed against the particular employer may be a legitimate justification reason for refusal to hire.

and forcibly retained an employer's factory buildings in an illegal sit-down strike, the Court noted pertinently: "We are unable to conclude that Congress intended to compel employers to retain persons in their employ regardless of their unlawful conduct, — to invest those who go on strike with an immunity from discharge for acts of trespass or violence against the employer's property. . . . Apart from the question of the constitutional validity of an enactment of that sort, it is enough to say that such a legislative intention should be found in some definite and unmistakable expression." *NLRB v. Fansteel Corp.*, 306 U.S. 240, 255 (1939).

Petitioner's reason for rejection thus suffices to meet the prima facie case, but the inquiry must not end here. While Title VII does not, without more, compel rehiring of respondent, neither does it permit petitioner to use respondent's conduct as a pretext for the sort of discrimination prohibited by §703(a)(1). On remand, respondent must, as the Court of Appeals recognized, be afforded a fair opportunity to show that petitioner's stated reason for respondent's rejection was in fact pretext. Especially relevant to such a showing would be evidence that white employees involved in acts against petitioner of comparable seriousness to the "stall-in" were nevertheless retained or rehired. Petitioner may justifiably refuse to rehire one who was engaged in unlawful, disruptive acts against it, but only if this criterion is applied alike to members of all races.

Other evidence that may be relevant to any showing of pretext includes facts as to the petitioner's treatment of respondent during his prior term of employment; petitioner's reaction, if any, to respondent's legitimate civil rights activities; and petitioner's general policy and practice with respect to minority employment. On the latter point, statistics as to petitioner's employment policy and practice may be helpful to a determination of whether petitioner's refusal to rehire respondent in this case conformed to a general pattern of discrimination against blacks. *Jones v. Lee Way Motor Freight, Inc.*, 431 F.2d 245 (C.A. 10 1970); *Blumrosen, Strangers in Paradise:* Griggs v. Duke Power Co., *and the Concept of Employment Discrimination*, 71 MICH. L. REV. 59, 91-94 (1972).[19] In short, on the retrial respondent must be given a full and fair opportunity to demonstrate by competent evidence that the presumptively valid reasons for his rejection were in fact a cover-up for a racially discriminatory decision.

The court below appeared to rely upon *Griggs v. Duke Power Co.*, in which the Court stated: "If an employment practice which operates to exclude Negroes cannot be shown to be related to job performance, the practice is prohibited." But *Griggs* differs from the instant case in important respects. It dealt with standardized testing devices which, however neutral on their face, operated to exclude many blacks who were capable of performing effectively in the desired positions. *Griggs* was rightly concerned that childhood deficiencies in the education and background of minority citizens, resulting from forces beyond their control, not be allowed to work a cumulative and invidious burden on such citizens for the remainder of their lives. Respondent, however, appears in different clothing. He had engaged in a seriously disruptive act against the very one from whom he now seeks employment. And petitioner does not seek his exclusion on the basis of a testing device which overstates what is

[handwritten marginalia: distinguish from Griggs]

19. The District Court may, for example, determine, after reasonable discovery that "the [racial] composition of defendant's labor force is itself reflective of restrictive or exclusionary practices." We caution that such general determinations, while helpful, may not be in and of themselves controlling as to an individualized hiring decision, particularly in the presence of an otherwise justifiable reason for refusing to rehire.

necessary for competent performance, or through some sweeping disqualification of all those with any past record of unlawful behavior, however remote, insubstantial, or unrelated to applicant's personal qualifications as an employee. Petitioner assertedly rejected respondent for unlawful conduct against it and in the absence of proof or pretext or discriminatory application of such a reason, this cannot be thought the kind of "artificial, arbitrary, and unnecessary barriers to employment" which the Court found to be the intention of Congress to remove.[21] . . .

NOTES

1. *A Surprising Decision?* The evidence Green presented showed simply that he had not been hired for a job that he applied for, a job he had previously performed successfully for the same employer. There was no unequal treatment evidence, no admissions testimony, no showing the employer acted on racial stereotypes. Further, the employer asserted that it had a good reason for not rehiring Green that had nothing directly to do with his race — Green's prior criminal activity aimed at it. Looking at the case from that perspective, was it a surprise that the trial court rejected Green's Title VII case? Nevertheless, do you think that race was a factor in the employer's action?

2. *The Mantra.* In employment discrimination law, "*McDonnell Douglas*" is more a mantra than a decision. That may not be a surprise since it was the first Supreme Court decision involving what we now refer to as "individual disparate treatment," the most common kind of discrimination claim. For example, in 2016, it was cited by the federal courts 2,795 times. While *McDonnell Douglas* is iconic, its meaning can be understood at several levels. At the most general level, *McDonnell Douglas* establishes a three-step structure: (1) the plaintiff must establish a prima facie case of discrimination, which creates a "presumption" that the employer discriminated. Once the prima facie case is established, the employer (2) has the burden of putting into evidence a nondiscriminatory reason for the alleged discriminatory decision. Carrying that burden destroys the presumption, but (3) the plaintiff has the opportunity to prove that the supposed reason was really a pretext for an underlying discriminatory motivation. This structure, however, does not reflect the steps in a Title VII trial — rather, it's merely a method of analyzing a claim — whether at summary judgment or at trial.

However, there are at least three other meanings of "*McDonnell Douglas*." First, the shorthand is also frequently cited for the case's four-pronged statement of what it takes to establish the plaintiff's prima facie case. Second, "*McDonnell Douglas*" is also invoked for the proposition that the plaintiff must prove that her protected characteristic was the determinative factor — the but-for cause — of the action the defendant took against her. Third, "*McDonnell Douglas*" is sometimes used to distinguish

---

21. It is, of course, a predictive evaluation, resistant to empirical proof, whether "an applicant's past participation in unlawful conduct directed at his prospective employer might indicate the applicant's lack of a responsible attitude toward performing work for that employer." But, in this case, given the seriousness and harmful potential of respondent's participation in the "stall-in" and the accompanying inconvenience to other employees, it cannot be said that petitioner's refusal to employ lacked a rational and neutral business justification. As the Court has noted elsewhere: "Past conduct may well relate to present fitness; past loyalty may have a reasonable relationship to present and future trust." *Garner v. Los Angeles Board*, 341 U.S. 716, 720 (1951).

a "circumstantial" method of proof from a more "direct" method. All too often, the several usages are not clearly differentiated.

3. *The First Step: The Prima Facie Case.* Citing *McDonnell Douglas* to mean its four-pronged specification of the prima facie case is questionable. While the Court framed the prima facie case in terms of four specific factual showings that seemed almost like "elements" necessary to make out a claim, the Court stressed in footnote 13 that these specific elements could not fit every fact situation. In *Teamsters v. United States*, 431 U.S. 324, 358 n.44 (1977), the Court departed from a by-the-numbers approach to describe the rationale for the prima facie case:

> Although the *McDonnell Douglas* formula does not require direct proof of discrimination, it does demand that the alleged discriminatee demonstrate at least that his rejection did not result from the two most common legitimate reasons on which an employer might rely to reject a job applicant: an absolute or relative lack of qualifications or the absence of a vacancy in the job sought. Elimination of these reasons for the refusal to hire is sufficient, absent other explanation, to create an inference that the decision was a discriminatory one.

To generalize from *Teamsters*, the *McDonnell Douglas* prima facie case proves discrimination by eliminating the most common, nondiscriminatory reasons for an employer's action, leaving for the factfinder to decide if plaintiff's claim of discrimination is the most likely reason for that action. In the case itself, a refusal to hire, the most common legitimate reasons would have been the lack of a job opening or plaintiff's lack of qualifications.

That's important because the particular four prongs of the *McDonnell Douglas* prima facie case are inapplicable to the vast majority of discrimination claims! In most hiring cases, after all, the position doesn't remain open. Rather, plaintiff loses out to another applicant. In most discharge cases, the plaintiff has worked for the employer and is let go.

4. *Other Versions of the Prima Face Case.* The courts applying the *McDonnell Douglas* prima facie case in fact adapt it in big and small ways that often vary between circuits and even within circuits. For example, in individual discharge cases, some courts have required the plaintiff to prove that she was doing "satisfactory work" in order to negate an obvious reason for termination, *Sheppard v. David Evans & Assoc.*, 694 F.3d 1045 (9th Cir. 2012); *cf. Zayas v. Rockford Mem'l Hosp.*, 740 F.3d 1154, 1158 (7th Cir. 2014) (prior satisfactory performance evaluations did not establish that plaintiff was meeting the employer's legitimate job expectations at the time she was fired given more recent disciplinary actions), and some require a showing of replacement by someone outside the plaintiff's protected group. *Shazor v. Prof'l Transit Mgmt.*, 744 F.3d 948, 957 (6th Cir. 2014).

In contrast, in "downsizing" or "reductions in force," where a number of employees are terminated simultaneously, the "legitimate, nondiscriminatory reason" — the need to reduce expenses — is apparent on its face. Because "positions" are being eliminated, the power of proof that the plaintiff is doing an apparently satisfactory job diminishes. Further, there is usually no "replacement" — younger or otherwise — for the plaintiff. In such cases, courts have altered *McDonnell Douglas* to require a plaintiff to produce other evidence, such as identifying younger workers who were retained when she was discharged. *E.g., Ward v. Int'l Paper Co.*, 509 F.3d 457, 460 (8th Cir. 2007); *Bellaver v. Quanex Corp./Nichols-Homeshield*, 200 F.3d 485, 494-95 (7th Cir. 2000).

Given these variations, courts are increasingly likely to describe the plaintiff's burden in tautological terms. *See Luster v. Vilsack*, 667 F.3d 1089, 1095 (10th Cir.

2011) ("To establish a prima facie disparate treatment claim, a plaintiff must present evidence that (1) she belongs to a protected class; (2) she suffered an adverse employment action; and (3) the adverse action occurred under circumstances giving rise to an inference of discrimination."). One court has treated the "inference of discrimination" prong as to essentially subsume the entire *McDonnell Douglas* litigation structure. *Young v. Builders Steel Co.*, 754 F.3d 573 (8th Cir. 2014) (plaintiff failed to prove a prima facie case because he could not establish the inference-of-discrimination element by showing that the defendant's reason was pretextual, which obviated the need to engage in the *McDonnell Douglas* burden-shifting analysis). *See also* Note on "Reverse" Discrimination, p. 43.

In short, the "*McDonnell Douglas* prima facie case" is an approach, not a set of elements. Further, since the purpose of the prima facie case is to eliminate at least some common nondiscriminatory reasons, the courts have often described the plaintiff's burden as very light, and they have stressed the importance of not shifting proof of pretext back into the prima facie case. *See Ruiz v. County of Rockland*, 609 F.3d 486 (2d Cir. 2010) (a defendant's claim of serious misconduct by the plaintiff does not bar his making out a prima facie case when his performance evaluations showed satisfactory work: "the step at which the court considers such evidence is important" because "no amount of evidence permits a plaintiff to overcome a failure to make out a prima facie case"); *Lake v. Yellow Transp., Inc.*, 596 F.3d 871, 874 (8th Cir. 2010) (a plaintiff is not required to disprove the asserted reason for firing him at the prima facie stage of the analysis since to do so would collapse the defendant's burden of production into the prima facie case). *Cf. Brady v. Office of the Sergeant at Arms*, 520 F.3d 490, 494 (D.C. Cir. 2008) (holding that district courts should not decide whether the plaintiff actually made out a *McDonnell Douglas* prima facie case in deciding an employer's motion for summary judgment or judgment as a matter of law once defendant has asserted a nondiscriminatory reason).

5. *The Prima Facie Case Does Not Shift the Burden of Persuasion.* While it may be easy to establish a prima facie case, a plaintiff does not get much reward for her efforts. The resulting "presumption" merely requires the employer to put into evidence its nondiscriminatory reason. In *Texas Department of Community Affairs v. Burdine*, 450 U.S. 248, 254 (1981), the Court described the consequences of proof of a prima facie case: "[i]f the trier of fact believes the plaintiff's evidence, and if the employer is silent in the face of the presumption, the court must enter judgment for the plaintiff because no issue of fact remains in the case." However, defendants *always* come up with some reason, and *Burdine* made clear that, when they do so, the presumption disappears (the "bubble bursts" as some Evidence sources describe it). Thus, only when an employer flunks a basic intelligence test and fails to put into evidence some explanation, will the plaintiff get judgment if the jury believes the evidence establishing the prima facie case.

In accompanying footnote 7, *Burdine* said the term "prima facie case" in *McDonnell Douglas* denoted "the establishment of a legally mandatory, rebuttable presumption," not a description of "the plaintiff's burden of producing enough evidence to permit the trier of fact to infer the fact at issue." *Id.* Isn't it odd that evidence could create a presumption of discrimination when it might not be enough to allow a jury to find that discrimination exists? While the distinction may seem subtle, it's incredibly important: since the prima facie case does not necessarily constitute a sufficient basis for the factfinder to infer discrimination, *proof of such a case does not mean that the plaintiff goes to the jury.* If *Burdine* had held the contrary, every Title VII case would warrant a jury trial when the plaintiff put in a prima facie case; the defendant's legitimate nondiscriminatory reason would, at most, give the jury a way to hold against the plaintiff. In fact, as we will see, getting to the jury turns less on the plaintiff's prima facie case than on the plaintiff's proof of pretext at the third step.

6. *The Second Step: Defendant's Easy Rebuttal.* The defendant may satisfy its burden of production to rebut a prima facie case by "articulat[ing] some legitimate, nondiscriminatory reason" for its action. *McDonnell Douglas* established that disloyalty is such a reason. But less rational or even illegal reasons also suffice. *See Biggins.* Suppose the court finds as a fact that Green was not rehired because he was a vegetarian? In *Purkett v. Elem,* 514 U.S. 765 (1995), a case dealing with peremptory challenges to jurors, the prosecutor explained its exclusion of several blacks because of their hair length and facial hair and not their race. The Supreme Court relied on Title VII analysis to indicate that even nonsensical explanations — "implausible," "silly," "fantastic," or "superstitious" — satisfied the defendant's burden of production. *Cf. Foster v. Chatman,* 136 S. Ct. 1737 (2016) (finding a state's explanations for striking two black prospective jurors motivated by discriminatory intent because of disparate treatment of other potential jurors as well as shifting explanations, misrepresentations of the record, and a persistent focus on race in documents in the prosecution's file). In *Forrester v. Rauland-Borg Corp.,* 453 F.3d 416, 418 (7th Cir. 2006), Judge Posner wrote: "the question is never whether the employer was mistaken, cruel, unethical, out of his head, or downright irrational in taking the action for the stated reason, but simply whether the stated reason *was* his reason: not a good reason, but a true reason."

7. *The Requirements for Defendant's Rebuttal Case.* Indeed, there are only two meaningful requirements for the defendant's rebuttal. First, the defendant must be able to put the reason into *evidence*; it is not enough to merely argue the possibility since the defendant has the burden of production. *See Burdine,* 450 U.S. at 254-55. Second, the defendant must provide a sufficiently specific reason to carry its burden of production. *See Alvarado v. Texas Rangers,* 492 F.3d 605 (5th Cir. 2007) (complete absence of explanation of criteria or basis for scores on interviews prevented employer from carrying its burden of production); *Iadimarco v. Runyon,* 190 F.3d 151, 166-67 (3d Cir. 1999) (to allow an assertion that the successful candidate was "the right person for the job" to rebut a prima facie case would be "tantamount to a judicial repeal of the very protections Congress intended under Title VII"). This specificity requirement can be drawn from footnote 8 of *Burdine,* where the Court described the purpose of the shifting burdens: "[i]n a Title VII case, the allocation of burdens and the creation of a presumption by the establishment of a prima facie case is intended progressively to sharpen the inquiry into the elusive factual question of intentional discrimination." 450 U.S. at 256 n.8.

8. *The Third Step: Proving Pretext.* A standard dictionary definition of "pretext" is "a reason given in justification of a course of action that is not the real reason." THE NEW OXFORD AMERICAN DICTIONARY 1350 (2001). Some lower courts, however, define "pretext" even more pointedly to mean that the defendant lied. For example, Judge Posner in *Forrester v. Rauland-Borg Corp.,* 453 F.3d 416, 419 (7th Cir. 2006), emphasized that evidence that the defendant's proffered reason was not factually correct was not necessarily probative of pretext because "[a] pretext is a deliberate falsehood. . . . An honest mistake, however dumb, is not."

A number of other courts have framed this in terms of an "honest belief" rule: the question is not whether the asserted reason is true but whether the defendant believed it to be true when it took the challenged action. *AT&T Corp.,* 422 F.3d 756, 762 (8th Cir. 2005) ("the proper inquiry is not whether AT&T was factually correct in determining that Johnson had made the bomb threats. Rather, the proper inquiry is whether AT&T honestly believed that Johnson had made the bomb threats").

Professor Katz agrees that proof of "pretext" requires proving that the defendant lied when it asserted its legitimate, nondiscriminatory reason, but he argues that a lie can be found from proof that the defendant's asserted reason was not true. Martin J. Katz, *Reclaiming* McDonnell Douglas, 83 Notre Dame L. Rev. 109, 122 n.56 (2007). This suggests that Posner is both right and wrong: a finding by the jury that the defendant's reason is not the real reason does not automatically justify a finding of pretext but would often (usually?) permit the inference that the defendant was lying by asserting it. Posner is wrong if he is insisting there must be evidence, separate from the evidence that the defendant's reason was not true, that the defendant lied about it being the reason. As we will soon see, this would resurrect in new language the "pretext-plus" rule repudiated in *Reeves v. Sanderson Plumbing Products, Inc.*, reproduced at p. 24.

Linda Hamilton Krieger and Susan T. Fiske, in *Behavioral Realism in Employment Discrimination Law: Implicit Bias and Disparate Treatment*, 94 Cal. L. Rev. 997, 1036 (2006), take a dramatically different approach to the whole truth-or-lie question. They criticize the "honest belief rule" as "plainly inconsistent with what empirical social psychologists have learned over the past twenty years about the manner in which stereotypes, functioning not as consciously held beliefs but as implicit expectancies, can cause a decisionmaker to discriminate against members of a stereotyped group." Thus, if acting on unconscious bias is nevertheless intentional discrimination, then the fact that the defendant acted on its "honest belief" is not determinative of whether there is discrimination. *See also* Natasha T. Martin, *Pretext in Peril*, 75 Mo. L. Rev. 313, 401 (2010).

9. *Pretext for Discrimination.* What about the possibility that the defendant lied, but not to conceal its discrimination? Suppose McDonnell Douglas's hiring officer did not rehire Green because he was saving the job for his nephew? The notion that the *McDonnell Douglas* proof structure was designed to progressively sharpen the inquiry might seem to require that a decision by the factfinder that the defendant lied mandates judgment for the plaintiff since, absent a remaining nondiscriminatory explanation in the record, a finding of discrimination seems mandated.

Despite that reasoning, the Supreme Court has held to the contrary. Proof of pretext, in the sense of proof that the defendant's asserted reason is not the real reason for the action is *not necessarily* sufficient to find for the plaintiff. Rather, the factfinder has to find both (1) the defendant's reason to be pretextual *and* (2) the pretext to be a cover-up for an underlying discriminatory motive. *St. Mary's Honor Center v. Hicks*, 509 U.S. 502, 511 (1993), held that "[t]he factfinder's disbelief of the reasons put forward by the defendant (particularly if disbelief is accompanied by a suspicion of mendacity) may, together with the elements of the prima facie case, suffice to show intentional discrimination. Thus, rejection of the defendant's proffered reasons will *permit* the trier of fact to infer the ultimate fact of intentional discrimination, and the Court of Appeals was correct when it noted that, upon such rejection, 'no additional proof of discrimination is *required*'" (emphasis added). However, *St. Mary's Honor Center* stressed that the factfinder must nevertheless find a discriminatory motivation. Another way to say it is that proof of pretext permits, but does not require, an inference of discriminatory intent.

10. *A Process of Elimination?* Professor Zimmer, drawing from *Teamsters*, has described *McDonnell Douglas* as a process of elimination: the plaintiff eliminates the most common legitimate nondiscriminatory reasons in proving his or her prima

*Pretext must be cover up for discrim. motive

facie case and then eliminates the defendant's asserted legitimate, nondiscriminatory reason. Since employers can be assumed to act for some reason, elimination of these reasons allows the factfinder to infer that discrimination is the remaining reason for its action. Michael J. Zimmer, *The New Discrimination Law*: Price Waterhouse *Is Dead, Whither* McDonnell Douglas?, 53 EMORY L.J. 1887, 1893-95 (2004). In *Furnco Constr. Corp. v. Waters*, 438 U.S. 567, 577 (1978), the Court wrote:

> A prima facie case under *McDonnell Douglas* raises an inference of discrimination only because we presume these acts, if otherwise unexplained, are more likely than not based on the consideration of impermissible factors. *See Teamsters v. United States.* And we are willing to presume this largely because we know from our experience that more often than not people do not act in a totally arbitrary manner, without any underlying reasons, especially in a business setting. Thus, when all legitimate reasons for rejecting an applicant have been eliminated as possible reasons for the employer's actions, it is more likely than not the employer, who we generally assume acts only with some reason, based his decision on an impermissible consideration such as race.

Indeed, Professor Corbett argues that "the *McDonnell Douglas* pretext proof structure is a thinly veiled version of res ipsa loquitur." William R. Corbett, *Unmasking a Pretext for Res Ipsa Loquitur: A Proposal to Let Employment Discrimination Speak for Itself*, 62 AM. U. L. REV. 447, 454-55 (2013).

Professor Martin Katz disagrees that *McDonnell Douglas* is a process of elimination, arguing that it does not depend on eliminating every reason other than discrimination. Rather, it is a process of proving causation by a chain of inferences. The defendant's nondiscriminatory reason is a target, which gives the plaintiff a chance to win if she can convince the factfinder, whether or not all possible nondiscriminatory reasons are eliminated, that "(1) the proffered reason was factually erroneous, (2) the error was a lie [not a mistake], (3) the lie was a cover-up, and (4) the cover-up was designed to conceal discrimination," not to conceal a benign or embarrassing reason such as nepotism. See Figure 1.1 on the next page for Katz's diagram of the process. *Reclaiming* McDonnell Douglas, 83 NOTRE DAME L. REV. at 129. Are the Zimmer and Katz positions so far apart? While it is logically possible that a nondiscriminatory motive explains the employer's action even if the "most common" reasons and the employer's supposed reason are eliminated, isn't it far less likely than a discriminatory motive in this setting? *See also* Martin Katz, *Unifying Disparate Treatment (Really)*, 59 HASTINGS L.J. 643 (2008).

11. *A Mixed-Motive or a But-For Case?* Green did not contest that he had engaged in the "stall-in" protesting the defendant's discrimination, and McDonnell Douglas claimed that was the reason for not rehiring him. That seems to establish one motivation of the employer beyond much doubt — it's hard to believe a factfinder would find it a complete lie. The question was whether, given Green's participation in the illegal protest (a legitimate nondiscriminatory reason), Green's race nevertheless was a factor in the defendant's not rehiring him. Even were the factfinder to find that Green's race partly motivated the employer's decision, was it the but-for reason for the defendant's action? As in *Biggins*, such a finding would not be precluded by another obvious reason (Green's protest activities), but it might be difficult to make given the strong non-racial motivation that existed. Michael J. Zimmer, A *Chain of Inferences Proving Discrimination*, 79 U. COLO. L. REV. 1243, 1257 (2008) (arguing against characterizing *McDonnell Douglas* cases as "single-motive" cases because "liability can be made out using the 'but-for' test even if some additional reason, such as the employer's explanation, played a role in its decision"). *See also* Peter Siegelman, *Protecting the*

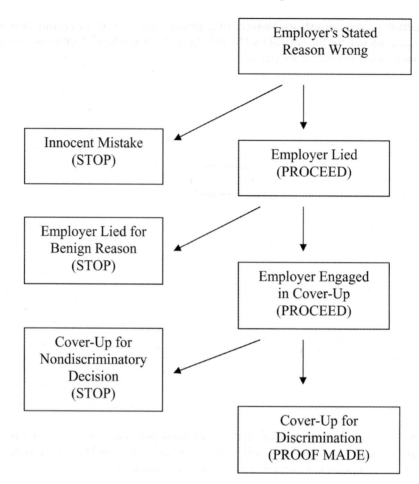

Figure 1.1.

Compromised Worker: A Challenge for Employment Discrimination Law, 64 Buff. L. Rev. 565 (2016).

12. *Retaliation.* Although *McDonnell Douglas* focuses on §703(a), the Court also noted that the plaintiff asserted a cause of action under §704(a), Title VII's antiretaliation provision. Didn't the defendant admit to discriminating against Green on the basis of his "opposition" conduct by asserting that the reason for not rehiring him was his participation in activities protesting its discrimination? We will examine that provision in Chapter 6, p. 407.

Pretext only
~~false~~ Rule

see pg 3̶0̶ 33

REEVES v. SANDERSON PLUMBING PRODUCTS, INC.
530 U.S. 133 (2000)

Justice O'Connor delivered the opinion of the Court.

This case concerns the kind and amount of evidence necessary to sustain a jury's verdict that an employer unlawfully discriminated on the basis of age. Specifically, we must resolve whether a defendant is entitled to judgment as a matter of law when the plaintiff's case consists exclusively of a prima facie case of discrimination and sufficient evidence for the trier of fact to disbelieve the defendant's legitimate, nondiscriminatory explanation for its action. . . .

Not Pretext

I

In October 1995, petitioner Roger Reeves was 57 years old and had spent 40 years in the employ of respondent, Sanderson Plumbing Products, Inc., a manufacturer of toilet seats and covers. Petitioner worked in a department known as the "Hinge Room," where he supervised the "regular line." Joe Oswalt, in his mid-thirties, supervised the Hinge Room's "special line," and Russell Caldwell, the manager of the Hinge Room and age 45, supervised both petitioner and Oswalt. Petitioner's responsibilities included recording the attendance and hours of those under his supervision, and reviewing a weekly report that listed the hours worked by each employee.

In the summer of 1995, Caldwell informed Powe Chesnut, the director of manufacturing and the husband of company president Sandra Sanderson, that "production was down" in the Hinge Room because employees were often absent and were "coming in late and leaving early." Because the monthly attendance reports did not indicate a problem, Chesnut ordered an audit of the Hinge Room's timesheets for July, August, and September of that year. According to Chesnut's testimony, that investigation revealed "numerous timekeeping errors and misrepresentations on the part of Caldwell, Reeves, and Oswalt." Following the audit, Chesnut, along with Dana Jester, vice president of human resources, and Tom Whitaker, vice president of operations, recommended to company president Sanderson that petitioner and Caldwell be fired. In October 1995, Sanderson followed the recommendation and discharged both petitioner and Caldwell.

At trial, respondent contended that it had fired petitioner due to his failure to maintain accurate attendance records, while petitioner attempted to demonstrate that respondent's explanation was pretext for age discrimination. Petitioner introduced evidence that he had accurately recorded the attendance and hours of the employees under his supervision, and that Chesnut, whom Oswalt described as wielding "absolute power" within the company had demonstrated age-based animus in his dealings with petitioner.

[The jury returned a verdict for Reeves of $35,000 in compensatory damages, which the judge doubled as "liquidated damages" pursuant to the jury's finding that the employer's age discrimination was "willful." The judge also awarded plaintiff $28,490.80 in front pay for two years' lost future income.]

The Court of Appeals for the Fifth Circuit reversed, holding that petitioner had not introduced sufficient evidence to sustain the jury's finding of unlawful discrimination. After noting respondent's proffered justification for petitioner's discharge, the court acknowledged that petitioner "very well may" have offered sufficient evidence for "a reasonable jury [to] have found that [respondent's] explanation for its employment decision was pretextual." The court explained, however, that this was "not dispositive" of the ultimate issue — namely, "whether Reeves presented sufficient evidence that his age motivated [respondent's] employment decision." Addressing this question, the court weighed petitioner's additional evidence of discrimination against other circumstances surrounding his discharge. Specifically, the court noted that Chesnut's age-based comments "were not made in the direct context of Reeves's termination"; there was no allegation that the two other individuals who had recommended that petitioner be fired (Jester and Whitaker) were motivated by age; two of the decision

Procedure

makers involved in petitioner's discharge (Jester and Sanderson) were over the age of 50; all three of the Hinge Room supervisors were accused of inaccurate record keeping; and several of respondent's management positions were filled by persons over age 50 when petitioner was fired. On this basis, the court concluded that petitioner had not introduced sufficient evidence for a rational jury to conclude that he had been discharged because of his age. . . .

II . . .

When a plaintiff alleges disparate treatment, "liability depends on whether the protected trait (under the ADEA, age) actually motivated the employer's decision." *Hazen Paper Co. v. Biggins.* That is, the plaintiff's age must have "actually played a role in [the employer's decisionmaking] process and had a determinative influence on the outcome." . . . [The Court assumed that the *McDonnell Douglas* framework, applicable to claims brought under §703(a)(1) of Title VII, also applied, and concluded that, under that framework, petitioner established a prima facie case and respondent rebutted it.] Although intermediate evidentiary burdens shift back and forth under this framework, "the ultimate burden of persuading the trier of fact that the defendant intentionally discriminated against the plaintiff remains at all times with the plaintiff." And in attempting to satisfy this burden, the plaintiff — once the employer produces sufficient evidence to support a nondiscriminatory explanation for its decision — must be afforded the "opportunity to prove by a preponderance of the evidence that the legitimate reasons offered by the defendant were not its true reasons, but were a pretext for discrimination." That is, the plaintiff may attempt to establish that he was the victim of intentional discrimination "by showing that the employer's proffered explanation is unworthy of credence." Moreover, although the presumption of discrimination "drops out of the picture" once the defendant meets its burden of production, the trier of fact may still consider the evidence establishing the plaintiff's prima facie case "and inferences properly drawn therefrom . . . on the issue of whether the defendant's explanation is pretextual."

In this case, the evidence supporting respondent's explanation for petitioner's discharge consisted primarily of testimony by Chesnut and Sanderson and documentation of petitioner's alleged "shoddy record keeping." Chesnut testified that a 1993 audit of Hinge Room operations revealed "a very lax assembly line" where employees were not adhering to general work rules. As a result of that audit, petitioner was placed on 90 days' probation for unsatisfactory performance. In 1995, Chesnut ordered another investigation of the Hinge Room, which, according to his testimony, revealed that petitioner was not correctly recording the absences and hours of employees. Respondent introduced summaries of that investigation documenting several attendance violations by 12 employees under petitioner's supervision, and noting that each should have been disciplined in some manner. Chesnut testified that this failure to discipline absent and late employees is "extremely important when you are dealing with a union" because uneven enforcement across departments would keep the company "in grievance and arbitration cases, which are costly, all the time." He and Sanderson also stated that petitioner's errors, by failing to adjust for hours not worked, cost the company overpaid wages. Sanderson testified that she accepted the recommendation to discharge petitioner because he had "intentionally falsified company pay records."

Petitioner, however, made a substantial showing that respondent's explanation was false. First, petitioner offered evidence that he had properly maintained the attendance records. Most of the timekeeping errors cited by respondent involved employees who were not marked late but who were recorded as having arrived at the plant at 7 A.M. for the 7 A.M. shift. Respondent contended that employees arriving at 7 A.M. could not have been at their workstations by 7 A.M., and therefore must have been late. But both petitioner and Oswalt testified that the company's automated timeclock often failed to scan employees' timecards, so that the timesheets would not record any time of arrival. On these occasions, petitioner and Oswalt would visually check the workstations and record whether the employees were present at the start of the shift. They stated that if an employee arrived promptly but the timesheet contained no time of arrival, they would reconcile the two by marking "7 A.M." as the employee's arrival time, even if the employee actually arrived at the plant earlier. On cross-examination, Chesnut acknowledged that the timeclock sometimes malfunctioned, and that if "people were there at their work stations" at the start of the shift, the supervisor "would write in seven o'clock." Petitioner also testified that when employees arrived before or stayed after their shifts, he would assign them additional work so they would not be overpaid.

Petitioner similarly cast doubt on whether he was responsible for any failure to discipline late and absent employees. Petitioner testified that his job only included reviewing the daily and weekly attendance reports, and that disciplinary write-ups were based on the monthly reports, which were reviewed by Caldwell. Sanderson admitted that Caldwell, and not petitioner, was responsible for citing employees for violations of the company's attendance policy. Further, Chesnut conceded that there had never been a union grievance or employee complaint arising from petitioner's record keeping, and that the company had never calculated the amount of overpayments allegedly attributable to petitioner's errors. Petitioner also testified that, on the day he was fired, Chesnut said that his discharge was due to his failure to report as absent one employee, Gina Mae Coley, on two days in September 1995. But petitioner explained that he had spent those days in the hospital, and that Caldwell was therefore responsible for any overpayment of Coley. Finally, petitioner stated that on previous occasions that employees were paid for hours they had not worked, the company had simply adjusted those employees' next paychecks to correct the errors.

Based on this evidence, the Court of Appeals concluded that petitioner "very well may be correct" that "a reasonable jury could have found that [respondent's] explanation for its employment decision was pretextual." Nonetheless, the court held that this showing, standing alone, was insufficient to sustain the jury's finding of liability: "We must, as an essential final step, determine whether Reeves presented sufficient evidence that his age motivated [respondent's] employment decision." And in making this determination, the Court of Appeals ignored the evidence supporting petitioner's prima facie case and challenging respondent's explanation for its decision. The court confined its review of evidence favoring petitioner to that evidence showing that Chesnut had directed derogatory, age-based comments at petitioner, and that Chesnut had singled out petitioner for harsher treatment than younger employees. It is therefore apparent that the court believed that only this additional evidence of discrimination was relevant to whether the jury's verdict should stand. That is, the Court of Appeals proceeded from the assumption that a prima facie case of discrimination, combined with sufficient evidence for the trier of fact to disbelieve the defendant's legitimate, nondiscriminatory reason for its decision, is insufficient as a matter of law to sustain a jury's finding of intentional discrimination.

In so reasoning, the Court of Appeals misconceived the evidentiary burden borne by plaintiffs who attempt to prove intentional discrimination through indirect evidence. This much is evident from our decision in *St. Mary's Honor Center* [*v. Hicks*, 509 U.S. 502 (1993)]. There we held that the factfinder's rejection of the employer's legitimate, nondiscriminatory reason for its action does not compel judgment for the plaintiff. The ultimate question is whether the employer intentionally discriminated, and proof that "the employer's proffered reason is unpersuasive, or even obviously contrived, does not necessarily establish that the plaintiff's proffered reason . . . is correct." In other words, "it is not enough . . . to disbelieve the employer; the factfinder must believe the plaintiff's explanation of intentional discrimination."

In reaching this conclusion, however, we reasoned that it is permissible for the trier of fact to infer the ultimate fact of discrimination from the falsity of the employer's explanation. Specifically, we stated:

> The factfinder's disbelief of the reasons put forward by the defendant (particularly if disbelief is accompanied by a suspicion of mendacity) may, together with the elements of the prima facie case, suffice to show intentional discrimination. Thus, rejection of the defendant's proffered reasons will permit the trier of fact to infer the ultimate fact of intentional discrimination.

Proof that the defendant's explanation is unworthy of credence is simply one form of circumstantial evidence that is probative of intentional discrimination, and it may be quite persuasive. [*St. Mary's Honor Center.*] ("Proving the employer's reason false becomes part of (and often considerably assists) the greater enterprise of proving that the real reason was intentional discrimination"). In appropriate circumstances, the trier of fact can reasonably infer from the falsity of the explanation that the employer is dissembling to cover up a discriminatory purpose. Such an inference is consistent with the general principle of evidence law that the factfinder is entitled to consider a party's dishonesty about a material fact as "affirmative evidence of guilt." *Wright v. West*, 505 U.S. 277 (1992); 2 J. WIGMORE, EVIDENCE §278(2), p. 133 (J. Chadbourn rev. ed. 1979). Moreover, once the employer's justification has been eliminated, discrimination may well be the most likely alternative explanation, especially since the employer is in the best position to put forth the actual reason for its decision. *Cf. Furnco Constr. Corp. v. Waters*, 438 U.S. 567, 577 (1978) ("When all legitimate reasons for rejecting an applicant have been eliminated as possible reasons for the employer's actions, it is more likely than not the employer, who we generally assume acts with some reason, based his decision on an impermissible consideration"). Thus, a plaintiff's prima facie case, combined with sufficient evidence to find that the employer's asserted justification is false, may permit the trier of fact to conclude that the employer unlawfully discriminated.

This is not to say that such a showing by the plaintiff will always be adequate to sustain a jury's finding of liability. Certainly there will be instances where, although the plaintiff has established a prima facie case and set forth sufficient evidence to reject the defendant's explanation, no rational factfinder could conclude that the action was discriminatory. For instance, an employer would be entitled to judgment as a matter of law if the record conclusively revealed some other, nondiscriminatory reason for the employer's decision, or if the plaintiff created only a weak issue of fact as to whether the employer's reason was untrue and there was abundant and uncontroverted independent evidence that no discrimination had occurred. To hold otherwise would be effectively to insulate an entire category of employment discrimination cases from review under Rule 50, and we have reiterated that trial courts should not "'treat discrimination differently from other ultimate questions of fact.'" *St. Mary's Honor Center.*

Whether judgment as a matter of law is appropriate in any particular case will depend on a number of factors. Those include the strength of the plaintiff's prima facie case, the probative value of the proof that the employer's explanation is false, and any other evidence that supports the employer's case and that properly may be considered on a motion for judgment as a matter of law. For purposes of this case, we need not — and could not — resolve all of the circumstances in which such factors would entitle an employer to judgment as a matter of law. It suffices to say that, because a prima facie case and sufficient evidence to reject the employer's explanation may permit a finding of liability, the Court of Appeals erred in proceeding from the premise that a plaintiff must always introduce additional, independent evidence of discrimination.

Reversal of CAA holding re burden of p re burden

III

A

The remaining question is whether, despite the Court of Appeals' misconception of petitioner's evidentiary burden, respondent was nonetheless entitled to judgment as a matter of law. Under Rule 50, a court should render judgment as a matter of law when "a party has been fully heard on an issue and there is no legally sufficient evidentiary basis for a reasonable jury to find for that party on that issue." . . .

[In entertaining a motion for judgment as a matter of law, the court should review all of the evidence in the record.] In doing so, however, the court must draw all reasonable inferences in favor of the nonmoving party, and it may not make credibility determinations or weigh the evidence. . . . That is, the court should give credence to the evidence favoring the non-movant as well as that "evidence supporting the moving party that is uncontradicted and unimpeached, at least to the extent that that evidence comes from disinterested witnesses."

B

Applying this standard here, it is apparent that respondent was not entitled to judgment as a matter of law. In this case, in addition to establishing a prima facie case of discrimination and creating a jury issue as to the falsity of the employer's explanation, petitioner introduced additional evidence that Chesnut was motivated by age-based animus and was principally responsible for petitioner's firing. Petitioner testified that Chesnut had told him that he "was so old [he] must have come over on the Mayflower" and, on one occasion when petitioner was having difficulty starting a machine, that he "was too damn old to do [his] job." According to petitioner, Chesnut would regularly "cuss at me and shake his finger in my face." Oswalt, roughly 24 years younger than petitioner, corroborated that there was an "obvious difference" in how Chesnut treated them. He stated that, although he and Chesnut "had [their] differences," "it was nothing compared to the way [Chesnut] treated Roger." Oswalt explained that Chesnut "tolerated quite a bit" from him even though he "defied" Chesnut "quite often," but that Chesnut treated petitioner "in a manner, as you would . . . treat . . . a child when . . . you're angry with [him]." Petitioner also demonstrated that, according to company records, he and Oswalt had nearly identical rates of productivity in 1993. Yet respondent conducted an efficiency study of only the regular line, supervised by petitioner, and placed only petitioner on probation. Chesnut conducted that efficiency study and, after having testified to the contrary on direct examination, acknowledged on cross-examination that he had recommended that petitioner be placed on probation following the study.

evidence corroborating age discrimination animus

Further, petitioner introduced evidence that Chesnut was the actual decision-maker behind his firing. Chesnut was married to Sanderson, who made the formal decision to discharge petitioner. Although Sanderson testified that she fired petitioner because he had "intentionally falsified company pay records," respondent only introduced evidence concerning the inaccuracy of the records, not their falsification. A 1994 letter authored by Chesnut indicated that he berated other company directors, who were supposedly his co-equals, about how to do their jobs. Moreover, Oswalt testified that all of respondent's employees feared Chesnut, and that Chesnut had exercised "absolute power" within the company for "as long as [he] can remember."

In holding that the record contained insufficient evidence to sustain the jury's verdict, the Court of Appeals misapplied the standard of review dictated by Rule 50. Again, the court disregarded critical evidence favorable to petitioner — namely, the evidence supporting petitioner's prima facie case and undermining respondent's non-discriminatory explanation. The court also failed to draw all reasonable inferences in favor of petitioner. For instance, while acknowledging "the potentially damning nature" of Chesnut's age-related comments, the court discounted them on the ground that they "were not made in the direct context of Reeves's termination." And the court discredited petitioner's evidence that Chesnut was the actual decisionmaker by giving weight to the fact that there was "no evidence to suggest that any of the other decisionmakers were motivated by age." Moreover, the other evidence on which the court relied — that Caldwell and Oswalt were also cited for poor record keeping, and that respondent employed many managers over age 50 — although relevant, is certainly not dispositive. In concluding that these circumstances so overwhelmed the evidence favoring petitioner that no rational trier of fact could have found that petitioner was fired because of his age, the Court of Appeals impermissibly substituted its judgment concerning the weight of the evidence for the jury's.

The ultimate question in every employment discrimination case involving a claim of disparate treatment is whether the plaintiff was the victim of intentional discrimination. . . . The District Court plainly informed the jury that petitioner was required to show "by a preponderance of the evidence that his age was a determining and motivating factor in the decision of [respondent] to terminate him." The court instructed the jury that, to show that respondent's explanation was a pretext for discrimination, petitioner had to demonstrate "1, that the stated reasons were not the real reasons for [petitioner's] discharge; and 2, that age discrimination was the real reason for [petitioner's] discharge." Given that petitioner established a prima facie case of discrimination, introduced enough evidence for the jury to reject respondent's explanation, and produced additional evidence of age-based animus, there was sufficient evidence for the jury to find that respondent had intentionally discriminated. The District Court was therefore correct to submit the case to the jury, and the Court of Appeals erred in overturning its verdict.

NOTES

1. *The Significance of* Reeves. It is hard to overestimate the significance of *Reeves*, which makes three important points. First, discrimination is a question of fact to be based on all the evidence in the record and the inferences that can be drawn from that evidence. Second, as part of that holistic viewpoint, ageist comments that did not qualify as "direct" evidence (because not directly related to the challenged decision) nevertheless could support drawing the inference of discrimination. Third, the

Court rejected the so-called pretext-plus rule that, to prevail, plaintiff had to adduce evidence over and above the prima facie case and prove that supposed nondiscriminatory reason was pretextual.

2. *It's All Pretext*. Given that the Court was reviewing a judgment as a matter of law, the three steps of *McDonnell Douglas* were less important than the ultimate question of whether a reasonable jury could find discrimination on the basis of all the evidence submitted. While cases might start as three-step *McDonnell Douglas* cases, given the ease with which the two parties can carry their step one and step two burdens, they tend to end up, like *Reeves*, as pretext cases. And the Court makes clear that, in deciding whether the defendant discriminated, it is necessary to look at all the evidence, regardless of what step in the analysis it arrived.

Looking at all the evidence favoring plaintiff, Justice O'Connor relied on the ageist comments as evidence of discriminatory motive both in its sense of admissions and acting on age stereotypes. Lower courts have since found "stray comments," that is, comments indicating bias but not made in the context of the decision at issue, to be probative of discrimination. *E.g., Gorence v. Eagle Food Ctrs., Inc.*, 242 F.3d 759, 763 (7th Cir. 2001) ("evidence of inappropriate remarks not shown to be directly related to the employment decision may not support a direct-method-of-proof case, but might support a case under *McDonnell Douglas*"); *Fisher v. Pharmacia & Upjohn*, 225 F.3d 915, 922 (8th Cir. 2000) ("Stray remarks therefore constitute circumstantial evidence of age discrimination"). There was also testimony in *Reeves* that Chesnut changed his tune when his original reason for terminating Reeves proved untenable: Reeves had been in the hospital and not at work when his alleged infractions occurred. Finally, the Court discusses the testimony of Reeve's co-worker, Oswalt, as supporting an unequal treatment claim as well as showing that Chesnut was out to get Reeves.

3. *Rejecting the Lower Court's "Direct" Evidence Rule*. The lower court in *Reeves* had viewed the comments regarding Reeves's age as essentially irrelevant because they were not "direct evidence" of discrimination. We'll explore the significance of "direct evidence" later in this chapter, see Note 5, p. 74, but for the moment assume it means something like statements by the decisionmaker in the context of the decision that manifest bias. Think Pohasky. The Supreme Court, however, viewed the evidence of Chesnut's ageist remarks to be probative circumstantial evidence supporting drawing the inference of discrimination. Of course, the probative strength varies along several axes, including whether it was said by the decisionmaker, how close to the decision it was uttered, and how clearly it evinces bias. *See Reed v. Neopost USA, Inc.*, 701 F.3d 434, 441 (5th Cir. 2012) (distinguishing different standards for the use of biased remarks as "direct evidence" and as circumstantial evidence).

4. *Inferring Discrimination*. In *O'Connor v. Consolidated Coin Caterers Corp.*, 517 U.S. 308, 311-12 (1996), the Court brought some clarity to when age differences may be suggestive of discrimination. There a 56-year-old plaintiff had been replaced by someone over 40 and therefore in the same protected group as plaintiff:

> As the very name "prima facie case" suggests, there must be at least a logical connection between each element of the prima facie case and the illegal discrimination for which it establishes a "legally mandatory, rebuttable presumption." The element of replacement by someone under 40 fails this requirement. The discrimination prohibited by the ADEA is discrimination "because of [an] individual's age," though the prohibition is "limited to individuals who are at least 40 years of age." This language does not ban discrimination because they are aged 40 or over; it bans discrimination against employees because of their age, but limits the protected class to those who are 40 or older. The fact that one person in the protected class has lost out to another person in the protected

class is thus irrelevant, so long as he has lost out because of his age. Or to put the point more concretely, there can be no greater inference of age discrimination (as opposed to "40 or over" discrimination) when a 40 year-old is replaced by a 39 year-old than when a 56 year-old is replaced by a 40 year-old.

The Court went on to deal with the hypotheticals of a 68-year-old replaced by a 65-year-old and a 40-year-old replaced by a 39-year-old and indicated that it would not be proper to draw an inference of discrimination in either case. An inference of age discrimination "cannot be drawn from the replacement of one worker with another worker insignificantly younger. Because the ADEA prohibits discrimination on the basis of age and not class membership, the fact that a replacement is substantially younger than the plaintiff is a far more reliable indicator of age discrimination than is the fact that the plaintiff was replaced by someone outside the protected class." 517 U.S. at 313. Presumably, as the difference in ages between the two workers increases, so does the reasonableness of drawing the inference that age was a factor in the decisionmaking. See p. 90.

5. *Rejecting the "Pretext-Plus" Rule.* In *St. Mary's Honor Center v. Hicks,* the Court held that a plaintiff was not entitled to judgment as a matter of law merely because the factfinder determined that the defendant's asserted nondiscriminatory reason was false. Rather, the plaintiff could prevail only if the trier of fact made the further finding on the ultimate question of whether the defendant discriminated against the plaintiff. There the plaintiff, an African American supervisor at a correctional facility, was discharged after a new management team took over the facility. At the rebuttal stage of *McDonnell Douglas,* the defendant asserted that Hicks had been discharged because of rules violations, but the trial judge not only found these reasons not the real reason but also found that the plaintiff failed to prove that race was the determining factor in his discharge: "although plaintiff has proven a crusade to terminate him, he has not proven that the crusade was racially rather than personally motivated." In short, the judge found that personal animosity, not race, motivated the supervisor.

What was disconcerting about this was that the only evidence relating to personal hostility between plaintiff and his new supervisor was the *denial* by the supervisor of any such hostility. From a doctrinal perspective, the litigation process had not narrowed the dispute to whether the defendant's asserted reason or discrimination motivated the defendant's action; rather, the judge found for the defendant based on the conclusion, not supported, and even controverted, by the evidence in the record, that the defendant was motivated by personal hostility and therefore not by race. The court of appeals, concluding that asserting reasons that were not true was the equivalent of not offering any reason at all (which, under *McDonnell Douglas* would require a judgment for the plaintiff), held that the plaintiff was entitled to judgment as a matter of law.

The Supreme Court reversed, reinstating the trial judge's dismissal, holding that a judgment for the plaintiff must rest on an affirmative finding of discrimination. That was because the presumption of discrimination arising from the establishment of a prima facie case simply disappears once the defendant carries its burden of production, and the trier of fact must still "decide the ultimate question" — whether plaintiff has proven discrimination because of race. *Id.* at 511.

Although this language requires a finding of discrimination, not merely a finding of pretext in the sense that the defendant's reason was untrue, it seemed very clearly to allow the factfinder to infer discrimination based on finding the defendant's asserted reason to be false. Despite that, some courts read *Hicks* as adopting a "pretext-plus" rule, which required the plaintiff to introduce *additional* evidence of discrimination, even if she had established a prima facie case and shown that the defendant's reason was not true. *Reeves* laid any such view to rest, essentially establishing a "pretext only" rule under which the plaintiff has the burden of proving a prima facie case and the burden of proving the defendant's asserted reason to be a pretext for discrimination. That should usually be sufficient because, as the Court says, "a plaintiff's prima facie case, combined with sufficient evidence to find that the employer's asserted justification is false, may permit the trier of fact to conclude that the employer unlawfully discriminated." *See Griffin v. Finkbeiner*, 689 F.3d 584 (6th Cir. 2012) (error to require plaintiff to adduce evidence in addition to the prima facie case and pretext to avoid summary judgment).

6. *The Plausibility of Alternative Explanations.* While a showing that a reason is "mistaken, ill-considered or foolish," *Millbrook v. IBP, Inc.*, 280 F.3d 1169, 1175 (7th Cir. 2002) (2-1), is not per se proof of discrimination, it certainly raises the possibility, and therefore may permit the inference that discrimination is at work. Another way to say this is that a jury confronted with a choice between the possibility of a defendant acting on some irrational (but nondiscriminatory) basis and its acting from bias might be permitted to find the former but certainly should be allowed to find the latter. Employers, after all, should not be viewed as likely to act irrationally. The same should be true when the employer claims to have made a mistake. Again, that would be, as a matter of law, a good defense to a charge of discrimination but, as a matter of fact, the jury should be permitted to determine whether an employer indeed made a mistake or discriminated. And the less reasonable the mistake, the more likely the inference of discrimination. *See DeJesus v. WP Co. LLC*, 841 F.3d 527, 535 (D.C. Cir. 2016) (a jury could find a supervisor's interpretation of plaintiff's actions as insubordination to be "so unreasonable that it could not be honestly held"); *Latowski v. Northwoods Nursing Ctr.*, 549 F. App'x 478, 484 (6th Cir. 2013) (while "a policy is not necessarily pretext for discrimination merely because we find it ill-advised," an unreasonable decision might suggest discriminatory motivation).

But what about motivations that do not appear to advance the employer's business interests at all yet are common human impulses? In *St. Mary's Honor Center*, the trial court found the adverse decision to be based on personal animosity, presumably an animosity the court believed to be totally unconnected with race. *See also Johnson v. Koppers, Inc.*, 726 F.3d 910, 915 (7th Cir. 2013) (even assuming a co-worker made a false report regarding plaintiff, there was no evidence it was racially motivated, given a long-standing dislike between the two). *See generally* Chad Derum & Karen Engle, *The Rise of the Personal Animosity Presumption in Title VII and the Return to "No Cause" Employment*, 81 Tex. L. Rev. 1177 (2003). Other courts have found decisions to be the result of the converse, favoritism, again presumably unconnected to race. *See* Ann C. McGinley, *The Emerging Cronyism Defense and Affirmative Action: A Critical Perspective on the Distinction Between Color-Blind and Race Conscious Decision Making Under Title VII*, 39 Ariz. L. Rev. 1003 (1997). Are these motivations common enough to be more likely explanations for decisions than discrimination?

NOTE ON LITIGATING INDIVIDUAL DISPARATE TREATMENT CASES

At this point, we pause in our discussion to note how the proof structures we have seen so far play out in terms of the litigation process.

Pleading. Obviously, the first step in any litigation is the filing of a complaint. While Title VII suits can be brought in either federal or state courts, we'll focus on federal courts, where there have been dramatic changes in pleading requirements. In *Swierkiewicz v. Sorema N.A.*, 534 U.S. 506 (2002), a unanimous Supreme Court applied a highly permissive "notice pleading" standard in analyzing complaints under Fed. R. Civ. P. 8(a) in response to a Rule 12(b)(6) motion to dismiss for "failure to state a claim upon which relief can be granted." The Court rejected any requirement that a plaintiff plead even the four prongs of a prima facie case under *McDonnell Douglas* because "the prima facie case relates to the employee's burden of presenting evidence that raises an inference of discrimination" and does not "apply to the pleading standard that plaintiffs must satisfy in order to survive a motion to dismiss." *Id.* at 511. One lower court colorfully summarized *Swierkiewicz*'s mandate: "Because racial discrimination in employment is 'a claim upon which relief can be granted,' this complaint could not be dismissed under Rule 12(b)(6). 'I was turned down for a job because of my race' is all a complaint has to say." *Bennett v. Schmidt*, 153 F.3d 516, 518 (7th Cir. 1998). That may be a bit of an overstatement (the complaint might well have to say what job and when in order to give the employer the requisite notice), but it does convey the permissiveness of notice pleading as it was traditionally conceived.

No longer. While the Court has denied requiring "heightened pleading," two landmark cases, *Bell Atl. Corp. v. Twombly*, 550 U.S. 544 (2007), and *Ashcroft v. Iqbal*, 556 U.S. 662 (2009), changed pleading standards dramatically. "To survive a motion to dismiss, a complaint must contain sufficient factual matter, accepted as true, to 'state a claim to relief that is plausible on its face.' A claim has facial plausibility when the plaintiff pleads factual content that allows the court to draw the reasonable inference that the defendant is liable for the misconduct alleged." *Id.* at 678. One could well ask whether a Title VII complaint has facial plausibility when it does not even plead a prima facie case. In other words, does *Swierkiewicz* survive plausible pleading? There are arguments both ways. *See McCleary-Evans v. Md. DOT*, 780 F.3d 582, 587-88 (4th Cir. 2015) (plaintiff's averments of discrimination were mere conclusions when she failed to allege either a prima facie case or other basis for inferring more than the possibility of discrimination); *Connelly v. Lane Constr. Corp.*, 809 F.3d 780, 791 (3d Cir. 2016) (at the pleading stage, plaintiff "is not obliged to choose whether she is proceeding under a mixed-motive or pretext theory, nor is she required to establish a prima facie case, much less to engage in the sort of burden-shifting rebuttal that *McDonnell Douglas* requires at a later stage in the proceedings").

Littlejohn v. City of New York, 795 F.3d 297, 310 (2d Cir. 2015), agreed that *Iqbal* applied to Title VII complaints but found it not to affect

> the benefit to plaintiffs pronounced in the *McDonnell Douglas* quartet. To the same extent that the *McDonnell Douglas* temporary presumption reduces the facts a plaintiff would need to *show* to defeat a motion for summary judgment prior to the defendant's furnishing of a non-discriminatory motivation, that presumption also reduces the facts needed to be *pleaded* under *Iqbal*. . . . The facts alleged must give plausible support to the reduced requirements that arise under *McDonnell Douglas* in the initial phase of a Title VII litigation. The facts required by *Iqbal* to be alleged in the complaint need not give plausible support to the ultimate question of whether the adverse employment action was attributable to discrimination. They need only give plausible support to a minimal inference of discriminatory motivation.

While this suggests that alleging a prima facie case will suffice, *Swierkiewicz* had not required that pleading, and it's unclear, even in the Second Circuit, what else might work. *See generally* Michael J. Zimmer, *Title VII's Last Hurrah: Can Discrimination*

Be Plausibly Pled?, 2014 U. CHI. LEGAL F. 19; Charles A. Sullivan, *Plausibly Pleading Employment Discrimination*, 52 WM. & MARY L. REV. 1613 (2011); Joseph A. Seiner, *After* Iqbal, 45 WAKE FOREST L. REV. 179, 194 (2010); Joseph A. Seiner, *Pleading Disability*, 51 B.C. L. REV. 95 (2010); Suzette M. Malveaux, *Front Loading and Heavy Lifting: How Pre-Dismissal Discovery Can Address the Detrimental Effect of* Iqbal *on Civil Rights Cases*, 14 LEWIS & CLARK L. REV. 65, 82 (2010); Suja A. Thomas, *The New Summary Judgment Motion: The Motion to Dismiss Under* Iqbal *and* Twombly, 14 LEWIS & CLARK L. REV. 15 (2010); Joseph A. Seiner, *The Trouble with* Twombly: *A Proposed Pleading Standard for Employment Discrimination Cases*, 2009 U. ILL. L. REV. 101.

Judgment as a Matter of Law. Under the Federal Rules, a court may enter judgment as a matter of law against a plaintiff at any of several points. The standard is always the same — whether, under the facts, a party is entitled by the governing legal principles to a judgment. When there is "a genuine dispute as to any material fact," no such judgment is appropriate and a trial is necessary. Despite the identity of the underlying issue, the point in the proceedings at which the question arises can be critical. There are basically three stages where a defendant may seek judgment as a matter of law: first, at summary judgment under Rule 56; second, after the plaintiff rests (traditionally called "directed verdict,") under Rule 50(a); and, third, after a jury verdict under Rule 50(b) (now called a "renewed judgment as a matter of law" but traditionally referred to as "jnov" or judgment notwithstanding the verdict). *Reeves* is an example, although the Court reversed the jnov. In the first two situations, the court decides whether a hypothetical reasonable jury *could* reach a verdict for plaintiff and, in the latter, whether the verdict the actual jury handed down could be reached by a reasonable jury. Notice that, at summary judgment, the court is predicting what a hypothetical trial would look like on the basis of the parties' submissions; in the other two instances, the court is not forecasting what the proof will be but rather looking to the evidence actually admitted.

Summary judgment under Rule 56(b) of the Federal Rules is commonly granted to defendants in antidiscrimination cases and almost always turns on whether a reasonable jury could find the defendant's asserted nondiscriminatory reason to be a pretext for discrimination under *McDonnell Douglas. See generally* Henry L. Chambers, Jr., *Recapturing Summary Adjudication Principles in Disparate Treatment Cases*, 58 SMU L. REV. 103 (2005); Ann C. McGinley, *Credulous Courts and the Tortured Trilogy: The Improper Use of Summary Judgment in Title VII and ADEA Cases*, 34 B.C. L. REV. 203, 210 (1993).

Although jury trials have been the rule for Title VII cases since 1991 (and existed for §1981 and the ADEA before that), cases may still be tried to a judge if no party demands a jury. In such cases, a judge's findings of fact are entitled to great deference and must be respected unless they are "clearly erroneous." *Anderson v. City of Bessemer City*, 470 U.S. 564 (1985). Similar deference is accorded to jury verdicts in the more common jury trial, but it is done under the "no reasonable jury" standard for judgment as a matter of law.

Increased use of jury trials introduced another complication for discrimination suits: what instructions should be given to the jury to decide the case? Having worked your way through the complexities of this chapter, you will probably not be surprised to learn that juries are not typically instructed in the exact *McDonnell Douglas* methodology. *E.g., Whittington v. Nordam Group Inc.*, 429 F.3d 986, 998 (10th Cir. 2005).

2. *Everyone Is Protected by Title VII*

Whites are protected under Title VII and §1981 of 42 USC

McDONALD v. SANTA FE TRAIL TRANSPORTATION CO.
427 U.S. 273 (1976)

Justice MARSHALL delivered the opinion of the Court.

. . . On September 26, 1970, petitioners, both white, and Charles Jackson, a Negro employee of Santa Fe, were jointly and severally charged with misappropriating 60 one-gallon cans of antifreeze which was part of a shipment Santa Fe was carrying for one of its customers. Six days later, petitioners were fired by Santa Fe, while Jackson was retained. . . .

[The plaintiffs sued their employer under both Title VII and §1981, but the district court dismissed the complaint because "the dismissal of white employees charged with misappropriating company property while not dismissing a similarly charged Negro employee" violated neither statute.]

II

Title VII

Holding

Title VII of the Civil Rights Act of 1964 prohibits the discharge of "any individual" because of "such individual's race." Its terms are not limited to discrimination against members of any particular race. Thus, although we were not there confronted with racial discrimination against whites, we described the Act in *Griggs v. Duke Power Co.* [reproduced at p. 167, as prohibiting "[d]iscriminatory preference for *any* [racial] group, *minority* or *majority*" (emphasis added).[6] Similarly the Equal Employment Opportunity Commission (EEOC), whose interpretations are entitled to great deference, has consistently interpreted Title VII to proscribe racial discrimination in private employment against whites on the same terms as racial discrimination against non-whites. . . . EEOC Decision No. 74-31, 7 FEP 1326, 1328, CCH EEOC Decisions ¶6404, p. 4084 (1973). This conclusion is in accord with uncontradicted legislative history to the effect that Title VII was intended to "cover white men and white women and all Americans," 110 Cong. Rec. 2578 (1964) (remarks of Rep. Celler), and create an "obligation not to discriminate against whites," *id.*, at 7218 (memorandum of Sen. Clark); *id.*, at 8912 (remarks of Sen. Williams). We therefore hold today that Title VII prohibits racial discrimination against the white petitioners in this case upon the same standards as would be applicable were they Negroes and Jackson white. . . .[8]

Respondents contend that, even though generally applicable to white persons, Title VII affords petitioners no protection in this case, because their dismissal was based upon their commission of a serious criminal offense against their employer. We think this argument is foreclosed by our decision in *McDonnell Douglas Corp. v. Green.* . . .

---

6. Our discussion in *McDonnell Douglas Corp. v. Green* of the means by which a Title VII litigant might make out a prima facie case of racial discrimination is not contrary. . . . As we particularly noted, however, this "specification . . . of the prima facie proof required . . . is not necessarily applicable in every respect to differing factual situations." Requirement (i) of this sample pattern of proof was set out only to demonstrate how the racial character of the discrimination could be established in the most common sort of case, and not as an indication of any substantive limitation of Title VII's prohibition of racial discrimination.

8. . . . Santa Fe disclaims that the actions challenged here were any part of an affirmative action program, and we emphasize that we do not consider here the permissibility of such a program, whether judicially required or otherwise prompted.

We find this case indistinguishable from *McDonnell Douglas*. Fairly read, the complaint asserted that petitioners were discharged for their alleged participation in a misappropriation of cargo entrusted to Santa Fe, but that a fellow employee, likewise implicated, was not so disciplined, and that the reason for the discrepancy in discipline was that the favored employee is Negro while petitioners are white.[11] While Santa Fe may decide that participation in a theft of cargo may render an employee unqualified for employment, this criterion must be "applied, alike to members of all races," and Title VII is violated if, as petitioners alleged, it was not.

We cannot accept respondents' argument that the principles of *McDonnell Douglas* are inapplicable where the discharge was based, as petitioners' complaint admitted, on participation in serious misconduct or crime directed against the employer. The Act prohibits all racial discrimination in employment, without exception for any group of particular employees, and while crime or other misconduct may be a legitimate basis for discharge, it is hardly one for racial discrimination. Indeed, the Title VII plaintiff in *McDonnell Douglas* had been convicted for a nontrivial offense against his former employer. It may be that theft of property entrusted to an employer for carriage is a more compelling basis for discharge than obstruction of an employer's traffic arteries, but this does not diminish the illogic in retaining guilty employees of one color while discharging those of another color. . . .

III

. . . We have previously held, where discrimination against Negroes was in question, that §1981 affords a federal remedy against discrimination in private employment on the basis of race, and respondents do not contend otherwise. *Johnson v. Railway Express Agency*, 421 U.S. 454 (1975). The question here is whether §1981 prohibits racial discrimination in private employment against whites as well as nonwhites.

While neither of the courts below elaborated its reasons for not applying §1981 to racial discrimination against white persons, respondents suggest two lines of argument to support that judgment. First, they argue that by operation of the phrase "as is enjoyed by white citizens," §1981 unambiguously limits itself to the protection of nonwhite persons against racial discrimination. Second, they contend that such a reading is consistent with the legislative history of the provision, which derives its operative language from §1 of the Civil Rights Act of 1866. The 1866 statute, they assert, was concerned predominantly with assuring specified civil rights to the former Negro slaves freed by virtue of the Thirteenth Amendment, and not at all with protecting the corresponding civil rights of white persons.

We find neither argument persuasive. Rather, our examination of the language and history of §1981 convinces us that §1981 is applicable to racial discrimination in private employment against white persons.

First, we cannot accept the view that the terms of §1981 exclude its application to racial discrimination against white persons. On the contrary, the statute explicitly

---

11. Santa Fe contends that petitioners were required to plead with "particularity" the degree of similarity between their culpability in the alleged theft and the involvement of the favored co-employee, Jackson. [But] precise equivalence in culpability between employees is not the ultimate question: as we indicated in *McDonnell Douglas*, an allegation that other "employees involved in acts against [the employer] of *comparable seriousness* . . . were nevertheless retained . . ." is adequate to plead an inferential case that the employer's reliance on his discharged employee's misconduct as grounds for terminating him was merely a pretext (emphasis added).

applies to "*all* persons" (emphasis added), including white persons. While a mechanical reading of the phrase "as is enjoyed by white citizens" would seem to lend support to respondents' reading of the statute, we have previously described this phrase simply as emphasizing "the racial character of the rights being protected." *Georgia v. Rachel*, 384 U.S. 780, 791 (1966). In any event, whatever ambiguity there may be in the language of §1981 is clarified by an examination of the legislative history of §1981's language as it was originally forged in the Civil Rights Act of 1866. It is to this subject that we now turn.

The bill ultimately enacted as the Civil Rights Act of 1866 was introduced by Senator Trumbull of Illinois as a "bill . . . to protect *all* persons in the United States in their civil rights. . . ." (emphasis added), and was initially described by him as applying to "every race and color." Cong. Globe, 39th Cong., 1st Sess., 211 (1866) (hereinafter Cong. Globe). Consistent with the views of its draftsmen, and the prevailing view in the Congress as to the reach of its powers under the enforcement section of the Thirteenth Amendment, the terms of the bill prohibited any racial discrimination in the making and enforcement of contracts against whites as well as nonwhites. . . .

While it is, of course, true that the immediate impetus for the bill was the necessity for further relief of the constitutionally emancipated former Negro slaves, the general discussion of the scope of the bill did not circumscribe its broad language to that limited goal. On the contrary, the bill was routinely viewed, by its opponents and supporters alike, as applying to the civil rights of whites as well as nonwhites. . . .

It is clear, thus, that the bill, as it passed the Senate, was not limited in scope to discrimination against nonwhites. Accordingly, respondents pitch their legislative history argument largely upon the House's amendment of the Senate bill to add the "as is enjoyed by white citizens" phrase. But the statutory history is equally clear that that phrase was not intended to have the effect of eliminating from the bill the prohibition of racial discrimination against whites. . . .

This cumulative evidence of congressional intent makes clear, we think, that the 1866 statute, designed to protect the "same right . . . to make and enforce contracts" of "citizens of every race and color" was not understood or intended to be reduced by Representative Wilson's amendment, or any other provision, to the protection solely of nonwhites. Rather, the Act was meant, by its broad terms, to proscribe discrimination in the making or enforcement of contracts against, or in favor of, any race. Unlikely as it might have appeared in 1866 that white citizens would encounter substantial racial discrimination of the sort proscribed under the Act, the statutory structure and legislative history persuade us that the 39th Congress was intent upon establishing in the federal law a broader principle than would have been necessary simply to meet the particular and immediate plight of the newly freed Negro slaves. And while the statutory language has been somewhat streamlined in re-enactment and codification, there is no indication that §1981 is intended to provide any less than the Congress enacted in 1866 regarding racial discrimination against white persons. Thus, we conclude that the District Court erred in dismissing petitioners' claims under §1981 on the ground that the protections of that provision are unavailable to white persons.

NOTES

1. *Meet §1981.* This is the first time we've encountered 42 U.S.C. §1981 in any detail, and we should note that, despite its Reconstruction origins, it was not generally thought to reach private conduct until *Johnson v. Railway Express Agency,* 421

U.S. 454 (1975), 10 years after Title VII became effective. The result is that "although related, and although directed to most of the same ends, [the two statutes] are separate, distinct, and independent" remedies for *race* discrimination in employment. *Id.* at 461. Nevertheless, the courts have generally read the substantive prohibitions of §1981 and Title VII to be identical. *See Patterson v. McLean Credit Union*, reproduced at p. 45 (applying the *McDonnell Douglas* approach in a §1981 case). We'll explore the meaning of "race" under §1981 in Note 5.

As compared to Title VII, §1981 has procedural advantages, which are explored in Chapter 8, including a generally longer statute of limitations and no requirement to file a charge with the EEOC. Section 1981 remedies also are broader than those available under Title VII, mostly due to the absence of a statutory cap on damages. See Chapter 9, p. 593. A third advantage of §1981 is that, unlike Title VII, its coverage is not expressly limited to employment, which means that discrimination against independent contractors is actionable. See Chapter 5B, p. 273. Indeed, it has also been held to bar racially motivated third party interference with a contract. *Moore v. Grady Mem'l Hosp. Corp.*, 834 F.3d 1168 (11th Cir. 2016) (a physician could premise a §1981 claim hospital's interference by a hospital with his employment contract with a medical school by restricting his privileges at the hospital).

2. *Good Cause vs. At-Will.* After *Santa Fe*, it is clear that whites are protected against race discrimination under both Title VII and §1981. It is equally clear that men are protected against sex discrimination in employment under Title VII. *Slack, McDonnell Douglas*, and *Santa Fe* all mean that *any* racial or gender motivation that results in an adverse employment action is unlawful. Indeed, the case makes clear that pervasive descriptions of "protected classes" under that statute are problematic. *See generally* Jessica A. Clarke, *Protected Class Gatekeeping*, 92 N.Y.U. L. Rev. 101 (2017) (requiring a focus on whether plaintiff is a member of a "protected class" is not based in Title VII's language and also distorts court decision across a variety of areas, including misperception and intersectional cases).

Doctrinally, that is quite a bit more limited than a general good cause standard. But from a risk management perspective, isn't it still a good idea for an employer to have a defensible reason for any significant employment action? After all, majority and minority men and all women are protected against discrimination, and beginning at 40, all workers are protected against age discrimination. Isn't the absence of a good reason risky because every employee can sue?

3. *Legitimate Nondiscriminatory Reason?* Surely Santa Fe had a nondiscriminatory reason for firing plaintiffs. The plaintiffs admitted participating in the thefts that the defendant claimed to be the basis for their discharge, yet the Court finds the case "indistinguishable from *McDonnell Douglas*" — there was a good reason for discharge in both cases. Given their admitted theft, how could the defendant's acting on that be a "pretext" for discrimination? Is *Santa Fe* really a mixed-motives case, with good reasons and bad reasons intertwined?

How would you frame the proof structure in *Santa Fe*? One could try to shoehorn it into *McDonnell Douglas*'s four requirements for a prima facie case, but isn't a more straightforward way to describe *Santa Fe* as an unequal treatment case? "It may be that theft of property entrusted to an employer for carriage is a . . . compelling basis for discharge . . . but this does not diminish the illogic in retaining guilty employees of one color while discharging those of another color." As in *Slack*, the unequal treatment is powerful evidence to establish liability. If you represented the defendant, what evidence would you look for to rebut plaintiffs' prima facie case? The best would be evidence that the black co-worker had not been involved in the theft. Then the decision is a guilt/innocence one, not a black/white one. Even if the black co-worker participated in the theft, maybe another non-racial difference might be past conduct: if the plaintiffs had long records of disciplinary actions against them but this was the black worker's first offense, the racial motivation might be undercut. Does this all take us back to *McDonnell Douglas*'s three-part approach: the apparent unequal treatment gives rise to a presumption of discrimination, which can be rebutted by a non-racial explanation, which, in turn, can be proven to be pretext?

4. *Comparator Cases.* Another way to view cases like *Santa Fe* is as literally "disparate treatment" cases: a plaintiff prevails by proving that she was treated differently than a "comparator" (a similarly situated person of the other sex or a different race). And that difference in treatment supports the inference that the different treatment was because of race. Most lower courts try to frame the analysis in *McDonnell Douglas* terms rather than as straightforward unequal treatment; under this approach, the similarities establish the prima facie case and the asserted differences between plaintiff and the comparator are the nondiscriminatory reasons that plaintiff must prove to be pretext. *See Baker v. Macon Rest., Inc.*, 750 F.3d 674 (7th Cir. 2014). But can it be argued that the difference in treatment of a sufficiently close comparator is enough to infer discrimination?

In any event, the problem is less the label than how close a comparator must be in order to count. Some lower courts seem to require the comparator to be "nearly identical" to the plaintiff, *e.g.*, *Castillo v. Roche Labs., Inc.*, 467 F. App'x 859, 862 (11th Cir. 2012) ("To prevent courts from second-guessing employers' reasonable decisions and confusing apples with oranges, the quantity and quality of the comparator's misconduct must be nearly identical"); *Lee v. Kan. City S. Ry. Co.*, 574 F.3d 253, 260 (5th Cir. 2009) (the plaintiff's conduct "must have been 'nearly identical' to that of the proffered comparator"). However, *Crawford v. Indiana Harbor Belt R.R. Co.*, 461 F.3d 844, 846 (7th Cir. 2006), disapproved of a trend "to require closer and closer comparability between the plaintiff and the members of the comparison group." Rather, "the plaintiff should have to show only that the members of the comparison group are sufficiently comparable to her to suggest that she was singled out for worse treatment."

[handwritten margin note: should consider characterized who reported the misconduct— was a minority's conduct defined in worse terms?]

The cases that require the same supervisor may make more sense than others requiring near identity precisely because they focus on the intent of the individual decisionmaker. The argument is that supervisor A's intent can't be inferred from what Supervisor B did. So if A thinks tardiness is a firing offense for an African American, the fact that B allows her white workers to be tardy does not prove that A had any discriminatory intent. This "me too" proof issue is treated in more detail in Note on Special Issues of Proof at p. 89. More detailed analyses of comparator proof are found in Charles A. Sullivan, *The Phoenix from the Ash: Proving Discrimination by Comparators*, 60 Ala. L. Rev. 191 (2009); Suzanne Goldberg, *Discrimination by Comparison*, 120 Yale L.J. 728 (2011).

5. *What Is "Race"?* It may seem odd to wait until this point in the course to ask what we mean by race, but it turns out that, however intuitive the meaning of the word, it has generated complications, especially under §1981 where the discrimination must be race-based to be actionable. The Supreme Court addressed the question in *Saint Francis College v. Al-Khazraji*, 481 U.S. 604 (1987), a suit by a United States citizen who had been born in Iraq and claimed that he was denied tenure at the college based on his Arab ancestry. The district court rejected his §1981 claim because Arabs are generally considered Caucasians. The Supreme Court reversed; it held Arabs to be a race, at least for purposes of §1981:

There is a common popular understanding that there are three major human races — Caucasoid, Mongoloid, and Negroid. Many modern biologists and anthropologists, however, criticize racial classifications as arbitrary and of little use in understanding the variability of human beings. It is said that genetically homogeneous populations do not exist and traits are not discontinuous between populations; therefore, a population can only be described in terms of relative frequencies of various traits. Clear-cut categories do not exist. The particular traits which have generally been chosen to characterize races have been criticized as having little biological significance. It has been found that differences between individuals of the same race are often greater than the differences between the "average" individuals of different races. These observations and others led some, but not all, scientists to conclude that racial classifications are for the most part sociopolitical, rather than biological, in nature. S. MOLNAR, HUMAN VARIATION (2d ed. 1983); S. GOULD, THE MISMEASURE OF MAN (1981); M. BANTON & J. HARWOOD, THE RACE CONCEPT (1975); A. MONTAGU, MAN'S MOST DANGEROUS MYTH (1974).

Id. at 610 n.4. Current scientific thinking on race, however, was ultimately irrelevant to the Court. Even if Arabs are now considered Caucasians, that was not the understanding in the nineteenth century when §1981 was enacted:

[Dictionaries commonly referred to race as a "continued series of descendants from a parent who is called the *stock*," "[t]he lineage of a family," or "descendants of a common ancestor."] The 1887 edition of Webster's expanded the definition somewhat: "The descendants of a common ancestor; a family, tribe, people or nation, believed or presumed to belong to the same stock." It was not until the 20th century that dictionaries began referring to the Caucasian, Mongolian and Negro races, or to race as involving divisions of mankind based upon different physical characteristics. Even so, modern dictionaries still include among the definitions of race as being "a family, tribe, people, or nation belonging to the same stock." Webster's Third New International Dictionary 1870 (1971); Webster's Ninth New Collegiate Dictionary 969 (Springfield, Mass. 1986).

Id. at 611. The Court noted references to "race" for groups such as Finns, gypsies, Basques, Hebrews, Scandinavians, Chinese, Mongolians, Spanish, and Anglo-Saxons. In this light, it concluded:

Congress intended to protect from discrimination identifiable classes of persons who are subjected to intentional discrimination solely because of their that Congress intended §1981 to forbid, whether or not it would be classified as racial in terms of modern scientific theory. The Court of Appeals was thus quite right in holding that §1981, "at a minimum," reaches discrimination against an individual "because he or she is genetically part of an ethnically and physiognomically distinctive sub-grouping of homo sapiens." It is clear from our holding, however, that a distinctive physiognomy is not essential to qualify for §1981 protection.

Id. at 613. *See also Shaare Tefila Congregation v. Cobb*, 481 U.S. 615, 617 (1987) (§1982 suit by a synagogue for defacement of its walls with anti-Semitic slogans permissible because, when §1982 was adopted, "Jews and Arabs were among the people then considered to be distinct races and hence within the protection of the statute"). This expansive definition of race has been applied in a variety of settings by the lower courts. *E.g.*, *Abdullahi v. Prada USA Corp.*, 520 F.3d 710, 712 (7th Cir. 2008) (Iranians within the "loose" meaning of race for §1981 purposes). *Pena-Rodriguez v. Colorado*, 137 S. Ct. 855, 863 (2017) (referring to anti-Hispanic statements in jury deliberations as "racial"). *Cf. Salas v. Wisconsin Dep't of Corrections*, 483 F.3d 913 (7th Cir. 2007) ("Hispanics" denotes a national origin).

Under Title VII, such questions are rarely important. Although the statute was enacted nearly a century after §1981 at a time when race had more or less its current meaning, Title VII also bars religious and national origin discrimination (although both can be justified by a bona fide occupational qualification, while race discrimination cannot). That means that, even if, say, discrimination against an Arab-American does not count as "race" bias it might be challenged as national origin or religious discrimination. Nevertheless, the increasing numbers of individuals of mixed races may pose challenges to application of traditional concepts. *See* Nancy Leong, *Judicial Erasure of Mixed-Race Discrimination*, 59 Am. U. L. Rev. 469 (2010).

6. *Colorism.* The question of what is "race" triggers a related inquiry: what is discrimination because of "color"? Section 1981, which is framed in terms of equal treatment with "whites," certainly implicates that question, and Title VII explicitly bars discrimination on account of color. §703(a). In many cases, color and race are perceived as synonymous, but a few cases have challenged discrimination based on darker skin, either by whites or lighter-skinned members of the plaintiff's own race. *See generally* Taunya Lovell Banks, *Colorism Among South Asians: Title VII and Skin Tone Discrimination*, 14 Wash. U. Global Stud. L. Rev. 665 (2015); Cynthia E. Nance, *The Continuing Significance of Color Under Title VII Forty Years After Its Passage*, 26 Berkeley J. Emp. & Lab. L. 435 (2005); Taunya Lovell Banks, *Colorism: A Darker Shade of Pale*, 47 UCLA L. Rev. 1705 (2000); Trina Jones, *Shades of Brown: The Law of Skin Color*, 49 Duke L.J. 1487 (2000). *See also* Tanya Katerí Hernández, *Latino Inter-Ethnic Employment Discrimination and the "Diversity" Defense*, Harv. C.R-C.L. L. Rev. 259 (2007) (exploring discrimination by some Latinos against others, whether on racial or national origin grounds).

7. *Intersectionalism.* A few cases have explored "intersectionality," that is, discrimination not because of one protected trait (such as race) but rather because two (such as race and sex) intersect. In *Lam v. University of Hawaii*, 40 F.3d 1551, 1562 (9th Cir. 1994), the court acknowledged that a claim brought by an Asian woman might be based upon multiple factors. *See also Shazor v. Prof'l Transit Mgmt.*, 744 F.3d 948, 958 (6th Cir. 2014) ("African American women are subjected to unique stereotypes that neither African American men nor white women must endure."). *See generally* Minna J. Kotkin, *Diversity and Discrimination: A Look at Complex Bias*, 50 Wm. & Mary L. Rev. 1439, 1440 (2009); Nicole Buonocore Porter, *Sex Plus Age Discrimination: Protecting Older Women Workers*, 81 Denv. U. L. Rev. 79 (2003). Rachel Kahn Best, Linda Hamilton Krieger, Lauren B. Edelman & Scott R. Eliason, *Multiple Disadvantages: An Empirical Test of Intersectionality Theory in EEO Litigation*, 5 Law & Soc'y Rev. 991 (2011); Jennifer Bennett Shinall, *The Substantially Impaired Sex: Uncovering the Gendered Nature of Disability Discrimination*, 101 Minn. L. Rev. 1099 (2017).

8. *Discrimination by Mistake.* Suppose a white applicant for employment is discriminated against because she is mistakenly perceived to be African American. Does she have a claim under Title VII? *See* D. Wendy Greene, *Categorically Black, White, or Wrong: "Misperception Discrimination" and the State of Title VII Protection*, 47 U. Mich. J.L. Reform 87 (2013); Angela Onwuachi-Willig & Mario L. Barnes, *By Any Other Name?: On Being "Regarded As" Black, and Why Title VII Should Apply Even If Lakisha and Jamal Are White*, 2005 Wis. L. Rev. 1283; Craig Robert Senn, *Perception over Reality: Extending the ADA's Concept of "Regarded as" Protection Under Federal Employment Discrimination Law*, 36 Fla. St. U. L. Rev. 827 (2009). Reconsider this question when you have read *EEOC v. Abercrombie & Fitch Stores*, reproduced at p. 369.

9. *Relationship-Based Race Discrimination.* In *Holcomb v. Iona College*, 521 F.3d 130 (2d Cir. 2008), the court found that discrimination because a white man was married to an African American woman was actionable under Title VII. *See also Ellis v. UPS, Inc.*, 523 F.3d 823, 828 (7th Cir. 2008) (applying an anti-fraternization policy more harshly to interracial associations than to intraracial ones would be actionable). In other words, discrimination on the bias of interracial association is also prohibited by the statute.

NOTE ON "REVERSE" DISCRIMINATION

Santa Fe makes clear that "reverse" discrimination is cognizable under both Title VII and §1981, although the affirmative action plan question, reserved in footnote 8 in *Santa Fe*, was resolved in favor of the voluntary use of some racial and gender preferences. See *Johnson v. Transportation Agency of Santa Clara County*, reproduced at p. 152. Thus, some racial preferences are permissible and some are not under those statutes, and, oddly enough, ad hoc discrimination seems actionable while more systemic preferences may not be. In any event, how does a white or male plaintiff make out a prima facie case? Where white plaintiffs were "minorities" in the institution or occupation where they sought work, *McDonnell Douglas* applies with little adjustment. *See Lincoln v. Board of Regents*, 697 F.2d 928 (11th Cir. 1983) (affirming judgment against a predominately black university in an action brought by a white faculty member). Similarly, the fact that African Americans are the decisionmakers may be an important factor in making out a prima facie case by a white plaintiff. *See Hague v. Thompson Distrib. Co.*, 436 F.3d 816, 822 (7th Cir. 2006) (white plaintiffs' proof that their black boss fired them and replaced them with blacks or left the position open was sufficient).

In some cases, of course, there is "direct evidence." *See Deets v. Massman Constr. Co.*, 811 F.3d 978 (7th Cir. 2016) (white construction worker who was told when laid off that the employer's "minority numbers" were too low produced direct evidence). But, absent that, where a white plaintiff challenges an employment decision by a white-dominated employer, it is difficult to draw the inference that the employer discriminated against whites, even where the most common, legitimate reasons for the decision are negated. This has led a number of courts to require that such a plaintiff show something more than a minority plaintiff or a woman would need to prove. A typical formulation is that, to establish a prima facie case, a reverse discrimination plaintiff must present evidence of "background circumstances" that establish that the defendant is that "unusual employer who discriminates against the majority." *Parker v. Balt. & Ohio R.R. Co.*, 652 F.2d 1012, 1017 (D.C. Cir. 1981). Most circuits continue to use the "background circumstances" label, but some view a wide range of circumstances as qualifying. *E.g.*, *Mastro v. Potomac Elec. Power Co.*, 447 F.3d 843, 852-53 (D.C. Cir. 2006) (a "nominally expired" consent decree was a background circumstance such that, when coupled with evidence that the employer was reluctant to discipline black workers, even for serious offenses, plaintiff stated a prima facie case); *Rudin v. Lincoln Land Cmty. College*, 420 F.3d 712, 722 (7th Cir. 2005) (evidence of LLCC's practice of inserting minorities into the interview pool plus an affirmative action plan sufficed).

Other courts have rejected the background circumstances test, although it is not clear whether they are really applying an undiluted *McDonnell Douglas* approach. In *Iadimarco v. Runyon*, 190 F.3d 151, 158 (3d Cir. 1999), the Third Circuit held that

[handwritten margin note: something more req. of white p to show prima facie for disc.]

a prima facie case of "reverse" discrimination requires that the plaintiff present sufficient evidence to allow a fact finder to conclude that the employer is treating some people less favorably than others based upon a trait that is protected under Title VII. But the court then held that this test was not satisfied by showing that the managers who made the decision plaintiff challenged were African American. Other circumstances, however, were sufficient to raise "material issues of fact as to whether the proffered explanation for not hiring him was a pretext for illegal discrimination." *Id.* at 167. Even in the Third Circuit, is it still harder for a white plaintiff than for an African American to make out a prima facie case?

Some courts find an affirmative action plan to assist a white plaintiff to establish discrimination. In *Bass v. Board of County Commissioners*, 256 F.3d 1095 (11th Cir. 2001), the court held that, where the employer does not seek to justify a decision as made pursuant to an affirmative action plan, a white plaintiff can prevail by showing both that the employer in fact relied on the plan in making the adverse decision and that the plan is invalid: "we hold that where there is an invalid affirmative action plan in effect relating to the employer's allegedly discriminatory actions, that plan constitutes direct evidence of discrimination if there is sufficient circumstantial evidence to permit a jury reasonably to conclude the employer acted pursuant to the plan when it took the employment actions in question." *Id.* at 1111. *See also Humphries v. Pulaski County Special Sch. Dist.*, 580 F.3d 688, 694 (8th Cir. 2009) (evidence that an employer followed an affirmative action plan in a consent decree in taking a challenged adverse employment action "may constitute direct evidence of unlawful discrimination"). *But see Mlynczak v. Bodman*, 442 F.3d 1050, 1058 (7th Cir. 2006) (neither the existence of an affirmative action policy nor ultimate decisionmaker being philosophically inclined toward hiring minorities was sufficient evidence of reverse discrimination). *See generally* Charles A. Sullivan, *Circling Back to the Obvious: The Convergence of Traditional and Reverse Discrimination in Title VII Proof*, 46 Wm. & Mary L. Rev. 1031 (2004). Revisit this question after you have studied affirmative action plans in Chapter 2.

NOTE ON PREFERENCES FOR OLDER WORKERS

"Affirmative action" is not a term often used in the ADEA context, but occasionally younger workers within the 40+ protected class sued for having been treated less favorably than older workers. However, *General Dynamics Land Systems, Inc. v. Cline*, 540 U.S. 581 (2004), rejected any such claim. There, the employer and its union agreed to "grandparent" incumbent workers over age 50 when the employer eliminated health benefits for retired workers. Plaintiffs, workers between 40 and 50 and denied grandparent status, claimed age discrimination. The Court concluded "that the ADEA was concerned to protect a relatively old worker from discrimination that works to the advantage of the relatively young." The effect of *Cline* is to eliminate any ADEA claim when the preferences challenged are for older workers, and there is nothing in the decision that would prevent more dramatic employment actions than the curtailing of benefits from also being permissible. For example, if the employer chose to lay off younger workers rather than older workers, the Court's reading of the statute would bar any suit by the younger workers, even if these younger workers were over age 40.

3. *Proving Pretext*

PATTERSON v. McLEAN CREDIT UNION
491 U.S. 164 (1989)

[handwritten: Petitioner can show ~~pretext~~]

Justice KENNEDY delivered the opinion of the Court. . . .

[handwritten: P is not limited to presenting a certain type of evidence to prove pretext]

I

[Brenda Patterson, a black woman, was employed by McLean Credit Union as a teller and a file coordinator from 1972 until 1982, when she was laid off. She sued, claiming that McLean had violated §1981 by harassing her, failing to promote her to an intermediate accounting clerk position, and then discharging her because of her race. The jury found for the defendant on the claims for discharge and the failure to promote. In a portion of the opinion since overturned by the Civil Rights Act of 1991, the Supreme Court limited §1981 in a number of respects. The part of the opinion reproduced below focuses on the plaintiff's challenge to the district court's jury instructions that, in order to prevail as to her promotion claim, she had to show that she was better qualified than her successful white competitor.]

. . . We think the District Court erred when it instructed the jury that petitioner had to prove that she was better qualified than the white employee who allegedly received the promotion. [The Court approved the application of the *McDonnell Douglas* structure to claims of "purposeful discrimination" under §1981, but found the court of appeals to have] erred in describing petitioner's burden. Under our well-established framework, the plaintiff has the initial burden of proving, by a preponderance of the evidence, a prima facie case of discrimination. *Burdine*. The burden is not onerous. Here, petitioner need only prove by a preponderance of the evidence that she applied for and was qualified for an available position, that she was rejected, and that after she was rejected respondent either continued to seek applicants for the position, or, as is alleged here, filled the position with a white employee. *McDonnell Douglas*. *[handwritten: ①]*

[handwritten: holding →]

Once the plaintiff establishes a prima facie case, an inference of discrimination arises. See *Burdine*. In order to rebut this inference, the employer must present evidence that the plaintiff was rejected, or the other applicant was chosen, for a legitimate nondiscriminatory reason. Here, respondent presented evidence that it gave the job to the white applicant because she was better qualified for the position, and therefore rebutted any presumption of discrimination that petitioner may have established. At this point, as our prior cases make clear, petitioner retains the final burden of persuading the jury of intentional discrimination. *[handwritten: ② ③]*

Although petitioner retains the ultimate burden of persuasion, our cases make clear that she must also have the opportunity to demonstrate that respondent's proffered reasons for its decision were not its true reasons. In doing so, petitioner is not limited to presenting evidence of a certain type. This is where the District Court erred. The evidence which petitioner can present in an attempt to establish that respondent's stated reasons are pretextual may take a variety of forms. *McDonnell Douglas*. Indeed, she might seek to demonstrate that respondent's claim to have promoted a better qualified applicant was pretextual by showing that she was in fact better qualified than the person chosen for the position. The District Court erred, however, in instructing the jury that in order to succeed petitioner was required to make such a showing. There are certainly other ways in which petitioner could seek to prove that respondent's reasons were pretextual. Thus, for example, petitioner could seek to persuade the jury that respondent had not offered the true reason for its promotion decision by presenting evidence of respondent's past treatment of petitioner, including the instances of the racial harassment which she alleges and respondent's failure to train her for an accounting position. While we do not intend to say this evidence necessarily would be sufficient to carry the day, it cannot be denied that it is one of the various ways in which petitioner might seek to prove intentional discrimination on the part of respondent. She may not be forced to pursue any particular means of demonstrating that respondent's stated reasons are pretextual. It was, therefore, error for the District Court to instruct the jury that petitioner could carry her burden of persuasion only by showing that she was in fact better qualified than the white applicant who got the job.

reject COA standard that P's qualifications must be so superior as to jump off the page in order to establish pretext.

ASH v. TYSON FOODS, INC.
546 U.S. 454 (2006)

[In a per curiam opinion, the Court reversed the lower court grant of summary judgment for the defendant. The] Court of Appeals erred in articulating the standard for determining whether the asserted nondiscriminatory reasons for Tyson's hiring decisions were pretextual. Petitioners had introduced evidence that their qualifications were superior to those of the two successful applicants. . . . The Court of Appeals, in finding petitioners' evidence insufficient, cited one of its earlier precedents and stated: "Pretext can be established through comparing qualifications only when 'the disparity in qualifications is so apparent as virtually to jump off the page and slap you in the face.'"

Rejects this

Under this Court's decisions, qualifications evidence may suffice, at least in some circumstances, to show pretext. See *Patterson v. McLean Credit Union* (indicating a plaintiff "might seek to demonstrate that respondent's claim to have promoted a better qualified applicant was pretextual by showing that she was in fact better qualified than the person chosen for the position"); *Texas Dep't of Community Affairs v. Burdine* ("The fact that a court may think that the employer misjudged the qualifications of the applicants does not in itself expose him to Title VII liability, although this may be probative of whether the employer's reasons are pretexts for discrimination").

in the same way that any pretext does not auto-matically est. liability, it may go to a jury who may infer that dishonesty sufficient to establish liability

The visual image of words jumping off the page to slap you (presumably a court) in the face is unhelpful and imprecise as an elaboration of the standard for inferring pretext from superior qualifications. Federal courts, including the Court of Appeals for the Eleventh Circuit in a decision it cited here, have articulated various other standards, see, e.g., *Cooper* [*v. Southern Co.*, 390 F.3d 695, 732 (CA11 2004)] (noting that "disparities in qualifications must be of such weight and significance that no reasonable person, in the exercise of impartial judgment, could have chosen the candidate selected over the plaintiff for the job in question") (internal quotation marks omitted)); *Raad v. Fairbanks North Star Borough School Dist.*, 323 F.3d 1185, 1194 (CA9 2003) (holding that qualifications evidence standing alone may establish pretext where the plaintiff's qualifications are "'clearly superior'" to those of the selected job applicant); *Aka v. Washington Hospital Center*, 156 F.3d 1284, 1294 (CADC 1998) (en banc) (concluding the factfinder may infer pretext if "a reasonable employer would have found the plaintiff to be significantly better qualified for the job"), and in this case the Court of Appeals qualified its statement by suggesting that superior qualifications may be probative of pretext when combined with other evidence. This is not the occasion to define more precisely what standard should govern pretext claims based on superior qualifications. Today's decision, furthermore, should not be read to hold that petitioners' evidence necessarily showed pretext. The District Court concluded otherwise. It suffices to say here that some formulation other than the test the Court of Appeals articulated in this case would better ensure that trial courts reach consistent results.

holding

NOTES

1. *Comparators as Proof of Pretext.* In *Patterson*, the defendant's asserted reason for not promoting plaintiff was that the person promoted in her stead was more qualified. In *Ash*, plaintiffs claimed discrimination because less qualified whites were promoted instead of them. In both situations, evidence of the qualifications of those promoted as compared to the plaintiffs' qualifications was important, perhaps critical: if defendant in fact promoted those with lesser qualifications than plaintiffs, a trier of fact could draw the inference that discrimination motivated the choice of less qualified whites. Indeed, proof of the plaintiff's superior qualifications, standing alone, may be sufficient evidence of pretext to go to a jury. *E.g., Raad v. Fairbanks North Star Borough Sch. Dist.*, 323 F.3d 1185 (9th Cir. 2003). *See also Wilson v. B/E Aero., Inc.*, 376 F.3d 1079, 1091 (11th Cir. 2004) (decisionmaker's admission that plaintiff was more qualified than the male selected).

2. Ash *as an Equal Treatment Case.* Both *Patterson* and *Ash* were argued as *McDonnell Douglas* cases. That is, the question of comparative qualifications entered in the pretext part of the analysis. But is there any need for the three-step mantra here? In other words, suppose the plaintiffs in *Ash* simply posed a straightforward unequal treatment claim: they were treated less favorably than comparable whites, leading to the inference that they would have been promoted had they been white. Under this approach, plaintiffs would bear the burden of proving that they were as or more qualified than those who were promoted.

3. *Role of Qualifications in* McDonnell Douglas *Cases.* Assuming *McDonnell Douglas* applies, "qualifications" can appear in both the prima facie case — plaintiff must prove she met the minimum qualifications for the job at issue — and at the pretext stage — an employer's promotion of someone less qualified than plaintiff may support the inference that discrimination was the real reason for the decision. While "qualifications" is a protean concept, it is critical for discrimination cases. As the Court in *Patterson* recognizes, evidence that plaintiff was *more* qualified would be potent evidence in proving pretext — that defendant's asserted reason for not promoting plaintiff was not true. But we saw in *Hicks*, see Note 5 on p. 32, that the plaintiff must prove more than that the defendant's asserted reason was not true. To be pretextual, the reason must be both inaccurate and conceal a discriminatory motive. Putting aside its purple prose, was the lower court in *Ash* suggesting that no reasonable person could find the defendant's asserted reason not to be the actual explanation for its decision? Or maybe that the marginal superiority of the plaintiff in qualifications would not support a finding of pretext for discrimination?

Brooks v. County Comm'n, 446 F.3d 1160, 1163 (11th Cir. 2006), decided in the wake of *Ash*, reaffirmed the *Cooper* standard referred to in *Ash*: "a plaintiff must show that the disparities between the successful applicant's and her own qualifications were 'of such weight and significance that no reasonable person, in the exercise of impartial judgment, could have chosen the candidate selected over the plaintiff.'" Is *Brooks* still too narrow a view? Wouldn't it be better to frame the question as whether it is more likely than not that a reasonable person would not have chosen the successful candidate over the plaintiff absent discrimination? *See White v. Baxter Healthcare Corp.*, 533 F.3d 381, 394 (6th Cir. 2008) (2-1) ("We find that this evidence of White's arguably superior qualifications . . . , in and of itself, could lead a jury to doubt the justifications given for Baxter's hiring decision").

4. *Methods of Proving Pretext.* In *Patterson*, the Court rejected the notion that proof of pretext in a promotion case was limited to evidence that plaintiff was more qualified than the person defendant had promoted. The most obvious type of pretext evidence is that the defendant is just wrong as to its reasons, *e.g.*, *Ridout v. JBS USA, LLC*, 716 F.3d 1079, 1084 (8th Cir. 2013) ("a strong showing that the plaintiff was meeting his employer's reasonable expectations at the time of termination may create a fact issue as to pretext when the employer claims that the employee was terminated for poor or declining performance"), although even here recall the honest belief rule, Note 8 on p. 21. Other types of evidence would also be admissible:

(a) *Prior Treatment of Plaintiff.* One possibility was the defendant's earlier treatment of the plaintiff in *Patterson*. Why would that help to prove that the defendant's asserted reason for not promoting her was a pretext for discrimination? Would earlier unfavorable treatment of her establish that the employer was discriminating against Brenda Patterson because she was black or merely because it did not like her or view her as competent?

(b) *Defendant's Stats.* The partial dissent of Justices Brennan and Stevens in *Patterson* argued that the jury instruction below was "much too restrictive," and it stressed that, *McDonnell Douglas* suggested that "a black plaintiff might be able to prove pretext . . . by proving the employer's 'general policy and practice with respect to minority employment.'" 491 U.S. at 217. Why would statistical evidence of the representation of women and minority men in the various jobs of the employer be relevant to whether the employer discriminated in a particular instance? Is an employer with "good stats" less likely to discriminate in any particular employment decision than one with "bad stats"? In later chapters we'll consider the relationship between individual and systemic claims of discrimination. See p. 230. But, for the moment, should bad stats be sufficient to establish pretext? Helpful?

(c) *Failure to Follow Procedures.* Can defects in the employer's approach to an employment decision be probative of intent to discriminate? In *Carter v. Three Springs Res. Treatment*, 132 F.3d 635, 644 (11th Cir. 1998), the court reversed summary judgment for the employer when it had failed to follow its usual policy of posting job vacancies: "the failure to promulgate hiring and promotion policies can be circumstantial evidence of discrimination. . . . Certainly, it is even more suspicious where it is alleged that established rules were bent or broken to give a non-minority applicant an edge in the hiring process." Not everyone agrees. In *Walker v. Abbott Laboratories*, 416 F.3d 641, 643-44 (7th Cir. 2005), Judge Posner denied the probative value of such evidence:

> This [evidence] makes it seem that Abbott complies with its personnel rules only when it wants to. Indeed so. And there is nothing wrong with that. Unless a rule is part of the company's contract with its employees, the company is free to create exceptions to it at will. . . . A well-managed company will not make exceptions to its personnel rules promiscuously because that will generate ill will among the employees; they will feel they're being subjected to arbitrary treatment, which nobody likes. . . . But neither will a well-managed company adhere to its personnel rules with a rigidity blind to circumstances that may make the rule occasionally wholly inapt. People in supervisory positions are not doing their best for the company if they are content to administer rules. Fairness,

consistency, and demonstrated interest in employee problems are the backbone of supervisory morale building. . . . No set of written policies should become a straitjacket on
management thinking.

This is a variation of the argument that the employer is free to act on any ground other
than a prohibited one. That may be true, but isn't the unexplained failure to follow
the normal procedures fishy? And might fishiness hide discrimination, not creative
administration à la Posner?

(d) *"Unreasonable" Decision vs. "Business Judgment."* We saw in Note 6, p. 33,
that there is dispute as to the extent to which courts should inquire into the reasonableness of employer decisions. They have sometimes recognized that the more unusual and
idiosyncratic a decision is — in terms of the way business is normally conducted — the
more appropriate it is to infer discrimination. This principle is in obvious tension with
what has sometimes been called the "business judgment" rule, which is that courts
should not second-guess business decisions. *Bagwe v. Sedgwick Claims Mgmt. Servs.*,
811 F.3d 866, 883 (7th Cir. 2016) ("we do not sit as a 'superpersonnel department[]'
that judges the wisdom of Sedgwick's decisions") (citation omitted).

One illustration of the conflict is *White v. Baxter Healthcare Corp.*, 533 F.3d 381,
394 (6th Cir. 2008) (2-1), where the majority reaffirmed that "the plaintiff may also
demonstrate pretext by offering evidence which challenges the reasonableness of the
employer's decision 'to the extent that such an inquiry sheds light on whether the
employer's proffered reason for the employment action was its actual motivation'"
(citation omitted). It went on:

> [O]ur Circuit has never adopted a "business-judgment rule" which requires us to defer
> to the employer's "reasonable business judgment" in Title VII cases. Indeed, in most
> Title VII cases the very issue in dispute is whether the employer's adverse employment
> decision resulted from an objectively unreasonable business judgment, *i.e.*, a judgment
> that was based upon an impermissible consideration such as the adversely affected em-
> ployee's race, gender, religion, or national origin. In determining whether the plaintiff
> has produced enough evidence to cast doubt upon the employer's explanation for its de-
> cision, we cannot . . . unquestionably accept the employer's own self-serving claim that
> the decision resulted from an exercise of "reasonable business judgment." Nor can we
> decide "as a matter of law" that "an employer's proffered justification is reasonable." The
> question of whether the employer's judgment was reasonable or was instead motivated
> by improper considerations is for the jury to consider.

5. *Several Nondiscriminatory Reasons.* When defendant has more than one supposed legitimate nondiscriminatory reason, some courts have required the plaintiff
to put in evidence of the pretextual nature of all the reasons. *See Crawford v. City
of Fairburn*, 482 F.3d 1305, 1308 (11th Cir. 2007) (plaintiff must rebut each reason
proffered by defendant). Other courts believe that proof that any reason is pretextual
may permit the jury to infer that the pretext conceals a discriminatory motive. *E.g.*,
Tomasso v. Boeing Co., 445 F.3d 702, 704 (3d Cir. 2006); *Jaramillo v. Colorado Judicial Dep't*, 427 F.3d 1303, 1310 (10th Cir. 2005). *See generally* Lawrence D. Rosenthal, *Motions for Summary Judgment When Employers Offer Multiple Justifications
for Adverse Employment Actions: Why the Exceptions Should Swallow the Rule*, 2002
Utah L. Rev. 335. Sometimes an employer's multiple reasons will conflict, thus providing another basis to infer pretext, *see Juarez v. AGS Gov't Solution Group*, 314 F.3d
1243 (10th Cir. 2003) (proof that manager's evaluation contained fraudulent data and
the employer's conflicting reasons for discharge were sufficient to establish pretext in

a race discrimination case), and a change in a defendant's rebuttal over time can be fatal to it. *See Foster v. Mt. Coal Co., LLC*, 830 F.3d 1178 (10th Cir. 2016) (a reasonable jury could find that the employer's proffered reason for terminating plaintiff unworthy of belief in light of the inconsistent justifications for terminating him).

6. *A Uniform Structure. Patterson* formally adopts the *McDonnell Douglas/Burdine* litigation structure for §1981 cases. The Supreme Court has several times employed this structure in ADEA cases, although, oddly enough, it has explicitly assumed the application rather than held it to apply. *E.g., Reeves v. Sanderson Plumbing Products, Inc.*, reproduced at p. 24. However, we will see that the causation question has grown more complicated and, at least in that regard, there is no unified approach to cases of individual disparate treatment under Title VII, §1981, and the ADEA.

4.　For Whose Actions Is the Employer Liable?

STAUB v. PROCTOR HOSPITAL
562 U.S. (2011)

Justice SCALIA delivered the opinion of the Court.

We consider the circumstances under which an employer may be held liable for employment discrimination based on the discriminatory animus of an employee who influenced, but did not make, the ultimate employment decision.

I

Petitioner Vincent Staub worked as an angiography technician for respondent Proctor Hospital until 2004, when he was fired. Staub and Proctor hotly dispute the facts surrounding the firing, but because a jury found for Staub in his claim of employment discrimination against Proctor, we describe the facts viewed in the light most favorable to him.

While employed by Proctor, Staub was a member of the United States Army Reserve, which required him to attend drill one weekend per month and to train full time for two to three weeks a year. Both Janice Mulally, Staub's immediate supervisor, and Michael Korenchuk, Mulally's supervisor, were hostile to Staub's military obligations. Mulally scheduled Staub for additional shifts without notice so that he would "'pa[y] back the department for everyone else having to bend over backwards to cover [his] schedule for the Reserves.'" She also informed Staub's coworker, Leslie Sweborg, that Staub's "'military duty had been a strain on th[e] department,'" and asked Sweborg to help her "'get rid of him.'" Korenchuk referred to Staub's military obligations as "'a b[u]nch of smoking and joking and [a] waste of taxpayers['] money.'" He was also aware that Mulally was "'out to get'" Staub.

In January 2004, Mulally issued Staub a "Corrective Action" disciplinary warning for purportedly violating a company rule requiring him to stay in his work area whenever he was not working with a patient. The Corrective Action included a directive requiring Staub to report to Mulally or Korenchuk "'when [he] ha[d] no patients and [the angio] cases [we]re complete[d].'" According to Staub, Mulally's justification for the Corrective Action was false for two reasons: First, the company rule invoked by Mulally did not exist; and second, even if it did, Staub did not violate it.

On April 2, 2004, Angie Day, Staub's co-worker, complained to Linda Buck, Proctor's vice president of human resources, and Garrett McGowan, Proctor's chief

[handwritten margin note: supervisors hostile toward Staub's military obligations]

operating officer, about Staub's frequent unavailability and abruptness. McGowan
directed Korenchuk and Buck to create a plan that would solve Staub's "'availability'
problems." But three weeks later, before they had time to do so, Korenchuk informed
Buck that Staub had left his desk without informing a supervisor, in violation of the
January Corrective Action. Staub now contends this accusation was false: he had
left Korenchuk a voice-mail notification that he was leaving his desk. Buck relied
on Korenchuk's accusation, however, and after reviewing Staub's personnel file, she
decided to fire him. The termination notice stated that Staub had ignored the directive issued in the January 2004 Corrective Action.

fired him for invalid reason

Staub challenged his firing through Proctor's grievance process, claiming that
Mulally had fabricated the allegation underlying the Corrective Action out of hostility toward his military obligations. Buck did not follow up with Mulally about this
claim. After discussing the matter with another personnel officer, Buck adhered to
her decision.

Staub sued Proctor under the Uniformed Services Employment and Reemployment Rights Act of 1994, 38 U.S.C. §4301 *et seq.*, claiming that his discharge was
motivated by hostility to his obligations as a military reservist. His contention was not
that Buck had any such hostility but that Mulally and Korenchuk did, and that their
actions influenced Buck's ultimate employment decision. A jury found that Staub's
"military status was a motivating factor in [Proctor's] decision to discharge him" and
awarded $57,640 in damages.

USERRA

Staub sues

The Seventh Circuit reversed, holding that Proctor was entitled to judgment as a
matter of law. The court observed that Staub had brought a "'cat's paw' case," meaning that he sought to hold his employer liable for the animus of a supervisor who was
not charged with making the ultimate employment decision.[1] It explained that under
Seventh Circuit precedent, a "cat's paw" case could not succeed unless the nondeci-
sionmaker exercised such "'singular influence'" over the decisionmaker that the decision to terminate was the product of "blind reliance." [For the circuit court, Buck had
looked beyond Mulally's and Korenchuk's statements so their statements were not a
"singular influence," even though her "investigation could have been more robust."]

didn't meet 7th circ. standard

II

[USERRA bars discrimination in employment on the basis of membership or an
obligation to perform service in a uniformed service. §4311(a). It has a structure similar to Title VII's 703(m) in that an employer violates the statute when uniformed service membership is "a motivating factor in the employer's action, unless the employer
can prove that the action would have been taken in the absence of such membership." §4311(c).]

USERRA is similar to Title VII

The central difficulty in this case is construing the phrase "motivating factor in
the employer's action." When the company official who makes the decision to take
an adverse employment action is personally acting out of hostility to the employee's
membership in or obligation to a uniformed service, a motivating factor obviously
exists. The problem we confront arises when that official has no discriminatory animus

similar to step 3 of McDonnell, have to show that the discriminatory reason was the actual reason

---

1. The term "cat's paw" derives from a fable conceived by Aesop, put into verse by La Fontaine in 1679,
and injected into United States employment discrimination law by [Judge] Posner in 1990. In the fable, a
monkey induces a cat by flattery to extract roasting chestnuts from the fire. After the cat has done so, burning its paws in the process, the monkey makes off with the chestnuts and leaves the cat with nothing. . . .

but is influenced by previous company action that is the product of a like animus in someone else.

In approaching this question, we start from the premise that when Congress creates a federal tort, it adopts the background of general tort law. See *Burlington Industries, Inc. v. Ellerth* [reproduced at p. 422]. Intentional torts such as this, "as distinguished from negligent or reckless torts, . . . generally require that the actor intend 'the *consequences* of an act,' not simply 'the act itself.'" *Kawaauhau v. Geiger*, 523 U.S. 57 (1998).

Staub contends that the fact that an unfavorable entry on the plaintiff's personnel record was caused to be put there, with discriminatory animus, by Mulally and Korenchuk, suffices to establish the tort, even if Mulally and Korenchuk did not intend to cause his dismissal. But discrimination was no part of Buck's reason for the dismissal; and while Korenchuk and Mulally acted with discriminatory animus, the act they committed — the mere making of the reports — was not a denial of "initial employment, reemployment, retention in employment, promotion, or any benefit of employment," as liability under USERRA requires. If dismissal was not the object of Mulally's and Korenchuk's reports, it may have been their result, or even their foreseeable consequence, but that is not enough to render Mulally or Korenchuk responsible.

Here, however, Staub is seeking to hold liable not Mulally and Korenchuk, but their employer. Perhaps, therefore, the discriminatory motive of one of the employer's agents (Mulally or Korenchuk) can be aggregated with the act of another agent (Buck) to impose liability on Proctor. Again we consult general principles of law, agency law, which form the background against which federal tort laws are enacted. See *Burlington*. Here, however, the answer is not so clear. The Restatement of Agency suggests that the malicious mental state of one agent cannot generally be combined with the harmful action of another agent to hold the principal liable for a tort that requires both. *See* RESTATEMENT (SECOND) AGENCY §275, Illustration 4 (1958). Some of the cases involving federal torts apply that rule. But another case involving a federal tort, and one involving a federal crime, hold to the contrary. Ultimately, we think it unnecessary in this case to decide what the background rule of agency law may be, since the former line of authority is suggested by the governing text, which requires that discrimination be "a motivating factor" *in the adverse action*. When a decision to fire is made with no unlawful animus on the part of the firing agent, but partly on the basis of a report prompted (unbeknownst to that agent) by discrimination, discrimination might perhaps be called a "factor" or a "causal factor" in the decision; but it seems to us a considerable stretch to call it "a motivating factor."

Proctor, on the other hand, contends that the employer is not liable unless the *de facto* decisionmaker (the technical decisionmaker or the agent for whom he is the "cat's paw") is motivated by discriminatory animus. This avoids the aggregation of animus and adverse action, but it seems to us not the only application of general tort law that can do so. Animus and responsibility for the adverse action can both be attributed to the earlier agent (here, Staub's supervisors) if the adverse action is the intended consequence of that agent's discriminatory conduct. So long as the agent intends, for discriminatory reasons, that the adverse action occur, he has the scienter required to be liable under USERRA. And it is axiomatic under tort law that the exercise of judgment by the decisionmaker does not prevent the earlier agent's action (and hence the earlier agent's discriminatory animus) from being the proximate cause of the harm. Proximate cause requires only "some direct relation between the injury asserted and the injurious conduct alleged," and excludes only those "link[s] that are too remote, purely contingent, or indirect." *Hemi Group, LLC v. City of New York*, 559 U.S. 1, 9 (2010) (internal quotation marks omitted). We do not think that the ultimate decisionmaker's exercise of judgment automatically renders the link to the supervisor's bias "remote" or "purely contingent." The decisionmaker's exercise of judgment is *also* a proximate cause of the employment decision, but it is common for injuries to have multiple proximate causes. *See Sosa v. Alvarez-Machain*, 542 U.S. 692, 704 (2004). Nor can the ultimate decisionmaker's judgment be deemed a super-seding cause of the harm. A cause can be thought "superseding" only if it is a "cause of independent origin that was not foreseeable." *Exxon Co., U.S.A. v. Sofec, Inc.*, 517 U.S. 830, 837 (1996) (internal quotation marks omitted).

Moreover, the approach urged upon us by Proctor gives an unlikely meaning to a provision designed to prevent employer discrimination. An employer's author-ity to reward, punish, or dismiss is often allocated among multiple agents. The one who makes the ultimate decision does so on the basis of performance assessments by other supervisors. Proctor's view would have the improbable consequence that if an employer isolates a personnel official from an employee's supervisors, vests the deci-sion to take adverse employment actions in that official, and asks that official to review the employee's personnel file before taking the adverse action, then the employer will be effectively shielded from discriminatory acts and recommendations of supervisors that were *designed and intended* to produce the adverse action. That seems to us an implausible meaning of the text, and one that is not compelled by its words.

Proctor suggests that even if the decisionmaker's mere exercise of independent judgment does not suffice to negate the effect of the prior discrimination, at least the decisionmaker's independent investigation (and rejection) of the employee's allega-tions of discriminatory animus ought to do so. We decline to adopt such a hard-and-fast rule. As we have already acknowledged, the requirement that the biased supervi-sor's action be a causal factor of the ultimate employment action incorporates the traditional tort-law concept of proximate cause. Thus, if the employer's investigation results in an adverse action for reasons unrelated to the supervisor's original biased action (by the terms of USERRA it is the employer's burden to establish that), then the employer will not be liable. But the supervisor's biased report may remain a causal factor if the independent investigation takes it into account without determining that the adverse action was, apart from the supervisor's recommendation, entirely justi-fied. We are aware of no principle in tort or agency law under which an employer's mere conduct of an independent investigation has a claim-preclusive effect. Nor do we think the independent investigation somehow relieves the employer of "fault." The employer is at fault because one of its agents committed an action based on discriminatory animus that was intended to cause, and did in fact cause, an adverse employment decision. . . .

We therefore hold that if a supervisor performs an act motivated by antimilitary animus that is *intended* by the supervisor to cause an adverse employment action,[3] and if that act is a proximate cause of the ultimate employment action, then the employer is liable under USERRA.[4]

Held

3. Under traditional tort law, "'intent' . . . denote[s] that the actor desires to cause consequences of his act, or that he believes that the consequences are substantially certain to result from it." *Id.*, §8A.

4. Needless to say, the employer would be liable only when the supervisor acts within the scope of his employment, or when the supervisor acts outside the scope of his employment and liability would be imputed to the employer under traditional agency principles. See *Burlington Industries, Inc. v. Ellerth.* We express no view as to whether the employer would be liable if a co-worker, rather than a supervisor, committed a discriminatory act that influenced the ultimate employment decision. We also observe that Staub took advantage of Proctor's grievance process, and we express no view as to whether Proctor would have an affirmative defense if he did not. *Cf. Pa. State Police v. Suders*, 542 U.S. 129 (2004).

III

Applying our analysis to the facts of this case, it is clear that the Seventh Circuit's judgment must be reversed. Both Mulally and Korenchuk were acting within the scope of their employment when they took the actions that allegedly caused Buck to fire Staub. A "reprimand . . . for workplace failings" constitutes conduct within the scope of an agent's employment. *Faragher v. Boca Raton.* As the Seventh Circuit recognized, there was evidence that Mulally's and Korenchuk's actions were motivated by hostility toward Staub's military obligations. There was also evidence that Mulally's and Korenchuk's actions were causal factors underlying Buck's decision to fire Staub. Buck's termination notice expressly stated that Staub was terminated because he had "ignored" the directive in the Corrective Action. Finally, there was evidence that both Mulally and Korenchuk had the specific intent to cause Staub to be terminated. Mulally stated she was trying to "'get rid of'" Staub, and Korenchuk was aware that Mulally was "'out to get'" Staub. Moreover, Korenchuk informed Buck, Proctor's personnel officer responsible for terminating employees, of Staub's alleged noncompliance with Mulally's Corrective Action, and Buck fired Staub immediately thereafter; a reasonable jury could infer that Korenchuk intended that Staub be fired. The Seventh Circuit therefore erred in holding that Proctor was entitled to judgment as a matter of law.

[The Court reversed and remanded for Seventh Circuit to consider whether the jury instructions, which required a finding only of motivating factor, were harmless error.]

Justice ALITO, with whom Justice THOMAS joins, concurred in the judgment. Justice KAGAN took no part in the consideration or decision of the case.

NOTES

1. *Intent, Yet Again.* In footnote 3, Justice Scalia writes: "Under traditional tort law, 'intent' . . . denote[s] that the actor desires to cause consequences of his act, or that he believes that the consequences are substantially certain to result from it." Maybe that's true of "traditional tort law," but "intent" is often thought to require something more in the discrimination context — a result sought *because* not merely in spite of the prohibited characteristic. *See Personnel Administrator v. Feeney*, 429 U.S. 66 (1976), reproduced at p. 131. At first glance, then, *Staub* would then seem to expand the reach of the discrimination statutes, not something the current Court seems likely to do. But *Staub*'s expansion of intent to reach substantially certain consequences is coupled with the requirement of finding an impermissible motive. In other words, while "intent to discriminate" was previously thought to satisfy the statutes, Justice Scalia would seem to have disaggregated the two: the case requires both motive and intent, *i.e.*, motive to treat an employee differently because of his military service (or race) and intent that that difference in treatment result in an adverse employment action. *See Cherry v. Siemens Healthcare Diagnostics, Inc.*, 829 F.3d 974 (8th Cir. 2016) (plaintiff could not establish cat's paw liability when the supervisor, even assuming a racially motivated negative performance evaluation, did not know at the time of the planned reduction in force and therefore could not have intended the resultant adverse employment action).

2. *Whose Motive/Intent?* Given the Court's continued focus on intent for individual disparate treatment cases, it is not surprising for the majority to hold that an entity

can discriminate only if particular individuals within that entity have the requisite intent. But, of course, individual human beings did have the requisite mental state in *Staub* and, according to the Court, a jury could find not only that they were motivated by antimilitary bias but also that they desired to have their reports result in an adverse employment action. In other cases, the convergence of both mental states may not be so clear.

Staub seems likely to sharpen the focus from the employing entity to the particular manager whose decision (or influence) is claimed to be biased. *Sharp v. Aker Plant Servs. Group, Inc.*, 726 F.3d 789, 797 (6th Cir. 2013) (although a manager was not the ultimate decisionmaker, those who were relied solely on his forced rankings and recommendation of who could be fired); *Haire v. Bd. of Supervisors of La. State Univ. Agric. & Mech. Coll.*, 719 F.3d 356, 366-67 (5th Cir. 2013) (university chancellor could be found to be cat's paw for biased campus police officer who provided him misinformation regarding supposed violations of security policies).

However, employers have escaped liability when plaintiff could not establish the causal link between the actions of the biased subordinate and those of the actual decisionmaker. *E.g., Woods v. City of Berwyn*, 803 F.3d 865, 870 (7th Cir. 2015) (although an allegedly biased supervisor initiated disciplinary proceedings, the board made its determination to discharge after a full hearing and without relying on any of his statements); *Jones v. SEPTA*, 796 F.3d 323 (3d Cir. 2015) (the fact that a supervisor reported and initiated an investigation is not sufficient to establish that the subsequent adverse action was tainted when there was a subsequent investigation independent of the supervisor).

3. *Proximate Cause*. The Court thinks we don't need to look hard for a factor motivating the decisionmaker herself because, assuming one human being has the necessary mental state (bias plus intent to cause an adverse action), employer liability will follow from that adverse action — at least if the culpable human being is a "supervisor." Cause in fact seems requisite for such liability, and the Court has often stressed that in terms of "determinative factor" causation. Recall *Biggins*.

But why *proximate* cause? Prior to *Staub*, proximate cause had been conspicuously absent from discrimination jurisprudence, raising the question why the Court invoked it at this juncture, especially since it seems unnecessary to the decision. After all, how could there be any question of proximity when the Court requires the first actor to both have the requisite motivation and intent to cause the harm that in fact results? This is not the time to revisit the entire proximate cause concept, which probably confused you enough in Torts, but the doctrine is almost always used for negligence-based physical injuries. It fits poorly as applied to intentional torts and is perhaps even more maladapted as applied to discrimination law. *See generally* Charles A. Sullivan, *Tortifying Employment Discrimination*, 62 BU L. Rev. 1431 (2012); Sandra F. Sperino, *Discrimination Statutes, the Common Law, and Proximate Cause*, 2013 U. Ill. L. Rev. 1; Sandra F. Sperino, *Statutory Proximate Cause*, 88 Notre Dame L. Rev. 1199 (2013). Other articles on this topic appear in a symposium sponsored by the Ohio State Law Journal and appearing in in volume 75.

4. *Co-workers and Cat's Paws*. In footnote 4, the Court confines its opinion to situations where a supervisor's actions would be imputed to the employer under traditional agency principles. Further, it did not pass on employer liability when a co-worker, rather than a supervisor, caused the adverse action. In this context, "co-worker" probably includes someone higher in the corporate hierarchy but not above the plaintiff in her chain of command. That's because anyone outside that chain would not normally trigger imputed liability under agency law. Suppose another worker, maybe even a

higher level employee but not Staub's supervisor, falsely reported that Staub had left his station and made the report for discriminatory reasons in order to have Staub fired. Actionable if all other facts are the same? *Velázquez-Pérez v. Developers Diversified Realty Corp.*, 753 F.3d 265, 274 (1st Cir. 2014), said yes when a jilted co-worker's claims of plaintiff's poor job performance resulted in his termination. Statements motivated by bias and intended to cause the plaintiff's discharge are actionable when they "proximately cause the plaintiff to be fired, and the employer acts negligently by allowing the co-worker's acts to achieve their desired effect though it knows (or reasonably should know) of the discriminatory motivation."

5. *Is an Internal Grievance Necessary?* We will see that, in the harassment area, an employer may sometimes avoid imputed liability if the victim failed to resort to internal remedies. See p. 337. Footnote 4 also noted "Staub took advantage of Proctor's grievance process, and we express no view as to whether Proctor would have an affirmative defense if he did not." If he had not, what result?

C.   EMPLOYMENT TERMS, CONDITIONS, PRIVILEGES OF EMPLOYMENT, AND EMPLOYMENT PRACTICES

In an early encounter with what has come to be called the "adverse employment action" doctrine, the Court looked to the language of Title VII to explain its result. Section 703(a) bars such discrimination but only "with respect to his compensation, terms, conditions, or privileges of employment." In *Hishon v. King & Spalding*, 467 U.S. 69 (1984), the issue was whether an associate in a law firm of some 50 partners and 50 associates could sue for not being elevated to partner. While "partners" are not "employees" protected by Title VII, see Note 4, p. 270, plaintiff claimed that consideration for partnership was one of the "terms, conditions, or privileges of employment" as an associate. The Court agreed. Once an employment relationship is established, by a contract "written or oral, formal or informal," including "the simple act of handing a job applicant a shovel and providing a workplace," Title VII bars discrimination in the "terms, conditions, or privileges" of that employment. *Id.* at 74. And those terms include benefits that are part of an employment contract, such as being considered for partnership. However, Title VII goes beyond what an employer is contractually obligated to do:

> An employer may provide its employees with many benefits that it is under no obligation to furnish by an express or implied contract. Such a benefit, though not a contractual right of employment, may qualify as a "privileg[e]" of employment under Title VII. A benefit that is part and parcel of the employment relationship may not be doled out in a discriminatory fashion, even if the employer would be free under the employment contract simply not to provide the benefit at all. Those benefits that comprise the "incidents of employment," or that form "an aspect of the relationship between the employer and employees" may not be afforded in a manner contrary to Title VII.

Id. at 75. Plaintiff's complaint suggested that "the opportunity to become a partner was part and parcel of an associate's status as an employee" at the firm, independent of any contractual claim and, "if proved at trial, would suffice to show that partnership consideration was a term, condition, or privilege of an associate's employment at respondent's firm, and accordingly that partnership consideration must be without regard to sex." *Id.*

To this point, the cases we have studied have involved what have sometimes been called "ultimate employment actions." Both *Slack* and *Biggins* involve "ultimate" actions — the decision to terminate a worker. Another "ultimate" action is the decision not to hire in the first place, such as in *McDonnell Douglas*. For obvious reasons, plaintiffs are far more likely to sue when they are fired than when not hired or even when denied promotions or raises. *Hishon* is also toward the ultimate end of the spectrum since, at least at that time, the "up or out" rule prevailed and a decision not to promote a law firm associate to partner was almost always a decision to terminate the associate's services.

But *Hishon* illustrates that a failure to promote may be actionable independent of a discharge, and cases such as *Patterson* and *Ash* involved failures to promote. Again, pretty important decisions. But is every action an employer takes with respect to an employee covered by Title VII? Suppose the employees in *Slack* had complied with Pohasky's request and then sued for being discriminatorily assigned the work. Would they have a cause of action? The answer isn't as clear as you might think since the lower courts have developed doctrines that bar suit where the challenged decision is not, in the court's mind at least, sufficiently important. While most denials of promotion or raises are actionable, other kinds of discriminatory conduct may not be. Dean Rebecca Hanner White in *De Minimis Discrimination*, 47 EMORY L.J. 1121, 1151 (1998), takes issue with this approach, arguing that "Congress's use of the phrase 'compensation, terms, conditions, or privileges of employment' emphasizes the employment-related nature of the prohibited discrimination. The phrase is better read as making clear that an employer who discriminates against an employee in a non-job-related context would not run afoul of Title VII, rather than as sheltering employment discrimination that does not significantly disadvantage an employee." Reconsider this argument after you read the next case.

MINOR v. CENTOCOR, INC.
457 F.3d 632 (7th Cir. 2006)

EASTERBROOK, Circuit Judge.

M. Jane Minor was a sales representative for Centocor, pitching to physicians and hospitals that Centocor and its affiliates offered to treat vascular conditions. After Antonio Siciliano became her supervisor, Minor contends, she was put in an impossible situation — Siciliano required her to visit all of her accounts twice a month, and her major accounts more frequently. That led her to work 70 to 90 hours a week (much of it driving time); until then 50 to 55 hours had been enough. In August 2001, after two months of this regimen, Minor began to experience atrial fibrillation and depression. In October 2001 she stopped working. . . . She attributes her medical problems to Siciliano's demands. In this litigation Minor contends that those demands reflected both age and sex discrimination. . . .

The district court concluded, however, that Minor had not established a prima facie case . . . because Centocor did not take any "adverse employment action" against her. Minor was not fired or demoted; she is still Centocor's employee, welcome to resume work if her condition improves. The events of which she complains — not only the schedule for visiting accounts but also being bombarded by email messages

Dist court [margin annotation]

from Siciliano and subject to criticism and close supervision — are the ordinary incidents of employment rather than adverse actions. . . .

Although hundreds if not thousands of decisions say that an "adverse employment action" is essential to the plaintiff's prima facie case, that term does not appear in any employment discrimination statute . . . and the Supreme Court has never adopted it as a legal requirement. The statutory term is "discrimination," and a proxy such as "adverse employment action" often may help to express the idea — which the Supreme Court *has* embraced — that it is essential to distinguish between material differences and the many day-to-day travails and disappointments that, although frustrating, are not so central to the employment relation that they amount to discriminatory terms or conditions. *See, e.g., Burlington Northern & Santa Fe Ry. v. White* [reproduced at p. 422]. . . . Helpful though a judicial gloss such as "adverse employment action" may be, that phrase must not be confused with the statute itself or allowed to displace the Supreme Court's approach, which inquires whether the difference is material.

Extra work can be a material difference in the terms and conditions of employment. Minor contends that Siciliano required her to work at least 25% longer to earn the same income as before. That is functionally the same as a 30% reduction in Minor's hourly pay, a material change by any standard. And if Centocor requires women (or older workers) to work longer hours than men (or younger workers) to obtain the same remuneration, that material difference also is discriminatory and violates federal law. . . .

NOTES

1. *Docket Reduction and Narrowing Employers' Liability.* The court in *Minor* finds that the employer's treatment of plaintiff, if discriminatory, would be actionable because it had a substantial economic impact. But why isn't discrimination related to a job actionable, whether or not there is any economic impact on the employee? In *Ferrill v. The Parker Group, Inc.*, 168 F.3d 468 (11th Cir. 1999), a §1981 case, the Eleventh Circuit struck down an employer's policy of racially segregating telemarketers aimed at getting out the vote for an election, with blacks calling blacks and whites calling whites from separate "boiler rooms" for each group. No economic harm was involved, just the dignitary harm of being segregated by race.

Suppose an employer paints all the cubicles pink for women workers and blue for men. Might plaintiff lose a challenge to this practice because it has no discernible economic effect? If so, then the courts are qualifying the plain meaning of the statutory language of Title VII. Why? There are two obvious possibilities. One is to reduce the number of discrimination cases before the courts. The second is to provide employers with some elbow room free of any possibility of judicial second-guessing. Is either of these reasons sufficient?

2. *Materiality.* As *Minor* suggests, the lower courts have generally required more than a mere showing that the employer discriminated in order for its conduct to be actionable. They have required an "adverse employment action," usually defined to require some material effect on the terms and conditions of employment. Beyond "ultimate employment actions," the easy cases involve meaningful changes in compensation. *E.g., Davis v. N.Y.C. Dep't of Educ.*, 804 F.3d 231 (2d Cir. 2015) (denial of a discretionary bonus could be an adverse employment action based on a prohibited factor); *Alexander v. Casino Queen, Inc.*, 739 F.3d 972, 980 (7th Cir. 2014) (floor assignments

could constitute an adverse employment action because of the importance of tips for cocktail waitresses). The harder question arises when there are less direct economic effects on employees' lives, and the decisions are hard to reconcile.

Mere problematic job evaluations may not suffice, even when future prospects are hindered, *Davis v. Town of Lake Park, Fla.*, 245 F.3d 1232, 1242-43 (11th Cir. 2001), nor may employer investigations of plaintiff, *Kuhn v. Washtenaw Cnty.*, 709 F.3d 612 (6th Cir. 2013), even when the employee is placed on paid administrative leave. *Jones v. SEPTA*, 796 F.3d 323 (3d Cir. 2015).

More dramatically, some courts find that a "lateral transfer" (usually defined to mean no reduction in pay or title) is not actionable, *Ortiz-Diaz v. United States Dep't of Hous. & Urban Dev.*, 831 F.3d 488 (D.C. Cir. 2016) (2-1), even though the transfer might be to a distant location, *Reynolds v. Ethicon Endo-Surgery, Inc.*, 454 F.3d 868 (8th Cir. 2006); *see also Youssef v. F.B.I.*, 687 F.3d 397 (D.C. Cir. 2012) (transferring agent to less important work than counterterrorism not materially adverse). But other courts look beyond the fact of transfer to lost prestige or opportunities for promotion. *Burns v. Johnson*, 829 F.3d 1 (1st Cir. 2016); *Bonenberger v. St. Louis Metro. Police Dep't*, 810 F.3d 1103 (8th Cir. 2016). *See also Deleon v. Kalamazoo Cnty. Rd. Comm'n*, 739 F.3d 914, 919 (6th Cir. 2014) (a transfer may be a materially adverse employment action when it gives rise to "some level of objective intolerability," such as daily exposure to toxic fumes), *cert. denied*, 135 S. Ct. 783 (2015) (Alito, J. dissenting). *See generally* Kevin Woodson, *Human Capital Discrimination: Law Firm Inequality and the Limits of Title VII*, 38 CARDOZO L. REV. 183 (2016).

3. *Materiality = Economic Effects? Minor* might seem to be an easy case, especially for the economically oriented panel of the Seventh Circuit, which included Judge Posner along with Judge Easterbrook. *Minor* views requiring more work for the same pay as equivalent to a reduction in hourly pay, and appreciable decreases in pay have been found to be adverse employment actions. But the employer did not actually decrease plaintiff's compensation (she earned as much as she had before), and won't many employment actions be translatable into dollars? A transfer to a distant location might involve heavy commuting or moving expenses. In any event, as Dean White explains, the language "terms and conditions of employment" comes from the National Labor Relations Act, and unions have often focused collective bargaining on aspects of employment that do not directly implicate economic interests. *De Minimis Discrimination*, at 1190 n.367. Further, Congress seemed to intend to go even further in Title VII by adding "privileges" to the protection afforded.

4. *Adverse Employment Action Unnecessary When Discrimination Is Proven?* Dean White argued that requiring an "adverse employment action" might be appropriate when the question is whether the decision was impermissibly motivated, but she asserts there should be no such "adverse action" requirement when the discrimination is facial or proven and the action in question was employment related. *De Minimis Discrimination*, at 1173-74. *See Piercy v. Maketa*, 480 F.3d 1192 (10th Cir. 2007) (apparently applying a lesser materiality standard to a challenge to a facially discriminatory assignment policy). More recently, Professor Sandra Sperino, *Justice Kennedy's Big New Idea*, 96 BU L. Rev. 1789, 1791-92 (2017), argued that the Supreme Court's FHA decision in *Texas Department of Housing & Community Affairs v. Inclusive Cmtys. Project, Inc.*, 135 S. Ct. 2507, 2519 (2015), suggests the end of the adverse employment action doctrine. She writes that the Court read §703(a) (2) — prohibiting employer actions that "limit . . . employees . . . in any way which would deprive or tend to deprive any individual of employment opportunities or otherwise adversely

affect his status as an employee" — to reach beyond its traditional focus on disparate impact to also reach disparate treatment. The broader language of that provision, then, would seem to make actionable discrimination that does not have the immediate material effects the lower courts have traditionally required under §703(a)(1), which bars discrimination in hiring, firing, and terms and conditions of employment.

5. *Constructive Discharge and Contaminated Work Environment.* Some conduct by the employer may be so severe as to justify a reasonable employee in quitting. Such "constructive discharges" are the equivalent of formal discharges and are therefore adverse employment actions. *See Pennsylvania State Police v. Suders*, 542 U.S. 129, 134 (2004) (to establish "constructive discharge," the plaintiff must not only make a case of an abusive working environment but that that environment "became so intolerable that her resignation qualified as a fitting response"). Some courts required both intolerable working conditions and proof that such conditions were imposed in order to force plaintiff to leave for a constructive discharge. If this theory were ever tenable, it has likely been laid to rest by the Supreme Court's recent decision in *Green v. Brennan*, 136 S. Ct. 1769 (2016). See p. 534.

6. *Discrimination vs. Retaliation.* The issue of whether a plaintiff must prove that she has suffered an adverse employment action has also been raised in retaliation cases. In *Burlington Northern & Santa Fe Ry. v. White*, cited in *Minor* and reproduced in Chapter 6 at p. 422, the plaintiff claimed that, in retaliation for complaining about sexual harassment, she was taken off her job of driving a forklift and put to work doing laborer work on the tracks. She was then suspended, but later reinstated with full backpay. The employer argued that the reassignment was not an adverse employment action since both positions were in the same job classification and that any harm from the suspension was cured by plaintiff's reinstatement. The Court rejected more demanding tests used by some lower courts and allowed a plaintiff to sue for any retaliation, whether or not related to employment, so long as she can "show that a reasonable employee would have found the challenged action materially adverse." 548 U.S. at 68. This objective test was important because it "separates significant from trivial harms." *Id.* Thus:

> Context matters. . . . A schedule change in an employee's work schedule may make little difference to many workers, but may matter enormously to a young mother with school age children. . . . A supervisor's refusal to invite an employee to lunch is normally trivial, a nonactionable petty slight. But to retaliate by excluding an employee from a weekly training lunch that contributes significantly to the employee's professional advancement might well deter a reasonable employee from complaining about discrimination.

Id. Minor may have drawn its materiality test from *Burlington*, but the touchstone for retaliation is not the same for discrimination. As the quoted passage suggests, the test for materiality is whether the challenged action is likely to deter complaints about discrimination by a reasonable employer. How does that translate to a situation where an employer changes a worker's schedule because she is a woman? Should she be able to challenge that even if she would not object to the schedule change had it been made for a nondiscriminatory reason? Some subsequent decisions have read *Burlington Northern* as establishing a more permissive standard for retaliation cases than applies to discrimination claims. *See McCoy v. City of Shreveport*, 492 F.3d 551 (5th Cir. 2007) (continuing to apply an "ultimate employment action" test to claims of discrimination).

D. LINKING BIAS TO THE ADVERSE EMPLOYMENT ACTION

PRICE WATERHOUSE v. HOPKINS
490 U.S. 228 (1989)

Justice BRENNAN announced the judgment of the Court and delivered an opinion, in which Justice MARSHALL, Justice BLACKMUN, and Justice STEVENS join. . . .

. . . At Price Waterhouse, a nationwide professional accounting partnership, a senior manager becomes a candidate for partnership when the partners in her local office submit her name as a candidate. All of the other partners in the firm are then invited to submit written comments on each candidate — either on a "long" or a "short" form, depending on the partner's degree of exposure to the candidate. Not every partner in the firm submits comments on every candidate. After reviewing the comments and interviewing the partners who submitted them, the firm's Admissions Committee makes a recommendation to the Policy Board. This recommendation will be either that the firm accept the candidate for partnership, put her application on "hold," or deny her the promotion outright. The Policy Board then decides whether to submit the candidate's name to the entire partnership for a vote, to "hold" her candidacy, or to reject her. The recommendation of the Admissions Committee, and the decision of the Policy Board, are not controlled by fixed guidelines: a certain number of positive comments from partners will not guarantee a candidate's admission to the partnership, nor will a specific quantity of negative comments necessarily defeat her application. Price Waterhouse places no limit on the number of persons whom it will admit to the partnership in any given year.

Protocol for promotion

Ann Hopkins had worked at Price Waterhouse's Office of Government Services in Washington, D.C., for five years when the partners in that office proposed her as a candidate for partnership. Of the 662 partners at the firm at that time, 7 were women. Of the 88 persons proposed for partnership that year, only 1 — Hopkins — was a woman. Forty-seven of these candidates were admitted to the partnership, 21 were rejected, and 20 — including Hopkins — were "held" for reconsideration the following year. Thirteen of the 32 partners who had submitted comments on Hopkins supported her bid for partnership. Three partners recommended that her candidacy be placed on hold, eight stated that they did not have an informed opinion about her, and eight recommended that she be denied partnership.

Facts

In a jointly prepared statement supporting her candidacy, the partners in Hopkins' office showcased her successful 2-year effort to secure a $25 million contract with the Department of State, labeling it "an outstanding performance" and one that Hopkins carried out "virtually at the partner level." Despite Price Waterhouse's attempt at trial to minimize her contribution to this project, Judge Gesell specifically found that Hopkins had "played a key role in Price Waterhouse's successful effort to win a multi-million dollar contract with the Department of State." Indeed, he went on, "[n]one of the other partnership candidates at Price Waterhouse that year had a comparable record in terms of successfully securing major contracts for the partnership."

The partners in Hopkins' office praised her character as well as her accomplishments, describing her in their joint statement as "an outstanding professional" who had a "deft touch," a "strong character, independence and integrity." Clients appear to have agreed with these assessments. At trial, one official from the State Department described her as "extremely competent, intelligent," "strong and forthright, very productive, energetic and creative." Another high-ranking official praised Hopkins' decisiveness, broadmindedness, and "intellectual clarity"; she was, in his words, "a stimulating conversationalist." Evaluations such as these led Judge Gesell to conclude that Hopkins "had no difficulty dealing with clients and her clients appear to have been very pleased with her work" and that she "was generally viewed as a highly competent project leader who worked long hours, pushed vigorously to meet deadlines and demanded much from the multidisciplinary staffs with which she worked."

On too many occasions, however, Hopkins' aggressiveness apparently spilled over into abrasiveness. Staff members seem to have borne the brunt of Hopkins' brusqueness. Long before her bid for partnership, partners evaluating her work had counseled her to improve her relations with staff members. Although later evaluations indicate an improvement, Hopkins' perceived shortcomings in this important area eventually doomed her bid for partnership. Virtually all of the partners' negative remarks about Hopkins — even those of partners supporting her — had to do with her "interpersonal skills." Both "[s]upporters and opponents of her candidacy," stressed Judge Gesell, "indicated that she was sometimes overly aggressive, unduly harsh, difficult to work with and impatient with staff."

There were clear signs, though, that some of the partners reacted negatively to Hopkins' personality because she was a woman. One partner described her as "macho"; another suggested that she "overcompensated for being a woman"; a third advised her to take "a course at charm school." Several partners criticized her use of profanity; in response, one partner suggested that those partners objected to her swearing only "because it[']s a lady using foul language." Another supporter explained that Hopkins "ha[d] matured from a tough-talking somewhat masculine hard-nosed mgr to an authoritative, formidable, but much more appealing lady ptr candidate." But it was the man who, as Judge Gesell found, bore responsibility for explaining to Hopkins the reasons for the Policy Board's decision to place her candidacy on hold who delivered the coup de grace: in order to improve her chances for partnership, Thomas Beyer advised, Hopkins should "walk more femininely, talk more femininely, dress more femininely, wear make-up, have her hair styled, and wear jewelry."

Dr. Susan Fiske, a social psychologist and Associate Professor of Psychology at Carnegie-Mellon University, testified at trial that the partnership selection process at Price Waterhouse was likely influenced by sex stereotyping. Her testimony focused not only on the overtly sex-based comments of partners but also on gender-neutral remarks, made by partners who knew Hopkins only slightly, that were intensely critical of her. One partner, for example, baldly stated that Hopkins was "universally disliked" by staff, and another described her as "consistently annoying and irritating"; yet these were people who had had very little contact with Hopkins. According to Fiske, Hopkins' uniqueness (as the only woman in the pool of candidates) and the subjectivity of the evaluations made it likely that sharply critical remarks such as these were the product of sex stereotyping — although Fiske admitted that she could not say with certainty whether any particular comment was the result of stereotyping. Fiske based her opinion on a review of the submitted comments, explaining that it was commonly accepted practice for social psychologists to reach this kind of conclusion without having met any of the people involved in the decisionmaking process.

In previous years, other female candidates for partnership also had been evaluated in sex-based terms. As a general matter, Judge Gesell concluded, "[c]andidates were viewed favorably if partners believed they maintained their femin[in]ity while becoming effective professional managers"; in this environment, "[t]o be identified as a 'women's lib[b]er' was regarded as [a] negative comment." In fact, the judge found that in previous years "[o]ne partner repeatedly commented that he could not consider any woman seriously as a partnership candidate and believed that women were not even capable of functioning as senior managers — yet the firm took no action to discourage his comments and recorded his vote in the overall summary of the evaluations."

Judge Gesell found that Price Waterhouse legitimately emphasized interpersonal skills in its partnership decisions, and also found that the firm had not fabricated its complaints about Hopkins' interpersonal skills as a pretext for discrimination. Moreover, he concluded, the firm did not give decisive emphasis to such traits only because Hopkins was a woman; although there were male candidates who lacked these skills but who were admitted to partnership, the judge found that these candidates possessed other, positive traits that Hopkins lacked.

The judge went on to decide, however, that some of the partners' remarks about Hopkins stemmed from an impermissibly cabined view of the proper behavior of women, and that Price Waterhouse had done nothing to disavow reliance on such comments. He held that Price Waterhouse had unlawfully discriminated against Hopkins on the basis of sex by consciously giving credence and effect to partners' comments that resulted from sex stereotyping. Noting that Price Waterhouse could avoid equitable relief by proving by clear and convincing evidence that it would have placed Hopkins' candidacy on hold even absent this discrimination, the judge decided that the firm had not carried this heavy burden. . . . *didn't carry burden of rebutting pretext discrimination*

lower court

II . . .

In passing Title VII, Congress made the simple but momentous announcement that sex, race, religion, and national origin are not relevant to the selection, evaluation, or compensation of employees. Yet, the statute does not purport to limit the other qualities and characteristics that employers may take into account in making employment decisions. The converse, therefore, of "for cause" legislation, Title VII eliminates certain bases for distinguishing among employees while otherwise preserving employers' freedom of choice. This balance between employee rights and employer prerogatives turns out to be decisive in the case before us.

Congress' intent to forbid employers to take gender into account in making employment decisions appears on the face of the statute. In now-familiar language, the statute forbids an employer to "[discriminate] *because of* such individual's . . . sex" (emphasis added). We take these words to mean that gender must be irrelevant to employment decisions. To construe the words "because of" as colloquial shorthand for "but-for causation," as does Price Waterhouse, is to misunderstand them.

But-for causation is a hypothetical construct. In determining whether a particular factor was a but-for cause of a given event, we begin by assuming that that factor was present at the time of the event, and then ask whether, even if that factor had been absent, the event nevertheless would have transpired in the same way. The present, active tense of the operative verbs of §703(a)(1) ("to fail or refuse"), in contrast, turns our attention to the actual moment of the event in question, the adverse employment decision. The critical inquiry, the one commanded by the words of §703(a)(1), is whether gender was a factor in the employment decision *at the moment it was made*. Moreover, since we know that the words "because of" do not mean "solely because of,"[7] we also know that Title VII meant to condemn even those decisions based on a mixture of legitimate and illegitimate considerations. When, therefore, an employer

---

7. Congress specifically rejected an amendment that would have placed the word "solely" in front of the words "because of." 110 Cong. Rec. 2728, 13837 (1964).

considers both gender and legitimate factors at the time of making a decision, that decision was "because of" sex and the other, legitimate considerations — even if we may say later, in the context of litigation, that the decision would have been the same if gender had not been taken into account.

To attribute this meaning to the words "because of" does not, as the dissent asserts, divest them of causal significance. A simple example illustrates the point. Suppose two physical forces act upon and move an object, and suppose that either force acting alone would have moved the object. As the dissent would have it, neither physical force was a "cause" of the motion unless we can show that but for one or both of them, the object would not have moved; to use the dissent's terminology, both forces were simply "in the air" unless we can identify at least one of them as a but-for cause of the object's movement. Events that are causally overdetermined, in other words, may not have any "cause" at all. This cannot be so.

[marginalia: does not have to be "but-for," just "because of," a force in the decision-making]

[Congress did not intend to require a plaintiff "to identify the precise causal role played by legitimate and illegitimate motivations"; it meant only to require her "to prove that the employer relied upon sex-based considerations" in its decision.]

To say that an employer may not take gender into account is not, however, the end of the matter, for that describes only one aspect of Title VII. The other important aspect of the statute is its preservation of an employer's remaining freedom of choice. We conclude that the preservation of this freedom means that an employer shall not be liable if it can prove that, even if it had not taken gender into account, it would have come to the same decision regarding a particular person. The statute's maintenance of employer prerogatives is evident from the statute itself and from its history, both in Congress and in this Court. . . .

[marginalia: Balance of rights]

The central point is this: while an employer may not take gender into account in making an employment decision . . . , it is free to decide against a woman for other reasons. We think these principles require that, once a plaintiff in a Title VII case shows that gender played a motivating part in an employment decision, the defendant may avoid a finding of liability only by proving that it would have made the same decision even if it had not allowed gender to play such a role. This balance of burdens is the direct result of Title VII's balance of rights. . . .[12]

C

In saying that gender played a motivating part in an employment decision, we mean that, if we asked the employer at the moment of the decision what its reasons were and if we received a truthful response, one of those reasons would be that the applicant or employee was a woman. In the specific context of sex stereotyping, an employer who acts on the basis of a belief that a woman cannot be aggressive, or that she must not be, has acted on the basis of gender.

. . . As to the existence of sex stereotyping in this case, we are not inclined to quarrel with the District Court's conclusion that a number of the partners' comments showed sex stereotyping at work. As for the legal relevance of sex stereotyping, we are beyond

12. Nothing in this opinion should be taken to suggest that a case must be correctly labeled as either a "pretext" case or a "mixed-motives" case from the beginning in the District Court; indeed, we expect that plaintiffs often will allege, in the alternative, that their cases are both. Discovery often will be necessary before the plaintiff can know whether both legitimate and illegitimate considerations played a part in the decision against her. At some point in the proceedings, of course, the District Court must decide whether a particular case involves mixed motives. If the plaintiff fails to satisfy the factfinder that it is more likely than not that a forbidden characteristic played a part in the employment decision, then she may prevail only if she proves . . . that the employer's stated reason for its decision is pretextual. . . .

the day when an employer could evaluate employees by assuming or insisting that they matched the stereotype associated with their group. . . . An employer who objects to aggressiveness in women but whose positions require this trait places women in an intolerable and impermissible Catch-22: out of a job if they behave aggressively and out of a job if they don't. Title VII lifts women out of this bind.

Remarks at work that are based on sex stereotypes do not inevitably prove that gender played a part in a particular employment decision. The plaintiff must show that the employer actually relied on her gender in making its decision. In making this showing, stereotyped remarks can certainly be evidence that gender played a part. In any event, the stereotyping in this case did not simply consist of stray remarks. On the contrary, Hopkins proved that Price Waterhouse invited partners to submit comments; that some of the comments stemmed from sex stereotypes; that an important part of the Policy Board's decision on Hopkins was an assessment of the submitted comments; and that Price Waterhouse in no way disclaimed reliance on the sex-linked evaluations. This is not, as Price Waterhouse suggests, "discrimination in the air"; rather, it is, as Hopkins puts it, "discrimination brought to ground and visited upon" an employee. By focusing on Hopkins' specific proof, however, we do not suggest a limitation on the possible ways of proving that stereotyping played a motivating role in an employment decision, and we refrain from deciding here which specific facts, "standing alone," would or would not establish a plaintiff's case, since such a decision is unnecessary in this case.

As to the employer's proof, in most cases, the employer should be able to present some objective evidence as to its probable decision in the absence of an impermissible motive.[15] Moreover, proving "that the same decision would have been justified . . . is not the same as proving that the same decision would have been made." An employer may not, in other words, prevail in a mixed-motives case by offering a legitimate and sufficient reason for its decision if that reason did not motivate it at the time of the decision. Finally, an employer may not meet its burden in such a case by merely showing that at the time of the decision it was motivated only in part by a legitimate reason. The very premise of a mixed-motives case is that a legitimate reason was present, and indeed, in this case, Price Waterhouse already has made this showing by convincing Judge Gesell that Hopkins' interpersonal problems were a legitimate concern. The employer instead must show that its legitimate reason, standing alone, would have induced it to make the same decision.

III

The courts below held that an employer who has allowed a discriminatory impulse to play a motivating part in an employment decision must prove by clear and convincing evidence that it would have made the same decision in the absence of discrimination. We are persuaded that the better rule is that the employer must make this showing by a preponderance of the evidence. . . .

IV

[Price Waterhouse challenged as clearly erroneous the district court's findings both that stereotyping occurred and that it played any part in the decision to place Hopkins' candidacy on hold. The plurality disagreed.]

---

15. Justice White's suggestion [in his concurring opinion] that the employer's own testimony as to the probable decision in the absence of discrimination is due special credence where the court has, contrary to the employer's testimony, found that an illegitimate factor played a part in the decision, is baffling.

In finding that some of the partners' comments reflected sex stereotyping, the District Court relied in part on Dr. Fiske's expert testimony. Without directly impugning Dr. Fiske's credentials or qualifications, Price Waterhouse insinuates that a social psychologist is unable to identify sex stereotyping in evaluations without investigating whether those evaluations have a basis in reality. This argument comes too late. At trial, counsel for Price Waterhouse twice assured the court that he did not question Dr. Fiske's expertise and failed to challenge the legitimacy of her discipline. Without contradiction from Price Waterhouse, Fiske testified that she discerned sex stereotyping in the partners' evaluations of Hopkins and she further explained that it was part of her business to identify stereotyping in written documents. We are not inclined to accept petitioner's belated and unsubstantiated characterization of Dr. Fiske's testimony as "gossamer evidence" based only on "intuitive hunches" and of her detection of sex stereotyping as "intuitively divined." Nor are we disposed to adopt the dissent's dismissive attitude toward Dr. Fiske's field of study and toward her own professional integrity.

Indeed, we are tempted to say that Dr. Fiske's expert testimony was merely icing on Hopkins' cake. It takes no special training to discern sex stereotyping in a description of an aggressive female employee as requiring "a course at charm school." Nor, turning to Thomas Beyer's memorable advice to Hopkins, does it require expertise in psychology to know that, if an employee's flawed "interpersonal skills" can be corrected by a soft-hued suit or a new shade of lipstick, perhaps it is the employee's sex and not her interpersonal skills that has drawn the criticism.

Price Waterhouse also charges that Hopkins produced no evidence that sex stereotyping played a role in the decision to place her candidacy on hold. As we have stressed, however, Hopkins showed that the partnership solicited evaluations from all of the firm's partners; that it generally relied very heavily on such evaluations in making its decision; that some of the partners' comments were the product of stereotyping; and that the firm in no way disclaimed reliance on those particular comments, either in Hopkins' case or in the past. Certainly a plausible — and, one might say, inevitable — conclusion to draw from this set of circumstances is that the Policy Board in making its decision did in fact take into account all of the partners' comments, including the comments that were motivated by stereotypical notions about women's proper deportment. . . .

V

Standard

Held ✱

We hold that when a plaintiff in a Title VII case proves that her gender played a motivating part in an employment decision, the defendant may avoid a finding of liability only by proving by a preponderance of the evidence that it would have made the same decision even if it had not taken the plaintiff's gender into account. . . .

Justice O'CONNOR concurring in the judgment.

I agree with the plurality that on the facts presented in this case, the burden of persuasion should shift to the employer to demonstrate by a preponderance of the evidence that it would have reached the same decision concerning Ann Hopkins' candidacy absent consideration of her gender. I further agree that this burden shift is properly part of the liability phase of the litigation. I thus concur in the judgment of the Court. My disagreement stems from the plurality's conclusions concerning the substantive requirement of causation under the statute and its broad statements regarding the applicability of the allocation of the burden of proof applied in this case. . . .

I

. . . The legislative history of Title VII bears out what its plain language suggests: a substantive violation of the statute only occurs when consideration of an illegitimate criterion is the "but-for" cause of an adverse employment action. The legislative history makes it clear that Congress was attempting to eradicate discriminatory actions in the employment setting, not mere discriminatory thoughts. Critics of the bill that became Title VII labeled it a "thought control bill," and argued that it created a "punishable crime that does not require an illegal external act as a basis for judgment." Senator Case . . . responded:

> The man must do or fail to do something in regard to employment. There must be some specific external act, more than a mental act. Only if he does the act because of the grounds stated in the bill would there be any legal consequences.

Thus, I disagree with the plurality's dictum that the words "because of" do not mean "but-for" causation; manifestly they do. We should not, and need not, deviate from that policy today. . . .

The evidence of congressional intent as to which party should bear the burden of proof on the issue of causation is considerably less clear. . . . [In the area of tort liability,] the law has long recognized that in certain "civil cases" leaving the burden of persuasion on the plaintiff to prove "but-for" causation would be both unfair and destructive of the deterrent purposes embodied in the concept of duty of care. Thus, in multiple causation cases, where a breach of duty has been established, the common law of torts has long shifted the burden of proof to multiple defendants to prove that their negligent actions were not the "but-for" cause of the plaintiff's injury. *See, e.g., Summers v. Tice,* 199 P.2d 1 (1948). The same rule has been applied where the effect of a defendant's tortious conduct combines with a force of unknown or innocent origin to produce the harm to the plaintiff. *See Kingston v. Chicago & N.W.R. Co.,* 211 N.W. 913, 915 (1927). . . .

. . . There is no doubt that Congress considered reliance on gender or race in making employment decisions an evil in itself. . . . Reliance on such factors is exactly what the threat of Title VII liability was meant to deter. While the main concern of the statute was with employment opportunity, Congress was certainly not blind to the stigmatic harm which comes from being evaluated by a process which treats one as an inferior by reason of one's race or sex. . . . At the same time, Congress clearly conditioned legal liability on a determination that the consideration of an illegitimate factor caused a tangible employment injury of some kind.

Where an individual disparate treatment plaintiff has shown by a preponderance of the evidence that an illegitimate criterion was a *substantial* factor in an adverse employment decision, the deterrent purpose of the statute has clearly been triggered. More importantly, as an evidentiary matter, a reasonable factfinder could conclude that absent further explanation, the employer's discriminatory motivation "caused" the employment decision. The employer has not yet been shown to be a violator, but neither is it entitled to the same presumption of good faith concerning its employment decisions which is accorded employers facing only circumstantial evidence of discrimination. Both the policies behind the statute, and the evidentiary principles developed in the analogous area of causation in the law of torts, suggest that at this point the employer may be required to convince the factfinder that, despite the smoke, there is no fire. . . .

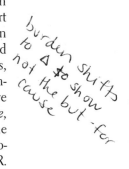

II . . .

[T]he facts of this case, and a growing number like it decided by the Courts of Appeals, convince me that the evidentiary standard I propose is necessary to make real the promise of *McDonnell Douglas*. . . . As the Court of Appeals characterized it, Ann Hopkins proved that Price Waterhouse "permitt[ed] stereotypical attitudes towards women to play a significant, though unquantifiable, role in its decision not to invite her to become a partner."

At this point Ann Hopkins had taken her proof as far as it could go. She had proved discriminatory input into the decisional process, and had proved that participants in the process considered her failure to conform to the stereotypes credited by a number of the decisionmakers had been a substantial factor in the decision. It is as if Ann Hopkins were sitting in the hall outside the room where partnership decisions were being made. As the partners filed in to consider her candidacy, she heard several of them make sexist remarks in discussing her suitability for partnership. As the decisionmakers exited the room, she was told by one of those privy to the decisionmaking process that her gender was a major reason for the rejection of her partnership bid. [If] "presumptions shifting the burden of proof are often created to reflect judicial evaluations of probabilities and to conform with a party's superior access to the proof," one would be hard pressed to think of a situation where it would be more appropriate to require the defendant to show that its decision would have been justified by wholly legitimate concerns. . . .

[The plurality, however, goes too far by holding that the burden shifts when "a decisional process is 'tainted' by awareness of sex or race in any way."]

In my view, in order to justify shifting the burden on the issue of causation to the defendant, a disparate treatment plaintiff must show by direct evidence that an illegitimate criterion was a substantial factor in the decision. . . . Requiring that the plaintiff demonstrate that an illegitimate factor played a substantial role in the employment decision identifies those employment situations where the deterrent purpose of Title VII is most clearly implicated. As an evidentiary matter, where a plaintiff has made this type of strong showing of illicit motivation, the factfinder is entitled to presume that the employer's discriminatory animus made a difference to the outcome, absent proof to the contrary from the employer. Where a disparate treatment plaintiff has made such a showing, the burden then rests with the employer to convince the trier of fact that it is more likely than not that the decision would have been the same absent consideration of the illegitimate factor. The employer need not isolate the sole cause for the decision; rather it must demonstrate that with the illegitimate factor removed from the calculus, sufficient business reasons would have induced it to take the same employment action. . . . If the employer fails to carry this burden, the factfinder is justified in concluding that the decision was made "because of" consideration of the illegitimate factor and the substantive standard for liability under the statute is satisfied.

Thus, stray remarks in the workplace, while perhaps probative of sexual harassment, see *Meritor Savings Bank v. Vinson* [reproduced at p. 326], cannot justify requiring the employer to prove that its hiring or promotion decisions were based on legitimate criteria. Nor can statements by nondecisionmakers, or statements by decisionmakers unrelated to the decisional process itself suffice to satisfy the plaintiff's burden in this regard. In addition, in my view testimony such as Dr. Fiske's in this case, standing alone, would not justify shifting the burden of persuasion to the employer. Race and gender always "play a role" in an employment decision in the benign sense that these are human characteristics of which decisionmakers are aware and may comment on in a perfectly neutral and nondiscriminatory fashion. For example, in the context of this case, a mere reference to "a lady candidate" might show that gender "played a role" in the decision, but by no means could support a rational factfinder's inference that the decision was made "because of" sex. What is required is what Ann Hopkins showed here: direct evidence that decisionmakers placed substantial negative reliance on an illegitimate criterion in reaching their decision.

It should be obvious that the threshold standard I would adopt for shifting the burden of persuasion to the defendant differs substantially from that proposed by the plurality, the plurality's suggestion to the contrary notwithstanding. . . . Under my approach, the plaintiff must produce evidence sufficient to show that an illegitimate criterion was a substantial factor in the particular employment decision such that a reasonable factfinder could draw an inference that the decision was made "because of" the plaintiff's protected status. Only then would the burden of proof shift to the defendant to prove that the decision would have been justified by other, wholly legitimate considerations. . . .

Holding / new suggested standard

[Justice White also concurred. Justice Kennedy, joined by Chief Justice Rehnquist and Justice Scalia, dissented. They viewed the plurality, despite its rhetoric, as adopting a but-for standard. "Labels aside, the import of today's decision is not that Title VII liability can arise without but-for causation, but that in certain cases it is not the plaintiff who must prove the presence of causation, but the defendant who must prove its absence."

The dissent was particularly critical of Dr. Fiske, who "purported to discern stereotyping in comments that were gender neutral — e.g., 'overbearing and abrasive' — without any knowledge of the comments' basis in reality and without having met the speaker or subject." It quoted a judge below to the effect that, "[t]o an expert of Dr. Fiske's qualifications, it seems plain that no woman could be overbearing, arrogant, or abrasive: any observations to that effect would necessarily be discounted as the product of stereotyping. If analysis like this is to prevail in federal courts, no employer can base any adverse action as to a woman on such attributes."]

NOTES

1. *Meet §703(m).* While *Price Waterhouse* was generally seen as plaintiff friendly, it was a splintered decision. Further, all the Justices had adopted a "no harm, no foul" rule: should the employer show that bias did not affect the final decision, there would be no liability even though the employer allowed bias to infect its decision processes. Congress addressed both problems by adding two new sections to the statute in the 1991 Civil Rights Act. Section 703(m) provides:

reason for 703(m)

> [A]n unlawful employment practice is established when the complaining party demonstrates that race, color, religion, sex, or national origin was a *motivating* factor for any employment practice, even though other factors also motivated the practice.

42 U.S.C §2000e-2(m). In other words, there's liability when a motivating factor is present, period.

2. *Meet §706(g)(2)(B).* But Congress simultaneously amended the statute to provide a *limited* affirmative defense: should defendant carry a burden of persuasion that it would have reached the same decision even had the illicit "motivating factor" not been present, the plaintiff's remedies are severely restricted. §706(g)(2)(B), 42 U.S.C. §706(g)(2)(B). But note the 1991 Civil Rights Act did not add similar provi-

sions to the ADEA or §1981, see p. 82, nor to the retaliation provision of Title VII. See p. 429.

These Title VII amendments had been operative for more than a decade before the Supreme Court finally construed them in the next principal case.

(handwritten margin note: female warehouse worker. fired while other party just suspended for 5 days. mixed-motive firing. P does not need to use direct evidence to establish 2000e-2(M) liability)

DESERT PALACE, INC. v. COSTA
539 U.S. 90 (2003)

Justice THOMAS delivered the opinion of the Court.

The question before us in this case is whether a plaintiff must present direct evidence of discrimination in order to obtain a mixed-motive instruction under Title VII of the Civil Rights Act of 1964, as amended by the Civil Rights Act of 1991. We hold that direct evidence is not required.

I

A

Since 1964, Title VII has made it an "unlawful employment practice for an employer . . . to discriminate against any individual . . . *because of* such individual's race, color, religion, sex, or national origin." (emphasis added). In *Price Waterhouse v. Hopkins* [reproduced at p. 61], the Court considered whether an employment decision is made "because of" sex in a "mixed-motive" case, *i.e.*, where both legitimate and illegitimate reasons motivated the decision. The Court concluded that, under §2000e-2(a)(1), an employer could "avoid a finding of liability . . . by proving that it would have made the same decision even if it had not allowed gender to play such a role." The Court was divided, however, over the predicate question of when the burden of proof may be shifted to an employer to prove the affirmative defense.

(handwritten margin note: (1) Burden shifts to A to show it would make same decision only when p has showed discrim was a motivating role. for P?)

Justice Brennan, writing for a plurality of four Justices, would have held that "when a plaintiff . . . proves that her gender played a *motivating* part in an employment decision, the defendant may avoid a finding of liability only by proving by a preponderance of the evidence that it would have made the same decision even if it had not taken the plaintiff's gender into account." The plurality did not, however, "suggest a limitation on the possible ways of proving that [gender] stereotyping played a motivating role in an employment decision."

Justice White and Justice O'Connor both concurred in the judgment. Justice White would have held that the case was governed by *Mt. Healthy City Bd. of Ed. v. Doyle*, 429 U.S. 274 (1977), and would have shifted the burden to the employer only when a plaintiff "showed that the unlawful motive was a *substantial* factor in the adverse employment action." Justice O'Connor, like Justice White, would have required the plaintiff to show that an illegitimate consideration was a "substantial factor" in the employment decision. But, under Justice O'Connor's view, "the burden on the issue of causation" would shift to the employer only where "a disparate treatment plaintiff [could] show by *direct evidence* that an illegitimate criterion was a substantial factor in the decision."

(handwritten margin note: (2) Burden shifts to D if P shows it was a substantial factor. (2A.) P must show w/ direct evidence)

Two years after *Price Waterhouse*, Congress passed the 1991 Act [which, in part,] "responded" to *Price Waterhouse* by "setting forth standards applicable in 'mixed motive' cases" in two new statutory provisions.[1] [The Court quoted §703(m) and went on to describe §706(g)(2)(B). With] respect to "a claim in which an individual proves

1. This case does not require us to decide when, if ever, [the amendments apply] outside of the mixed-motive context.

a violation under section 2000e-2(m)," the employer has a (limited) affirmative defense that does not absolve it of liability, but restricts the remedies available to a plaintiff. The available remedies include only declaratory relief, certain types of injunctive relief, and attorney's fees and costs. In order to avail itself of the affirmative defense, the employer must "demonstrate that [it] would have taken the same action in the absence of the impermissible motivating factor."

Since the passage of the 1991 Act, the Courts of Appeals have divided over whether plaintiff must prove by direct evidence that an impermissible consideration was a "motivating factor" in an adverse employment action. Relying primarily on Justice O'Connor's concurrence in *Price Waterhouse*, a number of courts have held that direct evidence is required to establish liability under §2000e-2(m). In the decision below, however, the Ninth Circuit concluded otherwise.

B

Petitioner Desert Palace, Inc., dba Caesar's Palace Hotel & Casino of Las Vegas, Nevada, employed respondent Catharina Costa as a warehouse worker and heavy equipment operator. Respondent was the only woman in this job and in her local Teamsters bargaining unit.

Respondent experienced a number of problems with management and her co-workers that led to an escalating series of disciplinary sanctions, including informal rebukes, a denial of privileges, and suspension. Petitioner finally terminated respondent after she was involved in a physical altercation in a warehouse elevator with fellow Teamsters member Herbert Gerber. Petitioner disciplined both employees because the facts surrounding the incident were in dispute, but Gerber, who had a clean disciplinary record, received only a 5-day suspension. . . .

. . . At trial, respondent presented evidence that (1) she was singled out for "intense 'stalking'" by one of her supervisors, (2) she received harsher discipline than men for the same conduct, (3) she was treated less favorably than men in the assignment of overtime, and (4) supervisors repeatedly "stacked" her disciplinary record and "frequently used or tolerated" sex-based slurs against her.

Based on this evidence, the District Court denied petitioner's motion for judgment as a matter of law, and submitted the case to the jury with instructions, two of which are relevant here. First, without objection from petitioner, the District Court instructed the jury that "the plaintiff has the burden of proving . . . by a preponderance of the evidence" that she "suffered adverse work conditions" and that her sex "was a motivating factor in any such work conditions imposed upon her."

Second, the District Court gave the jury the following mixed-motive instruction:

> You have heard evidence that the defendant's treatment of the plaintiff was motivated by the plaintiff's sex and also by other lawful reasons. If you find that the plaintiff's sex was a motivating factor in the defendant's treatment of the plaintiff, the plaintiff is entitled to your verdict, even if you find that the defendant's conduct was also motivated by a lawful reason.
>
> However, if you find that the defendant's treatment of the plaintiff was motivated by both gender and lawful reasons, you must decide whether the plaintiff is entitled to damages. The plaintiff is entitled to damages unless the defendant proves by a preponderance of the evidence that the defendant would have treated plaintiff similarly even if the plaintiff's gender had played no role in the employment decision.

Petitioner unsuccessfully objected to this instruction, claiming that respondent had failed to adduce "direct evidence" that sex was a motivating factor in her dismissal or in any of the other adverse employment actions taken against her. The jury rendered a verdict for respondent, awarding backpay, compensatory damages, and punitive damages. The District Court denied petitioner's renewed motion for judgment as a matter of law. . . .

II

This case provides us with the first opportunity to consider the effects of the 1991 Act on jury instructions in mixed-motive cases. Specifically, we must decide whether a plaintiff must present direct evidence of discrimination in order to obtain a mixed-motive instruction under 42 U.S.C. §2000e-2(m). Petitioner's argument on this point proceeds in three steps: (1) Justice O'Connor's opinion is the holding of *Price Waterhouse*; (2) Justice O'Connor's *Price Waterhouse* opinion requires direct evidence of discrimination before a mixed-motive instruction can be given; and (3) the 1991 Act does nothing to abrogate that holding. Like the Court of Appeals, we see no need to address which of the opinions in *Price Waterhouse* is controlling: the third step of petitioner's argument is flawed, primarily because it is inconsistent with the text of §2000e-2(m).

Our precedents make clear that the starting point for our analysis is the statutory text. And where, as here, the words of the statute are unambiguous, the "judicial inquiry is complete." Section 2000e-2(m) unambiguously states that a plaintiff need only "demonstrate" that an employer used a forbidden consideration with respect to "any employment practice." On its face, the statute does not mention, much less require, that a plaintiff make a heightened showing through direct evidence. Indeed, petitioner concedes as much.

Moreover, Congress explicitly defined the term "demonstrates" in the 1991 Act, leaving little doubt that no special evidentiary showing is required. Title VII defines the term "'demonstrates'" as to "meet the burdens of production and persuasion." §2000e(m). If Congress intended the term "'demonstrates'" to require that the "burdens of production and persuasion" be met by direct evidence or some other heightened showing, it could have made that intent clear by including language to that effect in §2000e(m). Its failure to do so is significant, for Congress has been unequivocal when imposing heightened proof requirements in other circumstances, including in other provisions of Title 42. . . . 42 U.S.C. §5851(b)(3)(D) (providing that "relief may not be ordered" against an employer in retaliation cases involving whistleblowers under the Atomic Energy Act where the employer is able to "*demonstrate by clear and convincing evidence* that it would have taken the same unfavorable personnel action in the absence of such behavior" (emphasis added)).

In addition, Title VII's silence with respect to the type of evidence required in mixed-motive cases also suggests that we should not depart from the "conventional rule of civil litigation [that] generally applies in Title VII cases." That rule requires a plaintiff to prove his case "by a preponderance of the evidence," using "direct or circumstantial evidence," *Postal Service Bd. of Governors v. Aikens*, 460 U.S. 711, 714, n.3 (1983). We have often acknowledged the utility of circumstantial evidence in discrimination cases. For instance, in *Reeves v. Sanderson Plumbing Products, Inc.* [reproduced at p. 24], we recognized that evidence that a defendant's explanation for an employment practice is "unworthy of credence" is "one form of *circumstantial evidence* that is probative of intentional discrimination" (emphasis added). The reason for treating circumstantial and direct evidence alike is both clear and deep-rooted: "Circumstantial evidence is not only sufficient, but may also be more certain, satisfying and persuasive than direct evidence." *Rogers v. Missouri Pacific R. Co.*, 352 U.S. 500, 508, n.17 (1957). . . .

For the reasons stated above, we agree with the Court of Appeals that no heightened showing is required under §2000e-2(m).

In order to obtain an instruction under §2000e-2(m), a plaintiff need only present sufficient evidence for a reasonable jury to conclude, by a preponderance of the evidence, that "race, color, religion, sex, or national origin was a motivating factor for any employment practice." Because direct evidence of discrimination is not required in mixed-motive cases, the Court of Appeals correctly concluded that the District Court did not abuse its discretion in giving a mixed-motive instruction to the jury. Accordingly, the judgment of the Court of Appeals is affirmed. . . .

[Justice O'Connor concurred, agreeing that evidentiary rule she adopted in *Price Waterhouse* had been superseded by the Civil Rights Act of 1991.]

NOTES

1. *How Does* Price Waterhouse *Differ?* Most cases before *Price Waterhouse* were viewed as "single motive" cases — the employer had either acted from discriminatory motives or it had acted because of its asserted "legitimate, nondiscriminatory reason." But the trial judge found that Hopkins did in fact have serious interpersonal issues that an employer had taken into account in making the partnership decision. Thus, its nondiscriminatory reason was not a "pretext" for discrimination and, if a single motive paradigm applied, plaintiff would have lost. Plaintiff, however, prevailed because that legitimate reason for putting her partnership bid on hold existed together with gender bias. While finding that the defendant was motivated by sex, the trial judge did not determine whether discrimination or defendant's asserted reason was the but-for cause of defendant's action. The decision thus wrestles with how to analyze "mixed motive" cases.

2. *But-For Causation in* Price Waterhouse. For all the talk about different concepts of causation, all of the opinions in *Price Waterhouse* assume that but-for causation is necessary, that is, plaintiff loses unless gender is a determinative factor. What changed was the burden of persuasion. In *Price Waterhouse*, six Justices (the plurality and Justices White and O'Connor) would shift the burden of persuasion on causation. When plaintiff established by a preponderance of the evidence that sex was a "motivating factor" (for O'Connor and White, a "substantial factor"), the burden shifted to defendant to negate but-for causation by establishing, by a preponderance of the evidence, that it would have made the same decision anyway. In other words, if the employer does carry its burden, then sex is not the but-for cause, which means there was no liability under *Price Waterhouse*.

3. *Proving a Motivating Factor.* The trial court found that Ann Hopkins's sex entered into the consideration of her candidacy, whether or not it had a determinative influence. Beyer's advice certainly suggested he thought that Hopkins would have more success the next year if she conformed more closely to feminine stereotypes. Comments by others linked their criticism of her partnership bid to her sex. And then there was the partner who in the past said that he would never vote for a woman partner, period. But all of this proof turns on statements by the decisionmakers, and most of the statements concerned the decision in question. In other words, most proof of defendant's motivation was what Justice O'Connor called "direct evidence," a classification that proved important to what *Price Waterhouse* came to mean.

4. *Two Distinct Proof Methods?* Justice O'Connor's concurrence was thought by the lower courts to have stated the narrowest grounds on which *Price Waterhouse* was decided and therefore became the holding of the case. *See Marks v. United States,* 430 U.S. 188 (1977) (where no majority speaks for the Court, the holding is the narrowest point upon which five justices on the prevailing side agree). Therefore, after *Price Waterhouse* and before *Desert Palace,* two separate methods of proof applied to individual disparate treatment cases. Analytically, the first question for every case was whether plaintiff could point to "direct" evidence that discrimination was a "substantial factor" in the challenged decision. If so, then the "substantial factor" showing established a violation, albeit subject to the defendant's potential same-decision affirmative defense to liability. Lacking evidence that the court would be willing to characterize as "direct," the default analysis was *McDonnell Douglas,* requiring the plaintiff to carry the burden of proving that discrimination was the determinative factor in defendant's action, as we saw in *Biggins.* That imposed on the plaintiff a higher level of proof than required by *Price Waterhouse,* but, if successful, it necessarily prevented the defendant from showing that it would have made the same decision even absent discrimination.

5. *The Direct Evidence Requirement.* After *Price Waterhouse,* then, whether "direct evidence" existed was often outcome determinative. Where it existed, the burden of persuasion of discrimination effectively shifted: the plaintiff did not have to prove but-for causation; rather, she could prove something less than that and still establish liability if the employer failed to negate the but-for link between discrimination and the action. But Justice O'Connor in *Price Waterhouse* did not define what evidence was "direct," although the evidence in the case included statements (best described as employer "admissions") that gender influenced the decision to put plaintiff's candidacy on hold. In the wake of the decision, there was rampant confusion among the lower courts as to what counted as "direct" as opposed to "circumstantial" proof.

The classic notion of "direct" evidence is evidence that, if believed, proves the ultimate question at issue *without drawing any inferences.* Suppose you are standing on a street corner and a car races by. You notice the driver is texting on his iPhone and immediately crashes into a parked car. As an observer (an omniscient one), you have direct evidence that the driver's negligence caused the collision. On the other hand, suppose you see only the crash and run up to the car to see the phone with an unfinished text on the phone screen in the driver's lap. You might be pretty sure that he was texting while driving, but it would be an inference (admittedly, a pretty obvious one), not a direct observation of negligence.

The problem with applying this standard to discrimination cases is that the critical question is the state of mind of the employer, which means there can never be direct evidence in that classic sense. So determining that mental state usually depends on inferences from the employer's conduct, *i.e.,* "circumstantial" evidence. Even statements by the employer supposed revealing its state of mind to discriminate at the time it acted could be viewed as indirect since the factfinder would have to determine whether the speaker spoke accurately. Nevertheless, this kind of evidence is what Justice O'Connor viewed as "direct." Under this view, the direct evidence threshold to burden shifting meant that burdens rarely shifted and *Biggins*'s "determinative factor" remained the rule for both Title VII and the ADEA, with direct evidence cases providing a narrow exception.

6. *The Addition of a Motivating Factor Standard.* As we saw in *Desert Palace,* the 1991 Civil Rights Act changed all this. Direct evidence is no longer needed to establish a motivating factor. Section 703(m) clearly draws its "a motivating factor"

language from the *Price Waterhouse* plurality, and Justice Brennan defined the term: "[i]n saying that gender played a motivating part in an employment decision, we mean that, if we asked the employer at the moment of the decision what its reasons were and if we received a truthful response, *one of those reasons* would be that the applicant or employee was a woman" (emphasis added).

Linda Hamilton Krieger and Susan T. Fiske, in *Behavioral Realism in Employment Discrimination Law: Implicit Bias and Disparate Treatment*, 94 CAL. L. REV. 997, 1010 (2006), criticize this passage, in part because it assumes that "the discriminator is consciously aware . . . that he or she is discriminating," which contradicts the implicit bias literature we've studied. They also take issue with Justice Brennan's "moment of decision" language because "'motivating factor' is 'an internal mental state, a category that includes cognitive structures like implicit stereotypes or other social schema that influence social perception, judgment, and action. For race, color, sex, national origin, or other protected characteristics to 'motivate' an employment decision means that the characteristic served as a stimulus which, interacting with the decision maker's internal biased mental state, led the decision maker to behave toward the person differently than he otherwise would." *Id.* at 1056.

These scholars to the contrary notwithstanding, Justice Brennan did define motivating factor in the passage the authors criticize for not taking into account deeper psychological impulses. Why isn't it possible to interpret Congress as adopting Brennan's "common sense" view, even if that view would not be shared by psychologists? But he also wrote that "we are beyond the day when an employer could evaluate employees by assuming or insisting that they match the stereotype associated with their group." Was Brennan speaking only of consciously held stereotypes or does "truthfully" mean objectively the truth, whether or not the defendant is conscious of relying on stereotypes or not? In other words, what, if anything does *Price Waterhouse* and motivating factor analysis say about unconscious bias?

7. *Expert Testimony of Stereotyping*. As to statements that did not expressly refer to sex that nevertheless showed stereotyping in the testimony of the expert witness, Dr. Susan Fiske, the plurality in *Price Waterhouse* indicated that it might be "merely icing on the cake." Justice O'Connor was more skeptical of such testimony, and Justice Kennedy's dissent was scathing: "Fiske purported to discern stereotyping in comments that were gender neutral — e.g., 'overbearing and abrasive' — without any knowledge of the comments' basis in reality and without having met the speaker or subject." Is this criticism valid? May not certain statements be susceptible of varying meanings, with expert testimony helping the factfinder in deciding whether the statements are likely to reflect stereotyping?

In a portion of *Ash v. Tyson Foods, Inc.*, 546 U.S. 454, 456-57 (2006), that we have not reproduced, the Supreme Court suggests that the answer is yes. Language is a slippery tool, and statements may be ambiguous about their racial content:

> [T]here was evidence that Tyson's plant manager, who made the disputed hiring decisions, had referred on some occasions to each of the petitioners as "boy." Petitioners argued this was evidence of discriminatory animus. The Court of Appeals disagreed, holding that "while the use of 'boy' when modified by a racial classification like 'black' or 'white' is evidence of discriminatory intent, the use of 'boy' alone is not evidence of discrimination." Although it is true the disputed word will not always be evidence of racial animus, it does not follow that the term, standing alone, is always benign. The speaker's meaning may depend on various factors including context, inflection, tone of voice, local custom, and historical usage. Insofar as the Court of Appeals held that modifiers or

qualifications [such as "black boy"] are necessary in all instances to render the disputed term probative of bias, the court's decision is erroneous.

Presumably, expert testimony might help that process. *See* Leora F. Eisenstadt, *The N-Word at Work: Contextualizing Language in the Workplace*, 33 BERKELEY J. EMP. & LAB. L. 299, 303 (2012). On remand, the Eleventh Circuit ultimately found that a jury could reasonably find that the term had a derogatory racial meaning. 664 F.3d 883 (11th Cir. 2011). *See generally* Jeffrey A. Van Detta, *The Strange Career of Title VII's §703(m): An Essay on the Unfulfilled Promise of the Civil Rights Act of 1991*, 89 ST. JOHN'S L. REV. 883 (2016) (exploring the tortured history of *Ash* both before and after the Supreme Court's decision).

There has been concern about whether various kinds of expert testimony meet the Supreme Court's heightened standards under *Daubert v. Merrell Dow Pharmaceuticals, Inc.*, 509 U.S. 579 (1993), and its progeny. *See generally* Susan T. Fiske & Eugene Borgida, *Providing Expert Knowledge in an Adversarial Context: Social Cognitive Science in Employment Discrimination Cases*, 4 ANN. REV. L. SOC. SCI. 123 (2008). If, instead of accepting the testimony of Dr. Fiske at trial, the defendant had objected, how should the trial court have ruled as to its admissibility?

8. *The Facts of* Desert Palace. The Court's description of the facts in *Costa* is abstract and bloodless. To get a better sense of plaintiff's case, the Ninth Circuit offered a much more robust description:

> Catharina Costa is a trailblazer. She has worked most of her life in a male-dominated environment, driving trucks and operating heavy equipment. . . . [After some time on the job,] Costa began to notice that she was being singled out because she was a woman. Her concerns not only fell on deaf ears — "my word meant nothing" — but resulted in her being treated as an "outcast."
>
> In a series of escalating events that included informal rebukes, denial of privileges accorded her male co-workers, suspension, and finally discharge, Costa's efforts to solve problems were thwarted along the way. . . . [W]hen men came in late, they were often given overtime to make up the lost time; when Costa came in late, in one case, one minute late, she was issued a written reprimand, known as a record of counseling. When men missed work for medical reasons, they were given overtime to make up the lost time; when Costa missed work for medical reasons, she was disciplined. On one occasion, a warehouse supervisor actually suspended her because she had missed work while undergoing surgery to remove a tumor; only the intervention of the director of human resources voided this action. . . .
>
> Costa presented extensive evidence that she received harsher discipline than the men. For instance, she was frequently warned and even suspended for allegedly hazardous use of equipment and for use of profanity, yet other Teamsters engaged in this conduct with impunity. . . .
>
> [W]hen Costa asked her supervisors point blank about the differential treatment of another Teamster who was favored with [more] overtime assignments, [t]he response: He "has a family to support."
>
> Costa also presented evidence that she was penalized for her failure to conform to sexual stereotypes. Although her fellow Teamsters frequently lost their tempers, swore at fellow employees, and sometimes had physical altercations, it was Costa, identified in one report as "the lady Teamster," who was called a "bitch," and told "you got more balls than the guys." . . .
>
> Supervisors frequently used or tolerated verbal slurs that were sex-based or tinged with sexual overtones. Most memorably, one co-worker called her a "fucking cunt." When she wrote a letter to management expressing her concern with this epithet . . . she received a three-day suspension in response. Although the other employee admitted

using the epithet, Costa was faulted for "engaging in verbal confrontation with co-work-er in the warehouse resulting in use of profane and vulgar language by other employee."

299 F.3d 838, 844-45. Ms. Costa was finally discharged after a co-worker, upset about a report that Costa had snitched on him for taking unauthorized lunch breaks, "trapped Costa in an elevator and shoved her against the wall, bruising her arm." *Id.* at 846. Following an investigation that her supervisor said was inconclusive, Costa was fired and her assailant subjected to only a five-day suspension.

9. *The "Jerk" Possibility.* Ms. Costa claimed that she was subjected to unequal treat-ment because she was a woman. Further, it is at least plausible that the treatment was not based merely on implicit bias. Rather, her male co-workers may well have been consciously hostile to a woman's intrusion into their previously all-male enclave. Hos-tile work environment discrimination is prohibited by Title VII, as will be developed in Chapter 5. Because Costa was the only woman, she might have been subjected to the treatment she challenged precisely because she was a woman. But isn't it also possible that all the bad things that happened to her were not because of her sex but because she was a jerk? Were the gender-specific statements (even if not "direct evi-dence") critical to the jury's finding of liability? *See also Hall v. City of Chicago,* 713 F.3d 325 (7th Cir. 2013) (while mistreatment of the only female plumber was not suf-ficient to establish a gender basis. the harasser's statement about wanting to "slap that woman" allowed a jury to find a sex basis).

10. *"Direct" Evidence Not a Prerequisite to Motivating Factor Proof.* The unani-mous *Desert Palace* holding is a straightforward reading of §703(m). Since the statute by its terms does not include a requirement of "direct" evidence, none is necessary: "[i]n order to obtain an instruction under §2000e-2(m), a plaintiff need only pre-sent sufficient evidence for a reasonable jury to conclude, by a preponderance of the evidence, that race, color, religion, sex, or national origin was a motivating factor for any employment practice." This sentence may seem pretty innocuous — after all, isn't the question in any litigation whether the plaintiff can adduce sufficient evidence to make out the violation? In reality, however, this language is potentially paradigm-shifting: instead of needing direct evidence to make out a motivating factor, "suffi-cient evidence," however defined, will do. And a motivating factor is less than but-for causation. *See* Michael J. Zimmer, *A Chain of Inferences Proving Discrimination,* 79 U. COLO. L. REV. 1243, 1254 (2008).

Thus, in cases to which §703(m) applies, a plaintiff no longer need prove that race or sex was a determinative factor in an employment decision, and whatever proof she need adduce is okay if it is "sufficient." *Biggins* no longer controls all Title VII cases although we will see that it continues to govern Title VII retaliation cases and claims under the ADEA, neither of which were amended to add a provision like §703(m). See pp. 82 and 429. But don't bury "direct evidence" just yet. Some circuits now speak in terms of the "direct method of proof" and the "indirect method." As you might guess, the latter is *McDonnell Douglas.* The "direct method" is *Desert Palace* and includes not only what would have been "direct evidence" for Justice O'Connor, but also some kinds of circumstantial evidence.

For years Seventh Circuit decisions described proof of discrimination as being con-structed either by direct evidence or by a "convincing mosaic" of circumstantial evi-dence. A panel of the court, however, recently declared that district courts (and even other panels) had mistakenly viewed "convincing mosaic" as a legal test. *Ortiz v. Wer-ner Enters., Inc.,* 834 F.3d 760, 765 (7th Cir. 2016), rejected that view, holding that the real question is "simply whether the evidence would permit a reasonable factfinder to conclude that the plaintiff's [protected class] caused the discharge or other adverse employment action." Further, "[e]vidence must be considered as a whole, rather than asking whether any particular piece of evidence proves the case by itself — or whether just the 'direct' evidence does so, or the 'indirect' evidence. Evidence is evidence. Relevant evidence must be considered and irrelevant evidence disregarded, but no evidence should be treated differently from other evidence because it can be labeled 'direct' or 'indirect.'"

11. *Is a §703(m) Case Different from a §703(a) Case?* Reading the text of *Desert Palace*, one would think that the "a motivating factor" standard of liability would apply to all Title VII cases. There are, however, indications that the decision can be read narrowly. For example, footnote 1 says that the Court was not deciding the impact of this decision "outside of the mixed-motive context." Presumably, *Desert Palace* involved mixed motives because the plaintiff essentially conceded that her altercation with a co-worker had played a role in the termination decision. But don't all individual disparate treatment cases involve a claim of discrimination by the plaintiff and a rebuttal claim by the defendant that it acted for a reason other than discrimination? Wouldn't a jury usually (always?) be able to determine that the nondiscriminatory reason played a role. In other words, what's the difference between a §703(a) (read *McDonnell Douglas*) case and a §703(m) (read *Desert Palace*) case?

12. Desert Palace *as a §703(m) Case.* The jury was asked whether discrimination was "a motivating factor" in the employer's decision to fire Costa. Since it found sex to be such "a motivating factor," we don't know if it concluded that other factors were also involved. But we do know that the jury did not find that the employer "would have taken the same action in the absence of the impermissible motivating factor," as the §706(g)(2)(B) affirmative defense to full remedies requires. The point is, the jury could have given the verdict it did even if it had found that Costa's involvement in a fight on the job did in part motivate the employer to discharge her. Prior *to Desert Palace*, the existence of a "legitimate, nondiscriminatory reason" that in fact motivated the employer was often fatal to a plaintiff's case unless she could point to direct evidence of discrimination. That's clearly no longer true.

13. "A *Motivating Factor*" *Causation.* But what, exactly, is a motivating factor when it need not cause a particular decision? One author views it as "minimal causation," which he describes as having "some tendency to influence the event in question but still not rise to the level of necessity or sufficiency." Martin J. Katz, *The Fundamental Incoherence of Title VII: Making Sense of Causation in Disparate Treatment Law*, 94 Geo. L.J. 489, 498-99 (2006). The notion of "tendency" is probabilistic; the plaintiff does not have to prove that the factor made a difference, only that it was likely to make a difference. Does this help you? In A *Better Route Through the Swamp: Causal Coherence in Disparate Treatment Doctrine*, 65 Rutgers L. Rev. 723, 772-73 (2013), Professor Brian S. Clarke disagrees: both the Court and Congress used the term in the sense of playing a substantial part in the adverse employment action. He argues that minimal causation is "artificially narrow" since the intermediate stage between traditional but-for and "minimal causation" is found in the notion of "necessary element of a sufficient set" of factors causing a decision. Do you think that juries will be able to draw either distinction?

14. Desert Palace *and* McDonnell Douglas. Did the addition of §§703(m) and 706(g)(2)(B) to Title VII change all §703(a) or just create a second, alternative avenue for plaintiffs? One circuit chose the alternative reading, *see Fogg v. Gonzales*, 492 F.3d 447 (D.C. Cir. 2007), but the Supreme Court later wrote in *University of Texas*

Consequence of Desert Palace

Southwestern Medical Center v. Nassar, 133 S. Ct. 2517 (2013), reproduced at p. 429, that "§2000e-2(m) is not itself a substantive bar on discrimination. Rather, it is a rule that establishes the causation standard for proving a violation defined elsewhere in Title VII." *Id.* at 2530. Professor Sandra Sperino argues that this makes clear that §703(m) does not create an alternative theory of liability but merely describes one way to prove a violation of §703: "[t]hese sentences mean that there is no such thing as a 'mixed-motive' claim or a 'single-motive' claim. Courts and litigants are entitled to use the 'motivating factor' definition of causation found in §2000e-2(m) for all intentional discrimination claims." *Nassar's Hidden Message*, http://lawprofessors.typepad.com/laborprof_blog/2014/04/nassars-hidden-messag.html.

Even if that's correct, might some plaintiffs want to forgo the presumably less demanding motivating factor approach? *See Coe v. Northern Pipe Prods., Inc.*, 589 F. Supp. 2d 1055, 1097-98 (N.D. Iowa 2008) ("plaintiffs might well choose to avoid §703(m) because of the strong possibility that a jury verdict will result in liability but no backpay or damages). Think about the professional responsibility issues of deciding whether to ask for a *Desert Palace* jury instruction when it might enhance the chances of getting a judgment of liability (which ensures your attorneys' fees) but perhaps also decreases the probability of your client getting a damage award because of the "same-decision anyway" defense.

15. *Why Is* McDonnell Douglas *Still Around?* In the wake of *Desert Palace*, multiple commentators questioned the continued viability of *McDonnell Douglas*, *see* Michael J. Zimmer, *The New Discrimination Law:* Price Waterhouse *Is Dead, Whither* McDonnell Douglas?, 53 EMORY L.J. 1887 (2004), On one level, the answer is clear: in the year before *Desert Palace*, *McDonnell Douglas* was cited 1,446 times; in 2016, it was cited 2,795 times. Apparently, it remains alive and well — but why, given that *Desert Palace* seems to offer a more plaintiff-friendly approach?

The quick answer is that the courts have not applied "motivating factor" analysis very often. Consistent with *Desert Palace*, most recognize that mixed-motive analysis can be applied to circumstantial evidence cases. *E.g., Quigg v. Thomas Cnty. Sch. Dist.*, 814 F.3d 1227, 1232-33 (11th Cir. 2016); *White v. Baxter Healthcare Corp.*, 533 F.3d 381, 400 (6th Cir. 2008); *but see Griffith v. City of Des Moines*, 387 F.3d 733 (8th Cir. 2004) (refusing to apply *Desert Palace* in the summary judgment context). That, of course, raises the question of what makes a controversy a "mixed motive case."

One view looks back to *Desert Palace* itself where the Ninth Circuit sketched out a unitary approach, essentially allowing *McDonnell Douglas* analysis as well as all other theories allowed by the evidence with the ultimate question of liability to be determined by §703(m)'s "motivating factor" test. In other words, the single-motive approach of *McDonnell Douglas* is merged into the mixed-motive approach of §703(m) along with all other claims of disparate treatment. *Dominguez-Curry v. Nevada Transportation Dep't*, 424 F.3d 1040 (9th Cir. 2005), held that, under the "a motivating factor" test, the fact that the person promoted was more qualified did not justify granting summary judgment for the defendant. "Even if it were uncontested that Andrews' qualifications were superior, this would not preclude a finding of discrimination. An employer may be held liable under Title VII even if it had a legitimate reason for its employment decision, as long as an illegitimate reason was a motivating factor in the decision." *Id.* at 1040. *See also* Steven J. Kaminshine, *Disparate Treatment as a Theory of Discrimination: The Need for a Restatement, Not a Revolution*, 2 STAN. J. C.R. & C.L. 1, 7 (2006) (since "*McDonnell Douglas* is not dead, just wounded," courts should apply a serial approach with each case first analyzed with a pretext lens and then a mixed-motive lens).

16.   *"Direct" Evidence Is Still the Gold Standard.* The kind of evidence that might have been characterized as "direct" before *Desert Palace*, while no longer required for liability, remains very important as a means of proving discrimination. *See Tolbert v. Smith*, 790 F.3d 427 (2d Cir. 2015) (principal's pejorative references to an African American's cooking "black food" suggested racial bias and were related to plaintiff's qualifications as a teacher); *Etienne v. Spanish Lake Truck & Casino Plaza, L.L.C.*, 778 F.3d 473 (5th Cir. 2015) (general manager's repeated statements that waitress was "too black" to be promoted in a casino was direct evidence of discrimination necessitating a trial); *Wilson v. Cox*, 753 F.3d 244, 247 (D.C. Cir. 2014) (decisionmaker's statements that older worker "came here to retire" were sufficient evidence to require a trial on plaintiff's claim of discriminatory termination).

17. *Academic Response to* Desert Palace. There has been an outpouring of scholarship on the meaning of *Desert Palace* and its implications for the continued viability of *McDonnell Douglas*. In addition to the works already cited, here's a sampling of the commentary: Henry L. Chambers, Jr., *The Effect of Eliminating Distinctions Among Title VII Disparate Treatment Cases*, 57 SMU L. Rev. 83 (2004); Kenneth R. Davis, Price-*Fixing: Refining the* Price Waterhouse *Standard and Individual Disparate Treatment Law*, 31 Fla. St. U. L. Rev. 859 (2004); Marcia L. McCormick, *The Allure and Danger of Practicing Law as Taxonomy*, 58 Ark. L. Rev. 159 (2005); Melissa Hart, *Subjective Decisionmaking and Unconscious Discrimination*, 56 Ala. L. Rev. 741 (2005).

NOTE ON EVIDENCE ISSUES ABOUT ADMISSIONS TESTIMONY

The preceding Notes suggest that employment discrimination law and evidence law intersect in potentially critical ways. One such intersection is hearsay. When *A* testifies to his own motivations, there is no hearsay problem. When, however, *B* testifies as to what *A* said about *A*'s motivations, the testimony is technically hearsay if it is introduced for its truth, that is, that *A* had such motivations. An example from *Price Waterhouse* is the partner who stated that no woman should ever be promoted to partner. If this statement was introduced for its truth, that is, that he believed women cannot be partners, it is hearsay. If it were introduced merely for its effects on other partners, its truth would be irrelevant, and it would not be hearsay. The law of evidence admits such statements only if defined as "nonhearsay" or pursuant to some exception to the hearsay rule. As the *Price Waterhouse* example suggests, there is a further complication: in the usual case, the employer will be a corporation or other legal entity that can only act through its agents, and the threshold question is whether the statement in question was made within the scope of the agent's employment.

The most common basis for admission of such statements in Title VII cases is admissions of a party opponent (which, of course, includes a party's agents speaking within the scope of their agency). *See* Kenneth S. Broun, McCormick on Evidence, ch. 25 (7th ed. 2014). To the extent that the speaker was commenting about matters within the scope of his or her employment at the time of the statement, such comments would generally be admissible as nonhearsay. *See Marra v. Philadelphia Housing Auth.*, 497 F.3d 286 (3d Cir. 2007) (supervisor's statement concerning "repercussions" for employee who testified against the employer in a discrimination case was admissible because it was made within the scope of his employment); *Simple v. Walgreen Co.*, 511 F.3d 668, 672 (7th Cir. 2007) (remark by person involved in the decisionmaking process that a store "was possibly not ready to have a black manager" was made within the scope of her employment and therefore admissible). *Cf. Back v. Nestlé USA, Inc.*, 694 F.3d 571, 577-78 (6th Cir. 2012) (while evidence that a human resources director said there was a plan to get rid of the three oldest employees would be admissible since it was made within the scope of his employment, the particular statement was actually hearsay within hearsay since the director was saying that "higher management" had made the statement and there was no showing that the unidentified declarants were speaking on a matter within the scope of their employment).

It seems likely that Justice O'Connor's use of "direct evidence" of defendant's state of mind was intended to embrace employer admissions, but not all statements that are admissible are necessarily close enough in time and closely enough related to the at-issue decision to constitute direct evidence that would satisfy Justice O'Connor. In any event, admission evidence raises four questions:

(a) *What did the agent actually say?* Students sometimes think that for an "admission" by a party to exist, the party must make the statement in court or in pleadings. While such statements are admissions, any out-of-court statement by a party to a case may also be used against it. Thus, the plaintiff's testimony about an employer's admission alone may create a jury issue of mixed motives when it shows an illegitimate consideration in operation. *EEOC v. Warfield-Rohr Casket Co.*, 364 F.3d 160, 163-64 (4th Cir. 2004) ("there is no requirement that an employee's testimony [of the employer's admissions] be corroborated in order to apply the mixed-motive framework").

(b) *Does the statement show illegitimate considerations?* Some remarks seem to be pretty obviously pejorative on racial grounds, *King v. Hardesty*, 517 F.3d 1049, 1059 (8th Cir. 2008) (supervisor's comment to black teacher — that "white people teach black kids . . . better than someone from their own race" — was "evidence that may be viewed as directly reflecting Hardesty's alleged discriminatory attitude"). But a more refined analysis is sometimes necessary since language is a slippery tool, and statements may be ambiguous about their racial content. We saw that with *Ash v. Tyson Foods, Inc.*, see p. 46, where there was considerable debate as to whether the use of the word "boy" directed at an adult African American male was probative of bias. *See also Bailey v. USF Holland, Inc.*, 526 F.3d 880 (6th Cir. 2008) (continued use of the word "boy" after plaintiffs had objected and after the racial implications had been explained at sensitivity training sessions was part of a pattern of racial harassment). Some courts, however, have also held more ambiguous comments capable of being found racist. *See Abrams v. Dep't of Pub. Safety*, 764 F.3d 244 (2d Cir. 2014) (statements about plaintiff not "fitting in" could be found to refer to race in the context of an all-white elite unit); *McGinest v. GTE Serv. Corp.*, 360 F.3d 1103, 1116-17 (9th Cir. 2004) (calling the plaintiff a drug dealer might be found to be code words for race such that a jury could find intent to discriminate implicit in the comments). *But see Putman v. Unity Health Sys.*, 348 F.3d 732 (8th Cir. 2003) (comments about plaintiff not being "humble enough" and being "too prideful" not clearly linked to race).

(c) *Is the statement connected closely enough with the at-issue decision?* Even statements revealing bias, while admissions, may not constitute direct evidence as to any particular decision; Justice O'Connor and numerous circuits also required that the statement be closely enough related to the at-issue decision. *See also Jennings v. State Dep't of Corrections*, 496 F.3d 764 (7th Cir. 2007) (no causal connection shown between discriminatory attitudes of individuals and adverse action). But if the decisionmaker in question made racist statements, even if unconnected with the decision in question, isn't that evidence from which a jury *could* find that race "played a role"?

(d) *Did the speaker mean what he said?* Speakers joke or in other ways may not mean what they are heard to say. That does not affect admissibility, but a jury could conclude that a statement was made by the decisionmaker but that he did not mean it literally. *See Goodwin v. Circuit Court*, 729 F.2d 541, 546 (8th Cir. 1984) (while the defendant claimed that his statement, "This court will never run well so long as there are women in charge" was made in jest, "the jury could well have disbelieved him or have felt that jokes like these indicate a bias against women").

GROSS v. FBL FINANCIAL SERVICES, INC.
557 U.S. 167 (2009)

Justice THOMAS delivered the opinion of the Court. . . .

II

The parties have asked us to decide whether a plaintiff must "present direct evidence of discrimination in order to obtain a mixed-motive instruction in a non-Title VII discrimination case." Before reaching this question, however, we must first determine whether the burden of persuasion ever shifts to the party defending an alleged mixed-motives discrimination claim brought under the ADEA. We hold that it does not.

A

Petitioner relies on this Court's decisions construing Title VII for his interpretation of the ADEA. Because Title VII is materially different with respect to the relevant burden of persuasion, however, these decisions do not control our construction of the ADEA.

In *Price Waterhouse*, a plurality of the Court and two Justices concurring in the judgment determined that once a "plaintiff in a Title VII case proves that [the plaintiff's membership in a protected class] played a motivating part in an employment decision, the defendant may avoid a finding of liability only by proving by a preponderance of the evidence that it would have made the same decision even if it had not taken [that factor] into account." But as we explained in *Desert Palace*, Congress has since amended Title VII by explicitly authorizing discrimination claims in which an improper consideration was "a motivating factor" for an adverse employment decision.

This Court has never held that this burden-shifting framework applies to ADEA claims. And, we decline to do so now. When conducting statutory interpretation, we "must be careful not to apply rules applicable under one statute to a different statute without careful and critical examination." *Federal Express Corp. v. Holowecki*, 552 U.S. 389, 393 (2008). Unlike Title VII, the ADEA's text does not provide that a plaintiff may establish discrimination by showing that age was simply a motivating factor. Moreover, Congress neglected to add such a provision to the ADEA when it amended Title VII to add §§20002-2(m) and 20002-5(g)(2)(B) even though it contemporaneously amended the ADEA in several ways, see Civil Rights Act of 1991, §115, 105 Stat. 1079; *id.*, §302, at 1088.

We cannot ignore Congress' decision to amend Title VII's relevant provisions but not make similar changes to the ADEA. When Congress amends one statutory provision but not another, it is presumed to have acted intentionally. Furthermore, as the

Court has explained, "negative implications raised by disparate provisions are strongest" when the provisions were "considered simultaneously when the language raising the implication was inserted." As a result, the Court's interpretation of the ADEA is not governed by Title VII decisions such as *Desert Palace* and *Price Waterhouse*.[2]

B

Our inquiry therefore must focus on the text of the ADEA to decide whether it authorizes a mixed-motives age discrimination claim. It does not. . . . The ADEA provides, in relevant part, that "[i]t shall be unlawful for an employer . . . to fail or refuse to hire or to discharge any individual or otherwise discriminate against any individual with respect to his compensation, terms, conditions, or privileges of employment, *because of* such individual's age."

The words "because of" mean "by reason of: on account of." 1 WEBSTER'S THIRD NEW INTERNATIONAL DICTIONARY 194 (1966); see also 1 OXFORD ENGLISH DICTIONARY 746 (1933) (defining "because of" to mean "By reason *of*, on account *of*" (italics in original)); The RANDOM HOUSE DICTIONARY OF THE ENGLISH LANGUAGE 132 (1966) (defining "because" to mean "by reason; on account"). Thus, the ordinary meaning of the ADEA's requirement that an employer took adverse action "because of" age is that age was the "reason" that the employer decided to act. See *Hazen Paper Co. v. Biggins* [reproduced at p. 10] (explaining that the claim "cannot succeed unless the employee's protected trait actually played a role in [the employer's decisionmaking] process *and had a determinative influence on the outcome*"). To establish a disparate-treatment claim under the plain language of the ADEA, therefore, a plaintiff must prove that age was the "but-for" cause of the employer's adverse decision. . . .

It follows, then, that under §623(a)(1), the plaintiff retains the burden of persuasion to establish that age was the "but-for" cause of the employer's adverse action. Indeed, we have previously held that the burden is allocated in this manner in ADEA cases. *Reeves v. Sanderson Plumbing Products, Inc.* [reproduced at p. 24]. And nothing in the statute's text indicates that Congress has carved out an exception to that rule for a subset of ADEA cases. Where the statutory text is "silent on the allocation of the burden of persuasion," we "begin with the ordinary default rule that plaintiffs bear the risk of failing to prove their claims." *Schaffer v. Weast*, 546 U.S. 49, 56 (2005); see also *Meacham v. Knolls Atomic Power Laboratory*, 554 U.S. 84, 92 (2008) ("Absent some reason to believe that Congress intended otherwise, . . . we will conclude that the burden of persuasion lies where it usually falls, upon the party seeking relief.") We have no warrant to depart from the general rule in this setting.

Hence, the burden of persuasion necessary to establish employer liability is the same in alleged mixed-motives cases as in any other ADEA disparate-treatment action.

---

2. Justice Stevens argues that the Court must incorporate its past interpretations of Title VII into the ADEA because "the substantive provisions of the ADEA were derived *in haec verba* from Title VII," and because the Court has frequently applied its interpretations of Title VII to the ADEA. But the Court's approach to interpreting the ADEA in light of Title VII has not been uniform. In *General Dynamic Land Systems, Inc. v. Cline*, 540 U.S. 581 (2004), for example, the Court declined to interpret the phrase "because of . . . age" to bar discrimination against people of all ages, even though the Court had previously interpreted "because of . . . race [or] sex" in Title VII to bar discrimination against people of all races and both sexes. And the Court has not definitively decided whether the evidentiary framework of *McDonnell Douglas* utilized in Title VII cases is appropriate in the ADEA context. In this instance, it is the textual differences between Title VII and the ADEA that prevent us from applying *Price Waterhouse* and *Desert Palace* to federal age discrimination claims.

A plaintiff must prove by a preponderance of the evidence (which may be direct or circumstantial), that age was the "but-for" cause of the challenged employer decision.

III

Finally, we reject petitioner's contention that our interpretation of the ADEA is controlled by *Price Waterhouse*, which initially established that the burden of persuasion shifted in alleged mixed-motives Title VII claims.[5] In any event, it is far from clear that the Court would have the same approach were it to consider the question today in the first instance. . . .

Whatever the deficiencies of *Price Waterhouse* in retrospect, it has become evident in the years since that case was decided that its burden-shifting framework is difficult to apply. For example, in cases tried to a jury, courts have found it particularly difficult to craft an instruction to explain its burden-shifting framework. . . . Thus, even if *Price Waterhouse* was doctrinally sound, the problems associated with its application have eliminated any perceivable benefit to extending its framework to ADEA claims.[6]

IV

We hold that a plaintiff bringing a disparate-treatment claim pursuant to the ADEA must prove, by a preponderance of the evidence, that age was the "but-for" cause of the challenged adverse employment action. The burden of persuasion does not shift to the employer to show that it would have taken the action regardless of age, even when a plaintiff has produced some evidence that age was one motivating factor in that decision. . . .

Justice STEVENS, with whom Justice SOUTER, Justice GINSBURG, and Justice BREYER join, dissenting.

The Age Discrimination in Employment Act makes it unlawful for an employer to discriminate against any employee "because of" that individual's age. The most natural reading of this statutory text prohibits adverse employment actions motivated in whole or in part by the age of the employee. The "but-for" causation standard

---

5. Justice Stevens also contends that we must apply *Price Waterhouse* under the reasoning of *Smith v. City of Jackson*, 544 U.S. 228 (2005) [see p. 180]. In *Smith*, the Court applied to the ADEA its pre-1991 interpretation of Title VII with respect to disparate-impact claims despite Congress' 1991 amendment adding disparate-impact claims to Title VII but not the ADEA. But the amendments made by Congress in this same legislation, which added the "motivating factor" language to Title VII, undermine Justice Stevens' argument. Congress not only explicitly added "motivating factor" liability to Title VII, but it also partially abrogated *Price Waterhouse*'s holding by eliminating an employer's complete affirmative defense to "motivating factor" claims. If such "motivating factor" claims were already part of Title VII, the addition of §2000e-5(g)(2)(B) alone would have been sufficient. Congress' careful tailoring of the "motivating factor" claim in Title VII, as well as the absence of a provision parallel to §2000e-2(m) in the ADEA, confirms that we cannot transfer the *Price Waterhouse* burden-shifting framework into the ADEA.

6. Gross points out that the Court has also applied a burden-shifting framework to certain claims brought in contexts other than pursuant to Title VII, citing, *inter alia NLRB v. Transportation Management Corp.*, 462 U.S. 393, 401-403 (1983) (claims brought under the National Labor Relations Act (NLRA)); *Mt. Healthy City Bd. of Ed. v. Doyle*, 429 U.S. 274, 287 (1977) (constitutional claims). These cases, however, do not require the Court to adopt his contra statutory position. The case involving the NLRA did not require the Court to decide in the first instance whether burden shifting should apply as the Court instead deferred to the National Labor Relation Board's determination that such a framework was appropriate. And the constitutional cases such as *Mt. Healthy* have no bearing on the correct interpretation of ADEA claims, which are governed by statutory text.

endorsed by the Court today was advanced in Justice Kennedy's dissenting opinion in *Price Waterhouse*, a case construing identical language in Title VII. Not only did the Court reject the but-for standard in that case, but so too did Congress when it amended Title VII in 1991. Given this unambiguous history, it is particularly inappropriate for the Court, on its own initiative, to adopt an interpretation of the causation requirement in the ADEA that differs from the established reading of Title VII. . . .

. . . As we recognized in *Price Waterhouse* when we construed the identical "because of" language of Title VII, the most natural reading of the text proscribes adverse employment actions motivated in whole or in part by the age of the employee. . . .

Today, however, the Court interprets the words "because of" in the ADEA "as colloquial shorthand for 'but-for' causation." That the Court is construing the ADEA rather than Title VII does not justify this departure from precedent. The relevant language in the two statutes is identical, and we have long recognized that our interpretations of Title VII's language apply "with equal force in the context of age discrimination, for the substantive provisions of the ADEA 'were derived *in haec verba* from Title VII.'" *Trans World Airlines, Inc. v. Thurston*, 434 U.S. 575, 584 (1978). . . .

[The dissent distinguished *Hazen Paper Co.* and *Reeves* as "non-mixed-motives ADEA cases" following] the standards set forth in non-mixed-motives Title VII cases including *McDonnell Douglas* and *Burdine*. This by no means indicates, as the majority reasons, that *mixed-motives* ADEA cases should follow those standards. Rather, it underscores that ADEA standards are generally understood to conform to Title VII standards.

II

[The dissent dealt with the 1991 Act's failure to add motivating factor language to the ADEA by citing *Smith v. City of Jackson*, 544 U.S. 228 (2005). There, Congress also failed to amend the ADEA when it added disparate impact language to Title VII. Nevertheless, the "pre-1991 interpretation of Title VII's identical language remains applicable to the ADEA."]

Curiously, the Court reaches the opposite conclusion, relying on Congress' partial ratification of *Price Waterhouse* to argue against that case's precedential value. It reasons that if the 1991 amendments do not apply to the ADEA, *Price Waterhouse* likewise must not apply because Congress effectively codified *Price Waterhouse*'s holding in the amendments. This does not follow. To the contrary, the fact that Congress endorsed this Court's interpretation of the "because of" language in *Price Waterhouse* (even as it rejected the employer's affirmative defense to liability) provides all the more reason to adhere to that decision's motivating- factor test. . . .

Justice BREYER, with whom Justice SOUTER and Justice GINSBURG join, dissenting.

. . . It is one thing to require a typical tort plaintiff to show "but-for" causation. In that context, reasonably objective scientific or commonsense theories of physical causation make the concept of "but-for" causation comparatively easy to understand and relatively easy to apply. But it is an entirely different matter to determine a "but-for" relation when we consider, not physical forces, but the mind-related characterizations that constitute motive. Sometimes we speak of *determining* or *discovering* motives, but more often we *ascribe* motives, after an event, to an individual in light of the individual's thoughts and other circumstances present at the time of decision. In a case where we characterize an employer's actions as having been taken out of multiple motives, say, both because the employee was old and because he wore loud clothing, to apply "but-for" causation is to engage in a hypothetical inquiry about what would have happened if the employer's thoughts and other circumstances had been different. The answer to this hypothetical inquiry will often be far from obvious, and, since the employee likely knows less than does the employer about what the employer was thinking at the time, the employer will often be in a stronger position than the employee to provide the answer.

All that a plaintiff can know for certain in such a context is that the forbidden motive did play a role in the employer's decision. And the fact that a jury has found that age did play a role in the decision justifies the use of the word "because," *i.e.*, the employer dismissed the employee because of his age (and other things). I therefore would see nothing wrong in concluding that the plaintiff has established a violation of the statute [subject to the affirmative defense recognized in *Price Waterhouse*]. The law permits the employer this defense, not because the forbidden motive, age, had no role in the *actual* decision, but because the employer can show that he would have dismissed the employee anyway in the *hypothetical* circumstance in which his age-related motive was absent. And it makes sense that this would be an affirmative defense, rather than part of the showing of a violation, precisely because the defendant is in a better position than the plaintiff to establish how he would have acted in this hypothetical situation. I can see nothing unfair or impractical about allocating the burdens of proof in this way. . . .

NOTES

1. *The Holding.* The Court decided that in ADEA individual disparate treatment cases the plaintiff must carry the burden of production and of persuasion that age was the but-for cause of the adverse employment action that is challenged. However, the circuit courts read *Gross* not to affect the application of the *McDonnell Douglas* framework in ADEA cases in carrying that burden. *E.g., Jones v. Okla. City Pub. Schs.,* 617 F.3d 1273 (10th Cir. 2010). They have also continued to look to something like "direct evidence" — not as a burden-shifting device but rather as a reason to find that age was a determinative factor. *E.g., Soto-Feliciano v. Villa Cofresí Hotels, Inc.,* 779 F.3d 19 (1st Cir. 2015) (negative age-related comments directed at plaintiff, including by the key decisionmaker in a performance evaluation within two weeks of his termination created a fact question as to pretext); *Scheick v. Tecumseh Pub. Schs.,* 766 F.3d 523 (6th Cir. 2014) (plaintiff's testimony as to the school board's expressed desire for a younger worker was sufficient to deny summary judgment to the employer despite real questions about both plaintiff's performance and the existence of a budget crisis).

But even where there is direct evidence, the causation requirement can be a daunting challenge for plaintiffs. *E.g., Arthur v. Pet Dairy,* 593 F. App'x 211, 221 (4th Cir. 2015) (while a supervisor's comments were direct evidence of age bias, summary judgment for the employer was still appropriate because no reasonable jury could find but-for causation in light of record evidence demonstrating that his employer terminated plaintiff for other lawful reasons); *Johnson v. Securitas Sec. Servs. USA, Inc.,* 769 F.3d 605, 614 (8th Cir. 2014) (age-related comments — at the time of plaintiff's termination — were not enough to create a jury question as to pretext when he left the scene of an accident and delayed reporting it).

2. *Three-Step Rationale.* The first step toward the majority's holding in *Gross* was that the amendment of Title VII in the 1991 Act to add the "a motivating factor" standard of liability in §703(m) did not apply to the ADEA. Given the decision in *Smith*

v. City of Jackson that the 1991 amendment to Title VII to codify disparate impact analysis did not apply in age discrimination cases, this step was not surprising.

The second step, however, is startling. The Court held that the burden-shifting approach established for Title VII in *Price Waterhouse* did not apply. The majority's approach seems directly at odds with the Court's methodology in *Smith v. City of Jackson*, which held that Title VII's disparate impact analysis, as developed by the Court in *Wards Cove* before the 1991 amendments, controlled the ADEA.

The third step was even more bizarre: *Gross* appeared to, sort of, overrule *Price Waterhouse*, even though it had just found it inapplicable to the ADEA and, as to Title VII, it had already been superseded by the 1991 amendments. If there is a point to this, it might be to foreclose the application of *Price Waterhouse* to any other statute without explicit "motivating factor" language. *See generally* Michael C. Harper, *The Causation Standard in Federal Employment Law*: Gross v. FBL Financial Services, Inc., *and the Unfulfilled Promise of the Civil Rights Act of 1991*, 58 BUFF. L. REV. 69 (2010); Martin J. Katz, Gross *Disunity*, 114 PENN ST. L. REV. 857 (2010).

3. *Gross's Effect on Other Discrimination Statutes.* *Desert Palace* and *Gross* create separate analytic regimes for Title VII and the ADEA respectively. But the world did not have long to wait before the reverberations of *Gross* were felt across the spectrum of antidiscrimination laws. The most dramatic manifestation was within Title VII itself, where a majority of the Court in *University of Texas Southwestern Medical Center v. Nassar*, 133 S. Ct. 2517 (2013), reproduced at p. 429, held that even the Title VII prohibition of retaliation, which is found in a separate section from its prohibitions of "status-based" discrimination, is subject to but-for causation analysis. Given *Gross* and *Nassar*, it seems likely that that will be the default rule across a range of antidiscrimination laws, including §1981. However, some have argued that *Gross/Nassar* will not apply to ADA cases because that statute incorporates Title VII procedures and remedies by reference. See p. 439.

4. *Trying Title VII and Age Act Issues in One Case.* Following *Gross*, plaintiffs claiming both age and, say, sex discrimination will now have two very different sets of instructions to the jury (or standards of liability for the trial judge). While direct and/or circumstantial evidence apparently can be used to support both claims, a plaintiff must prove her age claim with evidence strong enough to support drawing the inference that age was the but-for cause of the action. Failing to establish that means there is no liability under the ADEA. But, even if the factfinder finds but-for linkage as to age, a plaintiff might still also prevail if the factfinder is convinced that sex was also "a motivating factor." It is logically possible to find sex was implicated even though age was the but-for reason since a but-for finding allows other reasons to be involved.

NOTE ON SPECIAL ISSUES OF PROOF

Some scenarios have generated a number of lower court decisions regarding the inference (or not) of discrimination. These include the "same actor" and the "same supervisor" questions that, despite their similar labels, reflect very different concerns, the question of how large an age difference is necessary in ADEA cases to infer discrimination, and, more generally, whether replacements in race or sex cases by members of the plaintiff's own class prevent an inference of discrimination.

1. *"Same Actor" Rule vs. Inference.* Courts have sometimes dismissed a plaintiff's discrimination case when the person who hired the plaintiff was also the person who discharged him relatively soon after the hiring decision. The rationale is that, had the

employer held stereotypical views, he would not have hired the plaintiff in the first place. *E.g., Schechner v. KPIX-TV & CBS Broad., Inc.*, 686 F.3d 1018, 1026 (9th Cir. 2012). This principle applies under all the antidiscrimination statutes.

While some courts have described "same actor" as a "presumption," it is more accurately viewed as an inference, that is, as a basis for making it less likely that a given situation involves intent to discriminate. *Compare Fitzgerald v. Action, Inc.*, 521 F.3d 867, 877 (8th Cir. 2008) ("Under different circumstances, the remarks attributed to Easley might create an inference of discrimination. In this instance, however, they are insufficient to overcome the presumption created by the fact Action hired Fitzgerald at age fifty" when it fired him at 52), *with Waldron v. SL Industries, Inc.*, 56 F.3d 491 (3d Cir. 1995) (that hirer and firer are the same and discharge occurred shortly after hiring is simply evidence like any other and should not be accorded any presumptive value). This means that the factfinder can enter this factor into its calculus when making the ultimate determination. But should the same-actor inference play much of a role in deciding whether a reasonable jury could find discrimination in circumstances that would otherwise raise a jury question?

One court thought that would not often be appropriate. *Johnson v. Zema Systems Corp.*, 170 F.3d 734, 745 (7th Cir. 1999), explained that the inference was unlikely to make a difference in many cases:

> The psychological assumption underlying the same-actor inference [that it does not make sense to hire workers from a group one dislikes] may not hold true on the facts of the particular case. For example, a manager might hire a person of a certain race expecting them not to rise to a position in the company where daily contact with the manager would be necessary. Or an employer might hire an employee of a certain gender expecting that person to act, or dress, or talk in a way that employer deems acceptable for that gender and then fire that employee if she fails to comply with the employer's gender stereotypes.

See also Wexler v. White's Fine Furniture, 317 F.3d 564, 573-74 (6th Cir. 2003) (en banc) (even if the same-actor inference is appropriate, "it is insufficient to warrant summary judgment for the defendant if the employee has otherwise raised a genuine issue of material fact") *But see Coghlan v. American Seafoods Co. LLC*, 413 F.3d 1090 (9th Cir. 2005) (stronger evidence of discrimination is needed to defeat summary judgment when alleged discriminatory actor previously selected claimant for favorable treatment). *See also* Natasha T. Martin, *Immunity for Hire: How the Same-Actor Doctrine Sustains Discrimination in the Contemporary Workplace*, 40 CONN. L. REV. 1117, 1121 (2008).

Consistent with the Seventh Circuit's view that it really isn't "common sense" that someone who hires a protected class member is unlikely to harbor bias against that group, Linda Hamilton Krieger & Susan T. Fiske, in *Behavioral Realism in Employment Discrimination Law: Implicit Bias and Disparate Treatment*, 94 CAL. L. REV. 997, 1048 (2006), argue that "empirical research suggests that 'dispositionism,' the common-sense model of behavioral consistency on which the same-actor inference is based, is deeply flawed, and that human behavior is far less consistent across situations than lay people tend to believe." *See also* Victor D. Quintanilla & Cheryl R. Kaiser, *The Same-Actor Inference of Nondiscrimination: Moral Credentialing and the Psychological and Legal Licensing of Bias*, 104 CALIF. L. REV. 1 (2016) (same-actor evidence should be viewed as merely one datum in the analysis partly due to empirical evidence suggesting that non-biased actions (such as hiring a minority or woman) can actually establish a kind of "moral licensing" that privileges subsequent manifestations of bias).

Professor Kerri Lynn Stone, in *Taking in Strays: A Critique of the Stray Comment Doctrine in Employment Discrimination Law*, 77 Mo. L. Rev. 149 (2012), argues that the stray-comment doctrine, which views attitudes as not fixed, contradicts the dispositional underpinning of the same-actor inference, and at least one court has taken up this theme. *See Perez v. Thorntons, Inc.*, 731 F.3d 699, 710 (7th Cir. 2013) (noting the "disconnect" between the same actor inference and the "stray remark" doctrine since the former assumes that "if a person was unbiased at Time A (when he decided to hire the plaintiff), he was also unbiased at Time B (when he fired the plaintiff)," but the latter posits that "if a person was racist or sexist at Time A (time of the remark), it is *not* reasonable to infer that the person was still racist or sexist at Time B (when he made or influenced the decision to fire the plaintiff)").

2. *Same Supervisor.* A second recurring situation arises when the plaintiff attempts to bolster her case by adducing evidence of discrimination against other members of her class, derogatorily called "me too" evidence. There has been considerable resistance to its use when the alleged discrimination was by a different supervisor than the one accused of discriminating against plaintiff. In *Sprint/United Management Co. v. Mendelsohn*, 552 U.S. 379 (2007), a reduction-in-force case, the plaintiff wanted to call as witnesses five other older workers who claimed that they, too, were discriminated against because of their age in the downsizing. The defendant objected because none had worked under the same supervisor as the plaintiff. The Supreme Court did not decide the admissibility question but rather required the district court to determine admissibility on a case-by-case basis since "such evidence is neither *per se* admissible nor *per se* inadmissible." *Id.* at 381. Emphasizing the broad discretion accorded trial courts' evidentiary rulings — reviewable under a deferential abuse of discretion standard — the trial court should make the admissibility determination: "[w]ith respect to evidentiary questions in general [including relevance under Federal Rule of Evidence 401 and the possibility of excluding even relevant evidence because of the risk of undue prejudice under Rule 403] the district court virtually always is in the better position to assess the admissibility of the evidence in the context of the case before it." *Id.* at 387. Discrimination cases are well suited to this generally applicable approach since

> [t]he question whether evidence of discrimination by other supervisors is relevant in an individual ADEA case is fact based and depends on many factors, including how closely related the evidence is to the plaintiff's circumstances and theory of the case. Applying Rule 403 to determine if evidence is prejudicial also requires a fact-intensive, context-specific inquiry.

Id. at 388. *See also Dindinger v. Allsteel, Inc.*, 853 F.3d 414 (8th Cir. 2017) ("Me-too" evidence of other female employees' pay was properly admitted since it tended to demonstrate that the employer did not uniformly set the wages of more senior employees higher than the wages of less senior employees, and thus rebutted the employer's affirmative defense that seniority explained the plaintiffs' lesser pay). Discrimination cases may be especially fact sensitive, but the focus on "insular individualism" of supervisors and managers is arguably inconsistent with how workplaces operate in practice since any particular decision is influenced by a web of other decisions and practices, sometimes in ways the decisionmakers themselves do not understand. Tristin Green, *Insular Individualism: Employment Discrimination Law After* Ledbetter v. Goodyear, 43 Harv. C.R.-C.L. L. Rev. 353 (2008). *See generally* Emma Pelkey,

Comment, *The "Not Me Too" Evidence Doctrine in Employment Law: Courts' Disparate Treatment of "Me Too" Versus "Not Me Too" Evidence in Employment Discrimination Cases*, 92 Or. L. Rev. 545 (2014).

How the *Mendelsohn* rule plays out in the district courts remains to be seen, but a few thoughts might help. Proof by the plaintiff of other older workers' treatment by their supervisors shows that the RIF plan, though age neutral on its face and, perhaps, in its intent, allowed for discrimination, conscious or unconscious, in application. But even if that's true, doesn't the question remain whether plaintiff's supervisor discriminated? If *A*, *B*, and *C* are each separate decisionmakers, how could the fact that *B* discriminated show that *A* did? Does it matter that the employer (writ large) could be found to have discriminated? Or does *Staub* requires us to look at some human being's motives? Even if there is some umbrella policy that allowed each of them freedom to make decisions? *See Mattenson v. Baxter Healthcare Corp.*, 438 F.3d 763, 770-71 (7th Cir. 2006) (in a division of 7,000 employees with hundreds of executives, the fact that some may dislike old workers and even fire old workers because of their age is weak evidence that a particular older employee was fired because of his age).

3. *Age Difference in ADEA Cases.* We saw in *O'Connor v. Consolidated Coin Caterers Corp.*, 517 U.S. 308 (1996), p. 31, that it is the differences in age that matters when a plaintiff claims to have been replaced by a younger worker, not whether that comparator is within the protected class. Building on this theme, courts require that replacements be *significantly younger* than the plaintiff before age discrimination can be inferred. In *Barber v. CSX Distribution Servs.*, 68 F.3d 694, 699 (3d Cir. 1995), the court, acknowledging there "is no magical formula to measure a particular age gap and determine if it is sufficiently wide to give rise to an inference of discrimination," found that an eight-year difference between the plaintiff and the beneficiary of the discrimination could support a finding that the beneficiary was "sufficiently younger" than the plaintiff to permit an inference of age discrimination. *Accord. Liebman v. Metro. Life Ins. Co.*, 808 F.3d 1294, 1299 (11th Cir. 2015) (seven years is sufficiently younger than plaintiff to establish this prong of the prima facie case). *Contra Richter v. Hook-SupeRx, Inc.*, 142 F.3d 1024 (7th Cir. 1998) (absent other evidence, a seven-year age difference was not enough to establish a prima facie case).

4. *Replacement by a Member of the Same Race or Sex.* Most courts of appeals have held that, in a termination case, the plaintiff need not prove as part of the prima facie case that she was replaced by someone outside the relevant class. In *Pivirotto v. Innovative Systems, Inc.*, 191 F.3d 344 (3d Cir. 1999), the court explained:

> An employer's failure to hire someone of a different class from the plaintiff, after the plaintiff's discharge, could be explained in many ways. . . . [A]n employer may treat women less favorably than men, but still be willing to hire a woman to fill a position left vacant by the firing of a discriminated-against woman. Or an employer may act on gender-based stereotypes, firing women it perceives as not feminine enough (or as too feminine), or discharging women who are too aggressive while not doing the same to male employees. Such an employer would not necessarily replace a discriminated-against female employee with a man. Indeed, some employers, anticipating litigation, may hire a woman solely to attempt to defeat a sex discrimination claim.

Id. at 355. *Cf. Miles v. Dell, Inc.*, 429 F.3d 480 (4th Cir. 2005) (while generally plaintiff must show replacement by someone outside protected class, this is not necessary when the discharge and hiring decisions were made by different decisionmakers). Of course, that doesn't mean that replacement by a member of the plaintiff's class is without probative value on the ultimate issue of discrimination. *See Walker v. St. Anthony's Med. Ctr.*, 881 F.2d 554, 558 (8th Cir. 1989) (while there is no *per se* requirement of replacement by an individual from outside the protected class, "this fact is relevant in evaluating the employer's motive"). *Cf. Riley v. Elkhart Cmty. Schs.*, 829 F.3d 886 (7th Cir. 2016) (seeming to suggest that another-race comparator was needed for a prima facie case under §1981).

5. *Good Stats and Good Acts.* Some courts have looked to evidence of an employer's nondiscriminatory acts, such as favoring older workers, to rebut the inference of age discrimination that the plaintiff is attempting to have the jury draw. *See Blasdel v. Nw. Univ.*, 687 F.3d 813, 822 (7th Cir. 2012) (dean had increased the hiring and promotion of tenure track female faculty in the medical school); *Onyiah v. St. Cloud State Univ.*, 684 F.3d 711 (8th Cir. 2012) (higher pay for other Nigerian-born professors tended to negate Nigerian plaintiff's claim of salary discrimination). However, such evidence must be balanced against other proof. *See Whitfield v. Int'l Truck & Engine Corp.*, 755 F.3d 438, 444 (7th Cir. 2014) (district court erred by "giving enormous weight" to the employer's hiring of another African American: hiring a member of the same protected class "does not magically negate" the inference of discrimination from other evidence).

6. *Decisionmaker Within the Same Protected Class.* It has sometimes been argued that the fact that the decisionmaker shares the same protected characteristic as the alleged victim precludes a finding of discrimination. The Supreme Court rejected this position as a matter of law in *Oncale v. Sundowner Offshore Servs.*, 523 U.S. 75, 79 (1998) ("nothing in Title VII necessarily bars a claim of discrimination 'because of . . . sex' merely because the plaintiff and the defendant (or the person charged with acting on behalf of the defendant) are of the same sex"), an opinion we will encounter at p. 275. *See also Jackson v. VHS Detroit Receiving Hosp., Inc.*, 814 F.3d 769, 783-85 (6th Cir. 2016) (although all of the decisionmakers were female, as were most employees in the hospital's crisis center, plaintiff was the only female in her job category, which might imply that males were favored for that position).

NOTE ON LITIGATION SCORECARD

There is strong empirical evidence that plaintiffs in employment discrimination cases have much lower success rates than plaintiffs in other kinds of cases. *E.g.*, Kevin M. Clermont & Stewart J. Schwab, *Employment Discrimination Plaintiffs in Federal Court: From Bad to Worse*, 3 HARV. L. & POL'Y REV. 103, 126 (2009) (district court win rates for plaintiffs from 1979-2006 was 15 percent, much lower than for non-job cases, 51 percent, and "appellate courts reverse plaintiffs' wins far more than the defendants' wins below"). If it is true that plaintiffs have a very hard time winning discrimination cases, why do you think that is? One possible explanation is that the really strong plaintiffs' cases settle early and so never get to trial or, maybe, even into the courts. *See* Minna J. Kotkin, *Outing Outcomes: An Empirical Study of Confidential Employment Discrimination Settlements*, 64 WASH & LEE L. REV. 111, 112 (2007) ("employment discrimination litigation results in a mean recovery of $54,651"). Another possible explanation is that many discrimination cases are brought by the plaintiff pro se, and the failure to have professional representation may take its toll. A third explanation may be that plaintiffs' cases are weak, at least in light of the difficulty posed in litigating them successfully. Might that be because, in the world of at-will employment, claiming discrimination is one of the few hooks employees have when they feel that they have been mistreated by their employers? Are there other reasons you can think of for the low success rate?

In light of this, are you surprised by a study finding that plaintiffs in discrimination cases often view the law as unfair? Ellen Berrey, Steve G. Hoffman & Laura Beth Nielsen, *Situated Justice: A Contextual Analysis of Fairness and Inequality in Employment Discrimination Litigation*, 46 LAW & SOC'Y REV. 1, 1 (2012). But it turns out that defendants' representatives do, too! "Rather than sharing a complaint, however, each side sees unfairness only in those aspects of the process that work to their disadvantage." Further, "the very notion of fairness can belie structural asymmetries that, overall, profoundly benefit employers in employment discrimination lawsuits."

PROBLEM 1.1

In response to a help-wanted ad, Jane Armstrong, a 38-year-old woman, applies for a job as a cab driver at the Hacker Cab Company. She has a valid driver's license and has driven extensively, but not for pay, for 20 years. She is a vegetarian and a Capricorn. After a brief interview, at which all these facts emerge, she is rejected by "Tip" O'Neill, Hacker's president. Armstrong comes to you for legal counsel. You do some investigation. The first call you make is to O'Neill, who admits that the job is still open but explains that he rejected Armstrong because "Capricorns make lousy drivers; besides she's too old to adjust to the rigors of cab driving, especially since she doesn't eat meat." When asked whether Armstrong's gender played a part in the decision, O'Neill replied, "Hell no. Some of my best friends are women. I don't care if my brother marries one. Har, har." A "windshield survey" of the Hacker Cab Company at shift-changing times reveals an almost total absence of women drivers. It is common knowledge that there is a heavy turnover in the cab-driving business.

How would you analyze this case based on the law of individual disparate treatment discrimination as you understand it?

Chapter 2

Systemic Disparate Treatment Discrimination

A. INTRODUCTION

Chapter 1 explored challenges to individual instances of discrimination, but plaintiffs can also challenge employment policies or practices that sweep more broadly. Thus, an employer's policy to hire only men, to fire older workers, or to separate employees by race, gender, or age raises systemic issues. This chapter will develop systemic disparate treatment, one of the two concepts of systemic discrimination governing Title VII actions. 42 U.S.C. §§2000e to 2000e-17 (2018). This theory is also available under the Age Discrimination in Employment Act (ADEA), 29 U.S.C. §§631-634 (2018), and under 42 U.S.C. §1981 (2018), *Anderson v. Fulton County, Ga.*, 207 F.3d 1303 (11th Cir. 2000). The other systemic concept, disparate impact, will be considered in Chapter 3.

Systemic disparate treatment can be proven in two ways. First, the plaintiff may demonstrate that the employer has an announced, formal policy of discrimination. Second, the plaintiff who cannot prove a formal policy may nevertheless establish that the employer's pattern of employment decisions reveals that a practice of disparate treatment exists. Although these two methods parallel the direct and inferential proof of individual disparate treatment examined in Chapter 1, there are significant differences between the individual and systemic theories.

B.   FORMAL POLICIES OF DISCRIMINATION

The employer in *Slack v. Havens*, reproduced at p. 3, violated Title VII by requiring employees to perform a cleaning job because they were black. If such a requirement is part of a policy that regularly segregates black workers into unfavorable jobs, a systemic claim of discrimination could be established. Historically, formal systems excluding women and minority group members or segregating them into inferior jobs were common. During much of the twentieth century, employers, particularly in the South, segregated jobs by race, with blacks typically consigned to lower-paying, less attractive jobs. We will see, for example, in *Griggs v. Duke Power Co.*, reproduced at p. 167, that the employer formally restricted African Americans to the lowest-level positions prior to the passage of Title VII. Most employers also segregated many jobs by gender, again with lower-level jobs assigned to female workers. Newspaper help-wanted advertisements prior to 1965 were commonly broken down into male and female jobs. Similarly, before the Age Discrimination in Employment Act, employers frequently had formal policies mandating retirement at age 65. In the wake of the antidiscrimination statutes, most such formal discriminatory policies have disappeared. Nevertheless, not all formal policies were rescinded without court intervention.

LOS ANGELES DEPARTMENT OF WATER & POWER v. MANHART
435 U.S. 702 (1978)

Justice STEVENS delivered the opinion of the Court.

. . . For many years the [Los Angeles Department of Water and Power] had administered retirement, disability, and death-benefit programs for its employees. Upon retirement each employee is eligible for a monthly retirement benefit computed as a fraction of his or her salary multiplied by years of service. The monthly benefits of men and women of the same age, seniority and salary are equal. Benefits are funded entirely by contributions from the employees and the Department, augmented by the income earned on those contributions. No private insurance company is involved in the administration or payment of benefits.

Based on a study of mortality tables and its own experience, the Department determined that its 2,000 female employees, on the average, will live a few years longer than its 10,000 male employees. The cost of a pension for the average retired female is greater than for the average male retiree because more monthly payments must be made to the average woman. The Department therefore required female employees to make monthly contributions to the fund which were 14.84% higher than the contributions required of comparable male employees. Because employee contributions were withheld from paychecks, a female employee took home less pay than a male employee earning the same salary.[5] . . .

_____

5. The significance of the disparity is illustrated by the record of one woman whose contributions to the fund (including interest on the amount withheld each month) amounted to $18,171.40; a similarly situated male would have contributed only $12,843.53.

I

There are both real and fictional differences between women and men. It is true that the average man is taller than the average woman; it is not true that the average woman driver is more accident prone than the average man. Before the Civil Rights Act of 1964 was enacted, an employer could fashion his personnel policies on the basis of assumptions about the differences between men and women, whether or not the assumptions were valid.

It is now well recognized that employment decisions cannot be predicated on mere "stereotyped" impressions about the characteristics of males or females. Myths and purely habitual assumptions about a woman's inability to perform certain kinds of work are no longer acceptable reasons for refusing to employ qualified individuals, or for paying them less. This case does not, however, involve a fictional difference between men and women. It involves a generalization that the parties accept as unquestionably true: Women, as a class, do live longer than men. The Department treated its women employees differently from its men employees because the two classes are in fact different. It is equally true, however, that all individuals in the respective classes do not share the characteristic that differentiates the average class representatives. Many women do not live as long as the average man and many men outlive the average woman. The question, therefore, is whether the existence or non-existence of "discrimination" is to be determined by comparison of class characteristics or individual characteristics. A "stereotyped" answer to that question may not be the same as the answer that the language and purpose of the statute command.

The statute makes it unlawful "to discriminate against any *individual* with respect to his compensation, terms, conditions, or privileges of employment, because of such *individual's* race, color, religion, sex, or national origin (emphasis added). The statute's focus on the individual is unambiguous. It precludes treatment of individuals as simply components of a racial, religious, sexual, or national class. If height is required for a job, a tall woman may not be refused employment merely because, on the average, women are too short. Even a true generalization about the class is an insufficient reason for disqualifying an individual to whom the generalization does not apply.

That proposition is of critical importance in this case because there is no assurance that any individual woman working for the Department will actually fit the generalization on which the Department's policy is based. Many of those individuals will not live as long as the average man. While they were working, those individuals received smaller paychecks because of their sex, but they will receive no compensating advantage when they retire.

It is true, of course, that while contributions are being collected from the employees, the Department cannot know which individuals will predecease the average woman. Therefore, unless women as a class are assessed an extra charge, they will be subsidized, to some extent, by the class of male employees. It follows, according to the Department, that fairness to its class of male employees justifies the extra assessment against all of its female employees.

But the question of fairness to various classes affected by the statute is essentially a matter of policy for the legislature to address. Congress has decided that classifications based on sex, like those based on national origin or race, are unlawful. Actuarial studies could unquestionably identify differences in life expectancy based on race or national origin, as well as sex.[15] But a statute that was designed to make race irrelevant

---

15. For example, the life expectancy of a white baby in 1973 was 72.2 years; a nonwhite baby could expect to live 65.9 years, a difference of 6.3 years.

in the employment market could not reasonably be construed to permit a take-home-pay differential based on a racial classification.

Even if the statutory language were less clear, the basic policy of the statute requires that we focus on fairness to individuals rather than fairness to classes. Practices that classify employees in terms of religion, race, or sex tend to preserve traditional assumptions about groups rather than thoughtful scrutiny of individuals. The generalization involved in this case illustrates the point. Separate mortality tables are easily interpreted as reflecting innate differences between the sexes; but a significant part of the longevity differential may be explained by the social fact that men are heavier smokers than women.

Finally, there is no reason to believe that Congress intended a special definition of discrimination in the context of employee group insurance coverage. It is true that insurance is concerned with events that are individually unpredictable, but that is characteristic of many employment decisions. Individual risks, like individual performance, may not be predicted by resort to classifications proscribed by Title VII. Indeed, the fact that this case involves a group insurance program highlights a basic flaw in the Department's fairness argument. For when insurance risks are grouped, the better risks always subsidize the poorer risks. Healthy persons subsidize medical benefits for the less healthy; unmarried workers subsidize the pensions of married workers; persons who eat, drink, or smoke to excess may subsidize pension benefits for persons whose habits are more temperate. Treating different classes of risks as though they were the same for purposes of group insurance is a common practice that has never been considered inherently unfair. To insure the flabby and the fit as though they were equivalent risks may be more common than treating men and women alike; but nothing more than habit makes one "subsidy" seem less fair than the other.[20]

An employment practice that requires 2,000 individuals to contribute more money into a fund than 10,000 other employees simply because each of them is a woman, rather than a man, is in direct conflict with both the language and the policy of the Act. Such a practice does not pass the simple test of whether the evidence shows "treatment of a person in a manner which but for that person's sex would be different." It constitutes discrimination and is unlawful unless exempted by the Equal Pay Act of 1963 or some other affirmative justification.

III . . .

[T]he Department argues that the absence of a discriminatory effect on women as a class justifies an employment practice which, on its face, discriminated against individual employees because of their sex. But even if the Department's actuarial evidence is sufficient to prevent plaintiffs from establishing a prima facie case on

---

20. A variation on the Department's fairness theme is the suggestion that a gender-neutral pension plan would itself violate Title VII because of its disproportionately heavy impact on male employees. *Cf. Griggs v. Duke Power Co.* This suggestion has no force in the sex discrimination context because each retiree's total pension benefits are ultimately determined by his actual life span; any differential in benefits paid to men and women in the aggregate is thus "based on [a] factor other than sex," and consequently immune from challenge under the Equal Pay Act, 29 U.S.C. §206(d). Even under Title VII itself — assuming disparate-impact analysis applies to fringe benefits, *cf. Nashville Gas Co. v. Satty*, 434 U.S. 136, 144-145 — the male employees would not prevail. Even a completely neutral practice will inevitably have some disproportionate impact on one group or another. *Griggs* does not imply, and this Court has never held, that discrimination must always be inferred from such consequences.

the theory that the effect of the practice on women as a class was discriminatory, that evidence does not defeat the claim that the practice, on its face, discriminated against every individual woman employed by the Department.[30]

In essence, the Department is arguing that the prima facie showing of discrimination based on evidence of different contributions for the respective sexes is rebutted by its demonstration that there is a like difference in the cost of providing benefits for the respective classes. That argument might prevail if Title VII contained a cost-justification defense comparable to the affirmative defense available in a price discrimination suit. But neither Congress nor the courts have recognized such a defense under Title VII.

Although we conclude that the Department's practice violated Title VII, we do not suggest that the statute was intended to revolutionize the insurance and pension industries. All that is at issue today is a requirement that men and women make unequal contributions to an employer-operated pension fund. Nothing in our holding implies that it would be unlawful for an employer to set aside equal retirement contributions for each employee and let each retiree purchase the largest benefit which his or her accumulated contributions could command in the open market. Nor does it call into question the insurance industry practice of considering the composition of an employer's work force in determining the probable cost of a retirement or death benefit plan.[34] Finally, we recognize that in a case of this kind it may be necessary to take special care in fashioning appropriate relief. . . .

NOTES

1. *Why Did the City Discriminate?* Why would the city adopt a facially discriminatory plan? First, perhaps it believed that, although the plan technically discriminated on gender grounds, no court would find it to be sex discrimination. Second, whether or not it is sex discrimination, the city may have believed that it fit within a statutory exception. The possibility is not as far-fetched as one might think. Sex distinctions in employer dress and grooming codes generally have been held not to constitute illegal sex discrimination under Title VII when they treat male and female employees separately, but equally. See p. 300. *See also Bauer v. Lynch*, 812 F.3d 340 (4th Cir. 2016) (upholding gender-normed physical fitness tests for FBI trainees by rejecting the simple *Manhart* test of whether "the evidence shows treatment of a person in a

---

30. Some amici suggest that the Department's discrimination is justified by business necessity. They argue that, if no gender distinction is drawn, many male employees will withdraw from the plan, or even the Department, because they can get a better pension plan in the private market. But the Department has long required equal contributions to its death-benefit plan, and since 1975 it has required equal contributions to its pension plan. Yet the Department points to no "adverse selection" by the affected employees, presumably because an employee who wants to leave the plan must also leave his job, and few workers will quit because one of their fringe benefits could theoretically be obtained at a marginally lower price on the open market. In short, there has been no showing that sex distinctions are reasonably necessary to the normal operation of the Department's retirement plan.

34. Title VII bans discrimination against an "individual" because of "such individual's" sex, 42 U.S.C. §2000e-2(a)(1). The Equal Pay Act prohibits discrimination "within any establishment," and discrimination is defined as "paying wages to employees . . . at a rate less than the rate at which [the employer] pays wages to employees of the opposite sex" for equal work. 29 U.S.C. §206(d)(1). Neither of these provisions makes it unlawful to determine the funding requirements for an establishment's benefit plan by considering the composition of the entire force.

manner which but for that person's sex would be different" in favor of asking whether the test imposes a greater burden on one sex than the other). We also will encounter racial and gender preferences that sometimes are permissible under Title VII as part of valid affirmative action plans. See p. 151.

The city may have thought that the gender distinction would not be viewed as discriminatory because, while it seems unfair that women receive less take-home pay than men paid the same salary, women, as a group, will receive more months of retirement pay because, as a group, they live longer than men. In group terms, lower monthly salary is offset by more months of coverage. But any individual female may get the short end of the stick: if she does not live as long as predicted, she will earn less each month while working but will not be compensated by more months of coverage once retired. While insurance risks are, individually, unpredictable, this woman's disadvantage results solely from her sex. Despite this reality, the city might have hoped that the courts would accept what the Court termed a "cost justification" defense. Should the courts recognize such defense? We will see that, where age is concerned, the ADEA has an explicit cost justification defense for fringe benefits. See p. 403.

Another possibility is that the city thought it could not be guilty of sex discrimination because it was motivated neither by animus nor by a desire to disadvantage women — it merely used gender as a proxy for longevity. That might be called a stereotype, but, if so, it's one of those "true" stereotypes — one that's accurate across the genders although not true of every woman. Is that disparate treatment? *Manhart* tells us the answer is yes. In other words, the employer's motivation is irrelevant if it intends to treat women differently than men. *Cf. Kentucky Retirement Systems v. EEOC*, 554 U.S. 135 (2008) (holding 5-4 that a benefit scheme that facially differentiated on the basis of age was permissible when there was no motivation to disadvantage older workers).

2. *A BFOQ?* Even if the conduct was sex discrimination and otherwise actionable, Title VII offers a statutory defense, the bona fide occupational qualification (BFOQ). Because the employer concededly used gender to classify pension contributions, why couldn't it claim a BFOQ defense? Back in the day, there were "flight engineers" on large passenger planes in addition to the pilot and co-pilot. In *Trans World Airlines, Inc. v. Thurston*, 469 U.S. 111 (1985), plaintiffs challenged a rule that discriminated on the basis of age for transfer from pilot to flight engineer jobs: pilots forced to retire by the FAA age-60 (now 65) rule could not "bump" down into the flight engineer job, while those disqualified for any other reason could bump and continue as flight engineers past age 60. The Court held that the ADEA's BFOQ did not apply: "TWA's discriminatory transfer policy is not permissible under §4(f)(1) because age is not a BFOQ for the 'particular' position of flight engineer." *Id.* at 122. Similarly, all women workers in *Manhart* were the victims of the sex discrimination, without regard to the particular jobs they performed or their abilities. See p. 94.

3. *Disparate Treatment to Avoid Disparate Impact?* The city might also have hoped to convince the courts that its conduct was not discriminatory by arguing that it was damned if it did and damned if it didn't: requiring females to make larger contributions than males would establish disparate treatment discrimination but collecting equal contributions from all employees would provide retired women as a group more than retired men as a group, thereby creating an adverse impact on males. How did the Court avoid this dilemma? Does footnote 20 help? In *Ricci v. DeStefano*, 557 U.S.

[handwritten margin note, left:] all positions were disc., not just one where employer might claim BFOQ

[handwritten note, bottom:] Its not adverse if they're setting a limit on how many months they dood! Its not based on life can collect in total expectancy - theres no guarantee of who will collect what

557 (2009), the Court found a city liable for disparate treatment discrimination when it decided not to use the results of a promotion test because their use would result in disparate impact on African American and Hispanic test takers. This question is further discussed in Chapter 4 at p. 245.

4. *The Equal Pay Act and the Bennett Amendment.* Title VII is not the only federal statute dealing with sex discrimination in employment. A much narrower enactment, the Equal Pay Act of 1963, 29 U.S.C. §206(d) (2013), bars discrimination in pay on account of sex where members of each gender are doing "equal work." The Bennett Amendment to Title VII declares discrimination authorized by the Equal Pay Act to be legal under Title VII. The city might have hoped to bring its plan within the EPA provision allowing differentials based on a factor "other than sex." But how can something that is sex discrimination under Title VII be "other than sex" within the EPA? In any event, because of both its limitations to discrimination in "equal work" and its validation of compensation differences based on any other factor other than sex, the EPA has been relatively ineffective as a tool to attach compensation disparities. *See generally* Deborah L Brake, *Reviving Paycheck Fairness: Why and How the Factor-Other-Than-Sex Defense Matters*, 52 Idaho L. Rev. 889 (2016); Deborah Thompson Eisenberg, *Money, Sex, and Sunshine: A Market-Based Approach to Pay Discrimination*, 43 Ariz. St. L.J. 951, 990 (2011); Deborah Thompson Eisenberg, *Shattering the Equal Pay Act's Glass Ceiling*, 63 SMU L. Rev. 17 (2010).

5. *Partial Remedy Only. Manhart* established that gender-explicit classifications in pension *contributions* violate Title VII. A subsequent decision, *Arizona Governing Committee v. Norris*, 463 U.S. 1073 (1983), held that Title VII was violated by offering women lower monthly retirement *benefits* than men who contributed the same amount. However, a majority decided that only retirement benefits attributed to contributions made after the date of the decision had to be calculated without regard to the gender of the beneficiary. That limitation of remedies insulated all of the earlier unlawful pay discrimination. Why should the victims of defendant's discrimination be made only partially whole?

6. *Effect on Insurance Annuities.* A twist in *Norris* was the defendant's argument that it was not responsible for the discrimination: the employer collected employee contributions, but the plan was administered and all benefits paid by private insurance companies. The employer argued that it acted within the language in *Manhart* suggesting that an employer would not be liable if it set aside contributions and paid them in a lump sum upon retirement. The defendant also stressed that all the available annuities sold by insurance companies used sex-segregated life expectancy tables. The Court rejected those arguments: "[h]aving created a plan whereby employees can obtain the advantages of using deferred compensation to purchase an annuity only if they invest in one of the companies specifically selected by the State, the State cannot disclaim responsibility for the discriminatory features of the insurers' options." 463 U.S. at 1088-89.

7. *The Rise of the 401(k) and the Demise of Sex Neutrality.* The principle animating *Manhart* — that differentiating on the basis of a prohibited characteristic is impermissible unless within a statutory exception — remains robust. However, the actual holding of the case has diminished in importance. When *Manhart* was decided, "defined benefit" retirement plans were the norm, and, as the name suggests, such plans require employers to provide a specified level of benefits. The department was thus faced with the "damned if you do, damned if you don't" problem discussed in

Note 3. Such plans are diminishing even in the public sector and have largely disappeared in the private sector. Instead, employers offer "defined contribution" plans, of which the "401(k)" is the most common. Such plans in essence create individual retirement accounts for each worker, with the workers getting what has accumulated in their accounts once they retire. Employers can make equal contributions for all workers, usually a percentage of income. Will women seeking to buy an annuity with their accumulated contributions face sex-segregated mortality labels? The answer seems clearly yes. Accordingly, the plaintiffs in *Manhart* won the battle but may have lost the war as to retirement benefits. However, women at least have the individual choice to take an annuity or a lump sum at retirement instead. And the *Manhart* decision may deter employers who might have offered other benefits — such as health insurance — on a gender-differentiated basis.

Probability theory in using statistics

C. PATTERNS AND PRACTICES OF DISCRIMINATION

TEAMSTERS v. UNITED STATES
431 U.S. 324 (1977)

Refined by Hazelwood (same year)

Justice STEWART delivered the opinion of the Court.

. . . I

[The United States brought two actions, which were consolidated for trial. The first was against T.I.M.E.-D.C., charging discriminatory hiring, assignment, and promotion policies against Negroes at its Nashville terminal in violation of §707(a). The second action against the company charged a pattern and practice of employment discrimination against Negroes and Spanish-surnamed persons throughout the company's transportation system. The International Brotherhood of Teamsters union was also named a defendant.] The central claim in both lawsuits was that the company had engaged in a pattern or practice of discriminating against minorities in hiring so-called line drivers. Those Negroes and Spanish-surnamed persons who had been hired, the Government alleged, were given lower paying, less desirable jobs as servicemen or local city drivers, and were thereafter discriminated against with respect to promotions and transfers. . . .

II . . .

A

Consideration of the question whether the company engaged in a pattern or practice of discriminatory hiring practices involves controlling legal principles that are relatively clear. The Government's theory of discrimination was simply that the company, in violation of §703(a) of Title VII, regularly and purposefully treated Negroes and Spanish-surnamed Americans less favorably than white persons. The disparity in treatment allegedly involved the refusal to recruit, hire, transfer, or promote minority group members on an equal basis with white people, particularly with respect to line-driving positions. The ultimate factual issues are thus simply whether there was a

BFOQ?

△ arg

pattern or practice of such disparate treatment and, if so, whether the differences were "racially premised." *McDonnell Douglas Corp. v. Green.*[15]

As the plaintiff, the Government bore the initial burden of making out a prima facie case of discrimination. *Albermarle Paper Co. v. Moody*, 422 U.S. 405, 425; *McDonnell Douglas Corp. v. Green.* And, because it alleged a systemwide pattern or practice of resistance to the full enjoyment of Title VII rights, the Government ultimately had to prove more than the mere occurrence of isolated or "accidental" or sporadic discriminatory acts. It had to establish by a preponderance of the evidence that racial discrimination was the Company's standard operating procedure — the regular rather than the unusual practice.

We agree with the District Court and the Court of Appeals that the Government carried its burden of proof. As of March 31, 1971, shortly after the Government filed its complaint alleging systemwide discrimination, the company had 6,472 employees. Of these, 314 (5%) were Negroes and 257 (4%) were Spanish-surnamed Americans. Of the 1,828 line drivers, however, there were only 8 (0.4%) Negroes and 5 (0.3%) Spanish-surnamed persons, and all of the Negroes had been hired after the litigation had commenced. With one exception — a man who worked as a line driver at the Chicago terminal from 1950 to 1959 — the company and its predecessors did not employ a Negro on a regular basis as a line driver until 1969. And, as the Government showed, even in 1971 there were terminals in areas of substantial Negro population where all of the Company's line drivers were white.[17] A great majority of the Negroes (83%) and Spanish-surnamed Americans (78%) who did work for the company held the lower paying city operations and serviceman jobs, whereas only 39% of the non-minority employees held jobs in those categories.

The Government bolstered its statistical evidence with the testimony of individuals who recounted over 40 specific instances of discrimination. Upon the basis of his testimony the District Court found that "[n]umerous qualified black and Spanish-surnamed American applicants who sought line driving jobs at the company over the

---

15. "Disparate treatment" such as is alleged in the present case is the most easily understood type of discrimination. The employer simply treats some people less favorably than others because of their race, color, religion, sex, or national origin. Proof of discriminatory motive is critical, although it can in some situations be inferred from the mere fact of differences in treatment. See, e.g., *Arlington Heights v. Metropolitan Housing Dev. Corp.*, 429 U.S. 252, 265-266. Undoubtedly disparate treatment was the most obvious evil Congress had in mind when it enacted Title VII. See, e.g., 110 Cong. Rec. 13088 (1964) (remarks of Sen. Humphrey) ("What the bill does . . . is simply to make it an illegal practice to use race as a factor in denying employment. It provides that men and women shall be employed on the basis of their qualifications, not as Catholic citizens, not as Protestant citizens, not as Jewish citizens, not as colored citizens, but as citizens of the United States."). Claims of disparate treatment may be distinguished from claims that stress "disparate impact." The latter involve employment practices that are facially neutral in their treatment of different groups but that in fact fall more harshly on one group than another and cannot be justified by business necessity. Proof of discriminatory motive, we have held, is not required under a disparate-impact theory. Compare, e.g., *Griggs v. Duke Power Co.*, with *McDonnell Douglas Corp. v. Green.* See generally B. SCHLEI & P. GROSSMAN, EMPLOYMENT DISCRIMINATION LAW 1-12 (1976); Blumrosen, *Strangers in Paradise:* Griggs v. Duke Power Co. *and the Concept of Employment Discrimination,* 71 MICH. L. REV. 59 (1972). Either theory may, of course, be applied to a particular set of facts.

17. In Atlanta, for instance, Negroes composed 22.35% of the population in the surrounding metropolitan area and 51.3% of the population in the city proper. The company's Atlanta terminal employed 57 line drivers. All were white. In Los Angeles, 10.84% of the greater metropolitan population and 17.88% of the city population were Negro. But at the company's two Los Angeles terminals there was not a single Negro among the 374 line drivers. The proof showed similar disparities in San Francisco, Denver, Nashville, Chicago, Dallas, and at several other terminals.

years had either their requests ignored, were given false or misleading information about requirements, opportunities, and application procedures, or were not considered and hired on the same basis that whites were considered and hired." Minority employees who wanted to transfer to line-driver jobs met with similar difficulties.[19]

A's response, which court rejects

The company's principal response to this evidence is that statistics can never in and of themselves prove the existence of a pattern or practice of discrimination, or even establish a prima facie case shifting to the employer the burden of rebutting the inference raised by the figures. But, as even our brief summary of the evidence shows, this was not a case in which the Government relied on "statistics alone." The individuals who testified about their personal experiences with the company brought the cold numbers convincingly to life.

statistics can be helpful but rebuttable

In any event, our cases make it unmistakably clear that "[s]tatistical analyses have served and will continue to serve an important role" in cases in which the existence of discrimination is a disputed issue. We have repeatedly approved the use of statistical proof, where it reached proportions comparable to those in this case, to establish a prima facie case of racial discrimination in jury selection cases, see, e.g., *Turner v. Fouche*, 396 U.S. 346; *Hernandez v. Texas*, 347 U.S. 475; *Norris v. Alabama*, 294 U.S. 587. Statistics are equally competent in proving employment discrimination.[20] We caution only that statistics are not irrefutable; they come in infinite variety and, like any other kind of evidence, they may be rebutted. In short, their usefulness depends on all of the surrounding facts and circumstances.

[The defendants also argue that statistics showing racial imbalance failed to focus on the company's actions after the effective date of Title VII. However, this was not an employer that had done virtually no new hiring since the effective date of the statute. The] record shows that many line drivers continued to be hired throughout this period, and that almost all of them were white.

[While there were recent efforts to eradicate the effects of past discrimination, the lower courts both] found upon substantial evidence that the Company had engaged in a course of discrimination that continued well after the effective date of Title VII.

19. Two examples are illustrative: George Taylor, a Negro, worked for the company as a city driver in Los Angeles, beginning late in 1966. In 1968, after hearing that a white city driver had transferred to a line-driver job, he told the terminal manager that he also would like to consider line driving. The manager replied that there would be "a lot of problems on the road . . . with different people, Caucasian, et cetera," and stated: "I don't feel that the company is ready for this right now. . . . Give us a little time. It will come around, you know." Mr. Taylor made similar requests some months later and got similar responses. He was never offered a line-driving job or an application. Feliberto Trujillo worked as a dockman at the company's Denver terminal. When he applied for a line-driver job in 1967, he was told by a personnel officer that he had one strike against him. He asked what that was and was told: "You're a Chicano, and as far as we know, there isn't a Chicano driver in the system."

20. Petitioners argue that statistics, at least those comparing the racial composition of an employer's work force to the composition of the population at large, should never be given decisive weight in a Title VII case because to do so would conflict with §703(j) of the Act [barring preferential treatment because of demographic underrepresentation.] The argument fails in this case because the statistical evidence was not offered or used to support an erroneous theory that Title VII requires an employer's work force to be racially balanced. Statistics showing racial or ethnic imbalance are probative in a case such as this one only because such imbalance is often a telltale sign of purposeful discrimination; absent explanation, it is ordinarily to be expected that nondiscriminatory hiring practices will in time result in a work force more or less representative of the racial and ethnic composition of the population in the community from which employees are hired. Evidence of longlasting and gross disparity between the composition of a work force and that of the general population thus may be significant even though §703(j) makes clear that Title VII imposes no requirement that a work force mirror the general population. . . .

The company's later changes in its hiring and promotion policies could be of little comfort to the victims of the earlier post-Act discrimination, and could not erase its previous illegal conduct or its obligation to afford relief to those who suffered because of it.[23]

The District Court and the Court of Appeals, on the basis of substantial evidence, held that the Government had proved a prima facie case of systematic and purposeful employment discrimination, continuing well beyond the effective date of Title VII. The company's attempts to rebut that conclusion were held to be inadequate.[24] For the reasons we have summarized, there is no warrant for this Court to disturb the findings of the District Court and the Court of Appeals on this basic issue. . . .

[handwritten: upholds lower court decisions]

[handwritten: P.P. DOJ Company failed step 2 of rebutting in McDonnell test]

NOTES

1. *Proving a Pattern or Practice Case.* The Department of Justice, which at the time had authority that is now vested in the EEOC to bring "pattern or practice" cases, used a "snapshot" of the defendant's employment statistics on one particular day, March 31, 1971. How can statistical evidence prove discriminatory intent? If a plaintiff's evidence simply proved that over 99 percent of underground coal miners were men, would that establish a prima facie case?

Footnotes 20 and 23 sketch the rationale for the use of such statistics in systemic disparate treatment cases. Those footnotes in turn look to probability theory. The plaintiff must show that a particular group, such as African Americans, Latinos, or women, is underrepresented in the employer's work force. "Underrepresentation," in turn, means that there are fewer of such individuals than we would expect if the employer chose his workers without regard to race, national origin, or sex. Thus, the plaintiff must also establish the percentage of such individuals who would be employed absent such discrimination. The discrepancy between the "observed" and the "expected" can give rise to a finding of discrimination, but even then, for "disparate treatment" there

---

23. The company's narrower attacks upon the statistical evidence — that there was no precise delineation of the areas referred to in the general population statistics, that the Government did not demonstrate that minority populations were located closer to terminals or that transportation was available, that the statistics failed to show what portion of the minority population was suited by age, health, or other qualifications to hold trucking jobs, etc. — are equally lacking in force. At best, these attacks go only to the accuracy of the comparison between the composition of the company's work force at various terminals and the general population of the surrounding communities. They detract little from the Government's further showing that Negroes and Spanish-surnamed Americans who were hired were overwhelmingly excluded from line-driver jobs. . . . In any event, fine-tuning of the statistics could not have obscured the glaring absence of minority line drivers. As the Court of Appeals remarked, the company's inability to rebut the inference of discrimination came not from a misuse of statistics but from "the inexorable zero."

24. The company's evidence, apart from the showing of recent changes in hiring and promotion policies, consisted mainly of general statements that it hired only the best qualified applicants. But "affirmations of good faith in making individual selections are insufficient to dispel a prima facie case of systematic exclusion." *Alexander v. Louisiana*, 405 U.S. 625, 632. The company also attempted to show that all of the witnesses who testified to specific instances of discrimination either were not discriminated against or suffered no injury. The Court of Appeals correctly ruled that the trial judge was not bound to accept this testimony and that it committed no error by relying instead on the other overpowering evidence in the case. The Court of Appeals was also correct in the view that individual proof concerning each class member's specific injury was appropriately left to proceedings to determine individual relief. In a suit brought by the Government under §707(a) of the Act, the District Court's initial concern is in deciding whether the Government has proved that the defendant has engaged in a pattern or practice of discriminatory conduct.

has to be a further finding that the underrepresentation was the result of intentional discrimination. Look at the anecdotal evidence described in footnote 19. Coupled with the statistical data, it certainly suggests that intentional discrimination explains the underrepresentation. But is such evidence necessary to establish systemic disparate treatment or is it simply confirmatory of what the statistical evidence shows? In other words, can the inference be drawn from the statistics alone?

Maybe? It depends on the surrounding facts and circumstances

2. *Defendant's Rebuttal.* While rejecting the defendant's broad attack on the use of statistical evidence, the Court accepts the possibility that the defendant could rebut the government's prima facie case with evidence that it had not done any hiring of line drivers since Title VII became effective. The Court held that the defendant failed to make such a showing. But suppose it had. The defendant would not have shown that it did not discriminate; rather, it would have shown that it did not discriminate after July 2, 1965, the date Title VII became effective!

How else can the defendant rebut a systemic case? The Court, in footnote 24, rejected defendant's claim that it hired "only the best qualified applicants," as an affirmation of "good faith" that would not rebut the prima facie case. The defendant also tried to introduce evidence that the workers who testified that they had been discriminated against were not in fact victims of discrimination. While the Court upheld the trial court's rejection of that evidence at this stage in the case, defendants found liable for systemic disparate treatment discrimination can limit individualized relief by proving that they would have made the same decision in any event for any given member of the class allegedly discriminated against. See Chapter 8. There's an obvious parallel to a §706(k) case. See Note 2, p. 69.

3. *Shifting Burdens.* This litigation structure seems very strange to one familiar with the *McDonnell Douglas* proof structure. Other than rebutting the plaintiff's proof, a defendant seems to have no defense. It can, at the remedies stage, try to establish that a particular individual was not the victim of discrimination, but this seems much like the "same decision anyway" defense for individual cases — the defendant is guilty of discrimination, but its intent didn't harm this particular person. We will see, however, that the defendant can argue something akin to the "legitimate nondiscriminatory reason" in *McDonnell Douglas* cases: it can offer an explanation as to how the underrepresentation could have occurred even if the employer were not discriminating in its hiring. Can you think of what kinds of explanation T.I.M.E.-D.C. could have offered? Note also that this is not, strictly speaking, a defense: the plaintiff bears the burden of proof of intent to discriminate, and the employer's nondiscriminatory explanation is a way to challenge the inference of intent that might otherwise be drawn from the plaintiff's statistical proof.

4. *Justification for Different Approaches.* What justification is there for treating systemic cases more permissively than individual ones? Is it that we are more confident of our conclusions as to the existence of discriminatory intent when a cluster of employment decisions is involved? Put simply, one might, with greater reason, suspect the fairness of a coin that yielded 60 "heads" in 100 tosses than one that comes up "heads" 6 times out of 10. But perhaps even with larger numbers, the inference of intentional discrimination is not always as strong as may first appear.

5. *Individual vs. Systemic Cases. Teamsters* differs from *Manhart* by not requiring proof of a facially discriminatory policy to establish liability. Is *Teamsters* to *McDonnell Douglas* as *Manhart* is to *Price Waterhouse*? The systemic theory is usually asserted either in a government enforcement action (as in *Teamsters*) or in a private class action. Given the advantages of the systemic theory, may a plaintiff bring an individual disparate treatment case but employ the systemic disparate treatment theory to obtain the advantage of the shift in burdens? See Note 3, p. 233, Chapter 4.

No. systemic treatment is a class concept and therefore applicable only in class actions

6. *Easy vs. Harder Cases.* In part because discrimination in the unionized trucking industry was so notorious and pervasive, *Teamsters* presented a relatively easy systemic case because the statistics were so stark: virtually no minority group members were assigned line-driver positions anywhere in the industry. What must a plaintiff do to establish systemic disparate treatment when the numbers are not so stark and the discriminatory reputation of the defendants not so clear?

[handwritten: Refines Teamsters   compare observed w/ expected in labor mkt.]

HAZELWOOD SCHOOL DISTRICT v. UNITED STATES
433 U.S. 299 (1977)

[handwritten right margin: Note 2 — stats must consider the year Title VII was passed. Once Step 1 Prima facie is established Δ has chance to rebut by showing that its based on Pre-Act practices not Post-Act]

Justice STEWART delivered the opinion of the Court.

[Hazelwood School District is in the northern part of St. Louis County, Missouri. The Attorney General sued Hazelwood, alleging a "pattern or practice" of employment discrimination in violation of Title VII.]

Hazelwood was formed from 13 rural school districts between 1949 and 1951 by a process of annexation. By the 1967-1968 school year, 17,550 students were enrolled in the district, of whom only 59 were Negro; the number of Negro pupils increased to 576 of 25,166 in 1972-1973, a total of just over 2%.

From the beginning, Hazelwood followed relatively unstructured procedures in hiring its teachers. Every person requesting an application for a teaching position was sent one, and completed applications were submitted to a central personnel office, where they were kept on file. During the early 1960s the personnel office notified all applicants whenever a teaching position became available, but as the number of applications on file increased in the late 1960s and early 1970s, this practice was no longer considered feasible. The personnel office thus began the practice of selecting anywhere from 3 to 10 applicants for interviews at the school where the vacancy existed. The personnel office did not substantively screen the applicants in determining which of them to send for interviews, other than to ascertain that each applicant, if selected, would be eligible for state certification by the time he began the job. *[handwritten margin: → interview procedure]* Generally, those who had most recently submitted applications were most likely to be chosen for interviews.

Interviews were conducted by a department chairman, program coordinator, or the principal at the school where the teaching vacancy existed. Although those conducting the interviews did fill out forms rating the applicants in a number of respects, it is undisputed that each school principal possessed virtually unlimited discretion in hiring teachers for his school. The only general guidance given to the principals was to hire the "most competent" person available, and such intangibles as "personality, disposition, appearance, poise, voice, articulation, and ability to deal with people" counted heavily. The principal's choice was routinely honored by Hazelwood's Superintendent and the Board of Education. *[handwritten margin: hiring of teachers left to principal's discretion]*

In the early 1960s Hazelwood found it necessary to recruit new teachers, and for that purpose members of its staff visited a number of colleges and universities in Missouri and bordering States. All the institutions visited were predominantly white, and Hazelwood did not seriously recruit at either of the two predominantly Negro four-year colleges in Missouri. As a buyer's market began to develop for public school teachers, Hazelwood curtailed its recruiting efforts. For the 1971-1972 school year, 3,127 persons applied for only 234 teaching vacancies; for the 1972-1973 school year, there were 2,373 applications for 282 vacancies. A number of the applicants who were not hired were Negroes.

Hazelwood hired its first Negro teacher in 1969. The number of Negro faculty members gradually increased in successive years: 6 of 957 in the 1970 school year; 16 of 1,107 by the end of the 1972 school year; 22 of 1,231 in the 1973 school year. By comparison, according to 1970 census figures, of more than 19,000 teachers employed in that year in the St. Louis area, 15.4% were Negro. That percentage figure included the St. Louis City School District, which in recent years has followed a policy of attempting to maintain a 50% Negro teaching staff. Apart from that school district, 5.7% of the teachers in the county were Negro in 1970.

Drawing upon these historic facts, the Government mounted its "pattern or practice" attack in the District Court upon four different fronts. It adduced evidence of (1) a history of alleged racially discriminatory practices, (2) statistical disparities in hiring, (3) the standardless and largely subjective hiring procedures, and (4) specific instances of alleged discrimination against 55 unsuccessful Negro applicants for teaching jobs. Hazelwood offered virtually no additional evidence in response, relying instead on evidence introduced by the Government, perceived deficiencies in the Government's case, and its own officially promulgated policy "to hire all teachers on the basis of training, preparation and recommendations, regardless of race, color or creed."

[The District Court found no pattern or practice of discrimination. No dual school system ever existed in Hazelwood and the number of African Americans employed as teachers was proportionate to the number of African American pupils. The Eighth Circuit reversed.] After suggesting that the District Court had assigned inadequate weight to evidence of discriminatory conduct on the part of Hazelwood before [March 24, 1972] the effective date of Title VII [for public employment], the Court of Appeals rejected the trial court's analysis of the statistical data as resting on an irrelevant comparison of Negro teachers to Negro pupils in Hazelwood. The proper comparison, in the appellate court's view, was one between Negro teachers in Hazelwood and Negro teachers in the relevant labor market area. Selecting St. Louis County and St. Louis City as the relevant area,[8] the Court of Appeals compared the 1970 census figures, showing that 15.4% of teachers in that area were Negro, to the racial composition of Hazelwood's teaching staff. In the 1972-1973 and 1973-1974 school years, only 1.4% and 1.8%, respectively, of Hazelwood's teachers were Negroes. This statistical disparity, particularly when viewed against the background of the teacher-hiring procedures that Hazelwood had followed, was held to constitute a prima facie case of a pattern or practice of racial discrimination.

In addition, the Court of Appeals reasoned that the trial court had erred in failing to measure the 55 instances in which Negro applicants were denied jobs against the four-part standard for establishing a prima facie case of individual discrimination set out in this Court's opinion in *McDonnell Douglas Corp. v. Green.* Applying that standard, the appellate court found 16 cases of individual discrimination, which "buttressed" the statistical proof. Because Hazelwood had not rebutted the Government's prima facie case of a pattern or practice of racial discrimination, the Court of Appeals directed judgment for the Government. . . .

The petitioners primarily attack the judgment of the Court of Appeals for its reliance on "undifferentiated work force statistics to find an unrebutted prima facie case of employment discrimination." The question they raise, in short, is whether a basic component in the Court of Appeals' finding of a pattern or practice of discrimination — the comparatively small percentage of Negro employees on Hazelwood's teaching staff — was lacking in probative force.

---

8. The city of St. Louis is surrounded by, but not included in, St. Louis County.

This Court's recent consideration in *Teamsters v. United States* of the role of statistics in pattern-or-practice suits under Title VII provides substantial guidance in evaluating the arguments advanced by the petitioners. In that case we stated that it is the Government's burden to "establish by a preponderance of the evidence that racial discrimination was the [employer's] standard operating procedure — the regular rather than the unusual practice." We also noted that statistics can be an important source of proof in employment discrimination cases, since "absent explanation, it is ordinarily to be expected that nondiscriminatory hiring practices will in time result in a work force more or less representative of the racial and ethnic composition of the population in the community from which employees are hired. Evidence of long lasting and gross disparity between the composition of a work force and that of the general population thus may be significant even though §703(j) makes clear that Title VII imposes no requirement that a work force mirror the general population." Where gross statistical disparities can be shown, they alone may in a proper case constitute prima facie proof of a pattern or practice of discrimination. *Teamsters.*

[margin note: court looks to Teamsters]

There can be no doubt, in light of the *Teamsters* case, that the District Court's comparison of Hazelwood's teacher work force to its student population fundamentally misconceived the role of statistics in employment discrimination cases. The Court of Appeals was correct in the view that a proper comparison was between the racial composition of Hazelwood's teaching staff and the racial composition of the qualified public school teacher population in the relevant labor market.[13] See *Teamsters.* The percentage of Negroes on Hazelwood's teaching staff in 1972-1973 was 1.4%, and in 1973-1974 it was 1.8%. By contrast, the percentage of qualified Negro teachers in the area was, according to the 1970 census, at least 5.7%.[14] Although these differences were on their face substantial, the Court of Appeals erred in substituting its judgment for that of the District Court and holding that the Government had conclusively proved its "pattern or practice" lawsuit.

[margin note: relevant population for comparison]

[margin note: despite disparity, CoA in error to conclude that P met burden of proving pattern bc it did not consider the Post-Act stats in the record]

13. In *Teamsters*, the comparison between the percentage of Negroes on the employer's work force and the percentage in the general areawide population was highly probative, because the job skill there involved — the ability to drive a truck — is one that many persons possess or can fairly readily acquire. When special qualifications are required to fill particular jobs, comparisons to the general population (rather than to the smaller group of individuals who possess the necessary qualifications) may have little probative value. The comparative statistics introduced by the Government in the District Court, however, were properly limited to public school teachers. . . .

Although the petitioners concede as a general matter the probative force of the comparative work force statistics, they object to the Court of Appeals' heavy reliance on these data on the ground that applicant-flow data, showing the actual percentage of white and Negro applicants for teaching positions at Hazelwood, would be firmer proof. . . . [T]here was no clear evidence of such statistics. We leave it to the District Court on remand to determine whether competent proof of those data can be adduced. If so, it would, of course, be very relevant. *Cf. Dothard v. Rawlinson* [reproduced at p. 195].

14. As is discussed below, the Government contends that a comparative figure of 15.4%, rather than 5.7%, is the appropriate one. But even assuming, arguendo, that the 5.7% figure urged by the petitioners is correct, the disparity between that figure and the percentage of Negroes on Hazelwood's teaching staff would be more than fourfold for the 1972-1973 school year, and threefold for the 1973-1974 school year. A precise method of measuring the significance of such statistical disparities was explained in *Castaneda v. Partida*, 430 U.S. 482, 496-497, n.17 [(1977]. It involves calculation of the "standard deviation" as a measure of predicted fluctuations from the expected value of a sample. Using the 5.7% figure as the basis for calculating the expected value, the expected number of Negroes on the Hazelwood teaching staff would be roughly 63 in 1972-1973 and 70 in 1973-1974. The observed number in those years was 16 and 22, respectively. The difference between the observed and expected values was more than six standard deviations in 1972-1973 and more than five standard deviations in 1973-1974. The Court in *Castaneda* noted that "[a]s a general rule for such large samples, if the difference between the expected value and the observed number is greater than two or three standard deviations," then the hypothesis that teachers were hired without regard to race would be suspect. 430 U.S. at 497 n.17.

The Court of Appeals totally disregarded the possibility that this prima facie statistical proof in the record might at the trial court level be rebutted by statistics dealing with Hazelwood's hiring after it became subject to Title VII. Racial discrimination by public employers was not made illegal under Title VII until March 24, 1972. A public employer who from that date forward made all its employment decisions in a wholly nondiscriminatory way would not violate Title VII even if it had formerly maintained an all-white work force by purposefully excluding Negroes. For this reason, the Court cautioned in the *Teamsters* opinion that once a prima facie case has been established by statistical work force disparities, the employer must be given an opportunity to show that "the claimed discriminatory pattern is a product of pre-Act hiring rather than unlawful post-Act discriminations."

The record in this case showed that for the 1972-1973 school year, Hazelwood hired 282 new teachers, 10 of whom (3.5%) were Negroes; for the following school year it hired 123 new teachers, 5 of whom (4.1%) were Negroes. Over the two-year period, Negroes constituted a total of 15 of the 405 new teachers hired (3.7%). . . .

What the hiring figures prove obviously depends upon the figures to which they are compared. The Court of Appeals accepted the Government's argument that the relevant comparison was to the labor market area of St. Louis County and the city of St. Louis, in which, according to the 1970 census, 15.4% of all teachers were Negro. The propriety of that comparison was vigorously disputed by the petitioners, who urged that because the city of St. Louis has made special attempts to maintain a 50% Negro teaching staff, inclusion of that school district in the relevant market area distorts the comparison. Were that argument accepted, the percentage of Negro teachers in the relevant labor market area (St. Louis County alone) as shown in the 1970 census would be 5.7% rather than 15.4%.

The difference between these figures may well be important; the disparity between 3.7% (the percentage of Negro teachers hired by Hazelwood in 1972-1973 and 1973-1974) and 5.7% may be sufficiently small to weaken the Government's other proof, while the disparity between 3.7% and 15.4% may be sufficiently large to reinforce it.[17] In determining which of the two figures — or, very possibly, what intermediate figure — provides

---

17. Indeed, under the statistical methodology explained in *Castaneda v. Partida*, involving the calculation of the standard deviation as a measure of predicted fluctuations, the difference between using 15.4% and 5.7% as the areawide figure would be significant. If the 15.4% figure is taken as the basis for comparison, the expected number of Negro teachers hired by Hazelwood in 1972-1973 would be 43 (rather than the actual figure of 10) of a total of 282, a difference of more than five standard deviations; the expected number in 1973-1974 would be 19 (rather than the actual figure 5) of a total of 123, a difference of more than three standard deviations. For the two years combined, the difference between the observed number of 15 Negro teachers hired (of a total of 405) would vary from the expected number of 62 by more than six standard deviations. Because a fluctuation of more than two or three standard deviations would undercut the hypothesis that decisions were being made randomly with respect to race, each of these statistical comparisons would reinforce rather than rebut the Government's other proof. If, however, the 5.7% areawide figure is used, the expected number of Negro teachers hired in 1972-1973 would be roughly 16, less than two standard deviations from the observed number of 10; for 1973-1974, the expected value would be roughly seven, less than one standard deviation from the observed value of 5; and for the two years combined, the expected value of 23 would be less than two standard deviations from the observed total of 15. A more precise method of analyzing these statistics confirms the results of the standard deviation analysis. See F. MOSTELLER, R. ROURKE, & G. THOMAS, PROBABILITY WITH STATISTICAL APPLICATIONS 494 (2d ed. 1970).

These observations are not intended to suggest that precise calculations of statistical significance are necessary in employing statistical proof, but merely to highlight the importance of the choice of the relevant labor market area.

the most accurate basis for comparison to the hiring figures at Hazelwood, it will be necessary to evaluate such considerations as (i) whether the racially based hiring policies of the St. Louis City School District were in effect as far back as 1970, the year in which the census figures were taken; (ii) to what extent those policies have changed the racial composition of that district's teaching staff from what it would otherwise have been; (iii) to what extent St. Louis' recruitment policies have diverted to the city, teachers who might otherwise have applied to Hazelwood; (iv) to what extent Negro teachers employed by the city would prefer employment in other districts such as Hazelwood; and (v) what the experience in other school districts in St. Louis County indicates about the validity of excluding the City School District from the relevant labor market. . . .

We hold, therefore, that the Court of Appeals erred in disregarding the post-Act hiring statistics in the record, and that it should have remanded the case to the District Court for further findings as to the relevant labor market area and for an ultimate determination of whether Hazelwood engaged in a pattern or practice of employment discrimination after March 24, 1972. . . .

Justice WHITE, concurring.

I join the Court's opinion . . . but with reservations with respect to the relative neglect of applicant pool data in finding a prima facie case of employment discrimination and heavy reliance on the disparity between the areawide percentage of black public school teachers and the percentage of blacks on Hazelwood's teaching staff. . . .

Justice STEVENS, dissenting. . . .

II . . .

The petitioners offered no evidence concerning wage differentials, commuting problems, or the relative advantages of teaching in an inner-city school as opposed to a suburban school. Without any such evidence in the record, it is difficult to understand why the simple fact that the city was the source of a third of Hazelwood's faculty should not be sufficient to demonstrate that it is a part of the relevant market. The city's policy of attempting to maintain a 50/50 ratio clearly does not undermine that conclusion, particularly when the record reveals no shortage of qualified black applicants in either Hazelwood or other suburban school districts. Surely not all of the 2,000 black teachers employed by the city were unavailable for employment in Hazelwood at the time of their initial hire.

But even if it were proper to exclude the city of St. Louis from the market, the statistical evidence would still tend to prove discrimination. With the city excluded, 5.7% of the teachers in the remaining market were black. On the basis of a random selection, one would therefore expect 5.7% of the 405 teachers hired by Hazelwood in the 1972-1973 and 1973-1974 school years to have been black. But instead of 23 black teachers, Hazelwood hired only 15, less than two-thirds of the expected number. Without the benefit of expert testimony, I would hesitate to infer that the disparity between 23 and 15 is great enough, in itself, to prove discrimination.[5] It is perfectly

5. After I had drafted this opinion, one of my law clerks advised me that, given the size of the two-year sample, there is only about a 5% likelihood that a disparity this large would be produced by a random selection from the labor pool. If his calculation (which was made using the method described in H. BLALOCK, SOCIAL STATISTICS 151-173 (1972)) is correct, it is easy to understand why Hazelwood offered no expert testimony.

clear, however, that whatever probative force this disparity has, it tends to prove dis-crimination and does absolutely nothing in the way of carrying Hazelwood's burden of overcoming the Government's prima facie case.

Absolute precision in the analysis of market data is too much to expect. We may fairly assume that a nondiscriminatory selection process would have resulted in the hiring of somewhere between the 15% suggested by the Government and the 5.7% suggested by petitioners, or perhaps 30 or 40 black teachers, instead of the 15 actu-ally hired. On that assumption, the Court of Appeals' determination that there were 16 individual cases of discriminatory refusal to hire black applicants in the post-1972 period seems remarkably accurate.

In sum, the Government is entitled to prevail on the present record. It proved a prima facie case, which Hazelwood failed to rebut. Why, then, should we burden a busy federal court with another trial? . . .

NOTES

1. *Refining* Teamsters. *Hazelwood* confirms the statistical approach in *Teamsters* but refines it. But the case lacked either the notorious history of discrimination in the trucking industry or the "inexorable zero." Start simple: do you understand why the district court was wrong in comparing the ratio of black teachers to the ratio of black students in the school district? The right approach is to compare the representation of African Americans in the employer's work force with the percentage of African Americans available to be hired by the employer. How much disparity must be shown to establish that it is "gross"? The "inexorable zero" in *Teamsters* suffices simply by "eyeballing" the numbers, but what if the comparison is not that stark? Look at foot-notes 14 and 17 for the Court's discussion of more sophisticated statistical techniques. Must there be expert testimony showing that the difference based on race is "statisti-cally significant"? And do you understand what that means?

2. *Defining Underrepresentation.* In order to determine whether blacks are under-represented at an employer such as Hazelwood, we must compare the "observed" (*i.e.*, the percentage now employed) with the "expected" (the percentage who would be employed absent discrimination). Another way to say that is that we must ascer-tain the racial composition of the labor market from which the employer draws its work force. This comparison must be considered in three dimensions — time, geog-raphy, and skill.

3. *Post-Act Hiring. Hazelwood* itself turned on whether it was appropriate to use a "snapshot" of the employer's work force composition on a particular day as the basis for comparison with the relevant labor market. Because Title VII had only recently been extended to state and local government employees, this approach risked showing that any resulting discriminatory pattern was the product of pre-Act hiring, rather than unlawful post-Act discrimination. Thus, "flow" statistics, or movements in and out of jobs over time, are relevant to show whether the snapshot statistics incorporate pre-Act conduct. Since it has now been decades since the last major expansion of Title VII coverage, you might think the temporal dimension of the labor market is no longer of consequence, but you'd be wrong, since statutes of limitations continue to effectively insulate employers from the consequences of prior discriminatory acts.

4. *Applicant Pool.* Justice White complained about the "relative neglect" of applicant pool data. The most intuitive way to ascertain the "relevant labor market" is to look at the actual applicants. In *Teamsters*, the company had hired African Americans and Latinos but had segregated them out of the line driver jobs. Since the actual work was quite similar — truck driving is truck driving — the comparison of racial representation of city drivers and line drivers was powerful comparative evidence. The applicants for city jobs weren't actual applicants for line driver jobs but they constituted a pretty good proxy pool.

Hazelwood involved the absence of minority teachers, not their segregation. Thus, to find an appropriate comparison, it was necessary to look beyond the incumbent work force of the defendant. Justice White is surely correct when he suggests that applicant flow data can be very useful for a comparison. Looking only at actual applicants for the job in question eliminates many problems: it is unlikely that persons lacking minimal skills will apply, and, by definition, those who apply are interested in the work and willing to consider the location. *See Paige v. California*, 291 F.3d 1141 (9th Cir. 2002) (actual pool of promotional applicants is the correct comparison group for plaintiffs' claim of systemic disparate treatment in the promotion process). But employers such as Hazelwood do not always keep applications, and Hazelwood's haphazard method of dealing with applications might make such data suspect.

But, assuming accurate data, is the applicant pool always the correct comparison? In *EEOC v. Joe's Stone Crab, Inc.*, 220 F.3d 1263 (11th Cir. 2000), the at-issue jobs were wait staff positions at a popular Miami Beach restaurant. The number of women hired approximated their representation in the applicant pool, those who showed up for a "roll call." But the court rejected this actual applicant pool as the appropriate comparison because there was reason to believe that women were deterred from applying by Joe's reputation for hiring only male wait staff.

5. *Qualified Labor Pool: Skills and Interest.* Looking beyond either the incumbent work force or applicant flow, *Hazelwood* focuses on those qualified to teach. In contrast, *Teamsters* looked at general population figures. Can you explain why? A variation on this occurred in *Joe's Stone Crab, Inc.* After rejecting the applicant pool comparison, the court did not use general population figures (presumably about 50 percent female) but turned to the pool of food servers in Miami Beach. But rather than looking to the 44.1 percent representation of women in that entire group, the district court "refined" that pool to include only "servers who lived or worked in Miami Beach and earned between $25,000 and $50,000 . . . thereby using past earnings as a proxy for experience, and by extension, experience as a proxy for qualification." *Id.* at 1272. The resulting pool was 31.1 percent female, which resulted in a disparity that "bordered on statistical significance" and supported a prima facie case. Why discount the pool by income? Wouldn't lower-income food servers be exactly the people you would expect to apply for higher-paying jobs, such as at Joe's Stone Crab? For wait staff jobs, shouldn't general population statistics be used — can't most everyone learn that job?

6. *Qualified Labor Pool: Geography.* Defining the geographic labor market was the turning point in *Hazelwood*. Should teachers in the city of St. Louis be included? Sometimes a picture is worth a thousand words:

St. Louis Area School Districts

Is it possible that Hazelwood drew its teachers from, say, Mehlville rather than St. Louis City? Justice Stevens stressed that the high number of actual Hazelwood teachers who resided in the city mandated the inclusion of the city as part of the appropriate labor pool.

The defendant, however, claimed that St. Louis City hired to meet a goal of 50 percent black teachers. What is the significance of such a hiring pattern? Maybe St. Louis pays more; therefore, Hazelwood cannot attract St. Louis teachers. Factually, one would have expected Hazelwood to have made this argument the first time if that had been true. Analytically, is it a reason to exclude the whole St. Louis pool or merely to discount it somewhat? Might not some teachers prefer the suburbs, even at lower pay? Or maybe the implication was that St. Louis hires unqualified persons for affirmative action purposes. In that case, the pool of qualified teachers may not be as large as it first appears. But is that true? Even if some less-qualified persons were hired, should the St. Louis pool be discounted, or eliminated?

Presumably, the geographic labor pool should be the area from which the employer recruits employees or would do so but for discrimination. That was a complicated inquiry in *Hazelwood* but, for many jobs, recruitment is national or even global. Perhaps the statistics should be weighted to take account of different rates of representation in the local versus the national market.

7. *Statistical Techniques.* The *Hazelwood* Court uses binomial distribution as a way of determining whether the defendant acted with the intent to discriminate. Be clear what this means: if a certain result is "statistically significant," it is unlikely to be the result of chance. Actually, we will see that there are different levels of significance, but all of

them, to a greater or lesser degree, rule out chance as an explanation for certain results. However, ruling out chance merely allows a statistician to conclude that race (or sex) is related to a particular situation. If the results in *Hazelwood* were statistically significant, we could be pretty confident that there was something about being black that correlated with not being employed by the school district. That "something" might, of course, be intent by the employer to discriminate against blacks. The finder of fact is permitted to infer that the defendant's "standard operating procedure — the regular rather than the unusual practice" — was to discriminate. That shifts at least a burden of production to the employer to provide a nondiscriminatory explanation. *See generally* Jason Bent, *The Telltale Sign of Discrimination: Probabilities, Information Asymmetries, and the Systemic Disparate Treatment Theory*, 44 U. Mich. J.L. Reform 797 (2011).

8. *Systemic Age Cases.* Systemic disparate treatment cases can also be litigated under the ADEA, typically in the context of large-scale reductions in force. In *Adams v. Ameritech Servs., Inc.*, 231 F.3d 414 (7th Cir. 2000), the employer substantially reduced its personnel, eliminating some 2,500 of 21,000 management employees "either by persuasion or by force." The Seventh Circuit reaffirmed the admissibility of statistical evidence in systemic discrimination cases, found the statistical evidence plaintiffs had proffered admissible, and held that this evidence, together with plaintiffs' other proof, precluded summary judgment. As the court summarized the statistical evidence against one of the defendants: "ASI selected for termination 12.63% of those aged 40-44, 16.71% of those aged 45-49, 24.58% of those aged 50-54, and 29.19% of those aged 55 and older." 231 F.3d at 419-20. Plaintiff's statistician found that, within each 10-year age cohort, older workers were more likely to be terminated than younger ones, and these findings were statistically significant. *Adams* thus illustrates how a large-scale reduction in force can become a textbook exercise in the application of statistical analysis to prove a correlation between age and layoff in order to make out a prima facie case of systemic disparate treatment.

By contrast, *Aliotta v. Bair*, 614 F.3d 556, 566 (D.C. Cir. 2010), rejected a class systemic disparate treatment and disparate impact attack because plaintiffs' statistical evidence was lacking. Their expert combined the effects of the involuntary terminations with the effects of "voluntary" retirements to find an age effect, but the court found this inappropriate: "class members cannot include as evidence of discrimination the statistics of a group of employees who, because they voluntarily accepted a buyout, suffered no adverse employment action." Does this make sense to you when the question in the first instance is whether the employer acted adversely to the class of older workers? It's one thing to say that potential class members have waived their rights by accepting the employer's buyout and another thing to say that older workers weren't targeted or adversely affected by the riffing.

WAL-MART STORES, INC. v. DUKES
564 U.S. 338 (2011)

Scalia, J.

[The question before the Court involved whether to certify a class of about a million and a half women workers claiming pay and promotion discrimination because of sex. The Ninth Circuit had ruled *en banc* for certification. Rule 23 of the Federal Rules of Civil Procedure specifies several requirements for class certification, one of which is paragraph (a)(2), which requires that "there are questions of law or fact common to the class." The plaintiffs' core claim was that Wal-Mart's policy of granting unstructured and unreviewed discretion to store managers to make pay and promotion decisions was a practice of systemic disparate treatment discrimination. As for "commonality," the argument was that all women employees faced the risk of discrimination in pay and promotion because Wal-Mart's central management authorized its store managers to make those decisions but did not review them or otherwise intervene despite clear evidence of discrimination by the managers. The portion of the opinion reproduced below deals with the majority's treatment of this commonality question. Chapter 8, p. 547, deals with other aspects of the case.]

II . . .

A

The crux of this case is commonality — the rule requiring a plaintiff to show that "there are questions of law or fact common to the class." Rule 23(a)(2). . . . Commonality requires the plaintiff to demonstrate that the class members "have suffered the same injury." This does not mean merely that they have all suffered a violation of the same provision of law. Title VII, for example, can be violated in many ways — by intentional discrimination, or by hiring and promotion criteria that result in disparate impact, and by the use of these practices on the part of many different superiors in a single company. Quite obviously, the mere claim by employees of the same company that they have suffered a Title VII injury, or even a disparate-impact Title VII injury, gives no cause to believe that all their claims can productively be litigated at once. Their claims must depend upon a common contention — for example, the assertion of discriminatory bias on the part of the same supervisor. That common contention, moreover, must be of such a nature that it is capable of classwide resolution — which means that determination of its truth or falsity will resolve an issue that is central to the validity of each one of the claims in one stroke. . . .

In this case, proof of commonality necessarily overlaps with respondents' merits contention that Wal-Mart engages in a pattern or practice of discrimination. That is so because, in resolving an individual's Title VII claim, the crux of the inquiry is "the reason for a particular employment decision," *Cooper v. Federal Reserve Bank of Richmond*, 467 U.S. 867, 876 (1984). Here respondents wish to sue about literally millions of employment decisions at once. Without some glue holding the alleged reasons for all those decisions together, it will be impossible to say that examination of all the class members' claims for relief will produce a common answer to the crucial question why was I disfavored.

B . . .

[There is a "wide gap" between an individual's claim and the existence of a class of persons who have suffered the same injury as that individual. *Gen. Tel. Co. of the Southwest v. Falcon*, 457 U.S. 147 (1982)] suggested two ways in which that conceptual gap might be bridged. First, if the employer "used a biased testing procedure to evaluate both applicants for employment and incumbent employees, a class action on behalf of every applicant or employee who might have been prejudiced by the test clearly would satisfy the commonality and typicality requirements of Rule 23(a)." Second, "[s]ignificant proof that an employer operated under a general policy of discrimination conceivably could justify a class of both applicants and employees if the discrimination manifested itself in hiring and promotion practices in the same general fashion, such as through entirely subjective decisionmaking processes." *Ibid.* We think that statement precisely describes respondents' burden in this case. The first manner of bridging the gap obviously has no application here; Wal-Mart has no testing procedure or other companywide evaluation method that can be charged with bias. The whole point of permitting discretionary decisionmaking is to avoid evaluating employees under a common standard.

The second [possibility] requires "significant proof" that Wal-Mart "operated under a general policy of discrimination." That is entirely absent here. Wal-Mart's announced policy forbids sex discrimination, and as the district court recognized the company imposes penalties for denials of equal employment opportunity. The only evidence of a "general policy of discrimination" respondents produced was the testimony of Dr. William Bielby, their sociological expert. Relying on "social framework" analysis, Bielby testified that Wal-Mart has a "strong corporate culture," that makes it "'vulnerable'" to "gender bias." He could not, however, "determine with any specificity how regularly stereotypes play a meaningful role in employment decisions at Wal-Mart. At his deposition . . . Dr. Bielby conceded that he could not calculate whether 0.5 percent or 95 percent of the employment decisions at Wal-Mart might be determined by stereotyped thinking. . . . If Bielby admittedly has no answer to that question, we can safely disregard what he has to say. It is worlds away from "significant proof" that Wal-Mart "operated under a general policy of discrimination."

C

The only corporate policy that the plaintiffs' evidence convincingly establishes is Wal-Mart's "policy" of *allowing discretion* by local supervisors over employment matters. On its face, of course, that is just the opposite of a uniform employment practice that would provide the commonality needed for a class action; it is a policy *against having* uniform employment practices. It is also a very common and presumptively reasonable way of doing business — one that we have said "should itself raise no inference of discriminatory conduct." *Watson v. Ft. Worth Bank & Trust,* 487 U.S. 977 (1988) [reproduced at p. 183].

To be sure, we have recognized that, "in appropriate cases," giving discretion to lower-level supervisors can be the basis of Title VII liability under a disparate-impact theory — since "an employer's undisciplined system of subjective decisionmaking [can have] precisely the same effects as a system pervaded by impermissible intentional discrimination." *Watson.* But the recognition that this type of Title VII claim "can" exist does not lead to the conclusion that every employee in a company using a system of discretion has such a claim in common. To the contrary, left to their own devices most managers in any corporation — and surely most managers in a corporation that forbids sex discrimination — would select sex-neutral, performance-based criteria for hiring and promotion that produce no actionable disparity at all. Others may choose to reward various attributes that produce disparate impact — such as scores on general aptitude tests or educational achievements, see *Griggs v. Duke Power Co.* And still other managers may be guilty of intentional discrimination that produces a sex-based disparity. In such a company, demonstrating the invalidity of one manager's use of discretion will do nothing to demonstrate the invalidity of another's. A party seeking to certify a nationwide class will be unable to show that all the employees' Title VII claims will in fact depend on the answers to common questions.

Respondents have not identified a common mode of exercising discretion that pervades the entire company — aside from their reliance on Dr. Bielby's social frameworks analysis that we have rejected. In a company of Wal-Mart's size and geographical scope, it is quite unbelievable that all managers would exercise their discretion in a common way without some common direction. Respondents attempt to make that showing by means of statistical and anecdotal evidence, but their evidence falls well short.

The statistical evidence consists primarily of regression analyses performed by Dr. Richard Drogin, a statistician, and Dr. Marc Bendick, a labor economist. Drogin conducted his analysis region-by-region, comparing the number of women promoted into management positions with the percentage of women in the available pool of hourly workers. After considering regional and national data, Drogin concluded that "there are statistically significant disparities between men and women at Wal-Mart . . . [and] these disparities . . . can be explained only by gender discrimination." Bendick compared work force data from Wal-Mart and competitive retailers and concluded that Wal-Mart "promotes a lower percentage of women than its competitors."

Even if they are taken at face value, these studies are insufficient to establish that respondents' theory can be proved on a classwide basis. In *Falcon*, we held that one named plaintiff's experience of discrimination was insufficient to infer that "discriminatory treatment is typical of [the employer's employment] practices." A similar failure of inference arises here. . . . A regional pay disparity, for example, may be attributable to only a small set of Wal-Mart stores, and cannot by itself establish the uniform, store-by-store disparity upon which the plaintiffs' theory depends.

Even if it established (as it does not) a pay or promotion pattern that differs from the nationwide figures or the regional figures in *all* of Wal-Mart's 3,400 stores, that would still not demonstrate that commonality of issue exists. Some managers will claim that the availability of women, or qualified women, or interested women, in their stores' area does not mirror the national or regional statistics. And almost all of them will claim to have been applying some sex-neutral, performance-based criteria — whose nature and effects will differ from store to store. In the landmark case of ours which held that giving discretion to lower-level supervisors can be the basis of Title VII liability under a disparate-impact theory, the plurality opinion *conditioned* that holding on the corollary that merely proving that the discretionary system has produced a racial or sexual disparity *is not enough*. "[T]he plaintiff must begin by identifying the specific employment practice that is challenged." *Watson*.

Other than the bare existence of delegated discretion, respondents have identified no "specific employment practice" — much less one that ties all their 1.5 million claims together. Merely showing that Wal-Mart's policy of discretion has produced an overall sex-based disparity does not suffice.

Respondents' anecdotal evidence suffers from the same defects, and in addition is too weak to raise any inference that all the individual, discretionary personnel decisions are discriminatory. . . .

NOTES

1. *What Happened to Systemic Disparate Treatment?* In sketching the substantive law underpinning plaintiffs' claim, Justice Scalia posits only two possible bases for commonality — an employer using employment tests or its having a general policy of discriminating. In doing so, he overlooks a third option. In *Teamsters'* terms, the claim is that the employer has a *practice* of discriminating even in the absence of an express *policy* of discrimination. Presumably, in *Teamsters*, the practice of discriminating was based on the aggregation of the individual decisions of individual terminal managers who assigned drivers either to the city or to the over-the-road jobs. If there was a company policy, it was to permit the managers to make such decisions. The same was true in *Hazelwood*: the district would be responsible for rubber-stamping the decisions of individual principals.

See generally Tristin K. Green, *Title VII and the Mirage of the* "Monell *Analogue*," 95 B.U. L. REV. 1077, 1097-98 (2015) (rejecting the argument that systemic disparate treatment discrimination should be actionable only if it results from a policy or practice of a corporate employer rather than actions of individual employees).

Of course, in *Teamsters*, the collective decisions resulted in the "inexorable zero" of minority representation while in *Wal-Mart* not all women were discriminated against in pay and promotion. But *Hazelwood* seemingly solved that problem through statistical analysis supporting an inference of discriminatory intent — exactly the kind of evidence the plaintiffs adduced in *Wal-Mart*. Is the Court's ostensibly procedural decision one that really overturns systemic disparate treatment theory as it has been understood for more than three decades?

2. *A Closer Look at the Statistics.* What about the statistical evidence suggesting that the policy of letting store managers (who were, after all, agents of Wal-Mart) make the decisions that could be aggregated to draw the inference that the company's "standard operating procedure" included a considerable amount of discrimination? That evidence, cited in more detail by Justice Ginsburg in dissent, was that 70 percent of the hourly employees but only 33 percent of the managerial employees at the stores were women and that women were paid less than men, with the salary gap widening over time even for men and women hired into the same jobs. This dramatic shortfall for women in promotion and pay does not, by itself, prove intentional discrimination, but surely it raises the real possibility that the statistical profile is, at least partially, due to discrimination by managers. Further, the possibility of some other explanation for the underrepresentation was questionable in light of evidence that Wal-Mart did much worse than other big-box competitors. Why wasn't that the common question of law or fact justifying a Rule 23(a) class action?

In *Hazelwood*, the Court used the binomial distribution to reject the null hypothesis that race and hiring were not related. In *Wal-Mart*, the plaintiffs relied on multiple regression analysis, a different but judicially accepted, statistical technique, *Bazemore v. Friday*, 478 U.S. 385 (1986), to reject the null hypothesis that discretion in setting pay and making promotions was not related to sex. Further, Dr. Bielby testified that managerial discretion enabled stereotyping because of sex. Finally, as in *Teamsters*, there was anecdotal evidence that individual women had been the victims of pay and promotion discrimination. In light of this, is the majority's "procedural" decision really a redefinition of the theories available to eliminate an employer's practice (but not policy) of intentionally discriminating in its employment decisions? In short, what happened to systemic disparate treatment, at least absent a facially discriminatory policy?

3. *A Few Bad Apples?* Does the Court's apparent undermining of systemic disparate treatment discrimination result from its belief that whatever discrimination may exist is committed by a few bad apple store managers? Revealing the Court's mindset that discrimination is limited to a few individual wrongdoers is a statement completely unsupported by the facts of the case, or perhaps anywhere else: "left to their own devices most managers in any corporation — and surely most managers in a corporation that forbids sex discrimination — would select sex-neutral, performance-based criteria for hiring and promotion that produce no actionable disparity at all." Is this consistent with what you have learned so far in this course?

This individualized conception of discrimination has been the subject of intense scholarly analysis. *See* Noah D. Zatz. *Introduction: Working Group on the Future of Systemic Disparate Treatment Law*, 32 BERKELEY J. EMP. & LAB. L. 387 (2011); Tristin K. Green, *The Future of Systemic Disparate Treatment Law*, 32 BERKELEY J. EMP. & LAB. L. 395 (2011); Melissa Hart, *Civil Rights and Systemic Wrongs*, 32 BERKELEY J.

EMP. & LAB. L. 455 (2011); Michael Selmi, *Theorizing Systemic Disparate Treatment Law: After* Wal-Mart v. Dukes, 32 BERKELEY J. EMP. & LAB. L. 477 (2011). *See also* Leslie Wexler, Wal-Mart *Matters*, 46 WAKE FOREST L. REV. 95 (2011) (arguing that discrimination can persist at firms like Wal-Mart because of various market failures, despite the company's relentless pursuit of efficiency).

4. *The Bottom Line.* While large class actions will be rarer in the wake of *Wal-Mart* (see Chapter 8), whether *Wal-Mart* is "just" a "procedural" decision or redefines substantive theories remains important for whether the EEOC can sue. Put simply, suppose the agency files a pattern and practice suit against Wal-Mart relying on essentially the same proof as plaintiffs?

5. *Taking on an Industry.* At least during the Obama administration, the EEOC seemed prepared to undertake such challenges. In a setting getting enormous attention for obvious reasons, the agency responded to an ACLU letter raising serious claims of discrimination against women for director positions in films and television by launching an investigation and, reportedly, engaging in settlement discussion. David Robb, *EEOC: Major Studios Failed to Hire Female Directors; Lawsuit Looms*, Deadline Hollywood, Feb. 15, 2017 https://deadline.com/2017/02/hollywood-studios-female-directors-eeoc-investigation-1201912590. The statistics adduced by the ACLU were compelling and were buttressed by considerable anecdotal reports about bias against women. However, the fragmented legal structure of the industry poses additional complications should such a case go to court. *See generally* Michael J. Zimmer, Charles A. Sullivan & Rebecca Hanner White, *Taking on an Industry: Women and Directing in Hollywood*, 20 EMP. RTS. & EMP. POL'Y J. 229 (2016).

NOTE ON SOPHISTICATED STATISTICAL TECHNIQUES*

1. *Application of Statistical Analysis to Discrimination Litigation.* The basis for statistical evidence in employment discrimination litigation is, as the Court said in *Teamsters*, probability theory.

> [A]bsent explanation, it is ordinarily to be expected that non-discriminatory hiring practices will in time result in a work force more or less representative of the racial and ethnic composition of the population in the community from which employees are hired.

The converse of this is that a substantial departure from what is to be expected, absent discrimination, is so improbable that the trier of fact should conclude, at least prima facie, that discrimination explains the disparity.

---

* For a general study on the use of statistics in litigation, *see* DAVID W. BARNES, STATISTICS AS PROOF: FUNDAMENTALS OF QUANTITATIVE EVIDENCE (1983). Professor Barnes has also been kind enough to review this section and make some suggestions for improvement. *See also* RAMONA L. PAETZOLD & STEVEN L. WILLBORN, THE STATISTICS OF DISCRIMINATION (2008).

† Some of Professor Browne's objections can be met by the defendant's introduction of its own statistical proof. For example, Browne criticizes defining the relevant labor market in terms of those with minimal qualifications. If, however, the employer hires only (or disproportionately) persons with higher qualifications, a statistical study could show that it is qualifications, not race, that explain the makeup of the work force. Similarly, the defendant can proffer studies using other variables not reflected in plaintiff's analysis. It is true, however, that some factors — "subjective or otherwise unquantifiable" — will be hard to account for in this way.

This assumption has been controverted. Professor Kingsley R. Browne, in *Statistical Proof of Discrimination: Beyond "Damned Lies,"* 68 Wash. L. Rev. 477 (1993), questions what he calls the "Central Assumption" of statistical proof in employment discrimination: that different racial and ethnic groups and both genders have the same interests and abilities. Browne argues that this is at odds with the real world and inconsistent with the conceptual underpinnings of disparate impact theory, which assumes people have different interests and abilities related to ethnic, racial, and gender differences.

Professor Browne does recognize that, to some extent, these differences are taken into account in formulating the relevant labor market: the percentage of African American teachers in the labor market in *Hazelwood* was undoubtedly less than the percentage of African Americans in the general population. The comparison, therefore, filtered out — at least in gross terms — those whose abilities and interests were very different. But Browne doubts that abilities and interests are randomly distributed by race or sex even within the relevant labor market. Professor Browne also recognizes that the Central Assumption is only a tool for the plaintiff's prima facie case and that the defendant can, theoretically at least, rebut the inference of discrimination by showing factors other than the employer's discriminatory selection process that produce the nonrepresentative result. Nevertheless, he argues that the Central Assumption imposes an unfair burden on employers, a burden that is heightened by the tendency of some courts to require a strong rebuttal showing to defeat a systemic case. Reconsider this argument after you have read *EEOC v. Sears, Roebuck & Co.,* 839 F.2d 302 (7th Cir. 1988), reproduced at p. 133. The Supreme Court has, however, endorsed the Central Assumption, and the courts have refined it by looking increasingly to sophisticated statistical proofs.[†]

(a) *Probability Theory.* Probability is the basis of the science of statistics. As reflected in employment discrimination cases, probability theory starts with a comparison between the "observed" racial (or gender or age) distribution in the employer's work force and the "expected," that is, the racial distribution one would anticipate if race were not a factor in the selection of employees.

(b) *The Null Hypothesis.* To use probability theory to prove discrimination, a statistician would construct an assumption, called the null hypothesis, which would then be tested and either accepted or rejected. The null hypothesis, which states the opposite of what the plaintiff hopes to prove, is based on two assumptions: first, that there is no difference between the observed (the sample we are examining) and the expected, and, second, that any difference is the result of chance. The classic example is determining whether a coin is fair. A statistician would start with an assumption, the null hypothesis, that flipping a coin would result in no difference between the number of heads and the number of tails, and that, if there is a difference, it is due to chance.

In the employment context, this first means that the null hypothesis is that the employer does not discriminate, so that there will be no appreciable difference between the observed number of minorities employed and the expected number. Second, if there is a difference between the observed sample we are looking at (the employer's work force) and the expected, that difference is due to chance. The plaintiff obviously wants to rule out the null hypothesis — that is, to show that there is a difference and that difference is unlikely to be due to chance. The employer would prefer to confirm the null hypothesis — that is, to show that any difference is due to chance.

The statistician's job is to determine the probability that chance explains the difference. With a coin, the statistician could test the null hypothesis by counting the number of "heads" and "tails" when the coin is flipped. Suppose the statistician flips the coin 100 times, resulting in 49 heads and 51 tails. That outcome would be so close to what would be expected if the coin were fair (50 percent "heads," 50 percent "tails") that the statistician could accept the null hypothesis. Based on reason and logic, but not statistics, an observer would take the next step and conclude that, because it cannot be shown that the coin is unfair, it may be concluded that the coin is fair.

An example more attuned to the discrimination context is selection of marbles from a fishbowl. Suppose the statistician knows the racial composition of the relevant universe, that is, the percentages of white marbles and black marbles in the fishbowl — say, 80 percent white and 20 percent black. She can then make some probability judgments about the "fairness" of a drawing from the fishbowl a sample that yields 100 white marbles and no black ones.

Indeed, it should be apparent that *Teamsters* is simply a commonsense conclusion that the employer's draw of a sample (*i.e.*, its work force of line drivers) from the fishbowl (*i.e.*, the relevant labor market of city drivers) is sufficiently unlikely to require an explanation. Further, the *Hazelwood* use of standard deviation analysis is merely a way of quantifying the commonsense judgment for determining *how unlikely* it is that the draw of 100 white marbles could occur if being white were totally unconnected with the selection.

In short, a statistician can inform the court how probable it is that a certain pattern of selections would have occurred if color were not somehow influencing the selection decision.

(c) *Rejecting the Null Hypothesis.* Accepting or rejecting a null hypothesis, like making any decision, always entails a risk of being mistaken. Two possible errors may result from a decision based on sample information: a party who should not be found liable may be found liable (a "false inculpation"), and a party who should be found liable may be found not liable (a "false exculpation"). Statisticians have labeled false inculpation as "Type I error" and false exculpation as "Type II error." *See* Neil B. Cohen, *Confidence in Probability: Burdens of Persuasion in a World of Imperfect Knowledge*, 60 N.Y.U. L. Rev. 385, 410 (1985). In law, a jury that finds a defendant guilty of a crime when he is innocent commits what statisticians would call a Type I error, false inculpation. Juries in criminal cases are instructed to test the evidence under the "beyond a reasonable doubt" standard. This reflects the legal policy decision that it is much worse to convict an innocent person, a Type I false inculpation error, than it is to commit a Type II false exculpation error by letting a guilty person go free. In terms of probability theory, the criminal law sets the test of proof so that, if error is made, it is more likely to be a Type II error, freeing the guilty, than a Type I error, convicting the innocent. This is a deliberate policy decision that Type I errors are worse than Type II errors: many guilty people should go free, rather than one innocent person be convicted.

Statisticians address the probability of error in rejecting a null hypothesis based on a particular observation in terms of "significance level" or "p-value," terms that are used interchangeably. The threshold or critical significance level specifies the degree of risk of error the decisionmaker is willing to accept. The higher the p-value, therefore, the greater the risk of error. Once the level of significance is set, the null hypothesis will be rejected only if the calculated significance level (or p-value) is less than the threshold level.

By setting the level of confidence before a probability estimate is accepted, statisticians are directly deciding the risk of Type I error. The level is set by hundredths from zero to one. If it is very important to avoid Type I errors, that is, to avoid incorrectly finding an innocent employer guilty of discrimination, statisticians would set the level of statistical significance very high. Setting the level of significance at 0.05 means that a Type I error is made in only 5 percent of the cases, that is, 5 in 100 times.* As we will see, the 0.05 level is the one typically chosen for discrimination litigation.

In *Statistical Proof of Discrimination: Beyond "Damned Lies,"* Professor Browne argues that courts and commentators have erred by confusing a particular employer's work force statistics with the overall probabilities. The problem is a "base rate" one, and the standard illustration is testing for diseases. A test that is 99 percent accurate in positive results will still yield more false positive than true ones if the disease is very rare. The population of the United States is over 300 million, so that a disease so rare that only one person in a million suffers from it, would result in the number of afflicted persons in the United States being 300. But if the test is to be administered to the entire population of this country, its 99 percent accuracy rate would result in about 3,000,000 positives, of which all but 300 would be false. Professor Browne argues that a similar problem exists with the use of the 5 percent level in employment discrimination, but he fails to demonstrate why the legal system should conclude that base-rate discrimination is especially rare and he may not adequately take into account the fact that statistics merely prove a prima facie case—the defendant still has an opportunity to rebut.

Professor Jason Bent, in *Hidden Priors: Toward a Unifying Theory of Systemic Disparate Treatment Law,* 91 DENV. U. L. REV. 807 (2014), agrees with Professor Browne that the current use of statistics necessarily incorporates a view of discrimination as being relatively common. In other words, the theory supposes that the base rate is high, thus permitting the statistical proof to allow the factfinder to infer intentional discrimination by the particular defendant from a statistically significant underrepresentation. Looking to Bayesian analysis, Professor Bent argues that the base rate question should be analyzed as a "prior" and that expert testimony should be allowed to inform jury decisions on the level of such priors before analyzing the claim of discrimination based on statistics in the case at hand. *See also* Jason R. Bart, *P-Values, Priors and Procedure in Administration Law,* 63 BUFF. L. REV. 85 (2015).

In sum, probability theory suggests a basis for the use of statistical evidence in disparate treatment discrimination cases. Within probability theory, there are numerous statistical techniques available to analyze whether a null hypothesis should be accepted or rejected. When any one of these techniques is used to conclude that the null hypothesis (that race is not involved because any difference between the observed and the expected is the result of chance) should be rejected, the next step, based on reason and logic, should be to draw the inference that systemic disparate treatment discrimination has occurred. While the employer will have an opportunity to rebut that conclusion, the prima facie case will be established.

---

* The risk to innocent defendants is actually somewhat higher than 5 percent. Statistics only suggest a connection between race and employment decisions. They do not determine whether that connection is intentional discrimination. Statistical significance set at .05 means that in 5 percent of the cases, statistics will find a correlation between race and employment decisions when there is, in fact, no relationship (*e.g.,* the defendant is innocent). Even if there is a relationship, however, that relationship could result from some reason other than intentional discrimination. Thus, some defendants will be innocent even though statistics have accurately identified a relationship. In order to simplify the discussion of Type I and Type II errors, however, we will assume that whenever there is a relationship between race and employment decisions, this relationship results from intentional discrimination.

2. *Binomial Distribution and the Two- or Three-Standard Deviations Test.* The Supreme Court decided two cases in 1977 that used binomial distribution. The first, *Castaneda v. Partida*, 430 U.S. 482, 496 n.17 (1977), involved the exclusion of Mexican Americans from juries. The null hypothesis was that the juries are randomly drawn, without regard to whether a person picked was Mexican American. The probability, or expected outcome given random selection, was based on the percentage of Mexican Americans in the population, which was 79.1 percent. Among the 870 persons picked for juries over an 11-year period, some 688 would therefore be expected to be Mexican American. Over that period, only 339 of those selected were Mexican Americans. Figure 2.1 shows the expected outcome.

Each X plots the Mexican American representation in one jury panel. As the percentage of Mexican American representation in the panels departs from the expected outcome of 79.1 percent, fewer panels are represented. The "range" of the distribution is the spread of observed outcomes from highest to lowest. If samples are randomly drawn, some values will be higher and some lower than the expected value, so the range will include the expected value. In this example of an expected outcome, the range is between 66 and 92 percent, but in some other samples of jury panel selections, the range could be greater or smaller. For example, some juries may have no Mexican Americans, and others would be 100 percent Mexican American. In such a sample, the range would be from zero to 100 percent. To use the coin-flipping example, in some experimental runs the results will be bunched closer together than in other samples. In one sample, few, if any, outcomes of 100 flips will be more than 3 or 4 percent apart — say, 48 to 52 percent "heads" — while, in others, the variance might be much greater; some sample flips will be, say, 40 "heads" to 60 "tails."

Statisticians need some way of determining what kind of deviations from the expected value are likely, and how much deviation from the expected value can be viewed as due to chance. It is here that the concept of "standard deviation" is used. Standard deviation may be thought of as "normal" or "typical" or "average" deviation. Without regard to the exact variance along any baseline, 68 percent of all outcomes

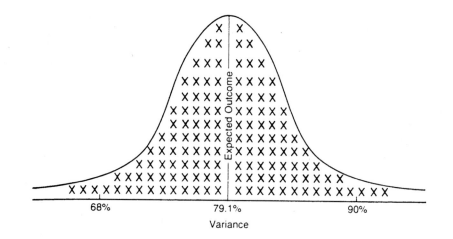

Figure 2.1

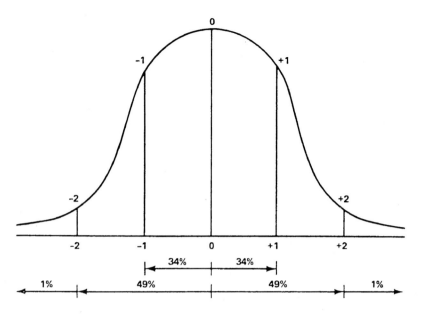

Figure 2.2

will fall between 1 and 2 "standard deviations" of the expected outcome. Only 2 per-cent of the outcomes will fall beyond 1 and 2 standard deviations from the expected outcome. Figure 2.2 illustrates this use of the standard deviation.

By characterizing data in terms of the number of standard deviations, it is possible to use standard deviation to decide whether to reject the null hypothesis. The test normally used is to reject the null hypothesis when an outcome falls more than 2 stan-dard deviations from the expected value. The reason for rejecting the null hypothesis in this situation is based on probability. The outcome is not likely to be the result of chance when a result is more than 2 standard deviations from the norm; in such a case, there are only 4 chances in 100 that the result is consistent with the null hypoth-esis, that the differences are the result of chance. As we have seen, there is a general statistical convention that the null hypothesis should be rejected when there is less than a 5 percent chance that the result could occur without there being a relationship between the two variables. Stated in terms of standard deviations, the 5 percent (or .05) level occurs when an outcome falls outside plus or minus 1.96 standard devia-tions. This .05 level of statistical significance as a basis for rejecting the null hypoth-esis is shown in Figure 2.3.

The outcome X casts doubt on the null hypothesis because that outcome could be consistent with the hypothesis less than 5 percent of the time if chance were the explanation. Rejecting the null hypothesis means that it is much more likely than not (though not certain) that the null hypothesis is incorrect. In the coin-flipping example, an outcome so far from the expected, as X is in Figure 2.3, is so unlikely if the coin is fair that it is a better judgment to reject the idea that the coin is fair.

So far, standard deviation has been described verbally and graphically, but it can also be performed mathematically. To calculate the probability of a Type I error in cases like *Castaneda*, statisticians start by calculating a "Z score." A Z score is simply

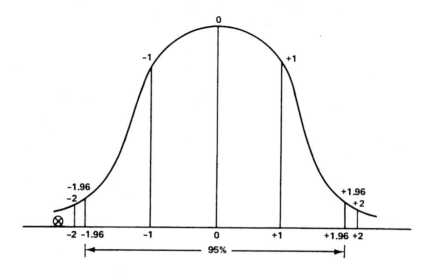

Figure 2.3

the number of standard deviations between the observed and the expected. In mathematical terms, the Z score is

$$Z = \frac{O - NP}{\sqrt{NP(1 - P)}}$$

where

Z = number of standard deviations
O = observed number of minority group members in the sample
N = size of the sample
P = minority percentage of the underlying population.
N × P, therefore, is the expected number of minorities in the sample.

In this formula, the top (or numerator) is the difference between the observed and the expected. The bottom (or denominator) is the formula for one standard deviation.

The facts of *Castaneda* can be plugged into the formula as follows:

$$Z = \frac{339 - (870 \times .79)}{\sqrt{(870 \times .79)(1 - .79)}} = \frac{339 - 687}{\sqrt{687 \times .21}} = \frac{-348}{\sqrt{144}} = \frac{-348}{12}$$

$$Z = -29$$

where

Z = unknown
O = 339 (observed number of Mexican American jurors)
N = 870 (total number of jurors selected)
P = .79 (the Mexican American population, the basis of the probability assumption).

With the outcome 29 standard deviations from the expected, the null hypothesis, that being a juror is unrelated to being a Mexican American, is rejected. The Court in *Castaneda* concluded:

Thus, in this case the standard deviation is approximately 29. As a general rule for such large samples, if the difference between the expected value and the observed number is greater than two or three standard deviations, then the hypothesis that the jury drawing was random would be suspect to a social scientist.

Id. The calculations for this formula are quite simple.

The result in *Castaneda* is shown graphically in Figure 2.4. The outcome X is –29 standard deviations from the expected result. The figure is a negative one because Mexican American representation on juries fell far short of the expected outcome. (Only if the representation of Mexican Americans exceeded the expected would a positive standard deviation figure be involved.) The chance that this outcome could occur with the null hypothesis being true, that is, that being Mexican American is unconnected with the chance of being selected for jury service, is infinitesimal.

Figure 2.4

The two- or three-standard deviation rule was accepted by the Supreme Court in *Hazelwood*. Surprisingly, the technique was not used by the Court in *Teamsters*, the case that set forth the probability assumptions underpinning the use of sophisticated statistical techniques such as binomial distribution. The almost total exclusion of minority group members from line-driver jobs, only 13 of 1,828, made statistical techniques unnecessary to show discrimination. But it is possible to work the analysis in terms of the facts given in the case for the defendant's employment in several cities where it operated. For employment at the defendant's Atlanta terminal, the number of standard deviations, the Z score, is calculated as follows:

$$Z = \frac{O - NP}{\sqrt{NP(1 - P)}} = \frac{0 - (57 \times .22)}{\sqrt{(57 \times .22)(1 - .22)}} = \frac{-12.54}{\sqrt{9.78}} = \frac{-12.54}{3.13}$$

$$Z = -4.01$$

where

   Z = unknown
   O = zero (no minority line drivers)
   N = 57 (number of Atlanta line drivers)
   P = .22 (using metropolitan minority population figures).

In Atlanta, the null hypothesis is rejected: the outcome of four standard deviations far exceeds the two or three standard deviations guideline. But note also that the probability was determined by the metropolitan area. Had only city population been used, the showing would have been even more dramatic. If the minority population of the city of Atlanta, which was 51.31 percent, is used to establish the probability, the observed outcome is 7.76 standard deviations from the expected.

The Supreme Court decision in *Hazelwood* added two refinements in the use of statistics that are of continuing significance. First, it distinguished between the use of general population statistics and the use of more limited labor pools reflecting the special qualifications needed for the job. In *Teamsters*, the general population was appropriate for comparison with the employer's work force because "the job skill there involved — the ability to drive a truck — is one that many persons possess or can fairly readily acquire." *Hazelwood*. In contrast, the jobs in *Hazelwood* were teaching positions. "When special qualifications are required to fill particular jobs, comparisons to the general population (rather than to the smaller group of individuals who possess the necessary qualifications) may have little probative value." Thus, the Court used the pool of qualified teachers as the basis for comparison with defendant's work force.

The second refinement in *Hazelwood* concerned the geographic area of concentration, the city of St. Louis. The plaintiff sought to use the entire metropolitan area. The Court remanded for a decision on what area was appropriate because the difference could determine the outcome. Assuming that post-Act hiring is the focus and further assuming that a pool of qualified teachers including those in the city of St. Louis is used as the basis for comparison, the expected percentage of minority group hires in 1972-1973 would be 15.4 percent. The Z score formula would yield a result of 5.6 standard deviations.

If the city of St. Louis is carved out of the geographic area, the qualified labor pool drops to 5.7 percent minority representation. With the new probability or expectancy of 5.7 percent, the result is a Z score of 1.5 standard deviations, which is less than the 1.96 cutoff showing statistical significance at the .05, or 1-chance-in-20, level. The 1.5 standard deviation figure means that there is a 14 percent chance that an outcome with this large a difference between the observed and the expected outcomes occurred randomly. The result is graphically shown in Figure 2.5, where X marks the observed outcome.

Statistical convention would have it that this showing is *not* sufficient to reject the null hypothesis. It could be accepted that race and teacher hiring were unrelated in staffing by the Hazelwood district in 1972-1973. However, the Court did not decide whether that statistical convention must be followed in Title VII litigation. The

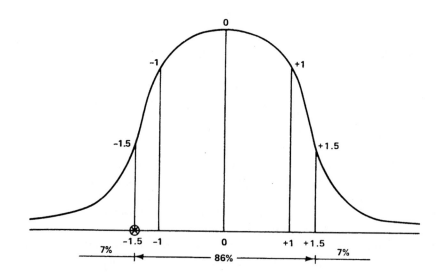

Figure 2.5

Hazelwood Court, after working through the above examples, noted: "These observations are not intended to suggest that precise calculations of statistical significance are necessary in employing statistical proof."

Subsequent cases have tended not to be much more definitive as to the level of statistical significance needed. The Supreme Court has recognized that, in relying on statistical evidence, courts are not bound by scientific tests of significance. In *Bazemore v. Friday*, 478 U.S. 385, 400 (1986), the Court said, "A plaintiff in a Title VII suit need not prove discrimination with scientific certainty; rather, his or her burden is to prove discrimination by a preponderance of evidence." The lower courts are in agreement that a showing of statistical significance at the 1.96 level will, at least in the normal case, suffice. *See Paige v. California*, 223 F. App'x 646 (9th Cir. 2007) (error for the district court to reject plaintiffs' statistical results showing a disparity of greater than 1.96 standard deviations although there were other deficiencies in the evidence).

But it is doubtful whether that level of significance is required. *Teamsters*, after all, did not rely on expert testimony of statistical significance; the "inexorable zero" may have made that unnecessary. And *Kadas v. MCI Systemhouse Corp.*, 255 F.3d 359, 362-63 (7th Cir. 2001), found "[t]he 5 percent test is arbitrary. . . . It is for the judge to say, on the basis of the evidence of a trained statistician, whether a particular significance level, in the context of a particular study in a particular case, is too low to make the study worth the consideration of judge or jury." *See also Chin v. Port Auth. of N.Y. & N.J.*, 685 F.3d 135, 153 (2d Cir. 2012) (a statistical analysis that concluded that underrepresentation of Asians in promotion decisions could have occurred by chance 13 percent of the time was not necessarily fatal to plaintiffs' case — "other evidence" could have been relied on by reasonable jurors "to find that an 87-percent likelihood that the disparity was not due to chance," including substantial evidence that the plaintiffs were more qualified than some white officers who were promoted).

Binomial distribution focuses on the relationship between two factors, the race or gender composition of the available labor pool versus that of the employer's work force. While powerful where applicable, this technique is limited because it cannot account for added variables sometimes involved in employment issues. For example, in *Hazelwood*, the Court used binomial distribution as a way of comparing the employer's work force with the pool of qualified teachers. While useful once the pool of those who were qualified is defined, binomial distribution cannot define what factors were considered in determining the qualifications relied on in hiring teachers.

3. *Multiple Regression.* Multiple regression is a technique used to study the influence of any number of factors, or variables. Its use in discrimination litigation was first approved by the Supreme Court in *Bazemore v. Friday*, a case involving race discrimination in salary. Multiple regression cannot show what qualifications are actually needed to do a job, but it can be useful in finding what factors an employer relied on in a particular employment setting and the weight given to each factor.

The core notion of multiple regression is an extension of the notion of matching pairs. Suppose two employees are so similarly situated in education, experience in the industry, seniority, job title, and work performed that they are a matched pair. It would be odd if these two employees do not receive the same pay. If they are of different races or genders and the pay difference is not otherwise explained, there would be a prima facie case of employment discrimination.

Multiple regression expands that notion so it is possible to compare the influence of many variables among a large group of employees. Once it is decided what variables are thought to bear on the employment situation, multiple regression makes it possible to hold these factors constant and then determine whether sex or race is also a statistically significant factor in setting salary.

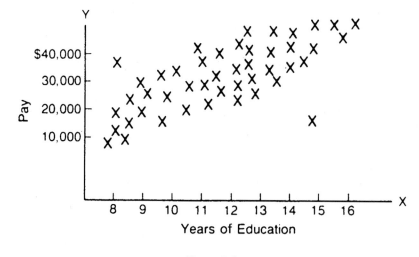

Figure 2.6

Multiple regression is beyond simple graphical or mathematical statement, but the following may help to develop the concept. Assume someone suggests that the relevant factor in determining salary for an employee is education: the more education, the higher the pay. Graphically, each person's pay and years of education would look like the scattergram in Figure 2.6, with each X representing a particular person plotted on the graph by years of education and salary.

Notice that there appears to be some relationship between salary and years of education, but no straight-line relationship exists. To say it another way, there is no automatic rule that causes salary to go up a set amount of dollars for each increase of a year in education for every employee. But statistically it is possible to draw a "regression line" that is the "best fit" line to describe all the individual cases. Figure 2.7 illustrates such a linear regression. The notion is to balance out all the employees above the line with those below the line. In Figure 2.7, employee 1 has higher pay for the same

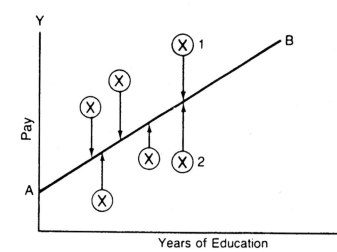

Figure 2.7

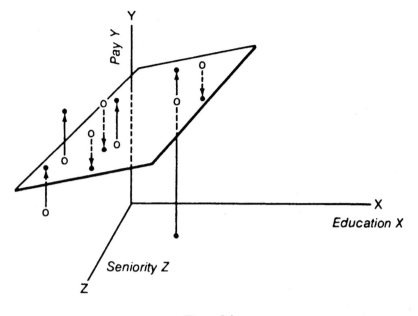

Figure 2.8

education as employee 2, but those differences balance out if each is "regressed" to line A-B, the regression line, sometimes called the line of best fit.

When another variable — say, seniority — is suggested as being relevant in determining salary, the graphic description requires three dimensions, as shown in Figure 2.8. Notice that, instead of a regression line, there is a three-dimensional plane that is the "best fit" description of the contribution of education and seniority to the determination of salary. Graphic demonstration stops at three dimensions, so it is not useful when more than two variables are to be taken into account in describing salary. Multiple regression can demonstrate how any number of independent variables affect a continuous variable like salary. It is "a method used to extract a systematic signal from the noise prescribed by the data." Franklin M. Fisher, *Multiple Regression in Legal Proceedings*, 80 COLUM. L. REV. 702, 706 (1980). Further, the result is quantifiable:

> The relationship between the dependent variable and the independent variable (race or sex) is then estimated by extracting the effects of the other major variables. When this has been done, one has the best available substitute for controlled experimentation. The results of multiple regression can be read as showing the effects of each variable on the dependent variable, holding the others constant. Moreover, those results allow one to make statements about the probability that the effect described has merely been observed as a result of chance fluctuation.

Multiple regression generates an equation that explains the relationship between the dependent variable (*e.g.*, salary) and the independent variables (*e.g.*, the factors used by the employer to determine salary). Note that the information used to generate the equation is drawn from the employer's own salary scheme. The resulting equation looks like this:

$$Y = a + b_1 x_1 + b_2 x_2 + b_3 x_3 + b_4 x_4 \ldots b_k x_k$$

In this equation, "Y" equals salary, "a" equals a constant dollar amount, "b_1" and "b_2" are dollar amounts, and "x_1" and "x_2" are factors relevant to the salary determination. For example, in an academic setting, "x_1" may equal number of years of seniority, while "x_2" equals number of years of education past undergraduate school, "x_3" equals number of articles written, and "x_4" equals number of committee chairs held. Each factor has a dollar value. Any individual faculty member's salary can be determined (approximately) by inserting that faculty member's characteristics into the equation. The factors and the dollar amounts associated with the factors are based on a study of the employer's salary system. If the factor "white" or "male" has a dollar value, we might suspect discrimination. An alternative approach is to generate two different equations — for example, one for women and another for men. Assuming statistical significance, if the factors have substantially different dollar values and/or the constant is different in the two different equations, we might again suspect discrimination.

One question that has emerged is whether a multiple regression analysis is probative of discrimination even though a variable that might influence salary is not included in the study. In *Bazemore*, the Court found that the absence of a variable does not necessarily destroy the probative value of a multiple regression. The multiple regression in that case used four variables that might influence salary — race, education, tenure, and job title. Though the study showed a statistically significant relationship between race and the dependent variable of salary, the lower courts rejected the study because it did not include all the possible variables that might have influenced salary. The unanimous Supreme Court rejected that view, holding that statistical evidence is to be evaluated as is all other evidence.

> While the omission of variables from a regression analysis may render the analysis less probative than it otherwise might be, it can hardly be said, absent some other infirmity, that an analysis which accounts for the major factors "must be considered unacceptable as evidence of discrimination." . . . Normally, failure to include variables will affect the analysis' probativeness, not its admissibility.
>
> Importantly, it is clear that a regression analysis that includes less than "all measurable variables" may serve to prove a plaintiff's case. A plaintiff in a Title VII suit need not prove discrimination with scientific certainty; rather, his or her burden is to prove discrimination by a preponderance of the evidence. . . . Whether, in fact, such a regression analysis does carry the plaintiffs' ultimate burden will depend in a given case on the factual context of each case in light of all the evidence presented by both the plaintiff and the defendant.

478 U.S. 400-01. The *Bazemore* Court did note that a multiple regression analysis could be so incomplete as to be inadmissible. Presumably, the question would be whether the analysis was so incomplete that no reasonable trier of fact could credit it. Suppose, in *Bazemore*, that the plaintiff's statistical analysis controlled only for race and education, omitting "tenure" and "job title." Should it nevertheless have been admitted into evidence? Professor Barnes has pointed out that the omission of a variable that does affect salary will make no difference unless the omitted variable is also correlated with race; only in that case would it tend to negate race as the explanation for the disparity shown. *See* David W. Barnes & John M. Conley, Statistical Evidence in Litigation, §8.16, and 1989 Supp. pp. 70-71.

Professor D. James Greiner, *Causal Inference in Civil Rights Litigation*, 122 Harv. L. Rev. 534 (2008), argues that multiple regression analysis should be rejected in favor of a "potential outcomes" approach, which asks the expert to decide what treatment the employees would have received if they were of the opposite sex or a different race and compares that with the treatment they actually received. It requires the expert to determine job-relevant characteristics for employees *before* the employer perceived their race or sex or were otherwise clearly independent of manipulation by the employer. *But see* Steven Willborn & Ramona Paetzold, *Statistics Is a Plural Word*, 122 HARV. L. REV. 48 (2009) (agreeing that potential outcomes is a useful technique but arguing that Professor Greiner overemphasizes both the deficiencies of multiple regression and the advantages of potential outcomes).

A final point concerns what statisticians call practical (as opposed to statistical) significance. It is possible that a statistical study will show a statistically significant relationship between gender and salary, but one at such a low level that it may not be cognizable. For example suppose the regression showed that, in a work force of thousands, women were underpaid relative to men by $5 a year. No matter how robust the statistical proof, it is questionable whether a finding of discrimination ought to follow because the difference is so small. *See Rudebusch v. Hughes*, 313 F.3d 506, 515 (9th Cir. 2002) (expressing "concern about inferring discrimination from a study in which the highest single pay disparity for ethnic minorities fell 2.0 standard deviations away from predicted salary — but produced a lowest statistically unexplainable difference of $87 between ethnic minorities and their Anglo counterparts"). In the disparate impact chapter, we address a similar question in discussing quantum of impact. See p. 200.

D. DEFENSES TO DISPARATE TREATMENT CASES

There are three approaches to defending a systemic disparate treatment case. The first is to challenge the factual basis on which the plaintiff's case is predicated. Where the plaintiff demonstrates a systemic practice-based case using statistics, the best defense might be statistical studies that counter the plaintiff's expert studies. The second line of defense is to challenge not the statistics the plaintiff uses but the inference of discriminatory intent the statistics raise. The third and final line of defense is to admit the discrimination but assert a recognized defense.

1. Rebutting the Inference of Discriminatory Intent

PERSONNEL ADMINISTRATOR v. FEENEY
442 U.S. 256 (1979)

[The Court was faced with a constitutional equal protection challenge to a Massachusetts law granting military veterans absolute preference for state jobs. Because at that time, 98 percent of the veterans were male, few women could realistically compete for jobs desired by veterans. The lower court found the consequences for women too inevitable to have been "unintended." The Supreme Court, per Justice Stewart, reversed the finding of unconstitutionality.]

The appellee's ultimate argument rests upon the presumption, common to the criminal and civil law, that a person intends the natural and foreseeable consequences of his voluntary actions. Her position was well stated in the concurring opinion in the District Court: "Conceding . . . that the goal here was to benefit the veteran, there is no reason to absolve the legislature from awareness that the means chosen to achieve this goal would freeze women out of all those state jobs actively sought by men. To be sure, the legislature did not wish to harm women. But the cutting-off of women's opportunities was an inevitable concomitant of the chosen scheme — as inevitable as the proposition that if tails is up, heads must be down. Where a law's consequences are that inevitable, can they meaningfully be described as unintended?"

This rhetorical question implies that a negative answer is obvious, but it is not. The decision to grant a preference to veterans was of course "intentional." So, necessarily, did an adverse impact upon nonveterans follow from that decision. And it cannot seriously be argued that the legislature of Massachusetts could have been unaware that most veterans are men. It would thus be disingenuous to say that the adverse consequences of this legislation for women were unintended, in the sense that they were not volitional or in the sense that they were not foreseeable.

"Discriminatory purpose," however, implies more than intent as volition or intent as awareness of consequences. It implies that the decisionmaker, in this case a state legislature, selected or reaffirmed a particular course of action at least in part "because of," not merely "in spite of," its adverse effects upon an identifiable group.[25] Yet, nothing in the record demonstrates that this preference for veterans was originally devised or subsequently re-enacted because it would accomplish the collateral goal of keeping women in a stereotypic and predefined place in the Massachusetts Civil Service.

To the contrary, the statutory history shows that the benefit of the preference was consistently offered to "any person" who was a veteran. That benefit has been extended to women under a very broad statutory definition of the term veteran. The preference formula itself, which is the focal point of this challenge, was first adopted — so it appears from this record — out of a perceived need to help a small group of older Civil War veterans. It has since been reaffirmed and extended only to cover new veterans. When the totality of legislative actions establishing and extending the Massachusetts veterans' preference are considered, the law remains what it purports to be: a preference for veterans of either sex over nonveterans of either sex, not for men over women.

NOTES

1. *Equal Protection vs. Title VII. Feeney* could not have been brought under Title VII because §712 explicitly excepts veterans' preference laws from attack under the statute. *Feeney* is consistent with *Washington v. Davis*, 426 U.S. 229 (1976), which had held that liability under the Equal Protection Clause depended on proving what would, in Title VII terms, be called disparate treatment. No disparate impact theory applies. But this does not mean that the effect or impact of an employer's actions is irrelevant to a disparate treatment case since that case also recognized that

[n]ecessarily, an invidious discriminatory purpose may often be inferred from the totality of the relevant facts, including the fact, if it is true, that the law bears more heavily

---

25. This is not to say that the inevitability or foreseeability of consequences of a neutral rule has no bearing upon the existence of discriminatory intent. Certainly, when the adverse consequences of a law upon an identifiable group are as inevitable as the gender-based consequences of [the veterans' preference] a strong inference that the adverse effects were desired can reasonably be drawn. But in this inquiry — made as it is under the Constitution — an inference is a working tool, not a synonym for proof. When, as here, the impact is essentially an unavoidable consequence of a legislative policy that has in itself always been deemed to be legitimate, and when, as here, the statutory history and all of the available evidence affirmatively demonstrate the opposite, the inference simply fails to ripen into proof.

on one race than another. It is also not infrequently true that the discriminatory impact . . . may for all practical purposes demonstrate unconstitutionality because in various circumstances the discrimination is very difficult to explain on nonracial grounds. . . . Disproportionate impact is not irrelevant, but it is not the sole touchstone of an invidious racial discrimination forbidden by the Constitution.

Id. at 242. In a concurring opinion in *Washington v. Davis,* Justice Stevens described a rationale for using impact data to show intent to discriminate: "Frequently the most probative evidence of intent will be objective evidence of what actually happened rather than evidence describing the subjective state of mind of the actor. For normally the actor is presumed to have intended the natural consequences of his deeds." *Id.* at 253. Thus, where disparate treatment is concerned, the statutory and constitutional approaches are similar, and underrepresentation is relevant to the extent it casts light on the motive underlying policies or practices.

2. *No Intent to Discriminate Shown?* The Court in *Feeney* rejected the natural and probable consequences test of "intent" for purposes of liability under the Equal Protection Clause, but it probably meant "motive," a clarification we saw in *Staub v. Proctor Hospital* in Chapter 1, p. 50. While consequences can be probative of the underlying motive, there must be a motive to discriminate on a prohibited ground for any disparate treatment claim. In this case, the Court was apparently convinced that, whatever the impact, gender discrimination was the last thing that motivated the legislature when it enacted the veterans' preference. *Cf.* footnote 24 in *Teamsters* on p. 103.

Can you imagine anything that might rebut the inference of discriminatory intent (without challenging the underlying statistics) in *Teamsters* or *Hazelwood*? In *Hazelwood*, for example, suppose the defendant claimed that residents of the school district were given preference as teachers so that it was Hazelwood's mostly white population that explained the scarcity of black teachers.

EEOC v. SEARS, ROEBUCK & CO.
839 F.2d 302 (7th Cir. 1988)

H. Wood, Jr., Circuit Judge.

[The EEOC challenged Sears's hiring, promotion, and compensation practices as systemic disparate treatment on the basis of gender, with the principal issue being the concentration of men in higher-paying sales jobs compensated by commissions and the concentration of women in lower-paying sales jobs paid by the hour. Sears won in the trial court. The Seventh Circuit first held that the burden of persuasion on the issue of intent to discriminate remains at all times on the plaintiff. Second, the court reviewed the trial court's findings on that issue, using a clearly erroneous standard of review.]

The EEOC presented, almost exclusively, statistical evidence in the form of regression analyses based on information from employment applications of rejected sales applicants and Sears' computerized payroll records from 1973 through 1980. The EEOC based other regression analyses on information from Applicant Interview Guides Sears had administered at various times from 1978 through 1980 at two Sears stores in its Southwestern Territory. The EEOC attempted to bolster this statistical evidence through nonstatistical evidence regarding the subjective nature of Sears' selection process and allegedly discriminatory aspects of Sears' testing practices.

Sears did not respond with like regression analyses based on employment application and payroll records. Instead, most of Sears' evidence was directed at undermining

7th
burden held
stays always
w/ p's

Stats and
subjective
testimony

two assumptions Sears claimed were faulty and fatal to the validity of the EEOC's statistical analysis — the assumptions of equal interests and qualifications of applicants for commission sales positions. . . .

The EEOC argues that Sears' "generalized interest evidence" is inadequate as a matter of law to refute the EEOC's statistical presentation. . . . The EEOC implies that Sears had the burden of responding with a more probative statistical analysis. The Supreme Court in *Teamsters* specifically stated, however, that "we do not . . . suggest that there are any particular limits on the type of evidence an employer may use." An employer may attempt to show that plaintiffs' proof is "either inaccurate or insignificant," or the [employer] may attempt to provide a "nondiscriminatory explanation for the apparently discriminatory result." Then-Justice, now Chief Justice Rehnquist, concurring in *Dothard v. Rawlinson* [reproduced at p. 195], stated that defendants in a discrimination case "may endeavor [in rebuttal] to impeach the reliability of the statistical evidence, they may offer rebutting evidence, or they may disparage in arguments or in briefs the probative weight which the Plaintiffs' evidence should be accorded." . . . [While an employer is entitled to rebut plaintiff's statistical analysis "with more 'refined, accurate and valid' statistical evidence,"] statistical evidence is only one method of rebutting a statistical case. We therefore reject the EEOC's contention that Sears' interest evidence, consisting of testimony of Sears' store witnesses, external labor force data, national survey data, and data from surveys of Sears' employees, is insufficient as a matter of law to undermine the EEOC's statistical evidence. . . .

The district judge found a plethora of problems in the statistical analyses that the EEOC had offered to support the claim that Sears discriminated against women in hiring into commission sales positions from 1973 to 1980. Before addressing the EEOC's specific challenges to the district court's criticisms of its statistical evidence, it is helpful to discuss three key findings made by the district court, which we believe are not clearly erroneous. Those findings are that during the period at issue in this case (1973-1980): (1) commission selling was significantly different from noncommission selling at Sears; (2) women were not as interested in commission selling as were men; and (3) women were not as qualified for commission selling as were men.

The finding that colors the district court's entire treatment of the EEOC's hiring as well as its promotion claims is that selling on commission at Sears is a very different job from "regular," or noncommission selling at Sears. We cannot say that finding is clearly erroneous. The court's description of commission and noncommission selling at Sears indicates that the two forms of selling differed in the type of merchandise sold, the risk involved, which was reflected in the manner of compensation, and the technical knowledge, expertise, and motivation involved. The district court describes the differences at length, thus we need only mention major differences. As the district court found, commission selling at Sears usually involved selling "big ticket" items, which are high-cost merchandise such as major appliances, furnaces, roofing, and sewing machines. Merchandise sold on a noncommission basis understandably was generally low-cost and included apparel, paint, and cosmetics. Commission selling involved some risk, especially before 1977. During that period commission salespersons generally received a commission ranging from 6% to 9% percent [sic] plus a "draw" each week. The draw usually did not exceed 70% of average or estimated earnings, but was subject to reduction if the employee's commission did not equal the amount of the draw. There was always a risk that the employee could lose some of the draw if the commissions did not equal the amount of the draw. After 1977, commission salespersons no longer faced deficits. In what the court noted was an effort "to reduce the financial risk of selling on commission in an effort to attract more women to commission sales," Sears paid commission salespersons a nominal salary plus a 3% commission. Noncommission salespersons were paid on a straight hourly rate, and full-time salespersons received 1% commission on all sales until January 1979 when the practice was discontinued. The district court found that commission selling often required salespersons to be available after the normal working hours of 8:00 A.M. to 5:00 P.M., sometimes required that they sell in people's homes, might require a license depending on the products sold, and required qualities usually not as necessary in regular selling, including a high degree of technical knowledge, expertise, and motivation.

different risks, pay, hours, expertise, etc.

The court's next two major findings, that there were different interests and qualifications among men and women for commission selling, were grounded in part on the court's recognition of differences between noncommission and commission selling at Sears. The court based these findings on the large amount of evidence presented by Sears on these issues. The court extensively discusses this evidence. Again, we cannot say that these findings are clearly erroneous.

Regarding the question of differing interests in general among men and women in commission selling, [the district] court found that "[t]he most credible and convincing evidence offered at trial regarding women's interest in commission sales at Sears was the detailed, uncontradicted testimony of numerous men and women who were Sears store managers, personnel managers and other officials, regarding their efforts to recruit women into commission sales." These witnesses testified to their only limited success in affirmative action efforts to persuade women to sell on commission, and testified that women were generally more interested in product lines like clothing, jewelry, and cosmetics that were usually sold on a noncommission basis, than they were in product lines involving commission selling like automotives, roofing, and furnaces. The contrary applied to men. Women were also less interested in outside sales which often required night calls on customers than were men, with the exception of selling custom draperies. Various reasons for women's lack of interest in commission selling included a fear or dislike of what they perceived as cut-throat competition, and increased pressure and risk associated with commission sales. Noncommission selling, on the other hand, was associated with more social contact and friendship, less pressure and less risk. This evidence was confirmed by a study of national surveys and polls from the mid-1930s through 1983 regarding the changing status of women in American society, from which a Sears expert made conclusions regarding women's interest in commission selling; morale surveys of Sears employees, which the court found "demonstrate[d] that noncommission saleswomen were generally happier with their present jobs at Sears, and were much less likely than their male counterparts to be interested in other positions, such as commission sales"; a job interest survey taken at Sears in 1976; a survey taken in 1982 of commission and noncommission salespeople at Sears regarding their attitudes, interests, and the personal beliefs and lifestyles of the employees, which the court concluded showed that noncommission salesmen were "far more interested" in commission sales than were noncommission saleswomen, and national labor force data.

The court recognized the EEOC's expert witness testimony regarding women's general interests in employment, which essentially was that there were no significant differences between women and men regarding interests and career aspirations. We cannot determine the district court clearly erred in finding the evidence not credible, persuasive or probative. These expert witnesses used small samples of women who had taken traditional jobs when opportunities arose. Larger samples would have been more persuasive. In addition as the court found, "[n]one of these witnesses had any specific knowledge of Sears." The court found Sears' evidence clearly more persuasive on the issue of different interest in commission selling between men and women. The court also found significant Sears' evidence that women became increasingly willing to accept commission sales positions between 1970 and 1980 due to, among other things, changes in commission sales positions from mostly full-time to largely part-time (more women preferred part-time), change in compensation to salary plus commission (which eliminated a lot of risk), increased availability of day care, and a group of successful saleswomen who served as role models. . . .

In short, we hold that the district court did not clearly err in finding that women were not as interested in commission sales positions as were men.

We similarly find that the district court did not clearly err in concluding that women applicants had different qualifications than did men applicants. The court noted that the EEOC's Commission Sales Report indicated that "on average, female applicants in the 'sales' pool were younger, less educated, less likely to have commission sales experience, and less likely than male applicants to have prior work experience with the products sold on commission at Sears." The EEOC does not challenge this finding.

All three of the court's findings discussed above — that commission selling is significantly different from noncommission selling, that women were not equally interested with men in commission selling at Sears, and that women applicants were not equally qualified with men for commission selling at Sears — form the bases for the court's criticisms of the EEOC's statistics regarding hiring at Sears. . . .

CUDAHY, Circuit Judge, concurring in part and dissenting in part. . . .

Perhaps the most questionable aspect of the majority opinion is its acceptance of women's alleged low interest and qualifications for commission selling as a complete explanation for the huge statistical disparities favoring men. The adoption by the district court and by the majority of Sears' analysis of these arguments strikes me as extremely uncritical. Sears has indeed presented varied evidence that these gender-based differences exist, both in our society as a whole and in its particular labor pool. But it remains a virtually insuperable task to overcome the weight of the statistical evidence marshalled by the EEOC or the skepticism that courts ought to show toward defenses to Title VII actions that rely on unquantifiable traits ascribed to protected groups.

[T]he majority's more benign view tends to minimize the significance of Sears' contentions that women lack the interest and qualifications to sell on commission. Women, as described by Sears, the district court and the majority, exhibit the very same stereotypical qualities for which they have been assigned low-status positions throughout history. . . .

These conclusions, it seems to me, are of a piece with the proposition that women are by nature happier cooking, doing the laundry and chauffeuring the children to softball games than arguing appeals or selling stocks. The stereotype of women as less greedy and daring than men is one that the sex discrimination laws were intended to address. It is disturbing that this sort of thinking is accepted so uncritically by the district court and by the majority. Perhaps they have forgotten that women have been hugely successful in such fields as residential real estate, and door-to-door and other direct outside merchandising. There are abundant indications that women lack neither the desire to compete strenuously for financial gain nor the capacity to take risks.

Sears, the district court and the majority hang much of their refutation of the EEOC's hiring and promotion claims on the putative difference between men's and women's interest in undertaking commission sales. Huge statistical disparities in participation in various commission selling jobs are ascribed to differences in interest. Yet there is scarcely any recognition of the employer's role in shaping the interests of applicants. Even the majority is willing to concede that lack of opportunity may drive lack of interest, but dismisses the matter as a "chicken-egg" problem. . . .

NOTES

1. *A Prima Facie Case?* The record in *Sears* revealed that, across the entire company and over a period of many years, women constituted 61 percent of the *applicants* for full-time sales jobs at Sears, but only 27 percent of the newly hired commission salespeople. Women made up 75 percent of the non-commission sales force. Median hourly wages were about twice as high for commission as non-commission salespeople. *See* Vicki Schultz, *Telling Stories About Women and Work: Judicial Interpretation of Sex Segregation in the Workplace in Title VII Cases Raising the Lack of Interest Argument*, 103 Harv. L. Rev. 1749, 1752 nn.5-6 (1990). *See also* Vicki Schultz & Stephen Petterson, *Race, Gender, and Choice: An Empirical Study of the Lack of Interest Defense in Title VII Cases Challenging Job Segregation*, 59 U. Chi. L. Rev. 1073 (1992). Using the applicant pool meant that all in the pool had expressed an interest in the jobs and likely thought they met the minimal job qualifications. Would these figures by themselves, without the use of any sophisticated statistical studies, show a gross enough disparity to establish a prima facie case? In other words, is this a *Teamsters* case?

The EEOC, however, failed to bring those cold statistics to life with anecdotal evidence of discrimination against individual women applicants. Why? The government in both *Teamsters* and *Hazelwood* deployed evidence of individual instances of discrimination, and plaintiffs have learned from the EEOC's debacle in *Sears* and have bulwarked statistical evidence with other proof. Nevertheless, it remains possible that a prima facie case could be established solely on the basis of statistical evidence. *See Kadas v. MCI Systemhouse*, 255 F.3d 359, 363 (7th Cir. 2001).

2. *Defense or Rebuttal?* The EEOC factored into its regression analyses the fact that women as a group had less interest in commission sales jobs than did men as a group. The studies still found a statistically significant relationship between gender and commission sales jobs. In other words, the parties were not disputing that women were less interested, but only how much less interested they were.

Further, Sears failed to introduce its own studies to contradict the EEOC's, surely a remarkable strategy if such studies would have undercut the inference of discrimination. Does Sears's failure to do so mean that it conceded the prima facie showing of intent to discriminate? In any event, Sears escaped liability by offering a nondiscriminatory explanation for the gender correlation that the EEOC apparently had established. It offered proof that women had different interests than men, that commission selling was different from non-commission selling, and that women were not as qualified for nor as interested in commission sales jobs as were men.

Having offered a nondiscriminatory explanation for the apparently damning data, Sears won because the EEOC failed to disprove that explanation. But should Sears have been able to respond to a statistically based prima facie case without statistically demonstrating how the nondiscriminatory explanation dispelled the disparity?

3. *Feminist Theory in Litigation Context.* One of the more controversial aspects of the case was Sears's success in using feminist theory to defend itself from liability. The

[handwritten margin notes: does using non-stats to rebut in some way concede the PF establishment of stat based discrimination? P failed at step 3 of McDonnell Douglas]

case involved two different themes in feminist thought, with Sears splitting the seam between the two:

(a) *Difference Theory.* Sears relied on one school of feminist thinking that stresses the differences between men and women. The divergent life experiences of men and women lead them to develop different perspectives and attitudes. Carol Gilligan, IN A DIFFERENT VOICE (1982), is the most prominent spokesperson for this view. Sears called Dr. Rosalind Rosenberg, a feminist historian at Barnard College, to make the point. In an offer of proof to the court, she stressed that women internalized the "feminine" values reinforced by society, through its customs, its culture, and its laws. They "tend to be more relationship centered and men tend to be more work centered," and "are seen by themselves and society as less competitive than men and more concerned with protecting personal relationships." Similarly, "[m]en's more extensive experience in competitive sports prepares them for the competitiveness, aggressiveness, teamwork, and leadership required for many jobs." Should this testimony rebut the inference of intent to discriminate in a systemic disparate treatment case? Would this evidence alone be sufficient to explain away the statistical evidence presented by the EEOC? Or would there have to be some quantification of the male/female differences?

Fast-forward many years and a related issue arose again with the remarks of the then-president of Harvard, Lawrence Summers, regarding the relative paucity of women in the academic sciences. Although most of the resultant outcry focused on his suggesting that there might be a biological basis for the underrepresentation of women, *see* Owen D. Jones, *The Causation Equation: Summers on Science*, 11 CARDOZO WOMEN'S L.J. 577 (2005), Dr. Summers also referred to cultural differences that Dr. Rosenberg had identified, and which many feminists have also noted. *See generally* Ellen M. Bublick, *Summers' Personal as Political: Reasoning Without Effort from Stereotypes*, 11 CARDOZO WOMEN'S L.J. 529 (2005).

Does Sears's argument amount to little more than blaming the victim? But if women are the victims, who is the victimizer? If society has socialized women in certain ways, why is that Sears's fault? Does Title VII impose an affirmative duty on employers to resocialize women or to alter job requirements to meet women's needs?

(b) *Equality Theory.* The EEOC countered with its own historian, Dr. Alice Kessler-Harris, who represents the equality vision of feminism, *i.e.*, that for purposes of employment women and men are basically alike. In her written testimony to the court, she responded to Dr. Rosenberg:

> A more accurate interpretation of the history of women's work in the U.S. would take the following form. The structure of the labor force is the product of a complex interaction between labor force needs and a socialization process that reinforces desirable roles. Women's "interests" as well as their expectations are thus a consequence of life experiences that are reinforced or discouraged by the larger society. In an industrial society, a major part of the cycle of reinforcement is played by employers whose hiring policies significantly influence women's self-perception, their assessment of reasonable aspirations, and their announced goals. What appear to be women's choices, and what are characterized as women's "interests" are, in fact, heavily influenced by the opportunities for work made available to them. In the past, opportunities offered to women have been conditioned by society's perceptions of women and assumptions about them. Thus, women have been hired into limited numbers of jobs, and discriminated against in the work force generally. The resulting profile of "women's work" has been then perceived to be what the women "chose."

See also Schultz, *supra* Note 1, at 1851. *Cf.* Scott A. Moss, *Women Choosing Diverse Workplaces: A Rational Preference with Disturbing Implications for Both Occupational Segregation and Economic Analysis of Law*, 27 Harv. Women's L.J. 1, 5 (2004) (gender segregated workplaces beget more segregation, without the need for employer discrimination because "women rationally use the level of diversity as a proxy for discrimination, which is more difficult to observe").

4. *Failure to Redress as Intentional Discrimination.* Taking Dr. Rosenberg's approach, what aspects of work culture would prove that Sears intended to keep women out of commission-paying sales jobs? Would evidence that competitive sales contests were used to motivate the workers be enough for a finding that Sears intended to discriminate on the basis of gender? Professor Ann McGinley, in Masculinity at Work 158-71 (2016), argues that hypercompetitive workplaces are "gendered male," and that such a work culture can be intentional discrimination. Do you agree?

Chapter 3 deals with disparate impact discrimination, which is a way to attack an employer's practices that have an adverse effect on women or minority men and that are not job related and necessary for business. Intent to discriminate is not an element. Should the EEOC have used the disparate impact theory to attack these practices that had the effect of making the jobs much less attractive to women than to men? Disparate impact theory requires the employer to take account of differences among workers to the extent that its practices weigh more heavily on one group or another. Would Dr. Rosenberg's testimony have helped the EEOC in a disparate impact case? Is there a downside to this approach? *See* Naomi Schoenbaum, *The Family and the Market at Wal-Mart*, 23 DePaul L. Rev. 769 (2013) (arguing that disparate impact suits may tend to reinforce stereotypes of women as less committed to the job market than men).

Handwritten margin note: can be. Women who are competitive or assertive are seen or bitchy or arrogant or undesirably non-feminine.

NOTE ON NATURE VERSUS NURTURE

The question whether differences among the races and between the sexes is inherent or genetic is always explosive, in part because claimed differences have all too frequently been used to justify denying full equality. The concurring opinion of Justice Bradley in the 1873 decision in *Bradwell v. Illinois*, 83 U.S. (16 Wall.) 130, 141, defended the exclusion of women from the practice of law, because the "paramount destiny and mission of women are to fulfill the noble and benign offices of wife and mother. This is the law of the creator." Add to this the long, ugly history of eugenics, typified by *Buck v. Bell*, 274 U.S. 200, 202 (1927), in which Justice Oliver Wendell Holmes made the stunning statement justifying sterilizations on the ground that "[t]hree generations of imbeciles are enough." More recently, the former president of Harvard, Lawrence Summers, began his fall from power by suggesting that the shortfall of women in the sciences might be based on biology. *See* Lawrence H. Summers, President, Harvard University, Remarks at NBER Conference on Diversifying the Science & Engineering Workforce (Jan. 14, 2005).

Originating around the turn of the twentieth century, efforts to differentiate the races were characterized by attempts to demonstrate the racial inferiority of nonwhite groups. *See generally* Stephen Jay Gould, The Mismeasure of Man (1981). Such efforts were cast into disrepute by a variety of scientific developments capped by charges of fraud leveled at Sir Cyril Burt, who had published a study of twins separated early in life purporting to show that 80 percent of IQ is inherited. In the

1970s, doubts about the validity of the study led the British Psychological Society to find that Burt had been guilty of fraud. In any event, others have also pressed genetic explanations for differences between scores of blacks as a group and whites as a group on IQ and other tests. Arthur Jensen, in *How Much Can We Boost IQ and Scholastic Achievement?*, 39 HARV. EDUC. REV. 1, 82 (1969); William Shockley, in *Dysgenics, Geneticity and Raceology: A Challenge to the Intellectual Responsibility of Educators*, 72 PHI DELTA KAPPAN 297 (1972).

The debate over genetic racial differences in intelligence broke out anew with the publication in 1994 of THE BELL CURVE: INTELLIGENCE AND CLASS STRUCTURE IN AMERICAN LIFE by Richard Herrnstein and Charles Murray. This book's central thesis is that social ills can largely be traced to low intelligence and that intelligence is largely inherited. Because blacks consistently score lower than whites on standard intelligence tests and other criteria, the book also argues that blacks as a race are significantly less intelligent than whites as a race. Needless to say, THE BELL CURVE prompted an enormous amount of criticism of its methods and conclusions. *E.g.*, STEPHEN J. GOULD, THE MISMEASURE OF MAN 367 (rev. ed. 1996). While the genetic link of "intelligence" has been less studied recently, the stunning advances in DNA research resulting in the mapping of the human genome have led to an increasing scientific focus on racial differences for medical research and treatments. *See generally* Erik Lillquist & Charles A. Sullivan, *The Law and Genetics of Racial Profiling in Medicine*, 39 HARV. C.R.-C.L. L. REV. 391 (2004).

There is more scientific basis for sex-linked differences beyond those obviously related to reproduction, but considerably less consensus about their significance. *See generally* Deborah Weiss, *The Annoyingly Indeterminate Effects of Sex Differences*, 19 TEX. J. WOMEN & L. 99 (2010); CYNTHIA FUCHS EPSTEIN, DECEPTIVE DISTINCTIONS: SEX, GENDER, AND THE SOCIAL ORDER (1988). Dr. Summers's controversial remarks suggested a biological cause for the lower representation of women in elite science positions because of what he described as the greater variability of male intelligence compared to females. That is, the male curve has longer tails on both ends of the spectrum. Males therefore have more geniuses but also more low-scoring individuals. Lawrence H. Summers, President, Harvard University, Remarks at NBER Conference on Diversifying the Science & Engineering Workforce (Jan. 14, 2005). In the wake of Dr. Summers's questioning whether the paucity of women in the sciences was genetic, the whole issue again reached national prominence. *See also* Julie A. Seaman, *Form and (Dys)Function in Sexual Harassment Law: Biology, Culture, and the Spandrels of Title VII*, 37 ARIZ. ST. L.J. 321 (2005).

While many feminists and others resist biological explanations for race or sex differences, some advocates of gay rights seemed to welcome them, perhaps because "immutability" would strengthen the case for treating sexual orientation as a suspect or quasi-suspect class. *See generally* Jessica Clarke, *Against Immutability*, 125 YALE L.J. 2, 4-7 (2015); Edward Stein, *Mutability and Innateness Arguments About Lesbian, Gay, and Bisexual Rights*, 89 CHI.-KENT L. REV. 597 (2014); Janet E. Halley, *Sexual Orientation and the Politics of Biology: A Critique of the Argument from Immutability*, 46 STAN. L. REV. 503 (1994).

PROBLEM 2.1

Reread Problem 1.1, p. 92. Can Jane Armstrong recover in a systemic disparate treatment case?

2. *Bona Fide Occupational Qualifications*

Section 703(e) of Title VII provides:

> Notwithstanding any other provision of this title . . . it shall not be an unlawful employment practice for an employer to hire and employ employees . . . on the basis of religion, sex, or national origin in those certain instances where religion, sex, or national origin is a bona fide occupational qualification reasonably necessary to the normal operation of that particular business or enterprise.

Although the bona fide occupational qualification (BFOQ) defense does not reach race discrimination, it constitutes a potentially large loophole in Title VII's general prohibition of employment discrimination on the other three grounds. The Age Discrimination in Employment Act also provides a BFOQ defense in language identical to Title VII. 29 U.S.C.S. §623(f)(1). As we will see, however, BFOQ has become mostly a sideshow in the broader antidiscrimination project.

The Court's first meaningful treatment of the defense was in *Dothard v. Rawlinson*, 433 U.S. 321 (1977). Although the Court's language was restrictive, indicating that the BFOQ is "an extremely narrow exception to the general prohibition of discrimination on the basis of sex," *id.* at 334, it nevertheless upheld a rule requiring prison guards in "contact" positions to be of the same gender as the inmates they guarded. The majority stressed that Alabama's penitentiaries had been held unconstitutional because of their dangerous and inhumane conditions. Since there was no attempt to segregate inmates according to dangerousness, the 20 percent of male prisoners who were sex offenders were scattered throughout the dormitories. "In this environment of violence and disorganization, it would be an over-simplification to characterize [the rule against women] as an exercise in Romantic paternalism." *Id.* at 335. While Title VII normally allows individual women to decide for themselves whether jobs are too dangerous, in the Alabama prisons it was likely that women could not perform the essence of the correctional counselor's job — to maintain security because the "employee's very womanhood" would lead to assaults and thus undermine her ability to do the job. *Id.* at 336. The dissent of Justice Marshall protested that this analysis justified discrimination because of the barbaric state of the prisons. Further, the notion that "the employee's very womanhood" makes assaults more likely "regrettably perpetuates one of the most insidious of the old myths about women — that women, wittingly or not, are seductive sexual objects." He stressed that the decision effectively punished women by making them "pay the price in lost job opportunities for the threat of depraved conduct by prison inmates." *Id.* at 345.

The Supreme Court's next encounter with the BFOQ defense was in a suit under the Age Discrimination in Employment Act, which permits discrimination where age is "a bona fide occupational qualification." In *Western Air Lines v. Criswell*, 472 U.S. 400 (1985), the Court adopted a uniform analysis applicable to both statutes. At issue was whether the airline's age-60 rule was a BFOQ for flight engineers, the third "pilot" who monitored side-facing instrument panels in larger commercial aircraft of that era. An FAA regulation banned people over age 60 from the other two pilot jobs — captain and first officer — but did not set any standard for flight engineers.

The defendant's evidence focused on the possibility that flight engineers would suffer a heart attack, the risks of which generally increased with age. The plaintiff's evidence focused on the fact that physiological deterioration was individualized and could be discovered through physical examinations that the FAA required for all flight engineers. Other airlines allowed flight engineers over age 60 to continue to fly without any apparent reduced safety records.

[handwritten margin note: Dothard → Title VII]

The Supreme Court approved a jury instruction that allowed the airline to establish a BFOQ by showing both that (1) "it was highly impractical for Western to deal with each second officer over age 60 on an individualized basis to determine his particular ability to perform his job safely"; and that (2) "some second officers over age 60 possess traits of a physiological, psychological or other nature which preclude safe and efficient job performance that cannot be ascertained by means other than knowing their age." *Id.* at 416. An alternative test would also find a BFOQ if "all or substantially all" persons in the disfavored group "would be unable to perform safely and efficiently the duties of the job involved." *Id.* at 414.

Colleges and universities cannot now retire tenured faculty at a given age unless they can establish a BFOQ. Do you think that a college with a mandatory retirement age could prevail in an ADEA suit? At what age?

INTERNATIONAL UNION, UAW v. JOHNSON CONTROLS, INC.
499 U.S. 187 (1991)

Justice BLACKMUN delivered the opinion of the Court. . . .

I

Respondent Johnson Controls, Inc., manufactures batteries. In the manufacturing process, the element lead is a primary ingredient. Occupational exposure to lead entails health risks, including the risk of harm to any fetus carried by a female employee.

[Johnson Controls originally did not employ any woman in a battery-manufacturing job; later it discouraged them from taking jobs with lead exposure but left the decision to the employees. In 1982, however,] Johnson Controls shifted from a policy of warning to a policy of exclusion. Between 1979 and 1983, eight employees became pregnant while maintaining blood lead levels in excess of 30 micrograms per deciliter. This appeared to be the critical level noted by the Occupational Safety and Health Administration (OSHA) for a worker who was planning to have a family. See 29 C.F.R. §1910.1025 (1989). The company responded by announcing a broad exclusion of women from jobs that exposed them to lead:

> [I]t is [Johnson Controls'] policy that women who are pregnant or who are capable of bearing children will not be placed into jobs involving lead exposure or which could expose them to lead through the exercise of job bidding, bumping, transfer or promotion rights.

The policy defined "women . . . capable of bearing children" as "all women except those whose inability to bear children is medically documented." It further stated that an unacceptable work station was one where, "over the past year," an employee had recorded a blood lead level of more than 30 micrograms per deciliter or the work site had yielded an air sample containing a lead level in excess of 30 micrograms per cubic meter.

II

[Plaintiffs filed a Title VII class action challenging the fetal-protection policy.] Among the individual plaintiffs were petitioners Mary Craig, who had chosen to be sterilized in order to avoid losing her job; Elsie Nason, a 50-year-old divorcee, who had suffered a loss in compensation when she was transferred out of a job where she was exposed to lead; and Donald Penney, who had been denied a request for a leave of absence for the purpose of lowering his lead level because he intended to become a father. . . .

[The district court granted summary judgment for the defendant. The Seventh Circuit, en banc, affirmed by a seven-to-four vote. The majority relied on the business necessity defense, while all the dissenters thought that only the BFOQ defense applied when a systemic policy of disparate treatment discrimination was proven. Two dissenters thought that the defendant would not be able to prove the BFOQ defense because concern for the health of the unborn was irrelevant to Johnson Controls' business.]

lower court) Reverses

III

The bias in Johnson Controls' policy is obvious. Fertile men, but not fertile women, are given a choice as to whether they wish to risk their reproductive health for a particular job. Section 703(a) prohibits sex-based classifications in terms and conditions of employment, in hiring and discharging decisions, and in other employment decisions that adversely affect an employee's status. Respondent's fetal-protection policy explicitly discriminates against women on the basis of their sex. The policy excludes women with childbearing capacity from lead-exposed jobs and so creates a facial classification based on gender. Respondent assumes as much in its brief before this Court.

overt policy of sex discrimination

Nevertheless, the Court of Appeals assumed, as did the two appellate courts who already had confronted the issue, that sex-specific fetal-protection policies do not involve facial discrimination. These courts analyzed the policies as though they were facially neutral, and had only a discriminatory effect upon the employment opportunities of women. Consequently, the courts looked to see if each employer in question had established that its policy was justified as a business necessity. The business necessity standard is more lenient for the employer than the statutory BFOQ defense. The Court of Appeals . . . assumed that because the asserted reason for the sex-based exclusion (protecting women's unconceived offspring) was ostensibly benign, the policy was not sex-based discrimination. That assumption, however, was incorrect.

First, Johnson Controls' policy classifies on the basis of gender and childbearing capacity, rather than fertility alone. Respondent does not seek to protect the unconceived children of all its employees. Despite evidence in the record about the debilitating effect of lead exposure on the male reproductive system, Johnson Controls is concerned only with the harms that may befall the unborn offspring of its female employees. . . . This Court faced a conceptually similar situation in *Phillips v. Martin Marietta Corp.*, 400 U.S. 542 (1971), and found sex discrimination because the policy established "one hiring policy for women and another for men — each having pre-school-age children." Johnson Controls' policy is facially discriminatory because it requires only a female employee to produce proof that she is not capable of reproducing.

→ doesnt apply to both sexes

Our conclusion is bolstered by the Pregnancy Discrimination Act of 1978 (PDA) in which Congress explicitly provided that, for purposes of Title VII, discrimination "on the basis of sex" includes discrimination "because of or on the basis of pregnancy, childbirth, or related medical conditions." "The Pregnancy Discrimination Act has now made clear that, for all Title VII purposes, discrimination based on a woman's pregnancy is, on its face, discrimination because of her sex." *Newport News Shipbuilding &*

Dry Dock Co. v. EEOC, 462 U.S. 669, 684 (1983). In its use of the words "capable of bearing children" in the 1982 policy statement as the criterion for exclusion, Johnson Controls explicitly classifies on the basis of potential for pregnancy. Under the PDA, such a classification must be regarded, for Title VII purposes, in the same light as explicit sex discrimination. Respondent has chosen to treat all its female employees as potentially pregnant; that choice evinces discrimination on the basis of sex.

We concluded above that Johnson Controls' policy is not neutral because it does not apply to the reproductive capacity of the company's male employees in the same way as it applies to that of the females. Moreover, the absence of a malevolent motive does not convert a facially discriminatory policy into a neutral policy with a discriminatory effect. Whether an employment practice involves disparate treatment through explicit facial discrimination does not depend on why the employer discriminates but rather on the explicit terms of the discrimination. . . . The beneficence of an employer's purpose does not undermine the conclusion that an explicit gender-based policy is sex discrimination under §703(a) and thus may be defended only as a BFOQ. . . .

In sum, Johnson Controls' policy "does not pass the simple test of whether the evidence shows 'treatment of a person in a manner which but for that person's sex would be different.'" *Los Angeles Dept. of Water & Power v. Manhart*. We hold that Johnson Controls' fetal-protection policy is sex discrimination forbidden under Title VII unless respondent can establish that sex is a "bona fide occupational qualification."

IV . . .

The BFOQ defense is written narrowly, and this Court has read it narrowly. *See, e.g., Dothard v. Rawlinson; Trans World Airlines, Inc. v. Thurston*, 469 U.S. 111 (1985). We have read the BFOQ language of §4(f) of the Age Discrimination in Employment Act of 1967 (ADEA), which tracks the BFOQ provision in Title VII, just as narrowly. *See Western Air Lines, Inc. v. Criswell*. Our emphasis on the restrictive scope of the BFOQ defense is grounded on both the language and the legislative history of §703.

The wording of the BFOQ defense contains several terms of restriction that indicate that the exception reaches only special situations. The statute thus limits the situations in which discrimination is permissible to "certain instances" where sex discrimination is "reasonably necessary" to the "normal operation" of the "particular" business. Each one of these terms — certain, normal, particular — prevents the use of general subjective standards and favors an objective, verifiable requirement. But the most telling term is "occupational"; this indicates that these objective, verifiable requirements must concern job-related skills and aptitudes.

The concurrence defines "occupational" as meaning related to a job. According to the concurrence, any discriminatory requirement imposed by an employer is "job-related" simply because the employer has chosen to make the requirement a condition of employment. In effect, the concurrence argues that sterility may be an occupational qualification for women because Johnson Controls has chosen to require it. This reading of "occupational" renders the word mere surplusage. "Qualification" by itself would encompass an employer's idiosyncratic requirements. By modifying "qualification" with "occupational," Congress narrowed the term to qualifications that affect an employee's ability to do the job.

Johnson Controls argues that its fetal-protection policy falls within the so-called safety exception to the BFOQ. Our cases have stressed that discrimination on the basis of sex because of safety concerns is allowed only in narrow circumstances. In *Dothard v. Rawlinson*, this Court indicated that danger to a woman herself does not justify discrimination. We there allowed the employer to hire only male guards in contact areas of maximum-security male penitentiaries only because more was at stake than the "individual woman's decision to weigh and accept the risks of employment." We found sex to be a BFOQ inasmuch as the employment of a female guard would create real risks of safety to others if violence broke out because the guard was a woman. Sex discrimination was tolerated because sex was related to the guard's ability to do the job — maintaining prison security. We also required in *Dothard* a high correlation between sex and ability to perform job functions and refused to allow employers to use sex as a proxy for strength although it might be a fairly accurate one.

Similarly, some courts have approved airlines' layoffs of pregnant flight attendants at different points during the first five months of pregnancy on the ground that the employer's policy was necessary to ensure the safety of passengers. *See*[, *e.g.*,] *Harriss v. Pan American World Airways, Inc.*, 649 F.2d 670 (CA9 1980). In these cases, the courts pointedly indicated that fetal, as opposed to passenger, safety was best left to the mother.

We considered safety to third parties in *Western Airlines, Inc. v. Criswell* in the context of the ADEA. We focused upon "the nature of the flight engineer's tasks," and the "actual capabilities of persons over age 60" in relation to those tasks. Our safety concerns were not independent of the individual's ability to perform the assigned tasks, but rather involved the possibility that, because of age-connected debility, a flight engineer might not properly assist the pilot, and might thereby cause a safety emergency. Furthermore, although we considered the safety of third parties in *Dothard* and *Criswell*, those third parties were indispensable to the particular business at issue. In *Dothard*, the third parties were the inmates; in *Criswell*, the third parties were the passengers on the plane. We stressed that in order to qualify as a BFOQ, a job qualification must relate to the "essence," or to the "central mission of the employer's business."

The concurrence ignores the "essence of the business" test and so concludes that "the safety to fetuses in carrying out the duties of battery manufacturing is as much a legitimate concern as is safety to third parties in guarding prisons (*Dothard*) or flying airplanes (*Criswell*)." By limiting its discussion to cost and safety concerns and rejecting the "essence of the business" test that our case law has established, the concurrence seeks to expand what is now the narrow BFOQ defense. Third-party safety considerations properly entered into the BFOQ analysis in *Dothard* and *Criswell* because they went to the core of the employee's job performance. Moreover, that performance involved the central purpose of the enterprise. . . . The concurrence attempts to transform this case into one of customer safety. The unconceived fetuses of Johnson Controls' female employees, however, are neither customers nor third parties whose safety is essential to the business of battery manufacturing. No one can disregard the possibility of injury to future children; the BFOQ, however, is not so broad that it transforms this deep social concern into an essential aspect of batterymaking.

Our case law, therefore, makes clear that the safety exception is limited to instances in which sex or pregnancy actually interferes with the employee's ability to perform the job. This approach is consistent with the language of the BFOQ provision itself, for it suggests that permissible distinctions based on sex must relate to ability to perform the duties of the job. Johnson Controls suggests, however, that we expand the exception to allow fetal-protection policies that mandate particular standards for pregnant or fertile women. We decline to do so. Such an expansion contradicts not only the language of the BFOQ and the narrowness of its exception but the plain language and history of the Pregnancy Discrimination Act.

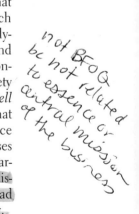
not BFOQ bc not related to essence or central mission of the business

doesn't that language leave a lot of latitude for an employer to say she is under-performing?

The PDA's amendment to Title VII contains a BFOQ standard of its own: unless pregnant employees differ from others "in their ability or inability to work," they must be "treated the same" as other employees "for all employment-related purposes." This language clearly sets forth Congress' remedy for discrimination on the basis of pregnancy and potential pregnancy. Women who are either pregnant or potentially pregnant must be treated like others "similar in their ability . . . to work." In other words, women as capable of doing their jobs as their male counterparts may not be forced to choose between having a child and having a job. . . .

We conclude that the language of both the BFOQ provision and the PDA which amended it, as well as the legislative history and the case law, prohibit an employer from discriminating against a woman because of her capacity to become pregnant unless her reproductive potential prevents her from performing the duties of her job. We reiterate our holdings in *Criswell* and *Dothard* that an employer must direct its concerns about a woman's ability to perform her job safely and efficiently to those aspects of the woman's job-related activities that fall within the "essence" of the particular business.

V

good summary

We have no difficulty concluding that Johnson Controls cannot establish a BFOQ. Fertile women, as far as appears in the record, participate in the manufacture of batteries as efficiently as anyone else. Johnson Controls' professed moral and ethical concerns about the welfare of the next generation do not suffice to establish a BFOQ of female sterility. Decisions about the welfare of future children must be left to the parents who conceive, bear, support, and raise them rather than to the employers who hire those parents. Congress has mandated this choice through Title VII, as amended by the Pregnancy Discrimination Act. Johnson Controls has attempted to exclude women because of their reproductive capacity. Title VII and the PDA simply do not allow a woman's dismissal because of her failure to submit to sterilization.

Nor can concerns about the welfare of the next generation be considered a part of the "essence" of Johnson Controls' business. Judge Easterbrook in this case pertinently observed: "It is word play to say that 'the job' at Johnson [Controls] is to make batteries without risk to fetuses in the same way 'the job' at Western Air Lines is to fly planes without crashing."

Johnson Controls argues that it must exclude all fertile women because it is impossible to tell which women will become pregnant while working with lead. This argument is somewhat academic in light of our conclusion that the company may not exclude fertile women at all; it perhaps is worth noting, however, that Johnson Controls has shown no "factual basis for believing that all or substantially all women would be unable to perform safely and efficiently the duties of the job involved." . . .

VI

A word about tort liability and the increased cost of fertile women in the workplace is perhaps necessary. [At the Seventh Circuit, Judge Posner] expressed concern about an employer's tort liability and concluded that liability for a potential injury to a fetus is a social cost that Title VII does not require a company to ignore. It is correct to say that Title VII does not prevent the employer from having a conscience. The statute, however, does prevent sex-specific fetal-protection policies. These two aspects of Title VII do not conflict.

[The majority recognized that more than 40 states currently recognized a right to recover for a prenatal injury based either on negligence or on wrongful death. But

Johnson Controls purportedly complied with OSHA lead standards and also warned its female employees about the damaging effects of lead. This would seem to preclude negligence, and "[w]ithout negligence, it would be difficult for a court to find liability on the part of the employer." Further, while the Court stressed that "the issue is not before us," it also suggested that, should tort liability "punish employers for complying with Title VII's clear command," federal law would preempt state tort law. Nevertheless, because] Johnson Controls has not argued that it faces any costs from tort liability, not to mention crippling ones, the pre-emption question is not before us. We therefore say no more than that the concurrence's speculation appears unfounded as well as premature.

The tort-liability argument reduces to two equally unpersuasive propositions. First, Johnson Controls attempts to solve the problem of reproductive health hazards by resorting to an exclusionary policy. Title VII plainly forbids illegal sex discrimination as a method of diverting attention from an employer's obligation to police the workplace. Second, the spectre of an award of damages reflects a fear that hiring fertile women will cost more. The extra cost of employing members of one sex, however, does not provide an affirmative Title VII defense for a discriminatory refusal to hire members of that gender. See *Manhart.* Indeed, in passing the PDA, Congress considered at length the considerable cost of providing equal treatment of pregnancy and related conditions, but made the "decision to forbid special treatment of pregnancy despite the social costs associated therewith."

We, of course, are not presented with, nor do we decide, a case in which costs would be so prohibitive as to threaten the survival of the employer's business. We merely reiterate our prior holdings that the incremental cost of hiring women cannot justify discriminating against them. . . .

Justice WHITE, with whom The Chief Justice and Justice KENNEDY join, concurring in part and concurring in the judgment.

The Court properly holds that Johnson Controls' fetal protection policy overtly discriminates against women, and thus is prohibited by Title VII unless it falls within the bona fide occupational qualification (BFOQ) exception. . . . The Court erroneously holds, however, that the BFOQ defense is so narrow that it could never justify a sex-specific fetal protection policy. I nevertheless concur in the judgment of reversal because on the record before us summary judgment in favor of Johnson Controls was improper. . . .

[A] fetal protection policy would be justified under the terms of the statute if, for example, an employer could show that exclusion of women from certain jobs was reasonably necessary to avoid substantial tort liability. . . .

Dothard and *Criswell* also confirm that costs are relevant in determining whether a discriminatory policy is reasonably necessary for the normal operation of a business. In *Dothard,* the safety problem that justified exclusion of women from the prison guard positions was largely a result of inadequate staff and facilities. If the cost of employing women could not be considered, the employer there should have been required to hire more staff and restructure the prison environment rather than exclude women. Similarly, in *Criswell* the airline could have been required to hire more pilots and install expensive monitoring devices rather than discriminate against older employees. The BFOQ statute, however, reflects "Congress' unwillingness to require employers to change the very nature of their operations." *Price Waterhouse v. Hopkins* (plurality opinion). . . .

Justice SCALIA, concurring in the judgment.

I generally agree with the Court's analysis, but have some reservations, several of which bear mention.

First, I think it irrelevant that there was "evidence in the record about the debilitating effect of lead exposure on the male reproductive system." Even without such evidence, treating women differently "on the basis of pregnancy" constitutes discrimination "on the basis of sex," because Congress has unequivocally said so. Pregnancy Discrimination Act of 1978.

Second, the Court points out that "Johnson Controls has shown no factual basis for believing that all or substantially all women would be unable to perform safely . . . the duties of the job involved." In my view, this is not only "somewhat academic in light of our conclusion that the company may not exclude fertile women at all"; it is entirely irrelevant. By reason of the Pregnancy Discrimination Act, it would not matter if all pregnant women placed their children at risk in taking these jobs, just as it does not matter if no men do so.

Third, [as to possible liability under state tort law,] all that need be said in the present case is that Johnson has not demonstrated a substantial risk of tort liability — which is alone enough to defeat a tort-based assertion of the BFOQ exception.

Last, the Court goes far afield, it seems to me, in suggesting that increased cost alone — short of "costs . . . so prohibitive as to threaten survival of the employer's business" — cannot support a BFOQ defense. I agree with Justice White's concurrence that nothing in our prior cases suggests this, and in my view it is wrong. I think, for example, that a shipping company may refuse to hire pregnant women as crew members on long voyages because the on-board facilities for foreseeable emergencies, though quite feasible, would be inordinately expensive. In the present case, however, Johnson has not asserted a cost-based BFOQ. . . .

NOTES

1. *A Policy of Sex Discrimination*. While not all women were prevented from working in lead exposure jobs, the Court found the employer's rule to be a policy that discriminated because of sex. That is because all those excluded from working in the at-issue jobs were women, even though the exclusion did not apply to sterile women. The rule did not exclude any men, fertile or not. Here the challenged rule is sex discrimination, even without the need to consider the PDA, but that statute reinforces the Court's analysis. *Johnson Controls* is also important for its holding that disparate treatment analysis (and, therefore, the BFOQ defense) applies whenever an employer facially discriminates or acts on the basis of gender, regardless of whether it is motivated by animus.

2. *The BFOQ Defense*. *Johnson Controls* rejected an attempt to sidestep the rigors of the BFOQ as developed in *Dothard* and *Criswell* by employing the more lenient business necessity test, which is available in disparate impact cases (see Chapter 3). The Civil Rights Act of 1991 codified *Johnson Controls* in this respect by adding subsection (k)(2) to §703 of Title VII: "A demonstration that an employment practice is required by business necessity may not be used as a defense against a claim of intentional discrimination under this title."

Assuming BFOQ is the appropriate analysis, is *Johnson Controls* consistent with *Dothard*? In both cases, third parties (fetuses or other prison guards and prisoners) could be affected by a woman's decision to perform a certain job. Is the difference that the third parties affected in *Dothard* are the essence of the business? Who defines that? The "essence" of a business test originated in *Diaz v. Pan American Airways, Inc.*, 442 F.2d 385 (5th Cir. 1971). There the district court had, shockingly by present standards, found that stewardesses were superior to male stewards by being sexually attractive to male passengers and comforting to female passengers. The court of appeals avoided this factfinding by saying that only superiority in aspects of the job that went to the essence of the business counted; the supposed female superiority was in aspects of the job peripheral to the airline's essential concern with safe transportation.

Perhaps because of this stringent standard, few cases have found BFOQs established. One exception is *Healey v. Southwood Psychiatric Hospital*, 78 F.3d 128 (3d Cir. 1996), where the plaintiff challenged a gender-specific rule for assigning child care specialists at a hospital for emotionally disturbed children and adolescents, some of whom had been sexually abused. The court upheld summary judgment for the employer because of expert testimony about how the patients would react to staff of the two sexes and therefore the necessity of having "at least one member of each sex available to the patients at all times." *Id.* at 132-33.

3. *Customer Preference as a BFOQ.* When, if ever, is "customer preference" a basis for a BFOQ? When framed this broadly, the courts have tended to answer this question "never." For example, the Ninth Circuit rejected a BFOQ claim in *Fernandez v. Wynn Oil Co.*, 653 F.2d 1273 (9th Cir. 1981), where the defendant argued that the plaintiff could not be made vice-president of international operations because Latin American clients would react negatively to a woman in such a position. The Ninth Circuit held a "customer preference" defense inadequate as a matter of law. But couldn't *Healey* be described as an extreme case of customer preference?

In any event, *Fernandez* involved an explicit preference for men based on the (perceived) preferences of customers. Can customer preferences influence employment in more subtle ways, even if there's no explicit gender-based policy? There's increasing concern with employers, in effect, catering to racial and gender customer preferences when continued employment and compensation is linked to "customer satisfaction," given strong indications of bias in such feedback. *See generally* Dallan F. Flake, *When Should Employers Be Liable for Factoring Biased Customer Feedback into Employment Decisions?*, 102 MINN. L. REV. (forthcoming 2018); Lu-in Wang, *When the Customer Is King*, 23 VA. J. SOC. POL'Y & L. 249 (2016); Naomi Schoenbaum, *The Law of Intimate Work*, 90 WASH. L. REV. 1167 (2015). Note in such cases the problem for plaintiffs is not the BFOQ defense but proving discrimination in the first place. Would the disparate impact theory help?

4. *Sexualized Businesses and Sex Work.* A continuing customer preference issue arises in sexualized businesses. Two decades ago, the EEOC dropped its investigation against Hooters, a restaurant chain characterized by "Hooter Girls" clad in revealing outfits, after the company launched a massive public relations campaign against the Commission. Although a private action was then settled, under terms that allowed Hooters to continue to hire only women as wait staff, the male plaintiffs received monetary compensation. *Hooters to Pay $3.75 Million in Sex Suit*, USA TODAY, Oct. 1, 1997, at 1A. Had either matter gone to trial, the question would be whether selling female sex appeal is a BFOQ. *See generally* Kimberly A. Yuracko, *Private Nurses and Playboy Bunnies: Explaining Permissible Sex Discrimination*, 92 CAL. L. REV. 147, 151-52 (2004). Even if so, would the defense extend to sexual harassment against employees in such settings? *See* Ann C. McGinley, *Harassing "Girls" at the Hard Rock: Masculinities in Sexualized Environments*, 2007 U. ILL. L. REV. 1229. See Chapter 5.

5. *Privacy BFOQs.* In an omitted footnote, the majority in *Johnson Controls* refused to address privacy-based BFOQs but stressed that "[n]othing in our discussion of the

'essence of the business test,' however, suggests that sex could not constitute a BFOQ when privacy interests are implicated." 499 U.S. at 206 n.4. The Court has not since revisited this, and the lower courts have reached mixed results. There are only a scattering of cases outside the prison context, but in that setting there is considerable litigation. Generally, the courts have been sympathetic to narrowly tailored rules restricting prison guard jobs to members of the same sex as the inmate, especially when female inmates are involved, although one might have thought that inmate privacy was not a very compelling basis for restricting employment opportunities by sex. Disparate results from two recent Ninth Circuit cases illustrate the complications. *Compare Teamsters Local Union No. 117 v. Wash. Dep't of Corr.*, 789 F.3d 979 (9th Cir. 2015) (a plan designating 110 female-only correctional positions was a valid BFOQ since it reflected an individualized, well-researched response to problems in women's prisons of sexual abuse and misconduct by prison guards, breaches of inmate privacy, and security gaps) *with Ambat v. City & Cnty. of S.F.*, 757 F.3d 1017 (9th Cir. 2014) (triable issue as to whether an employer's policy of prohibiting male deputies from supervising female jail inmates was a BFOQ). *See* Kim Shayo Buchanan, *Beyond Modesty: Privacy in Prison and the Risk of Sexual Abuse*, 88 MARQ. L. REV. 751, 756 (2005) ("when women prisoners are sexually exploited by guards, they are victims of sexual aggression; feminists do them no favor by pretending that they are not").

6. *BFOQ for Race?* Title VII contains no BFOQ for race, and there is no doubt that the omission was intentional. *See Chaney v. Plainfield Healthcare Ctr.*, 612 F.3d 908 (7th Cir. 2010) (honoring a patient's request for white caregivers did not justify discrimination in job assignments). In *Ferrill v. The Parker Group, Inc.*, 168 F.3d 468 (11th Cir. 1999), a §1981 case, the Eleventh Circuit rejected a BFOQ for racially segregating telemarketers aimed at getting out the vote for an election, with blacks calling blacks and whites calling whites. In contrast, the results are more mixed under the Equal Protection Clause. *Compare Wittner v. Peters*, 87 F.3d 916 (7th Cir. 1996) (allowing requirement for a black lieutenant at a prison run like a boot camp), *with Patrolmen's Benevolent Ass'n v. City of New York*, 310 F.3d 43 (2d Cir. 2002) (upholding jury verdict finding city had not demonstrated that transferring minority police officers to a racially troubled precinct was narrowly tailored to the justification for doing so). Could First Amendment concerns sometimes limit Title VII's prescription? *See* Russell K. Robinson, *Casting and Caste-ing: Reconciling Artistic Freedom and Antidiscrimination Norms*, 95 CAL. L. REV. 1 (2007) (First Amendment would justify limited use of race/sex classifications). *See also* Samira Paydar, Note, *Boys Club Behind the Scenes: Using Title VII to Remedy Gender Discrimination in Hollywood*, 47 SETON HALL L. REV. (forthcoming 2017).

7. *No Adverse Employment Action?* We saw in Chapter 1 that the circuits have differing standards with respect to what constitutes an adverse employment action. For many, a "lateral transfer," that is, one that does not result in loss of pay or a demotion, is not actionable. In jurisdictions with stringent definitions of adverse employment action, an employer may be able to assign individuals by sex, age, or even race without having to establish a BFOQ. *See Tipler v. Douglas County*, 482 F.3d 1023, 1025 (8th Cir. 2007) (BFOQ analysis "unnecessary if (1) the policy requiring female-only supervision of female inmates is reasonable, and (2) such a policy imposes only a 'minimal restriction' on the employee"); *but see Piercy v. Maketa*, 480 F.3d 1192 (10th Cir. 2007) (facial discrimination might be actionable when it was not clear that assignments were purely lateral). In *Breiner v. Nevada Dep't of Corr.*, 610 F.3d 1202, 1208 (9th Cir. 2010), the court rejected the employer's argument that reserving several promotions for women had only a "de minimis" impact on the plaintiffs and thus

did not violate Title VII; "[i]t is beyond dispute that the denial of a single promotion opportunity such as the one here at issue is actionable under Title VII."

3.   Voluntary Affirmative Action

In *United Steelworkers of America v. Weber*, 443 U.S. 193 (1979), a five-to-two majority upheld the employer's use of a voluntary affirmative action plan negotiated with the union representing its workers to create a training program for incumbent unskilled workers to fill skilled job categories. Until this plan was adopted, craft positions were filled by men with craft experience, typically learned through the apprentice system of craft unions in the area that historically excluded blacks from membership. Hiring skilled craft workers for the employer's plant meant that thcsc job categories were all white. In order to address this problem, the plan reserved for black employees 50 percent of the openings in these newly created in-plant training programs until the percentage of black skilled craftworkers approximated the percentage of blacks in the local labor force. Brian Weber, an unskilled white worker in the plant, sued because some black workers with less plant seniority were accepted into the craft training program.

After holding that Title VII's prohibition against racial discrimination does not condemn all private, voluntary, race-conscious affirmative action plans, the Court upheld the particular plan:

> We need not today define in detail the line of demarcation between permissible and impermissible affirmative action plans. It suffices to hold that the challenged Kaiser-USWA affirmative action plan falls on the permissible side of the line. The purposes of the plan mirror those of the statute. Both were designed to break down old patterns of racial segregation and hierarchy. Both were structured to "open unemployment opportunities for Negroes in occupations which have been traditionally closed to them."
>
> At the same time, the plan does not unnecessarily trammel the interests of the white employees. The plan does not require the discharge of white workers and their replacement with new black hires. . . . Nor does the plan create an absolute bar to the advancement of white employees; half of those trained in the program will be white. Moreover, the plan is a temporary measure; it is not intended to maintain racial balance, but simply to eliminate a manifest racial imbalance.

Id. at 208. *See generally* Kenneth R. Davis, *Wheel of Fortune: A Critique of the "Manifest Imbalance" Requirement for Race-Conscious Affirmative Action*, 43 GA. L. REV. 993 (2009). Justice Rehnquist, joined by then-Chief Justice Burger, dissented.

> The operative sections of Title VII prohibit racial discrimination in employment *simpliciter*. Taken in its normal meaning, and as understood by all Members of Congress who spoke to the issue during the legislative debates, this language prohibits a covered employer from considering race when making an employment decision, whether the race be black or white. . . . We have never wavered in our understanding that Title VII "prohibits all racial discrimination in employment, without exception for any group of particular employees." . . .
>
> Thus, by a tour de force reminiscent not of jurists such as Hale, Holmes, and Hughes, but of escape artists such as Houdini, the Court eludes clear statutory language, "uncontradicted" legislative history, and uniform precedent in concluding that employers are, after all, permitted to consider race in making employment decisions.

Id. at 220-22. The next case revisited the issue.

JOHNSON v. TRANSPORTATION AGENCY
OF SANTA CLARA COUNTY
480 U.S. 616 (1987)

Justice BRENNAN delivered the opinion of the Court.

Respondent, Transportation Agency of Santa Clara County, California, unilaterally promulgated an Affirmative Action Plan applicable, inter alia, to promotions of employees. In selecting applicants for the promotional position of road dispatcher, the Agency, pursuant to the Plan, passed over petitioner Paul Johnson, a male employee, and promoted a female employee applicant, Diane Joyce. The question for decision is whether in making the promotion the Agency impermissibly took into account the sex of the applicants in violation of Title VII of the Civil Rights Act of 1964. . . .

I

A

[The Santa Clara County Transit District Board of Supervisors adopted an Affirmative Action Plan for the County Transportation Agency. It] provides that, in making promotions to positions within a traditionally segregated job classification in which women have been significantly underrepresented, the Agency is authorized to consider as one factor the sex of a qualified applicant.

In reviewing the composition of its work force, the Agency noted in its Plan that women were represented in numbers far less than their proportion of the County labor force in both the Agency as a whole and in five of seven job categories. Specifically, while women constituted 36.4% of the area labor market, they composed only 22.4% of Agency employees. Furthermore, women working at the Agency were concentrated largely in EEOC job categories traditionally held by women: women made up 76% of Office and Clerical Workers, but only 7.1% of Agency Officials and Administrators, 8.6% of Professionals, 9.7% of Technicians, and 22% of Service and Maintenance Workers. As for the job classification relevant to this case, none of the 238 Skilled Craft Worker positions was held by a woman. The Plan noted that this underrepresentation of women in part reflected the fact that women had not traditionally been employed in these positions, and that they had not been strongly motivated to seek training or employment in them "because of the limited opportunities that have existed in the past for them to work in such classifications." . . .

The Agency stated that its Plan was intended to achieve "a statistically measurable yearly improvement in hiring, training and promotion of minorities and women throughout the Agency in all major job classifications where they are underrepresented." As a benchmark by which to evaluate progress, the Agency stated that its long-term goal was to attain a work force whose composition reflected the proportion of minorities and women in the area labor force. Thus, for the Skilled Craft category in which the road dispatcher position at issue here was classified, the Agency's aspiration was that eventually about 36% of the jobs would be occupied by women.

The Plan acknowledged that a number of factors might make it unrealistic to rely on the Agency's long-term goals in evaluating the Agency's progress in expanding job opportunities for minorities and women. Among the factors identified were low turnover rates in some classifications, the fact that some jobs involved heavy labor, the small number of positions within some job categories, the limited number of entry positions leading to the Technical and Skilled Craft classifications, and the limited number of minorities and women qualified for positions requiring specialized training and experience. As a result, the Plan counseled that short-range goals be established and annually adjusted to serve as the most realistic guide for actual employment decisions. . . .

The Agency's Plan thus set aside no specific number of positions for minorities or women, but authorized the consideration of ethnicity or sex as a factor when evaluating qualified candidates for jobs in which members of such groups were poorly represented. One such job was the road dispatcher position that is the subject of the dispute in this case.

had no specific # set out, just trying to hire more women

B

[In 1979, the Agency announced a vacancy for dispatcher in the Roads Division. Dispatchers assign road crews, equipment, and materials and maintain records. The position required a minimum of four years' experience with Santa Clara County. Twelve county employees applied, including Joyce and Johnson.] Joyce had worked for the County since 1970, serving as an account clerk until 1975. She had applied for a road dispatcher position in 1974, but was deemed ineligible because she had not served as a road maintenance worker. In 1975, Joyce transferred from a senior account clerk position to a road maintenance worker position, becoming the first woman to fill such a job. During her four years in that position, she occasionally worked out of class as a road dispatcher.

she was qualified + even worked as road mgmt. b/c wanted the job

Petitioner Johnson began with the County in 1967 as a road yard clerk, after private employment that included working as a supervisor and dispatcher. He had also unsuccessfully applied for the road dispatcher opening in 1974. In 1977, his clerical position was downgraded, and he sought and received a transfer to the position of road maintenance worker. He also occasionally worked out of class as a dispatcher while performing that job.

Johnson also qualified

Nine of the applicants, including Joyce and Johnson, were deemed qualified for the job, and were interviewed by a two-person board. Seven of the applicants scored above 70 on this interview, which meant that they were certified as eligible for selection by the appointing authority. The scores awarded ranged from 70 to 80. Johnson was tied for second with a score of 75, while Joyce ranked next with a score of 73. A second interview was conducted by three Agency supervisors, who ultimately recommended that Johnson be promoted. Prior to the second interview, Joyce had contacted the County's Affirmative Action Office because she feared that her application might not receive disinterested review.[5] The Office in turn contacted the Agency's Affirmative Action Coordinator, whom the Agency's Plan makes responsible for, inter alia, keeping the Director informed of opportunities for the Agency to accomplish its objectives under the Plan. At the time, the Agency employed no women in any Skilled Craft position, and had never employed a woman as a road dispatcher. The Coordinator recommended to the Director of the Agency, James Graebner, that Joyce be promoted.

interviews

AA committee

Graebner, authorized to choose any of the seven persons deemed eligible, thus had the benefit of suggestions by the second interview panel and by the Agency

---

5. Joyce testified that she had had disagreements with two of the three members of the second interview panel. [One had refused to issue coveralls when she began work as a road maintenance worker, resulting in her ruining her clothes on four occasions. A second had several differences in opinion with her about safety and may have tried to sabotage her interview by scheduling it at the same time as a disaster preparedness class.] This same panel member had earlier described Joyce as a "rebel-rousing, skirt-wearing person."

Coordinator in arriving at his decision. After deliberation, Graebner concluded that the promotion should be given to Joyce. As he testified: "I tried to look at the whole picture, the combination of her qualifications and Mr. Johnson's qualifications, their test scores, their expertise, their background, affirmative action matters, things like that. . . . I believe it was a combination of all those."

The certification for naming Joyce as the person promoted to the dispatcher position stated that both she and Johnson were rated as well qualified for the job. . . . Graebner testified that he did not regard as significant the fact that Johnson scored 75 and Joyce 73. . . .

Dist Court

. . . The District Court found that Johnson was more qualified for the dispatcher position than Joyce, and that the sex of Joyce was the "*determining factor* in her selection." [While a valid Affirmative Action Plan would justify the choice, the court found the Agency's Plan invalid because it was not temporary.]

II

As a preliminary matter, we note that petitioner bears the burden of establishing the invalidity of the Agency's Plan. [This case] fits readily within the analytical framework set forth in *McDonnell Douglas Corp. v. Green.* Once a plaintiff establishes a prima facie case that race or sex has been taken into account in an employer's employment decision, the burden shifts to the employer to articulate a nondiscriminatory rationale for its decision. The existence of an affirmative action plan provides such a rationale. If such a plan is articulated as the basis for the employer's decision, the burden shifts to the plaintiff to prove that the employer's justification is pretextual and the plan is invalid. As a practical matter, of course, an employer will generally seek to avoid a charge of pretext by presenting evidence in support of its plan. That does not mean, however, as petitioner suggests, that reliance on an affirmative action plan is to be treated as an affirmative defense requiring the employer to carry the burden of proving the validity of the plan. The burden of proving its invalidity remains on the plaintiff.

Analysis under McDonnell Douglas

The assessment of the legality of the Agency Plan must be guided by our decision in *Weber.*[6] [The majority rehearsed the facts of that case, quoting a passage in *Weber* stressing that "[i]t would be ironic indeed if a law triggered by a Nation's concern over centuries of racial injustice and intended to improve the lot of those who had 'been excluded from the American dream for so long' constituted the first legislative prohibition of all voluntary, private, race-conscious efforts to abolish traditional patterns of racial segregation and hierarchy."[7] The Court also noted that the plan in *Weber* neither unnecessarily trammeled the interests of the white employees nor

---

6. [The majority rejected Justice Scalia's argument in dissent that Title VII standards should be identical to those of the Constitution for public employers] because, as noted in *Weber*, "Title VI was an exercise of federal power 'over a matter in which the Federal Government was already directly involved,' since Congress 'was legislating to assure federal funds would not be used in an improper manner.'" In contrast, Title VII "was enacted pursuant to the commerce power to regulate purely private decisionmaking" and not intended to incorporate constitutional commands.

7. Justice Scalia's dissent maintains that *Weber*'s conclusion that Title VII does not prohibit voluntary affirmative action programs "rewrote the statute it purported to construe." [But not only was that decision sound, but Congress has made no effort to correct the result], and we therefore may assume that our interpretation was correct. . . . The fact that inaction may not always provide crystalline revelation, however, should not obscure the fact that it may be probative to varying degrees. *Weber*, for instance, was a widely publicized decision that addressed a prominent issue of public debate. Legislative inattention thus is not a plausible explanation for congressional inaction. . . .

created "an absolute bar to the advancement of white employees." And it quoted Justice Blackmun's *Weber* concurrence to the effect that "an employer seeking to justify the adoption of a plan need not point to its own prior discriminatory practices, nor even to evidence of an 'arguable violation' on its part": a "conspicuous . . . imbalance in traditionally segregated job categories" was all that was required since] voluntary employer action can play a crucial role in furthering Title VII's purpose of eliminating the effects of discrimination in the workplace, and that Title VII should not be read to thwart such efforts.[8]

. . . The first issue is therefore whether consideration of the sex of applicants for Skilled Craft jobs was justified by the existence of a "manifest imbalance" that reflected underrepresentation of women in "traditionally segregated job categories." In determining whether an imbalance exists that would justify taking sex or race into account, a comparison of the percentage of minorities or women in the employer's work force with the percentage in the area labor market or general population is appropriate in analyzing jobs that require no special expertise [citing *Teamsters* and *Weber*]. Where a job requires special training, however, the comparison should be with those in the labor force who possess the relevant qualifications [citing *Hazelwood*]. The requirement that the "manifest imbalance" relate to a "traditionally segregated job category" provides assurance both that sex or race will be taken into account in a manner consistent with Title VII's purpose of eliminating the effects of employment discrimination, and that the interests of those employees not benefiting from the plan will not be unduly infringed.

A manifest imbalance need not be such that it would support a prima facie case against the employer, as suggested in Justice O'Connor's concurrence, since we do not regard as identical the constraints of Title VII and the Federal Constitution on voluntarily adopted affirmative action plans. Application of the "prima facie" standard in Title VII cases would be inconsistent with *Weber*'s focus on statistical imbalance,[10] and could inappropriately create a significant disincentive for employers to adopt an affirmative action plan. A corporation concerned with maximizing return on investment, for instance, is hardly likely to adopt a plan if in order to do so it must compile evidence that could be used to subject it to a colorable Title VII suit.

8. Justice Scalia's suggestion that an affirmative action program may be adopted only to redress an employer's past discrimination was rejected in *Steelworkers v. Weber* because the prospect of liability created by such an admission would create a significant disincentive for voluntary action. . . .

10. The difference between the "manifest imbalance" and "prima facie" standards is illuminated by *Weber*. Had the Court in that case been concerned with past discrimination by the employer, it would have focused on discrimination in hiring skilled, not unskilled, workers, since only the scarcity of the former in Kaiser's work force would have made it vulnerable to a Title VII suit. In order to make out a prima facie case on such a claim, a plaintiff would be required to compare the percentage of black skilled workers in the Kaiser work force with the percentage of black skilled craft workers in the area labor market.

Weber obviously did not make such a comparison. Instead, it focused on the disparity between the percentage of black skilled craft workers in Kaiser's ranks and the percentage of blacks in the area labor force. Such an approach reflected a recognition that the proportion of black craft workers in the local labor force was likely as miniscule as the proportion in Kaiser's work force. The Court realized that the lack of imbalance between these figures would mean that employers in precisely those industries in which discrimination has been most effective would be precluded from adopting training programs to increase the percentage of qualified minorities. Thus, in cases such as *Weber*, where the employment decision at issue involves the selection of unskilled persons for a training program, the "manifest imbalance" standard permits comparison with the general labor force. By contrast, the "prima facie" standard would require comparison with the percentage of minorities or women qualified for the job for which the trainees are being trained, a standard that would have invalidated the plan in *Weber* itself.

It is clear that the decision to hire Joyce was made pursuant to an Agency Plan that directed that sex or race be taken into account for the purpose of remedying underrepresentation. . . .

As an initial matter, the Agency adopted as a benchmark for measuring progress in eliminating underrepresentation the long-term goal of a work force that mirrored in its major job classifications the percentage of women in the area labor market.[13] Even as it did so, however, the Agency acknowledged that such a figure could not by itself necessarily justify taking into account the sex of applicants for positions in all job categories. For positions requiring specialized training and experience, the Plan observed that the number of minorities and women "who possess the qualifications required for entry into such job classifications is limited." The Plan therefore directed that annual short-term goals be formulated that would provide a more realistic indication of the degree to which sex should be taken into account in filling particular positions. The Plan stressed that such goals "should not be construed as 'quotas' that must be met," but as reasonable aspirations in correcting the imbalance in the Agency's work force. . . . From the outset, therefore, the Plan sought annually to develop even more refined measures of the underrepresentation in each job category that required attention.

[When Joyce was selected for the road dispatcher position, the Agency was still in the process of refining its short-term goals for Skilled Craft Workers in accordance with the Plan. However, the Court rejected the argument that the Plan could not be taken into account in filling the dispatcher position since only the long-term goal was in place at that time. The Plan itself] emphasized that the long-term goals were not to be taken as guides for actual hiring decisions, but that supervisors were to consider a host of practical factors in seeking to meet affirmative action objectives, including the fact that in some job categories women were not qualified in numbers comparable to their representation in the labor force.

By contrast, had the Plan simply calculated imbalances in all categories according to the proportion of women in the area labor pool, and then directed that hiring be governed solely by those figures, its validity fairly could be called into question. This is because analysis of a more specialized labor pool normally is necessary in determining underrepresentation in some positions. If a plan failed to take distinctions in qualifications into account in providing guidance for actual employment decisions, it would dictate mere blind hiring by the numbers. . . .

The Agency's Plan emphatically did *not* authorize such blind hiring. . . .

Furthermore, in considering the candidates for the road dispatcher position in 1980, the Agency hardly needed to rely on a refined short-term goal to realize that it had a significant problem of underrepresentation that required attention. Given the obvious imbalance in the Skilled Craft category, and given the Agency's commitment to eliminating such imbalances, it was plainly not unreasonable for the Agency to determine that it was appropriate to consider as one factor the sex of Ms. Joyce in making its decision.[14] The promotion of Joyce thus satisfies the first requirement enunciated in *Weber*,

---

13. Because of the employment decision at issue in this case, our discussion henceforth refers primarily to the Plan's provisions to remedy the underrepresentation of women. Our analysis could apply as well, however, to the provisions of the Plan pertaining to minorities.

14. In addition, the Agency was mindful of the importance of finally hiring a woman in a job category that had formerly been all male. The Director testified that, while the promotion of Joyce "made a small dent, for sure, in the numbers," nonetheless "philosophically it made a larger impact in that it probably has encouraged other females and minorities to look at the possibility of so-called 'non-traditional' jobs as areas where they and the agency both have samples of a success story."

since it was undertaken to further an affirmative action plan designed to eliminate Agency work force imbalances in traditionally segregated job categories.

We next consider whether the Agency Plan unnecessarily trammeled the rights of male employees or created an absolute bar to their advancement. In contrast to the plan in *Weber*, which provided that 50% of the positions in the craft training program were exclusively for blacks . . . , the Plan sets aside no positions for women. The Plan expressly states that "[the] 'goals' established for each Division should not be construed as 'quotas' that must be met." Rather, the Plan merely authorizes that consideration be given to affirmative action concerns when evaluating qualified applicants. As the Agency Director testified, the sex of Joyce was but one of numerous factors he took into account in arriving at his decision. . . . [T]he Agency Plan requires women to compete with all other qualified applicants. No persons are automatically excluded from consideration; all are able to have their qualifications weighed against those of other applicants.

In addition, petitioner had no absolute entitlement to the road dispatcher position. Seven of the applicants were classified as qualified and eligible, and the Agency Director was authorized to promote any of the seven. Thus, denial of the promotion unsettled no legitimate, firmly rooted expectation on the part of petitioner. Furthermore, while petitioner in this case was denied a promotion, he retained his employment with the Agency, at the same salary and with the same seniority, and remained eligible for other promotions.

[Finally, "the Plan was intended to *attain* a balanced work force, not to maintain one," despite the absence of an explicit end date.]

III

. . . We therefore hold that the Agency appropriately took into account as one factor the sex of Diane Joyce in determining that she should be promoted to the road dispatcher position. Accordingly, the judgment of the Court of Appeals is Affirmed.

Held

[Justice Stevens concurred, essentially on the grounds of stare decisis. In light of "the authoritative construction" of *Bakke* and *Weber*, he was compelled to accept this view even if he thought it "at odds with [his] understanding of the actual intent of the authors of the legislation."]

Justice O'CONNOR, concurring in the judgment. . . .

In my view, the proper initial inquiry in evaluating the legality of an affirmative action plan by a public employer under Title VII is no different from that required by the Equal Protection Clause. In either case, consistent with the congressional intent to provide some measure of protection to the interests of the employer's nonminority employees, the employer must have had a firm basis for believing that remedial action was required. An employer would have such a firm basis if it can point to a statistical disparity sufficient to support a prima facie claim under Title VII by the employee beneficiaries of the affirmative action plan of a pattern or practice claim of discrimination. . . .

The *Weber* view of Congress' resolution of the conflicting concerns of minority and nonminority workers in Title VII appears substantially similar to this Court's resolution of these same concerns in *Wygant* [*v. Jackson Bd. of Ed.*, 476 U.S. 267 (1986)] which involved the claim that an affirmative action plan by a public employer violated the Equal Protection Clause. In *Wygant*, the Court was in agreement that remedying past or present racial discrimination by a state actor is a sufficiently weighty interest to warrant the remedial use of a carefully constructed affirmative action plan. The Court also concluded, however, that "[societal] discrimination, without more, is too amorphous a basis for imposing a racially classified remedy." Instead, we determined that affirmative action was valid if it was crafted to remedy past or present discrimination by the employer. Although the employer need not point to any contemporaneous findings of actual discrimination, I concluded in *Wygant* that the employer must point to evidence sufficient to establish a firm basis for believing that remedial action is required, and that a statistical imbalance sufficient for a Title VII prima facie case against the employer would satisfy this firm basis requirement. . . .

[Justice O'Connor thought *Wygant* was "entirely consistent with *Weber*" even though there was no evidence of intentional discrimination by Kaiser, but she believed the evidence of past discrimination in the present case to be] more complex. The number of women with the qualifications for entry into the relevant job classification was quite small. A statistical imbalance between the percentage of women in the work force generally and the percentage of women in the particular specialized job classification, therefore, does not suggest past discrimination for purposes of proving a Title VII prima facie case.

Unfortunately, the Court today gives little guidance for what statistical imbalance is sufficient to support an affirmative action plan. Although the Court denies that the statistical imbalance need be sufficient to make out a prima facie case of discrimination against women, the Court fails to suggest an alternative standard. Because both *Wygant* and *Weber* attempt to reconcile the same competing concerns, I see little justification for the adoption of different standards for affirmative action under Title VII and the Equal Protection Clause.

While employers must have a firm basis for concluding that remedial action is necessary, neither *Wygant* nor *Weber* places a burden on employers to prove that they actually discriminated against women or minorities. Employers are "trapped between the competing hazards of liability to minorities if affirmative action is not taken to remedy apparent employment discrimination and liability to nonminorities if affirmative action is taken." *Wygant* (O'Connor, J., concurring in part and concurring in judgment). Moreover, this Court has long emphasized the importance of voluntary efforts to eliminate discrimination. . . .

The long-term goal of the plan was "to attain a work force whose composition in all job levels and major job classifications approximates the distribution of women . . . in the Santa Clara County work force." If this long-term goal had been applied to the hiring decisions made by the Agency, in my view, the affirmative action plan would violate Title VII. "[I]t is completely unrealistic to assume that individuals of each [sex] will gravitate with mathematical exactitude to each employer . . . absent unlawful discrimination." *Sheet Metal Workers* (O'Connor, J., concurring in part and dissenting in part). [However, this long-range goal] was never used as a guide for actual hiring decisions. Instead, the goal was merely a statement of aspiration wholly without operational significance. [While no short-term goal had been fully developed for the position in question, the Agency] had determined that progress should be judged by a comparison to the qualified women in the area work force. As I view the record, the promotion decision in this case was entirely consistent with the philosophy underlying the development of the short-term goals. . . .

The ultimate decision to promote Joyce rather than petitioner was made by James Graebner, the Director of the Agency. As Justice Scalia views the record in this case, the Agency Director made the decision to promote Joyce rather than petitioner solely on the basis of sex and with indifference to the relative merits of the two applicants. In my view, however, the record simply fails to substantiate the picture painted by Justice Scalia. The Agency Director testified that he "tried to look at the whole picture, the combination of [Joyce's] qualifications and Mr. Johnson's qualifications, their test scores, their experience, their background, affirmative action matters, things like that." . . . While I agree with Justice Scalia's dissent that an affirmative action program that automatically and blindly promotes those marginally qualified candidates falling within a preferred race or gender category, or that can be equated with a permanent plan of "proportionate representation by race and sex," would violate Title VII, I cannot agree that this is such a case. Rather, as the Court demonstrates, Joyce's sex was simply used as a "plus" factor.

Justice SCALIA, with whom The Chief Justice joins, and with whom Justice WHITE joins in Parts I and II, dissenting.
. . . The Court today completes the process of converting [Title VII] from a guarantee that race or sex will not be the basis for employment determinations, to a guarantee that it often will. Ever so subtly, without even alluding to the last obstacles preserved by earlier opinions that we now push out of our path, we effectively replace the goal of a discrimination-free society with the quite incompatible goal of proportionate representation by race and by sex in the workplace.

I . . .

Several salient features of the plan should be noted. Most importantly, the plan's purpose was assuredly not to remedy prior sex discrimination by the Agency. It could not have been, because there was no prior sex discrimination to remedy. The majority, in cataloging the Agency's alleged misdeeds, neglects to mention the District Court's finding that the Agency "has not discriminated in the past, and does not discriminate in the present against women in regard to employment opportunities in general and promotions in particular." This finding was not disturbed by the Ninth Circuit.

Not only was the plan not directed at the results of past sex discrimination by the Agency, but its objective was not to achieve the state of affairs that this Court has dubiously assumed would result from an absence of discrimination — an overall work force "more or less representative of the racial and ethnic composition of the population in the community." *Teamsters*. Rather, the oft-stated goal was to mirror the racial and sexual composition of the entire county labor force, not merely in the Agency work force as a whole, but in each and every individual job category at the Agency. In a discrimination-free world, it would obviously be a statistical oddity for every job category to match the racial and sexual composition of even that portion of the county work force qualified for that job; it would be utterly miraculous for each of them to match, as the plan expected, the composition of the entire work force. Quite obviously, the plan did not seek to replicate what a lack of discrimination would produce, but rather imposed racial and sexual tailoring that would, in defiance of normal expectations and laws of probability, give each protected racial and sexual group a governmentally determined "proper" proportion of each job category. . . .

The fact of discrimination against Johnson is much clearer, and its degree more shocking, than the majority and Justice O'Connor's concurrence would suggest . . . . Worth mentioning, for example, is the trier of fact's determination that, if the Affirmative Action Coordinator had not intervened, "the decision as to whom to promote

. . . would have been made by [the Road Operations Division Director]," who had recommended that Johnson be appointed to the position. Likewise, the even more extraordinary findings that James Graebner, the Agency Director who made the appointment, "did not inspect the applications and related examination records of either [Paul Johnson] or Diane Joyce before making his decision," and indeed "did little or nothing to inquire into the results of the interview process and conclusions which [were] described as of critical importance to the selection process." In light of these determinations, it is impossible to believe (or to think that the District Court believed) Graebner's self-serving statements. . . . It was evidently enough for Graebner to know that both candidates (in the words of Johnson's counsel, to which Graebner assented) "met the M. Q.'s, the minimum. Both were minimally qualified." When asked whether he had "any basis," for determining whether one of the candidates was more qualified than the other, Graebner candidly answered, "No. . . . As I've said, they both appeared, and my conversations with people tended to corroborate, that they were both capable of performing the work."

After a 2-day trial, the District Court concluded that Diane Joyce's gender was "the determining factor," in her selection for the position. . . .

II

The most significant proposition of law established by today's decision is that racial or sexual discrimination is permitted under Title VII when it is intended to overcome the effect, not of the employer's own discrimination, but of societal attitudes that have limited the entry of certain races, or of a particular sex, into certain jobs. Even if the societal attitudes in question consisted exclusively of conscious discrimination by other employers, this holding would contradict a decision of this Court rendered only last Term. *Wygant v. Jackson Board of Education* held that the objective of remedying societal discrimination cannot prevent remedial affirmative action from violating the Equal Protection Clause. While Mr. Johnson does not advance a constitutional claim here, it is most unlikely that Title VII was intended to place a lesser restraint on discrimination by public actors than is established by the Constitution. . . .

[T]oday's decision goes well beyond merely allowing racial or sexual discrimination in order to eliminate the effects of prior societal discrimination. The majority opinion often uses the phrase "traditionally segregated job category" to describe the evil against which the plan is legitimately (according to the majority) directed. As originally used in *Weber* that phrase described skilled jobs from which employers and unions had systematically and intentionally excluded black workers — traditionally segregated jobs, that is, in the sense of conscious, exclusionary discrimination. But that is assuredly not the sense in which the phrase is used here. It is absurd to think that the nationwide failure of road maintenance crews, for example, to achieve the Agency's ambition of 36.4% female representation is attributable primarily, if even substantially, to systematic exclusion of women eager to shoulder pick and shovel. It is a "traditionally segregated job category" not in the *Weber* sense, but in the sense that, because of longstanding social attitudes, it has not been regarded by women themselves as desirable work. . . . There are, of course, those who believe that the social attitudes which cause women themselves to avoid certain jobs and to favor others are as nefarious as conscious, exclusionary discrimination. Whether or not that is so (and there is assuredly no consensus on the point equivalent to our national consensus against intentional discrimination), the two phenomena are certainly distinct. And it is the alteration of social attitudes, rather than the elimination of discrimination, which today's decision approves as justification for state-enforced discrimination. This is an enormous expansion, undertaken without the slightest justification or analysis. . . .

NOTES

1. *Litigation Structure.* Affirmative action plans are sometimes described as "defenses" to claims of disparate treatment, but after *Johnson* it is clear that no burden of persuasion ever shifts to defendant. Once put in issue, the *plaintiff* has the burden of showing that an affirmative action plan is invalid. At most, the employer must put into evidence facts going to the validity of its plan. *See Shea v. Kerry,* 796 F.3d 42 (D.C. Cir. 2015) (employer carried its burden of production by proof that the plan addressed manifest imbalances in senior-level positions in the Foreign Service Officer corps and that it refrained from unnecessarily trammeling the rights of nonminority candidates). *See generally* Cynthia L. Estlund, *Putting* Grutter *to Work: Diversity, Integration, and Affirmative Action in the Workplace,* 26 BERKELEY J. EMP. & LAB. L. 1, 35 (2005) ("The existence of a valid affirmative action plan operates not as an affirmative defense along the lines of 'business necessity' or a 'bona fide occupational qualification'; it is treated as a legitimate, nondiscriminatory basis for the challenged employment decision. *Johnson* thus makes room in the statute for affirmative action not by creating an affirmative defense but by narrowing the scope of what courts view as 'intentional discrimination'").

But not all "reverse discrimination" results from affirmative action plans. As we saw in Chapter 1, whites and males can bring disparate treatment cases, and in such situations the plaintiff may prove that (1) he was the victim of an ad hoc but intentional racial or gender preference; (2) he was the victim of a systematic preference where no affirmative action plan is involved; or (3) he was a victim of a preference pursuant to an affirmative action plan that he also proves is invalid. The first two theories require proof of the employer's discrimination only; the latter requires proof that the affirmative action plan was invalid. A plaintiff would presumably shoulder this burden only if it were the only way to prove discrimination in the first place. Absent that, plaintiffs presumably would challenge discrimination as ad hoc, leaving the employer to plead and put into evidence that the challenged decision was the result of an affirmative action plan. After all, that's now a "legitimate, nondiscriminatory reason" unless the plaintiff proves its invalidity.

Does *Price Waterhouse* or its codification in the 1991 Civil Rights Act alter the proof scheme *Johnson* established? No majority emerged on the question in *Price Waterhouse,* but Justice O'Connor and the three dissenters believed the burden-shifting approach should be fully applicable to reverse discrimination cases. The actual decision in *Johnson* to name Joyce was made by Graebner. Under *Price Waterhouse* analysis, does his quoted testimony show "direct evidence" of discrimination in favor of Joyce because she is a woman? If so, presumably one way that the county could limit remedies is to persuade the trier of fact that Joyce would have been hired in any event. But another way is to show that favoring Joyce was pursuant to a valid affirmative action plan. As to the latter, does the burden of persuasion still rest on the plaintiff in accordance with *Johnson?*

2. *§1981.* As might be expected, courts have applied affirmative action concepts developed under Title VII to §1981 claims alleging reverse discrimination. Thus, according to *Schurr v. Resorts International Hotel, Inc.,* 196 F.3d 486 (3d Cir. 1999), if an affirmative action plan is valid under Title VII, then actions based upon it will not

violate §1981; however, a plan that is invalid under Title VII will not excuse racially motivated decisions challenged under §1981.

3. *Diversity?* The two cases approved affirmative action plans, but only as remedial measures. Neither addressed the possibility of diversity as a justification for racial or gender preferences, and the first circuit to consider that issue rejected expanding the aims of affirmative action in that direction. *United States v. Board of Educ. of the Township of Piscataway*, 91 F.3d 1547 (3d Cir. 1996) (en banc), *cert. dismissed*, 522 U.S. 1010 (1997) (the school district's purpose of maintaining diversity in the work force was not one of the remediation purposes for affirmative action approved in *Weber* and *Johnson*). *See generally* Deborah C. Malamud, *The Strange Persistence of Affirmative Action Under Title VII*, 118 W. Va. L. Rev. 1, 23 (2015); Kingsley R. Browne, *Title VII and Diversity*, 14 Nev. L.J. 806, 829 (2014). The *Taxman* issue has not arisen frequently since that case in large part because, while workplace diversity efforts continue to be common, they rarely take the form of explicit racial or gender preferences, as opposed to race- or gender-conscious efforts to increase the numbers of underrepresented groups in the workplace. *See generally* Stacy L. Hawkins, *The Long Arc of Diversity Bends Towards Equality: Deconstructing the Progressive Critique of Workplace Diversity Efforts*, 16 U. Md. L. J. Race, Religion, Gender & Class 2 (2016).

4. *What About §116?* *Weber/Johnson* were arguably approved — or at least acquiesced in — by Congress in the Civil Rights Act of 1991, which amended Title VII by adopting a provision that "[n]othing in the amendments made by this title shall be construed to affect court-ordered remedies, affirmative action, or conciliation agreements, that are in accordance with the law." Pub. L. No. 102-166, Title I, §116, 105 Stat. 1071. *See* Michael J. Zimmer, Taxman: *Affirmative Action Dodges Five Bullets*, 1 U. Pa. J. Lab. & Emp. L. 229, 235 (1998) ("under any view, §116 bolsters *Weber/Johnson* and the stare decisis effect that the courts should give to that law").

5. *And What About* Ricci? But *Ricci v. DeStefano*, 557 U.S. 557 (2009), reproduced at p. 245, arguably casts doubt on the continued vitality of the doctrine. As we will study in more detail in Chapter 4, the Court there held that an employer could invalidate a test with disparate impact only if it had a strong basis in evidence for believing that it was in fact illegal, *i.e.*, that it was neither job related nor consistent with business necessity. Otherwise, reliance on disparate racial impact to reject a test would be actionable disparate treatment. While *Ricci* did not expressly discuss the validity of affirmative action under the *Weber/Johnson* analysis, there is at least considerable tension between its analysis and that of the earlier cases. *See* Sachin S. Pandya, *Detecting the Stealth Erosion of Precedent: Affirmative Action After* Ricci, 31 Berkeley J. Emp. & Lab. L. 285 (2011).

This has left the circuits to parse the two lines of authority. In *United States v. Brennan*, 650 F.3d 65 (2d Cir. 2011), the Second Circuit distinguished between the affirmative action defense under *Weber/Johnson* and *Ricci*'s "strong basis in evidence" defense: the threshold determination is now "whether the race- and sex-conscious action constitutes an affirmative action plan at all." *Id.* at 97. In its view,

> when an employer, acting ex ante, although in the light of past discrimination, establishes hiring or promotion procedures designed to promote equal opportunity and eradicate future discrimination, that may constitute an affirmative action plan. But where an employer, already having established its procedures in a certain way — such as through a seniority system — throws out the results of those procedures ex post because of the racial or gender composition of those results, that constitutes an individualized grant of employment benefits which must be individually justified, and not affirmative action.

Id. at 99-100. Thus, where only "ex post" actions are at issue, the employer may not invoke *Weber/Johnson. See also Shea v. Kerry*, 796 F.3d 42, 54 (D.C. Cir. 2015) (finding *Weber/Johnson* to control a challenge to an affirmative action plan, despite *Ricci*, because those opinion "are directly applicable to this case" and the Supreme Court has cautioned against the lower courts finding its decisions overruled by implication).

6. *On the Ground.* Whatever the doctrinal fate of *Weber/Johnson*, they have become less important on the ground because affirmative action plans used by public employers tend to be attacked under the more demanding standards of the Equal Protection Clause, and few private employers look explicitly to affirmative action plans to justify racial or gender preferences. To the extent the issue arises, it's likely to be when a plaintiff uses such a plan to establish the requisite racial intent behind an employment action. *See Humphries v. Pulaski County Special Sch. Dist.*, 580 F.3d 688, 697 (8th Cir. 2009) (plaintiff produced sufficient evidence that the district acted pursuant to invalid affirmative action policies in failing to promote her). See p. 43.

7. *Joyce as Victim of Discrimination.* Obviously, Johnson believed that Joyce received a preference because she was a woman. Is that so clear? Read footnote 10 concerning the second interview panel. Might not the hiring of Joyce have reflected merely an effort to remove disadvantages imposed on Joyce because she was a woman? If so, rather than "affirmative action," wouldn't that be only nondiscrimination? Justice O'Connor concludes that Joyce's sex was a "plus factor" in her hiring. Is she saying that sex discrimination did not occur? It would certainly violate Title VII for a man's sex to be a "plus factor," at least if it affected the decision and probably even if it were a motivating factor under *Desert Palace.* Is that Justice Scalia's point? The actual decision to name Joyce was made by Graebner. Does his quoted testimony amount to an admission of discrimination in favor of Joyce because she was a woman?

8. *"Affirmative Action" Under the ADEA.* While not normally denominated "affirmative action" when the Age Discrimination in Employment Act is concerned, one might so describe preferences for older workers as opposed to younger workers. As we saw in Chapter 1, such practices are simply not illegal under the Supreme Court's construction of the statute. See p. 44.

NOTE ON AFFIRMATIVE ACTION AND THE CONSTITUTION

As you undoubtedly learned in Constitutional Law, the Supreme Court has developed an elaborate jurisprudence about the legitimacy of racial preferences in the public sector. At the risk of being reductive, the Court's formal analysis is straightforward: any racial classification (whether or not "benign") is subject to strict scrutiny, *Adarand Constructors v. Pena*, 515 U.S. 200 (1995); *Richmond v. J.A. Croson*, 488 U.S. 469 (1989), which means they can stand only if they are narrowly tailored to achieve a compelling governmental interest. *Adarand*, 515 U.S. at 237.

To this point, the Supreme Court has approved of only two justifications as sufficiently compelling — redressing prior discrimination by the state actor in question and diversity in higher education. The first point was at issue in *Wygant v. Jackson Board of Education*, 476 U.S. 267 (1986), where the Court unanimously reaffirmed that race-conscious decisionmaking used to provide a remedy for the victims of proven discrimination was a sufficiently important governmental interest to withstand constitutional attack. While *Wygant* indicated that a state actor need not prove itself guilty of past discrimination to use this justification, 476 U.S. at 277, there are obvious disincentives to taking this path; in any event, the government must have convincing evidence of prior discrimination before embarking on an affirmative action program. Finally, *Croson* later found that an interest in remedying the effects of societal discrimination was not compelling enough to satisfy strict scrutiny. 488 U.S. at 505.

The second interest held to be sufficiently compelling is diversity in higher education. *Grutter v. Bollinger*, 539 U.S. 306 (2003), and *Gratz v. Bollinger*, 539 U.S. 244 (2003), both found diversity to be a compelling governmental interest justifying the consideration of race in university admissions decisions. However, the fact that an interest is compelling is only the beginning of the analysis, since the policy at issue has to be narrowly tailored to that interest. That was the basis for the different results in the two Michigan cases. *Grutter* upheld the law school's admissions policy as narrowly tailored, while *Gratz* struck down the undergraduate admissions policy. The essential difference between the two was that the law school assessed the complete admissions file of each individual applicant, including membership in underrepresented minority groups, while the undergraduate admissions committee mechanically awarded points to members of such underrepresented groups.

The Court's two subsequent encounters with diversity in the university admissions setting were in successive considerations of one controversy. While *Fisher v. University of Texas at Austin*, 133 S. Ct. 2411 (2013) (*"Fisher I"*), required a searching review of how "narrowly tailored" the university's plan was to the diversity goal, *Fisher II*, 136 S. Ct. 2198 (2016), found the plan at issue satisfied that standard even though the university's formulation of its goals was at a high level of generality. The majority opinion in *Fisher II*, written by Justice Kennedy, approved race as "a factor of a factor of a factor" in individualized admissions decisions. 136 S. Ct. at 2207. *Fisher II* is also notable for its recognition, and apparent acceptance, of the race-consciousness of Texas's facially neutral Top Ten Percent Plan, which, without individual consideration, guaranteed admission to approximately 10 percent of the graduating class of each high school in the state.

However, despite *Grutter* and *Fisher*, the limits of affirmative action are not far to seek. In *Parents Involved in Community Schools v. Seattle School Dist. No. 1*, 551 U.S. 701 (2007), the Supreme Court rejected the use of race as a tiebreaker by two school districts for assigning pupils to elementary and secondary schools. Writing for the plurality, Chief Justice Roberts found that neither the justification of remedying past intentional discrimination nor that of diversity applied to the cases before the Court. As for the latter, race was not "part of a broader effort to achieve 'exposure to widely diverse people, cultures, ideas, and viewpoints,'" and it was not simply one factor as in *Grutter* but "*the* factor." *Id.* at 723. Although siding with the majority, Justice Kennedy's decisive concurrence, perhaps signaling the stance he would later take in *Fisher II*, disapproved the plurality's "all-too-unyielding insistence that race cannot be a factor." *Id.* at 787. While voting to invalidate the policies, he would have allowed the districts to take account of race as one component in its decisionmaking process because avoiding racial isolation is a compelling governmental interest. *Id.* at 788.

The significance of these cases for public employment is uncertain. Some circuits have approved of public employer affirmative action plans, *see Petit v. City of Chicago*, 352 F.3d 1111 (7th Cir. 2003) (the city had a compelling operational need for a diverse police department given the size of the police force and its charge to protect a racially and ethnically divided major city), but more recent decisions have rejected race-consciousness, *see Rothe Dev. Corp. v. DOD*, 545 F.3d 1023, 1040 (Fed. Cir. 2008); *Alexander v. Milwaukee*, 474 F.3d 437 (7th Cir. 2007). That may be in part because *Grutter/Fisher II* seem of uncertain application in most employment settings. *See Lomack v. City of Newark*, 463 F.3d 303, 309 (3d Cir. 2006) ("While *Grutter* established that educational benefits are compelling *in a law school context*, we do not find its holding applicable in the firefighting context.") (emphasis in original). *See generally* Rebecca Hanner White, *Affirmative Action in the Workplace: The Significance of* Grutter?, 92 Ky. L.J. 263 (2003). *See also* Michael J. Yelnosky, *The Prevention Justification for Affirmative Action*, 64 Ohio St. L.J. 1385, 1387 (2003).

All of these cases involved race, but what about sex? The employer in *Johnson* was a public employer. If *Johnson* returned to the Supreme Court as a case raising the constitutional question of affirmative action based on sex, what standard would apply? While governmental racial classifications are subject to strict scrutiny, sex classifications are subject to more relaxed review, *United States v. Virginia*, 518 U.S. 515 (1996), at least in theory. *But see H.B. Rowe Co., Inc. v. Tippett*, 615 F.3d 233, 257 (4th Cir. 2010) (approving contracting preferences for African Americans and Native Americans but striking down such preferences for Hispanics, Asians, and women).

Chapter 3

Systemic Disparate Impact Discrimination

In contrast to disparate treatment, disparate impact discrimination has no intent requirement: it applies to employment practices that adversely affect one group more than another and cannot be adequately justified. This chapter presents the structure of disparate impact analysis, the policies subject to disparate impact analysis, and defenses to a disparate impact case.

define

As we will see, the disparate impact theory applies under Title VII of the Civil Rights Act of 1964 and the Americans with Disabilities Act (ADA). It also operates, albeit in a considerably diluted form, under the Age Discrimination in Employment Act (ADEA), but it is *not* available under 42 U.S.C. §1981 (2018), *General Bldg. Contractors Ass'n v. Pennsylvania*, 458 U.S. 375 (2002), or under 42 U.S.C. §1983 (2018) in suits enforcing the Equal Protection Clause of the United States Constitution, *e.g.*, *Washington v. Davis*, 426 U.S. 229 (1976).

A. THE CONCEPT OF DISPARATE IMPACT DISCRIMINATION

GRIGGS v. DUKE POWER CO.
401 U.S. 424 (1971)

Chief Justice BURGER delivered the opinion of the Court.

We granted the writ in this case to resolve the question whether an employer is prohibited by the Civil Rights Act of 1964, Title VII, from requiring a high school education or passing of a standardized general intelligence test as a condition of employment in or transfer to jobs when (a) neither standard is shown to be significantly related to successful job performance, (b) both requirements operate to disqualify Negroes at a substantially higher rate than white applicants, and (c) the jobs in question formerly had been filled only by white employees as part of a longstanding practice of giving preference to whites. . . .

All the petitioners are employed at the Company's Dan River Steam Station, a power generating facility located at Draper, North Carolina. At the time this action was instituted, the Company had 95 employees at the Dan River Station, 14 of whom were Negroes; 13 of these are petitioners here.

The District Court found that prior to July 2, 1965, the effective date of the Civil Rights Act of 1964, the company openly discriminated on the basis of race in the hiring and assigning of employees at its Dan River plant. The plant was organized into five operating departments: (1) Labor, (2) Coal Handling, (3) Operations, (4) Maintenance, and (5) Laboratory and Test. Negroes were employed only in the Labor Department where the highest paying jobs paid less than the lowest paying jobs in the other four "operating" departments in which only whites were employed. Promotions were normally made within each department on the basis of job seniority. Transferees into a department usually began in the lowest position.

In 1955 the Company instituted a policy of requiring a high school education for initial assignment to any department except Labor, and for transfer from the Coal Handling to any "inside" department (Operations, Maintenance, or Laboratory). When the Company abandoned its policy of restricting Negroes to the Labor Department in 1965, completion of high school also was made a prerequisite to transfer from Labor to any other department. From the time the high school requirement was instituted to the time of trial, however, white employees hired before the time of the high school education requirement continued to perform satisfactorily and achieve promotions in the "operating" departments. Findings on this score are not challenged.

The Company added a further requirement for new employees on July 2, 1965, the date on which Title VII became effective. To qualify for placement in any but the Labor Department it became necessary to register satisfactory scores on two professionally prepared aptitude tests, as well as to have a high school education. Completion of high school alone continued to render employees eligible for transfer to the four desirable departments from which Negroes had been excluded if the incumbent had been employed prior to the time of the new requirement. In September 1965 the Company began to permit incumbent employees who lacked a high school education to qualify for transfer from Labor or Coal Handling to an "inside" job by passing two tests — the Wonderlic Personnel Test, which purports to measure general intelligence, and the Bennett Mechanical Comprehension Test. Neither was directed or intended to measure the ability to learn to perform a particular job or category of jobs. The requisite scores used for both initial hiring and transfer approximated the national median for high school graduates.[3]

The District Court had found that while the Company previously followed a policy of overt racial discrimination in a period prior to the Act, such conduct had ceased. . . .

The Court of Appeals noted . . . that the District Court was correct in its conclusion that there was no showing of a racial purpose or invidious intent in the adoption of the high school diploma requirement or general intelligence test and that these standards had been applied fairly to whites and Negroes alike. It held that, in the absence of

---

3. The test standards are thus more stringent than the high school requirement, since they would screen out approximately half of all high school graduates.

a discriminatory purpose, use of such requirements was permitted by the Act. In so doing, the Court of Appeals rejected the claim that because these two requirements operated to render ineligible a markedly disproportionate number of Negroes, they were unlawful under Title VII unless shown to be job related. . . .

The objective of Congress in the enactment of Title VII is plain from the language of the statute. It was to achieve equality of employment opportunities and remove barriers that have operated in the past to favor an identifiable group of white employees over other employees. Under the Act, practices, procedures, or tests neutral on their face, and even neutral in terms of intent, cannot be maintained if they operate to "freeze" the status quo of prior discriminatory employment practices.

The Court of Appeals' [judges] agreed that, on the record in the present case, "whites register far better on the Company's alternative requirements" than Negroes.[6] This consequence would appear to be directly traceable to race. Basic intelligence must have the means of articulation to manifest itself fairly in a testing process. Because they are Negroes, petitioners have long received inferior education in segregated schools and this Court expressly recognized these differences in *Gaston County v. United States*, 395 U.S. 285 (1969). There, because of the inferior education received by Negroes in North Carolina, this Court barred the institution of a literacy test for voter registration on the ground that the test would abridge the right to vote indirectly on account of race. Congress did not intend by Title VII, however, to guarantee a job to every person regardless of qualifications. In short, the Act does not command that any person be hired simply because he was formerly the subject of discrimination, or because he is a member of a minority group. Discriminatory preference for any group, minority or majority, is precisely and only what Congress has proscribed. What is required by Congress is the removal of artificial, arbitrary, and unnecessary barriers to employment when the barriers operate invidiously to discriminate on the basis of a racial or other impermissible classification.

Congress has now provided that tests or criteria for employment or promotion may not provide equality of opportunity merely in the sense of the fabled offer of milk to the stork and the fox. On the contrary, Congress has now required that the posture and condition of the job-seeker be taken into account. It has — to resort again to the fable — provided that the vessel in which the milk is proffered be one all seekers can use. The Act proscribes not only overt discrimination but also practices that are fair in form, but discriminatory in operation. The touchstone is business necessity. If an employment practice which operates to exclude Negroes cannot be shown to be related to job performance, the practice is prohibited.

On the record before us, neither the high school completion requirement nor the general intelligence test is shown to bear a demonstrable relationship to successful performance of the jobs for which it was used. Both were adopted, as the Court of Appeals noted, without meaningful study of their relationship to job-performance ability. Rather, a vice president of the Company testified, the requirements were instituted on the Company's judgment that they generally would improve the overall quality of the work force.

6. In North Carolina, 1960 census statistics show that, while 34% of white males had completed high school, only 12% of Negro males had done so. U.S. Bureau of the Census, U.S. Census of Population: 1960, Vol. 1, Characteristics of the Population, pt. 35, Table 47. Similarly, with respect to standardized tests, the EEOC in one case found that use of a battery of tests, including the Wonderlic and Bennett tests used by the Company in the instant case, resulted in 58% of whites passing the tests as compared with only 6% of the blacks. Decision of EEOC, CCH Empl. Prac. Guide, para. 17,304.53 (Dec. 2, 1966). See also Decision of EEOC 70-552, CCH Empl. Prac. Guide, para. 6139 (Feb. 19, 1970).

people not meeting 2 criteria do just fine @ job

intent doesn't matter in disparate impact cases

evid suff: to relationship to job performance

The evidence, however, shows that employees who have not completed high school or taken the tests have continued to perform satisfactorily and make progress in departments for which the high school and test criteria are now used. The promotion record of present employees who would not be able to meet the new criteria thus suggests the possibility that the requirements may not be needed even for the limited purpose of preserving the avowed policy of advancement within the Company. In the context of this case, it is unnecessary to reach the question whether testing requirements that take into account capability for the next succeeding position or related future promotion might be utilized upon a showing that such long-range requirements fulfill a genuine business need. In the present case the Company has made no such showing.

The Court of Appeals held that the Company had adopted the diploma and test requirements without any "intention to discriminate against Negro employees." We do not suggest that either the District Court or the Court of Appeals erred in examining the employer's intent; but good intent or absence of discriminatory intent does not redeem employment procedures or testing mechanisms that operate as "built-in headwinds" for minority groups and are unrelated to measuring job capability.

The Company's lack of discriminatory intent is suggested by special efforts to help the undereducated employees through Company financing of two-thirds the cost of tuition for high school training. But Congress directed the thrust of the Act to the *consequences* of employment practices, not simply the motivation. More than that, Congress has placed on the employer the burden of showing that any given requirement must have a manifest relationship to the employment in question.

The facts of this case demonstrate the inadequacy of broad and general testing devices as well as the infirmity of using diplomas or degrees as fixed measures of capability. History is filled with examples of men and women who rendered highly effective performance without the conventional badges of accomplishment in terms of certificates, diplomas, or degrees. Diplomas and tests are useful servants, but Congress has mandated the common sense proposition that they are not to become masters of reality.

The Company contends that its general intelligence tests are specifically permitted by §703(h) of the Act.[8] That section authorizes the use of "any professionally developed ability test" that is not "designed, intended or *used* to discriminate because of race. . . ." (Emphasis added.)

The Equal Employment Opportunity Commission, having enforcement responsibility, has issued guidelines interpreting Section 703(h) to permit only the use of job-related tests.[9] The administrative interpretation of the Act by the enforcing agency

---

8. Section 703(h) applies only to tests. It has no applicability to the high school diploma requirement.
9. EEOC Guidelines on Employment Testing Procedures, issued August 24, 1966, provide:

The Commission accordingly interprets "professionally developed ability test" to mean a test which fairly measures the knowledge or skills required by the particular job or class of jobs which the applicant seeks, or which fairly affords the employer a chance to measure the applicant's ability to perform a particular job or class of jobs. The fact that a test was prepared by an individual or organization claiming expertise in test preparation does not, without more, justify its use within the meaning of Title VII.

The EEOC position has been elaborated in the new Guidelines on Employee Selection Procedures, 29 C.F.R. §1607, 35 Fed. Reg. 12333 (Aug. 1, 1970). These guidelines demand that employers using tests have available "data demonstrating that the test is predictive of or significantly correlated with important elements of work behavior which comprise or are relevant to the job or jobs for which candidates are being evaluated." *Id.*, at §1607.4(c).

is entitled to great deference. Since the Act and its legislative history support the Commission's construction, this affords good reason to treat the guidelines as expressing the will of Congress.

Section 703(h) was not contained in the House version of the Civil Rights Act but was added in the Senate during extended debate. For a period, debate revolved around claims that the bill as proposed would prohibit all testing and force employers to hire unqualified persons simply because they were part of a group formerly subject to job discrimination. Proponents of Title VII sought throughout the debate to assure the critics that the Act would have no effect on job-related tests. Senators Case of New Jersey and Clark of Pennsylvania, co-managers of the bill on the Senate floor, issued a memorandum explaining that the proposed Title VII "expressly protects the employer's right to insist that any prospective applicant, Negro or white, *must meet the applicable job qualifications*. Indeed, the very purpose of Title VII is to promote hiring on the basis of job qualifications, rather than on the basis of race or color." 110 Cong. Rec. 7247.[11] (Emphasis added.) Despite these assurances, Senator Tower of Texas introduced an amendment authorizing "professionally developed ability tests." Proponents of Title VII opposed the amendment because, as written, it would permit an employer to give any test, "whether it was a good test or not, so long as it was professionally designed. Discrimination could actually exist under the guise of compliance with the statute." 110 Cong. Rec. 13504 (remarks of Sen. Case).

The amendment was defeated and two days later Senator Tower offered a substitute amendment which was adopted verbatim and is now the testing provision of §703(h). Speaking for the supporters of Title VII, Senator Humphrey, who had vigorously opposed the first amendment, endorsed the substitute amendment, stating: "Senators on both sides of the aisle who were deeply interested in Title VII have examined the text of this amendment and have found it to be in accord with the intent and purpose of that title." 110 Cong. Rec. 13724. The amendment was then adopted. From the sum of the legislative history relevant in this case, the conclusion is inescapable that the EEOC's construction of §703(h) to require that employment tests be job related comports with congressional intent.

[handwritten: employment tests must be job-related]

Nothing in the Act precludes the use of testing or measuring procedures; obviously they are useful. What Congress has forbidden is giving these devices and mechanisms controlling force unless they are demonstrably a reasonable measure of job performance. Congress has not commanded that the less qualified be preferred over the better qualified simply because of minority origins. Far from disparaging job qualifications as such, Congress has made such qualifications the controlling factor, so that race, religion, nationality, and sex become irrelevant. What Congress has commanded is that any tests used must measure the person for the job and not the person in the abstract. . . . *[handwritten: these tests are measuring the person in the abstract]*

[handwritten: cannot be arbitrary]

11. The Court of Appeals majority, in finding no requirement in Title VII that employment tests be job related, relied in part on a quotation from an earlier Clark-Case interpretive memorandum [which allowed an employer to "set his qualifications as high as he likes," and test for "which applicants have these qualifications." The Court found this consistent with the "later memorandum dealing specifically with employer testing." That was because the first memorandum spoke in terms of "using tests that determine *qualifications*" and a "*reasonable* interpretation of what the Senators meant, in light of the subsequent memorandum directed specifically at employer testing, was that nothing in the Act prevents employers from requiring that applicants be fit for the job]."

NOTES

PF

1. *The* Griggs *"Structure."* The Court's approach to the structure of a disparate impact case seems reasonably clear. If a selection device — in *Griggs*, the high school diploma credential and passing two standardized tests — has a greater adverse impact on African American workers than on whites, see footnote 6, they are presumptively impermissible. Nevertheless, the defendant can prevail by justifying these selection devices, although in *Griggs* itself Duke Power had not shown that the requirements measured the ability to perform the jobs in question, and thus their use violated Title VII: "The touchstone is business necessity. If an employment practice which operates to exclude Negroes cannot be shown to be related to job performance, the practice is prohibited." *See generally* ROBERT BELTON, THE CRUSADE FOR EQUALITY IN THE WORK- PLACE: THE *Griggs v. Duke Power* STORY (Stephen L. Wasby ed., 2014).

2. *"Tests" vs. Other Employer Practices.* The diploma requirement is, presumably, subject to this straightforward analysis. The Wonderlic and Bennett tests, however, introduce a twist because of §703(h), which permits any "professionally developed ability test" that is not "designed, intended or *used* to discriminate because of race" (emphasis added). Look at the EEOC test Guidelines in footnote 9, which we'll explore further at p. 219. Do they suggest that "business necessity" is especially hard to show in that context? By the way, the *Griggs* Court accorded the EEOC's testing guidelines "great deference," but we'll see that that overstates a relatively complex relationship between courts and the Commission. See Note on Deference to the EEOC, Chapter 7 at p. 506.

3. *The Scope of Practices Subject to the Disparate Impact Theory.* The early dispa- rate impact cases before the Supreme Court, like *Griggs*, all involved "standardized employment tests or criteria," such as written tests, height and weight requirements, and a rule against employing drug addicts. *Watson v. Fort Worth Bank & Trust*, 487 U.S. 977, 988 (1988), addressed whether subjective employment practices were also subject to the disparate impact theory. Because "our decisions in *Griggs* and succeed- ing cases could largely be nullified if disparate impact analysis were applied only to standardized selection practices," the Court concluded that "subjective or discretion- ary employment practices may be analyzed under the disparate impact approach in appropriate cases." *Id.* at 989.

Watson seemed to be a high-water mark for disparate impact since the range of the theory had been expanded to cover all employment practices. However, in a part of her opinion that was joined only by a plurality, Justice O'Connor tempered her expan- sion of the theory by recasting *Griggs* in a manner that substantially weakened it. A majority of the Court adopted that approach the next year.

WARDS COVE PACKING CO. v. ATONIO
490 U.S. 642 (1989)

Justice WHITE delivered the opinion of the Court.

. . . I

The claims before us are disparate-impact claims, involving the employment prac- tices of petitioners, two companies that operate salmon canneries in remote and widely separated areas of Alaska. The canneries operate only during the salmon runs in the summer months. They are inoperative and vacant for the rest of the year. In May or

June of each year, a few weeks before the salmon runs begin, workers arrive and prepare the equipment and facilities for the canning operation. Most of these workers possess a variety of skills. When salmon runs are about to begin, the workers who will operate the cannery lines arrive, remain as long as there are fish to can, and then depart. The canneries are then closed down, winterized, and left vacant until the next spring. . . .

Jobs at the canneries are of two general types: "cannery jobs" on the cannery line, which are unskilled positions; and "noncannery jobs," which fall into a variety of classifications. Most noncannery jobs are classified as skilled positions. Cannery jobs are filled predominantly by nonwhites: Filipinos and Alaska Natives. The Filipinos are hired through, and dispatched by, Local 37 of the International Longshoremen's and Warehousemen's Union pursuant to a hiring hall agreement with the local. The Alaska Natives primarily reside in villages near the remote cannery locations. Noncannery jobs are filled with predominantly white workers, who are hired during the winter months from the companies' offices in Washington and Oregon. Virtually all of the noncannery jobs pay more than cannery positions. The predominantly white noncannery workers and the predominantly nonwhite cannery employees live in separate dormitories and eat in separate mess halls.

In 1974, respondents, a class of nonwhite cannery workers who were (or had been) employed at the canneries, brought this Title VII action against petitioners. Respondents alleged that a variety of petitioners' hiring/promotion practices — e.g., nepotism, a rehire preference, a lack of objective hiring criteria, separate hiring channels, a practice of not promoting from within — were responsible for the racial stratification of the work force and had denied them and other nonwhites employment as noncannery workers on the basis of race. Respondents also complained of petitioners' racially segregated housing and dining facilities. . . .

II

In holding that respondents had made out a prima facie case of disparate impact, the Court of Appeals relied solely on respondents' statistics showing a high percentage of nonwhite workers in the cannery jobs and a low percentage of such workers in the noncannery positions. Although statistical proof can alone make out a prima facie case, the Court of Appeals' ruling here misapprehends our precedents and the purposes of Title VII, and we therefore reverse.

"There can be no doubt," as there was when a similar mistaken analysis had been undertaken by the courts below in *Hazelwood*, "that the . . . comparison . . . fundamentally misconceived the role of statistics in employment discrimination cases." The "proper comparison [is] between the racial composition of [the at-issue jobs] and the racial composition of the qualified . . . population in the relevant labor market." It is such a comparison — between the racial composition of the qualified persons in the labor market and the persons holding at-issue jobs — that generally forms the proper basis for the initial inquiry in a disparate impact case. Alternatively, in cases where such labor market statistics will be difficult if not impossible to ascertain, we have recognized that certain other statistics — such as measures indicating the racial composition of "otherwise-qualified applicants" for at-issue jobs — are equally probative for this purpose. See, e.g., *New York City Transit Authority v. Beazer*, 440 U.S. 568 (1979).[6]

---

6. In fact, where "figures for the general population might . . . accurately reflect the pool of qualified job applicants," we have even permitted plaintiffs to rest their prima facie cases on such statistics as well. See, e.g., *Dothard v. Rawlinson*.

It is clear to us that the Court of Appeals' acceptance of the comparison between the racial composition of the cannery work force and that of the noncannery work force, as probative of a prima facie case of disparate impact in the selection of the latter group of workers, was flawed for several reasons. Most obviously, with respect to the skilled non-cannery jobs at issue here, the cannery work force in no way reflected "the pool of *qualified* job applicants" or the *"qualified* population in the labor force." Measuring alleged discrimination in the selection of accountants, managers, boat captains, electricians, doctors, and engineers — and the long list of other "skilled" noncannery positions found to exist by the District Court, by comparing the number of nonwhites occupying these jobs to the number of nonwhites filling cannery worker positions is nonsensical. If the absence of minorities holding such skilled positions is due to a dearth of qualified non-white applicants (for reasons that are not petitioners' fault), petitioners' selection methods or employment practices cannot be said to have had a "disparate impact" on nonwhites.

One example illustrates why this must be so. Respondents' own statistics concerning the noncannery work force at one of the canneries at issue here indicate that approximately 17% of the new hires for medical jobs, and 15% of the new hires for officer worker positions, were nonwhite. If it were the case that less than 15 to 17% of the applicants for these jobs were nonwhite and that nonwhites made up a lower percentage of the relevant qualified labor market, it is hard to see how respondents, without more, would have made out a prima facie case of disparate impact. Yet, under the Court of Appeals' theory, simply because nonwhites comprise 52% of the cannery workers at the cannery in question respondents would be successful in establishing a prima facie case of racial discrimination under Title VII.

Such a result cannot be squared with our cases or with the goals behind the statute. The Court of Appeals' theory, at the very least, would mean that any employer who had a segment of his work force that was — for some reason — racially imbalanced, could be haled into court and forced to engage in the expensive and time-consuming task of defending the "business necessity" of the methods used to select the other members of his work force. The only practicable option for many employers would be to adopt racial quotas, insuring that no portion of their work forces deviated in racial composition from the other portions thereof; this is a result that Congress expressly rejected in drafting Title VII. See 42 U.S.C. §2000e-2(j). . . .

The Court of Appeals also erred with respect to the unskilled noncannery positions. Racial imbalance in one segment of an employer's work force does not, without more, establish a prima facie case of disparate impact with respect to the selection of workers for the employer's other positions, even where workers for the different positions may have somewhat fungible skills (as is arguably the case for cannery and unskilled noncannery workers). As long as there are no barriers or practices deterring qualified nonwhites from applying for noncannery positions, if the percentage of selected applicants who are nonwhite is not significantly less than the percentage of qualified applicants who are nonwhite, the employer's selection mechanism probably does not operate with a disparate impact on minorities.[8] Where this is the case,

---

8. We qualify this conclusion — observing that it is only "probable" that there has been no disparate impact on minorities in such circumstances — because bottom-line racial balance is not a defense under Title VII. See *Connecticut v. Teal*, 457 U.S. 440 (1982) [reproduced at p. 189]. Thus, even if petitioners could show that the percentage of selected applicants who are nonwhite is not significantly less than the percentage of qualified applicants who are nonwhite, respondents would still have a case under Title VII, if they could prove that some particular hiring practice has a disparate impact on minorities, notwithstanding the bottom-line racial balance in petitioners' work force.

the percentage of nonwhite workers found in other positions in the employer's labor force is irrelevant to the question of a prima facie statistical case of disparate impact. As noted above, a contrary ruling on this point would almost inexorably lead to the use of numerical quotas in the workplace, a result that Congress and this Court have rejected repeatedly in the past.

Moreover, isolating the cannery workers as the potential "labor force" for unskilled noncannery positions is at once both too broad and too narrow in its focus. It is too broad because the vast majority of these cannery workers did not seek jobs in unskilled noncannery positions; there is no showing that many of them would have done so even if none of the arguably "deterring" practices existed. Thus, the pool of cannery workers cannot be used as a surrogate for the class of qualified job applicants because it contains many persons who have not (and would not) be noncannery job applicants. Conversely, if respondents propose to use the cannery workers for comparison purposes because they represent the "qualified labor population" generally, the group is too narrow because there are obviously many qualified persons in the labor market for noncannery jobs who are not cannery workers. . . .

Consequently, we reverse the Court of Appeals' ruling that a comparison between the percentage of cannery workers who are nonwhite and the percentage of noncannery workers who are nonwhite makes out a prima facie case of disparate impact. . . .

III

Since the statistical disparity relied on by the Court of Appeals did not suffice to make out a prima facie case, any inquiry by us into whether the specific challenged employment practices of petitioners caused that disparity is pretermitted, as is any inquiry into whether the disparate impact that any employment practice may have had was justified by business considerations.[9] Because we remand for further proceedings, however, on whether a prima facie case of disparate impact has been made in defensible fashion in this case, we address two other challenges petitioners have made to the decision of the Court of Appeals.

A

First is the question of causation in a disparate-impact case. The law in this respect was correctly stated by Justice O'Connor's opinion last Term in *Watson v. Fort Worth Bank & Trust* [requiring the plaintiff to "isolate[e] and identify[]] the specific employment practices that are allegedly responsible for any observed statistical disparities."

. . . Our disparate-impact cases have always focused on the impact of *particular* hiring practices on employment opportunities for minorities. Just as an employer cannot escape liability under Title VII by demonstrating that, "at the bottom line," his work force is racially balanced (where particular hiring practices may operate to deprive minorities of employment opportunities), *see Connecticut v. Teal*, a Title VII plaintiff

---

9. As we understand the opinions below, the specific employment practices were challenged only insofar as they were claimed to have been responsible for the overall disparity between the number of minority cannery and noncannery workers. The Court of Appeals did not purport to hold that any specified employment practice produced its own disparate impact that was actionable under Title VII. This is not to say that a specific practice, such as nepotism, if it were proved to exist, could not itself be subject to challenge if it had a disparate impact on minorities. Nor is it to say that segregated dormitories and eating facilities in the workplace may not be challenged under 42 U.S.C. §2000e-2(a)(2) without showing a disparate impact on hiring or promotion.

does not make out a case of disparate impact simply by showing that, "at the bottom line," there is racial imbalance in the work force. As a general matter, a plaintiff must demonstrate that it is the application of a specific or particular employment practice that has created the disparate impact under attack. Such a showing is an integral part of the plaintiff's prima facie case in a disparate-impact suit under Title VII.

Here, respondents have alleged that several "objective" employment practices (e.g., nepotism, separate hiring channels, rehire preferences), as well as the use of "subjective decision making" to select noncannery workers, have had a disparate impact on nonwhites. Respondents base this claim on statistics that allegedly show a disproportionately low percentage of nonwhites in the at-issue positions. However, even if on remand respondents can show that nonwhites are underrepresented in the at-issue jobs in a manner that is acceptable under the standards set forth above, this alone will not suffice to make out a prima facie case of disparate impact. Respondents will also have to demonstrate that the disparity they complain of is the result of one or more of the employment practices that they are attacking here, specifically showing that each challenged practice has a significantly disparate impact on employment opportunities for whites and nonwhites. To hold otherwise would result in employers being potentially liable for "the myriad of innocent causes that may lead to statistical imbalances in the composition of their work forces." *Watson.* . . .

B

If, on remand, respondents meet the proof burdens outlined above, and establish a prima facie case of disparate impact with respect to any of petitioners' employment practices, the case will shift to any business justification petitioners offer for their use of these practices. This phase of the disparate-impact case contains two components: first, a consideration of the justifications an employer offers for his use of these practices; and second, the availability of alternative practices to achieve the same business ends, with less racial impact. *See, e.g., Albemarle Paper Co. v. Moody.* We consider these two components in turn.

(1)

Though we have phrased the query differently in different cases, it is generally well established that at the justification stage of such a disparate-impact case, the dispositive issue is whether a challenged practice serves, in a significant way, the legitimate employment goals of the employer. The touchstone of this inquiry is a reasoned review of the employer's justification for his use of the challenged practice. A mere insubstantial justification in this regard will not suffice, because such a low standard of review would permit discrimination to be practiced through the use of spurious, seemingly neutral employment practices. At the same time, though, there is no requirement that the challenged practice be "essential" or "indispensable" to the employer's business for it to pass muster: this degree of scrutiny would be almost impossible for most employers to meet, and would result in a host of evils we have identified above.

. . . We acknowledge that some of our earlier decisions can be read as suggesting otherwise. But to the extent that those cases speak of an employers' "burden of proof" with respect to a legitimate business justification defense, they should have been understood to mean an employer's production — but not persuasion — burden. The persuasion burden here must remain with the plaintiff, for it is he who must prove that it was "because of such individual's race, color," etc., that he was denied a desired employment opportunity. See 42 U.S.C. §2000e-2(a).

(2)

Finally, if on remand the case reaches this point, and respondents cannot persuade the trier of fact on the question of petitioners' business necessity defense, respondents may still be able to prevail. To do so, respondents will have to persuade the factfinder that "other tests or selection devices, without a similarly undesirable racial effect, would also serve the employer's legitimate [hiring] interest[s]"; by so demonstrating, respondents would prove that "[petitioners were] using [their] tests merely as a 'pretext' for discrimination." *Albemarle Paper Co.; see also Watson.* If respondents, having established a prima facie case, come forward with alternatives to petitioners' hiring practices that reduce the racially disparate impact of practices currently being used, and petitioners refuse to adopt these alternatives, such a refusal would belie a claim by petitioners that their incumbent practices are being employed for nondiscriminatory reasons.

Of course, any alternative practices which respondents offer up in this respect must be equally effective as petitioners' chosen hiring procedures in achieving petitioners' legitimate employment goals. Moreover, "[f]actors such as the cost or other burdens of proposed alternative selection devices are relevant in determining whether they would be equally as effective as the challenged practice in serving the employer's legitimate business goals." *Watson.* "Courts are generally less competent than employers to structure business practices," *Furnco Construction Corp. v. Waters,* 438 U.S. 567 (1978); consequently, the judiciary should proceed with care before mandating that an employer must adopt a plaintiff's alternative selection or hiring practice in response to a Title VII suit. . . .

[Justice Stevens, joined by Justice Brennan, Justice Marshall, and Justice Blackmun, dissented, being especially critical of what they saw as the Court's dilution of business necessity by shifting the burden of persuasion of lack of business necessity back to plaintiffs and placing only a burden of production on employers.]

NOTES

1. Wards Cove *Remakes* Griggs. The *Wards Cove* majority remodeled disparate impact law (1) by requiring a highly focused showing that *particular* employment practices caused a disparate impact; (2) by reducing the employer's rebuttal obligations from a showing of job-relatedness and business necessity to "a reasoned review of the employer's justification"; and (3) by redefining the rebuttal stage to involve a burden of production, not of persuasion. It also reformulated an element added in *Albemarle Paper Co. v. Moody* — a final surrebuttal step that allows plaintiffs to win if they can show an "alternative practice" to the one challenged. After *Wards Cove,* disparate impact law looked more like individual disparate treatment law as set forth in *McDonnell Douglas v. Green,* though still without an intent to discriminate element.

2. *What's the Rationale for the Disparate Impact Theory?* Can you figure out the underlying basis for the theory? A number of possibilities exist.

(a) Smoke Out Animus. The *Wards Cove* Court's remaking of disparate impact law in the image of disparate treatment may have been driven by the majority's view that disparate impact is justified as attacking intentional but unprovable discrimination, the problem of the "discreet discriminator" we encountered earlier. *Griggs* itself can be viewed as precisely such a case: despite the district court's finding of no intent to

discriminate, the new selection criteria may have been adopted to effectively continue the prior formal exclusion of blacks from the better jobs.

(b) *Redress Unconscious Bias.* Perhaps relatedly, disparate impact could be justified as addressing the problems of unconscious bias. Justice O'Connor in *Watson* had noted that "even if one assumed that any such discrimination can be adequately policed through disparate treatment analysis, the problem of subconscious stereotypes and prejudices would remain." 487 U.S. at 990. And the Court in *Texas Department of Housing & Community Affairs v. Inclusive Cmtys. Project, Inc.*, 135 S. Ct. 2507, 2511-12 (2014), a case considering disparate impact under the Fair Housing Act, noted that the theory "plays an important role in uncovering discriminatory intent: it permits plaintiffs to counteract unconscious prejudices and disguised animus that escape easy classification as disparate treatment." *See generally* Charles A. Sullivan, *Disparate Impact: Looking Past the* Desert Palace *Mirage*, 47 Wm. & Mary L. Rev. 911 (2005) (disparate impact offers an opportunity to explicitly weigh the necessity of current practices that are shown to enable bias).

(c) *Remedy De Jure Discrimination.* A more limited rationale emerges from the *Griggs* Court's reference to racial segregation in North Carolina, where Duke Power was located. However, other cases applied disparate impact to the gender context, *e.g.*, *Dothard v. Rawlinson*, 433 U.S. 321 (1977) (height and weight minimum subject to disparate impact attack by women), thus establishing that the theory was neither confined to de jure segregation nor limited to racial discrimination.

(d) *Protect Subordinated Groups.* These cases, however, suggest a more expansive justification that would look at not just de jure discrimination as in *Griggs*, but to a history of discrimination and subordination of the group in question. In *Dothard v. Rawlinson*, while women's shorter stature and lower weight as compared to men were not the result of discrimination, women had a long history of legal and societal subordination that might justify removing unnecessary barriers to their advancement. *See* Julie Chi-hye Suk, *Antidiscrimination Law in the Administrative State*, 2006 U. Ill. L. Rev. 405; Stacy E. Seicshnaydre, *Is the Road to Disparate Impact Paved with Good Intentions? — Stuck on State of Mind in Antidiscrimination Law*, 42 Wake Forest L. Rev. 1141 (2007). *Texas Department of Housing & Community Affairs v. Inclusive Cmtys. Project, Inc.*, 135 S. Ct. 2507, 2521-22 (2014), affirms this approach, albeit in the context of the Fair Housing Act. It approved of the theory not just as dealing with unconscious and covert motivations but also as a mechanism to deal with arbitrary barriers. But the case also suggested some potential limitations on the theory. See Note 8, p. 195.

(e) *Maximize Individual "Capabilities."* Nobel economist Amertya Sen, in The Idea of Justice (2009), defines justice as systematically maximizing the capabilities of all. Is that the ultimate justification for disparate impact? If so, isn't it closely related to protecting subordinated groups? *See also* Professor Paulette Caldwell, *Reaffirming the Disproportionate Effects Standard of Liability in Title VII Litigation*, 46 U. Pitt. L. Rev. 555 (1985). Is this what Chief Justice Burger meant when he wrote in *Griggs* that "[h]istory is filled with examples of men and women who rendered highly effective performance without the conventional badges of accomplishment in terms of certificates, diplomas, and degrees"?

3. *Losing Its Normative Way?* While all these approaches provide justifications for disparate impact, they progressively depart from the strong normative force underlying Title VII. As "discrimination" moves along a spectrum from animus to conscious intent to unconscious intent to antisubordination to expanding labor pools, its moral force becomes progressively weaker. While the statute can be justified even if the discrimination is simply a form of negligence, see pp. 9-10, some have argued that

the attenuated way in which such theories define discrimination undercuts Title VII's legitimacy.

4. *Clash Between Disparate Treatment and Disparate Impact.* Whatever the underlying justifications, is the disparate impact theory at odds with the basic premise of antidiscrimination legislation — because members of protected groups are indistinguishable from similarly situated members of the majority, they ought not be treated differently in the workplace? Skin color does not make a worker less effective, nor does advancing age necessarily make her less efficient. While group differences may exist, disparate treatment ignores those differences and focuses instead on members of the protected group who are similarly situated to other individuals.

In contrast, impact analysis is dependent on differences between and among the groups. Individuals will be entitled to a remedy precisely because they are members of a group that is different. The impact approach, however, does not abandon the equality principle that similarly situated individuals should be treated equally. The business necessity defense is designed to permit the employer to rely on differences between employees when those differences are relevant to the job. Employers are prohibited only from considering differences not related to job performance. Thus, for purposes of qualifying for work, the underlying premise remains true: protected group members should be treated equally when their work qualifications are the same.

5. *Identifying the Practice That Produces the Impact.* The *Wards Cove* Court lists some practices that plaintiffs were challenging: "nepotism, a rehire preference, a lack of objective hiring criteria, separate hiring channels, a practice of not promoting from within." All but the last two seem unrelated to the different racial composition of the cannery and noncannery jobs. The employer's practices of using separate hiring channels, segregating the workers hired in the separate channels, and not promoting from cannery to noncannery jobs produced the impact. Therefore, one practice that should have been the focus was failing to recruit for the unskilled noncannery jobs from the same sources — the union hiring hall and the local areas close to the canneries — that the defendants used to hire for the unskilled cannery jobs. For unskilled noncannery jobs, a court could find that the failure to recruit from the heavily minority sources for the cannery jobs was a specific employment practice that had a disparate impact.

6. *Causation and Disparate Impact.* Ramona L. Paetzold & Steven L. Willborn, in *Deconstructing Disparate Impact: A View of the Model Through New Lenses,* 74 N.C. L. REV. 325, 356 (1995), argue that the plaintiff in a disparate impact case need not prove actual causation:

> [D]isparate impact cases . . . [do] not require that the plaintiff prove that the employer's criterion has actually produced a disparate impact in the workplace. In *Griggs*, for example, the same disparate impact on blacks may have occurred even if the employer had not utilized the high school diploma requirement. Employees applying for the jobs at issue in *Griggs* also had to attain a certain score on a general "intelligence" test that approximated the national median score for high school graduates. Blacks as a class may have suffered from the same (or even a greater) disparate impact as a result of the test requirement. The disparate impact model as applied in *Griggs*, then, did not require any proof that the criterion at issue actually produced a disparate impact; it merely required proof that the criterion at issue would have screened out protected class members disproportionately if applied independently of any other factors at play in the selection process.

7. *Disparate Impact and the "Q" Word.* *Wards Cove* generated a national controversy about the continued viability of the disparate impact theory that was ultimately resolved by the enactment of the Civil Rights Act of 1991. While that statute also

overrode other Supreme Court decisions that Congress viewed as cutting back on civil rights protection, the focus of the debate was on "quotas," *Wards Cove*, and the appropriate structure of the disparate impact theory. During the debates, proponents argued that a strong impact theory was needed to open up job opportunities to minorities and women. Opponents vociferously claimed that disparate impact would result in quotas by encouraging employers to hire minorities and women, without regard to qualifications, merely to avoid potential liability. Did *Griggs* encourage quota hiring? The research suggests not, but also questions the effectiveness of the theory in encouraging hiring of underrepresented groups. *See* Paul E. Oyer & Scott Schaefer, *The Unintended Consequences of the '91 Civil Rights Act*, 26 REGULATION 42 (2003); Paul Oyer & Scott Schaefer, *Sorting, Quotas, and the Civil Rights Act of 1991: Who Hires When It's Hard to Fire?*, 45 J.L. & ECON. 41 (2002); Ian Ayres & Peter Siegelman, *The Q-Word as Red Herring: Why Disparate Impact Liability Does Not Induce Hiring Quotas*, 74 TEX. L. REV. 1487 (1996).

NOTE ON DISPARATE IMPACT UNDER THE ADEA

For most of its history, it was unclear whether the Age Discrimination in Employment Act incorporated a disparate impact theory. However, the Supreme Court ultimately handed down two decisions establishing that such claims were viable under the ADEA, albeit in a diluted form. *Smith v. City of Jackson*, 544 U.S. 228, 232 (2005), held that "the ADEA does authorize recovery in 'disparate-impact' cases comparable to *Griggs*," although it found against plaintiffs on the facts. The case arose when police officers claimed that salary increases violated the statute "because they were less generous to officers over the age of 40 than to younger officers." *Id.* at 239. While all officers received raises designed to bring up salaries to competitive levels, those with less than five years of tenure received proportionately greater raises, and most older officers had longer service.

In a portion of the opinion written by Justice Stevens and joined only by three other Justices, the plurality looked to the similarity of the language of the ADEA and Title VII for their result since "when Congress uses the same language in two statutes having similar purposes, particularly when one is enacted shortly after the other, it is appropriate to presume that Congress intended that text to have the same meaning in both statutes." *Id.* at 233. The language of both laws "prohibits such actions that 'deprive any individual of employment opportunities or *otherwise adversely affect* his status as an employee, because of such individual's'" protected characteristic (emphasis in original). *Id.* at 235. This "focuses on the *effects* of the action on the employee rather than the motivation for the action of the employer." *Id.* at 236 (emphasis in original). Thus, *Griggs* "strongly suggests that a disparate-impact theory should be cognizable under the ADEA." *Id.* at 236.

The ADEA also has a provision — without any parallel in Title VII — that declares it permissible for an employer "to take any action otherwise prohibited under subsection (a) . . . where the differentiation is based on reasonable factors other than age discrimination . . . ." 29 U.S.C. §623(f). For Stevens, the RFOA would be pure surplusage if the ADEA could be violated only by disparate treatment since there would be no violation in the first place "if the employer in fact acted on a factor other than age." *Id.* at 238. It is precisely in disparate impact cases that "the RFOA provision plays its principal role by precluding liability if the adverse impact was attributable to a non-age factor that was 'reasonable.'" *Id.* at 239. Justice Scalia agreed with the plurality's analysis, but he would have preferred to rest that result on deference to the EEOC's interpretation of this effect since "[t]his is an absolutely classic case for deference to agency interpretation." *Id.* at 243.

Why? lc of expertise?

However, in a portion of the opinion joined by five Justices, the Court stressed that two textual differences between the ADEA and Title VII rendered "the scope of disparate-impact liability under ADEA . . . narrower than under Title VII." *Id.* at 240. The first was the RFOA, which reflected Congress's belief that "age, unlike race or other classifications protected by Title VII, not uncommonly has relevance to an individual's capacity to engage in certain types of employment." *Id.* As a result, "it is not surprising that certain employment criteria that are routinely used may be reasonable despite their adverse impact on older workers as a group." *Id.* at 241. The second textual difference was the 1991 Civil Rights Act's amendment to Title VII modifying the Court's holding in *Wards Cove.* Since the Act did not amend the ADEA, "*Wards Cove*'s pre-1991 interpretation of Title VII's identical language remains applicable to the ADEA." *Id.* at 240.

It was this latter point that proved fatal to the plaintiffs' claim since they had "not identified any specific test, requirement, or practice within the pay plan that has an adverse impact on older workers." *Id.* at 241. In any event, the City's plan was justified by reasonable factors other than age since any "disparate impact is attributable to the City's decision to give raises based on seniority and position [and r]eliance on seniority and rank is unquestionably reasonable given the City's goal of raising employees' salaries to match those in surrounding communities." *Id.* at 242.

City of Jackson left somewhat confused the relationship between the *Wards Cove* business necessity and the RFOA defenses. *Meacham v. Knolls Atomic Power Laboratory,* 554 U.S. 84 (2008), clarified the point by holding that the RFOA displaced business necessity under the ADEA. This paved the way for *Meacham*'s second holding, which was to find the RFOA to be an affirmative defense. Therefore, an employer planning to defend a disparate impact claim on the basis of the RFOA "must not only produce evidence raising the defense, but also persuade the factfinder of its merit." *Id.* at 87.

RFOA is an affirmative defense. ADEA replaced "business necessity" in ADEA

However, what makes a factor "reasonable" remains largely undefined. Is it that it serves the employer's legitimate goals? In a significant way? And what about alternative business practices? Is a practice nevertheless "reasonable" if it serves legitimate goals even though another equally effective alternative would also do so? Depending on the answer to these kinds of questions, it is unclear how significant shifting the burden of persuasion will be to the outcome in many cases. The EEOC has since promulgated regulations to clarify the meaning of the RFOA defense. 29 C.F.R. §1625.7 (2018). *See generally* Judith J. Johnson, *Reasonable Factors Other Than Age: The Emerging Specter of Ageist Stereotypes,* 33 SEATTLE U. L. REV. 49 (2009).

define reasonable?

City of Jackson was trumpeted by some as a victory for plaintiffs and as creating serious problems for employers. But the Court applied the *Wards Cove* version of disparate impact to the ADEA, and *Wards Cove* was pretty unanimously viewed as a defeat for plaintiffs because it freed employers from some of the strictures of *Griggs.* In the years since, it seems clear that the latter is the more accurate view.

Although *Smith* approved disparate impact suits, it arguably did so only for those within §623(a)(2), which bars actions against "employees" that "would deprive or tend to deprive" them of job opportunities. In contrast, §623(1)(2) bars discrimination against any "individual," but it lacks the "tend to" language. Some cases prior to *Smith* accordingly recognized the disparate impact theory as available in suits by employees but not in those brought by applicants. In a post-*Smith* case, the divided en banc Eleventh Circuit held that job applicants could not bring disparate impact claims under the ADEA. *Villarreal v. R.J. Reynolds Tobacco Co.*, 839 F.3d 958 (11th Cir. 2016). Relying on the textual distinction between "employees" and "individuals," the court rejected textual arguments to the contrary raised by the dissent and refused to consider legislative history or defer to the EEOC's contrary interpretation.

As for application of the doctrine, *City of Jackson* avoided an in-depth analysis of the disparate impact claim because it found the plaintiffs to have not identified a particular employment practice causing the impact. But that seems odd: modeling compensation on the pay of competing employers seems like a specific practice. How could the plaintiffs have done better? *See also Allen v. Highlands Hosp. Corp.*, 545 F.3d 387, 404 (6th Cir. 2008) (plaintiffs failed to establish that the employer's desire to reduce personnel costs "evolved into an identifiable practice that disproportionately harms" older workers). In any event, it's not so clear that compensation and benefits are the kind of employment practice that should be subject to disparate impact attack. In *Finnegan v. Trans World Air Lines, Inc.*, 967 F.2d 1161 (7th Cir. 1992), the court viewed changes in fringe benefits as not susceptible to impact analysis: any percentage reduction in compensation or certain types of fringe benefits, such as the vacation pay in *Finnegan*, will necessarily impact workers differently when they are paid at different levels. Paying older workers the same dollar amount will tend to give them lower percentage raises since they are generally higher paid. Is the employer required to use equal percentage wage increases (and therefore higher dollar amounts) to avoid causing disparate impact on older workers? Does that make sense even though it would be legal under that statute? See p. 44. *See also* Jonah B. Gelbach, Jonathan Klick & Lesley Wexler, *Passive Discrimination: When Does It Make Sense to Pay Too Little?*, 76 U. CHI. L. REV. 797 (2009) (arguing that it is difficult to regulate employer use of fringe benefit structures that tend to sort employees by race and sex when such groups systematically differ in their preferences).

Regardless of whether a plaintiff can make out a prima facie impact case, *City of Jackson* does not bode well for her on the employer's justification. After *Meacham*, it is clear that the right doctrine is "RFOA," but *Smith* approved the defendant's reliance on the salary structures of other employers in fashioning its own compensation structure. Is that because it was a normal way for employers to operate? That didn't work in *Griggs*! Or because it was "obviously" necessary for Jackson to compete for police officers?

One problem peculiar to disparate impact under the ADEA is whether the plaintiff must show an impact on the entire over-40 group or whether it is sufficient to demonstrate that a particular subgroup, say, employees over 60, is disproportionately impacted. Earlier courts rejected subgroup analysis, *see, e.g., EEOC v. McDonnell Douglas Corp.*, 191 F.3d 948 (8th Cir. 1999), but a recent Third Circuit case creates a circuit split. *Karlo v. Pittsburgh Glass Works, LLC*, 849 F.3d 61 (3d Cir. 2017) (allowing a disparate impact claim where the subgroup was at the upper end of the protected range).] *See generally* Sandra F. Sperino, *The Sky Remains Intact: Why Allowing Subgroup Evidence Is Consistent with the Age Discrimination in Employment Act*, 90 MARQ. L. REV. 227 (2006).

B.   DISPARATE IMPACT LAW AFTER THE 1991 CIVIL RIGHTS ACT

Section 703(k) was added to Title VII by the 1991 Amendments to provide a statutory basis for disparate impact law. It is a complex provision that legislatively overrules much of *Wards Cove* while simultaneously codifying some of its analysis. Section 703(k)(1) sets forth the current rules for plaintiff's proof:

> (A) An unlawful employment practice based on disparate impact is established under this title only if —
>
> (i) a complaining party demonstrates that a respondent uses a particular employment practice that causes a disparate impact on the basis of race, color, religion, sex, or national origin and the respondent fails to demonstrate that the challenged practice is job related for the position in question and consistent with business necessity; or
>
> (ii) the complaining party makes the demonstration described in subparagraph (C) with respect to an alternative employment practice and the respondent refuses to adopt such alternative employment practice.
>
> (B)(i) With respect to demonstrating that a particular employment practice causes a disparate impact as described in subparagraph (A)(i), the complaining party shall demonstrate that each particular challenged employment practice causes a disparate impact, except that if the complaining party can demonstrate to the court that the elements of a respondent's decisionmaking process are not capable of separation for analysis, the decisionmaking process may be analyzed as one employment practice.
>
> (ii) If the respondent demonstrates that a specific employment practice does not cause the disparate impact, the respondent shall not be required to demonstrate that such practice is required by business necessity.

[handwritten margin note: Severability of discriminatory practices?]

As was discussed in Chapter 1, §701(m) defines "demonstrates" as carrying the burden of production and persuasion.

1. Plaintiff's Proof of a Prima Facie Case

a. A Particular Employment Practice

Section 703(k)(1)(A)(i) states the general rule for a disparate impact case by accepting part of *Wards Cove*: the plaintiff carries the burden of persuasion that the employer "uses a particular employment practice that causes disparate impact on the basis of race, color, religion, sex, or national origin." This embraces two questions that arose before the 1991 Amendments: (1) is every employment-related action of an employer a qualifying "employment practice"?, and (2) how does a plaintiff establish that a disparate impact resulted from a "particular" practice as opposed to a congeries of causes? The former question was addressed by the next principal case, and the latter by *Wards Cove*.

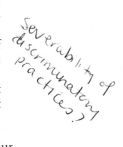

[handwritten margin note: 1. what qualifies as a practice vs an action? 2. how does P particularize the practice sufficiently]

[handwritten note: subjective or discretionary employment practices maybe analyzed under disparate impact theory → objective or subjective ok]

WATSON v. FORT WORTH BANK & TRUST
487 U.S. 977 (1988)

Justice O'CONNOR announced the judgment of the Court [and delivered its opinion with respect to the portions reproduced below]:

. . . I

Petitioner Clara Watson, who is black, was hired by respondent Fort Worth Bank and Trust (the Bank) as a proof operator in August 1973. In January 1976, Watson was promoted to a position as teller in the Bank's drive-in facility. In February 1980, she sought to become supervisor of the tellers in the main lobby; a white male, however, was selected for this job. Watson then sought a position as supervisor of the drive-in bank, but this position was given to a white female. In February 1981, after Watson had served for about a year as a commercial teller in the Bank's main lobby, and informally as assistant to the supervisor of tellers, the man holding that position was promoted. Watson applied for the vacancy, but the white female who was the supervisor of the drive-in bank was selected instead. Watson then applied for the vacancy created at the drive-in; a white male was selected for that job. The Bank, which has about 80 employees, had not developed precise and formal criteria for evaluating candidates for the positions for which Watson unsuccessfully applied. It relied instead on the subjective judgment of supervisors who were acquainted with the candidates and with the nature of the jobs to be filled. All the supervisors involved in denying Watson the four promotions at issue were white. . . .

were these different positions lateral moves or promotions in their own right?

II

A

. . . This Court has repeatedly reaffirmed the principle that some facially neutral employment practices may violate Title VII even in the absence of a demonstrated discriminatory intent. We have not limited this principle to cases in which the challenged practice served to perpetuate the effects of pre-Act intentional discrimination. Each of our subsequent decisions, however, like *Griggs* itself, involved standardized employment tests or criteria [including tests, height and weight requirements, and a rule against employing drug addicts]. In contrast, we have consistently used conventional disparate treatment theory, in which proof of intent to discriminate is required, to review hiring and promotion decisions that were based on the exercise of personal judgment or the application of inherently subjective criteria. *See, e.g., McDonnell Douglas Corp. v. Green.* . . .

Our decisions have not addressed the question whether disparate impact analysis may be applied to cases in which subjective criteria are used to make employment decisions. . . .

new combo

B . . .

We are persuaded that our decisions in *Griggs* and succeeding cases could largely be nullified if disparate impact analysis were applied only to standardized selection practices. . . .

We are also persuaded that disparate impact analysis is in principle no less applicable to subjective employment criteria than to objective or standardized tests. In either case, a facially neutral practice, adopted without discriminatory intent, may have effects that are indistinguishable from intentionally discriminatory practices. It is true, to be sure, that an employer's policy of leaving promotion decisions to the unchecked discretion of lower level supervisors should itself raise no inference of discriminatory conduct. Especially in relatively small businesses like respondent's, it may be customary and quite reasonable simply to delegate employment decisions to those employees who are most familiar with the jobs to be filled and with the candidates for those jobs. It does not follow, however, that the particular supervisors to whom this discretion is delegated always act without discriminatory intent. Furthermore, even if one assumed that any such discrimination can be adequately policed through disparate treatment analysis, the problem of subconscious stereotypes and prejudices would remain. In this case, for example, petitioner was apparently told at one point that the teller position was a big responsibility with "a lot of money . . . for blacks to have to count." Such remarks may not prove discriminatory intent, but they do suggest a lingering form of the problem that Title VII was enacted to combat. If an employer's undisciplined system of subjective decisionmaking has precisely the same effects as a system pervaded by impermissible intentional discrimination, it is difficult to see why Title VII's proscription against discriminatory actions should not apply. In both circumstances, the employer's practices may be said to "adversely affect [an individual's] status as an employee, because of such individual's race, color, religion, sex, or national origin." 42 U.S.C. §2000e-2(a)(2). We conclude, accordingly, that subjective or discretionary employment practices may be analyzed under the disparate impact approach in appropriate cases.

[Since the lower court had not evaluated the statistical evidence to determine if a prima facie disparate impact case was made out, the case was remanded with the caution that "[i]t may be that the relevant data base is too small to permit any meaningful statistical analysis . . . ."]

Rationale

Holding

NOTES

1. *Employer Practices Subject to Disparate Impact.* Section 703(k) apparently codifies *Watson*'s extension of disparate impact to both objective and subjective practices insofar as it applies to "a particular employment practice" without qualification as to the practice's objective or subjective characteristics. However, *Wards Cove* required that a plaintiff show a causal connection between the particular policy identified and the racial imbalance shown, and the amended statute codifies that requirement. *See Cooper v. Southern Co.*, 390 F.3d 695, 726 (11th Cir. 2004) (the plaintiffs "failed to demonstrate a causal nexus between any statistical disparities in the defendants' workforce and the practice of using partially subjective hiring criteria by some managers in some of the defendants' facilities"). In addition, a plaintiff cannot challenge an identified policy unless she was herself injured by it. *E.g., Welch v. Eli Lilly & Co.*, 585 F. App'x 911, 913 (7th Cir. 2014).

Standing issue?

2. *Retreating from* Watson? We saw in *Wal-Mart Stores, Inc. v. Dukes*, reproduced at p. 113, that the Court cast doubt on the use of systemic disparate treatment to attack Wal-Mart's practice of granting unstructured and unreviewed discretion to store managers to make pay and promotion decisions. Turning to disparate impact, Justice Scalia did acknowledge the possibility of a class action challenge, but stressed the necessity of plaintiffs' identifying a "specific employment practice":

> In the landmark case of ours [*Watson*] which held that giving discretion to lower-level supervisors can be the basis of Title VII liability under a disparate-impact theory, the plurality opinion conditioned that holding on the corollary that merely proving that the discretionary system has produced a racial or sexual disparity *is not enough.* "[T]he plaintiff must begin by identifying the specific employment practice that is challenged." That is all the more necessary when a class of plaintiffs is sought to be certified. Other than the bare existence of delegated discretion, respondents have identified no "specific employment practice" — much less one that ties all their 1.5 million claims together. Merely showing that Wal-Mart's policy of discretion has produced an overall sex-based disparity does not suffice.

564 U.S. at 357. Do you understand why a policy of delegated discretion is not an "employment practice" for purposes of establishing a disparate impact claim?

Justice Ginsburg's *Wal-Mart* dissent stressed that, in *Watson*, while four different supervisors rejected the plaintiff's repeated attempts to be promoted to a number of different job openings, the Court permitted her claim based on a disparate impact theory. Would Watson have been precluded from bringing a class action claiming disparate impact discrimination even though the Court upheld her individual claim of disparate impact discrimination? In other words, is *Wal-Mart* only about class action law and not about disparate impact law?

If a potential client asks you to represent her because her employer, a large company, had a policy of giving discretion to lower-level managers who had exercised that discretion by denying her attempts to be promoted and that the use by managers of that discretion had an adverse impact on women, would you advise her that:

1. Subjective employment decisions made pursuant to a policy allowing discretion cannot be challenged using disparate impact theory;
2. Subjective employment decisions made pursuant to a policy allowing discretion can be challenged in an individual disparate impact case but not in a class action; or
3. A company policy authorizing the use of subjective decisionmaking by managers insulates the decisions of those managers from challenge under any systemic theory of discrimination?

3. *Affirmative vs. Negative Practices.* In *EEOC v. Chicago Miniature Lamp Works*, 947 F.2d 292 (7th Cir. 1991), the employer relied on "word-of-mouth" recruitment by incumbent workers to fill job openings. Citing *Wards Cove*, the court reversed the finding of disparate impact liability.

> The EEOC does not allege that Miniature affirmatively engaged in word-of-mouth recruitment of the kind where it told or encouraged its employees to refer applicants for entry-level jobs. Instead, it is uncontested that Miniature passively waited for applicants who typically learned of opportunities from current Miniature employees. The court erred in considering passive reliance on employee word-of-mouth recruiting as a particular employment practice for the purposes of disparate impact. The practices here are undertaken solely by employees. Therefore, disparate impact liability against Miniature must be reversed.

Perhaps the Seventh Circuit has reconsidered. In *DeClue v. Central Ill. Light Co.*, 223 F.3d 434 (7th Cir. 2000), the employer's failure to provide restroom facilities for its employees was found to have a disparate impact on women. Would that have fallen within a "passivity" exception?

4. *Choice of Labor Market as a Particular Practice.* Is an employer's use of a particular labor market to recruit workers a particular employment practice within the general rule of §703(k)(1)(A)(i)? Lower courts have found such practices to be subject to disparate impact attack. In *NAACP, Newark Branch v. Town of Harrison*, 940 F.2d 792 (3d Cir. 1991), the town's residents-only rule had a disparate impact because Harrison was almost exclusively white, while adjacent areas, such as Newark, were predominately black. In short, Harrison had defined a geographic labor market, but the plaintiff challenged that very definition as creating an adverse impact.

5. *Subjective Employment Practices.* In a portion of her opinion in *Watson* joined by only a plurality of the Court, Justice O'Connor expressed concern that "validating" subjective employment criteria could prove to be nearly impossible:

Some qualities — for example, common sense, good judgment, originality, ambition, loyalty, and tact — cannot be measured accurately through standardized testing techniques. Moreover, success at many jobs in which such qualities are crucial cannot itself be measured directly. Opinions often differ when managers and supervisors are evaluated, and the same can be said for many jobs that involve close cooperation with one's co-workers or complex and subtle tasks like the provision of professional services or personal counseling. Because of these difficulties, we are told, employers will find it impossible to eliminate subjective selection criteria and impossibly expensive to defend such practices in litigation.

487 U.S. at 991-92. For O'Connor, this was not fatal to applying disparate impact because she would have simultaneously diluted the business necessity defense, as a majority later did in *Wards Cove*. After §703(k), however, this problem clearly exists. Do you think that that explains the reluctance of some courts to apply disparate impact? Does it explain *Wal-Mart? See also Morgan v. UPS of Am., Inc.*, 380 F.3d 459, 465 n.2 (8th Cir. 2004) (finding it "difficult to understand" a challenge to a subjective decisionmaking process as one of disparate impact).

6. *Pleading a Disparate Impact Case.* With the coming of "plausibility" pleading, see Note on Litigating Individual Disparate Treatment Cases, p. 33, the question arises as to what a plaintiff must plead to state a plausible claim of disparate impact. *See Adams v. City of Indianapolis*, 742 F.3d 720, 733 (7th Cir. 2014) (complaint properly dismissed for failure to allege facts showing that the city's testing process caused a disparity between black and white applicants for promotion). *See generally* Joseph A. Seiner, *Plausibility and Disparate Impact*, 64 HASTINGS L. REV. 287 (2013).

7. *New Structuralism and Debiasing Subjectivity.* Assume that on remand in *Watson* the court found that the practice of relying on subjective supervisor evaluations had a disparate impact on African Americans. How could the employer go about proving that the practice was job related and consistent with business necessity? Must it prove that the employer had made a reasonable effort to structure the exercise of that subjective decisionmaking to minimize the possibility that bias, either conscious or unconscious, could enter the system? Professor Susan Sturm, in *Second Generation Employment Discrimination: A Structural Approach*, 101 COLUM. L. REV. 458, 485-90 (2001), argues for an inquiry into "whether the degree of unaccountable or unstructured exercise of discretion is warranted," which in turn requires examining available alternatives to "minimize the expression of bias." Consistent with this approach, in *Malave v. Potter*, 320 F.3d 321 (2d Cir. 2003), the plaintiff successfully relied on the disparate impact theory to attack the employer's subjective promotion practices as contaminated with favoritism, friendship, and ethnic loyalty.

Professor Tristin Green, although agreeing with Professor Sturm about the employer's responsibility to minimize bias in individual decisions, doubts that disparate impact theory is capable of supporting the inquiry needed for change. She argues that the problem is not the use of identifiable subjective criteria per se, such as "friendliness" or "leadership ability," which may indeed be job related and justified by business necessity, but rather with the application of such criteria: "[r]ather than requiring the elimination of the practice itself, we need to begin exploring the ways in which employers can be held accountable for managing diversity within modern structures and practices to minimize the operation of discriminatory bias." *Discrimination in Workplace Dynamics: Toward a Structural Account of Disparate Treatment Theory*, 38 HARV. C.R.-C.L. L. REV. 91, 142-43 (2002). These theories may fit better into the systemic disparate treatment paradigm than into disparate impact, although they can perhaps best be described as urging a new conceptualization of discrimination rather than being shoehorned into any existing paradigm.

8. *Volitional Exception?* Some cases seem to recognize a "volitional exception" to disparate impact discrimination, sometimes formulated as an employee duty to make reasonable efforts to qualify. *See generally* Peter Siegelman, *Contributory Disparate Impacts in Employment Law*, 49 Wm. & Mary L. Rev. 515, 568 (2007). The core notion is that some employer requirements ought not to be subject to disparate impact analysis because employees or applicants can, more or less easily, conform their conduct to the requirement. The classic example is *Garcia v. Spun Steak Co.*, 998 F.2d 1480, 1483 (9th Cir. 1993), in which the employer required its bilingual employees to speak only English on the job. Although the rule fell more harshly on employees of Mexican origin than others, the Ninth Circuit found it immune from disparate impact attack. Bilingual employees could comply with the rule and thus could avoid discipline.

A volitional exception is more or less problematic depending on what conduct is defined as volitional, but it is scarcely well established. *Spun Steak* was decided before the 1991 Amendments, but a post-Act decision, *Lanning v. SEPTA*, 308 F.3d 286 (3d Cir. 2002), revived the notion. In that case, employment as a transit police officer was dependent upon each candidate running 1.5 miles within 12 minutes. Although the requirement had a disparate impact on female applicants, the Third Circuit upheld the policy, in part because nearly all women would be able to pass after only a moderate amount of training. The court did not think it unreasonable to expect women to train prior to applying; doing so, the court said, would demonstrate their commitment to the job. Obviously, this suggests some version of a volitional exception to disparate impact analysis.

9. *Disparate Impact and Hostile Environment.* In *Maldonado v. City of Altus*, 433 F.3d 1294, 1304-05 (10th Cir. 2006), the court faced a challenge by Hispanic workers to an English-only rule. In contrast to *Spun Steak*, see Note 8, the focus of this attack on an English-only policy was predicated on the hostile work environment that the policy allegedly generated. See Chapter 5 for a full discussion of hostile environment law. The court reversed summary judgment for the defendant on both disparate treatment and disparate impact grounds. As to the latter,

> [t]he policy itself, and not just the effect of the policy in evoking hostility by co-workers [of which plaintiffs had produced evidence], may create or contribute to the hostility of the work environment. A policy requiring each employee to wear a badge noting his or her religion, for example, might well engender extreme discomfort in a reasonable employee who belongs to a minority religion, even if no co-worker utters a word on the matter. Here, the very fact that the City would forbid Hispanics from using their preferred language could reasonably be construed as an expression of hostility to Hispanics. At least that could be a reasonable inference if there was no apparent legitimate purpose for the restrictions. . . . The less the apparent justification for mandating English, the more reasonable it is to infer hostility toward employees whose ethnic group or nationality favors another language. For example, Plaintiffs presented evidence that the English-only policy extended beyond its written terms to include lunch hours, breaks, and even private telephone conversations, if non-Spanish-speaking co-workers were nearby. Absent a legitimate reason for such a restriction, the inference of hostility may be reasonable.

Is the point that this is a disparate impact case because, although the policy makers had no intent to discriminate, adverse consequences would follow, at least if co-workers were reasonable, even if wrong, in inferring hostility by those in charge?

[handwritten margin note: bottom-line defense okay not]

CONNECTICUT v. TEAL
457 U.S. 440 (1982)

[handwritten margin note: Title VII cares about the individual's opportunity]

Justice BRENNAN delivered the opinion of the Court.

We consider here whether an employer sued for violation of Title VII of the Civil Rights Act of 1964 may assert a "bottom line" theory of defense. Under that theory, as asserted in this case, an employer's acts of racial discrimination in promotions — effected by an examination having disparate impact — would not render the employer liable for the racial discrimination suffered by employees barred from promotion if the "bottom line" result of the promotional process was an appropriate racial balance. We hold that the "bottom line" does not preclude respondent-employees from establishing a prima facie case, nor does it provide petitioner-employer with a defense to such a case.

[handwritten margin note: Holding]

Four of the respondents, Winnie Teal, Rose Walker, Edith Latney, and Grace Clark, are black employees of the Department of Income Maintenance of the State of Connecticut. Each was promoted provisionally to the position of Welfare Eligibility Supervisor and served in that capacity for almost two years. To attain permanent status as supervisors, however, respondents had to participate in a selection process that required, as the first step, a passing score on a written examination. This written test was administered . . . to 329 candidates. Of these candidates, 48 identified themselves as black and 259 identified themselves as white. . . . With the passing score set at 65,[3] 54.17 percent of the identified black candidates passed. This was approximately 68 percent of the passing rate for the identified white candidates. The four respondents were among the blacks who failed the examination, and they were thus excluded from further consideration for permanent supervisory positions. . . .

[handwritten margin note: Qs: is employer arguing that its test doesn't matter that impact be the selection process for those who pass is generous to black applicants? Also, confused about the focus on the individual in a disparate impact theme that focuses on the greater protected class]

[The state later] made promotions from the eligibility list generated by the written examination. In choosing persons from that list, petitioners considered past work performance, recommendations of the candidates' supervisors and, to a lesser extent, seniority. Petitioners then applied what the Court of Appeals characterized as an affirmative action program in order to ensure a significant number of minority supervisors. Forty-six persons were promoted to permanent supervisory positions, 11 of whom were black and 35 of whom were white. The overall result of the selection process was that, of the 48 identified black candidates who participated in the selection process, 22.9 percent were promoted and of the 259 identified white candidates, 13.5 percent were promoted. It is this "bottom-line" result, more favorable to blacks than to whites, that petitioners urge should be adjudged to be a complete defense to respondents' suit. . . .

[handwritten margin note: arg/defense re: bottom line theory - it was using an affirmative action policy, more favorable to black candidates so it should be a complete defense]

II

A

. . . The suggestion that disparate impact should be measured only at the bottom line ignores the fact that Title VII guarantees these individual respondents the *opportunity* to compete equally with white workers on the basis of job-related criteria [as provided in §703(a)(2)]. Title VII strives to achieve equality of opportunity by rooting out "artificial, arbitrary and unnecessary" employer-created barriers to professional development that have a discriminatory impact upon individuals. Therefore,

---

3. The mean score on the examination was 70.4 percent. However, because the black candidates had a mean score 6.7 percentage points lower than the white candidates, the passing score was set at 65, apparently in an attempt to lessen the disparate impact of the examination.

respondents' rights under §703(a)(2) have been violated, unless petitioners can demonstrate that the examination given was not an artificial, arbitrary, or unnecessary barrier, because it measured skills related to effective performance in the role of Welfare Eligibility Supervisor. . . .

III

Having determined that respondents' claim comes within the terms of Title VII, we must address the suggestion of petitioners and some *amici curiae* that we recognize an exception, either in the nature of an additional burden on plaintiffs seeking to establish a prima facie case or in the nature of an affirmative defense, for cases in which an employer has compensated for a discriminatory pass-fail barrier by hiring or promoting a sufficient number of black employees to reach a nondiscriminatory "bottom line." We reject this suggestion, which is in essence nothing more than a request that we redefine the protections guaranteed by Title VII.

Section 703(a)(2) prohibits practices that would deprive or tend to deprive "*any individual* of employment opportunities." The principal focus of the statute is the protection of the individual employee, rather than the protection of the minority group as a whole. Indeed, the entire statute and its legislative history are replete with references to protection for the individual employee.

In suggesting that the "bottom line" may be a defense to a claim of discrimination against an individual employee, petitioners and *amici* appear to confuse unlawful discrimination with discriminatory intent. The Court has stated that a nondiscriminatory "bottom line" and an employer's good faith efforts to achieve a nondiscriminatory work force, might in some cases assist an employer in rebutting the inference that particular action had been intentionally discriminatory: "Proof that [a] work force was racially balanced or that it contained a disproportionately high percentage of minority employees is not wholly irrelevant on the issue of intent when that issue is yet to be decided." *Furnco Construction Corp. v. Waters. See also Teamsters v. United States,* n.20. But resolution of the factual question of intent is not what is at issue in this case. Rather, petitioners seek simply to justify discrimination against respondents, on the basis of their favorable treatment of other members of respondents' racial group. Under Title VII, "A racially balanced work force cannot immunize an employer from liability for specific acts of discrimination." *Furnco Construction Corp. v. Waters.* . . .

It is clear that Congress never intended to give an employer license to discriminate against some employees on the basis of race or sex merely because he favorably treats other members of the employees' group. We recognized in *Los Angeles Dept. of Water & Power v. Manhart* [reproduced at p. 94], that fairness to the class of women employees as a whole could not justify unfairness to the individual female employee because the "statute's focus on the individual is unambiguous." . . .

Petitioners point out that [cases such as *Furnco* and *Manhart*] involved facially discriminatory policies, while the claim in the instant case is one of discrimination from a facially neutral policy. The fact remains, however, that irrespective of the form taken by the discriminatory practice, an employer's treatment of other members of the plaintiffs' group can be "of little comfort to the victims of . . . discrimination." *Teamsters v. United States.* Title VII does not permit the victim of a facially discriminatory policy to be told that he has not been wronged because other persons of his or her race or sex were hired. That answer is no more satisfactory when it is given to victims of a policy that is facially neutral but practically discriminatory. Every *individual* employee is protected against both discriminatory treatment and against "practices that are fair in form, but discriminatory in operation." *Griggs*. Requirements and tests that have a discriminatory impact are merely some of the more subtle, but also the more pervasive, of the "practices and devices which have fostered racially stratified job environments to the disadvantage of minority citizens." *McDonnell Douglas Corp.* . . .

   Justice POWELL, with whom The Chief Justice, Justice REHNQUIST, and Justice O'CONNOR join, dissenting.
   . . . Although [the language of §703(a)(2)] suggests that discrimination occurs only on an individual basis, . . . our disparate impact cases consistently have considered whether the result of an employer's *total selection process* had an adverse impact upon the protected group. If this case were decided by reference to the total process — as our cases suggest that it should be — the result would be clear. Here 22.9 percent of the blacks who entered the selection process were ultimately promoted, compared with only 13.5 percent of the whites. To say that this selection process had an unfavorable "disparate impact" on blacks is to ignore reality.
   [While "the aim of Title VII is to protect individuals, not groups," its goals are achieved by "two distinct methods of proof." The disparate impact theory] invites the plaintiff to prove discrimination by reference to the group rather than to the allegedly affected individual. There can be no violation of Title VII on the basis of disparate impact in the absence of disparate impact on a *group*.
   In this case the plaintiff seeks to benefit from a conflation of "discriminatory treatment" and "disparate impact" theories. But he cannot have it both ways. Having undertaken to prove discrimination by reference to one set of group figures (used at a preliminary point in the selection process), the plaintiff then claims that *non*discrimination cannot be proved by viewing the impact of the entire process on the group as a whole. The fallacy of this reasoning — accepted by the Court — is transparent. It is to confuse the individualistic *aim* of Title VII with the methods of proof by which Title VII rights may be vindicated. The respondent, as an individual, is entitled to the full personal protection of Title VII. But, having undertaken to prove a violation of his rights by reference to group figures, respondent cannot deny petitioner the opportunity to rebut his evidence by introducing figures of the same kind. Having pleaded a disparate impact case, the plaintiff cannot deny the defendant the opportunity to show that there was no disparate impact. . . .

III

   Today's decision takes a long and unhappy step in the direction of confusion. . . . By its holding today, the Court may force employers either to eliminate tests or rely on expensive, job-related, testing procedures, the validity of which may or may not be sustained if challenged. For state and local governmental employers with limited funds, the practical effect of today's decision may well be the adoption of simple quota hiring.[8] . . . This arbitrary method of employment is itself unfair to individual

   8. Another possibility is that employers may integrate consideration of test results into one overall hiring decision based on that "factor" *and* additional factors. Such a process would not, even under the Court's reasoning, result in a finding of discrimination on the basis of disparate impact unless the actual hiring decisions had a disparate impact on the minority group. But if employers integrate test results into a single-step decision, they will be free to select *only* the number of minority candidates proportional to their representation in the work force. If petitioner had used this approach, it would have been able to hire substantially fewer blacks without liability on the basis of disparate impact. The Court hardly could have intended to encourage this.

applicants, whether or not they are members of minority groups. And it is not likely to produce a competent workforce. Moreover, the Court's decision actually may result in employers employing *fewer* minority members [by discouraging voluntary affirmative action plans].

NOTES

1. *The Employment Practice Plaintiffs Challenged.* The plaintiffs had successfully performed the job that they sought but lost their positions when they failed a civil service test used to fill the job permanently. Since the test knocked them out of further consideration in the selection process, its use was the practice that plaintiffs challenged. The data on the racial impact of the test was clear. In a sense, this is simply a *Griggs* case; the twist is that this test was part of a multistep selection process. The only question was whether the fact that, at the end of the process, African Americans did not experience any negative impact was significant, though that fact would be small comfort to the plaintiffs who lost their jobs. *Teal* permits an attack on any practice with an identifiable impact and, just as importantly, renders a nondiscriminatory bottom line no defense to the impact of a particular practice.

2. *Hoist with Their Own Petard? Teal* was a victory for the plaintiffs, and the "liberal" wing of the Court was in the majority in allowing a challenge to a particular practice. But in *Wards Cove*, the plaintiffs lost because they focused on the bottom line and could not identify a particular practice that caused the impact. The "conservative" wing was in the ascendancy. How could the same principle cut so severely both ways? Maybe the majority in *Teal* believed that the plaintiffs could have their cake and eat it, too; that is, they could focus on any stage in the selection process or the bottom line, wherever there was an impact. After *Wards Cove*, however, plaintiffs could challenge only the effects of a particular employment practice. Bottom-line results were, presumably, subject to attack only under systemic disparate treatment.

3. *Multicomponent Selection Processes Under §703(k).* The 1991 Amendments struck a compromise between the extremes marked out by *Teal* and *Wards Cove*. The term "particular employment practice" in §703(k) suggests the necessity of separating multicomponent selection processes into their individual parts. But the section also allows a disparate impact attack on the "bottom line" result of the process if the data are not available to analyze the separate parts of the process. Thus, §703(k)(1)(B) normally requires the plaintiff to show that "each particular challenged employment practice" causes an impact. However, it creates an exception when "the complaining party can demonstrate to the court that the elements of [an employer's] decisionmaking process cannot be separated for analysis"; in that event, "the decisionmaking process may be analyzed as one employment practice." Thus, the plaintiffs in *Teal* could use the general rule of new §703(k) because the data concerning the racial impact of the test were available. If that data were unavailable and if there was no disparate impact on blacks at the end of the selection process, then these plaintiffs would now be out of luck. But, if, at the end of the process, there was impact, even though the source of that impact could not be identified, the plaintiff would then have a "bottom line" case — that is, the plaintiff could establish liability by showing that the proportion of women or minority men who were successful getting through the selection process was lower than for white males.

4. *Incapable of Separation for Analysis.* The employer in *Teal* used a sequential, multistep procedure: passing the test was a condition for being considered at the next

level, and the "particular employment practice" of new §703(k)(1)(B) deals with these situations. In the last footnote of his dissent in *Teal*, however, Justice Powell suggested that disparate impact attack could be avoided by integrating the test into a single, but multifactored, decision. Under his view, the bottom line would then become the only focus. Presumably to deal with such situations, §703(k)(1)(B)'s language about processes "not capable of separation for analysis" allows attacks on the "bottom line." And that section explicitly puts the burden of showing such incapability on the plaintiff.

However, all the data concerning the selection process will be maintained by the employer. An employer who resists discovery may well provide the plaintiff with "incapable of being separated for analysis" on a silver platter. This also should be true if the employer simply doesn't preserve the data. But if full information is turned over, the question of "separation for analysis" is likely to depend on the plaintiff's expert testimony. *See Chin v. Port Auth. of N.Y. & N.J.*, 685 F.3d 135, 154-55 (2d Cir. 2012) (while a promotion process formally involved three steps, the first two steps could not be separated from the rest for statistical analysis since both played an indeterminate role); *McClain v. Lufkin Indus.*, 519 F.3d 264, 279 (5th Cir. 2008) (no error in analyzing several employment practices as one where the seniority system and the treatment of absenteeism were subject to considerable managerial discretion).

5. *Employer Defenses to Bottom-Line Proof.* Whenever a plaintiff makes out a case of disparate impact, the defendant may defend by carrying the burden of persuasion that (1) the practices that do cause an impact are justified as job related and consistent with business necessity; or (2) those practices fall within the §703(h) defenses. If, however, plaintiff uses the "incapable of separation for analysis" avenue, §703(k)(1)(B)(ii) provides the employer another defense: "[i]f the respondent demonstrates that a specific employment practice does not cause the disparate impact, the respondent shall not be required to demonstrate that such practice is required by business necessity." How that allocation of the burden of proof meshes with placing the burden on plaintiff of showing "incapable of separation for analysis" is by no means clear.

6. *Impact on a "Protected Group."* The statistics in *Teal* show that, at the end of the selection process — the "bottom line" — the overall selection process had an adverse impact on whites: 22.9 percent of blacks who applied were promoted while only 13.5 percent of whites were. It is possible, of course, that disappointed white applicants could claim intentional discrimination in favor of blacks during the latter part of the process, especially given the majority's reference to "an affirmative action program." But what if whites argued disparate impact against their race in one or more subsequent steps of the process? Such impact clearly existed, right?

While Title VII protects all persons against disparate treatment because of race, color, sex, religion, and national origin, *McDonald v. Santa Fe Trail Transp. Co.*, reproduced at p. 36, it is not clear that disparate impact theory is available to whites or males. All of the disparate impact cases decided by the Supreme Court under Title VII involved claims by women or minority men. And *Griggs* emphasized that Title VII was "to achieve equality of employment opportunities and remove barriers that have operated in the past to favor an identifiable group of white employees over other employees." 401 U.S. at 429-30. The strong suggestion is that whites and males could not utilize the theory. And in *Manhart*, 435 U.S. at 710 n.20, the Court suggested that men (or whites) would not be able to use the disparate impact theory. "Even a completely neutral practice will inevitably have some disproportionate impact on one group or another. *Griggs* does not imply, and this Court has never held, that discrimination must always be inferred from such consequences." Nevertheless, a few lower courts have allowed disparate impact claims by whites. *See Meditz v. City of Newark*,

658 F.3d 364 (3d Cir. 2011) (white plaintiff permitted to attack a city's residency requirement because of its disparate impact on whites).

The answer to the question of whether whites (and males) can use disparate impact could depend on the language of the statute, the rationale underlying the theory, and the constitutionality of providing a cause of action to minorities and not to whites. *See generally* Charles A. Sullivan, *The World Turned Upside Down?: Disparate Impact Claims by White Males*, 98 Nw. U. L. Rev. 1505 (2004) (applying disparate impact beyond minorities and women is profoundly ahistorical and inconsistent with the theoretic underpinnings of the theory; nevertheless, limiting the theory to minorities and women cannot survive equal protection analysis. Accordingly, Title VII should be read to avoid the constitutional question by interpreting disparate impact as available to all races and both sexes).

7. *Exception for Drug Use Rules.* The 1991 Civil Rights Act created a specific exception to disparate impact attack for employment practices dealing with illegal drug use. Section 703(k)(3) provides that "a rule barring the employment of an individual who currently and knowingly uses or possesses a controlled substance . . . other than the use or possession of a drug taken under the supervision of a licensed health care professional," is unlawful only if it was adopted or applied with an intent to discriminate. This addresses an issue that divided the Court in *New York City Transit Auth. v. Beazer*, 440 U.S. 568 (1979), which involved a disparate impact challenge to an employer's rule prohibiting employment of individuals on methadone maintenance. Ironically, §703(k)(3) would not exempt the rule in *Beazer* since that rule involved the *legal* use of drugs.

8. *Is Disparate Impact Constitutional?* In *Ricci v. DeStefano*, 557 U.S. 557 (2009), reproduced at p. 245, the employer, the City of New Haven, administered a civil service test for promotions in its fire department. The results showed a disparate impact against minorities, leading the city to invalidate the test and not make any promotions based on it. White firefighters sued under both Title VII and the Equal Protection Clause, claiming that the decision was racially motivated. The Supreme Court held that avoidance of disparate impact liability could justify disparate treatment only if the employer had a "strong basis in evidence" for disparate impact liability. Finding no such basis, the majority granted summary judgment to the white firefighters on the Title VII claim, which allowed it to avoid the equal protection question. However, Justice Scalia, concurring, questioned whether disparate impact would survive constitutional scrutiny because it requires the employer to know the racial consequences of its practices, which violates his color-blind equal protection standard. *See* Sullivan, *The World Turned Upside Down*, Note 6 *supra. See also* Lawrence Rosenthal, *Saving Disparate Impact*, 34 Cardozo L. Rev. 2157 (2013); Eng L. Ngov, *When "the Evil Day" Comes, Will Title VII's Disparate Impact Provision Be Narrowly Tailored to Survive an Equal Protection Clause Challenge?*, 60 Am. U. L. Rev. 535 (2011); Richard Primus, *The Future of Disparate Impact*, 108 Mich. L. Rev. 1341 (2010).

However, doubts about the constitutional viability of disparate impact were assuaged by the Supreme Court's decision in *Texas Department of Housing & Community Affairs v. Inclusive Cmtys. Project, Inc.*, 135 S. Ct. 2507 (2014), which found the disparate impact theory applicable under the Fair Housing Act. However, in the process it suggested narrowing interpretations that might be necessary for its constitutionality as applied. Samuel R. Bagenstos, in *Disparate Impact and the Role of Classification and Motivation in Equal Protection Law After* Inclusive Communities, 101 Cornell L. Rev. 1115 (2015), views the case as reviving, as a constitutional matter, some of the limitations the Court imposed as a matter of statutory interpretation in *Wards Cove*:

> The principal tool the Court employed in *Inclusive Communities* to ensure that disparate impact did not violate the Constitution was to require plaintiffs to identify a particular practice or set of practices imposed by the defendant that caused the disparate impact. The Court stated that "a disparate-impact claim that relies on a statistical disparity must fail if the plaintiff cannot point to a defendant's policy or policies causing that disparity." As the next two sentences of the Court's opinion make clear, that "causality" requirement comes directly from *Wards Cove*.

Id. at 1138. This suggests that the statutory "incapable of separation for analysis" avenue is constitutionally questionable. Professor Bagenstos also argues that the *Inclusive Communities* opinion's mixed signals regarding justifications for housing policies with a disparate impact might portend some weakening of the business necessity standard for Title VII, perhaps along the lines signaled by *Wards Cove*. *Id.* at 1141. *See also Abril-Rivera v. Johnson*, 806 F.3d 599 (1st Cir. 2015) (when defendants present "legitimate business justifications for their actions," the disparate impact theory requires the plaintiff to prove a viable less discriminatory alternative; any other rule would too much constrain both business and government decisions and create the danger of racial quotas).

[handwritten margin note: Is that too much of a burden on P? P is just trying to establish liability to the business, not run the business]

PROBLEM 3.1

Fogey.com is a rapidly expanding e-commerce business. Alice Aortop is in charge of hiring, and she says she interviews every applicant and subjectively evaluates each one looking for "creativity, decisiveness, ambition, loyalty, and ability to create buzz!" Assuming that comparatively few of the African American and Latino applicants are hired, can the "bottom-line" number of minority group members be used to make out a prima facie case of disparate impact discrimination since the subjective evaluation system is a particular employment practice? Or since factors such as creativity, decisiveness, etc., are relied upon, must the plaintiff first convince the judge that these elements are not capable of separation for analysis because he is using bottom-line statistics to prove disparate impact?

b. The Employer Uses the Practice

Section 703(k)(1)(A)(i) requires that the plaintiff prove that the employer "*uses* a particular employment practice that causes a disparate impact."

DOTHARD v. RAWLINSON
433 U.S. 321 (1977)

Justice STEWART delivered the opinion of the Court. . . .

I

At the time she applied for a position as correctional counselor trainee, Rawlinson was a 22-year-old college graduate whose major course of study had been correctional psychology. She was refused employment because she failed to meet the minimum

120-pound weight requirement established by an Alabama statute. The statute also establishes a height minimum of 5 feet 2 inches. . . .

A correctional counselor's primary duty within these institutions is to maintain security and control of the inmates by continually supervising and observing their activities. To be eligible for consideration as a correctional counselor, an applicant must possess a valid Alabama driver's license, have a high school education or its equivalent, be free from physical defects, be between the ages of 20 ½ years and 45 years at the time of appointment, and fall between the minimum height and weight requirements of 5 feet 2 inches, and 120 pounds, and the maximum of 6 feet 10 inches, and 300 pounds. Appointment is by merit, with a grade assigned each applicant based on experience and education. No written examination is given. . . .

II . . .

A

The gist of the claim that the statutory height and weight requirements discriminate against women does not involve an assertion of purposeful discriminatory motive. It is asserted, rather, that these facially neutral qualification standards work in fact disproportionately to exclude women from eligibility for employment by the Alabama Board of Corrections. We dealt in *Griggs* and *Albemarle Paper* with similar allegations that facially neutral employment standards disproportionately excluded Negroes from employment, and those cases guide our approach here.

Those cases make clear that to establish a prima facie case of discrimination, a plaintiff need only show that the facially neutral standards in question select applicants for hire in a significantly discriminatory pattern. Once it is thus shown that the employment standards are discriminatory in effect, the employer must meet "the burden of showing that any given requirement [has] . . . a manifest relationship to the employment in question." *Griggs.* If the employer proves that the challenged requirements are job related, the plaintiff may then show that other selection devices without a similar discriminatory effect would also "serve the employer's legitimate interest in 'efficient and trustworthy workmanship.'" *Albemarle Paper,* quoting *McDonnell Douglas.*

Although women 14 years of age or older compose 52.75% of the Alabama population and 36.89% of its total labor force, they hold only 12.9% of its correctional counselor positions. In considering the effect of the minimum height and weight standards on this disparity in rate of hiring between the sexes, the District Court found that the 5'2" requirement would operate to exclude 33.29% of the women in the United States between the ages of 18-79, while excluding only 1.28% of men between the same ages. The 120-pound weight restriction would exclude 22.29% of the women and 2.35% of the men in this age group. When the height and weight restrictions are combined, Alabama's statutory standards would exclude 41.13% of the female population while excluding less than 1% of the male population.[12] Accordingly, the District Court found that Rawlinson had made out a prima facie case of unlawful sex discrimination.

The appellants argue that a showing of disproportionate impact on women based on generalized national statistics should not suffice to establish a prima facie case.

12. Affirmatively stated, approximately 99.76% of the men and 58.87% of the women meet both these physical qualifications. . . .

They point in particular to Rawlinson's failure to adduce comparative statistics concerning actual applicants for correctional counselor positions in Alabama. There is no requirement, however, that a statistical showing of disproportionate impact must always be based on analysis of the characteristics of actual applicants. *See Griggs v. Duke Power Co.* The application process itself might not adequately reflect the actual potential applicant pool, since otherwise qualified people might be discouraged from applying because of a self-recognized inability to meet the very standards challenged as being discriminatory. *See Teamsters v. United States.* A potential applicant could easily determine her height and weight and conclude that to make an application would be futile. Moreover, reliance on general population demographic data was not misplaced where there was no reason to suppose that physical height and weight characteristics of Alabama men and women differ markedly from those of the national population.

For these reasons, we cannot say that the District Court was wrong in holding that the statutory height and weight standards had a discriminatory impact on women applicants. The plaintiffs in a case such as this are not required to exhaust every possible source of evidence, if the evidence actually presented on its face conspicuously demonstrates a job requirement's grossly discriminatory impact. If the employer discerns fallacies or deficiencies in the data offered by the plaintiff, he is free to adduce countervailing evidence of his own. In this case no such effort was made.

B

We turn, therefore, to the appellants' argument that they have rebutted the prima facie case of discrimination by showing that the height and weight requirements are job related. These requirements, they say, have a relationship to strength, a sufficient but unspecified amount of which is essential to effective job performance as a correctional counselor. In the District Court, however, the appellants produced no evidence correlating the height and weight requirements with the requisite amount of strength thought essential to good job performance. Indeed, they failed to offer evidence of any kind in specific justification of the statutory standards.

If the job-related quality that the appellants identify is bona fide, their purpose could be achieved by adopting and validating a test for applicants that measures strength directly. Such a test, fairly administered, would fully satisfy the standards of Title VII because it would be one that "measure[s] the person for the job and not the person in the abstract." *Griggs.* But nothing in the present record even approaches such a measurement. . . .

[Justice Rehnquist, joined by The Chief Justice and Justice Blackmun, filed a concurring opinion.]

Justice WHITE, dissenting.
. . . I have . . . trouble agreeing that a prima facie case of sex discrimination was made out by statistics showing that the Alabama height and weight requirements would exclude a larger percentage of women in the United States than of men. As in *Hazelwood*, the issue is whether there was discrimination in dealing with actual or potential applicants; but in *Hazelwood* there was at least a colorable argument that the racial composition of the area-wide teacher work force was a reasonable proxy for the composition of the relevant applicant pool and hence that a large divergence between the percentage of blacks on the teaching staff and the percentage in the teacher work force raised a fair inference of racial discrimination in dealing with the applicant

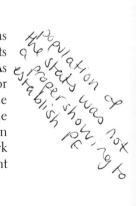

[Handwritten margin notes:] Improper standard be it assumes a strength based on other factors rather than testing strength directly. It also does not set out how much strength is actually required.

[Handwritten margin notes:] Population of the stats was proper showing not established pertaining to

pool. In *Dothard*, however, I am unwilling to believe that the percentage of women applying or interested in applying for jobs as prison guards in Alabama approximates the percentage of women either in the national or state population. A plaintiff could, of course, show that the composition of the applicant pool was distorted by the exclusion of nonapplicants who did not apply because of the allegedly discriminatory job requirement. But no such showing was made or even attempted here; and although I do not know what the actual fact is, I am not now convinced that a large percentage of the actual women applicants, or of those who are seriously interested in applying, for prison guard positions would fail to satisfy the height and weight requirements. . . .

NOTES

1. *The Employer "Used" the Challenged Practices.* There was no doubt in *Dothard* that the employer had "used" height and weight thresholds in selecting prison guards because it was a written employment policy. But there was a question, which would arise today under §703(k)(1)(A)(i), whether the practice the employer "uses" in fact produces the impact. Justice White's dissent would require the plaintiff to do so by showing the impact on those who applied. His point may be that only taller, heavier women are interested in prison guard positions in the first place, so that there is no actual (as opposed to theoretic) impact by the employer's policy. Is the Court correct in essentially assuming that a cross-section of the population will apply for this job? Presumably, the employer could prove the contrary, but does this assumption effectively shift the burden of proof to defendant or merely rebut plaintiffs' prima facie case?

[handwritten margin note: arguably merely rebuts it be of the discouragement factor]

2. *Back to General Population Statistics.* *Dothard* approves general population statistics, as opposed to applicant flow, but the Court has not been consistent as to the use of such statistics. In *New York City Transit Auth. v. Beazer*, 440 U.S. 568 (1979), the plaintiffs invoked Title VII to challenge an employer's rule disqualifying people taking methadone, a drug used in the treatment of heroin addiction. The plaintiffs showed that 81 percent of all Transit Authority (TA) employees suspected of drug use were black or Hispanic and, less certainly, that between 62 percent and 65 percent of all methadone-maintained people in New York City were black or Hispanic. The Supreme Court rejected that challenge in part because of the inadequate showing of impact.

> [The statistics about overall drug use tell] us nothing about the racial composition of the employees suspected of using methadone. Nor does the record give us any information about the number of black, Hispanic, or white persons who were dismissed for using methadone. . . . We do not know . . . how many of these persons [in methadone maintenance programs] ever worked or sought to work for TA. This statistic therefore reveals little if anything about the racial composition of the class of TA job applicants and employees receiving methadone treatment.

Id. at 585. Was the majority too demanding? Could an inference be drawn from these statistics that the methadone rule had a racial impact? The lesson seems to be that plaintiffs must introduce data that focus more directly on the effect of defendants' use of the challenged rule. The Court suggests that the relevant group for deriving impact statistics is the Transit Authority's applicant pool. But, as in *Dothard*, wouldn't individuals on methadone who are aware of the TA's methadone restriction not bother to apply?

3. *Who's Who?* Whatever the problems of counting, there was, until recently, little problem with plaintiffs' proof of impact in terms of who counts as a member of a particular race. But *EEOC v. Kaplan Higher Educ. Corp.*, 748 F.3d 749 (6th Cir. 2014), raised precisely that question when the EEOC failed to prove the racial effects of a particular practice because of difficulties in identifying the race of affected individuals. The Sixth Circuit upheld dismissal of EEOC's disparate impact complaint when the agency could not prove that defendant's credit check policy had a disparate impact on blacks after the lower court appropriately excluded an expert report using "race raters" to ascertain the supposed race of rejected applicants on the basis of drivers' license photographs. *See generally* Charles A. Sullivan, *Who Counts as Black?*, WORKPLACE PROF BLOG (Apr. 23, 2014), http://lawprofessors.typepad.com/laborprof_blog/2014/04/whats-race-once-again-.html.

4. *The Problem of Small Numbers.* We saw in *Watson*, see p. 183, that only about 80 employees worked at the bank, and Justice O'Connor suggested that the numbers might be too small to support a finding of impact at the bank. As you may have guessed, the "small numbers" problem is a statistical one. Even if there's a clear impact on the group in question, statistically speaking, the probability that these results could have happened by chance was quite high. While the "small numbers" difficulty can be a serious obstacle to proof of disparate impact, *see Mems v. City of St. Paul*, 224 F.3d 735 (8th Cir. 2000) (rejecting a claim because the sample sizes, ranging from three to seven, were too small to be statistically significant), it is not always fatal. In *Pietras v. Board of Fire Comm'rs*, 180 F.3d 468 (2d Cir. 1999), the plaintiff challenged a physical agility test used by a fire department when 63 out of 66 males passed (95%), but only 4 out of 7 females (57%). Acknowledging the small numbers, the court nevertheless upheld a finding of disparate impact based on expert testimony of the practices of other fire departments. Liability then attached because there was no evidence that the physical ability test was job related.

5. *The Defendant's Rebuttal of the Impact Showing.* In *Espinoza v. Farah Mfg. Co.*, 414 U.S. 86, 93 (1973), the Court allowed the employer to rebut the plaintiff's showing that a rule requiring American citizenship had a disparate impact on those born outside the United States by presenting statistics that the rule did not have that effect at its plant:

> [P]ersons of Mexican ancestry make up more than 96% of the employees at the company's San Antonio division, and 97% of those doing the work for which Mrs. Espinoza applied. While statistics such as these do not automatically shield an employer from a charge of unlawful discrimination, the plain fact of the matter is that Farah does not discriminate against persons of Mexican national origin with respect to employment in the job Mrs. Espinoza sought.

See also Newark Branch, NAACP v. City of Bayonne, 134 F.3d 113 (3d Cir. 1998) (no error in refusing to enjoin residency requirement when statistics showed that, during the years when the rule was suspended, representation of minorities had decreased rather than increased).

Section 703(k)(1)(B)(ii) now provides that if the employer "demonstrates that a specific employment practice does not cause the disparate impact, the [employer] shall not be required to demonstrate that such practice is required by business necessity." This subsection creates an affirmative defense to a prima facie case based on bottom-line statistics pursuant to subsection (i).

The broader question is whether subsection (ii) also creates an affirmative defense to the general rule of §703(k)(1)(A)(i). That is, where the plaintiff identifies a particular employment practice used by the employer that causes a disparate impact, can the employer prevail by demonstrating that the practice does not cause the impact? The argument against applying the subsection (ii) affirmative defense to this is that the burden of persuasion on the same point — whether the challenged practice causes a disparate impact — would then be on both parties. A response is that these two provisions, when read together, first require the plaintiff to carry the burden of persuasion that the employer used a practice that causes a disparate impact, which burden can be satisfied with national statistics as in *Dothard* and *Griggs*. Once the plaintiff satisfies that burden, the employer may prevail by proving the affirmative defense created by §703(k)(1)(B)(ii), as the employer did in *Espinoza*, that its own use of the practice did not cause a disparate impact. Note, however, that, even if such employer proof is not an affirmative defense, it clearly can operate as a rebuttal to the plaintiff's case of disparate impact.

PROBLEM 3.2

The Naperville police department chief wants to replace the traditional police revolver used as standard equipment with the much more powerful Smith & Wesson Model 59 semi-automatic. The Model 59 is quite large, with a wide hand grip. National data show that more than 50 percent of all women and about 10 percent of all men would be unable to handle the gun because of the size of the hand grip. Assume the police chief asks you if there would be any legal problem with the department adopting the Model 59. Is this an "employment practice" to begin with? Even if it is not, is hiring only those who can use the weapon such a practice or does this push the disparate impact theory too far? Assuming that theory applies, what more facts would you like to know before you render an opinion? Would you recommend that the department take any steps before requiring that the Model 59 be used by all department officers that might help insulate the department from disparate impact liability?

c.   The Quantum of Impact

Section 703(k)(1)(A)(i) requires a plaintiff to prove that the practice she challenges "causes a disparate impact," but it does not define "disparate" in terms of the quantum of impact that suffices. Obviously, to show impact, it is necessary to compare the impact on the protected group with the impact on others. This question actually involves two issues. The first is the "small numbers" problem we encountered in Note 5. The second question, however, goes not to whether there is an impact but rather the *amount* of impact. The Uniform Guidelines on Employee Selection Procedures, 29 C.F.R. §1607.4D (2018), adopted by federal civil rights enforcement agencies, including the EEOC, create a standard to trigger enforcement efforts:

> A selection rate for any race, sex, or ethnic group which is less than four-fifths (4/5) (or eighty percent) of the rate for the group with the highest rate will generally be regarded by the Federal enforcement agencies as evidence of adverse impact, while a greater than four-fifths rate will generally not be regarded by Federal enforcement agencies as evidence of adverse impact.

In other words, the agencies will not challenge an impact that is not substantial. *See Watson v. Ft. Worth Bank & Trust*, 487 U.S. 977, 995 n.3 (1988) (describing the Guidelines as providing "a rule of thumb" for the courts). But courts do not view the four-fifths rule as providing a safe harbor for private suits. In *Jones v. City of Boston*, 752 F.3d 38 (1st Cir. 2014), plaintiffs challenged the police department's use of hair samples to test for illegal drug use. While 98 percent of blacks passed the test, 99 percent of whites did so. Despite the argument that the difference was not cognizable, the First Circuit held this proof sufficient: the data was statistically significant, and there is no requirement that plaintiffs must also prove "practical significance," *i.e.*, that the size of the disparity is large enough to matter. *See also Stagi v. AMTRAK*, 391 F. App'x 133 (3d Cir. 2010) (a showing of "statistical significance" regarding the sex impact of the challenged rule sufficient to avoid summary judgment even absent a finding of "practical significance"). *But see Apsley v. Boeing Co.*, 691 F.3d 1184 (10th Cir. 2012) (statistical significance not sufficient to avoid summary judgment in light of practical insignificance). *See generally* Kevin Tobia, Note, *Disparate Statistics*, 126 YALE L. J. (forthcoming 2017).

To understand the concern, suppose the difference is real but quite small. Test A yields two curves of performance, one for men and one for women. There is obviously a gender impact, the female median being 20 points lower than the male median. If a passing score is set at the male median, 75, half the men would be qualified, but a much smaller percentage of the women would be. The curves in Figure 3.1 might reflect something like the situation in *Dothard*.*

Suppose, however, that Test B yields disparate gender impact, but with a much smaller margin, such as that shown in Figure 3.2. Given the fact that the whole universe is represented, there is no doubt as to the gender correlation, but the impact adverse to women is slight. If a passing score is set at the male median — so that 50

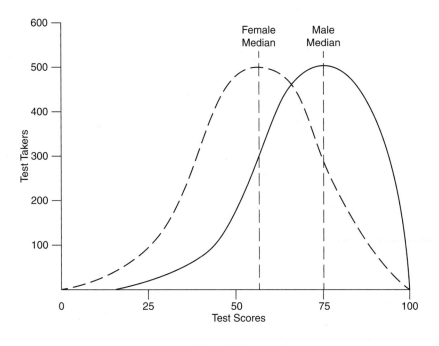

Figure 3.1

* The curves have been drawn to reflect equal numbers of test takers, which may be true where sex discrimination is concerned. In the typical race case, however, the universe of blacks is smaller than the universe of whites, which would require the black curve to be smaller than the white curve.

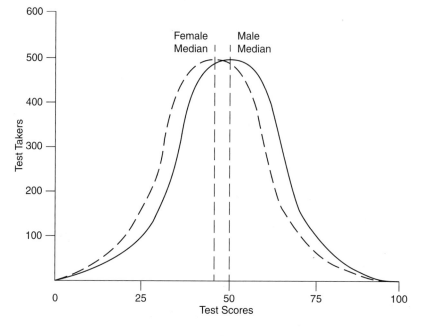

Figure 3.2

percent of males are hired — 49 percent of females will also qualify; the impact is real but the difference may be too small to matter.

2. Defendant's Options

There are five rebuttal possibilities available to the employer to respond to a case of disparate impact discrimination, several of which are affirmative defenses. The general defense is simply rebutting the showing of impact. The affirmative defenses include proving that the practice is job related and consistent with business necessity under §703(k) or showing that the practice is a professionally developed test, a bona fide seniority system, or a bona fide merit system under §703(h), as treated in section C.

a.   Rebuttal: The Employer's Use Does Not Cause Impact

An employer may try to undermine the plaintiff's showing of a prima facie case by introducing evidence that the data the plaintiff relied on were flawed. In *Council 31, AFSCME v. Doherty*, 169 F.3d 1068 (7th Cir. 1999), the plaintiff presented evidence that an employer's layoff criteria had a disparate impact on black employees, but the defendant rebutted by showing that the plaintiff had not accounted for all persons who were subject to the challenged practice, and, when all persons were included, no disparate impact existed. This rebuttal possibility does not change the basic rule that the plaintiff has the burden of persuasion to prove a prima facie case. Section 703(k)(1)(A)(i) states the general rule that "a complaining party demonstrates that a respondent uses a particular employment practice that causes a disparate impact," with "demonstrate" being separately defined in §701(m) as "meets the burdens of production and persuasion."

Section 703(k)(1)(B)(ii), however, appears to create an affirmative defense that imposes on the employer the burden of persuasion in one situation: when the plaintiff uses bottom-line data under the "incapable of separation for analysis" heading, the defendant may seek to prove that "a specific employment practice does not cause the disparate impact." As we noted previously, this seems to put the burden of persuasion on both the plaintiff and the defendant on the same issue, a logical impossibility that we suggested could be avoided by looking to the types of proof each may use. See Note 5, p. 200.

b. Business Necessity and Job Relatedness

EL v. SOUTHEASTERN PENNSYLVANIA TRANSPORTATION AUTHORITY
479 F.3d 232 (3d Cir. 2007)

AMBRO, Circuit Judge.

This appeal arises out of a Title VII action alleging employment discrimination based on race. Plaintiff Douglas El claims that the Southeastern Pennsylvania Transportation Authority (SEPTA) unnecessarily disqualifies applicants because of prior criminal convictions — a policy that he argues has a disparate impact on minority applicants because they are more likely than white applicants to have convictions on their records.

The Court granted summary judgment, however, in favor of SEPTA, concluding that it had borne the burden of proving that its policy is consistent with business necessity. Though we have reservations about such a policy in the abstract, we affirm here because El did not present any evidence to rebut SEPTA's expert testimony.

[handwritten margin note: P did not meet its burden to rebut defense of business necessity]

I. FACTUAL BACKGROUND AND PROCEDURAL HISTORY

In January 2000, King Paratransit Services, Inc. conditionally hired El to drive paratransit buses. The position involves providing door-to-door and curb-to-curb transportation service for people with mental and physical disabilities. King subcontracted with SEPTA to provide paratransit services on SEPTA's behalf. King's subcontract with SEPTA disallowed hiring anyone with, among other things, a violent criminal conviction. Accordingly, among the conditions stipulated in El's offer was successful completion of a criminal background check. Within the first few weeks of El's employment, King discovered that El had a 40-year-old conviction for second-degree murder.[2] Following the terms of King's subcontract with SEPTA and El's employment offer, King terminated his employment. According to King personnel, the murder conviction was their sole reason.

As the background check revealed, El was convicted of second-degree murder in 1960. According to his testimony, the murder took place in the context of a gang-related fight in which the victim was shot and died. El was 15 years old at the time, and the victim was 16. El claims not to have been the triggerman, and, indeed, he was not the only person convicted of the murder, but no objective report of the circumstances appears in the record before us. Following his conviction, El served three-and-a-half years for his crime. This now 47-year-old conviction is El's only violent offense.

According to the contract in place between King and SEPTA in 2000, King was required to ensure that anyone in SEPTA service as a driver or attendant have:

2. El actually had disclosed the conviction on his application, but King personnel apparently did not notice it until they examined the criminal background report.

e. no record of driving under [the] influence (DUI) of alcohol or drugs, and no record of any felony or misdemeanor conviction for any crime of moral turpitude or of
violence against any person(s);

f. have no record of any conviction within the last seven (7) years for any other felony
or any other misdemeanor [as defined], and not be on probation or parole for any such
crime, no matter how long ago the conviction for such crime may be. . . .

[El sued, arguing that the policy had a disparate impact because African Americans
and Hispanics were more likely to have a criminal record and thus be excluded by the
policy. Because SEPTA sought and was granted summary judgment on its affirmative
defense of business necessity, on which it would bear the burden of proof at trial, it
had to show that it had produced enough evidence that a reasonable factfinder would
be compelled to find for it.]

III. Discussion

A. THE BUSINESS NECESSITY DEFENSE . . .

[The court briefly reviewed the rebuttal discussions in *Griggs, Albemarle Paper Co.,*
and *Dothard,* and then went on to note that] two aspects of these cases are noteworthy.
First, the Court refused to accept bare or "common-sense"-based assertions of business
necessity and instead required some level of empirical proof that challenged hiring criteria accurately predicted job performance. *Dothard* is particularly noteworthy because the
Court rejected an employer's common-sense argument that prison guards must be relatively strong to justify criteria that roughly measured strength. The lesson is that employers cannot rely on rough-cut measures of employment-related qualities; rather they must
tailor their criteria to measure those qualities accurately and directly for each applicant.

Second, the Court did not allow employers to rely on "more is better"-style reasoning to justify their policies. In *Griggs, Albemarle,* and *Dothard,* the employers argued
that the challenged criteria were justified by the fact that one would naturally prefer
smarter or stronger employees to less intelligent or weaker ones, and so it was of no
moment that the criteria might be set a bit higher than strictly necessary. The Court
held, however, that some abstract notion that more of a given quality is better is insufficient to justify a discriminatory policy under Title VII; rather, the employer must
present real evidence that the challenged criteria "'measure[s] the person for the job
and not the person in the abstract.'" *Dothard* (quoting *Griggs*). . . .

Unfortunately, as numerous courts and commentators have noted, *Griggs* and
its progeny did not provide a precise definition of business necessity. *See, e.g., Lanning v. Southeastern Pa. Transp. Auth.,* 181 F.3d 478, 488 (3d Cir. 1999) (*Lanning
I*) (noting that the Act was so unclear that both proponents and opponents of a strict
business necessity standard claimed victory); Susan S. Grover, *The Business Necessity Defense in Disparate Impact Discrimination Cases,* 30 GA. L. REV. 387, 391-93
(1996); Andrew C. Spiropoulos, *Defining the Business Necessity Defense to the Disparate Impact Cause of Action: Finding the Golden Mean,* 74 N.C. L. REV. 1479, 1520
(1996). Normally, we would look to additional legislative history to determine if it
clarifies what Congress meant by business necessity. However, Congress stipulated
that courts may not consider any document other than [an interpretive memoran-
dum] as the Act's legislative history. In *Lanning I* and *II* [308 F.3d 286 (3d Cir. 2002)],
we heeded Congress's instruction and looked no further than the memorandum.

While some may be skeptical of Congress's power to instruct courts what legislative
history they may take into account when interpreting a statute, we need not consider
anything beyond the interpretive memorandum because doing so would be unhelpful

in this case.[10] Members of Congress simply could not agree on a precise definition of business necessity; all they could agree upon was overruling *Wards Cove* and reinstating the Supreme Court's somewhat conflicting post-*Griggs* and pre-*Wards Cove* jurisprudence. Thus, our task is to be as faithful to that intent as possible.

Attempting to implement the *Griggs* standard, we have held that hiring criteria must effectively measure the "minimum qualifications for successful performance of the job in question." See *Lanning I*. This holding reflects the *Griggs/Albemarle/Dothard* rejection of criteria that are overbroad or merely general, unsophisticated measures of a legitimate job-related quality. It is also consistent with the fact that Congress continues to call the test "business necessity," not "business convenience" or some other weaker term.

However, hiring policies need not be perfectly tailored to be consistent with business necessity. As we held in *Lanning II*, employers need not set the bar so low that they consider an applicant with some, but unreasonably low, probability of successful performance. *Lanning II* ("It would clearly be unreasonable to require SEPTA applicants to score so highly on the run test that their predicted rate of [job] success be 100%. It is perfectly reasonable, however, to demand a chance of success that is better than 5% to 20%."). After all, the Supreme Court has held that Title VII never forces an employer to accept an unqualified — or even less qualified — applicant in the name of nondiscrimination. *Griggs* ("Congress has not commanded that the less qualified be preferred over the better qualified simply because of minority origins"). Moreover, the Supreme Court has noted that bright-line criteria, such as aptitude tests, are legitimate and useful hiring tools so long as they accurately measure a person's qualifications. *Id.*

Putting these standards together, then, we require that employers show that a discriminatory hiring policy accurately — but not perfectly — ascertains an applicant's ability to perform successfully the job in question. In addition, Title VII allows the employer to hire the applicant most likely to perform the job successfully over others less likely to do so.

2. Applying the Defense to Criminal Conviction Policies . . .

The standards set out in *Griggs* and its progeny (including the standards noted by our Court in *Lanning I* and *II*) do not parallel the facts of this case. In the cases cited above, the hiring policies at issue were tests designed or used — at least allegedly — to measure an employee's ability to perform the relevant jobs. Here, however, the hiring policy has nothing to do with the applicant's ability to drive a paratransit bus; rather, it seeks to exclude applicants who, while able to drive a bus, pose too much of a risk of potential harm to the passengers to be trusted with the job. Thus, our standard of "minimum qualifications necessary for successful performance of the job in question" is appropriate in test-score cases, but awkward here because "successful performance of the job" in the usual sense is not at issue. SEPTA could argue that successful performance of the job includes not attacking a passenger and, therefore, that the standard is still appropriate. However, the standard is worded to address ability, not risk. Yet, the issue before us is the risk that the employee will harm a passenger, and the phrase "minimum qualification" simply does not fit, as it is hard to articulate the minimum qualification for posing a low risk of attacking someone.

The only reported appellate level case to address squarely the issue of exclusions from eligibility on the basis of prior convictions is *Green v. Missouri Pac. R.R. Co.,* 523

---

10. Even if we did review additional legislative history, it would not clarify the issue. . . .

F.2d 1290 (8th Cir. 1975). There the employer refused to hire anyone for any position who had been convicted of any offense other than a minor traffic violation. Green had applied for an office job, and he was not considered because of a previous conviction for refusing to answer the draft (after failing to qualify as a conscientious objector). The Court held that the employer's policy was too broad to be justified by business necessity.

distinguish from Green

   Green, however, presented materially different facts than those before us in two respects. First, the job in *Green* was an office job at a corporate headquarters; it did not require the employee to be alone with and in close proximity to vulnerable members of society. The public safety concern is of more moment in our case. Second, the hiring policy in *Green* prevented hiring a person with any criminal conviction, "no matter how remote, insubstantial, or unrelated to [the] applicant's personal qualifications as an employee." Here, SEPTA's policy only prevents consideration of people with certain types of convictions — those that it argues have the highest and most unpredictable rates of recidivism and thus present the greatest danger to its passengers. In this context, *Green* was an easier case insofar as the Supreme Court has held firmly that an employer with an extremely broad exclusionary policy that fails to offer any empirical justification for it is unable to make out a successful business necessity defense, *Dothard*, whereas SEPTA has a narrower policy for a position in which criminal convictions are more job-related.

   The EEOC has spoken to the issue in its Compliance Manual, which states that an applicant may be disqualified from a job on the basis of a previous conviction only if the employer takes into account:

     1. The nature and gravity of the offense or offenses;
     2. The time that has passed since the conviction and/or completion of the sentence; and
     3. The nature of the job held or sought.

Equal Empl. Opp. Comm. Compliance Manual §605 App. The EEOC clarifies that "nature and gravity of the offense" means for employers to consider the circumstances of that offense. The EEOC's Guidelines, however, do not speak to whether an employer can take these factors into account when crafting a bright-line policy, nor do they speak to whether an employer justifiably can decide that certain offenses are serious enough to warrant a lifetime ban. SEPTA's policy arguably takes into account the sensitive nature of the job and sorts applicants by type of offense. For some offenses, it considers the time since the conviction; for others, it does not. . . .

   Considering the dearth of authority directly on point, we believe that our standards from *Lanning I* and *II* — namely that discriminatory hiring policies accurately but not perfectly distinguish between applicants' ability to perform successfully the job in question — can be adapted to fit the context of criminal conviction policies. In a broad sense, hiring policies, such as the one at issue here, ultimately concern the management of risk. In *Lanning I & II*, we dealt with how employers manage the risk that applicants will be unable to perform the job in question. Here we deal with the risk that an applicant will endanger the employer's patrons. In both cases, it is impossible to measure the risk perfectly,[12] and in both cases Title VII does not ask the impossible. It does, however, as in the case of performance-related policies, require

---

12. As SEPTA discovered in the tragic case of paratransit driver David deSouza, even applicants with clean criminal records sometimes endanger passengers. At the time of his hire by King, deSouza had no prior criminal convictions. Nevertheless, he attacked and raped a passenger while serving as a SEPTA driver.

that the policy under review accurately distinguish between applicants that pose an unacceptable level of risk and those that do not.[13]

El urges us to go further and hold that Title VII prohibits any bright-line policy with regard to criminal convictions; he argues, rather, that Title VII requires that each applicant's circumstances be considered individually without reference to any bright-line rules. We decline to go so far. If a bright-line policy can distinguish between individual applicants that do and do not pose an unacceptable level of risk, then such a policy is consistent with business necessity. Whether a policy can do so is most often a question of fact that the district courts — and juries — must resolve in specific cases.[14]

3. Could a Reasonable Juror Find that SEPTA's Policy Is Not Consistent with Business Necessity?

In arguing that its policy is consistent with business necessity, SEPTA claims that it has presented evidence such that a reasonable juror must find that: (1) the job of a paratransit driver requires that the driver be in very close contact with passengers, (2) the job requires that the driver often be alone with passengers, (3) paratransit passengers are vulnerable because they typically have physical and/or mental disabilities, (4) disabled people are disproportionately targeted by sexual and violent criminals, (5) violent criminals recidivate at a high rate, (6) it is impossible to predict with a reasonable degree of accuracy which criminals will recidivate, (7) someone with a conviction for a violent crime is more likely than someone without one to commit a future violent crime irrespective of how remote in time the conviction is, and (8) SEPTA's policy is the most accurate way to screen out applicants who present an unacceptable risk.

As an initial matter, we agree with SEPTA that these facts, if proved, would be sufficient to show that its policy is consistent with business necessity, at least as it applies to a person with a violent criminal conviction like El.[15] If someone with a violent conviction presents a materially higher risk than someone without one, no matter which other factors an employer considers, then SEPTA is justified in not considering people with those convictions.[16] For example, SEPTA may be able to show that a policy excluding all violent offenders is justified by business necessity because other factors — such as age at conviction, the number of violent convictions, and/or the remoteness of that conviction — are unreliable or otherwise fail to reduce the risk to an acceptable level.

[handwritten margin note: how does one prove that? → P could have rebutted w/ an alternative method of accounting for the risk]

---

13. It may seem odd to speak of an acceptable level of risk in this context, given the horrors that drivers can inflict on disabled passengers, but, as the deSouza case demonstrates, some level of risk is inevitable, see *supra* note 12. SEPTA may minimize that risk to the extent reasonably possible, but whatever criteria it uses must distinguish with sufficient accuracy between those who pose that minimal level of risk and those who pose a higher level.

14. In this case, we have no occasion to hold that bright-line policies in the criminal conviction context are per se invalid. Indeed, we have upheld policies in other Title VII contexts that effectively bar an applicant from employment on the basis of a single, bright-line test result, but whatever criteria it uses must distinguish with sufficient accuracy between those who pose that minimal level of risk and those who do not. *Lanning II* (affirming SEPTA's use of a bright-line aerobic capacity test to bar applicants from employment as transit police officers).

15. [The court had "no occasion to determine" whether the SEPTA perpetual ban on those with convictions for crimes of moral turpitude is justified.]

16. SEPTA too heavily emphasizes the sixth alleged fact: that it is impossible to predict which criminal will recidivate. This fact, if proved, is of little use because it is also impossible to predict which non-criminal will commit a crime. What matters is the risk that the individual presents, taking into account whatever aspects of the person's criminal history are relevant. Thus, if screening out applicants with very old violent criminal convictions accurately distinguishes between those who present an unacceptable risk, then reliance on this factor is appropriate; if the criterion is inaccurate or overbroad in the case of very old convictions, then it is inappropriate for Title VII purposes.

In support of its summary judgment motion, SEPTA submitted the reports of three experts. All three rely heavily on data from the Department of Justice that tracked recidivism of prisoners within three years of their release from prison. Indeed, those data show relatively high rates of recidivism in those first three years. But what about someone who has been released from prison and violence-free for 40 years? The DOJ statistics do not demonstrate that someone in this position — or anything like it — is likely to recidivate.

One of SEPTA's experts was Dr. Alfred Blumstein, a noted authority on recidivism. He stated:

> It is also the case that an individual's propensity to commit a future violent crime decreases as that individual's crime-free duration increases. That is, an individual with a prior violent conviction who has been crime-free in the community for twenty years is less likely to commit a future crime than one who has been crime-free in the community for only ten years. But neither of these individuals can be judged to be less or equally likely to commit a future violent act than comparable individuals who have no prior violent history. It is possible that those differences might be small, but making such predictions of comparable low-probability events is extremely difficult, and the criminological discipline provides no good basis for making such predictions with any assurance that they will be correct.

This statement bridges, as best it can, the gap between the three-year statistics and El's 40-year-old conviction. Because Dr. Blumstein is a duly qualified professional criminologist and because nothing in the record rebuts his statement, we must take him at his word that former violent criminals who have been crime free for many years are at least somewhat more likely than members of the general population to commit a future violent act. He notes that the difference between the probability that someone with a remote conviction and someone with no conviction will commit a future violent crime "might be small," but given the marked sensitivity of the paratransit position at issue, a small but extant difference is sufficient. It is also noteworthy that Dr. Blumstein reports that the criminological discipline is incapable of distinguishing accurately between violent criminals who are and are not likely to commit future violent crimes. In other words, he believes that SEPTA's policy distinguishes as accurately as the criminological discipline allows. Again, because we see nothing in the record rebutting this statement, we must take Dr. Blumstein at his word.

SEPTA also submitted the report of Dr. Dick Sobsey, an education psychologist. Dr. Sobsey reported that disabled people are proportionately more likely than others to be the victims of violent or sexual crimes. He further reported that employees of transportation providers commit a disproportionate share of those crimes against disabled people. Like Dr. Blumstein, Dr. Sobsey claims that the strength of violent criminal activity as a predictor of future criminal activity "moderates over time but remains regardless of how much time passes." Dr. Sobsey's report, therefore, provides evidence for SEPTA's argument that paratransit positions are extraordinarily sensitive, and that screening out individuals with violent convictions — no matter how remote — is appropriate.

Thus, on this record, we have little choice but to conclude that a reasonable juror would necessarily find that SEPTA's policy is consistent with business necessity. This is not to say that we are convinced that SEPTA's expert reports are ironclad in the abstract. But El chose neither to hire an expert to rebut SEPTA's experts on the issue of business necessity nor even to depose SEPTA's experts. These choices are fatal to his claim [since there is nothing that a reasonable jury could rely on to find against SEPTA].

Had El produced evidence rebutting SEPTA's experts, this would be a different case. Had he, for example, hired an expert who testified that there is a time at which a former criminal is no longer any more likely to recidivate than the average person, then there would be a factual question for the jury to resolve. Similarly, had El deposed SEPTA's experts and thereby produced legitimate reasons to doubt their credibility, there would be a factual question for the jury to resolve. Here, however, he did neither, and he suffers pre-trial judgment for it.

This inability is particularly striking given that the policy SEPTA claims it applied makes distinctions among crimes, setting apart some crimes for a lifetime ban from SEPTA employment and applying a seven-year ban to others. If the policy were developed with anything approaching the level of care that *Griggs*, *Albemarle*, and *Dothard* seem to contemplate, then we would expect that someone at SEPTA would be able to explain how it decided which crimes to place into each category, how the seven-year number was selected, and why SEPTA thought a lifetime ban was appropriate for a crime like simple assault. Almost all of El's relevant questions about the policy were met with silence from SEPTA personnel, suggesting the reasonable inference that SEPTA has no real basis for asserting that its policy accurately distinguishes between applicants that do and do not present an unacceptable level of risk.

Title VII, however, does not measure care in formulating hiring policies; rather, it requires that an employer be able to show that its policy is consistent with business necessity when challenged. Granted, the two will typically go hand-in-hand. Here, however, for all of SEPTA's apparent loose manner in formulating and defending its policy, it produced credible expert testimony that its policy accurately screened out applicants too likely to commit acts of violence against paratransit passengers. . . .

Taking all of the record evidence into account, there is no substantive evidence on which a reasonable juror could find that SEPTA's policy is inconsistent with business necessity. Summary judgment in SEPTA's favor was, therefore, appropriate. . . .

NOTES

1. *The Burden of Proof of Business Necessity.* The synthesis that the *El* court draws from *Lanning I* and *II* is that the practice is a business necessity if the employer can show that it "accurately — but not perfectly — ascertains an applicant's ability to perform successfully the job in question." *El*'s standard links the practice at issue to the accuracy of its prediction of job-related performance and thus seems to merge "job related" and "business necessity," although the language of the statute requires an employer showing of both. Recall Chapter 2's discussion of the BFOQ defense to disparate treatment. *Johnson Controls* made clear the BFOQ is narrower, and harder for a defendant to establish, than *El*'s version of business necessity. Finally, assuming *El* correctly states the rule, does the court apply it correctly? The chance that any paratransit driver will attack a passenger is very remote, without regard to the driver's criminal record. Even assuming some (slightly?) increased risk of a driver with a criminal record engaging in such an unlikely occurrence, does business necessity mean much if such a rule is valid?

2. *The Business Necessity Standard and* Lanning I. The court in *El* refers to two earlier decisions that also involved SEPTA. *Lanning I — Lanning v. Southeastern Pennsylvania Transportation Authority*, 181 F.3d 478 (3d Cir. 1999) — involved a physical exertion test for candidates to become SEPTA transit police officers; it required them to be able to run 1.5 miles in 12 minutes. The test had a drastic impact on women: in two years, 6.7 percent and 12 percent of women passed it as compared with 55.6 percent and 60 percent of male applicants. The court reviewed the development of

[handwritten margin note: accuracy of the Prediction of the]

business necessity from *Griggs* through *Wards Cove* and then concluded that Congress had intended to reject the *Wards Cove* approach in favor of a return to *Griggs*. "[B]ecause the Act clearly chooses *Griggs* over *Wards Cove*, the Court's interpretation of the business necessity standard in *Wards Cove* does not survive the Act." 181 F.3d at 488. Looking to *Griggs* and other pre-*Wards Cove* cases, *Lanning I* summarized what the defense required in the case before it: "a discriminatory cutoff score [must] be shown to measure the minimum qualifications necessary for the successful performance of the job in question in order to survive a disparate impact challenge." If *Lanning I* is correct as to the standard, is *El* consistent with it? Is a "minimum qualification" for a paratransit driver that he or she pose *no* risk to passengers? Or perhaps that the driver pose no unavoidable risk? Note that in *El* the proof was from criminologists, not the employer's own experiences.

3. *The Business Necessity Standard and* Lanning II. SEPTA transit police did not undertake 1.5 mile runs in the performance of their jobs; in fact, the jobs rarely required any running at all. The prescribed run, however, concededly measured aerobic capacity, and SEPTA argued that this capacity was necessary for the job. That, too, seemed doubtful since SEPTA required only new officers to meet this level; incumbent officers were encouraged, but not required, to do so. Quite literally, it was not necessary to have that aerobic capacity to work as a transit police officer. Nevertheless, SEPTA introduced further testimony on remand comparing the performance of transit police based on their times running the 1.5 miles.

In *Lanning II*, 308 F.3d 286, 290 (3d Cir. 2002), the court upheld the test: "The study found that individuals who passed the run test had a success rate on the job standard ranging from 70% to 90%. The success rate of individuals who failed the run test ranged from 5% to 20%." Given that SEPTA wanted to improve the fitness and "crime fighting ability" of its police and that "the business necessity takes public safety into consideration," the test satisfied the standard, especially since women applicants could undertake aerobic training that would significantly improve their chances of passing it. *See also IBEW v. Miss. Power & Light Co.*, 442 F.3d 313 (5th Cir. 2006) (increasing a cut-off score was a business necessity in light of evidence that a passing applicant had a 50 percent chance of developing into an above-average worker, as compared with a 39 percent chance for passing applicants under the prior cut-off). *Lanning II* seems to hold that a selection device that measurably and substantially increases the likelihood of job success is a business necessity. But, accepting SEPTA's numbers, the increased success rate was very substantial. *El*, in contrast, does not quantify, or even suggest ranges, for the increased likelihood of violence at issue.

4. *More Is Better?* There has been recurrent debate about whether "more is better" in business necessity determinations. In other words, the question has been not merely whether some increase in performance (or, in *El*, some decrease in risk) is sufficient but whether some requirement of quantitative substantiality is required. *See Lanning v. SEPTA*, 308 F.3d 286, 292 (3d Cir. 2002) ("We are not saying . . . that 'more is better.' While, of course, a higher aerobic capacity will translate into better field performance — at least as to many job tasks which entail physical capability — to set an unnecessarily high cutoff score would contravene *Griggs*"). Isn't *El* saying exactly that — more (safety) is better? Why does setting an unnecessarily rigorous criterion for hiring not also contravene *Griggs*?

5. *Judge Trial.* Although the 1991 Civil Rights Act amended Title VII to provide a right to a jury trial in disparate treatment cases, it did not do so for disparate impact cases, which means that juries are either not used at all or are "advisory." See Chapter 8. So don't be confused by the recurrent references in *El* (and we'll soon see, in *Jones*

Is that contrary to Griggs?

v. City of Boston) to the "reasonable jury." However, the ADEA does not distinguish between judge and jury trials on the basis of the theory being litigated, so jury instructions can be important under that statute.

6. *No Battle of the Experts.* The plaintiff lost his case because of the experts — his failure to call any experts for his side and his failure even to depose SEPTA's experts. An expert on one side almost always begets an expert witness on the other. Why didn't the plaintiff hire experts to counter the defendant's experts? The answer is probably the economics of practice: plaintiff could not afford them. But why did the plaintiff's lawyers not depose the defendant's witnesses? What questions could be asked to create a genuine issue of material fact in order to avoid summary judgment? Note also that the plaintiff did depose SEPTA management employees, who all testified that they did not know why SEPTA had adopted the bright-line rule challenged in the case. Do you agree with the court that the lack of procedural regularity is irrelevant to the ultimate determination of business necessity?

7. *Criminal Records and Discrimination.* Despite the result in *El*, the EEOC launched a major initiative designed to alter the way American businesses treat arrest and conviction records because of the likely impact of such practices on minorities. *See* EEOC Enforcement Guidance on the Consideration of Arrest and Conviction Records in Employment Decisions Under Title VII of the Civil Rights Act of 1964 (Apr. 25, 2012), http://www.eeoc.gov/laws/guidance/arrest_conviction.cfm; the EEOC has filed several suits challenging such use. There has been substantial pushback, *see, e.g., Texas v. EEOC,* 838 F.3d 511 (5th Cir. 2016) (state attorney general challenge to EEOC guidance), but no clear resolution. Further, the change in presidential administrations may put the whole initiative in doubt.

Ironically, employer policies regarding conviction records may not have the adverse effects on black employment that one might expect from *El*. For example, Harry J. Holzer & Steven Raphael, *Perceived Criminality, Criminal Background Checks, and the Racial Hiring Practices of Employers,* 49 J.L. & ECON. 451, 473 (2006), find that employers who perform criminal background checks are more likely to hire black applicants than employers that do not. They believe the potential adverse consequence of such checks in terms of the likelihood of hiring African Americans are more than offset by the positive effect of eliminating "statistical discrimination." Even if this is true, it does not alter the fact that some individuals, like El, are excluded by the policy. And *Teal* would allow El to attack this screening device, even if the bottom line is that blacks are proportionately represented among SEPTA paratransit drivers. *See generally* Tammy R. Pettinato, *Employment Discrimination Against Ex-Offenders: The Promise and Limits of Title VII Disparate Impact Theory,* 98 MARQ. L. REV. 831 (2014). Disparate impact challenges are only one manifestation of the current movement to reduce barriers to employment for ex-offenders. *See also* Dallon Flake, *When Any Sentence Is a Life Sentence: Employment Discrimination Against Ex-Offenders,* 93 WASH. U. L. REV. 45 (2015).

8. *Unemployment and Credit Scores.* There is also some concern about discrimination on the basis of being unemployed or of having low credit scores (probably correlated phenomena). While there have been limited efforts on the state level to address "currently employed" requirements directly, *e.g.,* N.J. Stat. §34:8B-1, both grounds could be the basis of a disparate impact challenge. *See generally* Lea Shepard, *Seeking Solutions to Financial History Discrimination,* 46 CONN. L. REV. 993, 1000 (2014); Lea Shepard, *Toward a Stronger Financial History Antidiscrimination Norm,* 53 B.C. L. REV. 1695 (2012); Jennifer Jolly-Ryan, *Have a Job to Get a Job: Disparate Treatment and Disparate Impact of the "Currently Employed" Requirement,* 18 MICH. J. RACE & L. 189 (2012).

9. *Employer "Tournaments."* Some employers engage in forced "ranking" of workers against each other, with those ranked near the bottom (and thus the losers in the tournament) terminated. Assuming that such rankings have a disparate impact on protected groups, are they justified by a business necessity of enhancing employee effectiveness? Nancy Levit, June Carbone, & Naomi R. Cahn, *Gender and the Tournament: Reinventing Antidiscrimination Law in an Age of Inequality*, 96 Tex. L. Rev. (forthcoming 2017), argue no, looking to managerial literature findings that such techniques are ill-advised and declining and that there are less restrictive alternatives available.

10. *Big Data.* There is increasing concern among commentators that developments in the use of "big data" for employment decisions raises discrimination possibilities. *See generally* Pauline T. Kim, *Data-Driven Discrimination at Work*, 58 Wm. & Mary L. Rev. 857 (2017); Solon Barocas & Andrew D. Selbst, *Big Data's Disparate Impact*, 104 Calif. L. Rev. 671 (2016); Alan G. King & Marko J. Mrkonich, *"Big Data" and the Risk of Employment Discrimination*, 68 Okla. L. Rev. 555 (2016). While some argue that data-driven decisions are preferable to biased human decisionmaking, others warn that not only could algorithms using workforce analytics be structured to intentionally discriminate against protected classes but that, even absent such influences, big data threatens to have a disparate impact. A number of factors, including errors in the underlying data, programmer coding choices, unrepresentative samples, or the selection of variables for exclusion or inclusion, might produce results that adversely affect protected classes.

Such impact, however, seems at first blush justifiable. As Barocas and Selbst point out, "[b]y definition, data mining is always a form of statistical (and therefore seemingly rational) discrimination. Indeed, the very point of data mining is to provide a rational basis upon which to distinguish between individuals and to reliably confer to the individual the qualities possessed by those who seem statistically similar." 104 Calif. L. Rev. at 677. In other words, the point of data mining is to discover statistically significant correlations between the "target variables" (the sought-after characteristics of better workers) and whatever traits of potential workers lurk in the data. And, assuming that the target variable is itself job related (say to job tenure), the algorithm will identify traits that correlate with that variable — even though there may be, literally, no causal explanation for why that might be true. Thus, traditional validation techniques are likely to be satisfied. As the two commentators conclude, "[d]ata mining will likely only be used if it is actually predictive of something, so the business necessity defense solely comes down to whether the trait sought is important enough to job performance to justify its use in any context." *Id.* at 709. In the job tenure example, that would be whether an employer is justified in putting so much weight on predictions of longer job tenure given all the other aspects of job performance. But, as target variables increase, the likelihood that employers will be able to establish business necessity by their use of data analytics to select employees may increase despite problems such as unrepresentative samples. Further, given the nature of data mining, it will often be difficult, if not impossible, for plaintiffs to prove the alternative employment practices surrebuttal. *But see* James Grimmelmann & David Westreich, *Incomprehensible Discrimination*, 7 Cal. L. Rev. Online 164 (2017).

11. *The Universal Turn.* Some commentators have argued that it is politically more feasible to challenge objectionable practices without invoking race. *E.g.*, Katie R. Eyer, *That's Not Discrimination: American Beliefs and the Limits of Anti-Discrimination Law*, 96 Minn. L. Rev. 1275, 1280 (2012) (arguing in favor of "litigation-based approaches that do not focus on group-based discrimination claims"). For example, prisoner re-entry has often been a subject of concern without focusing on the racial disparities of prison populations. Under this view, disparate impact challenges may be misguided if the real

goal is systemic changes. Other scholars question this "universal turn." *E.g.*, Zev J. Eigen, Camille Gear Rich & Charlotte Alexander, *Post-Racial Hydraulics: The Hidden Danger of the Universal Turn*, 91 N.Y.U. L. Rev. 1 (2016); Jessica A. Clarke, *Beyond Equality? Against the Universal Turn in Workplace Protections*, 86 Ind. L.J. 1219, 1240-51 (2011).

12. *Challenging State Licensing Rules.* Direct suits against licensing agencies because their practices had a disparate impact on racial grounds have been unsuccessful. *E.g., Fields v. Hallsville Indep. Sch. Dist.*, 906 F.2d 1017 (5th Cir. 1990); *George v. New Jersey Bd. of Veterinary Med. Exam'rs*, 794 F.2d 113 (3d Cir. 1986). The major exception to this is where the requirements are imposed by a state agency that the court views as essentially an employer because its rules apply only to public, as opposed to private, schools. *Ass'n of Mexican Am. Educators v. California*, 231 F.3d 572, 582 (9th Cir. 2000) (en banc). However, the Second Circuit held that a city board of education would have to validate a test with a disparate impact even though the test was required by state law for "permanent" city teachers. *Gulino v. N.Y. State Educ. Dep't*, 460 F.3d 361 (2d Cir. 2006). The argument can be framed as whether Title VII preempts state law that would require discrimination in employment by the use of practices with a disparate impact. *See* 42 U.S.C. §2000e-7 (2018).

PROBLEM 3.3

Kaplan offers undergraduate and graduate degrees to students across the country. Some of its students obtain financial aid through programs operated by the Department of Education; consequently, some employees have access to those students' financial information. The Department has regulations that circumscribe the manner in which Kaplan can access and use students' information. Violations of those regulations can bring severe penalties.

About a decade ago, Kaplan discovered that some of its financial aid officers had stolen payments that belonged to students and that some executives had engaged in self-dealing, by hiring relatives as vendors. In response, Kaplan implemented a number of measures, one of which was to run credit checks on applicants for senior-executive positions, accounting and other positions with access to company financials or cash, and positions with access to student financial aid information. The credit checks are performed by a third-party vendor, which reports, among other things, whether the applicant has ever filed for bankruptcy, is delinquent on child-support payments, has any garnishments on earnings, or has outstanding civil judgments exceeding $2,000. If an applicant's credit history includes any of the enumerated items, the vendor flags the applicant's file for "review." At that point, Kaplan reviews the file and makes an ad hoc decision as to whether to move forward with the application. The credit-check process is racially blind: the vendor does not report the applicant's race with her other information.

The EEOC has launched an investigation of whether Kaplan's use of credit checks screens out more African American applicants than white applicants, creating a disparate impact in violation of Title VII. Assume that such an impact can be proved and that it is substantial. If you were representing Kaplan, how would you establish the business necessity of this practice? Are you assisted by the fact that the EEOC itself uses this kind of credit check for 84 of the agency's 97 positions, noting that "overdue just debts increase temptation to commit illegal or unethical acts as a means of gaining funds to meet financial obligations"?

These facts are drawn from *EEOC v. Kaplan Higher Educ. Corp.*, 748 F.3d 749 (6th Cir. 2014), although the court there never reached the business necessity question.

3.   *Alternative Employment Practices*

Early disparate impact cases, particularly *Albemarle Paper Co. v. Moody*, 422 U.S. 405, 425 (1975), described the litigation structure of a disparate impact case as including a plaintiff's surrebuttal, even if the employer proves the challenged practice is justified as job related and consistent with business necessity:

> If an employer does then meet the burden of proving that its tests are "job related," it remains open to the complaining party to show that other tests or selection devices, without a similarly undesirable racial effect, would also serve the employer's legitimate interest in "efficient and trustworthy workmanship." Such a showing would be evidence that the employer was using its tests merely as a "pretext" for discrimination.

It was not clear whether "pretext" was used as a state-of-mind concept, as in *McDonnell Douglas*, or merely as a kind of shorthand for a "less restrictive alternative" analysis, but the Civil Rights Act of 1991 resolved this problem. While a plaintiff presumably can always prevail by establishing intent to discriminate, "pretext" is not a formal part of disparate impact analysis.

Rather, the new statute adds §703(k)(1)(A) to Title VII. The first prong provides that a violation occurs when the plaintiff proves the employer uses a particular employment practice with a disparate impact, and the employer fails to establish job relation and business necessity. §703(k)(1)(A)(i). But a violation can also exist when, despite the employer's successfully establishing business necessity, the plaintiff "makes the demonstration described in subparagraph C with respect to an alternative employment practice and the [employer] refuses to adopt such alternative employment practice." §703(k)(1)(A)(ii). This language places the burden of persuasion on the plaintiff. *IBEW v. Miss. Power & Light Co.*, 442 F.3d 313 (5th Cir. 2006), but what does that entail?

Subparagraph (C) defines the plaintiff's surrebuttal burden as in "accordance with the law as it existed on June 4, 1989, with respect to the concept of 'alternative employment practice.'" The Court's decision in *Wards Cove* was issued on June 5, 1989, suggesting Congress meant "alternative employment practice" to embrace the law *prior* to *Wards Cove*, as it had explicitly provided with respect to business necessity and job relatedness.

So far, so good. But it was *Wards Cove* that first spoke of "alternative business practices" with a less discriminatory impact. Further, that case viewed the failure to adopt such alternatives as raising doubts about the employer's intent. On June 4, 1989, that is, prior to *Wards Cove*, the closest phrase to "alternative employment practices" was Justice O'Connor's plurality opinion in *Watson v. Fort Worth Bank & Trust*, 487 U.S. 977 (1988), which had permitted the plaintiff to demonstrate less discriminatory "alternative selection devices" in response to the defendant's business necessity showing. Justice O'Connor went on to note that "[f]actors such as the cost or other burdens of proposed alternative selection devices are relevant in determining whether they would be equally as effective as the challenged practice in serving the employer's legitimate business goals." *Id.* at 998.

Some light is cast on this concept by *Adams v. City of Chicago*, 469 F.3d 609 (7th Cir. 2006), where the parties agreed that promotions to sergeant based on an examination had a disparate impact on black and Hispanic law enforcement officers. Plaintiffs conceded the test was valid but pitched their claim on the alternative employment practice prong of the statute. Prior to the promotions, a mayoral task force had recommended using a heavier weight for "merit," defined as officers' on-the-job performance as rated by their supervisors. Plaintiffs argued that Chicago should have instituted the recommended merit component, contending it had previously done so for other departmental positions — both detectives and lieutenants — and did so after the promotions in question for the sergeant position. In short, they urged that the city had refused to adapt an equally valid, less discriminatory method of promotion.

The panel majority rejected this argument despite a concession by Chicago that the merit alternative was "of substantial equal validity as assessment-based promotions." It did so because the officers did not show that the alternative process was available at the time such that Chicago could be found to have refused to adopt it. *Id.* at 613. There was no extant *validated* merit procedure for potential sergeants: the task force's recommendation that one be developed was prospective only, and the sergeant's examination that ultimately emerged from that recommendation and included merit took months to develop and implement. The merit evaluation system for detectives could not be a basis for finding that alternative available since the sergeant position involved supervisory duties absent from the detective position. As for a lieutenants' exam using merit, there were far more individuals seeking the promotion to sergeant than to lieutenant, which meant plaintiffs did not show that a valid evaluation method was available "on this large scale."

Judge Williams dissented from the panel's result because she did not find anything in §2000e-2(k)(1)(A)(ii) that required an alternative to be validated in order to be "available." For the dissent, "[a]n alternative is unavailable when, for verifiable reasons, the defendant cannot adopt it. A reasonable alternative is not unavailable simply because the defendant has not completed its own inquiry into the viability of the alternative." *Id.* at 617. She cited *Fitzpatrick v. City of Atlanta*, 2 F.3d 1112 (11th Cir. 1993), as "a true situation of no viable alternative being available." 469 F.3d at 617. There, the plaintiffs failed to show that "shadow beards" were a plausible alternative to the Atlanta Fire Department's clean-shaven rule. That rule, which had a discriminatory impact on African American men (who are more likely to suffer from a bacterial disorder, pseudofolliculitis barbae, than white males), was justified by the need for firefighters to wear close-fitting breathing apparatus.

Adams did not bode well for alternative employment practices claim, and, in fact, other circuits have rejected the claim when it is raised. *See Johnson v. City of Memphis*, 770 F.3d 464, 467 (6th Cir. 2014); *IBEW v. Mississippi Power & Light Co.*, 442 F.3d 313 (5th Cir. 2006). *But see* Elizabeth Tippett, *Robbing a Barren Vault: The Implications of* Dukes v. Wal-Mart *for Cases Challenging Subjective Employment Practices*, 29 HOFSTRA LAB. & EMP. L.J. 433, 435-36 (2012) (at least where subjective practices are involved, disparate impact challenges are rare and, employers rarely assert the business necessity defense, resulting in plaintiffs being rarely required to show a less discriminatory alternative). But a recent decision may have breathed new life into the theory.

JONES v. CITY OF BOSTON
845 F.3d 28 (2016)

KAYATTA, Circuit Judge.

[Several police officers brought a disparate impact case against the Boston Police Department challenging a hair drug test that had resulted in them not being employed. In a prior opinion, *Jones v. City of Boston* ("*Jones I*"), 752 F.3d 38, 60 (1st Cir. 2014), the court had held that the test caused a cognizable disparate impact, but it remanded for the district court to consider the department's business necessity defense and the officers' alternative employment practice argument. The district court found against the plaintiffs on both remaining points.]

in the abstract

I. BACKGROUND

Our prior opinion details much of the relevant factual background. In a nutshell, from 1999 to 2006, the Department administered a hair drug test to thousands of officers, cadets, and job applicants. The testing procedure called for the gathering of a hair sample, which was then "washed" and analyzed for the presence of cocaine, marijuana, opiates, PCP, and amphetamines. Upon detecting cocaine in a hair sample, a licensed physician would determine whether legally administered medication could have caused the positive result. The individual who tested positive was also permitted to submit a second sample for a so-called "safety-net" test.

The results were negative for over 99% of the white individuals tested and over 98% of the black individuals tested. The Officers now before us, however, were among the fewer than two percent of black individuals who tested positive for cocaine. As a result, nine lost a job or job offer, and one received an unpaid suspension subject to participation in a drug rehabilitation and testing program.

statistically significant is sufficient

[The earlier opinion had held there was a disparate impact, rejecting the argument that the EEOC's four-fifth's "rule of thumb" precluded such an attack "because the one-percent difference in pass rates between white and black officers was so minuscule as to be of no practical significance." For the First Circuit, the difference in exam results by race was indisputably statistically significant, which sufficed.]

A. JOB-RELATEDNESS AND CONSISTENCY WITH BUSINESS NECESSITY

Reliability of the test in furthering the necessity

[There was no dispute as to the necessity of having police officers abstain from drug use. The question was whether the hair drug test was too unreliable to meaningfully further the department's legitimate need for a drug-abstaining police force. A reasonable jury could find the test not 100 percent reliable because "it could not always distinguish between ingestion of drugs and contamination of the hair by environmental exposure to drugs"; further, false positives could well have occurred because "black hair, especially if damaged by some cosmetic treatments more commonly used by black individuals, is more likely to absorb and retain contaminants to which the hair might be exposed." Nevertheless, such shortfalls did not undercut the value of the test, given that negative results were accurate and thus ensured that thousands of officers were drug free. The test, therefore, was job related and consistent with business necessity.]

B. REFUSAL TO ADOPT AVAILABLE ALTERNATIVE THAT WOULD HAVE MET EMPLOYER'S LEGITIMATE NEEDS WITH LESS DISPARATE IMPACT

1. does an alt method exist
2. is it less discriminatory or have less disparate impact?
3. showing that ∆ refused to adopt that method?

[Application of the alternative employment practice prong of disparate impact liability inquiry] turns on the answers to three questions: First, does the record contain evidence that would allow a jury to find that there was an "alternative" method of meeting the Department's legitimate needs? Second, does the record also allow a jury to find that adopting that alternative method would have had less of a disparate impact? And finally, could a jury find that the Department "refuses to adopt" that alternative method? We consider each question in turn.

1. Could a Reasonable Jury Find That an Alternative Drug-Testing Method Would Have Met the Department's Legitimate Needs?

[The proposed alternative was] "hair testing plus urinalysis." By this, the Officers mean the following: first, administer the hair test to all officers (which will clear over

98% of the individuals tested); then, administer a follow-up series of random urinalysis tests only to those officers who receive positive results on the hair test; and discharge (or suspend, pending rehabilitation and further drug testing) only those who flunk one of the follow-up random urinalysis tests.[2]

This approach would have fully replicated the results of the hair test alone except, a jury might find, it would have cleared those who received a positive hair test yet were likely not using cocaine. And if the urinalysis tests continued randomly over the course of more than ninety days, they would have confirmed a period of drug abstention equal to that confirmed by a negative hair test.

Would this alternative have equally met the Department's needs? A reasonable jury might so find. Keep in mind that the Department already used a series of negative urinalysis tests as a basis to reinstate suspended officers who tested positive on the hair test: officers who tested positive on the hair test under the challenged practice could choose to admit to drug use; receive a forty-five day unpaid suspension; undergo drug rehabilitation; and submit to frequent, random urinalysis for three years. The only difference between the challenged practice and the proposed "hair testing plus urinalysis" alternative is that firing (or suspension and drug rehabilitation) preceded the urinalysis testing in the actual regime, whereas no change in employment status would have occurred until after urinalysis confirmation in the alternative scheme. [This] naturally suggests that the Department viewed random urinalysis as an acceptably reliable method for detecting drug use on a targeted (rather than mass) basis.[3] To the extent that a concern with urinalysis is its manipulability, a jury could find that the more frequent and randomized nature of the Officers' proposed urinalysis program would have sufficiently minimized such a concern.

Crucially, the alternative would have retained the main benefit of the challenged drug testing program: using a relatively unintrusive, easy-to-supervise hair test to generate the negative results that confirm that almost all officers, regardless of race, do not use illegal drugs. All in all, we think that this is a close enough call that a jury could conclude that the Officers' proffered alternative equally would have met the Department's needs. Indeed, if a jury believed the thrust of the Officers' evidence, it might conclude that the alternative test method would have saved the Department from losing several veteran officers who were not using cocaine.

2.   Could a Reasonable Jury Find That the Alternative Would Have Generated Less of a Disparate Impact?

. . . Here, if the jury were to believe the Officers and their experts rather than the Department and its experts, it would be self-evident that the "hair testing plus urinalysis" alternative would have generated less of a disparate impact than that revealed by the large-sample statistical analysis of the hair drug test results. The jury could find that the hair test alone can generate false positives for some black individuals, that

---

2. The district court found that the Officers failed to show that use of urinalysis testing in lieu of hair testing would have sufficed. Urinalysis detects only very recent cocaine use (within two days), whereas hair testing detects cocaine use for a much longer period (within as many as ninety days). [Further, administering urinalysis frequently to all officers might be prohibitively expensive and easier to tamper with. Finally, it might well be legally problematic.]

3. Similarly, while it may be within the scope of inquiry to consider the putative costs of the Officers' proposed alternative, a reasonable jury could find that there would have been no material cost differential, especially given that the Department had shown a willingness to assume those costs by virtue of the rehabilitation option that it offered (and continues to offer) to all officers who tested positive on the hair test.

black individuals have no greater likelihood of receiving a false positive result from urinalysis than do white individuals, and that the Officers (who swear that they did not use cocaine) more likely than not received false positive results that urinalysis would have identified as such. Given such findings, the alternative would necessarily have resulted in the termination of a lower ratio of black officers to white officers. That is, because the statistical analysis of the challenged practice shows an overall disparate impact of X, where the number of black officers with positive results was Y, a reduction in Y alone would necessarily have resulted in an overall disparate impact of less than X. . . .

3.   Could a Reasonable Jury Find That the Department "Refuses" to Adopt the Alternative?

Title VII requires as an element of a successful disparate impact claim a finding that "the [employer] refuses to adopt such alternative employment practice." 42 U.S.C. §2000e-2(k)(1)(A)(ii). This language is susceptible to a number of different readings. Does an employer only "refuse to adopt" an alternative practice if the employer knows it will meet its needs and have less of a disparate impact? If this were a correct reading, then a finding for plaintiffs on the third prong of the disparate impact inquiry would effectively constitute a finding of intentional discrimination. *Cf. Wards Cove Packing Co. v. Atonio* (observing that a refusal to adopt an alternative "would belie a claim by petitioners that their incumbent practices are being employed for nondiscriminatory reasons"); *Albemarle Paper Co.* ("Such a showing would be evidence that the employer was using its tests merely as a 'pretext' for discrimination."). As we have previously observed, however, "proof of a disparate impact claim requires no proof of intentional discrimination." *Jones I.*

Other possible readings of the statute remain. Is it enough that the alternative was available and not used, or must its availability have been known? Must it be specifically proposed, like a dinner special at a restaurant, or is it enough that it was on the known menu of options and not selected? What are we to make of the statute's use of the present tense ("refuses")? The parties provide no express discussion of these nuances. Indeed, their briefs contain no acknowledgement that there are meaningfully different possible readings of the statutory text. [Both plaintiffs and defendant cited only the Seventh Circuit's decisions in *Adams v. City of Chicago*, 469 F.3d 609 (7th Cir. 2006), and *Allen v. City of Chicago*, 351 F.3d 306 (7th Cir. 2003).] The formulation employed in *Allen* and repeated in *Adams* is that "the statutory scheme requires plaintiffs to demonstrate a viable alternative and give the employer an opportunity to adopt it." *Adams* elsewhere seems to suggest that the employer is given an opportunity to adopt the alternative if the employer "had an opportunity" to adopt it, and that such an "opportunity" existed if the alternative was "available," and the employer was free to adopt it.

Confronted with the limited briefing on point, and the parties' consensus in pointing to Seventh Circuit precedent, we will follow the path of *Allen* and *Adams* by default (rather than by decision). We asked at oral argument whether there was evidence in the record that the "hair testing plus urinalysis" alternative was available to the Department at a time relevant to this lawsuit. The Officers' counsel directed us only to the fact that in 2003, they gave the Department an affidavit signed by their expert, Dr. Kidwell, proposing the alternative. . . . The affidavit appears to be an expert disclosure detailing Dr. Kidwell's opinions on hair testing as well as "more enlightened approach[es] to drug testing," which include hair testing followed by random, frequent urinalysis. . . . The Officers make no claim that the alternative was otherwise "available" before Dr. Kidwell proposed it. [T]he affidavit does indeed propose that the Department could use what we refer to as the "hair testing plus urinalysis" alternative.

Accordingly, we agree with the Officers that the summary judgment record reveals a material dispute of fact concerning whether, sometime in 2003, the Department, by continuing to administer the challenged hair test, "necessarily . . . refused to adopt" the alternative made available to it by the suggestion of Dr. Kidwell. . . .

NOTES

1. *Knowing Use = Intent to Discriminate?* Notice that the court seems to think that an employer's refusal to adopt an alternative known to have a disparate impact that will meet its needs "would effectively constitute a finding of intentional discrimination." Do you agree? What happened to *Feeney's* "'because of,' not merely 'in spite of'" distinction? See p. 131. Anyway, if the trier of fact does find in favor of plaintiffs, wouldn't that result be fairly so described? Would plaintiffs then be entitled to more generous disparate treatment recoveries?

2. *Did Plaintiffs Need an Expert?* The court relies heavily on the expert affidavit, and, in fact, the timing of the submission of that affidavit might pose some problems for plaintiffs whose claims arose before it was given to the city. But, really, isn't the proffered alternative a common sense one? Was an expert needed at all? Even if not, did the plaintiffs have to call the alternative explicitly to the department's attention before it could be said to have refused to adopt it? Is the court putting too much weight on the word "refuses"?

C.   SECTION 703(h) EXCEPTIONS

In addition to undermining the plaintiff's showing of impact or showing the job relatedness/business necessity defense, Title VII offers three other statutory defenses in disparate impact cases. Section 703(h) creates exceptions for professionally developed employment tests, for bona fide seniority systems, and for bona fide merit systems.

1.   *Professionally Developed Tests*

Section 703(h) provides that, "notwithstanding any other provision of Title VII, it shall not be an unlawful employment practice for an employer to give and to act upon the results of any professionally developed ability test provided that such test, its administration or action upon the results is not designed, intended or used to discriminate because of race, color, religion, sex or national origin." *Griggs* accepted the EEOC's position that, where there was a disparate impact, §703(h) incorporated the strict validation standards that industrial psychologists established for themselves for any test or selection device. Ironically, that holding means that §703(h) operates less as an exception than as a more demanding subset of the general business necessity defense where a "test" is involved.

ALBEMARLE PAPER CO. v. MOODY
422 U.S. 405 (1975)

Justice STEWART delivered the opinion of the Court.

. . . Like the employer in *Griggs*, Albemarle uses two general ability tests, the Beta Examination, to test nonverbal intelligence, and the Wonderlic Test (Forms A and B), the purported measure of general verbal facility which was also involved in the *Griggs* case. Applicants for hire into various skilled lines of progression at the plant are required to score 100 on the Beta Exam and 18 on one of the Wonderlic Test's two alternative forms.

The question of job relatedness must be viewed in the context of the plant's operation and the history of the testing program. The plant, which now employs about 650 persons, converts raw wood into paper products. It is organized into a number of functional departments, each with one or more distinct lines of progression, the theory being that workers can move up the line as they acquire the necessary skills. The number and structure of the lines have varied greatly over time. For many years, certain lines were themselves more skilled and paid higher wages than others, and until 1964 these skilled lines were expressly reserved for white workers. In 1968, many of the unskilled "Negro" lines were "end-tailed" onto skilled "white" lines, but it apparently remains true that at least the top jobs in certain lines require greater skills than the top jobs in other lines. In this sense, at least, it is still possible to speak of relatively skilled and relatively unskilled lines.

In the 1950's while the plant was being modernized with new and more sophisticated equipment, the Company introduced a high school diploma requirement for entry into the skilled lines. Though the Company soon concluded that this requirement did not improve the quality of the labor force, the requirement was continued until the District Court enjoined its use. In the late 1950's the Company began using the Beta Examination and the Bennett Mechanical Comprehension Test (also involved in the *Griggs* case) to screen applicants for entry into the skilled lines. The Bennett Test was dropped several years later, but use of the Beta Test continued.

The Company added the Wonderlic Tests in 1963, for the skilled lines, on the theory that a certain verbal intelligence was called for by the increasing sophistication of the plant's operations. The Company made no attempt to validate the test for job relatedness, and simply adopted the national "norm" score of 18 as a cut-off point for new job applicants. After 1964, when it discontinued overt segregation in the lines of progression, the Company allowed Negro workers to transfer to the skilled lines if they could pass the Beta and Wonderlic Tests, but few succeeded in doing so. Incumbents in the skilled lines, some of whom had been hired before adoption of the tests, were not required to pass them to retain their jobs or their promotion rights. The record shows that a number of white incumbents in high-ranking job groups could not pass the tests. . . .

Four months before this case went to trial, Albemarle engaged an expert in industrial psychology to "validate" the job relatedness of its testing program. He spent a half day at the plant and devised a "concurrent validation" study, which was conducted by plant officials, without his supervision. The expert then subjected the results to statistical analysis. The study dealt with 10 job groupings, selected from near the top of nine of the lines of progression. Jobs were grouped together solely by their proximity in the line of progression; no attempt was made to analyze jobs in terms of the particular skills they might require. All, or nearly all, employees in the selected groups participated in the study — 105 employees in all, but only four Negroes. Within each job grouping, the study compared the test scores of each employee with an independent "ranking" of the employee, relative to each of his coworkers, made by two of the employee's supervisors. . . .

For each job grouping, the expert computed the "Phi coefficient" of statistical correlation between the test scores and an average of the two supervisorial rankings. Consonant with professional conventions, the expert regarded as "statistically significant" any correlation that could have occurred by chance only five times, or fewer, in 100 trials. On the basis of these results, the District Court found that "[t]he personnel tests administered at the plant have undergone validation studies and have been proven to be job related." Like the Court of Appeals, we are constrained to disagree.

The EEOC has issued "Guidelines" for employers seeking to determine, through professional validation studies, whether their employment tests are job related. 29 C.F.R. pt. 1607. These Guidelines draw upon and make reference to professional standards of test validation established by the American Psychological Association. The EEOC Guidelines are not administrative "regulations" promulgated pursuant to formal procedures established by the Congress. But, as this Court has heretofore noted, they do constitute "[t]he administrative interpretation of the Act by the enforcing agency," and consequently they are "entitled to great deference."

The message of these Guidelines is the same as that of the *Griggs* case — that discriminatory tests are impermissible unless shown, by professionally acceptable methods, to be "predictive of or significantly correlated with important elements of work behavior which comprise or are relevant to the job or jobs for which candidates are being evaluated." 29 C.F.R. §1607.4(c).

Measured against the Guidelines, Albemarle's validation study is materially defective in several respects:

(1) Even if it had been otherwise adequate, the study would not have "validated" the Beta and Wonderlic test battery for all of the skilled lines of progression for which the two tests are, apparently, now required. The study showed significant correlations for the Beta Exam in only three of the eight lines. Though the Wonderlic Test's Form A and Form B are in theory identical and interchangeable measures of verbal facility, significant correlations for one form but not for the other were obtained in four job groupings. In two job groupings neither form showed a significant correlation. Within some of the lines of progression, one form was found acceptable for some job groupings but not for others. Even if the study were otherwise reliable, this odd patchwork of results would not entitle Albemarle to impose its testing program under the Guidelines. A test may be used in jobs other than those for which it has been professionally validated only if there are "no significant differences" between the studied and unstudied jobs. 29 C.F.R. §1607.4(c)(2). The study in this case involved no analysis of the attributes of, or the particular skills needed in, the studied job groups. There is accordingly no basis for concluding that "no significant differences" exist among the lines of progression, or among distinct job groupings within the studied lines of progression. Indeed, the study's checkered results appear to compel the opposite conclusion.

(2) The study compared test scores with subjective supervisorial rankings. While they allow the use of supervisorial rankings in test validation, the Guidelines quite plainly contemplate that the rankings will be elicited with far more care than was demonstrated here. Albemarle's supervisors were asked to rank employees by a "standard" that was extremely vague and fatally open to divergent interpretations. As previously noted, each "job grouping" contained a number of different jobs, and the supervisors were asked, in each grouping, to "determine which [employees] they felt

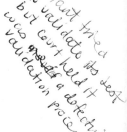

(handwritten margin note) Plant tried to validate its test but Court held it was a defective validation process

(handwritten margin note) Prediction of job performance is key

(handwritten margin note) the job positions themselves must be studied before a test can be validated as being predictive of performance

irrespective of the job that they were actually doing, but in their respective jobs, did a better job than the person they were rating against . . . ." There is no way of knowing precisely what criteria of job performance the supervisors were considering, whether each of the supervisors was considering the same criteria or whether, indeed, any of the supervisors actually applied a focused and stable body of criteria of any kind.[32] There is, in short, simply no way to determine whether the criteria *actually* considered were sufficiently related to the Company's legitimate interest in job-specific ability to justify a testing system with a racially discriminatory impact.

(3) The Company's study focused, in most cases, on job groups near the top of the various lines of progression. [The Court endorsed the Guidelines' "sensible approach" to the issue of whether a test valid for higher level positions can be used for lower level ones, which basically allows such use only when "job progression structures and seniority provisions are so established that new employees will probably, within a reasonable period of time and in a great majority of cases, progress to a higher level." 29 C.F.R. §1607.4(c)(1).] The fact that the best of those employees working near the top of a line of progression score well on a test does not necessarily mean that that test, or some particular cutoff score on the test, is a permissible measure of the minimal qualifications of new workers entering lower level jobs. [However, the] District Court made no findings on these issues. The issues take on special importance in a case, such as this one, where incumbent employees are permitted to work at even high-level jobs without passing the company's test battery. *See* 29 C.F.R. §1607.11. . . .

NOTES

1. *The Terrain.* "Aptitude," "intelligence," or "achievement" tests like those in *Griggs* and *Albemarle Paper* were frequently used in both the public and private sectors at the time the Civil Rights Act was passed, and, as indicated by those cases, typically had a greatly disproportionate impact. Perhaps because of the difficulties and expense of establishing business necessity by validating tests along the lines *Albemarle* suggested, they have largely fallen out of favor in the private sector over the last few decades. As a result, the law regarding such tests is mostly a subspecialty dealing with civil service jobs where tests — especially for police and firefighters — continue to be regularly given and regularly litigated.

However, many employer do give "honesty," "integrity," or "personality" tests, and they have generated very few Title VII challenges, perhaps because they do not have a markedly disparate impact. *See Reynolds v. Arizona*, 1993 U.S. App. LEXIS 9915 (9th Cir. Nov. 4, 1993) (plaintiff failed to prove a gender disparate impact of personality tests). We will also see that the Americans with Disabilities Act has special rules dealing with another kind of test — medical examinations — which has been held to apply to some psychological screening instruments. *See Karraker v. Rent-A-Center, Inc.*, 411 F.3d 831 (7th Cir. 2005). See p. 516. *See generally* Susan J. Stabile, *The Use of Personality Tests as a Hiring Tool: Is the Benefit Worth the Cost?*, 4 U. PA. J. LAB. & EMP. L. 279 (2002); David C. Yamada, *The Regulation of Pre-Employment Honesty Testing: Striking a Temporary (?) Balance Between Self-Regulation and Prohibition*, 39 WAYNE L. REV. 1549 (1993).

---

32. It cannot escape notice that Albemarle's study was conducted by plant officials, without neutral, on-the-scene oversight, at a time when this litigation was about to come to trial. Studies so closely controlled by an interested party in litigation must be examined with great care.

2. *Evolution of the Guidelines. Albemarle's* close comparison of the employer's validation study to the EEOC Uniform Guidelines provoked strong criticism from the testing community as unrealistic and unattainable because few employment tests would satisfy the rigorous requirements of the Guidelines. In response, the current version of the Guidelines was adopted. 29 C.F.R. §§1607.1 *et seq.* (2018). They now provide that any one of the three generally accepted validation strategies is acceptable: criterion, content, or construct. As a practical matter, however, almost all employers who attempt validation rely on content validation. As one court said, "[c]ontent validation is generally feasible while [criterion] validation is frequently impossible." *Guardians Ass'n v. Civil Service Comm.*, 630 F.2d 79, 92 (2d Cir. 1980). Further, most tests facing disparate impact challenges have been found to be valid in recent years, which may be a marker of the success of the theory: *Griggs* may be invalidating fewer tests because employment testing is now more rigorously designed. *But see Ernst v. City of Chi.*, 837 F.3d 788 (7th Cir. 2016) (rejecting a criterion-related validity study because there was no showing that it actually measured skills needed to perform the job and the population used to establish physical standards did not represent the relevant paramedic labor market).

3. *Content Validation.* Content validation is intuitively appealing because, at its simplest, it uses a sample of the work done on the job as the test. If the sample is really representative of the job, success on the test necessarily implies success on the job. Take a job in which typing is a major function. Obviously, a typing test can be content validated if it reflects the kind of typing the job requires. However, content validation as it operates in practice is far removed from the typing test paradigm. *See Association of Mexican-American Educators v. State of California*, 183 F.3d 1055 (9th Cir. 1999) (the California teaching credential exam was content valid because the skills the test addressed were necessary for teachers, even though there was no showing that the test was in any way a sample of the job of teaching).

Like all validation, content validation starts with a job analysis, whose function is to identify the KSAs (knowledge, skills, and abilities) entailed in the particular job. Unlike the minimal effort we saw in *Albemarle*, a good job analysis requires substantial time and effort by the test designer to ascertain what job incumbents actually do. *See Bryant v. City of Chi.*, 200 F.3d 1092 (7th Cir. 2000); *cf. M.O.C.H.A. Soc'y, Inc. v. City of Buffalo*, 689 F.3d 263, 286 (2d Cir. 2012) (2-1) (allowing the Buffalo Fire Department to rely on a statewide job analysis when fire lieutenants across New York "performed the same critical tasks and required the same critical skills").

Once the analysis is complete, the designer then constructs a test to determine whether the candidates possess the relevant KSAs. The test need not try to assess performance on all aspects of the job but is supposed to test "critical" and "important" KSAs as identified in the job analysis. *Lopez v. City of Lawrence*, 823 F.3d 102 (1st Cir. 2016) (2-1). "Knowledge" is perhaps the easiest aspect to test, although the designer should not seek to test knowledge easily and quickly learned on the job. Skills and abilities are more difficult. For example, one police lieutenant's test was constructed in three parts. The first part was a job-knowledge test consisting of 150 multiple choice questions. The second was an "In-Basket Exercise" designed to test a candidate's skills in responding to a packet of information simulating a lieutenant's in-basket. And the third component simulated a Chicago Police Lieutenant's responsibilities at roll call, an exercise intended to demonstrate a candidate's analytical abilities and oral communication skills. *Bryant*, 200 F.3d 1096-97.

The Seventh Circuit in *Bryant* affirmed the district court's finding that the test was content valid because it "measured a significant portion of the knowledge, skills, and abilities necessary for a police lieutenant." *Id.* at 1099. Further, it approved not only the use of the test generally but also using the resulting scores to make promotions in rank order. In theory, a test might be valid enough to be used for promotions but not reliable enough to use it for rank-ordered promotions, but the court found this test to be sufficiently reliable for such use, in part because the designer had pre-tested its various components. *Id.* Other recent decisions also uphold rank-ordering use of tests. *See Lopez v. City of Lawrence, supra; Johnson v. City of Memphis,* 770 F.3d 464, 482 (6th Cir. 2014).

4. *Differential Validation.* In a portion of the opinion not reproduced, *Albemarle* referred to EEOC guidelines requiring differential validation by race, thus suggesting that different scores could predict different levels of performance for blacks and whites. This technique was invalidated by the Civil Rights Act of 1991, which prohibited "race norming." Section 703(l) now provides:

> It shall be an unlawful employment practice for a respondent, in connection with the selection or referral of applicants or candidates for employment or promotion, to adjust the scores of, use different cutoff scores for, or otherwise alter the results of, employment related tests on the basis of race, color, religion, sex, or national origin.

In *Ricci v. DeStefano,* 557 U.S. 557, 584 (2009), reproduced at p. 245, the Court wrote: "If an employer cannot rescore a test based on the candidates' race, §2000e-2(l), then it follows *a fortiori* that it may not take the greater step of discarding the test altogether to achieve a more desirable racial distribution of promotion-eligible candidates — absent a strong basis in evidence that the test was deficient and that discarding the results is necessary to avoid violating the disparate-impact provision."

5. *Is the Disparate Impact Testing Game Worth the Candle?* Professor Amy Wax challenged the use of the disparate impact theory for testing in *Individual Rights: Disparate Impact Realism,* 53 WM. & MARY L. REV. 621, 621 (2011):

> Social science research casts doubt on . . . *Griggs.* First, research in industrial and organizational psychology (IOP) has repeatedly documented that, despite their imperfections, tests and criteria such as those at issue in *Griggs* (which are heavily "g"-loaded [g = general intellectual ability] and thus dependent on cognitive ability) remain the best predictors of performance for jobs at all levels of complexity. Second, work in psychometrics, educational demography, and labor economics indicates that blacks, and to a lesser extent Hispanics, currently lag behind whites both in cognitive ability test performance and in the skills needed for success on the job. These gaps are reflected in lower scores on the types of g-loaded job screens that best predict job success. The combination of well-documented racial differences in cognitive ability and the consistent link between ability and job performance generates a pattern that experts term the "validity-diversity tradeoff": the most effective job selection criteria consistently generate the smallest number of minority hires.

Although Professor Wax cited a number of industrial psychological sources, the notion of a "validity/diversity tradeoff" had not previously appeared in the legal literature and is still rare. Does it seem likely that enhanced cognitive abilities better predict laboring jobs like those at Duke Power or paper-making jobs like Albemarle? The argument seems more plausible for police lieutenants, but even here there was reason to believe that job performance (the "merit" factor in *Adams*) showed differing results. *See also* Kimberly West-Faulcon, *Fairness Feuds: Competing Conceptions of Title VII Discriminatory Testing,* 46 WAKE FOREST L. REV. 1035, 1039 (2011).

2. *Bona Fide Seniority Systems*

Section 703(h) also provides an exception to Title VII liability for seniority systems:

> [I]t shall not be an unlawful employment practice for an employer to apply different standards of compensation, or different terms, conditions, or privileges of employment pursuant to a bona fide seniority or merit system . . . provided that such differences are not the result of an intention to discriminate because of race, color, religion, sex, or national origin.

Seniority systems tend to reify the status quo by preferring more senior workers to ones hired more recently. Where racial or gender discrimination had been common in the past, seniority systems tended to freeze that status quo. For example, requiring an employee in a low-paid line of progression to forfeit her seniority there in order to pursue work in a higher-paid one would often be a severe disincentive to advancement, and some early authority drew on this kind of reasoning to conclude that Title VII was not "intend[ed] to freeze an entire generation of Negro employees into discriminatory patterns that existed before the act" by immunizing extant seniority systems, *Quarles v. Philip Morris*, 279 F. Supp. 505 (E.D. Va. 1968).

However, the Supreme Court disavowed this approach in *International Brotherhood of Teamsters v. United States*, 431 U.S. 324 (1977). In a portion of *Teamsters* we have not encountered before, the Court considered a collective bargaining agreement that created separate seniority lines for city driver jobs and line driver jobs. Blacks had been confined to the city driver jobs and excluded from the better line driver positions. To move to the better jobs, minority drivers would have to surrender their city driver seniority. The Supreme Court held that the mere perpetuation of earlier discrimination does not make a seniority provision in a collective bargaining agreement illegal. "[A]n otherwise neutral, legitimate seniority system does not become unlawful under Title VII simply because it may perpetuate pre-Act discrimination." Because of §703(h), Title VII does not invalidate a seniority system even where, owing to discrimination that occurred before Title VII became effective, women and minority males were handicapped in their present ability to compete for jobs. "[T]hat conclusion is inescapable even in a case, such as this one, where the pre-Act discriminatees are incumbent employees who accumulated seniority in other bargaining units." Just as important, the *Teamsters* Court also treated §703(h) as creating a defense to disparate impact claims for actions taken pursuant to a bona fide seniority system. "Were it not for §703(h), the seniority system in this case would seem to fall under the *Griggs* rationale." *Id.* at 349.

The early seniority cases involved collective bargaining systems. More recently the Supreme Court recognized a seniority defense even where no collective bargaining agreement was involved. In *US Airways, Inc. v. Barnett*, 535 U.S. 391 (2002) (reproduced at p. 476), the defendant had unilaterally promulgated a seniority system. Although the suit was brought under the Americans with Disabilities Act, which, unlike Title VII, has no explicit seniority exception, the Court not only read a seniority exception into the statute but also held that, "in the run of cases," a requested disability accommodation that would conflict with the rules of a seniority system is not reasonable. Whether or not a seniority system is the product of collective bargaining, such systems generally create expectations by employees of fair treatment and encourage employee loyalty that were to be respected.

While seniority necessarily relates to length of service, the Supreme Court has rejected any bright-line test of what is sheltered by §703(h) in favor of a broader test set

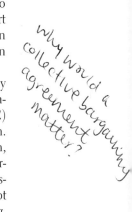

I thought impact didn't consider intention.

Why would a collective bargaining agreement matter?

by commonly accepted notions of what constitutes a seniority system. In *California Brewers Ass'n v. Bryant*, 444 U.S. 598, 605-06 (1980), while the Court viewed "seniority" as connoting length of employment, a "'seniority system' is a scheme that, alone or in tandem with non-'seniority' criteria, allots to employees ever improving employment rights and benefits as their relative lengths of pertinent employment increase." Since §703(h) by its terms protects seniority *systems* and Title VII was passed against a backdrop of labor policy favoring unregulated bargaining between labor and management, even those parts of a seniority system that do not turn on length of service are sheltered from disparate impact liability.

Given the broad protection of §703(h), a seniority system can be overturned only if it was put in place to intentionally discriminate. That is a question of fact, not of law, *Pullman-Standard v. Swint*, 456 U.S. 273 (1982), and few disparate treatment seniority cases are brought.

3. *Bona Fide Merit and Piecework Systems*

Section 703(h) not only creates an exception to disparate impact liability for seniority systems but also for a "bona fide . . . merit system, or a system which measures earnings by quantity or quality of production." Systems that measure compensation by quantity of production are piecework systems: the more a worker produces, the more he or she is paid. Since quantity of production obviously is a factor in determining a quality of a worker, piecework systems (sometimes called incentive systems) are one type of merit system. A system that measures compensation by quality of production may also be part of a piecework system in the sense that rejects do not count for pay. A quality-of-production system might be broader, however, in that it involves the evaluation of the quality-of-worker performance. In that sense, the quality-of-production notion is really just another name for a merit system. The general concept of this exception is that better job performance is rewarded. There are few cases interpreting these exceptions. *See McReynolds v. Merrill Lynch & Co.*, 694 F.3d 873 (7th Cir. 2012) (retention program that relied on race-neutral levels of production was protected by §703(h)).

NOTE ON LITIGATION SCORECARD

The Supreme Court's decision in 1989 in *Wards Cove* provoked general outrage at the Court's dilution of the disparate impact theory. While other anti–civil rights decisions in that same term also generated resistance, overturning *Wards Cove* was the driving force for what became the Civil Rights Act of 1991. Ironically, disparate impact is still not often invoked despite the pro-plaintiff provisions of §703(k). Elaine W. Shoben, *Disparate Impact Theory in Employment Discrimination: What's* Griggs *Still Good For? What Not?*, 42 BRANDEIS L.J. 597, 598-99 (2004), details possible reasons for this underutilization:

> First, it is a less desirable claim for plaintiffs than intent-based claims because there are no compensatory or punitive damages available for disparate impact claims. . . . Second, the theory is underutilized because it is inherently a class-based theory and class actions are difficult, if not impossible, for private plaintiffs to undertake unless they involve the possibility of very large damage awards. . . . Third, the world has changed in the last thirty-two years and employers now know the rules. . . .

Professor Charles A. Sullivan, however, has called for a revival of disparate impact theory in substantial part because intentional discrimination has become so hard to prove. *See* Charles A. Sullivan, *Disparate Impact: Looking Past the* Desert Palace *Mirage*, 47 WM. & MARY L. REV. 911 (2006). In contrast, Professor Michael L. Selmi, in *Was the Disparate Impact Theory a Mistake?*, 53 UCLA L. REV. 701, 701 (2006), argues disparate impact caused the problem: "by pushing an expansive theory of impact we were left with a truncated theory of intentional discrimination, one that continues to turn on animus and motive." After studying this chapter, do you think it is likely that plaintiffs' disparate impact cases will have any better chance of success than disparate treatment cases?

Chapter 4

The Interrelation of the Three Theories
of Discrimination

The individual disparate treatment, systemic disparate treatment, and disparate impact approaches to discrimination each developed separately and their intersection has generated both confusion and controversy, particularly the relationship between disparate treatment and disparate impact that crystallized in *Ricci v. DeStefano*, 557 U.S. 557 (2009), with which this chapter concludes. But before examining the various possibilities, test your understanding of the three theories by addressing the fact scenario below under each line of analysis.

PROBLEM 4.1

You are an attorney who has been visited by a potential client, Ann Abalos, who claims she was denied a promotion because she is Latina. The employer, Shuffled Papers Inc., hires many people for entry-level clerical jobs. In a metropolitan area with an 18 percent Latino population, the entry level is made up of 16 percent Latinos — 160 of the 1,000 clericals. Persons promoted to supervisor come from the pool of clericals; other than promoting from within, no announced policy describes the promotion process. Openings are not posted, and people apparently are simply picked for promotion by the managers, who are predominately white and male. Only two of the 50 supervisors are Latinos.

Abalos asked her supervisor, Bernie Baker, if she could be promoted. He told her that he thought she was well qualified and that he would suggest her name to his manager. After several other people were promoted, Abalos asked Baker why she had not been chosen. He told her that she was "in the running" but had to wait until her turn came.

In your initial discussions with the lawyer for Shuffled Papers, you were told that, to be considered for promotion to supervisor, a clerical employee must have two years of college and three years of experience. All of the supervisors satisfy those prerequisites, but some clericals, including Abalos, also satisfy them. Twenty percent of the white clerical workers meet these minimum requirements, while only 10 percent of the Latino clerical workers have both three years of experience and two years of college.

A.   THE INTERRELATIONSHIP OF INDIVIDUAL AND SYSTEMIC DISPARATE TREATMENT

Perhaps the easiest interrelationship question is that between individual and systemic disparate treatment. In terms of Problem 4.1, the question is how Abalos's individual case fits into a more systemic attack on intentional discrimination. A plaintiff such as Abalos can, of course, claim individual disparate treatment, focusing on only her own situation without bringing in evidence of other actions against other members of her protected group. At the opposite extreme, Abalos might try to put into evidence the kind of proof that would make out a systemic case. What is the effect of such proof?

mitigated by

In *McDonnell Douglas Corp. v. Green*, reproduced at p. 14, the Supreme Court invited systemic proof as evidence of pretext in an individual disparate treatment case: such evidence may include facts about the "general policy and practice with respect to minority employment. On the latter point, statistics as to petitioner's employment policy and practice may be helpful to a determination of whether petitioner's refusal to rehire respondent in this case conformed to a general pattern of discrimination against blacks." But the Court simultaneously dropped a footnote warning against giving this proof too much weight: such evidence, "while helpful, may not be in and of [itself] controlling as to an individualized hiring decision, particularly in the presence of an otherwise justifiable reason for refusing to rehire." 411 U.S. at 806 n.19. The following case explores that possibility.

BAYLIE v. FEDERAL RESERVE BANK OF CHICAGO
476 F.3d 522 (7th Cir. 2007)

EASTERBROOK, Chief Judge.

This appeal presents the tail end of a class action in which employees accused the Federal Reserve Bank of Chicago of race, sex, and age discrimination. Four years ago the district court decertified the class and allowed employees to pursue individual claims. Only two remain for resolution on this appeal. The district judge concluded that these two had not established even a *prima facie* case of discrimination and granted summary judgment to the Bank.

Although only two employees' claims remain for decision, their brief proceeds largely as if a class continued to seek systemic relief. Plaintiffs rely heavily on the report of an expert who concluded that black employees were less likely to be promoted than white employees. They maintain that this report is enough by itself to require a trial. Going to the opposite extreme, the Bank contends that statistical evidence is never relevant outside a class action or a suit by a public agency on behalf of employees as a group. Both of these positions misunderstand the role of statistical inference.

self-evident or unquestionable

Most contentions in litigation are empirical rather than (axiomatic.) Propositions of fact are arrived at by inductive rather than deductive means. All inferences are statistical — whether implicitly or explicitly does not matter. A plaintiff who accuses Supervisor X of discrimination because he never has promoted a black person, and often says disparaging things about black workers, is drawing a statistical inference: that if X has been indifferent to race, then selections from the pool of employees eligible for promotion would have included some black workers, and in particular would have included the plaintiff. Likewise the proposition "9 of 10 people exposed to sarin die within 20 minutes, so sarin is deadly" is a statistical inference, one so obvious that no expert is needed to show causation. But the inference often may be elusive, and then someone trained in the analysis of numbers will help.

Professional statistics is a rigorous means to analyze large numbers of events and inquire whether what appear to be patterns really are the result of chance (and, if not, which variables are associated with which outcomes). Suppose we know that 20,000 of 100,000 persons exposed to high dosage x-rays eventually develop cancer, and that 19,500 of 100,000 persons not so exposed develop cancer. Should we attribute the apparent excess risk of 500 cancers to the x-ray, or might it have some other cause? Is this excess risk real or an illusion caused by errors in measurement and analysis, the sort of variance that may occur by chance? A statistical analysis may be able to answer these questions — and, if the answer is yes, the knowledge that high-dosage x-rays increase the risk of cancer may inform a decision whether the benefits of the procedure are worth the extra risk. But it will not tell us whether a given person who develops cancer did so because of the x-ray; only 2.5% of cancers can be attributed to the radiation, so 97.5% of all cancers, even among persons exposed to high-dosage x-rays, have other causes. This is the sense in which statistics are more helpful in a pattern-or-practice case, where a judge will be asked to direct the employer to change how it makes hiring or promotion decisions.

stats helpful

In individual cases, studies of probabilities are less helpful. Suppose 1,000 employees apply for 100 promotions; 150 of the workers are black and 850 white. If all are equally qualified and the employer ignores race, then 85 white workers and 15 black workers will be promoted, plus or minus some variation that can be chalked up to chance. Suppose only 10 black workers are promoted. Is that the result of discrimination or chance? Econometric analysis (an application of statistical techniques) may suggest the answer by taking into account both other potentially explanatory variables and the rate of random variance.

When the answer is positive (discrimination occurred; the conclusion is statistically significant) it cannot reveal with certainty whether any given person suffered. In this example, 150 black workers applied for promotion; 10 were promoted and the other 140 were not. But for discrimination, 15 would have been promoted and 135 not. Which of the 140 non-promoted employees would have received the other 5 promotions? The statistical analysis does not tell us — and in civil litigation, where the plaintiff's burden is to show more likely than not that he was harmed by a legal wrong, data of this kind will not get a worker over that threshold.

Statistical analysis is relevant in the technical sense that it "has a tendency to make the existence of [a material] fact . . . more probable or less probable than it would be without the evidence." Fed. R. Evid. 401. But data showing a small increase in the probability of discrimination cannot by itself get a plaintiff over the more-likely-than-not threshold; it must be coupled with other evidence, which does most of the work. A disappointed worker could ask for damages measured by the lost opportunity: each of the 140 disappointed workers might receive as damages 5/140 of the extra income

stats not always enough

enjoyed by those who received promotions. That's the loss-of-a-chance measure of damages. *See Doll v. Brown*, 75 F.3d 1200 (7th Cir. 1996). But it is more suited to classwide litigation, and our two plaintiffs have not requested this remedy.

What statistics did these plaintiffs offer — the kind that permit a sound inference in an individual case (our examples of Supervisor X and exposure to sarin) or the kind that may support class-wide equitable relief but are only marginally relevant when an individual plaintiff seeks an award of damages? Plaintiffs' expert analyzed all non-managerial workers at the Bank between 1995 and 2000. Workers as a whole enjoyed a probability of about 0.25 of being promoted to a higher pay grade each year (stated otherwise, the average worker was promoted once every four years). Coefficients in an econometric regression implied that black workers had about a 0.20 probability and white workers about a 0.27 probability, and after controlling for other variables the expert concluded that 5/7 of this difference (or a 0.05 chance of promotion each year) was unaccounted for by any hypothesis other than race. In other words, the average white worker received an extra promotion every 20th year compared with the average black worker, holding constant factors (such as education) other than race. The Bank's experts questioned whether this result is statistically significant (that is, whether the difference is a result of chance rather than race) and whether it is meaningful for most of the workers. It turns out that the most frequent "promotion" is from temporary to full-time work. If the analysis is limited to persons (such as plaintiffs) already working at the Bank full time, then black workers are slightly more likely than white workers to be promoted in any given year.

stats just not enough here for the two Ps

Given the consequence of restricting the data set to full-time workers, this econometric analysis offers our two plaintiffs no support. Even presented as plaintiffs' expert did, rolling the temporary-to-full-time promotions into the data, the study doesn't provide plaintiffs with much assistance. These two plaintiffs applied for several promotions annually. If race affects one promotion every 20 years, and workers seek three promotional opportunities a year, then there is one chance in 60 that a given application would have been successful if the applicant were white rather than black. Over many years and many employees this effect could be substantial — which is why such analysis is helpful in class actions — but in a single employee's case it does very little to get the claim over the more-likely-than-not threshold. A worker can't say simply: "I've been here 20 years, so I'm entitled to one extra promotion." All of that time except the most recent 300 days falls outside Title VII's statute of limitations. *See National Railroad Passenger Corp. v. Morgan*, 536 U.S. 101 (2002). Analysis thus must proceed vacancy-by-vacancy in an individual case, not career-by-career.

more likely than not threshold = 50% +

If a plaintiff had evidence suggesting that the probability that race accounted for a given turn-down was (say) 49.8%, then the addition of the statistical analysis would push the probability past 50%. In other words, the expert's conclusion in this litigation could serve as a tie-breaker. But first there would have to *be* a tie — and plaintiffs' evidence does not come close to making this case a tossup that statistics might decide in their favor.

NOTES

1. *The Role of Statistics in Individual Disparate Treatment Cases.* Judge Easterbrook does not rule out the use of statistics in individual disparate treatment cases, but he assigns it a very limited role. Unless the plaintiff's case is otherwise very close to

establishing intent to discriminate by a preponderance of the evidence, it will not tip the balance. Statistical evidence is, at most, a tie-breaker. Other courts may be somewhat more hospitable to such proof. *See Walsh v. N.Y. City Hous. Auth.*, 828 F.3d 70, 77-78 (2d Cir. 2016) (2-1) ("The finder of fact may properly consider the dearth of female bricklayers as one component of its cumulative inquiry" in an individual disparate treatment suit); *Schechner v. KPIX-TV & CBS Broad., Inc.*, 686 F.3d 1018 (9th Cir. 2012) (statistics may be used to establish a prima facie case under *McDonnell Douglas*, at least if they show a "sharp pattern" even though they do not take into account the employer's articulated nondiscriminatory reason). If the plaintiff's case goes to the jury without considering the statistics, however, Judge Easterbrook's opinion suggests that the evidence is probative (even if of slight value), which should mean it is admissible. Might such evidence make a big difference with the jury? If it would likely do so, however, maybe that's a basis to exclude it under FRE 403 because its potential for prejudice would exceed its probative value.

[handwritten margin note: scarcity or lack of something]

2. *What If This Were a Systemic Case?* The litigation in *Baylie* started as a class action. While we will not meet the requirements of class actions until Chapter 8, had the case continued as a class action the plaintiffs' statistical proof would have played an entirely different role. We encountered this in *Teamsters* and *Hazelwood*, but it most clearly emerges in *Franks v. Bowman Transp. Co.*, 424 U.S. 747 (1976), which held that demonstrating a systemic pattern of intentional discrimination creates a presumption that the individual members of the racial group in question had themselves been discriminated against on account of race. Thus, the employer can avoid granting relief to individual members of the class only if it can carry the burden of persuasion that each individual was *not* a victim of discrimination. As applied to *Baylie*, *Franks* means that, had the class action continued and the statistics sufficed to prove systemic disparate treatment, the two individual plaintiffs would have been presumed to have been victims. It would then have been the Federal Reserve Board's burden to prove that they would not have been promoted in any event. While Judge Easterbrook found that neither plaintiff carried her burden, there would have been no burden to carry in a successful systemic case.

[handwritten margin note: when a class action presumption that each member has disp. treatment, suffered otherwise burden to show]

3. *Why Isn't* Baylie *a Systemic Case?* The Seventh Circuit does not explicitly address the issue, but *Baylie* implies that systemic disparate treatment can be invoked only in a class action or a government enforcement action. These are, in fact, the two situations in which the theory has been applied by the Supreme Court in *Teamsters/ Hazelwood* and *Franks*. Some courts have explicitly held that systemic disparate treatment is limited to these settings. *E.g., Daniels v. UPS*, 701 F.3d 620, 632-33 (10th Cir. 2012); *Chin v. Port Auth. of N.Y. & N.J.*, 685 F.3d 135, 147 (2d Cir. 2012). The rationale appears to be that systemic treatment is a class concept and therefore applicable only in class actions. *See generally* Jason R. Bent, *The Telltale Sign of Discrimination: Probabilities, Information Asymmetries, and the Systemic Disparate Treatment Theory*, 44 U. MICH. J.L. REFORM 797 (2011).

4. *Loss of Chance.* Is the individual/systemic question related to the "loss-of-a-chance" measure of damages? *Baylie* suggests that, in the hypothetical of 140 disappointed workers, each "might receive as damages 5/140 of the extra income enjoyed by those who received promotions." The opinion goes on to say that this measure "is more suited to class-wide litigation, and our two plaintiffs have not requested this remedy." Is that a sufficient reason to deny them a remedy that would otherwise be appropriate? Suppose they *had* asked for loss-of-chance damages? Why shouldn't it be awarded, assuming there was sufficient evidence to find discrimination against the group? We will revisit this measure in Chapter 9, Note 5, pp. 570-571.

5. *Nonstatistical Systemic Proof.* The logic of *Baylie* is that "nonstatistical" proof of other discriminatory decisions is admissible but may lack the power of statistical proof. Another way to say the same thing is that evidence that four out of five whites were promoted while only one of five blacks were is probative of discrimination. Such proof is not "statistical" in the sense that the numbers are too small to yield statistical significance, and no expert is needed; but the proof is admissible and may be a factor in the plaintiff establishing his case by a preponderance of the evidence. *See Sun v. Board of Trustees*, 473 F.3d 799, 813 (7th Cir. 2007) ("Although the sample size is insufficient to provide statistically reliable evidence, the PTC's voting pattern [against Asians and in favor of Caucasians] has some probative value regarding discriminatory employment practices").

NOTE ON THE RELATION BETWEEN INDIVIDUAL CASES AND UNSUCCESSFUL CLASS ACTIONS

We have seen that individuals in successful class actions have the advantage of being presumptively found to have suffered from discrimination. In *Baylie*, the class action was decertified before any classwide decision was made; thus the individual plaintiffs were neither helped nor hurt. But what about a class action in which the defendant prevails? *Cooper v. Federal Reserve Bank of Richmond*, 467 U.S. 867 (1984), held that failure of the systemic claims does not cut off the right of individuals making up the class to advance claims of individual disparate treatment. Thus, the members of the class are barred by res judicata from bringing another class action against the employer alleging systemic disparate treatment discrimination for the time period as are the individual claims of the class representative. But because the claims of individual disparate treatment made by unnamed class members have never been litigated, they are not precluded.

B.   THE RELATIONSHIP BETWEEN INDIVIDUAL DISPARATE TREATMENT AND DISPARATE IMPACT

Although litigants often try to use both theories, disparate impact analysis is neither necessary nor relevant in a pure disparate treatment case. The point is obvious with respect to individual disparate treatment: a plaintiff typically will present her case by focusing on facts relevant to her situation; there will be no need to develop broader theories. Similarly, the employer will not seek to justify, in business necessity terms, an individual employment decision. Under individual disparate treatment analysis, the employer's usual strategy will be to show a "legitimate, nondiscriminatory reason" for its actions. Because this is far easier to establish than "business necessity," employers will not try to shoulder the heavier burden.

This was confirmed by *Raytheon Co. v. Hernandez*, 540 U.S. 44 (2003), where the Court held that an individual disparate treatment case focuses on whether the defendant's explanation was a "legitimate, nondiscriminatory reason," which makes the business necessity defense irrelevant. Had Hernandez also pled a disparate impact claim and made out a prima facie case, then the business necessity defense would be appropriate. In *Raytheon*, the employer's asserted reason for not rehiring plaintiff was his earlier termination for violation of personal conduct rules, which the employer claimed to be its policy. Since misconduct was broader than drug- or alcohol-related disability, such a rule was facially disability-neutral. While neutrality would not itself make such a rule job related or necessary for business, that's unimportant in a disparate treatment case.

It is true that a plaintiff bringing an individual case of disparate treatment might try to establish that the employer's "legitimate, nondiscriminatory reason" has a disparate impact. Such a case, however, will then become a garden-variety disparate impact case. The only difference is that, by asserting the reason as the basis for its decision to take an adverse employment action, the employer will have eliminated the potential argument that the policy in issue was not what caused the adverse employment action against plaintiff.

C. THE RELATIONSHIP BETWEEN SYSTEMIC DISPARATE TREATMENT AND DISPARATE IMPACT

1. *Disparate Impact Analysis Inapplicable to Systemic Disparate Treatment Cases*

Disparate impact analysis is not applicable to systemic disparate treatment claims. With respect to formal systems of disparate treatment, the Supreme Court has several times spoken directly, most definitively in *International Union, UAW v. Johnson Controls, Inc.*, reproduced at p. 142, where the Court rejected an asserted "business necessity" justification for fetal-protection policies: such policies facially discriminate on the basis of sex and pregnancy, and business necessity is not a defense to intentional discrimination. Rather, business necessity can be employed only to defend a disparate impact attack.

The Court's position in *Johnson Controls* was codified by the Civil Rights Act of 1991, which added §703(k)(2) to Title VII: "A demonstration that an employment practice is required by business necessity may not be used as a defense against a claim of intentional discrimination under this title." This amendment also confirmed the approach of systemic disparate treatment cases relying on a pattern or practice of conduct to give rise to an inference of intentional discrimination. *Teamsters v. United States*, reproduced at p. 100. The language of §703(k)(2) makes clear that the employer in such a case may not prevail by proving business necessity. Rather, as we have seen, it may win only by disproving the pattern or by offering an alternative explanation for the inference of discriminatory intent the plaintiff seeks to draw.

2. *Intent to Discriminate: The Dividing Line Between the Two Systemic Theories*

The lower courts have repeatedly confused systemic disparate treatment and disparate impact. As we've seen, *Johnson Controls* rejected importing the business necessity defense from disparate impact law into a systemic disparate treatment case. The intentional use of a prohibited characteristic (in that case, sex) by the employer is disparate treatment, and thus the employer had engaged in unlawful discrimination unless it could prove a BFOQ.

More recently, in the context of the Americans with Disabilities Act, the Court again rejected an effort to blend the two analyses. *Raytheon Co. v. Hernandez*, 540 U.S. 44 (2003), involved a claim by a former employee that he had been discriminatorily denied reemployment by Raytheon because of his disability. Plaintiff had resigned, in lieu of being fired, for drug use. When he applied for reemployment two years later, his application was rejected. According to the company, the rejection was pursuant to its policy not to rehire employees who left the company for violating personal conduct rules. While we will study the ADA in more detail in Chapter 7, it is impermissible to discriminate against qualified individuals with a disability on the basis of their addiction or record of addiction, but it is legal to discriminate on the basis of their current illegal use of drugs. Thus, the original discharge was legal but a refusal to rehire because Hernandez was, or was believed to be, a recovering addict would not have been. See p. 515.

In *Raytheon* itself, however, the employer claimed that the person in its Labor Relations Department who reviewed Hernandez's application and rejected him did not know that he was a former drug addict when she made the decision to turn him down. She knew only that he had been discharged for violating "personal conduct" rules, and she rejected him because of that in accordance with Raytheon's (admittedly unwritten) policy to that effect. The Ninth Circuit, however, found that the "no rehire rule," at least as applied to former drug addicts, was not a legitimate, nondiscriminatory reason for a disparate treatment claim because of its disparate effects in screening out those with a record of drug addiction.

The Supreme Court reversed because this "improperly applied a disparate-impact analysis in a disparate-treatment case." *Id.* at 55. It went on:

> Had the Court of Appeals correctly applied the disparate-treatment framework, it would have been obliged to conclude that a neutral no-rehire policy is, by definition, a legitimate, nondiscriminatory reason under the ADA. And thus the only remaining question would be whether respondent could produce sufficient evidence from which a jury could conclude that "petitioner's stated reason for respondent's rejection was in fact pretext."

Id. at 51-52. The defendant's putting into evidence its neutral no-rehire policy satisfied its burden under *McDonnell Douglas*; indeed, the "no-rehire policy is a quintessential legitimate, nondiscriminatory reason for refusing to rehire an employee who was terminated for violating workplace conduct rules." *Id.* at 45. The only appropriate inquiry at that stage, therefore, was whether that reason was a pretext for discrimination. The Court suggested that the policy could have been challenged as having a disparate impact on disability grounds, but the plaintiff had not asserted that theory in a timely fashion. *But see* Elizabeth Roseman, Comment, *A Phoenix from the Ashes? Heightened Pleading Requirements in Disparate Impact Cases*, 36 Seton Hall L. Rev. 1043 (2005) (arguing that the disparate impact claim had in fact been properly pled); see Note 6, p. 187.

Raytheon reinforces the intent notion and sets out a litmus test: an employer cannot intentionally discriminate on the basis of a particular trait if it does not know of the trait. Obviously, the absence of knowledge is more likely with many disabilities and with religion as opposed to race, age, or sex, but *Raytheon* can apply even in the latter cases (as where a higher-level manager makes a decision without knowing the race of those affected). *See Fagerstrom v. City of Savannah*, 627 F. App'x 803 (11th Cir. 2015) (plaintiff could not show racial discrimination against Asians, despite self-identifying as Asian based on his mother's ethnicity, when the decisionmaker believed him to be white when he chose two white captains for the promotion); *McDowell v. T-Mobile USA, Inc.*, 307 F. App'x 531, 533 (2d Cir. 2009) (decision made by a high-level manager who had never met the plaintiff and was unaware of his race). One way to overcome the lack of knowledge by the decisionmaker is to show that the information that the decisionmaker relied on was the product of subordinates who were discriminating. *See Staub v. Proctor Hospital*, reproduced at p. 50.

3.   *Applying the Two Systemic Theories in One Case*

Pleading problems aside, it's easy to see how, in a case like *Raytheon Co. v. Hernandez*, a plaintiff could deploy both individual disparate treatment and disparate impact in one case. Mr. Hernandez could have claimed that the supposed nondiscriminatory reason was pretext because the Raytheon decisionmaker knew of his record of disability and acted on that basis; in fact, on remand, the Ninth Circuit required a trial on just this theory. *Hernandez v. Hughes Missile Sys. Co.*, 362 F.3d 564, 566 (9th Cir. 2004). Simultaneously, the plaintiff could have asserted that, if the no-hire policy were, in reality, the basis for the decision, it had a disparate impact on disability grounds.

Suppose, however, there is no formal policy but that the plaintiff proved that addicts were disproportionately denied employment. Is such proof systemic disparate treatment, disparate impact, or both? Bismarck is reputed to have said, "Laws are like sausages, it is better not to see them being made." The next principal case offers a unique opportunity for students to answer this question while seeing law and sausages being made simultaneously.

EEOC v. DIAL CORPORATION
469 F.3d 735 (8th Cir. 2006)

Murphy, Circuit Judge.

The Equal Employment Opportunity Commission (EEOC) brought this sex discrimination action against The Dial Corporation under Title VII of the Civil Rights Act of 1964 on behalf of a number of women who had applied for work but were not hired. A jury found that Dial had engaged in a pattern or practice of intentional discrimination against women and awarded compensatory damages, and the district court concluded that Dial's use of a preemployment strength test had an unlawful disparate impact on female applicants and awarded back pay and benefits. . . . [Dist. court]

Dial is an international company with a plant located in Fort Madison, Iowa, that produces canned meats. Entry level employees at the plant are assigned to the sausage packing area where workers daily lift and carry up to 18,000 pounds of sausage, walking the equivalent of four miles in the process. They are required to carry approximately 35 pounds of sausage at a time and must lift and load the sausage to heights between 30 and 60 inches above the floor. Employees who worked in the sausage packing area experienced a disproportionate number of injuries as compared to the rest of the workers in the plant.

Dial implemented several measures to reduce the injury rate starting in late 1996. These included an ergonomic job rotation, institution of a team approach, lowering the height of machines to decrease lifting pressure for the employees, and conducting periodic safety audits. In 2000 Dial also instituted a strength test used to evaluate potential employees, called the Work Tolerance Screen (WTS). In this test job applicants were asked to carry a 35-pound bar between two frames, approximately 30 and 60 inches off the floor, and to lift and load the bar onto these frames. The applicants were told to work at their "own pace" for seven minutes. An occupational therapist watched the process, documented how many lifts each applicant completed, and recorded her own comments about each candidate's performance. Starting in 2001, the plant nurse, Martha Lutenegger, also watched and documented the process. From the inception of the test, Lutenegger reviewed the test forms and had the ultimate hiring authority.

strength test

For many years women and men had worked together in the sausage packing area doing the same job. Forty-six percent of the new hires were women in the three years before the WTS was introduced, but the number of women hires dropped to fifteen percent after the test was implemented. During this time period the test was the only change in the company's hiring practices. The percentage of women who passed the test decreased almost each year the test was given, with only eight percent of the women applicants passing in 2002. The overall percentage of women who passed was thirty-eight percent while the men's passage rate was ninety-seven percent. While overall injuries and strength related injuries among sausage workers declined consistently after 2000 when the test was implemented, the downward trend in injuries had begun in 1998 after the company had instituted measures to reduce injuries.

[The EEOC brought suit on behalf of 54 women who had been denied employment after taking the WTS; 24 of these applicants had been unable to complete the test.]

half the women passed the test but still were not hired?

A jury trial was held in August 2004, and EEOC and Dial offered testimony by competing experts. EEOC presented an expert on industrial organization who testified that the WTS was significantly more difficult than the actual job workers performed at the plant. He explained that although workers did 1.25 lifts per minute on average and rested between lifts, applicants who took the WTS performed 6 lifts per minute on average, usually without any breaks. He also testified that in two of the three years before Dial had implemented the WTS, the women's injury rate had been lower than that of the male workers. EEOC's expert also analyzed the company's written evaluations of the applicants and testified that more men than women were given offers of employment even when they had received similar comments about their performance. EEOC also introduced evidence that the occupational nurse marked some women as failing despite their having completed the full seven minute test.

π EEOC evidence

Dial presented an expert in work physiology, who testified that in his opinion the WTS effectively tested skills which were representative of the actual job, and an industrial and organizational psychologist, who testified that the WTS measured the requirements of the job and that the decrease in injuries could be attributed to the test. Dial also called plant nurse Martha Lutenegger who testified that although she and other Dial managers knew the WTS was screening out more women than men, the decrease in injuries warranted its continued use.

Dial Δ

[The jury found that Dial had engaged in a pattern or practice of intentional discrimination. The trial judge then found that "the WTS had had a discriminatory impact, that Dial had not demonstrated that the WTS was a business necessity or shown either content or criterion validity, and that Dial had not effectively controlled

trial court

for other variables which may have caused the decline in injuries, including other safety measures that Dial had implemented." The judge assessed backpay for individual applicants ranging from $120,236 to $920 and health benefits ranging from $30,385 to $882.]

On appeal Dial challenges the district court's denial of its motion for judgment as a matter of law, arguing there was insufficient evidence for a jury to find intentional discrimination. Dial also attacks the district court's findings of disparate impact and claims it proved that the WTS was a business necessity because it drastically decreased the number of injuries in the sausage production area of the plant. . . .   *Δ's appeal*

A pattern or practice of intentional sex discrimination must be shown by proving "regular and purposeful" discrimination by a preponderance of the evidence, *Int'l Brotherhood of Teamsters v. United States.* EEOC must show that more than an isolated act of discrimination occurred and that "discrimination was the company's standard operating procedure," but statistics combined with anecdotal examples of discrimination may establish a pattern or practice of regular, purposeful discrimination. *Morgan v. United Parcel Service of America, Inc.*, 380 F.3d 459, 463-64 (8th Cir. 2004). Moreover, discriminatory intent can be inferred from the mere fact of differences in treatment, *Teamsters.*

Statistical disparities are significant if the difference between the expected number and the observed number is greater than two or three standard deviations. *Hazelwood Sch. Dist. v. U.S.* Here, the disparity between hiring of men and women showed nearly ten standard deviations. The percentage of women who passed the WTS declined with each implementation of the test. Despite knowing about the statistical difference, Dial continued to use the WTS. Dial argues that EEOC's statistics are inapplicable because men and women are not similarly situated and have profound physiological differences. There was evidence, however, that women and men worked the same job together for many years before the WTS was instituted. There was also evidence of women and men receiving similar comments on their test forms, but only the males receiving offers of employment.

. . . A reasonable jury could discredit Lutenegger's testimony that the decrease in injuries was the company's motivation for continuing to use the WTS. A reasonable jury could also have found that the differing treatment of males and females supported an inference of intentional discrimination. We conclude that the evidence was sufficient for a reasonable jury to find that there was a pattern and practice of intentional discrimination against women and that the district court did not err by denying Dial's motion for judgment as a matter of law.

Dial objects to the district court's findings of disparate impact and its conclusion that the company failed to prove the WTS was necessary to establish effective and safe job performance. We review the district court's factual findings regarding disparate impact for clear error and its legal findings de novo. Fed. R. Civ. P. 52(a). . . .

Dial contends the WTS was shown by its experts to have both content and criterion validity. Under EEOC guidelines, "A content validity study should consist of data showing that the content of the selection procedure is representative of important aspects of performance on the job for which the candidates are to be evaluated." 29 C.F.R. §1607.5(B). Dial's physiology expert testified that the WTS was highly representative of the actions required by the job, and Dial claims that his testimony was not rebutted by EEOC which had no physiology witness. The district court was persuaded by EEOC's expert in industrial organization and his testimony "that a crucial aspect of the WTS is more difficult than the sausage making jobs themselves" and that the average applicant had to perform four times as many lifts as current employees and had no rest breaks. There was also evidence that in a testing environment where hiring is contingent upon test performance, applicants tend to work as fast as possible during the test in order to outperform the competition.

Dial argues the WTS was criterion valid because both overall injuries and strength related injuries decreased dramatically following the implementation of the WTS. The EEOC guidelines establish that criterion validity can be shown by "empirical data demonstrating that the selection procedure is predictive of or significantly correlated with important elements of job performance." 29 C.F.R. §1607.5(B). Although Dial claims that the decrease in injuries shows that the WTS enabled it to predict which applicants could safely handle the strenuous nature of the work, the sausage plant injuries started decreasing before the WTS was implemented. Moreover, the injury rate for women employees was lower than that for men in two of the three years before Dial implemented the WTS. The evidence did not require the district court to find that the decrease in injuries resulted from the implementation of the WTS instead of the other safety mechanisms Dial started to put in place in 1996. . . .

NOTES

1. *Systemic Proof and the Overlap of the Two Theories.* The *Dial* opinion starts by noting the statistical significance of "the disparity between hiring of men and women" of nearly 10 standard deviations. But the disparity was not in overall hiring practices — it was the effects of the administration of the WTS. In other words, the court begins its systemic disparate treatment analysis with proof that would satisfy the disparate impact theory: a showing that a particular employment practice (here, the WTS) has a disparate impact on a protected group (here women).

This shouldn't seem so unusual. The common thread to both systemic theories, disparate treatment and disparate impact, is finding discrimination from the effects of an employer's decisions. In disparate treatment, of course, the effects create an inference of discriminatory intent; in disparate impact, the effects by themselves establish a violation unless the defendant can show business necessity. Both theories, therefore, begin with disparate effects. We'll encounter this again in the pregnancy context in *Young v. UPS*, 135 S. Ct. 1338 (2015), reproduced at p. 307.

2. Dial *as a Systemic Disparate Treatment Case.* It is no accident that, immediately after reporting the statistical proof of disparate effects, the *Dial* court stresses the declining success of women and Dial's knowledge of this fact. Remember *Personnel Administrator v. Feeney*, p. 131: "[c]ertainly, when the adverse consequences of a law upon an identifiable group are as inevitable as the gender-based consequences of [the veterans' preference], a strong inference that the adverse effects were desired can reasonably be drawn." But *Feeney* also held that knowledge of such an adverse impact doesn't necessarily prove the policy was adopted "because of, not despite" that impact. Is *Dial* different? Since the test seemed to be the only cause for the decline in women's employment, would a jury be reasonable in drawing the inference of discrimination in this case? What other evidence may have been critical in justifying that verdict?

3. Dial *as a Disparate Impact Case.* Given the statistical evidence of the test's impact, there could be no serious question that the EEOC made out its case of disparate impact discrimination. But the real question was whether the WTS was a business necessity. The answer seems to depend on a single, albeit crucial, aspect of test validation: the test was harder than the job.

4. *Judge and Jury Roles.* As we have seen, Title VII accords a jury trial right to disparate treatment claims but not to disparate impact claims. Since both were involved in *Dial*, both the jury and the judge engaged in factfinding. In such situations, any findings of fact by the jury bind the judge. *Lytle v. Household Mfg., Inc.*, 494 U.S. 545 (1990) (when judge-tried and jury-tried claims are both involved, the jury should decide its issues first, which finding will bind the judge on all facts so found). See Chapter 9 for the division of functions with respect to remedies.

5. *Another Two-Front Case.* In Chapter 3, we met *Maldonado v. City of Altus*, 433 F.3d 1294 (10th Cir. 2006), see Note 9, p. 188, where the court viewed a city's English-only policy for employees as potentially violating Title VII under both the disparate treatment and disparate impact theories. With regard to disparate treatment, "the disparate impact of the English-only rule (creation of a hostile work environment) is in itself evidence of intent," *id.* at 1308. Further, there was other proof of intent, including evidence that management realized that the policy was likely to lead to taunting Hispanic employees. Finally, "a jury could find that there were no substantial work-related reasons for the policy . . . suggesting that the true reason was illegitimate." *Id.* As for disparate impact, and even assuming no discriminatory motive, the policy itself "could reasonably be construed as an expression of hostility to Hispanics" when there was "no apparent legitimate purpose for the restrictions." *Id.* at 1305. In short, when an employer adopts a policy that is likely to result in disparate treatment by co-workers, it can be viewed as having a disparate impact, even if the employer does not wish for such consequences to follow.

6. *The Atmospherics of Discrimination.* We've also encountered another decision involving both theories. *EEOC v. Joe's Stone Crab, Inc.*, 220 F.3d 1263 (11th Cir. 2000), involved a famous Miami Beach seafood restaurant with an "'Old World' European tradition, in which the highest level of food service is performed by [tuxedo-clad] men, in order to create an ambience of 'fine dining' for its customers." *Id.* at 1270. There was no underrepresentation of women in hiring from an "open roll call," but there was reason to believe that women's lack of interest was due to Joe's business model: Old World dining didn't include waitresses. Conceptually, this scenario did not fit either of the systemic theories well. As for disparate impact, there was no facially neutral employment practice: "reputation" isn't a practice at all and atmosphere doesn't seem to be an *employment* practice. However, the Eleventh Circuit found sufficient evidence of systemic disparate treatment to justify a remand:

> [I]n light of the district court's findings that "Joe's management acquiesced in and gave silent approbation to the notion that male food servers were preferable to female food servers," and that "what prevailed at Joe's, albeit not mandated by written policy or verbal direction, was the ethos that female food servers were not to be hired," we also emphasize that under our controlling case law, either under a disparate treatment or a pattern or practice theory, Plaintiff need not show that hiring decisions were made pursuant to an *express* policy or directive from Joe's owners.

Id. at 1285. On remand, the district court found that Joe's had "engaged in intentional disparate treatment sex discrimination." 136 F. Supp. 2d 1311, 1313 (S.D. Fla. 2001). Joe's may not be alone since there is reason to believe that upper-crust restaurants tend to favor male wait staff. *See* Christine Jolls, *Is There a Glass Ceiling?*, 25 Harv. Women's L.J. 1, 5-7 (2002) (describing a restaurant audit study of wait staff selection that showed identical "female resumes" lead to fewer than half the interviews offered to "male resumes").

4. *The Relationship of the Systemic Theories*

a. When Can the Theories Be Deployed?

Dial and *Maldonado* both suggest that the two systemic theories can work together. Most obviously, proof of impact can not only make out the plaintiff's disparate impact case (thus shifting to the defendant the burden of persuasion) but also be evidence in the plaintiff's systemic disparate treatment case. With regard to the latter, however, it will rarely be sufficient by itself to create a jury question of intentional discrimination. It is possible that the impact will be so extreme as to warrant a finding of intent, but in most cases there will have to be additional evidence. In *Dial*, the additional evidence included the declining injury rate before the institution of the test, the employer's knowledge of its dramatic impact on women, the fact that women had had lower injury rates than men, and the lack of evenhandedness in administering the test. In *Maldonado*, it was evidence that the city expected the taunting that resulted and that it had no good business reasons for the policy.

But the possibility that a showing of impact can be critical to both theories does not change one distinction between the two systemic models: a plaintiff can use the impact theory to challenge any employment practice, whether "objective" or "subjective," but only so long as she can identify the practice and show that it (as distinguished from other components of the process) has a disparate impact. A plaintiff may, however, utilize bottom-line or "snapshot" statistics to make out a disparate treatment case.

The sharpness of any such distinction, however, is blunted by two further considerations. First, we have seen that, even in a disparate impact case, bottom-line results can be used if the elements of the employer's decisionmaking process "are not capable of separation for analysis." See Note 4, pp. 192-193. Second, as *Dial* and *Maldonado* hold, the disparate effects of a particular employment practice can be relevant to proving disparate treatment. It was the disparate impact of the particular employment practice that the EEOC successfully deployed in *Dial* as part of its proof of systemic disparate treatment. Thus, the requisites of each theory must be met, but both have potentially broad application.

b. Out of the Disparate Treatment Pan into the Disparate Impact Fire?

One other relationship between the two systemic theories may not be immediately apparent, and that is that an employer's defense to a disparate treatment claim can establish a plaintiff's disparate impact claim! Suppose a plaintiff puts forth statistical proof of a statistically significant underrepresentation of African Americans at the bottom line of the employer's selection process. The defendant must then respond either by refuting the claim that any disparity exists or by offering an explanation that rebuts the inference of bias that the plaintiff is asking the factfinder to draw. *But as Segar v. Smith*, 738 F.2d 1249 (D.C. Cir. 1984), points out, such an "explanatory defense" has further implications:

> To rebut a disparate treatment challenge the employer can argue that the observed disparity between the plaintiff class and the majority group does not support an inference of intentional discrimination because there is a legitimate, nondiscriminatory explanation for the disparity. For example, the defendant might come forward with some additional job qualifi-

[handwritten margin note: stats are more helpful in class cases (Bayli e)]

cation — not sufficiently perceptible to plaintiffs to have permitted them to account for it in their initial proof — that the plaintiff class lacks, thus explaining the disparity. . . .

[T]he employer's effort to rebut the pattern or practice claim by articulating a legitimate nondiscriminatory explanation may have the effect of putting before the court all elements of a traditional disparate impact case. By its explanation of an observed disparity the employer will typically pinpoint an employment practice (or practices) having a disparate impact on a protected class. And to rebut plaintiffs' case the employer will typically be required to introduce evidence showing that the employment practice in fact caused the observed disparity. In this situation, between the plaintiffs' prima facie showing of disparity and the defendant's rebuttal explanation of the disparity, the essential elements of a disparate impact case will have been placed before the trier of fact. Such a case is ripe for resolution using disparate impact analysis. Though the plaintiffs in a disparate treatment case bear the burden of persuasion as to the existence of a disparity, the defendant bears the burden of proving the business necessity of the practices causing the disparity. Thus when an employer defends a disparate treatment challenge by claiming that a specific employment practice causes the observed disparity, and this defense sufficiently rebuts the plaintiffs' initial case of disparate treatment, the defendant should at this point face a burden of proving the business necessity of the practice.

The only difference between this situation and the traditional disparate impact case is that in the latter the plaintiff articulates the employment practice causing the adverse impact and forces the employer to defend it, while in the former the employer articulates the employment practice and must then go on to defend it.

Id. at 1268-70.

To appreciate this, consider a simple hypothetical. The plaintiff shows that the employer's work force, which consists of non-skilled workers, is 99 percent white in a geographic labor market that is 23 percent minority. Her statistician finds the correlation between race and employment statistically significant. The defendant responds by arguing that it does not intentionally discriminate in hiring; rather, it employs only workers who reside in the town in which it is located, and the town happens to be 99 percent white. *See NAACP, Newark Branch v. Town of Harrison*, 940 F.2d 792 (3d Cir. 1991). In statistical terms, the defendant is showing a co-variable — residence — that is related to race and is arguing that residence, not race, explains its actions.

Of course, the employer might have chosen to employ only town residents precisely because this policy would exclude blacks. This was the EEOC's theory in *Dial*. But even if we accept the employer's explanation as a nondiscriminatory motivation, its proof makes out a disparate impact case. In other words, the defendant's rebuttal of the inference of discrimination raised by plaintiff's statistics turns entirely on whether the employer utilizes an intent-neutral practice that happens to have a disparate impact on blacks. Proof of that, as *Segar v. Smith* suggests, may mean that the defendant can avoid disparate treatment liability, but only by, in effect, conceding a prima facie case of disparate impact liability — although it can avoid both if it also shows that the policy producing the impact is justified by business necessity.

Segar is a relatively straightforward meshing of the two theories. Indeed, it is difficult to avoid the conclusion that, no matter who proves the various elements of a disparate impact claim, once it is shown, the employer can defend only by establishing business necessity. *Segar* preceded the Civil Rights Act of 1991, which generally restricted disparate impact to "a particular employment practice" but does not bar the plaintiff from using such proof to make out a systemic disparate treatment case, and that's the main thrust of *Segar*. Presumably, then, the defendant is left under the current statute basically where it was when *Segar v. Smith* was decided: to avoid a finding of disparate treatment, it can prove a practice giving rise to disparate impact.

If this is correct, why would an employer come forth with a "neutral" reason for a statistical disparity? Remember that the only defense to disparate treatment is the BFOQ, which is difficult to establish. And in race cases, the statute theoretically provides no exception at all except for affirmative action. Thus, it may be important for the defendant to shift the analysis from disparate treatment to disparate impact, where it has the defense of business necessity.

A plaintiff's incentives are the reverse: disparate treatment attacks will typically be preferred because prevailing on this issue effectively wins the case, while proof of disparate impact leaves the defendant able to prevail by showing business necessity. Further, the plaintiff has a right to a jury trial and compensatory and punitive damages for disparate treatment; nevertheless, disparate impact may be a fall-back theory even though it lacks a provision for compensatory damages.

D.   RECONCILING THE TENSION BETWEEN DISPARATE TREATMENT AND DISPARATE IMPACT

A simple way to sum up discrimination law is that employers may not intentionally use prohibited factors; employers may use any other criteria unless they have a disparate impact, in which case they may be used only if justified. Another way to say the same thing is that disparate treatment is not allowed because discriminatory intent is not a permissible basis for denying employment opportunities to individuals in our society; but even a nondiscriminatory motivation will not save practices that are not justified by business necessity and that have the effect of falling more harshly on a protected group. So stated, disparate treatment and disparate impact principles seem to work in conjunction to achieve the basic goals of Title VII.

But are the principles always consistent? Might they come into conflict? One possibility was raised in *Los Angeles Dep't of Water & Power v. Manhart*, reproduced at p. 94, where the Supreme Court held that the lack of disparate impact on one gender does not justify disparate treatment of that group. But what of the other side of that coin? Might eliminating any disparate treatment of women result in a disparate impact on men? In *Manhart*, had the employer collected equal pension contributions from men and women and paid out equal monthly retirement benefits, women as the longer-lived class would collect more total benefits than would the class of men. That would seem to show an adverse impact on males. Footnote 20 of *Manhart* tries to resolve this tension:

> Even under Title VII itself — assuming disparate-impact analysis applies to fringe benefits, the male employees would not prevail. Even a completely neutral practice will inevitably have some disproportionate impact on one group or another. *Griggs* does not imply, and this Court has never held, that discrimination must always be inferred from such consequences.

Id. at 710 n.20. The meaning of this passage is far from clear. It might imply that there is no tension between the two theories because disparate impact is not available to men (and, by implication, whites). We have explored this issue in Chapter 3 at p. 98, Note 3, and the answer is unclear. Were the theory available to both races, the disparate impact theory would create a dilemma. Imagine a new employer who is considering what employee selection procedure to adopt, and suppose further that using a written test will result in 90 percent white employees and 10 percent black employees. In contrast, a structured interview will result in 70 percent whites and 30 percent blacks. Isn't it clear that whether the employer picks the test or the structured interview, there will be a disparate impact on some group? Does that mean that, except for devices that are neutral along all axes, every selection device must be job related and a business necessity?

In any event, *Manhart's* footnote identified a tension between the two theories that came to a head in the next principal case.

RICCI v. DeSTEFANO
557 U.S. 557 (2009)

Justice KENNEDY delivered the opinion of the Court.

In the fire department of New Haven, Connecticut — as in emergency-service agencies throughout the Nation — firefighters prize their promotion to and within the officer ranks. An agency's officers command respect within the department and in the whole community; and, of course, added responsibilities command increased salary and benefits. Aware of the intense competition for promotions, New Haven, like many cities, relies on objective examinations to identify the best qualified candidates.

In 2003, 118 New Haven firefighters took examinations to qualify for promotion to the rank of lieutenant or captain. Promotion examinations in New Haven (or City) were infrequent, so the stakes were high. The results would determine which firefighters would be considered for promotions during the next two years, and the order in which they would be considered. Many firefighters studied for months, at considerable personal and financial cost.

When the examination results showed that white candidates had outperformed minority candidates, the mayor and other local politicians opened a public debate that turned rancorous. Some firefighters argued the tests should be discarded because the results showed the tests to be discriminatory. They threatened a discrimination lawsuit if the City made promotions based on the tests. Other firefighters said the exams were neutral and fair. And they, in turn, threatened a discrimination lawsuit if the City, relying on the statistical racial disparity, ignored the test results and denied promotions to the candidates who had performed well. In the end the City took the side of those who protested the test results. It threw out the examinations.

Certain white and Hispanic firefighters who likely would have been promoted based on their good test performance sued the City and some of its officials. . . .

We conclude that race-based action like the City's in this case is impermissible under Title VII unless the employer can demonstrate a strong basis in evidence that, had it not taken the action, it would have been liable under the disparate impact statute. The respondents, we further determine, cannot meet that threshold standard. As a result, the City's action in discarding the tests was a violation of Title VII. In light of our ruling under the statutes, we need not reach the question whether respondents' actions may have violated the Equal Protection Clause.

I . . .

[The promotion process in New Haven was governed by the city charter, which included a civil service merit system as determined by job-related tests. A collective bargaining agreement with the firefighters' union required any written promotion examination to account for 60 percent and an oral examination 40 percent of each applicant's total score. To sit for the examinations, the agreement set certain experience and education requirements. For promotion, test takers were ranked by score, and the city charter imposed a "rule of three" — whoever was promoted had to be among the top three scorers.]

After reviewing bids from various consultants, the City hired Industrial/Organizational Solutions, Inc. (IOS) to develop and administer the examinations, at a cost to the City of $100,000. IOS is an Illinois company that specializes in designing entry-level and promotional examinations for fire and police departments. In order to fit the examinations to the New Haven Department, IOS began the test-design process by performing job analyses to identify the tasks, knowledge, skills, and abilities that are essential for the lieutenant and captain positions. IOS representatives interviewed incumbent captains and lieutenants and their supervisors. They rode with and observed other on-duty officers. Using information from those interviews and ride-alongs, IOS wrote job-analysis questionnaires and administered them to most of the incumbent battalion chiefs, captains, and lieutenants in the Department. At every stage of the job analyses, IOS, by deliberate choice, oversampled minority firefighters to ensure that the results — which IOS would use to develop the examinations — would not unintentionally favor white candidates.

With the job-analysis information in hand, IOS developed the written examinations to measure the candidates' job-related knowledge. For each test, IOS compiled a list of training manuals, Department procedures, and other materials to use as sources for the test questions. IOS presented the proposed sources to the New Haven fire chief and assistant fire chief for their approval. Then, using the approved sources, IOS drafted a multiple-choice test for each position. Each test had 100 questions, as required by CSB rules, and was written below a 10th-grade reading level. After IOS prepared the tests, the City opened a 3-month study period. It gave candidates a list that identified the source material for the questions, including the specific chapters from which the questions were taken.

IOS developed the oral examinations as well. These concentrated on job skills and abilities. Using the job-analysis information, IOS wrote hypothetical situations to test incident-command skills, firefighting tactics, interpersonal skills, leadership, and management ability, among other things. Candidates would be presented with these hypotheticals and asked to respond before a panel of three assessors.

IOS assembled a pool of 30 assessors who were superior in rank to the positions being tested. At the City's insistence (because of controversy surrounding previous examinations), all the assessors came from outside Connecticut. IOS submitted the assessors' resumes to City officials for approval. They were battalion chiefs, assistant chiefs, and chiefs from departments of similar sizes to New Haven's throughout the country. Sixty-six percent of the panelists were minorities, and each of the nine three-member assessment panels contained two minority members. IOS trained the panelists for several hours on the day before it administered the examinations, teaching them how to score the candidates' responses consistently using checklists of desired criteria.

Candidates took the examinations in November and December 2003. Seventy-seven candidates completed the lieutenant examination — 43 whites, 19 blacks, and 15 Hispanics. Of those, 34 candidates passed — 25 whites, 6 blacks, and 3 Hispanics. Eight lieutenant positions were vacant at the time of the examination. As the rule of three operated, this meant that the top 10 candidates were eligible for an immediate promotion to lieutenant. All 10 were white. Subsequent vacancies would have allowed at least 3 black candidates to be considered for promotion to lieutenant.

Forty-one candidates completed the captain examination — 25 whites, 8 blacks, and 8 Hispanics. Of those, 22 candidates passed — 16 whites, 3 blacks, and 3 Hispanics. Seven captain positions were vacant at the time of the examination. Under the rule of three, 9 candidates were eligible for an immediate promotion to captain — 7 whites and 2 Hispanics.

[After five public meetings with each including testimony in favor and against using the tests, the Civil Service Board deadlocked 2-2, which resulted in not certifying the examination results, which in turn led to this lawsuit.] The plaintiffs — who are the petitioners here — are 17 white firefighters and 1 Hispanic firefighter who passed the examinations but were denied a chance at promotions when the CSB refused to certify the test results. They include the named plaintiff, Frank Ricci, who addressed the CSB at multiple meetings. . . .

[The District Court granted summary judgment for City, and the Second Circuit affirmed.] We now reverse.

II . . .

B

Petitioners allege that when the CSB refused to certify the captain and lieutenant exam results based on the race of the successful candidates, it discriminated against them in violation of Title VII's disparate-treatment provision. The City counters that its decision was permissible because the tests "appear[ed] to violate Title VII's disparate-impact provisions."

Our analysis begins with this premise: The City's actions would violate the disparate-treatment prohibition of Title VII absent some valid defense. All the evidence demonstrates that the City chose not to certify the examination results because of the statistical disparity based on race — i.e., how minority candidates had performed when compared to white candidates. As the District Court put it, the City rejected the test results because "too many whites and not enough minorities would be promoted were the lists to be certified." Without some other justification, this express, race-based decisionmaking violates Title VII's command that employers cannot take adverse employment actions because of an individual's race.

The District Court did not adhere to this principle, however. It held that respondents' "motivation to avoid making promotions based on a test with a racially disparate impact . . . does not, as a matter of law, constitute discriminatory intent." And the Government makes a similar argument in this Court. It contends that the "structure of Title VII belies any claim that an employer's intent to comply with Title VII's disparate-impact provisions constitutes prohibited discrimination on the basis of race." But both of those statements turn upon the City's objective — avoiding disparate-impact liability — while ignoring the City's conduct in the name of reaching that objective. Whatever the City's ultimate aim — however well intentioned or benevolent it might have seemed — the City made its employment decision because of race. The City rejected the test results solely because the higher scoring candidates were white. The question is not whether that conduct was discriminatory but whether the City had a lawful justification for its race-based action.

We consider, therefore, whether the purpose to avoid disparate-impact liability excuses what otherwise would be prohibited disparate-treatment discrimination. . . . [O]ur decision must be consistent with the important purpose of Title VII — that the workplace be an environment free of discrimination, where race is not a barrier to opportunity.

With these principles in mind, we turn to the parties' proposed means of reconciling the statutory provisions. . . . Petitioners would have us hold that, under Title VII, avoiding unintentional discrimination cannot justify intentional discrimination. That assertion, however, ignores the fact that, by codifying the disparate-impact provision in 1991, Congress has expressly prohibited both types of discrimination. We must interpret the statute to give effect to both provisions where possible. We cannot accept petitioners' broad and inflexible formulation.

Petitioners next suggest that an employer in fact must be in violation of the disparate-impact provision before it can use compliance as a defense in a disparate-treatment suit. Again, this is overly simplistic and too restrictive of Title VII's purpose. The rule petitioners offer would run counter to what we have recognized as Congress's intent that "voluntary compliance" be "the preferred means of achieving the objectives of Title VII." *Firefighters v. Cleveland*, 478 U.S. 501, 515 (1986). Forbidding employers to act unless they know, with certainty, that a practice violates the disparate-impact provision would bring compliance efforts to a near standstill. Even in the limited situations when this restricted standard could be met, employers likely would hesitate before taking voluntary action for fear of later being proven wrong in the course of litigation and then held to account for disparate treatment.

At the opposite end of the spectrum, respondents and the Government assert that an employer's good-faith belief that its actions are necessary to comply with Title VII's disparate-impact provision should be enough to justify race-conscious conduct. But the original, foundational prohibition of Title VII bars employers from taking adverse action "because of . . . race." §2000e-2(a)(1). And when Congress codified the disparate-impact provision in 1991, it made no exception to disparate-treatment liability for actions taken in a good-faith effort to comply with the new, disparate-impact provision in subsection (k). Allowing employers to violate the disparate-treatment prohibition based on a mere good-faith fear of disparate-impact liability would encourage race-based action at the slightest hint of disparate impact. A minimal standard could cause employers to discard the results of lawful and beneficial promotional examinations even where there is little if any evidence of disparate-impact discrimination. That would amount to a *de facto* quota system, in which a "focus on statistics . . . could put undue pressure on employers to adopt inappropriate prophylactic measures." *Watson* [*v. Fort Worth Bank & Trust*, reproduced at p. 183]. Even worse, an employer could discard test results (or other employment practices) with the intent of obtaining the employer's preferred racial balance. That operational principle could not be justified, for Title VII is express in disclaiming any interpretation of its requirements as calling for outright racial balancing. §2000e-2(j). The purpose of Title VII "is to promote hiring on the basis of job qualifications, rather than on the basis of race or color." *Griggs*.

In searching for a standard that strikes a more appropriate balance, we note that this Court has considered cases similar to this one, albeit in the context of the Equal Protection Clause of the Fourteenth Amendment. The Court has held that certain government actions to remedy past racial discrimination — actions that are themselves based on race — are constitutional only where there is a "'strong basis in evidence'" that the remedial actions were necessary. *Richmond v. J.A. Croson Co.*, 488 U.S. 469, 500 (1989). This suit does not call on us to consider whether the statutory constraints under Title VII must be parallel in all respects to those under the Constitution. That does not mean the constitutional authorities are irrelevant, however. Our cases discussing constitutional principles can provide helpful guidance in this statutory context. . . .

The same interests [as operated in *Wygant* and *Croson*] are at work in the interplay between the disparate-treatment and disparate-impact provisions of Title VII. Congress has imposed liability on employers for unintentional discrimination in order to rid the workplace of "practices that are fair in form, but discriminatory in operation." *Griggs.* But it has also prohibited employers from taking adverse employment actions "because of" race. Applying the strong-basis-in-evidence standard to Title VII gives effect to both the disparate-treatment and disparate-impact provisions, allowing violations of one in the name of compliance with the other only in certain, narrow circumstances. The standard leaves ample room for employers' voluntary compliance efforts, which are essential to the statutory scheme and to Congress's efforts to eradicate workplace discrimination. And the standard appropriately constrains employers' discretion in making race-based decisions: It limits that discretion to cases in which there is a strong basis in evidence of disparate-impact liability, but it is not so restrictive that it allows employers to act only when there is a provable, actual violation.

Resolving the statutory conflict in this way allows the disparate-impact prohibition to work in a manner that is consistent with other provisions of Title VII, including the prohibition on adjusting employment-related test scores on the basis of race. *See* §2000e-2(*l*). Examinations like those administered by the City create legitimate expectations on the part of those who took the tests. As is the case with any promotion exam, some of the firefighters here invested substantial time, money, and personal commitment in preparing for the tests. Employment tests can be an important part of a neutral selection system that safeguards against the very racial animosities Title VII was intended to prevent. Here, however, the fire-fighters saw their efforts invalidated by the City in sole reliance upon race-based statistics.

If an employer cannot rescore a test based on the candidates' race, §2000e-2(*l*), then it follows *a fortiori* that it may not take the greater step of discarding the test altogether to achieve a more desirable racial distribution of promotion-eligible candidates — absent a strong basis in evidence that the test was deficient and that discarding the results is necessary to avoid violating the disparate-impact provision. Restricting an employer's ability to discard test results (and thereby discriminate against qualified candidates on the basis of their race) also is in keeping with Title VII's express protection of bona fide promotional examinations. *See* §2000e-2(h); *cf. AT&T Corp. v. Hulteen*, 556 U.S. 701 (2009).

For the foregoing reasons, we adopt the strong-basis-in-evidence standard as a matter of statutory construction to resolve any conflict between the disparate-treatment and disparate-impact provisions of Title VII. . . .

Our statutory holding does not address the constitutionality of the measures taken here in purported compliance with Title VII. We also do not hold that meeting the strong-basis-in-evidence standard would satisfy the Equal Protection Clause in a future case. As we explain below, because respondents have not met their burden under Title VII, we need not decide whether a legitimate fear of disparate impact is ever sufficient to justify discriminatory treatment under the Constitution.

[We do not] question an employer's affirmative efforts to ensure that all groups have a fair opportunity to apply for promotions and to participate in the process by which promotions will be made. But once that process has been established and employers have made clear their selection criteria, they may not then invalidate the test results, thus upsetting an employee's legitimate expectation not to be judged on the basis of race. Doing so, absent a strong basis in evidence of an impermissible disparate impact, amounts to the sort of racial preference that Congress has disclaimed, §2000e-2(j), and is antithetical to the notion of a work-place where individuals are guaranteed equal opportunity regardless of race.

Title VII does not prohibit an employer from considering, before administering a test or practice, how to design that test or practice in order to provide a fair opportunity for all individuals, regardless of their race. And when, during the test-design stage, an employer invites comments to ensure the test is fair, that process can provide a common ground for open discussions toward that end. We hold only that, under Title VII, before an employer can engage in intentional discrimination for the asserted purpose of avoiding or remedying an unintentional disparate impact, the employer must have a strong basis in evidence to believe it will be subject to disparate-impact liability if it fails to take the race-conscious, discriminatory action.

C

The City argues that, even under the strong-basis-in-evidence standard, its decision to discard the examination results was permissible under Title VII. That is incorrect. Even if respondents were motivated as a subjective matter by a desire to avoid committing disparate-impact discrimination, the record makes clear there is no support for the conclusion that respondents had an objective, strong basis in evidence to find the tests inadequate, with some consequent disparate-impact liability in violation of Title VII.

On this basis, we conclude that petitioners have met their obligation to demonstrate that there is "no genuine issue as to any material fact" and that they are "entitled to judgment as a matter of law." Fed. Rule Civ. Proc. 56(c). . . .

The racial adverse impact here was significant, and petitioners do not dispute that the City was faced with a prima facie case of disparate-impact liability. [For example, on the captain exam, whites had a 64 percent pass rate as compared with a 37.5 percent for both black and Hispanic candidates. Since the pass rates of minorities were approximately one-half the pass rates for white candidates, they met the EEOC's 80-percent rule of thumb. Under the governing] "rule of three," certifying the examinations would have meant that the City could not have considered black candidates for any of the then-vacant lieutenant or captain positions.

Based on the degree of adverse impact reflected in the results, respondents were compelled to take a hard look at the examinations to determine whether certifying the results would have had an impermissible disparate impact. The problem for respondents is that a prima facie case of disparate-impact liability — essentially, a threshold showing of a significant statistical disparity, *Connecticut v. Teal*, and nothing more — is far from a strong basis in evidence that the City would have been liable under Title VII had it certified the results. That is because the City could be liable for disparate-impact discrimination only if the examinations were not job related and consistent with business necessity, or if there existed an equally valid, less-discriminatory alternative that served the City's needs but that the City refused to adopt. We conclude there is no strong basis in evidence to establish that the test was deficient in either of these respects. . . .

1

There is no genuine dispute that the examinations were job-related and consistent with business necessity. The City's assertions to the contrary are "blatantly contradicted by the record" [including the statements of IOS vice president Chad Legel and city officials outlining the detailed steps taken to develop and administer the examinations. The only outside witness who reviewed the examinations in any detail was the only one with any firefighting experience, and he stated that the "questions were relevant for both exams." Further, the City "turned a blind eye to evidence" supporting the exams' validity, including never asking IOS for a technical report about the exam's consistency with EEOC guidelines, which IOS stood ready to provide].

2

Respondents also lacked a strong basis in evidence of an equally valid, less-discriminatory testing alternative that the City, by certifying the examination results, would necessarily have refused to adopt. Respondents raise three arguments to the contrary, but each argument fails. First, respondents refer to testimony before the CSB that a different composite-score calculation — weighting the written and oral examination scores 30/70 — would have allowed the City to consider two black candidates for then-open lieutenant positions and one black candidate for then-open captain positions. (The City used a 60/40 weighting as required by its contract with the New Haven firefighters' union.) But respondents have produced no evidence to show that the 60/40 weighting was indeed arbitrary. In fact, because that formula was the result of a union-negotiated collective-bargaining agreement, we presume the parties negotiated that weighting for a rational reason. Nor does the record contain any evidence that the 30/70 weighting would be an equally valid way to determine whether candidates possess the proper mix of job knowledge and situational skills to earn promotions. Changing the weighting formula, moreover, could well have violated Title VII's prohibition of altering test scores on the basis of race. *See* §2000e-2(*l*). On this record, there is no basis to conclude that a 30/70 weighting was an equally valid alternative the City could have adopted.

Second, respondents argue that the City could have adopted a different interpretation of the "rule of three" [by "banding," that is, "rounding scores to the nearest whole number and considering all candidates with the same whole-number score as being of one rank." There was some question as to whether state law barred banding, but in any event it] was not a valid alternative for this reason: Had the City reviewed the exam results and then adopted banding to make the minority test scores appear higher, it would have violated Title VII's prohibition of adjusting test results on the basis of race. §2000e-2(*l*); *see also Chicago Firefighters Local 2 v. Chicago*, 249 F.3d 649, 656 (CA7 2001) (Posner, J.) ("We have no doubt that if banding were adopted in order to make lower black scores seem higher, it would indeed be . . . forbidden"). As a matter of law, banding was not an alternative available to the City when it was considering whether to certify the examination results.

Third, and finally, respondents refer to statements by [Christopher Hornick, an organizational psychologist and competitor of IOS] in his telephone interview with the CSB regarding alternatives to the written examinations. Hornick stated his "belie[f]" that an "assessment center process," which would have evaluated candidates' behavior in typical job tasks, "would have demonstrated less adverse impact." But Hornick's brief mention of alternative testing methods, standing alone, does not raise a genuine issue of material fact that assessment centers were available to the City at the time of the examinations and that they would have produced less adverse impact. . . .

3

On the record before us, there is no genuine dispute that the City lacked a strong basis in evidence to believe it would face disparate-impact liability if it certified the examination results. In other words, there is no evidence — let alone the required strong basis in evidence — that the tests were flawed because they were not job-related or because other, equally valid and less discriminatory tests were available to the City. Fear of litigation alone cannot justify an employer's reliance on race to the detriment of individuals who passed the examinations and qualified for promotions. The City's discarding the test results was impermissible under Title VII, and summary judgment is appropriate for petitioners on their disparate-treatment claim. . . .

* * *

The record in this litigation documents a process that, at the outset, had the potential to produce a testing procedure that was true to the promise of Title VII: No individual should face workplace discrimination based on race. Respondents thought about promotion qualifications and relevant experience in neutral ways. They were careful to ensure broad racial participation in the design of the test itself and its administration. As we have discussed at length, the process was open and fair.

The problem, of course, is that after the tests were completed, the raw racial results became the predominant rationale for the City's refusal to certify the results. The injury arises in part from the high, and justified, expectations of the candidates who had participated in the testing process on the terms the City had established for the promotional process. Many of the candidates had studied for months, at considerable personal and financial expense, and thus the injury caused by the City's reliance on raw racial statistics at the end of the process was all the more severe. Confronted with arguments both for and against certifying the test results — and threats of a lawsuit either way — the City was required to make a difficult inquiry. But its hearings produced no strong evidence of a disparate-impact violation, and the City was not entitled to disregard the tests based solely on the racial disparity in the results.

Our holding today clarifies how Title VII applies to resolve competing expectations under the disparate-treatment and disparate-impact provisions. If, after it certifies the test results, the City faces a disparate-impact suit, then in light of our holding today it should be clear that the City would avoid disparate-impact liability based on the strong basis in evidence that, had it not certified the results, it would have been subject to disparate-treatment liability. . . .

Justice SCALIA, concurring.

I join the Court's opinion in full, but write separately to observe that its resolution of this dispute merely postpones the evil day on which the Court will have to confront the question: Whether, or to what extent, are the disparate-impact provisions of Title VII of the Civil Rights Act of 1964 consistent with the Constitution's guarantee of equal protection? The question is not an easy one. *See generally* Primus, *Equal Protection and Disparate Impact: Round Three*, 117 HARV. L. REV. 493 (2003).

The difficulty is this: Whether or not Title VII's disparate-treatment provisions forbid "remedial" race-based actions when a disparate-impact violation would *not* otherwise result — the question resolved by the Court today — it is clear that Title VII not only permits but affirmatively *requires* such actions when a disparate-impact violation *would* otherwise result. But if the Federal Government is prohibited from discriminating on the basis of race, *Bolling v. Sharpe*, 347 U.S. 497, 500 (1954), then surely it is also prohibited from enacting laws mandating that third parties — *e.g.*, employers, whether private, State, or municipal — discriminate on the basis of race. As the facts of these cases illustrate, Title VII's disparate-impact provisions place a racial thumb on the scales, often requiring employers to evaluate the racial outcomes of their policies, and to make decisions based on (because of) those racial outcomes. That type of racial decisionmaking is, as the Court explains, discriminatory.

To be sure, the disparate-impact laws do not mandate imposition of quotas, but it is not clear why that should provide a safe harbor. Would a private employer not be guilty of unlawful discrimination if he refrained from establishing a racial hiring quota but intentionally designed his hiring practices to achieve the same end? Surely he would. Intentional discrimination is still occurring, just one step up the chain. Government compulsion of such design would therefore seemingly violate equal protection principles. . . .

It might be possible to defend the law by framing it as simply an evidentiary tool used to identify genuine, intentional discrimination — to "smoke out," as it were, disparate treatment. Disparate impact is sometimes a signal of something illicit, so a regulator might allow statistical disparities to play some role in the evidentiary process. But arguably the disparate-impact provisions sweep too broadly to be fairly characterized in such a fashion — since they fail to provide an affirmative defense for good-faith (*i.e.*, nonracially motivated) conduct, or perhaps even for good faith plus hiring standards that are entirely reasonable. This is a question that this Court will have to consider in due course. It is one thing to free plaintiffs from proving an employer's illicit intent, but quite another to preclude the employer from proving that its motives were pure and its actions reasonable.

The Court's resolution of these cases makes it unnecessary to resolve these matters today. But the war between disparate impact and equal protection will be waged sooner or later, and it behooves us to begin thinking about how — and on what terms — to make peace between them.

Justice ALITO, with whom Justice SCALIA and Justice THOMAS join, concurring.

[The concurrence "join[ed] the Court's opinion in full" but wrote separately to correct what it viewed as important omissions in Justice Ginsburg's dissent. In particular, it concluded that, even if Justice Ginsburg's "good cause" (as opposed to the majority's "strong basis in evidence") test were adopted, the decision below would still have to be reversed. That is because "I assume that the dissent would not countenance summary judgment for respondents if respondents' professed concern about disparate-impact litigation was simply a pretext." In the concurrences' view, the record would permit a reasonable jury to find "that the City's asserted reason for scrapping its test — concern about disparate-impact liability — was a pretext and that the City's real reason was illegitimate, namely, the desire to placate a politically important racial constituency." This did not, contrary to the dissent's rejoinder, "equat[e] political considerations with unlawful discrimination"; whatever the appropriateness of many efforts by a politician can attempt to win over a constituency, "there are some things that a public official cannot do, and one of those is engaging in intentional racial discrimination when making employment decisions."]

Justice GINSBURG, with whom Justice STEVENS, Justice SOUTER, and Justice BREYER join, dissenting.

[In assessing race discrimination claims, context matters, and, in 1972 when Congress extended Title VII to public employment, municipal fire departments across the country, including New Haven's, pervasively discriminated against minorities. It took decades of litigation to open firefighting posts to members of racial minorities.]

The white firefighters who scored high on New Haven's promotional exams understandably attract this Court's sympathy. But they had no vested right to promotion. Nor have other persons received promotions in preference to them. New Haven maintains that it refused to certify the test results because it believed, for good cause, that it would be vulnerable to a Title VII disparate-impact suit if it relied on those results. The Court today holds that New Haven has not demonstrated "a strong basis in evidence" for its plea. In so holding, the Court pretends that "[t]he City rejected the test results solely because the higher scoring candidates were white." That pretension, essential to the Court's disposition, ignores substantial evidence of multiple flaws in the tests New Haven used. The Court similarly fails to acknowledge the better tests used in other cities, which have yielded less racially skewed outcomes.

By order of this Court, New Haven, a city in which African-Americans and Hispanics account for nearly 60 percent of the population, must today be served — as it was in the days of undisguised discrimination — by a fire department in which members of racial and ethnic minorities are rarely seen in command positions. . . .

I

A

[The dissent traced a history of racial discrimination in firefighting in the nation as documented by the U.S. Commission on Civil Rights. In New Haven in the early 1970s, African Americans and Hispanics composed 30 percent of the population, but only 3.6 percent of the City's 502 firefighters. By 2003, African Americans and Hispanics constituted 30 percent and 16 percent of the City's firefighters, respectively, when New Haven's population was nearly 40 percent African American and more than 20 percent Hispanic. But significant disparities remained in supervisory positions: the rank of captain and higher comprised only 9 percent African American and 9 percent Hispanic.] It is against this backdrop of entrenched inequality that the promotion process at issue in this litigation should be assessed.

B

[All agree that stark disparities in the results of the selection process sufficed to state a prima facie case under Title VII's disparate impact provision and to give New Haven "cause for concern about the prospect of Title VII litigation and liability," which in turn led to the referral to the New Haven Civil Service Board and the public meetings. Justice Ginsburg recounted some of the basis of the opposition to certifying the test, including the failure "for security reasons" to have Department officials check the content of the questions prior to their administration. There was also testimony that "contrasted New Haven's experience with that of nearby Bridgeport, where minority firefighters held one-third of lieutenant and captain positions," in large part because Bridgeport gave more weight to the oral examination. In addition, Dr. Hornick testified that an assessment center would enable New Haven to better "identif[y] the best possible people" and "demonstrate dramatically less adverse impacts." She quoted Hornick as also saying "I think a person's leadership skills, their command presence, their interpersonal skills, their management skills, their tactical skills could have been identified and evaluated in a much more appropriate way."]

II . . .

B

Neither Congress' enactments nor this Court's Title VII precedents (including the now-discredited decision in *Wards Cove*) offer even a hint of "conflict" between an employer's obligations under the statute's disparate-treatment and disparate-impact provisions. Standing on an equal footing, these twin pillars of Title VII advance the same objectives: ending workplace discrimination and promoting genuinely equal opportunity. See *McDonnell Douglas Corp. v. Green.*

Yet the Court today sets at odds the statute's core directives. When an employer changes an employment practice in an effort to comply with Title VII's disparate-impact provision, the Court reasons, it acts "because of race" — something Title VII's disparate-treatment provision generally forbids. This characterization of an employer's compliance-directed action shows little attention to Congress' design or to the *Griggs* line of cases Congress recognized as pathmarking. . . . [Because a court is bound to read the provisions of any statute as harmonious] Title VII's disparate-treatment and disparate-impact proscriptions must be read as complementary.

In codifying the *Griggs* and *Albemarle* instructions, Congress declared unambiguously that selection criteria operating to the disadvantage of minority group members can be retained only if justified by business necessity.[5] In keeping with Congress' design, employers who reject such criteria due to reasonable doubts about their reliability can hardly be held to have engaged in discrimination "because of" race. A reasonable endeavor to comply with the law and to ensure that qualified candidates of all races have a fair opportunity to compete is simply not what Congress meant to interdict. I would therefore hold that an employer who jettisons a selection device when its disproportionate racial impact becomes apparent does not violate Title VII's disparate-treatment bar automatically or at all, subject to this key condition: The employer must have good cause to believe the device would not withstand examination for business necessity. . . .

This litigation does not involve affirmative action. But if the voluntary affirmative action at issue in *Johnson* [*v. Transportation Agency, Santa Clara Cty.*, reproduced at p. 152] does not discriminate within the meaning of Title VII, neither does an employer's reasonable effort to comply with Title VII's disparate-impact provision by refraining from action of doubtful consistency with business necessity.

C. . .

2. . .

As a result of today's decision, an employer who discards a dubious selection process can anticipate costly disparate-treatment litigation in which its chances for success — even for surviving a summary-judgment motion — are highly problematic. Concern about exposure to disparate-impact liability, however well grounded, is insufficient to insulate an employer from attack. Instead, the employer must make a "strong" showing that (1) its selection method was "not job related and consistent with business necessity," or (2) that it refused to adopt "an equally valid, less-discriminatory alternative." It is hard to see how these requirements differ from demanding that an employer establish "a provable, actual violation" *against itself.* There is indeed a sharp conflict here, but it is not the false one the Court describes between Title VII's core provisions. It is, instead, the discordance of the Court's opinion with the voluntary compliance ideal.[7]

5. What was the "business necessity" for the tests New Haven used? How could one justify, *e.g.*, the 60/40 written/oral ratio under that standard? Neither the Court nor the concurring opinions attempt to defend the ratio.

7. Notably, prior decisions applying a strong-basis-in-evidence standard have not imposed a burden as heavy as the one the Court imposes today. In *Croson*, the Court found no strong basis in evidence because the City had offered "nothing approaching a prima facie case." *Richmond v. J.A. Croson Co.*, 488 U.S. 469, 500 (1989). The Court did not suggest that anything beyond a prima facie case would have been required. . . .

3

The Court's additional justifications for announcing a strong-basis-in-evidence standard are unimpressive. First, discarding the results of tests, the Court suggests, calls for a heightened standard because it "upset[s] an employee's legitimate expectation." This rationale puts the cart before the horse. The legitimacy of an employee's expectation depends on the legitimacy of the selection method. If an employer reasonably concludes that an exam fails to identify the most qualified individuals and needlessly shuts out a segment of the applicant pool, Title VII surely does not compel the employer to hire or promote based on the test, however unreliable it may be. Indeed, the statute's prime objective is to prevent exclusionary practices from "operat[ing] to 'freeze' the status quo." *Griggs.*

Second, the Court suggests, anything less than a strong-basis-in-evidence standard risks creating "a *de facto* quota system, in which . . . an employer could discard test results . . . with the intent of obtaining the employer's preferred racial balance." Under a reasonableness standard, however, an employer could not cast aside a selection method based on a statistical disparity alone.[8] The employer must have good cause to believe that the method screens out qualified applicants and would be difficult to justify as grounded in business necessity. Should an employer repeatedly reject test results, it would be fair, I agree, to infer that the employer is simply seeking a racially balanced outcome and is not genuinely endeavoring to comply with Title VII.

D

The Court stacks the deck further by denying respondents any chance to satisfy the newly announced strong-basis-in-evidence standard. . . .

III

A

Applying what I view as the proper standard to the record thus far made, I would hold that New Haven had ample cause to believe its selection process was flawed and not justified by business necessity. Judged by that standard, petitioners have not shown that New Haven's failure to certify the exam results violated Title VII's disparate-treatment provision.

didn't really make an effort to modify the weighing)

. . . Chief among the City's problems was the very nature of the tests for promotion. In choosing to use written and oral exams with a 60/40 weighting, the City simply adhered to the union's preference and apparently gave no consideration to whether the weighting was likely to identify the most qualified fire-officer candidates.[11] There is strong reason to think it was not.

---

8. Infecting the Court's entire analysis is its insistence that the City rejected the test results "in sole reliance upon race-based statistics." But as the part of the story the Court leaves out plainly shows — the long history of rank discrimination against African-Americans in the firefighting profession, the multiple flaws in New Haven's test for promotions — "sole reliance" on statistics certainly is not descriptive of the CSB's decision.

11. This alone would have posed a substantial problem for New Haven in a disparate-impact suit, particularly in light of the disparate results the City's scheme had produced in the past. Under the Uniform Guidelines on Employee Selection Procedures (Uniform Guidelines), employers must conduct "an investigation of suitable alternative selection procedures." It is no answer to "presume" that the two-decades-old 60/40 formula was adopted for a "rational reason" because it "was the result of a union-negotiated collective bargaining agreement." That the parties may have been "rational' says nothing about whether their agreed-upon selection process was consistent with business necessity. . . .

Relying heavily on written tests to select fire officers is a questionable practice, to say the least. Successful fire officers, the City's description of the position makes clear, must have the "[a]bility to lead personnel effectively, maintain discipline, promote harmony, exercise sound judgment, and cooperate with other officials." These qualities are not well measured by written tests. Testifying before the CSB, Christopher Hornick, an exam-design expert with more than two decades of relevant experience, was emphatic on this point: Leadership skills, command presence, and the like "could have been identified and evaluated in a much more appropriate way."

Hornick's commonsense observation is mirrored in case law and in Title VII's administrative guidelines. Courts have long criticized written firefighter promotion exams for being "more probative of the test-taker's ability to recall what a particular text stated on a given topic than of his firefighting or supervisory knowledge and abilities." . . .

Given these unfavorable appraisals, it is unsurprising that most municipal employers do not evaluate their fire-officer candidates as New Haven does. [There was also testimony before the CSB that "alternative methods were both more reliable and notably less discriminatory in operation."] Considering the prevalence of these proven alternatives, New Haven was poorly positioned to argue that promotions based on its outmoded and exclusionary selection process qualified as a business necessity. . . .

That IOS representative Chad Legel and his team may have been diligent in designing the exams says little about the exams' suitability for selecting fire officers. IOS worked within the City's constraints. Legel never discussed with the City the propriety of the 60/40 weighting and "was not asked to consider the possibility of an assessment center." The IOS exams, Legel admitted, had not even attempted to assess "command presence": "[Y]ou would probably be better off with an assessment center if you cared to measure that."

In addition to the highly questionable character of the exams and the neglect of available alternatives, the City had other reasons to worry about its vulnerability to disparate-impact liability. Under the City's ground rules, IOS was not allowed to show the exams to anyone in the New Haven Fire Department prior to their administration. This "precluded [IOS] from being able to engage in [its] normal subject matter expert review process" — something Legel described as "very critical." As a result, some of the exam questions were confusing or irrelevant, and the exams may have over-tested some subject-matter areas while missing others. Testimony before the CSB also raised questions concerning unequal access to study materials and the potential bias introduced by relying principally on job analyses from nonminority fire officers to develop the exams.[16] . . .

In sum, the record solidly establishes that the City had good cause to fear disparate-impact liability. Moreover, the Court supplies no tenable explanation why the evidence of the tests' multiple deficiencies does not create at least a triable issue under a strong-basis-in-evidence standard.

16. The I-O Psychologists Brief identifies still other, more technical flaws in the exams that may well have precluded the City from prevailing in a disparate-impact suit. Notably, the exams were never shown to be suitably precise to allow strict rank ordering of candidates. A difference of one or two points on a multiple-choice exam should not be decisive of an applicant's promotion chances if that difference bears little relationship to the applicant's qualifications for the job. Relatedly, it appears that the line between a passing and failing score did not accurately differentiate between qualified and unqualified candidates. A number of fire-officer promotional exams have been invalidated on these bases. *See, e.g., Guardians Assn. [of New York City Police Dept., Inc. v. Civil Service Com.,* 630 F.2d 79, 105 (2d Cir. 1980)] ("When a cutoff score unrelated to job performance produces disparate racial results, Title VII is violated.").

B

[Addressing the argument in Justice Alito's concurrence that there was at least a triable issue of whether the City's "stated desire to comply with Title VII was insincere, a mere 'pretext' for discrimination against white firefighters," the dissent found most of the evidence adduced to be irrelevant because "the relevant decision was made by the CSB, an unelected, politically insulated body." Further, "Justice Alito's analysis contains a more fundamental flaw: It equates political considerations with unlawful discrimination."]

* * *

This case presents an unfortunate situation, one New Haven might well have avoided had it utilized a better selection process in the first place. But what this case does not present is race-based discrimination in violation of Title VII. I dissent from the Court's judgment, which rests on the false premise that respondents showed "a significant statistical disparity," but "nothing more."

NOTES

1. *Putting It All Together or Tearing It All Apart?* If you want an opportunity to think about big concepts spread across the entire course, *Ricci* has it all: systemic disparate treatment (Chapter 2), disparate impact (Chapter 3), testing (Chapter 3), affirmative action from a statutory or constitutional perspective (Chapter 2), and pretext (again, mostly from Chapter 1). What more could a professor (or student) ask for? The other perspective on *Ricci*, however, is that it tears apart quite a lot of what you've learned to this point. Indeed, there were those who thought that it signaled the end of disparate impact liability. That was an overstatement, but *Ricci* remains an important decision.

2. *The Holding.* The majority was clear: the defendants' decision not to use test results because that would have meant no promotions for African Americans and only two for Hispanics, who together made up over half of the test takers, was intentional disparate treatment discrimination against the white test takers who would have been promoted had the test been certified. Further, the fact that granting promotions on the basis of the test results amounted to a prima facie case of disparate impact discrimination was not itself a defense to a disparate treatment case; the employer also needed a strong basis in evidence to believe that it would be liable under the disparate impact theory, which means that it needed a strong basis to believe both that it lacked a business necessity/job relation for the practice and that there was no viable alternative employment practice.

3. *Does Knowledge Equal Intentional Discrimination?* The Court was firm that the decision not to certify the examination results because of the disparate racial impact was necessarily "because of" race. But is there a difference between intending not to disadvantage African American and Hispanic candidates and intending to discriminate against white candidates? This takes us back to *Personnel Administrator v. Feeney*, p. 131, where the Court said, admittedly in the equal protection context, that "'[d]iscriminatory purpose,' however, implies more than intent as volition or intent as awareness of consequences. It implies that the decisionmaker . . . selected or reaffirmed a particular course of action at least in part 'because of,' not merely 'in spite of,' its adverse effects upon an identifiable group." Did New Haven invalidate the test in order to deprive whites of promotions? Or was that merely a foreseeable consequence? Michael J. Zimmer, *Ricci's Color-Blind Standard in a Race Conscious*

Society: A Case of Unintended Consequences?, 2010 BYU L. Rev. 1257, 1301, warned that after *Ricci*, "[k]nowing the racial consequences of an action now violates this 'color-blind' approach and anyone adversely affected by that action could bring a challenge." Other commentators agreed. *See* Kerri Stone, *The Unexpected Appearance of Transferred Intent in Title VII*, 55 Loy. L. Rev. 752 (2010); Helen Norton, *The Supreme Court's Post-Racial Turn Towards a Zero-Sum Understanding of Equality*, 52 Wm. & Mary L. Rev. 197, 200 (2010); *but see* Ann C. McGinley, Ricci v. DeStefano: *Diluting Disparate Impact and Redefining Disparate Treatment*, 12 Nev. L.J. 626, 637 (2012). However, the Supreme Court's subsequent decision in *Texas Department of Housing & Community Affairs v. Inclusive Communities Project, Inc.*, 135 S. Ct. 2507, 2525 (2015), seems to reject such a reading: "[w]hen setting their larger goals, local housing authorities may choose to foster diversity and combat racial isolation with race-neutral tools, and mere awareness of race in attempting to solve the problems facing inner cities does not doom that endeavor at the outset." See Note 8, p. 194.

4. *A Hierarchy of Theories?* The majority thinks that disparate treatment is the main evil that Congress proscribed; disparate impact is a late addition to the statute, and must be tailored to minimize any conflict with the disparate treatment bar. In other words, for the majority, disparate treatment can be sacrificed to disparate impact only if the "strong basis in evidence" test is met, thus ensuring that disparate treatment is generally avoided. Under Justice Ginsburg's opposing view, *Griggs* made clear that disparate impact was implicit in Title VII from the beginning; in any event, by codifying disparate impact in 1991, Congress necessarily intended to allow race consciousness to avoid an unjustified racial impact. To put it another way, such race consciousness could not be the kind of disparate treatment Title VII meant to proscribe. We leave it to you to decide whether the majority or the dissent has the better view of history.

5. *What's the Disagreement on the Standard?* The various opinions disagree about a lot, especially about the application of the appropriate standard to the facts of the case. But Supreme Court decisions are usually more about law than facts, and is there all that much difference between the majority and the Ginsburg dissent? The majority articulates the "strong basis in evidence" standard. Justice Ginsburg would permit only "good cause to believe [a selection] device would not withstand examination for business necessity." So the difference is "strong basis" vs. "good cause." A tempest in a teapot? In any event, do you understand the dissent's concerns regarding the need for employers to "establish 'a provable, actual violation' *against itself*" (emphasis in original)? That comes out of the affirmative action cases, where such a requirement would discourage the adoption of such plans. See Chapter 2. But how does this argument apply here? By definition, if there is such a "strong basis," the employer can scrub the test. There will then be no disparate impact liability because the test is never used, and there will be no disparate treatment liability because of the strong basis for disparate impact liability.

6. *What's a Strong Enough Basis?* In *United States v. Brennan*, 650 F.3d 65, 109-10 (2d Cir. 2011), the Second Circuit tried to explain: "we hold that, under *Ricci*, a 'strong basis in evidence' of non-job-relatedness or of a less discriminatory alternative requires more than speculation, more than a few scattered statements in the record, and more than a mere fear of litigation, but less than the preponderance of the evidence that would be necessary for actual liability. This is what it means when courts say that the employer must have an objectively reasonable fear of disparate-impact liability." *See generally* Herman N. Johnson, Jr., *The Evolving Strong-Basis-in-Evidence Standard*, 32 Berkeley J. Emp. & Lab. L. 347 (2011).

7. *A Business Necessity as a Matter of Law?* Given the result, the majority must have concluded that the promotion tests were valid as a matter of law on the facts before the Court. The process of test construction and administration in *Ricci* should be familiar to you from Chapter 3. Under the Uniform Guidelines, IOS constructed a test that was supposedly content validated, *i.e.*, that it was a sample of the job. Even though taking written or oral exams was not a part of the jobs in question, we've seen that content validation has been stretched pretty far. Do you think the exam was content valid under the precedents we've studied — or at least valid enough that the CSB had no strong basis in evidence to doubt its validity? A number of scholars have supported the dissent, basically challenging the Court's equating merit with exam success, without regard to whether an exam actually predicts job performance. Ann C. McGinley, *Cognitive Illiberalism, Summary Judgment, and Title VII: An Examination of* Ricci v. DeStefano, 57 N.Y.L. Sch. L. Rev. 865, 889 (2012-2013); Mark S. Brodin, Ricci v. DeStefano: *The New Haven Firefighters Case and the Triumph of White Privilege*, 20 S. Cal. Rev. L. & Soc. Justice 161 (2011); Melissa Hart, *From* Wards Cove *to* Ricci: *Struggling Against the "Built-in-Headwinds" of a Skeptical Court*, 46 Wake Forest L. Rev. 261 (2011); Nancy L. Zisk, *Failing the Test: How* Ricci v. DeStefano *Failed to Clarify Disparate Impact and Disparate Treatment Law*, 34 Hamline L. Rev. 27 (2011); Cheryl I. Harris & Kimberly West-Faulcon, *Reading* Ricci: *White(ning) Discrimination, Race-ing Test Fairness*, 58 UCLA L. Rev. 73, (2010).

8. *Alternative Employment Practices.* We've also seen that even a valid test can't be used if there's an alternative employment practice that achieves the same purposes with less racial impact. The record before the CSB showed alternatives that were less discriminatory — simply altering the ratio of written to oral scores (as did Bridgeport, a city just down the interstate from New Haven), using "assessment centers," or altering the "rule of three" to a banding approach — all were alternatives that may have had less impact and that may have equally served the employer's needs. So why not remand on this question?

[handwritten margin note: because altering the test bc of the racial result would still be disparate treatment?]

9. *Back in the Frying Pan?* The New Haven saga did not end with *Ricci*. Although Frank Ricci obtained his promotion after remand, a black firefighter, Michael Briscoe, sued the city, claiming the promotion test had an unjustified disparate impact. New Haven promptly moved to dismiss, relying on this sentence in Justice Kennedy's opinion:

> If, after it certifies the test results, the City faces a disparate-impact suit, then in light of our holding today it should be clear that the City would avoid disparate-impact liability based on the strong basis in evidence that, had it not certified the results, it would have been subject to disparate-treatment liability.

The district court agreed, but the Second Circuit reversed. Normal preclusion principles prevent a judgment from binding a nonparty. *Briscoe v. City of New Haven*, 654 F.3d 200 (2d Cir. 2011). Although there are exceptions to this rule, including a provision in Title VII itself dealing with the effect of judgments in federal civil rights suits, *see* Charles A. Sullivan, Ricci v. DeStefano: *End of the Line or Just Another Turn on the Disparate Impact Road?*, 104 Nw. U. L. Rev. Colloquy 201 (2009), the Second Circuit held no such exception applied. In short, if Briscoe could persuade the court in his lawsuit that the test was in fact invalid, he would be entitled to a promotion. That case, however, was ultimately settled.

10. *A New Defense to Impact Claims?* Looking at the same convoluted sentence in Justice Kennedy's majority opinion, while the *Ricci* majority *allows* an employer

to take race into account when it has the requisite strong basis, does that sentence suggest that the employer can *choose* never to apply disparate impact analysis because doing so will always be disparate treatment? Under this view, avoidance of disparate treatment is always a complete defense to disparate impact. Or does the sentence make sense only when the employer does not (as New Haven didn't) have a strong basis to believe that it was subject to disparate impact liability? Under this view, an employer *must* avoid a practice with a disparate impact, even if it results in disparate treatment, so long as it has the requisite strong basis in evidence. But hold it — that can't be right. Before *Ricci*, an employer could prevail in a suit by black firefighters only by proving that it had a business necessity for its practice, not by showing that it had a strong basis in evidence that it had a business necessity.

The problem is the circularity of Justice Kennedy's sentence: there's no disparate treatment liability when avoidance of disparate impact is sufficiently shown, but avoidance of disparate impact liability seems to turn on whether the employer can avoid disparate treatment liability. Is your head hurting yet?

11. *Is* Ricci *Limited to End-Game Decisions?* The *Ricci* opinions focus on the decision whether to certify the test. At that point, the CSB had to favor either those who were successful or those who were not, with obvious racial consequences. But the majority also recognized that, in deciding whether or what to test, and before the competing expectations crystallized, potential racial effects can be taken into account; "an employer's affirmative efforts to ensure that all groups have a fair opportunity to apply for promotions" and therefore "how to design [a] test or practice in order to provide a fair opportunity for all individuals, regardless of their race." *See also Maraschiello v. City of Buffalo Police Dep't*, 709 F.3d 87, 95 (2d Cir. 2013) (proof that adoption of a new test was partially motivated by a desire for more racially balanced results would not establish that "the generalized overhaul of departmental promotional requirements amounted to the sort of race-based adverse action discussed in *Ricci*"). This is consistent with *Texas Department of Housing & Community Affairs v. Inclusive Communities Project, Inc.*, 135 S. Ct. 2507 (2015), discussed at Note 8, p. 194, and with recent constitutional affirmative action decisions. See p. 163.

12. *Relation to Affirmative Action.* Only Justice Ginsburg in dissent puts *Ricci* in context with the Court's Title VII affirmative action decisions. Recall that under *Weber/Johnson*, see p. 152, a prima facie case of disparate treatment is not required to justify an affirmative action plan; all that is necessary is a manifest imbalance in a traditionally segregated job category and no unnecessary trammeling of majority rights. In *Ricci*, however, even an uncontested prima facie case of disparate impact is not enough to permit the employer to take steps to reduce or eliminate the impact.

The parallels between affirmative action analysis under Title VII and *Ricci's* approach to the intersection of disparate treatment and disparate impact are obvious. In both, race is allowed to influence an employer's decision but only under certain circumstances. For a valid affirmative action plan, there must be a manifest imbalance and majority interests must not be unduly trammeled. For tests with a disparate impact, the test may be thrown out because of that impact, but only under a strong basis in evidence test. So both doctrines allow disparate treatment under more-or-less tight constraints.

Prior to *Ricci*, some wondered if the Roberts Court would overrule *Weber/Johnson's* approval of voluntary affirmative action. Does *Ricci* suggest that the answer is no because it allows some systemic disparate treatment? On the other hand, *Ricci* was not an affirmative action case, at least not as that term is normally used. No one was preferred over anyone else, although white firefighters lost promotions they would otherwise have gotten. Since the majority condemned actions taken for racial reasons absent a strong basis in evidence for disparate impact liability, *Ricci* can be viewed as harsher than the affirmative action cases. And the "strong basis in evidence test" clearly requires more in the way of proof than "manifest imbalance" does in the affirmative action context. *See generally* Roberto L. Corrada, Ricci's *Dicta: Signaling a New Standard for Affirmative Action Under Title VII?*, 46 WAKE FOREST L. REV. 241 (2011); Sachin S. Pandya, *Detecting the Stealth Erosion of Precedent: Affirmative Action After* Ricci, 31 BERKELEY J. EMP. & LAB. L. 285 (2010); George Rutherglen, Ricci v. DeStefano: *Affirmative Action and the Lessons of Adversity*, 2009 SUP. CT. REV. 83.

PROBLEM 4.2

Assume you hang out your shingle to practice law and you are open to taking plaintiffs' employment discrimination cases. If a potential client came through the door, what approach would you take to make sure that you did not miss any possible theories of recovery? What information would you try to find out that might support what theories? Starting at the broadest theory, what information would you want to have to support a systemic disparate treatment claim? While that information is also relevant to a disparate impact claim and to an individual disparate treatment claim, what information would you want to know that might support a claim based on the disparate impact theory? What information about possible defenses to all three theories would be desirable?

Assume you represent employers in employment discrimination cases. How would you go about creating a strategy that would successfully defend your clients as to each theory, taking into account the interrelationships among the three main theories?

In approaching these questions from either side, reconsider the facts of Problem 4.1.

Chapter 5

Special Problems in Applying Title VII, Section 1981, and the ADEA

A. INTRODUCTION

The broad theories developed in Chapters 1 through 4 generally control any Title VII suit. Distinctive problems, however, have arisen in applying these concepts to different types of discrimination.

This chapter considers the following topics. Section B treats the threshold question of coverage of Title VII, §1981, and the Age Discrimination in Employment Act (ADEA). The next five sections deal with distinctive problems under Title VII. Thus, Section C addresses issues concerning gender discrimination, including pregnancy, sexual harassment, grooming and dress codes, and sexual orientation. Section D focuses on discrimination on the basis of religion, including the duty to accommodate. Section E examines national origin discrimination and alienage restrictions. Section F considers questions of union liability. Finally, Section G treats distinctive problems that arise under the ADEA.

B. COVERAGE OF TITLE VII, THE ADEA, AND SECTION 1981

Only "employees" are protected by most of the antidiscrimination laws, and only "employers" (and labor organizations and employment agencies) fall within their prohibitions. This relatively simple statement conceals numerous problems concerning coverage of these statutes. Neither employment agencies nor labor organizations have caused much interpretive difficulty, but questions of "employment" have generated considerable litigation.

The starting point is the statutory language: an "employer" under Title VII means "a person engaged in an industry affecting commerce who has fifteen or more employees for each working day in each of twenty or more calendar weeks in the current or preceding calendar year, and any agent of such person." 42 U.S.C. §2000e(b), §701(b). The ADEA is phrased identically, except that an employer must have 20 or more employees. 29 U.S.C. §630(b). However, these definitions are circular. An "employer" must have "employees," but the statutes define "employee" as "an individual employed by an employer." §2000e(f); 29 U.S.C. §630(f). (The ADA, as we will see in Chapter 6, prohibits discrimination by a "covered entity" but that term also embraces "employers" as defined in the other statutes.) The critical question for all these statutes, then, is what constitutes "employment," And that term is not defined by either Title VII or the ADEA, leaving courts to struggle with where "employment" begins and other legal relationships end.

Counterintuitively, the fact that one person works for another does not necessarily create an employment relationship. Think of your college and law school unpaid externships! And on the other side of the coin, your doctor works for you, but isn't your employee. Nor is the local mechanic fixing your car or the electrician repairing your lights. The latter individuals are likely to be viewed by the law as "independent contractors." Oddly enough, the distinction between employees and independent contractors grew up for reasons far removed from discrimination questions. When a third party was injured by the negligence of an actor, tort law extended the liability to his "employer" (originally "master") under the label "respondeat superior"; "employees" (originally "servants") were often judgment-proof, which meant that vicarious liability was necessary to ensure any recovery at all for the harm. At the same time, tort law refused to extend such liability to "independent contractors." That distinction was justified because the employer had a right to control the work of its employees, and therefore was fairly held responsible for any torts committed within the scope of the worker's employment. There was no right to control the work of independent contractors and therefore no basis for such respondeat superior liability. Such a line might make sense when the question was who was responsible to the visitor harmed by negligent electrical work on the door bell, but it has less obvious application when it comes to discrimination.

Nevertheless, when federal regulation of work relationships began in earnest, the relevant statutes all adopted "employee" from tort law, which the Supreme Court has interpreted to indicate that Congress intended the word to have its common law meaning, *Nationwide Mutual Insurance Co. v. Darden*, 503 U.S. 318 (1992) (ERISA). And it has looked to the 1958 Restatement (Second) of Agency and its multifactor test to determine when an employment relationship exists. *Cmty. for Creative Non-Violence v. Reid*, 490 U.S. 730 (1989) (Copyright Act). We'll meet that test shortly.

However, since that time, the notion of employee has changed substantially. One example is the ALI's Restatement of Employment Law. Section 1.01 generally describes an employee as one who renders service for another without doing so as part of an independent business, which in turn depends on whether the service-renderer exercises "entrepreneurial control" over "important business decisions, including whether to hire and where to assign assistants, whether to purchase and where to deploy equipment, and whether and when to service customers." If the Restatement has the better view of the distinction, does that mean that the statutory definition of "employee" should shift to conform to it? Under the Supreme Court's approach, doesn't Congress adopt the common law definition as of the time it uses a common law term? Would it make any difference in the following case?

LEROHL v. FRIENDS OF MINNESOTA SINFONIA
322 F.3d 486 (8th Cir. 2003)

LOKEN, J.

[Tricia Lerohl and Shelley Hanson commenced separate actions against the Friends of the Minnesota Sinfonia, a nonprofit corporation that governs the Sinfonia. They alleged that they were terminated as regular members of the Sinfonia in violation of, respectively, Title VII and the ADA. Both complaints were dismissed on summary judgment on the basis that neither statute applied to the plaintiffs because they were independent contractors, not employees of either the Sinfonia or its conductor, defendant Jay Fishman.]

I. BACKGROUND

The Sinfonia was formed in 1989 by Fishman and other former members of the Minneapolis Chamber Symphony Orchestra. Its mission is to perform free classical music concerts in inner-city public schools and other locations accessible to inner-city youth, families with young children, and people of limited means. In its first decade of operation, the Sinfonia grew from thirty-two to seventy concerts per year. Fishman conducts the Sinfonia and acts as its executive and artistic director. Sinfonia concerts are performed by twenty-five to thirty professional musicians. Fishman and all Sinfonia players are members of Local 30-73 of the American Federation of Musicians. The Sinfonia advertises that its musicians are "the best of the area's freelance pool."

After scheduling a series of Sinfonia concerts, Fishman prepares a list of musicians eligible to play for that series. The schedule is mailed to eligible "regular" or "first call" players who then advise the Sinfonia whether they agree to play that series. The Sinfonia's free-lance musicians also perform for other organizations and as solo performers. They may even opt out of Sinfonia concerts they have agreed to play, so long as they give two weeks notice and arrange for an eligible substitute to perform. However, to remain a Sinfonia "regular," which ensures being invited to play in most if not all Sinfonia concerts, Fishman's policy is that a musician must "accept the vast majority of the work."

All Sinfonia players, and Fishman as conductor, are paid on a per-concert basis at the union scale. The Sinfonia does not withhold income or FICA taxes on these payments, instead documenting the payments for tax purposes on an IRS Form 1099. The Sinfonia does not provide musicians annual leave, health or life insurance, worker's compensation coverage, or other fringe benefits except that it does contribute an agreed percentage of the union scale payments to the musicians union pension fund. The parties dispute whether Fishman was required to agree to these contributions to remain in good standing as a union member. The Sinfonia also pays Fishman lump sums for his work as executive and artistic director. For tax and other purposes, he is treated as an employee with respect to these payments.

From 1990 to 1999, Lerohl and Hanson were "regular" players at Sinfonia concerts. Lerohl plays the French horn and Hanson plays the clarinet. In mid-1999, the Sinfonia stopped offering work to Lerohl and Hanson. Lerohl alleges the Sinfonia and

Fishman violated Title VII by terminating her in retaliation for complaining about sexual harassment by Fishman. Hanson alleges defendants violated the ADA by ending her long-standing working relationship when she sought to resume playing after being absent several months while recovering from injuries sustained during a Sinfonia rehearsal. Both statutes protect "employees" but not independent contractors.

II.   THE RELEVANT LEGAL STANDARD

The issue whether a person is an employee or an independent contractor arises in many legal contexts. When the issue concerns the scope of a federal statute, we must first examine the relevant statutory language. In both Title VII and the ADA, Congress adopted a circular definition of "employee" — an employee is an "individual employed by an employer." See 42 U.S.C. §§2000e(f), 12111(4). In such cases, the Supreme Court applies the general common law of agency to determine whether a hired party is an employee or an independent contractor. See *Nationwide Mut. Ins. Co. v. Darden*, 503 U.S. 318 (1992) (ERISA). In applying this test, the Court has instructed us to consider a nonexhaustive list of factors derived primarily from the Restatement (Second) of Agency §220(2) (1958):

> In determining whether a hired party is an employee under the general common law of agency, we consider the hiring party's right to control the manner and means by which the product is accomplished. Among the other factors relevant to this inquiry are the skill required; the source of the instrumentalities and tools; the location of the work; the duration of the relationship between the parties; whether the hiring party has the right to assign additional projects to the hired party; the extent of the hired party's discretion over when and how long to work; the method of payment; the hired party's role in hiring and paying assistants; whether the work is part of the regular business of the hiring party; whether the hiring party is in business; the provision of employee benefits; and the tax treatment of the hired party. . . . No one of these factors is determinative.

Cmty. for Creative Non-Violence v. Reid, 490 U.S. 730[, 751-52 (1989)] (footnotes omitted). In weighing these factors, "all of the incidents of the relationship must be assessed and weighed with no one factor being decisive." *Darden* (quotation omitted). The district court may properly consider economic aspects of the parties' relationship. "Our inquiry . . . requires more than simply tallying factors on each side and selecting the winner on the basis of a point score." *Schwieger v. Farm Bureau Ins. Co. of Neb.*, 207 F.3d 480, 487 (8th Cir. 2000).

On appeal, Lerohl, Hanson, and the EEOC primarily argue that, in the EEOC's words, "it is critical that 'control' be given primary consideration." They then state the control issue in terms of individual Sinfonia concerts and conclude, not surprisingly, that Fishman as conductor "controlled" the rehearsals and concerts, and therefore all Sinfonia musicians are employees. We emphatically reject that approach. First, it is contrary to the Supreme Court's repeated admonition that no factor is determinative and all aspects of the parties' relationship must be considered. See *Darden* (expressly rejecting a similar contention by the United States as amicus curiae); *Reid*.

Second, on a more practical level, the notion that musicians are always employees when they perform in a conducted band or orchestra flies in the face of both common sense and undisputed facts in this record, such as plaintiff Hanson's affidavit reciting that she is not an employer when she hires musicians to play while she records a musical composition. Work by independent contractors is often, if not typically, performed to the exacting specifications of the hiring party. In *Reid*, for example, the Supreme Court determined that a sculptor was an independent contractor for the purposes of the Copyright Act of 1976 even though the nonprofit association that hired him defined the scene to be sculpted and specified most of the details of the sculpture's appearance, including its scale and the materials to be used. Thus, although one relevant factor was Fishman's undisputed control in selecting the music to be played, scheduling Sinfonia rehearsals and concerts, and determining the manner in which the concert music was collectively played, that factor is not determinative of the common-law agency issue.

III.   Prior Musician Case Law

There are surprisingly few cases addressing whether musicians who played in a band or orchestra were employees of either the entity that engaged the performance, or the musicians' band leader or orchestra conductor. *Hilton Int'l Co. v. NLRB*, 690 F.2d 318 (2d Cir. 1982), a National Labor Relations Act case, held that the members of "steady engagement" bands were not employees of the casino hotels that engaged them. The decision confirms that the question is thorny, but it is not particularly relevant because the musicians were admittedly employees of someone (their independent band leaders), as were the musicians in *Associated Musicians of Greater Newark, Local 16*, 206 N.L.R.B. 581 (1973), *aff'd per curiam*, 512 F.2d 991 (D.C. Cir. 1975). Here, on the other hand, the issue is whether the musicians were free-lance independent contractors, or were employees of either Fishman, the orchestra conductor, *or* his employer, the Sinfonia.

A more relevant labor law case is *Seattle Opera v. NLRB*, 292 F.3d 757 (D.C. Cir. 2002), where a divided panel upheld the NLRB's determination that the Seattle Opera's auxiliary choristers were employees of the Opera. But the majority relied heavily on the deference due the NLRB's decision, consistent with *NLRB v. Town & Country Elec., Inc.*, 516 U.S. 85 (1995). On the control theory urged by Lerohl, Hanson, and the EEOC, we find Judge Randolph's dissent more persuasive:

> The Board and the majority find it significant in determining whether the auxiliary choristers are employees rather than volunteers that the Opera "has the power or right to control and direct the person in the material details of how such work is to be performed." This is outright silly. Are we to suppose that volunteer firefighters or volunteer rescue workers become "employees" because the fire chief or the head of the rescue squad directs them? . . . Auxiliary choristers join other singers to perform musical works. . . . Rehearsal cannot be done independently. Choir members need to know not only the notes and the words, but they must also blend their voices together into a single sound.

. . . IV.   Analysis . . .

Like the sculptor in *Reid*, Sinfonia musicians such as Lerohl and Hanson are highly skilled professionals who own their own instruments and need no on-the-job training other than rehearsals to perform in a variety of musical settings. Obviously, professional musicians have the option of becoming employees of a particular band or orchestra. The record in this case suggests that is true of the musicians who play for the Minnesota Orchestra, the St. Paul Chamber Orchestra, and the Minnesota Opera.

But other musicians may prefer to remain "free-lance," committing themselves fully to no client and retaining the discretion to pick and choose among available engagements, much like lawyers, accountants, and business consultants who choose private practice instead of "in-house" employment.

Our cases applying the common-law agency test have recognized this freedom-of-choice principle in determining whether a skilled professional was an employee or an independent contractor in a particular case. In our view, this is the relevant control issue, not whether Fishman could tell Lerohl and Hanson where to sit and when to play during a concert or a rehearsal. Thus, the "key distinction" is whether Sinfonia musicians retained the discretion to decline particular Sinfonia concerts and play elsewhere. *Berger Transfer & Storage v. Cent. States, S.E. & S.W. Areas Pension Fund*, 85 F.3d 1374, 1380 (8th Cir. 1996) (truck owner-operators who drove for more than one company were independent contractors); accord *Kirk v. Harter*, 188 F.3d 1005, 1008-09 (8th Cir. 1999) (computer programmer).

Here, it is undisputed that Lerohl, Hanson, and the other "regular" Sinfonia musicians retained the discretion to perform elsewhere and to accept or reject playing in a particular concert series. Indeed, they were permitted to back out of specific performances after agreeing to perform in a series if they arranged for suitable substitutes. Though the Sinfonia understandably offered inducements to preferred performers, such as "regular" status, the musicians retained control over the extent to which they committed their available professional time to the Sinfonia.

It is also highly significant that the Sinfonia withheld no income or FICA taxes, documented musician payments on an IRS Form 1099, and provided no employee benefits other than contributions to an independent union pension fund. "Every case since *Reid* that has applied the [common-law] test has found the hired party to be an independent contractor where the hiring party failed to extend benefits or pay social security taxes." *Kirk*. A recent exception is *Eisenberg v. Advance Relocation & Storage, Inc.*, 237 F.3d 111, 118 (2d Cir. 2000), but *Eisenberg* is readily distinguishable because it involved an hourly full-time warehouse worker, not a consultant or free-lance professional. Here, the Sinfonia's professional musicians retained the discretion to perform elsewhere and accepted payments structured in a manner that confirmed their independent contractor status. In such a case, we are loath to destroy the parties' freedom to choose that form of relationship by deciding, after the fact, that they were required to contract as employer and employees, particularly when Congress remains free to extend Title VII and the ADA to this kind of independent contractor relationship if it determines that to be in the public interest.

[Thus,] the undisputed facts in this case establish that Lerohl and Hanson were independent contractors as a matter of law, and the disputed facts, viewed most favorably to Lerohl and Hanson, do not affect that conclusion.

Finally, Lerohl and Hanson object that the district courts improperly dismissed Fishman as a separate defendant sua sponte, citing cases in which independent band leaders have been found to be employers. . . . Here, Fishman was not an independent orchestra conductor; he was an employee of the Sinfonia. If Lerohl and Hanson were employees of Fishman, they were employees of the Sinfonia. Thus, when the district courts concluded that Lerohl and Hanson were *not* employees, despite Fishman's control over their musical performances, that determination necessarily encompassed any separate claim against Fishman, whose relevant actions were taken on behalf of his employer. In these circumstances, the courts properly granted summary judgment in favor of Fishman as well as the Sinfonia.

NOTES

1. *Employment vs. Other Relationships.* The principal case makes clear that working for someone does not mean you are that person's employee, and that's true even if the worker views herself as employed. *See Delia v. Verizon Commc'ns Inc.*, 656 F.3d 1 (1st Cir. 2011) (worker's subjective belief insufficient to create a triable issue regarding her status). Further, given the multiple factors that go into the determination, the worker's status will be uncertain in many situations. The plaintiffs in *Lehrol* were not employees, but performers for other orchestras are. In short, the antidiscrimination law and most other employment regulations are predicated on the existence of a relationship the law has left largely indeterminate.

2. *Independent Contractors.* Given the tort origin of the concept, it's understandable why "employment" turns on "control": if the employer can't control the worker, maybe it shouldn't be vicariously liable for any torts that worker commits. Thus, the passage *Lerohl* quoted from *Reid* begins by saying "[i]n determining whether a hired party is an employee under the general common law of agency, we consider the hiring party's right to control the manner and means by which the product is accomplished." Under this reading, the two plaintiffs in *Lerohl* were clearly employees because their work was very closely controlled — a conductor not only dictates when and where an orchestra member plays, but also how she plays, what she wears, and even her facial expressions. If we apply the negligence concept, shouldn't the Sinfonia be liable for a player's tort, say, dropping a large instrument off the stage onto a member of the audience?

But the *Lerohl* court does not stop with the generic notion of "control"; rather, it looks to the multiple factors stated in *Reid*, and, using some undefined weighting scheme, concludes the performers were not employees. Under this view, which seems to be the more common, the question is less "control" in the abstract than adding and subtracting factors. *E.g., Brown v. J. Kaz, Inc.*, 581 F.3d 175 (3d Cir. 2009) (sales representatives were independent contractors: the firm made only general suggestions as to sales pitches; representatives had to provide their own equipment, office supplies, and transportation; and they were provided no office space and paid only on commission). Does this map onto tort law's concerns? And does either approach make sense in terms of the aims of the antidiscrimination laws?

3. *Avoiding Liability by Using Independent Contractors.* The "independent contractor" possibility potentially opens a huge loophole in the antidiscrimination laws. Did Sinfonia plan its relationships with its musicians to avoid being covered by employment laws? Some companies have radically restructured their operations by converting "employees" to "independent contractors." *See Isbell v. Allstate Ins. Co.*, 418 F.3d 788, 795 (7th Cir. 2005) (considering legal issues when Allstate eliminated all employee-agent positions and offered its former employees new positions as independent contractors). *See generally* Charlotte Alexander, *Misclassification and Antidiscrimination: An Economic Analysis*, 101 MINN. L. REV. 907 (2017); Richard R. Carlson, *Why the Law Still Can't Tell an Employee When It Sees One and How It Ought to Stop Trying*, 22 BERKELEY J. EMP. & LAB. L. 295 (2001); Lewis L. Maltby & David C. Yamada, *Beyond "Economic Realities": The Case for Amending Federal Employment Discrimination Laws to Include Independent Contractors*, 38 BC L. REV. 239 (1997).

4. *Owners as Employees.* Another recurrent question is whether owners of a business entity can also be employees. Small business owners often work for the business,

whether they are denominated "partners" or, in the case of some professional corporations, "shareholders." This issue is important not only for the individuals in question but also for individuals who are true employees. A case in point is *Clackamas Gastroenterology Assocs., P.C. v. Wells*, 538 U.S. 440 (2003), where the professional corporation, a medical clinic, had 14 employees and four physician-owners who also worked for the clinic. When the plaintiff sued under the ADA, the question was whether the statute applied: only if at least one owner was also an employee would the ADA's minimum of 15 employees be satisfied.

Although the doctors were formally employees, apparently to qualify for tax benefits under ERISA, the Court reiterated that "the common-law element of control is the principal guidepost that should be followed in this case." *Id.* at 448. More specifically, as to when partners, members of boards of directors, and major shareholders qualify as employees, the issue is "'whether the individual acts independently and participates in managing the organization, or whether the individual is subject to the organization's control.'" *Id., quoting* EEOC *Compliance Manual* §605:0009 (2000). To answer this question, the Compliance Manual suggests six factors, which include the organization's ability to hire or fire the individual or set the rules for, or otherwise supervise the work of, the individual. Other factors include whether the individual reports to someone higher in the organization and whether individual is able to influence the organization. Finally, the parties' intent as to status "as expressed in written agreements or contracts" is relevant, as is whether the individual shares in the organization's "profits, losses, and liabilities." *Id.* at 550. *See also Mariotti v. Mariotti Bldg. Prods.*, 714 F.3d 761 (3d Cir. 2013). As is the case with independent contractors, the multifactor analysis means that many cases will be indeterminate.

One continuing area of dispute is whether "partners" in large law firms are employees under the ADEA and therefore cannot be mandatorily retired. The focus has generally been on whether the partners in question have sufficient power to control the firm or are functionally more like associates. *E.g., EEOC v. Sidley Austin Brown & Wood*, 315 F.3d 696 (7th Cir. 2002); *see also Bluestein v. Cent. Wis. Anesthesiology, S.C.*, 769 F.3d 944, 948 (7th Cir. 2014) (anesthesiologist properly found to have been an employer rather than an employee of a corporation as a shareholder and member of the board of directors and entitled to vote on all issues, including her own termination). *See generally* Ann C. McGinley, *Functionality or Formalism? Partners and Shareholders as "Employees" Under the Anti-Discrimination Laws*, 57 SMU L. Rev. 3 (2004); Leonard Bierman & Rafael Gely, *So, You Want to Be a Partner at Sidley & Austin?*, 40 Hous. L. Rev. 969 (2003). *But see* Frank J. Menetrez, *Employee Status and the Concept of Control in Federal Employment Discrimination Law*, 63 SMU L. Rev. 137 (2010) (given that common law agency principles control, the case law regarding whether owners can also be employees must be rethought since the common law often viewed employers also as employees).

5. *The Numbers Game.* As *Clackamas* indicates, even assuming an employment relationship and that the plaintiff is an employee, the antidiscrimination statutes do not apply unless the employer is large enough to be a statutory employer, that is, unless it has the requisite number of employees (15 for Title VII and the ADA and 20 for the ADEA) for the requisite time ("each working day in each of twenty or more calendar weeks in the current or preceding calendar year"). *Bridge v. New Holland Logansport, Inc.*, 815 F.3d 356 (7th Cir. 2016) (plaintiff did not adduce sufficient evidence to allow jury to find it had at least 20 employees at the relevant time). The employer must also be "engaged in an industry affecting commerce," but this has rarely posed a separate obstacle. Hourly, part-time, and on-leave employees count

towards the total. *Walters v. Metro. Educ. Enters.*, 519 U.S. 202 (1997). However, the requirement of a minimum number of employees is not "jurisdictional" under the antidiscrimination statutes. *Arbaugh v. Y & H Corp.*, 546 U.S. 500 (2006).

6. *Integrated Enterprises and Joint Employers.* Sometimes two or more formally distinct legal entities are viewed as being in reality a single employer, thus allowing the employees of all to be aggregated to reach the required minimum number; this is referred to as the "integrated enterprise" or "single employer" doctrine. *See Davis v. Ricketts*, 765 F.3d 823 (8th Cir. 2014) (2-1) (despite evidence of common control and financial backing, two entities were not a single employer when there was little inter-relation of operations or shared control of labor relations); *Arculeo v. On-Site Sales & Mktg., L.L.C.*, 425 F.3d 193, 199 (2d Cir. 2005) ("although nominally and techni-cally distinct, several entities [may be] properly seen as a single integrated entity").

Distinct from the single-employer doctrine is "joint employment," under which an employee of one entity may hold another entity liable; the premise is not that two enti-ties are one but rather that they co-determine terms and conditions of employment. This, again, is often a multifactor analysis. *See, e.g., Butler v. Drive Auto. Indus. of Am.*, 793 F.3d 404, 413 (4th Cir. 2015). Joint employment can arise in a number of set-tings. One common scenario is when firms use staffing agencies to provide workers; in such cases, both the agency and its client can be found to be employers when both exercise sufficient control over the worker and regardless of who formally pays her. *E.g., Faush v. Tuesday Morning, Inc.*, 808 F.3d 208 (3d Cir. 2015); *Burton v. Freescale Semiconductor, Inc.*, 798 F.3d 222 (5th Cir. 2015). Joint employment can also arise in other settings, such as contractor/subcontractor relationships. *E.g., EEOC v. Skanska USA Bldg., Inc.*, 550 F. App'x 253 (6th Cir. 2013) (finding contractor the joint employer of employees of a subcontractor when it did virtually all the supervision of the workers at the site), *but see Knitter v. Corvias Military Living, LLC*, 758 F.3d 1214, 1228 (10th Cir. 2014) (defendant not joint employer when it lacked authority to supervise, discipline, or terminate plaintiff's employment). Another setting where joint employment issues arise is when affiliated but legally distinct corporate entities merge their employment practices. *Cf. Bridge v. New Holland Logansport, Inc.*, 815 F.3d 356 (7th Cir. 2016) (three individuals who formally worked for a sister firm were not in reality employees of the defendant).

However, a finding of joint employment does not automatically render one employer liable for the violations of the other. *See Whitaker v. Milwaukee Cnty.*, 772 F.3d 802, 811-12 (7th Cir. 2014) (a joint employer is liable for actions taken by the other employer only if it participates in the other employer's discrimination or if it knew or should have known about the other's discrimination and failed to take appro-priate corrective measures); *Burton v. Freescale Semiconductor, Inc.*, 798 F.3d 222 (5th Cir. 2015) (same).

Finally, in some cases, a corporate employer goes out of business only to have its operations taken over by a second company. Some courts allow liability for discrimi-nation to pass to the successor. *See EEOC v. Northern Star Hospitality, Inc.*, 777 F.3d 898, 902 (7th Cir. 2015) (permissible to impose liability on the successor for discrimi-nation by the predecessor in light of factors such as the successor's notice of the pend-ing lawsuit; whether the predecessor could have provided the relief sought before or after the transition; and whether there is continuity between the operations and work force of the two entities).

7. *What Do Volunteers, Interns, and Prisoners Have in Common?* In *Lerohl*, the court quotes approvingly an earlier case finding "silly" the claim that volunteer fire-fighters or volunteer rescue workers are employees "because the fire chief or the head

of the rescue squad directs them." It may in fact be silly, but perhaps because "employment" entails both control and compensation. In other words, the firefighters are not employees because they are unpaid, even assuming their work is controlled by the putative employer. In such settings, the courts have generally looked to remuneration either as an absolute requirement for employment or as an important factor in the determination. *See Marie v. Am. Red Cross*, 771 F.3d 344, 359 (6th Cir. 2014) (Catholic nuns claiming religious discrimination could not show they were employees even if compensation is not a threshold requirement for Title VII coverage); *Juino v. Livingston Parish Fire Dist. No. 5*, 717 F.3d 431 (5th Cir. 2013) ("remuneration" for volunteer firefighters is a threshold requirement to finding employment rather than merely one factor in the analysis). *But see Bryson v. Middlefield Volunteer Fire Dep't, Inc.*, 656 F.3d 348 (6th Cir. 2011) (given various benefits, volunteer firefighters might be employees even though not receiving compensation). *See generally* Lawrence D. Rosenthal, *No Good Deed Goes Unpunished: The Lack of Protection for Volunteers Under the Federal Anti-Discrimination Statutes*, 2016 BYU L. Rev. 117.

This means, for example, while graduate assistants in universities may be employees, *Cuddeback v. Florida Bd. of Educ.*, 381 F.3d 1230, 1234 (11th Cir. 2004), students interning at outside employers typically lacked statutory protection under the antidiscrimination laws. *See generally* David C. Yamada, *The Employment Law Rights of Student Interns*, 35 Conn. L. Rev. 215 (2002). That may be changing in light both of recent decisions and state legislation providing interns with protection at least from discrimination and harassment. *See* Stephanie A. Pisko, Comment, *Great Expectations, Grim Reality: Unpaid Interns and the Dubious Benefits of the DOL Pro Bono Exception*, 45 Seton Hall L. Rev. 613 (2015).

Then there's the question of prisoners, who are typically held not to be employees even when "leased" to private employers. *See Castle v. Eurofresh, Inc.*, 731 F.3d 901 (9th Cir. 2013) (prisoner not an "employee" of a state contractor under the ADA because his labor belonged to the State of Arizona, which put him to work at the contractor in order to comply with its statutory obligations). *See generally* Noah D. Zatz, *Working at the Boundaries of Markets: Prison Labor and the Economic Dimension of Employment Relationships*, 61 Vand. L. Rev. 857 (2008).

8. *Governmental Employment.* Title VII, the ADEA, and the ADA generally reach state and local governmental employers. Similarly, almost all federal civilian employment is also covered by Title VII and the ADEA through separate provisions in each law. 42 U.S.C. §2000e-16, §717; 29 U.S.C. §633(a). See p. 559. The ADA covers state and local employment, certainly under Title I but probably not under Title II. *See, e.g., Reyazuddin v. Montgomery Cnty.*, 789 F.3d 407 (4th Cir. 2015). However, the ADA does not itself reach federal governmental employment although substantially similar protection is accorded by its predecessor, the Rehabilitation Act. 29 U.S.C. §794 (2018). There are, however, special exemptions and Eleventh Amendment limitations on private suits under the ADEA and the ADA. See p. 557.

9. *Extraterritorial Effect.* The antidiscrimination laws have extraterritorial reach. 42 U.S.C. §2000e(f), §701(f); 29 U.S.C. §623(h). As a result, U.S. citizens abroad are protected, but only against discrimination by U.S.-owned or controlled employers. However, such companies are permitted to discriminate if compliance with the American statute would require the employer to violate the law of the foreign country where the work is performed. *See Mahoney v. RFE/RL, Inc.*, 47 F.3d 447 (D.C. Cir. 1995). Foreign companies acting abroad are expressly excluded from coverage.

10. *Exemptions.* Title VII exempts a "bona fide private membership club," 42 U.S.C. §2000e(b)(2), §701(b)(2), and Indian tribes, 42 U.S.C. §2000e(b), §701(b). Other exceptions may be found in other federal laws or treaties. *See Sumitomo Shoji,*

Am., Inc. v. Avagliano, 457 U.S. 176 (1982) (considering the effect of a treaty between the United States and Japan on suits against "companies of Japan" for discrimination in favor of Japanese employees); *Brzak v. U.N.*, 597 F.3d 107, 111 (2d Cir. 2010) (the U.N. and its officers immune from Title VII suit).

The denial of a security clearance may also effectively preclude Title VII suit. §2000e-2(g), §703(g). *See Toy v. Holder*, 714 F.3d 881 (5th Cir. 2013) (refusing to allow Title VII review of a denial of an FBI contract employee's access to a building based on national security considerations); *but see Rattigan v. Holder*, 689 F.3d 764 (D.C. Cir. 2012) (a decision to refer knowingly false information regarding a security clearance for discriminatory reasons could be challenged even if the clearance itself could not be reviewed).

11. *Pushing the Coverage Envelope.* Some courts expand Title VII's reach in ways that are not obvious. Thus, entities that exercise control over another entity's employees are sometimes held to be "indirect employers." This can apply to state agencies, *compare Ass'n of Mexican-Am. Educators v. California*, 231 F.3d 572 (9th Cir. 2000) (en banc) (Title VII applied to a California state credentialing agency in light of the power such agency exerted over employment as a teacher), *with Gulino v. N.Y. State Educ. Dep't*, 460 F.3d 361, 375 (2d Cir. 2006) (state defendants were not employers because the relationship between New York and its local school districts differed from that in California), *and Lopez v. Massachusetts*, 588 F.3d 69 (1st Cir. 2009) (state agency that administered promotional exams for local police officers under state civil service system was not a Title VII "employer" when acting in that capacity). But it can also apply in the private sector. *See Love v. JP Cullen & Sons, Inc.*, 779 F.3d 697, 701-02 (7th Cir. 2015) (applying a five-factor test, the court held that a prime contractor was not an indirect employer of its subcontractor's employees even though it retained the right to exclude such persons from the job site when there was otherwise minimal control and the exclusion did not require the sub to discharge the employee).

In another context, physicians with clinical privileges have traditionally been found not to be employees of the hospitals where they worked, *e.g., Shah v. Deaconess Hosp.*, 355 F.3d 496, 500 (6th Cir. 2004), but the expanding control hospitals exercise over such physicians led one circuit to alter this. *See Salamon v. Our Lady of Victory Hosp.*, 514 F.3d 217 (2d Cir. 2008). More recent cases have not followed *Salamon's* lead. *Ashkenazi v. S. Broward Hosp. Dist.*, 607 F. App'x 968 (11th Cir. 2015) (physician not an employee under the ADEA even though hospital radically increased supervision of his work); *Alexander v. Avera St. Luke's Hosp.*, 768 F.3d 756 (8th Cir. 2014) (pathologist not an employee of the hospital).

NOTE ON COVERAGE OF §1981

Questions of "employment" as such do not arise under §1981 because that statute reaches all "contract" relations, not merely employment. *See Runyon v. McCrary*, 427 U.S. 160 (1976). Thus, §1981 embraces relationships such as partnership or independent contractor status. *E.g., Brown v. J. Kaz, Inc.*, 581 F.3d 175 (3d Cir. 2009) (independent contractor may sue for race discrimination). The statute has been held applicable to at-will employment, despite the argument that, in some states, such employment is not contractual under state law. *Walker v. Abbott Labs.*, 340 F.3d 471 (7th Cir. 2003). *But see Jimenez v. Wellstar Health Sys.*, 596 F.3d 1304 (11th Cir. 2010) (because a doctor's hospital privileges were not contractual in nature under Georgia law, §1981 offered no relief from a discriminatory suspension of them).

Section 1981 does not reach federal employment, *Brown v. General Services Administration*, 425 U.S. 820, 825 (1976) (Title VII is exclusive discrimination remedy for federal employment within its scope), and perhaps not state and local government. Although one circuit has read §1981(c), "[t]he rights protected by this section are protected against . . . impairment under color of State law," to reach local governments although not the state, *see Fed'n of African Am. Contractors v. City of Oakland*, 96 F.3d 1204 (9th Cir. 1996), most circuit courts have refused to apply it to local governments. *E.g., McCormick v. Miami Univ.*, 693 F.3d 654 (6th Cir. 2012); *McGovern v. City of Phila.*, 554 F.3d 114 (3d Cir. 2009).

NOTE ON CONSTITUTIONAL LIMITATIONS ON THE REACH OF THE ANTIDISCRIMINATION LAWS

A number of efforts have been made to limit the reach of antidiscrimination laws by invoking various constitutional provisions. We will examine in more detail a narrow, but well-established limitation on these statutes, the "ministerial exception," which is predicated on the religion clauses of the First Amendment, see p. 583, and there is currently a debate about the extent to which the Religious Freedom Restoration Act will create broader exemptions where antidiscrimination principles collide with religious beliefs. See p. 393.

More general attempts to invoke the Constitution to immunize certain activities from attack have mostly failed. Freedom of association claims, for example, were rejected in *Roberts v. United States Jaycees*, 468 U.S. 609 (1984) (upholding decision that Jaycees had to admit women). *See also Runyon v. McCrary*, 427 U.S. 160 (1976) (no constitutional right for a private school to exclude black children in violation of §1981). However, *Boy Scouts of America v. Dale*, 530 U.S. 640 (2000), suggested that the First Amendment right of expressive association somewhat limits the reach of antidiscrimination laws, holding that right to insulate the Boy Scouts from New Jersey's ban on sexual orientation discrimination in public accommodations. At issue was whether "a private, not-for-profit organization engaged in instilling its system of values in young people," *id.* at 644, could be required to accept a gay scoutmaster. The Court held no: the BSA persuaded it both that homosexual conduct was inconsistent with scouting values and that having "an avowed homosexual and gay rights activist," *id.*, would impair the BSA's ability to impart those values.

While *Dale* could be read broadly, it has thus far not generated any sweeping exception to the antidiscrimination laws. First, to fall within the *Dale* rule, "a group must engage in some form of expression, whether it be public or private," *id.* at 648, and, other than the conflict between religious principles and LGBTQ rights, rarely do groups espouse beliefs at odds with the core protections of the antidiscrimination laws. Second, the Supreme Court's only expressive association decision after *Dale* suggests that the Court will avoid finding a conflict with the laws where it can. In *Rumsfeld v. Forum for Academic & Institutional Rights, Inc. FAIR*, 547 U.S. 47, 69 (2006), a group of law schools invoked *Dale* to resist the "Solomon Amendment," which required educational institutions receiving federal financial aid to allow access to military recruiters at a time when the military limited service by gays and lesbians. Although the law schools were expressive associations and the values they imparted included nondiscrimination on the basis of sex orientation, *FAIR* found no threat to the schools' expressive purpose since military recruiters "are not part of the law school. Recruiters are, by definition, outsiders who come onto campus for the limited purpose of trying to hire students — not to become members of the school's expressive association." *Id.* at 69. *FAIR* suggests that the post-*Dale* scholarship, from both the right and the left, overstated the potential implications of the doctrine. *Compare* Richard A. Epstein, *The Constitutional Perils of Moderation: The Case of the Boy Scouts*, 74 S. CAL. L. REV. 119, 142 (2000), *with* Andrew Koppelman, *Signs of the Times:* Dale v. Boy Scouts of America *and the Changing Meaning of Nondiscrimination*, 23 CARDOZO L. REV. 1819, 1819-20 (2002).

C. SEX DISCRIMINATION

In prior chapters, we've explored what is meant by "discrimination," as well as the proof structures involved in determining whether discrimination occurred. We now turn to what is or is not encompassed within the various protected classifications under Title VII. Sex discrimination claims, in particular, have raised difficult problems of what it means to discriminate "because of sex." Subsection 1 begins by exploring the meaning of "sex" under the statute. For example, is discrimination on the basis of sexual orientation or transgender discrimination actionable? What about claims of sex stereotyping? Is giving preferential treatment on the job to one's paramour cognizable under Title VII? And what about the separate dress and grooming codes for men and women that are common in the working world? How can those be squared with Title VII's antidiscrimination mandate? Finally, is discrimination because of "pregnancy, childbirth or related medical conditions" sex discrimination? Each of these questions is explored below.

Subsection 2 then turns to sexual harassment, which has raised difficult interpretive issues for the courts. Because most of the law dealing with racial and other discriminatory harassment originated with sexual harassment cases, these topics are also treated in this part.

1. Discrimination "Because of Sex"

Petitioner ONCALE v. SUNDOWNER OFFSHORE SERVICES, INC. Respondent
523 U.S. 75 (1998)

Justice SCALIA delivered the opinion of the Court.

This case presents the question whether workplace harassment can violate Title VII's prohibition against "discrimination . . . because of . . . sex," when the harasser and the harassed employee are of the same sex.

I

The District Court having granted summary judgment for respondent, we must assume the facts to be as alleged by petitioner Joseph Oncale. The precise details are irrelevant to the legal point we must decide, and in the interest of both brevity and dignity we shall describe them only generally. In late October 1991, Oncale was working

Q: does the harasser have to be in a supervisory position?

for respondent Sundowner Offshore Services on a Chevron U.S.A., Inc., oil platform in the Gulf of Mexico. He was employed as a roustabout on an eight-man crew which included respondents John Lyons, Danny Pippen, and Brandon Johnson. Lyons, the crane operator, and Pippen, the driller, had supervisory authority. On several occasions, Oncale was forcibly subjected to sex-related, humiliating actions against him by Lyons, Pippen, and Johnson in the presence of the rest of the crew. Pippen and Lyons also physically assaulted Oncale in a sexual manner, and Lyons threatened him with rape.

Oncale's complaints to supervisory personnel produced no remedial action; in fact, the company's Safety Compliance Clerk, Valent Hohen, told Oncale that Lyons and Pippen "picked [on] him all the time too," and called him a name suggesting homosexuality. Oncale eventually quit — asking that his pink slip reflect that he "voluntarily left due to sexual harassment and verbal abuse." When asked at his deposition why he left Sundowner, Oncale stated "I felt that if I didn't leave my job, that I would be raped or forced to have sex."

procedure

[The district court held that "Mr. Oncale, a male, has no cause of action under Title VII for harassment by male co-workers." The Fifth Circuit affirmed.]

II . . .

Title VII's prohibition of discrimination "because of . . . sex" protects men as well as women, *Newport News* [*Shipbuilding & Dry Dock Co. v. EEOC*, 462 U.S. 669 (1983)], and in the related context of racial discrimination in the workplace we have rejected any conclusive presumption that an employer will not discriminate against members of his own race. "Because of the many facets of human motivation, it would be unwise to presume as a matter of law that human beings of one definable group will not discriminate against other members of that group." *Castaneda v. Partida*, 430 U.S. 482 (1977). In *Johnson v. Transportation Agency, Santa Clara County* [reproduced at p. 152], a male employee claimed that his employer discriminated against him because of his sex when it preferred a female employee for promotion. Although we ultimately rejected the claim on other grounds, we did not consider it significant that the supervisor who made that decision was also a man. If our precedents leave any doubt on the question, we hold today that nothing in Title VII necessarily bars a claim of discrimination "because of . . . sex" merely because the plaintiff and the defendant (or the person charged with acting on behalf of the defendant) are of the same sex.

Courts have had little trouble with that principle in cases like *Johnson*, where an employee claims to have been passed over for a job or promotion. But when the issue arises in the context of a "hostile environment" sexual harassment claim, the state and federal courts have taken a bewildering variety of stances. Some, like the Fifth Circuit in this case, have held that same-sex sexual harassment claims are never cognizable under Title VII. Other decisions say that such claims are actionable only if the plaintiff can prove that the harasser is homosexual (and thus presumably motivated by sexual desire). Compare *McWilliams v. Fairfax County Board of Supervisors*, 72 F.3d 1191 (4th Cir. 1996), with *Wrightson v. Pizza Hut of America*, 99 F.3d 138 (4th Cir. 1996). Still others suggest that workplace harassment that is sexual in content is always actionable, regardless of the harasser's sex, sexual orientation, or motivations. See *Doe v. Belleville*, 119 F.3d 563 (7th Cir. 1997).

We see no justification in the statutory language or our precedents for a categorical rule excluding same-sex harassment claims from the coverage of Title VII. As some courts have observed, male-on-male sexual harassment in the workplace was assuredly not the principal evil Congress was concerned with when it enacted Title VII. But statutory prohibitions often go beyond the principal evil to cover reasonably comparable evils, and it is ultimately the provisions of our laws rather than the principal concerns of our legislators by which we are governed. Title VII prohibits "discrimination . . . because of . . . sex" in the "terms" or "conditions" of employment. Our holding that this includes sexual harassment must extend to sexual harassment of any kind that meets the statutory requirements.

Respondents and their amici contend that recognizing liability for same-sex harassment will transform Title VII into a general civility code for the American workplace. But that risk is no greater for same-sex than for opposite-sex harassment, and is adequately met by careful attention to the requirements of the statute. Title VII does not prohibit all verbal or physical harassment in the workplace; it is directed only at "discrimination . . . because of . . . sex." We have never held that workplace harassment, even harassment between men and women, is automatically discrimination because of sex merely because the words used have sexual content or connotations. "The critical issue, Title VII's text indicates, is whether members of one sex are exposed to disadvantageous terms or conditions of employment to which members of the other sex are not exposed." *Harris v. Forklift Systems, Inc.*, 510 U.S. 17 (1993) [reproduced at p. 331].

Courts and juries have found the inference of discrimination easy to draw in most male-female sexual harassment situations, because the challenged conduct typically involves explicit or implicit proposals of sexual activity; it is reasonable to assume those proposals would not have been made to someone of the same sex. The same chain of inference would be available to a plaintiff alleging same-sex harassment, if there were credible evidence that the harasser was homosexual. But harassing conduct need not be motivated by sexual desire to support an inference of discrimination on the basis of sex. A trier of fact might reasonably find such discrimination, for example, if a female victim is harassed in such sex-specific and derogatory terms by another woman as to make it clear that the harasser is motivated by general hostility to the presence of women in the workplace. A same-sex harassment plaintiff may also, of course, offer direct comparative evidence about how the alleged harasser treated members of both sexes in a mixed-sex workplace. Whatever evidentiary route the plaintiff chooses to follow, he or she must always prove that the conduct at issue was not merely tinged with offensive sexual connotations, but actually constituted "discrimination . . . because of . . . sex."

And there is another requirement that prevents Title VII from expanding into a general civility code: As we emphasized in *Meritor* [*Sav. Bank, FSB v. Vinson*, 477 U.S. 57 (1986), reproduced at p. 326] and *Harris*, the statute does not reach genuine but innocuous differences in the ways men and women routinely interact with members of the same sex and of the opposite sex. The prohibition of harassment on the basis of sex requires neither asexuality nor androgyny in the workplace; it forbids only behavior so objectively offensive as to alter the "conditions" of the victim's employment. "Conduct that is not severe or pervasive enough to create an objectively hostile or abusive work environment — an environment that a reasonable person would find hostile or abusive — is beyond Title VII's purview." *Harris*. We have always regarded that requirement as crucial, and as sufficient to ensure that courts and juries do not mistake ordinary socializing in the workplace — such as male-on-male horseplay or intersexual flirtation — for discriminatory "conditions of employment."

We have emphasized, moreover, that the objective severity of harassment should be judged from the perspective of a reasonable person in the plaintiff's position, considering "all the circumstances." *Harris.* In same-sex (as in all) harassment cases, that inquiry requires careful consideration of the social context in which particular behavior occurs and is experienced by its target. A professional football player's working environment is not severely or pervasively abusive, for example, if the coach smacks him on the buttocks as he heads onto the field — even if the same behavior would reasonably be experienced as abusive by the coach's secretary (male or female) back at the office. The real social impact of workplace behavior often depends on a constellation of surrounding circumstances, expectations, and relationships which are not fully captured by a simple recitation of the words used or the physical acts performed. Common sense, and an appropriate sensitivity to social context, will enable courts and juries to distinguish between simple teasing or roughhousing among members of the same sex, and conduct which a reasonable person in the plaintiff's position would find severely hostile or abusive. . . .

How to

NOTES

1. *Same-Sex Discrimination Is Actionable.* We will consider claims of sexual harassment later in this chapter, but for present purposes it is sufficient to understand that the Supreme Court had previously recognized that both quid pro quo and hostile work environment claims could be actionable under Title VII as sex discrimination. Those cases, however, had all involved claims by women accusing male supervisors of harassment, and the Fifth Circuit in *Oncale* concluded that, when the allegations involved male-on-male harassment, no claim could be brought. *Oncale* makes clear that, regardless of the genders of the harasser and victim, the central issue for purposes of establishing liability under Title VII is whether the terms and conditions of the victim's employment were altered because of sex.

landmark case — regardless of gender if the treatment was because of sex

2. *Harassment Need Not Be "Sexual" to Be Actionable.* Justice Scalia's opinion in *Oncale* states that harassment not based on sexual desire can be actionable under Title VII *if* the victim has been targeted because of her sex. It seems unlikely that the harassment in *Oncale* was predicated on a desire of the harassers to have sex with their victim. And a number of cases have found nonsexual harassment to be discriminatory when it is directed only at female employees. *E.g., Boumehdi v. Plastag Holdings LLC,* 489 F.3d 781, 788 (7th Cir. 2007) ("[a]lthough most of Vega's alleged comments were sexist rather than sexual, our precedent does not limit hostile environment claims to situations in which the harassment was based on sexual desire"). And even when conduct occurs in mixed-sex workplaces, profanity and other "sex-specific" language and conduct may be deemed harassment "based on sex." In *Gallagher v. C.H. Robinson Worldwide, Inc.,* 567 F.3d 263, 271 (6th Cir. 2009), the Sixth Circuit reasoned that "[t]he natural effect of exposure to such offensive conduct is embarrassment, humiliation and degradation, irrespective of the harasser's motivation — especially and all the more so if the captive recipient of the harassment is a woman."

3. *Proving the Harassment Was "Because of Sex."* Although *Oncale* establishes that same-sex harassment may be actionable, the question remains, how can a factfinder determine whether the harassment is because of sex? The Court confirms prior opinions in which an inference of sex-based discrimination was based on sexual advances made by a heterosexual toward a victim of the opposite sex. *See Furcron v. Mail Ctrs. Plus, LLC,* 843 F.3d 1295 (11th Cir. 2016) (factual issue as to whether certain conduct was based on sex in light of evidence that alleged harasser stared at

her in a constant state of arousal, an allegation supported by a female co-worker's declaration). Consistent with this logic, the Court indicates that sexual advances by a homosexual toward an individual of the same sex also may give rise to the inference that such action is "because of sex." Moreover, harassment that is sexual in nature is powerful evidence the harassment is because of sex, but, as *Oncale* demonstrates, the sexual form of the harassment is not conclusive. On remand, what evidence would you look for to establish that Oncale's co-workers were harassing him *because of* his sex? What evidence would you seek for the employer to prove an alternative motivation such as jealousy or dislike or, as we will see below, suspicions of sexual orientation?

In the same-sex setting, courts have read *Oncale* to allow a finding of "because of sex" by three evidentiary paths: (1) "the harasser was homosexual and motivated by sexual desire"; (2) "the harassment was framed 'in such sex-specific and derogatory terms . . . as to make it clear that the harasser [was] motivated by general hostility to the presence' of a particular gender in the workplace"; and (3) "comparative evidence about how the harasser treated members of both sexes." *EEOC v. Boh Bros. Constr. Co., L.L.C.*, 731 F.3d 444, 455-56 (5th Cir. 2013). The first route is perhaps most often pursued, *see, e.g., Redd v. N.Y. State Div. of Parole*, 678 F.3d 166 (2d Cir. 2012) (a female supervisor's repeated touching of the plaintiff's breasts could be found by a jury to constitute sexual advances), but the other routes have also been successful. *See Smith v. Rock-Tenn Servs.*, 813 F.3d 298 (6th Cir. 2016) (harassment could be found to be "because of sex" when supposed "horseplay" was aimed only at men in a mixed-sex workplace and included sexualized actions). But these three paths are not exclusive, and most circuits have recognized a fourth path: harassment for failure to conform to gender stereotypes. *See Boh Bros.*, 731 F.3d at 456 ("the EEOC may rely on evidence that Wolfe viewed Woods as insufficiently masculine to prove its Title VII claim"). We'll explore this at greater length shortly.

4. *The "Equal Opportunity" Harasser.* What about the "equal opportunity harasser," the person who directs offensive conduct and remarks against both men and women? At least under the "equality" approach, such a person is not guilty of sex discrimination under Title VII. Nor is this merely a law school hypothetical. *See Smith v. Hy-Vee, Inc.*, 622 F.3d 904, 908 (8th Cir. 2010) (despite evidence that harasser touched plaintiff and made sexual references, there was not sufficient basis to infer that she was motivated by sexual desire because she subjected both men and women to the same behavior). However, a number of cases have found harassment because of sex even when both genders were subjected to similar abuse. *See Beckford v. Dep't of Corr.*, 605 F.3d 951, 960 (11th Cir. 2010) ("equal opportunity harasser" defense rejected because epithets were gender-specific and targeted at female guards, although males were present); *Gallagher v. C.H. Robinson Worldwide, Inc.*, 567 F.3d 263, 272 (6th Cir. 2009) (even though male and female employees were exposed to the same offensive circumstances, sex-specific profanity that is more degrading to women than men is properly deemed "based on sex"). *See generally* Martin J. Katz, *Reconsidering Attraction in Sexual Harassment*, 79 IND. L.J. 101, 125-39 (2004); Ronald Turner, *Title VII and the Inequality-Enhancing Effects of the Bisexual and Equal Opportunity Harasser Defenses*, 7 U. PA. J. LAB. & EMP. L. 341, 342, 345 (2005); David S. Schwartz, *When Is Sex Because of Sex? The Causation Problem in Sexual Harassment Law*, 150 U. PA. L. REV. 1697 (2002). *See also* Ann C. McGinley, *Creating Masculine Identities: Bullying and Harassment "Because of Sex,"* 79 U. COLO. L. REV. 1151 (2008).

[handwritten margin note: So a degree difference in the treatment can establish sex discrimination?]

a.   Discrimination on the Basis of Sexual Orientation

Numerous decisions hold that harassment based on failure to conform to sex stereotypes is because of sex. *See EEOC v. Boh Bros. Constr. Co., L.L.C.*, 731 F.3d 444, 456 (5th Cir. 2013) (en banc) ("nothing in *Oncale* overturns or otherwise upsets the Court's holding in *Price Waterhouse*: a plaintiff may establish a sexual harassment claim with evidence of sex-stereotyping. Thus, the EEOC may rely on evidence that Wolfe viewed Woods as insufficiently masculine to prove its Title VII claim."); *Lewis v. Heartland Inns of Am., L.L.C.*, 591 F.3d 1033, 1039 (8th Cir. 2010) (discrimination based on sex stereotyping, in this case criticisms of the plaintiff for being tomboyish, could be actionable); *Nichols v. Azteca Rest. Enters., Inc.*, 256 F.3d 864 (9th Cir. 2001) ("because of sex" element was established where a male employee was subject to verbal abuse because of his "feminine mannerisms"). *See generally* Luke A. Boso, *Real Men*, 37 HAW. L. REV. 107, 108 (2015).

Despite this consensus, however, there long was an equally firm consensus that Title VII does not bar discrimination on the basis of sexual orientation, a rule that reaches far back in the history of the statute, *e.g., DeSantis v. Pacific Telephone & Telegraph Co.*, 608 F.2d 327 (9th Cir. 1979), and continued unbroken until relatively recently. When sex stereotyping was in evidence, this required courts to distinguish between harassment on account of sex (illegal) and on account of sexual orientation (legal). Many commentators found the distinction incoherent. Cary Franklin, *Inventing the "Traditional Concept" of Sex Discrimination*, 125 HARV. L. REV. 1307 (2012); Ann McGinley, *Erasing Boundaries: Masculinities, Sexual Minorities and Employment Discrimination*, 43 U. MICH. J.L. REFORM 713 (2010); L. Camille Hébert, *Transforming Transsexual and Transgender Rights*, 15 WM. & MARY J. WOMEN & L. 535, 989-90 (2009). *See also* Leora F. Eisenstadt, *Fluid Identity Discrimination*, 52 AM. BUS. L.J. 789 (2015). They also found it inconsistent with a long line of cases that have held that whites who are discriminated against because of interracial associations, including marriage, are the victims of race discrimination. Nevertheless, and despite some district court decisions to the contrary, the consensus held at the circuit level until the next case.

HIVELY v. IVY TECH COMMUNITY COLLEGE OF INDIANA
853 F.3d 339 (7th Cir. 2017) (en banc)

Chief Justice WOOD.

. . . For many years, the courts of appeals of this country understood [Title VII's] prohibition against sex discrimination to exclude discrimination on the basis of a person's sexual orientation. The Supreme Court, however, has never spoken to that question. In this case, we have been asked to take a fresh look at our position in light of developments at the Supreme Court extending over two decades. We have done so, and we conclude today that discrimination on the basis of sexual orientation is a form of sex discrimination. We therefore reverse the district court's judgment dismissing Kimberly Hively's suit against Ivy Tech Community College and remand for further proceedings.

I

Hively is openly lesbian. She began teaching as a part-time, adjunct professor at Ivy Tech Community College's South Bend campus in 2000. Hoping to improve her lot, she applied for at least six full-time positions between 2009 and 2014. These efforts were unsuccessful; worse yet, in July 2014 her part-time contract was not renewed.

Believing that Ivy Tech was spurning her because of her sexual orientation, she filed a pro se charge [with the EEOC discrimination "based on my sexual orientation." Her subsequent suit was dismissed by the district court, which relied on a line of circuit cases exemplified by *Hamner v. St. Vincent Hosp. and Health Care Ctr., Inc.*, 224 F.3d 701 (7th Cir. 2000), finding such discrimination not actionable. On appeal, the panel affirmed, looking to a long line of circuit authority and the uniform holdings of almost all of the circuits, and citing, inter alia, *Prowel v. Wise Bus. Forms, Inc.*, 579 F.3d 285, 290 (3d Cir. 2009); *Kalich v. AT&T Mobility, LLC*, 679 F.3d 464, 471 (6th Cir. 2012); *Evans v. Georgia Reg'l Hosp.*, 850 F.3d 1248 (11th Cir. 2017).] On the other hand, the Second Circuit recently found that an openly gay male plaintiff pleaded a claim of gender stereotyping that was sufficient to survive dismissal. The court observed that one panel lacked the power to reconsider the court's earlier decision holding that sexual orientation discrimination claims were not cognizable under Title VII. *Christiansen v. Omnicom Group, Inc.*, 852 F.3d 195 (2d Cir. 2017) (per curiam). Nonetheless, two of the three judges, relying on many of the same arguments presented here, noted in concurrence that they thought their court ought to consider revisiting that precedent in an appropriate case. Id. at 2 (Katzmann, J., concurring). Notable in its absence from the debate over the proper interpretation of the scope of Title VII's ban on sex discrimination is the United States Supreme Court.

That is not because the Supreme Court has left this subject entirely to the side. To the contrary, as the panel recognized, over the years the Court has issued several opinions that are relevant to the issue before us. Key among those decisions are *Price Waterhouse v. Hopkins* and *Oncale v. Sundowner Offshore Servs., Inc. Price Waterhouse* held that the practice of gender stereotyping falls within Title VII's prohibition against sex discrimination, and *Oncale* clarified that it makes no difference if the sex of the harasser is (or is not) the same as the sex of the victim. Our panel frankly acknowledged how difficult it is "to extricate the gender nonconformity claims from the sexual orientation claims." [Among other anomalies and given *Obergefell v. Hodges*, 135 S. Ct. 2584 (2015), the panel noted "a paradoxical legal landscape in which a person can be married on Saturday and then fired on Monday for just that act"; however, the panel was nevertheless correct in finding itself bound by the circuit's precedents on the precise point.] In light of the importance of the issue, and recognizing the power of the full court to overrule earlier decisions and to bring our law into conformity with the Supreme Court's teachings, a majority of the judges in regular active service voted to rehear this case en banc.

Supreme court precedent

II

A

The question before us is not whether this court can, or should, "amend" Title VII to add a new protected category to the familiar list of "race, color, religion, sex, or national origin." 42 U.S.C. § 2000e-2(a). Obviously that lies beyond our power. We must decide instead what it means to discriminate on the basis of sex, and in particular, whether actions taken on the basis of sexual orientation are a subset of actions taken on the basis of sex.[1] This is a pure question of statutory interpretation and thus well within the judiciary's competence.

---

1. For present purposes, we have no need to decide whether discrimination on the basis of "gender" is for legal purposes the same as discrimination on the basis of "sex," which is the statutory term. Many courts, including the Supreme Court, appear to have used "sex" and "gender" synonymously. . . .

methods of statutory interp.

Much ink has been spilled about the proper way to go about the task of statutory interpretation. One can stick, to the greatest extent possible, to the language enacted by the legislature; one could consult the legislative history that led up to the bill that became law; one could examine later actions of the legislature (*i.e.* efforts to amend the law and later enactments) for whatever light they may shed; and one could use a combination of these methods.

Few people would insist that there is a need to delve into secondary sources if the statute is plain on its face. Even if it is not pellucid, the best source for disambiguation is the broader context of the statute that the legislature — in this case, Congress — passed. This is uncontroversial when the reading seems consistent with the conventional wisdom about the reach of the law. It becomes somewhat harder to swallow if the language reveals suspected or actual unintended consequences. It is then that some have thought that legislative history should be used to block a particular reading of a statute. Legislative history, however, is notoriously malleable. Even worse is the temptation to try to divine the significance of unsuccessful legislative efforts to change the law. Those failures can mean almost anything, ranging from the lack of necessity for a proposed change because the law already accomplishes the desired goal, to the undesirability of the change because a majority of the legislature is happy with the way the courts are currently interpreting the law, to the irrelevance of the non-enactment, when it is attributable to nothing more than legislative logrolling or gridlock that had nothing to do with its merits.

Ivy Tech argues congress has consid. adding "orientation" but never has. court says legis. history can mean anything

Ivy Tech sets great store on the fact that Congress has frequently considered amending Title VII to add the words "sexual orientation" to the list of prohibited characteristics, yet it has never done so. Many of our sister circuits have also noted this fact. In our view, however, it is simply too difficult to draw a reliable inference from these truncated legislative initiatives to rest our opinion on them. The goalposts have been moving over the years, as the Supreme Court has shed more light on the scope of the language that already is in the statute: no *sex* discrimination.

The dissent makes much of the fact that Congresses acting more than thirty years after the passage of Title VII made use of the term "sexual orientation" to prohibit discrimination or violence on that basis in statutes such as the Violence Against Women Act and the federal Hate Crimes Act. But this gets us no closer to answering the question at hand, for Congress may certainly choose to use both a belt and suspenders to achieve its objectives, and the fact that "sex" and "sexual orientation" discrimination may overlap in later statutes is of no help in determining whether sexual orientation discrimination *is* discrimination on the basis of sex for the purposes of Title VII.

Moreover, the agency most closely associated with this law, the Equal Employment Opportunity Commission, in 2015 announced that it now takes the position that Title VII's prohibition against sex discrimination encompasses discrimination on the basis of sexual orientation. *See Baldwin v. Foxx*, EEOC Appeal No. 0120133080, 2015 WL 4397641 (July 15, 2015). Our point here is not that we have a duty to defer to the EEOC's position. We assume for present purposes that no such duty exists. But the Commission's position may have caused some in Congress to think that legislation is needed to carve sexual orientation *out* of the statute, not to put it *in*. In the end, we have no idea what inference to draw from congressional inaction or later enactments, because there is no way of knowing what explains each individual member's votes, much less what explains the failure of the body as a whole to change this 1964 statute.

Our interpretive task is guided instead by the Supreme Court's approach in the closely related case of *Oncale*, [which said that "statutory prohibitions often go beyond the principal evil to cover reasonably comparable evils, and it is ultimately the provisions of our laws rather than the principal concerns of our legislators by which we are governed"]. The Court could not have been clearer: the fact that the enacting Congress may not have anticipated a particular application of the law cannot stand in the way of the provisions of the law that are on the books.

It is therefore neither here nor there that the Congress that enacted the Civil Rights Act in 1964 and chose to include sex as a prohibited basis for employment discrimination (no matter why it did so) may not have realized or understood the full scope of the words it chose. . . .

B

Hively offers two approaches in support of her contention that "sex discrimination" includes discrimination on the basis of sexual orientation. The first relies on the tried-and-true comparative method in which we attempt to isolate the significance of the plaintiff's sex to the employer's decision: has she described a situation in which, holding all other things constant and changing only her sex, she would have been treated the same way? The second relies on the *Loving v. Virginia*, 388 U.S. 1 (1967), line of cases, which she argues protect her right to associate intimately with a person of the same sex. Although the analysis differs somewhat, both avenues end up in the same place: sex discrimination.

Hively's arguments

1

It is critical, in applying the comparative method, to be sure that only the variable of the plaintiff's sex is allowed to change. . . . The counterfactual we must use is a situation in which Hively is a man, but everything else stays the same: in particular, the sex or gender of the partner.

Hively alleges that if she had been a man married to a woman (or living with a woman, or dating a woman) and everything else had stayed the same, Ivy Tech would not have refused to promote her and would not have fired her. . . . This describes paradigmatic sex discrimination. . . . Nothing in the complaint hints that Ivy Tech has an anti-marriage policy that extends to heterosexual relationships, or for that matter even an anti-partnership policy that is gender-neutral.

①

Viewed through the lens of the gender non-conformity line of cases, Hively represents the ultimate case of failure to conform to the female stereotype (at least as understood in a place such as modern America, which views heterosexuality as the norm and other forms of sexuality as exceptional): she is not heterosexual. Our panel described the line between a gender nonconformity claim and one based on sexual orientation as gossamer-thin; we conclude that it does not exist at all. Hively's claim is no different from the claims brought by women who were rejected for jobs in traditionally male workplaces, such as fire departments, construction, and policing. The employers in those cases were policing the boundaries of what jobs or behaviors they found acceptable for a woman (or in some cases, for a man).

just like gender-non-conformity cases

This was the critical point that the Supreme Court was making in *Hopkins*. . . . [And as] far back as 1971, the Supreme Court held that Title VII does not permit an employer to refuse to hire women with pre-school-age children, but not men. *Phillips v. Martin Marietta Corp.*, 400 U.S. 542 (1971). Around the same time, this court held that Title VII "strike[s] at the entire spectrum of disparate treatment of men and women resulting from sex stereotypes," *Sprogis v. United Air Lines, Inc.*, 444 F.2d 1194, 1198 (7th Cir. 1971), and struck down a rule requiring only the female employees to be unmarried. In both those instances, the employer's rule did not affect every woman in the work-force. Just so here: a policy that discriminates on the basis of sexual

If all we changed was her sex, she would not have been treated same way ✸

orientation does not affect every woman, or every man, but it is based on assumptions about the proper behavior for someone of a given sex. The discriminatory behavior does not exist without taking the victim's biological sex (either as observed at birth or as modified, in the case of transsexuals) into account. Any discomfort, disapproval, or job decision based on the fact that the complainant — woman or man — dresses differently, speaks differently, or dates or marries a same-sex partner, is a reaction purely and simply based on sex. That means that it falls within Title VII's prohibition against sex discrimination, if it affects employment in one of the specified ways.

The virtue of looking at comparators and paying heed to gender non-conformity is that this process sheds light on the interpretive question raised by Hively's case: is sexual-orientation discrimination a form of sex discrimination, given the way in which the Supreme Court has interpreted the word "sex" in the statute? The dissent criticizes us for not trying to *rule out* sexual-orientation discrimination by controlling for it in our comparator example and for not placing any weight on the fact that if someone had asked Ivy Tech what its reasons were at the time of the discriminatory conduct, it probably would have said "sexual orientation," not "sex." We assume that this is true, but this thought experiment does not answer the question before us — instead, it begs that question. It commits the logical fallacy of assuming the conclusion it sets out to prove. It makes no sense to control for or rule out discrimination on the basis of sexual orientation if the question before us is *whether* that type of discrimination is nothing more or less than a form of sex discrimination. Repeating that the two are different, as the dissent does at numerous points, also does not advance the analysis.

2

As we noted earlier, Hively also has argued that action based on sexual orientation is sex discrimination under the associational theory. It is now accepted that a person who is discriminated against because of the protected characteristic of one with whom she associates is actually being disadvantaged because of her own traits. This line of cases began with *Loving*, in which the Supreme Court held that "restricting the freedom to marry solely because of racial classifications violates the central meaning of the Equal Protection Clause." The Court rejected the argument that miscegenation statutes do not violate equal protection because they "punish equally both the white and the Negro participants in an interracial marriage." . . .

In effect, both parties to the interracial marriage were being denied important rights by the state solely on the basis of their race. This point by now has been recognized for many years [in the employment context. The court cited in *Parr v. Woodmen of the World Life Ins. Co.*, 791 F.2d 888 (11th Cir. 1986), and *Holcomb v. Iona Coll.*, 521 F.3d 130 (2d Cir. 2008), both involving claims of discrimination on the basis of interracial marriage.]

. . . The dissent implies that we are adopting an anachronistic view of Title VII, enacted just three years before *Loving*, but it is the dissent's understanding of *Loving* and the miscegenation laws that is an anachronism. Thanks to *Loving* and the later cases we mentioned, society understands now that such laws are (and always were) inherently racist. But as of 1967 (and thus as of 1964), Virginia and 15 other states had anti-miscegenation laws on the books. *Loving*. These laws were long defended and understood as non-discriminatory because the legal obstacle affected *both* partners. The Court in *Loving* recognized that equal application of a law that prohibited conduct only between members of different races did not save it. Changing the race of one partner made a difference in determining the legality of the conduct, and so the law rested on "distinctions drawn according to race," which were unjustifiable and racially discriminatory.[4] *Loving*. So too, here. If we were to change the sex of one partner in a lesbian relationship, the outcome would be different. This reveals that the discrimination rests on distinctions drawn according to sex.

The dissent would instead have us compare the treatment of men who are attracted to members of the male sex with the treatment of women who are attracted to members of the female sex, and ask whether an employer treats the men differently from the women. But even setting to one side the logical fallacy involved, *Loving* shows why this fails. In the context of interracial relationships, we could just as easily hold constant a variable such as "sexual or romantic attraction to persons of a different race" and ask whether an employer treated persons of different races who shared that propensity the same. That is precisely the rule that *Loving* rejected, and so too must we, in the context of sexual associations.

The fact that *Loving, Parr,* and *Holcomb* deal with racial associations, as opposed to those based on color, national origin, religion, or sex, is of no moment. The text of the statute draws no distinction, for this purpose, among the different varieties of discrimination it addresses — a fact recognized by the *Hopkins* plurality. This means that to the extent that the statute prohibits discrimination on the basis of the race of someone with whom the plaintiff associates, it also prohibits discrimination on the basis of the national origin, or the color, or the religion, or (as relevant here) the sex of the associate. No matter which category is involved, the essence of the claim is that the *plaintiff* would not be suffering the adverse action had his or her sex, race, color, national origin, or religion been different.

III

Today's decision must be understood against the backdrop of the Supreme Court's decisions, not only in the field of employment discrimination, but also in the area of broader discrimination on the basis of sexual orientation. [The majority cited and described the holdings in *Romer v. Evans*, 517 U.S. 620 (1996), *Lawrence v. Texas*, 539 U.S. 558 (2003), *United States v. Windsor*, 133 S. Ct. 2675 (2013), and *Obergefell*, all of which struck down laws that discriminated on the basis of sexual orientation, but it did not explicitly link their analysis to sex discrimination.]

It would require considerable calisthenics to remove the "sex" from "sexual orientation." The effort to do so has led to confusing and contradictory results, as our panel opinion illustrated so well.[5] The EEOC concluded, in its *Baldwin* decision,

4. The dissent seems to imply that the discrimination in *Loving* was problematic because the miscegenation laws were designed to maintain the supremacy of one race — and by extension that sexual orientation discrimination is not a problem because it is not designed to maintain the supremacy of one sex. But while this was certainly a repugnant feature of Virginia's law, it was not the basis of the holding in *Loving*. Rather, the Court found the racial classifications to be at odds with the Constitution, "even assuming an even-handed state purpose to protect the 'integrity' of all races." *Loving*.

5. The dissent contends that a fluent speaker of the English language would understand that "sex" does not include the concept of "sexual orientation," and this ought to demonstrate that the two are easily distinguishable and not the same. But this again assumes the answer to the question before us: how to interpret the statute in light of the guidance the Supreme Court has provided. The dissent is correct that the term "sexual orientation" was not defined in the dictionary around the time of Title VII's enactment, but neither was the term "sexual harassment" — a concept that, although it can be distinguished from "sex," has at least since 1986 been included by the Supreme Court under the umbrella of sex discrimination. The dissent postulates that it is implausible that a reasonable person in 1964 could have understood discrimination based on sex to include sexual orientation discrimination. But that reasonable person similarly may not have understood it to include sexual harassment (and, by extension, not male-on-male sexual harassment). As *Oncale* said, we are concerned with the provisions of the law, not the principal concerns of those who wrote it. The approach we have taken does just that.

that such an effort cannot be reconciled with the straightforward language of Title VII. Many district courts have come to the same conclusion. Many other courts have found that gender-identity claims are cognizable under Title VII. *See, e.g., Barnes v. City of Cincinnati*, 401 F.3d 729 (6th Cir. 2005); *Smith v. City of Salem, Ohio*, 378 F.3d 566 (6th Cir. 2004).

This is not to say that authority to the contrary does not exist. As we acknowledged at the outset of this opinion, it does. But this court sits en banc to consider what the correct rule of law is now in light of the Supreme Court's authoritative interpretations, not what someone thought it meant one, ten, or twenty years ago. The logic of the Supreme Court's decisions, as well as the common-sense reality that it is actually impossible to discriminate on the basis of sexual orientation without discriminating on the basis of sex, persuade us that the time has come to overrule our previous cases that have endeavored to find and observe that line. . . .

POSNER, Circuit Judge, concurring.

I agree that we should reverse, and I join the majority opinion, but I wish to explore an alternative approach that may be more straightforward.

It is helpful to note at the outset that the interpretation of statutes comes in three flavors. The first and most conventional is the extraction of the original meaning of the statute — the meaning intended by the legislators — and corresponds to interpretation in ordinary discourse. Knowing English I can usually determine swiftly and straightforwardly the meaning of a statement, oral or written, made to me in English (not always, because the statement may be garbled, grammatically intricate or inaccurate, obtuse, or complex beyond my ability to understand).

The second form of interpretation, illustrated by the commonplace local ordinance which commands "no vehicles in the park," is interpretation by unexpressed intent, whereby we understand that although an ambulance is a vehicle, the ordinance was not intended to include ambulances among the "vehicles" forbidden to enter the park. . . .

Finally and most controversially, interpretation can mean giving a fresh meaning to a statement (which can be a statement found in a constitutional or statutory text) — a meaning that infuses the statement with vitality and significance to-day. An example of this last form of interpretation — the form that in my mind is most clearly applicable to the present case — is the Sherman Antitrust Act, enacted in 1890, long before there was a sophisticated understanding of the economics of monopoly and competition. Times have changed; and for more than thirty years the Act has been interpreted in conformity to the modern, not the nineteenth-century, understanding of the relevant economics. The Act has thus been updated by, or in the name of, judicial interpretation-the form of interpretation that consists of making old law satisfy modern needs and understandings. And a common form of interpretation it is, despite its flouting "original meaning." Statutes and constitutional provisions frequently are interpreted on the basis of present need and present understanding rather than original meaning — constitutional provisions even more frequently, because most of them are older than most statutes.

Title VII of the Civil Rights Act of 1964, now more than half a century old, invites an interpretation that will update it to the present, a present that differs markedly from the era in which the Act was enacted. But I need to emphasize that this third form of interpretation — call it judicial interpretive updating — presupposes a lengthy interval between enactment and (re)interpretation. A statute when passed has an understood meaning; it takes years, often many years, for a shift in the political and cultural environment to change the understanding of the statute.

. . . The argument that firing a woman on account of her being a lesbian does *not* violate Title VII is that the term "sex" in the statute, when enacted in 1964, undoubtedly meant "man or woman," and so at the time people would have thought that a woman who was fired for being a lesbian was not being fired for being a woman unless her employer would not have fired on grounds of homosexuality a man he knew to be homosexual; for in that event the only difference between the two would be the gender of the one he fired. Title VII does not mention discrimination on the basis of sexual orientation, and so an explanation is needed for how 53 years later the meaning of the statute has changed and the word "sex" in it now connotes both gender *and* sexual orientation.

It is well-nigh certain that homosexuality, male or female, did not figure in the minds of the legislators who enacted Title VII. I had graduated from law school two years before the law was enacted. Had I been asked then whether I had ever met a male homosexual, I would have answered: probably not; had I been asked whether I had ever met a lesbian I would have answered "only in the pages of À *la recherche du temps perdu*." Homosexuality was almost invisible in the 1960s. It became visible in the 1980s as a consequence of the AIDS epidemic; today it is regarded by a large swathe of the American population as normal. But what is certain is that the word "sex" in Title VII had no immediate reference to homosexuality; many years would elapse before it could be understood to include homosexuality.

A diehard "originalist" would argue that what was believed in 1964 defines the scope of the statute for as long as the statutory text remains unchanged, and therefore until changed by Congress's amending or replacing the statute. But as I noted earlier, statutory and constitutional provisions frequently are interpreted on the basis of present need and understanding rather than original meaning. [The concurrence ranged over a variety of non-originalist interpretations of the Constitution, including flag burning, a warrant requirement for searching homes, the "cruel and unusual punishments" prohibition and the Second Amendment.] Over and over again, old statutes, old constitutional provisions, are given new meaning. . . .

[As for Title VII, it] receives today a new, a broader, meaning. Nothing has changed more in the decades since the enactment of the statute than attitudes toward sex. 1964 was more than a decade before Richard Raskind underwent male-to-female sex reassignment surgery and took the name Renée Richards, becoming the first transgender celebrity; now of course transgender persons are common.

In 1964 (and indeed until the 2000s), and in some states until the Supreme Court's decision in *Obergefell v. Hodges*, men were not allowed to marry each other, nor women allowed to marry each other. If in those days an employer fired a lesbian because he didn't like lesbians, he would have said that he was not firing her because she was a woman — he would not have fired her had she been heterosexual — and so he was not discriminating on the basis of sex as understood by the authors and ratifiers of Title VII. But today "sex" has a broader meaning than the genitalia you're born with. In *Baskin v. Bogan*, 766 F.3d 648 (7th Cir. 2014), our court, anticipating *Obergefell* by invalidating laws in Indiana and Wisconsin that forbade same-sex marriage, discussed at length whether homosexual orientation is innate or chosen, and found that the scientific literature strongly supports the proposition that it is biological and innate, not a choice like deciding how to dress. The position of a woman discriminated against on account of being a lesbian is thus analogous to a woman's being discriminated against on account of being a woman. That woman didn't choose to be a woman; the lesbian didn't choose to be a lesbian. I don't see why firing a lesbian because she is in the subset of women who are lesbian should

"sex discrimination is broad"

be thought any less a form of sex discrimination than firing a woman because she's a woman.

But it has taken our courts and our society a considerable while to realize that sexual harassment, which has been pervasive in many workplaces (including many Capitol Hill offices and, notoriously, Fox News, among many other institutions), is a form of sex discrimination. It has taken a little longer for realization to dawn that discrimination based on a woman's failure to fulfill stereotypical gender roles is also a form of sex discrimination. And it has taken still longer, with a substantial volume of cases struggling and failing to maintain a plausible, defensible line between sex discrimination and sexual-orientation discrimination, to realize that homosexuality is nothing worse than failing to fulfill stereotypical gender roles.

It's true that even today if asked what is the sex of plaintiff Hively one would answer that she is female or that she is a woman, not that she is a lesbian. Lesbianism denotes a form of sexual or romantic attraction; it is not a physical sex identifier like masculinity or femininity. A broader understanding of the word "sex" in Title VII than the original understanding is thus required in order to be able to classify the discrimination of which Hively complains as a form of sex discrimination. That broader understanding is essential. Failure to adopt it would make the statute anachronistic, just as interpreting the Sherman Act by reference to its nineteenth-century framers' understanding of competition and monopoly would make the Sherman Act anachronistic.

We now understand that homosexual men and women (and also bisexuals, defined as having both homosexual and heterosexual orientations) are normal in the ways that count, and beyond that have made many outstanding intellectual and cultural contributions to society (think for example of Tchaikovsky, Oscar Wilde, Jane Addams, André Gide, Thomas Mann, Marlene Dietrich, Bayard Rustin, Alan Turing, Alec Guinness, Leonard Bernstein, Van Cliburn, and James Baldwin — a very partial list). We now understand that homosexuals, male and female, play an essential role, in this country at any rate, as adopters of children from foster homes — a point emphasized in our *Baskin* decision. The compelling social interest in protecting homosexuals (male and female) from discrimination justifies an admittedly loose "interpretation" of the word "sex" in Title VII to embrace homosexuality: an interpretation that cannot be imputed to the framers of the statute but that we are entitled to adopt in light of (to quote Holmes) *"what this country has become,"* or, in Blackstonian terminology, to embrace as a sensible deviation from the literal or original meaning of the statutory language.

I am reluctant however to base the new interpretation of discrimination on account of sex in Title VII on such cases as *Oncale v. Sundowner Offshore Services, Inc.* [because its reference to being bound by "the provisions of our laws," could be thought to be "originalism," if "provisions" meant statutory language]. Rather, "we're back to the essential issue in this case, which is whether passage of time and concomitant change in attitudes toward homosexuality and other unconventional forms of sexual orientation can justify a fresh interpretation of the phrase "discriminat[ion] . . . because of . . . sex" in Title VII, which fortunately however is a half-century-old statute ripe for reinterpretation.

Another decision we should avoid in ascribing present meaning to Title VII is *Loving v. Virginia*, which Hively argues protects her right to associate intimately with a person of the same sex. That was a constitutional case, based on race. It outlawed state prohibitions of interracial marriage. It had nothing to do with the recently enacted Title VII.

. . . The most tenable and straightforward ground for deciding in favor of Hively is that while in 1964 sex discrimination meant discrimination against men or women as such and not against subsets of men or women such as effeminate men or mannish women, the concept of sex discrimination has since broadened in light of the recognition, which barely existed in 1964, that there are significant numbers of both men and women who have a sexual orientation that sets them apart from the heterosexual members of their genetic sex (male or female), and that while they constitute a minority their sexual orientation is not evil and does not threaten our society. Title VII in terms forbids only sex discrimination, but we now understand discrimination against homosexual men and women to be a form of sex discrimination. . . .

The majority opinion states that Congress in 1964 "may not have realized or understood the full scope of the words it chose." This could be understood to imply that the statute forbade discrimination against homosexuals but the framers and ratifiers of the statute were not smart enough to realize that. I would prefer to say that theirs was the then-current understanding of the key word-sex. "Sex" in 1964 meant gender, not sexual orientation. What the framers and ratifiers understandably didn't understand was how attitudes toward homosexuals would change in the following half century. They shouldn't be blamed for that failure of foresight. We understand the words of Title VII differently not because we're smarter than the statute's framers and ratifiers but because we live in a different era, a different culture. Congress in the 1960s did not foresee the sexual revolution of the 2000s. . . .

I would prefer to see us acknowledge openly that today we, who are judges rather than members of Congress, are imposing on a half-century-old statute a meaning of "sex discrimination" that the Congress that enacted it would not have accepted. This is something courts do fairly frequently to avoid statutory obsolescence and concomitantly to avoid placing the entire burden of updating old statutes on the legislative branch. We should not leave the impression that we are merely the obedient servants of the 88th Congress (1963-1965), carrying out their wishes. We are not. We are taking advantage of what the last half century has taught.

FLAUM, Circuit Judge, joined by RIPPLE, Circuit Judge, concurring.

I join Parts I and II of the majority opinion and agree that Title VII . . . does not preclude Professor Hively's claim that Ivy Tech Community College engaged in unlawful employment discrimination. I find the issue before us is simply whether discriminating against an employee for being homosexual violates Title VII's prohibition against discriminating against that employee because of their sex. In my view, the answer is yes, and the statute's text commands as much. . . .

Setting aside the treatment in the majority and dissenting opinions of sexual orientation as a freestanding concept, I conclude discrimination against an employee on the basis of their homosexuality is necessarily, in part, discrimination based on their sex. Fundamental to the definition of homosexuality is the sexual attraction to individuals of the "same sex." [citing several dictionaries.] One cannot consider a person's homosexuality without also accounting for their sex: doing so would render "same" and "own" meaningless. As such, discriminating against that employee because they are homosexual constitutes discriminating against an employee because of (A) the employee's sex, *and* (B) their sexual attraction to individuals of the *same sex*. And "sex," under Title VII, is an enumerated trait.

This raises the question: Does Title VII's text require a plaintiff to show that an employer discriminated against them *solely* "because of" an enumerated trait? Again, I turn to the text, which clearly states:

> Except as otherwise provided in this subchapter, an unlawful employment practice is established when the complaining party demonstrates that . . . sex . . . was *a motivating factor for any employment practice, even though other factors also motivated the practice.*

42 U.S.C. §2000e-2(m) (emphasis added). [Judge Flaum traced the history of that provision to *Price Waterhouse*, where the plurality stated that the critical inquiry was whether gender was *a factor* in the adverse decision.] So if discriminating against an employee because she is homosexual is equivalent to discriminating against her because she is (A) a woman who is (B) sexually attracted to women, then it is motivated, in part, by an enumerated trait: the employee's sex. That is all an employee must show to successfully allege a Title VII claim.[2]

Cases analyzing employment actions based on interracial relationships provide an apt illustration. Although this Circuit has not yet addressed whether claims based on a theory of associational discrimination are cognizable under Title VII, I agree with the majority that the Second Circuit's analysis in *Holcomb v. Iona College*, 521 F.3d 130 (2d Cir. 2008), is persuasive. . . .

SYKES, Circuit Judge, with whom BAUER and KANNE, Circuit Judges, join, dissenting.

Any case heard by the full court is important. This one is momentous. All the more reason to pay careful attention to the limits on the court's role. The question before the en banc court is one of statutory interpretation. The majority deploys a judge-empowering, common-law decision method that leaves a great deal of room for judicial discretion. So does Judge Posner in his concurrence. Neither is faithful to the statutory text, read fairly, as a reasonable person would have understood it when it was adopted. The result is a statutory amendment courtesy of unelected judges. Judge Posner admits this; he embraces and argues for this conception of judicial power. The majority does not, preferring instead to smuggle in the statutory amendment under cover of an aggressive reading of loosely related Supreme Court precedents. Either way, the result is the same: the circumvention of the legislative process by which the people govern themselves.

Respect for the constraints imposed on the judiciary by a system of written law must begin with fidelity to the traditional first principle of statutory interpretation: When a statute supplies the rule of decision, our role is to give effect to the enacted text, interpreting the statutory language as a reasonable person would have understood it at the time of enactment. We are not authorized to infuse the text with a new or unconventional meaning or to update it to respond to changed social, economic, or political conditions.

In a handful of statutory contexts, Congress has vested the federal courts with authority to consider and make new rules of law in the common-law way. The Sherman Act is the archetype of the so-called "common-law statutes," but there are very few of these and Title VII is not one of them. So our role is interpretive only; we lack the discretion to ascribe to Title VII a meaning it did not bear at its inception. Sitting en banc permits us to overturn our own precedents, but in a statutory case, we do not sit as a

---

2. The foregoing analysis should obtain even if an employer allegedly discriminates against all homosexual employees. In that case, the employer's discrimination across sexes does not demonstrate that sex is irrelevant, but rather that each individual has a plausible sex-based discrimination claim. When confronting claims that are inherently based in part on sex, such as discrimination against homosexuals, each employee's claim satisfies Title VII on its face, no matter the sex of any other employee who experienced discrimination.

common-law court free to engage in "judicial interpretive updating," as Judge Posner calls it, or to do the same thing by pressing hard on tenuously related Supreme Court opinions, as the majority does.

Judicial statutory updating, whether overt or covert, cannot be reconciled with the constitutional design [because it bypasses the Constitution's procedure for enacting and amending statutes].

I

. . . Today the court jettisons the prevailing interpretation and installs the polar opposite. Suddenly sexual-orientation discrimination *is* sex discrimination and thus is actionable under Title VII. What justification is offered for this radical change in a well-established, uniform interpretation of an important — indeed, transformational — statute? My colleagues take note of the Supreme Court's "absence from the debate." What debate? There is no debate, at least not in the relevant sense. Our long-standing interpretation of Title VII is not an outlier. From the statute's inception to the present day, the appellate courts have unanimously and repeatedly read the statute the same way, as my colleagues must and do acknowledge. The Supreme Court has had no need to weigh in, and the unanimity among the courts of appeals strongly suggests that our long-settled interpretation is correct.

Of course there *is* a robust debate on this subject in our culture, media, and politics. Attitudes about gay rights have dramatically shifted in the 53 years since the Civil Rights Act was adopted. Lambda Legal's proposed new reading of Title VII — offered on behalf of plaintiff Kimberly Hively at the appellate stage of this litigation — has a strong foothold in current popular opinion.

This striking cultural change informs a case for legislative change and might eventually persuade the people's representatives to amend the statute to implement a new public policy. But it does not bear on the sole inquiry properly before the en banc court: Is the prevailing interpretation of Title VII — that discrimination on the basis of sexual orientation is different in kind and not a form of sex discrimination — *wrong as an original matter?*

A

On that question Lambda Legal has not carried its burden of legal persuasion. To be clear, I agree with my colleagues that the proposed new interpretation is not necessarily incorrect simply because no one in the 1964 Congress that adopted Title VII intended or anticipated its application to sexual-orientation discrimination. The subjective intentions of the legislators do not matter. Statutory interpretation is an objective inquiry that looks for the meaning the statutory language conveyed to a reasonable person at the time of enactment. . . .

B

That is where our agreement ends. The en banc majority rests its new interpretation of sex discrimination on a thought experiment drawn from the "tried-and-true" comparative method of proof often used by plaintiffs in discrimination cases. The majority also invokes *Loving v. Virginia*, 388 U.S. 1 (1967), the Supreme Court's historic decision striking down Virginia's miscegenation laws under the Fourteenth Amendment's Equal Protection Clause, as well as cases involving sex stereotyping, most prominently *Price Waterhouse v. Hopkins*.

But the analysis must begin with the statutory text; it largely ends there too. Is it even remotely plausible that in 1964, when Title VII was adopted, a reasonable person competent in the English language would have understood that a law banning employment discrimination "because of sex" also banned discrimination because of sexual orientation? The answer is no, of course not.

[The dissent looked to the "fundamental canon of statutory construction that, unless otherwise defined, words will be interpreted as taking their ordinary, contemporary, common meaning," which required looking to "the original public meaning of the statutory text." Since Title VII does not define discrimination "because of sex," the courts must look to "common, ordinary usage," which, "in 1964 — and now, for that matter" — means "biologically *male* or *female*; it does not also refer to sexual orientation."]

To a fluent speaker of the English language — then and now — the ordinary meaning of the word "sex" does not fairly include the concept of "sexual orientation." The two terms are never used interchangeably, and the latter is not subsumed within the former; there is no overlap in meaning. Contrary to the majority's vivid rhetorical claim, it does not take "considerable calisthenics" to separate the two. The words plainly describe different traits, and the separate and distinct meaning of each term is easily grasped. More specifically to the point here, discrimination "because of sex" is not reasonably understood to include discrimination based on sexual orientation, a different immutable characteristic. Classifying people by sexual orientation is different than classifying them by sex. The two traits are categorically distinct and widely recognized as such. There is no ambiguity or vagueness here. . . .

C

This commonsense understanding is confirmed by the language Congress uses when it *does* legislate against sexual-orientation discrimination. For example, the Violence Against Women Act prohibits funded programs and activities from discriminating "on the basis of actual or perceived race, color, religion, national origin, *sex*, gender identity, . . . *sexual orientation*, or disability." 42 U.S.C. §13925(b)(13)(A) (emphases added). If sex discrimination is commonly understood to encompass sexual-orientation discrimination, then listing the two categories separately, as this statute does, is needless surplusage. [The dissent also cited the federal Hate Crimes Act and other federal statutes as well as state and local antidiscrimination laws that "likewise distinguish between sex discrimination and sexual-orientation discrimination by listing them separately as distinct forms of unlawful discrimination.]

I could go on, but the point has been made. This uniformity of usage is powerful objective evidence that sexual-orientation discrimination is broadly recognized as an independent category of discrimination and is *not* synonymous with sex discrimination.

II

My colleagues in the majority superficially acknowledge [the] "truism" that sex discrimination is discrimination based on a person's biological sex. As they see it, however, even if sex discrimination is understood in the ordinary way, sexual-orientation discrimination *is* sex discrimination because "it is actually impossible to discriminate on the basis of sexual orientation without discriminating on the basis of sex."

Not true. An employer who refuses to hire homosexuals is not drawing a line based on the job applicant's sex. He is not excluding gay men because they are men and lesbians because they are women. His discriminatory motivation is independent of and unrelated to the applicant's sex. Sexism (misandry and misogyny) and homophobia are separate kinds of prejudice that classify people in distinct ways based on different immutable characteristics. Simply put, sexual-orientation discrimination doesn't classify people by sex; it doesn't draw male/female distinctions but instead targets homosexual men and women for harsher treatment than heterosexual men and women.

The majority opinion merges these two distinct categories of discrimination by misapplying the comparative method of proof often used by plaintiffs in discrimination cases. [The dissent viewed the comparative method as "a *method of proof* or a technique for evaluating the sufficiency of the plaintiff's allegations or evidence," not as a method for ascertaining the meaning of the word "sex" in the statute. In contrast,] Lambda Legal is advancing a creative new *legal* argument for *reinterpreting* Title VII, deploying the comparative method not as a method of proof (its normal and intended function) but as a thought experiment with the end of imbuing the statute with a new meaning that it did not bear at its inception. . . .

The comparative method of proof is a useful technique for uncovering the employer's real motive for taking the challenged action. Comparing the plaintiff to a similarly situated employee of the opposite sex can help the fact finder determine whether the employer was actually motivated by the plaintiff's sex or acted for some other reason. It's a device for ferreting out a prohibited discriminatory motive as an actual cause of the adverse employment action; it does this by controlling for other possible motives. If a female plaintiff can point to a male employee who is identical to her in every material respect and was treated more favorably, then the fact finder can draw an inference that the unfavorable treatment was actually motivated by the plaintiff's sex.

Here the majority is not using the comparative method to isolate whether Ivy Tech was *actually* motivated by Hively's sex when it refused to promote her to full-time professor and canceled her part-time teaching contract. To repeat, Hively does not make that allegation. Her factual claim is that Ivy Tech refused to promote her and canceled her contract because she is a lesbian. The only question for us is whether *that* claim — her *real* claim — is actionable under Title VII *as a matter of law*. That's a pure question of statutory interpretation.

But the comparative method of proof is an evidentiary test; it is not an interpretive tool. It tells us *nothing* about the meaning or scope of Title VII. In ordinary English usage, sexual-orientation discrimination is a distinct form of discrimination and is not synonymous with sex discrimination. That's the plain meaning of Title VII's text as originally understood. An *evidentiary test* like the comparative method of proof has no work to do here and is utterly out of place.

Moreover, the majority distorts the comparative method by opportunistically framing the comparison. If the aim is to isolate actual discriminatory motive based on the plaintiff's sex, then we must hold everything constant *except* the plaintiff's sex. But my colleagues load the dice by changing *two* variables — the plaintiff's sex *and* sexual orientation — to arrive at the hypothetical comparator. The court's reasoning essentially distills to this: If we compare Hively, a homosexual woman, to hypothetical Professor A, a heterosexual man, we can see that Ivy Tech is actually disadvantaging Hively because she is a woman.

As a test for isolating an *actual* case of *sex* discrimination, that way of framing the comparative question doesn't do the trick. Simply put, the comparison can't do its job of *ruling in* sex discrimination as the actual reason for the employer's decision (by *ruling out* other possible motivations) if we're not scrupulous about holding *everything* constant except the plaintiff's sex. That includes the plaintiff's sexual orientation. If we're really serious about trying to isolate whether sex discrimination played a role in a specific employment decision, the test must exclude other factors that may have been decisive.

For the comparison to be valid as a test for the role of sex discrimination in this employment decision, the proper comparison is to ask how Ivy Tech treated qualified gay men. If an employer is willing to hire gay men but not lesbians, then the comparative method has exposed an actual case of sex discrimination. If, on the other hand, an employer hires only heterosexual men and women and rejects all homosexual applicants, then no inference of sex discrimination is possible, though we could perhaps draw an inference of sexual-orientation discrimination.

But of course my colleagues are not actually trying to isolate sex discrimination as the *real* motivation for Ivy Tech's decision. They are not, that is, testing for a *true* case of sex discrimination. They are using the comparative method as a rhetorical device to conjure an entirely new understanding of the term "sex discrimination" for use in the Title VII context, one that denies the reality that sex and sexual orientation are different traits and that classifying people by sexual orientation is not the same as classifying them by sex. This is artifice, not interpretation. . . .[5]

III

A

The majority also draws on *Loving*, the Supreme Court's iconic decision invalidating Virginia's miscegenation statutes on equal-protection grounds. This case is not a variant of *Loving*. Miscegenation laws plainly employ invidious racial classifications; they are inherently racially discriminatory. In contrast, sexual-orientation discrimination springs from a wholly different kind of bias than sex discrimination. The two forms of discrimination classify people based on different traits and thus are not the same. . . .

As these passages from the Court's opinion make clear, *Loving* rests on the inescapable truth that miscegenation laws are inherently racist. They are premised on invidious ideas about white superiority and use racial classifications toward the end of racial purity and white supremacy. Sexual-orientation discrimination, on the other hand, is not inherently *sexist*. No one argues that sexual-orientation discrimination aims to promote or perpetuate the supremacy of one sex. In short, *Loving* neither compels nor supports the majority's decision to upend the long-settled understanding that sex discrimination and sexual-orientation discrimination are distinct.

For the same reason, the majority's reliance on *Parr* [and] *Holcomb*, which translated *Loving* to the Title VII context, is entirely inapt. An employer who refuses to hire

---

5. Judge Flaum's concurrence offers a somewhat different way to think about sexual-orientation discrimination: "Fundamental to the definition of homosexuality is the sexual attraction to individuals of the 'same sex.' . . . One cannot consider a person's homosexuality without also accounting for their sex: doing so would render 'same' . . . meaningless." But an employer who categorically won't hire homosexuals is not "accounting for" a job applicant's sex in the sense meant by antidiscrimination law; a hiring policy of "no homosexuals need apply" is gender blind. The next sentence in the analysis likewise doesn't follow: "As such, discriminating against that employee because they are homosexual constitutes discriminating against an employee because of (A) the employee's sex, *and* (B) their sexual attraction to individuals of the *same sex*." Part (B) is true; part (A) is not. An employer who refuses to hire a lesbian applicant because she is a lesbian only "accounts for" her sex in the limited sense that he notices she is a woman. But that's not the object of the employer's discriminatory intent, not even in part. Her sex isn't a motivating factor for the employer's decision; the employer objects only to her sexual orientation. This attempt to conceptually split homosexuality into two parts — a person's sex and his or her sexual attraction to persons of the same sex — doesn't make sexual-orientation discrimination actionable as sex discrimination.

or fires an employee based on his interracial marriage is obviously drawing invidious racial classifications akin to those inherent in Virginia's miscegenation laws. . . .

B

The majority also relies on cases involving sex stereotyping, most notably the Supreme Court's decision in *Price Waterhouse v. Hopkins*. More specifically, my colleagues conclude that a claim of sexual-orientation discrimination is indistinguishable from a claim involving sex stereotyping. I disagree. Nothing in *Hopkins* altered the traditional understanding that sexual-orientation discrimination is a distinct type of discrimination and is not synonymous with sex discrimination.

As a preliminary matter, neither *Hopkins* nor any other decision of the Supreme Court establishes an independent cause of action for, or "doctrine" or "theory" of, "sex stereotyping."[7] *Hopkins* held only that the presence of sex stereotyping by an employer "can certainly be *evidence*" of sex discrimination; to prove her case, the plaintiff must always prove that "the employer *actually* relied on her gender in making its decision." (second emphasis added). . . .

To put the matter plainly, heterosexuality is not a *female* stereotype; it is not a *male* stereotype; it is not a *sex-specific* stereotype at all. An employer who hires only heterosexual employees is neither assuming nor insisting that his female and male employees match a stereotype specific to their sex. He is instead insisting that his employees match the dominant sexual orientation *regardless of their sex*. Sexual-orientation discrimination does not classify people according to invidious or idiosyncratic *male* or *female* stereotypes. It does not spring from a sex-specific bias at all.

The point is easy to see if we take the question posed by the plurality opinion in *Hopkins* and map it onto this case. Hively suspects that the real reason Ivy Tech rejected her repeated applications for promotion is her sexual orientation. Assume for the moment that her suspicion is correct. If we asked Ivy Tech "at the moment of the decision what its reasons were and if we received a truthful response," would it be reasonable to expect Ivy Tech to respond that it rejected her applications because she is a woman? No. If Ivy Tech responded truthfully, it would confess that its decisions were based on Hively's sexual orientation, not her sex.

So it's a serious mistake to think that *Hopkins* either supports or requires a new interpretation of Title VII that equates sexual-orientation discrimination with sex discrimination. To the contrary, *Hopkins* does not even gesture in that direction. If the lower-court decisions involving "sex stereotyping" are a confusing hodgepodge — and I agree that they are — the confusion stems from an unfortunate tendency to read *Hopkins* for more than it's worth. That's not a reason to embed the confusion in circuit law.

C

Neither does *Oncale* compel or support today's decision. *Oncale* held only that same-sex sexual harassment may, in an appropriate case, support a claim under Title VII *provided* that it "meets the statutory requirements." The Court reiterated that in *all* sex-discrimination cases, including sexual-harassment cases, "[t]he critical issue, Title VII's text indicates, is whether members of one sex are exposed to

---

7. Some lower courts use the phrase "gender nonconformity" interchangeably with "sex stereotyping," but the Supreme Court has never used that term.

disadvantageous terms or conditions of employment to which members of the other sex are not exposed." (quotation marks omitted).

[The dissent recited the facts and reasoning of *Oncale*, concluding that] in authorizing claims of same-sex harassment as a theoretical matter, the Court carefully tethered *all* sexual-harassment claims to the statutory requirement that the plaintiff prove discrimination "because of sex." Nothing in *Oncale* eroded the distinction between sex discrimination and sexual-orientation discrimination or opened the door to a new interpretation of Title VII.

Oncale was not a revolutionary decision. In contrast, today's decision by the en banc court works a profound transformation of Title VII by any measure.

D

The majority also finds support for its decision in "the backdrop of the Supreme Court's decisions . . . in the area of broader discrimination on the basis of sexual orientation," citing *Romer v. Evans*; *Lawrence v. Texas*; *United States v. Windsor*; and *Obergefell v. Hodges*

But the majority's position is actually irreconcilable with these cases. First, *Lawrence* was decided solely under the Due Process Clause; it was not an equal-protection case. In the other cases, far from collapsing the well-understood distinction between sex discrimination and sexual-orientation discrimination, the Court actually preserved it. The Court assigned these two distinct forms of discrimination to different analytical categories for purposes of equal-protection scrutiny. If sex discrimination and sexual-orientation discrimination were really one and the same, then the Court would have applied the intermediate standard of scrutiny that governs judicial review of laws that classify people by sex. *See United States v. Virginia*, 518 U.S. 515, 531 (1996). It did not do so.

E

Finally, drawing especially on *Obergefell*, my colleagues worry that adhering to the long-settled interpretation of Title VII "creates 'a paradoxical legal landscape in which a person can be married on Saturday and then fired on Monday for just that act.'" The concern is understandable, but my colleagues conflate the distinction between state action, which is subject to constitutional limits, and private action, which is regulated by statute. The Due Process and Equal Protection Clauses are constitutional restraints on government. Title VII is a statutory restraint on employers. The legal regimes differ accordingly. Any discrepancy is a matter for legislative, not judicial, correction.

* * *

If Kimberly Hively was denied a job because of her sexual orientation, she was treated unjustly. But Title VII does not provide a remedy for this kind of discrimination. The argument that it *should* must be addressed to Congress. . . .

* * *

In the end, today's decision must be recognized for what it is: a new form of Title VII liability based on *imputed* motive, not *actual* motive. The majority's new rule — that sexual-orientation discrimination = sex discrimination — imputes to the employer a motive that is not, and need not be, present in fact. Liability under this new "theory" of sex discrimination does not require the jury to find that the employer's decision was *actually* motivated by the plaintiff's sex. That's a necessary predicate for liability in all other sex-discrimination cases, but not here. Discrimination "because of sex" need not be found as a fact; instead, the court will impute the statutorily forbidden motive to the employer if the plaintiff proves discrimination "because of sexual orientation." . . .

NOTES

1. *Distinguishing Sexual Orientation from Sex Stereotyping.* Prior to *Hively*, the lower courts generally rejected claims based on sexual orientation per se, but in the wake of that decision another circuit has taken the issue en banc. *Zarda v. Altitude Express*, 855 F.3d 76 (2d Cir. 2017), *reh'g granted*. However, many courts, relying on *Price Waterhouse*, also upheld claims based on a failure to conform to sex stereotypes. Thus, a number of cases would have permitted a plaintiff like Hively to state a claim if she asserted she was discriminated against on the basis of gender nonconformity rather than sexual orientation as such. Such a rule has the somewhat odd result of providing more protection to gays who "manifest traits coded as gay" than to those merely cognitively perceived to be gay. *See* Brian Soucek, *Perceived Homosexuals: Looking Gay Enough for Title VII*, 63 Am. U. L. Rev. 715 (2014). *See also* Zachary A. Kramer, *Heterosexuality and Title VII*, 103 Nw. U. L. Rev. 205, 227-30 (2009); Kimberly A. Yuracko, *The Sex Stereotyping Prohibition at Work*, 161 U. Pa. L. Rev. 757 (2013).

Even though *Hively* remains an outlier, those decisions mean that plaintiffs in the position of Ms. Hively may well be able to pursue claims in other circuits under the gender nonconformity theory rather than claim discrimination based on sexual orientation. See *Evans v. Georgia Reg'l Hosp.*, 850 F.3d 1248 (11th Cir. 2017). But this path is by no means easy, *see Vickers v. Fairfield Med. Ctr.*, 453 F.3d 757, 762 (6th Cir. 2006), and plaintiffs are open to the rebuttal that the employer discriminated against gays as such.

2. *"Sex Stereotyping" Claims by Transsexuals.* Even before *Hively*, courts seemed more sympathetic to another kind of LGBT claims — those of transsexuals. In *Smith v. City of Salem*, 378 F.3d 566, 572 (6th Cir. 2004), a transsexual stated a Title VII claim by alleging that he (the pronoun used by the court) was a victim of discrimination because his conduct and mannerisms "did not conform to his employers' and co-workers' sex stereotypes of how a man should look and behave." The comments about him not being sufficiently masculine culminated in his supervisors seeking to compel his resignation "by forcing him to undergo multiple psychological evaluations of his gender non-conforming behavior." *Smith* wrote:

> After *Price Waterhouse*, an employer who discriminates against women because, for instance, they do not wear dresses or makeup, is engaging in sex discrimination because the discrimination would not occur but for the victim's sex. It follows that employers who discriminate against men because they do wear dresses and makeup, or otherwise act femininely, are also engaging in sex discrimination, because the discrimination would not occur but for the victim's sex. . . .
>
> Yet some courts have held that this latter form of discrimination is of a different and somehow more permissible kind. For instance, the man who acts in ways typically associated with women is not described as engaging in the same activity as a woman who acts in ways typically associated with women, but is instead described as engaging in the different activity of being a transsexual (or in some instances, a homosexual or transvestite). Discrimination against the transsexual is then found not to be discrimination "because of . . . sex," but rather, discrimination against the plaintiff's unprotected status or mode of self-identification. In

other words, these courts superimpose classifications such as "transsexual" on a plaintiff, and then legitimize discrimination based on the plaintiff's gender non-conformity by formalizing the non-conformity into an ostensibly unprotected classification. . . .

Such analyses cannot be reconciled with *Price Waterhouse*, which does not make Title VII protection against sex stereotyping conditional or provide any reason to exclude Title VII coverage for non sex-stereotypical behavior simply because the person is a transsexual.

Id. at 574. *See also Glenn v. Brumby*, 663 F.3d 1312 (11th Cir. 2011) (a violation of the Equal Protection Clause's prohibition of sex discrimination to fire a transgender or transsexual employee because of his or her gender nonconformity). What about bisexuals? How does current law protect, or not protect them? *See* Elizabeth M. Glazer, *Sexual Reorientation*, 100 Geo. L.J. 997 (2012).

3. *The Majority's Analysis.* The first edition of this book, published in 1982, essentially asked why it isn't sex discrimination to fire a male for having sex with a man when a woman would not be fired for that conduct. While that may not have been an original argument, it was viewed by many as naïve — an exercise in sterile logic divorced from an interpretation of the law more in line with Congress's purposes. Fast forward 35 years and *Hively* relies in large part on that analysis. Why did the argument fail to obtain traction for 35 years? Does it tell you something about the art of statutory interpretation?

The majority also bought Lambda's associational argument: discrimination on the basis of the gender of those who one marries or otherwise romantically associates with is sex discrimination. This *Loving* argument was accepted by several circuits in the race context but, until *Hively*, had no success in the gender setting. What led to its acceptance now?

4. *Original Public Meaning vs. Judicial Interpretive Updating.* The most radical of the four opinions is Judge Posner's, who urges a dramatic interpretive role for court, one that is the polar opposite of dissenting Judge Syke's "original public meaning" approach to statutes. Which do you prefer? When the Supreme Court reaches this issue — obviously more likely now that *Hively* has created a circuit split — what will it do? Does Sykes adequately explain why the comparative and associational theories don't trump what she thinks would be the interpretation of a reasonable observer in 1964? Even if so, does she sufficiently account for the "expansion" of Title VII to reach sexual harassment, a cause of action which most agree would not have been anticipated by those who wrote the statute?

5. *The EEOC.* As the majority noted, the EEOC got there first. In *Macy v. Holder*, No. 0120120821, 2012 EEOPUB LEXIS 1181 (E.E.O.C. Apr. 20, 2012), it found that discrimination against transgender individuals based on their transgender status constituted sex-based discrimination in violation of Title VII, and, in 2015, in a claim involving alleged discrimination in federal employment, the EEOC ruled (3-2) that discrimination on the basis of sexual orientation is sex discrimination within the meaning of Title VII. See *Complainant v. Foxx*, 2015 WL 4397641 (E.E.O.C. July 15, 2015).

6. *Protection Beyond Title VII.* The majority lists the Supreme Court's constitutional decisions regarding sexual orientation. Although hard to classify doctrinally, they nevertheless clearly view classifications based on sexual orientation with hostility. *United States v. Windsor*, 133 S. Ct. 2675 (2013), struck down the federal Defense of Marriage Act which barred same-sex partners from a wide array of federal benefits offered to married couples. While it was widely believed to have portended a more sweeping invalidation of state prohibitions on same-sex marriage, that did not occur until *Obergefell v. Hodges*, 135 S. Ct. 2584 (2015), in which a majority of the

Court struck down such laws. *Obergefell* was grounded primarily in the Due Process Clause but also looked to the Equal Protection Clause for its holding.

While the *Hively* majority cited those opinions, it failed to explain their significance for Title VII analysis, and the Sykes dissent made much of the fact that the Court created a separate strand of analysis rather than simply applying its sex discrimination precedents. What do you think the role of those precedents should be in this debate? *See generally* Keith Cunningham-Parmeter, *Marriage Equality, Workplace Inequality: The Next Gay Rights Battle*, 67 FLA. L. REV. 1099 (2015); Stephen F. Befort & Michael J. Vargas, *Same-Sex Marriage and Title VII*, 56 SANTA CLARA L. REV. 207 (2016).

In response to the current lack of statutory protection for gays under federal law, a number of states have enacted their own civil rights legislation expressly covering sexual orientation. According to the ACLU, as of March 2017, 19 states prohibit discrimination based on sexual orientation and/or gender identity. http://www.aclu.org/maps/non-discrimination-laws-state-state-information-map. And a decade ago, *See* Ian Ayres & Jennifer Gerarda Brown, *Mark(et)ing Nondiscrimination: Privatizing ENDA with A Certification Mark*, 104 MICH. L. REV. 1639, 1712 n.98 (2006), reported that "47% of the U.S. population lives in jurisdictions that have adopted nondiscrimination laws. This includes 38% who live in states with such laws; another 9% are covered by city or county law." Such statutes typically protect against discrimination on the basis of sexual orientation, normally defined as including heterosexuality, bisexuality, and homosexuality. And increasingly states are adding gender identity to the list of protected classifications.

b. Personal Relationships

What happens when an employee uses his or her sexual attractiveness or a sexual relationship to obtain an advantage relative to other employees? Is this actionable under Title VII? In *DeCintio v. Westchester County Medical Center*, 807 F.2d 304 (2d Cir. 1986), male respiratory therapists complained that their department head discriminated against them by adopting promotion standards designed to disqualify them and to favor a female applicant with whom he was romantically involved. The court found no Title VII violation:

> Ryan's conduct, although unfair, simply did not violate Title VII. Appellees were not prejudiced because of their status as males; rather, they were discriminated against because Ryan preferred his paramour. Appellees faced exactly the same predicament as that faced by any woman applicant for the promotion: No one but Guagenti could be considered for the appointment because of Guagenti's special relationship to Ryan. That relationship forms the basis of appellees' sex discrimination claims. Appellees' proffered interpretation of Title VII prohibitions against sex discrimination would involve the EEOC and federal courts in the policing of intimate relationships. Such a course, founded on a distortion of the meaning of the word "sex" in the context of Title VII, is both impracticable and unwarranted.

Id. at 308. The court emphasized that Title VII protects individuals from discrimination on the basis of status, "not on his or her sexual affiliations." *Id.* at 306-07. As we will see later in this section, this reasoning led to early Title VII decisions declining to find liability for quid pro quo sexual harassment. That, of course, is no longer true for such harassment but seems to remain true for "paramour" favoritism.

The court in *DeCintio* distinguished sexual harassment claims because the issue there is "the coercive nature of the employer's acts, rather than the fact of the relationship itself." *Id.* at 307. But doesn't *Oncale* confirm that the basis of sexual harassment liability is the notion that, "but for" an individual's sex, he or she would not be subjected to harassment? Didn't the plaintiffs in *DeCintio* lose a job opportunity that, "but for" their gender, they may have had? However problematic the analysis, *DeCintio* continues to control. *E.g., Tenge v. Phillips Modern Ag Co*, 446 F.3d 903 (8th Cir. 2006); *Preston v. Wisconsin Health Fund*, 397 F.3d 539, 541 (7th Cir. 2005). Might *Hively* change that?

Did the plaintiffs in *DeCintio* lose because the court was unwilling to recognize a Title VII discrimination claim for an employee because he was *not* a victim of sexual harassment? What if a female plaintiff had complained about Ryan's actions? *See Miller v. Dep't of Corr.*, 115 P.3d 77, 80 (Cal. 2005) (distinguishing isolated instances of sexual favoritism from workplaces where sexual favoritism is sufficiently widespread to create a hostile work environment by conveying the demeaning message to female employees that "they are viewed by management as 'sexual playthings' or that the way required for women to get ahead in the workplace is by engaging in sexual conduct with their supervisors").

Suppose Guagenti, after being hired by Ryan, refused to continue their romantic relationship and Ryan discharged her. Would she have a discrimination claim? In *Green v. Administrators of Tulane Educational Fund*, 284 F.3d 642, 650 (5th Cir. 2002), the court rejected Tulane's argument that harassment triggered by the ending of a consensual relationship was merely "personal animosity" and not actionable. The harassing behavior was causally related to the plaintiff's gender; the plaintiff was harassed because she refused to continue to have a "casual" sexual relationship after the breakup. What if there had been no demand for sex after the breakup? Would harassing her simply because she was once a consensual sexual partner be actionable? *See also Forrest v. Brinker Int'l Payroll Co., LP*, 511 F.3d 225, 229 (1st Cir. 2007) ("since the prior relationship would not have existed had the victim not been a member of the harasser's preferred sex, "the victim's sex is inextricably linked to the harasser's decision to harass" once the relationship turned sour). *Cf. Pipkins v. City of Temple Terrace*, 267 F.3d 1197 (11th Cir. 2001) (disappointment in failed relationship was not discrimination because of sex).

c.   Grooming and Dress Codes

JESPERSEN v. HARRAH'S OPERATING COMPANY, INC.
444 F.3d 1104 (9th Cir. 2006) (en banc)

SCHROEDER, Chief Judge. . . .

I.   BACKGROUND

Plaintiff Darlene Jespersen worked successfully as a bartender at Harrah's for twenty years and compiled what by all accounts was an exemplary record. During Jespersen's entire tenure with Harrah's, the company maintained a policy encouraging female beverage servers to wear makeup. The parties agree, however, that the policy was not enforced until 2000. In February 2000, Harrah's implemented a "Beverage Department Image Transformation" program at twenty Harrah's locations, including its casino in Reno. Part of the program consisted of new grooming and appearance standards, called the "Personal Best" program. The program contained certain appearance standards that applied equally to both sexes, including a standard uniform of black pants, white shirt, black vest, and black bow tie. Jespersen has never objected to any of these policies. The program also contained some sex-differentiated appearance requirements as to hair, nails, and makeup.

In April 2000, Harrah's amended that policy to require that women wear makeup. Jepersen's only objection here is to the makeup requirement. . . .

II. UNEQUAL BURDENS . . .

In this case, Jespersen argues that the makeup requirement itself establishes a prima facie case of discriminatory intent and must be justified by Harrah's as a bona fide occupational qualification. Our settled law in this circuit, however, does not support Jespersen's position that a sex-based difference in appearance standards alone, without any further showing of disparate effects, creates a prima facie case.

In *Gerdom v. Cont'l Airlines, Inc.*, 692 F.2d 602 (9th Cir. 1982), we considered the Continental Airlines policy that imposed strict weight restrictions on female flight attendants, and held it constituted a violation of Title VII. We did so because the airline imposed no weight restriction whatsoever on a class of male employees who performed the same or similar functions as the flight attendants. Indeed, the policy was touted by the airline as intended to "create the public image of an airline which offered passengers service by thin, attractive women, whom executives referred to as Continental's 'girls.'" In fact, Continental specifically argued that its policy was justified by its "desire to compete [with other airlines] by featuring attractive female cabin attendants[,]" a justification which this court recognized as "discriminatory on its face." The weight restriction was part of an overall program to create a sexual image for the airline.

In contrast, this case involves an appearance policy that applied to both male and female bartenders, and was aimed at creating a professional and very similar look for all of them. All bartenders wore the same uniform. The policy only differentiated as to grooming standards.

In *Frank v. United Airlines, Inc.*, 216 F.3d 845 (9th Cir. 2000), we dealt with a weight policy that applied different standards to men and women in a facially unequal way. The women were forced to meet the requirements of a medium body frame standard while men were required to meet only the more generous requirements of a large body frame standard. In that case, we recognized that "an appearance standard that imposes different but essentially equal burdens on men and women is not disparate treatment." The United weight policy, however, did not impose equal burdens. On its face, the policy embodied a requirement that categorically "'applied less favorably to one gender[,]'" and the burdens imposed upon that gender were obvious from the policy itself. (quoting *Gerdom*) (alteration omitted).

This case stands in marked contrast, for here we deal with requirements that, on their face, are not more onerous for one gender than the other [no pun intended]. Rather, Harrah's "Personal Best" policy contains sex-differentiated requirements regarding each employee's hair, hands, and face. While those individual requirements differ according to gender, none on its face places a greater burden on one gender than the other. Grooming standards that appropriately differentiate between the genders are not facially discriminatory.

We have long recognized that companies may differentiate between men and women in appearance and grooming policies, and so have other circuits. *See, e.g., Fountain v. Safeway Stores, Inc.*, 555 F.2d 753, 755 (9th Cir. 1977); *Barker v. Taft Broad. Co.*, 549 F.2d 400, 401 (6th Cir. 1977); *Earwood v. Cont'l Southeastern Lines, Inc.*, 539 F.2d 1349, 1350 (4th Cir. 1976). The material issue under our settled law is not whether the policies are different, but whether the policy imposed on the plaintiff creates an "unequal burden" for the plaintiff's gender. *See Frank; Gerdom.*

Not every differentiation between the sexes in a grooming and appearance policy creates a "significantly greater burden of compliance[.]" *Gerdom.* For example, in *Fountain,* this court upheld Safeway's enforcement of its sex-differentiated appearance standard, including its requirement that male employees wear ties, because the company's actions in enforcing the regulations were not "overly burdensome to its employees[.]" *See also Barker.* Similarly, as the Eighth Circuit has recognized, "where, as here, such [grooming and appearance] policies are reasonable and are imposed in an evenhanded manner on all employees, slight differences in the appearance requirements for males and females have only a negligible effect on employment opportunities." *Knott* [*v. Missouri P.R. Co.,* 527 F.2d 1249, 1252 (8th Cir. 1975)]. Under established equal burdens analysis, when an employer's grooming and appearance policy does not unreasonably burden one gender more than the other, that policy will not violate Title VII.

Jespersen asks us to take judicial notice of the fact that it costs more money and takes more time for a woman to comply with the makeup requirement than it takes for a man to comply with the requirement that he keep his hair short, but these are not matters appropriate for judicial notice. Judicial notice is reserved for matters "generally known within the territorial jurisdiction of the trial court" or "capable of accurate and ready determination by resort to sources whose accuracy cannot reasonably be questioned." Fed. R. Evid. 201. The time and cost of makeup and haircuts is in neither category. . . .

Having failed to create a record establishing that the "Personal Best" policies are more burdensome for women than for men, Jespersen did not present any triable issue of fact. The district court correctly granted summary judgment on the record before it with respect to Jespersen's claim that the makeup policy created an unequal burden for women.

III.   Sex Stereotyping

[The plaintiff claimed that the makeup requirement constituted unlawful sex stereotyping under *Price Waterhouse.* The en banc court rejected this argument as well.]

The stereotyping in *Price Waterhouse* interfered with Hopkins' ability to perform her work; the advice that she should take "a course at charm school" was intended to discourage her use of the forceful and aggressive techniques that made her successful in the first place. Impermissible sex stereotyping was clear because the very traits that she was asked to hide were the same traits considered praiseworthy in men.

Harrah's "Personal Best" policy is very different. The policy does not single out Jespersen. It applies to all of the bartenders, male and female. It requires all of the bartenders to wear exactly the same uniforms while interacting with the public in the context of the entertainment industry. It is for the most part unisex, from the black tie to the non-skid shoes. There is no evidence in this record to indicate that the policy was adopted to make women bartenders conform to a commonly-accepted stereotypical image of what women should wear. The record contains nothing to suggest the grooming standards would objectively inhibit a woman's ability to do the job. The only evidence in the record to support the stereotyping claim is Jespersen's own subjective reaction to the makeup requirement.

Judge Pregerson's dissent improperly divides the grooming policy into separate categories of hair, hands, and face, and then focuses exclusively on the makeup requirement to conclude that the policy constitutes sex stereotyping. This parsing, however, conflicts with established grooming standards analysis. *See, e.g., Knott* ("Defendant's hair length requirement for male employees is *part of a comprehensive personal grooming code* applicable to all employees.") (Emphasis added). The requirements must be viewed in the context of the overall policy. The dissent's conclusion that the unequal burdens analysis allows impermissible sex stereotyping to persist if imposed equally on both sexes is wrong because it ignores the protections of *Price Waterhouse* our decision preserves. If a grooming standard imposed on either sex amounts to impermissible stereotyping, something this record does not establish, a plaintiff of either sex may challenge that requirement under *Price Waterhouse*.

We respect Jespersen's resolve to be true to herself and to the image that she wishes to project to the world. We cannot agree, however, that her objection to the makeup requirement, without more, can give rise to a claim of sex stereotyping under Title VII. If we were to do so, we would come perilously close to holding that every grooming, apparel, or appearance requirement that an individual finds personally offensive, or in conflict with his or her own self-image, can create a triable issue of sex discrimination.

This is not a case where the dress or appearance requirement is intended to be sexually provocative, and tending to stereotype women as sex objects. *See, e.g., EEOC v. Sage Realty Corp.*, 507 F. Supp. 599 (S.D.N.Y. 1981). In *Sage Realty*, the plaintiff was a lobby attendant in a hotel that employed only female lobby attendants and required a mandatory uniform. The uniform was an octagon designed with an opening for the attendant's head, to be worn as a poncho, with snaps at the wrists and a tack on each side of the poncho, which was otherwise open. The attendants wore blue dancer pants as part of the uniform but were prohibited from wearing a shirt, blouse, or skirt under the outfit. There, the plaintiff was required to wear a uniform that was "short and revealing on both sides [such that her] thighs and portions of her buttocks were exposed." Jespersen, in contrast, was asked only to wear a unisex uniform that covered her entire body and was designed for men and women. The "Personal Best" policy does not, on its face, indicate any discriminatory or sexually stereotypical intent on the part of Harrah's. . . .

We emphasize that we do not preclude, as a matter of law, a claim of sex-stereotyping on the basis of dress or appearance codes. Others may well be filed, and any bases for such claims refined as law in this area evolves. This record, however, is devoid of any basis for permitting this particular claim to go forward, as it is limited to the subjective reaction of a single employee, and there is no evidence of a stereotypical motivation on the part of the employer. This case is essentially a challenge to one small part of what is an overall apparel, appearance, and grooming policy that applies largely the same requirements to both men and women. As we said in *Nichols* in commenting on grooming standards, the touchstone is reasonableness. A makeup requirement must be seen in the context of the overall standards imposed on employees in a given workplace.

[Dissenting opinions omitted.]

NOTES

1. *Separate But Equal.* Perhaps the most blatant remaining form of gender discrimination in employment is dress and grooming codes, which frequently have disparate standards for males and females. The *Jespersen* court correctly observed that different grooming codes or appearance standards for men and women have routinely been upheld by the courts, despite being facially discriminatory. Why? In *Willingham v.*

[Handwritten margin notes:] Is Price Waterhouse the right test? A policy can apply equally to both genders but it can be reinforcement of sex stereotypes. However if a policy applied, per se, would no longer then implicate hair length, that standards of beauty norms. There does not need to be control on appearance of women. Such the life of his own the appearance has over liable for he is not continuously for discrimination connection

[Handwritten margin note:] Interesting emphasis on the individual

Macon Telegraph Publishing Co., 507 F.2d 1084, 1091-92 (5th Cir. 1975) (en banc), the Fifth Circuit denied a man's challenge to an employer's rule prohibiting male (but not female) employees from having hair longer than shoulder length:

> Equal employment *opportunity* may be secured only when employers are barred from discriminating against employees on the basis of immutable characteristics, such as race and national origin. Similarly, an employer cannot have one hiring policy for men and another for women *if* the distinction is based on some fundamental right. But a hiring policy that distinguishes on some other ground, such as grooming codes or length of hair, is related more closely to the employer's choice of how to run his business than to equality of employment opportunity. In [*Phillips v. Martin Marietta*, 400 U.S. 532 (1971),] the Supreme Court condemned a hiring distinction based on having pre-school age children, an existing condition not subject to change. In *Sprogis v. United Air Lines*[, 444 F.2d 1194 (7th Cir. 1971)], the Seventh Circuit reached a similar result with respect to marital status. We have no difficulty with the result reached in those cases; but nevertheless perceive that a line must be drawn between distinctions grounded on such fundamental rights as the right to have children or to marry and those interfering with the manner in which an employer exercises his judgment as to the way to operate a business. Hair length is not immutable and in the situation of employer vis à vis employee enjoys no constitutional protection. If the employee objects to the grooming code he has the right to reject it by looking elsewhere for employment. . . .
>
> We adopt the view, therefore, that distinctions in employment practices between men and women on the basis of something other than immutable or protected characteristics do not inhibit employment *opportunity* in violation of Sec. 703(a). Congress sought only to give all persons equal access to the job market, not to limit an employer's right to exercise his informed judgment as to how best to run his shop.

Willingham's holding that the mere fact of gender-specific differences in dress and grooming codes does not violate Title VII is the accepted view, as the *Jespersen* court notes.

No one seems to doubt that permitting female, but not male, employees to have shoulder-length hair is sex discrimination in an analytic sense. What, then, is the justification for permitting it? Does *Willingham* establish a de minimis test: if the sex distinctions in question are too trivial, they do not warrant federal court intervention? That would explain the court's distinction between cases involving hair length and cases involving "fundamental rights," a concept borrowed from constitutional law. Remember, also, as we saw in Chapter 1, that courts have required different treatment to have material adverse effects in order to constitute discrimination, and *Jespersen* is consistent with that view: the only job requirement she challenged was not a material difference in the terms and conditions of her employment. Moreover, declining protection because the different treatment is considered trivial is consistent with the law's treatment of sexual harassment that is not sufficiently "severe or pervasive," as we shall see in the next section. But sexual harassment becomes actionable when job benefits are contingent on acceptance of the discriminatory remarks or conduct, and here Jespersen lost her job over her refusal to conform to the casino's grooming code. How can this be viewed as trivial?

2. *Separate But Unequal.* While "separate but equal" grooming codes have not been considered illegal, "separate but unequal" requirements have been. Do you agree with *Jespersen* that a grooming code that requires women, but not men, to wear makeup imposes equal burdens on men and women? Do the cases where treatment was found to be unequal help you? In *Carroll v. Talman Federal Savings & Loan Ass'n*, 604 F.2d 1028, 1033 (7th Cir. 1979), the court struck down a policy allowing males to wear "customary business attire," but requiring women to wear uniforms. Different

dress norms were found to be offensive because of "the assumption on which the employer openly admits that rule is based: that women cannot be expected to exercise good judgment in choosing business apparel, whereas men can." What about good judgment regarding facial appearance?

Do you think Jespersen's "unequal burden" claim failed because the court believed the differences in the grooming standards for men and women were really not that significant or because Jespersen failed to introduce evidence of the cost and time involved in applying makeup? Judge Kozinski's dissenting opinion would have upheld Jespersen's "unequal burden" claim, finding that "Harrah's overall grooming policy is substantially more burdensome for women than for men. . . . The requirement that women spend time and money applying full facial makeup has no corresponding requirement for men, making the 'overall policy' more burdensome for the former than for the latter." 444 F.3d at 1117.

We earlier encountered *Bauer v. Lynch*, 812 F.3d 340, 342 (4th Cir. 2016), see p. 97, where the Fourth Circuit found no violation in gender-differentiated FBI standards for recruits training at Quantico, with women required to meet lower levels of specified performance than men. Is that because the standards tried to "normalize testing standards between men and women in order to account for their innate physiological differences"? Why didn't it matter that, unlike dress and grooming codes, meeting the standards was difficult or impossible for the plaintiff? *a man*

3. *Grooming Codes as "Sex Stereotyping."* In addition to her claim that the makeup requirement was facially discriminatory, Jespersen also argued sex stereotyping, relying on *Price Waterhouse*. Why did that claim fail? After all, the casino was requiring its employees to adhere to a stereotypical view of masculine and feminine appearances. Women must wear makeup, and men must not. Judge Pregerson's dissenting opinion found that the plaintiff "articulated a classic case of *Price Waterhouse* discrimination"; as he observed, "[t]he inescapable message is that women's undoctored faces compare unfavorably to men's, not because of a physical difference between men's and women's faces, but because of a cultural assumption — and gender-based stereotype — that women's faces are incomplete, unattractive or unprofessional without full makeup." 444 F.3d at 1116.

What about the flip side of *Jespersen* — women being fired for being too attractive? *Nelson v. James H. Knight DDS, P.C.*, 834 N.W.2d 64 (Iowa 2013), held that an employer did not engage in sex discrimination when he fired a female employee at the request of his wife due to her concerns about the sexual attractiveness of the fired worker, not her involvement in any affair with the boss. Do you agree that this would not violate Title VII? If so, is it because a male could be fired for such a reason? *See* William R. Corbett, *Hotness Discrimination: Appearance Discrimination as a Mirror for Reflecting on the Body of Employment-Discrimination Law*, 60 CATH. U. L. REV. 615 (2011) (discussing an allegation by an employee that she was fired for being "too hot").

4. *The Scholarship.* There is an enormous literature concerning grooming codes and potential race as well as sex discrimination. A few examples include Angela Onwuachi-Willig, *Another Hair Piece, Exploring New Strands of Analysis*, 98 GEO. L.J. 1079, 1087 (2010); D. Wendy Greene, *Black Women Can't Have Blonde Hair . . . in the Workplace*, 14 GENDER, RACE & JUST. 405 (2011); Michael Selmi, *The Many Faces of Darlene Jespersen*, 14 DUKE J. GENDER L. & POL'Y 467 (2007); Dianne Avery & Marion Crain, *Branded: Corporate Image, Sexual Stereotyping, and the New Face of Capitalism*, 14 DUKE J. GENDER L. & POL'Y 13 (2007); Dianne Avery, *The Great American Makeover: The Sexing Up and Dumbing Down of Women's Work After* Jespersen v. Harrah's

Operating Company, Inc., 42 U.S.F. L. Rev. 299 (2007); Kimberly A. Yuracko, *Trait Discrimination as Race Discrimination: An Argument About Assimilation*, 74 Geo. Wash. L. Rev. 365 (2006). There is also scholarship favoring at least a limited right of personal autonomy in dress and grooming apart from any concerns with discrimination. Catherine L. Fisk, *Privacy, Power, and Humiliation at Work: Re-Examining Appearance Regulation as an Invasion of Privacy*, 66 La. L. Rev. 1111 (2006); Gowri Ramachandran, *Freedom of Dress: State and Private Regulation of Clothing, Hairstyle, Jewelry, Makeup, Tattoos, and Piercing*, 66 Md. L. Rev. 11 (2006).

5. *Other Sources of Protection.* Litigants with complaints regarding grooming and dress codes should also explore the possibility of a claim under state or local antidiscrimination provisions. *See generally* Jennifer Bennett Shinall, *Less Is More: Procedural Efficacy in Vindicating Civil Rights*, 68 Ala. L. Rev. 49 (2016).

d.   Discrimination Because of Pregnancy

The central theme of employment discrimination law is the notion that similarly situated individuals should receive equal treatment by employers. But sometimes treating people equally will disadvantage particular groups, which has led to efforts at amelioration by statutory requirements of "reasonable accommodation," treated later in this chapter for religious discrimination and in Chapter 7 for disabilities. In both cases, equal treatment is viewed as not yielding equal outcomes so limited special treatment is required. Disparate impact can also be viewed as a recognition of the reality that equal treatment does not always mean equal opportunity.

These exceptions to the equality principle reflect an alternative theme for employment discrimination law: *equalizing employment opportunity* even for groups who are different in some respects. Title VII's prohibition against discrimination on the basis of pregnancy highlights the tension between equal treatment and equal opportunity inherent in the antidiscrimination project. Pregnancy, childbirth, and related medical conditions affect a woman's ability to work. Most women who carry a child to term will require at least six to eight weeks of leave to deliver the child and physically recover from childbirth. Women who work in jobs that require physical exertion also may be impaired during the latter months of their pregnancy. Given these differences, what constitutes discrimination on the basis of pregnancy? What is *equal* treatment and will it provide pregnant women with equal employment opportunities?

This section will first explore Title VII's response to discrimination on the basis of pregnancy, reflected largely in the Pregnancy Discrimination Act, and will then consider whether Title VII adequately addresses the problems faced by fertile women in the workplace. In this latter regard, we will briefly examine the federal statute most directly addressing this and similar problems, the Family and Medical Leave Act of 1993.

The Supreme Court's first encounter with the question of pregnancy discrimination was not auspicious. In *General Electric Co. v. Gilbert*, 429 U.S. 125 (1976), the Court concluded that discrimination on the basis of pregnancy was *not* discrimination on the basis of sex within the meaning of Title VII. *Gilbert* involved an employer-sponsored disability insurance plan that excluded pregnancy from coverage. The Court followed Fourteenth Amendment equal protection precedent established in *Geduldig v. Aiello*, 417 U.S. 484 (1974), holding that pregnancy classifications are not gender classifications. In reaching its result, the *Gilbert* Court quoted from a footnote in *Geduldig*:

> The lack of identity between the excluded disability [pregnancy] and gender as such . . . becomes clear upon the most cursory analysis. The program divides potential recipients

into two groups — pregnant women and nonpregnant persons. While the first group is exclusively female, the second includes members of both sexes.

429 U.S. at 135. *See also AT&T Corp. v. Hulteen*, 556 U.S. 701 (2009) (since the PDA was not retroactive, a policy providing less retirement credit for pre-PDA pregnancy leave than for other medical leave was permissible under *Gilbert* and so not discriminatory within the meaning of Title VII).

Public reaction to what was seen as a contrived distinction led Congress to soon overrule *Gilbert* by passing the Pregnancy Discrimination Act of 1978, Pub. L. No. 95-555, 92 Stat. 2076 (Oct. 31, 1978), which amended Title VII to include a new §701(k):

> The terms "because of sex" or "on the basis of sex" include, but are not limited to, because of or on the basis of pregnancy, childbirth, or related medical conditions; and women affected by pregnancy, childbirth, or related medical conditions shall be treated the same for all employment-related purposes, including receipt of benefits under fringe benefit programs, as other persons not so affected but similar in their ability or inability to work, and nothing in section 703(h) of this title shall be interpreted to permit otherwise. . . .

[handwritten margin note: unclear wording]

This seemingly simple sentence generated enormous confusion in the courts, in part because of the relationship between the two clauses. The Supreme Court's most important encounter with the statute did not occur until nearly 40 years after its passage.

YOUNG v. UPS
135 S. Ct. 1338 (2015)

[handwritten margin note: disparate treatment → needs to show intent]

Justice BREYER delivered the opinion of the Court.

The Pregnancy Discrimination Act makes clear that Title VII's prohibition against sex discrimination applies to discrimination based on pregnancy. It also says that employers must treat "women affected by pregnancy . . . the same for all employment-related purposes . . . as other persons not so affected but similar in their ability or inability to work." 42 U.S.C. §2000e(k). We must decide how this latter provision applies in the context of an employer's policy that accommodates many, but not all, workers with nonpregnancy-related disabilities.

In our view, the Act requires courts to consider the extent to which an employer's policy treats pregnant workers less favorably than it treats nonpregnant workers similar in their ability or inability to work. And here — as in all cases in which an individual plaintiff seeks to show disparate treatment through indirect evidence — it requires courts to consider any legitimate, nondiscriminatory, nonpretextual justification for these differences in treatment. See *McDonnell Douglas Corp. v. Green*. Ultimately the court must determine whether the nature of the employer's policy and the way in which it burdens pregnant women shows that the employer has engaged in intentional discrimination. The Court of Appeals here affirmed a grant of summary judgment in favor of the employer. Given our view of the law, we must vacate that court's judgment.

I

A

[Peggy Young was informed by her doctor that she should not lift more than 20 pounds during the first 20 weeks of her pregnancy or more than 10 pounds thereafter. Drivers like Young are normally required to be able to lift parcels weighing up to 70 pounds (and up to 150 pounds with assistance), and UPS told Young she could not work while under a lifting restriction, which caused her loss of pay and eventual loss of medical coverage. She sued, claiming that UPS was required to accommodate her pregnancy-related lifting restriction. She argued both that her co-workers were willing to help her with heavy packages and that UPS accommodated other drivers "similar in their . . . inability to work."]

UPS responded that the "other persons" whom it had accommodated were (1) drivers who had become disabled on the job, (2) those who had lost their Department of Transportation (DOT) certifications, and (3) those who suffered from a disability covered by the Americans with Disabilities Act of 1990. UPS said that, since Young did not fall within any of those categories, it had not discriminated against Young on the basis of pregnancy but had treated her just as it treated all "other" relevant "persons."

B

[The Court noted a tension between the PDA's first clause — providing that "because of sex" includes "because of or on the basis of pregnancy, childbirth, or related medical conditions" — and its second clause — requiring that women affected by those conditions "shall be treated the same for all employment-related purposes . . . as other persons not so affected but similar in their ability or inability to work. . . ."]

This case requires us to consider the application of the second clause to a "disparate-treatment" claim — a claim that an employer intentionally treated a complainant less favorably than employees with the "complainant's qualifications" but outside the complainant's protected class. *McDonnell Douglas.* We have said that "[l]iability in a disparate-treatment case depends on whether the protected trait actually motivated the employer's decision." *Raytheon Co. v. Hernandez*, 540 U.S. 44, 52 (2003). We have also made clear that a plaintiff can prove disparate treatment either (1) by direct evidence that a workplace policy, practice, or decision relies expressly on a protected characteristic, or (2) by using the burden-shifting framework set forth in *McDonnell Douglas.* See *Trans World Airlines, Inc. v. Thurston*, 469 U.S. 111 (1985).

[Noting that Young had not alleged either a disparate impact or a "pattern-or-practice" claim, the majority described the *McDonnell Douglas* litigation structure, and went on:] Young pointed to favorable facts that she believed were either undisputed or that, while disputed, she could prove. They include the following:

1. Young worked as a UPS driver, picking up and delivering packages carried by air.

2. Young was pregnant in the fall of 2006.

3. Young's doctor recommended that she "not be required to lift greater than 20 pounds for the first 20 weeks of pregnancy and no greater than 10 pounds thereafter."

4. UPS required drivers such as Young to be able to "[l]ift, lower, push, pull, leverage and manipulate . . . packages weighing up to 70 pounds" and to "[a]ssist in moving packages weighing up to 150 pounds."

5. UPS' occupational health manager, the official "responsible for most issues relating to employee health and ability to work" at Young's UPS facility, told Young that she could not return to work during her pregnancy because she could not satisfy UPS' lifting requirements.

6. The manager also determined that Young did not qualify for a temporary alternative work assignment.

7. UPS, in a collective-bargaining agreement, had promised to provide temporary alternative work assignments to employees "unable to perform their normal work assignments due to an *on-the-job* injury." (emphasis added).

8. The collective-bargaining agreement also provided that UPS would "make a good faith effort to comply . . . with requests for a reasonable accommodation because of a permanent disability" under the ADA.

9. The agreement further stated that UPS would give "inside" jobs to drivers who had lost their DOT certifications because of a failed medical exam, a lost driver's license, or involvement in a motor vehicle accident.

10. When Young later asked UPS' Capital Division Manager to accommodate her disability, he replied that, while she was pregnant, she was "too much of a liability" and could "not come back" until she "'was no longer pregnant.'"

11. Young remained on a leave of absence (without pay) for much of her pregnancy.

12. Young returned to work as a driver in June 2007, about two months after her baby was born.

As direct evidence of intentional discrimination, Young relied, in significant part, on the statement of the Capital Division Manager (10 above). As evidence that she had made out a prima facie case under *McDonnell Douglas*, Young relied, in significant part, on evidence showing that UPS would accommodate workers injured on the job (7), those suffering from ADA disabilities (8), and those who had lost their DOT certifications (9). That evidence, she said, showed that UPS had a light-duty-for-injury policy with respect to numerous "other persons," but not with respect to pregnant workers.

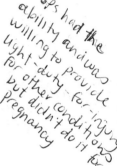

UPS had the ability and was willing to provide light-duty-for-injury for other conditions but didn't do it for Pregnancy

Young introduced further evidence indicating that UPS had accommodated several individuals when they suffered disabilities that created work restrictions similar to hers. [Viewed in the light most favorable to Young in the summary judgment context, this evidence was:]

13. Several employees received accommodations while suffering various similar or more serious disabilities incurred on the job [a 10-pound lifting limitation, foot injury, and an arm injury].

14. Several employees received accommodations following injury, where the record is unclear as to whether the injury was incurred on or off the job [recurring knee injury, ankle injury, knee injury, stroke, and leg injury].

15. Several employees received "inside" jobs after losing their DOT certifications [for a DUI conviction, high blood pressure, and sleep apnea diagnosis].

accommodation for poor outside choices

16. Some employees were accommodated despite the fact that their disabilities had been incurred off the job.

17. According to a deposition of a UPS shop steward who had worked for UPS for roughly a decade, "the only light duty requested [due to physical] restrictions that became an issue" at UPS "were with women who were pregnant."

[The District Court granted UPS's motion for summary judgment and the Fourth Circuit affirmed.]

D

[The majority noted that the ADA Amendments Act of 2008 "may limit the future significance of our interpretation" of the PDA by expanding the definition of "disability" to require employers to accommodate employees whose temporary lifting restrictions originate off the job. *See* 29 C.F.R. pt. 1630, App., §1630.2(j)(1)(ix). But it "express[ed] no view on these statutory and regulatory changes." See p. 445.]

II

Issue

The parties disagree about the interpretation of the Pregnancy Discrimination Act's second clause. As we have said, the Act's first clause specifies that discrimination "'because of sex'" includes discrimination "because of . . . pregnancy." But the meaning of the second clause is less clear; it adds: "[W]omen affected by pregnancy, childbirth, or related medical conditions shall be treated the same for all employment-related purposes . . . as *other persons* not so affected but *similar in their ability or inability to work*." 42 U.S.C. §2000e(k) (emphasis added). Does this clause mean that courts must compare workers *only* in respect to the work limitations that they suffer? Does it mean that courts must ignore all other similarities or differences between pregnant and nonpregnant workers? Or does it mean that courts, when deciding who the relevant "other persons" are, may consider other similarities and differences as well? If so, which ones?

The differences between these possible interpretations come to the fore when a court, as here, must consider a workplace policy that distinguishes between pregnant and nonpregnant workers in light of characteristics not related to pregnancy. Young poses the problem directly in her reply brief when she says that the Act requires giving "the same accommodations to an employee with a pregnancy-related work limitation as it would give *that employee* if her work limitation stemmed from a different cause but had a similar effect on her inability to work." Suppose the employer would not give "*that [pregnant] employee*" the "same accommodations" as another employee, but the employer's reason for the difference in treatment is that the pregnant worker falls within a facially neutral category (for example, individuals with off-the-job injuries). What is a court then to do?

P's interpret of 2nd clause

Court says it is too broad

The parties propose very different answers to this question. Young and the United States believe that the second clause of the Pregnancy Discrimination Act "requires an employer to provide the same accommodations to workplace disabilities caused by pregnancy that it provides to workplace disabilities that have other causes but have a similar effect on the ability to work." In other words, Young contends that the second clause means that whenever "an employer accommodates only a subset of workers with disabling conditions," a court should find a Title VII violation if "pregnant workers who are similar in the ability to work" do not "receive the same [accommodation] even if still other non-pregnant workers do not receive accommodations."

π's arg.

UPS takes an almost polar opposite view. It contends that the second clause does no more than define sex discrimination to include pregnancy discrimination. Under this view, courts would compare the accommodations an employer provides to pregnant women with the accommodations it provides to others *within* a facially neutral category (such as those with off-the-job injuries) to determine whether the employer has violated Title VII. Cf. (Scalia, J., dissenting) (hereinafter the dissent).

Δ's arg

A

We cannot accept either of these interpretations. Young asks us to interpret the second clause broadly and, in her view, literally. As just noted, she argues that, as long as "an employer accommodates only a subset of workers with disabling conditions," "pregnant workers who are similar in the ability to work [must] receive the same treatment even if still other nonpregnant workers do not receive accommodations." She adds that, because the record here contains "evidence that pregnant and nonpregnant workers were not treated the same," that is the end of the matter, she must win; there is no need to refer to *McDonnell Douglas*.

The problem with Young's approach is that it proves too much. It seems to say that the statute grants pregnant workers a "most-favored-nation" status. As long as an employer provides one or two workers with an accommodation — say, those with particularly hazardous jobs, or those whose workplace presence is particularly needed, or those who have worked at the company for many years, or those who are over the age of 55 — then it must provide similar accommodations to *all* pregnant workers (with comparable physical limitations), irrespective of the nature of their jobs, the employer's need to keep them working, their ages, or any other criteria.

Lower courts have concluded that this could not have been Congress' intent in passing the Pregnancy Discrimination Act. [Young conceded that the statute did not require pregnant workers to get benefits "based on the employee's tenure or position within the company," such as seniority, full-time work, and different job classifications, but the Court did not see why (other than the statutory protection of seniority) these should be treated differently than,] say, extra-hazardous duty[.] If Congress intended to allow differences in treatment arising out of special duties, special service, or special needs, why would it not also have wanted courts to take account of differences arising out of special "causes" — for example, benefits for those who drive (and are injured) in extra-hazardous conditions?

We agree with UPS to this extent: We doubt that Congress intended to grant pregnant workers an unconditional most-favored-nation status. The language of the statute does not require that unqualified reading. The second clause, when referring to nonpregnant persons with similar disabilities, uses the open-ended term "other persons." It does not say that the employer must treat pregnant employees the "same" as "*any* other persons" (who are similar in their ability or inability to work), nor does it otherwise specify *which* other persons Congress had in mind.

Moreover, disparate-treatment law normally permits an employer to implement policies that are not intended to harm members of a protected class, even if their implementation sometimes harms those members, as long as the employer has a legitimate, nondiscriminatory, nonpretextual reason for doing so. See, *e.g.*, *Raytheon*; *Burdine*; *McDonnell Douglas*. There is no reason to believe Congress intended its language in the Pregnancy Discrimination Act to embody a significant deviation from this approach. Indeed, the relevant House Report specifies that the Act "reflect[s] no new legislative mandate." H.R. Rep. No. 95-948, pp. 3-4 (1978) (hereinafter H.R. Rep.). And the Senate Report states that the Act was designed to "reestablis[h] the law as it was understood prior to" this Court's decision in *General Electric Co. v. Gilbert*. S. Rep. No. 95-331, p. 8 (1978) (hereinafter S. Rep.).

B

[The Court traced the somewhat inconsistent history of EEOC pronouncements. After certiorari had been granted in *Young*, the EEOC promulgated a guideline barring employers from looking to the source of an employee's limitations in any policy regarding accommodations. The majority refused to defer to this guidance in part because it seemed tailored to the present case, in part because its position was inconsistent with those the government has long advocated, and in part because the position was insufficiently rationalized.]

C

We find it similarly difficult to accept the opposite interpretation of the Act's second clause. UPS says that the second clause simply defines sex discrimination to include ∆'s arg pregnancy discrimination. But that cannot be so.

The first clause accomplishes that objective when it expressly amends Title VII's definitional provision to make clear that Title VII's words "because of sex" and "on the basis of sex" "include, but are not limited to, because of or on the basis of pregnancy, childbirth, or related medical conditions." 42 U.S.C. §2000e(k). We have long held that "'a statute ought, upon the whole, to be so construed that, if it can be prevented, no clause'" is rendered "'superfluous, void, or insignificant.'" *TRW Inc. v. Andrews*, 534 U.S. 19, 31 (2001). But that is what UPS' interpretation of the second clause would do.

The dissent, basically accepting UPS' interpretation, says that the second clause is not "superfluous" because it adds "clarity." It makes "plain," the dissent adds, that unlawful discrimination "includes disfavoring pregnant women relative to other workers of similar inability to work." Perhaps we fail to understand. *McDonnell Douglas* itself makes clear that courts normally consider how a plaintiff was treated relative to other "persons of [the plaintiff's] qualifications" (which here include disabilities). If the second clause of the Act did not exist, we would still say that an employer who disfavored pregnant women relative to other workers of similar ability or inability to work had engaged in pregnancy discrimination. In a word, there is no need for the "clarification" that the dissent suggests the second sentence provides.

Moreover, the interpretation espoused by UPS and the dissent would fail to carry out an important congressional objective. [The PDA was designed to overturn both the holding and the reasoning of *Gilbert*, which had upheld a plan denying pregnancy-related health benefits because pregnancy was not comparable to the conditions covered by the plan since it was not a "disease" nor necessarily a result of accident.] In short, the *Gilbert* majority reasoned in part just as the dissent reasons here. The employer did "not distinguish between pregnant women and others of similar ability or inability *because of pregnancy*." It distinguished between them on a neutral ground — *i.e.*, it accommodated only sicknesses and accidents, and pregnancy was neither of those.

Simply including pregnancy among Title VII's protected traits (*i.e.*, accepting UPS' interpretation) would not overturn *Gilbert* in full — in particular, it would not respond to *Gilbert*'s determination that an employer can treat pregnancy less favorably than diseases or disabilities resulting in a similar inability to work. . . .

III

The statute lends itself to an interpretation other than those that the parties advocate and that the dissent sets forth. Our interpretation minimizes the problems we have discussed, responds directly to *Gilbert*, and is consistent with longstanding interpretations of Title VII.

In our view, an individual pregnant worker who seeks to show disparate treatment through indirect evidence may do so through application of the *McDonnell Douglas* framework. That framework requires a plaintiff to make out a prima facie case of discrimination. But it is "not intended to be an inflexible rule." *Furnco Constr. Corp. v. Waters*, 438 U.S. 567, 575 (1978). Rather, an individual plaintiff may establish a prima facie case by "showing actions taken by the employer from which one can infer, if such actions remain unexplained, that it is more likely than not that such actions were based on a discriminatory criterion illegal under" Title VII. *Id*. The burden of making this showing is "not onerous." *Burdine*. In particular, making this showing is not as burdensome as succeeding on "an ultimate finding of fact as to" a discriminatory employment action. *Furnco*. Neither does it require the plaintiff to show that those whom the employer favored and those whom the employer disfavored were similar in all but the protected ways. See *McDonnell Douglas* (burden met where plaintiff showed that employer hired other "qualified" individuals outside the protected class); *Furnco* (same); *Burdine* (same). Cf. *Reeves v. Sanderson Plumbing Products, Inc.*, 530 U.S. 133, 142 (2000) (similar).

Thus, a plaintiff alleging that the denial of an accommodation constituted disparate treatment under the Pregnancy Discrimination Act's second clause may make out a prima facie case by showing, as in *McDonnell Douglas*, that she belongs to the protected class, that she sought accommodation, that the employer did not accommodate her, and that the employer did accommodate others "similar in their ability or inability to work."

The employer may then seek to justify its refusal to accommodate the plaintiff by relying on "legitimate, nondiscriminatory" reasons for denying her accommodation. But, consistent with the Act's basic objective, that reason normally cannot consist simply of a claim that it is more expensive or less convenient to add pregnant women to the category of those ("similar in their ability or inability to work") whom the employer accommodates. After all, the employer in *Gilbert* could in all likelihood have made just such a claim.

If the employer offers an apparently "legitimate, non-discriminatory" reason for its actions, the plaintiff may in turn show that the employer's proffered reasons are in fact pretextual. We believe that the plaintiff may reach a jury on this issue by providing sufficient evidence that the employer's policies impose a significant burden on pregnant workers, and that the employer's "legitimate, nondiscriminatory" reasons are not sufficiently strong to justify the burden, but rather — when considered along with the burden imposed — give rise to an inference of intentional discrimination.

The plaintiff can create a genuine issue of material fact as to whether a significant burden exists by providing evidence that the employer accommodates a large percentage of nonpregnant workers while failing to accommodate a large percentage of pregnant workers. Here, for example, if the facts are as Young says they are, she can show that UPS accommodates most nonpregnant employees with lifting limitations while categorically failing to accommodate pregnant employees with lifting limitations. Young might also add that the fact that UPS has multiple policies that accommodate nonpregnant employees with lifting restrictions suggests that its reasons for failing to accommodate pregnant employees with lifting restrictions are not sufficiently strong — to the point that a jury could find that its reasons for failing to accommodate pregnant employees give rise to an inference of intentional discrimination.

This approach, though limited to the Pregnancy Discrimination Act context, is consistent with our longstanding rule that a plaintiff can use circumstantial proof to rebut an employer's apparently legitimate, nondiscriminatory reasons for treating individuals within a protected class differently than those outside the protected class. See *Burdine*. In particular, it is hardly anomalous (as the dissent makes it out to be) that a plaintiff may rebut an employer's proffered justifications by showing how a policy operates in practice. In *McDonnell Douglas* itself, we noted that an employer's "general policy and practice with respect to minority employment" — including "statistics as to" that policy and practice — could be evidence of pretext. Moreover, the continued focus on whether the plaintiff has introduced sufficient evidence to give rise to an inference of *intentional* discrimination avoids confusing the disparate-treatment and disparate-impact doctrines. . . .

IV

[Under this interpretation, there was adequate evidence to deny the defendant summary judgment.] Viewing the record in the light most favorable to Young, there is a genuine dispute as to whether UPS provided more favorable treatment to at least some employees whose situation cannot reasonably be distinguished from Young's. In other words, Young created a genuine dispute of material fact as to the fourth prong of the *McDonnell Douglas* analysis.

Young also introduced evidence that UPS had three separate accommodation policies (on-the-job, ADA, DOT). Taken together, Young argued, these policies significantly burdened pregnant women. [Citing shop steward's testimony that "the only light duty requested [due to physical] restrictions that became an issue" at UPS "were with women who were pregnant."] The Fourth Circuit did not consider the combined effects of these policies, nor did it consider the strength of UPS' justifications for each when combined. That is, why, when the employer accommodated so many, could it not accommodate pregnant women as well?

just reverses summary judgment

We do not determine whether Young created a genuine issue of material fact as to whether UPS' reasons for having treated Young less favorably than it treated these other nonpregnant employees were pretextual. We leave a final determination of that question for the Fourth Circuit to make on remand, in light of the interpretation of the Pregnancy Discrimination Act that we have set out above. . . .

Justice ALITO, concurring in the judgment.

[The concurrence read the first clause to require "an employer's intent to discriminate because of or on the basis of pregnancy." The second clause "raises more difficult questions of interpretation," but "does not merely explain but instead adds to the language that precedes it," a reading consistent with the statutory text's use of the word "and." Further, the "second clause makes no reference to intent": it "is an affirmative command (an employer 'shall' provide equal treatment), while the first clause is negative (it prohibits discrimination)." Finally, if the second clause does not set out an additional restriction on employer conduct, it would appear to be largely, if not entirely, superfluous.]

job-dependent, not disability-dependent

This leads to the second question: In determining whether pregnant employees have been given the equal treatment that this provision demands, with whom must the pregnant employees be compared? I interpret the second clause to mean that pregnant employees must be compared with employees performing the same or very similar jobs. Pregnant employees, the second provision states, must be given the same treatment as other employees who are "similar in their ability or inability to work." An employee's ability to work — despite illness, injury, or pregnancy — often depends on the tasks that the employee's job includes. Different jobs have different tasks, and different tasks require different abilities. Suppose that an employer provides a period of leave with pay for employees whose jobs require tasks, *e.g.*, lifting heavy objects, that they cannot perform because of illness or injury. Must the employer provide the same benefits for pregnant employees who are unable to lift heavy objects but have desk jobs that do not entail heavy lifting? The answer is no. The treatment of pregnant employees must be compared with the treatment of nonpregnant employees whose jobs involve the performance of the same or very similar tasks. . . .

This conclusion leads to a third, even more difficult question: When comparing pregnant employees to nonpregnant employees in similar jobs, which characteristics of the pregnant and nonpregnant employees must be taken into account? The answer, I believe, must be found in the reference to "other employees who are similar in their ability or inability to work." I see two possible interpretations of this language. The first is that the capacity to perform the tasks required by a job is the only relevant characteristic, but like the Court, I cannot accept this "most favored employee" interpretation. . . .

Recall that the second clause of §2000e(k) requires that pregnant women "be treated the same for all employment-related purposes . . . as *other persons* not so affected but similar in their ability or inability to work." (Emphasis added.) Therefore, UPS could say that its policy treated the pregnant employees the same as "other persons" who were similar in their ability or inability to work, namely, those nonpregnant employees [who were not accommodated]. But at the same time, the pregnant drivers like petitioner could say that UPS did not treat them the same as "other employees" who were similar in their ability or inability to work, namely, the nonpregnant employees [who were accommodated]. An interpretation that leads to such a problem cannot be correct.

I therefore turn to the other possible interpretation of the phrase "similar in their ability or inability to work," namely, that "similar in the ability or inability to work" means "similar *in relation* to the ability or inability to work." Under this interpretation, pregnant and nonpregnant employees are not similar in relation to the ability or inability to work if they are unable to work for different reasons. And this means that these two groups of employees are not similar in the relevant sense if the employer has a neutral business reason for treating them differently. I agree with the Court that a sufficient reason "normally cannot consist simply of a claim that it is more expensive or less convenient to add pregnant women to the category of those . . . whom the employer accommodates."[5] Otherwise, however, I do not think that the second clause of the PDA authorizes courts to evaluate the justification for a truly neutral rule. The language used in the second clause of the PDA is quite different from that used in other anti-discrimination provisions that require such an evaluation. Cf. §12112(b)(5)(A) [ADA provision requiring reasonable accommodation of disabilities]; §2000e(j) [Title VII prohibition requiring reasonable accommodation of religion]; §2000e-2(k)(1)(A)(i) (business necessity defense in Title VII disparate-impact cases).

III

[Justice Alito agreed with the majority that the record was "sufficient (albeit barely)" to survive summary judgment under the first clause, but also agreed that summary judgement should be denied under the second clause. Under the UPS policy, drivers physically unable to perform the usual tasks of the position fell into three groups.]

First, some drivers were reassigned to less physically demanding positions. Included in this group were (a) those who were unable to work as drivers due to an injury incurred on the job, (b) those drivers who were unable to work as drivers due to a disability as defined by the Americans With Disabilities Act of 1990 (ADA), and (c) those drivers who, as the result of a medical condition or injury, lost the Department of Transportation (DOT) certification needed to work in that capacity.

The second group of drivers consisted of those who were not pregnant and were denied transfer to a light-duty job. Drivers who were injured off the job fell into this category. The third group was made up of pregnant drivers like petitioner.

It is obvious that respondent had a neutral reason for providing an accommodation when that was required by the ADA. Respondent also had neutral grounds for providing special accommodations for employees who were injured on the job [since otherwise they would been eligible for workers' compensation benefits].

---

5. If cost alone could justify unequal treatment of pregnant employees, the plan at issue in *General Electric Co. v. Gilbert* would be lawful. But this Court has repeatedly said that the PDA rejected "'both the holding and the reasoning'" in *Gilbert*.

The accommodations that are provided to drivers who lost their DOT certifications, however, are another matter. A driver may lose DOT certification for a variety of reasons, including medical conditions or injuries incurred off the job that impair the driver's ability to operate a motor vehicle. Such drivers may then be transferred to jobs that do not require physical tasks incompatible with their illness or injury. It does not appear that respondent has provided any plausible justification for treating these drivers more favorably than drivers who were pregnant.

The Court of Appeals provided two grounds for distinguishing petitioner's situation from that of the drivers who had lost their DOT certifications, but neither is adequate. First, the Court of Appeals noted that "no legal obstacle [stood] between [petitioner] and her work." But the legal obstacle faced by drivers who have lost DOT certification only explains why those drivers could not continue to perform all the tasks required by their ordinary jobs; it does not explain why respondent went further and *provided such drivers with a work accommodation.* Petitioner's pregnancy prevented her from continuing her normal work as a driver, just as is the case for a driver who loses DOT certification. But respondent had a policy of accommodating drivers who lost DOT certification but not accommodating pregnant women, like petitioner. The legal obstacle of lost certification cannot explain this difference in treatment.

[The concurrence doubted that all workers who lost DOT certification maintained the ability to perform any number of demanding physical tasks. Despite that, UPS's policy was to transfer them to available "inside" jobs. Since UPS presumably did not assign these drivers to jobs that they were physically unable to perform] in at least some instances, they must have been assigned to jobs that did not require them to perform tasks that they were incapable of performing due to the medical condition that caused the loss of DOT certification. Respondent has not explained why pregnant drivers could not have been given similar consideration. . . .

Justice SCALIA, with whom Justice KENNEDY and Justice THOMAS join, dissenting.

Faced with two conceivable readings of the Pregnancy Discrimination Act, the Court chooses neither. It crafts instead a new law that is splendidly unconnected with the text and even the legislative history of the Act. To "treat" pregnant workers "the same . . . as other persons," we are told, means refraining from adopting policies that impose "significant burden[s]" upon pregnant women without "sufficiently strong" justifications. Where do the "significant burden" and "sufficiently strong justification" requirements come from? Inventiveness posing as scholarship — which gives us an interpretation that is as dubious in principle as it is senseless in practice.

I . . .

[Plaintiff did not establish liability under either the disparate treatment or disparate impact theories, which forced Young and the Court to turn to §2000e(k). But the] most natural way to understand the same-treatment clause is that an employer may not distinguish between pregnant women and others of similar ability or inability *because of pregnancy.* Here, that means pregnant women are entitled to accommodations *on the same terms* as other workers with disabling conditions. If a pregnant woman is denied an accommodation under a policy that does not discriminate against pregnancy, she *has* been "treated the same" as everyone else. UPS's accommodation for drivers who lose their certifications illustrates the point. A pregnant woman who loses her certification gets the benefit, just like any other worker who loses his. And a pregnant woman who keeps her certification does not get the benefit, again just like any other worker who keeps his. That certainly sounds like treating pregnant women and others the same. . . .

. . . The point of Title VII's bans on discrimination is to prohibit employers from treating one worker differently from another *because of a protected trait*. It is not to prohibit employers from treating workers differently for reasons that have nothing to do with protected traits. . . .

Prohibiting employers from making *any* distinctions between pregnant workers and others of similar ability would elevate pregnant workers to most favored employees. If Boeing offered chauffeurs to injured directors, it would have to offer chauffeurs to pregnant mechanics. And if Disney paid pensions to workers who can no longer work because of old age, it would have to pay pensions to workers who can no longer work because of childbirth. It is implausible that Title VII, which elsewhere creates guarantees of *equal* treatment, here alone creates a guarantee of *favored* treatment. . . .

II

The Court agrees that the same-treatment clause is not a most-favored-employee law, but at the same time refuses to adopt the reading I propose — which is the only other reading the clause could conceivably bear. The Court's reasons for resisting this reading fail to persuade.

The Court starts by arguing that the same-treatment clause must do more than ban distinctions on the basis of pregnancy, lest it add nothing to the part of the Act defining pregnancy discrimination as sex discrimination. Even so read, however, the same-treatment clause *does* add something: clarity. Just defining pregnancy discrimination as sex discrimination does not tell us what it means to discriminate because of pregnancy. Does pregnancy discrimination include, in addition to disfavoring pregnant women relative to the workplace in general, disfavoring them relative to disabled workers in particular? Concretely, does an employer engage in pregnancy discrimination by excluding pregnancy from an otherwise complete disability-benefits program? Without the same-treatment clause, the answers to these questions would not be obvious. . . .

[handwritten margin note: Supports that 2nd arg to clarify the 1st that pregnancy = sex]

This clarifying function easily overcomes any charge that the reading I propose makes the same-treatment clause "'superfluous, void, or insignificant.'" Perhaps, as the Court suggests, even without the same-treatment clause the best reading of the Act would prohibit disfavoring pregnant women relative to disabled workers. But laws often make explicit what might already have been implicit, "for greater caution" and in order "to leave nothing to construction." . . .

That brings me to the Court's remaining argument: the claim that the reading I have set forth would not suffice to overturn our decision in *Gilbert*. Wrong. *Gilbert* upheld an otherwise comprehensive disability-benefits plan that singled pregnancy out for disfavor. The most natural reading of the Act overturns that decision, because it prohibits singling pregnancy out for disfavor.

The Court goes astray here because it mistakenly assumes that the *Gilbert* plan excluded pregnancy on "a neutral ground" — covering sicknesses and accidents but nothing else. In reality, the plan in *Gilbert* was not neutral toward pregnancy [citing the dissenters in *Gilbert* to this effect].

III

Dissatisfied with the only two readings that the words of the same-treatment clause could possibly bear, the Court decides that the clause means something in-between. It takes only a couple of waves of the Supreme Wand to produce the desired result.

Poof!: The same-treatment clause means that a neutral reason for refusing to accommodate a pregnant woman is pretextual if "the employer's policies impose a significant burden on pregnant workers." Poof!: This is so only when the employer's reasons "are not sufficiently strong to justify the burden."

How we got here from the same-treatment clause is anyone's guess. There is no way to read "shall be treated the same" — or indeed anything else in the clause — to mean that courts must balance the significance of the burden on pregnant workers against the strength of the employer's justifications for the policy. That is presumably why the Court does not even *try* to connect the interpretation it adopts with the text it purports to interpret. The Court has forgotten that statutory purpose and the presumption against superfluity are tools for choosing among competing reasonable readings of a law, not authorizations for making up new readings that the law cannot reasonably bear.

The fun does not stop there. Having ignored the terms of the same-treatment clause, the Court proceeds to bungle the dichotomy between claims of disparate treatment and claims of disparate impact. Normally, liability for disparate treatment arises when an employment policy has a "discriminatory motive," while liability for disparate impact arises when the effects of an employment policy "fall more harshly on one group than another and cannot be justified by business necessity." *Teamsters*. In the topsy-turvy world created by today's decision, however, a pregnant woman can establish disparate *treatment* by showing that the *effects* of her employer's policy fall more harshly on pregnant women than on others (the policies "impose a significant burden on pregnant workers," and are inadequately justified (the "reasons are not sufficiently strong to justify the burden"). The change in labels may be small, but the change in results assuredly is not. Disparate-treatment and disparate-impact claims come with different standards of liability, different defenses, and different remedies. §§1981a, 2000e-2(k). For example, plaintiffs in disparate-treatment cases can get compensatory and punitive damages as well as equitable relief, but plaintiffs in disparate impact cases can get equitable relief only. See §§1981a, 2000e-5(g). A sound reading of the same-treatment clause would preserve the distinctions so carefully made elsewhere in the Act; the Court's reading makes a muddle of them.

But (believe it or not) it gets worse. In order to make sense of its conflation of disparate impact with disparate treatment, the Court claims that its new test is somehow "limited to the Pregnancy Discrimination Act context," yet at the same time "consistent with" the traditional use of circumstantial evidence to show intent to discriminate in Title VII cases. A court in a Title VII case, true enough, may consider a policy's effects and even its justifications — along with "'all of the [other] surrounding facts and circumstances'" — when trying to ferret out a policy's motive. *Hazelwood School Dist. v. United States*. The Court cannot possibly think, however, that its newfangled balancing test reflects this conventional inquiry. It has, after all, just marched up and down the hill telling us that the same-treatment clause is not (no-no!) "'superfluous, void, or insignificant.'" If the clause merely instructed courts to consider a policy's effects and justifications the way it considers other circumstantial evidence of motive, it *would* be superfluous. So the Court's balancing test must mean something else. Even if the effects and justifications of policies are not enough to show intent to discriminate under ordinary Title VII principles, they could (Poof!) still show intent to discriminate for purposes of the pregnancy same-treatment clause. Deliciously incoherent.

And all of this to what end? The difference between a routine circumstantial-evidence inquiry into motive and today's grotesque effects-and-justifications inquiry into motive, it would seem, is that today's approach requires judges to concentrate on effects and justifications to the exclusion of other considerations. But Title VII *already* has a framework that allows judges to home in on a policy's effects and justifications — disparate impact. Under that framework, it is *already* unlawful for an employer to use a practice that has a disparate impact on the basis of a protected trait, unless (among other things) the employer can show that the practice "is job related . . . and consistent with business necessity." §2000e-2(k)(1)(A)(i). The Court does not explain why we need (never mind how the Act could possibly be read to contain) today's ersatz disparate-impact test, under which the disparate-impact element gives way to the significant-burden criterion and the business-necessity defense gives way to the sufficiently-strong-justification standard. Today's decision can thus serve only one purpose: allowing claims that belong under Title VII's disparate-impact provisions to be brought under its disparate-treatment provisions instead.

[handwritten margin note: this should be disparate impact, not disparate treatment]

IV

[The dissent also took issue with Justice Alito's concurrence for allowing an employer to] deny a pregnant woman a benefit granted to workers who perform similar tasks only on the basis of a "neutral business ground." This requirement of a "business ground" shadows the Court's requirement of a "sufficiently strong" justification, and, like it, has no footing in the terms of the same-treatment clause. . . . [His] need to engage in this text-free broadening in order to make the concurrence's interpretation work is as good a sign as any that its interpretation is wrong from the start. . . .

Justice KENNEDY, dissenting.

[Although joining Justice Scalia's dissent, Justice Kennedy's separate dissent had "little doubt that women who are in the work force — by choice, by financial necessity, or both — confront a serious disadvantage after becoming pregnant." This reality is partially addressed by the PDA and the parental leave provisions of the FMLA, and perhaps by the ADA Amendments Act of 2008, whose implementing regulations "may require accommodations for many pregnant employees, even though pregnancy itself is not expressly classified as a disability. Additionally, many states have enacted laws providing certain accommodations for pregnant employees. "These Acts honor and safeguard the important contributions women make to both the workplace and the American family."]

NOTES

1. *The First Clause.* The *Young* case is all about the significance of the second clause of the PDA, but that might suggest that the first clause is a model of clarity. It isn't. The equation of discrimination on account of pregnancy with sex discrimination implies that any pregnancy-based decision is impermissible — at least absent a BFOQ, and you'll recall how hard that is to establish from *International Union, United Auto. Workers v. Johnson Controls, Inc.*, in Chapter 2 at p. 142. However, circuit cases did not adopt that literal reading. For example, in *Marafino v. St. Louis County Circuit Court*, 707 F.2d 1005 (8th Cir. 1983), a court's failure to hire a pregnant woman as a judicial law clerk because she would require a leave of absence soon after starting work was held lawful because the employer presumably would not have hired *anyone* who required a leave of absence shortly after beginning work. Similarly,

in *Troupe v. May Department Store Co.*, 20 F.3d 734, 738 (7th Cir. 1994), the court believed that discharge of a woman who was repeatedly late due to morning sickness was not actionable since a male with a comparable absentee record would presumably also have been fired.

The Seventh Circuit later retreated somewhat from this position, upholding a suit by a discharged bank teller when "the bank simply assumed that, because of her pregnancy, Maldonado would be absent from work for an indeterminate period sometime in the future." *Maldonado v. United States Bank*, 186 F.3d 759, 766 (7th Cir. 1999). The court recognized that "[t]here might be some limited circumstances in which an employer could be justified in taking anticipatory adverse action against a pregnant employee," but held that "an employer cannot take anticipatory action unless it has a good faith basis, supported by sufficiently strong evidence, that the normal inconveniences of an employee's pregnancy will require special treatment." *Id.* at 767. Although *Maldonado* was more demanding than the earlier decisions, all three cases permit adverse actions based on pregnancy, and *Marafino* and *Troupe* reached their conclusions based on an intuition, more than proof, that similarly situated nonpregnant persons would be similarly treated. Further, only *Maldonado* made any effort to justify this departure from the plain language of the statute and it did so by a glancing reference to BFOQ. Of course, maybe the justification for so reading the first clause is the second clause: if similarly situated males (say, those temporarily disabled) would also be fired, there's no violation.

In any event, what's apparent in all three cases is that the most that an employer is obligated to do is treat all employees equally when they are similarly situated. *Maldonado* could not have been clearer that the plaintiff could have been discharged had she asked for maternity leave during a time when she was required to work: "the bank did not have sufficient specific evidence (apart from general assumptions about pregnancy) that Maldonado would require special treatment. Absent such evidence, the bank cannot terminate Maldonado simply because it 'anticipated' that she would be unable to fulfill its job expectations." *Id.* at 768.

That means that there is no duty to accommodate pregnancy per se, a standard view of the PDA before *Young*. *See also Serednyj v. Beverly Healthcare, LLC*, 656 F.3d 540, 548 (7th Cir. 2011) (modified work policy "complies with the PDA because it does, in fact, treat nonpregnant employees the same as pregnant employees — both are denied an accommodation of light duty work for non-work-related injuries. This is all the PDA requires"). Thus, plaintiffs could look to the first clause mainly for protection against discrimination not rooted in inability to work, *see Hitchcock v. Angel Corps, Inc.*, 718 F.3d 733 (7th Cir. 2013); *Holland v. Gee*, 677 F.3d 1047 (11th Cir. 2012), but only the second clause provides a basis for mandating pregnancy accommodations and only then when other employees have also been accommodated.

2. *The Second Clause.* The critical statutory language is "women affected by pregnancy, childbirth, or related medical condition shall be treated the same for all employment-related purposes as other persons not so affected but similar in their ability or inability to work." Thus, any duty to accommodate pregnancy depends on whether other workers (male or female) are accommodated. *See generally* Deborah A. Widiss, Gilbert *Redux: The Interaction of the Pregnancy Discrimination Act and the Amended Americans with Disabilities Act after* Young v. UPS, 46 U.C. Davis L. Rev. 961 (2013). *See also* Nicole Buonocore Porter, *Mutual Marginalization: Individuals with Disabilities and Workers with Caregiving Responsibilities*, 66 Fla. L. Rev. 1099, 1135-38 (2014).

But *which* other workers? All the Justices reject the "most-favored nation" reading of this second clause of the PDA, which would allow a pregnant woman to compare herself with any other person accommodated by her employer. The majority so holds because such a reading would write intent to discriminate out of the statute for these disparate treatment cases. It then applies *McDonnell Douglas*, which is all about intent, to the question of pregnancy accommodations while making clear that this analysis applies only to pregnancy claims, not other kinds of discrimination. In short, the Court seems to be defining what it means to intend to discriminate, but only for cases of pregnancy accommodation.

3. *The Test.* The critical sentence seems to be: "[w]e believe that the plaintiff may reach a jury on this issue by providing sufficient evidence that the employer's policies impose a significant burden on pregnant workers, and that the employer's 'legitimate, nondiscriminatory' reasons are not sufficiently strong to justify the burden, but rather — when considered along with the burden imposed — give rise to an inference of intentional discrimination." So the factfinder still has to find intent, but that issue gets to the jury when there's evidence of "a significant burden" and evidence that the employer's reasons are not "sufficiently strong."

Up to this point, you've learned that intent to discriminate requires, well, intent. The strength or weakness of the employer's reasons is irrelevant so long as the factfinder determines that a prohibited characteristic did not play a role in the decision. Of course, very weak reasons might allow a jury to infer intent since the jury might not credit that an employer in fact acted for what seemed a silly or irrational reason. Does *Young* change this? If it doesn't, why did the majority limit its rule to pregnancy? If it does, what does intent mean in the pregnancy setting? *See* William Corbett, Young v. United Parcel Service, Inc.: McDonnell Douglas *to the Rescue?*, 92 Wash. U. L. Rev. 1683, 1686-87 (2015) (arguing that the Court's use of pretext analysis will probably revive the distinction between claims based on direct evidence and those based on circumstantial evidence that the Court seemed to have laid to rest in *Desert Palace, Inc. v. Costa*). Professor Deborah Brake, *The Shifting Sands of Employment Discrimination: From Unjustified Impact to Disparate Treatment in Pregnancy and Pay*, 105 Geo. L. J. 559, 584-85 (2017), finds *Young* remarkable. First, the demand for sufficiently strong reasons "rips the seams out of the traditional understanding of what separates impact from treatment claims. Time and again, the Court has reiterated that proof that a practice has a disparate impact does not establish proof of intent to discriminate." Secondly, the plaintiff now need not prove pretext in its original meaning, "that the employer's reason was not its genuine motivation for acting. Rather, the plaintiff need show only that it was not a 'strong' enough reason 'to justify the burden' on pregnant women."

4. *Significant Burden and Sufficiently Strong.* The Court provided some guidance on the two key concepts for its new test. A plaintiff can get to the jury on a significant burden "by providing evidence that the employer accommodates a large percentage of nonpregnant workers while failing to accommodate a large percentage of pregnant workers." As applied to the case before it, a showing would suffice that "UPS accommodates most nonpregnant employees with lifting limitations while categorically failing to accommodate pregnant employees with lifting limitations." The second half of the statement is certainly true, but did Young show that UPS accommodated "most nonpregnant employees with lifting limitations"? If so, is that because having a lifting limitation is an ADA-defined disability? And what happens if the employer errs on the side of accommodation for injured workers, even if they are not "disabled" within the meaning of the ADA? *See* Deborah A. Widiss, *The Interaction of the Pregnancy Discrimination Act with the Americans with Disabilities Act after* Young v. UPS, 50 U.C Davis L. Rev. 1423 (2017) (most pregnancy accommodation cases will be influenced by ADA-mandated accommodations since a prima facie case can be established

[handwritten marginal note: treatment cases get a jury and have the opportunity for more damages for more significant]

by looking to any group of favored workers and a pretext finding is possible even for workers favored by statutory mandate because the employer will have to explain why if did not extent such accommodations to pregnant workers).

As for the strength of the employer's reasons, the majority noted, and Justice Alito agreed, that "consistent with the Act's basic objective, that reason normally cannot consist simply of a claim that it is more expensive or less convenient to add pregnant women to the category of those ('similar in their ability or inability to work') whom the employer accommodates." As for Young's claim, she could argue that UPS's multiple policies accommodating nonpregnant employees with lifting restrictions suggest that its reasons for failing to accommodate pregnant employees "are not sufficiently strong — to the point that a jury could find that its reasons for failing to accommodate pregnant employees give rise to an inference of intentional discrimination."

But check out Justice Alito's concurrence. He would find compliance with the ADA and accommodations for those injured on the job to be sufficiently strong. Only the DOT disqualification apparently suffices as not strong enough. Do you think the majority would agree if forced to confront the issue? If so, is the decision really so sweeping?

In a post-*Young* decision, *Legg v. Ulster Cnty.*, 820 F.3d 67 (2d Cir. 2016), the court overturned defendant's post-trial judgment as a matter of law. Plaintiff had established a prima facie case by showing that she was denied light duty accommodation for her pregnancy when workers injured on the job were accommodated. While the employer's duty under state law to continue to pay those workers was a neutral reason, a reasonable jury could find it to be pretextual when a large number of other workers were accommodated and one woman was not. In addition, such a jury could also find the defendants' reasons not "sufficiently strong," when there was only one pregnant worker and the cost of the accommodation could have been found to be a factor, contrary to *Young*'s teaching. *But see Jackson v. J.R. Simplot Co.*, 666 F. App'x 739 (10th Cir. 2016) (pregnant employee not treated less favorably than other workers when there was no showing that other workers were accommodated because of their sensitivity to chemicals present in the chemical plant).

5. *What's Next for Accommodation?* Whatever the doctrinal implications of *Young* for either the pregnancy context or more broadly, the significance of the case for at least larger employers is clear: failing to accommodate pregnant workers when other workers are so accommodated is risky under Title VII. Add to that the spread of state laws requiring accommodation of pregnancy, *see* http://www.abetterbalance.org/web/ourissues/fairness-for-pregnant-workers/310, and the ADA's treatment of pregnancy as a temporary disability, see p. 445, and the stars seem to have realigned so that accommodation is now the best risk management strategy. *See generally* Joanna L. Grossman, *Expanding the Core: Pregnancy Discrimination Law as It Approaches Full Term*, 52 Idaho L. Rev. 825 (2016); Bradley A. Areheart, *Accommodating Pregnancy*, 67 Ala. L. Rev. 1125 (2016).

But can robustly accommodating pregnant women raise reverse discrimination problems? In *California Federal Savings & Loan Assoc. v. Guerra*, 479 U.S. 272 (1987), the Supreme Court held that a California statute mandating unpaid pregnancy disability leave, but not leave for other disabling conditions, was not preempted by Title VII. In so holding, the Court described the PDA as a "floor, not a ceiling," thus permitting states to provide preferential treatment to pregnancy. *Cal Fed* likely also permits employers to provide such "special treatment" even absent state compulsion although at some point extended child-*rearing* leave for mothers may raise claims of sex discrimination if paternity leave is not similarly offered fathers. *See Schafer v. Bd. of Pub. Educ. of Sch. Dist.*, 903 F.2d 243 (3d Cir. 1990). *See also* Keith

also have state law!

Cunningham-Parmeter, *Men at Work, Fathers at Home: Uncovering the Masculine Face of Caregiver Discrimination*, 24 COLUM. J. GENDER & L. 253 (2013).

6. *Merging Disparate Treatment and Disparate Impact. Young's* looking to the strength of the employer's reasons (rather than merely their honesty) is a radical shift in approach to disparate treatment. Indeed, Justice Scalia's dissent accused the majority of importing disparate impact analysis into a disparate treatment framework. Is that a fair observation? Although we have seen that factfinders could always draw an inference of intent to discriminate from the use of a practice with a disparate impact, see Chapter 4, that was rare in the lower courts absent sophisticated statistical evidence. If Scalia is right, is that a bad thing? In any event, will this change in the pregnancy context leak out to other disparate treatment cases?

7. *Systemic Cases?* The majority views *Young* under the *McDonnell Douglas* framework — individual disparate treatment. It also goes out of its way to state that no systemic disparate treatment claim is before it ("Nor has she asserted what we have called a 'pattern-or-practice' claim."). But how can that be? The challenge isn't to an ad hoc decision but rather to the operation of an employer policy. And the proof is, at least in part, the effects of that policy.

And then there's disparate impact. Although the Scalia dissent believes the majority's analysis mimics disparate impact, the Court is explicit that no such claim is at issue. Suppose plaintiff had asserted disparate impact. Does Scalia's dissent suggest she would have a good claim? There is some question whether the second clause of the PDA bars application of that theory under the PDA. *Cal. Fed. Sav. & Loan Ass'n v. Guerra*, 479 U.S. 272, 298 n.1 (1987) (White, J., dissenting), although that was prior to the codification of disparate impact by the Civil Rights Act of 1991. A few courts have recognized the possibility of an impact claim if a practice disproportionately disadvantages *pregnant* women. *See Garcia v. Woman's Hosp. of Tex.*, 97 F.3d 810 (5th Cir. 1996). *But see Stout v. Baxter Healthcare Corp.*, 282 F.3d 856, 861 (5th Cir. 2002) (refusing to extend *Garcia* to claims that sick leave "is insufficient to accommodate the time off required in a typical pregnancy"). *See generally* L. Camille Hébert, *Disparate Impact and Pregnancy: Title VII's Other Accommodation Requirement*, 24 AM. U. J. GENDER SOC. POL'Y & L. 107 (2015); Deborah Dinner, *The Costs of Reproduction: History and the Legal Construction of Sexual Equality*, 46 HARV. C.R.-C.L. L. REV. 415, 485-89 (2011).

[handwritten margin note: Court says not a disparate impact claim]

8. *The "Immorality" Defense.* Suppose an employer fires an unmarried pregnant woman. May it escape liability under §701(k) by claiming that it discriminated not because of pregnancy, but because of "immorality"? The courts seem to believe it permissible to do so as long as the employer does (or would) also discharge men who engaged in premarital sex. *E.g., Cline v. Catholic Diocese*, 206 F.3d 651, 658 (6th Cir. 2000) *Cf. Hamilton v. Southland Christian School, Inc.*, 680 F.3d 1316 (11th Cir. 2012) (teacher allegedly fired for premarital sex raised a material factual dispute about whether the school terminated her because of her pregnancy or because she sinned in conceiving a child before marriage). If the employer is a church, its "ministerial employees" are exempt from employment discrimination laws. See p. 383.

9. *Related Medical Conditions.* The PDA protects against discrimination not only on account of pregnancy but also on account of "childbirth and related medical conditions." As a result, Title VII bars discrimination based on a woman having an in vitro procedure, *Hall v. Nalco Co.*, 534 F.3d 644, 645 (7th Cir. 2008), or an abortion, *Doe v. C.A.R.S. Prot. Plus*, 527 F.3d 358 (3d Cir. 2008). *See also Kocak v. Community Health Ptnrs. of Ohio, Inc.*, 400 F.3d 466 (6th Cir. 2005) (employer's failure to rehire

an applicant because of scheduling complications caused by her prior pregnancy). While most courts have not read the statute to require accommodation of breast feeding, *see, e.g., Puente v. Ridge*, 324 F. App'x 423 (5th Cir. 2009), it nevertheless seems likely that discrimination against women on this basis is illegal. *See EEOC v. Houston Funding II, Ltd.*, 717 F.3d 425 (5th Cir. 2013). Outside of Title VII, the Affordable Care Act amended the Fair Labor Standards Act to provide for some accommodations for nursing mothers. 29 U.S.C. §207(r) (2018). The section requires "reasonable break time" and a private place other than a bathroom when a worker needs to express breast milk for a year after the child's birth. However, an employer is not required to compensate employees during these periods beyond any compensation ordinarily provided for break time, and employers with fewer than 50 employees may be exempt from this requirement if it would impose an undue hardship.

10. *Health Insurance.* In *Newport News Shipbuilding & Dry Dock Co. v. EEOC*, 462 U.S. 669 (1983), the Court confronted an employer-sponsored medical plan that provided the same hospitalization coverage for male and female employees but differentiated between female employees and spouses of male employees by imposing a cap on the pregnancy-related hospital benefits for spouses of male workers. The Court held that the employer's plan failed the "simple test of Title VII discrimination that we enunciated in *Los Angeles Department of Water & Power v. Manhart*," reproduced at p. 94. While a female employee's spouse had hospitalization coverage for all conditions, a male employee's spouse was covered for all conditions except pregnancy. The PDA "makes clear that it is discriminatory to treat pregnancy-related conditions less favorably than other medical conditions. Thus, petitioner's plan unlawfully gives married male employees a benefit package for their dependents that is less inclusive than the dependency coverage provided to married female employees." *Id.* at 684. But the Court stressed that the issue was not pregnancy coverage per se: Title VII imposes no requirement that an employer provide any medical insurance at all. If an employer fails to insure its workers, it is treating them all equally, and there can be no violation of Title VII.

NOTE ON CHILDREARING

Suppose medical testimony establishes that a pregnant woman is unable to work for only six weeks. If she asks for more time, isn't she seeking leave not for *childbearing*, but for *childrearing*? Does Title VII require employers to grant such leave? It seems clear that childrearing is not "pregnancy, childbirth, or related medical conditions." *See Fisher v. Vassar Coll.*, 70 F.3d 1420 (2d Cir. 1995). However, employer fears that such flexibility will impact production, *see Phillips v. Martin Marietta Corp.*, 400 U.S. 861 (1970) (employer policy against hiring women with preschool-age children), can create what Professor Joan Williams calls the "maternal wall" to barriers to workplace advancement of women with childcare responsibilities. *See* Joan C. Williams & Nancy Segal, *Beyond the Maternal Wall: Relief for Family Caregivers Who Are Discriminated Against on the Job*, 26 HARV. WOMEN'S L.J. 77 (2003). She argues that Title VII has been more effective in dealing with "maternal wall" cases than is often realized, *e.g., Walsh v. National Computer Sys.*, 332 F.3d 1150 (8th Cir. 2003) (upholding verdict in favor of a plaintiff who had been discriminated against because she had been pregnant, had taken a maternity leave, and might become pregnant again). *See also* Joan C. Williams & Stephanie Bornstein, *The Evolution of "FReD": Family Responsibilities Discrimination and Developments in the Law of Stereotyping and Implicit Bias*, 59 HASTINGS L.J. 1311 (2008); Joan C. Williams, *Using Social Science to Litigate Gender Discrimination Cases and Defang the "Cluelessness" Defense*, 7 EMP. RTS. & EMP. POL'Y J. 401 (2003). The EEOC issued an Enforcement Guidance in this area, www.eeoc.gov/policy/docs/caregiving. html, which recognizes that caregivers are not per se protected under Title VII, but exploring when discrimination against caregivers might constitute unlawful disparate treatment under Title VII or the ADA. *See also EEOC, Employer Best Practices for Workers with Caregiving Responsibilities (2009)*, http://www.eeoc.gov/policy/docs/ caregiver-best-practices.html.

Should employers ask, or women raise, questions about pregnancy and family responsibilities? A counterintuitive article suggests that open discussions about family status in the hiring context are likely to assist women in returning to the job market; current practice, which discourage both employers and employees from raising the topic, *see EEOC Best Practices, supra*, plays into employer "ambiguity aversion." *See* Jodi Herch & Jennifer Bennett Shinall, *Something to Talk About: Information Exchange Under Employment Law*, 165 U. PA. L. REV. 49 (2016).

NOTE ON THE FAMILY AND MEDICAL LEAVE ACT

Some of the problems faced by pregnant women and parents of small children are addressed by the Family and Medical Leave Act of 1993 (FMLA), 29 U.S.C. §§2601 et seq. (2018), 29 C.F.R. §§825.120, 825.121 (2018), which ensures up to 12 weeks of unpaid leave for a variety of purposes, including the birth or adoption of a child. The Department of Labor recognizes that "[c]ircumstances may require that leave for the birth of a child, or for placement for adoption or foster care, be taken prior to the actual birth or placement." §825.120. *See generally* Julie C. Suk, *Are Gender Stereotypes Bad for Women? Rethinking Antidiscrimination Law and Work-Family Conflict*, 110 COLUM. L. REV. 1 (2010) (arguing that grouping family and medical leave into a single legal regime may limit more generous pregnancy leave for many women).

The FMLA reduces, but by no means eliminates, the importance of the PDA for pregnant workers. The FMLA applies only to employers with 50 or more employees. Furthermore, to be eligible, an employee must have worked for the employer (1) for at least 12 months, (2) for at least 1,250 hours during the year preceding the start of the leave, and (3) be employed at a worksite where the employer employs at least 50 employees within a 75-mile radius. §825.110. Thus, part-time employees, first-year employees, and employees who work for smaller employers are not entitled to leave. Additionally, the FMLA does not require any pregnancy accommodations other than unpaid leave. The FMLA is also discussed on p. 521.

PROBLEM 5.1

Charlene works in a company mail room for an employer that is not covered by the FMLA. Her duties include helping to unload bags of mail from the mail trucks. She also sorts mail and works at the front counter serving customers. Charlene is in her sixth month of pregnancy and has been advised by her doctor not to lift the heavy mailbags at work. When she asked her employer to permit her to limit her work to sorting mail and working at the counter for the remaining period of her pregnancy, the employer refused and put her on leave without pay, promising to return her to her job after the baby was delivered and she became well enough to perform all of the duties of her job. Charlene's employer has no pregnancy leave policy and no long-term disability policy. The employer permits employees to take two weeks of sick leave each year. Employees who require more than two weeks of sick leave are discharged. The only exception is for workers injured on the job, who are assigned "light duty work as available." Charlene filed suit under the PDA, alleging discrimination on the basis of her pregnancy. A male employee who recently suffered injuries in a car accident also has filed suit, complaining that, rather than receiving leave without pay and a promise of reinstatement, he was discharged after using up his allotted two weeks of sick leave. What rights and remedies (if any) do these employees have?

2.   *Sexual and Other Discriminatory Harassment*

In this section, we consider employees' rights to a workplace free from sexual and other discriminatory harassment. As suggested by *Oncale v. Sundowner Offshore Servs.*, reproduced at p. 275, Title VII provides employees with a cause of action for harassment when it is based on membership in a protected group. Sexual harassment imposes different conditions of employment on women or men because of their gender, but harassment is also actionable when aimed at racial, religious, or ethnic groups or at older or disabled workers. Sexual harassment is unique, however, because unlike other discriminatory behavior, sexual harassment involves some conduct that, in other times and settings, is perfectly appropriate.

As we have seen, most claims under the antidiscrimination laws are based on an "adverse employment action," some tangible change in compensation or position; in contrast, harassment can violate the law even if the victim suffers no such harm. Moreover, harassment typically occurs in violation of, rather than in compliance with, company policy, and harassers typically are satisfying their own personal interests, rather than seeking to further their employer's interests. This aspect of discriminatory harassment generates an additional question: what is the employer's liability for harassment by supervisors and co-workers in violation of company policy?

"severe or pervasive"

MERITOR SAVINGS BANK v. VINSON
477 U.S. 57 (1986)

Justice REHNQUIST delivered the opinion of the Court.

I

[In 1974, Michelle Vinson met Sidney Taylor, a vice president of Meritor Savings Bank and manager of one of its branch offices. Taylor hired her and became her supervisor. Vinson started as a trainee, but ultimately was promoted to assistant branch manager, working at the same branch until her discharge in 1978. "[I]t is undisputed that her advancement there was based on merit alone." In late 1978, Vinson took sick leave and finally was discharged for excessive use of that leave. Vinson sued both Taylor and the bank, claiming that she had "constantly been subjected to sexual harassment" by Taylor during her four years of employment.]

At . . . trial, the parties presented conflicting testimony about Taylor's behavior during respondent's employment. Respondent testified that during her probationary

period as a teller-trainee, Taylor treated her in a fatherly way and made no sexual
advances. Shortly thereafter, however, he invited her out to dinner and, during the
course of the meal, suggested that they go to a motel to have sexual relations. At first she
refused, but out of what she described as fear of losing her job she eventually agreed.
According to respondent, Taylor thereafter made repeated demands upon her for sexual favors, usually at the branch, both during and after business hours; she estimated
that over the next several years she had intercourse with him some 40 or 50 times.
In addition, respondent testified that Taylor fondled her in front of other employees,
followed her into the women's restroom when she went there alone, exposed himself
to her, and even forcibly raped her on several occasions. These activities ceased after
1977, respondent stated, when she started going with a steady boyfriend.

[Vinson "testified that Taylor touched and fondled other women employees of the
bank," but was not allowed "to present wholesale evidence of a pattern and practice
relating to sexual advances to other female employees in her case in chief." She also
testified that "because she was afraid of Taylor she never reported his harassment to
any of his supervisors and never attempted to use the bank's complaint procedure."]

Taylor denied respondent's allegations of sexual activity, testifying that he never
fondled her, never made suggestive remarks to her, never engaged in sexual intercourse with her, and never asked her to do so. He contended instead that respondent made her accusations in response to a business-related dispute. The bank also
denied respondent's allegations and asserted that any sexual harassment by Taylor was
unknown to the bank and engaged in without its consent or approval.

The District Court denied relief, but did not resolve the conflicting testimony
about the existence of a sexual relationship between respondent and Taylor. It found
instead that:

> [i]f [respondent] and Taylor did engage in an intimate or sexual relationship during the
> time of [respondent's] employment with [the bank], that relationship was a voluntary
> one having nothing to do with her continued employment at [the bank] or her advance-
> ment or promotions at that institution.

The court ultimately found that respondent "was not the victim of sexual harassment
and was not the victim of sexual discrimination" while employed at the bank. . . .

II . . .

Respondent argues, and the Court of Appeals held, that unwelcome sexual advances
that create an offensive or hostile working environment violate Title VII. Without
question, when a supervisor sexually harasses a subordinate because of the subordinate's sex, that supervisor "discriminate[s]" on the basis of sex. Petitioner apparently
does not challenge this proposition. It contends instead that in prohibiting discrimination with respect to "compensation, terms, conditions, or privileges" of employment,
Congress was concerned with what petitioner describes as "tangible loss" of "an economic character," not "purely psychological aspects of the workplace environment."
In support of this claim petitioner observes that in both the legislative history of Title
VII and this Court's Title VII decisions, the focus has been on tangible, economic
barriers erected by discrimination.

We reject petitioner's view. First, the language of Title VII is not limited to "economic" or "tangible" discrimination. The phrase "terms, conditions, or privileges of
employment" evinces a congressional intent "'to strike at the entire spectrum [of]
disparate treatment of men and women'" in employment. *Los Angeles Dept. of Water*

and Power v. Manhart. Petitioner has pointed to nothing in the Act to suggest that Congress contemplated the limitation urged here.

[Second, the 1980 EEOC Guidelines providing that "sexual harassment" is a form of sex discrimination constituted "a body of experience and informed judgment to which courts and litigants may properly resort for guidance" and "fully support the view that harassment leading to noneconomic injury can violate Title VII."]

In defining "sexual harassment," the Guidelines first describe the kinds of workplace conduct that may be actionable under Title VII. These include "[u]nwelcome sexual advances, requests for sexual favors, and other verbal or physical conduct of a sexual nature." 29 C.F.R. §1604.11(a) (1985). Relevant to the charges at issue in this case, the Guidelines provide that such sexual misconduct constitutes prohibited "sexual harassment," whether or not it is directly linked to the grant or denial of an economic quid pro quo, where "such conduct has the purpose or effect of unreasonably interfering with an individual's work performance or creating an intimidating, hostile, or offensive working environment." §1604.11(a)(3).

In concluding that so-called "hostile environment" (*i.e.,* non-quid pro quo) harassment violates Title VII, the EEOC drew upon a substantial body of judicial decisions and EEOC precedent holding that Title VII affords employees the right to work in an environment free from discriminatory intimidation, ridicule, and insult. *Rogers v. EEOC,* 454 F.2d 234 (5th Cir. 1971), was apparently the first case to recognize a cause of action based upon a discriminatory work environment.

In *Rogers,* the Court of Appeals for the Fifth Circuit held that a Hispanic complainant could establish a Title VII violation by demonstrating that her employer created an offensive work environment for employees by giving discriminatory service to its Hispanic clientele. The court explained that an employee's protections under Title VII extend beyond the economic aspects of employment:

> [T]he phrase "terms, conditions or privileges of employment" in [Title VII] is an expansive concept which sweeps within its protective ambit the practice of creating a working environment heavily charged with ethnic or racial discrimination. . . . One can readily envision working environments so heavily polluted with discrimination as to destroy completely the emotional and psychological stability of minority group workers. . . .

Courts applied this principle to harassment based on race, religion, and national origin. Nothing in Title VII suggests that a hostile environment based on discriminatory sexual harassment should not be likewise prohibited. The Guidelines thus appropriately drew from, and were fully consistent with, the existing case law.

Since the Guidelines were issued, courts have uniformly held, and we agree, that a plaintiff may establish a violation of Title VII by proving that discrimination based on sex has created a hostile or abusive work environment. As the Court of Appeals for the Eleventh Circuit wrote in *Henson v. Dundee,* 682 F.2d 897, 902 (1982):

> Sexual harassment which creates a hostile or offensive environment for members of one sex is every bit the arbitrary barrier to sexual equality at the workplace that racial harassment is to racial equality. Surely, a requirement that a man or woman run a gauntlet of sexual abuse in return for the privilege of being allowed to work and make a living can be as demeaning and disconcerting as the harshest of racial epithets.

Of course, as the courts in both *Rogers* and *Henson* recognized, not all workplace conduct that may be described as "harassment" affects a "term, condition, or privilege" of employment within the meaning of Title VII. For sexual harassment to be actionable, it must be sufficiently severe or pervasive "to alter the conditions of [the victim's] employment and create an abusive working environment." Respondent's allegations in this case — which include not only pervasive harassment but also criminal conduct of the most serious nature — are plainly sufficient to state a claim for "hostile environment" sexual harassment.

[The District Court's ultimate finding that Vinson "was not the victim of sexual harassment" was likely based on one or both of two errors of law. First, a sexual harassment claim will not lie absent an economic effect on the employment; second, the court's view that any sexual relationship was "voluntary."] But the fact that sex-related conduct was "voluntary," in the sense that the complainant was not forced to participate against her will, is not a defense to a sexual harassment suit brought under Title VII. The gravamen of any sexual harassment claim is that the alleged sexual advances were "unwelcome." 29 C.F.R. §1604.11(a) (1985). While the question whether particular conduct was indeed unwelcome presents difficult problems of proof and turns largely on credibility determinations committed to the trier of fact, the District Court in this case erroneously focused on the "voluntariness" of respondent's participation in the claimed sexual episodes. The correct inquiry is whether respondent by her conduct indicated that the alleged sexual advances were unwelcome, not whether her actual participation in sexual intercourse was voluntary.

Petitioner contends that even if this case must be remanded to the District Court, the Court of Appeals erred in one of the terms of its remand. Specifically, the Court of Appeals stated that testimony about respondent's "dress and personal fantasies," which the District Court apparently admitted into evidence, "had no place in this litigation." The apparent ground for this conclusion was that respondent's voluntariness vel non in submitting to Taylor's advances was immaterial to her sexual harassment claim. While "voluntariness" in the sense of consent is not a defense to such a claim, it does not follow that a complainant's sexually provocative speech or dress is irrelevant as a matter of law in determining whether he or she found particular sexual advances unwelcome. To the contrary, such evidence is obviously relevant. The EEOC Guidelines emphasize that the trier of fact must determine the existence of sexual harassment in light of "the record as a whole" and "the totality of circumstances, such as the nature of the sexual advances and the context in which the alleged incidents occurred." 29 C.F.R. §1604.11(b) (1985). Respondent's claim that any marginal relevance of the evidence in question was outweighed by the potential for unfair prejudice is the sort of argument properly addressed to the District Court. In this case the District Court concluded that the evidence should be admitted, and the Court of Appeals' contrary conclusion was based upon the erroneous, categorical view that testimony about provocative dress and publicly expressed sexual fantasies "had no place in this litigation." While the District Court must carefully weigh the applicable considerations in deciding whether to admit evidence of this kind, there is no per se rule against its admissibility. . . .

NOTES

1. *What Constitutes Harassment?* Because the alleged conduct by Taylor was so egregious, it may not be clear from *Meritor* that one central theoretical problem with the sexual harassment cause of action is deciding what constitutes harassment. At one extreme, a violation will be established if accepting sexual advances is an explicit or implicit "quid pro quo" for obtaining, retaining, or advancing in a job. *See McMiller v. Metro,* 738 F.3d 185, 189 (8th Cir. 2013) (although sexual advances were not sufficiently severe or pervasive to contaminate plaintiff's work environment, a reasonable

jury could find quid pro quo harassment in her discharge for refusing to accede to her supervisors advances). The Court in *Meritor* goes beyond this scenario, holding that contaminating a work environment is also prohibited.

At the other extreme, however, the Court emphasized in *Oncale that* Title VII is not a "civility code." Is every "pass" a Title VII violation? Every pass by a supervisor? Does harassment by co-workers (or even subordinates) violate Title VII? Is mere exposure to raw language harassment? What about compliments or criticisms regarding an employee's appearance? These questions will be explored in the materials following.

what is sufficiently or pervasive offensive?

2. *Fed. R. Evid. 412.* The *Meritor* Court admitted evidence of Vinson's dress and sexual fantasies. In rape cases, defendants commonly seek to put in issue the character of the victim. If such a defense is raised in a sexual harassment case, what is the appropriate judicial response? Consider the relevance of dress or past conduct to the question whether sexual advances were unwelcome. Rule 412 of the Federal Rules of Evidence regulates the admissibility of evidence of past sexual conduct. In trials relating to sexual misconduct, it makes inadmissible

> evidence offered to prove a victim engaged in other sexual behavior . . . [or] . . . to prove a victim's sexual predisposition . . . [unless] its probative value substantially outweighs the danger of harm to any victim and of unfair prejudice to any party. The court may admit evidence of a victim's reputation only if the victim has placed it in [controversy].

See Rodriguez-Hernandez v. Miranda-Valez, 132 F.3d 848 (1st Cir. 1998) (plaintiff's sexual history properly excluded under Rule 412). *But see Wilson v. City of Des Moines,* 442 F.3d 637 (8th Cir. 2006) (admission of testimony of plaintiff's workplace behavior and sexually charged comments was not abuse of discretion, despite the trial court failing to hold a required Rule 412 hearing where testimony was highly probative of "welcomeness"). *See generally* Theresa M. Beiner, *Sexy Dressing Revisited: Does Target Dress Play a Part in Sexual Harassment Cases?,* 14 Duke J. Gender L. & Pol'y 125 (2007) (finding very few cases where the target's dress was relevant and even fewer where it was used to argue that the target welcomed the sexually harassing behavior).

3. *Remedial Issues.* The 1991 Civil Rights Act expanded the remedies available in Title VII cases to include compensatory and punitive damages and damages for emotional distress. This was largely due to the controversy generated by Anita Hill's accusations of harassment during the confirmation hearings for Justice Clarence Thomas. The debate highlighted the fact that Title VII as originally enacted provided only equitable remedies, which were largely ineffective in hostile environment cases because plaintiffs could often secure only attorneys' fees and injunctive relief against further violations. By providing emotional distress and punitive damages, the 1991 Act reinvigorated Title VII's prohibition of harassment. The amount of damages available is limited, however, depending on the size of the plaintiff's employer. See Chapter 9. Further, courts may hold, as they have in tort suits, that a plaintiff seeking damages for mental and emotional distress places her mental state in controversy, justifying an order to undergo psychiatric examination.

NOTE ON OTHER DISCRIMINATORY HARASSMENT

Sexual harassment claims have predominated among the hostile environment cases under Title VII, but, as the Court noted in *Meritor,* the first case to recognize hostile environment as a basis for liability under Title VII concerned an employer who "created an offensive work environment for employees by giving discriminatory service to its Hispanic clientele." Such cases continue to arise in the race context.

See, e.g., Ellis v. Houston, 742 F.3d 307 (8th Cir. 2014) (pattern of harassment suffered by African American prison guards actionable, especially since supervisors made or condoned racist comments on nearly a daily basis); *Lambert v. Peri Formworks Sys., Inc.*, 723 F.3d 863, 868-69 (7th Cir. 2013) (racial harassment could be found even though the most offensive statements — reference to workers as "donkeys" and a "gorilla" and the use of "nigger" — occurred over a period of several years, were not physically threatening, and did not affect Lambert's work performance); *Ayissi-Etoh v. Fannie Mae*, 712 F.3d 572 (D.C. Cir. 2013) (a reasonable jury could find supervisors' behavior sufficiently severe or pervasive when one "used a deeply offensive racial epithet when yelling at [plaintiff] to get out of the office" and another explicitly linked his race to the denial of a raise). In addition, claims based on age, *Dediol v. Best Chevrolet, Inc.*, 655 F.3d 435 (5th Cir. 2011), religion, *Griffin v. City of Portland*, 2013 U.S. Dist. LEXIS 154204 (D. Or. Oct. 25, 2013), and retaliation have been upheld. *Gowski v. Peake*, 682 F.3d 1299 (11th Cir. 2012).

While any harassment claim under Title VII must allege harassment based on a protected status or activity, complaints of other kinds of discriminatory harassment involve many of the same issues as sexual harassment. In *National Railroad Passenger Corp. v. Morgan*, 536 U.S. 101, 116 n.10 (2002), the Court asserted that "[h]ostile work environment claims based on racial harassment are reviewed under the same standard as those based on sexual harassment." As we will see, the core question is frequently whether the conduct in question was "severe or pervasive" enough to contaminate the work environment, and that issue is as important for other discriminatory harassment as it is in sexual harassment cases. *E.g., Nichols v. Mich. City Plant Planning Dep't*, 755 F.3d 594 (7th Cir. 2014) (one-time use of a racial epithet is not severe enough to trigger liability, and six incidents of harassment within a two-and-a-half-week period not sufficiently pervasive); *Colenburg v. Starcon Int'l, Inc.*, 619 F.3d 986 (8th Cir. 2010) (racial harassment not severe or pervasive even though it included supervisor's comments to plaintiff analogizing pace of his work to speed at which black man in Texas had been dragged to death behind truck); *but see* Pat K. Chew, *Freeing Racial Harassment from the Sexual Harassment Model*, 85 Or. L. Rev. 615 (2006).

a. Severe or Pervasive Harassment

HARRIS v. FORKLIFT SYSTEMS, INC.
510 U.S. 17 (1993)

requires objective and subjective determination of abuse

O'CONNOR, J., delivered the opinion for a unanimous Court. . . .

I

Teresa Harris worked as a manager at Forklift Systems, Inc., an equipment rental company, from April 1985 until October 1987. Charles Hardy was Forklift's president.

The Magistrate found that, throughout Harris' time at Forklift, Hardy often insulted her because of her gender and often made her the target of unwanted sexual innuendos. Hardy told Harris on several occasions, in the presence of other employees, "You're a woman, what do you know" and "We need a man as the rental manager"; at least once, he told her she was "a dumb ass woman." Again in front of others, he suggested that the two of them "go to the Holiday Inn to negotiate [Harris'] raise." Hardy occasionally asked Harris and other female employees to get coins from his front pants pocket. He threw objects on the ground in front of Harris and other women, and asked them to pick the objects up. He made sexual innuendos about Harris' and other women's clothing.

In mid-August 1987, Harris complained to Hardy about his conduct. Hardy said he was surprised that Harris was offended, claimed he was only joking, and apologized. He also promised he would stop, and based on this assurance Harris stayed on the job. But in early September, Hardy began anew: While Harris was arranging a deal with one of Forklift's customers, he asked her, again in front of other employees, "What did you do, promise the guy . . . some [sex] Saturday night?" On October 1, Harris collected her paycheck and quit.

Harris then sued Forklift, claiming that Hardy's conduct had created an abusive work environment for her because of her gender. The [district court] found this to be "a close case," but held that Hardy's conduct did not create an abusive environment. The court found that some of Hardy's comments "offended [Harris], and would offend the reasonable woman," but that they were not "so severe as to be expected to seriously affect [Harris'] psychological well-being." A reasonable woman manager under like circumstances would have been offended by Hardy, but his conduct would not have risen to the level of interfering with that person's work performance.

Neither do I believe that [Harris] was subjectively so offended that she suffered injury. . . . Although Hardy may at times have genuinely offended [Harris], I do not believe that he created a working environment so poisoned as to be intimidating or abusive to [Harris].

. . . We granted certiorari to resolve a conflict among the Circuits on whether conduct, to be actionable as "abusive work environment" harassment (no quid pro quo harassment issue is present here), must "seriously affect [an employee's] psychological well-being" or lead the plaintiff to "suffer injury." . . .

II

Title VII of the Civil Rights Act of 1964 makes it "an unlawful employment practice for an employer . . . to discriminate against any individual with respect to his compensation, terms, conditions, or privileges of employment, because of such individual's race, color, religion, sex, or national origin." As we made clear in *Meritor*, this language "is not limited to 'economic' or 'tangible' discrimination. The phrase 'terms, conditions, or privileges of employment' evinces a congressional intent 'to strike at the entire spectrum of disparate treatment of men and women' in employment," which includes requiring people to work in a discriminatorily hostile or abusive environment. When the workplace is permeated with "discriminatory intimidation, ridicule, and insult," that is "sufficiently severe or pervasive to alter the conditions of the victim's employment and create an abusive working environment," Title VII is violated.

This standard, which we reaffirm today, takes a middle path between making actionable any conduct that is merely offensive and requiring the conduct to cause a tangible psychological injury. As we pointed out in *Meritor*, "mere utterance of an . . . epithet which engenders offensive feelings in an employee," does not sufficiently affect the conditions of employment to implicate Title VII. Conduct that is not severe or pervasive enough to create an objectively hostile or abusive work environment — an environment that a reasonable person would find hostile or abusive — is beyond Title VII's purview. Likewise, if the victim does not subjectively perceive the

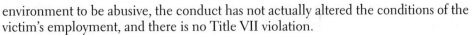

environment to be abusive, the conduct has not actually altered the conditions of the victim's employment, and there is no Title VII violation.

But Title VII comes into play before the harassing conduct leads to a nervous breakdown. A discriminatorily abusive work environment, even one that does not seriously affect employees' psychological well-being, can and often will detract from employees' job performance, discourage employees from remaining on the job, or keep them from advancing in their careers. Moreover, even without regard to these tangible effects, the very fact that the discriminatory conduct was so severe or pervasive that it created a work environment abusive to employees because of their race, gender, religion, or national origin offends Title VII's broad rule of workplace equality. The appalling conduct alleged in *Meritor*, and the reference in that case to environments "'so heavily polluted with discrimination as to destroy completely the emotional and psychological stability of minority group workers,'" quoting *Rogers v. EEOC*, merely present some especially egregious examples of harassment. They do not mark the boundary of what is actionable.   *psych not even required*   *meritor is not the min. threshold*

We therefore believe the District Court erred in relying on whether the conduct "seriously affected plaintiff's psychological well-being" or led her to "suffer injury." Such an inquiry may needlessly focus the factfinder's attention on concrete psychological harm, an element Title VII does not require. Certainly Title VII bars conduct that would seriously affect a reasonable person's psychological well-being, but the statute is not limited to such conduct. So long as the environment would reasonably be perceived, and is perceived, as hostile or abusive, there is no need for it also to be psychologically injurious.   *Title VII does not require psych harm*   * *Standard*

This is not, and by its nature cannot be, a mathematically precise test. We need not answer today all the potential questions it raises [but] we can say that whether an environment is "hostile" or "abusive" can be determined only by looking at all the circumstances. These may include the frequency of the discriminatory conduct; its severity; whether it is physically threatening or humiliating, or a mere offensive utterance; and whether it unreasonably interferes with an employee's work performance. The effect on the employee's psychological well-being is, of course, relevant to determining whether the plaintiff actually found the environment abusive. But while psychological harm, like any other relevant factor, may be taken into account, no single factor is required. . . .   *totality test Factors*

NOTES

1. *How Bad Is Bad Enough?* Harris reaffirms the *Meritor* "severe or pervasive" standard, but does the standard go very far in helping to draw the line between acceptable social behavior and actionable sexual harassment? Does *Harris* make the standard *any* clearer than it was after *Meritor*? Justice Scalia's concurrence stressed its vagueness, leaving "virtually unguided juries [to] decide whether sex-related conduct engaged in (or permitted by) an employer is egregious enough to warrant an award of damages." However, because "I know of no test more faithful to the inherently vague statutory language than the one the Court today adopts," he joined the Court's opinion. 510 U.S. at 24. What should the district court find on remand? Was Hardy's conduct "severe" or "pervasive" or both? If none of the acts of harassment in this case was severe, when did they become pervasive enough to be actionable?

A quarter century after *Harris*, courts are still struggling to apply its standard and, somewhat surprisingly in light of Justice Scalia's emphasis on juries, the decisions often find conduct not sufficiently severe or pervasive to even raise a jury question. It is true that many decisions have found the at-issue conduct actionable, usually because it was "pervasive." *Zetwick v. Cnty. of Yolo*, 850 F.3d 436 (9th Cir. 2017) (a reasonable juror could find sheriff's conduct sufficiently severe or pervasive in light of plaintiff's testimony that he hugged her more than 100 times over a 13 year period and that he hugged female employees much more often than males; while cross-gender hugging may be common in some workplaces, that does not establish beyond need for a trial that it was ordinary workplace socializing); *Gerald v. Univ. of P.R.*, 707 F.3d 7 (1st Cir. 2013) (testimony that her supervisor grabbed plaintiff's breasts, sexually propositioned her, and crassly asked in front of others why she would not have sex with him could be found sufficiently egregious to be actionable). However, some decisions find very questionable conduct not to be actionable. *See Watson v. Heartland Health Labs., Inc.*, 790 F.3d 856 (8th Cir. 2015) (a single racial slur, a sexual touching, four sexual slurs, and a threat from a patient with whom plaintiff had to deal at a facility over a 10-day period not sufficient to require a jury trial). The cases tend to be fact-bound, which makes generalizations difficult. However, in addition to the raw number of incidents, *King v. Acosta Sales & Mktg.*, 678 F.3d 470, 472 (7th Cir. 2012), touching is more likely to be associated with a finding of liability than mere language, *Ladd v. Grand Trunk Western R.R.*, 552 F.3d 495, 501 (6th Cir. 2009), and sexual propositions seem to count more than sexualized language, *Henthorn v. Capitol Commc'ns, Inc.*, 359 F.3d 1021 (8th Cir. 2004).

2. *Severe or Pervasive.* Since conduct need be either severe *or* pervasive, doesn't that mean that in appropriate circumstances, a single incident will be enough to constitute actionable harassment? A few courts have found single incidents sufficient to establish liability under Title VII, usually when it involves physical contact. *See, e.g., Berry v. Chi. Transit Auth.*, 618 F.3d 688 (7th Cir. 2010) (supervisor grabbed plaintiff's breasts, lifted her, and rubbed her body against his); *Little v. Windermere Relocation, Inc.*, 301 F.3d 958 (9th Cir. 2002) (rape by client and employer's subsequent reinforcement of the harassment satisfied severity requirement). *But see Paul v. Northrop Grumman Ship Sys.*, 309 F. App'x 825 (5th Cir. 2009) (single incident of "chesting up" to plaintiff and rubbing pelvic region across her hips and buttocks in confrontation lasting some 90 seconds not sufficient). In particularly egregious cases, even a single instance of *verbal* harassment can be enough. *See, e.g., Howley v. Town of Stratford*, 217 F.3d 141 (2d Cir. 2000) (references to plaintiff as a "fucking whining cunt" who received her job because she performed oral sex were enough to send the case to a jury).

3. *Non-Targeted Harassment.* Whether offensive conduct is targeted at the plaintiff or merely "in the air" may be relevant to whether it is viewed as sufficiently severe or pervasive, but the cases have generally found the absence of targeting not fatal to a claim. *See Gallagher v. C.H. Robinson Worldwide, Inc.*, 567 F.3d 263, 273 (6th Cir. 2009) (even if not intentionally directed at plaintiff, "she had no means of escaping her coworkers' loud insulting language and degrading conversations"); *Hoyle v. Freightliner, LLC*, 650 F.3d 321 (4th Cir. 2011) (photos of women nude or in sexually provocative poses could be found detrimental to female employees since such action was particularly offensive to women and could signal hostility to women in the workplace); *Patane v. Clark*, 508 F.3d 106 (2d Cir. 2007) (sexual harassment claim stated by secretary with regard to a professor's watching pornographic videos; the mere presence of pornography in the workplace can alter the status of women). *See also Reeves v. C.H. Robinson Worldwide, Inc.*, 594 F.3d 798 (11th Cir. 2010) (vulgar language was not generally targeted at plaintiff, but "a substantial corpus of gender-derogatory language [was] addressed specifically to women as a group in the workplace").

Relatedly, harassment of other women may be relevant to establishing that harassment of the plaintiff is actionable. That is in part because, if the plaintiff knows that the same individual committed offending acts in the past, the employer's leaving "a serial harasser . . . free to harass again leaves the impression that acts of harassment are tolerated at the workplace and supports a plaintiff's claim that the workplace is both objectively and subjectively hostile." *Hawkins v. Anheuser-Busch, Inc.*, 517 F.3d 321, 336-37 (6th Cir. 2008). *See also Ziskie v. Mineta*, 547 F.3d 220 (4th Cir. 2008) (evidence of harassment of other women could lend credence to plaintiff's claims, show the harassment was pervasive, or support a finding that she was treated poorly by co-workers because of her sex, and not some other reason); *See generally* Kerri Lynn Stone, *License to Harass: Holding Defendants Accountable for Retaining Recidivist Harassers*, 41 AKRON L. REV. 1059 (2008); Kelly Cahill Timmons, *Sexual Harassment and Disparate Impact: Should Non-Targeted Workplace Sexual Conduct Be Actionable Under Title VII?*, 81 NEB. L. REV. 1152, 1155 (2003).

Pre-req that no consequence was given to the offender? otherwise any harasser is vulnerable in any workplace to this argument

4. *Pervasiveness and Timeliness.* Contaminated workplace sexual harassment is often "pervasive" precisely because a number of incidents — no one of which may suffice — occur over a period of time and collectively alter the plaintiff's terms and conditions of employment. Title VII, however, has a very short period in which to file a charge with the EEOC — usually 300 days from a violation. This raises a question of whether events occurring before that period can be the basis of a sexual harassment claim. In *National R.R. Passenger Corp. v. Morgan*, 536 U.S. 101 (2002), the Supreme Court held that "the entire scope of a hostile work environment claim, including behavior alleged outside the statutory time period, is permissible for the purposes of assessing liability, so long as any act contributing to that same hostile environment takes place within the statutory time period." *Id.* at 117. See Note 2, p. 531.

Confused here

5. *Harassment BFOQ?* Is conduct that would otherwise constitute harassment ever permissible because of the necessities of the employment at question? In *Lyle v. Warner Brothers Television Productions*, 132 P.3d 211 (Cal. 2006), the California Supreme Court upheld summary judgment in favor of the employer, finding that in the context of the television show on which plaintiff was working (*Friends*), the language used by the writers could not reasonably be viewed as harassment of the plaintiff. If such conduct is justifiable, is it because sexualized activity is a BFOQ in such settings? *Lyle* analogized the argument to the "business necessity" defense in disparate impact cases. Was that an appropriate analogy? *See* Ann C. McGinley, *Harassment of Sex(y) Workers: Applying Title VII to Sexualized Industries*, 18 YALE J.L. & FEMINISM 65, 108 (2006). These issues often arise in institutions whose inmates or patients harass their guards or caregivers. Even in such settings, employers may be held liable if they do not take reasonable steps to protect their employees. *See Beckford v. Dep't of Corr.*, 605 F.3d 951, 953 (11th Cir. 2010) (upholding jury verdict when prison unreasonably failed to remedy sexual harassment by inmates, including the frequent use of gender-specific abusive language and openly masturbating toward female staff); *Randolph v. Ohio Dep't of Youth Servs.*, 453 F.3d 724, 732 (6th Cir. 2006) (plaintiff's "allegations are so serious that they satisfy the hostile work environment prong despite the mitigating consideration of the prison work environment"). *But see Vajdl v. Mesabi Acad. of Kidspeace, Inc.*, 484 F.3d 546 (8th Cir. 2007) (those who choose to work in a prison accept the probability of facing inappropriate and socially deviant behavior"); *EEOC v. Nexion Health at Broadway, Inc.*, 199 F. App'x 351, 354 (5th Cir. 2006) (it was objectively unreasonable for plaintiff, who worked in a nursing home, "to perceive a racially hostile work environment based solely on statements made by those who are mentally impaired").

Expectation/ assumption/ risk? of

b.   The "Reasonable Person" Requirement

Harris judges harassment in part by an objective standard. Thus, the fact that the victim feels harassed is not sufficient: the conduct must *reasonably* be perceived as hostile. But reasonably be perceived by whom? Presumably, by a reasonable person in the victim's shoes. However, studies have shown that men and women may react differently to harassing conduct. Does that suggest that, if the victim is a woman, the conduct should be evaluated from the perspective of a reasonable woman? Prior to *Harris*, the Ninth Circuit adopted such an approach in *Ellison v. Brady*, 924 F.2d 872, 878 (9th Cir. 1991), looking to Professor Kathryn Abrams's article, *Gender Discrimination and the Transformation of Workplace Norms*, 42 VAND. L. REV. 1183, 1205 (1989). There she noted that the characteristically male view depicts sexual harassment as comparatively harmless amusement but that women's "greater physical and social vulnerability to sexual coercion can make women wary of sexual encounters," especially "in a society where rape and sex-related violence have reached unprecedented levels, and a vast pornography industry creates continuous images of sexual coercion, objectification and violence."

After *Harris*, the Ninth Circuit modified its standard for evaluating sexual harassment in an attempt to reconcile *Ellison* with the standard applied in *Harris*: "[w]hether the workplace is objectively hostile must be determined from the perspective of a reasonable person with the same fundamental characteristics." *Fuller v. City of Oakland*, 47 F.3d 1522, 1527 (9th Cir. 1995). But in *McGinest v. GTE Service Corp.*, 360 F.3d 1103, 1115 (9th Cir. 2004), a racially hostile work environment case, the Ninth Circuit reasserted the *Ellison* holding, saying when "evaluating the significance of the statements in question, [the court considers] the hostility of the workplace from the perspective of the . . . reasonable person belonging to the racial or ethnic group of the plaintiff." The court did note that other courts have read *Harris* to reject a "reasonable person standard based on the perspective of a person sharing the characteristics of the plaintiff." Which is the better reading of *Harris*?

c.   "Unwelcome" Conduct

Harris also made clear that it is not enough for the conduct to reasonably be perceived as hostile or abusive; the victim herself must *subjectively* perceive the conduct to be abusive for a Title VII violation to exist. In contrast, *Meritor* spoke in terms of the harassment being "unwelcome." Are the two standards simply different ways of saying the same thing?

Either way, it should usually be sufficient for this prong for a plaintiff to testify she found the conduct unwelcome or offensive. Occasionally, however, defendants have attempted to rebut the claim that the conduct was unwelcome by introducing evidence of the plaintiff's behavior, language, or appearance. Recall that in *Meritor*, the Court stated that Vinson's style of dress was "obviously relevant" to the question whether she welcomed Taylor's sexual advances. Does this mean that an employee who dresses in a sexually provocative manner can lose her right to be free of sexual harassment? Surely not! And the Seventh Circuit rejected a "welcoming" argument by defendant when the girl in question was underage when the harassment occurred, *Doe v. Oberweis Dairy*, 456 F.3d 704, 714 (7th Cir. 2006), and thus legally precluded from welcoming it.

But the possibility remains that a woman's conduct might justify conduct that would otherwise be impermissible. In other words, maybe "welcoming" refers not to the victim's subjective feelings but to what a reasonable man might perceive she welcomed. *See EEOC v. Prospect Airport Servs.*, 621 F.3d 991, 997-98 (9th Cir. 2010) (while "welcomeness is inherently subjective," for the conduct to impose employer's liability, unwelcomeness has to be communicated).

In any event, while *Meritor* seems to require the plaintiff to prove unwelcomeness and/or subjective offense, the next principal case suggests that the burden of proof on the question of whether the victim subjectively viewed the conduct as hostile and offensive may, as a practical matter, have been shifted to the defendant. As you read it, ask yourself whether the affirmative defense makes a separate "welcomeness" inquiry unnecessary in most sexual harassment cases because of the importance of whether the plaintiff complained. *See* Henry L. Chambers, Jr., *(Un)Welcome Conduct and the Sexually Hostile Work Environment*, 53 ALA. L. REV. 733 (2002).

d. Vicarious Liability

BURLINGTON INDUSTRIES, INC. v. ELLERTH
524 U.S. 742 (1998)

S.Ct. 1998

Justice KENNEDY delivered the opinion of the Court.

We decide whether, under Title VII of the Civil Rights Act of 1964, an employee who refuses the unwelcome and threatening sexual advances of a supervisor, yet suffers no adverse, tangible job consequences, can recover against the employer without showing the employer is negligent or otherwise at fault for the supervisor's actions.

issue

I

Summary judgment was granted for the employer, so we must take the facts alleged by the employee to be true. The employer is Burlington Industries, the petitioner. The employee is Kimberly Ellerth, the respondent. From March 1993 until May 1994, Ellerth worked as a salesperson in one of Burlington's divisions in Chicago, Illinois. During her employment, she alleges, she was subjected to constant sexual harassment by her supervisor, one Ted Slowik.

In the hierarchy of Burlington's management structure, Slowik was a mid-level manager. . . . He had authority to make hiring and promotion decisions subject to the approval of his supervisor, who signed the paperwork. According to Slowik's supervisor, his position was "not considered an upper-level management position," and he was "not amongst the decision-making or policy-making hierarchy." Slowik was not Ellerth's immediate supervisor. Ellerth worked in a two-person office in Chicago, and she answered to her office colleague, who in turn answered to Slowik in New York.

Against a background of repeated boorish and offensive remarks and gestures which Slowik allegedly made, Ellerth places particular emphasis on three alleged incidents where Slowik's comments could be construed as threats to deny her tangible job benefits. In the summer of 1993, while on a business trip, Slowik invited Ellerth to the hotel lounge, an invitation Ellerth felt compelled to accept because Slowik was her boss. When Ellerth gave no encouragement to remarks Slowik made about her breasts, he told her to "loosen up" and warned, "[y]ou know, Kim, I could make your life very hard or very easy at Burlington."

In March 1994, when Ellerth was being considered for a promotion, Slowik expressed reservations during the promotion interview because she was not "loose enough." The comment was followed by his reaching over and rubbing her knee. Ellerth did receive the promotion; but when Slowik called to announce it, he told

Ellerth, "you're gonna be out there with men who work in factories, and they certainly like women with pretty butts/legs."

③ In May 1994, Ellerth called Slowik, asking permission to insert a customer's logo into a fabric sample. Slowik responded, "I don't have time for you right now, Kim — unless you want to tell me what you're wearing." Ellerth told Slowik she had to go and ended the call. A day or two later, Ellerth called Slowik to ask permission again. This time he denied her request, but added something along the lines of, "are you wearing shorter skirts yet, Kim, because it would make your job a whole heck of a lot easier."

A short time later, Ellerth's immediate supervisor cautioned her about returning telephone calls to customers in a prompt fashion. In response, Ellerth quit. She faxed a letter giving reasons unrelated to the alleged sexual harassment we have described. About three weeks later, however, she sent a letter explaining she quit because of Slowik's behavior.

she did not report

During her tenure at Burlington, Ellerth did not inform anyone in authority about Slowik's conduct, despite knowing Burlington had a policy against sexual harassment. In fact, she chose not to inform her immediate supervisor (not Slowik) because "'it would be his duty as my supervisor to report any incidents of sexual harassment.'" On one occasion, she told Slowik a comment he made was inappropriate.

Dist. Court

. . . The District Court granted summary judgment to Burlington. The Court found Slowik's behavior, as described by Ellerth, severe and pervasive enough to create a hostile work environment, but found Burlington neither knew nor should have known about the conduct. . . .

Appellate

The Court of Appeals en banc reversed in a decision which produced eight separate opinions and no consensus for a controlling rationale. . . .

II

At the outset, we assume an important proposition yet to be established before a trier of fact. It is a premise assumed as well, in explicit or implicit terms, in the various opinions by the judges of the Court of Appeals. The premise is: a trier of fact could find in Slowik's remarks numerous threats to retaliate against Ellerth if she denied some sexual liberties. The threats, however, were not carried out or fulfilled. Cases based on threats which are carried out are referred to often as *quid pro quo* cases, as distinct from bothersome attentions or sexual remarks that are sufficiently severe or pervasive to create a hostile work environment. The terms *quid pro quo* and hostile work environment are helpful, perhaps, in making a rough demarcation between cases in which threats are carried out and those where they are not or are absent altogether, but beyond this are of limited utility. [They "do not appear in the statutory text" but rather] appeared first in the academic literature, found their way into decisions of the Courts of Appeals, and were mentioned in this Court's decision in *Meritor*.

In *Meritor*, the terms served a specific and limited purpose. There we considered whether the conduct in question constituted discrimination in the terms or conditions of employment in violation of Title VII. We assumed, and with adequate reason, that if an employer demanded sexual favors from an employee in return for a job benefit, discrimination with respect to terms or conditions of employment was explicit. Less obvious was whether an employer's sexually demeaning behavior altered terms or conditions of employment in violation of Title VII. We distinguished between *quid pro quo* claims and hostile environment claims, and said both were cognizable under Title VII, though the latter requires harassment that is severe or pervasive. The principal significance of the distinction is to instruct that Title VII is violated by either explicit or constructive alterations in the terms or conditions of employment and to explain the latter must be severe or pervasive. The distinction was not discussed for its bearing upon an employer's liability for an employee's discrimination. On this question *Meritor* held, with no further specifics, that agency principles controlled.

[Nevertheless, in the wake of *Meritor*, the terms acquired their own significance, with vicarious employer liability turning on whether plaintiff established a quid pro quo claim. The point is clear in this case where the question presented] is whether Ellerth can state a claim of quid pro quo harassment, but the issue of real concern to the parties is whether Burlington has vicarious liability for Slowik's alleged misconduct, rather than liability limited to its own negligence. . . .

We do not suggest the terms *quid pro quo* and hostile work environment are irrelevant to Title VII litigation. To the extent they illustrate the distinction between cases involving a threat which is carried out and offensive conduct in general, the terms are relevant when there is a threshold question whether a plaintiff can prove discrimination in violation of Title VII. When a plaintiff proves that a tangible employment action resulted from a refusal to submit to a supervisor's sexual demands, he or she establishes that the employment decision itself constitutes a change in the terms and conditions of employment that is actionable under Title VII. For any sexual harassment preceding the employment decision to be actionable, however, the conduct must be severe or pervasive. Because Ellerth's claim involves only unfulfilled threats, it should be categorized as a hostile work environment claim which requires a showing of severe or pervasive conduct. For purposes of this case, we accept the District Court's finding that the alleged conduct was severe or pervasive. The case before us involves numerous alleged threats, and we express no opinion as to whether a single unfulfilled threat is sufficient to constitute discrimination in the terms or conditions of employment.

Held: can have claim even if threats unfulfilled

When we assume discrimination can be proved, however, the factors we discuss below, and not the categories *quid pro quo* and hostile work environment, will be controlling on the issue of vicarious liability. That is the question we must resolve.

III

We must decide, then, whether an employer has vicarious liability when a supervisor creates a hostile work environment by making explicit threats to alter a subordinate's terms or conditions of employment, based on sex, but does not fulfill the threat. We turn to principles of agency law, for the term "employer" is defined under Title VII to include "agents." . . .

issue

As *Meritor* acknowledged, the RESTATEMENT (SECOND) OF AGENCY (1957) (hereinafter Restatement), is a useful beginning point for a discussion of general agency principles. . . .

A

Section 219(1) of the Restatement sets out a central principle of agency law:

A master is subject to liability for the torts of his servants committed while acting in the scope of their employment.

An employer may be liable for both negligent and intentional torts committed by an employee within the scope of his or her employment. Sexual harassment under

Title VII presupposes intentional conduct. While early decisions absolved employers of liability for the intentional torts of their employees, the law now imposes liability where the employee's "purpose, however misguided, is wholly or in part to further the master's business." W. KEETON, D. DOBBS, R. KEETON & D. OWEN, PROSSER AND KEETON ON LAW OF TORTS §70, p. 505 (5th ed. 1984) (hereinafter Prosser and Keeton on Torts). In applying scope of employment principles to intentional torts, however, it is accepted that "it is less likely that a willful tort will properly be held to be in the course of employment and that the liability of the master for such torts will naturally be more limited." F. MECHEM, OUTLINES OF THE LAW OF AGENCY §394, p. 266 (P. Mechem 4th ed., 1952). The Restatement defines conduct, including an intentional tort, to be within the scope of employment when "actuated, at least in part, by a purpose to serve the [employer]," even if it is forbidden by the employer. Restatement §§228(1)(c), 230.

As Courts of Appeals have recognized, a supervisor acting out of gender-based animus or a desire to fulfill sexual urges may not be actuated by a purpose to serve the employer. The harassing supervisor often acts for personal motives, motives unrelated and even antithetical to the objectives of the employer. There are instances, of course, where a supervisor engages in unlawful discrimination with the purpose, mistaken or otherwise, to serve the employer.

The general rule is that sexual harassment by a supervisor is not conduct within the scope of employment.

B

Scope of employment does not define the only basis for employer liability under agency principles. In limited circumstances, agency principles impose liability on employers even where employees commit torts outside the scope of employment. The principles are set forth in the much-cited §219(2) of the Restatement:

> (2) A master is not subject to liability for the torts of his servants acting outside the scope of their employment, unless:
>   (a) the master intended the conduct or the consequences, or
>   (b) the master was negligent or reckless, or
>   (c) the conduct violated a non-delegable duty of the master, or
>   (d) the servant purported to act or to speak on behalf of the principal and there was reliance upon apparent authority, or he was aided in accomplishing the tort by the existence of the agency relation.

Subsection (a) addresses direct liability, where the employer acts with tortious intent, and indirect liability, where the agent's high rank in the company makes him or her the employer's alter ego. None of the parties contend Slowik's rank imputes liability under this principle. There is no contention, furthermore, that a non-delegable duty is involved. See §219(2)(c). So, for our purposes here, subsections (a) and (c) can be put aside.

Subsections (b) and (d) are possible grounds for imposing employer liability on account of a supervisor's acts and must be considered. Under subsection (b), an employer is liable when the tort is attributable to the employer's own negligence. Thus, although a supervisor's sexual harassment is outside the scope of employment because the conduct was for personal motives, an employer can be liable, nonetheless, where its own negligence is a cause of the harassment. An employer is negligent with respect to sexual harassment if it knew or should have known about the conduct and failed to stop it. Negligence sets a minimum standard for employer liability under Title VII; but Ellerth seeks to invoke the more stringent standard of vicarious liability.

Subsection 219(2)(d) concerns vicarious liability for intentional torts committed by an employee when the employee uses apparent authority (the apparent authority standard), or when the employee "was aided in accomplishing the tort by the existence of the agency relation" (the aided in the agency relation standard). As other federal decisions have done in discussing vicarious liability for supervisor harassment, we begin with §219(2)(d).

C

As a general rule, apparent authority is relevant where the agent purports to exercise a power which he or she does not have, as distinct from where the agent threatens to misuse actual power. In the usual case, a supervisor's harassment involves misuse of actual power, not the false impression of its existence. Apparent authority analysis therefore is inappropriate in this context. If, in the unusual case, it is alleged there is a false impression that the actor was a supervisor, when he in fact was not, the victim's mistaken conclusion must be a reasonable one. When a party seeks to impose vicarious liability based on an agent's misuse of delegated authority, the Restatement's aided in the agency relation rule, rather than the apparent authority rule, appears to be the appropriate form of analysis.

D

We turn to the aided in the agency relation standard. In a sense, most workplace tortfeasors are aided in accomplishing their tortious objective by the existence of the agency relation: Proximity and regular contact may afford a captive pool of potential victims. Were this to satisfy the aided in the agency relation standard, an employer would be subject to vicarious liability not only for all supervisor harassment, but also for all co-worker harassment, a result enforced by neither the EEOC nor any court of appeals to have considered the issue. The aided in the agency relation standard, therefore, requires the existence of something more than the employment relation itself.

At the outset, we can identify a class of cases where, beyond question, more than the mere existence of the employment relation aids in commission of the harassment: when a supervisor takes a tangible employment action against the subordinate. Every Federal Court of Appeals to have considered the question has found vicarious liability when a discriminatory act results in a tangible employment action. In *Meritor*, we acknowledged this consensus [and] we think it reflects a correct application of the aided in the agency relation standard.

In the context of this case, a tangible employment action would have taken the form of a denial of a raise or a promotion. . . . A tangible employment action constitutes a significant change in employment status, such as hiring, firing, failing to promote, reassignment with significantly different responsibilities, or a decision causing a significant change in benefits. Compare *Crady v. Liberty Nat. Bank & Trust Co. of Ind.*, 993 F.2d 132, 136 (7th Cir. 1993) ("A materially adverse change might be indicated by a termination of employment, a demotion evidenced by a decrease in wage or salary, a less distinguished title, a material loss of benefits, significantly diminished material responsibilities, or other indices that might be unique to a particular situation"), with *Flaherty v. Gas Research Institute*, 31 F.3d 451, 456 (7th Cir. 1994) (a "bruised ego" is not enough); *Kocsis v. Multi-Care Management, Inc.*, 97 F.3d 876, 887 (6th Cir. 1996) (demotion without change in pay, benefits, duties, or prestige insufficient); and *Harlston v. McDonnell Douglas Corp.*, 37 F.3d 379, 382 (8th Cir. 1994) (reassignment to more inconvenient job insufficient).

When a supervisor makes a tangible employment decision, there is assurance the injury could not have been inflicted absent the agency relation. A tangible employment action in most cases inflicts direct economic harm. As a general proposition, only a supervisor, or other person acting with the authority of the company, can cause this sort of injury. A co-worker can break a co-worker's arm as easily as a supervisor, and anyone who has regular contact with an employee can inflict psychological injuries by his or her offensive conduct. But one co-worker (absent some elaborate scheme) cannot dock another's pay, nor can one co-worker demote another. Tangible employment actions fall within the special province of the supervisor. The supervisor has been empowered by the company as a distinct class of agent to make economic decisions affecting other employees under his or her control.

Tangible employment actions are the means by which the supervisor brings the official power of the enterprise to bear on subordinates. A tangible employment decision requires an official act of the enterprise, a company act. The decision in most cases is documented in official company records, and may be subject to review by higher level supervisors. The supervisor often must obtain the imprimatur of the enterprise and use its internal processes.

tangible employment action requires an agency relationship

For these reasons, a tangible employment action taken by the supervisor becomes for Title VII purposes the act of the employer. Whatever the exact contours of the aided in the agency relation standard, its requirements will always be met when a supervisor takes a tangible employment action against a subordinate. In that instance, it would be implausible to interpret agency principles to allow an employer to escape liability, as *Meritor* itself appeared to acknowledge.

issue Whether the agency relation aids in commission of supervisor harassment which does not culminate in a tangible employment action is less obvious. [While "a supervisor's power and authority invests his or her harassing conduct with a particular threatening character," the "acts of harassment a supervisor might commit . . . might be the same acts a co-employee would commit, and there may be some circumstances where the supervisor's status makes little difference."]

It is this tension which, we think, has caused so much confusion among the Courts of Appeals which have sought to apply the aided in the agency relation standard to Title VII cases. The aided in the agency relation standard, however, is a developing feature of agency law, and we hesitate to render a definitive explanation of our understanding of the standard in an area where other important considerations must affect our judgment. In particular, we are bound by our holding in *Meritor* that agency principles constrain the imposition of vicarious liability in cases of supervisory harassment [especially since] Congress has not altered *Meritor*'s rule even though it has made significant amendments to Title VII in the interim. Although *Meritor* suggested the limitation on employer liability stemmed from agency principles, the Court acknowledged other considerations might be relevant as well. For example, Title VII is designed to encourage the creation of antiharassment policies and effective grievance mechanisms. Were employer liability to depend in part on an employer's effort to create such procedures, it would effect Congress' intention to promote conciliation rather than litigation in the Title VII context and the EEOC's policy of encouraging the development of grievance procedures. See 29 CFR §1604.11(f) (1997); EEOC Policy Guidance on Sexual Harassment, 8 BNA FEP Manual 405:6699 (Mar. 19, 1990). To the extent limiting employer liability could encourage employees to report harassing conduct before it becomes severe or pervasive, it would also serve Title VII's deterrent purpose. As we have observed, Title VII borrows from tort law the avoidable consequences doctrine, and the considerations which animate that doctrine would also support the limitation of employer liability in certain circumstances.

In order to accommodate the agency principles of vicarious liability for harm caused by misuse of supervisory authority, as well as Title VII's equally basic policies of encouraging forethought by employers and saving action by objecting employees, we adopt the following holding in this case and in *Faragher v. Boca Raton*, also decided today. An employer is subject to vicarious liability to a victimized employee for an actionable hostile environment created by a supervisor with immediate (or successively higher) authority over the employee. When no tangible employment action is taken, a defending employer may raise an affirmative defense to liability or damages, subject to proof by a preponderance of the evidence. The defense comprises two necessary elements: (a) that the employer exercised reasonable care to prevent and correct promptly any sexually harassing behavior, and (b) that the plaintiff employee unreasonably failed to take advantage of any preventive or corrective opportunities provided by the employer or to avoid harm otherwise. While proof that an employer had promulgated an anti-harassment policy with complaint procedure is not necessary in every instance as a matter of law, the need for a stated policy suitable to the employment circumstances may appropriately be addressed in any case when litigating the first element of the defense. And while proof that an employee failed to fulfill the corresponding obligation of reasonable care to avoid harm is not limited to showing any unreasonable failure to use any complaint procedure provided by the employer, a demonstration of such failure will normally suffice to satisfy the employer's burden under the second element of the defense. No affirmative defense is available, however, when the supervisor's harassment culminates in a tangible employment action, such as discharge, demotion, or undesirable reassignment.

[The Court remanded so that Ms. Ellerth would have an adequate opportunity to prove she has a claim for which Burlington is liable and Burlington would have an opportunity to prove its affirmative defense.]

NOTES

1. *Employer Liability and Harassment Claims.* In a part of *Meritor* not reproduced previously, the Court addressed, but did not fully resolve, the issue of *employer* liability for harassment in the workplace. It rejected holding employers "automatically liable" but also held that the "mere existence of a grievance procedure and a policy against discrimination" does not insulate an employer from liability if the plaintiff failed to invoke that procedure. 477 U.S. at 72-73. That left the question of employer liability law more than a little confused, but resolving that question was critical because, while Title VII defines "employer" to include "any agent" of an employer, courts have generally refused to hold individual employees personally liable for their discriminatory conduct. See Chapter 9 at p. 594. If, then, employers are not liable for their supervisors' conduct, there will typically be no liability for admittedly harassing conduct.

Ellerth, and *Faragher v. City of Boca Raton*, 524 U.S. 775 (1998), a companion case to *Ellerth*, attempted to resolve the issues *Meritor* left open. *Faragher* adopted the same holding as in *Ellerth*. *See id.* at 802-08. Did *Ellerth/Faragher* create a rule of employer liability that is fair to plaintiffs? Fair to defendants? Scholars critiqued the resulting structure from a variety of perspectives. *See Martha Chamallas, Two Very Different Stories: Vicarious Liability Under Tort and Title VII Law*, 75 Ohio St. L.J. 1315 (2014); Sandra F. Sperino, *A Modern Theory of Direct Corporate Liability for Title VII*, 61 Ala. L. Rev. 773, 774-75 (2010).

2. *The Use of Agency Principles.* Prior to *Ellerth*, courts held that, if the harasser is himself in a high enough position in the employer's hierarchy, the actions and

knowledge of the harasser are imputed to the employer, what *Ellerth* referred to as "alter ego" liability. *Faragher,* for example, viewed *Harris* as involving imputed liability because "the individual charged with creating the abusive atmosphere was the president of the corporate employer, who was indisputably within that class of an employer organization's officials who may be treated as the organization's proxy." 524 U.S. at 790. *Ellerth* also notes the possibility of "direct liability, where the employer acts with tortious intent, and indirect liability, where the agent's high rank in the company makes him or her the employer's alter ego." *Id.* at 758. Is the *Ellerth/Faragher* defense available in cases in which the harasser's actions are imputed to the employer under the "alter ego" or "proxy" approach? *See Townsend v. Benjamin Enters.,* 679 F.3d 41 (2d Cir. 2012) (holding no and noting that this holding is consistent with the determinations of every court of appeals to have considered the issue). *See generally* Curtis J. Bankers, *Identifying Employers' "Proxies" in Sexual-Harassment Litigation,* 99 Iowa L. Rev. 1785 (2014).

3. *Tangible Employment Actions.* A key holding of *Ellerth* and *Faragher* was that an employer is automatically liable when a "supervisor" takes a "tangible employment action" with respect to the plaintiff. While we will explore the definition of "supervisor" shortly, a key issue in the wake of the two cases was the definition of a tangible employment action. Finding a tangible employment action has occurred is often outcome determinative because the employer cannot assert the affirmative defense in such cases. But, as with its cousin concept the "adverse employment action," see p. 56, courts have reached somewhat disparate results on the question. Is a lateral transfer a tangible employment action if an employee's pay is not affected? Is being assigned different tasks? Being denied perks such as travel to conferences?

Some courts view the analysis of "tangible employment action" as parallel to "adverse employment action" because they focus on the effects on plaintiff. *See Dulaney v. Packaging Corp. of Am.,* 673 F.3d 323 (4th Cir. 2012) (if employee would have been discharged had she not signed severance agreement with waiver of rights, tangible job action occurred, precluding employer's assertion of the affirmative defense); *Roebuck v. Washington,* 408 F.3d 790 (D.C. Cir. 2005) (changing door locks, ordering a transfer and then rescinding it, and a lateral transfer of plaintiff were not tangible employment actions; it is not the "official" nature of the act that matters but whether it has a significant effect on the plaintiff's employment status); *Agusty-Reyes v. Dep't of Educ.,* 601 F.3d 45 (1st Cir. 2010) ("failure to grant tenure could also lead to a meaningful change in an employee's benefits in an up-or-out situation at a time when budgetary constraints loomed").

But one commentator, Rebecca Hanner White, in *De Minimis Discrimination,* 47 Emory L.J. 1121, 1158 (1998), asserts that the best way to determine whether an action is tangible within the meaning of *Ellerth* and *Faragher* is to look to the agency theory relied on in those cases and thus to examine whether the action is one the supervisor's authority *as supervisor* enabled him to take. If so, it should be deemed a tangible employment action:

> Only a supervisor can transfer, reassign, or negatively evaluate a worker, but supervisors and co-workers alike may use racial epithets, may hurt an employee's feelings, or smack an employee on the rear. . . . Accordingly, it is not the economic or materially adverse nature of the discrimination that makes [the employer vicariously liable] but the fact that it involves an action only supervisors can inflict on their subordinates.

Professor White's approach to "tangible employment actions" is broader than that followed by numerous lower courts. Is it too broad? Professor Michael Harper suggests a somewhat different analysis: a tangible employment action is any supervisory action that is recorded or reported, as it would be "readily available for review." Michael C. Harper, *Employer Liability for Harassment Under Title VII: A Functional Rationale for* Faragher *and* Ellerth, 36 SAN DIEGO L. REV. 41 (1999).

4. *Constructive Discharge.* In *Pennsylvania State Police v. Suders*, 542 U.S. 129 (2004), the Supreme Court considered whether a constructive discharge is by definition a tangible job action. The lower court had held categorically yes, thus rendering the *Ellerth/Faragher* affirmative defense unavailable. It reasoned that, because termination was unquestionably a tangible employment action, a constructive termination, carrying the same economic consequences, should be similarly viewed. The Supreme Court rejected that approach. Instead, whether a constructive discharge qualifies is to be resolved under the agency theories put forward in *Ellerth*. Accordingly, if it is only a hostile work environment that triggers the constructive discharge, the affirmative defense remains available to the employer.

5. *Scope of Employment.* After *Ellerth*, can sexual harassment by a supervisor be "within the scope of employment" of the supervisor? Suppose a supervisor, in order to boost sales, requires female employees to wear revealing attire that generates severe and pervasive responses by customers? *See EEOC v. Sage Realty Co.*, 507 F. Supp. 599 (S.D.N.Y. 1981). If employer liability can be based on harassment being "within the scope of employment" of a supervisor, is the defense created in *Ellerth* available, or is the defense available only when "agency" is based on the "aided in the agency relation" approach and no "tangible employment actions" are involved?

VANCE v. BALL STATE UNIVERSITY
133 S. Ct. 2434 (2013)

S. Ct. 2013

Justice ALITO delivered the opinion of the Court.

. . . We hold that [under the *Ellerth/Faragher* framework] an employee is a "supervisor" for purposes of vicarious liability under Title VII if he or she is empowered by the employer to take tangible employment actions against the victim. . . .

Held ✳

I

Maetta Vance, an African-American woman, began working for Ball State University (BSU) in 1989 as a substitute server in the University Banquet and Catering division of Dining Services. In 1991, BSU promoted Vance to a part-time catering assistant position, and in 2007 she applied and was selected for a position as a full-time catering assistant.

Over the course of her employment with BSU, Vance lodged numerous complaints of racial discrimination and retaliation, but most of those incidents are not at issue here. For present purposes, the only relevant incidents concern Vance's interactions with a fellow BSU employee, Saundra Davis.

During the time in question, [Saundra] Davis, a white woman, was employed as a catering specialist in the Banquet and Catering division. The parties vigorously dispute the precise nature and scope of Davis' duties, but they agree that Davis did not have the power to hire, fire, demote, promote, transfer, or discipline Vance.

In late 2005 and early 2006, Vance filed internal complaints with BSU and charges with the Equal Employment Opportunity Commission (EEOC), alleging racial harassment and discrimination, and many of these complaints and charges pertained to Davis. Vance complained that Davis "gave her a hard time at work by glaring at her, slamming

evidence of harassment

pots and pans around her, and intimidating her." She alleged that she was "left alone in the kitchen with Davis, who smiled at her"; that Davis "blocked" her on an elevator and "stood there with her cart smiling"; and that Davis often gave her "weird" looks.

Vance's workplace strife persisted despite BSU's attempts to address the problem. . . .

II . . .

B

[W]e have held that an employer is directly liable for an employee's unlawful harassment if the employer was negligent with respect to the offensive behavior. *Faragher*. Courts have generally applied this rule to evaluate employer liability when a co-worker harasses the plaintiff.

[The opinion then reiterated the differing analysis "where the harassing employee is the plaintiff's 'supervisor,'" looking to §219(2) of the Restatement (Second) of Agency, which articulates the aided-in-the-accomplishment rule. That rule warrants employer liability even absent negligence in two situations, both of which involve harassment by a "supervisor," as opposed to a co-worker. The first was the vicarious liability "when a supervisor takes a tangible employment action." Second, even absent a tangible employment action, "the employer can be vicariously liable for the supervisor's creation of a hostile work environment if the employer is unable to establish an affirmative defense.]³

III . . .

We hold that an employer may be vicariously liable for an employee's unlawful harassment only when the employer has empowered that employee to take tangible employment actions against the victim, *i.e.*, to effect a "significant change in employment status, such as hiring, firing, failing to promote, reassignment with significantly different responsibilities, or a decision causing a significant change in benefits." *Ellerth*. We reject the nebulous definition of a "supervisor" advocated in the EEOC Guidance and substantially adopted by several courts of appeals. Petitioner's reliance on colloquial uses of the term "supervisor" is misplaced, and her contention that our cases require the EEOC's abstract definition is simply wrong.

As we will explain, the framework set out in *Ellerth* and *Faragher* presupposes a clear distinction between supervisors and co-workers. Those decisions contemplate a unitary category of supervisors, *i.e.*, those employees with the authority to make tangible employment decisions. There is no hint in either decision that the Court had in mind two categories of supervisors: first, those who have such authority and, second, those who, although lacking this power, nevertheless have the ability to direct a co-worker's labor to some ill-defined degree. On the contrary, the *Ellerth/Faragher* framework is one under which supervisory status can usually be readily determined, generally by written documentation. The approach recommended by the EEOC Guidance, by contrast, would make the determination of supervisor status depend on a highly case-specific evaluation of numerous factors.

The *Ellerth/Faragher* framework represents what the Court saw as a workable compromise between the aided-in-the-agency theory of vicarious liability and the legitimate interests of employers. The Seventh Circuit's understanding of the concept of a "supervisor," with which we agree, is easily workable; it can be applied without undue

---

3. . . . Neither party in this case challenges the application of *Faragher* and *Ellerth* [both of which involved sexual harassment] to race-based hostile environment claims, and we assume that the framework announced in *Faragher* and *Ellerth* applies to cases such as this one.

difficulty at both the summary judgment stage and at trial. The alternative, in many cases, would frustrate judges and confound jurors.

A

[The majority recognized that the term "supervisor" has "varying meanings both in colloquial usage and in the law," but, in any event, is not a term chosen by Congress in Title VII but rather adopted by *Ellerth* and *Faragher* "as a label for the class of employees whose misconduct may give rise to vicarious employer liability," which requires "the interpretation that best fits within the highly structured framework that those cases adopted."]

"supervisor"

B

[The Court rejected] petitioner's argument that the question before us in the present case was effectively settled in her favor by our treatment of the alleged harassers in *Ellerth* and *Faragher*. [It went on to state that as] *Ellerth* recognized, "most workplace tortfeasors are aided in accomplishing their tortious objective by the existence of the agency relation," and consequently "something more" is required in order to warrant vicarious liability. The ability to direct another employee's tasks is simply not sufficient. Employees with such powers are certainly capable of creating intolerable work environments, but so are many other co-workers. Negligence provides the better framework for evaluating an employer's liability when a harassing employee lacks the power to take tangible employment actions.

C

Although our holdings in *Faragher* and *Ellerth* do not resolve the question now before us, we believe that the answer to that question is implicit in the characteristics of the framework that we adopted.

To begin, there is no hint in either *Ellerth* or *Faragher* that the Court contemplated anything other than a unitary category of supervisors, namely, those possessing the authority to effect a tangible change in a victim's terms or conditions of employment. The *Ellerth/Faragher* framework draws a sharp line between co-workers and supervisors. Co-workers, the Court noted, "can inflict psychological injuries" by creating a hostile work environment, but they "cannot dock another's pay, nor can one co-worker demote another." *Ellerth.* Only a supervisor has the power to cause "direct economic harm" by taking a tangible employment action. . . . The strong implication . . . is that the authority to take tangible employment actions is the defining characteristic of a supervisor, not simply a characteristic of a subset of an ill-defined class of employees who qualify as supervisors. . . .

[The *Ellerth/Faragher* framework was designed to be workable and to balance the legitimate interests of employers and employees. Rather than "the wholesale incorporation" of the aided-in-the-accomplishing rule into Title VII, *Ellerth*] also considered the objectives of Title VII, including "the limitation of employer liability in certain circumstances." *Id.*

The interpretation of the concept of a supervisor that we adopt today is one that can be readily applied. . . . By contrast, under the approach advocated by petitioner and the EEOC, supervisor status would very often be murky — as this case well illustrates.[12]

a Court can make a finding of sex discr. or harassment w/out economic tangible consequences (ie psych) but there we use a diff. liability theory so the tangibility test is used diff'ly in this context

---

12. The dissent attempts to find ambiguities in our holding, but it is indisputable that our holding is orders of magnitude clearer than the nebulous standard it would adopt. . . .

π argue Davis counts as supervisor

U.S. argues she does NOT count

According to petitioner, the record shows that Davis, her alleged harasser, wielded enough authority to qualify as a supervisor. Petitioner points in particular to Davis' job description, which gave her leadership responsibilities, and to evidence that Davis at times led or directed Vance and other employees in the kitchen. The United States, on the other hand, while applying the same open-ended test for supervisory status, reaches the opposite conclusion. At least on the present record, the United States tells us, Davis fails to qualify as a supervisor. Her job description, in the Government's view, is not dispositive, and the Government adds that it would not be enough for petitioner to show that Davis "occasionally took the lead in the kitchen."

This disagreement is hardly surprising since the EEOC's definition of a supervisor, which both petitioner and the United States defend, is a study in ambiguity. . . . We read the EEOC Guidance as saying that the number (and perhaps the importance) of the tasks in question is a factor to be considered in determining whether an employee qualifies as a supervisor. And if this is a correct interpretation of the EEOC's position, what we are left with is a proposed standard of remarkable ambiguity.

The vagueness of this standard was highlighted at oral argument when the attorney representing the United States was asked to apply that standard to the situation in *Faragher*, where the alleged harasser supposedly threatened to assign the plaintiff to clean the toilets in the lifeguard station for a year if she did not date him. Since cleaning the toilets is just one task, albeit an unpleasant one, the authority to assign that job would not seem to meet the more-than-a-limited-number-of-tasks requirement in the EEOC Guidance. Nevertheless, the Government attorney's first response was that the authority to make this assignment would be enough. He later qualified that answer by saying that it would be necessary to "know how much of the day's work [was] encompassed by cleaning the toilets." He did not explain what percentage of the day's work (50%, 25%, 10%?) would suffice.

The Government attorney's inability to provide a definitive answer to this question was the inevitable consequence of the vague standard that the Government asks us to adopt. . . .

MOL

Under the definition of "supervisor" that we adopt today, the question of supervisor status, when contested, can very often be resolved as a matter of law before trial. The elimination of this issue from the trial will focus the efforts of the parties, who will be able to present their cases in a way that conforms to the framework that the jury will apply. The plaintiff will know whether he or she must prove that the employer was negligent or whether the employer will have the burden of proving the elements of the *Ellerth/Faragher* affirmative defense. Perhaps even more important, the work of the jury, which is inevitably complicated in employment discrimination cases, will be simplified. . . .

The alternative approach advocated by petitioner and the United States would make matters far more complicated and difficult. . . .

Contrary to the dissent's suggestions, this approach will not leave employees unprotected against harassment by co-workers who possess the authority to inflict psychological injury by assigning unpleasant tasks or by altering the work environment in objectionable ways. In such cases, the victims will be able to prevail simply by showing that the employer was negligent in permitting this harassment to occur, and the jury should be instructed that the nature and degree of authority wielded by the harasser is an important factor to be considered in determining whether the employer was negligent. The nature and degree of authority possessed by harassing employees varies greatly, and as we explained above, the test proposed by petitioner and the United States is ill equipped to deal with the variety of situations that will inevitably

arise. This variety presents no problem for the negligence standard, which is thought
to provide adequate protection for tort plaintiffs in many other situations. There is no
reason why this standard, if accompanied by proper instructions, cannot provide the
same service in the context at issue here.

D

The dissent argues that the definition of a supervisor that we now adopt is out of
touch with the realities of the workplace, where individuals with the power to assign
daily tasks are often regarded by other employees as supervisors. But in reality it is the
alternative that is out of touch. Particularly in modern organizations that have abandoned a highly hierarchical management structure, it is common for employees to
have overlapping authority with respect to the assignment of work tasks. Members of
a team may each have the responsibility for taking the lead with respect to a particular
aspect of the work and thus may have the responsibility to direct each other in that
area of responsibility.

[addressing dissent]

Finally, petitioner argues that tying supervisor status to the authority to take tangible employment actions will encourage employers to attempt to insulate themselves
from liability for workplace harassment by empowering only a handful of individuals
to take tangible employment actions. But a broad definition of "supervisor" is not
necessary to guard against this concern.

As an initial matter, an employer will always be liable when its negligence leads to
the creation or continuation of a hostile work environment. And even if an employer
concentrates all decisionmaking authority in a few individuals, it likely will not isolate itself from heightened liability under *Faragher* and *Ellerth*. If an employer does
attempt to confine decisionmaking power to a small number of individuals, those
individuals will have a limited ability to exercise independent discretion when making
decisions and will likely rely on other workers who actually interact with the affected
employee. Under those circumstances, the employer may be held to have effectively
delegated the power to take tangible employment actions to the employees on whose
recommendations it relies. See *Ellerth*.

IV

[The majority responded to the dissent's claim that in many cases the Court's holding would preclude employer liability, but, even assuming "that a harasser is not a
supervisor, a plaintiff could still prevail by showing that his or her employer was negligent." Further, the standard the majority adopted "has been the law for quite some
time in the First, Seventh, and Eighth Circuits." Finally, the majority "skeptical that
there are a great number of" cases in which negligence liability would not attach for
the actions of an employee who cannot take tangible employment actions but who
does direct the victim's daily work activities in a meaningful way. In any event, "we are
confident that, in every case, the approach we take today will be more easily administrable than the approach advocated by the dissent."]

* * *

We hold that an employee is a "supervisor" for purposes of vicarious liability under
Title VII if he or she is empowered by the employer to take tangible employment
actions against the victim. Because there is no evidence that BSU empowered Davis
to take any tangible employment actions against Vance, the judgment of the Seventh
Circuit is affirmed. . . .

[Held]

Justice THOMAS, concurring.

I continue to believe that *Burlington Industries, Inc. v. Ellerth* and *Faragher v. Boca Raton* were wrongly decided. However, I join the opinion because it provides the narrowest and most workable rule for when an employer may be held vicariously liable for an employee's harassment.

Justice GINSBURG, with whom Justice BREYER, Justice SOTOMAYOR, and Justice KAGAN join, dissenting.

. . . The Court today strikes from the supervisory category employees who control the day-to-day schedules and assignments of others, confining the category to those formally empowered to take tangible employment actions. The limitation the Court decrees diminishes the force of *Faragher* and *Ellerth*, ignores the conditions under which members of the work force labor, and disserves the objective of Title VII to prevent discrimination from infecting the Nation's workplaces. I would follow the EEOC's Guidance and hold that the authority to direct an employee's daily activities establishes supervisory status under Title VII.

I

[handwritten: supervisory authority should not be limited to ability to make tangible employment actions. scheduling, assignments, etc are not properly acknowledged in this standard by the majority]

[The dissent summarized the employer liability structure of *Harris v. Forklift Systems, Inc.*, §219(2)(d) of the Restatement (Second) of Agency, *Faragher*, and *Ellerth* and then wrote that the] distinction *Faragher* and *Ellerth* drew between supervisors and co-workers corresponds to the realities of the workplace. Exposed to a fellow employee's harassment, one can walk away or tell the offender to "buzz off." A supervisor's slings and arrows, however, are not so easily avoided. An employee who confronts her harassing supervisor risks, for example, receiving an undesirable or unsafe work assignment or an unwanted transfer. She may be saddled with an excessive workload or with placement on a shift spanning hours disruptive of her family life. And she may be demoted or fired. Facing such dangers, she may be reluctant to blow the whistle on her superior, whose "power and authority invests his or her harassing conduct with a particular threatening character." *Ellerth.* See also *Faragher.* In short, as *Faragher* and *Ellerth* recognized, harassment by supervisors is more likely to cause palpable harm and to persist unabated than similar conduct by fellow employees.

II

[handwritten: Court should've deferred to EEOC guidance]

[The Court's view that supervisors are only those authorized to take tangible employment actions] is out of accord with the agency principles that, *Faragher* and *Ellerth* affirmed, govern Title VII. It is blind to the realities of the workplace, and it discounts the guidance of the EEOC, the agency Congress established to interpret, and superintend the enforcement of, Title VII. . . .

[After arguing that both *Faragher* and *Pennsylvania State Police v. Suders* involved employees who lacked the authority the majority now requires, the dissent went on to claim that w]orkplace realities fortify my conclusion that harassment by an employee with power to direct subordinates' day-to-day work activities should trigger vicarious employer liability. The following illustrations, none of them hypothetical, involve in-charge employees of the kind the Court today excludes from supervisory status.]

Yasharay Mack, an African-American woman, worked for the Otis Elevator Company as an elevator mechanic's helper at the Metropolitan Life Building in New York City. James Connolly, the "mechanic in charge" and the senior employee at the site, targeted Mack for abuse. He commented frequently on her "fantastic ass," "luscious lips," and "beautiful eyes," and, using deplorable racial epithets, opined that minorities and women did not "belong in the business." Once, he pulled her on his lap, touched her buttocks, and tried to kiss her while others looked on. Connolly lacked authority to take tangible employment actions against mechanic's helpers, but he did assign their work, control their schedules, and direct the particulars of their workdays. When he became angry with Mack, for example, he denied her overtime hours. And when she complained about the mistreatment, he scoffed, "I get away with everything." [*Mack v. Otis Elevator Co.*, 326 F.3d 116, 127 (CA2 2003).]

[The dissent then recounted the facts of *Rhodes v. Ill. Dep't of Transp.*, 359 F.3d 498, 501-03, 506-07 (CA7 2004), and *Whitten v. Fred's, Inc.*, 601 F.3d 231, 245-47 (CA4 2010).]

Monika Starke: CRST Van Expedited, Inc., an interstate transit company, ran a training program for newly hired truckdrivers requiring a 28-day on-the-road trip. Monika Starke participated in the program. Trainees like Starke were paired in a truck cabin with a single "lead driver" who lacked authority to hire, fire, promote, or demote, but who exercised control over the work environment for the duration of the trip. Lead drivers were responsible for providing instruction on CRST's driving method, assigning specific tasks, and scheduling rest stops. At the end of the trip, lead drivers evaluated trainees' performance with a nonbinding pass or fail recommendation that could lead to full driver status. Over the course of Starke's training trip, her first lead driver, Bob Smith, filled the cabin with vulgar sexual remarks, commenting on her breast size and comparing the gear stick to genitalia. A second lead driver, David Goodman, later forced her into unwanted sex with him, an outrage to which she submitted, believing it necessary to gain a passing grade. See *EEOC v. CRST Van Expedited, Inc.*, 679 F.3d 657 (CA8 2012).

In each of these cases, a person vested with authority to control the conditions of a subordinate's daily work life used his position to aid his harassment. But in none of them would the Court's severely confined definition of supervisor yield vicarious liability for the employer. The senior elevator mechanic in charge, the Court today tells us, was Mack's co-worker, not her supervisor. . . . So were the lead drivers who controlled all aspects of Starke's working environment. . . .

As anyone with work experience would immediately grasp, [the harassers in the four cases] wielded employer-conferred supervisory authority over their victims. Each man's discriminatory harassment derived force from, and was facilitated by, the control reins he held. Under any fair reading of Title VII, in each of the illustrative cases, the superior employee should have been classified a supervisor whose conduct would trigger vicarious liability.[3]

C

[The dissent argued in favor of "*Skidmore* deference" to the EEOC's definition of supervisor, deference that had been accorded other EEOC interpretations.]

---

3. The Court misses the point of the illustrations. Even under a vicarious liability rule, the Court points out, employers might escape liability for reasons other than the harasser's status as supervisor. . . . That, however, is no reason to restrict the definition of supervisor in a way that leaves out those genuinely in charge.

III . . .

A

[Turning to the majority's stress on sharp lines and workable standards, the dissent doubted] just how "clear" and "workable" the Court's definition is. A supervisor, the Court holds, is someone empowered to "take tangible employment actions against the victim, i.e., to effect a 'significant change in employment status, such as hiring, firing, failing to promote, reassignment with significantly different responsibilities, or a decision causing a significant change in benefits.'" Whether reassignment authority makes someone a supervisor might depend on whether the reassignment carries economic consequences. The power to discipline other employees, when the discipline has economic consequences, might count, too. So might the power to initiate or make recommendations about tangible employment actions. And when an employer "concentrates all decisionmaking authority in a few individuals" who rely on information from "other workers who actually interact with the affected employee," the other workers may rank as supervisors (or maybe not; the Court does not commit one way or the other).

not as workable of a standard as the court makes it out to be

Someone in search of a bright line might well ask, what counts as "significantly different responsibilities"? Can any economic consequence make a reassignment or disciplinary action "significant," or is there a minimum threshold? How concentrated must the decisionmaking authority be to deem those not formally endowed with that authority nevertheless "supervisors"? The Court leaves these questions unanswered, and its liberal use of "mights" and "mays," dims the light it casts.

That the Court has adopted a standard, rather than a clear rule, is not surprising, for no crisp definition of supervisor could supply the unwavering line the Court desires. Supervisors, like the workplaces they manage, come in all shapes and sizes. Whether a pitching coach supervises his pitchers (can he demote them?), or an artistic director supervises her opera star (can she impose significantly different responsibilities?), or a law firm associate supervises the firm's paralegals (can she fire them?) are matters not susceptible to mechanical rules and on-off switches. One cannot know whether an employer has vested supervisory authority in an employee, and whether harassment is aided by that authority, without looking to the particular working relationship between the harasser and the victim. That is why *Faragher* and *Ellerth* crafted an employer liability standard embracive of all whose authority significantly aids in the creation and perpetuation of harassment.

The Court's focus on finding a definition of supervisor capable of instant application is at odds with the Court's ordinary emphasis on the importance of particular circumstances in Title VII cases. . . .

B . . .

The negligence standard allowed by the Court scarcely affords the protection the *Faragher* and *Ellerth* framework gave victims harassed by those in control of their lives at work. [An employer is negligent only if it knew or should have known of the harassment but failed to take appropriate corrective action, but it "is not uncommon for employers to lack actual or constructive notice of a harassing employee's conduct.] An employee may have a reputation as a harasser among those in his vicinity, but if no complaint makes its way up to management, the employer will escape liability under a negligence standard.

Faragher is illustrative. After enduring unrelenting harassment, Faragher reported Terry's and Silverman's conduct informally to Robert Gordon, another immediate supervisor. But the lifeguards were "completely isolated from the City's higher management," and it did not occur to Faragher to pursue the matter with higher ranking city officials distant from the beach. Applying a negligence standard, the Eleventh Circuit held that, despite the pervasiveness of the harassment, and despite Gordon's awareness of it, Boca Raton lacked constructive notice and therefore escaped liability. Under the vicarious liability standard, however, Boca Raton could not make out the affirmative defense, for it had failed to disseminate a policy against sexual harassment.

[In addition, a negligence approach "saddles plaintiffs" with the burden of proof in contrast to *Faragher* and *Ellerth*, which placed the burden squarely on the employer to make out the affirmative defense. This allocation was "both sensible and deliberate: An employer has superior access to evidence bearing on whether it acted reasonably to prevent or correct harassing behavior, and superior resources to marshal that evidence."]

IV

[While the dissent would remand for application of the proper standard, the record gave it "cause to anticipate that Davis would not qualify as Vance's supervisor."]

NOTES

1. *Fewer Supervisors = More Negligence Claims.* The majority's narrow definition of "supervisor" means that far fewer cases will trigger the strict or presumptive employer liability structure of *Faragher/Ellerth*. Instead, most harassment cases will proceed as negligence claims, which means that the employee has the burden of proving the employer knew (or should have known) of the harassment and failed to respond reasonably. That means many cases will turn on employer knowledge. *See Lambert v. Peri Formworks Sys., Inc.*, 723 F.3d 863, 867 (7th Cir. 2013) (while "yard leads" were not supervisors, they may have had authority to report harassment to satisfy the knowledge requirement). Effectively, that eliminates strict liability and shifts the burden of proof from the employer's establishing an affirmative defense to the employee to establish both elements of her claim.

Is negligence truly "the better framework" for employer's liability when the harasser can't take tangible employment actions? At one point, the majority seems to argue that its decision will have little effect in the real world because victims can show employer negligence, with "the nature and degree of authority wielded by the harasser" an important factor in that determination. Further, while the EEOC's test is too vague to support the *Faragher/Ellerth* structure of strict or presumptive liability, these aren't "a problem for the negligence standard," which "provide[s] adequate protection for tort plaintiffs in many other situations." If the court or jury is going to weigh all the same factors under either approach, the only effect of *Vance's* restrictive definition of supervisor is to shift the burden of persuasion from employer to employee. Is that really so important? In *Velázquez-Pérez v. Developers Diversified Realty Corp.*, 753 F.3d 265 (1st Cir. 2014), the court, relying on both *Staub* and *Vance*, held that an employer could be liable in negligence when a co-worker's biased allegations against another employee resulted in her termination. When the jilted co-worker intended to cause the employee's firing, her allegations were the proximate cause of the firing, and the employer knew or should have known the co-worker's allegations were discriminatorily motivated.

2. *Delegating Decisionmaking.* In response to the argument that an employer might try to "isolate itself from heightened liability" by limiting decisionmaking power to a small number of individuals, Justice Alito noted that "those individuals will have a limited ability to exercise independent discretion when making decisions and will likely rely on other workers who actually interact with the affected employee. Under those circumstances, the employer may be held to have effectively delegated the power to take tangible employment actions to the employees on whose recommendations it relies." Note that the possibility of concentrating decisionmaking in a few individuals is not far-fetched: in most large firms, the human resources department has the formal power to hire and fire (and much in between), although in practice HR is likely to accord great deference to line managers. In any event, this delegation argument echoes possibilities raised in *Staub v. Proctor Hospital*, reproduced at p. 50. Does it also suggest that the bright line the Court drew isn't so bright after all? Presumably, the point is that there are supervisors in practice who are not supervisors on paper.

Speaking of *Staub*, recall that the Court there decided only that where "supervisors" influenced a decisionmaker, cat's paw liability can follow. But were the two individuals who influenced Buck, Mulally and Korenchuk, both "supervisors" under *Vance*? They certainly didn't have the power to fire Staub since they had to influence Buck in order to do so. Of course, they may have had other supervisory power (maybe they hired Staub), but, if not, *Vance* raises the question of whether *Staub's* holding retains much significance. After all, the Court went out of its way to note that it wasn't deciding whether subordinate bias liability applied to acts of "co-workers," 562 U.S. at 422 n.4, and *Vance* renders far more harassers co-workers. Could the same statute have two different definitions of supervisor — a narrower one for harassment liability and a broader one for subordinate bias liability? *See generally* Charles A. Sullivan, WORKPLACE PROF BLOG, Vance *Negates* Staub?, http://lawprofessors.typepad.com/laborprof_blog/2014/03/vance-or-staub-or-both.html.

This issue came to the fore in *Kramer v. Wasatch County Sheriff's Office*, 743 F.3d 726, 741 (10th Cir. 2014), where the court recognized that, where the "harasser is empowered to effect significant changes in employment status indirectly through recommendations, performance evaluations, and the like, and where the person with final decision-making power does not work directly with the plaintiff, the harasser may be a 'supervisor' under Title VII." Applying that principle, the court found a triable issue of fact whether the sheriff's department "effectively delegated to Sergeant Benson the power to cause tangible employment actions regarding Ms. Kramer by providing for reliance on recommendations from sergeants such as Benson when making decisions regarding firing, promotion, demotion, and reassignment." *Id.* Further, plaintiff need not prove that the sheriff followed Benson's recommendations blindly; even "if he undertook *some* independent analysis" when considering Benson's recommendations, "Benson would qualify as a supervisor so long as his recommendations were among the proximate causes of the Sheriff's decision-making." *Id. See also Velázquez-Pérez v. Developers Diversified Realty Corp.*, 753 F.3d 265 (1st Cir. 2014) (relying on *Vance* to find biased individual was a co-worker, not a supervisor, but relying on *Staub* to find employer could be liable for co-worker's impermissibly motivated allegations that were the proximate cause of an employee's termination, where employer knew or should have known her allegations were impermissibly motivated).

3. *Workability.* If there is a single theme to the majority's opinion in *Vance*, it is that its approach is workable and the dissent's (and EEOC's) is not. Justice Ginsburg's dissent, in turn, criticizes the majority's standard for its vagueness. But isn't Title VII riddled with general standards whose application is intensely fact-specific? One

example is the definition of harassment itself; a second is the standard for actionable retaliation. Is there a simpler way to approach the liability question? *See* Samuel R. Bagenstos, *Formalism and Employer Liability Under Title VII*, 2014 U. CHI. LEGAL F. 145 (urging Congress to make employers liable for any severe or pervasive harassment in the workplace).

When no tangible employment action has occurred, *Ellerth* permits the employer to assert an affirmative defense. What facts must a defendant prove to establish this defense?

EEOC v. MANAGEMENT HOSPITALITY OF RACINE, INC.
666 F.3d 422 (7th Cir. 2012)

YOUNG, District Judge.

The Equal Employment Opportunity Commission ("EEOC") brought this action on behalf of two servers, Katrina Shisler and Michelle Powell, who were employed at an International House of Pancakes franchise in Racine, Wisconsin (the "Racine IHOP"), alleging that the servers were sexually harassed in violation of Title VII. A jury found in favor of Shisler and Powell on the hostile work environment claim, and against the Defendants, Management Hospitality of Racine, Inc. ("MHR") d/b/a International House of Pancakes, Flipmeastack, Inc., and Salauddin Janmohammed. The jury awarded compensatory damages to Shisler and Powell, and awarded punitive damages to Powell. . . .

I.   BACKGROUND . . .

A.   THE DEFENDANTS

Janmohammed was the principal owner and franchisee of twenty-one IHOPs, including the Racine IHOP. He operated the Racine IHOP under the franchise name of MHR and was its president and sole share-holder. MHR contracted with Flipmeastack, a company solely owned by Janmohammed's wife, Victoria Janmohammed, to provide management consulting services for his IHOPs. . . . Flipmeastack hired the district managers, who, in turn, hired the general managers of each restaurant in the district, and oversaw the day-to-day operations of those particular restaurants. In 2005, Steve Smith was the district manager of the Racine IHOP, Michelle Dahl was the general manager, and Nadia Del Rio and Rosalio "Junior" Gutierrez were the assistant managers. The employees of each restaurant, including the general manager, assistant managers, and servers, were employees of MHR.

B.   THE SEXUAL HARASSMENT POLICY

In 2005, Flipmeastack formulated and updated the Sexual Harassment and Diversity Policy for managers and employees of MHR. The policy indicated that "any form of unlawful harassment of co-workers or members of the public is absolutely forbidden, regardless of whether it is verbal, physical, or visual harassment." It also stated that employees "will report any instances of improper behavior to my manager or company representative." Victoria Janmohammed confirmed that Gutierrez, Del Rio, and Dahl were managers or "company representatives" within the meaning of the policy, and that a complaint to any one of those three would be effective. As the general manager, Dahl was responsible for maintaining a workplace free of sexual harassment and for reporting instances of sexual harassment to upper management, and Del Rio was responsible for training all new hires. This training consisted of showing all new hires a sexual harassment videotape, handing them a copy of the sexual harassment policy, and asking them to read and sign it. Both Shisler and Powell viewed the videotape and signed Flipmeastack's sexual harassment policy. . . .

C. THE CLAIMANTS

Shisler, a teenager, worked at the Racine IHOP on two different occasions. . . . Her second term of employment began on March 3, 2005. By this time, Dahl served as the general manager of the Racine IHOP. Gutierrez, who was approximately 10 years older than Shisler, was relatively new to the position and worked as the night manager (5:00 P.M. to 3:00 A.M.), while Shisler worked the second shift (3:00 P.M. to 11:00 P.M.); consequently, their schedules overlapped. Shisler testified that whenever she worked with Gutierrez, he made sexually charged comments to her, including, "I want to take you in the back and fuck you over the pancake batter," "I bet you're kinky," and "you like it rough." Gutierrez even propositioned her for three-way sex with his (allegedly) bisexual girlfriend. Gutierrez stared at her body, breasts and buttocks, like she was "a piece of meat," rubbed her shoulders and pressed his body up against hers, and made her feel very "uncomfortable." Shisler "told him to get the fuck away from [her]." She felt "bullied" by him and felt "dirty" after he told the cooks in Spanish that he wanted to have sex with her. On March 18, 2005, Shisler, along with two other servers, reported Gutierrez's behavior to Del Rio. Shisler told Del Rio that she would have to be "blind" if she did not "see it going on." Del Rio "blew [them] off," shook her head, and called them "silly girls."

At some point after Shisler reported Gutierrez's behavior to Del Rio, Gutierrez "slap groped" her buttocks as she was bending over to pick up hot sauce from the floor. Shisler told Gutierrez to "get the fuck off [her]." On March 27, 2005, Shisler reported Gutierrez's behavior to Dahl, who said that this was "none of [her] concern" and then said "we're done here." After her complaints fell on deaf ears, Shisler "gave up" and kept working "because [she] needed the money." On April 3, 2005, Dahl terminated Shisler for violating the Racine IHOP's coupon policy, which barred servers from possessing coupons and giving them to customers.

[Powell, another teenager, had similar or worse experiences with Gutierrez and testified that] during the first week of April 2005, she complained to Dahl that Gutierrez was "sexually and physically abusing [her] and other female workers" and "grabbing us and saying dirty things to us." Although Dahl said she "would take care of it," Dahl did nothing to address her complaints. Powell also testified that Del Rio, prompted by the complaints from other servers, asked Powell if Gutierrez was treating her in an inappropriate way. Although Powell responded "yes," Del Rio did not report these complaints to upper management. When Gutierrez continued with his harassing behavior, Powell reported his inappropriate conduct to Dahl again, but Dahl cut her off by saying that "[she] didn't need to hear it." Eventually, like Shisler, Powell "learned not to say anything."

D. THE INVESTIGATION

[Shisler's attorney hired a private investigator and after she interviewed servers of the Racine IHOP, Gutierrez quit his position as assistant manager. Del Rio informed Smith about the private investigator's inquiry, which prompted Smith to conduct his own investigation. Gutierrez had already quit, but after determining that Shisler and Powell had complained to Dahl, he terminated her for not investigating their complaints.]

II. ANALYSIS

[The court found sufficient evidence to support the jury's finding that the conduct was sufficiently severe and/or pervasive.]

2. *The* Faragher/Ellerth *Affirmative Defense*

An employer can be held vicariously liable for a supervisor's sexual harassment of a subordinate. Generally, an employer may avoid liability if it can prove the two elements of the *Faragher/Ellerth* affirmative defense: "(a) that the employer exercised reasonable care to prevent and correct promptly any sexually harassing behavior, and (b) that the plaintiff employee unreasonably failed to take advantage of any preventive or corrective opportunities provided by the employer or to avoid harm otherwise." *Ellerth*; *Faragher*.

[Handwritten marginal notes: no tangible employment action against Powell so determine hostile work environment; tangible to be by the action home does by the harasser? have power supervisor? to effect action; employment]

a. Defendants' Preventative Measures

The Defendants contend that they took sexual harassment seriously, and instituted an effective sexual harassment policy to prevent and promptly correct any instances of sexual harassment occurring in the workplace. Victoria Janmohammed testified that the policy was a "zero tolerance" policy, meaning "we do not tolerate any sexual harassment, any discrimination. We don't even tolerate somebody not investigating." To this end, the Defendants required all of their new employees, including Shisler and Powell, to watch a video educating them on sexual harassment in the workplace, and to read and sign their sexual harassment policy. The Sexual Harassment and Diversity Policy that Shisler and Powell signed stated the following:

> I have watched the Sexual Harassment and Diversity videos. I am fully aware of our companies [sic] policies regarding both — zero tolerance for any type of unlawful discrimination and/or harassment. Our company is committed to providing a work environment that is free of unlawful behavior in any form. I will lead by example.
>
> . . .
>
> Any form of unlawful harassment of co-workers or members of the public is absolutely forbidden, regardless of whether it is verbal, physical, or visual harassment. You must be sensitive to the feelings of others and must not act in a way that might be considered offensive to someone else. I will report any instances of improper behavior to my manager or company representative. The company will take immediate and appropriate steps to investigate all reports of improper behavior.
>
> I also understand the severity of knowingly making false accusations of discrimination or harassment. Sexual Harassment and/or Discrimination are a serious charge and should be taken seriously.

In addition, the Defendants also note the presence of the Crisis Management Guidelines Poster in the employee break room that displayed, in part, Smith's cell phone number. Lastly, Defendants point out that as soon as Del Rio informed Smith that a private investigator was asking questions about sexual harassment at the Racine IHOP, he immediately conducted an investigation, took witness statements, determined that the policy had been violated, and took corrective action by firing Dahl for her failure to investigate the servers' allegations.

We find that a rational jury could have concluded that the Defendants exercised reasonable care by instituting a sexual harassment policy with a reasonable complaint mechanism, and by engaging in prompt and corrective action by investigating Shisler's and Powell's complaints of harassment and terminating Dahl. Like the district court, however, we find that the evidence was sufficient for a jury to find otherwise. Although the presence of a sexual harassment policy is encouraged by Title VII, "the mere creation of a sexual harassment policy will not shield a company from its responsibility to actively prevent sexual harassment in the workplace." *Gentry* [*v. Export Packaging Co.*, 238 F.3d 842, 847 (7th Cir. 2001)]. . . . Moreover, the policy must not only be reasonably effective on paper, but also reasonably effective in practice. *Clark v. United Parcel Serv., Inc.*, 400 F.3d 341, 350 (6th Cir. 2005).

Despite the fact that the Defendants had a sexual harassment policy in place, a rational jury could have found that the policy and complaint mechanism were not reasonably effective in practice. At trial, the jury heard evidence indicating that all managerial employees at the Racine IHOP failed to carry out their duties under the policy. For example, Gutierrez violated the policy by engaging in sexual harassment. The other assistant manager of the Racine IHOP, Del Rio, and the general manager of the Racine IHOP, Dahl, both failed to report Gutierrez's harassment after Shisler and Powell complained to them. Moreover, the jury heard evidence that Smith failed to investigate Shisler's prior complaint of harassment of another female server by the former general manager of the Racine IHOP, Hecker. The jury also heard evidence that Smith engaged in inappropriate conduct that could be described under the policy as sexual harassment, by rubbing his finger over the cleavage area of a picture of Dahl's teenage daughter and stating, "if only she was 18." Gutierrez testified that he witnessed this incident, but did not report it. A rational jury, faced with this evidence, could have found that none of the managers of the Racine IHOP took action under the policy that could be termed "corrective" or "effective."

Second, although management was required to take sexual harassment training, the evidence at trial suggested that the training was inadequate. Del Rio testified that she did not receive sexual harassment training when she became an assistant manager, even though she, as the assistant manager, was responsible for the orientation and training of new employees. Moreover, even though the policy stated that "any form of unlawful harassment of co-workers or members of the public is absolutely forbidden," Del Rio "blew off" Shisler's and Powell's complaints. Del Rio knew that she had an absolute duty to report sexual harassment allegations to upper management, yet she did not report Powell's complaints because, in her opinion, Powell did not seem to be "afraid" of Gutierrez. Similarly, Dahl knew that she had an absolute duty to report such allegations to upper management. Yet, in the face of Powell's allegations that Gutierrez was "sexually and physically abusing [her] and other female servers," she failed to report Powell's complaints. On these facts, a rational jury could have concluded that, not only was the policy and the management training ineffective, but the protections offered by them were illusory.

Third, "[o]ur cases recognize prompt investigation of the alleged misconduct as a hallmark of reasonable corrective action." *Cerros v. Steel Techs., Inc.*, 398 F.3d 944, 954 (7th Cir. 2005) (citations omitted). Here, a rational jury could have concluded that Smith's investigation of Gutierrez's sexual harassment was not "prompt." Shisler complained to management of Gutierrez's harassment twice in March 2005, and Powell complained to management three times in April 2005. Smith did not commence his investigation until May 23, 2005. This is not the type of response "'reasonably likely to prevent the harassment from recurring.'" *Id.* (quoting *Williams v. Waste Mgmt. of Ill.,* 361 F.3d 1021, 1029 (7th Cir. 2004)). In addition, a rational jury could have believed that an investigation ensued only because Shisler's private investigator started making inquiries of other female servers at the Racine IHOP.

Further, a rational jury could have concluded that the policy was not reasonably effective on paper. As the district court observed, an employer's complaint mechanism must provide a clear path for reporting harassment, particularly where, as here, a number of the servers were teenagers. Flipmeastack's sexual harassment policy did not provide a point person to air complaints to. In fact, it provided no names or contact information at all. To the extent the Crisis Management Guidelines Poster was meant to supplement the sexual harassment policy in this regard, a rational jury could have concluded that it did not fulfill this role. [Neither Shisler nor Powell could recall the poster being actually displayed, and, in any event, it focused on dealing with natural disasters, fires, and events such as food-borne illness. While it contained the word "discrimination" under the heading "other emergencies," it did not inform employees whom to call regarding violations of the *sexual harassment* policy nor describe employees' Title VII rights or EEOC contact information.] These facts, and the inferences reasonably drawn from them, could have led a rational jury to conclude that the complaint mechanism provided by Flipmeastack's sexual harassment policy did not provide a clear path for reporting harassment. For all of these reasons, we find that the jury's determination that the Defendants did not discharge their duty to effectively prevent and correct promptly sexual harassment in the workplace, was not unreasonable.

Held: D did not meet duty to effectively prevent and correct promptly sexual harassment in the workplace.

b.   Shisler's and Powell's Preventative or Corrective Action

We now turn to the second element of the *Faragher/Ellerth* affirmative defense — i.e., whether Shisler and Powell unreasonably failed to take advantage of preventative or corrective measures. [Defendants argued that neither employee ever complained to Smith, who would have taken prompt corrective action had they done so. That] argument ignores the terms of the sexual harassment policy itself, which provided that an employee was to "report any instances of improper behavior to [the employee's] manager or company representative." As the creator of the policy, Victoria Janmohammed affirmed this fact at trial. Shisler and Powell utilized the complaint mechanism by first asking Gutierrez, an assistant manager, to stop his harassing behavior. When Gutierrez refused to stop his harassment, both Shisler and Powell reported Gutierrez's harassment to Del Rio and Dahl — each of whom were managers or company representatives within the meaning of the policy. . . . Given this evidence, a rational jury could have believed that Shisler did not act unreasonably by failing to report Gutierrez's conduct directly to Smith.

In addition, a rational jury could have believed that Shisler did not feel comfortable reporting Gutierrez's harassment to Smith. Shisler testified that Smith failed to respond to her prior complaint of harassment by Hecker toward another server in 2004. Shisler also testified that after she complained to Smith, Hecker began to treat her more harshly. In light of this prior experience, a rational jury could have concluded that her decision not to contact Smith in 2005 was therefore justified.

[Much the same was true of Powell who complained to Dahl several times without response. In fact, the last time she complained, Dahl told her that she "didn't need to hear it." Further, a rational jury could have concluded that she did not act

[handwritten marginal note: Held: plaintiffs did not fail to reasonably take advantage of preventive or corrective measures provided by the employer]

unreasonably in failing to contact Smith during the time period.] For all of these reasons, we find that the jury's determination that Shisler and Powell took prompt and appropriate action under the policy was not unreasonable. . . .

NOTES

1. *What Does* Vance *Say About This Case?* The principal case was decided before *Vance*, which is why the court analyzed it as supervisory harassment, which means presumptive liability subject to the affirmative defense. It seems unlikely, post-*Vance*, that Gutierrez was a "supervisor." Is it likely the result would have been any different had negligence analysis been used?

2. *Reasonable Care to Prevent Harassment.* The employer in *Racine* had promulgated and disseminated an antiharassment policy that defined sexual harassment but failed to provide an adequate complaint procedure. In fact, the "policy did not provide a point person to air complaints to." The court also emphasized that the mere creation of a sexual harassment policy is insufficient: "the policy must not only be reasonably effective on paper, but also reasonably effective in practice." A policy that looks good on paper, accordingly, may not be sufficient proof that the employer has met this prong of the defense. *See also Bruno v. Monroe Cnty.*, 383 F. App'x 845, 849-50 (11th Cir. 2010) ("Although the express terms of Monroe County's sexual harassment policy clearly made it applicable to the county's 'agents,' such as elected commissioners, the evidence at trial showed that the policy could be considered largely ineffective as to them."); *Agusty-Reyes v. Dep't of Educ.*, 601 F.3d 45 (1st Cir. 2010) (no showing that the defendant communicated its policy to employees or supervisors; further, allowing the alleged harasser, but not the complainant, to appear at a hearing could be found inherently unreasonable). However, the occurrence of harassment, despite the employer's efforts, does not mean the employer failed to exercise reasonable care. *See Helm v. Kansas*, 656 F.3d 1277 (10th Cir. 2011) (employer exercised reasonable care by implementing a sexual harassment policy, distributing it as part of a 50-page handbook, and providing training to managers although no training was provided to non-management employees).

3. *Drafting an Effective Policy.* Although the Supreme Court has not demanded an antiharassment policy, employers rarely prevail on the affirmative defense absent such a policy. And while courts have not laid down a rigid list of requirements, it is advisable for such a policy not only to prohibit sexual harassment but also to give some explanation or description of what is included in the term. *See Molnar v. Booth*, 229 F.3d 593 (7th Cir. 2000). Particularly important are alternative avenues for reporting harassment; often it is the immediate supervisor who is engaging in the harassment, and thus a requirement that an employee report harassment to her supervisor will likely render the policy ineffective. *See Madray v. Publix Supermarkets, Inc.*, 208 F.3d 1290 (11th Cir. 2000). Moreover, as illustrated by *Racine*, clear identification of to whom within the organization complaints are to be made is important: even on paper, the antiharassment policy in *Racine* did not provide a clear path for reporting harassment. *See also Gentry v. Exp. Packing Co.*, 238 F.3d 842 (7th Cir. 2001). Some employers have adopted an "open door" program, which enables an employee "to speak with any other member of management"; that may suffice for the first prong but means that very informal complaints satisfy an employee's reporting obligation under the second prong. *Olson v. Lowe's Home Centers Inc.*, 130 F. App'x 380, 390 (11th Cir. 2005). A policy's assurance against retaliation for reporting has been important to some courts. *See, e.g.,*

Barrett v. ARECO, 240 F.3d 262 (4th Cir. 2000). One court has even required policies to be crafted for the understanding of the average teenager when a large number of such persons were in the employer's work force. *EEOC v. V&J Foods, Inc.*, 507 F.3d 575 (7th Cir. 2007). *See generally* Anne Lawton, *Operating in an Empirical Vacuum: The* Ellerth *and* Faragher *Affirmative Defense*, 13 COLUM. J. GENDER & L. 197, 266-67 (2004) (specifying optimal requirements for an adequate policy).

4. *Bullet-Proofing or Real Change?* Professor Susan Sturm, in *Second Generation Employment Discrimination: A Structural Approach*, 101 COLUM. L. REV. 458 (2001), approves the law's encouragement of employer initiatives aimed at achieving workplace equality. However, other commentators have questioned the Court's willingness to allow training programs to ground an affirmative defense, suggesting that the effectiveness of these programs in deterring harassing behavior (as opposed to limiting employer liability) has yet to be shown. *See* Linda Hamilton Krieger, Rachel Kahn Best & Lauren B. Edelman, *When "Best Practices" Win, Employees Lose: Symbolic Compliance and Judicial Inference in Federal Equal Employment Opportunity Cases*, 40 LAW & SOC. INQUIRY 843 (2015); Joanna L. Grossman, *The Culture of Compliance: The Final Triumph of Form over Substance in Sexual Harassment Law*, 26 HARV. WOMEN'S L.J. 3 (2003); Tristin K. Green, *Targeting Workplace Context: Title VII as a Tool for Institutional Reform*, 72 FORDHAM L. REV. 659 (2003); Susan Bisom-Rapp, *An Ounce of Prevention Is a Poor Substitute for a Pound of Cure: Confronting the Developing Jurisprudence of Education and Prevention in Employment Discrimination Law*, 22 BERKELEY J. EMP. & LAB. L. 1 (2001); Susan Bisom-Rapp, *Fixing Watches with Sledgehammers: The Questionable Embrace of Employee Sexual Harassment Training by the Legal Profession*, 24 U. ARK. LITTLE ROCK L. REV. 147 (2001). *See also* Anne Lawton, *The Bad Apple Theory in Sexual Harassment Law*, 13 GEO. MASON L. REV. 817 (2005) (reporting that the lower courts are allowing employers to create what are in effect statutes of limitations for sexual harassment claims via their affirmative defense policies).

5. *Reasonable Steps to Correct Harassment.* In addition to taking reasonable care to prevent harassment, the employer also must establish that it took reasonable steps to *correct* harassment when learns of it. The requisite knowledge could be the result of a report by the victim, as in *Racine. Cf. Jajeh v. Cty. of Cook*, 678 F.3d 560 (7th Cir. 2012) (reports of conflict with co-workers that did not link the conflict to a protected category did not place employer on notice); *Helm v. Kansas*, 656 F.3d 1277 (10th Cir. 2011) (employee's complaint failed to provide adequate notice when it stated only that a superior had done something inappropriate and made her feel uncomfortable). But even where a victim does not herself complain, the employer may learn of harassment by other means, which would likewise seem to trigger the duty to promptly correct harassment. But not all courts agree as to what kind of notice suffices. *See Chaloult v. Interstate Brands Corp.*, 540 F.3d 64 (1st Cir. 2008) (to hold that a policy requiring all supervisors to report harassment meant that any supervisor's knowledge was imputed to the employer as a matter of law would discourage employers from adopting such policies). *Accord Calloway v. Aerojet Gen. Corp.*, 419 F. App'x 840, 844 (10th Cir. 2011); *contra Clark v. United Parcel Serv., Inc.*, 400 F.3d 341 (6th Cir. 2005).

Once the employer knows, it must act promptly to correct any violation. The failure of the company in *Racine* to take action until the matter reached Smith's attention was obviously problematic, and delay can be fatal to the affirmative defense. *See Smith v. Rock-Tenn Servs.*, 813 F.3d 298 (6th Cir. 2016) (a reasonable jury could conclude that total inaction for 10 days was unreasonable in the circumstances); *Nichols v. Tri-Nat'l Logistics, Inc.*, 809 F.3d 981, 987 (8th Cir. 2016) (employer's failure to immediately respond to a complaint by a female long-haul truck driver about her co-driver's conduct could be found to be inadequate).

A reasonable response by an employer should provide adequate assurance to a complaining employee that her allegations are being properly investigated. Should the investigation confirm that harassment has occurred, termination of the harasser will generally constitute reasonable corrective action. *Green v. Franklin Nat'l Bank*, 459 F.3d 903, 912 (8th Cir. 2006). But even lesser discipline may suffice. *See Williams-Boldware v. Denton County*, 741 F.3d 635 (5th Cir. 2014) (harasser reprimanded and required to undergo training while plaintiff was insulated from any repercussions); *see also Sutherland v. Wal-Mart Stores, Inc.*, 632 F.3d 990, 994 (7th Cir. 2011) (drastic remedial measures not required when the misconduct at issue did not suggest that the harasser was likely to engage in sexual assault). It may well be reasonable to take no action against the accused when the investigation does not corroborate the plaintiff's complaint. *See Thornton v. Federal Express Corp.*, 530 F.3d 451, 457 (6th Cir. 2008) (when employer's investigation did not corroborate harassment, the employer's offer to transfer plaintiff to a different supervisor satisfied its responsibility to take reasonable steps to correct any harassment that may have occurred).

[handwritten margin note: indicates that as long as its not sexual assault its okay]

Employers who discipline harassers in order to avoid liability under Title VII must be careful to avoid liability to the harassing employee, who may have a variety of job protections. Moreover, there is even the possibility of Title VII suit by the alleged harasser. *See Sassaman v. Gamache*, 566 F.3d 307 (2d Cir. 2009) (while an employer is required to take charges of harassment seriously, it is sex discrimination to conclude that an accused male is a harasser because "you probably did what she said you did because you're male and nobody would believe you anyway"); *Russell v. City of Kansas City*, 414 F.3d 863, 868 (8th Cir. 2005) (white female demoted for allegedly fostering racially harassing workplace may have been the victim of discrimination when black and white males were given only a "slap on the wrist"). Usually, however, these claims have been unsuccessful. *See, e.g., Hawn v. Executive Jet Mgmt.*, 615 F.3d 1151 (9th Cir. 2010); *Farr v. St. Francis Hosp. & Health Ctrs.*, 570 F.3d 829 (7th Cir. 2009).

6. *Requests for Confidentiality.* A troubling question arises when the employee who complains about harassment also asks the employer to keep her complaint confidential. In *Torres v. Pisano*, 116 F.3d 625 (2d Cir. 1997), the Second Circuit ruled that an employee's confidentiality request insulated the employer from liability for its failure to act. *Id.* at 627. The court emphasized that some complaints, such as those alleging harassment of other employees, may require the employer to act but found that this was not such a case. *Id.* at 639. *See also Hardage v. CBS Broad. Inc.*, 436 F.3d 1050 (9th Cir. 2006) (plaintiff's statement to employer that he preferred to handle the matter himself meant that the defendant's failure to investigate was not unreasonable even though its policy required investigation). Are *Torres* and *Hardage* consistent with *Ellerth* and *Faragher*? Could there be a difference between liability to the employee who asks that no action be taken and liability to later victims of harassment if the complaining person's request is honored and no action is taken?

7. *Did the Employee Act Unreasonably?* Since both prongs of the affirmative defense must be satisfied, an employer that takes reasonable preventive and corrective action will still lose unless it also proves that the employee unreasonably failed to take advantage of preventive or corrective opportunities. In *Racine*, the employees' failure to report harassment to a district manager, instead of her store's general manager, was not unreasonable in the circumstances. But in many other cases, the plaintiff's delay in reporting has enabled the employer to prevail on this prong, even when the employee

claims to have feared retaliation, *see Crawford v. BNSF Ry. Co.*, 665 F.3d 978, 985 (8th Cir. 2012) (plaintiffs adduced no evidence that their fear of retaliation was either "genuine or reasonable," especially since the employer's antiharassment policy contained an antiretaliation provision), *but see Monteagudo v. Asociación de Empleados del Estado Libre Asociado*, 554 F.3d 164 (1st Cir. 2009) (a jury could find the plaintiff's failure to report reasonable when the harasser was close friends with the director of human resources to whom she would have reported under the employer's policy), or hoped to deal with the problem less formally. As we'll see, there is no doubt that women workers are generally reluctant to report harassment for a variety of reasons, and some courts have been more sympathetic to delays in doing so. For example, the court in *Watts v. Kroger Co.*, 170 F.3d 505, 510 (5th Cir. 1999), found it reasonable that Watts did not report her supervisor's harassment until it intensified after nearly a year.

In any event, when an employee does take action, some courts have required that it conform to the employer's policy. *See Taylor v. Solis*, 571 F.3d 1313 (D.C. Cir. 2009) (not reasonable for the plaintiff to notify her team leader when the employer's policy required her to contact an EEO counselor or manager). *See also Christian v. AHS Tulsa Regional Med. Ctr. LLC*, 430 F. App'x 694 (10th Cir. 2011) (summary judgment for employer when employee failed to cooperate with HR investigation by timely providing written details of the alleged incident.

Suppose the employee does complain to a supervisor. If nothing is done, is her failure to then complain to others also identified in the employer's policy unreasonable? *Racine* suggests no. *See also Gorzynski v. JetBlue Airways Corp.*, 596 F.3d 93, 104-05 (2d Cir. 2010) (not requiring plaintiff, who had complained to her manager pursuant to the employer's policy, to pursue alternate avenues when she received no response). *But see Lauderdale v. Texas Dep't of Crim. Justice*, 512 F.3d 157 (5th Cir. 2007) (in §1983 suit, a correctional officer's failure to make second complaint about sexual harassment by warden after her immediate supervisor refused to act on her first complaint established that prong of the affirmative defense).

Racine says that it's not unreasonable failure if the employee does not seek alternative avenues of reporting but some courts say it is

8. *Law Changing Norms?* As we've noted, women are frequently reluctant to report harassment, which makes the second prong of the employer's defense often easy to establish. *See* L. Camille Hébert, *Why Don't "Reasonable Women" Complain About Sexual Harassment?*, 82 IND. L.J. 711 (2007); Theresa M. Beiner, *Sex, Science and Social Knowledge: The Implications of Social Science Research on Imputing Liability to Employers for Sexual Harassment*, 7 WM. & MARY J. WOMEN & L. 273 (2001); Joanna L. Grossman, *The First Bite Is Free: Employer Liability for Sexual Harassment*, 61 U. PITT. L. REV. 671 (2000); Theresa M. Beiner, *Using Evidence of Women's Stories in Sexual Harassment Cases*, 24 U. ARK. LITTLE ROCK L. REV. 117 (2001); Linda Hamilton Krieger, *Employer Liability for Sexual Harassment — Normative, Descriptive, and Doctrinal Interactions: A Reply to Professors Beiner and Bisom-Rapp*, 24 U. ARK. LITTLE ROCK L. REV. 169 (2001).

Assuming that the research is correct as a descriptive matter that women are reluctant to report harassment until it becomes extreme, does this answer the normative question of whether their rights should depend on speedy reporting? The Supreme Court clearly intended to change employers' conduct through the affirmative defense; perhaps it also intended to change the conduct of women workers. The requirement of speedy reporting is often treated as a kind of mitigation of damages approach: there is no "duty" to report but a victim cannot recover for harm that would have been avoided had she acted "reasonably" and reported.

Even under this approach, however, the lower courts' requirement that plaintiffs speak up at the earliest opportunity is in some tension with the Supreme Court's decision in *Clark County v. Breeden*, reproduced at p. 412, holding that a complaint of sexual conduct that obviously was not severe or pervasive enough to state a claim for a hostile work environment was not protected from retaliation. For discussion of the interaction between the antiretaliation provisions of Title VII and the use of internal complaint procedures, see Note 2, p. 415. *See also* Elinor P. Schroeder, *Handbooks, Disclaimers, and Harassment Policies: Another Look at* Clark County School District v. Breeden, 42 BRANDEIS L.J. 581 (2004).

9. *Both Prongs of the Affirmative Defense Must Be Satisfied.* What happens if a supervisor commits a severe act of harassment, such as a rape or attempted rape, and the employee immediately reports the harassment to her employer? Assuming a strong antiharassment policy and prompt and effective corrective action, can the employer still be vicariously liable for the hostile work environment? Since it is the employer's burden to establish *both* prongs of the affirmative defense, the answer should be yes. The employer would be unable to establish the second prong of the defense because the employee has acted reasonably. *See Frederick v. Sprint/United Mgmt. Co.*, 246 F.3d 1305 (11th Cir. 2001); *Harrison v. Eddy Potash Inc.*, 248 F.3d 1014 (10th Cir. 2001); *Johnson v. West*, 218 F.3d 725 (7th Cir. 2000). However, one circuit has answered the question in the negative. *See McCurdy v. Arkansas State Police*, 375 F.3d 762, 771 (8th Cir. 2004). *See generally* Kerri Lynn Stone, *License to Harass*, 41 AKRON L. REV. 1059 (2008).

10. *Other Remedies.* Title VII is not the only source of remedies for sexual and other harassment in the employment setting. Such conduct can also be attacked under state employment discrimination statutes, and public employees may assert a violation of their federal or state constitutional rights. Such claims may avoid some of the technicalities of Title VII law, and resort to state tort claims, such as assault and intentional infliction of emotional distress, may avoid limitations on Title VII remedies. *See Seibert v. Jackson Cnty.*, 851 F.3d 430, 438 (5th Cir. 2017) (upholding jury verdict for intentional infliction of emotional distress despite jury not finding actionable sexual harassment under Title VII since the standards for both causes of action are different). See Chapter 9. *See generally* Martha Chamallas, *Discrimination and Outrage: The Migration from Civil Rights to Tort Law*, 48 WM. & MARY L. REV. 2115 (2007). In addition, such remedies may be critical should the harassment not be severe or pervasive enough to be actionable under Title VII or to hold an individual tortfeasor liable when the employer has a viable affirmative defense. In some jurisdictions, however, workers' compensation statutes may provide the exclusive remedy for intentional infliction of mental distress on the job. Note, also, that state law claims that cannot be resolved without interpreting a collective bargaining agreement may be preempted by federal law. *See* TIMOTHY P. GLYNN, CHARLES A. SULLIVAN & RACHEL ARNOW-RICHMAN, EMPLOYMENT LAW: PRIVATE ORDERING AND ITS LIMITATIONS 315-20 (3d ed. 2015).

NOTE ON EMPLOYER LIABILITY FOR HARASSMENT BY CO-WORKERS AND CUSTOMERS

Ellerth implied and *Vance* confirmed that an employer is liable for the harassing conduct of co-workers only if the employer knew or should have known of the harassment and failed to take adequate corrective action. As one circuit has observed, the difference between employer liability for supervisory harassment as opposed to co-worker harassment essentially reduces to which party bears the burden of proof. The factors examined in determining whether the affirmative defense has been satisfied are very similar to those involved in employer liability for co-worker harassment.

However, when it is a supervisor's harassment that is at issue, it is the employer that bears the burden of proving the affirmative defense. In co-worker harassment cases, it is the plaintiff's burden to prove the employer's knowledge and failure to take corrective action in order to establish its negligence. *See May v. Chrysler Group, LLC*, 692 F.3d 734 (7th Cir. 2012) (employer's minimal response to reported racist death threats was grossly inadequate since the appropriateness of a response is judged in part by the severity of the harassment). If adequate corrective action is taken immediately, however, there can be no negligence liability. *Chaib v. Indiana*, 744 F.3d 974, 985-86 (7th Cir. 2014); *Summa v. Hofstra Univ.*, 708 F.3d 115 (2d Cir. 2013).

But in a corporate setting, what humans need to know about the harassment for the "employer" to be viewed as having such knowledge? *See Huston v. P&G Paper Prods. Corp.*, 568 F.3d 100, 105 (3d Cir. 2009) (employer has constructive notice of a hostile work environment when "management level personnel" are provided "with enough information to raise a probability of harassment in the mind of a reasonable employer"); *Williamson v. City of Houston*, 148 F.3d 462 (5th Cir. 1998) (employer's policy directing employees to report harassment to supervisors establishes that supervisor's knowledge of harassment is imputed to the employer); *but see Wilson v. Gaston Cnty.*, No. 15-2522, 2017 U.S. App. LEXIS 6354, at *14 (4th Cir. Apr. 13, 2017) (employer not on notice of co-worker harassment when only mild teasing was witnessed by supervisors before a formal complaint by plaintiff); *Chaloult v. Interstate Brands Corp.*, 540 F.3d 64 (1st Cir. 2008) (a policy requiring all supervisors to report harassment did not result in imputing any supervisor's knowledge to the employer as a matter of law since that would discourage employers from adopting such policies); *Bombaci v. Journal Cmty. Publ'g Group, Inc.*, 482 F.3d 979 (7th Cir. 2007) (employee offered no evidence of the reasonableness of her belief that a certain individual was a "supervisor" and none of that individual's duties suggested that she could affect the terms of another person's employment in a way that could remedy sexual harassment).

Must the employer have knowledge that the plaintiff herself had been the victim of harassment? In *Faragher*, the Court commented on situations where knowledge of harassing behavior is widespread:

> There have . . . been myriad cases [that] have held employers liable on account of actual knowledge by the employer, or high-echelon officials of an employer organization, of sufficiently harassing action by subordinates, which the employer or its informed officers have done nothing to stop. In such instances, the combined knowledge and inaction may be seen as demonstrable negligence, or as the employer's adoption of the offending conduct and its results, quite as if they had been authorized affirmatively as the employer's policy.

524 U.S. at 788.

There is also the question of employer liability for sexual harassment by customers. Suppose a sales representative must regularly deal with a customer's purchasing agent who harasses her. Does her employer have a duty to protect her? How far does this duty reach? Must it cease doing business with the harasser's firm if other methods fail? *Quinn v. Green Tree Credit Corp.*, 159 F.3d 759, 766 (2d Cir. 1998), held that an employer's duty with respect to controlling harassment by customers is the same as its duty with respect to co-worker harassment — the employer is responsible for sexual harassment if it knows or should have known of it unless it can demonstrate immediate and appropriate corrective action. This is the approach taken in *Dunn v. Wash. County Hosp.*, 429 F.3d 689 (7th Cir. 2005), where the harasser was a doctor with admitting privileges at the hospital but who was not an employee. The court found the relationship of the harasser to the employer irrelevant:

Because liability is direct rather than derivative, it makes no difference whether the person whose acts are complained of is an employee, an independent contractor, or for that matter a customer. Ability to "control" the actor plays no role. Employees are not puppets on strings; employers have an arsenal of incentives and sanctions (including discharge) that can be applied to affect conduct. It is the use (or failure to use) these options that makes an employer responsible — and in this respect independent contractors are no different from employees. Indeed, it makes no difference whether the actor is human. Suppose a patient kept a macaw in his room, that the bird bit and scratched women but not men, and that the Hospital did nothing. The Hospital would be responsible for the decision to expose women to the working conditions affected by the macaw, even though the bird (a) was not an employee, and (b) could not be controlled by reasoning or sanctions. It would be the Hospital's responsibility to protect its female employees by excluding the offending bird from its premises. This is, by the way, the norm of direct liability in private law as well. . . .

Id. at 691. *See generally* Noah Zatz, *Managing the Macaw: Third-Party Harassers, Accommodation, and the Disaggregation of Discriminatory Intent*, 109 COLUM. L. REV. 1357 (2009). *See also* Dallan F. Flake, *Employer Liability for Nonemployee Discrimination*, 58 BC L. REV. (forthcoming 2017).

Can a supervisor sue for harassment by her subordinates? Can a school system be held liable for acts of sexual harassment against its teachers by students? One circuit so held, *Stewart v. Rise, Inc.*, 791 F.3d 849 (8th Cir. 2015), and others have suggested that theory in dicta. *See Lucero v. Nettle Creek Sch. Corp.*, 566 F.3d 720 (7th Cir. 2009); *Schroeder v. Hamilton Sch. Dist.*, 282 F.3d 946, 951 (7th Cir. 2002). *See generally* Ann Juliano, *Harassing Women with Power: The Case for Including Contra-Power Harassment Within Title VII*, 87 BU L. REV. 491 (2007).

NOTE ON FIRST AMENDMENT IMPLICATIONS OF SEXUAL HARASSMENT LIABILITY

The First Amendment implications of regulating sexual harassment in the workplace are broad-reaching and complex. This note provides no more than a brief introduction to the issue. One source of further information is Professor Eugene Volokh's website on free speech and workplace harassment, which is located at http://www2.law.ucla.edu/volokh/harass.

Sexist or racist speech in the workplace is relevant in employment discrimination litigation for a variety of reasons. Most obviously, sex or race stereotyping or expressions of bias and prejudice may provide evidence that an employer made decisions on the basis of sex or race, rather than for nondiscriminatory reasons. *See Price Waterhouse v. Hopkins*, reproduced at p. 61. However, the government, through Title VII, imposes liability in such cases not because of what was said but because of the discriminatory actions taken. The speech merely provides evidence of motive and does not, therefore, create First Amendment problems of restricting speech. Similarly, sexual propositions may be evidence of quid pro quo sexual harassment. The employer may inform a female employee, for example, that she will not receive an employment benefit unless she cooperates by providing him with sexual favors. If she rejects the advance and suffers an adverse action, the proposition evidences the Title VII violation in the same way an offer to sell a controlled substance may be criminalized.

In contrast to these uses of speech in discrimination litigation, sexist or racist speech may provide the basis for claiming that the employer is maintaining a hostile environment in violation of Title VII. The speech is not merely evidence of discriminatory conduct — it is prohibited because it is offensive enough to contaminate the work setting for women or minorities. In other words, the speech itself forms the basis of liability. Hostile environment cases that rely primarily on speech, rather than on actual or proposed conduct, most clearly implicate First Amendment rights.

Nevertheless, the First Amendment implications of sexual harassment liability are minimal when private employers voluntarily choose to regulate the speech absent any government coercion. In such cases, the actions of the private employer do not implicate the Constitution because no state action is involved. Of course, government employers who control the speech of their own employees are subject to some First Amendment restrictions. Moreover, when courts impose Title VII liability on private employers on the basis of their speech or their agents' speech, First Amendment concerns are implicated. Just as common law defamation is subject to First Amendment restrictions, *New York Times v. Sullivan*, 376 U.S. 254 (1964), so, too, is Title VII harassment law.

The Supreme Court has recognized categories of speech that the government may prohibit or restrict in some circumstances without violating the First Amendment. Several of these categories, including fighting words, offensive speech, and obscenity, are potentially analogous to speech that creates a hostile environment. While some speech at issue in sexual harassment cases readily fits within these categories, other speech does not.

Not only is classifying sexually harassing speech as an unprotected category of speech difficult, but prohibiting discriminatory harassing speech raises further First Amendment problems. Viewpoint restrictions have nearly always been considered violations of the First Amendment, and the Court specifically held that prohibiting discriminatory fighting words because they express a particular point of view violates the First Amendment. *See R.A.V. v. City of St. Paul*, 505 U.S. 377 (1992) (successful challenge to a statute on which a cross-burning prosecution was based; the statute prohibited symbols known to arouse "anger, alarm, or resentment in others on the basis of race, color, creed, religion, or gender"). Nevertheless, *R.A.V.* suggested that Title VII's prohibition of sexual harassment is distinguishable from the statute in question:

> [S]ince words can in some circumstances violate laws directed not against speech but against conduct (a law against treason, for example, is violated by telling the enemy the nation's defense secrets), a particular content-based subcategory of a proscribable class of speech can be swept up incidentally within the reach of a statute directed at conduct rather than speech. Thus, for example, sexually derogatory "fighting words," among other words, may produce a violation of Title VII's general prohibition against sexual discrimination in employment practices. Where the government does not target conduct on the basis of its expressive content, acts are not shielded from regulation merely because they express a discriminatory idea or philosophy.

505 U.S. at 389. *See also Virginia v. Black*, 538 U.S. 343 (2003) (upholding conviction for cross-burning). Does the Court's distinction apply to all hostile environment cases or only those based on "fighting words"? What does the Court mean by "'fighting words' among other words" in the context of sexual harassment? What about obscene and indecent speech? Could a court find that artwork depicting naked women creates a discriminatory environment without violating the First Amendment? What about statements like "there's nothing worse than having to work around women"? Does the Court's attempt to distinguish sexual harassment cases extend to other discriminatory hostile environment cases involving communicative "conduct"? Note that the *R.A.V.* Court's attempt to distinguish hostile environment liability clearly was dicta.

After *R.A.V.*, the Court decided *Harris v. Forklift Systems Inc.*, reproduced at p. 331, where the sexually harassing behavior in that case was primarily evidenced by offensive remarks. Although the constitutionality of imposing liability on the employer for those remarks was raised in briefs submitted in that case, the Court did not address the issue in its opinion. Are the remarks in *Harris* fighting words? Does the Court's dicta in *R.A.V.* explain why Hardy's statements are not protected by the First Amendment? *See also Booth v. Pasco Cnty.*, 757 F.3d 1198, 1214 (11th Cir. 2014) (upholding a jury verdict against a First Amendment challenge when the speech in question was "part and parcel" of retaliation and the jury found a union liable not merely for notifying its members of a charge of discrimination but for publishing a "call for reprisal").

In the public sector, the Supreme Court has, outside of the harassment context, developed First Amendment doctrine to accommodate both government employees' free speech rights and government employers' interest in controlling the behavior of their own employees in the work-place. In this context, the Court has ruled that generally, public employees may not be disciplined or discharged for engaging in speech on a matter of public concern unless the government can assert some interest in restricting that speech, such as disruption of the workplace, that outweighs the employees' interest in speaking. *Connick v. Meyers*, 461 U.S. 138 (1983); *Pickering v. Bd. of Educ.*, 391 U.S. 563 (1968). But not only have some courts have narrowly construed the "public concern" requirement, *see, e.g., Morris v. City of Colorado Springs*, 666 F.3d 654 (10th Cir. 2012), but the Supreme Court has held that, to be protected, the employee's speech must not be part of his job. *Garcetti v. Ceballos*, 547 U.S. 410 (2006). *But see Lane v. Franks*, 134 S. Ct. 2369 (2014) (holding that an employee's sworn testimony in a corruption trial was protected even if related to his job duties). *Garcetti* has been a major obstacle to public employee First Amendment claims. *See, e.g., Savage v. Gee*, 665 F.3d 732 (6th Cir. 2012) (librarian's speech unprotected when made in his role as head librarian and as committee member selecting book for freshman students to read with "anti-gay" content). *See generally* Paul M. Secunda, *Neoformalism and the Reemergence of the Right-Privilege Distinction in Public Employment Law*, 48 San Diego L. Rev. 907 (2011); Lawrence Rosenthal, *The Emerging First Amendment Law of Managerial Prerogative*, 77 Fordham L. Rev. 33 (2008); Cynthia Estlund, *Free Speech Rights That Work at Work: From the First Amendment to Due Process*, 54 UCLA L. Rev. 1463 (2007). Does this suggest that a harasser who spoke in the workplace could not raise a First Amendment defense? Or maybe it suggests the opposite — such speech is never part of the job because it is prohibited by employer policies? *But see Nagle v. Marron*, 663 F.3d 100, 108 (2d Cir. 2011) (rejecting the argument that the teacher's report lost First Amendment protection because it violated employment protocols). *Cf. DeJohn v. Temple Univ.*, 537 F.3d 301 (3d Cir. 2008) (striking down university's harassment policy as facially invalid because it prohibited expression by students even in the absence of a hostile environment).

D.   DISCRIMINATION ON ACCOUNT OF RELIGION

Title VII prohibits discrimination because of religion, which, of course, includes what could be described as plain vanilla disparate treatment — taking an adverse employment action against an individual because of her religion. The statute, however, goes further to introduce an obligation we have not encountered before — the duty to reasonably accommodate religious practices and observances. Further, the statute permits religious discrimination by certain religious employers and also permits such discrimination when religion is a bona fide occupational qualification. Beyond Title VII, the religion clauses of the First Amendment have been held to limit the reach of the antidiscrimination statutes. Thus, the Free Exercise Clause can sometimes be invoked by employees and churches, and the Establishment Clause both limits the extent to which the state can intervene in church governance and the extent to which it may favor religion by its enactments in this area. And then there's the Religious Freedom Restoration Act. All in all, a complicated mix. But we'll begin with the core prohibition of Title VII.

EEOC v. ABERCROMBIE & FITCH STORES, INC.
135 S. Ct. 2028 (2015)

Justice SCALIA delivered the opinion of the Court.

Title VII of the Civil Rights Act of 1964 prohibits a prospective employer from refusing to hire an applicant in order to avoid accommodating a religious practice that it could accommodate without undue hardship. The question presented is whether this prohibition applies only where an applicant has informed the employer of his need for an accommodation.

I

We summarize the facts in the light most favorable to the Equal Employment Opportunity Commission (EEOC), against whom the Tenth Circuit granted summary judgment. Respondent Abercrombie & Fitch Stores, Inc., operates several lines of clothing stores, each with its own "style." Consistent with the image Abercrombie seeks to project for each store, the company imposes a Look Policy that governs its employees' dress. The Look Policy prohibits "caps" — a term the Policy does not define — as too informal for Abercrombie's desired image.

Samantha Elauf is a practicing Muslim who, consistent with her understanding of her religion's requirements, wears a headscarf. She applied for a position in an Abercrombie store, and was interviewed by Heather Cooke, the store's assistant manager. Using Abercrombie's ordinary system for evaluating applicants, Cooke gave Elauf a rating that qualified her to be hired; Cooke was concerned, however, that Elauf's headscarf would conflict with the store's Look Policy.

Cooke sought the store manager's guidance to clarify whether the headscarf was a forbidden "cap." When this yielded no answer, Cooke turned to Randall Johnson, the district manager. Cooke informed Johnson that she believed Elauf wore her headscarf because of her faith. Johnson told Cooke that Elauf's headscarf would violate the Look Policy, as would all other headwear, religious or otherwise, and directed Cooke not to hire Elauf. . . .

II

[Section 2000e-2(a)(1) and (2)], often referred to as the "disparate treatment" (or "intentional discrimination") provision and the "disparate impact" provision, are the only causes of action under Title VII. The word "religion" is defined to "includ[e] all aspects of religious observance and practice, as well as belief, unless an employer demonstrates that he is unable to reasonably accommodate to" a "religious observance or practice without undue hardship on the conduct of the employer's business." §2000e(j).[1]

Abercrombie's primary argument is that an applicant cannot show disparate treatment without first showing that an employer has "actual knowledge" of the applicant's need for an accommodation. We disagree. Instead, an applicant need only show that his need for an accommodation was a motivating factor in the employer's decision.[2]

The disparate-treatment provision forbids employers to: (1) "fail . . . to hire" an applicant (2) "because of" (3) "such individual's . . . religion" (which includes his religious practice). Here, of course, Abercrombie (1) failed to hire Elauf. The parties concede that (if Elauf sincerely believes that her religion so requires) Elauf's wearing of a headscarf is (3) a "religious practice." All that remains is whether she was not hired (2) "because of" her religious practice.

The term "because of" appears frequently in antidiscrimination laws. It typically imports, at a minimum, the traditional standard of but-for causation. *University of Tex. Southwestern Medical Center v. Nassar* [reproduced at p. 429]. Title VII relaxes this standard, however, to prohibit even making a protected characteristic a "motivating factor" in an employment decision. 42 U.S.C. §2000e-2(m). "Because of" in §2000e-2(a)(1) links the forbidden consideration to each of the verbs preceding it; an individual's actual religious practice may not be a motivating factor in failing to hire, in refusing to hire, and so on.

It is significant that §2000e-2(a)(1) does not impose a knowledge requirement. As Abercrombie acknowledges, some antidiscrimination statutes do. For example, the Americans with Disabilities Act of 1990 defines discrimination to include an employer's failure to make "reasonable accommodations to the *known* physical or mental limitations" of an applicant. §12112(b)(5)(A) (emphasis added). Title VII contains no such limitation.

Instead, the intentional discrimination provision prohibits certain *motives*, regardless of the state of the actor's knowledge. Motive and knowledge are separate concepts. An employer who has actual knowledge of the need for an accommodation does not violate Title VII by refusing to hire an applicant if avoiding that accommodation is not his *motive*. Conversely, an employer who acts with the motive of avoiding accommodation may violate Title VII even if he has no more than an unsubstantiated suspicion that accommodation would be needed.

---

1. For brevity's sake, we will in the balance of this opinion usually omit reference to the §2000e(j) "undue hardship" defense to the accommodation requirement, discussing the requirement as though it is absolute.

2. The concurrence mysteriously concludes that it is not the plaintiff's burden to prove failure to accommodate. But of course that *is* the plaintiff's burden, if failure to hire "because of" the plaintiff's "religious practice" is the gravamen of the complaint. Failing to hire for that reason is *synonymous* with refusing to accommodate the religious practice. To accuse the employer of the one is to accuse him of the other. If he is willing to "accommodate" — which means nothing more than allowing the plaintiff to engage in her religious practice despite the employer's normal rules to the contrary — adverse action "because of" the religious practice is not shown. "The clause that begins with the word 'unless,'" as the concurrence describes it, has no function except to place upon the employer the burden of establishing an "undue hardship" defense. The concurrence provides no example, not even an unrealistic hypothetical one, of a claim of failure to hire because of religious practice that does not say the employer refused to permit ("failed to accommodate") the religious practice. In the nature of things, there cannot be one.

Thus, the rule for disparate-treatment claims based on a failure to accommodate a religious practice is straightforward: An employer may not make an applicant's religious practice, confirmed or otherwise, a factor in employment decisions. For example, suppose that an employer thinks (though he does not know for certain) that a job applicant may be an orthodox Jew who will observe the Sabbath, and thus be unable to work on Saturdays. If the applicant actually requires an accommodation of that religious practice, and the employer's desire to avoid the prospective accommodation is a motivating factor in his decision, the employer violates Title VII.

Abercrombie urges this Court to adopt the Tenth Circuit's rule "allocat[ing] the burden of raising a religious conflict." This would require the employer to have actual knowledge of a conflict between an applicant's religious practice and a work rule. The problem with this approach is the one that inheres in most incorrect interpretations of statutes: It asks us to add words to the law to produce what is thought to be a desirable result. That is Congress's province. We construe Title VII's silence as exactly that: silence. Its disparate-treatment provision prohibits actions taken with the *motive* of avoiding the need for accommodating a religious practice. A request for accommodation, or the employer's certainty that the practice exists, may make it easier to infer motive, but is not a necessary condition of liability.[3]

Abercrombie argues in the alternative that a claim based on a failure to accommodate an applicant's religious practice must be raised as a disparate-impact claim, not a disparate-treatment claim. We think not. That might have been true if Congress had limited the meaning of "religion" in Title VII to religious *belief* — so that discriminating against a particular religious *practice* would not be disparate treatment though it might have disparate impact. In fact, however, Congress defined "religion," for Title VII's purposes, as "includ[ing] all aspects of religious observance and practice, as well as belief." 42 U.S.C. §2000e(j). Thus, religious practice is one of the protected characteristics that cannot be accorded disparate treatment and must be accommodated.

Nor does the statute limit disparate-treatment claims to only those employer policies that treat religious practices less favorably than similar secular practices. Abercrombie's argument that a neutral policy cannot constitute "intentional discrimination" may make sense in other contexts. But Title VII does not demand mere neutrality with regard to religious practices — that they be treated no worse than other practices. Rather, it gives them favored treatment, affirmatively obligating employers not "to fail or refuse to hire or discharge any individual . . . because of such individual's" "religious observance and practice." An employer is surely entitled to have, for example, a no-headwear policy as an ordinary matter. But when an applicant requires an accommodation as an "aspec[t] of religious . . . practice," it is no response that the subsequent "fail[ure] . . . to hire" was due to an otherwise-neutral policy. Title VII requires otherwise-neutral policies to give way to the need for an accommodation. . . .

Justice ALITO, concurring in the judgment.

[The concurrence reframed the statutory language as yielding the following "somewhat simplified" rule: "An employer may not take an adverse employment action

---

3. While a knowledge requirement cannot be added to the motive requirement, it is arguable that the motive requirement itself is not met unless the employer at least suspects that the practice in question is a religious practice — *i.e.*, that he cannot discriminate "because of" a "religious practice" unless he knows or suspects it to be a religious practice. That issue is not presented in this case, since Abercrombie knew — or at least suspected — that the scarf was worn for religious reasons. The question has therefore not been discussed by either side, in brief or oral argument. It seems to us inappropriate to resolve this unargued point by way of dictum, as the concurrence would do.

against an applicant or employee because of any aspect of that individual's religious observance or practice unless the employer demonstrates that it is unable to reasonably accommodate that observance or practice without undue hardship." It then rejected the Tenth Circuit's requirement that applicants inform employers of religious practices that conflict with a work requirement and their need for an accommodation. While it interpreted the statute] to require proof that Abercrombie knew that Elauf wore the headscarf for a religious reason, the evidence of Abercrombie's knowledge is sufficient to defeat summary judgment.

The opinion of the Court states that "§2000e-2(a)(1) does not impose a knowledge requirement," but then reserves decision on the question whether it is a condition of liability that the employer know or suspect that the practice he refuses to accommodate is a religious practice, n.3, but in my view, the answer to this question, which may arise on remand, is obvious. I would hold that an employer cannot be held liable for taking an adverse action because of an employee's religious practice unless the employer knows that the employee engages in the practice for a religious reason. If §2000e-2(a)(1) really "does not impose a knowledge requirement," it would be irrelevant in this case whether Abercrombie had any inkling that Elauf is a Muslim or that she wore the headscarf for a religious reason. That would be very strange.

[The concurrence went on to stress that, had the person who interviewed Elauf had no reason to suspect that she was a Muslim or was wearing the scarf for a religious reason, it would be "surely wrong" to conclude that Abercrombie would still be liable under the disparate treatment theory. Such an interpretation is "surely wrong" since "an employer cannot be liable for taking adverse action because of a religious practice if the employer does not know that the practice is religious."]

A plaintiff need not show, however, that the employer took the adverse action because of the religious nature of the practice. Cf. (Thomas, J., concurring in part and dissenting in part). Suppose, for example, that an employer rejected all applicants who refuse to work on Saturday, whether for religious or nonreligious reasons. Applicants whose refusal to work on Saturday was known by the employer to be based on religion will have been rejected because of a religious practice.

This conclusion follows from the reasonable accommodation requirement imposed by §2000e(j). If neutral work rules (e.g., every employee must work on Saturday, no employee may wear any head covering) precluded liability, there would be no need to provide that defense, which allows an employer to escape liability for refusing to make an exception to a neutral work rule if doing so would impose an undue hardship.

[Justice Alito then rejected the majority's statement that the plaintiff has the burden to prove failure to accommodate, which he argued "blatantly contradicts the language of the statutes," which require the employer to "demonstrate[ ] that he is unable to reasonably accommodate to [the] employee's or prospective employee's religious observance or practice without undue hardship on the conduct of the employer's business." §2000e(j).]

Justice THOMAS, concurring in part and dissenting in part.

I agree with the Court that there are two — and only two — causes of action under Title VII of the Civil Rights Act of 1964 as understood by our precedents: a disparate-treatment (or intentional-discrimination) claim and a disparate-impact claim. Our agreement ends there. Unlike the majority, I adhere to what I had thought before today was an undisputed proposition: Mere application of a neutral policy cannot constitute "intentional discrimination." Because the [EEOC] can prevail here only if Abercrombie engaged in intentional discrimination, and because Abercrombie's application of its neutral Look Policy does not meet that description, I would affirm the judgment of the Tenth Circuit.

[Justice Thomas criticized the majority for "expand[ing] the meaning of 'intentional discrimination' to include a refusal to give a religious applicant 'favored treatment,'" which he found "not commanded by the relevant statutory text." The statute's language — prohibiting adverse actions "because of such individual's religious practice" — should be interpreted to reach actions "taken because of the religious nature of an employee's particular practice rather than prohibit[ing] adverse actions 'because of an employee's practice that *happens* to be religious'"; this "second, more expansive reading . . . would punish employers who have no discriminatory motive," a result "plainly at odds with the concept of intentional discrimination." The possibility of this strict-liability theory is surprisingly left open by the majority, but even its holding — that employers who act with the motive of avoiding accommodation are liable — is unjustifiable. That is because an employer who is aware that strictly applying a neutral policy will have an adverse effect on a religious group, and applies the policy anyway, is not engaged in intentional discrimination, at least as that term has traditionally been understood. As the Court explained many decades ago, "Discriminatory purpose" — *i.e.*, the purpose necessary for a claim of intentional discrimination — demands "more than . . . awareness of consequences. It implies that the decisionmaker . . . selected or reaffirmed a particular course of action at least in part 'because of,' not merely 'in spite of,' its adverse effects upon an identifiable group." *Personnel Administrator of Mass. v. Feeney* [reproduced at p. 131].

[While an employer may be liable for intentional discrimination in refusing to accommodate a religious practice, when it accommodates similar secular practices, "merely refusing to create an exception to a neutral policy for a religious practice cannot be described as treating a particular applicant 'less favorably than others.'"]

The Court today rightly puts to rest the notion that Title VII creates a freestanding religious-accommodation claim, but creates in its stead an entirely new form of liability: the disparate-treatment-based-on-equal-treatment claim. . . .

NOTES

1. *Discrimination vs. Accommodation.* We haven't yet studied the Americans with Disabilities Act, but you should know that there are three theories of discrimination under that statute — disparate treatment, disparate impact, and failure to reasonably accommodate a disability unless such accommodation poses an undue hardship. See Chapter 7. So it was not such a surprise that the lower courts saw a similar structure for religious discrimination under Title VII. But the *Abercrombie* majority rejects failure to accommodate as a separate liability theory for Title VII religious discrimination, and Justice Thomas concurs in the rejection of a "freestanding" accommodation theory. That would have led him to find for the employer — because no headwear was allowed for anyone, there could be no liability under the statute (absent disparate impact). But wouldn't a third theory of discrimination — a failure to accommodate claim — be both statutorily rooted and fill the gap between the disparate treatment and disparate impact theories? Why did no Justice support such an approach?

2. *Does It Make a Difference?* For the majority, the duty to accommodate is wrapped up in the duty not to intentionally discriminate. Look at footnote 2: "Failing to hire [because of plaintiff's religious practice] is *synonymous* with refusing to accommodate the religious practice. To accuse the employer of the one is to accuse him

of the other." Justice Scalia then goes on to lambaste Justice Alito for not providing any example, "not even an unrealistic hypothetical one, of a claim of failure to hire because of religious practice that does not say the employer refused to permit ('failed to accommodate') the religious practice. In the nature of things, there cannot be one."

That can't be right, can it? Suppose an employer is revolted by animal sacrifice and for that reason refuses to hire a practitioner of Santeria. The would-be employee requires nothing we would usually call a workplace accommodation; rather, it seems like plain vanilla discrimination. Or maybe the majority believes that hiring an animal-killer whose conduct is religious-based is an accommodation when the employer would not otherwise hire anyone who kills animals? At any rate, the merging of the accommodation and discrimination theories raises issues the Court did not address. Employers are normally permitted to discriminate when religion is a BFOQ, see p. 382. But employers are permitted not to accommodate when accommodation would pose an undue hardship. Going forward, are both defenses applicable or only one?

3. *Burdens of Proof.* Under Scalia's unified approach, the plaintiff has the burden of proving discrimination (including a failure to accommodate). However, the lower courts developed two different proof schemes for the two situations. Discrimination was usually proven pursuant to a version of *McDonnell Douglas* with causation typically the outcome-determinative question. In other words, plaintiffs in these situations were trying to prove that, say, being Jewish was the basis for an adverse action when the defendant claimed a nondiscriminatory reason explained the decision. In accommodation cases, however, causation was rarely at issue: the plaintiff typically asked for an exemption from a work rule, and the only question was whether the request was reasonable or would pose an undue hardship. Regardless of the *Abercrombie*, unified structure, the two very different factual scenarios will continue to confront the lower courts.

The majority also makes clear that the plaintiff bears the burden of proving some accommodation is reasonable. Presumably, where the employee is not asking for any dispensation from a work rule but merely seeking for her religion not to be held against her, reasonableness will be apparent (subject perhaps to the BFOQ defense). Where, however, the plaintiff wants some relief from a work rule of general application, the plaintiff will have the initial burden of showing that the accommodation is reasonable while the employer can still escape liability by showing that, albeit reasonable, the accommodation will cause it an undue hardship. These seem like two sides of the same coin, but, under the Americans with Disabilities Act, the Court has reconciled the allocation of burdens by requiring the plaintiff to show only that an accommodation "seems reasonable on its face, i.e., ordinarily or in the run of cases," leaving the employer to show "special (typically case-specific) circumstances that demonstrate undue hardship in the particular circumstances." *US Airways, Inc. v. Barnett*, 535 U.S. 391, 401-02 (2002). See p. 476. Presumably, that allocation of burdens will apply under Title VII.

Try to apply this to *Abercrombie* itself. Suppose that accommodating a headscarf would be reasonable for the average retailer; Abercrombie would still have the opportunity to show that its business model, *i.e.*, its Look Policy, would render it an "undue hardship" for it to allow her to do so. Could it be that not hiring Ms. Elauf would be a violation even if Abercrombie had the hardship defense? Maybe the answer is yes: that would at least have given the applicant the opportunity to choose. But if the applicant chose not to comply with a work rule that the employer was not required to change, should the employer be liable? Is this where motivating factor/same decision anyway comes into play — Abercrombie would violate the statute by taking Elauf's religion into account, but not owe her damages because she would never have been employed for failure to follow the Look policy?

4. *Knowledge*. Whatever the analysis, the Court's holding is "straightforward" and employee-friendly: "[a]n employer may not make an applicant's religious practice, confirmed or otherwise, a factor in employment decisions." But where does employer knowledge fit in? While the majority rejected any requirement that the employer have "actual knowledge" of the need for an accommodation, Abercrombie had at least a suspicion that Elauf was Muslim and that she would insist on wearing her headscarf if hired. See footnote 3. That sufficed for proof of religion being a motivating factor in the employer's decision.

But Justice Alito's concurrence views any possible liability without employer knowledge as "very strange." Does the majority's opinion suggest that an employer is liable if it applies a neutral workplace rule to reject an applicant with no reason to believe that there is a religious basis to the "issue" the applicant poses? If that's correct, it has to be disparate impact, right? But does it follow that there's necessarily an impact from such rules? For example, are most of those who would be excluded by a no-beard rule Muslim?

The majority also finds that the employer must be *motivated* by the religion (or suspected religion) of the applicant to be liable. How can that be true if it doesn't "know" about that religion? Is this all a convoluted way of saying that "know" has a very low threshold here? After all, the Court writes that an employer who acts on the basis of "no more than an unsubstantiated suspicion" may be liable. That language casts into doubt several lower court decisions that seemed to require much more proof of employer knowledge of religious belief. *See Reed v. Great Lakes Cos.*, 330 F.3d 931 (7th Cir. 2003) (finding no violation when plaintiff was fired for refusing to pray with the Gideons). *But see Nobach v. Woodland Village Nursing Center*, 799 F.3d 374 (5th Cir. 2015) (post-*Abercrombie* decision holding that firing an employee for refusing to pray the rosary with a patient was not religious discrimination when there was no evidence that plaintiff ever advised anyone that such prayer was against her religion or that anyone involved in the discharge suspected that her refusal was motivated by a religious belief).

Of course, plaintiffs seeking an accommodation would be well advised to make clear the religious basis of their request, which may not be obvious to the employer. *See Adeyeye v. Heartland Sweeteners, LLC*, 721 F.3d 444, 450-51 (7th Cir. 2013) (even though plaintiff's religious practices were not as familiar as others closer to the modern American mainstream, his request for leave to attend his father's funeral gave sufficient notice of its religious nature when it referred to a "funeral ceremony," a "funeral rite," and animal sacrifice). Does the possibility of liability for acting on "an unsubstantiated suspicion" in effect put the employer to the choice of inquiring further or not rejecting the applicant for reasons which may have a religious basis?

By the way, what happens when an employer takes an adverse action against an employee because of a misperception about her religion? *See* Dallan F. Flake, *Religious Discrimination Based on Employer Misperception*, 2016 Wis. L. Rev. 87. See Note 8 on p. 42.

NOTE ON "RELIGION" AND SINCERITY

Although central to Title VII's prohibition, "religion" is neither self-defining nor in any meaningful way defined by the statute — although the statute does tell us that, whatever counts as religion "includes all aspects of religious observance and practice, as well as belief." Courts have considered, for example, whether the vegan belief system is a religion. *Friedman v. S. Cal. Permanente Med. Grp.*, 125 Cal. Rptr. 2d 663 (Ct. App. 2002) (veganism is a secular philosophy, not a religion).

What, then, is a "religion"? The law is not at all clear on this point. The Supreme Court has addressed this in detail only in connection with conscientious objector status. The relevant statute exempted from service in the armed forces anyone who, "by reason of religious training and belief, is conscientiously opposed to participation in war in any form." Construing that statute, the Supreme Court first formulated a definition of a religious-based belief as a "sincere and meaningful belief which occupies in the life of its possessor a place parallel to that filled by the God of those admittedly qualifying for the exemption." *United States v. Seeger*, 380 U.S. 163, 176 (1965). Later, it expanded the definition to include moral and ethical beliefs that assumed the function of a religion in the registrant's life. Only if the belief "rests solely upon considerations of policy, pragmatism, or expediency" does it fail to qualify. *Welsh v. United States*, 398 U.S. 333, 342-43 (1970). This expansive approach to the meaning of religion may well have been driven by constitutional concerns of not overly favoring religion and thereby violating the Establishment Clause, but those concerns also seem applicable to Title VII.

The EEOC has adopted an expansive definition in accordance with *Seeger/Welsh.* 29 C.F.R. §1605.1 (2012). Perhaps because of the breadth of this definition, few cases find the claimed belief system not to be religious, even in relatively extreme situations such as the Church of Body Modification, which celebrates piercings, *Cloutier v. Costco Wholesale Corp.*, 390 F.3d 126 (1st Cir. 2004), and the World Church of the Creator, which preaches white supremacy. *Peterson v. Wilmur Commn'cs, Inc.*, 205 F. Supp. 2d 1014, 1015 (E.D. Wis. 2002). Perhaps counterintuitively, however, the courts have generally viewed "religion" as including atheism — the absence of a religious belief. *See EEOC v. Townley Engineering & Mfg. Co.*, 859 F.2d 610 (9th Cir. 1988); *Young v. Southwestern Savings & Loan Ass'n*, 509 F.2d 140, 142 (5th Cir. 1975). As Judge Posner wrote, "[a]nd so an atheist . . . cannot be fired because his employer dislikes atheists. If we think of religion as taking a position on divinity, then atheism is indeed a form of religion." *Reed v. Great Lakes Cos.*, 330 F.3d 931, 934 (7th Cir. 2003).

However, Posner also cautioned that "an employee is not permitted to redefine a purely personal preference or aversion as a religious belief," citing a case involving alleged belief in the deeply spiritual effects of eating Kozy Kitten People/Cat Food. *Id.* at 935 (citing *Seshadri v. Kasraian*, 130 F.3d 798 (7th Cir. 1997)). Otherwise, such an employee "could announce without warning that white walls or venetian blinds offended his 'spirituality,' and the employer would have to scramble to see whether it was feasible to accommodate him by repainting the walls or substituting curtains for venetian blinds." *Id.* But see *Davis v. Fort Bend Cnty.*, 765 F.3d 480, 486-87 (5th Cir. 2014) (2-1) (the fact that others might view an activity as only a social commitment is irrelevant if the employee sincerely viewed it as religious).

Of course, Judge Posner's hypothetical white wall worshipper might be dealt with not by debating whether the asserted belief is religious in nature but rather with whether the believer was sincere about it. It is well established that, while there can be no inquiry into the rationality of a particular belief, a court can determine whether the asserted belief is sincerely held. Relevant to that determination is whether the employee's conduct is consistent with the professed belief. *See EEOC v. Union Independiente de la Autoridad de Acueductos y Alcantarillados de P.R.*, 279 F.3d 49, 56-57 (1st Cir.

2002) (summary judgment denied where the sincerity of a claimed Seventh-day Adventist was challenged by evidence of his conduct contrary to the tenets of his professed religious belief). Nevertheless, just as there are relatively few cases holding that a particular belief is not religious, there are very few cases successfully challenging an employee's sincerity. *See Tagore v. United States*, 735 F.3d 324, 328 (5th Cir. 2013) (despite arguments that a slightly shorter blade length would satisfy plaintiff's religion, there was a genuine issue of material fact on the sincerity of Tagore's practice of wearing a kirpan with a three-inch blade).

A final issue regarding religion is whether a practice needs to be important or central to religious belief to be accommodated or at least in some sense required. Some courts seem to weigh the importance of the religious practice in approaching these cases. *See Davis v. Fort Bend Cty.*, 765 F.3d 480, 486 (5th Cir. 2014) ("the issue here is whether there exists a genuine dispute of material fact whether Davis sincerely felt that she was religiously compelled to attend and participate in a special service at church"). But the statute does not say that a religious practice or observance must be "compelled" to be accommodated. In fact, the notion of "required" religious observances seems to reflect a very Western, even Christian, view of religion since many religions are less commandment-oriented. Other courts have rejected any requirement that the observance or practice be required or central. *E.g., Heller v. EBB Auto Co.*, 8 F.3d 1433, 1438 (9th Cir. 1993) (upholding a claim for failure to accommodate an employee's attendance at his wife's conversion ceremony; a court should not inquire whether a particular practice is mandated or prohibited by a religion because that would involve deciding religious questions).

NOTE ON JUSTIFYING RELIGIOUS DISCRIMINATION

Suppose the defendant discriminated against the plaintiff on the basis of his religion. Is that ever permissible? A few possibilities suggest yes. First, normal "mixed motives" analysis means that, even when religion is found to be a motivating factor in an employment decision, an employer may limit the plaintiff's remedies by demonstrating that it would have taken the same action for nondiscriminatory reasons. *See Cowan v. Strafford R-VI Sch. Dist.*, 140 F.3d 1153, 1158 (8th Cir. 1998). Second, Title VII contains several exemptions permitting discrimination on account of religion. One permits certain religious organizations to discriminate on account of religion (but not on the basis of race, sex, or other prohibited ground). See p. 381. The ADA has a similar exemption. 42 U.S.C. §12113(d). Third, the bona fide occupational qualification defense permits some religious discrimination although the exemption of religious institutions from the prohibition of religious discrimination obviates the application of the BFOQ in the most likely cases when it might apply. See p. 382.

Fourth, religion-based restrictions by public employers have also been upheld when necessary to avoid constitutional problems. Thus, claims by public employees under Title VII are frequently joined with §1983 claims based on the Free Exercise Clause (even though there is no free exercise duty of accommodation), *see Shrum v. City of Coweta*, 449 F.3d 1132, 1143 (10th Cir. 2006) ("the mere failure of a government employer to accommodate the religious needs of an employee, where the need for accommodation arises from a conflict with a neutral and generally applicable employment requirement, does not violate the Free Exercise Clause"), but both kinds of claims are often defeated by an Establishment Clause justification for restrictions on employees. *See Grossman v. S. Shore Pub. Sch. Dist.*, 507 F.3d 1097 (7th Cir. 2007) (when a Lutheran guidance counselor's contract was not renewed because she threw out literature on condom use, taught abstinence, and prayed with students, there was no discrimination because of her Christian beliefs and Establishment Clause concerns justified limitations on her belief-inspired conduct); *Berry v. Dep't of Soc. Servs.*, 447 F.3d 642 (9th Cir. 2006) (neither the Constitution nor Title VII was violated by the employer's ban on the plaintiff discussing religion with the employer's clients or displaying religious items in his cubicle because of the risk of Establishment Clause violations). *But see Wigg v. Sioux Falls Sch. Dist. 49-5*, 382 F.3d 807, 815 (8th Cir. 2004) (Establishment Clause did not justify school district's flat prohibition of teachers participating in religious-based programs held on school grounds when no reasonable observer would perceive such participation as state endorsement of religion).

THE DUTY OF REASONABLE ACCOMMODATION

The duty to accommodate religious practices reflects a congressional concern with the problems of those whose religions forbid work on their Sabbath or other holy day. For example, both Seventh-day Adventists and Orthodox Jews have strict limitations on the kinds of work they can perform on their Sabbaths. In fact, the vast majority of "accommodation" cases involve refusals by employers to adjust work schedules to the religious observances of particular employees. But the language of the statute is not limited to excusing employees from work when their religion forbids labor (or demands religious practices). It reaches a broad spectrum of other activities, which may range from wearing distinctive clothes to not shaving to displaying religious symbols.

The broad formulation of the reasonable accommodation provision suggests that religious observances are privileged as opposed to secular practice. But the law on reasonable accommodation of religion has evolved in a much less stringent fashion than the statute's language might suggest, and much less stringently than has the similar reasonable accommodation requirement under the Americans with Disabilities Act. See Chapter 7. Despite its broad language, the Supreme Court has read the §701(j) provision quite narrowly.

Thus, in *Trans World Airlines, Inc. v. Hardison*, 432 U.S. 63 (1977), the Court defined undue hardship sweepingly. The facts involved a Saturday Sabbatarian who asked that a shift schedule requiring Saturday work be modified for him. He proposed a number of alternatives, but the Court found each to involve an "undue hardship" under a remarkably deferential definition: "[t]o require TWA to bear more than a de minimis cost in order to give Hardison Saturdays off is an undue hardship." *Id.* at 84. Hardship would flow either from TWA paying other employees premium rates to do Hardison's work or from TWA allocating days off on a religious basis: if Hardison were given Saturdays off for religious reasons, other employees would lose their opportunity to have Saturdays off. The Court concluded:

> . . . Title VII does not contemplate such unequal treatment. The repeated, unequivocal emphasis of both the language and the legislative history of Title VII is on eliminating discrimination in employment, and such discrimination is proscribed when it is directed against majorities as well as minorities. Indeed, the foundation of Hardison's claim is that TWA and IAM engaged in religious discrimination in violation of §703(a)(1) when they failed to arrange for him to have Saturdays off. It would be anomalous to conclude that by "reasonable accommodation" Congress meant that an employer must deny the shift and job preference of

some employees, as well as deprive them of their contractual rights, in order to accommodate or prefer the religious needs of others, and we conclude that Title VII does not require an employer to go that far.

. . . Like abandonment of the seniority system, to require TWA to bear additional costs when no such costs are incurred to give other employees the days off that they want would involve unequal treatment of employees on the basis of their religion. By suggesting that TWA should incur certain costs in order to give Hardison Saturdays off the Court of Appeals would in effect require TWA to finance an additional Saturday off and then to choose the employee who will enjoy it on the basis of his religious beliefs. While incurring extra costs to secure a replacement for Hardison might remove the necessity of compelling another employee to work involuntarily in Hardison's place, it would not change the fact that the privilege of having Saturdays off would be allocated according to religious beliefs.

As we have seen, the paramount concern of Congress in enacting Title VII was the elimination of discrimination in employment. In the absence of clear statutory language or legislative history to the contrary, we will not readily construe the statute to require an employer to discriminate against some employees in order to enable others to observe their Sabbath.

Id. at 80-85. And when the employer does offer a reasonable accommodation, that satisfies its Title VII duty even if another accommodation might be viewed as better responding to the employee's religious needs. *See Ansonia Bd. of Educ. v. Philbrook,* 479 U.S. 60, 86 (1986) ("We find no basis in either the statute or its legislative history for requiring an employer to choose any particular reasonable accommodation. By its very terms the statute directs that any reasonable accommodation by the employer is sufficient to meet its accommodation obligation.").

Taking their lead from these Supreme Court cases, the lower courts have often refused to require proposed accommodations, either because they are not reasonable to begin with or because they would impose an undue hardship. *E.g., Yeager v. FirstEnergy Generation Corp.,* 777 F.3d 362, 363 (6th Cir. 2015) (an employer need not accommodate an employee's religious beliefs by violating a federal statute," such as the requirement that employers provide the Social Security numbers of their workers); *Tagore v. United States,* 735 F.3d 324, 329-30 (5th Cir. 2013) (a Sikh fired because she could not enter her IRS workplace because her kirpan violated federal office security rules need not be accommodated by being allowed to work from her home or assigned elsewhere); *EEOC v. Geo Grp., Inc.,* 616 F.3d 265 (3d Cir. 2010) (a prison need not accommodate female Muslim guards' religious-based desire to wear khimars when the policy against headgear was justified by security concerns). *But see Adeyeye v. Heartland Sweeteners, LLC,* 721 F.3d 444, 455-56 (7th Cir. 2013) (employer failed to show that allowing worker to take several weeks of unpaid leave would have caused it an undue hardship when there was high turnover of workers in any event).

And where some accommodation is offered, the courts have typically found it to be reasonable. *Telfair v. Fed. Express Corp.,* 567 F. App'x 681 (11th Cir. 2014) (employer's offer to transfer employees to lower-paid positions when shift reassignments would have required them to work on their Sabbath was a reasonable accommodation, thus pretermitting any need to explore any further accommodations); *Sánchez-Rodríguez v. AT&T Mobility P.R., Inc.,* 673 F.3d 1, 12-13 (1st Cir. 2012) (taken together the employer's offer of a different position, allowing plaintiff to swap shifts and refraining from disciplining him for absenteeism satisfied its statutory obligations).

Where an employee's preferred accommodation collides with a collective bargaining agreement, the courts often find for the employer. *E.g., Virts v. Consolidated Freightways Corp. of Del.,* 285 F.3d 508 (6th Cir. 2002) (undue hardship for trucking company to accommodate a Christian truck driver who refused to make overnight runs with female drivers because it would require violating a collective bargaining agreement under which drivers are dispatched in the order of seniority). Even where a collective bargaining agreement does not control, courts have been reluctant to require accommodations that burden co-workers. *E.g., Broff v. N. Miss. Health Servs., Inc.*, 244 F.3d 495 (5th Cir. 2001) (undue hardship to accommodate counselor's religious beliefs by assigning to other counselors her patients who wished help involving homosexual or extramarital relations).

While many of these cases involve a tangible impact on other workers' jobs, the courts have also denied accommodation claims when the impact was on other employees' feelings and beliefs. A prime example is *Wilson v. U.S. West Communications*, 58 F.3d 1337 (8th Cir. 1995), which involved a Roman Catholic plaintiff who had made a religious vow to wear an anti-abortion button, one that was two inches in diameter and showed a color photograph of an 18- to 20-week-old fetus. This resulted in disruption at work, with co-workers testifying that they found the button offensive for reasons not related to abortion or religion. Although U.S. West suggested accommodations, plaintiff viewed them as inconsistent with her vow. She was ultimately was fired for refusing to comply with instructions not to wear the button. Ultimately, the court found that the accommodations the employer did offer — essentially wearing the button only in her work cubicle, covering it while at work, or wearing a similar button without the photograph — were reasonable. That exhausted the employer's duty and pretermitted any need to explore the undue hardship defense. Although Wilson argued that it was not her conduct but her co-workers' response to her beliefs that caused the workplace disruption, the court was unpersuaded: accepting Wilson's position "would require U.S. West to allow Wilson to impose her beliefs as she chooses." *Id.* at 1341. *See* Dallan F. Flake, *Bearing Burdens: Religious Accommodations That Adversely Affect Coworker Morale*, 76 OHIO ST. L.J. 169 (2015) (harm to employee morale from an accommodation should be accepted as sufficient to prove undue hardship).

Now that you've explored the duty of reasonable accommodation, how would these principles apply in *Abercrombie*? In other words, supposing the employer suspected both that Elauf was a Muslim and would want to wear a headscarf, is that the end of the case? Must it hire her? Presumably not — questions would remain as to whether exempting her from the Look Policy would be a reasonable accommodation for her religion or would pose an undue hardship. *See Cloutier v. Costco Wholesale Corp.*, 390 F.3d 126 (1st Cir. 2004) (it was undue hardship to defendant's public image for it to accommodate plaintiff's religious beliefs as a member of the Church of Body Modification by allowing her to wear her facial jewelry, even though there were no complaints and other employees' piercings went unnoticed); *Peterson v. Hewlett-Packard Co.*, 358 F.3d 599, 606-07 (9th Cir. 2004) (it would be an undue hardship to either permit plaintiff to post anti-gay scriptural passages that demeaned co-workers or to exclude sexual orientation from the employer's workplace diversity program); *Brown v. Polk County*, 61 F.3d 650, 655 (8th Cir. 1995) (en banc) (suggesting that the employer could prevail if it could show that any accommodation of the plaintiff's religious expression would be an undue hardship).

NOTE ON RELIGIOUS-BASED HARASSMENT

Harassment based on religion is certainly actionable. *See EEOC v. Sunbelt Rentals, Inc.*, 521 F.3d 306, 311 (4th Cir. 2008) (severe or pervasive harassment of plaintiff, a Muslim, which included "a steady stream of demeaning comments and degrading actions," including "religiously charged epithets" such as "Taliban" and "towel head," was actionable religious harassment). However, courts have not viewed situations as harassing where observant individuals were offended by conduct that was not motivated by religion. *See Rivera v. P.R. Aqueduct & Sewers Auth.*, 331 F.3d 183, 190 (1st Cir. 2003) (there "is a conceptual gap between an environment that is offensive to a person of strong religious sensibilities and an environment that is offensive because of hostility to the religion guiding those sensibilities").

But can a religious observer be viewed as herself "harassing" others because of her religious beliefs, as by proselytizing? *See Anderson v. U.S.F. Logistics (IMC), Inc.*, 274 F.3d 470 (7th Cir. 2001) (affirming denial of a preliminary injunction to employee that would have permitted her to wish a "Blessed Day" to a customer who objected). *But see Peterson v. Hewlett-Packard Co.*, 358 F.3d 599, 607 (9th Cir. 2004) ("That is not to say that accommodating an employee's religious beliefs creates undue hardship for an employer merely because the employee's co-workers find his conduct irritating or unwelcome. Complete harmony in the workplace is not an objective of Title VII."). If co-worker reaction against having a female or an African American supervisor is not a justification for an employer's race or gender discrimination, why is co-worker backlash relevant in a religious discrimination case? In the *U.S. West* case, suppose Wilson had merely worn a crucifix, a Star of David, or a head scarf and other workers had objected?

We examined sexual and other kinds of harassment in the preceding section, but religious harassment raises some distinctive issues. Indeed, the EEOC has attempted to formulate guidelines for such harassment without success. *See generally* Nantiya Ruan, *Accommodating Respectful Religious Expression in the Workplace*, 92 MARQ. L. REV. 1, 31-32 (2008); Theresa M. Beiner & John M.A. DiPappa, *Hostile Environments and the Religious Employee*, 19 U. ARK. LITTLE ROCK L.J. 577 (1997); David L. Gregory, *Religious Harassment in the Workplace: An Analysis of the EEOC's Proposed Guidelines*, 56 MONT. L. REV. 119 (1995).

NOTE ON RELIGIOUS INSTITUTIONS' EXEMPTION FROM THE PROHIBITION OF RELIGIOUS DISCRIMINATION

Some religious entities are exempted from Title VII's prohibition of discrimination on the basis of religion. *See Corporation of the Presiding Bishop v. Amos*, 483 U.S. 327 (1987). Even religious employers, however, are barred from discriminating on the other grounds prohibited by Title VII (subject, as we will see, to the constitutional "ministerial exception"). See p. 383. The statutory exemption raises several questions, two of which frequently arise in tandem: is an employer "religious," and, if so, is the discrimination it practices "religious" in nature?

With regard to those exempted, §2000e-1(a), §702(a), provides that "[t]his title shall not apply . . . to a religious corporation, association, educational institution, or society with respect to the employment of individuals of a particular religion to perform work connected with carrying on" the activities of such an entity. Although there is an obvious overlap, §2000e-1(e) has a similar exemption for "educational institutions" employing individuals "of a particular religion." *See Killinger v. Samford Univ.*, 113 F.3d 196 (11th Cir. 1997). The Americans with Disabilities Act also has similar provisions, §12113(d)(1) and (2), but the ADEA does not.

The courts are divided as to what makes an employer "religious" for the purposes of this exemption. *Compare LeBoon v. Lancaster Jewish Cmty. Ctr. Ass'n*, 503 F.3d 217 (3d Cir. 2007) (finding nonprofit community center within exception after applying multifactor test), *with Spencer v. World Vision, Inc.*, 633 F.3d 723 (9th Cir. 2011) (panel divided three ways as to the appropriate test for the exemption but nevertheless decided 2-1 that a nonprofit humanitarian aid organization was exempted even though it was not a church or church-affiliated); *see also EEOC v. Kamehameha Schs./Bishop Estate*, 990 F.2d 458 (9th Cir. 1993) (nominally religious school not exempted).

While these exemptions allow such institutions to employ "individuals of a particular religion," this has been read not merely to permit religious institutions to prefer members of their own faiths but also to allow such institutions to exclude individuals who, while claiming to be of the same faith of the institution, have violated some of its tenets. *See Hall v. Baptist Mem'l Health Care Corp.*, 215 F.3d 618 (6th Cir. 2000).

NOTE ON BFOQ DEFENSE TO RELIGIOUS DISCRIMINATION

Because of the exemptions for religious institutions, church-related organizations rarely need to rely on the BFOQ defense. In some cases, however, institutions that were not within the exemption, but were nevertheless religiously oriented, have used the defense. For example, *Pime v. Loyola University*, 803 F.2d 351 (7th Cir. 1986), found a BFOQ established for tenured lines reserved for Jesuits in Loyola's philosophy department, although it did not find Loyola to be a religious employer. *Pime* was decided before *International Union, UAW v. Johnson Controls*, reproduced at p. 142, which narrowed the BFOQ exemption. Is *Pime* still good law? *EEOC v. Kamehameha Schools/Bishop Estate*, 990 F.2d 458, 466 (9th Cir. 1993), doubted that and, in any event, rejected a BFOQ for hiring Protestants to teach in the Kamehameha schools, which it viewed as merely nominally religious.

NOTE ON THE ESTABLISHMENT CLAUSE

Constitutional objections to Title VII's treatment of religion have not been well received. The Supreme Court rejected a challenge to the exemption of religious institutions from the statute's prohibition on religious discrimination. *Corporation of the Presiding Bishop v. Amos*, 483 U.S. 327 (1987), involved the Deseret Gymnasium in Salt Lake City, a nonprofit facility, open to the public but operated by two religious corporations, both associated with the Church of Jesus Christ of Latter-day Saints. A building engineer sued when he was discharged because he failed to qualify for "a temple recommend, that is, a certificate that he is a member of the Church and eligible to attend its temples." *Id.* at 330. When the defendants moved to dismiss on the basis that §702 shielded them from liability, the plaintiff contended that §702 would violate the Establishment Clause if it were construed to allow religious employers to discriminate in hiring for nonreligious jobs. The Supreme Court upheld the §702 exemption: "This Court has long recognized that the government may (and sometimes must) accommodate religious practices and that it may do so without violating the Establishment Clause," and that such accommodation can exceed what is required by the Free Exercise Clause. *Id.* at 334.

A second constitutional challenge on Establishment Clause grounds has been to the notion of reasonable accommodation for secular employers. An unqualified duty to accommodate employees' religious beliefs goes too far. In *Estate of Thornton v. Caldor, Inc.*, 472 U.S. 703 (1985), the Court struck down a Connecticut statute that prohibited employers from requiring an employee to work on his Sabbath. That statute was not limited to "reasonable" accommodation, but required accommodation by the employer regardless of the burden imposed. *Amos* described the statute struck down in *Thornton* as effectively having given "the force of law to an employee's designation of his Sabbath day and required accommodation by the employer regardless of the burden that constituted for the employer or other employees." *Amos*, 483 U.S. at 337-38, n.15.

Title VII, of course, requires only "reasonable" accommodation and provides employers protection for undue hardship. Thus, *Thornton* is distinguishable. *See Protos v. Volkswagen of Am., Inc.*, 797 F.2d 129 (3d Cir. 1986); *see also Cutter v. Wilkinson*, 544 U.S. 709 (2005) (upholding the Religious Land Use and Institutionalized Persons Act as applied to state prisons as not impermissibly advancing religion). It may be that these kinds of Establishment Clause concerns led the Supreme Court to so narrowly construe the duty of reasonable accommodation in *Hardison*. *See also NLRB v. Catholic Bishop*, 440 U.S. 490 (1979) (interpreting National Labor Relations Act not to reach religiously affiliated schools in order to avoid free exercise problems).

* * *

We have seen that religious institutions have also been exempted from Title VII's prohibition on religious discrimination. But Title VII does not exempt religious institutions from its other prohibitions. Thus, a church or religious educational institution is barred from discriminating on the grounds of race, sex, and national origin by Title VII; it is also barred from discrimination on account of age or disability by the ADEA and the ADA. In a number of cases, religious employers have claimed a free exercise right to do exactly what these statutes proscribe.

HOSANNA-TABOR EVANGELICAL LUTHERAN CHURCH AND SCHOOL v. EEOC
565 U.S. 171 (2012)

Chief Justice ROBERTS delivered the opinion of the Court.

Certain employment discrimination laws authorize employees who have been wrongfully terminated to sue their employers for reinstatement and damages. The question presented is whether the Establishment and Free Exercise Clauses of the First Amendment bar such an action when the employer is a religious group and the employee is one of the group's ministers.

I

A

Petitioner Hosanna-Tabor Evangelical Lutheran Church and School is a member congregation of the Lutheran Church-Missouri Synod, the second largest Lutheran denomination in America. Hosanna-Tabor operated a small school in Redford, Michigan, offering a "Christ-centered education" to students in kindergarten through eighth grade.

The Synod classifies teachers into two categories: "called" and "lay." "Called" teachers are regarded as having been called to their vocation by God through a congregation. To be eligible to receive a call from a congregation, a teacher must satisfy certain academic requirements. One way of doing so is by completing a "colloquy" program at a Lutheran college or university. The program requires candidates to take eight courses of theological study, obtain the endorsement of their local Synod district, and pass an oral examination by a faculty committee. A teacher who meets these requirements may be called by a congregation. Once called, a teacher receives the formal title "Minister of Religion, Commissioned." A commissioned minister serves for an open-ended term; at Hosanna-Tabor, a call could be rescinded only for cause and by a supermajority vote of the congregation.

"Lay" or "contract" teachers, by contrast, are not required to be trained by the Synod or even to be Lutheran. At Hosanna-Tabor, they were appointed by the school board, without a vote of the congregation, to one-year renewable terms. Although teachers at the school generally performed the same duties regardless of whether they were lay or called, lay teachers were hired only when called teachers were unavailable.

[Cheryl Perich was first employed by Hosanna-Tabor as a lay teacher but when she completed her colloquy she become a called teacher. She taught kindergarten and fourth grade, including math, language arts, social studies, science, gym, art, and music.] She also taught a religion class four days a week, led the students in prayer and devotional exercises each day, and attended a weekly school-wide chapel service. Perich led the chapel service herself about twice a year.

Perich became ill in June 2004 with what was eventually diagnosed as narcolepsy. Symptoms included sudden and deep sleeps from which she could not be roused. Because of her illness, Perich began the 2004-2005 school year on disability leave. [Although she desired to return in February, the school had already contracted with a lay teacher to fill her position and was concerned that Perich was not yet ready to return to the classroom. On January 30, the congregation] voted to offer Perich a "peaceful release" from her call, whereby the congregation would pay a portion of her health insurance premiums in exchange for her resignation as a called teacher. Perich refused to resign and produced a note from her doctor stating that she would be able to return to work on February 22. The school board urged Perich to reconsider, informing her that the school no longer had a position for her, but Perich stood by her decision not to resign.

On the morning of February 22 — the first day she was medically cleared to return to work — Perich presented herself at the school. [Principal] Hoeft asked her to leave but she would not do so until she obtained written documentation that she had reported to work. Later that afternoon, Hoeft called Perich at home and told her that she would likely be fired. Perich responded that she had spoken with an attorney and intended to assert her legal rights.

Following a school board meeting that evening, board chairman Scott Salo sent Perich a letter stating that Hosanna-Tabor was reviewing the process for rescinding her call in light of her "regrettable" actions. Salo subsequently followed up with a letter advising Perich that the congregation would consider whether to rescind her call at its next meeting. As grounds for termination, the letter cited Perich's "insubordination and disruptive behavior" on February 22, as well as the damage she had done to her "working relationship" with the school by "threatening to take legal action." The congregation voted to rescind Perich's call on April 10, and Hosanna-Tabor sent her a letter of termination the next day.

B

[Perich sued under the ADA claiming discriminating on the basis of disability and retaliation for opposing discrimination. Although the ADA itself provides religious entities with exemptions from claims of religious discrimination, 42 U.S.C.A. §§12113(d)(1), §12113(d)(2), Hosanna-Tabor did not argue that these defenses barred retaliation claims. The EEOC brought suit against Hosanna-Tabor and Perich intervened. The district court found the suit barred by the "ministerial exception," but the Sixth Circuit disagreed because Perich did not qualify as a "minister" since her duties as a called teacher were identical to her duties as a lay teacher.]

II

The First Amendment provides, in part, that "Congress shall make no law respecting an establishment of religion, or prohibiting the free exercise thereof." . . . Both Religion Clauses bar the government from interfering with the decision of a religious group to fire one of its ministers.

A

[Chief Justice Roberts traced the history of "controversy between church and state over religious offices," noting that any freedom of the church from state control "did not survive the reign of Henry VIII, even in theory." During his reign and thereafter, various statutes made the monarch the supreme head of the Church and gave him the right to appoint its high officials.]

Seeking to escape the control of the national church, the Puritans fled to New England, where they hoped to elect their own ministers and establish their own modes of worship. *See* T. CURRY, THE FIRST FREEDOMS: CHURCH AND STATE IN AMERICA TO THE PASSAGE OF THE FIRST AMENDMENT 3 (1986); McConnell, *The Origins and Historical Understanding of Free Exercise of Religion*, 103 HARV. L. REV. 1409, 1422 (1990). William Penn, the Quaker proprietor of what would eventually become Pennsylvania and Delaware, also sought independence from the Church of England. The charter creating the province of Pennsylvania contained no clause establishing a religion. *See* S. COBB, THE RISE OF RELIGIOUS LIBERTY IN AMERICA 440-441 (1970).

Colonists in the South, in contrast, brought the Church of England with them. But even they sometimes chafed at the control exercised by the Crown and its representatives over religious offices. In Virginia, for example, the law vested the governor with the power to induct ministers presented to him by parish vestries, but the vestries often refused to make such presentations and instead chose ministers on their own. *See* H. ECKENRODE, SEPARATION OF CHURCH AND STATE IN VIRGINIA 13-19 (1910). Controversies over the selection of ministers also arose in other Colonies with Anglican establishments. . . .

It was against this background that the First Amendment was adopted. Familiar with life under the established Church of England, the founding generation sought to foreclose the possibility of a national church. See 1 Annals of Cong. 730-731 (1789) (noting that the Establishment Clause addressed the fear that "one sect might obtain a pre-eminence, or two combine together, and establish a religion to which they would compel others to conform" (remarks of J. Madison)). By forbidding the "establishment of religion" and guaranteeing the "free exercise thereof," the Religion Clauses ensured that the new Federal Government — unlike the English Crown — would have no role in filling ecclesiastical offices. The Establishment Clause prevents the

Government from appointing ministers, and the Free Exercise Clause prevents it from interfering with the freedom of religious groups to select their own.

This understanding of the Religion Clauses was reflected in two events involving James Madison, "'the leading architect of the religion clauses of the First Amendment." [The first event was refusing a solicitation from John Carroll, the first Catholic bishop in the United States, for the executive's opinion on who should be appointed to direct the Church affairs in the newly acquired Louisiana Purchase. The "scrupulous policy of the Constitution in guarding against a political interference with religious affairs," Madison explained, prevented the government from rendering an opinion on the "selection of ecclesiastical individuals." The second episode occurred in 1811 when Madison vetoed a bill incorporating the Protestant Episcopal Church in what was then the District of Columbia because it violated the Establishment Clause. He stressed that the bill established by law rules that reached "even the election and removal of the Minister" of the church.]

B

Given this understanding of the Religion Clauses — and the absence of government employment regulation generally — it was some time before questions about government interference with a church's ability to select its own ministers came before the courts. This Court touched upon the issue indirectly, however, in the context of disputes over church property. Our decisions in that area confirm that it is impermissible for the government to contradict a church's determination of who can act as its ministers.

In *Watson v. Jones*, 80 U.S. 679 (1872), the Court considered a dispute between antislavery and proslavery factions over who controlled the property of the Walnut Street Presbyterian Church in Louisville, Kentucky. The General Assembly of the Presbyterian Church had recognized the antislavery faction, and this Court — applying not the Constitution but a "broad and sound view of the relations of church and state under our system of laws" — declined to question that determination. . . . As we would put it later, our opinion in *Watson* "radiates . . . a spirit of freedom for religious organizations, an independence from secular control or manipulation — in short, power to decide for themselves, free from state interference, matters of church government as well as those of faith and doctrine." *Kedroff v. Saint Nicholas Cathedral of Russian Orthodox Church in North America*, 344 U.S. 94 (1952).

Confronting the issue under the Constitution for the first time in *Kedroff*, the Court recognized that the "[f]reedom to select the clergy, where no improper methods of choice are proven," is "part of the free exercise of religion" protected by the First Amendment against government interference. At issue in *Kedroff* was the right to use a Russian Orthodox cathedral in New York City. The Russian Orthodox churches in North America had split from the Supreme Church Authority in Moscow, out of concern that the Authority had become a tool of the Soviet Government. . . . New York's highest court ruled in favor of the North American churches, based on a state law requiring every Russian Orthodox church in New York to recognize the determination of the governing body of the North American churches as authoritative.

This Court reversed, concluding that the New York law violated the First Amendment. We explained that the controversy over the right to use the cathedral was "strictly a matter of ecclesiastical government, the power of the Supreme Church Authority of the Russian Orthodox Church to appoint the ruling hierarch of the archdiocese of North America." By "pass[ing] the control of matters strictly ecclesiastical from one church authority to another," the New York law intruded the "power of the state into the forbidden area of religious freedom contrary to the principles of the First Amendment." Accordingly, we declared the law unconstitutional because it "directly prohibit[ed] the free exercise of an ecclesiastical right, the Church's choice of its hierarchy."

This Court reaffirmed these First Amendment principles in *Serbian Eastern Orthodox Diocese for United States and Canada v. Milivojevich*, 426 U.S. 696 (1976), a case involving a dispute over control of the American-Canadian Diocese of the Serbian Orthodox Church, including its property and assets. The Church had removed Dionisije Milivojevich as bishop of the American-Canadian Diocese because of his defiance of the church hierarchy. Following his removal, Dionisije brought a civil action in state court challenging the Church's decision, and the Illinois Supreme Court "purported in effect to reinstate Dionisije as Diocesan Bishop," on the ground that the proceedings resulting in his removal failed to comply with church laws and regulations.

Reversing that judgment, this Court explained that the First Amendment "permit[s] hierarchical religious organizations to establish their own rules and regulations for internal discipline and government, and to create tribunals for adjudicating disputes over these matters." When ecclesiastical tribunals decide such disputes, we further explained, "the Constitution requires that civil courts accept their decisions as binding upon them." We thus held that by inquiring into whether the Church had followed its own procedures, the State Supreme Court had "unconstitutionally undertaken the resolution of quintessentially religious controversies whose resolution the First Amendment commits exclusively to the highest ecclesiastical tribunals" of the Church.

C

Until today, we have not had occasion to consider whether this freedom of a religious organization to select its ministers is implicated by a suit alleging discrimination in employment. The Courts of Appeals, in contrast, have had extensive experience with this issue. Since the passage of Title VII of the Civil Rights Act of 1964 and other employment discrimination laws, the Courts of Appeals have uniformly recognized the existence of a "ministerial exception," grounded in the First Amendment, that precludes application of such legislation to claims concerning the employment relationship between a religious institution and its ministers.

We agree that there is such a ministerial exception. The members of a religious group put their faith in the hands of their ministers. Requiring a church to accept or retain an unwanted minister, or punishing a church for failing to do so, intrudes upon more than a mere employment decision. Such action interferes with the internal governance of the church, depriving the church of control over the selection of those who will personify its beliefs. By imposing an unwanted minister, the state infringes the Free Exercise Clause, which protects a religious group's right to shape its own faith and mission through its appointments. According the state the power to determine which individuals will minister to the faithful also violates the Establishment Clause, which prohibits government involvement in such ecclesiastical decisions.

The EEOC and Perich acknowledge that employment discrimination laws would be unconstitutional as applied to religious groups in certain circumstances. They grant, for example, that it would violate the First Amendment for courts to apply such laws to compel the ordination of women by the Catholic Church or by an Orthodox

Jewish seminary. According to the EEOC and Perich, religious organizations could successfully defend against employment discrimination claims in those circumstances by invoking the constitutional right to freedom of association — a right "implicit" in the First Amendment. *Roberts v. United States Jaycees*, 468 U.S. 609. The EEOC and Perich thus see no need — and no basis — for a special rule for ministers grounded in the Religion Clauses themselves.

We find this position untenable. The right to freedom of association is a right enjoyed by religious and secular groups alike. It follows under the EEOC's and Perich's view that the First Amendment analysis should be the same, whether the association in question is the Lutheran Church, a labor union, or a social club. That result is hard to square with the text of the First Amendment itself, which gives special solicitude to the rights of religious organizations. We cannot accept the remarkable view that the Religion Clauses have nothing to say about a religious organization's freedom to select its own ministers.

The EEOC and Perich also contend that our decision in *Employment Div., Dept. of Human Resources of Ore. v. Smith*, 494 U.S. 872 (1990), precludes recognition of a ministerial exception. In *Smith*, two members of the Native American Church were denied state unemployment benefits after it was determined that they had been fired from their jobs for ingesting peyote, a crime under Oregon law. We held that this did not violate the Free Exercise Clause, even though the peyote had been ingested for sacramental purposes, because the "right of free exercise does not relieve an individual of the obligation to comply with a valid and neutral law of general applicability on the ground that the law proscribes (or prescribes) conduct that his religion prescribes (or proscribes)."

It is true that the ADA's prohibition on retaliation, like Oregon's prohibition on peyote use, is a valid and neutral law of general applicability. But a church's selection of its ministers is unlike an individual's ingestion of peyote. *Smith* involved government regulation of only outward physical acts. The present case, in contrast, concerns government interference with an internal church decision that affects the faith and mission of the church itself. The contention that *Smith* forecloses recognition of a ministerial exception rooted in the Religion Clauses has no merit.

III

Having concluded that there is a ministerial exception grounded in the Religion Clauses of the First Amendment, we consider whether the exception applies in this case. We hold that it does.

Every Court of Appeals to have considered the question has concluded that the ministerial exception is not limited to the head of a religious congregation, and we agree. We are reluctant, however, to adopt a rigid formula for deciding when an employee qualifies as a minister. It is enough for us to conclude, in this our first case involving the ministerial exception, that the exception covers Perich, given all the circumstances of her employment.

To begin with, Hosanna-Tabor held Perich out as a minister, with a role distinct from that of most of its members. When Hosanna-Tabor extended her a call, it issued her a "diploma of vocation" according her the title "Minister of Religion, Commissioned." She was tasked with performing that office "according to the Word of God and the confessional standards of the Evangelical Lutheran Church as drawn from the Sacred Scriptures." The congregation prayed that God "bless [her] ministrations to the glory of His holy name, [and] the building of His church." In a supplement to the diploma, the congregation undertook to periodically review Perich's "skills of ministry" and "ministerial responsibilities," and to provide for her "continuing education as a professional person in the ministry of the Gospel."

Perich's title as a minister reflected a significant degree of religious training followed by a formal process of commissioning. To be eligible to become a commissioned minister, Perich had to complete eight college-level courses in subjects including biblical interpretation, church doctrine, and the ministry of the Lutheran teacher. She also had to obtain the endorsement of her local Synod district by submitting a petition that contained her academic transcripts, letters of recommendation, personal statement, and written answers to various ministry-related questions. Finally, she had to pass an oral examination by a faculty committee at a Lutheran college. It took Perich six years to fulfill these requirements. And when she eventually did, she was commissioned as a minister only upon election by the congregation, which recognized God's call to her to teach. At that point, her call could be rescinded only upon a supermajority vote of the congregation — a protection designed to allow her to "preach the Word of God boldly."

Perich held herself out as a minister of the Church by accepting the formal call to religious service, according to its terms. She did so in other ways as well. For example, she claimed a special housing allowance on her taxes that was available only to employees earning their compensation "'in the exercise of the ministry.'" In a form she submitted to the Synod following her termination, Perich again indicated that she regarded herself as a minister at Hosanna-Tabor, stating: "I feel that God is leading me to serve in the teaching ministry. . . . I am anxious to be in the teaching ministry again soon."

Perich's job duties reflected a role in conveying the Church's message and carrying out its mission. Hosanna-Tabor expressly charged her with "lead[ing] others toward Christian maturity" and "teach[ing] faithfully the Word of God, the Sacred Scriptures, in its truth and purity and as set forth in all the symbolical books of the Evangelical Lutheran Church." In fulfilling these responsibilities, Perich taught her students religion four days a week, and led them in prayer three times a day. Once a week, she took her students to a school-wide chapel service, and — about twice a year — she took her turn leading it, choosing the liturgy, selecting the hymns, and delivering a short message based on verses from the Bible. During her last year of teaching, Perich also led her fourth graders in a brief devotional exercise each morning. As a source of religious instruction, Perich performed an important role in transmitting the Lutheran faith to the next generation.

In light of these considerations — the formal title given Perich by the Church, the substance reflected in that title, her own use of that title, and the important religious functions she performed for the Church — we conclude that Perich was a minister covered by the ministerial exception.

In reaching a contrary conclusion, the Court of Appeals committed three errors. First, the Sixth Circuit failed to see any relevance in the fact that Perich was a commissioned minister. Although such a title, by itself, does not automatically ensure coverage, the fact that an employee has been ordained or commissioned as a minister is surely relevant, as is the fact that significant religious training and a recognized religious mission underlie the description of the employee's position. It was wrong for the Court of Appeals . . . to say that an employee's title does not matter.

Second, the Sixth Circuit gave too much weight to the fact that lay teachers at the school performed the same religious duties as Perich. We express no view on whether someone with Perich's duties would be covered by the ministerial exception in the absence of the other considerations we have discussed. But though relevant, it cannot be dispositive that others not formally recognized as ministers by the church perform the same functions — particularly when, as here, they did so only because commissioned ministers were unavailable.

Third, the Sixth Circuit placed too much emphasis on Perich's performance of secular duties. It is true that her religious duties consumed only 45 minutes of each work-day, and that the rest of her day was devoted to teaching secular subjects. The EEOC regards that as conclusive, contending that any ministerial exception "should be limited to those employees who perform exclusively religious functions." We cannot accept that view. Indeed, we are unsure whether any such employees exist. The heads of congregations themselves often have a mix of duties, including secular ones such as helping to manage the congregation's finances, supervising purely secular personnel, and overseeing the upkeep of facilities.

Although the Sixth Circuit did not adopt the extreme position pressed here by the EEOC, it did regard the relative amount of time Perich spent performing religious functions as largely determinative. The issue before us, however, is not one that can be resolved by a stopwatch. The amount of time an employee spends on particular activities is relevant in assessing that employee's status, but that factor cannot be considered in isolation, without regard to the nature of the religious functions performed and the other considerations discussed above.

[The suit originally sought to reinstate Perich to her former position as a called teacher, which "would have plainly violated the Church's freedom under the Religion Clauses to select its own ministers," but even the monetary award now sought] would operate as a penalty on the Church for terminating an unwanted minister, and would be no less prohibited by the First Amendment than an order overturning the termination. Such relief would depend on a determination that Hosanna-Tabor was wrong to have relieved Perich of her position, and it is precisely such a ruling that is barred by the ministerial exception.

The EEOC and Perich suggest that Hosanna-Tabor's asserted religious reason for firing Perich — that she violated the Synod's commitment to internal dispute resolution — was pretextual. That suggestion misses the point of the ministerial exception. The purpose of the exception is not to safeguard a church's decision to fire a minister only when it is made for a religious reason. The exception instead ensures that the authority to select and control who will minister to the faithful — a matter "strictly ecclesiastical," *Kedroff*.[4]

IV

[The Court noted the broader issues it did not address, for example, whether a ministerial exception protects religious organizations from liability for retaliating against employees for reporting criminal misconduct, or for testifying in criminal proceedings or whether it freed such organizations to hire children or unauthorized aliens. However, it went on to limit its decision:] The case before us is an employment

---

4. A conflict has arisen in the Courts of Appeals over whether the ministerial exception is a jurisdictional bar or a defense on the merits. We conclude that the exception operates as an affirmative defense to an otherwise cognizable claim, not a jurisdictional bar. That is because the issue presented by the exception is "whether the allegations the plaintiff makes entitle him to relief," not whether the court has "power to hear [the] case." District courts have power to consider ADA claims in cases of this sort, and to decide whether the claim can proceed or is instead barred by the ministerial exception.

discrimination suit brought on behalf of a minister, challenging her church's decision to fire her. Today we hold only that the ministerial exception bars such a suit. We express no view on whether the exception bars other types of suits, including actions by employees alleging breach of contract or tortious conduct by their religious employers. There will be time enough to address the applicability of the exception to other circumstances if and when they arise. . . .

THOMAS, J., concurring

[While agreeing with the Court on the facts before it as to Perich's ministerial role, it would be sufficient for Justice Thomas that the defendant "sincerely considered Perich a minister."]

Justice ALITO, with whom Justice KAGAN joins, concurring.

I join the Court's opinion, but I write separately to clarify my understanding of the significance of formal ordination and designation as a "minister" in determining whether an "employee"[1] of a religious group falls within the so-called "ministerial" exception. The term "minister" is commonly used by many Protestant denominations to refer to members of their clergy, but the term is rarely if ever used in this way by Catholics, Jews, Muslims, Hindus, or Buddhists. In addition, the concept of ordination as understood by most Christian churches and by Judaism has no clear counterpart in some Christian denominations and some other religions. [For example, Jehovah's Witnesses consider all baptized disciples to be ministers, while in Islam, "every Muslim can perform the religious rites, so there is no class or profession of ordained clergy. Yet there are religious leaders who are recognized for their learning and their ability to lead communities of Muslims in prayer, study, and living according to the teaching of the Qur'an and Muslim law."]

The First Amendment protects the freedom of religious groups to engage in certain key religious activities, including the conducting of worship services and other religious ceremonies and rituals, as well as the critical process of communicating the faith. Accordingly, religious groups must be free to choose the personnel who are essential to the performance of these functions.

The "ministerial" exception should be tailored to this purpose. It should apply to any "employee" who leads a religious organization, conducts worship services or important religious ceremonies or rituals, or serves as a messenger or teacher of its faith. If a religious group believes that the ability of such an employee to perform these key functions has been compromised, then the constitutional guarantee of religious freedom protects the group's right to remove the employee from his or her position. . . .

[The ministerial exception applies to Perich because, as the Court notes, she played a substantial role in "conveying the Church's message and carrying out its mission."] It makes no difference that respondent also taught secular subjects. While a purely secular teacher would not qualify for the "ministerial" exception, the constitutional protection of religious teachers is not somehow diminished when they take on secular functions in addition to their religious ones. What matters is that respondent played

---

1. It is unconventional to refer to many persons who clearly fall within the "ministerial" exception, such as Protestant ministers, Catholic priests, and Jewish rabbis, as "employees," but I use the term in the sense in which it is used in the antidiscrimination laws that are often implicated in cases involving the exception.

an important role as an instrument of her church's religious message and as a leader of its worship activities. Because of these important religious functions, Hosanna-Tabor had the right to decide for itself whether respondent was religiously qualified to remain in her office.

NOTES

1. *The Significance of the Opinion.* In a rare show of unanimity, all nine Justices agreed that Perich was not protected by the ADA. The majority opinion not only recognized the ministerial exception but adopted a broad view of it. Even more strikingly, the three Justices concurring would have adopted an even broader view, and the majority did not so much reject their analyses as find it unnecessary to reach the question. It seems clear that churches have considerably more freedom to pick and choose "ministers" than one might have believed prior to *Hosanna-Tabor.*

2. *The Fate of* Smith. Although you can't tell from the opinions, one of the biggest problems for the lower courts in continuing to recognize the ministerial exception was *Employment Division, Department of Human Resources v. Smith*, 494 U.S. 872 (1990). Prior to 1990, the question of whether the Free Exercise Clause was violated by the antidiscrimination statutes would have been analyzed in terms of whether they imposed a "substantial burden" on the church and could not be justified by a "compelling state interest." The plaintiffs in *Smith* challenged the state's denial of unemployment compensation benefits after they had been fired from their private-sector jobs because of their sacramental use of the drug peyote. Writing for the Court, Justice Scalia rejected the substantial burden analysis. Regardless of burdens, he held that neutral laws of general application simply did not implicate free exercise concerns. Rather, for the Free Exercise Clause to apply, a law must be aimed at religious practices. *Cf. Church of Lukumi Babalu Aye v. Hialeah*, 508 U.S. 520 (1993) (ordinance prohibiting ritual animal sacrifice targets religion and violates the First Amendment because it is not narrowly tailored to serve the asserted government interests).

Although *Smith* itself suggested some potential exceptions, *see Fraternal Order of Police Newark Lodge No. 12 v. City of Newark*, 170 F.3d 359 (3d Cir. 1999) (city's refusal to accommodate officers whose religion required them to wear beards violated the Free Exercise Clause, at least where the city permitted officers with medical conditions that limited shaving to wear beards), none seemed to reach the ministerial exception scenario. Nevertheless, the lower courts continued to apply the exception and *Hosanna-Tabor* confirmed that line of cases. It distinguished *Smith* by saying that a church's selection of its ministers is "unlike an individual's ingestion of peyote. *Smith* involved government regulation of only outward physical acts. The present case, in contrast, concerns government interference with an internal church decision that affects the faith and mission of the church itself." Does the government ever regulate anything other than "outward physical acts"? In any event, does this passage undercut *Smith*'s general thrust or just mean that there's a church autonomy exception to *Smith*? Of course, *Hosanna-Tabor* is also premised in part on the Establishment Clause so maybe the tension with free exercise jurisprudence is less problematic.

3. *Who's a Minister?* The principal case suggests a broad view of the exemption, and lower court decisions the wake of *Hosanna-Tabor* confirm that approach. For example, the Sixth Circuit in *Cannata v. Catholic Diocese of Austin*, 700 F.3d 169 (5th Cir. 2012), held that, although plaintiff was neither ordained nor formally trained in religion, his role as music director for the church's liturgy and his playing the piano

at Mass brought him within the ministerial exception. *See also Conlon v. Intervarsity Christian Fellowship/USA*, 777 F.3d 829 (6th Cir. 2015) (a "religious group," although not a "church," could claim the ministerial exception even though not tied to a particular denomination; the exception applies when a formal title and religious function are both present). *But see Kant v. Lexington Theological Seminary*, 26 S.W.3d 587 (Ky. 2014) (holding a Jewish professor at a Christian seminary not to be a minister and thus able to pursue a contract claim for discharge in violation of his tenure contract).

4. *A Law-Free Zone?* Prior to *Hosanna-Tabor*, some courts, while recognizing the ministerial exception, viewed it as not foreclosing all inquiry into church employment practices. *See Elvig v. Calvin Presbyterian Church*, 375 F.3d 951, 964 (9th Cir. 2004) (review of a church's decision to terminate plaintiff's ministry foreclosed, but plaintiff's hostile environment claims may be pursued since this inquiry "does not require interpretations of religious doctrine or scrutiny of the Defendants' ministerial choices"). *Hosanna-Tabor* clearly render such decisions questionable, but the majority conspicuously avoided deciding how far the Constitution would go in immunizing church choice of ministers from civil law.

5.   *Not Jurisdictional.* Another important aspect of *Hosanna-Tabor* was footnote 4, which states the ministerial exception is nonjurisdictional. That suggests that it is waivable, which raises the question of whether courts can adjudicate ministers' claims if the church did not raise the defense. Much prior scholarship had concluded that any such exception would be jurisdictional since courts are simply not competent, under the First Amendment, to decide religion questions, but *Hosanna-Tabor* requires a reconsideration of that position. *See generally* Michael A. Helfand, *Religion's Footnote Four: Church Autonomy as Arbitration*, 97 MINN. L. REV. 1891 (2013).

NOTE ON THE RELIGIOUS FREEDOM RESTORATION ACT

While *Hosanna-Tabor* recognizes a significant exception to *Smith*'s rule, it is not the only such exception. An earlier congressional response to *Smith* was the Religious Freedom Restoration Act (RFRA), 42 U.S.C. §2000bb (2018), whose stated purpose was to reinstate the substantial burden/compelling governmental interest analysis to neutral laws of general application as a matter of statute, not constitutional law. In *City of Boerne v. Flores*, 521 U.S. 507 (1997), however, the Supreme Court found RFRA unconstitutional as applied to the states. This, in turn, led to a number of states passing "little RFRAs." More important for our purposes, *City of Boerne* implied that RFRA remained valid as applied to the federal government, which the Court confirmed in *Gonzales v. O Centro Espírita Beneficente União do Vegetal*, 546 U.S. 418 (2006) (upholding preliminary injunction against federal government enforcement of the Controlled Substances Act when the sacramental use of hoasca was thereby burdened).

This means that federal employees have potential RFRA protections (as may state and local employees in jurisdictions with little RFRAs), which might be broader than the crabbed interpretation the courts have accorded Title VII's duty of accommodation. *See Tagore v. United States*, 735 F.3d 324, 330-32 (5th Cir. 2013) (under RFRA, while the government has a compelling interest in protecting federal buildings, the need for uniform security rules may not satisfy the "least restrictive means" test for strict scrutiny in light of numerous exceptions to the general rule); *Potter v. District of Columbia*, 558 F.3d 542, 547 (D.C. Cir. 2009) (while firefighter safety was a compelling state interest, the District failed to show why safety would be threatened by using the breathing equipment sought by plaintiffs as an accommodation).

Before *Hosanna-Tabor*, there was also a question as to whether RFRA limited what would otherwise be the reach of federal statutes such as Title VII when a religious institution was burdened. Under this view, RFRA pro tanto amended Title VII, the ADA, and the ADEA to limit the impact of the antidiscrimination laws on religious employers. There was considerable confusion in the lower courts as to the effects of RFRA. *See Harrell v. Donahue*, 638 F.3d 975, 984 (8th Cir. 2011) ("RFRA was not intended to broaden the remedies for federal employment discrimination beyond those that already existed under Title VII [which] provides the exclusive remedy for his claims of religious discrimination."); *Tomic v. Catholic Diocese of Peoria*, 442 F.3d 1036, 1042 (7th Cir. 2006) ("RFRA is applicable only to suits to which the government is a party"); *Hankins v. Lyght*, 441 F.3d 96 (2d Cir. 2006) (2-1) (RFRA's effect must be analyzed since it operates as an amendment to the ADEA, which would otherwise bar mandatory retirement). *Hosanna-Tabor* never mentioned RFRA, but it seems likely that the First Amendment now bars federal government intrusion into many of the kinds of decisions that RFRA might have insulated from court review, whatever RFRA might have to say on the matter. Indeed, the *Hosanna-Tabor* Court did not suggest a compelling state interest justification for intrusion into such decisions, which would mean that the religion clauses provide more protection than would RFRA.

As for RFRA itself, *Burwell v. Hobby Lobby Stores, Inc.*, 134 S. Ct. 2751 (2014), held that that statute barred application of regulations under the Affordable Care Act that would have required two for-profit corporations to either provide comprehensive health insurance for their workers or pay a tax. Comprehensive insurance included contraceptive coverage, which was objectionable on religious grounds to the individuals who controlled the two closely held corporations subject to the mandate.

The majority opinion, authored by Justice Alito and joined by the Chief Justice and Justices Scalia, Thomas, and Kennedy, found a RFRA violation. Although there had been considerable doubt whether the statute reached corporations in the first place and whether such entities could "exercise religion," the majority found that RFRA protects the religious interests of "persons" who direct closely held corporations, even if the corporations as such are for profit and not explicitly religious. That the corporations were for-profit did not mean that their owners could not simultaneously pursue their religious beliefs through the corporate form.

Second, the majority had "little trouble" determining that the ACA imposed substantial burdens on the plaintiffs. One of the plaintiff companies would have to pay as much as $475 million per year if it offered noncompliant health insurance. *Id.* at 2776. Even assuming the employer chose to pay the $2,000 per employee tax rather than provide insurance itself, the burden would be $26 million for the largest corporate plaintiff. *Id.* Nor did the majority pause long over the contention that providing required coverage had too "attenuated" a connection to the religious beliefs of the controlling individuals given the reality that any use of the objectionable contraceptives would require the actions of multiple other actors (insurers, doctors, employees). That argument dodged the RFRA question: "whether the HHS mandate imposes a substantial burden on the ability of the objecting parties to conduct business in accordance with their *religious beliefs*"; instead, it "addresses a very different question that the federal courts have no business addressing (whether the religious belief asserted in a RFRA case is reasonable)." *Id.* at 2778.

Applying the statute's language, the majority assumed, without deciding, that providing health insurance with contraceptive coverage furthered a compelling governmental interest. Nevertheless, it held that the ACA scheme violated RFRA by not using the least restrictive means of pursuing that objective. The Court flirted with the idea that government payment for such coverage was itself a viable less restrictive alternative, *id.* at 2780, but ultimately found a less dramatic alternative available, one that the government already employed for religious nonprofits. That allowed the organization to "self-certify that it opposes providing coverage for particular contraceptive services," which results in its issuer "excluding contraceptive coverage from group health insurance coverage, while providing separate payments for any contraceptive services required to be covered for employees." This would occur without "any cost-sharing requirements . . . on the eligible organization, the group health plan, or plan participants or beneficiaries." *Id.* at 2782.

HHS had essentially viewed this as a win-win-win for religious nonprofits: no need for payment by religious objectors, contraception without additional cost for female employees, and cost savings for insurance companies since contraception coverage costs less than pregnancy and childbirth. For the majority, this possibility, while not necessarily suitable for all RFRA objections, was a less restrictive alternative for close corporations like the plaintiffs' whose owners did not wish to be complicit in what they viewed as sinful. *See also Holt v. Hobbs,* 135 S. Ct. 853 (2015) (finding in a RLUIPA suit that a prison's no-beard policy was not the least restrictive means to ensure the state's compelling interest in prison security).

The principal dissent, authored by Justice Ginsburg and joined entirely by Justice Sotomayor and in most part by Justices Breyer and Kagan, parted company with the majority on most points. Most importantly, the dissent viewed RFRA as not reaching the case before the Court. Although for-profit corporations might be "persons" within the meaning of the statute, they could not, as such, exercise religion: "the Court forgets that religious organizations exist to serve a community of believers. For-profit corporations do not fit that bill." *Id.* at 2796.

Given the blurring of the for-profit/nonprofit line, the dissent was very concerned about the potential reach of the majority opinion. Although Justice Alito had thought it "unlikely" that "corporate giants" would be able to assert plausible RFRA claims, he did not rule out that possibility, *id.* at 2774, and the dissent thought the majority's language "extends to corporations of any size, public or private." *Id.* at 2797. Accordingly, it believed a large number of potential religious objectors would raise claims for "alternatives" under a great number of federal statutes. Citing prior cases, for example, it suggested claims for exemptions from the wage and hour laws and antidiscrimination statutes, *id.* at 2802. The majority, however, explicitly rejected this argument:

> The principal dissent raises the possibility that discrimination in hiring, for example on the basis of race, might be cloaked as religious practice to escape legal sanction. Our decision today provides no such shield. The Government has a compelling interest in providing an equal opportunity to participate in the workforce without regard to race, and prohibitions on racial discrimination are precisely tailored to achieve that critical goal.

Id. at 2783 (cross reference omitted).

Further, Justice Kennedy may provide another backstop. Although he joined the Alito opinion, thus ensuring a majority, his separate concurrence seemed to stress that the majority's opinion did not require the government to "create an additional program." *Id.* at 2786. Rather, all HHS needed to do was extend the accommodation already provided religious nonprofits to for-profit companies with religious objections. That was a very different matter from a situation "in which it is more difficult and expensive to accommodate a governmental program to countless religious claims." *Id.* at 2787.

Hobby Lobby was by no means the end of the dispute concerning the intersection of the Affordable Care Act and RFRA. In *Zubik v. Burwell*, 136 S. Ct. 1557 (2016), the Court sent back a number of cases for reconsideration as to how the objections of religiously affiliated organizations could be reconciled with the employer notice requirements of the ACA.

E.   NATIONAL ORIGIN AND ALIENAGE DISCRIMINATION

Americans have long had a complex love-hate relationship with immigrants to this country, no more so than at the present. It should be no surprise to find these tensions reflected in our laws. This section sketches the interrelationship of three statutes, Title VII, §1981, and the Immigration Reform and Control Act of 1986, which provide a complicated amalgam of legal approaches.

As for Title VII, "national origin" is listed as one of the prohibited classification, and, as the term suggests, focuses on an individual's country of origin — regardless of whether the individual is currently a citizen of the United States. It is also national origin discrimination to refuse to hire an individual because of his ancestry — the country of origin of his parents or more remote ancestors. National origin discrimination may or may not overlap with racial discrimination. *See Vill. of Freeport v. Barrella*, 814 F.3d 594, 606-07 (2d Cir. 2016) ("Hispanics" constitute a race for purposes of both §1981 and Title VII; accordingly, discrimination against an Italian American in favor of a Hispanic is actionable even though both are white). It may also overlap with religion, as when individuals are victims of discrimination because they are Arab and Muslim. *See Huri v. Office of the Chief Judge of the Circuit Court of Cook Cnty.*, 804 F.3d 826 (7th Cir. 2015).

However, Title VII has been held not to bar alienage discrimination, despite its close connection with national origin. In *Espinoza v. Farah Mfg. Co.*, 414 U.S. 86 (1973), the employer refused to hire a lawfully admitted resident alien, a citizen of Mexico, because she was not a citizen of the United States. The Court rejected her suit. Since "national origin" refers to the country from which a person or her ancestors came, it does not refer to a person's citizenship status. Further, there was no reason to believe that the employer discriminated against Mexican national origin from either a disparate treatment or disparate impact perspective because individuals of Mexican ancestry made up 97 percent of the workers in the job Espinosa sought. *See also Guimaraes v. SuperValu, Inc.*, 674 F.3d 962, 973 (8th Cir. 2012) (a "green card" statement might evince an intent to terminate plaintiff because she was not yet a lawful permanent resident, but discrimination on account of alienage is not illegal). This distinction sometimes poses difficulties, as when a charge is made that an employer discriminates against "Americans." If aimed at a national origin, such a complaint is valid, *see Brown v. Daikin Am.*, 756 F.3d 219 (2d Cir. 2014) (national origin and race discrimination claims stated when plaintiff's employment with a New York–based wholly owned subsidiary of a Japanese corporation was terminated), but if it refers only to American citizens, it does not.

As for §1981, we have seen that it prohibits much of what might now be called national origin discrimination as "racial" discrimination because, when the statute was first passed, "race" had a broader meaning than it does today. Recall *St. Francis College v. Al-Khazraji*, Note 5, p. 396. Unlike Title VII, §1981 has been held to prohibit alienage discrimination. *Anderson v. Conboy,* 156 F.3d 167 (2d Cir. 1998) (§1981 reaches alienage discrimination but not discrimination against aliens not authorized to work by other federal laws).

It was in this legal setting that the Immigration Reform and Control Act of 1986 (IRCA), Pub. L. No. 99-603, 100 Stat. 3359, was passed. IRCA was an attempted "grand compromise" to resolve an earlier iteration of the immigration "crisis." Like Title VII and §1981, IRCA bars national origin discrimination; unlike Title VII, but like §1981, it also bars some kinds of alienage discrimination (against those authorized to work). However, for the first time at the national level, IRCA also mandates employers not to hire workers who are in this country illegally — "undocumented workers." It's not hard to imagine the complications this welter of laws can create. Indeed, the risk that efforts to deter work by "illegals" will result in more national origin discrimination as employers avoid hiring workers who appear "foreign" explains much of the complicated structure of IRCA.

IRCA's grand compromise was, essentially, amnesty for those here in 1986 while, for the first time, making it illegal to employ new undocumented immigrants, thus hopefully cutting off the flow across the nation's southern border by reducing the incentives to come here. The failure to stem the tide of immigration explains much of what has happened since, *see generally* Kevin R. Johnson, *Possible Reforms of the U.S. Immigration Laws,* 18 CHAP. L. REV. 315 (2015), especially the disdain of many for "amnesty" for those in this country illegally. IRCA did, on the one hand, provide amnesty for most such individuals then in the United States, but two generations have passed and there continue to be millions of undocumented aliens whose presence has prompted a variety of state laws and federal efforts to build "a wall." State initiatives have had mixed success in the courts. *Compare Chamber of Commerce v. Whiting,* 563 U.S. 582 (2011) (upholding against a preemption challenge under IRCA the Legal Arizona Workers Act allowing suspension of employers' licenses to do business for knowingly employing unauthorized aliens and requiring all Arizona employers to use a federal electronic verification system to confirm legal authorization), *with Arizona v. United States,* 567 U.S. 387 (finding preempted a number of provisions in another Arizona law, including one declaring it a misdemeanor for an unauthorized alien to seek or engage in work in the state). The success, practically and legally, of executive orders by President Trump remains to be seen. *See, e.g., Hawaii v. Trump,* 2017 U.S. Dist. LEXIS 47042 (D. Hawaii Mar. 29, 2017).

At any rate, back to IRCA. That statute imposed sanctions on employers who hired undocumented workers without sufficient proof of work authorization. That provision, by itself, would have created incentives to discriminate on the basis of national origin — against those who looked or sounded "foreign," regardless of their citizenship or authorization status.

Thus, IRCA counterbalanced its prohibitions on hiring unauthorized workers by prohibitions on national origin discrimination, *see* 8 U.S.C. §1324b(a)(1), (g)(1)(B), and by specifying what kinds of documentation would suffice. You've probably encountered I-9; submission of the form certifies that the employer has examined relevant documents such as a passport or a driver's license along with a Social Security card to confirm the worker's identity and employability. Eventually, the federal government added the E-Verify system to assist employers in making hiring decisions. Use of these methods provides considerable assurance to employers that they will not be held liable even if the worker turns out to be unauthorized. *See* §§1324a(a)(3), 1324a(b)(6). At the same time, Congress defined the kinds of documents that could be required by the employer, §1324a(b)(1)(B), and limited employers' right to ask for "more or different documents" or to "refus[e] to honor documents tendered that on their face reasonably appear to be genuine." It did so by declaring that such actions are unfair immigration-related employment practices "if made for the purpose or with the intent of discriminating against an individual on the basis of either national origin or because of a lawfully admitted individual's citizenship status." §1324b(a)(6).

While IRCA's prohibition of hiring or retaining undocumented workers essentially requires employers to discriminate on account of alienage, the statute simultaneously declares it "an unfair immigration-related employment practice" to discriminate against any individual because of her national origin. 8 U.S.C. §1324b(a)(1)(A). Because IRCA applies to employers with between 4 and 14 employees, this effectively expands the federal prohibition to much smaller employers than covered by Title VII. However, unlike Title VII, IRCA is enforced through an administrative agency hearing in contrast to court suit. 8 U.S.C. §1324a(e)(3)(A). The effectiveness of IRCA in discouraging national origin discrimination, however, has been questioned. *See generally* Huyen Pham, *The Private Enforcement of Immigration Laws*, 96 GEO. L.J. 777, 780-82 (2008) (arguing that not only have employer sanctions proved ineffective but the result has been national origin discrimination against lawful workers). *See also* Juliet P. Stumpf, *Getting to Work: Why Nobody Cares About E-Verify (and Why They Should)*, 2 U.C. IRVINE L. REV. 381 (2012).

The simultaneous prohibitions of national origin discrimination and hiring unauthorized workers have posed challenges for some employers. *E.g., Zamora v. Elite Logistics, Inc.*, 478 F.3d 1160 (10th Cir. 2007) (en banc) (upholding summary judgment against plaintiff who brought a national origin suit after being suspended despite having produced a naturalization certificate because the employer was not unreasonable in questioning certain discrepancies in plaintiff's documentation). *See also New El Rey Sausage Co. v. INS*, 925 F.2d 1153 (9th Cir. 1991) (adopting a "constructive knowledge standard," under which "a deliberate failure to investigate suspicious circumstances imputes knowledge" to an employer of unauthorized status).

NOTE ON LANGUAGE AND NATIONAL ORIGIN DISCRIMINATION

National origin discrimination is distinctive from other bases of discrimination with respect to language. Policies requiring workers to be fluent in English are probably permissible under Title VII. *See Garcia v. Rush-Presbyterian-St. Luke's Med. Ctr.*, 660 F.2d 1217, 1222 (7th Cir. 1981) (finding no disparate treatment or disparate impact in a hospital's requirement that employees speak and read English, but also suggesting that such a requirement would be a BFOQ where most patients and staff of the hospital speak English); *De la Cruz v. New York City Human Res. Admin. Dep't Social Servs.*, 82 F.3d 16 (2d Cir. 1996) (lawful to replace bilingual Puerto Rican who had difficulty writing English with better writer when job requires good writing skills). However, discrimination because of a foreign accent may be actionable, *e.g., Gold v. FedEx Freight East, Inc.*, 487 F.3d 1001 (6th Cir. 2007) (comments about accent were direct evidence of national origin discrimination); *Hasham v. California State Bd. of Equalization*, 200 F.3d 1035 (7th Cir. 2000) (comment that foreign accent cannot be understood supports inference of national origin discrimination, unless the accent is sufficiently "thick" to impede communication important to the job). *See generally* Professor Mari J. Matsuda, *Voices of America: Accent, Antidiscrimination Law, and a Jurisprudence for the Last Reconstruction*, 100 YALE L.J. 1329, 1384-85 (1991).

These cases, however, are often confusing as to their rationale. In *Fragante v. City & Cnty. of Honolulu*, 888 F.2d 591 (9th Cir. 1989), the court held it permissible to reject an individual whose accent would have hindered his performance of a position requiring interaction with the public. However, the Ninth Circuit's opinion indicates that foreign accent discrimination constitutes national origin discrimination but then intermixes the BFOQ defense and *McDonnell Douglas* analysis, concluding that the plaintiff had failed to prove that the employer's job-related reason was a pretext. *See also Jianxin Fong v. Sch. Bd.*, 590 F. App'x 930, 933-34 (11th Cir. 2014) (while discrimination based on an employee's accent can be national origin discrimination, an employee's heavy accent can be a legitimate basis for adverse employment action where effective communication skills are related to job performance).

As for "English-only" policies, *i.e.*, requiring employees to speak only English on the job, the cases reflect mixed results. *Garcia v. Gloor*, 618 F.2d 264, 270 (5th Cir. 1980), upheld a rule requiring bilingual sales personnel to speak only English on the job, stressing that such persons could easily comply. Although the *Gloor* court believed that the language bilingual persons speak is volitional, socio-linguistic scholarship suggests that such individuals often "code switch," that is, speak a combination of languages without always being conscious of which language(s) they are using. *See also Garcia v. Spun Steak Co.*, 998 F.2d 1480 (9th Cir. 1993) (rejecting disparate impact and hostile work environment challenges to English-only rules). More recently, however, the Tenth Circuit has departed from the holdings of *Gloor* and *Spun Steak* by finding that an English-only rule could be challenged as both disparate treatment and disparate impact violations. *Maldonado v. City of Altus*, 433 F.3d 1294 (10th Cir. 2006). *Cf. Montes v. Vail Clinic, Inc.*, 497 F.3d 1160 (10th Cir. 2007) (upholding a narrow English-only rule against a harassment challenge). See Note 9, p. 188. *See also* EEOC Guidelines on Discrimination Because of National Origin, 29 C.F.R. §1606.7 (2018). *See generally* David Ruiz Cameron, *How the Garcia Cousins Lost Their Accents: Understanding the Language of Title VII Decisions Approving English-Only Rules as the Product of Racial Dualism, Latino Invisibility, and Legal Indeterminacy*, 85 CAL. L. REV. 1347 (1997). The continuing debate about English-only in the workplace is only a subset of recurring disputes about the extent to which the nation should encourage or discourage other languages. *See* James Leonard, *Title VII and the Protection of Minority Languages in the American Workplace: The Search for a Justification*, 72 MO. L. REV. 745 (2007).

Discrimination related to language is just a subset of a broader category sometimes described as trait discrimination, *i.e.*, discrimination on the basis of some trait highly associated with a protected class but not co-extensive with it. Trait discrimination can apply to race and sex as well as national origin. *See generally* Zachary A. Kramer, *The New Sex Discrimination*, 63 DUKE L.J. 891, 893 (2014) (modern sex discrimination targets men and women who do not conform to workplace norms); Kimberly A. Yuracko, *Trait Discrimination as Race Discrimination: An Argument About Assimilation*, 74 GEO. WASH. L. REV. 365 (2006) (employers should not be allowed to use invalid trait proxies at all and to use valid ones only if there is no disparate impact); Kimberly A. Yuracko, *Trait Discrimination as Sex Discrimination: An Argument Against Neutrality*, 83 TEX. L. REV. 167 (2004) (trait discrimination should be actionable sex discrimination "only when it stems from gender norms and scripts that are themselves incompatible with sex equality in the workplace"); Tristin Green, *Discomfort at Work: Workplace Assimilation Demands, Social Equality, and the Contact Hypothesis*, 86 N.C. L. REV. 379, 386 (2008) ("employees should be provided space to signal membership in groups protected by Title VII of the Civil Rights Act through employer accommodation of appearance"); D. Wendy Greene, *Title VII:*

What's Hair (and Other Race-Based Characteristics) Got to Do With It?, 79 U. Colo. L. Rev. 1355, 1393 (2008) (courts should expand the definition of race to include historical and contemporary understandings).

The more highly correlated, the more likely a court will view discrimination on the basis of that trait as being the same as discrimination on the protected basis with which it is correlated. But Justice O'Connor's opinion in *Biggins*, see p. 10, distinguishing between age discrimination and discrimination to avoid pension vesting, indicates that courts draw distinctions even between highly correlated factors. *See also EEOC v. Catastrophe Mgmt. Solutions*, 837 F.3d 1156 (11th Cir. 2016) (Title VII protects against discrimination on the basis of immutable characteristics, not traits culturally associated with race, such as dreadlocks).

Some have cautioned that overly broad attacks on trait discrimination tend to essentialize the group in question:

> Even if a court could resolve the conflicting claims over which traits are essential to a group's identity — and even if a court could separate the empowering narratives of identity from those that are repressive — recognizing cultural rights would nonetheless solidify one version of the group's identity over others and bolster the notion that groups have essences.

Roberto J. González, Note, *Cultural Rights and the Immutability Requirement in Disparate Impact Doctrine*, 55 Stan. L. Rev. 2195, 2198-99 (2003). *But see* Camille Gear Rich, *Performing Racial and Ethnic Identity: Discrimination by Proxy and the Future of Title VII*, 79 N.Y.U. L. Rev. 1134, 1239 (2004) (downplaying the risk that courts will recognize employees' race or ethnicity performance only when it "comports with stereotypical negative representations of minority communities").

NOTE ON LIMITING THE RIGHTS OF UNAUTHORIZED ALIENS

There are certainly reasons for employers to hire unauthorized aliens. A standard claim is that they will do work that native-born Americans will not. But beyond meeting demands for labor, undocumented workers are often willing to work "off the books" for less than minimum wage and without other protections employment laws might provide. It is generally thought that such workers' unwillingness to invoke the law's protection for fear of calling ICE's attention to them is a major barrier to enforcement of such laws. *See generally* Leticia M. Saucedo, *The Employer Preference for the Subservient Worker and the Making of the Brown Collar Workplace*, 67 Ohio St. L.J. 961 (2006).

Espinosa v. Farah, 414 U.S. 86 (1973), while holding that alienage discrimination is not within Title VII's prohibition of national origin discrimination, nevertheless stressed that aliens remain protected by Title VII from discrimination for race, sex, national origin, or religion. Subsequent developments, however, have cast doubt on that statement. It remains true that aliens who are authorized to work by the immigration laws are fully protected by Title VII. However, IRCA may provide the employer with a defense in an employment discrimination action by an unauthorized alien even if the challenged discrimination is, say, racial in character. *See Egbuna v. Time-Life Libraries, Inc.*, 153 F.3d 184 (4th Cir. 1998) (en banc) (affirming summary judgment for the defendant because IRCA rendered the plaintiff ineligible for employment and therefore beyond the protection of Title VII).

Even if *Egbuna* is not generally accepted and undocumented workers are not wholly outside the protections of the discrimination laws, their legal status may sharply limit the remedies available to them. In *Hoffman Plastic Compounds, Inc. v. NLRB*, 535 U.S. 137 (2002), the majority set aside an NLRB backpay award to an unauthorized alien who had fraudulently obtained employment, but who then had been unlawfully discharged due to his union activity: "allowing the Board to award backpay to illegal aliens would unduly trench upon explicit statutory prohibitions critical to federal immigration policy, as expressed in IRCA. It would encourage the successful evasion of apprehension by immigration authorities, condone prior violations of the immigration laws, and encourage future violations." *Id.* at 151. It is not clear whether *Hoffman* carries over to the antidiscrimination statutes. *See Rivera v. NIBCO, Inc.*, 364 F.3d 1057 (9th Cir. 2004) (believing it "unlikely that it applies in Title VII cases"). If it does, an unauthorized alien might be allowed to obtain a prohibitory injunction and attorneys' fees, but no other relief, under Title VII or §1981. *See generally* Keith Cunningham-Parmeter, *Redefining the Rights of Undocumented Workers*, 58 Am. U. L. Rev. 1361 (2009); Jarod S. Gonzalez, *Employment Law Remedies for Illegal Immigrants*, 40 Tex. Tech L. Rev. 987 (2008); Craig Robert Senn, *Proposing a Uniform Remedial Approach for Undocumented Workers Under Federal Employment Discrimination Law*, 77 Fordham L. Rev. 113 (2008).

F. UNION LIABILITY

In 1935, Congress passed the Wagner Act, which, as amended and now called the National Labor Relations Act (NLRA), 29 U.S.C. §§151 et seq. (2018), established the legal structure for the relationship between unions and employers. The Act made no provisions regarding race or gender discrimination and, as originally passed, did not include any direct control of the activities of unions.

Despite the absence of statutory language, one of the first theories of federal law available to attack employment discrimination was the duty of fair representation. In *Steele v. Louisville & Nashville R.R.*, 323 U.S. 192 (1944), the Court created a federal cause of action on behalf of black railroad employees who claimed that the union that was legally charged with representing them was bargaining with the employer to have them replaced. While the statute did not give these black workers the right to become members of the union, the Court found that a union granted exclusive bargaining representative status over some workers under the Railway Labor Act had the duty to represent them fairly. "While the majority of the craft chooses the bargaining representative, when chosen it represents, as the Act by its terms makes plain, the craft or class, and not the majority. The fair interpretation of the statutory language is that the organization chosen to represent a craft is to represent all its members, the majority as well as the minority, and it is to act for and not against those whom it represents." *Id.* at 202.

In 1964, in Title VII's §703, Congress directly barred discrimination by unions. Section 703(c)(1) prohibits a union from discriminating in union membership, "or otherwise to discriminate"; subsection (2) prohibits a union from limiting, segregating, or classifying members or applicants "in any way which would deprive or tend to deprive any individual of employment opportunities"; and subsection (3) prohibits a union from causing an employer to discriminate against an individual.

In *Goodman v. Lukens Steel Co.*, 482 U.S. 656 (1987), the Supreme Court construed §703(c). The lower court had found that the union had failed to challenge the employer's discriminatory discharge of black probationary employees, had failed to assert race discrimination as a ground for grievances, and had tolerated the employer's racial harassment. The union argued that it could be liable for an employer's action only if, under §703(c)(3), the union had caused the employer to discriminate. The Court rejected that narrow reading of Title VII and referred to §703(c)(1), which made it an unlawful practice for a union to "exclude or to expel from its membership, or *otherwise to discriminate against*" any individual (emphasis added). *See also Green v. AFT/Ill. Fed'n of Teachers Local 604*, 740 F.3d 1104 (7th Cir. 2014) (even absent any duty of fair representation for state employees, failure of union to process black plaintiff's grievance or represent him in legal proceedings grievance when it would have done so were he white would violate Title VII); *Stuart v. Local 727, Int'l Bhd. of Teamsters*, 771 F.3d 1014 (7th Cir. 2014) (a union's failure to refer a woman for employment on the basis of her sex would be actionable under Title VII); *Wells v. Chrysler Group LLC*, 559 F. App'x 512 (6th Cir. 2014) (union's duty not to discriminate and its duty of fair representation when predicated on failure to process racial grievances were essentially the same but neither was violated when the union failed to pursue a meritless grievance on behalf of the plaintiff). However, some courts have distinguished between a union's "causing" an employer to discriminate, as §703(c)(3) prohibits, and its mere failure to attempt to remediate any such discrimination. *See EEOC v. Pipefitters Ass'n Local Union 597*, 334 F.3d 656 (7th Cir. 2003) (employer, not union, responsible for removal of graffiti from the workplace and therefore union could not be liable for harassment); *Thorn v. Amalgamated Transit Union*, 305 F.3d 826 (8th Cir. 2002) (no affirmative duty for union to investigate and take steps to remedy employer discrimination).

G. AGE DISCRIMINATION

Treatment of the Age Discrimination in Employment Act has been largely integrated into the discussion of the theories of discrimination analyzed in earlier chapters, with differences between discrimination on account of age and discrimination on the grounds prohibited by Title VII noted throughout. For example, we saw in Chapter 1 that the *McDonnell Douglas* framework for individual disparate treatment cases has frequently been adapted to age cases, but that *Gross v. FBL Fin. Servs.*, 557 U.S. 167 (2009), rejected motivating factor analysis under the ADEA, reaffirming that a plaintiff claiming age discrimination must prove that discrimination was a determinative factor in a challenged decision. See p. 82. Similarly, we saw in Chapter 2 that the ADEA has a bona fide occupational qualification defense much like that of Title VII but that there is no need for a defense for "reverse discrimination" since favoring older members of the protected class over younger members is not prohibited by the ADEA. See p. 44. Finally, in Chapter 3, we learned that disparate impact, while actionable in the age context, is subject to a much looser scrutiny than would be true under Title VII because of the "reasonable factors other than age" language in the ADEA. See p. 180.

Yet another difference between the ADEA and Title VII is with respect to facial discrimination. Although both *Los Angeles Department of Water & Power v. Manhart*, reproduced at p. 94, and *International Union, UAW v. Johnson Controls*, reproduced at p. 142, suggest that facial discrimination is always illegal under Title VII (except when within a statutory exception), the Court refused to so hold with respect to the ADEA. *Kentucky Retirement System v. EEOC*, 554 U.S. 135 (2008), in a five-to-four opinion, upheld the use of age as a criterion for a pension essentially on the ground that the age criterion did not reflect age-based animus and dealt with "the quite special case of different treatment based on *pension status*, where pension status — with the explicit blessing of the ADEA itself turns, in part, on age." *Id.* at 148 (emphasis in original). *Cf. EEOC v. Baltimore Cnty.*, 747 F.3d 267 (4th Cir. 2010) (discriminatory for a retirement plan to require two new-hires, each with the same number of years until retirement age, to pay different contributions).

This section considers several additional differences between the ADEA and other antidiscrimination statutes, most notably with respect to exceptions from the statute's prohibitions.

1. Exception for Police and Firefighters

The only major sector of the economy exempted from the ADEA's general prohibition of age discrimination is state and municipal law enforcement and firefighting. The ADEA permits states or political subdivisions to set age limitations both for hire and for discharge after age 55 for individuals employed "as a firefighter or as a law enforcement officer." 29 U.S.C. §623(j) (2018). *See Jones v. City of Cortland Police Dep't*, 448 F.3d 369 (6th Cir. 2006) (no ADEA claim by 54-year-old applicant for police position since Ohio law requires police to be under age 35 at hiring and city was thereby protected by ADEA exemption). Both "firefighter" and "law enforcement officer" are defined broadly. *See EEOC v. Illinois*, 986 F.2d 187 (7th Cir. 1993) (special agents of Division of Criminal Investigation counted as state police and, therefore, were law enforcement officers). This exception is somewhat limited by the proviso that the action must be taken "pursuant to a bona fide hiring or retirement plan that is not a subterfuge to evade the purposes of this Act," §623(j)(2), but the courts have been very permissive on this criterion. *See Sadie v. City of Cleveland*, 718 F.3d 596, 601 (6th Cir. 2013) (not interpreting "subterfuge" to bar a preference for younger workers because that would "nullify the exemption"); *Kannady v. City of Kiowa*, 590 F.3d 1161, 1173 (10th Cir. 2010) (showing that the legislature's taking financial considerations into account in adopting a pension system's hiring-age ceiling did not demonstrate subterfuge).

2. Bona Fide Employee Benefit Plans

With respect to fringe benefits, perhaps the ADEA's most sweeping "exception" is the Supreme Court's decision in *General Dynamics Land Systems, Inc. v. Cline*, 540 U.S. 581 (2004), which held that favoring older workers over younger workers in the protected class is not prohibited by the statute. See p. 44. This decision permits skewing of fringe benefits (as well as other employment decisions) toward the older end of the work force spectrum with no liability.

However, even beyond *Cline*, the ADEA has a "bona fide employee benefit plan" provision that is a significant exception to the statute's general prohibition of age discrimination since it permits discrimination *against* older workers in some circumstances. While benefits law is a specialty unto itself, the ADEA's exemption permits age to be taken into account in a limited fashion. Where a "bona fide employee benefit plan" is involved, an employer will not violate the statute if it either (1) provides its workers equal benefits (in which case there is no discrimination) or (2) provides age-differentiated benefits but incurs equal costs in doing so. 29 U.S.C. §623(f)(2) (2018). This provision recognizes that the costs of some fringe benefits (typically life and health insurance) rise with the age of the worker and permits employers to take that into account. For example, suppose the cost of $100,000 of employer-provided life insurance is $1,000 for workers aged 40. If the same $1,000 will buy only $70,000 of insurance for workers aged 60, the employer may provide them that lesser benefit without violating the law. The ADEA also allows defined benefit plans to be "coordinated" with Social Security and Medicare and other benefit plans, thereby reducing employer costs. §4(*l*)(1), 29 U.S.C. §623(*l*). *See AARP v. EEOC*, 489 F.3d 558 (3d Cir. 2007) (upholding proposed EEOC regulation on coordination of benefits). *See also Fulghum v. Embarq Corp.*, 785 F.3d 395 (10th Cir. 2015) (employer's reduction of health benefits for Medicare-eligible retirees was permissible in light of EEOC regulation so allowing; its reduction of life insurance benefits was based on a reasonable factor other than age when the change was motivated by a desire to reduce costs and bring life insurance benefits in line with those provided by other companies).

3.   *Early Retirement Incentive Plans*

Early retirement incentive plans play a critical role in corporate downsizing, and the ADEA permits such plans subject to certain limitations. These plans typically involve both carrots and sticks. As for the carrot, the employer creates a "window of opportunity" during which employees can obtain greater benefits if they elect early retirement. When the window shuts, the enhanced benefits disappear. As for the stick, while retirement incentive plans do not explicitly threaten termination of those who do not accept, such plans are typically offered by companies in the process of downsizing. There typically is, therefore, an implicit threat that layoffs will follow if enough workers do not accept the early retirement incentive. *See generally* Michael C. Harper, *Age-Based Exit Incentives, Coercion, and the Prospective Waiver of ADEA Rights: The Failure of the Older Workers Benefit Protection Act*, 79 VA. L. REV. 1271 (1993).

The Older Workers Benefit Protection Act amended the ADEA to address this situation while striking a balance between employer and employee interests. First, the ADEA permits a benefit plan "that is a voluntary early retirement incentive plan" consistent with the purposes of the Act. §4(f)(2)(B)(ii), 29 U.S.C. §623(f)(2)(B)(ii) (2018). To qualify, any such plan "must make retirement a relatively more attractive option than continuing to work." *Abrahamson v. Bd. of Educ. of the Wappingers Falls Cent. Sch. Dist.*, 374 F.3d 66, 74 (2d Cir. 2004). Further, the requirement that the plan be "consistent with the purposes of the Act" tends to invalidate retirement incentive plans that exclude older workers. *See Jankovitz v. Des Moines Indep. Cmty.*, 421 F.3d 649, 655 (8th Cir. 2005) (school district's incentive plan not within the statutory safe harbor because it was inconsistent with the purposes of the ADEA by providing that "early retirement benefits drop to zero upon an employee's attainment of the age of 65"). The statute also provides that a pension plan will not violate the statute by providing a minimum age of eligibility, §4(*l*)(1)(a), 29 U.S.C. §623(*l*)(1)(a), but this provision is surplusage after *General Dynamics Land Systems, Inc. v. Cline*, 540 U.S. 581 (2004), which holds that it is not discriminatory to favor older workers.

Most significantly, employees who do not accept the incentive plan will rarely have standing to challenge it, and those who do sign may find themselves unable to attack even a plan that is, in some sense, illegal. That is because OWBPA also authorizes "knowing and voluntary" waivers of ADEA rights, and specifies a rigorous laundry list of substantive and procedural requirements before a waiver of ADEA rights will be deemed "knowing and voluntary." *E.g., Adams v. Lucent Techs., Inc.*, 284 F. App'x 296, 301-02 (6th Cir. 2008) (plaintiffs, who accepted an early retirement offer in the light of a pending merger, could not show constructive discharge since they were not certain to lose their jobs). The topic of OWBPA releases, as well as releases of rights under other antidiscrimination statutes, is taken up in Chapter 9.

4.   *Bona Fide Executive Exception*

Although mandatory retirement is generally prohibited by the ADEA, "bona fide executives" can be mandatorily retired at age 65 under certain circumstances:

> [A]ny employee who has attained 65 years of age, and who, for the 2-year period immediately before retirement, is employed in a bona fide executive or high policymaking position, if such employee is entitled to an immediate nonforfeitable annual retirement benefit from a pension, profit-sharing, savings or deferred compensation plan, or any combination of such plans, of the employer of such employee, which equals, in the aggregate, at least $44,000.

§12(c)(1), 29 U.S.C. §631(c)(1). *See also* 29 C.F.R. §1625.12 (2018). The exception obviously is highly qualified. First, a "bona fide executive" remains fully protected by the ADEA until age 65. Even thereafter, such an executive may not be discriminated against on age grounds except for mandatory retirement. Second, the statute's requirements for the exception are conjunctive: to be subject to the provision, the employee must both (1) be in a "bona fide executive" or "high policymaking position" and (2) receive the defined benefits of $44,000 a year. *See Morrissey v. Boston Five Cents Sav. Bank*, 54 F.3d 27 (1st Cir. 1995).

Chapter 6

Retaliation

A. INTRODUCTION

In addition to prohibiting discrimination on the grounds of race, sex, religion, national origin, and age, Title VII, §1981, and the ADEA also create a remedy for certain retaliatory conduct. Section 704(a) of Title VII, 42 U.S.C. §2000e-3(a), provides:

> It shall be an unlawful employment practice for an employer to discriminate against any of his employees or applicants for employment . . . because he has opposed any practice made an unlawful employment practice by this title, or because he has made a charge, testified, assisted, or participated in any manner in an investigation, proceeding, or hearing under this title.

The ADEA bars retaliation in substantially identical language. 29 U.S.C. §623(d). Retaliation is also prohibited by the Americans with Disabilities Act, albeit in slightly different language, and is covered in Chapter 7. Although §1981 does not expressly prohibit retaliation, the Supreme Court in *CBOCS West, Inc. v Humphries*, 553 U.S. 442 (2008), held that that statute's bar of race discrimination also encompasses retaliation claims.

This chapter will focus on retaliation claims under Title VII. As the text above indicates, that prohibition consists of two separate clauses that present distinct legal questions. The first bars retaliation for "oppos[ing] . . . any practice made an unlawful employment practice." This "opposition clause" encompasses more types of conduct than the second clause, the "free access" or "participation" clause, which proscribes retaliation "because [an employee or applicant] has made a charge, testified, assisted, or participated . . . in an investigation, proceeding, or hearing" under the relevant statute. *See generally* Richard Moberly, *The Supreme Court's Antiretaliation Principle*, 61 CASE W. RES. L. REV. 375 (2010).

Retaliation claims are ubiquitous under the antidiscrimination laws. One source reports that, over the last 10 years, they have increased "by over fifty percent (from 27.9% to 42.8%) and now rank as the single most popular claim filed with the EEOC under these laws." Craig Robert Senn, *Redefining Protected "Opposition" Activity in Employment Retaliation Cases*, 37 CARDOZO L. REV. 2035 (2016).

B.   WHO IS PROTECTED?

THOMPSON v. NORTH AMERICAN STAINLESS, LP
131 S. Ct. 863 (2011)

Justice SCALIA delivered the opinion of the Court.

[North American Stainless fired Eric Thompson three weeks after being notified that his fiancée, Miriam Regalado, filed a charge alleging sex discrimination with the EEOC. Thompson sued, claiming that he had been fired to retaliate for Regalado's charge.]

I . . .

It is undisputed that Regalado's filing of a charge with the EEOC was protected conduct under Title VII. In the procedural posture of this case, we are also required to assume that NAS fired Thompson in order to retaliate against Regalado for filing a charge of discrimination. This case therefore presents two questions: First, did NAS's firing of Thompson constitute unlawful retaliation? And second, if it did, does Title VII grant Thompson a cause of action?

II

With regard to the first question, we have little difficulty concluding that if the facts alleged by Thompson are true, then NAS's firing of Thompson violated Title VII. In *Burlington N. & S.F.R. Co. v. White* [reproduced at p. 422] we held that Title VII's antiretaliation provision must be construed to cover a broad range of employer conduct. We reached that conclusion by contrasting the text of Title VII's antiretaliation provision with its substantive antidiscrimination provision. Title VII prohibits discrimination on the basis of race, color, religion, sex, and national origin "'with respect to . . . compensation, terms, conditions, or privileges of employment,'" and discriminatory practices that would "'deprive any individual of employment opportunities or otherwise adversely affect his status as an employee.'" In contrast, Title VII's antiretaliation provision prohibits an employer from "'discriminat[ing] against any of his employees'" for engaging in protected conduct, without specifying the employer acts that are prohibited. Based on this textual distinction and our understanding of the antiretaliation provision's purpose, we held that "the anti-retaliation provision, unlike the substantive provision, is not limited to discriminatory actions that affect the terms and conditions of employment." Rather, Title VII's antiretaliation provision prohibits any employer action that "well might have dissuaded a reasonable worker from making or supporting a charge of discrimination."

We think it obvious that a reasonable worker might be dissuaded from engaging in protected activity if she knew that her fiancé would be fired. Indeed, NAS does not dispute that Thompson's firing meets the standard set forth in *Burlington*. NAS raises the concern, however, that prohibiting reprisals against third parties will lead to difficult line-drawing problems concerning the types of relationships entitled to protection. Perhaps retaliating against an employee by firing his fiancée would dissuade the employee from engaging in protected activity, but what about firing an employee's girlfriend, close friend, or trusted co-worker? Applying the *Burlington* standard to third-party reprisals, NAS argues, will place the employer at risk any time it fires any employee who happens to have a connection to a different employee who filed a charge with the EEOC.

Although we acknowledge the force of this point, we do not think it justifies a categorical rule that third-party reprisals do not violate Title VII. As explained above, we adopted a broad standard in *Burlington* because Title VII's antiretaliation provision is worded broadly. We think there is no textual basis for making an exception to it for third-party reprisals, and a preference for clear rules cannot justify departing from statutory text.

We must also decline to identify a fixed class of relationships for which third-party reprisals are unlawful. We expect that firing a close family member will almost always meet the *Burlington* standard, and inflicting a milder reprisal on a mere acquaintance will almost never do so, but beyond that we are reluctant to generalize. As we explained in *Burlington*, "the significance of any given act of retaliation will often depend upon the particular circumstances." Given the broad statutory text and the variety of workplace contexts in which retaliation may occur, Title VII's antiretaliation provision is simply not reducible to a comprehensive set of clear rules. We emphasize, however, that "the provision's standard for judging harm must be objective," so as to "avoi[d] the uncertainties and unfair discrepancies that can plague a judicial effort to determine a plaintiff's unusual subjective feelings."

III

The more difficult question in this case is whether Thompson may sue NAS for its alleged violation of Title VII. The statute provides that "a civil action may be brought . . . by the person claiming to be aggrieved." 42 U.S.C. §2000e-5(f)(1). . . .

We have suggested in dictum that the Title VII aggrievement requirement conferred a right to sue on all who satisfied Article III standing. *Trafficante v. Metropolitan Life Ins. Co.*, 409 U.S. 205 (1972), involved the "person aggrieved" provision of Title VIII (the Fair Housing Act) rather than Title VII. In deciding the case, however, we relied upon, and cited with approval, a Third Circuit opinion involving Title VII, which, we said, "concluded that the words used showed 'a congressional intention to define standing as broadly as is permitted by Article III of the Constitution.'" We think that dictum regarding Title VII was too expansive. . . .

We now find that this dictum was ill-considered, and we decline to follow it. If any person injured in the Article III sense by a Title VII violation could sue, absurd consequences would follow. For example, a shareholder would be able to sue a company for firing a valuable employee for racially discriminatory reasons, so long as he could show that the value of his stock decreased as a consequence. At oral argument Thompson acknowledged that such a suit would not lie. We agree, and therefore conclude that the term "aggrieved" must be construed more narrowly than the outer boundaries of Article III.

At the other extreme from the position that "person aggrieved" means anyone with Article III standing, NAS argues that it is a term of art that refers only to the employee who engaged in the protected activity. We know of no other context in which the words carry this artificially narrow meaning, and if that is what Congress intended it would more naturally have said "person claiming to have been discriminated against" rather than "person claiming to be aggrieved." We see no basis in text or prior practice for limiting the latter phrase to the person who was the subject of unlawful retaliation. Moreover, such a reading contradicts the very holding of *Trafficante*, which was that residents of an apartment complex were "person[s] aggrieved" by discrimination against prospective tenants. We see no reason why the same phrase in Title VII should be given a narrower meaning.

In our view there is a common usage of the term "person aggrieved" that avoids the extremity of equating it with Article III and yet is fully consistent with our application of the term in *Trafficante*. The Administrative Procedure Act, 5 U.S.C. §551 *et seq.*, authorizes suit to challenge a federal agency by any "person . . . adversely affected or aggrieved . . . within the meaning of a relevant statute." §702. We have held that this language establishes a regime under which a plaintiff may not sue unless he "falls within the 'zone of interests' sought to be protected by the statutory provision whose violation forms the legal basis for his complaint." *Lujan v. National Wildlife Federation*, 497 U.S. 871, 883 (1990). We have described the "zone of interests" test as denying a right of review "if the plaintiff's interests are so marginally related to or inconsistent with the purposes implicit in the statute that it cannot reasonably be assumed that Congress intended to permit the suit." *Clarke v. Securities Industry Assn.*, 479 U.S. 388, 399-400 (1987). We hold that the term "aggrieved" in Title VII incorporates this test, enabling suit by any plaintiff with an interest "arguably [sought] to be protected by the statutes," *National Credit Union Admin. v. First Nat. Bank & Trust Co.*, 522 U.S. 479, 495 (1998), while excluding plaintiffs who might technically be injured in an Article III sense but whose interests are unrelated to the statutory prohibitions in Title VII.

Applying that test here, we conclude that Thompson falls within the zone of interests protected by Title VII. Thompson was an employee of NAS, and the purpose of Title VII is to protect employees from their employers' unlawful actions. Moreover, accepting the facts as alleged, Thompson is not an accidental victim of the retaliation — collateral damage, so to speak, of the employer's unlawful act. To the contrary, injuring him was the employer's intended means of harming Regalado. Hurting him was the unlawful act by which the employer punished her. In those circumstances, we think Thompson well within the zone of interests sought to be protected by Title VII. He is a person aggrieved with standing to sue.

[Justices Ginsburg and Breyer concurred, essentially on the grounds that the EEOC's Compliance Manual so required and "statements in the Manual merit deference" under *Skidmore v. Swift & Co.*, 323 U.S. 134 (1944). Justice Kagan took no part in the case.]

NOTES

1. *Coordinating Wrong with Remedy.* To reach its result, the Court framed the issues as twofold: whether Thompson's firing constituted retaliation against Regalado in violation of Title VII and whether the statute granted Thompson a cause of action. If the court found that the firing violated Title VII but Thompson did *not* have a claim, Regalado's remedies would seem grossly inadequate to the harm caused — Thompson

would suffer loss of backpay and possible other damages but recover nothing. According Thompson the right to sue ensured that the wrong was better aligned with the remedy.

2. *The "Zone of Interests."* The Court's somewhat labored analysis regarding standing in *North American Stainless* suggests that it was concerned with a potentially overly broad application of "dictum" in earlier Fair Housing Act cases that suggested that Title VII "person aggrieved" standing reached as far as Article III would permit. Like Goldilocks, Scalia found Article III standing too broad but limiting standing to the employee who engaged in the protected conduct too narrow. Instead, the "just right" standard was drawn from the Administrative Procedure Act, permitting suit by those within the "zone of interests" the statute was designed to protect.

The "zone of interests" test is malleable, allowing the courts leeway to deny a right of review to any plaintiff with interests "so marginally related to or inconsistent with the purposes implicit in the statute that it cannot reasonably be assumed that Congress intended to permit the suit." *North American Stainless* itself suggested that a corporate shareholder whose stock has decreased in value after the company fired a valuable employee for racially discriminatory reasons is outside Title VII's zone of interests. On the other hand, Thompson fell within the zone of interests because he was not merely "collateral damage" of the employer's discriminatory act.

3. *Applications of the "Zone of Interests" Test.* In *North American Stainless*, the Court did not critique cases according standing to those denied the benefits of interracial association, and in fact seemed to reaffirm the holding of *Trafficante* to that effect. *See generally* Camille Gear Rich, *Marginal Whiteness*, 98 Calif. L. Rev. 1497, 1499 (2010); Noah D. Zatz, *Beyond the Zero-Sum Game: Toward Title VII Protection for Intergroup Solidarity*, 77 Ind. L.J. 63 (2002). Thus, a white may be able to sue for his employer's refusal to hire African Americans.

But what about more derivative claims? Consider plaintiffs who allege that the employer took an adverse action against them in order to discriminate against others. Thompson was not "an accidental victim of the retaliation — collateral damage, so to speak, of the employer's unlawful act," but is that an accurate description of the plaintiffs in *Anjelino v. New York Times Co.*, 200 F.3d 73, 79-80 (3d Cir. 2000)? There, the court found standing for male "extras" who alleged that the employer stopped assigning work when the next person on the priority list was female. Aren't these plaintiffs "collateral damage"? Should they have standing in any event? Recently, *Bank of Am. v. City of Miami*, 137 S. Ct. 1296 (2017), found that a city had standing to sue for Fair Housing violations against its residents. Does this help?

4. *How Close Is Close Enough?* The zone of interests test might suggest that whenever X is fired to punish Y for protected conduct, Title VII is violated and the discharged person has standing to bring suit. But *North American Stainless* avoided deciding which third parties are protected by its rule. *See also Zamora v. City of Houston*, 425 F. App'x 314 (5th Cir. 2011) (police officer may base retaliation claim on protected activity engaged in by his father, a police lieutenant). Context is apparently all. Presumably, then, some retaliatory action is not a violation — even if the employer's purpose is to retaliate. *See generally* Alex B. Long, *The Troublemaker's Friend: Retaliation Against Third Parties and the Right of Association in the Workplace*, 59 Fla. L. Rev. 931 (2007).

5. *A Managers Exception?* A few lower court decisions adopted what has been called the "managers rule" for Title VII cases. *See, e.g., Brush v. Sears Holdings Corp.*, 466 F. App'x 781 (11th Cir. 2012), which held that managerial employees, when acting in their capacity as managers, are not engaged in opposition conduct within

the meaning of the statute when they oppose their employer's decisions. This line of authority is similar to *Garcetti v. Ceballos*, 547 U.S. 410 (2006), where the Court held that the First Amendment did not protect employees whose speech is within the scope of their job responsibilities. Other statutory schemes have also adopted limitations along these lines, *see generally* Nancy M. Modesitt, *The* Garcetti *Virus*, 80 U. Cin. L. Rev. 137 (2011), although the federal Whistleblower Protection Enhancement Act of 2012, Pub. L. No 112-199, eliminated that defense for the WPA.

More recent decisions have cast doubt on any broad exception. *Littlejohn v. City of N.Y.*, 795 F.3d 297, 318 (2d Cir. 2015), agreed that opposition protection was not triggered merely because "an employee is required as part of her job duties to report or investigate other employees' complaints of discrimination"; however, "if an employee—even one whose job responsibilities involve investigating complaints of discrimination—actively 'support[s]' other employees in asserting their Title VII rights or personally 'complain[s]' or is 'critical' about the 'discriminatory employment practices' of her employer, that employee has engaged in a protected activity under §704(a)'s opposition clause." *See also DeMasters v. Carilion Clinic*, 796 F.3d 409, 413 (4th Cir. 2015) (finding that the manager rule "has no place in Title VII jurisprudence"). *See generally* Deborah L. Brake, *Retaliation in the EEO Office*, 50 Tulsa L. Rev. 1 (2014); Deborah L. Brake, *Tortifying Retaliation: Protected Activity at the Intersection of Fault, Duty, and Causation*, 75 Ohio St. L. Rev. 6 (2014). Will the *Littlejohn* distinction between bureaucratic processing and more active support or criticism be easy to draw?

C.   DISTINGUISHING PARTICIPATION FROM OPPOSITION

North American Stainless involved retaliation for filing a charge with the EEOC. Such activities, broadly, "participation" in formal challenges to discrimination, are one kind of conduct protected by Title VII, but §704(a) also safeguards other kinds of less formal challenges — "opposition" conduct. The following cases considers both branches.

CLARK COUNTY SCHOOL DISTRICT v. BREEDEN
532 U.S. 268 (2001)

Per Curiam.

. . . In 1997, respondent filed a §2000e-3(a) retaliation claim against petitioner Clark County School District. The claim as eventually amended alleged that petitioner had taken two separate adverse employment actions against her in response to two different protected activities in which she had engaged. . . .

participation

[R]espondent's male supervisor met with respondent and another male employee to review the psychological evaluation reports of four job applicants. The report for one of the applicants disclosed that the applicant had once commented to a co-worker, "I hear making love to you is like making love to the Grand Canyon." At the meeting respondent's supervisor read the comment aloud, looked at respondent and stated, "I don't know what that means." The other employee then said, "Well, I'll tell you later," and both men chuckled. Respondent later complained about the comment to the offending employee, to Assistant Superintendent George Ann Rice, the employee's supervisor, and to another assistant superintendent of petitioner. Her first claim of retaliation asserts that she was punished for these complaints.

The Court of Appeals for the Ninth Circuit has applied §2000e-3(a) to protect employee "opposition" not just to practices that are actually "made . . . unlawful" by Title VII, but also to practices that the employee could reasonably believe were unlawful. We have no occasion to rule on the propriety of this interpretation, because even assuming it is correct, no one could reasonably believe that the incident recounted above violated Title VII.

Title VII forbids actions taken on the basis of sex that "discriminate against any individual with respect to his compensation, terms, conditions, or privileges of employment." Just three Terms ago, we reiterated, what was plain from our previous decisions, that sexual harassment is actionable under Title VII only if it is "so 'severe or pervasive' as to 'alter the conditions of [the victim's] employment and create an abusive working environment.'" *Faragher v. Boca Raton*, 524 U.S. 775, 786 (1998). Workplace conduct is not measured in isolation; instead, "whether an environment is sufficiently hostile or abusive" must be judged "by 'looking at all the circumstances,' including the 'frequency of the discriminatory conduct; its severity; whether it is physically threatening or humiliating, or a mere offensive utterance; and whether it unreasonably interferes with an employee's work performance.'" *Faragher* (quoting *Harris v. Forklift Systems, Inc.*). Hence, "[a] recurring point in [our] opinions is that simple teasing, offhand comments, and isolated incidents (unless extremely serious) will not amount to discriminatory changes in the 'terms and conditions of employment.'" *Faragher.*

No reasonable person could have believed that the single incident recounted above violated Title VII's standard. The ordinary terms and conditions of respondent's job required her to review the sexually explicit statement in the course of screening job applicants. Her co-workers who participated in the hiring process were subject to the same requirement, and indeed, in the District Court respondent "conceded that it did not bother or upset her" to read the statement in the file. Her supervisor's comment, made at a meeting to review the application, that he did not know what the statement meant; her co-worker's responding comment; and the chuckling of both are at worst an "isolated incident" that cannot remotely be considered "extremely serious," as our cases require. *Faragher v. Boca Raton.* The holding of the Court of Appeals to the contrary must be reversed.

Besides claiming that she was punished for complaining to petitioner's personnel about the alleged sexual harassment, respondent also claimed that she was punished for filing charges against petitioner with the [state fair employment agency and the EEOC] and for filing the present suit. Respondent filed her lawsuit on April 1, 1997; on April 10, 1997, respondent's supervisor, Assistant Superintendent Rice, "mentioned to Allin Chandler, Executive Director of plaintiff's union, that she was contemplating transferring plaintiff to the position of Director of Professional Development Education"; and this transfer was "carried through" in May. In order to show, as her defense against summary judgment required, the existence of a causal connection between her protected activities and the transfer, respondent "relied wholly on the temporal proximity of the filing of her complaint on April 1, 1997 and Rice's statement to plaintiff's union representative on April 10, 1997 that she was considering transferring plaintiff to the [new] position." The District Court, however, found that respondent did not serve petitioner with the summons and complaint until April 11, 1997, one day after Rice had made the statement, and Rice filed an affidavit stating

[handwritten margin note: judge says comment wasn't Title VII violation]

that she did not become aware of the lawsuit until after April 11, a claim that respondent did not challenge. Hence, the court concluded, respondent "had not shown that any causal connection exists between her protected activities and the adverse employment decision."

The Court of Appeals reversed, relying on two facts: The EEOC had issued a right-to-sue letter to respondent three months before Rice announced she was contemplating the transfer, and the actual transfer occurred one month after Rice learned of respondent's suit. The latter fact is immaterial in light of the fact that petitioner concededly was contemplating the transfer before it learned of the suit. Employers need not suspend previously planned transfers upon discovering that a Title VII suit has been filed, and their proceeding along lines previously contemplated, though not yet definitively determined, is no evidence whatever of causality.

no causal connection b/t her complaints + her transfer As for the right-to-sue letter, [plaintiff had not relied on that below but, in any event, it "will not do" to draw the inference that the transfer proposal made three months later was the employer's reaction to the charge.] First, there is no indication that Rice even knew about the right-to-sue letter when she proposed transferring respondent. And second, if one presumes she knew about it, one must also presume that she (or her predecessor) knew *almost two years earlier* about the protected action (filing of the EEOC complaint) that the letter supposedly disclosed. . . . The cases that accept mere temporal proximity between an employer's knowledge of protected activity and an adverse employment action as sufficient evidence of causality to establish a prima facie case uniformly hold that the temporal proximity must be "very close," *Neal v. Ferguson Constr. Co.*, 237 F.3d 1248, 1253 (CA10 2001). See e.g., *Richmond v. Oneok, Inc.*, 120 F.3d 205, 209 (CA10 1997) (3-month period insufficient); *Hughes v. Derwinski*, 967 F.2d 1168, 1174-1175 (CA7 1992) (4-month period insufficient). Action taken (as here) 20 months later suggests, by itself, no causality at all. . . .

NOTES

1. *Broader Protection Under the Participation Clause.* Shirley Breeden presented two distinct claims of retaliation. One was for opposition conduct (her internal complaints), while the other was for participation conduct (her filing of charges with the state agency and the EEOC). There is a sharp distinction between the protections of the "opposition" clause as compared to the "participation" clause. While a plaintiff invoking the opposition clause must demonstrate, at the least, a reasonable, good faith belief that the conduct complained of is unlawful, the participation clause does not seem to have any such requirement. One of the first "participation" cases, *Pettway v. Am. Cast Iron Pipe Co.*, 411 F.2d 998 (5th Cir. 1969), set the tone for these decisions by finding actionable retaliation when a worker was fired for filing an allegedly false and malicious charge with the EEOC — namely, that the employer had bought off an EEOC investigator. The court wrote:

> There can be no doubt about the purpose of §704(a). In unmistakable language it is to protect the employee who utilizes the tools provided by Congress to protect his rights. The Act will be frustrated if the employer may unilaterally determine the truth or falsity of charges and take independent action.

Id. at 1004-05. *See also Ray v. Ropes & Gray LLP, 799 F.3d 99, 110 (1st Cir. 2015)* ("unlike opposition activity, a plaintiff who engages in participation activity need not hold a reasonable belief that his employer's actions actually violated Title VII"); *Glover v. S.C. Law Enf.*, 170 F.3d 411 (4th Cir. 1999) (unreasonable deposition testimony protected by participation clause); *Clover v. Total Sys. Serv., Inc.*, 176 F.3d 1346 (11th Cir. 1999) (reasonable belief not needed for participation clause protections to be triggered).

After the *Breeden* Court disposed of the plaintiff's "opposition clause" claim by deciding that no reasonable person could believe that she had been sexually harassed, it went on to consider the causation issue on her "participation" clause claim. *Breeden* thus strongly implies that the participation clause prohibits retaliation even where the underlying discrimination claim lacks a reasonable basis. Why should that be so? Bad faith lawsuits can be sanctioned by attorneys' fees awards to the employer. *Cf. Christiansburg Garment Co. v. EEOC*, 434 U.S. 412 (1978) (reproduced at p. 595). Isn't there an obvious reason to allow courts to decide bad faith while precluding employers from being judges in their own cases by taking adverse employment actions against employees they believe have filed claims in bad faith? *See generally* Lawrence D. Rosenthal, *Reading Too Much into What the Court Doesn't Write: How Some Federal Courts Have Limited Title VII's Participation Clause's Protections After* Clark County School District v. Breeden, 83 Wash. L. Rev. 345 (2008).

2. *Participation Conduct or Opposition Conduct?* Because the protections afforded by these two clauses differ, perhaps dramatically, what is the line between participation, as opposed to opposition, conduct? Internal complaints of discrimination, it appears from *Breeden*, are opposition, not participation, conduct and thus must meet the reasonable, good faith belief test. On the other hand, participation includes not only filing a charge or lawsuit but also testifying in court or at deposition. *See Long v. Ala. Dep't of Human Res.*, 650 F.3d 957 (11th Cir. 2016) (deposition testimony). *See also Rodríguez-Vives v. P.R. Firefighters Corps of P.R.*, 743 F.3d 278 (1st Cir. 2014) (a suit challenging sex discrimination under the Equal Protection Clause constitutes protected activity within the opposition clause of Title VII). What about answering questions in an employer's investigation of a complaint, perhaps one that appears to be conducted to provide the employer its *Ellerth* affirmative defense? In *Crawford v. Metro Gov't of Nashville & Davidson Counties*, 555 U.S. 271 (2009), the Supreme Court held that participation in an employer's internal investigation of a sexual harassment claim could be protected opposition conduct but declined to decide if it would be protected under the participation clause. In a later opinion, the Second Circuit held that the participation clause does not cover internal investigations that are not associated with a formal EEOC charge, *Townsend v. Benjamin Enterprises, Inc.*, 679 F.3d 41 (2d Cir. 2012), reserving judgment on whether participation in an internal investigation begun after a charge was filed would fall within the participation clause. *Cf. Deravin v. Kerik*, 335 F.3d 195 (2d Cir. 2003) (an employee defending himself against a formal charge of sexual harassment is engaged in protected activity under the participation clause).

What about rejecting a sexual advance? Is that protected conduct? The first precedential decision on the subject held it to be protected opposition even if the employee did nothing further in the way of complaint. *EEOC v. New Breed Logistics*, 783 F.3d 1057, 1067 (6th Cir. 2015) ("a demand that a supervisor cease his/her harassing conduct constitutes protected activity covered by Title VII"). *Contra Frank v. Harris County*, 118 F. App'x 799, 804 (5th Cir. 2004).

3. *Retaliation and the* Ellerth *Affirmative Defense.* Is *Breeden*'s classification of internal complaints as opposition, not participation, consistent with the affirmative

defense set forth in *Ellerth*, reproduced at p. 337? Since the affirmative defense encourages plaintiffs to utilize internal complaint mechanisms, perhaps before harassment becomes "severe or pervasive," why not protect employees from retaliation when they do so? At the very least, perhaps the notion of "reasonable belief" in illegality should be broadened. *See Boyer-Liberto v. Fontainebleau Corp.*, 786 F.3d 264 (4th Cir. 2015) (en banc) ("rather than encourage the early reporting vital to achieving Title VII's goal of avoiding harm, [too strict a standard of reasonableness] deters harassment victims from speaking up by depriving them of their statutory entitlement to protection from retaliation"). We'll revisit the reasonableness issue at p. 416.

[handwritten margin notes: broaden reasonable standard so that it is in harmony w/ affirmative ellerth affirmative defense that employer took reasonable care to prevent/correct and employee unreasonably failed to utilize the employer's prevent/correct measures]

D.   THE SCOPE OF PARTICIPATION PROTECTION

In *Crawford v. Metro. Gov't of Nashville and Davidson Counties*, 555 U.S. 271 (2009), the Court held that an employee who speaks out about discrimination in response to inquiries made during an employer's internal investigation is protected by the opposition clause. In so doing, it rejected the lower court's conclusion that, because the plaintiff had merely answered questions rather than initiated a complaint, she lacked protection against retaliation: "nothing in the statute requires a freakish rule protecting an employee who reports discrimination on her own initiative but not one who reports the same discrimination in the same words when her boss asks a question." *Id.* at 277-78. The Court noted that protecting the employee who speaks up when questioned by the employer was in keeping with the *Ellerth-Faragher* affirmative defense:

> The appeals court's rule would thus create a real dilemma for any knowledgeable employee in a hostile work environment if the boss took steps to assure a defense under our cases. If the employee reported discrimination in response to the enquiries, the employer might well be free to penalize her for speaking up. But if she kept quiet about the discrimination and later filed a Title VII claim, the employer might well escape liability, arguing that it "exercised reasonable care to prevent and correct [any discrimination] promptly" but "the plaintiff employee unreasonably failed to take advantage of . . . preventive or corrective opportunities provided by the employer." *Ellerth*. Nothing in the statute's text or our precedent supports this catch-22.

Id. at 279. While *Crawford* makes clear that an employee does not have to voluntarily step forward and oppose wrongful conduct, what if she just joins in a casual conversation critical of the employer? Does that suffice under the opposition clause? *See generally* Matthew W. Green, Jr., *Express Yourself: Striking a Balance Between Silence and Active, Purposive Opposition Under Title VII's Anti-Retaliation Provision*, 28 HOFSTRA LAB. & EMP. L.J. 107 (2010).

In any event, the significance of *Crawford* may be limited. As we have seen, a good faith, reasonable belief in the illegality of the conduct opposed is generally required under the opposition clause. After *Crawford*, is such a belief required when an employee answers questions in an internal investigation? *See EEOC v. Rite Way Serv.*, 819 F.3d 235(5th Cir. 2016) (even a plaintiff who is merely acting as a third-party witness to questions about possible discrimination must have a reasonable belief in the conduct's illegality to be protected from retaliation). *See generally* Deborah L. Brake, *Retaliation in an EEO World*, 89 IND. L.J. 115 (2014) (by deciding *Crawford* under the opposition clause rather than the participation clause, the Court left witnesses still subject to the requirement that their answers reflect a reasonable belief in illegality).

More generally, the reasonable belief requirement has often been an obstacle to plaintiffs' §704(a) suits. Indeed, the *Breeden* Court raised the question, although it did not decide, whether the opposition clause's protections even attach if the challenged practice is not *in fact* unlawful. In other words, will a reasonable, good faith belief that the employer has acted unlawfully ultimately suffice under the opposition clause? While the statutory language certainly supports limiting the statute's protections only to opposition to conduct that is actually unlawful, such an interpretation would likely be inconsistent with the policy objectives of §704. *See Robinson v. Shell Oil*, 519 U.S. 337 (1997) (since policy of §704 is furthered by including former employees within the protections of the statute, they are within the protected class). And there is a consensus in the lower courts to that effect. *E.g.*, *Clark v. Cache Valley Elec. Co.*, 573 F. App'x 693 (10th Cir. 2014). *See generally* Ernest F. Lidge, III, *The Necessity of Expanding Protection from Retaliation for Employees Who Complain About Hostile Environment Harassment*, 53 U. LOUISVILLE L. REV. 39 (2014); Matthew W. Green Jr., *What's So Reasonable About Reasonableness? Rejecting a Case Law-Centered Approach to Title VII's Reasonable Belief Doctrine*, 62 KAN. L. REV. 759, 763-64 (2014); Deborah L. Brake & Joanna L. Grossman, *The Failure of Title VII as a Rights Claiming System*, 86 N.C. L. REV. 859, 919 (2008).

At least that's the doctrine. In fact, however, the courts applying these tests often come perilously close to requiring "reasonable" employees to have fairly well-informed views of the law of employment discrimination, which seems very odd. *See Hatcher v. Bd. of Trs. of S. Ill. Univ.*, 829 F.3d 531 (7th Cir. 2016) (assisting a student in reporting sexual harassment was not protected conduct under Title VII). For example, a pair of cases, *Clark v. Cache Valley Elec. Co.*, 573 F. App'x 693 (10th Cir. 2014) and *Kelly v. Howard I. Shapiro & Assocs. Consulting Eng'rs, P.C.*, 716 F.3d 10 (2d Cir. 2013), found that complaints about "sexual favoritism" for paramours were not protected. Having studied Chapter 5, p. 297, you now know that, but would it have been so obvious before you enrolled in this course? And what about discrimination on the basis of sexual orientation? We've seen how this has evolved in recent years. See p. 280. Is it so clear, today, that opposition to discrimination against gays is not reasonably believed to be a violation of Title VII?

But perhaps the most dramatic example is opposition to sexual harassment where the lower courts, perhaps taking the lead from *Breeden*, have repeatedly found internal complaints unprotected when the conduct opposed is analytically harassment but has not yet come close enough to the "severe or pervasive" line. *See* Craig Robert Senn, *Redefining Protected "Opposition" Activity in Employment Retaliation Cases*, 37 CARDOZO L. REV. 2035 (2016). While commentators have long criticized these kinds of decisions, *see* Deborah L. Brake, *Retaliation in an EEO World, supra*; Russell Robinson, *Perceptual Segregation*, 108 COLUM. L. REV. 1093 (2008); Lawrence D. Rosenthal, *To Report or Not to Report: The Case for Eliminating the Objectively Reasonable Requirement for Opposition Activities Under Title VII's Anti-Retaliation Provision*, 39 ARIZ. ST. L.J. 1127 (2007), there are signs of liberalization in the courts. *See Kacian v. Postmaster Gen. of the United States*, 653 F. App'x 125, 128 (3d Cir. 2016) (the complained-of conduct involved a supervisor asking plaintiff for a photograph of her in a bikini more than once, making several unwelcome comments about her physical appearance and private life, and refusing her assistance in completing unfamiliar tasks); *Boyer-Liberto v. Fontainebleau Corp.*, 786 F.3d 264, 284 (4th Cir.

2015) (en banc) ("an employee will have a reasonable belief that a hostile work environment is occurring based on an isolated incident if that harassment is physically threatening or humiliating").

Opposition protection is different from participation protection in yet another important way. Participation involves *formal* activities, such as filing a charge or testifying. Courts are very protective of this kind of conduct and have found employers liable for unlawful retaliation when they take an adverse employment action based on such activities even if for otherwise defensible reasons. For example, *Greengrass v. Int'l Monetary Sys., Ltd.*, 776 F.3d 481 (7th Cir. 2015), held that an employer's naming of a female employee's charge to the EEOC in a required SEC filing could be actionable retaliation if done with the requisite intent to retaliate. *See generally* Jamie Darin Prenkert, Julie Manning Magid & Allison Fetter-Harrott, *Retaliatory Disclosure: When Identifying the Complainant Is an Adverse Action*, 91 N.C. L. REV. 889 (2013). *But see Benes v. A.B. Data, Ltd.*, 724 F.3d 752 (7th Cir. 2013) (misconduct during EEOC-sponsored mediation of a discrimination claim is a legitimate reason for discharging an employee); *Niswander v. Cincinnati Ins. Co.*, 529 F.3d 714, 722 (6th Cir. 2008) (plaintiff's intentional conduct in turning over confidential employment documents to her attorney in response to a discovery request was not protected under the participation clause when the documents were irrelevant to her claim); *Vaughn v. Villa*, 537 F.3d 1147 (10th Cir. 2008) (permitting discharge for providing unredacted patient record to EEOC when the employer would have terminated any other employee for violating patient confidentiality).

In contrast, opposition clause cases often ask whether the manner of the employee's opposition can take her out from under the protections of the Act. As should be obvious from *McDonnell Douglas Corp. v. Green*, reproduced at p. 14, the answer is yes. Recall that Green had engaged in a "stall in" to protest alleged discrimination by the company, and the company had asserted his participation in those activities as the explanation for why Green was not rehired. Although the Court did not directly rule on §704(a), as that claim was not before it, the Court, in language broad enough to embrace §704(a), wrote: "Nothing in Title VII compels an employer to absolve and rehire one who has engaged in such deliberate, unlawful activity against it." *Id.* at 803.

McDonnell Douglas could be read as permitting retaliation where the opposition violates criminal statutes, but the Court suggested a broader reading by looking to the "disloyalty doctrine" under the National Labor Relations Act. *NLRB v. Fansteel Metallurgical Corp.*, 306 U.S. 240 (1939) (some protests are sufficiently disloyal to justify discharge). Whatever *McDonnell Douglas* may have meant, lower courts have frequently found that opposition to what the employee reasonably and in good faith believes is unlawful discrimination is nevertheless outside the protection of the statute because of the manner of that opposition.

LAUGHLIN v. METROPOLITAN WASHINGTON AIRPORTS AUTHORITY
149 F.3d 253 (4th Cir. 1998)

WILLIAMS, Circuit Judge.

[Plaintiff sued for retaliation, claiming her conduct was protected under both the participation and opposition clauses of Title VII. The district court granted summary judgment to the employer, concluding that the plaintiff was not engaged in participation conduct and that conduct that is "surreptitious, dishonest and disloyal" is presumptively unprotected by the opposition clause, a presumption the plaintiff had not overcome.]

I . . .

Essential to understanding the incident that directly led to Laughlin's termination are the events related to another MWAA [Metropolitan Washington Airports Authority] employee. Kathy LaSauce, an operations officer at the MWAA, filed an informal complaint with the EEO officer at the MWAA against William Rankin, LaSauce's supervisor. In her complaint, she alleged that Rankin had retaliated against her for providing testimony in another operations officer's EEO action. Initially LaSauce took her complaint to the Washington National Airport manager, Augustus Melton, Jr., in April 1994. Melton took steps to settle the complaint informally. Those steps failed, and LaSauce filed a formal complaint with the MWAA EEO officer and tendered her resignation. In the process of investigating and attempting to settle the LaSauce/Rankin dispute, in September 1994, Melton drafted a written warning to Rankin regarding the inappropriate retaliatory actions that he had taken against LaSauce. The written warning, however, was never formalized; it was neither signed by Melton nor seen by Rankin, it was simply prepared and left on Melton's desk. At about the same time that LaSauce's resignation became effective and Melton had drafted the written warning, Rankin was selected for the job of El Paso Airport manager and tendered his resignation to the MWAA officials.

Meanwhile, Laughlin, a secretary to Melton, reported directly to the airport manager's staff assistant. During the course of her regular duties, on or about September 29, 1994, she discovered a copy of the unsigned written warning on Melton's desk addressed to Rankin. She noticed immediately that the written warning discussed the LaSauce dispute. The written warning was date-stamped September 8, 1994. Laughlin believed that the existence of the dated warning on the desk was highly irregular because correspondence was not generally date-stamped at the MWAA until it was in final form awaiting signature. Alongside the written warning she found Rankin's resignation letter explaining that he had been offered the position in El Paso, and a news clipping, predating the resignation letter, from an El Paso newspaper mentioning that Rankin was the front runner for the position in El Paso. Laughlin was so surprised to see the unsigned correspondence on her boss's desk that she immediately concluded that he was engaging in a coverup to prevent LaSauce from having adequate access to relevant documents for a future lawsuit. As a result of these suspicions, Laughlin removed the documents, photocopied them, and replaced the originals on her boss's desk. She sent the copies to LaSauce with a note stating that she thought LaSauce might find them interesting.

Laughlin's removal and copying of the documents was discovered in 1996 during a deposition in a civil suit filed by LaSauce. Laughlin was terminated as a result of removing the documents. Her termination notice stated in pertinent part that:

> 1) you are a confidential employee in that you are an employee who acts in a confidential capacity with respect to me, the Airport Manager, who effectuates management policies in labor-management relations; 2) you released a draft letter of reprimand, a personnel related document which is confidential by nature; 3) you released personal documents of Mr. William Rankin's, without his or my consent, that had been sent to me for my information; 4) you sent these documents to Ms. Kathy LaSauce on your own accord, without my consent; and 5) according to Ms. LaSauce's sworn deposition, she never asked you for these documents.

III . . .

On appeal, Laughlin contends that she forecasted sufficient evidence to establish a prima facie case of retaliation under Title VII and that the district court erred when it granted summary judgment to MWAA. To establish a prima facie case of retaliation, a plaintiff must prove three elements: (1) that she engaged in protected activity, (2) that an adverse employment action was taken against her, and (3) that there was a causal link between the protected activity and the adverse employment action. It is undisputed that Laughlin suffered an adverse employment action and therefore satisfies the second requirement of a prima facie case: She was terminated. Moreover, it is undisputed that Laughlin was terminated as a result of removing the documents in question. To survive summary judgment, therefore, Laughlin must have evidence that removing the documents was a protected activity.

Laughlin urges us to conclude that the district court erred when it did not characterize her removal of documents as participation in LaSauce's EEO claim. She argues that her actions were taken to assist LaSauce in her investigation. The evidence, however, does not support Laughlin's assertion. First, at the time the documents were removed from the desk, LaSauce was not involved in any ongoing investigation under Title VII. LaSauce had recently resigned from her position at the MWAA and had not yet filed suit. Second, LaSauce herself testified that she had not requested Laughlin's assistance and that she was surprised to receive the documents in the mail. There was quite simply no ongoing "investigation, proceeding or hearing" in which Laughlin could participate at the time she discovered the documents on her boss's desk. On that basis, we disagree with Laughlin's contention that her case should have been analyzed under the participation clause.[4]

Because Laughlin's actions are not cognizable as participation, they must be oppositional or her case fails as a matter of law. To qualify as opposition activity an employee need not engage in the formal process of adjudicating a discrimination claim. *See Armstrong v. Index Journal Co.*, 647 F.2d 441, 448 (4th Cir. 1981). Opposition activity encompasses utilizing informal grievance procedures as well as staging informal protests and voicing one's opinions in order to bring attention to an employer's discriminatory activities. *See id.* To determine whether an employee has engaged in legitimate opposition activity we employ a balancing test. *See id.* We "'balance the purpose of the Act to protect persons engaging reasonably in activities opposing . . . discrimination, against Congress' equally manifest desire not to tie the hands of employers in the objective selection and control of personnel.'" *Id.* (quoting *Hochstadt v. Worcester Found. for Experimental Biology*, 545 F.2d 222, 231 (1st Cir. 1976)).

The district court initially did not use this test, but rather determined that the circumstances of this case, in which an employee committed an egregious breach of confidentiality, mandated a rebuttable presumption that the activity was not protected under Title VII. Laughlin asserts that the district court erred by analyzing her case utilizing this rebuttable presumption that activity that constitutes a "breach of the employee's obligations of honest and faithful service" is not protected under the

---

4. The distinction between participation clause protection and opposition clause protection is significant because the scope of protection is different. Activities under the participation clause are essential to "'the machinery set up by Title VII.'" *Hashimoto v. Dalton*, 118 F.3d 671, 680 (9th Cir. 1997). As such, the scope of protection for activity falling under the participation clause is broader than for activity falling under the opposition clause. *See Booker v. Brown & Williamson Tobacco Co.*, 879 F.2d 1304, 1312 (6th Cir. 1989).

opposition clause. We believe that this Circuit's well-established balancing test provides an adequate, workable framework for assessing opposition clause claims and, thus, decline to adopt the district court's rationale. . . .

When we apply the balancing test to the facts of this case, we easily conclude that the employer's interest in maintaining security and confidentiality of sensitive personnel documents outweighs Laughlin's interest in providing those documents to LaSauce. Laughlin's reaction to the situation was disproportionate and unreasonable under the circumstances. This court has recognized that complaining to the employer, *see Hopkins v. Baltimore Gas & Elec., Co.*, 77 F.3d 745, 754 (1996); *Armstrong*, and participating in an employer's informal grievance procedures, *see Armstrong*, when done in a manner that is "not disruptive or disorderly," *id.*, constitute opposition activities that merit protection under Title VII. Laughlin's drastic actions are not akin to the measured responses to employer discrimination that we have approved in the past.

In contrast, the MWAA's decision to terminate Laughlin was sound. The MWAA had a reasonable and significant interest in preventing the dissemination of confidential personnel documents. *See Jefferies v. Harris County Community Action Ass'n*, 615 F.2d 1025, 1036-37 (5th Cir. 1980) ("[Employer] clearly had a legitimate and substantial interest in keeping its personnel records and agency documents confidential"). Laughlin had breached her employer's trust by copying confidential material and sending it to an outside party. Title VII was "not intended to immunize insubordinate, disruptive, or nonproductive behavior at work." *Armstrong*. Because the MWAA's strong interest in protecting sensitive records outweighs Laughlin's interest in this instance, the district court was correct in holding that Laughlin, as a matter of law, did not engage in protected oppositional activity and, therefore, did not establish a prima facie case of retaliatory discharge. . . .

NOTES

1. *Retaliation Claims and the* McDonnell Douglas *Proof Scheme. Laughlin* follows the approach adopted by the circuit courts in relying on the *McDonnell Douglas* burden-shifting method of drawing inferences to determine an employer's motivation when there is no direct evidence. As you'll recall from Chapter 1, this includes three stages: (1) the plaintiff establishes a prima facie case, (2) the employer articulates a nondiscriminatory reason for its actions, and (3) the plaintiff rebuts by proving pretext. This structure makes sense (at least if the second step is framed as a "nonretaliatory reason") when the issue is why the employer acted. *See Franklin v. Local 2 of the Sheet Metal Workers Ass'n*, 565 F.3d 508 (8th Cir. 2009) (fact question as to whether union's actions were pretextual when it claimed it was necessary to post and read out loud plaintiffs' names after they filed charges with the EEOC as part of its requirement to post all legal bills).

It's less obviously appropriate in cases like *Laughlin* where the employer was clearly retaliating for her plaintiff's conduct and the only issue was whether that conduct was too extreme to be protected. If the plaintiff has the burden of showing protected opposition, in cases like *Laughlin* that might mean showing that she fares well in balancing disruption with opposition. Nevertheless, the cases often speak as though the conduct is in some sense protected while going on to describe the employer's punishment of disruptive conduct as a nonretaliatory reason. *See Alvarez v. Royal Atl. Developers, Inc.*, 610 F.3d 1253, 1269 (11th Cir. 2010) (the case could be viewed as the employer firing plaintiff not because of her complaint about discrimination per se but rather because it "revealed that she was mad at the company"; alternatively, it could be viewed as an admission of firing because of her complaint but raising an affirmative defense that the termination was necessary to protect itself).

2. *Balancing?* As we've seen earlier and as *Laughlin* confirms, the protections of the opposition clause are far less sweeping than those of the participation clause. *McDonnell Douglas*, reproduced at p. 14, establishes that some conduct is too unreasonable to be protected. And in a footnote omitted from your text, *Laughlin* asserts it is "black letter law" that illegal actions are not protected by Title VII. But the case makes clear that even "legal" opposition can be viewed as sufficiently extreme to justify employer discipline, whether the case is analyzed at the prima facie stage or in determining whether the proffered reason is a legitimate, nonretaliatory one. But if the courts are balancing employer and employee interests, what goes on the scales? Violation of certain neutral workplace norms, like *Laughlin* itself, has been held to suffice. *See Argyropoulos v. City of Alton*, 539 F.3d 724 (7th Cir. 2008) (secretly recording plaintiff's meeting with supervisors not protected); *Cruz v. Coach Stores, Inc.*, 202 F.3d 560 (2d Cir. 2000) (slapping co-worker in response to sexual harassment not protected activity). But much opposition—such as picketing — would violate the norm in many workplaces against "rocking the boat," which suggests that's not much of a test. What about the extent of any resulting disruption? It's not clear there was any in *Laughlin*, as that term is often used, but could even substantial disruption be outweighed by employer provocation? Should the court consider whether the plaintiff was more disruptive than necessary or whether the plaintiff had ulterior motivations? *See generally* Leora Eisenstadt & Deanna Geddes, *Suppressed Anger, Retaliation Doctrine, and Workplace Culture*, SSRN abstract_id: 2928240; Terry Smith, *Everyday Indignities: Race, Retaliation, and the Promise of Title VII*, 34 Colum. Hum. Rts. L. Rev. 529 (2003) (criticizing the courts' reactions to opposition to "subtle discrimination").

What if an employer believes an employee lied during an investigation of sexual harassment? Will the employer's reasonable, good faith belief that the employee was not telling the truth constitute a legitimate, nondiscriminatory reason for firing her? Or is protection lost only if the employee in fact lied? Even after *Crawford*, courts have held that an employer can terminate a worker "based on its good-faith belief that the employee lied during an internal investigation." *Griffin v. City of Demorest*, 635 F. App'x 701, 707 (11th Cir. 2015).

E.   ADVERSE ACTION

As we saw in Chapter 1, the courts have required that discrimination be sufficiently "adverse" to be actionable. Even when an intent to discriminate is unquestionably present, courts nonetheless have required that there be an "adverse action" before a claim is stated. Is this "adverse action" a requirement of a retaliation claim as well? The Supreme Court addressed that question in the following case.

BURLINGTON NORTHERN AND SANTA FE RAILWAY CO. v. WHITE
548 U.S. 53 (2006)

Breyer, J.

Title VII of the Civil Rights Act of 1964 forbids employment discrimination against "any individual" based on that individual's "race, color, religion, sex, or national origin." A separate section of the Act — its anti-retaliation provision — forbids an employer from "discriminating against" an employee or job applicant because that individual "opposed any practice" made unlawful by Title VII or "made a charge, testified, assisted, or participated in" a Title VII proceeding or investigation.

The Courts of Appeals have come to different conclusions about the scope of the Act's anti-retaliation provision, particularly the reach of its phrase "discriminate against." Does that provision confine actionable retaliation to activity that affects the terms and conditions of employment? And how harmful must the adverse actions be to fall within its scope?

We conclude that the anti-retaliation provision does not confine the actions and harms it forbids to those that are related to employment or occur at the workplace. We also conclude that the provision covers those (and only those) employer actions that would have been materially adverse to a reasonable employee or job applicant. In the present context that means that the employer's actions must be harmful to the point that they could well dissuade a reasonable worker from making or supporting a charge of discrimination.

Held

[Shortly after Sheila White complained of harassment by her supervisor, she was reassigned from her position operating a forklift to a track laborer job, a more physically demanding and dirtier job. The pay and benefits, however, were the same. After White filed a charge of discrimination with the EEOC, she was suspended without pay for 37 days, supposedly for insubordination, and that suspension would have become a termination had she not filed a grievance. White did grieve her suspension, and the hearing officer found she had not been insubordinate and ordered her reinstated with backpay. Despite having suffered no economic harm, White filed suit, alleging that the change in her job responsibilities and her suspension constituted actionable retaliation under Title VII. A jury agreed with White. The Sixth Circuit, en banc, affirmed the judgment in White's favor.]

II

Title VII's anti-retaliation provision forbids employer actions that "discriminate against" an employee (or job applicant) because he has "opposed" a practice that Title VII forbids or has "made a charge, testified, assisted, or participated in" a Title VII "investigation, proceeding, or hearing." No one doubts that the term "discriminate against" refers to distinctions or differences in treatment that injure protected individuals. See *Jackson v. Birmingham Bd. of Ed.*, 544 U.S. 167, 174 (2005); *Price Waterhouse v. Hopkins* (plurality opinion); see also 4 Oxford English Dictionary 758 (2d ed. 1989) (def. 3b). But different Circuits have come to different conclusions about whether the challenged action has to be employment or workplace related and about how harmful that action must be to constitute retaliation.

[The Court trifurcated the approaches taken by the circuits. Some insisted on a close relationship between the retaliatory action and employment, such as a "materially adverse change in the terms and conditions" of employment. Other circuits had adopted a more restrictive approach, requiring an "ultimate employment decision," which limited actionable retaliation to acts such as hiring and firing. Still other circuits said that the plaintiff must show that the "employer's challenged action would have been material to a reasonable employee,"] which in contexts like the present one means that it would likely have "dissuaded a reasonable worker from making or supporting a charge of discrimination[,]" [although this test was sometimes phrased differently].

issue

We granted certiorari to resolve this disagreement. To do so requires us to decide whether Title VII's anti-retaliation provision forbids only those employer actions and resulting harms that are related to employment or the workplace. And we must characterize how harmful an act of retaliatory discrimination must be in order to fall within the provision's scope.

A

[The Court rejected the argument that Title VII's retaliation prohibition should be read *in pari materia* with its substantive antidiscrimination provision to require a link between "the challenged retaliatory action and the terms, conditions, or status of employment."] We cannot agree. The language of the substantive provision differs from that of the anti-retaliation provision in important ways. . . .

Section 704(a) sets forth Title VII's anti-retaliation provision in the following terms:

> It shall be an unlawful employment practice for an employer *to discriminate against* any of his employees or applicants for employment . . . because he has opposed any practice made an unlawful employment practice by this subchapter, or because he has made a charge, testified, assisted, or participated in any manner in an investigation, proceeding, or hearing under this subchapter.

(Emphasis added.)

[In contrast, the substantive provisions of §703 use words such as] "hire," "discharge," "compensation, terms, conditions, or privileges of employment," "employment opportunities," and "status as an employee" [which] explicitly limit the scope of that provision to actions that affect employment or alter the conditions of the workplace. No such limiting words appear in the anti-retaliation provision. Given these linguistic differences, the question here is not whether identical or similar words should be read *in pari materia* to mean the same thing. Rather, the question is whether Congress intended its different words to make a legal difference. We normally presume that, where words differ as they differ here, " 'Congress acts intentionally and purposely in the disparate inclusion or exclusion.' " *Russello v. United States*, 464 U.S. 16, 23 (1983).

There is strong reason to believe that Congress intended the differences that its language suggests, for the two provisions differ not only in language but in purpose as well. The anti-discrimination provision seeks a workplace where individuals are not discriminated against because of their racial, ethnic, religious, or gender-based status. See *McDonnell Douglas Corp. v. Green* [reproduced at p. 14]. The anti-retaliation provision seeks to secure that primary objective by preventing an employer from interfering (through retaliation) with an employee's efforts to secure or advance enforcement of the Act's basic guarantees. The substantive provision seeks to prevent injury to individuals based on who they are, *i.e.*, their status. The anti-retaliation provision seeks to prevent harm to individuals based on what they do, *i.e.*, their conduct.

To secure the first objective, Congress did not need to prohibit anything other than employment-related discrimination. The substantive provision's basic objective of "equality of employment opportunities" and the elimination of practices that tend to bring about "stratified job environments," would be achieved were all employment-related discrimination miraculously eliminated.

But one cannot secure the second objective by focusing only upon employer actions and harm that concern employment and the workplace. Were all such actions and harms eliminated, the anti-retaliation provision's objective would *not* be achieved. An employer can effectively retaliate against an employee by taking actions not directly related to his employment or by causing him harm *outside* the workplace. See, *e.g.,* *Rochon v. Gonzales*, 438 F.3d [1211, 1213 (CADC 2006)] (FBI retaliation against employee "took the form of the FBI's refusal, contrary to policy, to investigate death threats a federal prisoner made against [the agent] and his wife"); *Berry v. Stevinson Chevrolet*, 74 F.3d 980, 984, 986 (CA10 1996) (finding actionable retaliation where employer filed false criminal charges against former employee who complained about discrimination). A provision limited to employment-related actions would not deter the many forms that effective retaliation can take. Hence, such a limited construction would fail to fully achieve the anti-retaliation provision's "primary purpose," namely, "maintaining unfettered access to statutory remedial mechanisms." *Robinson v. Shell Oil Co.*, 519 U.S. 337 (1997).

Thus, purpose reinforces what language already indicates, namely, that the anti-retaliation provision, unlike the substantive provision, is not limited to discriminatory actions that affect the terms and conditions of employment. . . .

Finally, we do not accept the petitioner's and Solicitor General's view that it is "anomalous" to read the statute to provide broader protection for victims of retaliation than for those whom Title VII primarily seeks to protect, namely, victims of race-based, ethnic-based, religion-based, or gender-based discrimination. Congress has provided similar kinds of protection from retaliation in comparable statutes without any judicial suggestion that those provisions are limited to the conduct prohibited by the primary substantive provisions. [The Court cited cases under the National Labor Relations Act such as *Bill Johnson's Restaurants, Inc. v. NLRB*, 461 U.S. 731, 740 (1983), which construed that statute's antiretaliation provision to go far beyond work-related retaliation to bar even "'a wide variety of employer conduct that is intended to restrain, or that has the likely effect of restraining, employees in the exercise of protected activities,' including the retaliatory filing of a lawsuit against an employee."]

In any event, as we have explained, differences in the purpose of the two provisions remove any perceived "anomaly," for they justify this difference of interpretation. Title VII depends for its enforcement upon the cooperation of employees who are willing to file complaints and act as witnesses. "Plainly, effective enforcement could thus only be expected if employees felt free to approach officials with their grievances." *Mitchell v. Robert DeMario Jewelry, Inc.*, 361 U.S. 288 (1960). Interpreting the anti-retaliation provision to provide broad protection from retaliation helps assure the cooperation upon which accomplishment of the Act's primary objective depends.

For these reasons, we conclude that Title VII's substantive provision and its anti-retaliation provision are not coterminous. The scope of the anti-retaliation provision extends beyond workplace-related or employment-related retaliatory acts and harm. We therefore reject the standards applied in the Courts of Appeals that have treated the anti-retaliation provision as forbidding the same conduct prohibited by the anti-discrimination provision and that have limited actionable retaliation to so-called "ultimate employment decisions."

B

The anti-retaliation provision protects an individual not from all retaliation, but from retaliation that produces an injury or harm. [While the Circuits have used differing language, we] agree with the formulation set forth by the Seventh and the District of Columbia Circuits. In our view, a plaintiff must show that a reasonable employee would have found the challenged action materially adverse, "which in this context means it well might have 'dissuaded a reasonable worker from making or supporting a charge of discrimination.'" *Rochon.*

We speak of *material* adversity because we believe it is important to separate significant from trivial harms. Title VII, we have said, does not set forth "a general civility code for the American workplace." *Oncale v. Sundowner Offshore Services, Inc.* [reproduced at p. 275]; see *Faragher* (judicial standards for sexual harassment must "filter out complaints attacking 'the ordinary tribulations of the workplace, such as the sporadic use of abusive language, gender-related jokes, and occasional teasing'"). An employee's decision to report discriminatory behavior cannot immunize that employee from those petty slights or minor annoyances that often take place at work and that all employees experience. *See* 1 B. LINDEMANN & P. GROSSMAN, EMPLOYMENT DISCRIMINATION LAW 669 (3d ed. 1996) (noting that "courts have held that personality conflicts at work that generate antipathy" and "'snubbing' by supervisors and co-workers" are not actionable under §704(a)). The anti-retaliation provision seeks to prevent employer interference with "unfettered access" to Title VII's remedial mechanisms. *Robinson.* It does so by prohibiting employer actions that are likely "to deter victims of discrimination from complaining to the EEOC," the courts, and their employers. *Ibid.* And normally petty slights, minor annoyances, and simple lack of good manners will not create such deterrence. See 2 EEOC 1998 Manual §8, p. 8-13.

We refer to reactions of a *reasonable* employee because we believe that the provision's standard for judging harm must be objective. An objective standard is judicially administrable. It avoids the uncertainties and unfair discrepancies that can plague a judicial effort to determine a plaintiff's unusual subjective feelings. We have emphasized the need for objective standards in other Title VII contexts, and those same concerns animate our decision here. See, *e.g.*, [*Pa. State Police v.*] *Suders*, [542 U.S. 129, 141 (2004)] (constructive discharge doctrine); *Harris v. Forklift Systems, Inc.* [reproduced at p. 331] (hostile work environment doctrine).

We phrase the standard in general terms because the significance of any given act of retaliation will often depend upon the particular circumstances. Context matters. "The real social impact of workplace behavior often depends on a constellation of surrounding circumstances, expectations, and relationships which are not fully captured by a simple recitation of the words used or the physical acts performed." *Oncale.* A schedule change in an employee's work schedule may make little difference to many workers, but may matter enormously to a young mother with school age children. *Cf., e.g., Washington* [*v. Ill. Dep't of Revenue*, 420 F.3d 658, 661 (CA7 2005)] (finding flex-time schedule critical to employee with disabled child). A supervisor's refusal to invite an employee to lunch is normally trivial, a nonactionable petty slight. But to retaliate by excluding an employee from a weekly training lunch that contributes significantly to the employee's professional advancement might well deter a reasonable employee from complaining about discrimination. See 2 EEOC 1998 Manual §8, p. 8-14. Hence, a legal standard that speaks in general terms rather than specific prohibited acts is preferable, for an "act that would be immaterial in some situations is material in others." *Washington.*

Finally, we note that contrary to the claim of the concurrence, this standard does *not* require a reviewing court or jury to consider "the nature of the discrimination that led to the filing of the charge." Rather, the standard is tied to the challenged retaliatory act, not the underlying conduct that forms the basis of the Title VII complaint. By focusing on the materiality of the challenged action and the perspective of a reasonable person in the plaintiff's position, we believe this standard will screen out trivial conduct while effectively capturing those acts that are likely to dissuade employees from complaining or assisting in complaints about discrimination.

III

Applying this standard to the facts of this case, we believe that there was a sufficient evidentiary basis to support the jury's verdict on White's retaliation claim. [The instructions required the jury to find that White "suffered a materially adverse change in the terms or conditions of her employment." While today's decision makes clear that the jury was not required to find a relation to the terms or conditions of employment,] insofar as the jury also found that the actions were "materially adverse," its findings are adequately supported.

First, Burlington argues that a reassignment of duties cannot constitute retaliatory discrimination where, as here, both the former and present duties fall within the same job description. We do not see why that is so. Almost every job category involves some responsibilities and duties that are less desirable than others. Common sense suggests that one good way to discourage an employee such as White from bringing discrimination charges would be to insist that she spend more time performing the more arduous duties and less time performing those that are easier or more agreeable. That is presumably why the EEOC has consistently found "retaliatory work assignments" to be a classic and "widely recognized" example of "forbidden retaliation." 2 EEOC 1991 Manual §614.7, pp. 614-31 to 614-32. . . .

To be sure, reassignment of job duties is not automatically actionable. Whether a particular reassignment is materially adverse depends upon the circumstances of the particular case, and "should be judged from the perspective of a reasonable person in the plaintiff's position, considering 'all the circumstances.'" *Oncale*. But here, the jury had before it considerable evidence that the track labor duties were "by all accounts more arduous and dirtier"; that the "forklift operator position required more qualifications, which is an indication of prestige"; and that "the forklift operator position was objectively considered a better job and the male employees resented White for occupying it." Based on this record, a jury could reasonably conclude that the reassignment of responsibilities would have been materially adverse to a reasonable employee.

Second, Burlington argues that the 37-day suspension without pay lacked statutory significance because Burlington ultimately reinstated White with backpay.

. . . White did receive backpay. But White and her family had to live for 37 days without income. They did not know during that time whether or when White could return to work. Many reasonable employees would find a month without a paycheck to be a serious hardship. And White described to the jury the physical and emotional hardship that 37 days of having "no income, no money" in fact caused. ("That was the worst Christmas I had out of my life. No income, no money, and that made all of us feel bad. . . . I got very depressed.") Indeed, she obtained medical treatment for her emotional distress. A reasonable employee facing the choice between retaining her job (and paycheck) and filing a discrimination complaint might well choose the former. That is to say, an indefinite suspension without pay could well act as a deterrent, even if the suspended employee eventually received backpay. . . . Thus, the jury's conclusion that the 37-day suspension without pay was materially adverse was a reasonable one.

[Justice Alito's concurring opinion omitted.]

NOTES

1. *Section 703 vs. Section 704.* The Court holds that, while §703 reaches only actions that affect employment or that alter the conditions of the workplace, §704 is *not* limited to discriminatory acts that affect those terms and conditions. Given that the actions White complained of did affect her employment, it's not clear why the Court felt it necessary to decide that §704 applied to actions that did not affect the terms and conditions of employment. *See* Lisa Durham Taylor, *Parsing Supreme Court Dicta and the Example of Non-Workplace Harms,* 57 DRAKE L. REV. 75 (2008). Could the Court have reached out to decide this question because it did not believe the actions White complained of, even though arising from the workplace, would have been sufficient to state a claim under §703? Obviously, this would have important implications for the concept of "adverse employment action" we discussed in Chapter 1. In his concurring opinion, Justice Alito disagreed with the majority's analysis, believing that the scope of §§703 and 704 are the same and both reach only materially adverse employment actions. But he finds the actions White complained of were materially adverse within the meaning of either section.

2. *The Limits of Language.* Having looked to the text of §704 to distinguish it from §703, the Court then declines to apply the language of §704 literally. That is, instead of recognizing a cause of action for any discrimination based on protected conduct, it requires the discrimination to be sufficiently severe to deter a reasonable employee from engaging in that conduct. Why?

3. *Employer Liability.* Does the Court's opinion mean that employers are strictly liable for a supervisor's retaliation when a reasonable employee would have found the challenged action materially adverse? To borrow language from sexual harassment, is any conduct actionable under *Burlington* a tangible employment action when done by a supervisor? Isn't that the logical reading of *Burlington*? But if not, would the affirmative defense outlined in *Ellerth* apply to retaliation claims if the supervisor's action is not tangible but *is* sufficiently severe or pervasive? And what about actions taken by "co-workers" (remembering that under *Vance v. Ball State University,* reproduced at p. 345, many of them could be in a position to materially affect plaintiffs)? *See Shott v. Katz,* 829 F.3d 494 (7th Cir. 2016) (§1981 did not bar a plaintiff's fellow employees at a medical school from refusing to seek out the plaintiff to collaborate on professional projects, even for retaliatory reasons, especially in light of the First Amendment and implications of such a holding); *Spencer v. Schmidt Elec. Co.,* 576 F. App'x 442, 455 (5th Cir. 2014) (employer is not liable for retaliatory intimidation by its foremen). *See generally* Sandra Sperino, *The "Disappearing" Dilemma: Why Agency Principles Should Now Take Center Stage in Retaliation Cases,* 57 U. KAN. L. REV. 157 (2008).

4. *What's Materially Adverse?* In deciding what would deter a reasonable employee from opposing discrimination or participating in proceedings, some post-*Burlington* cases have viewed employees as being made of pretty stern stuff. *See, e.g., Wheat v. Fla. Parish Juvenile Justice Comm'n,* 811 F.3d 702 (5th Cir. 2016) (assigning a correctional officer to janitorial duties did not establish a triable issue of a materially adverse action); *AuBuchon v. Geithner,* 743 F.3d 638 (8th Cir. 2014) (no unlawful retaliation when sexual harassment allegations against plaintiff never resulted in harm and other acts constituted only petty slights or minor annoyances); *Tepperwien v. Entergy Nuclear Operations, Inc.,* 663 F.3d 556 (2d Cir. 2011) (no reasonable jury could find, singly or combined, nine alleged acts to be materially adverse, including three factfinding sessions; a counseling; threats of termination; and being forced to switch from a day shift to the night shift). Other courts are more sympathetic to workers.

See, e.g., Planadeball v. Wyndham Vacation Resorts, Inc., 793 F.3d 169, 178 (1st Cir. 2015) ("multiple, consecutive threats . . . could dissuade a reasonable employee from making or supporting a charge of discrimination"); *Laster v. City of Kalamazoo,* 746 F.3d 714, 732 (6th Cir. 2014) (heightened scrutiny, frequent reprimands for breaking selectively enforced policies, harsher discipline than comparators, and "a pre-termination hearing based on unfounded allegations of wrongdoing might well have dissuaded a reasonable worker from making or supporting a charge of discrimination"). *See generally* Sandra F. Sperino, *Retaliation and the Reasonable Person,* 67 FLA. L. REV. 2031 (2016); Ernest F. Lidge III, *What Types of Employer Actions Are Cognizable Under Title VII?: The Ramifications of* Burlington Northern & Santa Fe Railroad Co. v. White, 59 RUTGERS L. REV. 497 (2007); Lisa Durham Taylor, *Adding Subjective Fuel to the Vague-Standard Fire: A Proposal for Congressional Intervention After* Burlington Northern & Santa Fe Railway Co. v. White, 9 U. PA. J. LAB. & EMP. L. 533 (2007).

5. *Threats Just Fine?* One consequence of the Court's definition of actionable retaliation in *White* is that threats to retaliate are not necessarily actionable. Suppose White's boss threatened to fire her, but didn't; or suppose he just threatened to "get even," without being more specific? Although some of the decisions favoring employees take threats into the calculus, the Seventh Circuit seems to hold that an unfulfilled threat cannot violate the antiretaliation provisions of the federal statutes. *Poullard v. McDonald,* 829 F.3d 844, 857 (7th Cir. 2016) ("We do not doubt that threats of future discipline can cause stress or worry, but so too can 'petty slights or minor annoyances that often take place at work and that all employees experience,' which the Supreme Court has excluded from the bounds of materially adverse actions."). Similarly, in *EEOC v. Sundance Rehab. Corp.,* 466 F.3d 490 (6th Cir. 2006), the court found no facial violation of antiretaliation provisions in a severance pay agreement conditioned on not filing charges with the EEOC despite the implicit threat that suit might be brought to recover the payments. The agreement might have been unenforceable, which would have made the threat not meaningful. But is that true? Might a reasonable employee, who didn't want to risk her severance or retain an attorney to defend a suit, forbear from filing a charge? *See also Brandon v. Sage Corp.,* 808 F.3d 266, 271 (5th Cir. 2015) (while the threat of "a realistic, drastic pay cut" might deter protected conduct, the threat to plaintiff would not be seen as realistic given the relative positions of the two parties).

F.   CAUSATION

UNIVERSITY OF TEXAS SOUTHWESTERN
MEDICAL CENTER v. NASSAR
133 S. Ct. 2517 (2013)

Justice KENNEDY delivered the opinion of the Court.

. . . Title VII is central to the federal policy of prohibiting wrongful discrimination in the Nation's workplaces and in all sectors of economic endeavor. This opinion discusses the causation rules for two categories of wrongful employer conduct prohibited by Title VII. The first type is called, for purposes of this opinion, status-based discrimination. The term is used here to refer to basic workplace protection such as prohibitions against employer discrimination on the basis of race, color, religion, sex, or national origin, in hiring, firing, salary structure, promotion and the like. The second type of conduct is employer retaliation on account of an employee having opposed, complained of, or sought remedies for, unlawful workplace discrimination. An employee who alleges status-based discrimination under Title VII need not show that the causal link between injury and wrong is so close that the injury would not have occurred but for the act. So-called but-for causation is not the test. It suffices instead to show that the motive to discriminate was one of the employer's motives, even if the employer also had other, lawful motives that were causative in the employer's decision. This principle is the result of an earlier case from this Court, *Price Waterhouse v. Hopkins* [reproduced at p. 61] and an ensuing statutory amendment by Congress that codified in part and abrogated in part the holding in *Price Waterhouse*, see §§2000e-2(m), 2000e-5(g)(2)(B). The question the Court must answer here is whether that lessened causation standard is applicable to claims of unlawful employer retaliation under §2000e-3(a).

[The Court then cited *Gross v. FBL Financial Services, Inc.*, reproduced at p. 82, as concluding] that the ADEA requires proof that the prohibited criterion was the but-for cause of the prohibited conduct. The holding and analysis of that decision are instructive here.

I

Petitioner, the University of Texas Southwestern Medical Center (University), is an academic institution within the University of Texas system [which] has affiliated itself with a number of healthcare facilities including, as relevant in this case, Parkland Memorial Hospital (Hospital). [T]he Hospital permits the University's students to gain clinical experience working in its facilities. The agreement also requires the Hospital to offer empty staff physician posts to the University's faculty members, and, accordingly, most of the staff physician positions at the Hospital are filled by those faculty members.

Respondent is a medical doctor of Middle Eastern descent who specializes in internal medicine and infectious diseases [who was both an assistant professor at the University and a physician at the Hospital].

In 2004, Dr. Beth Levine was hired as the University's Chief of Infectious Disease Medicine. In that position Levine became respondent's ultimate (though not direct) superior. Respondent alleged that Levine was biased against him on account of his religion and ethnic heritage, a bias manifested by undeserved scrutiny of his billing practices and productivity, as well as comments that "'Middle Easterners are lazy.'" On different occasions during his employment, respondent met with Dr. Gregory Fitz, the University's Chair of Internal Medicine and Levine's supervisor, to complain about Levine's alleged harassment. Despite obtaining a promotion with Levine's assistance in 2006, respondent continued to believe that she was biased against him. So he tried to arrange to continue working at the Hospital without also being on the University's faculty. After preliminary negotiations with the Hospital suggested this might be possible, respondent resigned his teaching post in July 2006 and sent a letter to Dr. Fitz (among others), in which he stated that the reason for his departure was harassment by Levine. That harassment, he asserted, "'stems from . . . religious, racial and cultural bias against Arabs and Muslims.'" After reading that letter, Dr. Fitz expressed consternation at respondent's accusations, saying that Levine had been "publicly humiliated by th[e] letter" and that it was "very important that she be publicly exonerated."

Meanwhile, the Hospital had offered respondent a job as a staff physician, as it had indicated it would. On learning of that offer, Dr. Fitz protested to the Hospital, asserting that the offer was inconsistent with the affiliation agreement's requirement that all staff physicians also be members of the University faculty. The Hospital then withdrew its offer.

[Nassar sued claiming both status-based discrimination and retaliation and won a jury verdict on both claims. The Fifth Circuit vacated his discrimination verdict because of insufficient evidence to support constructive discharge, but it affirmed as to the finding of retaliation for Dr. Fitz's efforts to prevent the University from hiring him because retaliation claims] require only a showing that retaliation was a motivating factor for the adverse employment action, rather than its but-for cause. It further held that the evidence supported a finding that Dr. Fitz was motivated, at least in part, to retaliate against respondent for his complaints against Levine. . . .

II

A

This case requires the Court to define the proper standard of causation for Title VII retaliation claims. Causation in fact—i.e., proof that the defendant's conduct did in fact cause the plaintiff's injury—is a standard requirement of any tort claim, see Restatement of Torts §9 (1934) (definition of "legal cause"); §431, Comment a (same); §279, and Comment c (intentional infliction of physical harm); §280 (other intentional torts); §281(c) (negligence). This includes federal statutory claims of workplace discrimination. *Hazen Paper Co. v. Biggins* [reproduced at p. 10].

In the usual course, this standard requires the plaintiff to show "that the harm would not have occurred" in the absence of—that is, but for—the defendant's conduct. Restatement of Torts §431, Comment a (negligence); §432(1), and Comment a (same); see §279, and Comment c (intentional infliction of bodily harm); §280 (other intentional torts); Restatement (Third) of Torts: Liability for Physical and Emotional Harm §27, and Comment b (2010) (noting the existence of an exception for cases where an injured party can prove the existence of multiple, independently sufficient factual causes, but observing that "cases invoking the concept are rare"). See also Restatement (Second) of Torts §432(1) (1963 and 1964) (negligence claims); §870, Comment l (intentional injury to another); cf. §435A, and Comment a (legal cause for intentional harm). It is thus textbook tort law that an action "is not regarded as a cause of an event if the particular event would have occurred without it." W. Keeton, D. Dobbs, R. Keeton & D. Owen, Prosser and Keeton on Law of Torts 265 (5th ed. 1984). This, then, is the background against which Congress legislated in enacting Title VII, and these are the default rules it is presumed to have incorporated, absent an indication to the contrary in the statute itself.

B

Since the statute's passage in 1964, it has prohibited employers from discriminating against their employees on any of seven specified criteria. Five of them—race, color, religion, sex, and national origin—are personal characteristics and are set forth in §2000e-2. (As noted at the outset, discrimination based on these five characteristics is called status-based discrimination in this opinion.) And then there is a point of great import for this case: The two remaining categories of wrongful employer conduct— the employee's opposition to employment discrimination, and the employee's submission of or support for a complaint that alleges employment discrimination—are not wrongs based on personal traits but rather types of protected employee conduct. These latter two categories are covered by a separate, subsequent section of Title VII, §2000e-3(a).

[The Court traced the history of §2000e-2(m) in the 1991 Civil Rights Act, which it described as a "lessened-causation" standard.] So, in short, the 1991 Act substituted a new burden-shifting framework for the one endorsed by *Price Waterhouse*. Under that new regime, a plaintiff could obtain declaratory relief, attorney's fees and costs, and some forms of injunctive relief based solely on proof that race, color, religion, sex, or nationality was a motivating factor in the employment action; but the employer's proof that it would still have taken the same employment action would save it from monetary damages and a reinstatement order. See *Gross*.

[The Court then reviewed its decision in *Gross*, "[c]oncentrating first and foremost" on that opinion's reading of "*because of*" to indicate "but-for" causation. *Gross* declined to adopt the interpretation endorsed by the plurality and concurring opinions in *Price Waterhouse*. It] holds two insights for the present case. The first is textual and concerns the proper interpretation of the term "because" as it relates to the principles of causation underlying both §623(a) and §2000e-3(a). The second is the significance of Congress' structural choices in both Title VII itself and the law's 1991 amendments. These principles do not decide the present case but do inform its analysis, for the issues possess significant parallels.

III

A

[Section 704(a)], like the statute at issue in *Gross*, makes it unlawful for an employer to take adverse employment action against an employee "because" of certain criteria. Given the lack of any meaningful textual difference between the text in this statute and the one in *Gross*, the proper conclusion here, as in *Gross*, is that Title VII retaliation claims require proof that the desire to retaliate was the but-for cause of the challenged employment action.

The principal counterargument offered by respondent and the United States relies on their different understanding of the motivating-factor section, which—on its face—applies only to status discrimination, discrimination on the basis of race, color, religion, sex, and national origin. In substance, they contend that: (1) retaliation is defined by the statute to be an unlawful employment practice; (2) §2000e-2(m) allows unlawful employment practices to be proved based on a showing that race, color, religion, sex, or national origin was a motivating factor for—and not necessarily the but-for factor in—the challenged employment action; and (3) the Court has, as a matter of course, held that "retaliation for complaining about race discrimination is 'discrimination based on race.'"

There are three main flaws in this reading of §2000e-2(m). The first is that it is inconsistent with the provision's plain language. It must be acknowledged that because Title VII defines "unlawful employment practice" to include retaliation, the question presented by this case would be different if §2000e-2(m) extended its coverage to all unlawful employment practices. As actually written, however, the text of the motivating-factor provision, while it begins by referring to "unlawful employment practices," then proceeds to address only five of the seven prohibited discriminatory actions—actions based on the employee's status, i.e., race, color, religion, sex, and national origin. This indicates Congress' intent to confine that provision's coverage to only those types of employment practices. The text of

§2000e-2(m) says nothing about retaliation claims. Given this clear language, it would be improper to conclude that what Congress omitted from the statute is nevertheless within its scope.

The second problem with this reading is its inconsistency with the design and structure of the statute as a whole. See *Gross*. Just as Congress' choice of words is presumed to be deliberate, so too are its structural choices. When Congress wrote the motivating-factor provision in 1991, it chose to insert it as a subsection within §2000e-2, which contains Title VII's ban on status-based discrimination, and says nothing about retaliation. . . .

The third problem with respondent's and the Government's reading of the motivating-factor standard is in its submission that this Court's decisions interpreting federal antidiscrimination law have, as a general matter, treated bans on status-based discrimination as also prohibiting retaliation. [These include *CBOCS West, Inc. v. Humphries*, 553 U.S. 442, 452-53 (2008), which held] that 42 U.S.C. §1981—which declares that all persons "shall have the same right . . . to make and enforce contracts . . . as is enjoyed by white citizens"—prohibits not only racial discrimination but also retaliation against those who oppose it. And in *Gómez-Pérez v. Potter*, 553 U.S. 474 (2008), the Court likewise read a bar on retaliation into the broad wording of the federal-employee provisions of the ADEA. See also *Jackson v. Birmingham Bd. of Ed.*, 544 U.S. 167, 173, 179 (2005) (20 U.S.C. §1681(a) (Title IX)); *Sullivan v. Little Hunting Park, Inc.*, 396 U.S. 229, 235, n.3, 237 (1969) (42 U.S.C. §1982).

These decisions are not controlling here. It is true these cases do state the general proposition that Congress' enactment of a broadly phrased antidiscrimination statute may signal a concomitant intent to ban retaliation against individuals who oppose that discrimination, even where the statute does not refer to retaliation in so many words. What those cases do not support, however, is the quite different rule that every reference to race, color, creed, sex, or nationality in an antidiscrimination statute is to be treated as a synonym for "retaliation." For one thing, §2000e-2(m) is not itself a substantive bar on discrimination. Rather, it is a rule that establishes the causation standard for proving a violation defined elsewhere in Title VII. The cases cited by respondent and the Government do not address rules of this sort, and those precedents are of limited relevance here.

The approach respondent and the Government suggest is inappropriate in the context of a statute as precise, complex, and exhaustive as Title VII. As noted, the laws at issue in *CBOCS*, *Jackson*, and *Gómez-Pérez* were broad, general bars on discrimination. In interpreting them the Court concluded that by using capacious language Congress expressed the intent to bar retaliation in addition to status-based discrimination. See *Gómez-Pérez*. In other words, when Congress' treatment of the subject of prohibited discrimination was both broad and brief, its omission of any specific discussion of retaliation was unremarkable.

If Title VII had likewise been phrased in broad and general terms, respondent's argument might have more force. But that is not how Title VII was written, which makes it incorrect to infer that Congress meant anything other than what the text does say on the subject of retaliation. . . .

This fundamental difference in statutory structure renders inapposite decisions which treated retaliation as an implicit corollary of status-based discrimination.

Text may not be divorced from context. In light of Congress' special care in drawing so precise a statutory scheme, it would be improper to indulge respondent's suggestion that Congress meant to incorporate the default rules that apply only when Congress writes a broad and undifferentiated statute. . . .

B

The proper interpretation and implementation of §2000e-3(a) and its causation standard have central importance to the fair and responsible allocation of resources in the judicial and litigation systems. This is of particular significance because claims of retaliation are being made with ever-increasing frequency. . . .

In addition lessening the causation standard could also contribute to the filing of frivolous claims, which would siphon resources from efforts by employer, administrative agencies, and courts to combat workplace harassment. Consider in this regard the case of an employee who knows that he or she is about to be fired for poor performance, given a lower pay grade, or even just transferred to a different assignment or location. To forestall that lawful action, he or she might be tempted to make an unfounded charge of racial, sexual, or religious discrimination; then, when the unrelated employment action comes, the employee could allege that it is retaliation. If respondent were to prevail in his argument here, that claim could be established by a lessened causation standard, all in order to prevent the undesired change in employment circumstances. Even if the employer could escape judgment after trial, the lessened causation standard would make it far more difficult to dismiss dubious claims at the summary judgment stage. Cf. *Vance v. Ball State Univ.* [reproduced at p. 345]. It would be inconsistent with the structure and operation of Title VII to so raise the costs, both financial and reputational, on an employer whose actions were not in fact the result of any discriminatory or retaliatory intent. Yet there would be a significant risk of that consequence if respondent's position were adopted here.

The facts of this case also demonstrate the legal and factual distinctions between status-based and retaliation claims, as well as the importance of the correct standard of proof. Respondent raised both claims in the District Court. The alleged wrongdoer differed in each: In respondent's status-based discrimination claim, it was his indirect supervisor, Dr. Levine. In his retaliation claim, it was the Chair of Internal Medicine, Dr. Fitz. The proof required for each claim differed, too. For the status-based claim, respondent was required to show instances of racial slurs, disparate treatment, and other indications of nationality-driven animus by Dr. Levine. Respondent's retaliation claim, by contrast, relied on the theory that Dr. Fitz was committed to exonerating Dr. Levine and wished to punish respondent for besmirching her reputation. Separately instructed on each type of claim, the jury returned a separate verdict for each, albeit with a single damages award. And the Court of Appeals treated each claim separately, too, finding insufficient evidence on the claim of status-based discrimination.

If it were proper to apply the motivating-factor standard to respondent's retaliation claim, the University might well be subject to liability on account of Dr. Fitz's alleged desire to exonerate Dr. Levine, even if it could also be shown that the terms of the affiliation agreement precluded the Hospital's hiring of respondent and that the University would have sought to prevent respondent's hiring in order to honor that agreement in any event. That result would be inconsistent with both the text and purpose of Title VII.

[Based on the textual and structural indications, the Court concludes that] Title VII retaliation claims must be proved according to traditional principles of but-for causation, not the lessened causation test stated in §2000e-2(m). This requires proof that the unlawful retaliation would not have occurred in the absence of the alleged wrongful action or actions of the employer.

IV

[The majority rejected arguments for *Skidmore v. Swift & Co.*, 323 U.S. 134 (1944), deference to the EEOC's guidance manual, which endorsed a motivating factor analysis. Since *Skidmore* deference depends on the "persuasive force" of the agency interpretation, it was unavailable when the EEOC's rationale was unconvincing.]

Respondent's final argument . . . is that even if §2000e-2(m) does not control the outcome in this case, the standard applied by *Price Waterhouse* should control instead. That assertion is incorrect. First, this position is foreclosed by the 1991 Act's amendments to Title VII. . . . Given the careful balance of lessened causation and reduced remedies Congress struck in the 1991 Act, there is no reason to think that the different balance articulated by *Price Waterhouse* somehow survived that legislation's passage. Second, even if this argument were still available, it would be inconsistent with the *Gross* Court's reading (and the plain textual meaning) of the word "because" as it appears in both §623(a) and §2000e-3(a). For these reasons, the rule of *Price Waterhouse* is not controlling here. . . .

Justice GINSBURG, with whom Justice BREYER, Justice SOTOMAYOR, and Justice KAGAN join, dissenting.

. . . In so reining in retaliation claims, the Court misapprehends what our decisions teach: Retaliation for complaining about discrimination is tightly bonded to the core prohibition and cannot be disassociated from it. Indeed, this Court has explained again and again that "retaliation in response to a complaint about [proscribed] discrimination is discrimination" on the basis of the characteristic Congress sought to immunize against adverse employment action. *Jackson v. Birmingham Bd. of Ed.*

The Court shows little regard for the trial judges who will be obliged to charge discrete causation standards when a claim of discrimination "because of," e.g., race is coupled with a claim of discrimination "because" the individual has complained of race discrimination. And jurors will puzzle over the rhyme or reason for the dual standards. Of graver concern, the Court has seized on a provision, §2000e-2(m), adopted by Congress as part of an endeavor to strengthen Title VII, and turned it into a measure reducing the force of the ban on retaliation. . . .

II

This Court has long acknowledged the symbiotic relationship between proscriptions on discrimination and proscriptions on retaliation. . . .

Adverting to the close connection between discrimination and retaliation for complaining about discrimination, this Court has held, in a line of decisions unbroken until today, that a ban on discrimination encompasses retaliation. . . . There is no sound reason in this case to stray from the decisions in *Sullivan*, *Jackson*, *Gómez-Pérez*, and *CBOCS West*.

III . . .

[The dissent reviewed the history of §703(m), and then went on to argue that there] is scant reason to think that, despite Congress' aim to "restore and strengthen . . . laws that ban discrimination in employment," Congress meant to exclude retaliation claims from the newly enacted "motivating factor" provision. Section 2000e-2(m) provides that an "unlawful employment practice is established" when the plaintiff shows that a protected characteristic was a factor driving "any employment practice."

Title VII, in §2000e-3(a), explicitly denominates retaliation, like status-based discrimination, an "unlawful employment practice." Because "any employment practice" necessarily encompasses practices prohibited under §2000e-3(a), §2000e-2(m), by its plain terms, covers retaliation.

Notably, when it enacted §2000e-2(m), Congress did not tie the new provision specifically to §§2000e-2(a)-(d), which proscribes discrimination "because of" race, color, religion, gender, or national origin. Rather, Congress added an entirely new provision to codify the causation standard, one encompassing "any employment practice." §2000e-2(m).

Also telling, §2000e-2(m) is not limited to situations in which the complainant's race, color, religion, sex, or national origin motivates the employer's action. In contrast, Title VII's substantive antidiscrimination provisions refer to the protected characteristics of the complaining party. Congress thus knew how to limit Title VII's coverage to victims of status-based discrimination when it was so minded. It chose, instead, to bring within §2000e-2(m) "any employment practice." To cut out retaliation from §2000e-2(m)'s scope, one must be blind to that choice.

[The dissent also urged deference to the EEOC's position on the question under *Skidmore v. Swift & Co.*, 323 U.S. 134, 140 (1944).] If the breadth of §2000e-2(m) can be deemed ambiguous (although I believe its meaning is plain), the provision should be construed to accord with the EEOC's well-reasoned and longstanding guidance.

IV

The Court draws the opposite conclusion, ruling that retaliation falls outside the scope of §2000e-2(m). In so holding, the Court ascribes to Congress the unlikely purpose of separating retaliation claims from discrimination claims, thereby undermining the Legislature's effort to fortify the protections of Title VII. None of the reasons the Court offers in support of its restrictive interpretation of §2000e-2(m) survives inspection.

A

[The Court acknowledges that "the text of the motivating-factor provision . . . begins by referring to unlawful employment practices, a term that undeniably includes retaliation." While the text goes on to reference as motivating factors only the status-based consideration, the Court errs in viewing retaliation as a protected activity entirely discrete from status-based discrimination. This vision] of retaliation as a separate concept runs up against precedent. Until today, the Court has been clear eyed on just what retaliation is: a manifestation of status-based discrimination. As *Jackson* explained in the context of sex discrimination, "retaliation is discrimination 'on the basis of sex' because it is an intentional response to the nature of the complaint: an allegation of sex discrimination."

[The dissent criticized the majority's distinction of *Jackson* and other cases as not involving "a detailed statutory scheme." It] is strange logic indeed to conclude that when Congress homed in on retaliation and codified the proscription, as it did in Title VII, Congress meant protection against that unlawful employment practice to have less force than the protection available when the statute does not mention retaliation. It is hardly surprising, then, that our jurisprudence does not support the Court's conclusion. . . .

V . . .

The Court's decision to construe §2000e-3(a) to require but-for causation in line with *Gross* is even more confounding in light of *Price Waterhouse*. . . . It is wrong to revert to *Price Waterhouse*, the Court says, because the 1991 Civil Rights Act's amendments to Title VII abrogated that decision.

This conclusion defies logic. . . . Shut from the Court's sight is a legislative record replete with statements evincing Congress' intent to strengthen antidiscrimination laws and thereby hold employers accountable for prohibited discrimination. It is an odd mode of statutory interpretation that divines Congress' aim in 1991 by looking to a decision of this Court, *Gross*, made under a different statute in 2008, while ignoring the overarching purpose of the Congress that enacted the 1991 Civil Rights Act. . . .

VI

A

The Court's assertion that the but-for cause requirement it adopts necessarily follows from §2000e-3(a)'s use of the word "because" fails to convince. Contrary to the Court's suggestion, the word "because" does not inevitably demand but-for causation to the exclusion of all other causation formulations. When more than one factor contributes to a plaintiff's injury, but-for causation is problematic. See, e.g., 1 Restatement (Third) of Torts §27, Comment a, p. 385 (2005) (noting near universal agreement that the but-for standard is inappropriate when multiple sufficient causes exist) (hereinafter Restatement Third); Restatement of Torts §9, Comment b, p. 18 (1934) (legal cause is a cause that is a "substantial factor in bringing about the harm").

When an event is "overdetermined," i.e., when two forces create an injury each alone would be sufficient to cause, modern tort law permits the plaintiff to prevail upon showing that either sufficient condition created the harm. Restatement Third §27, at 376-377. In contrast, under the Court's approach (which it erroneously calls "textbook tort law"), a Title VII plaintiff alleging retaliation cannot establish liability if her firing was prompted by both legitimate and illegitimate factors.

Today's opinion rehashes arguments rightly rejected in *Price Waterhouse*. . . .

NOTES

1. *Two Insights and a Default Principle.* Although the *Nassar* Court stated that *Gross* did "not decide the present case," the "insights" of the earlier opinion came close to doing so: first, its reading of "because" seems to set the default principle for other statutes; second, "Congress' structural choices in both Title VII itself and the law's 1991 amendments" are significant. Needless to say, both "insights" cut strongly against motivating factor causation for §704(a) cases since that provision used the word "because" and §703(m) does not explicitly refer to retaliation. *See generally* Michael J. Zimmer, *Hiding the Statute in Plain View*: University of Texas Southwestern Medical Center v. Nassar, 14 NEV. L.J. 705 (2014).

2. *Retaliation Is Discrimination?* The path to avoiding this result, of course, was prior case law that had treated a ban on discrimination as necessarily including a ban on retaliation for opposing such discrimination. E.g., *CBOCS West, Inc. v. Humphries*, 553 U.S. 442 (2008). Are you persuaded by the Court's effort to distinguish them—that the earlier cases show that "a broadly phrased antidiscrimination

statute may signal a concomitant intent to ban retaliation" but that such an inference should not be drawn in a more detailed statute? What's the relevance of the fact that "§2000e-2(m) is not itself a substantive bar on discrimination. Rather, it is a rule that establishes the causation standard for proving a violation defined elsewhere in Title VII." And does that single sentence put to rest the dispute in the lower courts as to whether there is a single claim of discrimination? See pp. 78–79, Notes 11 and 14.

3. *Employees Gaming the System.* Although the Court's opinion seems to reach its result without relying on policy considerations, Part IIB stresses both the large number of retaliation claims and the risks of employees filing charges in order to "forestall" an employer's lawful adverse action. While this is a logical possibility, do you think it's a serious problem? Even if so, should the majority have been concerned, given proof problems, about the "false negatives" a stricter standard of causation will produce even when retaliation is the but-for cause of an adverse action? Is that what the Ginsburg dissent was saying? *See generally* Sandra F. Sperino & Suja A. Thomas, *Fakers and Floodgates*, 10 Stan. J. C.R. & C.L. 223 (2014) (finding no evidence of a significant number of spurious retaliation claims). *See also* Kerri Lynn Stone, *Reality's Bite*, 28 J. Civ. Rts. & Econ. Dev. 227 (2015). *But see* David Sherwyn, Michael Heise & Zev J. Eigen, *Experimental Evidence That Retaliation Claims Are Unlike Other Employment Discrimination Claims*, 44 Seton Hall L. Rev. 455 (2014) (justifying a stricter standard of proof for retaliation claims in part to encourage employers to try to assist struggling workers by reducing the risk of a successful retaliation suit).

4. *What About §706(g)?* In one passage, the majority suggests that applying the motivating factor standard to Dr. Nassar's retaliation claim might well subject the university to liability because of Dr. Fitz's desire to exonerate Dr. Levine, even if the affiliation agreement would have led to the university to prevent the hospital's hiring of Dr. Nassar in any event. It goes on: "That result would be inconsistent with both the text and purpose of Title VII." But is it? The university would be liable but, given the same decision defense, would not be subject to damages in this scenario. What's inconsistent with a declaratory judgment or even an injunction relating to the retaliation?

5. *Really?* The Court rejected the argument that, even if §703(m) did not govern this case, *Price Waterhouse* should control. Its basic response was that the 1991 Act's amendments displaced the *Price Waterhouse* burden-shifting framework: But, as the dissent stressed, Congress intended to give burden shifting *more* bite in the 1991 Amendments. How could the Court have read them to implicitly cut back on the preexisting regime? *See generally* Stephen M. Rich, *A Matter of Perspective: Textualism, Stare Decisis, and Federal Employment Discrimination Law*, 87 S. Cal. L. Rev. 1197, 1199 (2014).

6. *But-for Does Not Mean Sole Cause.* While *Nassar* undoubtedly increased plaintiff's burden, it did not render such cases impossible to prove. *Kwan v. Andalex Grp. LLC*, 737 F.3d 834 (2d Cir. 2013), stressed that "'but-for' causation does not require proof that retaliation was the only cause of the employer's action, but only that the adverse action would not have occurred in the absence of the retaliatory motive." That is because traditional tort principles establish that "a plaintiff's injury can have multiple 'but-for' causes, each one of which may be sufficient to support liability." *Id.* at 834 n.5, citing, inter alia, Fowler V. Harper et al., 4 Harper, James and Gray on Torts §20.2, at 100101 (3d ed. 2007). To that end, some courts have held that, "at the prima facie stage, a plaintiff need only proffer evidence sufficient to raise the inference that her engagement in a protected activity was the *likely reason* for the adverse employment action, not the but-for reason." *Carvalho-Grevious v. Del. State Univ.*, 851 F.3d 249, 253 (3d Cir. 2017); *accord Foster v. Univ. of Md.-E. Shore*, 787 F.3d 243

(4th Cir. 2015); *contra EEOC v. Ford Motor Co.*, 782 F.3d 753, 770 (6th Cir. 2015) (en banc); *Ward v. Jewell*, 772 F.3d 1199, 1203 (10th Cir. 2014).

7. Gross/Nassar *and Other Antidiscrimination Statutes. Desert Palace* and *Gross* create separate analytic regimes for Title VII and the ADEA, and *Nassar* holds that even Title VII does not have a single motivating factor standard. But what about other laws? It seems likely that *Gross/Nassar* pose a real obstacle for any lesser causation standard. *See Palmquist v. Shinseki*, 689 F.3d 66, 73-74 (1st Cir. 2012) (but-for causation applies to cases brought under the Rehabilitation Act). *But see Ford v. Mabus*, 629 F.3d 198 (D.C. Cir. 2010) (in a federal employee suit under ADEA §633a, plaintiffs need show only that age was a factor in the employer's decision in order to prevail as to liability). *See generally* Lawrence D. Rosenthal, *A Lack of "Motivation," or Sound Legal Reasoning? Why Most Courts Are Not Applying Either* Price Waterhouse's *or the* 1991 Civil Rights Act's *Motivating-Factor Analysis to Title VII Retaliation Claims in a Post-*Gross *World*, 64 ALA. L. REV. 1067 (2013).

However, some have argued that *Gross/Nassar* do not apply to ADA cases because that statute incorporates Title VII procedures and remedies by reference. *See* Melissa Hart, *Procedural Extremism: The Supreme Court's 2008-2009 Employment and Labor Cases*, 13 EMP. RTS. & EMP. POL'Y J. 253 (2009). *See also* Catherine T. Struve, *Shifting Burdens: Discrimination Law Through the Lens of Jury Instruction*, 51 BC L. REV. 279 (2010). There is also legislative history of the Civil Rights Act of 1991 to this effect: "Similarly, mixed motive cases involving disability under the ADA should be interpreted consistent with the prohibition against all intentional discrimination in Section 5 of this Act." H.R. Rep. No. 102-40 (II), at 4, 1991 U.S.C.C.A.N. 694, 697 (1991). But the first circuits to decide the issue held otherwise. *E.g., Gentry v. E.W. Partners Club Mgmt. Co.*, 816 F.3d 228 (4th Cir. 2016); *Lewis v. Humboldt Acquisition Corp.*, 681 F.3d 312 (6th Cir. 2012).

8. *Cat's Paws.* We have seen that a retaliation claim requires proof of protected conduct, an adverse action, and a causal link between the two. Some courts also add a fourth requirement, employer knowledge of the employee's protected activity. *See, e.g., Gordon v. New York City Bd. of Educ.*, 232 F.3d 111 (2d Cir. 2000). Others consider employer knowledge as embraced within the causation element. Either way, knowledge seems necessary, a point that *Breeden* made clear. In some retaliation cases, however, the knowledge requirement may be satisfied by application of the cat's paw doctrine, discussed at p. 50. *E.g., Fisher v. Lufkin Indus.*, 847 F.3d 752 (5th Cir. 2017) (a supervisor and co-worker's triggering an investigation of plaintiff out of retaliatory animus was the proximate cause of his dismissal; plaintiff's mild failure to cooperate in the investigation was not a sufficient superseding cause); *Zamora v. City of Houston*, 798 F.3d 326 (5th Cir. 2015); *EEOC v. New Breed Logistics*, 783 F.3d 1057 (6th Cir. 2015).

9. *Temporal Proximity.* Plaintiffs often rely on timing as evidence of causation. When an adverse action follows closely on the heels of protected conduct, it is not a difficult inferential leap to conclude that one may have been caused by the other — at least for purposes of a prima facie case. But how close in time must the adverse act and the protected conduct be? *Breeden* might be read to hold that the plaintiff always loses on a summary judgment motion where the employer has denied retaliation and the plaintiff's only evidence of causation is that the adverse employment action occurred three months or more after the decisionmaker learned of the protected activity. A closer temporal connection, however, will often suffice, at least for a prima facie case. *Kacian v. Postmaster Gen. of the United States*, 653 F. App'x 125, 128-29 (3d Cir. 2016) (sufficient evidence of a causal connection when plaintiff was fired within

a week of her protected conduct and there as evidence of employer antagonism after her complaint); *Wilson v. Ark. Dep't of Human Servs.*, 850 F.3d 368 (8th Cir. 2017) (2-1) (plaintiff properly pleaded retaliation when she alleged a short, six-week period between her charge and her termination; while her allegations may have been consistent with poor performance, they were not an "obvious alternative explanation" that rendered her claim implausible); *Littlejohn v. City of N.Y.*, 795 F.3d 297, 319-20 (2d Cir. 2015) (plaintiff's allegations that her demotion occurred "within days after her complaints of discrimination are sufficient to plausibly support an indirect inference of causation"). However, longer time periods may not suffice even for a prima facie case, and, of course, mere proximity in time will not suffice to meet the but-for causation standard at summary judgment. *Bird v. W. Valley City*, 832 F.3d 1188, 1204 (10th Cir. 2016) ("even though the timing leading up to an employee's termination is evidence of pretext, . . . it is not sufficient standing alone to establish pretext. Our cases regarding Title VII retaliation claims make this point clear."); *Abrams v. Dep't of Pub. Safety*, 764 F.3d 244, 254 (2d Cir. 2014) ("Though five months might be enough to establish a prima facie case, temporal proximity alone is not enough to establish pretext in this Circuit"). *See generally* Troy B. Daniels & Richard A. Bales, *Plus at Pretext: Resolving the Split Regarding the Sufficiency of Temporal Proximity Evidence in Title VII Retaliation Cases*, 44 Gonz. L. Rev. 493 (2008/2009).

10. *Back to Direct Evidence*. Although it remains possible to win a retaliation case by circumstantial evidence, "direct evidence" became more important after *Nassar*. While it will not shift a burden of persuasion, it can be very persuasive in carrying plaintiff's burden to establish but-for causation. *Compare Lors v. Dean*, 746 F.3d 857 (8th Cir. 2014) (summary judgment on ADA retaliation claim granted when there was only temporal proximity of discharge during appeal of a challenge to a transfer; "team leader's" statements indicating retaliatory intent were not made by decision-maker; and discharge letter, albeit referring to his continuing challenge to the transfer, specifically disclaimed retaliatory intent), *with Willis v. Cleco Corp.*, 749 F.3d 314, 323 (5th Cir. 2014) (overturning summary judgment on retaliation claim of an HR representative for reporting racially hostile statements in light of affidavit stating that the HR general manager stated that he was "very pissed" with Willis for reporting the conversation with Cooper and that "[i]f we have to find a reason, Ed [Taylor] and I have decided; we are going to terminate that nigger Greg Willis for reporting me and trying to burn my ass").

11. *Employer Mistake*. What happens if an employer mistakenly believes an employee has engaged in protected conduct and demotes the employee based on the mistaken belief? The Supreme Court faced this question in a case involving a First Amendment claim, holding that it is the employer's motive that matters; thus a claim is stated even if the employee had not actually engaged in conduct protected by the First Amendment. *Heffernan v. City of Paterson*, 136 S. Ct. 1412 (2016). Whether this reasoning will be imported into retaliation claims under Title VII and other employment discrimination statutes remains to be seen.

Chapter 7

Disability Discrimination

A. INTRODUCTION

The Americans with Disabilities Act of 1990 is a sweeping statute that prohibits discrimination against persons with disabilities in a variety of contexts, including public accommodations and services by state and local governments. We will mostly be concerned with Title I, 42 U.S.C. §§12111-12117 (2018), which covers most employment agencies, labor organizations, and employers, including state and local governments since employment claims against state and local governments likely cannot be pursued under Title II. *See, e.g., Brumfield v. City of Chicago*, 735 F.3d 619 (7th Cir. 2013) (employment discrimination can be challenged only under Title I, not Title II, of the ADA); *contra Bledsoe v. Palm Beach Cty. Soil & Water Conservation Dist.*, 133 F.3d 816 (11th Cir. 1998).

Although the ADA as originally enacted was hailed as a dramatic change in the nation's approach to disability, a number of restrictive court interpretations, especially in deciding who counted as disabled, cut back on that promise. That led Congress in 2008 to enact the Americans with Disabilities Amendments Act (ADAAA), Pub. L. No. 110-325, 122 Stat. 3553. Even before the original ADA, the Rehabilitation Act of 1973, 29 U.S.C. §§701 et seq. (2018), barred disability discrimination in most federal employment and by those doing business with the federal government or receiving financial assistance from it. That Act continues to govern in those settings although it is largely aligned with the ADA substantively.

The statutory scheme for protecting individuals with disabilities from discrimination in employment is somewhat more complicated than the other antidiscrimination statutes. Prohibiting discrimination because of disability poses difficult legal problems, largely because disabilities are sometimes relevant to an individual's ability to work. Some disabilities deprive people of the physical and/or mental prerequisites to perform essential job functions. Prohibiting disability-based "discrimination" against such individuals would unduly interfere with employers' ability to select a qualified work force. Other disabled individuals may be qualified to work but only if employers accommodate their disability in some way. These individuals, unlike most other statutorily protected groups, require some form of special treatment in order to enjoy equal access to employment opportunities and benefits.

The ADA seeks to deal with these problems in two separate ways. First, the statute protects only an individual with a disability who is *qualified*, which means that employers are permitted to engage in disparate treatment when the disabled employee is unable to perform the essential functions of the job with or without reasonable accommodation. In addition, employers are free to use qualification standards that screen out disabled individuals if those qualifications are job related and consistent with business necessity.

Counterbalancing this, disabled individuals have rights beyond those guaranteed to most other groups protected by antidiscrimination legislation. The centerpiece of disability discrimination law is the employer's affirmative duty to provide reasonable accommodation (short of "undue hardship") to ensure that individuals with disabilities secure equal employment opportunities and benefits. The focus of the duty to accommodate is on equal employment opportunity, rather than on equal treatment.

As a result, employers are legally obligated to treat covered employees equally or differently depending on the circumstances — employers *must treat individuals with disabilities equally* if they are qualified and their disabilities do not require accommodation; employers are *permitted to treat such individuals differently* if their disabilities cannot be accommodated; and employers *are required to treat such individuals differently* if reasonable accommodations are necessary to ensure equal employment opportunity and benefits.

The chapter will proceed as follows: Section B focuses on the threshold question of what constitutes a "disability" under the ADA; Section C then turns to what makes a disabled individual "qualified," in the process exploring the concepts of "essential function," "reasonable accommodation," and "undue hardship"; Section D examines discriminatory qualification standards, including the provision that permits employers to discriminate against employees who pose a "direct threat" to health or safety; and Section E addresses special problems under the ADA, including coverage for individuals addicted to drugs or alcohol, medical examinations and inquiries, retaliation, harassment, relationships with covered individuals, and rights under the Family and Medical Leave Act.

B. THE MEANING OF "DISABILITY"

In contrast to other statutes prohibiting discrimination in employment, establishing membership in the ADA's protected classification was often difficult under the original ADA and still requires attention under the ADAAA. Section 12103(1) defined "disability" as

    (A) a physical or mental *impairment* that *substantially limits* one or more of the *major life activities* of . . . [an] individual;

    (B) a record of such an impairment; or

    (C) being regarded as having such an impairment. . . .

(emphasis added). Defining the italicized terms is critical to defining protected individuals. However, other sections expressly exclude certain conditions from this definition. Many of these are sex-related, such as homosexuality, bisexuality, transvestism, transsexualism, pedophilia, exhibitionism, voyeurism, "gender identity disorders not resulting from physical impairments," and other sexual behavior disorders, but also excluded are compulsive gambling, kleptomania, pyromania, and disorders resulting from the current illegal use of psychoactive drugs. §§12208, 12211.

Subsection (A) deals with an actual, present disability, and the ADAAA made several modifications in the statute to overturn judicial decisions that Congress viewed as imposing too high a standard for this threshold requirement. Subsection (B) extends protection to those with a "record" of such a disability. Even if a person does not currently have such an impairment or was previously misclassified as having such an impairment, he is within the definition if he has a record of such an impairment. The final method of establishing a "disability" is in subsection (C) — that the employer "regarded" the individual as having a disability, and it is here that the ADAAA made a second major change. Contrary to prior law, an individual is regarded as having such an impairment when she has been subjected to an adverse action "because of an actual or perceived physical or mental impairment *whether or not* the impairment limits or is perceived to limit a major life activity." §12102(3)(A) (emphasis added). While there is an exception for "transitory and minor" impairments, §12102(3)(B), this change is highly significant since it obviates the need for a plaintiff to show that her impairment substantially limited a major life activity. All she need show is that her employer took a prohibited action because of the impairment, actual or perceived.

This change worked by the ADAAA essentially creates a two-tier liability structure. Individuals with actual disabilities must show substantial limitation in a major life activity but thereby become entitled to reasonable accommodations. In contrast, individuals who are merely regarded as disabled need not make such a showing, but the statute expressly provides that they are *not* entitled to reasonable accommodations. §12201(h). For that reason, it seems likely that most claims of plain vanilla discrimination — those where reasonable accommodation is *not* at issue — will proceed under the "regarded as" prong since that avoids the need to analyze whether the impairment substantially limits one or more major life activities. Rather, all plaintiff must show is that an employer took a prohibited action because of the real or perceived impairment.

1.   *Actual Disability*

The Supreme Court considered the meaning of the three-pronged definition of disability for the first time in *School Board of Nassau County v. Arline*, 480 U.S. 273 (1987). Although *Arline* was a Rehabilitation Act case, the definition of "handicapped" individual (the term used at the time) was identical to the definition of individual with a disability under the original ADA. In *Arline*, the school board had fired the plaintiff, an elementary school teacher, because it believed her active tuberculosis posed a threat to the health of others. The school board claimed that a person with a contagious disease was not protected by the Rehabilitation Act if the adverse employment action was based on the employee's contagiousness and not on the condition itself. The Supreme Court refused to allow the employer to disassociate the contagious effects of the teacher's impairment from the impairment: "Arline's contagiousness and her physical impairment each resulted from the same underlying condition, tuberculosis. It would be unfair to allow an employer to seize upon the distinction between the effects of a disease on others and the effects of a disease on a patient and use that distinction to justify discriminatory intent." *Id.* at 282.

In light of *Arline*'s holding that a contagious disease can be a "disability," a person who has developed acquired immune deficiency syndrome (AIDS) is undoubtedly an "individual with a disability" under both the Rehabilitation Act and the ADA. Active AIDS clearly qualifies as a physical impairment and also substantially limits major life activities. But *Arline* left open the question of whether a person can be considered "handicapped" purely on the basis of contagiousness alone. Is a person who tests positively for the antibodies produced in reaction to HIV, the virus that causes AIDS, an "individual with a disability"? The Supreme Court addressed this issue in its first ADA case confronting the definition of disability. Although *Bragdon v. Abbott*, 524 U.S. 624 (1998), was a Title III case involving public accommodation discrimination (a dentist refused to treat plaintiff outside of a hospital setting), the definition of disability also applies to Title I, and the Court's decision that the plaintiff was within the statute was a dramatic application of the ADA.

While plaintiff's impairment in *Bragdon* was her HIV status, the issue for the Court was whether that condition substantially limited a major life activity when the infection had not yet reached the symptomatic phase. The Court held that it did, in the process laying out a three-step structure for analyzing actual disability cases:

> First, we consider whether respondent's HIV infection was a physical impairment. Second, we identify the life activity upon which respondent relies (reproduction and child bearing) and determine whether it constitutes a major life activity under the ADA. Third, tying the two statutory phrases together, we ask whether the impairment substantially limited the major life activity.

Id. at 631. The decision was "informed by interpretations of parallel definitions in [the Rehabilitation Act] and the views of various administrative agencies which have faced this interpretive question," an approach that has continued in many ADA cases. *Id.*

With respect to impairment, the Court quoted regulations identical to those adopted by the EEOC, which define "physical or mental impairment" to mean:

(A) any physiological disorder or condition, cosmetic disfigurement, or anatomical loss affecting one or more of the following body systems: neurological; musculoskeletal; special sense organs; respiratory, including speech organs; cardiovascular; reproductive, digestive, genito-urinary; hemic and lymphatic; skin; and endocrine; or

(B) any mental or psychological disorder, such as mental retardation, organic brain syndrome, emotional or mental illness, and specific learning disabilities.

In light of the science regarding its development, "HIV infection must be regarded as a physiological disorder with a constant and detrimental effect on the infected person's hemic and lymphatic systems from the moment of infection." *Id.* at 637.

But an impairment does not suffice for an actual disability unless it substantially limits a major life activity. Plaintiff claimed such a limitation in terms of her ability to reproduce and to bear children. The Court had little difficulty concluding that reproduction qualified as a major life activity since "[r]eproduction and the sexual dynamics surrounding it are central to the life process itself." *Id.* at 638. It rejected the argument that the ADA should reach "only those aspects of a person's life which have a public, economic, or daily character" as inconsistent with the statutory language and the clear thrust of the regulations. *Id.* at 638.

Finally, the Court found a substantial limitation on plaintiff's ability to reproduce both because a woman infected with HIV "imposes on the man a significant risk of becoming infected" and, because an infected woman has a significant risk of infecting her child during gestation and childbirth. *Id.* at 640. "The Act addresses substantial limitations on major life activities, not utter inabilities. Conception and childbirth are not impossible for an HIV victim but, without doubt, are dangerous to the public health. This meets the definition of a substantial limitation." *Id.* at 641.

While *Bragdon* resolved the issue of ADA coverage for *most* individuals who are infected with HIV, it left some questions unresolved. For example, what about HIV-infected plaintiffs who are unable to bear children for reasons other than their HIV infection? Or an HIV-infected woman who had her fallopian tubes tied prior to her infection? In *Blanks v. Southwestern Bell Corp.*, 310 F.3d 398 (5th Cir. 2002), the court held that an HIV-positive worker who did not intend to have more children failed to establish a disability under the ADA. But doesn't the *Bragdon* opinion support an argument that HIV infection is substantially limiting because it restricts an individual's freedom to engage in sexual intercourse, surely a major life activity? In its regulations implementing the ADAAA, the EEOC makes clear that HIV infection will substantially limit immune function, thus making HIV an actual disability. *See* 29 C.F.R. §1630.3(iii).

NOTE ON "IMPAIRMENT"

As in *Bragdon*, whether an impairment exists is often not difficult to determine. But not every physical or mental condition is an impairment. In its Interpretive Guidance on Title I, the EEOC stated that the term "physical or mental impairment" does not include physical characteristics such as weight, height, and eye color that are in the "normal" range and are not the result of a physiological disorder. The Interpretive Guidance also excludes common personality traits, illiteracy, economic disadvantages, and temporary physical conditions. Advanced age also is excluded, although physical and mental impairments associated with aging are not. *See* 29 C.F.R. pt. 1630, app. §1630.2(h), (j). Is any physical characteristic outside the normal range an "impairment"? Consider unusual strength or high intelligence. Are these impairments (because they are out of the normal range), but not disabilities (because they do not substantially impair life activities)? Or are they not impairments at all because they are out of the normal range on the "positive" rather than the "negative" side? Other impairment issues have arisen.

Pregnancy. Pregnancy shares many of the characteristics of a disability as defined by the ADA. Nonetheless, the EEOC believes that pregnancy is not a disability covered by the statute because it is not an impairment. *See* 29 C.F.R. pt. 1630, app. §1630.2(h). However, conditions resulting from pregnancy can trigger the ADA's protections, especially lifting restrictions. *Id.* The Supreme Court referred to these regulations but did not pass on their validity in *Young v. UPS*, reproduced at p. 307. *But see Serednyj v. Beverly Healthcare, LLC*, 656 F.3d 540 (7th Cir. 2011) (plaintiff's pregnancy-related complications were not a disability under the ADA because they did not substantially limit her in the major life activities of reproduction or lifting since they were of limited duration and did not result in any long-term limitations).

See generally Jeannette Cox, *Pregnancy as "Disability" and the Amended Americans with Disabilities Act*, 53 BC L. Rev. 443 (2012).

Voluntary Conditions. Can a physical condition that is caused at least in part by voluntary conduct constitute an impairment? In *Cook v. Rhode Island Dep't of Mental Health*, 10 F.3d 17 (1st Cir. 1993), the First Circuit held, in a claim under the Rehabilitation Act, that morbid obesity could be an impairment, rejecting the defendant's argument that "mutable" conditions or those "caused, or at least exacerbated, by voluntary conduct," were not impairments. The Act "indisputably applies to numerous conditions that may be caused or exacerbated by voluntary conduct, such as alcoholism, AIDS, diabetes, cancer resulting from cigarette smoking, heart disease resulting from excesses of various types, and the like." *Id.* at 24. However, other pre-ADAAA cases excluded morbid obesity unless related to a psychological condition, and the first post-ADAAA circuit decision held it neither an actual disability nor a regarded as one unless plaintiff could show that his employer "perceived his obesity to be a condition that met the definition of 'physical impairment.'" *Morriss v. BNSF Ry. Co.*, 817 F.3d 1104, 1109 (8th Cir. 2016). *See generally* Jane Byeff Korn, *Too Fat*, 17 Va. J. Soc. Pol'y & L. 209 (2010).

Temporary Impairments. Another question is whether temporary impairments are covered by the ADA. In *Toyota Motor Manufacturing, Kentucky v. Williams*, 534 U.S. 184 (2002), the Supreme Court stated that, to substantially limit performance of manual tasks, "the impairment's impact must also be permanent or long-term." This seems to continue to be true. The ADAAA addresses a piece of this question: it provides that the "regarded as" prong does not apply to transitory and minor impairments and defines "transitory" as an actual or expected duration of less than six months. In *Summers v. Altarum Inst. Corp.*, 740 F.3d 325, 329-30 (4th Cir. 2014), plaintiff had a serious but temporary injury, one that left him unable to walk for seven months despite surgery, pain medication, and physical therapy. The court held he could be disabled within the meaning of the amended ADA: EEOC regulations providing that a short-term impairment may qualify if sufficiently severe were entitled to deference. See Note on Deference to the EEOC, p. 506. *But see Gecewicz v. Henry Ford Macomb Hosp. Corp.*, 683 F.3d 316, **322** (6th Cir. 2012) ("none of Rogers's statements shows that she believed Gecewicz had a physical or mental impairment of a duration longer than six months"). As for the actual and record of prongs, the EEOC views the six-month durational requirement as *not* applying, reasoning that if an impairment substantially limits a major life activity, the definition is met, even if the duration is less than six months. *See* 29 C.F.R. pt. 1630, app. §1630.2(j)(1)(ix).

In any event, the ADAAA amended the statute to provide that "an impairment that is episodic or in remission is a disability if it would substantially limit a major life activity when active." 42 U.S.C §12102(4)(D). *See, e.g., Gogos v. AMS Mech. Sys., Inc.*, 737 F.3d 1170, 1173 (7th Cir. 2013) (an episode of a blood-pressure spike and vision loss may be covered disabilities when both problems may be "episodic" manifestations of a long-standing blood-pressure condition); *Oehmke v. Medtronic, Inc.*, 844 F.3d 748, 756 (8th Cir. 2016) (a cancer survivor whose cancer was in remission was nevertheless disabled under the ADA since the statute clearly includes impairments in remission).

Genetic Conditions as Impairments. Is an individual with a genetic propensity to disease impaired within the meaning of the ADA? If so, does this impairment substantially limit any major life activity? A few diseases, like Huntington's disease, are inevitable for those with the allele although they may not manifest the symptoms until late in life. Most "genetic diseases," however, simply make individuals more susceptible to the condition (although sometimes increasing the risk factor enormously). Is someone with the Huntington's allele but no symptoms impaired? If so, does this impairment substantially limit any major life activity? Even if the answer is yes, what about those genetic diseases whose manifestation is not inevitable? *See* John V. Jacobi, *Genetic Discrimination in a Time of False Hopes*, 30 FLA. ST. U. L. REV. 363 (2003). Might a victim of discrimination on the basis of a genetic propensity be regarded as disabled even if not actually disabled? *See* EEOC's Compliance Manual, §902 (yes).

Some of these questions may be resolved by the 2008 Genetic Information Non-Discrimination Act, 42 U.S.C. §2000ff (2018). GINA prohibits discrimination by employers and health insurers based on genetic information. The EEOC is charged with enforcing the Act's employment provisions and has promulgated regulations to carry out Title II (the employment chapter). 29 C.F.R. pt. 1635 (2018). In a nutshell, Title II prohibits the use of genetic information in employment, generally prohibits the intentional acquisition of genetic information about applicants and employees, and imposes strict confidentiality requirements. It applies to employers, public and private, with 15 or more employees. The EEOC regards the protections of GINA as absolute when it comes to an employer's *use* of genetic information; any use is strictly prohibited. The acquisition of genetic information by employers is restricted but not prohibited. See the section on Medical Examinations and Inquiries, p. 516. *See generally* Jessica L. Roberts, *The Genetic Information Nondiscrimination Act as an Antidiscrimination Law*, 86 NOTRE DAME L. REV. 597 (2011).

Medical Evidence Needed? In *Felkins v. City of Lakewood*, 774 F.3d 647, 652 (10th Cir. 2014), plaintiff failed to produce any medical testimony that she had avascular necrosis, which proved fatal to her claim of actual disability. While her declarations were admissible in describing her injuries and symptoms, they were inadmissible "insofar as they diagnose her condition or state how that condition causes limitations on major life activities," both of which require an expert witness. Implementing regulations under the ADAAA, 29 C.F.R. §1630.2(j)(1)(v), were read to allow lay testimony as to plaintiff's performance of major life activities compared to others but not as to whether any limitations were caused by a particular disease.

NOTE ON BEING SUBSTANTIALLY LIMITED IN MAJOR LIFE ACTIVITIES

Although *Bragdon* held that reproduction is a major life activity, lower courts wrestled with determining what other life activities were major within the meaning of the original ADA, confronting, for example, whether the ability to work, eat, drink, sleep, drive a car, think, or get along with people were major life activities. That was in part because the original ADA did not define the term (although agency regulations did address the issue). The ADAAA filled that statutory gap, and its definition is sweeping. Major life activities "include but are not limited to, caring for oneself, performing manual tasks, seeing, hearing, eating, sleeping, walking, lifting, bending, speaking, breathing, reading, concentrating, thinking, communicating and working." §12102(2)(A). The term also includes "the operation of a major bodily function, including, but not limited to, functions of the immune system, normal cell growth, digestive, bowel, bladder, neurological, brain, respiratory, circulatory, endocrine, and reproductive functions." *Id.* at §12102(2)(B).

The ADAAA also doubled down on "*substantially limited.*" The amendments were driven in large part by *Toyota Motor Manufacturing, Kentucky v. Williams*, 534 U.S. 184 (2002), a unanimous opinion that was widely viewed as gutting the

ADA. Plaintiff was a Toyota employee working on the assembly line who sought an accommodation for her carpal tunnel syndrome. The parties agreed that plaintiff's medical conditions were physical impairments and that they limited her ability to do certain manual tasks related to her job. However, the Sixth Circuit erred in assessing whether plaintiff had a disability when "it analyzed only a limited class of manual tasks and failed to ask whether respondent's impairments prevented or restricted her from performing tasks that are of central importance to most people's daily lives." *Id.* at 187.

For the Court, the manual tasks "must be central to daily life [to constitute a disability]. If each of the tasks included in the major life activity of performing manual tasks does not independently qualify as a major life activity, then together they must do so." *Id.* at 197. It was only these activities that were "major" and which had to be "substantially" limited for a plaintiff to claim the protection of the ADA. No part of the opinion generated more criticism than its statement that both terms "need to be interpreted strictly to create a demanding standard for qualifying as disabled." *Id.*

The Court summarized its holding: "to be substantially limited in performing manual tasks, an individual must have an impairment that prevents or severely restricts the individual from doing activities that are of central importance to most people's daily lives. The impairment's impact must also be permanent or long-term." *Id.* at 198. To make such an assessment, evidence of a medical diagnosis of an impairment is not sufficient; a plaintiff must prove the substantial effects on her own lived experience. Such an individualized assessment "is particularly necessary when the impairment is one whose symptoms vary widely from person to person, such as plaintiff's carpal tunnel syndrome." *Id.* at 199. The Sixth Circuit erred in disregarding the evidence it should have focused upon: "household chores, bathing, and brushing one's teeth are among the types of manual tasks of central importance to people's daily lives, and should have been part of the assessment of whether respondent was substantially limited in performing manual tasks." *Id.* at 184.

The dramatic implications of *Toyota* are illustrated by the Catch-22 the Court's construction of "disability" posed for persons such as Williams. One who can perform basic life functions despite her impairment would have a difficult time establishing she is disabled. However, Williams's condition worsened to the point where she was placed on a "no work of any kind" restriction. Her termination at that point was held by both lower courts to be lawful because she was no longer a "qualified" individual, whether or not she had a disability.

Toyota led to a wide variety of lower court decisions finding plaintiff not to be actually disabled, sometimes in extreme circumstances. *See, e.g., Williams v. Excel Foundry & Machine, Inc.*, 489 F.3d 227 (7th Cir. 2007) (foundry worker with fractured spine unable to stand for more than 30-40 minutes was not substantially limited in major life activity of standing). Overriding *Toyota* was a major impetus for the statutory amendments, and Congress listed as a purpose for the ADAAA its intent to reject specifically the "demanding standard" language from *Toyota*. §2(a)(5), (7); (b)(4), (5), Pub. L. No. 110-325, 122 Stat. 3553, 3553-3554 (2008). Ironically, however, Congress did not define "substantially limits" in the ADAAA. Instead, it directed the EEOC to revise its regulations in a manner consistent with the purposes of the amendments. In its amended regulations, the EEOC, too, opted not to define "substantially limits," but it did direct the focus toward an individualized assessment of whether the impairment "limits the ability of an individual to perform a major life activity as compared to most people in the general population." 29 C.F.R. §1630.2(j)(1)(ii).

And it provided that no scientific, medical, or statistical evidence will usually be needed in making this comparison. 29 C.F.R. §1630.2(j)(1)(v). The agency also issued nine Rules of Construction to be used in construing the term, including the following:

- the term "substantially limits" requires a lower degree of functional limitation than that previously used by the courts
- the term "substantially limits" is to be construed broadly
- an individualized assessment is required to determine if an impairment is substantially limiting
- other than for eyeglasses or contacts, the assessment is to be made without regard to mitigating measures
- the determination of disability should not require extensive analysis

29 C.F.R. §1630.2(j). The thrust of the statute and the regulations, then, is clear — Congress has flatly rejected the *Toyota* Court's view that the path to disability status be a demanding one.

Additionally, the EEOC's regulations implementing the ADAAA provide examples of impairments that should almost always be found to substantially limit a major life activity. Thus:

it should easily be concluded that the following types of impairments will, at a minimum, substantially limit the major life activities indicated: Deafness substantially limits hearing; blindness substantially limits seeing; an intellectual disability (formerly termed mental retardation) substantially limits brain function; partially or completely missing limbs or mobility impairments requiring the use of a wheelchair substantially limit musculoskeletal function; autism substantially limits brain function; cancer substantially limits normal cell growth; cerebral palsy substantially limits brain function; diabetes substantially limits endocrine function; epilepsy substantially limits neurological function; Human Immunodeficiency Virus (HIV) infection substantially limits immune function; multiple sclerosis substantially limits neurological function; muscular dystrophy substantially limits neurological function; and major depressive disorder, bipolar disorder, post-traumatic stress disorder, obsessive compulsive disorder, and schizophrenia substantially limit brain function.

29 C.F.R. §1630.2(j)(3)(iii). The regulations provide that, "with respect to these types of impairments, the necessary individualized assessment should be particularly simple and straightforward." 29 C.F.R. §1630.2(j)(3).

Congress's aim of reducing the difficulty of proving an individual is disabled seems largely achieved. *See, e.g., Cannon v. Jacobs Field Servs. N. Am.,* 813 F.3d 586 (5th Cir. 2016) (plaintiff's shoulder injury, which prevented him from lifting his right arm above shoulder level and caused considerable difficulty in lifting, pushing, or pulling, was ample evidence of a disability under the ADAAA, which views lifting as a major life activity); *Jacobs v. N.C. Admin. Office of the Courts,* 780 F.3d 562, 573-74 (4th Cir. 2015) (since a "person need not live as a hermit in order to be 'substantially limited' in interacting with others, plaintiff's social anxiety disorder may be a protected disability even though she endured social situations, at least when they caused her 'intense anxiety'"). *See generally* Stephen F. Befort, *An Empirical Analysis of Case Outcomes Under the ADA Amendments Act,* 70 WASH. & LEE L. REV. 2027 (2013) (the empirical evidence reveals fewer dismissals for the plaintiff not being disabled and more plaintiff success in surviving various motions); Nicole B. Porter, *The New ADA Backlash*, 82 TENN. L. REV. 1 (2014) (empirical study showing courts are generally following the ADAAA's command to be more receptive to claims of disability).

NOTE ON MITIGATING MEASURES

The ADAAA also addressed an issue concerning "substantial limitation" that had arisen in *Sutton v. United Air Lines, Inc.*, 527 U.S. 471 (1999), and two companion cases, *Murphy v. United Parcel Service, Inc.*, 527 U.S. 516 (1999), and *Albertson's, Inc. v. Kirkingburg*, 527 U.S. 555 (1999), reproduced at p. 508. The essential question was whether a medical intervention or physiological adjustment should be considered in assessing whether that disability substantially limited a major life activity. *Sutton* involved twins who sought employment as commercial airline pilots. Each had severe myopia; without eyeglasses they were legally blind, but their vision was 20/20 when wearing their glasses. The Supreme Court concluded they were not disabled, rejecting the EEOC's position that individuals should be assessed in their "hypothetical uncorrected state" as an impermissible interpretation of the ADA.

Similarly, *Murphy* considered the claim of a mechanic discharged from his job because of high blood pressure. The plaintiff asserted that his disability should be assessed without reference to the medication he took to control his blood pressure, but the Court rejected this argument in light of its resolution of this issue in *Sutton*. Finally, in *Kirkingburg*, the plaintiff had monocular vision, but his brain had subconsciously adjusted to the impairment. The Supreme Court held that a body's coping mechanisms that mitigate an impairment must be considered in assessing disability status. "We see no principled basis for distinguishing between measures undertaken with artificial aids, like medications and devices, and measures undertaken, whether consciously or not, with the body's own systems." 527 U.S. at 565. The *Sutton* trilogy had enormous impact since it left employers free to discriminate against someone who had a corrected physical or mental impairment, even when the employer was taking action based on the impairment's unmitigated effects. As Justice Stevens pointed out in dissent, "the Court's approach would seem to allow an employer to refuse to hire every person who has epilepsy or diabetes that is controlled by medication, or every person who functions effectively with a prosthetic limb." 527 U.S. at 509.

Congress also responded to the *Sutton* trilogy in the ADAAA, which provided that "the determination of whether an impairment substantially limits a major life activity shall be made *without regard* to the ameliorative effects of mitigating measures" and lists a number of mitigating measures such as medication, prosthetics, and hearing aids. §12102(4)(E). However, the amended statute goes on to provide that "the ameliorative effects of the mitigating measures of ordinary eyeglasses or contact lenses shall be considered in determining whether an impairment substantially limits a major life activity." Accordingly, while Congress amended the statute in direct response to the result in *Sutton*, it essentially agreed that the *Sutton* plaintiffs were not persons with *actual* disabilities within the meaning of the ADA. Oddly enough, however, the ADAAA also requires any vision standard to be job related. 42 U.S.C. §12113(c). The twins, however, had also contended that, even if they were not actually disabled under the ADA, they were regarded as having a disability. This portion of *Sutton*, and Congress's response to it in the ADAAA, is discussed at p. 452.

But there remains a potential problem regarding those who do not use mitigating measures when they are available. Such individuals will be disabled (a matter that divided the courts prior to the ADAAA), but the failure to mitigate may sometimes make them unqualified. As we will see, a disabled person is otherwise qualified if she can perform the essential functions of the position with or without reasonable accommodation. The obvious question that will arise is the extent to which an employer must accommodate an individual who does not use mitigating measures that would enable her to do the job at issue. *See generally* Jeannette Cox, *"Corrective" Surgery and the Americans with Disabilities Act*, 46 SAN DIEGO L. REV. 113 (2009).

Finally, there is the question of whether the use of a mitigating measure might itself create a disability where none previously existed. *Sulima v. Tobyhanna Army Depot*, 602 F.3d 177, 187 (3d Cir. 2010), held that the side effects from medical treatment may themselves constitute an impairment under the ADA even if the condition treated is not itself disabling; however, since "'disability' connotes an involuntary condition," a plaintiff seeking protection on this theory must show both that the treatment was required in the "prudent judgment" of the medical profession and there was not an available alternative that is equally efficacious but lacks similarly disabling side effects.

PROBLEM 7.1

Sarah Smith is an assembly-line worker who is diabetic and dependent on insulin injections to maintain her glucose level. She must inject up to four times a day to maintain ideal glucose levels. If her glucose level drops too low, she will become hypoglycemic and go into a coma. If her glucose level is too high, it will cause long-term physical deterioration of numerous body systems. Eating increases glucose levels, so Sarah needs to inject one half-hour before eating larger meals. Her doctor has recommended that she eat smaller and more frequent meals to help her modulate variations in her glucose levels. Outside of work, Sarah leads an active life and exercises regularly. She must be careful to time her injections depending on her exercise and eating patterns. Exercise reduces glucose levels on a short-term basis and can upset the balance of insulin and glucose in the body, possibly resulting in a hypoglycemic reaction. Because Sarah is careful about her eating, exercise, and treatment regimen, her diabetes is reasonably well controlled. She does not yet exhibit any physical damage related to excess glucose levels. She carries small amounts of sugar with her to minimize the incidence of hypoglycemic reactions. Assembly-line workers operate on a very rigid schedule. Sarah wants to seek accommodations from her employer to make it easier for her to maintain her glucose levels while at work. Is Sarah an individual with a disability under the original ADA? *See Griffin v. UPS*, 661 F.3d 216 (5th Cir. 2011) (individual with well-controlled diabetes not disabled). Under the ADA as amended?

PROBLEM 7.2

Serum alpha-1 antitrypsin (SAT) is a serum protein that protects the lungs from proteolytic enzymes. Approximately 80 percent of individuals who inherit an SAT deficiency from both parents develop chronic obstructive pulmonary disease (COPD). Individuals who inherit the deficiency from only one parent have a much lower risk, but nevertheless have a higher risk than the general population of developing COPD (1 in 10), especially if they smoke or work in dusty environments. Tuan, who inherited SAT deficiency from both of his parents, does not yet suffer from any symptoms of COPD. Is Tuan impaired? Is he substantially limited with respect to a major life activity and, therefore, disabled under the ADA, either as originally enacted or as amended? Whether or not he is an individual with a disability within the meaning of the ADA, would he be entitled to the protections of GINA?

2.   *Record of Such an Impairment*

Section 3(2) of the ADA defines disability to include having a "record" of an impairment that substantially limits a major life activity. A variety of records contain such information, including employment records, medical records, and education records. Individuals with impairments that, as a result of successful treatment, are not currently substantially limiting may seek to establish that they are protected by the ADA based on a "record" of an impairment. However, "[t]he impairment indicated in the record must be an impairment that would substantially limit one or more of the individual's major life activities." 29 C.F.R. pt. 1630, app. §1630.2(k). The EEOC states that the ADA "protects former cancer patients from discrimination on the basis of their prior medical history," and also "ensures that individuals are not discriminated against because they have been misclassified as disabled." 29 C.F.R. pt. 1630, app. §1630.2(k).

Are individuals who establish coverage under the ADA by demonstrating a record of a substantially limiting impairment entitled to reasonable accommodations relating to continuing nonsubstantial limitations associated with their impairment? The EEOC says yes; an employer, for example, may need to accommodate an employee's need for periodic checkups related to the disability even if it's currently in remission. 29 C.F.R. pt. 1630, app. §1630.2(k). And to be liable, must the employer discriminate based on the record of disability rather than on the basis of continuing nonsubstantial limitations? In thinking about how best to answer these questions, reconsider *Arline*. *See generally* Alex B. Long, *(Whatever Happened to) The ADA's "Record of" Prong(?)*, 81 Wash. L. Rev. 669 (2006).

PROBLEM 7.3

Reconsider Problems 7.1 and 7.2. Could you make a "record of impairment" argument on behalf of Sarah or Tuan?

3.   *Regarded as Having Such an Impairment*

SUTTON v. UNITED AIR LINES, INC.
527 U.S. 471 (1999)

O'Connor, J. delivered the opinion of the Court.
[The facts of this case are summarized in the Note on Mitigating Measures, p. 450.]

IV

Our conclusion that petitioners have failed to state a claim that they are actually disabled under subsection (A) of the disability definition does not end our inquiry. Under subsection (C), individuals who are "regarded as" having a disability are disabled within the meaning of the ADA. *See* §12102(2)(C). Subsection (C) provides that having a disability includes "being regarded as having," §12102(2)(C), "a physical or mental impairment that substantially limits one or more of the major life activities of such individual," §12102(2)(A). There are two apparent ways in which individuals may fall within this statutory definition: (1) a covered entity mistakenly believes that a person has a physical impairment that substantially limits one or more major life activities, or (2) a covered entity mistakenly believes that an actual, nonlimiting impairment substantially limits one or more major life activities. In both cases, it is necessary that a covered entity entertain misperceptions about the individual — it must believe either that one has a substantially limiting impairment that one does not have or that one has a substantially limiting impairment when, in fact, the impairment is not so limiting. These misperceptions often "result from stereotypic assumptions not truly indicative of . . . individual ability." *See* 42 U.S.C. §12101(7).

There is no dispute that petitioners are physically impaired. Petitioners do not make the obvious argument that they are regarded due to their impairments as substantially limited in the major life activity of seeing. They contend only that respondent mistakenly believes their physical impairments substantially limit them in the major life activity of working. To support this claim, petitioners allege that respondent has a vision requirement, which is allegedly based on myth and stereotype. Further, this requirement substantially limits their ability to engage in the major life activity of working by precluding them from obtaining the job of global airline pilot, which they argue is a "class of employment." In reply, respondent argues that the position of global airline pilot is not a class of jobs and therefore petitioners have not stated a claim that they are regarded as substantially limited in the major life activity of working.

Standing alone, the allegation that respondent has a vision requirement in place does not establish a claim that respondent regards petitioners as substantially limited in the major life activity of working. By its terms, the ADA allows employers to prefer some physical attributes over others and to establish physical criteria. An employer runs afoul of the ADA when it makes an employment decision based on a physical or mental impairment, real or imagined, that is regarded as substantially limiting a major life activity. Accordingly, an employer is free to decide that physical characteristics or medical conditions that do not rise to the level of an impairment — such as one's height, build, or singing voice — are preferable to others, just as it is free to decide that some limiting, but not substantially limiting, impairments make individuals less than ideally suited for a job.

Considering the allegations of the amended complaint in tandem, petitioners have not stated a claim that respondent regards their impairment as substantially limiting their ability to work. . . .

When the major life activity under consideration is that of working, the statutory phrase "substantially limits" requires, at a minimum, that plaintiffs allege they are unable to work in a broad class of jobs. Reflecting this requirement, the EEOC uses a specialized definition of the term "substantially limits" when referring to the major life activity of working:

significantly restricted in the ability to perform either a class of jobs or a broad range of jobs in various classes as compared to the average person having comparable training, skills and abilities. The inability to perform a single, particular job does not constitute a substantial limitation in the major life activity of working.

§1630.2(j)(3)(i). The EEOC further identifies several factors that courts should consider when determining whether an individual is substantially limited in the major life activity of working, including the geographical area to which the individual has reasonable access, and "the number and types of jobs utilizing similar training, knowledge, skills or abilities, within the geographical area, from which the individual is also disqualified." §§1630.2(j)(3)(ii)(A), (B). To be substantially limited in the major life activity of working, then, one must be precluded from more than one type of job, a specialized job, or a particular job of choice. If jobs utilizing an individual's skills (but perhaps not his or her unique talents) are available, one is not precluded from a substantial class of jobs. Similarly, if a host of different types of jobs are available, one is not precluded from a broad range of jobs. . . .

Assuming without deciding that working is a major life activity and that the EEOC regulations interpreting the term "substantially limits" are reasonable, petitioners have failed to allege adequately that their poor eyesight is regarded as an impairment that substantially limits them in the major life activity of working. They allege only that respondent regards their poor vision as precluding them from holding positions as a "global airline pilot." Because the position of global airline pilot is a single job, this allegation does not support the claim that respondent regards petitioners as having a substantially limiting impairment. *See* 29 CFR §1630.2(j)(3)(i) ("The inability to perform a single, particular job does not constitute a substantial limitation in the major life activity of working"). Indeed, there are a number of other positions utilizing petitioners' skills, such as regional pilot and pilot instructor to name a few, that are available to them. Even under the EEOC's Interpretative Guidance, to which petitioners ask us to defer, "an individual who cannot be a commercial airline pilot because of a minor vision impairment, but who can be a commercial airline co-pilot or a pilot for a courier service, would not be substantially limited in the major life activity of working." 29 CFR pt. 1630, App. §1630.2.

Petitioners also argue that if one were to assume that a substantial number of airline carriers have similar vision requirements, they would be substantially limited in the major life activity of working. Even assuming for the sake of argument that the adoption of similar vision requirements by other carriers would represent a substantial limitation on the major life activity of working, the argument is nevertheless flawed. It is not enough to say that if the physical criteria of a single employer were *imputed* to all similar employers one would be regarded as substantially limited in the major life activity of working *only as a result of this imputation.* An otherwise valid job requirement, such as a height requirement, does not become invalid simply because it would limit a person's employment opportunities in a substantial way if it were adopted by a substantial number of employers. Because petitioners have not alleged, and cannot demonstrate, that respondent's vision requirement reflects a belief that petitioners' vision substantially limits them, we agree with the decision of the Court of Appeals affirming the dismissal of petitioners' claim that they are regarded as disabled.

NOTES

1. *Working as a Major Life Activity.* The *Sutton* Court reserved the question of whether "working" is a major life activity, as had *Toyota.* But Congress reacted by adding working to the list of major life activities in the ADAAA. §12102(2)(A). However, given the expansive definition of major life activity in the amended statute, it should be the unusual case where a plaintiff relies on working as the activity his impairment substantially limits.

2. *Substantially Limited in Ability to Work.* The *Sutton* Court's analysis of the plaintiffs' claim that they were regarded as substantially limited with respect to working is consistent with the EEOC regulations insofar as the Court requires the plaintiffs to establish that they were regarded as excluded from "either a class of jobs or a broad range of jobs" as compared to persons with "comparable training, skills and abilities." The opinion also rests comfortably within the EEOC's then-existing Interpretive Guidance in concluding that the plaintiffs were not substantially limited with respect to working because other airline positions were open to them.

What is a broad class or range of jobs? As we shall see below, this question is no longer important for "regarded as" claims, but it remains important for those (presumably now rare cases) claiming an actual disability when the major life activity in question is "working." In *Murphy v. United Parcel Service,* 527 U.S. 516 (1999), the plaintiff was denied DOT certification to drive a commercial truck because of his high blood pressure. UPS dismissed Murphy from his job because he could not obtain the certification. The Court held that the defendant did not regard Murphy as substantially limited in the activity of working but regarded Murphy only as unable to perform mechanics' jobs that required driving a commercial motor vehicle. Pre-ADAAA cases reached varying results on how broad a class of jobs must be to satisfy the standard. Firefighting is not, *Bridges v. City of Bossier,* 92 F.3d 329 (5th Cir. 1996); law enforcement may, *McKenzie v. Dovola,* 242 F.3d 967 (10th Cir. 2001), or may not, be, *Rossbach v. City of Miami,* 371 F.3d 1354 (11th Cir. 2004). Post-ADAAA cases tend to take a strict view. *See Ferrari v. Ford Motor Co.,* 826 F.3d 885 (6th Cir. 2016) (employer did not view plaintiff's opioid use as substantially limiting working since it restricted him only from jobs that required ladder climbing or working at heights); *Carothers v. Cnty. of Cook,* 808 F.3d 1140, 1147-48 (7th Cir. 2015) (anxiety about interacting with juvenile detainees merely affected "single specific job" at a juvenile correctional center).

NOTE ON "REGARDED AS" CLAIMS UNDER THE ADAAA

One of the most significant changes the ADAAA made is the definition of "regarded as" claims:

(A) An individual meets the requirement of "being regarded as having such an impairment" if the individual establishes that he or she has been subjected to an action prohibited under this Act because of an actual or perceived physical or mental impairment whether or not the impairment limits or is perceived to limit a major life activity.

(B) [The regarded as prong] shall not apply to impairments that are transitory and minor. A transitory impairment is an impairment with an actual or expected duration of 6 months or less.

42 U.S.C. §12102(3). The "regarded as" prong now provides the broadest protection under the statute. There need be no finding that the impairment, real or perceived, was regarded as substantially limiting a major life activity. Rather, all the plaintiff need show is that the employer took a prohibited action because of the impairment, which in turn can be either real or perceived. *See generally* Michelle A. Travis, *Impairment as a Protected Status: A New Universality of Disability Rights*, 46 GA. L. REV. 937 (2012); Kerri Lynn Stone, *Substantial Limitations: Reflections on the ADAAA*, 14 N.Y.U. J. LEGIS. & PUB. POL'Y 509, 542-43 (2011); Stephen F. Befort, *Let's Try This Again: The ADA Amendments Act of 2008 Attempts to Reinvigorate the "Regarded As" Prong of the Statutory Definition of Disability*, 2010 UTAH L. REV. 993.

Take, for example, the twins in *Sutton*. They presumably have no actual disability under the ADA, originally or as amended. Under both, corrective lenses may be taken into account in determining whether an impairment substantially limits one or more major life activities. But, corrected or not, the twins did have myopia, an impairment. And their prospective employer denied them employment because of their myopia. Each thus would be an individual with a disability under the "regarded as" prong under the amended statute.

But would they be "qualified"? The ADAAA also provides that an employer shall not use a qualification standard based on uncorrected vision unless that standard was job related for the position in question and consistent with business necessity. §12112(b)(6)-(7). Under the amended ADA, the twins' claims would have turned on this provision, that is, whether United's insistence that its pilots have uncorrected vision of at least 20/100 is job related for the position in question and consistent with business necessity.

Although the ADA amendments dramatically widen the class of protected persons by requiring only that the employer act on the basis of an impairment rather than a disability, the ADAAA simultaneously cut back on the protection accorded. The amendments provide that "regarded as" plaintiffs are *not* entitled to reasonable accommodation. Thus, such persons may not be discriminated against, but their impairments need not be accommodated; for this reason, the EEOC regulations state that "cases in which an applicant or employee does not require reasonable accommodation can be evaluated solely under the 'regarded as' prong." 29 C.F.R. §1630.2(g).

Moreover, a plaintiff cannot satisfy the "regarded as" prong if her impairments are minor or "transitory and minor," which seems to be an objective test with the burden of proving both on the employer. *Silk v. Bd. of Trs.*, 795 F.3d 698, 706-07 (7th Cir. 2015) (since bypass surgery "was the treatment, not the impairment," the employer did not establish that a heart condition was minor). The transitory prong is satisfied if the condition has "an actual or expected duration of six months or less." §12102(3)(B).

The following case provides an example of the correct analysis of all three prongs of the disability definition under the amended statute.

ALEXANDER v. WASH. METRO. AREA TRANSIT AUTH.
826 F.3d 544 (D.C. Cir. 2016)

PER CURIAM:

Carlos Alexander brought this disability discrimination action under Section 504 of the Rehabilitation Act of 1973, 29 U.S.C. §701 *et seq.*, against his former employer, the Washington Metropolitan Area Transit Authority ("Authority"). The district court granted summary judgment to the Authority on the ground that Alexander failed to come forward with sufficient evidence that he had a "disability" as defined in the Act. In so holding, however, the district court failed to properly consider the record evidence as applied to all three of the Act's alternative definitions of "disability." We accordingly reverse and remand.

I

Alexander has suffered from alcoholism since approximately 1980. The Authority hired him in 1999 as an Automatic Train Control Mechanic Helper. In 2007, he transferred to a Communications Mechanic Helper position. One day in April 2007, Alexander's supervisor smelled alcohol on his breath. A breathalyzer test came up positive for alcohol. Shortly thereafter, Alexander was suspended and referred to the Authority's Employee Assistance Program.

Alexander returned to work in December 2007, subject to periodic alcohol tests. In January 2009, Alexander proved unable to comply with the Authority's internal Employee Assistance Program as he again tested positive for alcohol while at work. As a result, he was terminated. During the exit interview, Alexander was told that he could apply to be rehired in one year if he completed an intensive alcohol dependency treatment program. Accordingly, Alexander enrolled in the Chemical Dependency Intensive Outpatient Program at Washington Hospital Center, completing it in January 2010. He then sought to be rehired by the Authority on several occasions, three of which are the subject of his complaint. . . .

[Alexander sued under the Rehabilitation Act, but the district court granted summary against him because plaintiff could not established he was an individual with a disability because he failed to adduce any evidence "demonstrat[ing] that his alcohol dependency substantially limits at least one of his major life activities."]

II . . .

A. DISABILITY DISCRIMINATION

Section 504 of the Rehabilitation Act provides that "[n]o otherwise qualified individual with a disability . . . shall, solely by reason of her or his disability, be excluded from the participation in, be denied the benefits of, or be subjected to discrimination under any program or activity receiving Federal financial assistance." 29 U.S.C. §794(a). The Act expressly incorporates the liability standards set out in the ADA. *See id.* §794(d); 29 C.F.R. §1614.203(b). Accordingly, to prevail on a claim of discrimination under the Rehabilitation Act, a plaintiff must first establish that he has a "disability" as defined in the ADA. . . .

The district court ruled that Alexander had failed to establish that he is disabled within the meaning of the Rehabilitation Act because he failed to come forward with sufficient evidence showing that his alcoholism "substantially limits one or more major life activities," 42 U.S.C. §12102(1)(A). The district court's analysis, however, focused on only the first definition of "disability" — an actual and substantially limiting "physical or mental impairment" — and failed to consider whether Alexander met either the record-of-impairment or regarded-as-impaired definitions of disability. Compounding the error, the district court also applied an outmoded statutory standard, overlooking material changes to the governing law worked by the 2008 Amendments.

The district court's central error was in failing to consider at all whether the Authority "regarded" Alexander as "having . . . an impairment," §12102(1)(C), or discriminated against him for having a "record of . . . impairment," §12102(1)(B), even though Alexander's claim implicated both definitions. . . .

Considering those alternative definitions was critical. In particular, after the 2008 Amendments, the regarded-as prong has become the primary avenue for bringing the type of discrimination claim that Alexander asserts. *See* 29 C.F.R. §1630.2(g)(3) ("Where an individual is not challenging a covered entity's failure to make reasonable accommodations[,] . . . it is generally unnecessary to proceed under the 'actual disability' or 'record of' prongs . . . . In these cases, the evaluation of coverage can be made solely under the 'regarded as' prong of the definition of disability[.]"). Critically, while the district court's decision relied heavily on what it deemed to be insufficient evidence that Alexander's alcoholism substantially limited any major life activity, the 2008 Amendments eliminate any such requirement for a regarded-as claim. *See* §12102(3); *see also* 29 C.F.R. §1630 app. at 380 (2009).

Instead, Alexander needed only to show that the Authority took "a prohibited action against [him] because of an actual or perceived impairment." 29 C.F.R. §1630.2(*l*)(2). There is no dispute in this case that Alexander's alcoholism is an "impairment" under the ADA and the Rehabilitation Act. *[S]ee also* H.R. Rep. No. 485, 101st Cong., 2d Sess. pt. 2, at 51 (1990) ("physical or mental impairment" under the ADA includes "drug addiction and alcoholism"); *Bailey v. Georgia-Pacific Corp.*, 306 F.3d 1162, 1167 (1st Cir. 2002) ("There is no question that alcoholism is an impairment for purposes of . . . analysis under the ADA.") (listing cases).

In addition, Alexander came forward with sufficient evidence from which a reasonable jury could conclude that the Authority refused to hire him because of his alcoholism. Alexander's deposition testimony and sworn affidavit attest that he was told by Authority representatives at the time of his termination that he would be eligible for rehire in one year's time if he successfully completed a substance abuse program, a contention supported by the Authority's written drug and alcohol policy itself, as well as a letter from a union official about the conversation. There also is no dispute that Alexander successfully completed the Washington Hospital Center's alcohol dependency treatment program and waited a year before applying to be rehired. Yet when he did apply, the Authority told him that he "couldn't come back . . . because [he] failed the [Employee Assistance] program that got [him] fired in the first place, and Metro don't have revolving doors."

Alexander further testified that, after applying for the Automatic Fare Collections Mechanic Helper position, he was pulled out of the line to take the practical entrance exam by Rita Watkins, an Authority human resources representative, who "remember[ed]" him as "the one that can't have safety-sensitive positions." But Alexander also produced evidence suggesting that Automatic Fare Collections Mechanic Helper was not a safety-sensitive position.

In addition, Alexander testified that, during a meeting with Dr. Lisa Cooper-Lucas, the Authority's medical office manager and the person who made the decision to disqualify him, she offered shifting reasons for the Authority's refusal to rehire Alexander. She initially said that Alexander had been disqualified for lying on his medical questionnaire form by marking a box indicating he had never been in a drug treatment program. When Alexander challenged that accusation, Cooper-Lucas asserted that the real reason for disqualification was that Alexander needed to wait two years, not one, before he could be rehired. When Alexander countered that version with the information he received from the union and other Authority personnel, Cooper-Lucas "got mad or upset" and upped the requirement to three years. Alexander questioned "how can it take three if it don't take two[?]," which led Cooper-Lucas to declare that he "can't come back at all." Alexander further testified that Cooper-Lucas's boss later informed him that, despite "no policy preventing [him] from coming back," he would not be rehired "because it will open the floodgates for people like [him]."

Deposition testimony from Authority witnesses likewise supports Alexander's claim. Cooper-Lucas confirmed that she presided over the Authority's Employee Assistance Program at the time of Alexander's participation, and thus was aware of Alexander's alcoholism before he was terminated. She admitted she had no reason to believe that Alexander was drinking at the time of his rehire applications "to the point where there is a concern about his ability to function in a safety-sensitive program," and that his physical exam revealed no evidence of drug or alcohol use. Yet she insisted that Alexander was nonetheless "too much of a risk for a safety sensitive position." Both Cooper-Lucas and Romina Parahoo, a human resources official, also conceded that they could not recall any employee who had been terminated for violating the substance abuse policy and was later rehired.

Further, the record calls into question the non-discriminatory reasons that the Authority asserted for refusing to rehire Alexander. Cooper-Lucas testified that she disqualified Alexander because he had falsified information on his pre-employment medical form and lacked required documentation showing he had been assessed by a substance abuse professional trained on U.S. Department of Transportation regulations. But she had no recollection of ever providing either of those reasons to Alexander. Moreover, the record indicates how a reasonable jury could conclude that Alexander's allegedly false answer on the medical form could have been accurate: he checked "no" for whether he had ever had "*drug* rehab/counseling" (emphasis added). Alexander also showed that nothing in the Authority's drug and alcohol policy requires that substance abuse programs be approved by the federal Department of Transportation.

Beyond those errors with respect to the regarded-as definition of disability, the district court further erred by enforcing too strict a definition of the "substantially limits" showing needed for Alexander's actual-disability and record-of-impairment claims. Under the 2008 Amendments, the substantially-limits requirement "is not meant to be a demanding standard," 29 C.F.R. §1630.2(j)(1)(i), or to require "extensive analysis," *id.* §1630.2(j)(1)(iii). *See also* §12101 note (one purpose of the 2008 Amendments is "to convey congressional intent that the standard created by the Supreme Court . . . for 'substantially limits' . . . ha[d] created an inappropriately high level of limitation necessary to obtain coverage under the ADA").

Given the legal standard prescribed by the 2008 Amendments, we hold that Alexander came forward with sufficient evidence to permit a reasonable jury to find that his alcoholism "substantially limit[ed]" major life activities "compared to most people in the general population." 29 C.F.R. §1630.2(j)(1)(ii). For example, Alexander stated in response to interrogatories that "sleeping, daily care activities[,] and depression" are the "major life activity or activities . . . affected by [his] disability." An expert medical report from Dr. Roberta Malone provides additional detail, explaining that Alexander has a "debilitating diagnosis of alcoholism," and his condition "dramatically [a]ffects major life activities, including the ability to care for himself, walking, concentrating, and communicating." The report catalogs Alexander's long and difficult history of alcohol dependency, including that Alexander had a "stated daily history of consuming a six-pack of beer or half a pint of rum"; that "[h]e also noted periods of time during which he could not recollect events following his consumption of alcohol (consistent with blackouts), as well as a more general deterioration in his ability to sleep regularly"; that he previously continued to use alcohol "despite a clearly declared motivation to re-commit himself to his work, and even in the face of the considerable occupational difficulties it presented"; and that he met the DSM-IV-TR criteria of "[i]mportant social, occupational, or recreational activities given up or reduced because of drinking." The report further indicates that Alexander had been assessed a DSM-IV-TR Axis V "Level of function" score of "55-60 (occupational difficulty)."

In sum, the district court erred in granting summary judgment because a reasonable jury considering the proffered evidence could conclude both that Alexander has a qualifying "disability" under all three definitions of the term in the Rehabilitation Act, and that the Authority refused to rehire him because of his disability. . . .

NOTES

1. *The Rehabilitation Act.* Although the case was decided under the Rehabilitation Act, the substantive standards to be applied are found in the ADA. As we noted at the outset, the Rehabilitation Act preceded the ADA but was limited to federal employment and federal contractors. Although the core prohibition of discrimination "solely" because of disability might suggest a very strict causation standard, it appears that the courts will apply the same but-for causation test they apply to the ADA generally. *See Palmquist v. Shinseki,* 689 F.3d 66 (1st Cir. 2012). See Note on Burdens of Production and Proof, p. 497.

2. *The Three Prongs.* The plaintiff in *Alexander* prevailed on all three prongs. With respect to the refusal to hire, he needed to survive a motion to dismiss on only one ground, and the court correctly suggests that "regarded as" may be the easiest route to success because it avoids the substantial limitation inquiry. But should plaintiff want accommodations after being hired, success on his actual disability claim would be critical, and the opinion suggests that might not be difficult. But isn't there a problem? Is Alexander a recovering alcoholic, one who isn't currently drinking? If so, is much of what the court relates a showing that he has an actual disability or merely that he has a record of one? Does it make any difference? Both actual and record of disabilities are entitled to reasonable accommodation, but how does an employer accommodate a record?

For regarded as cases, *Alexander* recognizes, in order to prove a claim, all a plaintiff need show is that she suffered an adverse action because of her impairment. There need be no finding that the employer regarded the impairment as substantially limiting. Nevertheless, there must be a finding of impairment, not merely lesser physical capacity. In the case itself, alcoholism sufficed. *But see Fischer v. Minneapolis Pub. Sch.,* 792 F.3d 985, 989 (8th Cir. 2015) ("MPS's belief that Fischer was capable of performing the physical labor of a medium strength worker is not equivalent to a belief that Fischer suffered a physical impairment such as a physiological disorder, cosmetic disfigurement, anatomical loss, or disease.").

3. *Causation. Alexander* is like many of the cases we studied in earlier sections of the book because the plaintiff had to prove discrimination on the basis of his protected status when the employer denied such action. The plaintiff lacked "direct evidence" of bias against alcoholics, *see Rodriguez v. Eli Lilly & Co.,* 820 F.3d 759 (5th Cir. 2016) (direct evidence requires proximity in time to the adverse employment action by an individual with authority over that action; a conversation about plaintiff's PTSD more than six months before his termination failed the proximity requirement), but the shifting explanations and misstatements of policy sufficed to

create a jury question. *See also Oehmke v. Medtronic, Inc.*, 844 F.3d 748, 757-58 (8th Cir. 2016) (the lack of medical evidence connecting her disability to illnesses causing her absences prevented plaintiff from establishing a causal link between her disability and the employer's reasons for terminating her). By the way, if you're wondering why plaintiff could have been legally discharged originally, recall he wasn't fired for being an alcoholic, he was fired for being intoxicated on the job. See p. 515.

4. *Adverse Employment Action.* Disability discrimination cases are also like others we have studied in another respect: the discrimination usually has to constitute an adverse employment action in order to be actionable. *See Kelleher v. Wal-Mart Stores, Inc.*, 817 F.3d 624 (8th Cir. 2016) (transfer to a position on the night shift was not an adverse employment action because it did not materially change the terms or conditions of her employment and was less physically strenuous than her prior position). We will see, however, that the duty of reasonable accommodation requires some qualification of this statement. See p. 493.

5. *"Regarded as" Claims and Stereotyping.* When plaintiffs prevailed in "regarded as" claims under the original ADA, it was usually when there was evidence that an employer was acting on the basis of bias, prejudice, or stereotypes. For example, in *Josephs v. Pacific Bell*, 443 F.3d 1050 (9th Cir. 2006), the Ninth Circuit upheld a jury verdict in favor of a service technician. Years before being hired by PacBell, the plaintiff had been found not guilty of attempted murder by reason of insanity and had been institutionalized. PacBell employees considered Josephs unemployable because he had spent time in a "mental ward" and might "go off" on a customer. Since Pac-Bell considered Josephs unfit for any job with the company, the jury could find that it viewed him as having a mental disability that "substantially limited" him in the "major life activity" of working. *See also EEOC v. Heartway Corp.*, 466 F.3d 1156 (10th Cir. 2006) (a nursing home cook with hepatitis C was regarded as disabled where an administrator's remarks indicated that he did not believe that she could work in any food-related position).

Bad faith or ill will, however, is not necessary for a violation. A good faith or "innocent misperception" can still result in liability under the "regarded as" prong. *See Taylor v. Pathmark Stores, Inc.*, 177 F.3d 180 (3d Cir. 1999). *See generally* Michelle A. Travis, *Perceived Disabilities, Social Cognition, and "Innocent Mistakes,"* 55 Vand. L. Rev. 481 (2002). *See also* Dale Larson, Comment, *Unconsciously Regarded as Disabled: Implicit Bias and the Regarded-As Prong of the Americans With Disabilities Act*, 56 UCLA L. Rev. 451, 477 (2008) (noting that studies find substantial implicit bias against the disabled coupled with a large discrepancy between express and implicit bias).

6. *Direct Threat to Others?* There was a dispute in *Alexander* about whether plaintiff applied for a "safety-sensitive" position, but suppose he had. Would it have been permissible to deny him that job because he was an alcoholic? As we will see later in this chapter, a defendant may discriminate against a disabled individual if he poses a direct threat to the health and safety of himself or others. But under the amended statute, claims like Alexander's will be decided under that rubric, not bounced out because his impairment is not regarded as precluding him from a broad range or class of jobs.

7. *Fitness for Duty Examinations.* The ADA regulates, but does not bar, medical examinations of prospective and current employees. There is an obvious tension between "regarded as" liability and permissible medical examinations, *see Coursey v. Univ. of Md. E. Shore*, 577 F. App'x 167 (4th Cir. 2014) (an employer's request for a medical evaluation of its employee is not, by itself, sufficient to show that the employer regarded the employee as disabled for purposes of the ADA), which we will explore later. See p. 516.

C.   THE MEANING OF "QUALIFIED INDIVIDUAL"

Establishing the existence of a disability is alone insufficient to bring an individual within Title I's protected class. The individual must also be "qualified," and, as with other antidiscrimination laws, the plaintiff must link his protected status to an adverse employment action. Section 12112(a) provides:

> No covered entity shall discriminate against a qualified individual on the basis of disability in regard to job application procedures, the hiring, advancement, or discharge of employees, employee compensation, job training and other terms, conditions and privileges of employment.

The concept of protecting only qualified individuals from disability discrimination is borrowed from §504 of the Rehabilitation Act of 1973, which protects only those disabled persons who are "otherwise qualified." 29 U.S.C. §794(a). In *Southeast Community College v. Davis*, 442 U.S. 397 (1979), a case decided under §504, the Supreme Court rejected a reading of "otherwise qualified" that would protect individuals who were qualified apart from their disability but limited the term to mean an individual who can meet the demands of the job or program *despite* the disability. The Court went on to hold, however, that an entity may be required to make changes in its program to accommodate the need of the disabled individual. As later described by the Court:

> *Davis* thus struck a balance between the statutory rights of the handicapped to be integrated into society and the legitimate interests of federal grantees in preserving the integrity of their programs: while a grantee need not be required to make "fundamental" or "substantial" modifications to accommodate the handicapped, it may be required to make reasonable ones.

Alexander v. Choate, 469 U.S. 287, 301 (1985).

This structure is carried over into Title I of the ADA. Title I defines a "qualified individual with a disability" as:

> an individual with a disability who, with or without reasonable accommodation, can perform the essential functions of the employment position that such individual holds or desires. For the purposes of this title, consideration shall be given to the employer's judgment as to what functions of a job are essential, and if an employer has prepared a written description before advertising or interviewing applicants for the job, this description shall be considered evidence of the essential functions of the job.

§12111(8). Thus, numerous decisions reject claims by disabled persons because their disabilities prevent them from performing essential functions and cannot be accommodated. *See, e.g., Williams v. AT&T Mobility Servs. LLC*, 847 F.3d 384 (6th Cir. 2017) (when depression and anxiety required a customer service representative to log off her workstation when random customer calls triggered anxiety attacks, the plaintiff was not capable of performing the essential job functions with or without an accommodation); *Williams v. J.B. Hunt Transp., Inc.*, 826 F.3d 806 (5th Cir. 2016) (rescission of plaintiff's certification to drive a truck rendered him unqualified to do so and thus outside of ADA's protection); *Jakubowski v. Christ Hosp., Inc.*, 627 F.3d 195 (6th Cir. 2010) (plaintiff with Asperger's did not propose an accommodation that would have improved his patient communication skills to render him otherwise qualified as a medical resident). However, the ADA protects disabled individuals who can perform the essential tasks of their jobs even if they cannot do the marginal or relatively unimportant aspects of the position. Accordingly, it is necessary to distinguish the essential functions of the job from those that are not.

1.   Essential Job Functions

REHRS v. THE IAMS COMPANY
486 F.3d 353 (8th Cir. 2007)

RILEY, Circuit Judge.

I.   BACKGROUND

Rehrs, who suffers from Type I diabetes, worked as a warehouse technician for the Iams Company (Iams) in Aurora, Nebraska, from 1997 until 2003. Iams operated the facility on a 24-hour basis using a straight-shift schedule, *i.e.*, three daily shifts. From 1997 until 1999, Rehrs worked a fixed schedule from 4 P.M. to midnight.

In August 1999, P&G [Procter & Gamble] acquired Iams, and in January 2000, P&G implemented a rotating-shift schedule for all warehouse technicians. The rotating-shift schedule consisted of two daily twelve-hour shifts, one from 6:00 A.M. to 6:00 P.M. and the other from 6:00 P.M. to 6:00 A.M. Employees on this schedule worked two days, were off two days, and worked alternating weekends. Every two weeks the first and second shift workers rotated.

Rehrs worked the rotating shift from January 2000 to February 2002 when he suffered a heart attack. Rehrs underwent bypass surgery and had a defibrillator and pacemaker implanted. Due to his medical condition, and at Rehrs's request, P&G placed Rehrs on short-term disability leave.

Rehrs returned to work by early August 2003. However, in September 2003, Rehrs's doctor submitted a letter to P&G, requesting Rehrs be placed on a fixed daytime schedule because his diabetes had become difficult to control. Rehrs's doctor believed a routine or fixed schedule would enhance the efforts to control Rehrs's blood sugar level. Rehrs was granted this accommodation and worked a straight eight-hour shift for sixty days. When P&G learned Rehrs's doctor intended for the requested accommodation to be permanent, P&G informed Rehrs that his accommodation would not continue because shift rotation was an essential part of his job. . . .

[The district court granted summary judgment to P&G, concluding that] Rehrs was not a qualified individual under the ADA because Rehrs could not perform an essential function of the job, specifically, shift rotation at the Aurora facility.

II.   DISCUSSION. . . .

An individual is qualified if he satisfies the requisite skill, experience, education, and other job-related requirements, and "can perform the essential job functions, with or without reasonable accommodation." *Cravens* [*v. Blue Cross & Blue Shield of Kan. City*, 214 F.3d 1011, 1016 (8th Cir. 2000)]. Essential functions are the fundamental job duties but not the marginal functions of a particular job. *Canny v. Dr. Pepper/Seven-Up Bottling Group*, 439 F.3d 894, 900 (8th Cir. 2006) (citing 29 C.F.R.

§1630.2(n)(1)). An employer has the burden of showing a particular job function is an essential function of the job. *Benson v. Nw. Airlines, Inc.*, 62 F.3d 1108, 1113 (8th Cir. 1995). . . .

P&G claims shift rotation was an essential function of the positions at the Aurora facility during the relevant period because all P&G subsidiaries operated under a High Performance Work System (HPWS), and shift rotation was a component of this system. According to P&G, it had employed shift rotation since the 1960s in its new production facilities, and in the 1980s began transitioning its existing production facilities from traditional work systems to HPWS. P&G contends shift rotation exposes employees to management, and to more resources, suppliers, and outside customers with whom the company only interfaces during the day shift. P&G believes this type of exposure provides all employees with additional opportunities for training and development to further their career opportunities in the company and, in turn, increases productivity. P&G asserts that not implementing shift rotation for all warehouse technicians would harm the company from a production standpoint and allowing an employee to work a straight shift would undermine the team concept. P&G further claims not enforcing shift rotation would adversely affect other technicians, creating inequities, because these other technicians would be forced to work the night shift exclusively or for longer periods and lose the benefits of shift rotation, thereby decreasing their opportunities for promotion and development.

All of these factors weigh heavily in favor of finding shift rotation in the P&G work culture is an essential function of working as a warehouse technician. Commencing in January 2000, the facility did not have a straight day-shift technician position — all technician positions were on rotating shifts. Allowing Rehrs to work a straight day-shift schedule would have placed a heavier or unfavorable burden on other technicians at the facility. Under the ADA, an accommodation that would cause other employees to work harder, longer, or be deprived of opportunities is not mandated. *Turco v. Hoechst Celanese Corp.*, 101 F.3d 1090, 1094 (5th Cir. 1996) (citing *Milton v. Scrivner, Inc.*, 53 F.3d 1118, 1125 (10th Cir. 1995), and 29 C.F.R. §1630.2(p)(2)(v)).

Based on the affidavits of two co-workers, Rehrs claims shift rotation is not an essential function of his warehouse technician job. Rehrs argues the plant operated on a straight-shift schedule before P&G's acquisition of the plant and again after P&G outsourced the facility to Excel, while all other functions of the facility, with the exception of the shift rotation, remained the same. However, as the district court noted, the fact that straight shifts were in effect at the Aurora facility before and after P&G ran the facility has little relevance. P&G does not have to exercise the same business judgment as other employers who may believe a straight shift is more productive. It is not the province of the court to question the legitimate operation of a production facility or determine what is the most productive or efficient shift schedule for a facility. See *Milton*.

Rehrs also contends the duties performed at the facility on the day shift were the same duties performed on the night shift. He contends essential functions are duties to be *performed* and a rotating shift is not *performed*. See 29 C.F.R. §1630.2(n)(1). Thus, Rehrs asserts, shift rotation is not an essential part of the job. However, the term essential function encompasses more than core job requirements; indeed, it also may include scheduling flexibility. *Laurin v. Providence Hosp.*, 150 F.3d 52, 59 n.6 (1st Cir. 1998).

Rehrs also argues P&G allowed him a temporary exception from shift rotation, which demonstrates shift rotation is not essential. However, "[a]n employer does not concede that a job function is 'non-essential' simply by voluntarily assuming the limited burden associated with a temporary accommodation, nor thereby acknowledge that the burden associated with a permanent accommodation would not be unduly onerous." *Id.* (citing *Shiring v. Runyon*, 90 F.3d 827, 831 (3d Cir. 1996)). "To find otherwise would unacceptably punish employers from doing more than the ADA requires, and might discourage such an undertaking on the part of employers." *Phelps v. Optima Health, Inc.*, 251 F.3d 21, 26 (1st Cir. 2001) (citations omitted).

Here, P&G required all employees in Rehrs's position to rotate shifts. Such a generally applicable requirement was not discriminatory. The ADA does not require P&G to create a new straight shift position for Rehrs. *Fjellestad v. Pizza Hut of Am., Inc.*, 188 F.3d 944, 950 (8th Cir. 1999) (holding an employer is not obligated to create a new position, or to transform a temporary position into a permanent position as an accommodation, or to eliminate or reallocate the essential functions of a job to accommodate its disabled employees); *Malabarba v. Chi. Tribune Co.*, 149 F.3d 690, 696 (7th Cir. 1998) ("[T]he ADA does not require that employers transform temporary work assignments into permanent positions."). "The [ADA] does not require affirmative action in favor of individuals with disabilities. It merely prohibits employment discrimination against qualified individuals with disabilities, no more and no less." *Turco*. . . .

Viewing the facts in the light most favorable to Rehrs, we conclude shift rotation was a nondiscriminatory essential function of Rehrs's technician job at P&G and Rehrs's restrictions to work only a straight shift rendered him unqualified to carry out all the essential functions of his P&G technician job. Thus, summary judgment was appropriate.

EEOC v. THE PICTURE PEOPLE, INC.
684 F.3d 981 (10th Cir. 2012)

Kelly, Circuit Judge. . . .

The district court granted summary judgment on the basis that Employee [Jessica Chrysler] could not establish an essential element of her case, that she was qualified — with or without accommodation — to perform an essential function of her job as a "performer" in Employer's store.

I. Background

Employee is a congenitally and profoundly deaf individual who communicates with hearing individuals by writing notes, gesturing, pointing, and miming. She can also type, text message, and use body language. According to the EEOC, "[s]he also uses basic American Sign Language ("ASL") signs that most people can understand and speaks some words." Employer maintains that Employee "cannot read lips effectively, nor can she speak except for a few words." It also claims that Employee's written communication skills are poor and that she scored below average on vocational tests administered by EEOC's expert. On October 23, 2007, Employer hired Employee to work in its Littleton, Colorado, store as a "performer." Employee's interview occurred in writing because she was not able to meaningfully participate in a group interview with four other prospective employees. Performers have four areas of responsibility: customer intake, sales, portrait photography, and laboratory duties. During peak (holiday) periods, the employer hires "seasonal" performers who are scheduled to work in one of the four "zones" of responsibility listed above. Arnold Aguilar, Employer's

studio manager, hired Employee to work primarily in the camera room doing photography. During non-peak periods, Employer schedules only one manager and one
performer to work at a time, termed "2-2 staff coverage." When 2-2 staff coverage is
used, "each Performer must be able to perform all four essential functions of the Performer job . . . ."

Employee had the opportunity to shoot photographs on 15-20 occasions with a
hearing performer; she attempted to conduct a shoot by herself on a couple of occasions. Employee communicated with subjects by writing notes, gesturing and miming. This was often difficult as photo subjects are usually young children. In order to
sell packages, Employee had to write notes, gesture, or "get somebody else that could
do it more efficiently . . . ."

In November 2007, Employer dispatched Master Photographer Libby Johnston
to the Littleton store to improve photography quality and sales in anticipation of the
holidays. Ms. Johnston "found [Employee's] written communications awkward, cumbersome, and *impractical* . . . ." She telephoned the District Manager, Candi Bryan;
they conferred and recommended that Employee be reassigned exclusively to the
photo lab. Thereafter, Employee was assigned almost exclusively to the lab.

After the 2007 holiday season, Employer instructed the local acting studio manager to cut the hours of or terminate seasonal performers. Employee complained
about her hours, and management explained in writing that all performers' hours
had been cut. On December 29, 2007, management notified Ms. Bryan that Employee's performance in the lab was deteriorating — Employee was coloring with pencils
instead of working, refusing to take legally required rest breaks, and demanding hours
with threats, when all Performers' hours were cut. With the assistance of the human
resources department, Ms. Bryan prepared a Performance Track Counseling statement to put Employee on notice of performance problems. Ms. Bryan also requested
a meeting with Employee on January 9, 2008, to administer a counseling statement.
The EEOC characterizes the notice as reprimanding Employee for the performance
deficiencies, and for becoming "angry" and "threaten[ing] to bring a grievance . . .
when [she] did not get her hours increased."

After the 2007 holiday season, Employee remained on the schedule as an employee,
but was not scheduled to work. Employer officially terminated Employee in October
2008.

I. DISCUSSION . . .

I. WAS EMPLOYEE QUALIFIED FOR THE PERFORMER POSITION? . . .

A. ARE VERBAL COMMUNICATION SKILLS AN ESSENTIAL FUNCTION OF THE
PERFORMER POSITION?

Employer maintains that strong verbal communication skills are an essential function of the performer position. Whether such skills are an essential function depends in
part upon whether Employer "actually requires all employees in the particular position
to satisfy the alleged job-related requirement." *Hennagir v. Utah Dep't of Corr.*, 587
F.3d 1255, 1262 (10th Cir. 2009). If so, the next inquiry is whether verbal communication skills are fundamental to the performer position. Factors to consider are:

   (i)   The employer's judgment as to which functions are essential;
   (ii) Written job descriptions prepared before advertising or interviewing applicants
         for the job;

    (iii) The amount of time spent on the job performing the function;
    (iv) The consequences of not requiring the incumbent to perform the function;
    (v) The terms of a collective bargaining agreement;
    (vi) The work experience of past incumbents in the job; and/or
    (vii) The current work experience of incumbents in similar jobs.

Id.; 29 C.F.R. §1630.2(n)(3). The essential function analysis "is not intended to second guess the employer or to require [it] to lower company standards. . . . Provided that any necessary job specification is job-related, uniformly enforced, and consistent with business necessity, the employer has a right to establish what a job is and what is required to perform it." *Hennagir; cf. Davidson v. Am. Online, Inc.*, 337 F.3d 1179, 1191 (10th Cir. 2003) (stating that evidence of what an employer thinks is an essential job function is important, but not conclusive).

    Using the criteria listed above, verbal communication skills are an essential function of the performer position. Employer explains that a performer must be able to verbally communicate with customers (many of whom are children), and it lists "[s]trong verbal communication skills" and "[s]trong customer service skills" as job qualifications for the performer position. According to Employer, "substituting written notes, gestures, and pointing for fast, efficient verbal cuing in the Camera Room is simply impractical in light of (a) the short attention span of most Picture People subjects . . . ; (b) the interruption to the flow of the photo shoot; (c) the inability to establish rapport with the parent and child and finally, (d) the quick 20-minute duration of each Camera Room sitting[.]"

    Employee is unable to fully perform three of the four duties of a performer. Although she can fully perform the lab function, her ability to (a) efficiently register and recruit customers, (b) instruct young children while taking their photos, and (c) sell photo packages by addressing customer critiques and concerns, is problematic, particularly given Employer's business model. Employer allows only 20 minutes for each Camera Room sitting — a relatively short period of time, especially when photographing young children.

    The only evidence of a verbally impaired employee in the performer position is not really comparable. Ms. Wendy Duke — a former employee — is also hearing impaired, but Ms. Duke is able to speak and can effectively read lips. Though the EEOC claims that a jury could find that the differences between Ms. Duke and Employee were not as significant as urged, the EEOC does not dispute that Ms. Duke could read lips and speak and that Employee does very little of either. Furthermore, when 2-2 staffing is employed during most of the year, Employee is unable to fully perform three of the four main duties of a performer, while Ms. Duke was able to converse with customers while selling photos, and while taking pictures, ("Every time I go into the camera shoot I use my voice"). Though the EEOC maintains that Employee could communicate non-verbally, nothing suggests that gestures, pantomime, and written communication are similarly effective and efficient for these tasks. When only one other staff member is present, it simply is not feasible to delegate all of these duties. Therefore, based on the factors outlined in 29 C.F.R. §1630.2(n)(3), we must conclude that verbal communication is an essential function of the performer position.

B. WERE REASONABLE ACCOMMODATIONS AVAILABLE?

    If an employee is unable to perform an essential function, the next inquiry is whether the employee could perform this job with reasonable accommodations. *See Davidson.* The EEOC first argues that Employer was required to modify how

Employee worked as a performer "to allow her to communicate with customers using non-verbal means of communication." It is axiomatic, however, that an employer is not required to relieve an employee of an essential job function. *See Mason v. Avaya Commc'ns, Inc.*, 357 F.3d 1114, 1122 (10th Cir. 2004) ("[A]n employee's request to be relieved from an essential function of her position is not, as a matter of law, a reasonable or even plausible accommodation"); *Hennagir*. Given that verbal communication is an essential job function, requiring Employer to eliminate this function cannot be a "reasonable accommodation" required under the ADA.

Next, the EEOC argues that Employer was required to provide ASL interpreters at staff meetings and training sessions. 42 U.S.C. §12111(9)(B). The EEOC relies upon cases in which a court held that an employer was required to provide an ASL interpreter for staff meetings. Those cases are readily distinguishable. [The court cited *EEOC v. UPS Supply Chain Solutions*, 620 F.3d 1103 (9th Cir. 2010); *EEOC v. Federal Express Corp.*, 513 F.3d 360 (4th Cir. 2008), and its own prior decision in *EEOC v. Wal-Mart Stores, Inc.*, 187 F.3d 1241 (10th Cir. 1999), but noted that in all three cases there was no indication that the employee needed accommodation to perform the essential functions of his job.]

This case is different. Employee's position as a performer required her to communicate extensively with customers and to conduct photo sessions with dispatch. Providing Employee with an ASL interpreter at staff meetings would not ameliorate her inability to interact verbally with customers — an essential function of the performer job. This difficulty would preclude Employer from scheduling her during non-peak periods with 2-2 staffing. No reasonable accommodation has been suggested that would allow Employee to perform her job given these constraints. . . .

[The court also affirmed summary judgment on the retaliation claim.]

HOLLOWAY, Circuit Judge, dissenting:

. . . Ms. Jessica Chrysler was hired as a photographer or "performer" at the Littleton, Colorado, studio of Defendant-Appellee The Picture People, Inc. (the Employer). The manager who hired her had full knowledge of her deafness and the means by which she can communicate, and he also had the experience to fully understand the requirements of the job.

When Ms. Chrysler was given an opportunity to conduct a photo session, her performance was given high praise by the customers. She conducted a number of other sessions as well, and there is no evidence that these sessions were less than successful in any way. Nevertheless, acting on what a jury could well determine was nothing more than a stereotyped view of the limitations of the deaf, the Employer first relegated Ms. Chrysler to work only in the lab, then eliminated all of her hours, and finally, after months of hollow promises that she would be given some opportunities, it fired her. Not only that, but the Employer explicitly chastised Ms. Chrysler for having the temerity to complain about her treatment. . . .

Despite substantial evidence that Ms. Chrysler had performed well, the district court granted summary judgment for the Employer, holding that Ms. Chrysler was unable to perform the "essential functions" of the job and thus was not a "qualified individual" entitled to the protection of the ADA. Thus, the judge concluded that she could not do that which she had in fact done.

The day after completing . . . training, Ms. Chrysler had a photo session with the Krol family and their infant. This went very well and the Krols were very pleased, so much so that they bought more pictures than they had planned to buy, and returned the next month for another session. At that time, they requested to work with Ms.

Chrysler again but were told that she was not available. In fact, she was available but the Employer had relegated her to lab work only at that time.

Just three days after the Krols' session with Chrysler, two managers visited the Littleton studio to conduct advanced training for the staff. Ms. Chrysler attended. She requested an interpreter, but none was provided. Consequently, she could not benefit from the training session. One of the managers providing the training contacted district manager Bryan to express concern about Chrysler. (Apparently the concern was not that Ms. Chrysler had not been provided an interpreter, but concern that she had been hired as a photographer.) The next day Ms. Bryan directed Mr. Aguilar to assign Ms. Chrysler to the lab. . . .

Ms. Chrysler testified in her deposition that she had conducted as many as 15 to 20 photo shoots for the Employer, most with other employees present and "a couple" by herself. She said that district manager Bryan was with her during one session. Most significantly, she testified that no one ever expressed concern to her about how those sessions had been conducted. On appeal, the Employer has not identified any evidence that there was any deficiency in Ms. Chrysler's performance during the times that she conducted photo sessions, and my search of the record has produced no such evidence. Accordingly, a jury could conclude that the decision to assign Ms. Chrysler to work only in the lab, where she would have no contact with customers, was based on nothing but stereotyped assumptions against the abilities of the deaf. This is what the ADA was intended to counter.

The studio occasionally held mandatory staff meetings. During the six weeks that Ms. Chrysler worked there, she requested an interpreter for the meetings, but none was ever provided. Instead, the Employer merely gave her a written outline or agenda. As a result, she was not able to benefit as intended from the discussions in the meetings.

The Employer's business is seasonal. Ms. Chrysler had been hired as part of a pre-holiday expansion of the work force because Christmas is one of the busiest seasons. Immediately after Christmas, business slowed down dramatically at least until Valentine's Day, with the result that most employees got substantially reduced hours. But Ms. Chrysler was never given another shift after Christmas Eve. . . .

Coverage under the ADA extends to one who is a "qualified person with a disability" and that in turn is defined as one who "with or without reasonable accommodation, can perform the essential functions" of the position in question. Therefore, a necessary first step is to identify the "essential functions" of the position. "Essential functions" are the fundamental duties, not the "marginal functions of the position." *Davidson v. America Online, Inc.*, 337 F.3d 1179, 1191 (10th Cir. 2003). Determining whether a particular duty is "essential" is a *factual* inquiry based on a number of factors, including but not limited to the employer's judgment as to what duties are essential and any written job description the employer prepared for the position. 42 U.S.C. §12111(8); *Davidson.* But the employer's judgment is not conclusive evidence. As this court has said, "an employer may not turn every condition of employment which it elects to adopt into a job function, let alone an essential job function, merely by including it in a job description." *Davidson.* More specifically, we deal here with a purported "essential function" that the Employer now seeks to define in such a way as to eliminate an entire class of disabled persons — those who do not communicate well orally. . . .

The Employer's primary contention is that the ability to communicate orally is an essential function of the position. The EEOC's primary contention is that ability to communicate orally is a *method* by which most employees perform the essential function of communicating with the customers.

The Employer offered two job descriptions in its materials supporting its motion for summary judgment, one for the position of "performer" and one for the position of "seasonal associate." Both listed as job duties making customers feel welcome and comfortable and providing customers with a variety of distinct portraits. The Employer's witnesses gave similar descriptions of the job duties, such as: greet customers as they arrive and check them in at the front desk (intake); ascertain the kind of pictures the customer wants and take pictures that satisfy the customer, which includes communicating with the customer on desired poses (photography); develop pictures in the lab; and sell the customer a package of pictures (sales). Notably, none of these descriptions includes as a job duty a requirement of oral communication. A jury could find from this evidence that oral communication is "*a useful skill or method* to perform the essential functions" of communicating with customers, but one that is "not in itself an essential function of the . . . position." *See Skerski v. Time Warner Cable Co.*, 257 F.3d 273 280 (3d Cir. 2001) (emphasis added). Significantly, *Skerski* noted that the legislative history of the ADA indicated that the "essential function requirement focuses on the desired result rather than the means of accomplishing it." *Id.* (quoting 136 Cong. Rec. 11,451 1990).

The majority says that Ms. Chrysler "is unable to fully perform three of the four main duties of a performer." Rejecting the EEOC's evidence that Ms. Chrysler can communicate effectively using her alternative means, the majority further says that "nothing suggests that gestures, pantomime, and written communication are similarly effective and efficient for these tasks." I strongly disagree. Considerable evidence was produced from which a jury could determine that Ms. Chrysler could communicate effectively.

Most notably, there was evidence that Ms. Chrysler not only could but *did* communicate effectively and efficiently. First, there is the evidence of the photo session with the Krol family, discussed *supra*. Only by ignoring this clear example of Ms. Chrysler's ability to perform the essential functions of photo shooting and sales can the majority find that "nothing suggests" that she could do that which she had in fact already done. Moreover, Ms. Chrysler conducted several other shoots, some by herself and some with another employee present. No evidence has been cited to us suggesting that there were any communication problems in conducting these sessions. Mr. Aguilar testified that he never received a complaint from a customer for whom Ms. Chrysler had taken photos.

It appears that none of the employees who worked with Ms. Chrysler in photo sessions testified; in any event, the Employer has not cited any record evidence that any of these persons observed deficiencies in her performance. Consequently, in the face of Ms. Chrysler's testimony that she had conducted 15 to 20 photo sessions, there is no evidence of any resulting communication problems.

As for the efficiency of the communication, again there is no evidence that any of Ms. Chrysler's sessions were out of the ordinary in duration. Of course the Employer's ultimate interest is sales. The only evidence in the record regarding Ms. Chrysler's performance in this area comes from her manager, Mr. Aguilar, who testified that Ms. Chrysler made a "huge sale" to the Krol family, successfully selling the Krols more photos than they had originally planned to purchase.

It is surely relevant also that Ms. Chrysler was, after all, hired by the branch's manager, Mr. Aguilar, with full awareness of both the job requirements and Ms. Chrysler's deafness. Mr. Aguilar had been with the Employer for some years and believed that Ms. Chrysler could perform the job. As noted, he had worked with a deaf performer in the past. A jury could find these facts highly relevant in determining whether the ability to communicate orally is indeed a business necessity.

The EEOC produced additional evidence of Ms. Chrysler's abilities. Her vocational rehabilitation counselor, Ms. Barbara Bryant, testified, based on her experience in working with the disabled, that deaf persons can perform a job calling for strong customer service skills and oral communication skills by using gestures, notes and so forth. The counselor also testified that, based on her experience working with her, Ms. Chrysler could communicate with customers in the Employer's setting and ensure that they had a pleasant experience. The EEOC's vocational expert, Mr. Newman, also testified that Ms. Chrysler could perform the essential functions of the performer position with reasonable accommodation.

In sum, substantial evidence was presented from which a jury could determine that oral communication is not an essential function of the job but a *method* for performing the essential function of communication, and that Ms. Chrysler could perform the essential function of communication with or without reasonable accommodation. Thus the summary judgment against the EEOC on the discrimination claims was clearly unjustified. . . .

A *jury* must decide whether oral communication skills are an essential function of the job or only the manner in which most hearing employees perform the job. Indeed, I find it astonishing that on this record the district court and the majority rule *as a matter of law* that Ms. Chrysler could not perform the essential functions of the position when in fact the evidence that she could do so was considerably stronger than the minimum necessary to submit these *factual* questions to the jury.

A jury could determine that the Employer's decisions were based on exactly the kind of stereotypes that the ADA was enacted to combat. . . .

NOTES

1. *The Employer's Judgment.* Recall that §12111(8) states that "consideration shall be given to the employer's judgment as to what functions of a job are essential" and that written job descriptions prepared prior to advertising or interviewing applicants "shall be considered evidence of the essential functions of the job." Does this allow employers too often to dictate the outcome of ADA claims by labeling tasks as "essential"? The *Rehrs* court gives consideration to the employer's judgment but claims not to view it as dispositive. At the same time, it declares it "not the province of the court to question the legitimate operation of a production facility or determine what is the most productive or efficient shift schedule for a facility." And in a statement omitted from *The Picture People* decision, the majority states, "A court should be hesitant in displacing the business judgment of an employer on how to run its business." Is deference to the employer why the majority reached the result it did despite the impassioned argument from the dissent? *See also Gratzl v. Office of the Chief Judges of the 12th, 18th, 19th & 22nd Judicial Circuits*, 601 F.3d 674, 679-80 (7th Cir. 2010) ("We presume that an employer's understanding of the essential functions of the job is correct, unless the plaintiff offers sufficient evidence to the contrary"). Is this too deferential an approach? *See generally* Michelle A. Travis, *Disqualifying Universality Under the Americans with Disabilities Act Amendments Act*, 2015 MICH. ST. L. REV. 1689.

In other cases, employer *claims* about what is an essential function have failed in light of what the employer in fact *treats* as essential. *See Camp v. Bi-Lo, LLC*, 662 F. App'x 357 (6th Cir. 2016) (despite job description requiring heavy lifting, evidence that plaintiff's actual performance as part of a shelf-stocking team created a fact issue on essentiality barring summary judgment for the employer); *Shell v. Smith*, 789 F.3d

715 (7th Cir. 2015) (despite a job description requiring a mechanic's helper to occasionally drive a bus, the employer's actual practice of not requiring plaintiff to do so for 12 years created a jury question as to whether driving was an essential function).

2. *Burden of Proof.* The *Rehrs* opinion states it is the employer's burden to prove that a job function is an essential one. Is that correct? Or is it the employee's burden to prove he can perform the essential functions of the job, with or without reasonable accommodation? *Cf. Hawkins v. Schwan's Home Serv.*, 778 F.3d 877, 879 (10th Cir. 2015) (the employer has the burden of production on essential functions, but plaintiff has the burden of persuasion that particular functions are not essential); *Bates v. UPS*, 511 F.3d 974 (9th Cir. 2007) (en banc) (the plaintiff bears the ultimate burden of persuading the factfinder that he can perform the job's essential functions, but an employer who disputes the point must introduce evidence of those functions).

3. *Defining the Term.* The EEOC's regulations, promulgated under Title I and quoted in *The Picture People*, define essential job function to mean the "fundamental job duties," as opposed to the "marginal functions" of the job. Those regulations also list the factors to be considered in the analysis. 29 C.F.R. §1630.2(n). Applying this standard, was communicating effectively (as the dissent claimed) or effective *verbal* communication (as the majority claimed) the essential job function in *The Picture People?* Did the majority give sufficient attention to the EEOC's distinction between the task to be done — communicating with customers — and the method of performing that task? Michelle A. Travis, *Recapturing the Transformative Potential of Employment Discrimination Law*, 62 Wash & Lee L. Rev. 3, 6 (2005), argues that "judges must be able — and willing — to parse out the malleable ways that job tasks are organized from the actual tasks that comprise the essence of the job."

As with any multifactored test, different courts reach different results in situations that are at least broadly similar. For example, while *Rehrs* found rotating shifts essential and *Dargis v. Sheahan*, 526 F.3d 981 (7th Cir. 2008), held that a corrections officer was required to rotate through positions requiring inmate contact, *Turner v. Hershey Chocolate USA*, 440 F.3d 604 (3d Cir. 2006), was not so sure: a jury should decide whether rotation among three production lines was essential despite employer's contentions that it reduced repetitive stress injuries, where neither job description nor collective bargaining agreement mentioned rotation, little time was spent rotating, and inspectors had not rotated in past. *See also Rorrer v. City of Stow*, 743 F.3d 1025 (6th Cir. 2014) (genuine issue of material fact existed as to whether driving fire apparatus during an emergency was essential for a firefighter when that function could have been easily performed by others).

4. *Attendance as an Essential Job Function.* Numerous courts have held that regular and timely attendance at work is an essential job function, and, therefore, a disabled individual who cannot meet that requirement is not "qualified" within the meaning of the ADA or the Rehabilitation Act. *See, e.g., EEOC v. Ford Motor Co.*, 782 F.3d 753 (6th Cir. 2015) (en banc) (regular and predictable on-site attendance was essential for a resale buyer position when technological shifts did not permit the work to be performed by telecommuting for up to four days per week); *Taylor-Novotny v. Health Alliance Med. Plans, Inc.*, 772 F.3d 478, 489-90 (7th Cir. 2014) (the fact that her employer allowed for work from home did not mean that attendance was not an essential function); *Samper v. Providence St. Vincent Med. Ctr.*, 675 F.3d 1233 (9th Cir. 2012) (scheduled attendance was an essential function of neonatal nurse job and absences could not be reasonably accommodated due to difficulty in finding last-minute replacements with her specific skills). Some courts have cautioned, however, that presuming uninterrupted attendance is essential improperly avoids the individualized assessment of accommodations required by

the ADA. *See Solomon v. Vilsack*, 763 F.3d 1 (D.C. Cir. 2014) (allowing an employee to vary the number of hours worked each day or week is not per se an unreasonable accommodation under the Rehabilitation Act); *McMillan v. City of New York*, 711 F.3d 120 (2d Cir. 2013) (while arrival on time might be essential for many, perhaps most, jobs, it may not have been an essential requirement of the plaintiff's position given past approval of his late arrivals and the employer's flex-time policy).

Is there a difference between an employee whose disability results in sporadic absences and one whose disability requires a medical leave? Leave as a reasonable accommodation is discussed further in subsection C2.

5. *Accommodations Impacting Other Workers.* If the plaintiff works only day shifts as an accommodation, then other employees necessarily will need to work more night and evening shifts. Is it appropriate to take this burden on other employees into account in determining whether a job function is essential? *See Hill v. Walker*, 737 F.3d 1209, 1217 (8th Cir. 2013) (plaintiff, a social worker, was not otherwise qualified when removing her from particularly stressful cases to accommodate her anxiety would "wreak havoc" with management of the agency). Or should that instead be considered a question of undue hardship? See p. 495.

6. *Quality and Quantity of Work.* Can the quantity or quality of work produced be an essential function of the job? The EEOC's Interpretive Guidance provides:

> [T]he inquiry into essential functions is not intended to second guess an employer's business judgment with regard to production standards, whether qualitative or quantitative, nor to require employers to lower such standards. . . . If an employer requires its typists to be able to accurately type 75 words per minute, it will not be called upon to explain why an inaccurate work product, or a typing speed of 65 words per minute, would not be adequate. . . . However, if an employer does require accurate 75 word per minute typing . . . , it will have to show that it actually imposes such requirements on its employees in fact, and not simply on paper.

29 C.F.R. pt. 1630, app. §1630.2(n). *See Milton v. Scrivner, Inc.*, 53 F.3d 1118 (10th Cir. 1995) (employer's new production standard constituted an essential function of the selector job). What arguments would you make on the issue of essential functions on behalf of a dyslexic lawyer who produces a good product but is denied partnership on the basis of low productivity? Is she a qualified individual with a disability? Note that the statute prohibits discriminatory qualification standards unless job related for the position in question and consistent with business necessity and the duty of reasonable accommodation. §12112(b)(6). Is the Interpretive Guidance consistent with this statutory provision?

7. *Essential Even If Infrequent.* While the frequency with which a job function is performed may be relevant to whether it is "essential," even rarely performed functions may be essential. In *Hennagir v. Utah Dep't of Corr.*, 587 F.3d 1255 (10th Cir. 2009), the court held that a physician's assistant who could not perform activities necessary for a prison's emergency-response training program was unable to perform an essential job function. Because the PAs had daily contact with inmates, the training was an essential, if rarely performed, function. *See also Adair v. City of Muskogee*, 823 F.3d 1297 (10th Cir. 2016) (although plaintiff's position as hazmat director did not require him to lift, as a firefighter he could be called upon to respond to a fire and required to lift heavy objects); *Scruggs v. Pulaski Cnty.*, 817 F.3d 1087, 1092-93 (8th Cir. 2016) (the ability to lift 40 pounds is an essential function of juvenile detention officer job, despite not being often required; officers sometimes had to lift detainees to restrain them, all of whom weigh more than 40 pounds).

8. *A More Refined Analysis.* Although these principles suggest that courts can be strict with respect to finding functions essential, a number of decisions have been more receptive to plaintiffs' claims. *E.g., Samson v. Fed. Express Corp.*, 746 F.3d 1196 (11th Cir. 2014) (despite Fed Ex's judgment and a job description, many licensed drivers in the terminal could test-drive trucks and the incumbent technician spent little time doing it); *Rorrer v. City of Stow*, 743 F.3d 1025 (6th Cir. 2014) (genuine dispute as to whether driving a fire apparatus was an essential function of a firefighter position given no evidence that the department utilized national guidelines so providing and the certifying physician did not rely on them in determining plaintiff's unfitness); *Keith v. County of Oakland*, 703 F.3d 918 (6th Cir. 2013) (genuine issue of material fact as to deaf lifeguard's ability to perform the essential function of communication while working at a wave pool given his visual scanning techniques and use of whistle and physical gestures).

PROBLEM 7.4

Sam is hearing impaired. He has applied for a secretarial job that includes answering phones. He asserts that he can perform all aspects of the job, except for answering the phone, without any accommodation. With respect to answering the phone, he has proposed two alternative accommodations: (1) eliminating the phone responsibilities, or (2) providing a telecommunications device (TDD) that would allow him to answer the phone. Is he qualified for this job? What arguments can he make? What arguments can the employer make? Do you need any additional information to answer these questions?

PROBLEM 7.5

Jan works as a supervisor for Acme Products, a small manufacturing company. Jan suffers from Tourette's syndrome, a disorder that causes some individuals to uncontrollably burst out with obscene or extremely insulting remarks. Jan's outbursts usually take the form of racial epithets. Fifty percent of Acme Products' employees are African Americans. Several of these employees have complained to the EEO officer at Acme about Jan's outbursts. Acme has consulted you for advice. What advice would you give?

2.   *The Duty of Reasonable Accommodation*

A qualified individual with a disability is one who can perform the essential functions of the job she holds or desires *with or without reasonable accommodation.* The concept of reasonable accommodation distinguishes the ADA from other antidiscrimination statutes. Under the ADA, it is *not* enough for an employer to treat its disabled employees the same — no better and no worse — than it treats its nondisabled employees. In appropriate circumstances, the employer must take affirmative steps that will allow disabled employees to perform their jobs. *See Cleveland v. Policy Mgmt. Sys. Corp.*, 526 U.S. 795, 803 (1999) (a Social Security claim of total and permanent disability is not necessarily inconsistent with an employee's ADA claim alleging plaintiff would be qualified had the employer accommodated his disability). *See also Holly v.*

Clairson Indus., 492 F.3d 1247, 1262 (11th Cir. 2007) (defendant "is not insulated from liability under the ADA by treating its nondisabled employees exactly the same as its disabled employees . . . the very purpose of reasonable accommodation laws is to *require* employers to treat disabled individuals differently in some circumstances"). It is often the accommodation that will allow the disabled employee who otherwise would be unable to work at all to perform the essential functions of the job.

Failing to provide reasonable accommodations constitutes one form of discrimination under the statute. Section 12112(b)(5) of the ADA defines discrimination to include:

> (A) not making reasonable accommodations to the known physical or mental limitations of an otherwise qualified individual with a disability who is an applicant or employee, unless such covered entity can demonstrate that the accommodation would impose an undue hardship on the operation of the business of such covered entity; or
> (B) denying employment opportunities to a job applicant or employee who is an otherwise qualified individual with a disability, if such denial is based on the need of such covered entity to make reasonable accommodation to the physical or mental impairments of the employee or applicant.

Thus, this section makes reasonable accommodation relevant both to establishing and defending against a discrimination claim based on the failure to accommodate. If a disabled individual can perform essential functions with reasonable accommodation, the employer has a duty to provide those accommodations. If the disabled individual requires accommodations that are not reasonable or that impose an undue hardship on the employer, disparate treatment on the basis of disability is permitted and accommodating the disability is not required. Recall, however, that after the ADAAA employers are not required to reasonably accommodate "regarded as" plaintiffs. Thus, under the amended statute, only plaintiffs who qualify as disabled under one of the first two prongs of "disability" may pursue a reasonable accommodation claim.

This section considers "reasonable accommodation" in the context of proving a disability discrimination claim of "not making reasonable accommodations." Reasonable accommodation goes beyond providing accommodations required to perform essential job functions. Employers also have a duty to provide accommodations that permit disabled individuals to enjoy equal access to the benefits and privileges of employment. *See Feist v. Louisiana, Dep't of Justice, Office of the Atty. Gen.*, 730 F.3d 450 (5th Cir. 2013). The ADA also requires employers to make "accommodations that are required to ensure equal opportunity in the application process." *See* 29 C.F.R. pt. 1630, app. §1630.2(o).

Section 12111(9) identifies some of the areas in which accommodation may be required:

> (A) making existing facilities used by employees readily accessible to and usable by individuals with disabilities; and
> (B) job restructuring, part-time or modified work schedules, reassignment to a vacant position, acquisition or modification of equipment or devices, appropriate adjustment or modifications of examinations, training materials or policies, the provision of qualified readers or interpreters, and other similar accommodations for individuals with disabilities.

Note that the issue in a "failure to accommodate" case is not whether the employer has treated the disabled individual differently. Nor is the question whether the employer has legitimate reasons for treating a disabled individual differently. In a reasonable accommodation case, the disabled individual is *requesting* different treatment, and the issue is whether providing it is reasonable or an undue hardship.

US AIRWAYS, INC. v. BARNETT
535 U.S. 391 (2002)

BREYER, J., delivered the opinion of the Court, in which REHNQUIST, C.J., and STEVENS, O'CONNOR, and KENNEDY, JJ., joined. STEVENS, J., and O'CONNOR, J., filed concurring opinions. SCALIA, J., filed a dissenting opinion, in which THOMAS, J., joined. SOUTER, J., filed a dissenting opinion, in which GINSBURG, J., joined.

The Americans with Disabilities Act of 1990 prohibits an employer from discriminating against an "individual with a disability" who, with "reasonable accommodation," can perform the essential functions of the job. This case, arising in the context of summary judgment, asks us how the Act resolves a potential conflict between: (1) the interests of a disabled worker who seeks assignment to a particular position as a "reasonable accommodation," and (2) the interests of other workers with superior rights to bid for the job under an employer's seniority system. In such a case, does the accommodation demand trump the seniority system?

In our view, the seniority system will prevail in the run of cases. As we interpret the statute, to show that a requested accommodation conflicts with the rules of a seniority system is ordinarily to show that the accommodation is not "reasonable." Hence such a showing will entitle an employer/defendant to summary judgment on the question — unless there is more. The plaintiff remains free to present evidence of special circumstances that make "reasonable" a seniority rule exception in the particular case. And such a showing will defeat the employer's demand for summary judgment.

I

In 1990, Robert Barnett, the plaintiff and respondent here, injured his back while working in a cargo-handling position at petitioner US Airways, Inc. He invoked seniority rights and transferred to a less physically demanding mailroom position. Under US Airways' seniority system, that position, like others, periodically became open to seniority-based employee bidding. In 1992, Barnett learned that at least two employees senior to him intended to bid for the mailroom job. He asked US Airways to accommodate his disability-imposed limitations by making an exception that would allow him to remain in the mailroom. After permitting Barnett to continue his mailroom work for five months while it considered the matter, US Airways eventually decided not to make an exception. And Barnett lost his job.

Barnett then brought this ADA suit claiming, among other things, that he was an "individual with a disability" capable of performing the essential functions of the mailroom job, that the mailroom job amounted to a "reasonable accommodation" of his disability, and that US Airways, in refusing to assign him the job, unlawfully discriminated against him. . . .

[US Airways' petition for certiorari asked whether] "the [ADA] requires an employer to reassign a disabled employee to a position as a 'reasonable accommodation' even though another employee is entitled to hold the position under the employer's bona fide and established seniority system." . . .

II

In answering the question presented, we must consider the following statutory provisions. First, the ADA says that an employer may not "discriminate against a qualified individual with a disability." §12112(a). Second, the ADA says that a "qualified" individual includes "an individual with a disability who, *with* or without *reasonable accommodation*, can perform the essential functions of" the relevant "employment position." §12111(8) (emphasis added). Third, the ADA says that "discrimination" includes an employer's "*not making reasonable accommodations* to the known physical or mental limitations of an otherwise qualified . . . employee, *unless* [the employer] can demonstrate that the accommodation would impose an *undue hardship* on the operation of [its] business." §12112(b)(5)(A) (emphasis added). Fourth, the ADA says that the term "'reasonable accommodation' may include . . . reassignment to a vacant position." §12111(9)(B).

The parties interpret this statutory language as applied to seniority systems in radically different ways. In US Airways' view, the fact that an accommodation would violate the rules of a seniority system always shows that the accommodation is not a "reasonable" one. In Barnett's polar opposite view, a seniority system violation never shows that an accommodation sought is not a "reasonable" one. Barnett concedes that a violation of seniority rules might help to show that the accommodation will work "undue" employer "hardship," but that is a matter for an employer to demonstrate case by case. . . .

A

US Airways' claim that a seniority system virtually always trumps a conflicting accommodation demand rests primarily upon its view of how the Act treats workplace "preferences." Insofar as a requested accommodation violates a disability-neutral workplace rule, such as a seniority rule, it grants the employee with a disability treatment that other workers could not receive. Yet the Act, US Airways says, seeks only "equal" treatment for those with disabilities. See, e.g., 42 U.S.C. §12101(a)(9). It does not, it contends, require an employer to grant preferential treatment. Cf. H.R. Rep. No. 101-485, pt. 2, p. 66 (1990); S. Rep. No. 101-116, pp. 26-27 (1989) (employer has no "obligation to prefer *applicants* with disabilities over other *applicants*" (emphasis added)). Hence it does not require the employer to grant a request that, in violating a disability-neutral rule, would provide a preference.

While linguistically logical, this argument fails to recognize what the Act specifies, namely, that preferences will sometimes prove necessary to achieve the Act's basic equal opportunity goal. The Act requires preferences in the form of "reasonable accommodations" that are needed for those with disabilities to obtain the *same* workplace opportunities that those without disabilities automatically enjoy. By definition any special "accommodation" requires the employer to treat an employee with a disability differently, *i.e.*, preferentially. And the fact that the difference in treatment violates an employer's disability-neutral rule cannot by itself place the accommodation beyond the Act's potential reach.

Were that not so, the "reasonable accommodation" provision could not accomplish its intended objective. Neutral office assignment rules would automatically prevent the accommodation of an employee whose disability-imposed limitations require him to work on the ground floor. Neutral "break-from-work" rules would automatically prevent the accommodation of an individual who needs additional breaks from work, perhaps to permit medical visits. Neutral furniture budget rules would automatically prevent the accommodation of an individual who needs a different kind of chair or desk. Many employers will have neutral rules governing the kinds of actions most needed to reasonably accommodate a worker with a disability. See 42 U.S.C. §12111(9)(b) (setting forth examples such as "job restructuring," "part-time or modified work schedules," "acquisition or modification of equipment or devices," "and other similar accommodations"). Yet Congress, while providing such examples, said nothing suggesting that the presence of such neutral rules would create an automatic exemption. . . .

In sum, the nature of the "reasonable accommodation" requirement, the statutory examples, and the Act's silence about the exempting effect of neutral rules together convince us that the Act does not create any such automatic exemption. The simple fact that an accommodation would provide a "preference" — in the sense that it would permit the worker with a disability to violate a rule that others must obey — cannot, *in and of itself*, automatically show that the accommodation is not "reasonable." As a result, we reject the position taken by US Airways and Justice Scalia to the contrary. . . .

B

Barnett argues that the statutory words "reasonable accommodation" mean only "effective accommodation," authorizing a court to consider the requested accommodation's ability to meet an individual's disability-related needs, and nothing more. On this view, a seniority rule violation, having nothing to do with the accommodation's effectiveness, has nothing to do with its "reasonableness." It might, at most, help to prove an "undue hardship on the operation of the business." . . . Barnett adds that any other view would make the words "reasonable accommodation" and "undue hardship" virtual mirror images — creating redundancy in the statute. And he says that any such other view would create a practical burden of proof dilemma.

The practical burden of proof dilemma arises, Barnett argues, because the statute imposes the burden of demonstrating an "undue hardship" upon the employer, while the burden of proving "reasonable accommodation" remains with the plaintiff, here the employee. This allocation seems sensible in that an employer can more frequently and easily prove the presence of business hardship than an employee can prove its absence. But suppose that an employee must counter a claim of "seniority rule violation" in order to prove that an "accommodation" request is "reasonable." Would that not force the employee to prove what is in effect an absence, *i.e.*, an absence of hardship, despite the statute's insistence that the employer "demonstrate" hardship's presence?

These arguments do not persuade us that Barnett's legal interpretation of "reasonable" is correct. For one thing, in ordinary English the word "reasonable" does not mean "effective." It is the word "accommodation," not the word "reasonable," that conveys the need for effectiveness. An *ineffective* "modification" or "adjustment" will not *accommodate* a disabled individual's limitations. Nor does an ordinary English meaning of the term "reasonable accommodation" make of it a simple, redundant mirror image of the term "undue hardship." The statute refers to an "undue hardship on the operation of the business." 42 U.S.C. §12112(b)(5)(A). Yet a demand for an effective accommodation could prove unreasonable because of its impact, not on business operations, but on fellow employees — say because it will lead to dismissals, relocations, or modification of employee benefits to which an employer, looking at the matter from the perspective of the business itself, may be relatively indifferent.

Neither does the statute's primary purpose require Barnett's special reading. The statute seeks to diminish or to eliminate the stereotypical thought processes, the thoughtless actions, and the hostile reactions that far too often bar those with disabilities from participating fully in the Nation's life, including the workplace. See generally §§12101(a) and (b). These objectives demand unprejudiced thought and reasonable responsive reaction on the part of employers and fellow workers alike. They will sometimes require affirmative conduct to promote entry of disabled people into the workforce. They do not, however, demand action beyond the realm of the reasonable. . . .

Finally, an ordinary language interpretation of the word "reasonable" does not create the "burden of proof" dilemma to which Barnett points. Many of the lower courts, while rejecting both US Airways' and Barnett's more absolute views, have reconciled the phrases "reasonable accommodation" and "undue hardship" in a practical way.

They have held that a plaintiff/employee (to defeat a defendant/employer's motion for summary judgment) need only show that an "accommodation" seems reasonable on its face, *i.e.*, ordinarily or in the run of cases. *See, e.g., Reed v. LePage Bakeries, Inc.*, 244 F.3d 254, 259 (CA1 2001) (plaintiff meets burden on reasonableness by showing that, "at least on the face of things," the accommodation will be feasible for the employer); *Borkowski v. Valley Central School Dist.*, 63 F.3d 131, 138 (CA2 1995) (plaintiff satisfies "burden of production" by showing "plausible accommodation").

Once the plaintiff has made this showing, the defendant/employer then must show special (typically case-specific) circumstances that demonstrate undue hardship in the particular circumstances. *See Reed* ("'undue hardship inquiry focuses on the hardships imposed . . . in the context of the particular [employer's] operations'"); *Borkowski* (after plaintiff makes initial showing, burden falls on employer to show that particular accommodation "would cause it to suffer an undue hardship").

Not every court has used the same language, but their results are functionally similar. In our opinion, that practical view of the statute, applied consistently with ordinary summary judgment principles, see Fed. Rule Civ. Proc. 56, avoids Barnett's burden of proof dilemma, while reconciling the two statutory phrases ("reasonable accommodation" and "undue hardship").

III

The question in the present case focuses on the relationship between seniority systems and the plaintiff's need to show that an "accommodation" seems reasonable on its face, *i.e.*, ordinarily or in the run of cases. We must assume that the plaintiff, an employee, is an "individual with a disability." He has requested assignment to a mailroom position as a "reasonable accommodation." We also assume that normally such a request would be reasonable within the meaning of the statute, were it not for one circumstance, namely, that the assignment would violate the rules of a seniority system. *See* §12111(9) ("reasonable accommodation" may include "reassignment to a vacant position"). Does that circumstance mean that the proposed accommodation is not a "reasonable" one?

In our view, the answer to this question ordinarily is "yes." The statute does not require proof on a case-by-case basis that a seniority system should prevail. That is because it would not be reasonable in the run of cases that the assignment in question trump the rules of a seniority system. To the contrary, it will ordinarily be unreasonable for the assignment to prevail.

A

Several factors support our conclusion that a proposed accommodation will not be reasonable in the run of cases. Analogous case law supports this conclusion, for it has recognized the importance of seniority to employee-management relations. [The Court cited numerous decisions issued under Title VII, the Rehabilitation Act, and the ADA holding that seniority systems found in collective bargaining agreements trump requested accommodations. It then noted that problems caused by violating seniority systems did not pertain merely to collectively bargained systems.]

For one thing, the typical seniority system provides important employee benefits by creating, and fulfilling, employee expectations of fair, uniform treatment. These benefits include "job security and an opportunity for steady and predictable advancement based on objective standards." They include "an element of due process," limiting "unfairness in personnel decisions." And they consequently encourage employees to invest in the employing company, accepting "less than their value to the firm early in their careers" in return for greater benefits in later years.

Most important for present purposes, to require the typical employer to show more than the existence of a seniority system might well undermine the employees' expectations of consistent, uniform treatment — expectations upon which the seniority system's benefits depend. That is because such a rule would substitute a complex case-specific "accommodation" decision made by management for the more uniform, impersonal operation of seniority rules. Such management decision making, with its inevitable discretionary elements, would involve a matter of the greatest importance to employees, namely, layoffs; it would take place outside, as well as inside, the confines of a court case; and it might well take place fairly often. We can find nothing in the statute that suggests Congress intended to undermine seniority systems in this way. And we consequently conclude that the employer's showing of violation of the rules of a seniority system is by itself ordinarily sufficient.

B

The plaintiff (here the employee) nonetheless remains free to show that special circumstances warrant a finding that, despite the presence of a seniority system (which the ADA may not trump in the run of cases), the requested "accommodation" is "reasonable" on the particular facts. That is because special circumstances might alter the important expectations described above. The plaintiff might show, for example, that the employer, having retained the right to change the seniority system unilaterally, exercises that right fairly frequently, reducing employee expectations that the system will be followed — to the point where one more departure, needed to accommodate an individual with a disability, will not likely make a difference. The plaintiff might show that the system already contains exceptions such that, in the circumstances, one further exception is unlikely to matter. We do not mean these examples to exhaust the kinds of showings that a plaintiff might make. But we do mean to say that the plaintiff must bear the burden of showing special circumstances that make an exception from the seniority system reasonable in the particular case. And to do so, the plaintiff must explain why, in the particular case, an exception to the employer's seniority policy can constitute a "reasonable accommodation" even though in the ordinary case it cannot.

IV

In its question presented, US Airways asked us whether the ADA requires an employer to assign a disabled employee to a particular position even though another employee is entitled to that position under the employer's "established seniority system." We answer that *ordinarily* the ADA does not require that assignment. Hence, a showing that the assignment would violate the rules of a seniority system warrants summary judgment for the employer — unless there is more. The plaintiff must present evidence of that "more," namely, special circumstances surrounding the particular case that demonstrate the assignment is nonetheless reasonable. . . .

[Justice O'Connor's concurring opinion omitted.]

Justice SCALIA, with whom Justice THOMAS joins, dissenting.

The principal defect of today's opinion . . . goes well beyond the uncertainty it produces regarding the relationship between the ADA and the infinite variety of seniority systems. The conclusion that any seniority system can ever be overridden is merely one consequence of a mistaken interpretation of the ADA that makes all employment rules and practices — even those which (like a seniority system) pose no *distinctive* obstacle to the disabled — subject to suspension when that is (in a court's view) a "reasonable" means of enabling a disabled employee to keep his job. That is a far cry from what I believe the accommodation provision of the ADA requires: the suspension (within reason) of those employment rules and practices *that the employee's disability prevents him from observing.* . . .

The Court begins its analysis by describing the ADA as declaring that an employer may not "discriminate against a qualified individual with a disability." In fact the Act says more: an employer may not "discriminate against a qualified individual with a disability *because of the disability* of such individual." 42 U.S.C. §12112(a) (1994 ed.) (emphasis added). It further provides that discrimination includes "not making reasonable accommodations *to the known physical or mental limitations* of an otherwise qualified individual with a disability." §12112(b)(5)(A) (emphasis added).

Read together, these provisions order employers to modify or remove (within reason) policies and practices that burden a disabled person "because of [his] disability." In other words, the ADA eliminates workplace barriers only if a disability prevents an employee from overcoming them — those barriers that would not be barriers *but for* the employee's disability. These include, for example, work stations that cannot accept the employee's wheelchair, or an assembly-line practice that requires long periods of standing. But they do not include rules and practices that bear no more heavily upon the disabled employee than upon others — even though an exemption from such a rule or practice might in a sense "make up for" the employee's disability. It is not a required accommodation, for example, to pay a disabled employee more than others at his grade level — even if that increment is earmarked for massage or physical therapy that would enable the employee to work with as little physical discomfort as his co-workers. That would be "accommodating" the disabled employee, but it would not be "making . . . accommodation *to the known physical or mental limitations*" of the employee, §12112(b)(5)(A), because it would not eliminate any workplace practice that constitutes an obstacle because of his disability.

So also with exemption from a seniority system, which burdens the disabled and nondisabled alike. In particular cases, seniority rules may have a harsher effect upon the disabled employee than upon his co-workers. If the disabled employee is physically capable of performing only one task in the workplace, seniority rules may be, for him, the difference between employment and unemployment. But that does not make the seniority system a disability-related obstacle, any more than harsher impact upon the more needy disabled employee renders the salary system a disability-related obstacle. When one departs from this understanding, the ADA's accommodation provision becomes a standardless grab bag — leaving it to the courts to decide which workplace preferences (higher salary, longer vacations, reassignment to positions to which others are entitled) can be deemed "reasonable" to "make up for" the particular employee's disability. . . .

Justice SOUTER, with whom Justice GINSBURG joins, dissenting.
[The dissent noted that the ADA listed "reassignment to a vacant position" as one method of reasonable accommodation and stressed that the ADA, unlike Title VII and the ADEA, did not have any explicit seniority exception. Thus, "consideration of facts peculiar to this very case is needed to gauge whether Barnett has carried the burden of showing his proposed accommodation to be a 'reasonable' one despite the policy in force at US Airways." In that analysis, highly relevant was the fact that Barnett was merely seeking to keep the mailroom job he had held for two years and was not seeking to bump any other employee. Further, "US Airways apparently took pains to ensure that its seniority rules raised no great expectations" since it insisted that its seniority system "was noncontractual and modifiable at will."]

NOTES

1. *Is There a Vacancy?* US Airways contended that a position that would be allocated under a seniority system's bumping or bidding provisions was not a "vacancy" within the meaning of the statute. The majority rejected that argument out of hand. But notice the predicate of the argument — an accommodation can't require bumping of a co-worker out of a position he or she already holds. *Barnett* strongly implies that is correct, and that may be true regardless of whether there is a seniority system. *See Dunderdale v. United Airlines, Inc.*, 807 F.3d 849, 851 (7th Cir. 2015) (while plaintiff could perform his job with an accommodation, reassignment was not required either to a position violating the seniority system or to positions not shown to be vacant).

2. *Reasonable Accommodation as Special Treatment.* The *Barnett* Court expressly acknowledged that the ADA will sometimes require that the disabled worker receive a preference. "By definition any special 'accommodation' requires the employer to treat an employee with a disability differently, *i.e.*, preferentially. And the fact that the difference in treatment violates an employer's disability-neutral rule cannot by itself place the accommodation beyond the Act's potential reach." Despite *Barnett*, however, we will see that there is still resistance to the notion of preferences for the disabled.

3. *Benefits to the Nondisabled?* The "special treatment" critique of the duty of reasonable accommodation often, as in *Barnett*, focuses on the costs that accommodation imposes on other workers. Left out of the equation, however, are the benefits that the ADA creates for nondisabled co-workers. *See generally* Michelle A. Travis, *Lashing Back at the ADA Backlash: How the Americans With Disabilities Act Benefits Americans Without Disabilities*, 76 TENN. L. REV. 311 (2009) (exploring the variety of ways in which the ADA aligns the interests of workers with and without disabilities, rather than pitting them against each other in a zero-sum game, thereby giving all workers a stake in the ADA's future); Elizabeth F. Emens, *Integrating Accommodation*, 156

U. PA. L. REV. 839 (2008) (while courts have recognized that accommodations may create third-party costs, they have overlooked the potential for third-party benefits).

4. *Preferential Reassignment? Barnett* was decided in the context of a seniority system dispute, but the issue of the conflicting interests of the disabled and their co-workers can arise where no such systems exist. Does reasonable accommodation mean that disabled workers must be preferred to their abled peers? One provision of the statute may suggest exactly that by stating that reasonable accommodation may include "reassignment to a vacant position." §12111(9). Assuming other competitors for such a position, must a disabled worker be given preference? Does it matter if the co-workers are better qualified so long as the disabled worker is also qualified?

In *Huber v. Wal-Mart*, 486 F.3d 480 (8th Cir. 2007), the Eighth Circuit held no, upholding an employer's policy of filling vacancies with the most qualified applicant. For Wal-Mart, the duty of reasonable accommodation was apparently satisfied because plaintiff could compete for the position — although the prohibition of discriminating on the basis of disability would require that in any event. The court concluded that "the ADA is not an affirmative action statute," and does not require an employer to "violate a legitimate nondiscriminatory policy of the employer to hire the most qualified candidate." *Id.* at 483. It found *Barnett* no obstacle to its result; indeed, to the extent that case allowed a seniority system to prevail over the duty to accommodate a disabled plaintiff, *Barnett* supported its result. *Id.* at 484.

Huber created a circuit split, with *Smith v. Midland Brake, Inc.*, 180 F.3d 1154, 1164-65 (10th Cir. 1999) (en banc). *See also Aka v. Washington Hospital Center*, 156 F.3d 1284 (D.C. Cir. 1998). More importantly, the Seventh Circuit did a U-turn after *Barnett* was decided. Although an earlier panel (in a decision much relied on by *Huber*) had held that the ADA does not require reassignment of a qualified disabled employee over a more qualified competitor, *EEOC v. United Airlines, Inc.*, 693 F.3d 760 (7th Cir. 2012), overruled that decision, reading *Barnett* as rejecting the "anti-preference interpretation of the ADA," and finding that "[m]erely following a 'neutral rule' did not allow U.S. Airways to claim an 'automatic exemption' from the accommodation requirement." *Id.* at 763. While *Barnett* did allow a seniority system to trump the accommodation duty, "a best-qualified selection policy" isn't equivalent because "violation of a best-qualified selection policy does not involve the property-rights and administrative concerns (and resulting burdens) presented by the violation of a seniority policy." *Id.* at 764. According to the *United Airlines* court, the employer could prevail only by following *Barnett*'s lead only if mandatory reassignment were not ordinarily a reasonable accommodation or, if so, whether there were consideration specific to United's situation that would make such an accommodation an undue hardship. Nevertheless, the next circuit to address the question sided with *Huber. United States EEOC v. St. Joseph's Hosp., Inc.*, 842 F.3d 1333, 1347 (11th Cir. 2016) (ADA does not require preferential noncompetitive reassignment).

5. *When Is a Position Vacant?* Whatever the parameters of the duty of reasonable accommodation when an employer has a vacant position, any such obligation depends on the position in fact being available. Thus, whatever the reassignment obligations of an employer might be to a disabled employee, they do not require creating a new job. *See Toronka v. Cont'l Airlines, Inc.*, 411 F. App'x 719 (5th Cir. 2011). Further, the time frame for an available vacancy has been treated as short. *See Turner v. City of Paris, Ky.*, 534 F. App'x 299, 303 (6th Cir. 2013) (a position is not vacant if it is not currently so or will be vacant within "a short period of time," perhaps a week). Finally, the courts have tended to view positions as not vacant for purposes of accommodation if any other worker has a claim to them. *E.g., McFadden v. Ballard Spahr Andrews &*

Ingersoll, LLP, 611 F.3d 1 (D.C. Cir. 2010) (failure to reassign plaintiff to a temporarily open receptionist position did not violate the duty to accommodate when it was occupied by a long-term permanent receptionist on disability leave who was expected to return); *Duvall v. Georgia-Pacific Consumer Prods., L.P.*, 607 1255 (10th Cir. 2010) (positions filled by "temporary" workers were not "vacant"). Finally, an employer is not required to promote a disabled individual if the only available jobs are higher level. *Bush v. Compass Grp. USA., Inc.*, No. 16-6258, 2017 U.S. App. LEXIS 5248, at *22 (6th Cir. Mar. 23, 2017).

6. *The Scholarship.* The notion that the ADA sometimes pits disabled workers against their abled peers rather than their employers has generated a wealth of scholarship. *See* Stacey M. Hickox, *Transfer as an Accommodation: Standards from Discrimination Cases and Theory*, 62 ARK. L. REV. 195 (2009); Nicole B. Porter, *Reasonable Burdens: Resolving the Conflict Between Disabled Employees and Their Coworkers*, 34 FLA. ST. U. L. REV. 313 (2007) Alex B. Long, *The ADA's Reasonable Accommodation Requirement and "Innocent Third Parties,"* 68 MO. L. REV. 863, 905 (2003); Stephen F. Befort, *Reasonable Accommodation and Reassignment Under the Americans with Disabilities Act: Answers, Questions and Suggested Solutions After* U.S. Airways, Inc. v. Barnett, 45 ARIZ. L. REV. 931 (2003); Cheryl L. Anderson, *"Neutral" Employer Policies and the ADA: The Implications of* U.S. Airways Inc. v. Barnett *Beyond Seniority Systems*, 51 DRAKE L. REV. 1 (2002).

VANDE ZANDE v. STATE OF WISCONSIN DEPARTMENT OF ADMINISTRATION
44 F.3d 538 (7th Cir. 1995)

POSNER, Chief Judge.

In 1990, Congress passed the Americans with Disabilities Act. The stated purpose is "to provide a clear and comprehensive national mandate for the elimination of discrimination against individuals with disabilities." . . . [Many] impairments are not in fact disabling but are believed to be so, and the people having them may be denied employment or otherwise shunned as a consequence. Such people, objectively capable of performing as well as the unimpaired, are analogous to capable workers discriminated against because of their skin color or some other vocationally irrelevant characteristic.

The more problematic case is that of an individual who has a vocationally relevant disability — an impairment such as blindness or paralysis that limits a major human capability, such as seeing or walking. In the common case in which such an impairment interferes with the individual's ability to perform up to the standards of the workplace, or increases the cost of employing him, hiring and firing decisions based on the impairment are not "discriminatory" in a sense closely analogous to employment discrimination on racial grounds. The draftsmen of the Act knew this. But they were unwilling to confine the concept of disability discrimination to cases in which the disability is irrelevant to the performance of the disabled person's job. Instead, they defined "discrimination" to include an employer's "not making reasonable accommodations to the known physical or mental limitations of an otherwise qualified individual with a disability who is an applicant or employee, unless . . . [the employer] can demonstrate that the accommodation would impose an undue hardship on the operation of the . . . [employer's] business." . . .

Lori Vande Zande, aged 35, is paralyzed from the waist down as a result of a tumor of the spinal cord. Her paralysis makes her prone to develop pressure ulcers, treatment of which often requires that she stay at home for several weeks. [The court rejected the argument that an intermittent impairment that "is a characteristic manifestation of an admitted disability" was not itself a disability that must be accommodated, a position later codified by the ADAAA. §12102(4)(D).]

Vande Zande worked for the housing division of the state's department of administration for three years, beginning in January 1990. . . . Her job was that of a program assistant, and involved preparing public information materials, planning meetings, interpreting regulations, typing, mailing, filing, and copying. In short, her tasks were of a clerical, secretarial, and administrative assistant character. In order to enable her to do this work, the defendants, as she acknowledges, "made numerous accommodations relating to the plaintiff's disability." As examples, in her words, "they paid the landlord to have bathrooms modified and to have a step ramped; they bought special adjustable furniture for the plaintiff; they ordered and paid for one-half of the cost of a cot that the plaintiff needed for daily personal care at work; they sometimes adjusted the plaintiff's schedule to perform backup telephone duties to accommodate the plaintiff's medical appointments; they made changes to the plans for a locker room in the new state office building; and they agreed to provide some of the specific accommodations the plaintiff requested in her October 5, 1992 Reasonable Accommodation Request."

But she complains that the defendants did not go far enough in two principal respects. One concerns a period of eight weeks when a bout of pressure ulcers forced her to stay home. She wanted to work full time at home and believed that she would be able to do so if the division would provide her with a desktop computer at home (though she already had a laptop). Her supervisor refused. . . . [S]he was able to work all but 16.5 hours in the eight-week period. She took 16.5 hours of sick leave to make up the difference. As a result, she incurred no loss of income, but did lose sick leave that she could have carried forward indefinitely. She now works for another agency of the State of Wisconsin, but any unused sick leave in her employment by the housing division would have accompanied her to her new job. Restoration of the 16.5 hours of lost sick leave is one form of relief that she seeks in this suit.

She argues that a jury might have found that a reasonable accommodation required the housing division either to give her the desktop computer or to excuse her from having to dig into her sick leave to get paid for the hours in which, in the absence of the computer, she was unable to do her work at home. No jury, however, could in our view be permitted to stretch the concept of "reasonable accommodation" so far. Most jobs in organizations public or private involve team work under supervision rather than solitary unsupervised work, and team work under supervision generally cannot be performed at home without a substantial reduction in the quality of the employee's performance. This will no doubt change as communications technology advances, but is the situation today. Generally, therefore, an employer is not required to accommodate a disability by allowing the disabled worker to work, by himself, without supervision, at home. This is the majority view, illustrated by *Tyndall v. National Education Centers, Inc.*, 31 F.3d 209 (4th Cir. 1994), and *Law v. United States Postal Service*, 852 F.2d 1278 (Fed. Cir. 1988) (per curiam). The District of Columbia Circuit disagrees. *Langon v. Dept. of Health & Human Services*, 959 F.2d 1053 (D.C. Cir. 1992); *Carr v. Reno*, 23 F.3d 525, 530 (D.C. Cir. 1994). But we think the majority view is correct. An employer is not required to allow disabled workers to work at home, where their productivity inevitably would be greatly reduced. No doubt to this as to any generalization about so complex and varied an activity as employment there are exceptions, but it would take a very extraordinary case for the employee to be able to create a triable issue of the employer's failure to allow the employee to work at home.

And if the employer, because it is a government agency and therefore is not under intense competitive pressure to minimize its labor costs or maximize the value of its output, or for some other reason, bends over backwards to accommodate a disabled worker — goes further than the law requires — by allowing the worker to work at home, it must not be punished for its generosity by being deemed to have conceded the reasonableness of so far-reaching an accommodation. That would hurt rather than help disabled workers. Wisconsin's housing division was not required by the Americans with Disabilities Act to allow Vande Zande to work at home; even more clearly it was not required to install a computer in her home so that she could avoid using up 16.5 hours of sick leave. It is conjectural that she will ever need those 16.5 hours; the expected cost of the loss must, therefore, surely be slight. An accommodation that allows a disabled worker to work at home, at full pay, subject only to a slight loss of sick leave that may never be needed, hence never missed, is, we hold, reasonable as a matter of law.

Her second complaint has to do with the kitchenettes in the housing division's building, which are for the use of employees during lunch and coffee breaks. Both the sink and the counter in each of the kitchenettes were 36 inches high, which is too high for a person in a wheelchair. The building was under construction, and the kitchenettes not yet built, when the plaintiff complained about this feature of the design. But the defendants refused to alter the design to lower the sink and counter to 34 inches, the height convenient for a person in a wheelchair. . . . [S]he argues that once she brought the problem to the attention of her supervisors, they were obliged to lower the sink and counter, at least on the floor on which her office was located but possibly on the other floors in the building as well, since she might be moved to another floor. All that the defendants were willing to do was to install a shelf 34 inches high in the kitchenette area on Vande Zande's floor. That took care of the counter problem. As for the sink, the defendants took the position that since the plumbing was already in place it would be too costly to lower the sink and that the plaintiff could use the bathroom sink, which is 34 inches high.

Apparently it would have cost only about $150 to lower the sink on Vande Zande's floor; to lower it on all the floors might have cost as much as $2,000, though possibly less. Given the proximity of the bathroom sink, Vande Zande can hardly complain that the inaccessibility of the kitchenette sink interfered with her ability to work or with her physical comfort. Her argument rather is that forcing her to use the bathroom sink for activities (such as washing out her coffee cup) for which the other employees could use the kitchenette sink stigmatized her as different and inferior; she seeks an award of compensatory damages for the resulting emotional distress. We may assume without having to decide that emotional as well as physical barriers to the integration of disabled persons into the workforce are relevant in determining the reasonableness of an accommodation. But we do not think an employer has a duty to expend even modest amounts of money to bring about an absolute identity in working conditions between disabled and nondisabled workers. The creation of such a duty would be the inevitable consequence of deeming a failure to achieve identical conditions "stigmatizing." That is merely an epithet. We conclude that access to a particular sink, when access to an equivalent sink, conveniently located, is provided, is not a legal duty of an employer. The duty of reasonable accommodation is satisfied when the employer does what is necessary to enable the disabled worker to work in reasonable comfort. . . .

NOTES

1. *Analogizing to Title VII.* Improving employment opportunities for disabled individuals required Congress to devise an antidiscrimination statute for individuals who are different from other employees in job-related ways. This problem is analogous to the problem of guaranteeing equal employment opportunity for pregnant women. Recall Title VII's approach in Chapter 5. Since pregnant women need be treated only like others similar in their ability or inability to work, Title VII permits different treatment if pregnancy alters women's ability to perform job functions; thus, Title VII does *not* require that pregnancy be accommodated unless comparable workers are also accommodated. In contrast, the ADA *requires* employers to accommodate individuals with disabilities to ensure equal employment opportunity. Which approach is the better policy?

While some commentators distinguish Title VII and the ADA because the latter's duty of accommodation makes it explicitly redistributivist, Samuel Issacharoff & Justin Nelson, *Discrimination with a Difference: Can Employment Discrimination Law Accommodate the Americans with Disabilities Act?*, 79 N.C. L. Rev. 307 (2001), others analogize the ADA duty to Title VII's disparate impact theory. Christine Jolls, *Antidiscrimination and Accommodation*, 115 Harv. L. Rev. 642 (2001). There is a lively literature on the subject. *See, e.g.*, Michael Ashley Stein, *The Law and Economics of Disability Accommodations*, 53 Duke L.J. 79 (2003); Samuel R. Bagenstos, *"Rational Discrimination," Accommodation, and the Politics of (Disability) Civil Rights*, 89 Va. L. Rev. 825 (2003); Stewart J. Schwab & Steven L. Willborn, *Reasonable Accommodation of Workplace Disabilities*, 44 Wm. & Mary L. Rev. 1197 (2003); Seth D. Harris, *Re-thinking the Economics of Discrimination*: US Airways v. Barnett, *the ADA, and the Application of Internal Labor Markets Theory*, 89 Iowa L. Rev. 123 (2003); Michael Ashley Stein, *Same Struggle, Different Difference: ADA Accommodations as Antidiscrimination*, 153 U. Pa. L. Rev. 579 (2004); J.H. Verkerke, *Disaggregating Antidiscrimination and Accommodation*, 44 Wm. & Mary L. Rev. 1385 (2003).

How would disparate impact work in Vande Zande's case? Could she have argued, for example, that requiring employees to work at the office has a disparate impact on individuals with disabilities or, more particularly, individuals suffering from pressure ulcers? Is working under supervision a business necessity? And what about the height of the sink? Is the argument that "standard" heights have a disparate impact on some disabled? Assuming so, again, is there a business necessity? The usual remedy for a successful disparate impact Title VII claim is to remove the barrier for everyone. In contrast, the duty of accommodation allows the employer to address only the situation of the disabled worker.

2. *Forms of Reasonable Accommodation.* In addition to the accommodations mentioned in the statutory definition, the ADA Interpretive Guidance suggests other accommodations that might be relevant to assisting an individual in performing essential job functions, including "making employer provided transportation accessible and providing reserved parking spaces," permitting "an individual who is blind to use a guide dog at work," and permitting "an employee with a disability that inhibits the ability to write . . . to computerize records that were customarily maintained manually." 29 C.F.R. pt. 1630, app. §1630.2(o).

Examples of accommodations that may be reasonable include *Spurling v. C & M Fine Pack, Inc.*, 739 F.3d 1055, 1061-62 (7th Cir. 2014) (further medical testing and prescription medication to control plaintiff's narcolepsy were obvious accommodation possibilities that should have been explored); *Ekstrand v. Sch. Dist. of Somerset*, 683 F.3d 826 (7th Cir. 2012) (transfer of an elementary school teacher with seasonal affective disorder to a classroom with natural light); *Colwell v. Rite Aid Corp.*, 602 F.3d 495 (3d Cir. 2010) (accommodating a shift change when the employee's vision disability prevents her from driving to work at night).

ADA §101(9) also states that providing readers or interpreters may be a reasonable accommodation. The Interpretive Guidance suggests additional accommodations that involve providing personal assistants such as a page turner for an employee with no hands or a travel attendant for an employee who is blind. Again, the concept of essential functions is critical: "[a]n employer would not have to provide [a security guard] who is legally blind with an assistant to look at the identification cards [because] the assistant would be performing the job for the individual with a disability rather than assisting the individual to perform the job." 29 C.F.R. pt. 1630, app. §1630.2(o). These provisions do not make it clear under what circumstances providing a reader, interpreter, page turner, or travel attendant would constitute "assisting the individual [with a disability] to perform the job" rather than "performing the job for the individual."

3. *Reasonable, Not Preferred.* Courts have not been sympathetic with employees who demand preferred accommodations when, in the court's judgment, the offered accommodation would suffice. *Bunn v. Khoury Enters.*, 753 F.3d 656 (7th Cir. 2014) (once an employer provided a reasonable accommodation, it had discharged its obligations under the law); *Yovtcheva v. City of Phila. Water Dep't*, 518 F. App'x 116 (3d Cir. 2013) (city did not need to transfer an asthmatic city chemist or use a solvent to which she was not sensitive when it offered her a reasonable accommodation by a partial-face respirator even though she refused to attempt to use it because she had suffered a panic attack while using a full-face device).

4. *Attendance Policies and the Duty of Reasonable Accommodation.* As we saw previously, courts have ruled that timely and regular attendance is an essential job function for most jobs. See Note 4, p. 472. If attending work regularly or starting work at a particular time of day or working full-time is an essential function, the employer need not offer part-time or modified work schedules as a reasonable accommodation. However, the FMLA and analog state laws provide some job protection, see p. 521, and, when the employer's own policies or practice make working time flexible, a modified work schedule may be a reasonable accommodation. *EEOC v. Convergys Mgmt. Group, Inc.*, 491 F.3d 790 (8th Cir. 2007) (not allowing wheelchair-bound plaintiff a 15-minute extension on lunch and starting time violated employer's duty of reasonable accommodation). Similarly, a short-term leave of absence often will be viewed as a reasonable accommodation, particularly when the employer's own policies provide for paid or unpaid leave as great as that requested by the disabled employee. However, the courts have generally not required either extended or open-ended leave. *See Whitaker v. Wis. Dep't of Health Servs.*, 849 F.3d 681, 686 (7th Cir. 2017) (absent evidence that additional unpaid leave would have enabled plaintiff to return to work on a regular basis, employer did not have to provide additional leave as a reasonable accommodation); *Hwang v. Kan. State Univ.*, 753 F.3d 1159, 1161 (10th Cir. 2014) (no accommodation required for an employee who cannot work for more than six months even in a university where sabbaticals often exceed that period). *See generally* Stacy A. Hickox & Joseph M. Guzman, *Leave as an Accommodation: When Is Enough, Enough?*, 62 CLEV. ST. L. REV. 437 (2014); Stephen F. Befort, *The Most*

Difficult Reasonable Accommodation Issues: Reassignment and Leave of Absence, 37 WAKE FOREST L. REV. 439 (2002).

5. *Withdrawn Accommodations.* Notice in *Vande Zande* that Posner stressed that an employer that "bends over backwards to accommodate a disabled worker . . . must not be punished for its generosity by being deemed to have conceded the reasonableness of so far-reaching an accommodation." This issue arises more often than you might think, and the courts have generally followed Judge Posner's lead despite the fact that the accommodation was offered would seem strong evidence of its reasonableness. *See, e.g., EEOC v. TriCore Reference Labs.*, 493 F. App'x 955, 960 n.7 (10th Cir. 2012). They seem concerned with the disincentives to accommodation that would follow from holding that providing an accommodation established its reasonableness and the absence of undue hardship. *See generally* Nicole Buonocore Porter, *Withdrawn Accommodations*, 63 DRAKE L. REV. 885 (2015).

6. *Conflicting Duties?* What about the situation where an accommodation for one disabled employee triggers a disability of another? *See* Steven Greenhouse, *When Treating One Worker's Allergy Sets Off Another's*, N.Y. TIMES, May 10, 2010, at A10, recounting how a service dog used by one employee to warn of the presence of paprika, to which she had a potentially fatal allergy, triggered another employee's asthma attack as an allergic reaction. "Legal experts say her case raises tough questions about how to balance the sometimes clashing interests of co-workers with disabilities and how far employers need to go to make reasonable accommodations for workers under the Americans with Disabilities Act." How would you resolve this conflict?

What happens when an employee engages in misconduct that is the product of the disability? Is the employer entitled to take action based on the misconduct, or is that in essence discrimination on the basis of the disability? Alternatively, does the duty of reasonable accommodation require the employer to excuse work rule violations by disabled workers that would result in discipline if engaged in by nondisabled employees? The Ninth Circuit faced the question of employee misconduct in a case arising under Washington's state disability law, but in so doing, made clear its analysis was based on the ADA.

GAMBINI v. TOTAL RENAL CARE, INC.
486 F.3d 1087 (9th Cir. 2007)

SHADUR, Senior District Judge:

. . . BACKGROUND

In November 2000 Gambini began working as a contracts clerk at DaVita, a company that provides dialysis to renal patients. It is undisputed that Gambini had a history of health problems that predated her employment at DaVita. After several months at DaVita she began to experience depression and anxiety, and in April 2001 she experienced an emotional breakdown at work. Gambini eventually met with a mental health provider at the community health clinic and was told that her symptoms were consistent with bipolar disorder.

Upon returning to work several days later, Gambini informed her supervisor Robin Warren ("Warren") that she was seeking medical treatment for bipolar disorder. When Warren was promoted in May 2001, DaVita replaced her with Carrie Bratlie ("Bratlie"), who became Gambini's new direct supervisor. Gambini also told Bratlie that she was suffering from bipolar disorder and requested several accommodations. In addition, Gambini told her co-workers that she was experiencing mood swings, which she was addressing with medications, and asked that they not be personally offended if she was irritable or short with them. Gambini privately divulged to Bratlie that she was seeing a therapist and struggling with some medication issues.

Gambini's bipolar symptoms grew more severe in April 2002 — she found herself increasingly irritable and easily distracted and began to have a hard time concentrating or assigning priorities as between her tasks. Gambini admitted to a fellow co-worker, who also suffered from bipolar disorder, that she was struggling to perform her job because of her symptoms. That co-worker recommended that Gambini seek treatment from psychiatric nurse practitioner Bobbie Fletcher ("Fletcher"), who confirmed Gambini's bipolar disorder based on Gambini's "short fuse," high energy, and propensity to exhibit anger and irritability.

During that period Gambini's current and former supervisors, Warren and Bratlie, convened to discuss Gambini's attitude and what they perceived as her poor job performance. Their meeting culminated in a decision to deliver a written performance improvement plan to Gambini at a later meeting that would include Bratlie, Gambini, and Gina Lovell ("Lovell"), the Supervisor of Payor Contracting. Accordingly, on July 11, 2002 Bratlie emailed Gambini, requesting that she come to Bratlie's office without indicating any specific purpose for the meeting.

Upon arriving at Bratlie's office Gambini was already agitated because she did not know the purpose of the meeting or why Lovell was in attendance. When Bratlie presented Gambini with the improvement plan, the first sentence of which stated, "[Gambini's] attitude and general disposition are no longer acceptable in the SPA department," Gambini began to cry. Reading the remainder of the document did not alleviate Gambini's symptoms — instead she found her face growing hot and felt a tightening feeling in her chest, as well as shortness of breath and shaking. When she had finished reading the performance plan, Gambini threw it across the desk and in a flourish of several profanities expressed her opinion that it was both unfair and unwarranted. Before slamming the door on her way out, Gambini hurled several choice profanities at Bratlie. There is a dispute about whether during her dramatic exit Gambini warned Lovell and Bratlie that they "will regret this," but Bratlie did observe Gambini kicking and throwing things at her cubicle after the meeting. Back at her cubicle, Gambini tried unsuccessfully to call Fletcher to tell her about how upset the meeting made her feel and about her ensuing suicidal thoughts. . . .

[Several days later], McLemore and Bratlie called Gambini on her cell phone to tell her that her employment was being terminated. Three days later Gambini sent DaVita a letter stating that her behavior during the July 11 meeting was a consequence of her bipolar disorder and asking DaVita to reconsider its decision to terminate her. When DaVita refused to reconsider, Gambini filed this action, which proceeded to trial in December 2004. [The jury returned a verdict in favor of DaVita on all claims.] . . .

INSTRUCTION AS TO CONDUCT RESULTING FROM DISABILITY

Gambini submitted and the trial court denied Prop. Instr. 26:

> Conduct resulting from a disability is part of the disability and not a separate basis for termination.

We conclude (1) that the district court abused its discretion when it declined to give that instruction and (2) that such exclusion was not harmless error.

Most significantly, the Washington Supreme Court has itself enunciated the rule embodied in that instruction. On that score *Riehl v. Foodmaker, Inc.*, 94 P.3d 930, 938 (Wash. 2004) (en banc) has stated explicitly [precisely the instruction Gambini sought].

In so doing *Riehl* drew on our own holding in *Humphrey v. Memorial Hospitals Ass'n*, 239 F.3d 1128, 1139-40 (9th Cir. 2001), which in the context of the Americans With Disabilities Act ("ADA") similarly articulated that "conduct resulting from a disability is considered part of the disability, rather than a separate basis for termination." As a practical result of that rule, where an employee demonstrates a causal link between the disability-produced conduct and the termination, a jury must be instructed that it may find that the employee was terminated on the impermissible basis of her disability.

Because of the Washington Supreme Court's express reliance on *Humphrey*, we may properly look to that decision in applying the Washington Law. Indeed, the facts in *Humphrey* are substantially analogous to Gambini's situation, and we held there that a jury could reasonably find the "requisite causal link between" the symptoms of obsessive compulsive disorder and Humphrey's inability to conform her behavior to her employer's expectations of punctuality and attendance, so that she was fired because of her disability.

. . . Failure to have instructed the jury on that score plainly requires reversal. At trial Gambini presented evidence that DaVita signed an interrogatory response, which stated that one of the reasons it terminated Gambini was because she had "frightened her co-workers with her violent outbursts," as "documented by emails to the People Services Department." Her "violent outbursts," . . . were arguably symptomatic of her bipolar disorder. Gambini had informed her supervisors about her condition and kept them apprised of her medication issues and the various accommodations she thought might reduce the chances of an outburst at work. When her temper erupted during the July 11 meeting, Gambini was in the throes of a medication change, which heightened the volatility of the mood swings that she and her health care providers were trying to get under control.

Under all the circumstances it was surely permissible for a properly instructed jury to review the events culminating in the July 11 meeting and Gambini's eventual termination and to conclude that it was her personality and not her work product that motivated DaVita. In fact, the very first sentence of the written performance improvement plan that Bratlie presented to Gambini on July 11 stated, "[Gambini's] attitude and general disposition are no longer acceptable in the SPA department." It is undisputed that people who suffer from bipolar disorder struggle to control their moods, which may vacillate wildly from deep depressions to wild frenzies of hypomania. Hence the record is replete with examples of how Gambini's bipolar disorder manifested itself through her irritability, her "short fuse" and her sometimes erratic emotions.

Accordingly the jury was entitled to infer reasonably that her "violent outburst" on July 11 was a consequence of her bipolar disorder, which the law protects as part and parcel of her disability. In those terms, if the law fails to protect the manifestations of her disability, there is no real protection in the law because it would protect the disabled in name only. As *School Board of Nassau County, Florida v. Arline* instructs, the disability discrimination laws are necessary because Congress acknowledged that "the American people are simply unfamiliar with and insensitive to the difficulties confront[ing] individuals with handicaps." . . .

That said, requiring Prop. Instr. 26 in no way provides employees with *absolute* protection from adverse employment actions based on disability-related conduct. Under the ADA a plaintiff must still establish that she is "an individual with a disability who, with or without reasonable accommodation, can perform the essential functions of the employment position that such individual holds or desires." Even if a plaintiff were to establish that she's qualified, under the ADA the defendant would still be entitled to raise a "business necessity" or "direct threat" defense against the discrimination claim (*see* 42 U.S.C. §12113(a)-(b)). Defendant may also raise the defense that the proposed reasonable accommodation poses an undue burden (*see id.* §12111(10)). . . .

NOTES

1. *Facially Discriminatory?* The Ninth Circuit holds that taking action based on misconduct that is a product of a known underlying disability is the same as acting on the basis of the disability itself. Remember the Seventh Circuit's treatment of symptoms of a disability in *Vande Zande*, reproduced at p. 484, and the Supreme Court's treatment of the same issue in *Arline*, discussed at p. 443. Is the Ninth Circuit correct in viewing misconduct as comparable to the contagiousness in *Arline* or the pressure ulcers in *Vande Zande?*

In cases with similar facts, most other circuits have reached a different result. *See Vannoy v. FRB of Richmond*, 827 F.3d 296, 305 (4th Cir. 2016) ("the ADA does not require an employer to simply ignore an employee's blatant and persistent misconduct, even where that behavior is potentially tied to a medical condition"); *Budde v. Kane Cnty. Forest Pres.*, 597 F.3d 860, 862 (7th Cir. 2010) (rejecting a police chief's ADA claim for being fired after having his license suspended for causing an accident by driving while intoxicated: "[v]iolation of a workplace rule, even if it is caused by a disability [here alcoholism], is no defense to discipline up to and including termination"); *Macy v. Hopkins County*, 484 F.3d 357 (6th Cir. 2007) ("this court has repeatedly stated that an employer may legitimately fire an employee for conduct, even conduct that occurs as a result of a disability, if that conduct disqualifies the employee from his or her job"). Which is the better view of the statute?

2. *The EEOC Weighs In.* In its Enforcement Guidance on Reasonable Accommodation, the EEOC takes the position that an employer need not excuse employee misconduct, even when it is the product of a disability, so long as the conduct rule is job related for the position in question and consistent with business necessity and the employer would impose the same discipline on a nondisabled worker. Which is the better rule — the EEOC's or the Ninth Circuit's?

Or are the two positions that far apart? After all, the Ninth Circuit recognized the employer would be entitled to rely on a business necessity defense. Wouldn't it be a business necessity in almost every workplace for an employee to refrain from the conduct Gambini engaged in? And is the EEOC's Guidance a way of requiring the employer to justify the conduct rule, even if it is applied uniformly? Perhaps the problem is that an occasional outburst might be tolerated by workers whom the employer did not view as suffering from a condition that would make them recur. *See generally* Kelly Cahill Timmons, *Accommodating Misconduct Under the Americans with Disabilities Act*, 57 FLA. L. REV. 187 (2005) ("employers may view misconduct committed by employees with mental disabilities more severely because of the stigma and stereotypes associated with such disabilities"). *See also* Elizabeth F. Emens, *The Sympathetic Discriminator: Mental Illness, Hedonic Costs and the ADA*, 94 GEO. L.J. 399 (2006) (understanding emotional contagion and hedonic costs is important for deciding claims brought by plaintiffs with mental illness).

3. *Essential Job Functions.* Alternatively, some courts have reasoned that individuals who pose a threat of violence to others are not "otherwise qualified" individuals. *See Williams v. Motorola, Inc.*, 303 F.3d 1284, 1290-91 (11th Cir. 2002); *Palmer v. Circuit Court of Cook Cnty.*, 117 F.3d 351 (7th Cir. 1997). Or should that approach work only if the employer establishes that the employee is a "direct threat"? See Section D, p. 499. But even less dramatic difficulties in working with others have resulted in a finding that the individual was not otherwise qualified when such interactions were essential to the position. *Walz v. Ameriprise Fin., Inc.*, 779 F.3d 842, 845-46 (8th Cir. 2015) (where plaintiff's bipolar disorder prevented her from working well with others, she could not perform the essential functions without accommodation and failed to request any accommodation that might allow her to do so).

4. *Failure of Accommodation and Constructive Discharge.* We explored constructive discharge in Chapter 1. In the ADA context, a variation on this theme occurs when an employer fails to provide a required accommodation, resulting in the employee resigning her position. While denial of some accommodations may not constitute a constructive discharge, other denials will leave the employee no reasonable choice. *See Talley v. Family Dollar Stores of Ohio, Inc.*, 542 F.3d 1099 (6th Cir. 2008) (failure to accommodate plaintiff's osteoarthritis by allowing her to sit while working could constitute a constructive discharge). An undeveloped issue under the ADA is whether all denials of reasonable accommodations are actionable or whether some may not be sufficiently serious to justify suit. Put differently, is there an adverse employment action requirement for such denials? Megan I. Brennan, *Need I Prove More: Why an Adverse Employment Action Prong Has No Place in a Failure to Accommodate Disability Claim*, 36 Hamline L. Rev. 497 (2013).

NOTE ON ACCOMMODATIONS NECESSARY TO ENJOY BENEFITS AND PRIVILEGES OF EMPLOYMENT

Beyond accommodations enabling employees to perform essential functions is the question of accommodations enabling disabled employees "to enjoy equal benefits and privileges of employment as are enjoyed by employees without disabilities." 29 C.F.R. pt. 1630, app. §1630.2(o). This includes, for example, accommodations designed to permit equal access to cafeterias, lounges, and restrooms. Recall Vande Zande's issues with the sink. While acknowledging that emotional barriers can threaten equal employment of disabled individuals and therefore are relevant to determining the reasonableness of an accommodation, the court ruled that the employer need not spend "even modest amounts of money to bring about an absolute identity in working conditions." Why not? Is an individual with a disability entitled to access to all unrestricted areas of the employer's business, even areas that relate neither to essential functions nor to specific job benefits? Is it a "privilege of employment" to have access to all unrestricted areas? What if a deaf employee requests an interpreter at workplace social events?

Of course, access to some facilities may be directly relevant to success on the job. Recall that in *The Picture People* the employer had not provided the deaf employee with an interpreter during training sessions and staff meetings, which the EEOC contended violated the employer's duty to provide accommodations necessary to enjoy equal benefits and privileges. *See also EEOC v. UPS Supply Chain Solutions*, 620 F.3d 1103 (9th Cir. 2010) (fact question as to whether employer-provided written materials were sufficient to enable a hearing-impaired person to enjoy the same benefits of weekly meetings as other employees).

Cases involving accommodations relating to the privileges and benefits of employment may also raise questions about the distinction between personal and work-related accommodations. The EEOC's Interpretive Guidance finds the duty of accommodation ends for "adjustments or modifications that are primarily for the personal benefit of the individual with a disability." The suggested test is whether it "assists the individual throughout his or her daily activities, on and off the job," in which case it falls on the personal side of the line. 29 C.F.R. pt. 1630, app. §1630.9.

The personal vs. employment related issue seems to arise mainly in getting to and from work. In *Lyons v. Legal Aid Soc'y*, 68 F.3d 1512 (2d Cir. 1995), a disabled attorney sought financial assistance to park her car near her office because injuries limited her mobility. Legal Aid, in defending its refusal to pay for parking, argued that the requested accommodation was merely "a matter of personal convenience" and therefore not within its obligation to provide accommodation. The Second Circuit ruled that a parking place was a work-related need, not merely a personal need. Lyons could not do her job without parking near the office, and there was no evidence that she planned to use the space for any other purpose. *Id.* at 1517. *But see Regan v. Faurecia Auto. Seating, Inc.*, 679 F.3d 475 (6th Cir. 2012) (plaintiff's request to commute during "lighter" rush hour traffic because of her narcolepsy was not a reasonable accommodation). *See generally* Kelly Cahill Timmons, *Limiting "Limitations": The Scope of the Duty of Reasonable Accommodation Under the Americans with Disabilities Act*, 57 S.C. L. Rev. 313 (2005). Was Vande Zande's request for accessible kitchen sinks a request for a personal benefit or was it job related?

NOTE ON KNOWING THAT ACCOMMODATION IS NEEDED AND THE INTERACTIVE PROCESS

The ADA provides that employers must make "reasonable accommodations to the *known* physical and mental limitations of an otherwise qualified individual with a disability." ADA §102(b)(5)(A) (emphasis added). The Interpretive Guidance reinforces that by providing that it is generally "the responsibility of the individual with a disability to inform the employer that an accommodation is needed," 29 C.F.R. pt. 1630, app. §1630.9, which makes sense in light of the statute's bar on inquiry into disabilities. *See Kobus v. Coll. of St. Scholastica, Inc.*, 608 F.3d 1034 (8th Cir. 2010) (employee who did not reveal his treatment for depression and whose limitations were not apparent at work had no failure to accommodate claim when he was fired for excessive absenteeism resulting from the depression). The Guidance does, however, note that "[i]f an employee with a known disability is having difficulty performing his or her job, an employer may inquire whether the employee is in need of a reasonable accommodation." *Id.* This seems to permit, but not require, an inquiry, thus leaving the ball squarely in the worker's court. *See EEOC v. Convergys Customer Mgmt. Grp. Inc.*, 491 F.3d 790 (8th Cir. 2007) (wheelchair-bound employee not required to request specific accommodations to trigger employer duty).

That said, what suffices as a request for an accommodation is not always clear. *See generally* EEOC Enforcement Guidance: Reasonable Accommodation and Undue Hardship Under the Americans with Disabilities Act (Oct. 17, 2002), available at http://www.eeoc.gov/policy/docs/accommodation.html ("To request accommodation, an individual may use 'plain English' and need not mention the ADA or use the phrase 'reasonable accommodation'"). In a number of cases the courts have imposed a duty to accommodate absent a formal employee request when the need was clear.

See Kowitz v. Trinity Health, 839 F.3d 742 (8th Cir. 2016) (although plaintiff did not ask for an accommodation in so many words, her written notification that she would be unable to complete the basic life support certification without medical clearance and her statement that she required four months of physical therapy before completing the certification could have been found to constitute such a request); *Snapp v. United Transp. Union*, 547 F. App'x 824, 826 (9th Cir. 2013) (a job application and a letter from plaintiff's physician referring to plaintiff's ongoing disability and need for accommodations created a fact question as to notification). Further, the accommodation must be requested in a timely fashion. *See Schaffhauser v. UPS*, 794 F.3d 899, 905 (8th Cir. 2015) (request for an accommodation based on a treatment for a medical condition that contributed to an inappropriate remark came too late when it attempted to deflect otherwise appropriate discipline for that remark).

The Interpretive Guidance contemplates that reasonable accommodation will be achieved through an "interactive process" by which disabled individuals and their employers meet and negotiate accommodations that satisfy the needs of both parties. 29 C.F.R. §1630.2(o)(3). Despite language in some cases suggesting otherwise, the lower courts generally have been unwilling to impose liability on an employer *solely* for failure to engage in the interactive process. There must also be a showing that a reasonable accommodation could have been found had the process been pursued. *See Stern v. St. Anthony's Health Ctr.*, 788 F.3d 276 (7th Cir. 2015) (failure to engage in the interactive process not independently actionable when plaintiff's cognitive difficulties prevented him from performing the essential functions of chief psychologist given the sensitive nature of the position and the potential safety and liability risks); *McBride v. BIC Consumer Prods. Mfg. Co.*, 583 F.3d 92, 97 (2d Cir. 2009) (where "plaintiff provided no evidence that there existed any potential accommodation that would have allowed her to continue to work," failure to engage in interactive process was not a violation).

Further, the duty to engage in an interactive process is not a one-way street. While an employer cannot be held liable merely for failures in such a process, an employee may forfeit a right to accommodation by failing to participate in discussions about what accommodations are appropriate. *See EEOC v. Kohl's Dep't Stores, Inc.*, 774 F.3d 127, 133-34 (1st Cir. 2014) (when an employer initiates an interactive dialogue, the employee must engage in a good faith effort to work out potential solutions); *Ward v. McDonald*, 762 F.3d 24, 32 (D.C. Cir. 2014) (when plaintiff resigned during the interactive process, she short-circuited the process and no reasonable juror could have found that the employer, rather than plaintiff, was responsible for the breakdown).

3.   Undue Hardship

Relatively few cases have examined closely the question of undue hardship; instead, as in *Barnett*, reproduced at p. 476, they have determined the proposed accommodation is unreasonable. However, a claimed failure to accommodate can be defended on the ground that even an otherwise reasonable accommodation would pose an "undue hardship" on the operation of the employer's business, ADA §102(b)(5)(A); 29 C.F.R. §1630.15(d). The ADA provides that an "undue hardship" is an accommodation requiring "significant difficulty or expense," which must be determined by considering all relevant factors, including the size and financial resources of the covered entity. *See* 29 C.F.R. §1630.2(p). Section 102(b)(5)(A) expressly states that the covered entity must "demonstrate" the existence of an "undue hardship." The ADAAA did not alter the definition.

The concepts of reasonable accommodation and undue hardship, as has been observed, go somewhat "hand in hand." *Riel v. Elec. Data Sys. Corp.*, 99 F.3d 678, 681 (5th Cir. 1996). But they are analytically distinct. Reasonable accommodation involves an assessment not only of whether the accommodation would enable the employee to do the job (or enjoy the benefits) but also whether it is facially reasonable. If this showing is made, the employer has the opportunity to prove that, under the facts and circumstances of the particular situation, the accommodation would pose an undue hardship. Reasonable accommodation is thus a more "generalized inquiry," while undue hardship focuses on the particular employer. *See Barnett*. Thus, while the plaintiff bears the burden of proving a reasonable accommodation exists, the burden of proving that an accommodation would pose an undue hardship is on the employer.

The Second Circuit in *Borkowski v. Valley Cent. Sch. Dist.*, 63 F.3d 131 (2d Cir. 1995), discussed the elements of "undue hardship," citing ADA provisions that define "undue hardship" to mean "an action requiring significant difficulty or expense, when considered in light of" the following factors:

(i)   the nature and cost of the accommodation needed under this Act;
(ii) the overall financial resources of the facility or facilities involved in the provision of the reasonable accommodation; the number of persons employed at such facility; the effect on expenses and resources, or the impact otherwise of such accommodation upon the operation of the facility;
(iii) the overall financial resources of the covered entity; the overall size of the business of a covered entity with respect to the number of its employees; the number, type, and location of its facilities; and
(iv) the type of operation or operations of the covered entity, including the composition, structure, and functions of the workforce of such entity; the geographic separateness, administrative, or fiscal relationship of the facility or facilities in question to the covered entity.

42 U.S.C. §12111(10). The issue, according to *Borkowski*, is one of degree: "even this list of factors says little about how great a hardship an employer must bear before the hardship becomes undue." The court held that employers are not required to show that they would be driven to the brink of insolvency. It relied on ADA legislative history rejecting a provision that would have defined an undue hardship as one that threatened the continued existence of the employer. *Borkowski*, 63 F.3d at 139. "Where the employer is a government entity, Congress could not have intended the only limit on the employer's duty to make reasonable accommodation to be the full extent of the tax base on which the government entity could draw." *Id.*

The court concluded that, in order to demonstrate both that the proposed accommodation is unreasonable and that the hardship it would impose is undue, the employer must "undertake a refined analysis" of the relative costs and benefits of the accommodation, considering both "the industry to which the employer belongs as well as the individual characteristics of the particular defendant-employer." *Id.* The court further noted that "mathematical precision" and "complex economic formulae" are not required. Rather "a common-sense balancing of the costs and benefits in light of the factors listed in the regulations is all that is expected." *Id.* at 140. Is a cost-benefit analysis appropriate under the ADA? *See Reyazuddin v. Montgomery Cnty.*, 789 F.3d 407, 418 (4th Cir. 2015) (summary judgment reversed when "the district court reduced a multi-factor analysis to a single factor — cost — that the court believed was simply too much for the County to bear. But while cost is important, it cannot be viewed in isolation. Rather, it is the relative cost, along with other factors, that matters.").

Is it an undue hardship if accommodations for one employee will have a negative effect on the morale of other employees? Should *Rehrs*, reproduced at p. 463, have been analyzed as an undue hardship case? What about *Barnett?* Can undue hardship be raised as an affirmative defense if plaintiff has not requested, or does not need, an accommodation? Doesn't the statutory structure suggest the answer is no?

NOTE ON BURDENS OF PRODUCTION AND PROOF

By now, it is obvious that disability discrimination claims often differ in significant ways from disparate treatment claims brought under Title VII, §1981, and the ADEA. For example, the ADA expressly permits employers to act on the basis of an employee's disability. Thus, for instance, if an individual's disability precludes him from performing the essential functions of a job, with or without reasonable accommodation, then the employer may disqualify him on that basis without incurring liability. Under Title VII, however, an employer could disqualify an employee because of her sex only in the rare instances where a bona fide occupational qualification can be established. See p. 142.

At the same time, as the statutory language makes clear and *Barnett* confirms, the ADA at times requires more than equal treatment; it expressly requires employers to treat individuals differently because of the disability by providing a reasonable accommodation. Given these differences, how do, or should, the burden of proof schemes devised under Title VII, the ADEA, and §1981 apply, if at all, to ADA claims?

The plaintiff bears the burden of proving he is an individual with a disability within the meaning of the ADA. *Barnett* also clarified that plaintiff has the burden of showing that a reasonable accommodation is available. *See also Horn v. Knight Facilities Mgmt.-GM*, 556 F. App'x 452, 455 (6th Cir. 2014) (plaintiff, a janitor with a sensitivity to cleaning fluids, did not identify a reasonable accommodation). But despite *Barnett*, the close connection of the notions of reasonable accommodation and undue hardship can confuse the courts. *Osborne v. Baxter Healthcare Corp.*, 798 F.3d 1260, 1278 (10th Cir. 2015), is an example. It first held that, to shift the burden of proving undue hardship to the employer, plaintiff "must show only that her proposed accommodation is reasonable on its face; that is, it would permit her to perform the essential function at issue — here, donor monitoring. She need not show that the accommodation would eliminate every de minimis health or safety risk that [the employer] can hypothesize." However, it was error for the district court to require plaintiff to also show that the accommodation would be "feasible" for the employer; "how much alarms would cost, when they could be added in the production process, and who would install them" are part of the employer's burden to "identify with specificity . . . why the proposed accommodation constitutes an undue hardship and is thus unreasonable." *Id.* at 1273.

But placement of the burdens is more complicated when considering whether the plaintiff is a *qualified* individual with a disability. We saw that the *Rehrs* opinion placed on the employer the burden to prove that a job function is an essential one, but other cases place the burden of persuasion on the plaintiff since being qualified is central to coverage. These courts, however, recognize a burden of production for employers. See Note 2, p. 472.

By the way, if you're wondering about the relationship of ADA claims to pursuit of various government and private disability benefits, it's complicated. *Cleveland v. Policy Mgmt. Sys. Corp.*, 526 U.S. 795 (1999), held that plaintiff's application for Social Security benefits based on a claim of total and permanent disability was not necessarily inconsistent with the employee's ADA claim: plaintiff could be unable to work without accommodation but able to do so had the employer accommodated her. *See also EEOC v. Vicksburg Healthcare, L.L.C.*, 663 F. App'x 331, (5th Cir. 2016) (the claim that an employee "was temporarily totally disabled for the purposes of private disability benefits is not inconsistent with the claim that she could work *if provided an accommodation*").

As we will see in the next section, the ADA also provides a "direct threat" defense to employers, and the statute also permits the use of other standards or selection criteria that screen out or tend to screen out individuals with disabilities so long as the standard is job related for the position in question and consistent with business necessity. As the cases below demonstrate, the Supreme Court *appears* to place the burden of persuasion on the employer in these cases.

In those cases where the issue is whether plaintiff's disability is causally related to the challenged action, which will usually be "regarded as" cases after the ADAAA, courts have frequently borrowed the *McDonnell Douglas* proof structure with its three stages — prima facie case, articulation of a legitimate, nondiscriminatory reason, and proof of pretext for discrimination — for ADA claims. While this may be correct, it seems increasingly likely that the causation showing is the higher but-for standard set by *Gross/Nassar* and not Title VII's relaxed "motivating factor." See Note 7, p. 439.

However, issues peculiar to the ADA arise. *See* Craig Robert Senn, *Minimal Relevance: Non-Disabled Replacement Evidence in ADA Discrimination Cases*, 66 BAYLOR L. REV. 64 (2014) (arguing that proof of a nondisabled replacement is neither necessary for a prima facie case nor sufficient to create a fact question as to intent). And many courts are unwilling to find a regarded as violation when the employer acts on the basis of potential medical problems. In *Ferrari v. Ford Motor Co.*, 826 F.3d 885 (6th Cir. 2016), the Sixth Circuit held that a plaintiff could not prove pretext when he was unable to raise a fact issue as to the "honest belief" of decisionmakers that a doctor's medical restrictions on his work because of risks posed by his opioid use reflected a reasonable medical judgment). *See also Dewitt v. Sw. Bell Tel. Co.*, 845 F.3d 1299 (10th Cir. 2017) (finding against plaintiff who claimed to have suffered from a hypoglycemic episode causing her to hang up on two customers when her supervisors reasonably believed she had intentionally, rather than accidentally, done so).

D.   DISCRIMINATORY QUALIFICATION STANDARDS

ADA §102(b) provides that "discriminate" includes

> (3) utilizing standards, criteria, or methods of administration . . . that have the effect of discrimination on the basis of disability . . .
> (6) using employment tests or other selection criteria that screen out or tend to screen out an individual with a disability or a class of individuals with disabilities unless the standard, test or other selection criteria, as used by the covered entity, is shown to be job-related for the position in question and is consistent with business necessity. . . .

Consistent with Title VII's approach to disparate impact, the ADA regulations indicate that both provisions are subject to a job-relatedness and business necessity defense. 29 C.F.R. §§1630.7, 1630.10. Further, §103(a), which sets forth defenses, provides that the use of criteria with a disparate impact on the basis of disability must also be consistent with the employer's duty to provide reasonable accommodation. *See* §1630.15(b)(1), (c). Standards or selection criteria may also be defended on the basis that they are permitted or required by another federal statute or regulation. *See* 29 C.F.R. §1630.15(e). Finally, ADA §103(b) provides that "[t]he term 'qualification standards' may include a requirement that an individual shall not pose a direct threat to the health or safety of other individuals in the workplace."

In its Interpretive Guidance, the EEOC further explains that selection criteria with a disparate impact that "do not concern an essential function of the job would not be consistent with business necessity." *See* 29 C.F.R. pt. 1630, app. §1630.10. The Interpretive Guidance goes on to suggest that most challenges to selection criteria can be resolved by reasonable accommodation. Finally, the EEOC interprets these provisions as "applicable to all types of selection criteria, including safety requirements, vision or hearing requirements, walking requirements, and employment tests," although the Commission notes that "production standards will generally not be subject to a challenge under this provision." *Id.*

In short, qualification standards that are either facially discriminatory or that have a disparate impact on disabled individuals can violate the ADA, but all discriminatory qualification standards are subject to the same defenses — they may be defended on the basis that they are job related and consistent with business necessity, permitted or required by another federal statute or regulation, or necessary to prevent a direct threat to health and safety.

Most challenges to qualification standards do not raise significant issues about whether the standard screens out disabled individuals. Challenged criteria frequently are facially discriminatory, such as vision requirements for drivers. Even standards or criteria that do not expressly address a disabling impairment generally are challenged on the ground that a disabled individual cannot meet the standard because of his or her disability. Thus, the fact that the standard or criterion screens out an individual with a disability is obvious. The primary issue in these cases, therefore, is whether the discriminatory standard or criterion can be defended.

This section first examines the "direct threat" defense. Second, it considers the job-relatedness and business necessity defense as it applies to qualification standards that screen out disabled individuals, including qualification standards promulgated by the federal government. Finally, we address the more general application of disparate impact theory in disability discrimination cases.

1.   Direct Threat

ADA §103(b) provides that "[t]he term 'qualification standards' may include a requirement that an individual shall not pose a direct threat to the health or safety of other individuals in the workplace." Direct threat is defined by §101(3) as a "significant risk to the health or safety of others" that cannot be eliminated by a reasonable accommodation. The ADAAA did not alter the definition of "direct threat." The EEOC requires the "direct threat" determination to be based on a reasonable medical judgment that considers such factors as the duration of the risk, the nature and severity of the potential harm, the likelihood of the potential harm, and the imminence of the potential harm. *See* 29 C.F.R. §1630.2(r). Direct threat is simultaneously relevant to whether the individual with a disability is "qualified" to perform essential functions, whether the employer is justified in basing an employment decision on the individual's disability, and whether the employer has a duty to accommodate the individual's disability.

The ADA's "direct threat" provision is derived from the Supreme Court's decision in *School Bd. of Nassau County v. Arline*, 480 U.S. 273 (1987). In *Arline*, a case decided under §504 of the Rehabilitation Act, the Court confronted the question of whether an individual with tuberculosis was otherwise qualified to be an elementary school teacher. The Court concluded the answer is no — if she poses a significant risk of transmitting the disease to others, and that risk cannot be eliminated through reasonable accommodation. In determining whether a significant risk exists, the Court explained that the inquiry

> should include [findings of] facts, based on reasonable medical judgments given the state of medical knowledge, about (a) the nature of the risk (how the disease is transmitted), (b) the duration of the risk (how long is the carrier infectious), (c) the severity of the risk (what is the potential harm to third parties) and (d) the probabilities the disease will be transmitted and will cause varying degrees of harm.

Id. at 288. In making this determination, courts were directed to defer to the "reasonable medical judgments of public health officials," with the Court reserving judgment on whether or not courts should defer to the judgment of private physicians.

In *Bragdon v. Abbott*, discussed at p. 444, the defendant, a dentist, asserted that a risk's significance should be assessed from the point of view of the person denying the service. The Court, however, confirmed that such assessments are to be made on the basis of medical or other objective evidence available at the time that the allegedly discriminatory action occurred. A good faith belief that a significant risk exists is not enough, nor would any special deference be afforded a defendant who is himself a medical professional.

The EEOC's regulation interpreting "direct threat" defines the term to include "a significant risk of substantial harm to the health or safety of *the individual* or others that cannot be eliminated or reduced by reasonable accommodation." 29 C.F.R. §1630.2(r) (emphasis added). The validity of that regulation was at issue in the following case.

CHEVRON U.S.A. INC. v. ECHAZABAL
536 U.S. 73 (2002)

Justice SOUTER delivered the opinion of the Court.

A regulation of the Equal Employment Opportunity Commission authorizes refusal to hire an individual because his performance on the job would endanger his own health, owing to a disability. The question in this case is whether the Americans with Disabilities Act of 1990 permits the regulation. We hold that it does.

I

Beginning in 1972, respondent Mario Echazabal worked for independent contractors at an oil refinery owned by petitioner Chevron U.S.A. Inc. Twice he applied for a job directly with Chevron, which offered to hire him if he could pass the company's physical examination. Each time, the exam showed liver abnormality or damage, the cause eventually being identified as Hepatitis C, which Chevron's doctors said would be aggravated by continued exposure to toxins at Chevron's refinery. In each instance, the company withdrew the offer, and the second time it asked the contractor employing Echazabal either to reassign him to a job without exposure to harmful chemicals or to remove him from the refinery altogether. The contractor laid him off in early 1996.

. . . Chevron defended [plaintiff's ADA suit] under a regulation of the Equal Employment Opportunity Commission permitting the defense that a worker's disability on the job would pose a "direct threat" to his health, *see* 29 CFR §1630.15(b)(2) (2001). Although two medical witnesses disputed Chevron's judgment that Echazabal's liver function was impaired and subject to further damage under the job conditions in the refinery, the District Court granted summary judgment for Chevron. It held that Echazabal raised no genuine issue of material fact as to whether the company acted reasonably in relying on its own doctors' medical advice, regardless of its accuracy.

On appeal, the Ninth Circuit asked for briefs on a threshold question not raised before, whether the EEOC's regulation recognizing a threat-to-self defense, exceeded the scope of permissible rulemaking under the ADA. The Circuit held that it did and reversed the summary judgment. The court rested its position on the text of the ADA itself in explicitly recognizing an employer's right to adopt an employment qualification barring anyone whose disability would place others in the workplace at risk, while saying nothing about threats to the disabled employee himself. The majority opinion reasoned that "by specifying only threats to 'other individuals in the workplace,' the statute makes it clear that threats to other persons — including the disabled individual himself — are not included within the scope of the [direct threat] defense," and it indicated that any such regulation would unreasonably conflict with congressional policy against paternalism in the workplace. . . .

II

Section 102 of the Americans with Disabilities Act of 1990 prohibits "discrimination against a qualified individual with a disability because of the disability . . . in regard to" a number of actions by an employer, including "hiring." 42 U.S.C. §12112(a). The statutory definition of "discrimination" covers a number of things an employer might do to block a disabled person from advancing in the workplace, such as "using qualification standards . . . that screen out or tend to screen out an individual with a disability." §12112(b)(6). By that same definition, as well as by separate provision, §12113(a), the Act creates an affirmative defense for action under a qualification standard "shown to be job-related for the position in question and . . . consistent with business necessity." Such a standard may include "a requirement that an individual shall not pose a direct threat to the health or safety of other individuals in the workplace," §12113(b), if the individual cannot perform the job safely with reasonable accommodation, §12113(a). By regulation, the EEOC carries the defense one step further, in allowing an employer to screen out a potential worker with a disability not only for risks that he would pose to others in the workplace but for risks on the job to his own health or safety as well: "The term 'qualification standard' may include a requirement that an individual shall not pose a direct threat to the health or safety of the individual or others in the workplace." 29 CFR §1630.15(b)(2) (2001).

Chevron relies on the regulation here, since it says a job in the refinery would pose a "direct threat" to Echazabal's health. In seeking deference to the agency, it argues that nothing in the statute unambiguously precludes such a defense, while the regulation was adopted under authority explicitly delegated by Congress, 42 U.S.C. §12116, and after notice-and-comment rulemaking. *See United States v. Mead Corp.*, 533 U.S. 218, 227 (2001); *Chevron U.S.A. Inc. v. Natural Resources Defense Council, Inc.*, 467 U.S. 837, 842-844 (1984). Echazabal, on the contrary, argues that as a matter of law the statute precludes the regulation, which he claims would be an unreasonable interpretation even if the agency had leeway to go beyond the literal text.

A

As for the textual bar to any agency action as a matter of law, Echazabal says that Chevron loses on the threshold question whether the statute leaves a gap for the EEOC to fill. Echazabal recognizes the generality of the language providing for a defense when a plaintiff is screened out by "qualification standards" that are "job-related and consistent with business necessity" (and reasonable accommodation would not cure the difficulty posed by employment). 42 U.S.C. §12113(a). Without more, those provisions would allow an employer to turn away someone whose work would pose a serious risk to himself. That possibility is said to be eliminated, however, by the further specification that " 'qualification standards' may include a requirement that an individual shall not pose a direct threat to the health or safety of other individuals in the workplace." §12113(b); *see also* §12111(3) (defining "direct threat" in terms of risk to others). Echazabal contrasts this provision with an EEOC regulation under the Rehabilitation Act of 1973, as amended, 29 U.S.C. §701 *et seq.*, antedating the ADA, which recognized an employer's right to consider threats both to other workers and to the threatening employee himself. Because the ADA defense provision recognizes threats only if they extend to another, Echazabal reads the statute to imply as a matter of law that threats to the worker himself cannot count.

The argument follows the reliance of the Ninth Circuit majority on the interpretive canon, *expressio unius exclusio alterius*, "expressing one item of [an] associated group or series excludes another left unmentioned." *United States v. Vonn*, 535 U.S. 55, 65 (2002). The rule is fine when it applies, but this case joins some others in showing when it does not.

The first strike against the expression-exclusion rule here is right in the text that Echazabal quotes. Congress included the harm-to-others provision as an example of legitimate qualifications that are "job-related and consistent with business necessity." These are spacious defensive categories, which seem to give an agency (or in the absence of agency action, a court) a good deal of discretion in setting the limits of permissible qualification standards. That discretion is confirmed, if not magnified, by the provision that "qualification standards" falling within the limits of job relation and business necessity "may include" a veto on those who would directly threaten others in the workplace. Far from supporting Echazabal's position, the expansive phrasing of "may include" points directly away from the sort of exclusive specification he claims. . . .

Just as statutory language suggesting exclusiveness is missing, so is that essential extrastatutory ingredient of an expression-exclusion demonstration, the series of terms from which an omission bespeaks a negative implication. The canon depends on identifying a series of two or more terms or things that should be understood to go hand in hand, which are abridged in circumstances supporting a sensible inference that the term left out must have been meant to be excluded. E. Crawford, Construction of Statutes 337 (1940) (*expressio unius* " 'properly applies only when in the natural association of ideas in the mind of the reader that which is expressed is so set over by way of strong contrast to that which is omitted that the contrast enforces the affirmative inference,'"); *United States v. Vonn, supra.*

Strike two in this case is the failure to identify any such established series, including both threats to others and threats to self, from which Congress appears to have made a deliberate choice to omit the latter item as a signal of the affirmative defense's scope. [The Rehabilitation Act tracked the current text of the ADA, excluding only threats to self. Under the Rehabilitation Act, however, the EEOC had adopted a regulation, like the one at issue here, which reached threat-to-self employment. Against this backdrop,] Echazabal argues that Congress's adoption only of the threat-to-others exception in the ADA must have been a deliberate omission of the Rehabilitation Act regulation's tandem term of threat-to-self, with intent to exclude it. . . .

Even if we . . . look no further than the EEOC's Rehabilitation Act regulation pairing self and others, the congressional choice to speak only of threats to others would still be equivocal. . . . Instead of making the ADA different from the Rehabilitation Act on the point at issue, Congress used identical language, knowing full well what the EEOC had made of that language under the earlier statute. Did Congress mean to imply that the agency had been wrong in reading the earlier language to allow it to recognize threats to self, or did Congress just assume that the agency was free to do under the ADA what it had already done under the earlier Act's identical language? There is no way to tell. Omitting the EEOC's reference to self-harm while using the very language that the EEOC had read as consistent with recognizing self-harm is equivocal at best. No negative inference is possible.

There is even a third strike against applying the expression-exclusion rule here. It is simply that there is no apparent stopping point to the argument that by specifying a threat-to-others defense Congress intended a negative implication about those whose safety could be considered. When Congress specified threats to others in the workplace, for example, could it possibly have meant that an employer could not defend a refusal to hire when a worker's disability would threaten others outside the workplace? If Typhoid Mary had come under the ADA, would a meat packer have been defenseless if Mary had sued after being turned away? *See* 42 U.S.C. §12113(d). *Expressio unius* just fails to work here.

B

Since Congress has not spoken exhaustively on threats to a worker's own health, the agency regulation can claim adherence under the rule in *Chevron*, so long as it makes sense of the statutory defense for qualification standards that are "job-related and consistent with business necessity." 42 U.S.C. §12113(a). Chevron's reasons for calling the regulation reasonable are unsurprising: moral concerns aside, it wishes to avoid time lost to sickness, excessive turnover from medical retirement or death, litigation under state tort law, and the risk of violating the national Occupational Safety and Health Act of 1970. Although Echazabal claims that none of these reasons is legitimate, focusing on the concern with OSHA will be enough to show that the regulation is entitled to survive.

Echazabal points out that there is no known instance of OSHA enforcement, or even threatened enforcement, against an employer who relied on the ADA to hire a worker willing to accept a risk to himself from his disability on the job. In Echazabal's mind, this shows that invoking OSHA policy and possible OSHA liability is just a red herring to excuse covert discrimination. But there is another side to this. The text of OSHA itself says its point is "to assure so far as possible every working man and woman in the Nation safe and healthful working conditions," §651(b), and Congress specifically obligated an employer to "furnish to each of his employees employment and a place of employment which are free from recognized hazards that are causing or are likely to cause death or serious physical harm to his employees," §654(a)(1). Although there may be an open question whether an employer would actually be liable under OSHA for hiring an individual who knowingly consented to the particular dangers the job would pose to him, there is no denying that the employer would be asking for trouble: his decision to hire would put Congress's policy in the ADA, a disabled individual's right to operate on equal terms within the workplace, at loggerheads with the competing policy of OSHA, to ensure the safety of "each" and "every" worker. Courts would, of course, resolve the tension if there were no agency action, but the EEOC's resolution exemplifies the substantive choices that agencies are expected to make when Congress leaves the intersection of competing objectives both imprecisely marked but subject to the administrative leeway found in 42 U.S.C. §12113(a).

Nor can the EEOC's resolution be fairly called unreasonable as allowing the kind of workplace paternalism the ADA was meant to outlaw. It is true that Congress had paternalism in its sights when it passed the ADA, see §12101(a)(5) (recognizing "overprotective rules and policies" as a form of discrimination). But the EEOC has taken this to mean that Congress was not aiming at an employer's refusal to place disabled workers at a specifically demonstrated risk, but was trying to get at refusals to give an even break to classes of disabled people, while claiming to act for their own good in reliance on untested and pretextual stereotypes.[5] Its regulation disallows just this sort of sham protection, through demands for a particularized enquiry into the harms the employee would probably face. The direct threat defense must be "based on a reasonable medical judgment that relies on the most current medical knowledge and/or the best available objective evidence," and upon an expressly "individualized assessment of the individual's present ability to safely perform the essential functions of the job," reached after considering, among other things, the imminence of the risk and the severity of the harm portended. 29 CFR §1630.2(r) (2001). The EEOC was certainly acting within the reasonable zone when it saw a difference between rejecting workplace paternalism and ignoring specific and documented risks to the employee himself, even if the employee would take his chances for the sake of getting a job.

Finally, our conclusions that some regulation is permissible and this one is reasonable are not open to Echazabal's objection that they reduce the direct threat provision

---

5. Echazabal's contention that the Act's legislative history is to the contrary is unpersuasive. Although some of the comments within the legislative history decry paternalism in general terms, *see, e.g.*, H.R. Rep. No. 101-485, pt. 2, p. 72 (1990) ("It is critical that paternalistic concerns for the disabled person's own safety not be used to disqualify an otherwise qualified applicant"), those comments that elaborate actually express the more pointed concern that such justifications are usually pretextual, rooted in generalities and misperceptions about disabilities. See, e.g., H.R. Rep. No. 101-485, at 74 ("Generalized fear about risks from the employment environment, such as exacerbation of the disability caused by stress, cannot be used by an employer to disqualify a person with a disability").

Similarly, Echazabal points to several of our decisions expressing concern under Title VII, which like the ADA allows employers to defend otherwise discriminatory practices that are "consistent with business necessity," 42 U.S.C. §2000e-2(k), with employers adopting rules that exclude women from jobs that are seen as too risky. See, e.g., *Dothard v. Rawlinson* [reproduced at p. 195]; *Automobile Workers v. Johnson Controls, Inc.* [reproduced at p. 142]. Those cases, however, are beside the point, as they, like Title VII generally, were concerned with paternalistic judgments based on the broad category of gender, while the EEOC has required that judgments based on the direct threat provision be made on the basis of individualized risk assessments.

to "surplusage," see *Babbitt v. Sweet Home Chapter, Communities for Great Ore.*, 515 U.S. 687, 698 (1995). The mere fact that a threat-to-self defense reasonably falls within the general "job related" and "business necessity" standard does not mean that Congress accomplished nothing with its explicit provision for a defense based on threats to others. The provision made a conclusion clear that might otherwise have been fought over in litigation or administrative rulemaking. It did not lack a job to do merely because the EEOC might have adopted the same rule later in applying the general defense provisions, nor was its job any less responsible simply because the agency was left with the option to go a step further. A provision can be useful even without congressional attention being indispensable. . . .

NOTES

1. *Individualized Medical Inquiry.* The Court did not decide whether Chevron had made the requisite individualized inquiry into Echazabal's medical condition that the EEOC's regulation required. That issue was left for the lower court on remand, and the Ninth Circuit then found a triable issue on that point. *Echazabal v. Chevron U.S.A., Inc.*, 336 F.3d 1023 (9th Cir. 2003). *See also Ollie v. Titan Tire Corp.*, 336 F.3d 680 (8th Cir. 2003) (doctor's report that individual "may have trouble working near dust or fumes" was insufficient basis to exclude him from employment; jury verdict on plaintiff's "regarded as" claim upheld). Nor did the *Echazabal* Court indicate whether the plaintiff or defendant had the burden of proof as to whether an employee posed a direct threat. Circuits have been split on this issue. *Compare Felix v. Wis. DOT*, 828 F.3d 560, 569 (7th Cir. 2016) ("Because the direct-threat defense is an affirmative defense, it is the employer that bears the burden of proving the defense"), *with EEOC v. Amego, Inc.*, 110 F.3d 135, 144 (1st Cir. 1997) (plaintiff must prove that he or she is qualified, and where essential job functions "necessarily implicate the safety of others, plaintiff must demonstrate that she can perform those functions in a way that does not endanger others"). At least one court, however, has watered down the necessary showing by requiring only that the employer show a reasonable belief as to direct threat. *EEOC v. Beverage Distribs. Co., LLC*, 780 F.3d 1018, 1019 (10th Cir. 2015).

2. *Extent of the Defense. Echazabal* involved a potentially life-threatening condition. Could Toyota have avoided the whole disability question by claiming that Mrs. Williams's employment posed a direct threat to her carpel tunnel condition?

3. *Special Treatment of Food Handlers.* After *Arline*, the Rehabilitation Act's definition of an "individual with a disability" was amended to exclude carriers of currently contagious disease or infection who pose a "direct threat" to the health or safety of others. *See* 29 U.S.C. §705(20)(D) (2018). And ADA §12113(e)(1)-(3) provides that a food-handling position may be denied to a person who has an infectious or communicable disease that is transmittable to others through food handling if the risk to others cannot be "eliminated" by a reasonable accommodation.

4. *Direct Threat Examples.* In *Den Hartog v. Wasatch Academy*, 129 F.3d 1076 (10th Cir. 1997), the court held that an employee's association with a disabled individual was a direct threat and therefore provided a defense to associational discrimination. In *Hartog*, the plaintiff was a boarding school teacher whose son suffered from psychiatric disorders that caused him to engage in threatening behavior toward other boarding school personnel and their families. *See also Darnell v. Thermafiber, Inc.*, 417 F.3d 657, 659 (7th Cir. 2005) ("uncontrolled" diabetes made plaintiff a direct

threat to safety at a plant that processed material at high temperatures when there was testimony that he would eventually pass out and therefore pose a risk to himself and others); *Moses v. American Nonwovens, Inc.*, 97 F.3d 446 (11th Cir. 1997) (epileptic worker with a significant risk of seizures on the job who worked close to fast-moving and high-temperature machinery was a direct threat).

A number of courts have considered the "direct threat" defense in cases involving persons infected with HIV, and several have found the defense satisfied where the risk of transmission was high. *See, e.g., Waddell v. Valley Forge Dental Assocs.*, 276 F.3d 1275 (11th Cir. 2001) (HIV-positive dental hygienist posed a direct threat to others); *Estate of Mauro v. Borgess Med. Ctr.*, 137 F.3d 398 (6th Cir. 1998) (surgical technician with HIV was a direct threat to others because his job required that he place his hands in patients' body cavities in the presence of sharp instruments). In contrast, the defense has been denied in less risky settings. *See Chalk v. United States Dist. Court*, 840 F.2d 701 (9th Cir. 1988) (teacher with AIDS did not pose a "significant risk" in the workplace); *Taylor v. Rice*, 451 F.3d 898 (D.C. Cir. 2006) (summary judgment overturned with regard to HIV-positive State Department employee on direct threat to oneself defense because it was not clear that the job entailed assignments that would put the individual at risk).

5. *Direct Threat and Mental Illness.* Recall *Gambini*, reproduced at p. **489.** If the case had been brought under the ADA and had a "direct threat" defense been asserted, what result? In *The ADA, The Workplace, and the Myth of the "Dangerous Mentally Ill,"* 34 U.C. Davis L. Rev. 849, 850-51 (2001), Professor Ann Hubbard addresses the direct threat defense in the context of mental disabilities. She notes that public fears concerning persons with mental disabilities are out of proportion to the risk of violence actually posed. In another article, *Understanding and Implementing the ADA's Direct Threat Defense*, 95 Nw. U. L. Rev. 1279 (2001), Professor Hubbard elaborates on the direct threat defense more generally. She contends that lower courts and employers tend to overestimate risk that is unfamiliar or uncontrollable or more publicized over risks that are known or within our control or less in the media spotlight. Do you agree? *See also* Susan D. Carle, *Analyzing Social Impairments Under Title I of the Americans with Disabilities Act*, 50 U.C. Davis L. Rev. 1109 (2017); Jane Byeff Korn, *Crazy (Mental Illness Under the ADA)*, 36 U. Mich. J.L. Reform 585 (2003).

NOTE ON DEFERENCE TO THE EEOC

The central question before the Court in *Echazabal* was whether the EEOC's regulations, which expanded the "direct threat" defense to include threats to an individual's own health and safety, was entitled to judicial deference. Indeed, the issue of deference to the EEOC was front and center at a number of the cases we have studied, and, of course, this chapter has repeatedly cited the regulations as establishing ADA "law." But, as *Echazabal* indicates, the fact that the EEOC issues a regulation does not necessarily resolve the matter. Although the *Echazabal* Court found that regulation valid, that has not always been true. The legislatively overruled *Sutton* decision, for example, rejected the EEOC's approach to mitigating measures.

Answering that question requires a consideration of administrative law and how its principles apply to the EEOC. The EEOC is charged with the administration and enforcement of Title VII, the ADEA, and the ADA. And while we will study the role of the Commission in enforcing these statutes when we reach Chapter 8, the EEOC, like other administrative agencies, also has a role as law interpreter. To what extent is it entitled to meaningful deference from the courts in its *interpretation* of the statutes it administers? As we have seen in earlier chapters, the Court's willingness to defer to EEOC interpretations of Title VII's substantive provisions has been limited. Although Congress gave the EEOC the power to issue procedural regulations under Title VII, it withheld from the agency the power to issue substantive regulations under that statute. But court deference to the EEOC should be greater under the Americans with Disabilities Act since Title I conferred substantive rule-making authority on the EEOC in §12116. The EEOC carried out that mandate, issuing regulations promulgated after notice and comment. The formal regulations also added an "Interpretive Guidance" as an appendix.

The Supreme Court's decision in *Bragdon v. Abbott*, discussed at p. **444** suggested the Court was willing to allow agencies a leading role in interpreting the statute, but that approach was called into question in *Sutton v. United Air Lines, Inc.*, which presented the question of what deference was due the EEOC's Interpretive Guidance, arguably agency action that was entitled to less deference than its "regulations." The basis of the argument for deference was *Chevron U.S.A., Inc. v. Natural Res. Def. Council, Inc.*, 467 U.S. 837 (1984), in which the Supreme Court recognized that agency interpretations of silent or ambiguous statutes are due deference from the courts when Congress has delegated law-interpreting power to the agency. *See also United States v. Mead Corp.*, 533 U.S. 218 (2001) (a delegation of rule-making or adjudicative authority to agency will support an implied delegation of interpretive authority). Other comparable indicia may also support an implied delegation of such authority. *Chevron* review will attach to such an agency's statutory interpretations, if the agency was exercising that authority when it promulgated the interpretation for which deference is claimed. Even when an agency has not been delegated interpretive authority, however, its interpretations of the statutes it administers still will merit attention from the courts. Such interpretations may be persuasive, depending on "the thoroughness evident in its consideration, the validity of its reasoning, its consistency with earlier and later pronouncements, and all [other] factors which give it power to persuade, if lacking power to control." *Skidmore v. Swift & Co.*, 323 U.S. 134 (1944). This is referred to as *Skidmore* deference.

In *Sutton*, the EEOC contended that its position on the mitigating measures question was deserving of heightened deference under *Chevron*. But the Supreme Court refused to defer to the agency's view as expressed in its Interpretive Guidance. It found the EEOC's reading was an impermissible interpretation of the statute because it was inconsistent with the statutory text. Under *Chevron*, a reviewing court will *not* defer to an agency's construction of a statute if it finds that Congress itself has spoken to the precise question at issue. In such cases, no implied delegation has occurred since Congress itself has made the policy choice. The *Sutton* Court, through its textualist approach, appeared to find that Congress had determined impairments are to be assessed in their mitigated state.

Sutton's substantive holding regarding mitigating measures, of course, has since been legislatively overruled by the ADAAA. Perhaps more important for present purposes, Congress also addressed *Sutton's* analytic framework. *Sutton* noted that the definition of disability was not contained within Title I but instead is in the generally applicable provisions of the Act; as to those, "no agency has been delegated authority to interpret the term 'disability.'" 527 U.S. at 479. That language called into question whether the EEOC's extensive regulations and Interpretive Guidance addressing what constitutes a disability were entitled to any deference at all. (Note that in

Echazabal, at issue were formal regulations interpreting a provision of Title I, the chapter on which the EEOC had been expressly delegated rule-making authority.) Congress, in enacting the ADAAA, responded to this aspect of *Sutton* as well, expressly giving the EEOC the authority to issue regulations implementing the definition of disability. §12205a. Thus, the EEOC now has the expressly delegated authority to interpret "disability," something the Court had found lacking in *Sutton*, along with the substantive rule-making authority it has had from the outset under Title I of the ADA. *See Echazabal.*

Another complicating factor in *Sutton*, however, was that the EEOC's position on mitigating measures was found not in the text of the regulation itself but in the Interpretive Guidance, which was issued as an appendix accompanying the regulations. That appendix, however, had also been subject to notice and comment proceedings. The *Sutton* Court noted, but did not resolve, the format issue. In other words, the Court may extend *Chevron* deference to the EEOC's disability regulations but not to its Interpretive Guidance. The EEOC also has issued various other interpretations in even more informal forms. Its Compliance Manual sets forth Enforcement Guidances, and it also has promulgated a Technical Assistance Manual. Although the failure to follow notice and comment procedures may deprive these interpretations of deference under *Chevron*, they still are entitled to deference under a *Skidmore* review standard. *See Nat'l R.R. Passenger Corp. v. Morgan*, 536 U.S. 101 (2002). For a discussion of judicial deference to the EEOC, *see generally* Rebecca Hanner White, *Deference and Disability Discrimination*, 99 Mich. L. Rev. 532 (2000); Melissa Hart, *Skepticism and Expertise: The Supreme Court and the EEOC*, 74 Fordham L. Rev. 1937 (2006). For criticism of *Echazabal's* inclusion of the threat-to-self in the ADA's direct threat defense, *see, e.g.*, Samuel R. Bagenstos, *The Supreme Court, the Americans with Disabilities Act, and Rational Discrimination*, 55 Ala. L. Rev. 923 (2004).

2.   *Job-Related and Consistent with Business Necessity*

ALBERTSON'S, INC. v. KIRKINGBURG
527 U.S. 555 (1999)

Justice Souter, delivered the opinion for a unanimous Court with respect to Parts I and III, and the opinion of the Court with respect to Part II, in which Chief Justice Rehnquist, and Justices O'Connor, Scalia, Kennedy, Thomas, and Ginsburg, joined.

The question posed is whether, under the Americans with Disabilities Act of 1990 an employer who requires as a job qualification that an employee meet an otherwise applicable federal safety regulation must justify enforcing the regulation solely because its standard may be waived in an individual case. We answer no.

I

In August 1990, petitioner, Albertson's, Inc., a grocery-store chain with supermarkets in several States, hired respondent, Hallie Kirkingburg, as a truck driver based at its Portland, Oregon, warehouse. Kirkingburg had more than a decade's driving experience and performed well when Albertson's transportation manager took him on a road test.

Before starting work, Kirkingburg was examined to see if he met federal vision standards for commercial truck drivers. For many decades the Department of Transportation or its predecessors has been responsible for devising these standards for individuals who drive commercial vehicles in interstate commerce. Since 1971, the basic vision regulation has required corrected distant visual acuity of at least 20/40 in each eye and distant binocular acuity of at least 20/40. Kirkingburg, however, suffers from amblyopia, an uncorrectable condition that leaves him with 20/200 vision in his left eye and monocular vision in effect. Despite Kirkingburg's weak left eye, the doctor erroneously certified that he met the DOT's basic vision standard, and Albertson's hired him.

In December 1991, Kirkingburg injured himself on the job and took a leave of absence. Before returning to work in November 1992, Kirkingburg went for a further physical as required by the company. This time, the examining physician correctly assessed Kirkingburg's vision and explained that his eyesight did not meet the basic DOT standards. The physician, or his nurse, told Kirkingburg that in order to be legally qualified to drive, he would have to obtain a waiver of its basic vision standards from the DOT. The doctor was alluding to a scheme begun in July 1992 for giving DOT certification to applicants with deficient vision who had three years of recent experience driving a commercial vehicle without a license suspension or revocation, involvement in a reportable accident in which the applicant was cited for a moving violation, conviction for certain driving-related offenses, citation for certain serious traffic violations, or more than two convictions for any other moving violations. A waiver applicant had to agree to have his vision checked annually for deterioration, and to report certain information about his driving experience to the Federal Highway Administration, the agency within the DOT responsible for overseeing the motor carrier safety regulations. Kirkingburg applied for a waiver, but because he could not meet the basic DOT vision standard Albertson's fired him from his job as a truck driver. In early 1993, after he had left Albertson's, Kirkingburg received a DOT waiver, but Albertson's refused to rehire him.

Kirkingburg sued Albertson's, claiming that firing him violated the ADA. . . .

III

Albertson's primary contention is that even if Kirkingburg was disabled, he was not a "qualified" individual with a disability because Albertson's merely insisted on the minimum level of visual acuity set forth in the DOT's Motor Carrier Safety Regulations. If Albertson's was entitled to enforce that standard as defining an "essential job function of the employment position," see 42 U.S.C. §12111(8), that is the end of the case, for Kirkingburg concededly could not satisfy it.

Under Title I of the ADA, employers may justify their use of "qualification standards . . . that screen out or tend to screen out or otherwise deny a job or benefit to an individual with a disability," so long as such standards are "job-related and consistent with business necessity, and . . . performance cannot be accomplished by reasonable accommodation. . . ." 42 U.S.C. §12113(a).

Kirkingburg and the Government argue that these provisions do not authorize an employer to follow even a facially applicable regulatory standard subject to waiver without making some enquiry beyond determining whether the applicant or employee meets that standard, yes or no. Before an employer may insist on compliance, they say, the employer must make a showing with reference to the particular job that the waivable regulatory standard is "job-related . . . and . . . consistent with business necessity," see §12112(b)(6), and that after consideration of the capabilities of the individual a reasonable accommodation could not fairly resolve the competing interests when an applicant or employee cannot wholly satisfy an otherwise justifiable job qualification.

The Government extends this argument by reference to a further section of the statute, which at first blush appears to be a permissive provision for the employer's and the public's benefit. An employer may impose as a qualification standard "a requirement that an individual shall not pose a direct threat to the health or safety of other individuals in the workplace," §12113(b), with "direct threat" being defined by the Act as "a significant risk to the health or safety of others, which cannot be eliminated by reasonable accommodation," §12111(3). The Government urges us to read subsections (a) and (b) together to mean that when an employer would impose any safety qualification standard, however specific, tending to screen out individuals with disabilities, the application of the requirement must satisfy the ADA's "direct threat" criterion. That criterion ordinarily requires "an individualized assessment of the individual's present ability to safely perform the essential functions of the job," 29 CFR §1630.2(r) (1998), "based on medical or other objective evidence," *Bragdon, see* 29 CFR §1630.2(r) (1998) (assessment of direct threat "shall be based on a reasonable medical judgment that relies on the most current medical knowledge and/or on the best available objective evidence.").[15]

Albertson's answers essentially that even assuming the Government has proposed a sound reading of the statute for the general run of cases, this case is not in the general run. It is crucial to its position that Albertson's here was not insisting upon a job qualification merely of its own devising, subject to possible questions about genuine appropriateness and justifiable application to an individual for whom some accommodation may be reasonable. The job qualification it was applying was the distant visual acuity standard of the Federal Motor Carrier Safety Regulations, 49 CFR §391.41(b)(10) (1998), which is made binding on Albertson's by §391.11: "a motor carrier shall not . . . permit a person to drive a commercial motor vehicle unless that person is qualified to drive," by, among other things, meeting the physical qualification standards set forth in §391.41. The validity of these regulations is unchallenged, they have the force of law, and they contain no qualifying language about individualized determinations.

If we looked no further, there would be no basis to question Albertson's' unconditional obligation to follow the regulation and its consequent right to do so. This, indeed, was the understanding of Congress when it enacted the ADA.[16] But there is more: the waiver program.

The Court of Appeals majority . . . assumed that the regulatory provisions for the waiver program had to be treated as being on par with the basic visual acuity regulation, as if the general rule had been modified by some different safety standard made applicable by grant of a waiver. On this reading, an individualized determination under a different substantive safety rule was an element of the regulatory regime,

---

15. This appears to be the position taken by the EEOC in the Interpretive Guidance promulgated under its authority to issue regulations to carry out Title I of the ADA, 42 U.S.C. §12116, see 29 CFR pt. 1630, App., §§1630.15(b) and (c) (1998) (requiring safety-related standards to be evaluated under the ADA's direct threat standard); *see also* App. §1630.10 (noting that selection criteria that screen out individuals with disabilities, including "safety requirements, vision or hearing requirements," must be job-related, consistent with business necessity, and not amenable to reasonable accommodation). Although it might be questioned whether the Government's interpretation, which might impose a higher burden on employers to justify safety-related qualification standards than other job requirements, is a sound one, we have no need to confront the validity of the reading in this case.

16. The implementing regulations of Title I also recognize a defense to liability under the ADA that "a challenged action is required or necessitated by another Federal law or regulation," 29 CFR §1630.15(e) (1998). As the parties do not invoke this specific regulation, we have no occasion to consider its effect.

which would easily fit with any requirement of 42 U.S.C. §§12113(a) and (b) to consider reasonable accommodation. An employer resting solely on the federal standard for its visual acuity qualification would be required to accept a waiver once obtained, and probably to provide an applicant some opportunity to obtain a waiver whenever that was reasonably possible. . . .

But the reasoning underlying the Court of Appeal's decision was unsound, for we think it was error to read the regulations establishing the waiver program as modifying the content of the basic visual acuity standard in a way that disentitled an employer like Albertson's to insist on it. . . .

Nothing in the waiver regulation, of course, required an employer of commercial drivers to accept the hypothesis and participate in the Government's experiment. The only question, then, is whether the ADA should be read to require such an employer to defend a decision to decline the experiment. Is it reasonable, that is, to read the ADA as requiring an employer like Albertson's to shoulder the general statutory burden to justify a job qualification that would tend to exclude the disabled, whenever the employer chooses to abide by the otherwise clearly applicable, unamended substantive regulatory standard despite the Government's willingness to waive it experimentally and without any finding of its being inappropriate? If the answer were yes, an employer would in fact have an obligation of which we can think of no comparable example in our law. The employer would be required in effect to justify de novo an existing and otherwise applicable safety regulation issued by the Government itself. The employer would be required on a case-by-case basis to reinvent the Government's own wheel when the Government had merely begun an experiment to provide data to consider changing the underlying specifications. And what is even more, the employer would be required to do so when the Government had made an affirmative record indicating that contemporary empirical evidence was hard to come by. It is simply not credible that Congress enacted the ADA (before there was any waiver program) with the understanding that employers choosing to respect the Government's sole substantive visual acuity regulation in the face of an experimental waiver might be burdened with an obligation to defend the regulation's application according to its own terms.

Justice Thomas, concurring. . . .

[The concurrence would have preferred resolving the case by finding that plaintiff failed to prove that he was a "qualified individual with a disability" since the "quintessential function" of a truck driving job is "to be able to drive a commercial truck in interstate commerce," which plaintiff could not legally do under federal law. While "[t]he waiver program might be thought of as a way to reasonably accommodate respondent," as the Court explained, that program "did nothing to modify the regulation's unconditional requirements." Justice Thomas joined the Court's opinion "only on the understanding that it leaves open the argument that federal laws such as DOT's visual acuity standards might be critical in determining whether a plaintiff is a 'qualified individual with a disability.'"]

NOTES

1. *Analogizing to Title VII's BFOQ.* Under the ADA, evaluating qualification standards — such as the DOT visual acuity standard that expressly screens out disabled individuals — to determine whether they are justified is somewhat analogous to establishing a bona fide occupational qualification defense in a gender discrimination case

under Title VII. What differences do you see? Why is disability discrimination treated differently than gender discrimination?

2. *A Higher Threshold for Safety Standards?* The Court notes that the regulations require an individualized determination when an employer asserts that an individual's disability constitutes a direct threat. Neither the statute nor the regulations mention individualized determinations in the context of job qualifications that are not based on the direct threat defense. Is the standard for establishing a safety qualification more stringent than the standard for establishing other qualifications that screen out those with disabilities? The Court questioned this interpretation. See footnote 15.

3. *Job Related to the Position in Question and Consistent with Business Necessity.* Is the ADA more or less burdensome on employers than Title VII in terms of the job-related and business necessity defense? On the one hand, under the ADA, employers may use the defense to justify facially discriminatory policies. On the other hand, does the ADA impose a more stringent evidentiary standard for the defense? In *Bates v. UPS*, 511 F.3d 974 (9th Cir. 2007) (en banc), the court wrote:

> To show "job-relatedness," an employer must demonstrate that the qualification standard fairly and accurately measures the individual's actual ability to perform the essential functions of the job. When every person excluded by the qualification standard is a member of a protected class — that is, disabled persons — an employer must demonstrate a predictive or significant correlation between the qualification and performance of the job's essential functions.
>
> To show that the disputed qualification standard is "consistent with business necessity" the employer must show that it "substantially promote[s]" the business's needs. "The 'business necessity' standard is quite high, and is not to be confused with mere expediency." For a safety-based qualification standard, "[i]n evaluating whether the risks addressed by . . . [the] qualification standard constitute a business necessity, the court should take into account the magnitude of possible harm as well as the probability of occurrence."
>
> Finally, to show that "performance cannot be accomplished by reasonable accommodation," the employer must demonstrate either that no reasonable accommodation currently available would cure the performance deficiency or that such reasonable accommodation poses an "undue hardship" on the employer.

Id. at 996 (citations and footnotes omitted). The court then turned to the qualification standard allocation of burdens of proof, which it viewed as parallel to those for the "direct threat" defense. It explained:

> Because UPS has linked hearing with safe driving, UPS bears the burden to prove that nexus as part of its defense to use of the hearing qualification standard. The employees, however, bear the ultimate burden to show that they are qualified to perform the essential function of safely driving a package car. . . .
>
> By requiring UPS to justify the hearing test under the business necessity defense, but also requiring plaintiffs to show that they can perform the essential functions of the job, we are not saying, nor does the ADA require, that employers must hire employees who cannot safely perform the job, particularly where safety itself is an essential function. Nor are we saying that an employer can never impose a safety standard that exceeds minimum requirements imposed by law. However, when an employer asserts a blanket safety-based qualification standard — beyond the essential job function — that is not mandated by law and that qualification standard screens out or tends to screen out an individual with a disability, the employer — not the employee — bears the burden of showing that the higher qualification standard is job-related and consistent with business necessity, and that performance cannot be achieved through reasonable accommodation.

Id. at 992. *See also Kapche v. San Antonio*, 304 F.3d 493 (5th Cir. 2002) (rejecting per se rule that persons with insulin-treated diabetes cannot perform essential job function of driving; individualized assessment of plaintiff required). *But see Parker v. Crete Carrier Corp.*, 839 F.3d 717 (8th Cir. 2016) (a trucking company that required drivers with a body mass index above 33 to participate in a sleep apnea study did not violate the ADA; the study was job related and consistent with business necessity insofar as it dealt with a condition that might impair drivers' abilities to operate vehicles safely and was no more intrusive than necessary because a lab was the best way to diagnose the condition); *Allmond v. Akal Sec. Inc.*, 558 F.3d 1312 (11th Cir. 2009) (hearing aid ban for federal marshals was valid when it was developed after a detailed analysis of the position to identify essential functions and the medical qualifications necessary to perform them given the possible harm that could result from a failure to perform essential hearing functions).

4. *Burdens of Proof.* Is it appropriate to refer to the proof of job relationship and business necessity as a "defense" when the statute defines covered individuals in terms of whether they are "qualified" to perform essential functions of the job? This is the point of Justice Thomas's concurrence in *Kirkingburg* — that it is the *plaintiff's* burden to prove that he is a qualified individual with a disability, which includes proof that he can perform the essential functions of driving trucks in interstate commerce; Thomas would hold it not the defendant's burden to prove he cannot. But the Court in *Echazabal*, reproduced at p. 500, repeatedly refers to the showing that a qualification standard that screens out a disabled person be job related for the position in question and consistent with business necessity as an affirmative defense. Don't *Echazabal* and *Kirkingburg* clearly contemplate placing the burden of proof on this issue on the employer?

5. *Standing to Sue.* At least one circuit has held that only individuals with a disability can challenge qualification standards under §12112(b)(6). In *Bates v. Dura Auto Sys.*, 625 F.3d 283 (6th Cir. 2010), the plaintiffs attacked their employer's prohibition against the use of certain legally prescribed drugs and their resulting termination for the use of such drugs, claiming the employer was using a qualification standard or test that screened out or tended to screen out the disabled and that was not justified by job-relatedness or business necessity. The court held the nondisabled plaintiffs could not proceed with a claim under this section of the ADA.

3. Disparate Impact

Many disparate impact claims under the ADA can be recast as reasonable accommodation claims and vice versa. Which approach is more advantageous to plaintiffs? Do you think undue hardship and direct threat are harder defenses for the employer to prove than job-relatedness and business necessity? How do the remedies differ?

Some reasonable accommodation claims, however, are more difficult to frame as disparate impact claims. Consider, for example, the request of a covered individual for extra sick leave to deal with medical problems. Restricting sick leave may not exclude the person from work, but it may make it more difficult for her to schedule doctor's appointments or more expensive because she must take unpaid personal days to see the doctor. This policy would "impact" individuals with disabilities because their needs differ from those of other individuals.

Is disparate impact designed to deal with claims like this? ADA §102(b)(3) provides that "discriminate" includes "utilizing standards, criteria, or methods of administration . . . that have the effect of discrimination on the basis of disability." The EEOC Guidance relating to disparate impact defenses seems to contemplate claims based on a variety of employer policies: "there may be uniformly applied standards, criteria and policies not relating to selection that may also screen out or tend to screen out [individuals with disabilities]. Like selection criteria that have a disparate impact, non-selection criteria having such an impact may also have to be job-related and consistent with business necessity, subject to consideration of reasonable accommodation." 29 C.F.R. pt. 1630, app. §1630.15(c) (2018).

Does the hypothetical leave policy violate this section? In *Alexander v. Choate*, 469 U.S. 287 (1985), a case decided under the Rehabilitation Act, the Supreme Court rejected the claim that the Tennessee Medicaid Program's 14-day limitation on inpatient coverage would have an unlawful disparate impact on the disabled. *Choate* seems most directly relevant to a claim by an individual with a disability for more sick leave than other individuals receive. Under the ADA, could a disabled employee attack a sick leave policy that restricts paid leave to 14 days as having a disparate impact on employees with disabilities? The EEOC suggests that such a claim is not viable but that an employee affected by such a policy may be entitled to leave as a reasonable accommodation:

> "No-leave" policies (*e.g.*, no leave during the first six months of employment) are . . . not subject to challenge under the adverse impact theory. However, an employer, in spite of its "no-leave" policy, may, in appropriate circumstances, have to consider the provision of leave to an employee with a disability as a reasonable accommodation, unless the provision of leave would impose an undue hardship.

29 C.F.R. pt. 1630, app. §1630.15(c). What does this mean?

What is the burden of proof required for ADA disparate impact claims? In *Lopez v. Pacific Maritime Ass'n*, 657 F.3d 762 (9th Cir. 2011), the Ninth Circuit ruled that the plaintiff must adduce statistically significant evidence to support his claim that the employer's "one-strike" rule, permanently eliminating from consideration for employment any applicant who tested positive for drug or alcohol use during a pre-employment screening process, discriminated against recovering addicts. The court acknowledged the plaintiff's concerns that the standard placed an unfair burden on him because "he has no way to know how many recovering or recovered drug addicts Defendant has disqualified. Neither can he determine the proportion of recovering or recovered drug addicts in the relevant labor market because, he argues, state law prevents him from inquiring into a person's history of drug abuse." *Id.* at 768. Nevertheless, it found statistical evidence required "under both logic and precedent." *Id.* However, in so ruling, the court refused to consider an argument, raised for the first time in a petition for rehearing, that the evidentiary burden on a disparate impact claim under the ADA is different than that under Title VII. The argument was that, because the ADA prohibits selection criteria that *tend to screen out* those with disabilities, no formal statistical showing is needed.

E. SPECIAL PROBLEMS OF DISABILITY DISCRIMINATION

The ADA contains detailed provisions relating to applicants and employees who use alcohol or illegal drugs and to employers who use medical examinations or inquiries.

In addition, the ADA prohibits retaliation, interference, and discrimination against someone who has a relationship with a person with a disability, and it has been interpreted to prohibit disability-based harassment. Finally, rights granted under the Family and Medical Leave Act may be a useful alternative to the ADA for individuals whose health problems make regular attendance at work difficult.

1.   Drug or Alcohol Users

Section 12114(a) provides that the term "qualified individual with a disability" shall not include a person "who is currently engaging in the illegal use of drugs" when the covered entity acts on the basis of such use. Such individuals simply are not covered by the statute. In contrast, the plain language of §12114(a) states that an alcoholic who is currently using alcohol may be disabled under the ADA. In any event, alcoholics and drug addicts are protected from discrimination on the basis of their addiction when they satisfy the statutory definition, which should be relatively easy after the ADAAA. See *Alexander v. Wash. Metro. Area Transit Auth.* at p. 456.

Further, §12114(b) provides that nothing in §12114(a) shall exclude from the definition of qualified individual with a disability an individual who:

> (1)   has successfully completed a supervised drug rehabilitation program and is no longer engaging in the illegal use of drugs, or has otherwise been rehabilitated successfully and is no longer engaging in such use;
> (2)   is participating in a supervised rehabilitation program and is no longer engaging in such use;
> (3)   is erroneously regarded as engaging in such use, but is not engaging in such use.

However, §12114(c) provides employers with a number of potential defenses against a person claiming disability discrimination because of drug or alcohol addiction or use. For example, subsection (c)(1)-(2) permits a covered entity to prohibit the *use* of illegal drugs or being under the influence of alcohol at the workplace, and subsection (c)(4) permits covered entities to "hold an employee who engages in the illegal use of drugs or who is an alcoholic to the same qualification standards for employment or job performance and behavior that such entity holds other employees, even if any unsatisfactory performance or behavior is related to the drug use or alcoholism of such employee."

As marijuana has increasingly been decriminalized in the states for medical or even recreational use, it has been argued that it is now a "legal" drug. Courts addressing the question, however, have concluded that the ADA's reference to "illegal drugs" refers to federal, rather than state, law and marijuana remains a federally controlled substance. *See James v. City of Costa Mesa*, 700 F.3d 394 (9th Cir. 2012). As for alcohol, courts have been permissive as to how employers may deal with individuals who are intoxicated on the job, generally approving "last chance" agreements and other restrictions when the employee could have been fired immediately for inebriation. *See Ostrowski v. Con-Way Freight, Inc.*, 543 F. App'x 128 (3d Cir. 2013); *Clifford v. Cnty. of Rockland*, 528 F. App'x 6 (2d Cir. 2013).

The statute's provisions can generate some complicated legal scenarios. For example, in *Zenor v. El Paso Health Care*, 176 F.3d 847 (5th Cir. 1999), the Fifth Circuit considered the meaning of the exclusion and the safe harbor. The court found that, in determining whether an individual is "currently" engaged in the illegal use of drugs, the operative moment is the time the employment decision is made, not when it goes into effect. In that case, at the time the company made the decision to fire a pharmacist, his illegal drug use had occurred roughly one month previously, which was "current" enough to deprive him of protection under the ADA. The court read "currently" to mean "sufficiently recent" to justify the employer's belief that the drug use was a continuing problem, and no doubt the fact that the plaintiff was a pharmacist made his employer's concerns about his drug use particularly credible. *See also Jarvela v. Crete Carrier Corp.*, 776 F.3d 822, 830 (11th Cir. 2015) ("a seven-day-old diagnosis is 'current'" under governing DOT regulations such that plaintiff was unqualified to drive a commercial motor vehicle).

As for the rehabilitation safe harbor, courts have not read it literally. *Zenor* held that "a plaintiff may not evade termination merely by entering into a rehabilitation program, without first showing a significant period of recovery." 176 F.3d at 858. *See also Shirley v. Precision Castparts Corp.*, 726 F.3d 675, 680-81 (5th Cir. 2013) (plaintiff not within the safe harbor when, although voluntarily entering an in-patient facility, he did not complete the program and remained on an opiate pain reliever); *Mauerhan v. Wagner Corp.*, 649 F.3d 1180 (10th Cir. 2011) (employee was not qualified for the safe harbor after a 30-day in-patient program in light of testimony that three months of treatment would be necessary for an addict like plaintiff to reach a "threshold of significant improvement").

2.   *Medical Examinations and Inquiries*

Section 12112(d)(1)-(4) contains a number of provisions restricting the use of medical examinations and inquiries.

a.   Pre-Employment Medical Examinations and Inquiries

An employer is prohibited from using a medical examination or inquiry to determine whether a job applicant has a disability or the nature and severity of such a disability. But the employer (1) may inquire into the applicant's ability to do the job before making a job offer and (2) may condition an offer of employment on the results of a medical examination if certain conditions are met. These conditions include subjecting all new employees to medical examinations and keeping the results confidential. Such medical examinations given *after* an offer of employment has been made but prior to the commencement of employment need not be job related or consistent with business necessity. However, the Genetic Information Non-Discrimination Act of 2008, 42 U.S.C. §2000ff, also restricts post-offer medical inquiries and examinations. GINA, with very limited exceptions, prohibits employers from requiring disclosure of genetic information, including family medical history. Nor may employers acquire genetic information in determining continuing fitness for duty.

The ADA itself, however, puts no restriction on the *scope* of such examinations — only on the *use* to which they are put. Of course, if they are used to exclude an individual because of disability, then the exclusionary criteria must be job related and consistent with business necessity. Presumably, Congress thought this somewhat cumbersome structure would force disability-related decisions out in the open and make employers think twice about whether their requirements were justified. And, of course, an employer must now comply not only with the ADA but with GINA as well.

In contrast to these provisions, §12114(d)(1) provides that testing for the illegal use of drugs shall not be considered a "medical examination." *Williams v. FedEx Corp. Servs.*, 849 F.3d 889, 901 (10th Cir. 2017) (while a test for "illegal use of drugs" is not a medical examination under the ADA, plaintiff may have a claim if the employer required him to disclose his use of legally-prescribed medications). Further, subsection (d)(2) provides that the ADA shall not be construed to "encourage, prohibit, or authorize" testing for the illegal use of drugs or making employment decisions based on the results of such tests. As you would expect, the ADA regulations contain lengthy and detailed interpretations of these provisions. *See* 29 C.F.R. §§1630.13, 1630.14, 1630.16(c). However, were an employer to test for drugs that are *legally* used, §12114(d)(1)'s safe harbor would not apply. *See Bates v. Dura Auto. Sys., Inc.*, 767 F.3d 566 (6th Cir. 2014).

The EEOC has issued detailed guidance on pre-employment questions. EEOC Notice 915.002 (Oct. 10, 1995). The document identifies as illegal any questions that seek information about whether the applicant is disabled including:

Do you have AIDS?
Have you ever filed for workers' compensation?
What prescription drugs are you currently taking?
Have you ever been treated for mental health problems?
How much alcohol do you drink each week?

On the other hand, the following questions are identified as lawful:

Can you perform the functions of this job with or without reasonable accommodation?
Please describe or demonstrate how you would perform these functions.
Can you meet the attendance requirements of the job?
Do you have the required licenses to perform these jobs?

As for tests, since pre-offer tests are prohibited if they are "medical," the definition of that term is critical. For the EEOC, prohibited "medical" tests are those that seek to reveal the existence of an impairment rather than measure an individual's performance of a task. Physical fitness tests, for example, are not medical examinations and are permitted, *cf. Indergard v. Georgia-Pacific Corp.*, 582 F.3d 1049 (9th Cir. 2009) ("physical capacity evaluation" of paper mill employee with knee injuries who sought to return to work after disability leave was medical examination under ADA since the broad range of tests allowed discovery of impairments beyond physical agility); but, since they will tend to screen out disabled applicants, they must be job related for the position in question and consistent with business necessity. *See also Bates v. Dura Auto. Sys., Inc.*, 767 F.3d 566 (6th Cir. 2014) (2-1) (fact question as to whether a company's testing program for drug use, including certain prescription drugs, qualified as "medical examination" or, alternatively, as a disability inquiry; if so, it was not justified by job relation or business necessity).

Under the EEOC's Enforcement Guidance, psychological tests that are "designed to identify a mental disorder or impairment" qualify as medical examinations, but psychological tests "that measure personality traits such as honesty, preferences, and habits" do not. http://eeoc.gov/policy/docs/ guidance-inquiries.html#7. *See Karraker v. Rent-A-Center, Inc.*, 411 F.3d 831 (7th Cir. 2005) (Minnesota Multiphasic Personality Inventory was a medical examination and not a test designed merely to identify personality traits and could not be administered in a pre-offer setting). *See also Kroll v. White Lake Ambulance Auth.*, 691 F.3d 809 (6th Cir. 2012) (psychological counseling required of employee was a medical examination because it was designed to reveal a mental health impairment).

If an employer asks an applicant questions that are *lawful* under the ADA and the applicant lies, the employer is justified in discharging the employee when the lie is discovered. *See Smith v. Chrysler Corp.*, 155 F.3d 799 (6th Cir. 1998). But what if the employer asks questions that are *unlawful* under the ADA and the applicant lies? Should she be permitted to sue under the ADA, or is she no longer qualified because she lied on the application? *See Leonel v. Am. Airlines, Inc.*, 400 F.3d 702 (9th Cir. 2005) (HIV-positive applicants for flight attendant positions whose job offers were rescinded for their failure to disclose that status raised factual issue as to whether airline violated ADA in requiring applicants to disclose medical information and undergo medical examinations before background checks had been completed).

Suppose an employer asks an applicant unlawful questions and the applicant is not hired. Must the applicant be a qualified disabled individual in order to sue? *See Wetherbee v. S. Co.*, 754 F.3d 901, 904 (11th Cir. 2014) (joining the Seventh and Tenth Circuits in holding that "an individual seeking relief under §12112(d)(3)(C) must demonstrate that he is a qualified individual with a disability"). Assuming nondisabled applicants can bring such claims, what remedy is appropriate?

b. Post-Employment Medical Examinations and Inquiries

Employers are prohibited from requiring medical examinations and inquiries of current employees, unless such examination or inquiry is job related and consistent with a business necessity. Fitness-for-duty examinations are common. The courts interpret the ADA to permit employers to require such examinations when they have reasonable, objective concerns about the employee's ability to perform the duties of his position. *See, e.g., Owusu-Ansah v. Coca-Cola Co.*, 715 F.3d 1306, 1312 (11th Cir. 2013) ("Coca-Cola had a reasonable, objective concern about Mr. Owusu-Ansah's mental state, which affected job performance and potentially threatened the safety of its other employees."); *Brownfield v. City of Yakima*, 612 F.3d 1140, 1146 (9th Cir. 2010) (finding an exam appropriate even absent a decline in performance "if the employer is faced with significant evidence that could cause a reasonable person to inquire as to whether an employee is still capable of performing his job"). Some courts have been deferential to employers. *E.g., Michael v. City of Troy Police Dep't*, 808 F.3d 304, 309 (6th Cir. 2015) (despite conflicting medical opinions, a city was entitled to rely on an objectively reasonable medical opinion that plaintiff was unfit for duty, especially when coupled with non-medical evidence of plaintiff's unusual conduct that raised grave concerns about his judgment).

However, a number of decisions suggest more demanding scrutiny. *See Wright v. Ill. Dep't of Children & Family Servs.*, 798 F.3d 513 (7th Cir. 2015) (jury question as to whether an examination was consistent with business necessity when, contrary to its practice, the employer continued to assign children's cases to plaintiff pending the examination); *Kroll v. White Lake Ambulance Auth.*, 763 F.3d 619, 625 (6th Cir. 2014) (while plaintiff's conduct might have justified disciplinary proceedings, it did not support the conclusion that she was experiencing emotional or psychological problems that affected her job performance). *See* Enforcement Guidance on Disability-Related Inquiries and Medical Examinations of Employees Under the Americans with Disabilities Act No. 915.002 (July 26, 2000) ("Enforcement Guidance on Employees").

Unlike the pre-employment provision of the ADA, the courts have generally interpreted §12112(d) to protect even nondisabled employees. That is true both for improper medical inquiries, *Harrison v. Benchmark Elecs. Huntsville, Inc.*, 593 F.3d 1206, 1214 (11th Cir. 2010), and the ADA's confidentiality provisions. *Cossette v. Minn. Power & Light*, 188 F.3d 964, 969 (8th Cir. 1999).

The ADA permits *voluntary* medical exams and inquiries of current employees as part of an employee health program. HIPAA and the Patient Protection and Affordable Care Act encourage "wellness" programs, permitting employers to offer incentives to employees to complete health risk assessments or to demonstrate healthy behaviors. At what point, however, does an incentive become great enough to render an employee's participation in the wellness program "involuntary"? *See Seff v. Broward Cnty.*, 691 F.3d 1221 (11th Cir. 2012) (the ADA was not violated by an employer's $20 bi-weekly penalty on employees who refused to complete a health risk assessment and undergo a biometric screening because the statute's prohibition on involuntary medical exams and inquiries does not apply to an employer's health plan that meets the ADA's safe harbor for bona fide benefit plans, §12201(c)(2)). The EEOC issued its final rule on Title I and wellness programs on May 17, 2016, https://www.eeoc. gov/laws/regulations/qanda-ada-wellness-final-rule.cfma. While its details are complicated, the rule would permit employers to offer incentives up to 30 percent of the total cost of employee-only coverage to promote participation in a wellness program and/or for achieving health outcomes. The rule describes what qualifies as a wellness program, defines what it means for a program to be voluntary, and addresses the confidentiality of medical information obtained through the program.

Wellness programs also implicate GINA, but that statute specifically permits an employer to request genetic information as part of a wellness program if the employee provides prior, knowing, *voluntary*, and written authorization. 29 C.F.R. §1635.8(b)(2). In its final regulations interpreting GINA, the EEOC provided that, if a financial inducement is offered to participate in a wellness program, the employer must make clear that the inducement will be made available whether or not the participant answers questions concerning genetic information. And the EEOC states that compliance with GINA does not necessarily satisfy the ADA.

3. *Retaliation and Interference*

Section 12203 prohibits certain acts of retaliation and interference. Subsection (a) essentially tracks the language of Title VII and the ADEA, which we explored in Chapter 6. However, subsection (b) adds a prohibition of coercing, intimidating, threatening, or interfering with the exercises of ADA rights for himself or another, which is considerably broader than the other statutes. The Third Circuit, in *Krouse v. American Sterilizer Co.*, 126 F.3d 494 (3d Cir. 1997), held that a plaintiff asserting a retaliation claim under the ADA need not establish that he or she is a qualified individual with a disability. *Accord Muller v. Costello*, 187 F.3d 298 (2d Cir. 1999). *See also EEOC v. The Picture People, Inc.*, 684 F.3d 981 (10th Cir. 2012) (affirming summary judgment against plaintiff on the retaliation claim on the merits, even after finding her unqualified within the meaning of the ADA).

While the other antidiscrimination statutes do not explicitly reach third-party retaliation claims, they have been held actionable under Title VII, *see Thompson v. North American Stainless, LP*, reproduced at p. 408, which may well apply under the ADA. But, as noted above, the ADA's antiretaliation provisions are in any event broader than those in Title VII or the ADEA. *See Fogelman v. Mercy Hosp., Inc.*, 283 F.3d 561 (3d Cir. 2002) (pre-*North American Stainless* decision finding a third-party retaliation claim by a son actionable under the ADA under §12203(b) and, alternatively, upholding an ADA "perception" claim if the employer mistakenly believed the plaintiff had assisted his father with his suit).

In analyzing claims under §12203(a), courts, consistent with their practice under Title VII and the ADEA, have insisted that the plaintiff identify an adverse action in order to state a retaliation claim. Presumably, however, the Supreme Court's decision in *Burlington Northern*, reproduced at p. 422, will govern analysis of the "adverse action" element in ADA §12203(a)'s retaliation claims as well. *See, e.g., Colón-Fontánez v. San Juan*, 660 F.3d 17 (1st Cir. 2011), but the broader language of subsection (b), barring, inter alia, "threats" suggests a more liberal approach under that provision.

4.   Harassment

The lower courts have either assumed or have expressly acknowledged that a claim for hostile work environment may be brought under the ADA. *See, e.g., Ryan v. Capital Contrs., Inc.*, 679 F.3d 772 (8th Cir. 2012); *Arrieta-Colon v. Wal-Mart P.R., Inc.*, 434 F.3d 75, 79 (1st Cir. 2006), although the "severe or pervasive" requirement may be difficult to meet. *See Colón-Fontánez v. San Juan*, 660 F.3d 17 (1st Cir. 2011) (co-workers calling plaintiff a hypochondriac, claiming she was "faking" her disability, and isolating her from workplace interaction were not sufficiently severe or pervasive); *Shaver v. Indep. Stave Co.*, 350 F.3d 716 (8th Cir. 2003) (two years of calling plaintiff "platehead" because of a metal appliance implanted in his skull to treat epilepsy not sufficient to be actionable).

A hostile work environment claim may arise when the plaintiff can show he was targeted for harassment either because of his disability or because of his request for an accommodation. When the hostile work environment claim is based on a request for accommodation, the line between a retaliation claim and a hostile work environment claim becomes murky. Courts have sometimes divided the allegations into two separate claims, looking to see whether there is a materially adverse job action to support a retaliation claim and then looking at taunts, threats, cartoons, and jokes to see if the conduct is sufficiently severe or pervasive to constitute harassment. *See Silk v. City of Chi.*, 194 F.3d 788 (7th Cir. 1999). Is this the correct approach? What about §12203(b)? *See Brown v. City of Tucson*, 336 F.3d 1181 (9th Cir. 2003). *See also* Mark C. Weber, *Exile and the Kingdom: Integration, Harassment, and the Americans with Disabilities Act*, 63 MD. L. REV. 162, 189-90 (2004) ("Verbal threats, which are commonly found in cases that courts throw out as inadequate to sustain a harassment claim, are specific violations of 12203(b)").

5.   Protected Relationships

Section 12112(b)(4) prohibits a covered entity from discriminating against a qualified individual "because of the known disability of an individual with whom the qualified individual is known to have a relationship or association." Section 504 of the Rehabilitation Act was amended to provide the same protection. The EEOC, however, believes that this prohibition does not entitle such an individual to reasonable accommodation so that he or she can attend to the needs of his or her relative or associate. *See* 29 C.F.R. pt. 1630, app. §1630.8. *See Tyndall v. National Educ. Ctrs.*, 31 F.3d

209 (4th Cir. 1994) (school not required to restructure an employee's work schedule to enable her to care for her disabled son).

In order to make out a case of associational discrimination, the plaintiff must show that the individual with whom she has a relationship is disabled and that the employer was aware of the third party's disability. *Ennis v. National Ass'n of Bus. & Educ. Radio, Inc.*, 53 F.3d 55 (4th Cir. 1995). Even if these minimum requirements are satisfied, the employee must be fired *because of* the relationship. In *Ennis*, the court concluded that the plaintiff was discharged for inadequate performance, not because of her relationship with her disabled son. *Graziadio v. Culinary Inst. of Am.*, 817 F.3d 415, 432 (2d Cir. 2016), recognized three kinds of association claims: adverse actions caused by (1) "expense," because the employer believes her association with a disabled person will generate insurance costs; (2) "disability by association," triggered by employer fears that the employee may contract or is genetically predisposed to develop the disability of the associated person; and (3) "distraction," instances in which the employer fears that the employee will be inattentive at work due to concerns about the disabled person.

An example of an expense case is *Dewitt v. Proctor Hosp.*, 517 F.3d 944 (7th Cir. 2008), where plaintiff's claim of discrimination on account of her association with her disabled husband was allowed to proceed where there was evidence that her discharge was an effort to avoid the high costs of her husband's cancer treatment; Judge Posner concurred, suggesting that, if the employer would have discriminated against anyone who ran up such high medical bills, there would have been no discrimination on the basis of disability. What do you think of that argument? *See also Trujillo v. Pacifi-Corp*, 524 F.3d 1149 (10th Cir. 2008) (married employees raised factual issue as to whether the alleged reason for their discharges was a pretext for avoiding the high costs of their son's medical expenses).

Cases of discrimination based on association are subject to ADA defenses, including the direct threat defense. *See Den Hartog v. Wasatch Academy*, 129 F.3d 1076 (10th Cir. 1997) (boarding school teacher lawfully discharged based on relationship with son who suffered from psychiatric disorder that caused the son to engage in threatening behavior toward other boarding school personnel and their families). *See generally* Lawrence D. Rosenthal, *Association Discrimination Under the Americans with Disabilities Act: Another Uphill Battle for Potential ADA Plaintiffs*, 22 HOFSTRA LAB. & EMP. L.J. 132 (2004).

6.   *Family and Medical Leave Act*

The Family and Medical Leave Act of 1993, 29 U.S.C. §§2601 et seq., requires covered employers to provide "eligible" employees with up to 12 weeks of unpaid leave per year when the employee is unable to work because of a "serious health condition." Other aspects of the FMLA are discussed in Chapter 5 at p. 325, including limitations on coverage. Employers also are required to maintain preexisting health insurance while the employee is on leave and to reinstate the employee to the same or an equivalent job when the leave period is over. An employer may require an employee to provide medical certification from a health care provider to demonstrate that the employee is suffering from a serious health condition that makes the employee unable to perform job functions and is, therefore, eligible for leave.

FMLA regulations define "serious health condition" as an illness, injury, impairment, or physical or mental condition that involves inpatient care or continuing treatment by a health care provider. 29 C.F.R. §825.113(a). The definition of "continuing treatment by a health care provider" in the regulations provides for five different types of continuing treatment: (a) a period of incapacity of more than three consecutive calendar days; (b) a period of incapacity due to pregnancy or prenatal care; (c) a period of incapacity due to a chronic serious health condition (*e.g.*, asthma, diabetes, epilepsy); (d) a period of incapacity that is permanent or long term due to a condition for which treatment may not be effective (*e.g.*, Alzheimer's, stroke, terminal illness); and (e) a period of absence to receive multiple treatments for necessary restorative surgery or for conditions such as cancer, arthritis, or kidney disease that, without treatment, would result in absences of more than three days. In order to qualify for FMLA leave, each of these situations must involve specified levels of active treatment or supervision by health care professionals. *See* 29 C.F.R. §825.115(a)-(e).

The regulations provide specific examples of conditions and treatments that are, and are not, eligible for FMLA leave. Routine physical, dental, or eye examinations are not covered. Cosmetic treatments not medically required do not constitute "serious health conditions," unless inpatient hospital care is required or complications arise. A variety of common short-term illnesses, such as colds and flu, do not qualify for FMLA leave, absent complications. On the other hand, surgery to remove cancerous growths and treatments for allergies, stress, or substance abuse are included if the other conditions of the regulation are met. *See* 29 C.F.R. §825.113(c)-(d). Treating substance abuse as a "serious health condition" should not prevent an employer from taking action against an employee whose abuse interferes with job performance as long as the employer complies with the ADA and does not take action against the employee because the employee has exercised his or her right to take FMLA leave for treatment of that condition. *See* 29 C.F.R. §825.119(b).

According to FMLA regulations, being "unable to perform the functions of the position of the employee" means: "where the health care provider finds that the employee is unable to work at all or is unable to perform any one of the essential functions of the employee's position" as defined by the ADA. *See* 29 C.F.R. §825.123. The FMLA regulations expressly provide that the FMLA does not modify the ADA in any way and that employers are obligated to comply with both statutes. *See* 29 C.F.R. §825.702.

With respect to the notice that employees must give in order to be eligible for FMLA leave, the statute provides that, when the need for leave is foreseeable, an employee must provide her employer with no less than 30 days' advance notice. *See* 29 U.S.C. §2612(e)(1) & (2)(B); *see also* 29 C.F.R. §825.302. When the need for leave is unforeseeable, the regulations provide that "an employee should give notice to the employer of the need for FMLA leave as soon as practicable," which should generally be "within the time prescribed by the employer's usual and customary notice requirements applicable to such leave." *See* 29 C.F.R. §825.303.

Individuals who are covered by both the ADA and the FMLA should be aware that, if they suffer from an impairment that necessitates frequent absence, they have more than one option for dealing with this issue. Even if accommodations with respect to leave are not reasonable given their employer's needs, leave without pay under the FMLA is a statutory right with no business necessity defense as long as the employer is provided with adequate notice. In addition, employees with attendance problems that are health related, but who do not meet the ADA definition of "disabled," will not be covered by the ADA. They will, however, be entitled to leave without pay if their health problem is a "serious health condition" under the FMLA.

Chapter 8

Procedures for Enforcing
Antidiscrimination Laws

A. INTRODUCTION

Title VII, 42 U.S.C. §§2000e et seq. (2018), the Age Discrimination in Employment Act, 29 U.S.C. §§621 et seq. (2018), and the Americans with Disabilities Act, 42 U.S.C. §§12101 et seq. (2018) all have complicated procedural requirements as a prerequisite to filing suit. The paradigm is Title VII, which Title I of the ADA incorporates by reference. §12117(a). The ADEA is aligned largely, but not perfectly, with Title VII. Because of the substantial identity of all three statutes, the following discussion will be framed in terms of Title VII, although relevant differences between it and the ADEA are noted.

Title VII creates a unique amalgam of methods — administrative and judicial — for enforcement of its substantive proscriptions. §706, 42 U.S.C. §2000e-5. Any suit must be preceded by a charge filed with the EEOC by a "person aggrieved" by the alleged act of discrimination, and that charge must be lodged within 300 days of the occurrence of the unfair employment practice. It must also be filed with any existing state antidiscrimination agency.[*]

The EEOC is directed by Title VII to serve notice of the charge on the respondent and then to conduct an investigation, culminating in a determination of whether there is reasonable cause to believe that the charge is true. If the EEOC finds no reasonable cause, it must dismiss the charge and notify the charging party, who may then bring

---

[*] In a few states, those without state fair employment practices agencies, the time limit is 180 days from the occurrence. *See* Charles A. Sullivan & Lauren M. Walter, Employment Discrimination Law and Practice ch. 12 (2008).

a private action within 90 days. If, however, the EEOC does find reasonable cause, it is directed first to attempt conciliation. If that fails to eliminate the alleged unlawful employment practice, the EEOC may bring a civil suit against the respondent in district court or send a "right to sue" letter to the charging party, who may then file her own suit within 90 days. If the EEOC does not sue within 180 days from the filing of the charge, the charging party may obtain a right-to-sue letter (receipt of which will start the 90 days running) to bring an action; or the charging party may permit EEOC processes to proceed to their conclusion and bring suit within 90 days of that point.

In short, Title VII has two separate time limitations a plaintiff must satisfy: filing an EEOC charge within 300 days of the violation and filing court suit within 90 days of the receipt of a notice of dismissal or of a right-to-sue letter.

B. THE ADMINISTRATIVE PHASE: CHARGE FILING

1. *Introduction*

Although Title VII envisions careful EEOC processing of charges, the only preconditions for private suit are timely resort to the EEOC and seasonable filing of a court suit thereafter. Even an EEOC finding of no reasonable cause to believe discrimination occurred does not bar suit. *McDonnell Douglas Corp. v. Green*, 411 U.S. 792, 798-99 (1972). Thus, defects in EEOC proceedings — such as failing to notify the defendant of a filed charge or failing to conduct conciliation efforts prior to private suit — do not prejudice the private plaintiff.

2. *Filing a Timely Charge*

a. What Constitutes a "Charge"?

Every private Title VII, ADA, and ADEA suit must begin with a charge under oath filed with the Equal Employment Opportunity Commission. §706(b), 42 U.S.C. §20003-5(b). Oddly, neither the statute nor the EEOC's regulations comprehensively define what constitutes a "charge." *See* 29 C.F.R. §1601.12(b) (2018). While the regulations identify desirable information, they also state that a charge is sufficient if it is in writing, names the alleged violator, and "generally allege[s] the discriminatory act[s]." *Federal Express Corp. v. Holowecki*, 552 U.S. 389, 396 (2008). Given these minimal requirements, issues arise as to whether an "inquiry" is in fact a charge. *Holowecki* held that a filing with the Commission is a "charge" if it has the minimal information required by the regulations and is "reasonably construed as a request for the agency to take remedial action to protect the employee's rights or otherwise settle a dispute between the employer and the employee." *Id.* at 402. In the case before it, the Court found an agency Intake Questionnaire insufficient by itself, but that the plaintiff's affidavit expressed a request that the agency take action to protect her rights. The EEOC has since revised its Intake Questionnaire to allow claimants to check a box to request that the EEOC take remedial action. When "Box 2" is checked, an employee "unquestionably files a charge of discrimination." *Hildebrand v. Allegheny Cnty.*, 757 F.3d 99, 113 (3d Cir. 2014). Even a bare-bones charge will satisfy the statutes' timeliness requirements since another EEOC regulation allows amendments to the first filing to "relate back to the date the charge was first received." §1601.12(b). *Edelman v. Lynchburg Coll.*, 535 U.S. 106, 114 (2002).

b.   When Does the Violation "Occur"?

Since Title VII requires filing a charge within 300 days "after the alleged unlawful employment practice occurred," 42 U.S.C. §2000e-5(e), §706(e), the filing must be timely as measured from when the challenged act of discrimination "occurs." In some cases, such as when a worker is discharged on the spot, the "occurrence" is easily identified: the act and its consequences occur simultaneously. In the employment context, however, decisions by the employer may not be transparent to an employee; for example, she may know that she received a 3 percent raise but not know that her male co-workers received a 5 percent increase. Further, employment decisions often have downstream consequences that may not become clear for years.

ALMOND v. UNIFIED SCHOOL DISTRICT #501
665 F.3d 1174 (10th Cir. 2011)

GORSUCH, Circuit Judge

Enacted in 2009, the Lilly Ledbetter Fair Pay Act governs how long parties have to file "discrimination in compensation" claims. This case requires us to consider what that phrase means. As it turns out, the phrase refers to situations in which a member of a protected class receives less pay than similarly situated colleagues — that is, unequal pay for equal work. Because the plaintiffs in this case don't raise an unequal pay for equal work claim, they do not benefit from the Act's comparatively generous deadlines and preexisting accrual rules apply. Under those rules, and as the district court observed, the plaintiffs' claims are untimely and must be dismissed.

This case stretches us back to 2003 when Kansas Unified School District #501 says it was facing serious budgetary straits. To help get back on course, the District claims, it decided to eliminate three positions, one of which was Dwight Almond's maintenance job. Rather than fire him, however, the District told Mr. Almond that he could transfer to a vacant custodial position at a lower pay grade. If Mr. Almond accepted the new position, the District promised, he could retain his current salary for two years before the lower pay associated with the new job kicked in. To all this Mr. Almond agreed in writing, and two years later the District reduced his salary just as it said it would.

[The district took similar action with respect to the other plaintiff, Kevin Weems.]

Eventually, Mr. Almond and Mr. Weems filed administrative charges alleging that the District's actions were motivated by unlawful age discrimination, not budget necessity. But with this came a wrinkle. The men didn't bring their administrative charges until 2006, even though the discrimination they alleged occurred in 2003 and 2004. And this fact posed a problem for the pair when they sought to take their claims to court. The district court held that the men had waited too long to seek administrative review — and that the delay had the effect of barring their lawsuits altogether.

[The district court reconsidered its ruling when Congress passed the Lilly Ledbetter Fair Pay Act, "a law specifically aimed at effecting changes to limitations law in the employment discrimination field," but it adhered to its original decision. This appeal required the court] to consider the timeliness of the plaintiffs' claims in light of both preexisting law and the Ledbetter Act.

We start with the first question first, asking whether preexisting law requires dismissal of the plaintiffs' claims. The Age Discrimination Employment Act ("ADEA") provides that "no civil action may be commenced" in federal court unless the would-be plaintiff first files a grievance with the appropriate administrative agency — and does so "within 300 days after the alleged unlawful practice occurred" where (as here) a state administrative agency process exists to remedy the alleged discrimination. 29 U.S.C. §626(d)(1)(B). Compliance with this administrative exhaustion requirement and its concomitant limitations period is a condition precedent to bringing suit.

But determining when exactly an "unlawful practice occur[s]" — when an ADEA claim accrues and the 300-day limitations clock starts running — isn't as simple as it might first appear. Does the clock start when the challenged employment practice is decided internally? When the decision is first announced to the plaintiff? When the plaintiff learns the decision was motivated by discriminatory animus? Or perhaps each and every time the plaintiff experiences some effect from the adverse decision?

In the absence of contrary directives from Congress, the Supreme Court has read into federal statutory limitations periods a relatively consistent rule. As formulated by the Court, the clock starts running when the plaintiff first knew or should have known of his injury, whether or not he realized the cause of his injury was unlawful.

As applied to the employment discrimination context, the Court has explained, this rule generally means that a claim accrues when the disputed employment practice — the demotion, transfer, firing, refusal to hire, or the like — is first announced to the plaintiff. *See Del. State Coll. v. Ricks*, 449 U.S. 250 (1980). Sometimes, of course, an adverse employment decision isn't announced and the employee doesn't learn of it until much later — and in those circumstances courts revert to asking when the plaintiff did or a reasonable employee would have known of the employer's decision. *See, e.g., Oshiver v. Levin, Fishbein, Sedran & Berman*, 38 F.3d 1380, 1386 (3d Cir. 1994). But in all events, and consistent with the general federal rule, an employee who discovers, or should have discovered, the *injury* (the adverse employment decision) need not be aware of the unlawful *discriminatory intent* behind that act for the limitations clock to start ticking. (Whether and when the limitations clock, once it has started, might be equitably tolled is, of course, another matter.)

With these principles in hand, the question for us becomes when Mr. Almond and Mr. Weems first had or should have taken notice of the District's allegedly discriminatory decision. The undisputed facts show that the answer is 2003 for Mr. Almond and 2004 for Mr. Weems. It was then that the District told the plaintiffs their jobs were being eliminated, then that the District announced the demotions, and then that the District revealed the future pay reduction associated with those demotions. And all this poses a problem for the plaintiffs, just as the district court held, because they filed their administrative charges in 2006, well past the 300-day deadline set by statute and much too late to be able to pursue their claims in federal court.

The plaintiffs respond by protesting that the most painful consequence of the District's transfer decision — the reduction in their pay — didn't take place in 2003 and 2004 but two years later, in 2005 and 2006, and so well within the 300-day statutory period. Because of this, they say, they should be able — at the very least — to contest their pay reduction in federal court.

We cannot agree. Some adverse employment actions — such as demotion to a lower position — can require more work of the employee for less pay on an ongoing basis. Other adverse employment actions can involve entirely deferred consequences — such as a delayed demotion, a deferred reduction in pay, or a notice of termination with a grace period before actual firing occurs. But whether the adverse consequences flowing from the challenged employment action hit the employee straight away or only much later, the "limitations period[] normally commence[s] when the employer's decision is made" and "communicated" to the employee. *Ricks*. Put differently, the "proper focus" is on the time that the employee has notice of "the *discriminatory acts*," not "the time at which the *consequences* of the acts became most painful." And in this case there is no question that the District's actions, including the planned pay reductions, were first announced to the plaintiffs in 2003 and 2004. The fact that some of those actions weren't implemented until later is immaterial.

Our conclusion in this case parallels (and is compelled by) the Supreme Court's decision in *Ricks*. The plaintiff there was a college professor whose employer denied him tenure but gave him a year to find new work. The Court held the limitations period began to run at the time the employer announced the adverse tenure decision, not when it ultimately terminated his employment a year later. The Court did so explaining that the challenged unlawful employment practice was the tenure decision and the plaintiff's eventual but deferred termination was only "a delayed . . . consequence of the denial of tenure." And as it was in *Ricks* so it must be here. The plaintiffs before us seek to challenge (among other things) the District's decision to reduce their pay, a decision known to them well before it happened to take effect.

Shifting ground, the plaintiffs contend that, however the limitations clock used to operate under *Ricks*, the Supreme Court's decision in *Nat'l R.R. Passenger Corp. v. Morgan*, 536 U.S. 101, 117 (2002), reset it. As they read *Morgan*, the §626 limitations clock now doesn't begin running until *all* acts contributing to an adverse employment practice cease. And, the plaintiffs say, this means their claims are timely because they continued to receive paychecks reflecting the District's alleged discrimination well into 2006.

Morgan, however, didn't so fundamentally rework how we measure time. To be sure, *Morgan* held that *hostile work environment* claims accrue each time acts contributing to that environment occur. And to be sure, this represents a deviation from the general *Ricks* accrual rule. But *Morgan* took great pains to reaffirm the *Ricks* rule and to draw only a narrow distinction for hostile work environment claims. *Morgan* [distinguished] hostile work environment claims from this general rule only because, unlike the mine run of employment discrimination claims, hostile work environment claims "cannot be said to occur on any particular day," and instead usually involve a pattern of acts that aren't "actionable on [their] own" but give rise to a legal violation only when assessed in their totality. By its own terms, then, *Morgan*, helps the plaintiffs in this case not at all. Mr. Almond and Mr. Weems don't seek to pursue a hostile work environment claim but wish instead to challenge the District's termination, transfer, and demotion decisions. And *Morgan* expressly held that those sorts of decisions remain subject to the *Ricks* rule.

[The court rejected plaintiffs' argument that the district's "temporizing" about the potential pay cuts, suggesting that they would not occur if financial conditions improved, changed the analysis.] Whatever other problems may attend this tack, a factual one surely does. Even straining to view the facts most favorably to the plaintiffs, the District in 2003 and 2004 didn't say it *might* or *could* reduce the plaintiffs' pay in the future. It said it *would* reduce their pay in two years' time, subject only to the possibility of later review or reconsideration. And the Supreme Court has instructed us in no uncertain terms that, when a challenged employment decision is merely subject to later review, reconsideration, or appeal, this does nothing to stop the clock from running. The limitations period still accrues with the employer's announcement and "the pendency of a grievance, or some other method of collateral review of an employment decision, does not toll the running of the limitations periods . . . [and neither does] [t]he existence of careful procedures to assure fairness." *Ricks.*

Having concluded that the district court was right and preexisting accrual doctrine renders the plaintiffs' claims untimely, and without any suggestion from the plaintiffs that equitable tolling doctrine might save their cause, our work is still only half finished. We still have to consider whether the Ledbetter Act changes the limitations equation in any way, whether it might save the plaintiffs' otherwise lost federal claims.

The Ledbetter Act came in response to the *Ledbetter* case. Lilly Ledbetter proved at trial that her supervisors gave her poor performance reviews because of her sex — and that these reviews, in turn, caused her employer to pay her less than similarly situated male workers. *Ledbetter v. Goodyear Tire & Rubber Co., Inc.*, 550 U.S. 618 (2007). The Supreme Court, however, reversed. It explained that Ms. Ledbetter's pay discrimination claim was untimely and the jury's verdict had to be overturned because Ms. Ledbetter filed her administrative charge more than 300 days after the announcement of the employer's relevant pay-setting decision.

Writing for herself and three others, Justice Ginsburg dissented. The dissent argued that the Court should treat compensation discrimination claims like it did hostile work environment claims in *Morgan.* The dissent emphasized that, while most adverse employment actions (firings, failures to hire, demotions, transfers) are communicated or quickly made obvious to employees, compensation discrimination (or unequal pay for equal work) claims and hostile work environment claims are different. In these two situations, the dissent explained, employers don't typically announce or communicate the injurious facts to the employee. In the pay discrimination context, workers like Ms. Ledbetter of course know their own salaries but they are rarely told what their co-workers earn. And this means that an employee may have no reason to know of the fact of his or her *injury* — the very existence of a pay disparity — for a long time. For this reason, Justice Ginsburg argued, pay discrimination claims shouldn't accrue when a particular pay decision is made and announced to an individual employee but should arise anew with each pay check, much as a hostile work environment claim accrues with each new act contributing to the unlawful environment. . . .

Enter the Ledbetter Act. In addition to modifying Title VII to overturn the Supreme Court's *Ledbetter* decision, the Act added new and parallel language to the ADEA:

> [f]or purposes of this section, an unlawful practice occurs, with respect to discrimination in compensation in violation of this chapter, when a discriminatory compensation decision or other practice is adopted, when a person becomes subject to a discriminatory compensation decision or other practice, or when a person is affected by application of a discriminatory compensation decision or other practice, including each time wages, benefits, or other compensation is paid, resulting in whole or in part from such a decision or other practice.

29 U.S.C. §626(d)(3).

The plaintiffs would have us believe this language saves their claims. In their view, an "unlawful practice" for purposes of §626(d) occurs anytime the employer adopts a "discriminatory compensation decision or other practice." And, in their view, the "other practice" language means the alleged act of discrimination need only *relate* to compensation. Though not *all* discriminatory employment decisions involve compensation decisions or practices, the plaintiffs acknowledge many (perhaps most) do. So it is that, in their estimation, the Ledbetter Act works a near total revolution in how we measure time, with a new claim arising — and the limitations clock resetting anew — each time an employer issues a new paycheck reflecting or effecting an act of discrimination. As applied to their own case, the plaintiffs say, the District's decision to transfer the plaintiffs to lower-paid positions is the "unlawful practice" and, because that decision eventually affected their compensation, a new cause of action arises for limitations purposes each and every time they receive a smaller paycheck in their new positions.

The Ledbetter Act, however, didn't go so far. By its express terms, the Act applies only to claims alleging "discrimination in compensation" — or, put another way, claims of unequal pay for equal work. The plaintiffs before us don't seek to bring such claims and so the Ledbetter Act offers them no help. Why all this is so takes a bit of unpacking, but it is revealed by Congress's particular choice of language in §626(d)(3) and amply confirmed by the Act's statutory cross-references and history and by the circumstances surrounding its adoption.

[The language of the amendment made clear that the new accrual rules it established pertain "only to 'discrimination in compensation' claims 'in violation of this chapter.'" And to] prove such a claim, it isn't enough for an employee to show that a discriminatory practice somehow affected his or her pay. Instead, the employee must show a discriminatory *pay disparity* between himself or herself and similarly situated but younger employees. *See, e.g., MacPherson v. Univ. of Montevallo*, 922 F.2d 766, 774 (11th Cir. 1991) (proof of "discrimination in compensation" under ADEA requires showing "similarly situated persons outside the protected age group received higher wages"); *Schuler v. PricewaterhouseCoopers, LLP*, 595 F.3d 370, 374-75 (D.C. Cir. 2010). In other words, "discrimination in compensation" requires not just *any* effect on pay, but one of a particular kind: unequal pay for equal work.

Parallel language added to Title VII underscores the point. To address the particular sex discrimination claim at issue in *Ledbetter*, the Act contains a new accrual rule for claims of "discrimination in compensation in violation of" Title VII. *See* §2000e-5(e)(3)(A). And like the ADEA, Title VII prohibits employers from "discriminating against any individual with respect to his compensation" because of membership in a protected class. 42 U.S.C. §2000e-2(a)(1). We have already interpreted this prohibition to require proof of unequal pay between the employee and co-workers outside the protected class doing the same work. *See, e.g., Johnson v. Weld Cnty., Colo.*, 594 F.3d 1202, 1215 (10th Cir. 2010) ("To establish a prima facie case of pay discrimination, [plaintiff must] adduce evidence tending to show that she occupied a job similar to that of a higher paid male" (quotation omitted)); *see also* 1 LARSON, EMPLOYMENT DISCRIMINATION, §13.01 (Title VII discrimination in compensation claims involve unequal pay for the same work); 1 BARBARA LINDEMANN AND PAUL GROSSMAN, EMPLOYMENT DISCRIMINATION LAW §18.I (4th ed. 2007) (similar). Of course, if there are no similarly situated co-workers, the employee may be able to make out a claim with evidence that a person outside the protected class *would have* been paid more for doing the same job. *See Washington Cnty. v. Gunther*, 452 U.S. 161, 166, 178-79 (1981). But in any case the key to a successful claim is a showing that the employer discriminatorily paid the employee too little for the position he or she occupies.

The plaintiffs' competing reading — that the Ledbetter Act applies to any "other practice" involving a discriminatory decision affecting pay — thus errs. It errs by ignoring the statute's first phrase expressly limiting the law's coverage to claims of "discrimination in compensation," as well as its clear cross-reference, "in violation of this chapter," directing us to a class of claims with a settled and statutorily precise meaning. And, in this way, the plaintiffs' proposed interpretation commits not one but two statutory interpretation sins — first by rendering a statutory phrase superfluous and then by failing to give effect to Congress's reference to a preexisting legal term with a well settled meaning.

Having said that, the question remains what work *does* the second statutory phrase on which the plaintiffs seek to rely do? The answer has nothing to do with *which* claims the Act covers but with *when* those claims accrue. *After* the first phrase of the Act defines *which* claims it affects (discrimination in compensation claims), the second phrase goes on to tell us *when* those claims accrue for limitations purposes. As a matter of plain linguistic direction, the second phrase tells us compensation discrimination claims accrue for limitations purposes "*when* a discrimination in compensation decision or other practice" is "adopted," or "*when*" someone becomes "subject to" or "affected by" its application. Of course, the word "discriminatory" must modify both "compensation decision" and "other practice" because the Supreme Court tells us that the Act doesn't permit a plaintiff to challenge a decision unless it involves unlawful discrimination. *AT&T Corp. v. Hulteen*, 556 U.S. 701 (2009). But the "other practice" phrase does real and important work of its own by making clear that the accrual period for covered compensation discrimination claims is triggered not only when the pay setting decision takes place (the "discriminatory compensation decision") but *also* when other discriminatory employment practices ("other practice[s]") that result in compensation discrimination are "adopted." So it is that the first statutory phrase tells us *which* claims are covered by the Act (those alleging unequal pay for equal work) and the second phrase, including the "other practice" language, tells us *when* those claims accrue for limitations purposes.

The Act's history erases any possible lingering questions. The Act's findings tell us that Congress's target was the *Ledbetter* majority and its purpose to undo the Court's treatment of "discrimination in compensation" claims. But while Justice Ginsburg in dissent in *Ledbetter* expressly advocated just such a statutory change, she never advocated a limitations revolution for any claim somehow touching on pay. To the contrary, Justice Ginsburg reaffirmed that hiring, firing, promotion, demotion, and transfer decisions, though often touching on pay, should and do accrue as soon as they are announced. *Ledbetter* (Ginsburg, J., dissenting). She sought to distinguish *only* compensation discrimination (or equal-pay-for-equal-work) claims from this rule. And it is hardly surprising that Congress would (and did) follow her lead.

Justice Ginsburg's dissent also helps confirm the (limited) significance of the "other practice" language. As Justice Ginsburg observed, the act of discrimination against Ms. Ledbetter wasn't in the pay-setting decision itself, but in the poor performance reviews given to her because of her gender that were later used to justify paying her less than her male colleagues. The *Ledbetter* dissent repeatedly emphasized that the pay differential, the unequal pay for equal work, Ms. Ledbetter experienced was *caused by* these earlier discriminatory acts. Ginsburg, J., dissenting) (Ledbetter's pay was "discriminatorily low due to a long series of decisions reflecting Goodyear's pervasive discrimination against women managers"). The dissent argued that the law should take account of these *other practices* when setting accrual rules for compensation discrimination claims. And it is once again hardly surprising that Congress would include language to do just that, to trigger the accrual of a compensation discrimination claim not only when employers intentionally discriminate in pay-setting decisions, but also when they discriminate in other ways that cause a discriminatory pay disparity.

Beyond language of §626(d)(3) itself, beyond its statutory references and history, lies the realm of legislative history. And any effort to venture so far would only serve to corroborate that the "other practice" phrase doesn't covertly convert the Ledbetter

Act into a Leviathan swallowing *Ricks*'s ordinary accrual rule. The House Committee Report tells us that the Act "is designed to be a narrow reversal of the *Ledbetter* decision, without upsetting any other current law." H.R. Rep. No. 110-237, at 17 (2007). The report proceeds to emphasize that the Act aims at compensation discrimination claims alone, emphasizing the unique nature of those claims and distinguishing them from other discriminatory practices. *See, e.g., id.* at 6 ("While workers know immediately when they are fired, refused employment or denied a promotion or transfer, the secrecy and confidentiality associated with employees' salaries make pay discrimination difficult to detect."). And in explaining why the committee rejected an amendment that sought to strike "other practice" from the legislation, the report tells us that the phrase was necessary to ensure the bill addressed "the fact pattern in [*Ledbetter*], where sex-based performance evaluations were used in conjunction with a performance-based pay system to effectuate the discriminatory pay." H.R. Rep. No. 110-237, at 5. The bill's sponsor, Senator Mikulski, made plain as well that the "other practice[s]" term does *not* embrace any "discrete personnel decisions like promotions and discharges," as the plaintiffs before us imagine — and that it does not precisely because, as we have explained, the use of the preceding phrase "discrimination in compensation . . . means that [the Act] already covers only such claims — nothing more, nothing less." 155 Cong. Rec. S757 (daily ed. Jan. 22, 2009).

In light of all this, we hold that §626(d)(3) of the Ledbetter Act governs the accrual only of discrimination in compensation (unequal pay for equal work) claims in violation of §623(a)(1) — nothing more, nothing less. The language does not affect the accrual of other cases alleging discrimination in hiring, firing, demotions, transfers, or the like. And having reached that conclusion, it follows ineluctably that the Act can't save the plaintiffs' claims in this case. That's because there's no pay discrimination claim here. True, the plaintiffs were transferred to lower paying positions. True, this had the knock on effect of lowering their compensation. True, we must assume that the transfer decision was discriminatory at this stage of the litigation. But none of this brings the plaintiffs' claim within the ambit of the Ledbetter Act because they don't contend they were ever paid less than others doing the same work. In fact, and though it is inessential to our decision, the plaintiffs acknowledge they were paid *more* for the first two years than their similarly situated co-workers, until their salaries were brought in line with everyone else in their pay grade. Put differently, the plaintiffs may have been discriminated against *in the transfer decision* but they were not discriminated against *in compensation.* Accordingly, the general *Ricks* accrual rule, not the Ledbetter Act's discrimination in compensation rule, governs this case and the plaintiffs' claims remain untimely. . . .

NOTES

1. *Notice of Adverse Action Rule.* The principal case correctly states the "notice of adverse action" rule that had been announced in a number of Supreme Court decisions, culminating with *Ledbetter v. Goodyear Tire & Rubber Co.,* 550 U.S. 618 (2007). In short, discrimination occurs for purposes of the filing requirement when the employee is notified of an adverse employment decision, not when it is effective.

2. *The Contaminated Environment Exception.* As the *Almond* court also notes, a major exception to this "notice of decision" rule is for contaminated work environment harassment, which may be charged to the EEOC within 300 days of any act constituting the same course of harassment. *Amtrak v. Morgan,* 536 U.S. 101

(2002). While not challenging prior cases holding that "discrete acts" must be charged within 300 days of their occurrence, the Court saw hostile environment sexual harassment claims as different because their "very nature involves repeated conduct." *Id.* at 103. It elaborated: "The 'unlawful employment practice' therefore cannot be said to occur on any particular day. It occurs over a series of days or perhaps years and, in direct contrast to discrete acts, a single act of harassment may not be actionable on its own. Such claims are based on the cumulative effect of individual acts." *Id.* at 115 (citations omitted). For that reason, "[p]rovided that an act contributing to the claim occurs within the filing period, the entire time period of the hostile environment may be considered by a court for the purposes of determining liability." *Id.* at 117.

The only limitation on this principle is that, for there to be "one" employment practice, there must be a sufficient relationship between the various acts that comprise the putative violation. *See Hansen v. SkyWest Airlines*, 844 F.3d 914, 923-24 (10th Cir. 2016) (when acts occurring outside 300-day window involved the same type of harassment by same harassers at same location, "abatement" of harassment for a six-month period did not prevented all acts from being part of one hostile environment). *See also Moll v. Telesector Res. Grp., Inc.*, 760 F.3d 198, 203-04 (2d Cir. 2014) ("both sexually overt and facially sex-neutral incidents" should be considered in assessing whether plaintiff alleged a timely hostile work environment claim). But some cases seem surprisingly unwilling to see such a relationship. *See Wilkie v. Dep't of Health and Human Servs.*, 638 F.3d 944 (8th Cir. 2011) (misconduct, including "sexual advances" and the harasser coming to plaintiff's home while intoxicated and passing out naked in her bed, was substantially different than the later misconduct and therefore not "similar in nature, frequency, and severity").

3. *Other Pre-Fair Pay Act Exceptions.* Two other exceptions to the notice of decision rule not mentioned by *Almond* have been recognized, but are rarely applicable. First, facially discriminatory practices can be challenged at any time, *see, e.g., Ledbetter*, 550 U.S. at 634; *Lorance v. AT&T Technologies*, 490 U.S. 900, 911-12 (1989); *see also Courtney v. La Salle University*, 124 F.3d 499 (3d Cir. 1997) (mandatory retirement policy could be challenged by a charge filed within 300 days of the policy's application to a particular professor). Second, pursuant to the 1991 Civil Rights Act, discriminatory seniority systems can be challenged whenever they affect individuals. *Ledbetter*, 550 U.S. at 627 n.2.

4. *The Lilly Ledbetter Fair Pay Act of 2009.* As Judge Gorsuch says, enter the Fair Pay Act, §2000e-5(e)(3)(A), which amended Title VII (and, as *Almond* indicates, the ADEA and other antidiscrimination statutes) to create a "paycheck" rule — a plaintiff who suffered discrimination in compensation can file a timely charge, *inter alia*, within 300 days of receiving a paycheck that is lower than it would have been but for the discrimination. The FPA was explicitly retroactive although it limits backpay recovery to no more than two years prior to the filing of a charge. §2000e-5(e)(3)(B).

5. *No Panacea.* As the *Almond* plaintiffs discovered, the Ledbetter Act did not resolve all problems. At first glance, it seems to consign to the scrap heap the Supreme Court's prior timeliness jurisprudence. Clearly, "compensation decisions" with present consequences on pay are actionable — no matter how far in the past they were made. Some have suggested that the amendment reaches beyond compensation decisions because of the references to "other practices." However, as Judge Gorsuch suggests, actionable discrimination must be "with respect to discrimination in compensation in violation of this title," although such discrimination may be "a discriminatory compensation decision or other practice."

But why isn't any employer action that affects compensation a "compensation decision"? If that were true, the *Almond* plaintiffs' demotions would be actionable. The court, however, adopts a narrower reading: "discriminatory compensation" modifies not just "decision" but also "other practices," which would mean that no action that is not a "compensation" action is within the FPA's expanded notion of "occurrence." This reading has been criticized, *see* Charles A. Sullivan, *Raising the Dead: The Lilly Ledbetter Fair Pay Act*, 84 TUL. L. REV. 499, 520-36 (2010); *see also* Deborah A. Widiss, *Shadow Precedents and the Separation of Powers: Statutory Interpretation of Congressional Overrides*, 84 NOTRE DAME L. REV. 511 (2009); but the circuits thus far are in line with *Almond*. *See Davis v. Bombardier Transp. Holdings (USA), Inc.*, 794 F.3d 266, 269 (2d Cir. 2015); *Schuler v. PricewaterhouseCoopers, LLP*, 595 F.3d 370 (D.C. Cir. 2010). So what is a "compensation decision"? A raise (or not), obviously. But if a demotion doesn't qualify, would a hiring decision that set initial salary?

By the way, don't be confused by *Almond's* repeated references to "unequal pay for equal work." "Equal work" is a term of art under the Equal Pay Act, 29 U.S.C.S. §206(d), which limits its prohibitions to "equal work" settings and therefore has very restricted application. *See Corning Glass Works v. Brennan*, 417 U.S. 188 (1974). While Title VII suits can be brought for equal work discrimination that would also violate the EPA, the Supreme Court held in *County of Washington. v. Gunther*, 452 U.S. 161 (1981), that Title VII can be used to challenge any sex discrimination in compensation. For example, in *City of L.A. Dep't of Water & Power v. Manhart*, 435 U.S. 702 (1978), reproduced at p. 94, the Court struck down differential pension contributions for men and women without worrying about whether the employees performed equal work.

6. *Decisions Needn't Be Final or Immediate.* As *Almond* makes clear, a decision needn't be final to trigger the filing period. In *Delaware State College v. Ricks*, 449 U.S. 250 (1980), the Court held that the filing period ran from the point where the employee was notified that the adverse action would be taken; it didn't matter that the termination was deferred until a year later. In *Almond* itself, the contingent nature of the financial harm was held irrelevant. Further, as *Almond* points out, *Ricks* held that the filing period would not be tolled by pursuit of internal remedies or grievance procedures.

7. *Nor Is Perpetuating Past Discrimination Enough.* In *United Air Lines, Inc. v. Evans*, 431 U.S. 553 (1977), the time period for filing suit for a discharge ran from the point when the plaintiff was forced from her position as a flight attendant in 1968 because of United Airlines' sex-discriminatory "no marriage" policy. The fact that Evans was later rehired by United without seniority credit did not make a difference, at least where the seniority system itself treated all rehired employees as starting the seniority clock anew. This was confirmed by *AT&T Corp. v. Hulteen*, 556 U.S. 701 (2009). At issue there was whether the employer's calculation of service time for retirement purposes discriminated by not crediting pregnancy leave while giving seniority credit to other short-term leaves. The leave for which credit had been denied was taken prior to the passage of the Pregnancy Discrimination Act, when, as we saw in Chapter 5, disfavoring pregnancy was not sex discrimination within the meaning of Title VII. For the *Hulteen* majority, this meant that there was no violation when AT&T's policy first denied credit for pregnancy leave. 556 U.S. at 712. The PDA reversed this interpretation prospectively but was not retroactive. Thus, the original denial of leave was not actionable. *Id.* at 712-13. As for the fact that the employer's seniority system carried forward the effects of this denial of credit past the PDA's effective date, the *Hulteen* majority held these consequences not actionable because of Title VII's exemption of seniority systems. This analysis

allowed the majority to skirt the Fair Pay Act, which it cited but found inapposite: "AT&T's pre-PDA decision not to award Hulteen service credit for pregnancy leave was not discriminatory [within the meaning of the Title VII], with the consequence that Hulteen has not been 'affected by application of a discriminatory compensation decision or other practice.'"*Id.* at 716.

8. *Constructive Discharge and the Filing Period.* A recent Supreme Court retaliation decision, *Green v. Brennan*, 136 S. Ct. 1769 (2016), can be viewed as creating another exception to the normal timeliness rules, although the Court did not conceptualize it that way. The issue was when the Title VII filing period "begins to run for an employee who was not fired, but resigns in the face of intolerable discrimination — a 'constructive' discharge." *Id.* at 1774. Reasoning that ordinarily limitations periods commence when the plaintiff has a viable cause of action, the majority held that "in the context of a constructive-discharge claim, a resignation is part of the 'complete and present cause of action' necessary before a limitations period ordinarily begins to run." *Id.* at 1776. That is because a claim of constructive discharge "has two basic elements. A plaintiff must prove first that he was discriminated against by his employer to the point where a reasonable person in his position would have felt compelled to resign. But he must also show that he actually resigned." *Id.* at 1777.

Justice Alito concurred in the result but viewed the majority's rule as "los[ing] sight of a bedrock principle of our Title VII cases: An act done with discriminatory intent must have occurred within the limitations period." *Id.* at 1782. The majority wrongly shifted the focus from the employer's acts (the only conduct that could violate the statute) to the employee's response. Nevertheless, he would have permitted plaintiffs to measure timeliness from the point the employee gave notice of resignation in those cases where the employer had the *"specific discriminatory intent of forcing the employee to resign." Id.* at 1785 (emphasis in original). Justice Thomas dissented, arguing that prior precedents, such as *Ricks* and *Evans*, required a focus on the present acts of the employer, not the later consequences of those acts. Although *Green* involved a federal employee suit, which is subject to somewhat different time limits and administrative procedures than are suits against other employers, the majority left little doubt that its rule would apply more generally.

9. *Stale Claims as Evidence.* Although the filing limitations will bar a cause of action based on incidents prior to the filing period, such incidents may be relevant to a suit challenging timely filed discrimination. *Evans* indicated that such events can be "relevant background evidence in a proceeding in which the status of a current practice is at issue." *Evans*, 431 U.S. at 558. It repeated the same point in *Morgan*, 536 U.S. at 113. *See also Malin v. Hospira, Inc.*, 762 F.3d 552, 561 (7th Cir. 2014) (older acts of retaliation could be used as circumstantial evidence that a later decision not to promote plaintiff was part of a retaliatory pattern).

10. *Summarizing Current Individual Disparate Treatment Law.* In brief, a hostile environment can be timely charged within 300 days of any act that contributes to that contaminated environment. The same may be true of any action taken pursuant to a facially discriminatory policy, whether compensation, seniority, or otherwise. However, all other discrete acts must be charged within 300 days of the time they occur, unless they fall within the Fair Pay Act. Acts that fall within the FPA are limited to those affecting compensation, and maybe even more limited to "compensation decisions." Qualifying acts may be challenged as late as 300 days from the last time "wages, benefits, or other compensation is paid, resulting in whole or in part from such a decision." A failure to timely challenge one discrete act of discrimination, however, will not bar a challenge to a later act that is timely charged. *Stuart v. Local 727,*

Int'l Bhd. of Teamsters, 771 F.3d 1014, 1018 (7th Cir. 2014) (a rule that time barred a plaintiff who has been repeatedly discriminated against by her employer from challenging later instances of discrimination when she failed to file a charge within 300 days of the first such act would be "absurd").

11. *Timeliness in Systemic Cases.* What about disparate impact challenges? In *Lewis v. City of Chicago*, 560 U.S. 205 (2010), the Supreme Court addressed whether a plaintiff who does not file a timely charge challenging the *adoption* of a practice by an employer may nevertheless assert a disparate impact claim in a timely charge challenging the employer's later *application* of the process. The Court unanimously held that, even though a civil service examination had been given years previously, applicants could bring a disparate impact suit as to any of the 10 rounds of selection from the list that occurred within the 300-day charging period. It focused on the fact that §2000e-2(k)(i) barred an employer's "use" of an employment practice with a disparate impact: a new violation occurred each time the city "used" the results of the test by hiring from the eligibility lists it established when the test was first given.

However, it appears likely that a different analysis applies when systemic disparate treatment is alleged, as in *Teamsters* and *Hazelwood*. Such policies can be viewed through two different lenses. Although it could be argued that the various acts of discrimination reflect an underlying policy, which can be attacked as long as it continues, the circuit authority goes the other way. *Chin v. Port Auth. of N.Y. & N.J.*, 685 F.3d 135, 157 (2d Cir. 2012) ("Discrete acts of this sort, which fall outside the limitations period, cannot be brought within it, even when undertaken pursuant to a general policy that results in other discrete acts occurring within the limitations period. . . . Each of our sister circuits has held that an allegation of an ongoing discriminatory policy does not extend the statute of limitations where the individual effects of the policy that give rise to the claim are merely discrete acts."). *See also Lewis*, 560 U.S. 214-15 ("For disparate-treatment claims — and others for which discriminatory intent is required — that means the plaintiff must demonstrate deliberate discrimination within the limitations period."). *See generally* Jason R. Bent, *What the Lilly Ledbetter Fair Pay Act Doesn't Do: "Discrete Acts" and the Future of Pattern or Practice Litigation*, 33 RUTGERS L. REV. 31 (2009).

NOTE ON STATE DEFERRAL REQUIREMENTS

We've referred to the filing period as 300 days, which is correct in the vast majority of states having fair employment practices agencies. These "deferral states" are so called because Title VII requires a filing both with the state agency and the EEOC and requires the EEOC to defer to the state agency for 60 days. In the few nondeferral states, the plaintiff has only 180 days to file with the EEOC.

The requirement of state filing in deferral states generates a few problems. Under Title VII and the ADA (which incorporates Title VII procedures by reference), not only must the plaintiff file with the state agency prior to filing with the EEOC, §2000e-5(c), §706(c), but the state must be accorded 60 days to act before the EEOC can commence its processes. That means that charges must normally be filed with the state agency within 240 days of the violation (in order to ensure compliance with the 60-day period for state deferral and the 300-day period for EEOC filing). *Mohasco Corp. v. Silver*, 447 U.S. 807 (1980). Obviously, a plaintiff would be well advised to file with both agencies as soon as practicable, in which case the EEOC will hold the charge in "suspended animation" until the required period of state deferral expires and the EEOC filing becomes effective. *Love v. Pullman*, 404 U.S. 522 (1972). The ADEA is more relaxed than Title VII because a charge of age discrimination may be filed simultaneously with the state and the federal agencies. *See Oscar Mayer & Co. v. Evans*, 441 U.S. 750, 765 (1979). The complications generated by these rules are typically ameliorated by "work-sharing" agreements between the EEOC and state agencies, which divide charge-processing responsibility between them. *See EEOC v. Commercial Office Prods. Co.*, 486 U.S. 107 (1988); *see also Velázquez-Pérez v. Developers Diversified Realty Corp.*, 753 F.3d 265 (1st Cir. 2014) (such agreements can automatically initiate state proceedings when the EEOC receives the charge). A filing need not be timely under state law to satisfy the federal statute. *Commercial Office Products; Oscar Mayer*.

While a state filing is necessary in order to bring a Title VII suit, it will typically also satisfy state exhaustion requirements. A subsequent suit (whether in state or federal court), then, can assert both federal and state claims, and state law may be more generous than federal law in a number of respects. *See generally* Sandra F. Sperino, *Revitalizing State Employment Discrimination Law*, 20 Geo. Mason L. Rev. 545, 546 (2013).

NOTE ON WAIVER, TOLLING, ESTOPPEL, AND LACHES

National R.R. Passenger Corp. v. Morgan noted that "the filing period is not a jurisdictional prerequisite to filing a Title VII suit. Rather, it is a requirement subject to waiver, estoppel, and equitable tolling 'when equity so requires.'" 536 U.S. 101, 121 (2002) (citing *Zipes v. Trans World Airlines, Inc.*, 455 U.S. 385 (1982)). It stressed, however, that such doctrines were "to be applied sparingly," *see Baldwin County Welcome Center v. Brown*, 466 U.S. 147, 152 (1984) (per curiam). But the Supreme Court has provided little further guidance, and the lower courts have not been very receptive, although they have provided some relief in limited situations.

Waiver. In *Zipes* itself, the issue was whether the defendants had waived the timely filing requirement by failing to assert it, and the Court merely remanded for a decision once it had decided that waiver might operate. A few cases have found objections to procedural requirements waived. *See Gad v. Kan. State Univ.*, 787 F.3d 1032 (10th Cir. 2015) (requirement of verification of charge may be waived in appropriate circumstances).

Discovery Rule. The Supreme Court has "declined to address" whether antidiscrimination statutes are subject to a "discovery" rule, which would toll the charge-filing period until the employee knew (or reasonably should have known) that an adverse action was discriminatory, *Ledbetter*, 550 U.S. at 642 n.10, although three Justices in *Morgan* endorsed "some version of the discovery rule," 536 U.S. at 114 (Justices O'Connor, Rehnquist, and Breyer). Any such rule would require deciding whether it is enough that the plaintiff knew (or should have known) that she has been treated differently than other employees or whether the plaintiff need also have reason to suspect discrimination before the statute begins to run. What does *Almond* suggest about this? *See Beamon v. Marshall & Ilsley Trust Co.*, 411 F.3d 854 (7th Cir. 2005) (no equitable tolling since a reasonable person would have been aware that discrimination could be one possible basis for the employer's actions).

Tolling and Estoppel. Even prior to *Morgan*, the lower courts sometimes mitigated the rigors of strict adherence to time limits although they used a variety of different nomenclatures and tests, sometimes speaking of tolling, sometimes of equitable estoppel, and sometimes of fraudulent concealment. Recently, the Supreme Court seemed to establish an overall structure for equitable tolling of a federal statute of limitation. *Menominee Indian Tribe of Wis. v. United States*, 136 S. Ct. 750, 755-56 (2016), comprises two elements, first, whether the party has been pursuing his rights diligently and, second, whether extraordinary circumstances prevent timely filing, which requires that the circumstances that caused the delay "are both extraordinary and beyond [the litigant's] control." *Menominee* did not involve the antidiscrimination laws and concerned tolling the time to bring court suit, not file an agency charge. Nevertheless, it seems likely to influence lower courts and, if anything, suggest a more rigorous standard than the already stringent requirements adopted by the lower courts for discrimination suits. Those cases tended to allow relief from the filing period in narrowly defined circumstances, such as defendant's intentional concealment of facts or plaintiffs being misled by the EEOC about their rights. Situations where such relief may be available include filing in the wrong court or being misled by the EEOC, *see Granger v. Aaron's, Inc.*, 636 F.3d 708, 712 (5th Cir. 2011), and when the employer failed to post notices required by the statutes. *E.g., Hammer v. Cardio*, 131 F. App'x 829, 831-32 (3d Cir. 2005). Other decisions reject seemingly appealing tolling arguments. For example, the Seventh Circuit concluded that threatened employer retaliation for filing a charge would not be a basis for equitable estoppel. *Beckel v. Wal-Mart Assocs.*, 301 F.3d 621, 624 (7th Cir. 2002).

Laches. While the doctrines we have just surveyed are beneficial to plaintiffs, the doctrine of laches is decidedly employer-friendly. *Morgan* stated that

> an employer may raise a laches defense, which bars a plaintiff from maintaining a suit if he unreasonably delays in filing a suit and as a result harms the defendant. This defense "requires proof of (1) lack of diligence by the party against whom the defense is asserted, and (2) prejudice to the party asserting the defense."

536 U.S. at 121-22. Laches would seem to be most likely applicable in contaminated work environment cases, which are the only cases where a plaintiff could otherwise long delay filing a charge and still bring a timely suit. *See Pruitt v. City of Chicago*, 472 F.3d 925, 927 (7th Cir. 2006) (laches barred harassment suit where plaintiffs alleged a hostile work environment dating back 20 years). Even in this context, however, the affirmative defense's requirement that a victim take advantage of the employer's corrective measures is likely to supplant laches. See p. 337. However, laches can also bar suit or at least limit recovery when a plaintiff files a timely charge with the EEOC but delays too long in bringing suit. *Compare Brown-Mitchell v. Kan. City Power & Light Co.*, 267 F.3d 825 (8th Cir. 2001) (six-year delay in bringing suit is "unreasonable" and justifies dismissal), *with EEOC v. Watkins Motor Lines, Inc.*, 463 F.3d 436 (6th Cir. 2006) (defendants could not demonstrate prejudice from two-year delay).

This authority, at least insofar as it reaches damages claims at law, may have been undercut by *Petrella v. MGM*, 134 S. Ct. 1962, 1975 n.16 (2014), holding that laches cannot preclude a legal claim for damages brought within a governing statute of limitations although the doctrine can be invoked to limit otherwise appropriate injunctive relief. The Court read *Morgan* as not to the contrary since it at most held that laches may "limit the continuing violation doctrine's potential to rescue *untimely* claims, not claims accruing separately within the limitations period" (emphasis in original). However, *Petrella's* application to backpay (as opposed to damages) is unclear: since backpay is an equitable remedy, laches may apply to limit recovery.

C. FILING SUIT

As we have seen, timely resort to the EEOC is a prerequisite to any court suit under Title VII, the ADA, and the ADEA. Under all three statutes, a timely charge of discrimination must be filed with the Commission before suit can be brought. Contrary to normal administrative law principles, however, "exhaustion" of agency remedies is *not* required. Nevertheless, it is still desirable that charging parties be permitted to exhaust EEOC processes if they so desire.

① Three principles have evolved to balance these concerns. First, a charging party must usually wait 180 days from filing with the Commission before bringing suit. §706(b); 42 U.S.C.S. §2000e-5(b). Mechanically, this is achieved by requiring a "right-to-sue" letter from the Commission as a condition for maintaining an action; the charging party may demand the suit letter from the EEOC once 180 days have passed.* Should the charging party wish to go to court more quickly, EEOC regulations allow the agency to terminate its proceedings early upon the charging party's request. 29 C.F.R. §91601.28(a)(2). Most courts have upheld the regulation. *E.g., Walker v. UPS*, 240 F.3d 1268 (10th Cir. 2001).

② Second, the charging party may elect to permit the EEOC's procedures to continue after the 180-day period, but she retains the power to demand a right-to-sue letter at any time. There is no specific time limit within which the EEOC must act, and the agency sometimes takes years to finish its proceedings. While there is no explicitly defined outer time limit for filing suit, we have seen that a charging party's decision to permit the EEOC to complete its charge processing may result in laches barring the suit or at least limiting defendant's backpay liability. See p. 537.

③ Third, if the charging party permits the agency to process the charge to conclusion, the EEOC will either (1) find no reasonable cause to believe a violation has occurred and issue a notice of dismissal; or (2) find reasonable cause, attempt conciliation, and, if that fails to resolve the matter, ultimately issue a right-to-sue letter. In either case, the charging party must file suit within 90 days or forfeit all power to sue on the basis of the subject charge.

Several issues have arisen under these three principles. Most obviously, the statute requires suit within 90 days after the EEOC gives its notice, 42 U.S.C. §2000e-5, which has been interpreted to mean the actual "receipt" of the right-to-sue letter by the charging party or by her attorney. *Loubriel v. Fondo del Seguro del Estado*, 694 F.3d 139 (1st Cir. 2012); *see also Irwin v. Veterans Admin.*, 498 U.S. 89 (1990) (notice to attorney qualified as notice to client for federal employees). Once the starting point is established, filing a complaint is normally necessary to satisfy the 90-day rule. *See Baldwin Cnty. Welcome Cent. v. Brown*, 466 U.S. 147 (1984) (filing right-to-sue letter and requesting appointment of attorney not sufficient to satisfy statute).

Like filing a charge with the EEOC within 300 days, filing suit in court within 90 days is subject to waiver, estoppel, and equitable tolling. *Baldwin County* so implied while finding no basis for tolling in the case before it. *See Gordon v. England*, 354 F. App'x 975, 980-81 (6th Cir. 2009) (finding tolling possible when the attorney's conduct went far beyond "garden variety" neglect). *But see Harris v. Boyd Tunica, Inc.*,

---

* Under the ADEA, a right-to-sue letter from the EEOC is not a prerequisite for suit, *Julian v. City of Houston*, 314 F.3d 721 (5th Cir. 2002), although the 90-day period for suit governs when the EEOC in fact sends such a letter. 29 U.S.C. §626.

628 F.3d 237 (5th Cir. 2010) (no tolling for ordinary neglect when plaintiff failed to timely file due to clerical error in her attorney's office).

Finally, state statutes of limitations have no applicability to private suits. Lower courts have built on *Occidental Life Insurance Co. v. EEOC*, 432 U.S. 355 (1977), which held that such state laws did not apply to suits by the EEOC, to find them also irrelevant to private suits. E.g., *Burgh v. Borough Council of Montrose*, 251 F.3d 465 (3d Cir. 2001).

PROBLEM 8.1

Susan Russo, 21 years old, completed secretarial school in June 2015. Shortly after graduating and before looking for employment, she was in a serious car accident. Although she has otherwise fully recovered, she lost the effective use of her legs and now relies on a wheelchair to get around. In early January 2016, she sent a letter and resume in response to a help-wanted advertisement placed in the *Gazette* by Firm Bodies Health Spa. She received a phone call scheduling an interview, and on January 15, 2016, she went to the spa to meet with the personnel director. The director seemed awkward during the interview, which Russo attributed to her being in a wheelchair. The interview ended with the director telling Russo that there were "many, many applicants for this job, but we'll get back to you." Russo heard nothing further until ~~December 15, 2016,~~ when she received a letter thanking her for "your interest in Firm Bodies," but informing her that "your interests and ours do not coincide at this time."   2/15/16

Russo, however, noticed that the help-wanted ad to which she had responded was republished every Sunday in the *Gazette* throughout January and February, last appearing on March 13, 2016. Russo was upset about this, but did not want to be paranoid. About April 15, she discovered that one of her friends was a member of Firm Bodies and asked her to "nose around." The friend reported back to Russo on May 15 the following information: a secretary was employed who had begun work around April 4. The new secretary had found out about the position through an ad in March. Firm Bodies must know about the Americans with Disabilities Act because there is a poster in the cafeteria listing individuals' rights under the ADA. The cafeteria, however, is upstairs from the business offices (including the office of the personnel director), and there is no elevator or ramp leading to the second floor.

Russo had first learned about the ADA from the physical therapist who had worked with her during her convalescence in the second half of 2015. At that time, however, she had not thought much about employment discrimination against individuals with disabilities. In the wake of her turndown from Firm Bodies, and unable to find another suitable job, Russo joined a support group. Over the next few months, she became more and more upset about what had happened. On August 16, 2016, Russo visited the office of the state fair employment practices agency. The intake officer there told her she could file a charge of discrimination if she wished, but they were overworked, and it would make more sense if she filed with the federal Equal Employment Opportunity Commission. Russo did not then file a charge with the state agency. On October 17, 2016, she went to the offices of the EEOC, where an investigator completed an intake questionnaire, informed her that "you have a good case," and promised to fill out a charge form for her signature. On December 16, not having heard anything further, Russo went to the EEOC office again. The investigator she had first met had, it turned out, been transferred. The new investigator reviewed the intake questionnaire in the file and helped Russo complete a charge, which she signed and he notarized on that date.

If the EEOC does not pursue this matter, may Russo bring a private suit under the Americans with Disabilities Act? Does 42 U.S.C. §12115 bear on the question? You may assume that the state fair employment practices agency in question has jurisdiction over disability claims and that it has a six-month statute of limitations for filing a state charge.

D.   RELATIONSHIP OF THE EEOC CHARGE TO PRIVATE SUIT

Since any Title VII action must be properly predicated on a charge filed with the EEOC, questions of the relationship between the charge and the suit have arisen along three axes: first, who may sue on the basis of a charge filed with the EEOC; second, what defendants may be sued on the basis of a charge; and, third, to what extent is the scope of the suit circumscribed by the content of the charge?

1.   *Proper Plaintiffs*

To bring a Title VII suit, the plaintiff must be what Title VII describes as a "person aggrieved." 42 U.S.C. §2000e-5(b) (2018). In the vast majority of cases, this is not an issue since current or former employees as well as applicants for employment clearly satisfy the statute. We've explored the outer reaches of the standing in *Thompson v. North American Stainless, LP*, 562 U.S. 170 (2011), reproduced at p. 408, which established a "zone of interests" test. In that case, the Court held that a person fired in retaliation for his fiancé's protected conduct had standing to sue.

Assuming proper standing under the statute, a plaintiff must also satisfy the charge-filing requirement we have seen. One question is whether a particular plaintiff must file his own charge or whether he can rely on a charge filed by someone else. In the class action context, persons who have not filed a charge with the EEOC may nevertheless be class members. See p. 545. But even where no class action is involved, some courts have adopted a "single filing" or "piggybacking" rule to allow persons who did not file charges to be named plaintiffs. *E.g.*, *Ariz. ex rel. Horne v. Geo Grp., Inc.*, 816 F.3d 1189, 1202 (9th Cir. 2016) ("an aggrieved employee who fails to file a timely charge with the EEOC may still be able to pursue a claim under the piggyback or single-filing rule, in which the employee 'piggyback[s]' onto the timely charge filed by another plaintiff for purposes of exhausting administrative remedies").

2.   *Proper Defendants*

Even when a plaintiff's suit is based on a charge filed with the EEOC, a question may arise about what parties may be named as defendants in the complaint. Title VII authorizes the bringing of a civil action "against the respondent named in the charge," §2000e-5(f)(1), §706(f)(1), but the courts have been more liberal than the statutory language might suggest. *E.g.*, *Peppers v. Cobb Cty., Georgia*, 651 F. App'x 415 (11th

Cir. 2016) (a party not named in the predicate EEOC charge could nevertheless be sued when it received notice of the charge, had at least a similarity of interest with the named party, and could have participated in the EEOC's process); *EEOC v. Simbaki, Ltd.*, 767 F.3d 475 (5th Cir. 2014) (describing different circuit tests for determining when an unnamed party may be sued under Title VII).

3. Scope of the Suit

We have seen the difficulties posed by "plausible pleading" for discrimination claims in Chapter 1, p. 33, but the requirement that every private Title VII, ADA, and ADEA suit be predicated on a charge properly filed with the EEOC raises another "pleading" issue — the extent to which the subsequent court complaint will be limited by the contents of the EEOC charge. The courts often articulate a liberal rule permitting a court suit to "encompass any kind of discrimination like or related to allegations contained in the charge and growing out of such allegations," on the theory that the purposes of charge filing are thereby satisfied, *Sanchez v. Standard Brands, Inc.*, 431 F.2d 455, 466 (5th Cir. 1970); *see also Sydnor v. Fairfax Cnty.*, 681 F.3d 591 (4th Cir. 2012), but numerous opinions narrow suits to conform to the scope of the EEOC charge. *E.g., Williams v. Milwaukee Health Servs.*, 562 F. App'x 523 (7th Cir. 2014) (plaintiff's ADA claim failed because the charge she filed with the EEOC did not mention disability discrimination). Special problems arise when a plaintiff claims to have been retaliated against on the basis of a filed EEOC charge. Some courts find that such retaliation can be challenged as within the scope of the original charge, *Hentosh v. Old Dominion Univ.*, 767 F.3d 413 (4th Cir. 2014) (retaliation claim based on the filing of a charge of discrimination is "reasonably related to" the charge), but other courts are not so liberal. *See generally* Lawrence D. Rosenthal, *To File or Not to File (Again): The Post-*Morgan *Circuit Split over the Duty to File an Amended or Second EEOC Charge of Claims of Post-Charge Employer Retaliation*, 66 BAYLOR L. REV. 531 (2014).

NOTE ON AVOIDING THE TITLE VII PROCEDURAL MAZE VIA §1981

Unlike the other antidiscrimination laws we have encountered, no federal agency is charged with enforcing 42 U.S.C. §1981. Thus, a plaintiff may prosecute such suits in either federal or state court without concern for the procedural niceties we have just studied. However, §1981 has its own complications in terms of the statute of limitations. For most of its history, state limitations periods were "borrowed" in such suits, *Goodman v. Lukens Steel Co.*, 482 U.S. 656 (1987) (§1981 suits subject to the state statute applicable to "personal injury" actions), including state rules concerning the accrual of the cause of action, continuing violation, and tolling, *Johnson v. Railway Express Agency, Inc.*, 421 U.S. 454, 463-64 (1975), although "considerations of state law may be displaced where their application would be inconsistent with the federal policy underlying the cause of action under consideration." *Id.* at 465.

This authority was dramatically altered by *Jones v. R.R. Donnelley & Sons Co.*, 541 U.S. 369 (2004), which created an exception to the borrowing principle. While borrowing continues to apply where the cause of action was created by §1981 as it was

originally passed after the Civil War, the Court held that 28 U.S.C. §1658 (2018) created an exception. Section 1658 established a four-year federal statute of limitations
for federal claims that do not otherwise have a specified limitations period, and *R.R.
Donnelley* held that it governs any causes of action that would not have been cognizable under the original version of §1981 but were actionable under the 1991 Civil
Rights Act's amendment of that statute. As a practical matter, that means that most
§1981 claims will be subject to a four-year filing period. *See, e.g., Johnson v. Lucent
Techs. Inc.*, 653 F.3d 1000 (9th Cir. 2011) (holding a §1981 retaliation claim subject
to the four-year statute of limitations in §1658).

E.   THE INTERRELATIONSHIP OF VARIOUS RIGHTS
AND REMEDIES

We have encountered separate federal remedies that address the same wrong. For
example, Title VII and §1981 overlap when race discrimination is involved. In addition, most states have laws prohibiting race, sex, age, and disability discrimination.
Finally, discrimination may be prohibited by collective bargaining agreements. The
interrelationship of these remedies has raised difficult questions.

Coordinating Federal Remedies. With respect to federal remedies, the Supreme
Court has generally treated them as separate and independent, *Johnson v. Railway
Express Agency*, 421 U.S. 454, 462 (1975), thus leaving coordination of separate suits
to the normal doctrines of res judicata (or claim preclusion) and collateral estoppel
(or issue preclusion). *See, e.g., Matusick v. Erie County Water Auth.*, 739 F.3d 51
(2d Cir. 2014) (preclusion barred relitigation of whether plaintiff actually engaged in
misconduct as found in a prior administrative proceeding but did not bar a jury from
determining that one of the reasons for his discharge was his romantic relationship
with an African American); *Adams v. FedEx Ground Package Sys., Inc.*, 546 F. App'x
772, 775 (10th Cir. 2013) (issue preclusion by prior arbitration agreement barred
subsequent suit on discrimination claims).

Coordinating State and Federal Remedies. State remedies for employment discrimination typically parallel federal prohibitions but may in fact go further than the federal law (in substantive protections and in remedies). The general rule is that federal
law does not preempt the "field" of discrimination, meaning that state laws are valid
so long as they do not actually conflict with federal law. Further, the courts are slow to
find a conflict. For example, *California Federal Savings & Loan Association v. Guerra*,
479 U.S. 272 (1987), concluded that a state statute requiring unpaid maternity leave
did not conflict with Title VII's prohibition of sex discrimination.

Because an employee has available both state and federal remedies for the same
wrong, coordination questions arise, especially since, as we have seen, Title VII
requires deferral to state agencies, an attack on discrimination can, in most states,
set in motion two separate proceedings against discriminatory employment practices.
These proceedings may converge in a single suit in either state court or federal court
asserting all claims. Thus, state courts have concurrent jurisdiction with federal courts
over Title VII claims, *e.g., Yellow Freight Systems, Inc. v. Donnelly*, 494 U.S. 820
(1990), so state and federal claims can be joined in state court. Similarly, supplemental jurisdiction will normally allow a plaintiff filing Title VII suit in federal court to
join state law claims. 28 U.S.C. §1367 (2018).

If a plaintiff chooses to proceed in state court, normal preclusion principles apply should she later file a second suit in federal court. *Kremer v. Chemical Construction Corp.*, 456 U.S. 461 (1982), held that a state *court judgment* precludes a subsequent Title VII suit in federal district court if the state in question would accord the decision preclusive effects in its courts. However, state *administrative determinations*, even those made upon a full hearing, are not entitled to full faith and credit in a Title VII or ADEA claim unless they have been reviewed by a state court. *Univ. of Tenn. v. Elliott*, 478 U.S. 788 (1986) (Title VII); *Astoria Fed. Sav. & Loan Ass'n v. Solimino*, 501 U.S. 104 (1991) (ADEA). Such state administrative determination may, however, preclude federal suits under §1981. *Elliott*, 478 U.S. at 793.

Collective Bargaining Agreements. Collective bargaining agreements typically contain both job security protections and nondiscrimination clauses, and a worker in a unionized setting may seek relief under the CBA's grievance procedure, typically culminating in binding arbitration. Should that be unsuccessful or should the worker prefer a judicial forum to pursuing arbitration, the question arises about the relationship between the two forums. See Chapter 9.

F.   CLASS ACTIONS

1.   Introduction

Class actions played an important role for much of the history of Title VII. As one early case put it, a "suit for violation of Title VII is necessarily a class action as the evil sought to be ended is discrimination on the basis of a class characteristic, *i.e.*, race, sex, religion or national origin." *Bowe v. Colgate-Palmolive Co.*, 416 F.2d 711, 719 (7th Cir. 1969). For example, *Griggs v. Duke Power Co.*, reproduced at p. 167, one of the iconic Title VII decisions, was brought as a class action. While government enforcement "pattern and practice" suits have tried to vindicate sweeping claims, *e.g.*, *Teamsters v. United States*, reproduced at p. 100, private class actions have played an important role in attacking both systemic disparate treatment and systemic disparate impact. *See generally* Tristin K. Green, *Targeting Workplace Context: Title VII as a Tool for Institutional Reform*, 72 FORDHAM L. REV. 659 (2003); Susan Sturm, *Second Generation Employment Discrimination: A Structural Approach*, 101 COLUM. L. REV. 458, 512-13 (2001); Nancy Levit, *MegaCases, Diversity, and the Elusive Goal of Workplace Reform*, 49 BC L. REV. 367 (2008); Michael Ashley Stein & Michael Evan Waterstone, *Disability, Disparate Impact, and Class Actions*, 56 DUKE L.J. 861 (2006). Although there have been questions raised about the effectiveness of private class actions in remedying discrimination, *see, e.g.*, Michael Selmi, *The Price of Discrimination: The Nature of Class Action Employment Discrimination Litigation and Its Effects*, 81 TEX. L. REV. 1249 (2003) (class actions and settlements have relatively little effect on shareholder value and frequently produce little to no substantive change), they remained a vital part of the employment discrimination landscape until they came under threat recently.

In 2011, the Supreme Court issued two decisions that led to substantial curbs on class actions. The first, *AT&T Mobility LLC v. Concepción*, 563 U.S. 333 (2011), while not a discrimination case, gave impetus to the growing tendency of employers to condition employment on workers agreeing to arbitrate their claims individually and thus foreclose either a class suit or class arbitration. The Court held that the Federal Arbitration Act prohibits states from invalidating arbitration agreements that deny a class alternative. While §2 of the FAA preserved generally applicable state contract defenses, it did not preserve state-law rules impeding the accomplishment of the FAA's objectives; thus, California's unconscionability doctrine barring waiver of the right to bring class claims was preempted. In short, *Concepcion* opened the door for employers to immunize themselves from broad challenges merely by requiring individual arbitration of employee claims. A later decision, *American Express Co. v. Italian Colors Restaurant*, 133 S. Ct. 2304, 2307 (2013), reinforced *Concepción* by finding that a contractual waiver of class arbitration is enforceable under the FAA even when the plaintiff's cost of individually arbitrating a federal statutory claim exceeds the potential recovery.

Concepción, however, arose in the consumer context, and it is possible it may be limited in the employment setting by the National Labor Relations Act. Although the NLRA is often viewed as concerned only with unionization and collective bargaining, it is framed in broader terms and protects the rights of covered workers to engage in collective action. In *D.R. Horton, Inc.*, 2012 NLRB LEXIS 11 (N.L.R.B. Jan. 3, 2012), the NLRB held that a company's arbitration agreement was an unfair labor practice in violation of §7 of the NLRA, which protects workers' right to engage in "concerted activities for mutual aid or protection" precisely because it barred collective action. Further, the Board found that the FAA, which was enacted earlier than the NLRA, did not affect the analysis. In part this was because the "[t]he right to engage in collective action — including collective *legal* action — is a core substantive right protected by the NLRA and is the foundation on which the Act and federal labor policy rests." *Id.* at 43. While a union might waive this right as part of a collective bargaining agreement, it could not be restricted by an agreement between an employer and an individual employee. Although this aspect of *D.R. Horton* was rejected on review by the Fifth Circuit, 737 F.3d 344 (5th Cir. 2013), and by other courts, two recent circuit decisions have looked to *D.R. Horton* to invalidate a bar on class relief for employees. Together with a contrary decision from the Fifth Circuit, both have led to grants of certiorari. *Morris v. Ernst & Young, LLP*, 834 F.3d 975 (9th Cir. 2016), *cert. granted*, 137 S. Ct. 809 (2017); *Lewis v. Epic Sys. Corp.*, 823 F.3d 1147 (7th Cir. 2016), *cert. granted*, 137 S. Ct. 809 (2017). *See generally* Charles A. Sullivan & Timothy P. Glynn, Horton *Hatches the Egg: Concerted Action Includes Concerted Dispute Resolution*, 64 Ala. L. Rev. 1013 (2013).

A second 2011 Supreme Court decision threatened to cut back radically on the possibilities of class actions even when no arbitration agreement exists. To understand the holdings of *Wal-Mart Stores, Inc. v. Dukes*, 564 U.S. 338 (2011), it is necessary to appreciate the requirements for federal class actions. While discrimination is necessarily a class evil, not every suit attacking such discrimination qualifies as a class action. Class actions under Title VII, §1981, or the ADA* must satisfy Rule 23 of the Federal Rules of Civil Procedure as applied in those contexts.

---

* The Age Discrimination in Employment and Equal Pay Acts are somewhat different since both expressly incorporate the enforcement provisions of the Fair Labor Standards Act, including 29 U.S.C. §216 (2018), which require each member of a "collective" or "representative" action to provide written consent. *See Hoffman-La Roche, Inc. v. Sperling*, 493 U.S. 165, 169 (1989) (upholding district court's notice to potential class members under §216(b)). *See generally* Scott A. Moss & Nantiya Ruan, *The Second-Class Class Action: How Courts Thwart Wage Rights by Misapplying Class Action Rules*, 61 Am. U. L. Rev. 523 (2012); Charlotte S. Alexander, *Would an Opt-in Requirement Fix the Class Action Settlement?: Evidence from the Fair Labor Standards Act*, 80 Miss. L.J. 443 (2010); Douglas D. Scherer & Robert Belton, *Handling Class Actions Under the ADEA*, 10 Emp. Rts. & Emp. Pol'y J. 553 (2006).

As a first step, Title VII and the ADA class suits must be properly predicated on a charge filed with the EEOC by the representative plaintiff. However, each class member need not file a charge with the EEOC because "[i]t would be wasteful, if not vain, for numerous employees, all with the same grievance, to have to process many identical complaints with the EEOC." *Oatis v. Crown Zellerbach Corp.*, 398 F.2d 496, 498 (5th Cir. 1968). Assuming a proper charge, a class action can be certified under Rule 23 of the Federal Rules of Civil Procedure only if it satisfies all the requirements of Rule 23(a) and falls into one of the categories of 23(b). *Wal-Mart* was a major blow to broad class certifications under both paragraphs.

2.   *Requirements of Rule 23*

Rule 23 establishes two sets of requirements that class actions must meet; the party seeking to maintain the suit as a class action has the burden of persuasion with respect to them. The first set is found in Rule 23(a), which sets forth the requirements for any class certification. The second set is found in Rule 23(b), which sets forth different kinds of certification, the central significance of which is whether class members need to be notified individually of the class certification and given the right to opt out of the class.

The four factors of Rule 23(a), all of which must be met, are:

(1)   the class is so numerous that joinder of all members is impracticable,
(2)   there are questions of law or fact common to the class,
(3)   the claims or defenses of the representative parties are typical of the claims or defenses of the class, and
(4)   the representative parties will fairly and adequately protect the interests of the class.

While each of these requirements must be satisfied, a mechanical analysis of the four categories risks overlooking the underlying concept of Rule 23(a): because class actions necessarily commit the rights of unnamed class members into the hands of the named plaintiff and her attorneys, the courts must ensure that a class action is both appropriate to the claims alleged and structured to maximize the quality of the representation of the interests of the unnamed class members.

To this end, (a)(1), "*numerosity*," focuses on whether the case is appropriate for class action treatment or whether traditional multiparty litigation is preferable. The remaining three parts of paragraph (a) examine facets of the adequacy of the named plaintiff (or her counsel) as a representative of the class. Thus, (a)(2), "*commonality*," and (3), "*typicality*," attempt to ensure that the named plaintiff will, in the course of representing her own interests, necessarily represent the other class members because her claims are identical or very similar to theirs. However, Rule 23(a)(2) requires only the existence of *some* common questions. The existence of noncommon questions does not preclude commonality. Typicality requires a closer fit between the representative plaintiff's claims and those of the unnamed class members.

Finally, (a)(4) considers adequacy of representation in terms of the qualifications of the class representative and possible conflicts of interest with other class members. The adequacy of class counsel was originally also considered under this prong, but is now analyzed under Rule 23(g), which codifies the various requirements regarding attorneys that are applicable to class actions.

While all four requirements can generate complications for discrimination suits,* "commonality" has been perhaps the biggest sticking point for large-scale employment discrimination class actions. Even before *Wal-Mart*, the Supreme Court in *General Telephone Co. of the Southwest v. Falcon*, 457 U.S. 147 (1982), found a lack of commonality between the named plaintiff's claims and those of the class. The plaintiff had been denied a promotion but the class certification he sought included Mexican Americans who were denied employment by the defendant. The district court certified a class including Mexican American employees and unsuccessful Mexican American applicants. It ultimately found that the employer had not discriminated against Falcon in hiring, but that it did discriminate against him in its promotion practices. "The court reached converse conclusions about the class, finding no discrimination in promotion practices, but concluding that petitioner had discriminated against Mexican Americans at its Irving facility in its hiring practices." 457 U.S. at 152. Rejecting the certification, the Court stressed the

> wide gap between (a) an individual's claim that he has been denied a promotion on discriminatory grounds, and his otherwise unsupported allegation that the company has a policy of discrimination, and (b) the existence of a class of persons who have suffered the same injury as that individual, such that the individual's claim and the class claims will share common questions of law or fact and that the individual's claim will be typical of the class claim.

Id. at 157. Proof that the named plaintiff was the victim of national origin discrimination in promotion "would not necessarily justify the additional inferences" that such discriminatory treatment was typical of the employer's promotion practices, or that such practices are motivated "by a policy of ethnic discrimination that pervades petitioner's Irving division," or that any such policy is reflected in other employment practices, such as hiring. *Id.* at 158. The Court noted that, "[a]s the District Court's bifurcated findings on liability demonstrate, the individual and class claims might as well have been tried separately." *Id.* at 159.

Falcon did indicate when a class suit might be appropriate:

> If petitioner used a biased testing procedure to evaluate both applicants for employment and incumbent employees, a class action on behalf of every applicant or employee who might have been prejudiced by the test clearly would satisfy the commonality and typicality requirements of Rule 23(a). Significant proof that an employer operated under a general policy of discrimination conceivably could justify a class of both applicants and employees if the discrimination manifested itself in hiring and promotion practices in the same general fashion, such as through entirely subjective decisionmaking processes.

Id. at 159, n.15. It was upon this passage that the landmark *Wal-Mart* case was pitched. What once seemed a highpoint of employment discrimination class actions instead became its nadir.

---

* For example, *East Texas Motor Freight Systems, Inc. v. Rodriguez*, 431 U.S. 395 (1977), overturned a class certification because the representatives had different claims than the class they sought to represent: they therefore did not possess the same interest and suffer the same injury as class members. Further, the individual plaintiffs' failure to move for certification as a class action strongly suggested that they would not be adequate representatives as did the named representatives' demand for relief that had been voted down by class members.

WAL-MART STORES, INC. v. DUKES
564 U.S. 338 (2011)

Justice Scalia's majority opinion is reproduced in Chapter 2, p. 113. The dissent is not reproduced there and follows below:

Justice GINSBURG, with whom Justice BREYER, Justice SOTOMAYOR, and Justice KAGAN join, concurring in part and dissenting in part. . . .

I . . .

B

Even a single question of law or fact common to the members of the class is sufficient for Rule 23(a) purposes. The District Court, recognizing that "one significant issue common to the class may be sufficient to warrant certification" found that the plaintiffs easily met that test. Absent an error of law or an abuse of discretion, an appellate tribunal has no warrant to upset the District Court's finding of commonality.

The District Court certified a class of "[a]ll women employed at any Wal-Mart domestic retail store at any time since December 26, 1998." The named plaintiffs, led by Betty Dukes, propose to litigate, on behalf of the class, allegations that Wal-Mart discriminates on the basis of gender in pay and promotions. They allege that the company "[r]eli[es] on gender stereotypes in making employment decisions such as . . . promotion[s] [and] pay." Wal-Mart permits those prejudices to infect personnel decisions, the plaintiffs contend, by leaving pay and promotions in the hands of "a nearly all male managerial workforce" using "arbitrary and subjective criteria." Further alleged barriers to the advancement of female employees include the company's requirement, "as a condition of promotion to management jobs, that employees be willing to relocate." Absent instruction otherwise, there is a risk that managers will act on the familiar assumption that women, because of their services to husband and children, are less mobile than men. See Dept. of Labor, Federal Glass Ceiling Commission, Good for Business: Making Full Use of the Nation's Human Capital 151 (1995).

Women fill 70 percent of the hourly jobs in the retailer's stores but make up only "33 percent of management employees." "[T]he higher one looks in the organization the lower the percentage of women." The plaintiffs' "largely uncontested descriptive statistics" also show that women working in the company's stores "are paid less than men in every region" and "that the salary gap widens over time even for men and women hired into the same jobs at the same time."

The District Court identified "systems for . . . promoting in-store employees" that were "sufficiently similar across regions and stores" to conclude that "the manner in which these systems affect the class raises issues that are common to all class members." The selection of employees for promotion to in-store management "is fairly characterized as a 'tap on the shoulder' process," in which managers have discretion about whose shoulders to tap. Vacancies are not regularly posted; from among those employees satisfying minimum qualifications, managers choose whom to promote on the basis of their own subjective impressions.

Wal-Mart's compensation policies also operate uniformly across stores, the District Court found. The retailer leaves open a $2 band for every position's hourly pay rate. Wal-Mart provides no standards or criteria for setting wages within that band, and thus does nothing to counter unconscious bias on the part of supervisors.

Wal-Mart's supervisors do not make their discretionary decisions in a vacuum. The District Court reviewed means Wal-Mart used to maintain a "carefully constructed . . . corporate culture," such as frequent meetings to reinforce the common way of thinking, regular transfers of managers between stores to ensure uniformity throughout the company, monitoring of stores "on a close and constant basis," and "Wal-Mart TV," "broadcas[t] . . . into all stores."

The plaintiffs' evidence, including class members' tales of their own experiences, suggests that gender bias suffused Wal-Mart's company culture. Among illustrations, senior management often refer to female associates as "little Janie Qs." One manager told an employee that "[m]en are here to make a career and women aren't." A committee of female Wal-Mart executives concluded that "[s]tereotypes limit the opportunities offered to women."

Finally, the plaintiffs presented an expert's appraisal to show that the pay and promotions disparities at Wal-Mart "can be explained only by gender discrimination and not by . . . neutral variables . . . ." Using regression analyses, their expert, Richard Drogin, controlled for factors including, inter alia, job performance, length of time with the company, and the store where an employee worked.[5] The results, the District Court found, were sufficient to raise an "inference of discrimination."

C

The District Court's identification of a common question, whether pay and promotions policies gave rise to unlawful discrimination, was hardly infirm. The practice of delegating to supervisors large discretion to make personnel decisions, uncontrolled by formal standards, has long been known to have the potential to produce disparate effects. Managers, like all humankind, may be prey to biases of which they are unaware.[6] The risk of discrimination is heightened when those managers are predominantly of one sex, and are steeped in a corporate culture that perpetuates gender stereotypes.

We have held that "discretionary employment practices" can give rise to Title VII claims, not only when such practices are motivated by discriminatory intent but also when they produce discriminatory results. See *Watson v. Fort Worth Bank & Trust* [reproduced at p. 183]. . . . In *Watson*, as here, an employer had given its managers large authority over promotions. An employee sued the bank under Title VII, alleging that the "discretionary promotion system" caused a discriminatory effect based on race. Four different supervisors had declined, on separate occasions, to promote the employee. Their reasons were subjective and unknown. The employer, we noted "not developed precise and formal criteria for evaluating candidates"; "[i]t relied instead on the subjective judgment of supervisors."

5. The Court asserts that Drogin showed only average differences at the "regional and national level" between male and female employees. In fact, his regression analyses showed there were disparities within stores. . . .

6. An example vividly illustrates how subjective decisionmaking can be a vehicle for discrimination. Performing in symphony orchestras was long a male preserve. Goldin and Rouse, *Orchestrating Impartiality: The Impact of "Blind" Auditions on Female Musicians*, 90 AM. ECON. REV. 715, 715-716 (2000). In the 1970's orchestras began hiring musicians through auditions open to all comers. Reviewers were to judge applicants solely on their musical abilities, yet subconscious bias led some reviewers to disfavor women. Orchestras that permitted reviewers to see the applicants hired far fewer female musicians than orchestras that conducted blind auditions, in which candidates played behind opaque screens.

Aware of "the problem of subconscious stereotypes and prejudices," we held that the employer's "undisciplined system of subjective decisionmaking" was an "employment practic[e]" that may be analyzed under the disparate impact approach. *See also Wards Cove Packing Co. v. Atonio* [reproduced at p. 172] (recognizing "the use of 'subjective decision making'" "as an "employment practic[e]" subject to disparate-impact attack).

The plaintiffs' allegations state claims of gender discrimination in the form of biased decisionmaking in both pay and promotions. The evidence reviewed by the District Court adequately demonstrated that resolving those claims would necessitate examination of particular policies and practices alleged to affect, adversely and globally, women employed at Wal-Mart's stores. Rule 23(a)(2), setting a necessary but not a sufficient criterion for class-action certification, demands nothing further.

II

A

[The dissent also criticized the majority for confusing the commonality inquiry under 23(a) with the "predominance" question when certification was sought under Rule 23(b)(3), which requires a determination that "questions of law or fact common to class members predominate over any questions affecting only individual members" and that "a class action is superior to other available methods for . . . adjudicating the controversy."]

B

The "dissimilarities" approach leads the Court to train its attention on what distinguishes individual class members, rather than on what unites them. Given the lack of standards for pay and promotions, the majority says, "demonstrating the invalidity of one manager's use of discretion will do nothing to demonstrate the invalidity of another's."

Wal-Mart's delegation of discretion over pay and promotions is a policy uniform throughout all stores. The very nature of discretion is that people will exercise it in various ways. A system of delegated discretion, *Watson* held, is a practice actionable under Title VII when it produces discriminatory outcomes. A finding that Wal-Mart's pay and promotions practices in fact violate the law would be the first step in the usual order of proof for plaintiffs seeking individual remedies for company-wide discrimination. *Teamsters v. United States*; see *Albemarle Paper Co. v. Moody* [reproduced at p. 561]. That each individual employee's unique circumstances will ultimately determine whether she is entitled to backpay or damages, §2000e-5(g)(2)(A) (barring backpay if a plaintiff "was refused . . . advancement . . . for any reason other than discrimination"), should not factor into the Rule 23(a)(2) determination. . . .

NOTES

1. *Procedure and Substance.* As Justice Scalia makes clear, the class action certification question is intimately bound up with the merits determination. This means that *Wal-Mart* is not merely a "procedural" case: the answer to the procedural question of whether there is a class sufficiently homogeneous to challenge a pattern of discrimination, in effect, requires answering the substantive question of whether, under either

systemic disparate treatment or systemic disparate impact theories, the requisite policy or practice of discrimination exists. The Court reaches its certification decision by clarifying (many would say changing) substantive theories. Ultimately, the majority rejects the two systemic theories on the facts before it and sees the named plaintiffs as asserting cases of individual disparate treatment, essentially unconnected to other class members' claims. See further discussion in Chapter 2, p. 116, and Chapter 3, pp. 185-186. Is *Wal-Mart* the *Iqbal* and *Twombly* of class actions?

2. *Bad Stats.* As the case reached the Court, there wasn't much dispute that Wal-Mart's gender profile of pay and promotions was very unfavorable to women. Although Wal-Mart had proffered its own statistical studies to the contrary, the lower court had accepted the plaintiffs' evidence in this regard. Dr. Drogin found statistical evidence of discrimination at the regional level by comparing male and female employees within Wal-Mart. Dr. Bendick conducted a "benchmarking" study comparing Wal-Mart with its big box competitors, with women faring worse at Wal-Mart in pay and promotions. Given the EEOC's failure in *EEOC v. Sears*, reproduced at p. 133, it's easy to see how important it was for the plaintiffs to rule out the "lack of interest" defense through Bendick's work. Thus, there was substantial statistical evidence that something was rotten in Wal-Mart.

But, these statistical showings weren't enough to certify a class that included every woman at every Wal-Mart store. The Court saw two problems. First, even taking these studies at face value, "[a] regional pay disparity, for example, may be attributable to only a small set of Wal-Mart stores, and cannot by itself establish the uniform, store-by-store disparity upon which the plaintiffs' theory of commonality depends." Second, and more fundamentally, even if this evidence proved a disparity in all 3,400 stores, commonality would still not be proven because of claimed differences in the availability of qualified or interested women and the possibility that each manager was applying "some sex-neutral, performance-based criteria — whose nature and effects will differ from store to store." In short, even if each store showed a statistical gender disparity, there might be varying explanations for those results, not all of which are discrimination.

3. *No More Disparate Treatment Class Actions?* Does this mean the end of systemic disparate treatment class actions, at least those not premised on a formal discriminatory policy like *Manhart* and *Johnson Controls?* It's true that, presumably, the workers in any one store might seek class certification based on the bias of a single manager who made all the promotion and pay decisions. But such a suit might well fall afoul of Rule 23(a)'s numerosity requirement — that the class be sufficiently large to justify class certification, rather than simple joinder of all plaintiffs. In any event, some authors doubt radical effects of the decision, given that prior law was not hospitable to class actions. *See* Michael Selmi & Sylvia Tsakos, *Employment Discrimination Class Actions After* Wal-Mart v. Dukes, 48 AKRON L. REV. 803 (2015); Michael C. Harper, *Class-Based Adjudication of Title VII Claims in the Age of the Roberts Court*, 95 BU L. REV. 1099, 1101 (2015); Elizabeth Tippett, *Robbing a Barren Vault: The Implications of* Dukes v. Wal-Mart *for Cases Challenging Subjective Employment Practices*, 29 HOFSTRA LAB. & EMP. L.J. 433 (2012). Other commentators urge that *Wal-Mart's* threat to systemic disparate treatment class actions should lead to an increased EEOC focus on systemic cases. *See* Joseph A. Seiner, *Weathering* Wal-Mart, 89 NOTRE DAME L. REV. 1343 (2014); Angela D. Morrison, Duke-*Ing Out Pattern or Practice After* Wal-Mart: *The EEOC as Fist*, 63 AM. U. L. REV. 87 (2013); *see also* Joseph A. Seiner, *The Issue Class*, 56 BC L. REV. 121 (2015).

4. *Decentralized Decisions as a Central Policy.* The plaintiffs sought to avoid the problem of multiple individual decisionmakers by pitching their commonality claims on a centralized, corporate-wide policy implicating Wal-Mart as a whole and thus justifying a firm-wide class action. And they sought to link that policy to the gender disparities the other experts had uncovered. Without a unifying policy, the statistical showing of female underrepresentation in higher-level positions and lower salaries would allow only a series of class actions against individual stores because the differentials were due to store-level decisions. The plaintiffs argued that the glue that tied the lower promotions and pay of women to the policy of giving store managers unstructured and unreviewed discretion in pay and promotions was that all the women faced the *same risk* that their managers would individually discriminate against them because the Wal-Mart policy enabled them to do so. They claimed that this constituted common questions of both disparate impact and disparate treatment.

The plaintiffs' strategy was clever, if ultimately unsuccessful. The lynchpin of their case was their social framework expert Dr. Bielby. He did not view the centralized policies as discriminatory per se, but he testified that, precisely by virtue of decentralizing decisionmaking, these policies enabled discrimination at the store level. This raised two questions. First, was Dr. Bielby's testimony admissible? Second, if so, did it support the class certification?

5. *Speaking of Experts.* The majority was quite disdainful of Bielby and, likely, his entire area of expertise. But a rich body of social science literature supports a social framework perspective; indeed, you have encountered these studies repeatedly in this book. Nor is there much doubt that Dr. Bielby was qualified to speak to that literature, at least in a general way. Further, the majority assumed the testimony to be admissible. However, in an omitted footnote, the Court cast doubt on future use of such experts by noting that "Bielby's conclusions in this case have elicited criticism from the very scholars on whose conclusions he relies for his social-framework analysis," citing John Monahan, Laurens Walker & Gregory Mitchell, *Contextual Evidence of Gender Discrimination: The Ascendance of Social Frameworks*, 94 VA. L. REV. 1715 (2008). The essential argument of these critics is that, before a social scientist can opine on such matters, he or she should conduct a detailed study of the institution in question, not merely rely on information obtained in discovery by attorneys who obviously have a predisposition to seek damaging data. *See* Gregory Mitchell, *Good Causes and Bad Science*, 63 VAND. L. REV. 133 (2010). There is, however, another side to the debate. *See* Melissa Hart & Paul M. Secunda, *A Matter of Context: Social Framework Evidence in Employment Discrimination Class Actions*, 78 FORDHAM L. REV. 37 (2009). While the *Wal-Mart* majority merely noted the expertise question and did not resolve it, the question will be more pointed in future cases. *See also* David L. Faigman, Nilanjana Dasgupta & Cecilia L. Ridgeway, *A Matter of Fit: The Law of Discrimination and the Science of Implicit Bias*, 59 HASTINGS L.J. 1389, 1431-32 (2008).

6. *Retreating from* Watson's *Approval of Disparate Impact.* In one sense, of course, *Wal-Mart* did worse than reject Bielby's expertise: it declared it essentially irrelevant by rejecting the core argument that a policy of delegating authority was actionable: "[i]t is also a very common and presumptively reasonable way of doing business — one that we have said 'should itself raise no inference of discriminatory conduct,'" citing *Watson v. Fort Worth Bank & Trust*, reproduced at p. 183. But we saw that *Watson* had held that subjective employment practices *can* be attacked if they result in disparate impact. Didn't Bielby's testimony, coupled with the statistical evidence, create a common question of whether Wal-Mart had a central policy with a disparate impact?

And Justice O'Connor in *Watson* had justified applying disparate impact theory to subjective policies in part because of the possibility that lower-level managers might be acting on the basis of stereotypical views.

The Court acknowledged *Watson* to be a "landmark case," but then proceeded to gut it. Justice Scalia noted that the *Watson* "plurality opinion *conditioned* that holding on the corollary that merely proving that the discretionary system has produced a racial or sexual disparity *is not enough.* '[T]he plaintiff must begin by identifying the specific employment practice that is challenged.'" Thus, Dr. Bielby may have identified a general policy of "delegated discretion, [but] respondents have identified no 'specific employment practice' — much less one that ties all their 1.5 million claims together. Merely showing that Wal-Mart's policy of discretion has produced an overall sex-based disparity does not suffice." *Id.*

What's left of *Watson*'s approval of disparate impact attacks on subjective practices? The Court writes that plaintiffs "have not identified a common mode of exercising discretion that pervades the entire company." Can you imagine what that "mode" might be? Suppose plaintiffs had claimed that the policy of requiring employees seeking promotion to be willing to relocate adversely affected promotion and pay. Would that suffice to create a common question if plaintiffs could adduce evidence of disparate impact? But notice, the challenge would no longer be to a subjective policy.

In any event, disparate impact class actions may still survive where the challenged policy is objective. In *Stockwell v. City & County of San Francisco*, 749 F.3d 1107, 1116 (9th Cir. 2014), the plaintiffs challenged a decision to abandon an examination as a basis for certain assignments, arguing that it created a disparate impact based on age. The court reversed the lower court's denial of class certification: "the officers are all challenging a single policy they contend has adversely affected them. The question whether the policy has an impermissible disparate impact on the basis of age necessarily has a single answer." The court stressed that in doing so it did not necessarily "approve of the statistical showing the officers have made as adequate to make out their merits case." Rather, it was merely identifying "a common question sufficient for Rule 23(a)(2) purposes."

BYE-BYE (b)(2)

Although the *Wal-Mart* majority's resolution of the commonality question was enough to require reversal, a portion of the opinion we have not reproduced went further to resolve a dispute that had been simmering in the lower courts for decades: assuming Rule 23(a), when can a Title VII class action be certified under Rule 23(b)(2) as opposed to (b)(3)? The majority stated that (b)(2) certification was generally inappropriate when the plaintiff sought monetary relief, and in this view was joined by the dissenters. Thus, the Court was unanimous on an issue that may be as significant in practical terms as the more publicized refusal to find commonality.

Without exploring all of the ins and outs of the question, plaintiffs generally prefer class certification under Rule 23(b)(2) to certification under (b)(3) because (b)(3) requires notice to class members and gives them the concomitant right to opt out while (b)(2) does not. Since plaintiffs' counsel would have to bear the costs of notice in the first instance, it seems unlikely that, even had commonality been found, Wal-Mart could have gone forward under (b)(3): imagine the costs of locating and mailing notices to more than a million women, most of whom probably no longer work for Wal-Mart.

Rule 23(b)(2) authorizes certification when "the party opposing the class has acted or refused to act on grounds that apply generally to the class, so that final injunctive relief or corresponding declaratory relief is appropriate respecting the class as a whole." In contrast, Rule 23(b)(3) requires that "the court find that the questions of law or fact common to the members of the class predominate over any questions affecting only individual members, and that a class action [be] superior to other available methods for the fair and efficient adjudication of the controversy."

Because of (b)(2)'s language focusing on injunctive and declaratory relief, there was a long-running dispute in the circuits as to whether class actions seeking monetary relief could ever be certified under (b)(2). Those who favored such certification argued that Title VII suits, being essentially equitable, could fall within the paragraph, at least if the monetary relief sought did not "predominate." The Court rejected that argument, with all the Justices agreeing that (b)(2) was inapplicable when monetary relief was more than incidental to equitable relief, regardless of whether the monetary relief was framed as legal (damages) or equitable (backpay):

> Rule 23(b)(2) applies only when a single injunction or declaratory judgment would provide relief to each member of the class. It does not authorize class certification when each individual class member would be entitled to a different injunction or declaratory judgment against the defendant. Similarly, it does not authorize class certification when each class member would be entitled to an individualized award of monetary damages.

564 U.S. at 360-61. The Court even questioned whether "incidental" monetary relief would be appropriate when a class is certified under (b)(2), although it did not decide that issue.

Reinforcing its reading of Rule 23(b), the Court reasoned that Wal-Mart "is entitled to individualized determinations of each employee's eligibility for backpay." *Id.* at 366. It looked to the statute's detailed remedial scheme, including the provision allowing an employer to avoid an order for "hiring, reinstatement, or promotion of an individual as an employee, or the payment to him of any backpay," §2000e-5(g)(2)(A), if it can show that it took an adverse employment action for any reason other than discrimination. The majority rejected the Ninth Circuit's suggestion of what Justice Scalia called "Trial by Formula," which involved hearings for a sample drawn from the class members, with the results being extrapolated across the class. "Because the Rules Enabling Act forbids interpreting Rule 23 to 'abridge, enlarge or modify any substantive right,' 28 U.S.C. §2072(b), a class cannot be certified on the premise that Wal-Mart will not be entitled to litigate its statutory defenses to individual claims." *Id.* at 367. *See* Melissa Hart, *Civil Rights and Systemic Wrongs*, 32 Berkeley J. Emp. & Lab. L. 455, 461 (2011) ("By rejecting statistical modeling as a permissible remedial approach, the Court reduces the structural and systemic claim to the sum of its individual parts and gives those individual parts the power to destroy the whole").

Despite *Wal-Mart*'s disapproval of "Trial by Formula," *Tyson Foods, Inc. v. Bouaphakeo*, 136 S. Ct 1036 (2016), approved expert proof of average times for donning and doffing in an FLSA class action in the face of the argument that the individual questions as to remedy meant that those questions predominated. The Court viewed such statistical proof as admissible in an individual case to establish each worker's harm and, accordingly, admissible in a class case. The employer's reliance on *Wal-Mart* for "the broad proposition that a representative sample is an impermissible means of establishing classwide liability" was misplaced because in *Wal-Mart* there was *no* common questions, and no employee "could have prevailed in an individual suit by relying on depositions detailing the ways in which other employees were discriminated against by their particular store managers." *Id.* at 1048. In contrast, the donning and doffing study in *Bouaphakeo* "could have been sufficient to sustain a jury finding as to hours worked if it were introduced in each employee's individual action." *Id.*

NOTE ON THE FUTURE OF ANTIDISCRIMINATION CLASS ACTIONS

As you're probably aware, class actions have been under attack across the legal landscape, not merely in the employment law arena. One major concern, which the *Wal-Mart* majority noted, is that class actions may be unfair to class members, who may find their claims lost by virtue of preclusion if they are not adequately represented in the litigation. To a considerable extent, however, these concerns are ameliorated by 23(b)(3) certifications with their concomitant notice and opt-out rights, and, as a practical matter, post-*Wal-Mart* class actions are almost certain to be brought under (b)(3). Further, preclusive effects on class members in the discrimination context are much more limited than might first appear. In *Cooper v. Federal Reserve Bank of Richmond*, 467 U.S. 867, 869 (1984), the Court held "a judgment in a class action determining that an employer did not engage in a general pattern or practice of racial discrimination against the certified class of employees [does not preclude] a class member from maintaining a subsequent civil action alleging an individual claim of racial discrimination against the employer."

A second concern is that class actions are unfair to defendants, who may be forced to settle regardless of the merits by the sheer magnitude of potential liability and costs of defense. This is because of a straightforward economic calculation: as exposure rises, even a very small risk of liability will push a rational defendant to settle. But given Wal-Mart's notorious success in obtaining price concessions from its vendors because of its huge buying power, do you find it odd to be concerned that the potential liability generated by its very size is problematic? And is there something wrong with a system that finds some defendants "too big to sue"?

The third set of concerns arises from fears that class actions may be inimical because they effectively divorce the attorney from her client. This is a standard objection to class actions, and there are certainly many instances where the major beneficiaries of a class action are not the class members but rather the attorneys.

Policy concerns aside, the clearest message of *Wal-Mart* is a practical one: plaintiffs need to first address the size of the class in terms of having the resources to provide notice. It's not impossible that the outer limits of classes will be defined by plaintiffs' attorneys' budgets. Second, plaintiffs must identify a classwide issue, and *Wal-Mart* makes it harder. It seems likely that traditional disparate impact attacks on objective measures such as tests can continue to be mounted. *See McReynolds v. Merrill Lynch, Pierce, Fenner & Smith, Inc.*, 672 F.3d 48 (7th Cir. 2012) (overturning a denial of certification to permit a class action on the employer's "teaming" and "account distribution" policies, which were claimed to have an adverse impact on black brokers). But recall the Court's notation that "the mere claim by employees of the same company that they have suffered a Title VII injury, or even a disparate-impact Title VII injury, gives no cause to believe that all their claims can productively be litigated at once." The class will be limited to those affected by the challenged policy.

The same would be true of systemic disparate treatment cases focused on policies of discrimination such as we saw in *Manhart* and *Johnson Controls*. Further, such suits should still be cognizable if focused on the bias of one decisionmaker (although these might pose numerosity problems). However, the extent to which plaintiffs can identify subjective policies that are nevertheless sufficiently specific under the *Wal-Mart* analysis to be subject to disparate impact analysis remains unclear. One commentator noted the potential of the ruling "to cut short a number of employment discrimination class actions premised on the theory of excessive subjectivity as a discriminatory policy." Suzette M. Malveaux, *How Goliath Won: The Future Implications of* Dukes v. Wal-Mart, 106 Nw. U. L. Rev. Colloquy 34, 44-45 (2011). Even beyond these problems, particular suits may simply be impossible to bring under Rule 23. *See Davis v. Cintas Corp.*, 717 F.3d 476, 489 (6th Cir. 2013) (affirming a district court's denial of certification because the named plaintiff failed to show that the class of women shared a common question of law or fact).

However, some recent cases reject the more extreme negative interpretations of *Wal-Mart*. In *Scott v. Family Dollar Stores, Inc.*, 733 F.3d 105, 114 (4th Cir. 2013) (2-1), the Fourth Circuit read *Wal-Mart* as limited to discretionary decisions by lower-level managers; when "high-level personnel exercise discretion, [the] resulting decisions affect a much larger group, and depending on their rank in the corporate hierarchy, all the employees in the company." *Id.* at 113-14. In other words, *Wal-Mart* did not "set out a per se rule against class certification where subjective decision-making or discretion is alleged." *Id.* at 113. The dissent of Judge Wilkerson complained that majority opinion drained *Wal-Mart* of meaning. *Id.* at 119. *See also Brown v. Nucor Corp.*, 785 F.3d 895 (4th Cir. 2015) (reversing decertification of plant-wide disparate treatment and disparate impact class action by black steel workers in light of statistical and substantial anecdotal evidence of discrimination in promotion decisions in multiple departments). And in *Chicago Teachers Union, Local No. 1 v. Bd. of Educ. of Chi.*, 797 F.3d 426, 437 (7th Cir. 2015), the court found a company-wide practice appropriate for class treatment "even where some decisions in the chain of acts challenged as discriminatory can be exercised by local managers with discretion — at least where the class at issue is affected in a common manner, such as where there is a uniform policy or process applied to all." Thus, subjective, discretionary decisions can share commonality "if they are, for example, the outcome of employment practices or policies controlled by higher-level directors, if all decision-makers exercise discretion in a common way because of a company policy or practice, or if all decision-makers act together as one unit." *Id.* at 438.

In any event, as we will see in the next section, the EEOC can bring the functional equivalent of class actions in some circumstances. Nevertheless, a shift from substantial private enforcement of systemic claims to predominantly public enforcement does not bode well for antidiscrimination law.

G.   FEDERAL GOVERNMENT ENFORCEMENT

Enforcement by the federal government of Title VII and the Americans with Disabilities Act is largely committed to the Equal Employment Opportunity Commission, although the Attorney General retains a role with respect to suits against state and local governments. 42 U.S.C. §2000e-5(f)(1, §706(f)(1). The Age Discrimination in Employment Act has a similar but slightly different enforcement scheme, but no government agency is charged with enforcing §1981.

The enforcement scheme we have examined means that the EEOC is the recipient of a huge number of charges of discrimination, recently exceeding 90,000 annually. The ability of the Commission to effectively process these charges and what that means for its enforcement strategy has been a subject of continued concern. *See generally* Pauline T. Kim, *Addressing Systemic Discrimination: Public Enforcement and the Role of the EEOC,* 95 BU L. Rev. 1133 (2015); Margo Schlanger & Pauline T. Kim, *The Equal Employment Opportunity Commission and Structural Reform of the American Workplace,* 91 Wash. U. L. Rev. 1519 (2014); Stephanie Bornstein, *Rights in Recession: Towards Administrative Antidiscrimination Law,* 33 Yale L. & Pol'y Rev. 119 (2014); Nancy M. Modesitt, *Reinventing the EEOC,* 63 SMU L. Rev. 1237 (2010); Marcia L. McCormick, *The Truth Is Out There: Revamping Federal Antidiscrimination Enforcement for the Twenty-First Century,* 30 Berkley J. Emp. & Lab. L. 193 (2009); Michael Selmi, *The Value of the EEOC: The Agency's Role in Employment Discrimination Law,* 57 Ohio St. L.J. 1 (1996).

Earlier sections exploring the relationship of this administrative procedure to private suits concluded that defects in EEOC charge processing do not affect the right of charging parties to sue employees. Such defects, however, may limit the EEOC when it attempts to sue the employer. For example, defendants in suits brought by the EEOC sometimes seek dismissal because the agency failed to conciliate. In *Mach Mining, LLC v. EEOC,* 135 S. Ct. 1645 (2015), the Court recognized that judicial review of EEOC conciliation efforts was appropriate, but it simultaneously framed the scope of review as exceedingly narrow. It is limited to whether the EEOC informed the employer about the specific allegations and whether the agency "tr[ied] to engage the employer in some form of discussion (whether written or oral), so as to give the employer an opportunity to remedy the allegedly discriminatory practice." *Id.* at 1656. And, should a court determine the EEOC had failed to satisfy these minimal standards, "the appropriate remedy is to order the EEOC to undertake the mandated efforts to obtain voluntary compliance." *Id.* It seems likely that *Mach Mining* will also control challenges to other aspects of agency charge processing. *See EEOC v. Sterling Jewelers Inc.,* 801 F.3d 96 (2d Cir. 2015) (judicial review of an EEOC investigation is similarly limited to whether the agency conducted an investigation, not its sufficiency). *Cf. CRST Van Expedited, Inc. v. EEOC,* 136 S. Ct. 642 (2016) (considering award of attorneys' fees to defendant based largely on the EEOC's failure to investigate before bringing suit).

In terms of investigation, the courts have generally been supportive of EEOC pre-suit efforts, upholding broad agency subpoenas. *See EEOC v. Shell Oil Co.,* 466 U.S. 54 (1984) (liberal approach to what constitutes a sufficient charge to support an agency subpoena); *see also McLane Co. v. EEOC,* 137 S. Ct. 1159 (2017) (district court decisions regarding EEOC subpoenas are reviewable under an abuse of discretion standard); *EEOC v. Aerotek, Inc.,* 815 F.3d 328, 334 (7th Cir. 2016) (upholding enforcement of EEOC administrative subpoena seeking staffing agency's client information in investigation of possible age discrimination). *See generally* Angela D. Morrison, *Misconstruing Notice in EEOC Administrative Processing and Conciliation,* 14 Nev. L.J. 785 (2014).

Defendants have also sought to limit EEOC suits on behalf of individual employees. In *EEOC v. Waffle House, Inc.,* 534 U.S. 279 (2002), the Court permitted the EEOC to obtain relief on behalf of employees even if those employees had agreed to arbitrate any claims against their employers. While recoveries by such employees, either after litigation or by arbitration, would presumably bar duplicate recovery in the EEOC action, the Commission cannot be foreclosed from suing by virtue of an arbitration agreement to which it is not a party. *See also EEOC v. Sidley Austin LLP*, 437 F.3d 695, 696 (7th Cir. 2006) (EEOC can seek damages on behalf of individuals who had agreed to arbitrate any claims against the firm so long as there is no double recovery); *EEOC v. Pemco Aeroplex*, 383 F.3d 1280, 1294 (11th Cir. 2004) (EEOC not bound by previous private action brought by 22 plaintiffs).

A final question concerning EEOC suits relates to the governing time limitations. *Occidental Life Insurance Co. v. EEOC*, 432 U.S. 355 (1977), effectively settled most such issues, holding that there was no statute of limitations for EEOC suits. However, the Court did suggest that laches, or some related doctrine, may limit such suits. *Id.* at 373. See p. 537.

H.   SUIT AGAINST GOVERNMENTAL EMPLOYERS

1.   *State and Local Government Employment*

a.   **Tenth and Eleventh Amendment Challenges**

The application of Title VII, as well as the Age Discrimination in Employment Act and the Americans with Disabilities Act, to state and local governments has survived constitutional challenge on Tenth Amendment grounds. *Garcia v. San Antonio Metro. Trans. Auth.*, 469 U.S. 528 (1985). However, the ADEA and ADA have not been as fortunate with regard to the Eleventh Amendment, which bars private suit against the state or its instrumentalities. Despite Congress's unequivocally expressed intent to override that immunity with respect to both laws, neither statute survived scrutiny insofar as it authorized private suit against the state. *Kimel v. Fla. Bd. of Regents*, 528 U.S. 62 (2000) (ADEA); *Board of Trustees v. Garrett*, 531 U.S. 356 (2001) (Title I of the ADA). *But see Tennessee v. Lane*, 541 U.S. 509 (2004) (upholding abrogation of state immunity in an ADA Title II suit for at least some applications).

Despite *Kimel* and *Garrett*, federal government enforcement is still allowed. *E.g., EEOC v. Bd. of Supervisors for Univ. of La. Sys.*, 539 F.3d 270 (5th Cir. 2009) (EEOC could sue a state to enforce the ADEA, without regard to Eleventh Amendment immunity, and could seek make-whole relief in that suit on behalf of individuals who would be barred by the Eleventh Amendment from suing the state themselves). Second, *Kimel* and *Garrett* do not bar suits against local governmental entities. They merely prohibit private suits against an employer that counts as the state, *see Mt. Healthy City Sch. Dist. Bd. of Ed. v. Doyle*, 429 U.S. 274, 280 (1977) (Eleventh Amendment immunity does not reach to counties and similar municipal corporations), and most public sector employment will remain actionable by private suit because the employers involved are local governmental units.

Third, Eleventh Amendment immunity may be waived by the state, *Lapides v. Board of Regents*, 535 U.S. 613 (2002) (a state can waive its Eleventh Amendment immunity by removing a state lawsuit from state court to federal court), and several circuits have held that state receipt of federal funds expressly conditioned on waiver of immunity does indeed waive that immunity. *E.g., Miller v. Tex. Tech Univ. Health Scis. Ctr.*, 421 F.3d 342 (5th Cir. 2005) (en banc) (a state waives its Eleventh Amendment immunity from suit in federal court under §504 of the Rehabilitation Act of 1973 when it accepts federal funds expressly conditioned on waiver of immunity). *But see Sossamon v. Texas*, 563 U.S. 277, 285 (2011) ("RLUIPA's authorization of 'appropriate relief against a government,' §2000cc-2(a), is not the unequivocal expression of state consent that our precedents require"). Fourth, injunctive relief may be available against state officials under *Ex parte Young*, 209 U.S. 123 (1980).

In contrast to the ADEA and ADA, Title VII was held to trump state Eleventh Amendment immunity in *Fitzpatrick v. Bitzer*, 427 U.S. 445 (1976). This authority was reinforced by *Nevada Department of Human Resources v. Hibbs*, 538 U.S. 721 (2003) (permitting private suit against the state under the Family and Medical Leave Act for family care leave). *Cf. Coleman v. Court of Appeals*, 566 U.S. 30 (rejecting private suit against the state for "self-care" leave under the FMLA).

The rationale for *Fitzpatrick* is that Title VII is partially based on §5 of the Fourteenth Amendment, which accords Congress the power "to enforce, by appropriate legislation, the provisions of this article." In the proper exercise of this power, Congress may abrogate what would otherwise be state immunity to private suit. The Court, however, had held Congress can only *enforce* Fourteenth Amendment rights, not define them. *City of Boerne v. Flores*, 521 U.S. 507, 517 (1997). It is possible, then, that some applications of Title VII suits are not sufficiently linked to the Fourteenth Amendment to be valid. However, the Court has, without noting any problem, enforced disparate impact claims against a state, *Connecticut. v. Teal*, 457 U.S. 440 (1982), and only one circuit has thus far rejected a private Title VII suit on Eleventh Amendment grounds. *See Holmes v. Marion Cnty. Office of Family & Children*, 349 F.3d 914, 921 (7th Cir. 2003) (private suits seeking to enforce a state employer's duty to reasonably accommodate religious beliefs not permitted under the Eleventh Amendment). *See generally* James M. Oleske, Jr., *Federalism, Free Exercise and Title VII: Reconsidering Reasonable Accommodations*, 6 U. Pa. J. Const. L. 525 (2004). While §1981(c) explicitly authorizes private suits against state and local governments, there is a question as to whether suits against such entities remain subject to the constraints applicable to §1983. See p. 274.

b. Exemptions

Remaining federalism concerns in the antidiscrimination statutes are reflected mainly in special statutory provisions and in judicial approaches to interpreting laws, such as exceptions for elected officials and their appointees. For example, Title VII excludes from the definition of "employee"

> any person elected to public office in any State or political subdivision of any State by the qualified voters thereof, or any person chosen by such officer to be on such officer's personal staff, or an appointee on the policymaking level or an immediate adviser with respect to the exercise of the constitutional or legal power of the office.

42 U.S.C. §2000e(f), §701(f). There is a comparable provision in the ADEA. 29 U.S.C. §630(f).

The Supreme Court construed the ADEA version of this exception in *Gregory v. Ashcroft*, 501 U.S. 452 (1991), and held that appointed state judges are within it, in part because Congress had not clearly enough included them in the statute. After *Ashcroft*, Congress passed the Government Employee Rights Act (GERA) to provide the "plain statement" of its intent to intrude into state operations that the Court had required. *See* 42 U.S.C. §2000e-16c. Given *Kimel v. Florida Board of Regents*, 528 U.S. 62 (1999), and *Board of Trustees v. Garrett*, 531 U.S. 356 (2001), the issue seems moot for most ADEA and ADA private suits against state officials. Neverthe-less, it remains a live one for Title VII claims and for ADEA and ADA suits where the employer is a political subdivision. *See Alaska v. EEOC*, 564 F.3d 1062 (9th Cir. 2009) (en banc) (when challenged action would violate the Fourteenth Amendment or First Amendment, GERA validly waived state Eleventh Amendment immunity).

GERA changed the ground rules somewhat. It left the original statutory exemp-tion technically intact but created a new statutory protection for appointed officials by which the EEOC adjudicates disputes through a formal agency hearing. The EEOC's decision is then subject to limited judicial review, rather than the trial de novo that exists in the private sector. *See Depriest v. Milligan*, 823 F.3d 1179 (8th Cir. 2016).

2.   *Federal Employment*

While neither Title VII nor the ADEA originally included the federal government, amendments to both statutes extended their reach to most federal workers. However, rather than merely adding federal employment to the statutes' coverage, Congress added a separate provision to each law, §717 of Title VII, 42 U.S.C. §2000e-16 and §15, 29 U.S.C. §633a, to the ADEA. Although these provisions do not speak expressly of retaliation, they have been held to bar not only discrimination on the prohibited grounds but also retaliation for opposing such discrimination. *Gomez-Perez v. Potter*, 553 U.S. 474 (2008) (ADEA). Most lower courts have also held that retaliation is ille-gal under §717. *E.g., Diggs v. HUD*, 670 F.3d 1353, 1357 (Fed. Cir. 2011), although the Supreme Court avoided deciding that question in *Green v. Brennan*, 136 S. Ct. 769, 774 n.1 (2016). The Americans with Disabilities Act does not generally reach federal employees, but these employees receive comparable protection under the Re-habilitation Act, which specifically adopts the "remedies, procedures, and rights" of §717. 29 U.S.C. §794(a). These procedures are the exclusive avenue for redress for federal employees for harms within their scope. *Brown v. Gen. Servs. Admin.*, 425 U.S. 820 (1976).

However, the procedures we have examined in this chapter do not apply to federal employees. Each statute created a slightly different scheme, both of which basically entrust enforcement to an administrative process. Employees file an administrative complaint with the agency responsible for the discrimination, and, after final agency action on that complaint, the charging party may either appeal to the EEOC or file suit in district court. If appeal to the EEOC does not resolve the matter, suit may then be brought in federal court, where trial is de novo. *Chandler v. Roudebush*, 425 U.S. 840 (1976). These statutes impose requirements, such as time limitations, that are analogous, but not identical, to those governing private sector suit. *See Irwin v. Dep't of Veterans Affairs*, 498 U.S. 89, 95-96 (1990).

Chapter 9

Judicial Relief

A. INTRODUCTION

This chapter explores the judicial relief available once a violation of Title VII, §1981, the ADEA, or the ADA has been proven. These statutes have similar, but distinct, remedial schemes. As a result, relief varies from statute to statute with little rationale other than history. For example, (1) compensatory (traditional tort) damages are available under Title VII, §1981, and the ADA but not under the ADEA; (2) a statutory maximum is placed on compensatory damages in Title VII and ADA actions, but not in §1981 suits.

When Title VII was originally enacted, its proponents did not want it to include compensatory damages because such relief would likely trigger a right to a jury trial at a time when there was rampant race discrimination in jury selection. *See Castenada v. Partida*, 430 U.S. 482 (1977) (systematic exclusion of Latinos from juries). Accordingly, equitable relief administered by a federal judge was believed to be a surer way of vindicating the rights Title VII created. However, compensatory and punitive damages, as well as a jury trial right for such claims, were added to Title VII by the Civil Rights Act of 1991, but only for disparate treatment discrimination; thus, there is neither a jury trial right nor compensatory or punitive damages available for disparate impact claims.

We begin with the policies served by the remedial schemes provided under the antidiscrimination statutes.

ALBEMARLE PAPER CO. v. MOODY
422 U.S. 405 (1975)

Justice STEWART delivered the opinion of the Court.

I

[The district court found that the employer's seniority system violated Title VII by locking black employees into low-level jobs. It ordered the employer to implement a system of "plantwide" seniority, but refused to award backpay.]

II . . .

Though at least some of the members of the plaintiff class obviously suffered a loss of wage opportunities on account of Albemarle's unlawfully discriminatory system of job seniority, the District Court decided that *no* backpay should be awarded to *anyone* in the class. The court declined to make such an award on two stated grounds: the lack of "evidence of bad faith non-compliance with the Act," and the fact that "the defendants would be substantially prejudiced" by an award of backpay that was demanded contrary to an earlier representation and late in the progress of the litigation. . . . [T]he Court of Appeals reversed, holding that backpay could be denied only in "special circumstances." The petitioners argue that the Court of Appeals was in error — that a district court has virtually unfettered discretion to award or deny backpay. . . .

. . . [B]ackpay is not an automatic or mandatory remedy; like all other remedies under the Act, it is one which the courts "may" invoke. The scheme implicitly recognizes that there may be cases calling for one remedy but not another, and — owing to the structure of the federal judiciary — these choices are, of course, left in the first instance to the district courts. However, such discretionary choices are not left to a court's "inclination, but to its judgment; and its judgment is to be guided by sound legal principles." The power to award backpay was bestowed by Congress, as part of a complex legislative design directed at a historic evil of national proportions. A court must exercise this power "in light of the large objectives of the Act." That the court's discretion is equitable in nature hardly means that it is unfettered by meaningful standards or shielded from thorough appellate review. . . .

"Equity eschews mechanical rules . . . [and] depends on flexibility." But when Congress invokes the Chancellor's conscience to further transcendent legislative purposes, what is required is the principled application of standards consistent with those purposes and not "equity [which] varies like the Chancellor's foot." Important national goals would be frustrated by a regime of discretion that "produce[d] different results for breaches of duty in situations that cannot be differentiated in policy."

The District Court's decision must therefore be measured against the purposes which inform Title VII. As the Court observed in *Griggs* [*v. Duke Power Co.*, reproduced at p. 167], the primary objective was a prophylactic one: "It was to achieve equality of employment opportunities and remove barriers that have operated in the past to favor an identifiable group of white employees over other employees." Backpay has an obvious connection with this purpose. If employers faced only the prospect of an injunctive order, they would have little incentive to shun practices of dubious legality. It is the reasonably certain prospect of a backpay award that "provide[s] the spur or catalyst which causes employers and unions to self-examine and to self-evaluate their employment practices and to endeavor to eliminate, so far as possible, the last vestiges of an unfortunate and ignominious page in this country's history."

It is also the purpose of Title VII to make persons whole for injuries suffered on account of unlawful employment discrimination. This is shown by the very fact that Congress took care to arm the courts with full equitable powers. For it is the historic purpose of equity to "secur[e] complete justice." "[W]here federally protected rights have been invaded, it has been the rule from the beginning that courts will be alert to adjust their remedies so as to grant the necessary relief." Title VII deals with legal injuries of an economic character occasioned by racial or other antiminority discrimination. The terms "complete justice" and "necessary relief" have acquired a clear meaning in such circumstances. Where racial discrimination is concerned, "the [district] court has not merely the power but the duty to render a decree which will so far as possible eliminate the discriminatory effects of the past as well as bar like discrimination in the future."

And where a legal injury is of an economic character, "[t]he general rule is, that when a wrong has been done, and the law gives a remedy, the compensation shall be equal to the injury. The latter is the standard by which the former is to be measured. The injured party is to be placed, as near as may be, in the situation he would have occupied if the wrong had not been committed." . . .

The District Court's stated grounds for denying backpay in this case must be tested against these standards. The first ground was that Albemarle's breach of Title VII had not been in "bad faith." This is not a sufficient reason for denying backpay. Where an employer *has* shown bad faith — by maintaining a practice which he knew to be illegal or of highly questionable legality — he can make no claims whatsoever on the Chancellor's conscience. But, under Title VII, the mere absence of bad faith simply opens the door to equity; it does not depress the scales in the employer's favor. If backpay were awardable only upon a showing of bad faith, the remedy would become a punishment for moral turpitude, rather than a compensation for workers' injuries. This would read the "make whole" purpose right out of Title VII, for a worker's injury is no less real simply because his employer did not inflict it in "bad faith." Title VII is not concerned with the employer's "good intent or absence of discriminatory intent" for "Congress directed the thrust of the Act to the *consequences* of employment practices, not simply the motivation." *Griggs*. To condition the awarding of backpay on a showing of "bad faith" would be to open an enormous chasm between injunctive and backpay relief under Title VII. There is nothing on the face of the statute or in its legislative history that justifies the creation of drastic and categorical distinctions between those two remedies.

The District Court also grounded its denial of backpay on the fact that the respondents initially disclaimed any interest in backpay, first asserting their claim five years after the complaint was filed. The court concluded that the petitioners had been "prejudiced" by this conduct. . . .

. . . Title VII contains no legal bar to raising backpay claims after the complaint for injunctive relief has been filed, or indeed after a trial on that complaint has been had. Furthermore, Fed. Rule Civ. Proc. 54(c) directs that "every final judgment shall grant the relief to which the party in whose favor it is rendered is entitled, even if the party has not demanded such relief in his pleadings." But a party may not be "entitled" to relief if its conduct of the cause has improperly and substantially prejudiced the other party. The respondents here were not merely tardy, but also inconsistent, in demanding backpay. To deny backpay because a *particular* cause has been prosecuted in an eccentric fashion, prejudicial to the other party, does not offend the broad purposes of Title VII. This is not to say, however, that the District Court's ruling was necessarily correct. . . .

[Concurring opinions omitted.]

NOTES

1. *The Statutory Objectives.* Based on the twin statutory objectives of Title VII — eliminating discrimination and making its victims whole — the Court created a presumption of full, make-whole relief: "given a finding of unlawful discrimination, backpay should be denied only for reasons which, if applied generally, would not frustrate the central statutory purposes of eradicating discrimination throughout the economy and making persons whole for injuries suffered through past discrimination." Notice, however, that "make-whole" was an overstatement of the Title VII remedial scheme when *Albemarle* was decided since no damages other than backpay were available. The 1991 Civil Rights Act's addition of compensatory damages to Title VII perfected the make-whole goal for disparate treatment, and its addition of punitive damages added a deterrent component that had previously been lacking.

2. *Limiting the Twin Objectives.* The Court cut back on *Albemarle* in *Los Angeles Dep't of Water & Power v. Manhart*, 435 U.S. 702, 719-21 (1978), reproduced in part at p. 94, which held the employer had violated Title VII when, pursuant to sex-based actuarial tables, female employees were required to contribute more than male employees to its retirement program. While this was discrimination in compensation against the women, the Court also held that the district court erred in ordering a refund of the excess contributions to the plaintiffs. After noting that "conscientious and intelligent administrators of pension funds" might have thought the program was legal and that there was no reason to think that they would not amend their practices without the threat of backpay liability, the Court stressed the potentially devastating effects on a pension fund, which "would fall in large part on innocent third parties" since the fund would be "forced to meet unchanged obligations with diminished assets." *Manhart* certainly sets a limit to *Albemarle*'s emphasis on the make-whole and prophylactic purposes of Title VII, but there has been little evidence that it has had much influence outside the context in which it arose. Still, aren't backpay awards payable by the employer, which would not put the retirement plan at risk?

3. *Equitable vs. Legal Remedies.* Section 706(g)(1), as interpreted by *Albemarle*, establishes that Title VII backpay is in some sense discretionary and thus an equitable remedy. In an omitted concurrence, Justice Rehnquist explained the importance of this characterization: the Seventh Amendment gives a right to trial by jury to "suits at common law" but not to claims in equity. The less discretionary and the more automatic the backpay award, the more it would resemble a legal award of damages and therefore trigger a right to jury trial. While the 1991 Civil Rights Act authorized compensatory and punitive damages for intentional discrimination claims under Title VII, with the concomitant right to a jury trial, the backpay remedy under that statute (and therefore under the ADA) remains equitable. In contrast, "unpaid wages" under the ADEA (the equivalent of "backpay") is a legal claim to which the right to jury trial attaches. *Lorillard v. Pons*, 434 U.S. 575 (1978).

B.   EQUITABLE RELIEF TO THE VICTIMS OF DISCRIMINATION

1.   *Reinstatement, Retroactive Seniority, and Injunctive Relief*

Albemarle establishes that backpay is an equitable remedy, but it is only one of a broad array of such remedies available in Title VII actions. Section 703(g) provides that, when a violation is established, "the court may enjoin the respondent from engaging in such unlawful employment practice, and order such affirmative action as may be appropriate, which may include, but is not limited to, reinstatement or hiring of employees, with or without back pay . . . or any other equitable relief as the court deems appropriate." Both prohibitory and restorative equitable relief may be ordered. The most common prohibitory relief is an injunction against the discriminatory practice, and a common form of restorative relief is an award of instatement or reinstatement — ordering the employer to hire or rehire the victim of discrimination. Another form of restorative equitable relief is an award of retroactive seniority — the seniority lost due to the discrimination.

As for future discrimination, there is said to be a presumption that the employer will be enjoined from further discrimination "absent clear and convincing proof of no reasonable probability of further noncompliance with the law." *EEOC v. Boh Bros. Constr. Co., L.L.C.*, 731 F.3d 444, 469-70 (5th Cir. 2013) (citation and internal quotation omitted). In *EEOC v. KarenKim, Inc.*, 698 F.3d 92 (2d Cir. 2012), the district court abused its discretion by declining to order injunctive relief to ensure that an individual found responsible for egregious acts of sexual harassment against multiple female employees could not continue his harassing conduct.

However, in remedying past discrimination, the interests of other workers are typically taken into account. In *Franks v. Bowman Transp. Co.*, 424 U.S. 747 (1976), the plaintiffs had all applied for but been denied over-the-road truck driving jobs because of their race. Having found Bowman liable, the trial court enjoined the defendant's discriminatory practices and ordered the victims to be hired to fill any vacancies. However, since there were not enough vacancies to ensure immediate employment to all of them, the court applied a "first available vacancy" rule under which each victim would receive front pay until he was hired as jobs opened up. This effectively meant that incumbent workers would not be bumped, or displaced, by successful plaintiffs. *See also Doll v. Brown*, 75 F.3d 1200, 1205 (7th Cir. 1996) (effects on innocent parties may be taken into account in deciding whether to bump them or instead to award front pay to victims of discrimination until a vacancy arises).

Franks also decided a related issue: whether, once hired, the plaintiffs were entitled to seniority retroactive to the time when they would have been hired absent discrimination. The Supreme Court held that the full remedial purpose of Title VII would not be achieved without a grant of what the Court called "rightful place" seniority. Echoing *Albemarle Paper*, it wrote: "the denial of seniority relief to victims of illegal racial discrimination in hiring is permissible "only for reasons which, if applied generally, would not frustrate the central statutory purposes of eradicating discrimination throughout the economy and making persons whole for injuries suffered through past discrimination." Since job assignment, and therefore to some extent pay depended on seniority as compared with other workers, a rehire order without seniority "falls far short of a 'make-whole' remedy." The Court went on:

> A concomitant award of the seniority credit [each victim] presumptively would have earned but for the wrongful treatment would also seem necessary in the absence of justification for denying that relief. Without an award of seniority dating from the time when he was discriminatorily refused employment, an individual who applies for and obtains employment as an OTR driver pursuant to the District Court's order will never obtain his rightful place in the hierarchy of seniority according to which these various employment benefits are distributed. He will perpetually remain subordinate to persons who, but for the illegal discrimination, would have been in respect to entitlement to these benefits his inferiors. . . .

424 U.S. at 767-68. The Court rejected the argument that rightful place seniority should be denied because it would conflict with the economic interest of the incumbent Bowman employees: "[i]f relief under Title VII can be denied merely because the majority group of employees, who have not suffered discrimination, will be unhappy about it, there will be little hope of correcting the wrongs to which the Act is directed." *Id.* at 774 (internal quotation omitted).

Justice Powell, joined by then-Justice Rehnquist, dissented in part. They would distinguish *benefits* seniority from *competitive* seniority. Granting vacations and other benefits does not interfere with the interest of other employees; in contrast, slotting plaintiffs into the seniority ladder for competitive purposes, such as layoff, imposes no cost on the employer but instead penalizes incumbent employees who have not been shown to have discriminated.

Although apparently aligned with *Albemarle Paper*, the *Franks* Court's remedial philosophy differs markedly from that expressed in the earlier case. The latter opinion grandly spoke of granting "complete justice" and said that courts have "the duty to render a decree which will so far as possible eliminate the discriminatory effects of the past." *Franks*, on the other hand, emphasized that the seniority relief sought in that case "in no sense constitutes 'complete relief,' " 424 U.S. at 776, because it did not grant the class members the positions they would have had in the absence of discrimination. Rather, individuals hired instead of these victims maintained their original date of hire as their date of seniority. Thus, in a future layoff, a victim of prior discrimination and the person hired instead of her would have equal seniority protection because they shared the same date of hire. Further, in a systemic case, any given victim of discrimination could be pushed well down the seniority ladder because those actually hired retained their seniority. Seth D. Harris, in *Innocence and The Sopranos*, 46 N.Y.L. Sch. L. Rev. 577, 580 (2004), argues that the Supreme Court "has repeatedly relied on the innocence of white and male workers to deprive African-American and female discrimination victims of complete relief from discrimination."

These kinds of issues have become less important as formal seniority systems have declined with the decline of the union movement, although employers sometimes impose such systems unilaterally. See *U.S. Airways v. Barnett*, reproduced at p. 474.

Can a court award tenure to a successful plaintiff in an academic setting? This is rare but not unknown. *See Brown v. Trs. of Boston Univ.*, 891 F.2d 337, 360 (1st Cir. 1989) (tenure awarded after court found university had "impermissibly discriminated in making a tenure decision"); *Kunda v. Muhlenberg Coll.*, 621 F.2d 532 (3d Cir. 1980) (tenure award appropriate, at least where district court did not have to evaluate plaintiff's teaching, scholarship, and service). *But see Gurmankin v. Costanzo*, 626 F.2d 1115 (3d Cir. 1980) (affirming the denial of a tenure award in a §1983 suit when the school district had not evaluated plaintiff's qualifications and performance). *See generally* Scott Moss, *Against "Academic Deference": How Recent Developments in Employment Discrimination Law Undercut an Already Dubious Doctrine*, 27 Berkeley J. Emp. & Lab. L. 1 (2006). What about ordering an employer to make an employee a partner? The trial court granted Ann Hopkins partnership on remand in *Price Waterhouse*, 737 F. Supp. 1202 (D.D.C. 1990).

2. Who Gets Retroactive Seniority and Backpay?

Awarding retroactive seniority and backpay can pose especially difficult problems in systemic cases where a large number of individuals have been the victims of various acts of discrimination extending over a long period of time and involving numerous employment decisions. Must the court determine the precise injuries suffered by each class member when a simpler and less burdensome alternative would provide substantial justice? What if individual determinations are highly impractical because of the factual complexities of the case?

TEAMSTERS v. UNITED STATES
431 U.S. 324 (1977)

Justice STEWART delivered the opinion of the Court. . . .

I

[After finding that the defendant had a standard operating procedure of discriminating against blacks and Latinos by not hiring them for line-driver jobs, the question was what relief was appropriate and to whom. The] Court of Appeals held that all Negro and Spanish-surnamed incumbent employees were entitled to bid for future line-driver jobs on the basis of their company seniority, and that once a class member had filled a job, he could use his full company seniority — even if it predated the effective date of Title VII — for all purposes, including bidding and layoff. . . .

III

[The Supreme Court held that individual post-Act discriminatees "may obtain full 'make-whole' relief, including retroactive seniority, but such seniority may not begin before the effective date of Title VII." The Court then turned to the relief awarded below.]

The petitioners argue generally that the . . . Court of Appeals' [seniority relief] sweeps with too broad a brush by granting a remedy to employees who were not shown to be actual victims of unlawful discrimination. Specifically, the petitioners assert that no employee should be entitled to relief until the Government demonstrates that he was an actual victim of the company's discriminatory practices; [and] that no employee who did not apply for a line-driver job should be granted retroactive competitive seniority. . . .

A

The petitioners' first contention is in substance that the Government's burden of proof in a pattern or practice case must be equivalent to that outlined in *McDonnell Douglas v. Green* [reproduced at p. 14]. Since the Government introduced specific evidence of company discrimination against only some 40 employees, they argue that the District Court properly refused to award retroactive seniority to the remainder of the class of minority incumbent employees. . . .

In *Franks v. Bowman Transportation Co*, we held that the trial court had erred in placing this burden on the individual plaintiffs [to show they were qualified and a vacancy had been available]. By "demonstrating the existence of a discriminatory hiring pattern and practice," the plaintiffs had made out a prima facie case of discrimination against individual class members; the burden therefore shifted to the employer "to prove that individuals who reapply were not in fact victims of previous hiring discrimination." The *Franks* case thus illustrates another means by which a Title VII plaintiff's initial burden of proof can be met. The class there alleged a broad-based

policy of employment discrimination; upon proof of that allegation there were reasonable grounds to infer that individual hiring decisions were made in pursuit of the
discriminatory policy and to require the employer to come forth with evidence dispel-
ling that inference.[45]

Although not all class actions will necessarily follow the *Franks* model, the nature
of a pattern-or-practice suit brings it squarely within our holding in *Franks*. . . .

. . . When the Government seeks individual relief for the victims of the discriminatory practice, a district court must usually conduct additional proceedings after the
liability phase of the trial to determine the scope of individual relief. The petitioners'
contention in this case is that if the Government has not, in the course of proving a
pattern or practice, already brought forth specific evidence that each individual was
discriminatorily denied an employment opportunity, it must carry that burden at the
second, "remedial" stage of trial. That basic contention was rejected in the *Franks*
case. As was true of the particular facts in *Franks*, and as is typical of Title VII pattern-or-practice suits, the question of individual relief does not arise until it has been
proved that the employer has followed an employment policy of unlawful discrimination. The force of that proof does not dissipate at the remedial stage of the trial. The
employer cannot, therefore, claim that there is no reason to believe that its individual
employment decisions were discriminatorily based; it has already been shown to have
maintained a policy of discriminatory decisionmaking.

The proof of the pattern or practice supports an inference that any particular
employment decision, during the period in which the discriminatory policy was in
force, was made in pursuit of that policy. The Government need only show that an
alleged individual discriminatee unsuccessfully applied for a job and therefore was a
potential victim of the proved discrimination. As in *Franks*, the burden then rests on
the employer to demonstrate that the individual applicant was denied an employment
opportunity for lawful reasons. . . .

On remand, therefore, every post-Act minority group applicant for a line-driver
position will be presumptively entitled to relief, subject to a showing by the company
that its earlier refusal to place the applicant in a line-driver job was not based on its
policy of discrimination.

B

. . . We now decide that an incumbent employee's failure to apply for a job is
not an inexorable bar to an award of retroactive seniority. Individual nonapplicants
must be given an opportunity to undertake their difficult task of proving that they
should be treated as applicants and therefore are presumptively entitled to relief
accordingly.

---

45. The holding in *Franks* that proof of a discriminatory pattern and practice creates a rebuttable
presumption in favor of individual relief is consistent with the manner in which presumptions are created generally. Presumptions shifting the burden of proof are often created to reflect judicial evaluations
of probabilities and to conform with a party's superior access to the proof. These factors were present in
Franks. Although the prima facie case did not conclusively demonstrate that all of the employer's decisions were part of the proved discriminatory pattern and practice, it did create a greater likelihood that
any single decision was a component of the overall pattern. Moreover, the finding of a pattern or practice
changed the position of the employer to that of a proved wrongdoer. Finally, the employer was in the best
position to show why any individual employee was denied an employment opportunity. . . .

(1)

[T]he company's assertion that a person who has not actually applied for a job can never be awarded seniority relief cannot prevail. The effects of and the injuries suffered from discriminatory employment practices are not always confined to those who were expressly denied a requested employment opportunity. A consistently enforced discriminatory policy can surely deter job applications from those who are aware of it and are unwilling to subject themselves to the humiliation of explicit and certain rejection.

If an employer should announce his policy of discrimination by a sign reading "Whites Only" on the hiring-office door, his victims would not be limited to the few who ignored the sign and subjected themselves to personal rebuffs. The same message can be communicated to potential applicants more subtly but just as clearly by an employer's actual practices — by his consistent discriminatory treatment of actual applicants, by the manner in which he publicizes vacancies, his recruitment techniques, his responses to casual or tentative inquiries, and even by the racial or ethnic composition of that part of his workforce from which he has discriminatorily excluded members of minority groups. When a person's desire for a job is not translated into a formal application solely because of his unwillingness to engage in a futile gesture he is as much a victim of discrimination as is he who goes through the motions of submitting an application. . . .

(2)

To conclude that a person's failure to submit an application for a job does not inevitably and forever foreclose his entitlement to seniority relief under Title VII is a far cry, however, from holding that nonapplicants are always entitled to such relief. A nonapplicant must show that he was a potential victim of unlawful discrimination. Because he is necessarily claiming that he was deterred from applying for the job by the employer's discriminatory practices, his is the not always easy burden of proving that he would have applied for the job had it not been for those practices. When this burden is met, the nonapplicant is in a position analogous to that of an applicant. . . .

While the scope and duration of the company's discriminatory policy can leave little doubt that the futility of seeking line-driver jobs was communicated to the company's minority employees, that in itself is insufficient. The known prospect of discriminatory rejection shows only that employees who wanted line-driving jobs may have been deterred from applying for them. It does not show which of the nonapplicants actually wanted such jobs, or which possessed the requisite qualifications.[53]

There are differences between city- and line-driving jobs, for example, but the desirability of the latter is not so self-evident as to warrant a conclusion that all employees would prefer to be line drivers if given a free choice. Indeed, a substantial number of white city drivers who were not subjected to the company's discriminatory practices were apparently content to retain their city jobs.

---

53. Inasmuch as the purpose of the nonapplicant's burden of proof will be to establish that his status is similar to that of the applicant, he must bear the burden of coming forward with the basic information about his qualifications that he would have presented in the application. . . . [T]he burden then will be on the employer to show that the nonapplicant was nonetheless not a victim of discrimination. For example, the employer might show that there were other, more qualified persons who would have been chosen for a particular vacancy, or that the nonapplicant's stated qualifications were insufficient.

[However, a nonapplicant's current willingness to transfer into a line-driver position does not necessarily show he would have applied earlier but for his knowledge of the company's discriminatory policy. That is because, should such a person be successful, he would become a line-driver with retroactive seniority. "A willingness to accept the job security and bidding power afforded by retroactive seniority says little about what choice an employee would have made had he previously been given the opportunity freely to choose a starting line-driver job" when he would have started with no seniority and the substantial risk of layoff or less lucrative assignments.]

NOTES

1. *Bifurcation of Systemic Litigation.* The Court envisions that systemic cases in which relief is sought for a group of victims should be tried in two stages: the first focuses on establishing liability and, if liability is found, the second stage determines the appropriate remedies. Systemic cases include both EEOC suits and class actions. One great advantage of a systemic case for plaintiffs is that, once liability is established, the defendant carries the burden of proving that the presumptive victims of that discrimination were, in fact, not discriminated against. But we've seen that most circuits do not allow the use of systemic disparate treatment by individuals except in class actions. See Note 3, p. 233.

2. *Identifying the Beneficiaries of the Presumption.* Who are the presumptive victims? In *Teamsters*, as in *Franks*, those African Americans and Latinos who applied for but were denied line-driver jobs were clearly victims. The Court also allowed nonapplicants to establish that they too were victims of defendant's practice of not hiring minority group members for the over-the-road jobs. But *Teamsters* held that a nonapplicant's present desire to become a line driver did not establish that he would have sought the position earlier. Would testimony that a person would have applied for an over-the-road job but for the defendant's known discrimination suffice?

3. *Rebutting the Presumption.* To escape liability to a presumptive victim, it seems likely that the employer will have to establish the "same decision anyway" defense. While the systemic cases we have examined precede the adoption of the "same decision" defense in §706(g)(2)(B) for "motivating factor" cases, see p. 69, the current statute seems to reflect what the Court held in the earlier systemic cases.

4. *Disparate Impact.* Is the *Teamsters* burden-shifting procedure applicable in disparate impact cases? It seems likely, with the twist that determining whether the presumptive victim is qualified can itself be problematic. Suppose the individual had been denied a position because she had failed a written examination with a disparate impact. Could the employer satisfy its burden by showing that she had later failed a written test that was job related? *Cf. Cohen v. West Haven Bd.*, 638 F.2d 496 (2d Cir. 1980) (failure of applicants to pass a nondiscriminatory agility test in 1978 did not demonstrate that they were disqualified after failing a discriminatory test in 1977).

5. *Is Each Victim Entitled to Full Relief?* The courts think the employer's liability cannot exceed the amount of backpay that was lost; that is, there is "one backpay award." E.g., *United States v. City of Miami*, 195 F.3d 1292 (11th Cir. 1999). That means that a court must either decide which of several competitors for a single position would have gotten the job absent discrimination or it must split the award among each presumptive victim. Suppose two employees were discriminatorily denied transfer to a vacant position that was filled by a third employee, but the court cannot determine who would have received the position in the absence of discrimination. *Doll v.*

Brown, 75 F.3d 1200 (7th Cir. 1996), raised, but did not decide, that in such cases each victim should receive the percentage of a backpay award that corresponds to the chance he had to obtain the position. *See generally* Paul M. Secunda, *A Public Interest Model for Applying Lost Chance Theory to Probabilistic Injuries in Employment Discrimination Cases*, 2005 Wis. L. Rev. 747. The need for probabilistic determinations stems from the "one backpay award" principle. Is that principle consistent with *Albemarle Paper* and *Teamsters?*

In any event, whether probabilistic awards are permissible without employer consent is doubtful after *Wal-Mart Stores, Inc. v. Dukes,* which held that a class action seeking individualized awards for class members could not be brought under Rule 23(b)(2). See p. 553. In the course of the opinion, the Court stated that "Wal-Mart is entitled to individualized determinations of each employee's eligibility for backpay," citing §2000e-5(g)(2)(A) (restricting remedies if the employer can show that it took an adverse employment action against an employee "for any reason other than discrimination"). 564 U.S. at 366. The Court then referred to *Teamsters*, noting that, in the remedies phase, "the burden of proof will shift to the company, but it will have the right to raise any individual affirmative defenses it may have, and to 'demonstrate that the individual applicant was denied an employment opportunity for lawful reasons.' " *Id. See* Melissa Hart, *Civil Rights and Systemic Wrongs*, 32 Berkeley J. Emp. & Lab. L. 455, 461 (2011) ("By rejecting statistical modeling as a permissible remedial approach, the Court reduces the structural and systemic claim to the sum of its individual parts and gives those individual parts the power to destroy the whole").

6. *Equal Protection and Remedying Discrimination.* Courts ordering remedies against defendants in discrimination cases obviously are governmental actors for the purpose of constitutional equal protection principles. Since the beneficiaries of hiring orders, awards of backpay, and grants of retroactive seniority are usually women and minority men — actions based on race or sex — how do those awards of remedies comport with equal protection? The problem arises largely because of the impossibility of identifying each victim of discrimination. Were each actual victim to be identified and instated with appropriate seniority, there would be no problem since the Court has held that remedying discrimination against actual victims is a compelling state interest. *Wygant v. Jackson Bd. of Educ.*, 476 U.S. 267, 274 (1986) ("the Court has insisted upon some showing of prior discrimination by the governmental unit involved before allowing limited use of racial classifications in order to remedy such discrimination"). *See also Parents Involved in Cmty. Schs. v. Seattle Sch. Dist. No. 1,* 551 U.S. 701 (2007) (all members of the Court appeared to accept the use of race to provide a remedy for the actual victims of the past intentional discrimination of the defendant).

In the real world, however, providing relief to identifiable victims will rarely, if ever, result in the employer's work force becoming reflective of the racial or gender composition it would have had absent discrimination. Is further relief permissible to achieve that goal? In *Local 28, Sheet Metal Workers' Int'l Ass'n v. EEOC*, 478 U.S. 421 (1986), the Court limited, but did not bar, the use of race by courts in remedying employment discrimination in such situations. Since the case involved a union that had long persisted in excluding African Americans from membership, such a remedy was appropriate only in light of (1) the pervasive and egregious discrimination of the defendant, and (2) its history of discouraging nonwhites from applying for membership. Even then, the remedy could not seek to *maintain* racial balancing, although using race as a benchmark for progress was permissible; thus, the court order to admit nonwhite applicants ended when the goal of minority membership matched the goal that had been established. Finally, the remedy must not trammel the rights of innocent third parties. The high-water mark of class race-based remedies is *United States v. Paradise*, 480 U.S. 149 (1987), which approved the use of race to order the one-for-one promotion of black and white state police officers to the position of sergeant, even though some of the African American beneficiaries of that relief had not themselves been shown to be victims of discrimination. *Paradise* was based not only on the proven disparate treatment by the defendant but also its repeated flouting of earlier, less drastic orders.

3.   *Limits on Backpay*

Each antidiscrimination statute permits the recovery of income lost due to the employer's discrimination. Under Title VII (and the ADA by incorporation), that is an award of "backpay," 42 U.S.C. §2000e-5(g)(1); under the ADEA, the equivalent award is for "unpaid wages," 29 U.S.C. §626. In both cases, recovery includes all the compensation the successful plaintiff would have received in the absence of discrimination — lost wages, raises, overtime compensation, bonuses, vacation pay, and retirement benefits. *E.g., United States v. Burke*, 504 U.S. 229 (1992). And the calculation is not necessarily predicated on what the plaintiff *was* earning when the discrimination occurred but rather on what she *would have* earned, *see Howe v. City of Akron*, 801 F.3d 718, 746 (6th Cir. 2015) (step raises should be factored in); one court even thought that backpay could be based on what another employer would have paid plaintiff but for the discrimination. *See Szeinbach v. Ohio State Univ.*, 820 F.3d 814 (6th Cir. 2016). Whatever the amount, prejudgment interest must be added to the award. *Howe, supra.*

Title VII limits backpay to "not more than two years prior to the filing of a charge with the Commission," §2000e-5(g)(1). *See* 29 U.S.C. §255. Although §1981 does not contain an express limitation on the beginning of the backpay period, the applicable statute of limitations operates to limit recovery. See pp. 541-542. The ADEA limitations period is less clear because it lacks a statute of limitations or backpay cutoff. *See* Charles A. Sullivan & Lauren Walter, Employment Discrimination Law and Practice §13.09[C] (2008).

All recoveries are subject to the plaintiff's duty to mitigate. Thus, Title VII provides that "[i]nterim earnings or amounts earnable with reasonable diligence . . . shall operate to reduce the backpay otherwise allowable." Although the ADEA does not have an explicit provision to that effect, mitigation is required. *E.g., Palasota v. Haggar Clothing Co.*, 499 F.3d 474, 486 (5th Cir. 2007).

a.   The Title VII and ADA Backpay Period

The beginning date of the Title VII backpay period is normally the date the plaintiff first lost wages due to the discrimination at issue so long as it is not more than two years prior to the filing of the predicate EEOC charge. *Howe v. City of Akron*, 801 F.3d 718, 746 (6th Cir. 2015). This may or may not be the same date the discriminatory act occurred for purposes of the EEOC filing period since, under the rules we studied in Chapter 8, the charge filing period may start running before any financial consequences are felt. *See Del. State Coll. v. Ricks*, 449 U.S. 250 (1980) (filing period began to run when plaintiff was informed that he would be terminated at the end of the following academic year).

The backpay period normally ends on the date of judgment, *e.g.*, *Walsdorf v. Bd. of Comm'rs*, 857 F.2d 1047 (5th Cir. 1988), but can terminate before this date. If, for example, the plaintiff has died or would have been permanently laid off prior to the date of judgment, the backpay period ends on the date his employment would have ceased. *See Zisumbo v. Ogden Reg'l Med. Ctr.*, 801 F.3d 1185, 1207 (10th Cir. 2015) (not an abuse of discretion for the district court to end backpay upon the plaintiff's conviction for a misdemeanor assault unconnected with work when the defendant would have terminated him for that conviction). More controversially, the backpay period may also end on the date the discriminate either resigns his position with the defendant or rejects the defendant's offer of employment.

FORD MOTOR CO. v. EEOC
458 U.S. 219 (1982)

Justice O'CONNOR delivered the opinion of the Court.

This case presents the question whether an employer charged with discrimination in hiring can toll the continuing accrual of backpay liability under §706(g) of Title VII simply by unconditionally offering the claimant the job previously denied, or whether the employer also must offer seniority retroactive to the date of the alleged discrimination. . . .

I

In June and July 1971, Judy Gaddis, Rebecca Starr, and Zettie Smith applied at a Ford Motor Company (Ford) parts warehouse located in Charlotte, North Carolina, for jobs as "picker-packers." . . . Gaddis and Starr recently had been laid off from equivalent jobs at a nearby General Motors (GM) warehouse, and Smith had comparable prior experience. . . . Ford, however, [discriminatorily] filled the three vacant positions with men. . . .

In January 1973, [GM] recalled Gaddis and Starr to their former positions at its warehouse. The following July, while they were still working at GM, a single vacancy opened up at Ford. Ford offered the job to Gaddis, without seniority retroactive to her 1971 application. Ford's offer, however, did not require Gaddis to abandon or compromise her Title VII claim against Ford. Gaddis did not accept the job, in part because she did not want to be the only woman working at the warehouse, and in part because she did not want to lose the seniority she had earned at [GM]. Ford then made the same unconditional offer to Starr, who declined for the same reasons. . . . [In 1974, Gaddis and Starr were again laid off by GM.]

[The Court of Appeals concluded that Ford's 1973 offer was "incomplete and unacceptable" without retroactive seniority and that Gaddis and Starr were entitled to backpay from 1971 through the 1977 trial.]

III

[T]he legal rules fashioned to implement Title VII should be designed, consistent with other Title VII policies, to encourage Title VII defendants promptly to make curative, unconditional job offers to Title VII claimants, thereby bringing defendants into "voluntary compliance" and ending discrimination far more quickly than could litigation proceeding at its often ponderous pace. Delays in litigation unfortunately are now commonplace, forcing the victims of discrimination to suffer years of under-employment or unemployment before they can obtain a court order awarding them the jobs unlawfully denied them. . . .

The rule tolling the further accrual of backpay liability if the defendant offers the claimant the job originally sought well serves the objective of ending discrimination through voluntary compliance, for it gives an employer a strong incentive to hire the Title VII claimant. While the claimant may be no more attractive than the other job applicants, a job offer to the claimant will free the employer of the threat of liability for further backpay damages. Since paying backpay damages is like paying an extra worker who never came to work, Ford's proposed rule gives the Title VII claimant a decided edge over other competitors for the job he seeks.

The rule adopted by the court below, on the other hand, fails to provide the same incentive, because it makes hiring the Title VII claimant more costly than hiring one of the other applicants for the same job. To give the claimant retroactive seniority before an adjudication of liability, the employer must be willing to pay the additional costs of the fringe benefits that come with the seniority that newly hired workers usu-ally do not receive. More important, the employer must also be prepared to cope with the deterioration in morale, labor unrest, and reduced productivity that may be engendered by inserting the claimant into the seniority ladder over the heads of the incumbents who have earned their places through their work on the job. In many cases, moreover, disruption of the existing seniority system will violate a collective bargaining agreement, with all that such a violation entails for the employer's labor relations. . . .

IV

Title VII's primary goal, of course, is to end discrimination; the victims of job dis-crimination want jobs, not lawsuits. But when unlawful discrimination does occur, Title VII's secondary, fallback purpose is to compensate the victims for their injuries. To this end, §706(g) aims "'to make the victims of unlawful discrimination whole'" by restoring them, "'so far as possible . . . to a position where they would have been were it not for the unlawful discrimination.'" We now turn to consider whether the rule urged by Ford not only better serves the goal of ending discrimination, but also properly compensates injured Title VII claimants.

A

If Gaddis and Starr had rejected an unconditional offer from Ford before they were recalled to their jobs at GM, tolling Ford's backpay liability from the time of Ford's offer plainly would be consistent with providing Gaddis and Starr full compensation for their injuries. An unemployed or underemployed claimant, like all other Title VII claimants, is subject to the statutory duty to minimize damages set out in §706(g). This duty, rooted in an ancient principle of law, requires the claimant to use reason-able diligence in finding other suitable employment. Although the un- or underem-ployed claimant need not go into another line of work, accept a demotion, or take a demeaning position, he forfeits his right to backpay if he refuses a job substantially equivalent to the one he was denied. Consequently, an employer charged with unlaw-ful discrimination often can toll the accrual of backpay liability by unconditionally offering the claimant the job he sought, and thereby providing him with an opportunity to minimize damages.[18]

An employer's unconditional offer of the job originally sought to an un- or underemployed claimant, moreover, need not be supplemented by an offer of retroactive seniority to be effective, lest a defendant's offer be irrationally disfavored relative to other employers' offers of substantially similar jobs. The claimant, after all, plainly would be required to minimize his damages by accepting another employer's offer even though it failed to grant the benefits of seniority not yet earned.[19] Of course, if the claimant fulfills the requirement that he minimize damages by accepting the defendant's unconditional offer, he remains entitled to full compensation if he wins his case. A court may grant him backpay accrued prior to the effective date of the offer, retroactive seniority, and compensation for any losses suffered as a result of his lesser seniority before the court's judgment.

In short, the un- or underemployed claimant's statutory obligation to minimize damages requires him to accept an unconditional offer of the job originally sought, even without retroactive seniority. Acceptance of the offer preserves, rather than jeopardizes, the claimant's right to be made whole; in the case of an un- or underemployed claimant, Ford's suggested rule merely embodies the existing requirement of §706(g) that the claimant minimize damages, without affecting his right to compensation. . . .

C

Therefore, we conclude that, when a claimant rejects the offer of the job he originally sought, as supplemented by a right to full court-ordered compensation, his choice can be taken as establishing that he considers the ongoing injury he has suffered at the hands of the defendant to have been ended by the availability of better opportunities elsewhere. For this reason, we find that, absent special circumstances,[27] the simple rule that the ongoing accrual of backpay liability is tolled when a Title VII claimant rejects the job he originally sought comports with Title VII's policy of making discrimination victims whole. . . .

Justice BLACKMUN, with whom Justice BRENNAN and Justice MARSHALL join, dissenting. . . .

. . . The Court's approach authorizes employers to . . . terminate their backpay liability unilaterally by extending to their discrimination victims offers they cannot reasonably accept. Once an employer has refused to hire a job applicant, and that applicant has mitigated damages by obtaining and accumulating seniority in another job, the employer may offer the applicant the same job that she was denied unlawfully several years earlier. In this very case, for example, Ford offered Gaddis and Starr jobs only after they had obtained employment elsewhere and only because they had filed charges with the EEOC. If, as here, the applicant declines the offer to preserve

18. The claimant's obligation to minimize damages in order to retain his right to compensation does not require him to settle his claim against the employer, in whole or in part. Thus, an applicant or discharged employee is not required to accept a job offered by the employer on the condition that his claims against the employer be compromised.

19. For the same reasons, a defendant's job offer is effective to force minimization of damages by an un- or underemployed claimant even without a supplemental offer of backpay. . . .

27. If, for example, the claimant has been forced to move a great distance to find a replacement job, a rejection of the employer's offer might reflect the costs of relocation more than a judgment that the replacement job was superior, all things considered, to the defendant's job. . . .

existing job security, the employer has successfully cut off all future backpay liability to the applicant. . . .

The Court's rule also violates Title VII's second objective — making victims of discrimination whole. . . . [I]f Gaddis and Starr had accepted those offers, they would not have been made whole. . . .

NOTES

1. *The Context.* To understand this case, it is essential to appreciate the cyclical fluctuations in employment in the automobile industry. Newer workers often go through a cycle of layoffs and recalls until they obtain sufficient seniority to have some meaningful job security. Accepting the offer Ford made to plaintiffs would have actually put them in a worse position than they had at GM in the sense that they would have no seniority at Ford while they had at least some at GM. Nevertheless, rejecting Ford's offer tolls the plaintiffs' backpay claim. Notice, however, the requirements: first, Ford did not require them to release their claims; second, Ford offered them work at their prior pay. Presumably, had Ford offered less, the question of whether plaintiffs would have been reasonable in staying at GM would have been more complicated and might turn on whether the GM or Ford compensation was higher. Had plaintiffs accepted the offer, they could have continued to litigate their claims, seeking accrued seniority and perhaps wage increases they would have received if they had not been laid off.

2. *Making an Offer Plaintiffs Will Refuse.* Once Ford knew the plaintiffs had accepted jobs at GM, it decided to offer to rehire plaintiffs. Do you think this was a strategic ploy designed to achieve exactly what happened — cutting off the plaintiffs' right to future backpay? As Justice O'Connor's opinion suggests, this is essentially costless to the employer, whether or not accepted. But the majority wants to encourage such offers by employers. Why? Mitigation kicked in when the plaintiffs started working at equivalent jobs at GM, so the plaintiffs lost backpay once they started working for GM (except for any difference in pay between the two jobs). Does the duty to mitigate serve whatever is the appropriate policy interest here without forcing the employee into an uncomfortable choice?

3. *Special Circumstances Exception.* The Court recognized that the rule tolling backpay does not apply when there are "special circumstances," but provided little further guidance. The Eighth Circuit interprets this as meaning only that the rejection must have been reasonable. *Smith v. World Ins. Co.*, 38 F.3d 1456 (8th Cir. 1994) (rejection reasonable where plaintiff thought that higher pay offered was not worth risk of being subjected to discrimination since he had no guarantees of how long he would be kept and his poor performance record would not be expunged). Was Gaddis reasonable in not accepting Ford's offer because "she did not want to be the only woman working in the warehouse"? *See Brown v. Ala. DOT*, 597 F.3d 1160 (11th Cir. 2010) (racially hostile environment could justify rejecting promotions).

McKENNON v. NASHVILLE BANNER PUBLISHING CO.
513 U.S. 352 (1995)

Justice KENNEDY delivered the opinion of the Court.

The question before us is whether an employee discharged in violation of the [ADEA] is barred from all relief when, after her discharge, the employer discovers evidence of wrongdoing that, in any event, would have led to the employee's termination on lawful and legitimate grounds. . . .

I

For some 30 years, petitioner Christine McKennon worked for respondent Nashville Banner Publishing Company. She was discharged, the Banner claimed, as part of a work force reduction plan necessitated by cost considerations. McKennon, who was 62 years old when she lost her job, thought another reason explained her dismissal: her age. She filed suit [seeking] a variety of legal and equitable remedies available under the ADEA, including backpay.

In preparation of the case, the Banner took McKennon's deposition. She testified that, during her final year of employment, she had copied several confidential documents bearing upon the company's financial condition. . . . McKennon took the copies home and showed them to her husband. Her motivation, she averred, was an apprehension she was about to be fired because of her age. When she became concerned about her job, she removed and copied the documents for "insurance" and "protection." A few days after these deposition disclosures, the Banner sent McKennon a letter declaring that removal and copying of the records was in violation of her job responsibilities and advising her (again) that she was terminated. . . .

II

We shall assume [for purposes of summary judgment] . . . that the misconduct revealed by the deposition was so grave that McKennon's immediate discharge would have followed its disclosure in any event. We do question the legal conclusion reached by [the lower] courts that after-acquired evidence of wrongdoing which would have resulted in discharge bars employees from any relief under the ADEA. That ruling is incorrect. . . .

The ADEA and Title VII share common substantive features and also a common purpose: "the elimination of discrimination in the workplace." Congress designed the remedial measures in these statutes to serve as a "spur or catalyst" to cause employers "to self-examine and to self-evaluate their employment practices and to endeavor to eliminate, so far as possible, the last vestiges" of discrimination. Deterrence is one object of these statutes. Compensation for injuries caused by the prohibited discrimination is another. . . . The private litigant who seeks redress for his or her injuries vindicates both the deterrence and the compensation objectives of the ADEA. It would not accord with this scheme if after-acquired evidence of wrongdoing that would have resulted in termination operates, in every instance, to bar all relief for an earlier violation of the Act.

The objectives of the ADEA are furthered when even a single employee establishes that an employer has discriminated against him or her. The disclosure through litigation of incidents or practices which violate national policies respecting nondiscrimination in the work force is itself important, for the occurrence of violations may disclose patterns of noncompliance resulting from a misappreciation of the Act's operation or entrenched resistance to its commands, either of which can be of industry-wide significance. The efficacy of its enforcement mechanisms becomes one measure of the success of the Act. . . .

[T]he case comes to us on the express assumption that an unlawful motive was the sole basis for the firing. McKennon's misconduct was not discovered until after she had been fired. The employer could not have been motivated by knowledge it did not have and it cannot now claim that the employee was fired for the nondiscrimina-tory reason. Mixed motive cases are inapposite here, except to the important extent they underscore the necessity of determining the employer's motives in ordering the discharge, an essential element in determining whether the employer violated the federal antidiscrimination law. As we have observed, "proving that the same decision would have been justified . . . is not the same as proving that the same decision would have been made."

Our inquiry is not at an end, however, for even though [for purposes of summary judgment we assume] the employer has violated the Act, we must consider how the after-acquired evidence of the employee's wrongdoing bears on the specific rem-edy to be ordered. [The Court rejected the equitable "unclean hands" doctrine as inapplicable "where Congress authorizes broad equitable relief to serve important national policies."] That does not mean, however, the employee's own misconduct is irrelevant to all the remedies otherwise available under the statute. . . . In giving effect to the ADEA, we must recognize the duality between the legitimate interests of the employer and the important claims of the employee who invokes the national employment policy mandated by the Act. The employee's wrongdoing must be taken into account, we conclude, lest the employer's legitimate concerns be ignored. . . . In determining appropriate remedial action, the employee's wrongdoing becomes rel-evant not to punish the employee, or out of concern "for the relative moral worth of the parties," but to take due account of the lawful prerogatives of the employer in the usual course of its business and the corresponding equities that it has arising from the employee's wrongdoing.

The proper boundaries of remedial relief in the general class of cases where, after termination, it is discovered that the employee has engaged in wrongdoing . . . will vary from case to case. We do conclude that here, and as a general rule in cases of this type, neither reinstatement nor front pay is an appropriate remedy. It would be both inequitable and pointless to order the reinstatement of someone the employer would have terminated, and will terminate, in any event and upon lawful grounds.

The proper measure of backpay presents a more difficult problem. Resolution of this question must give proper recognition to the fact that an ADEA violation has occurred which must be deterred and compensated without undue infringement upon the employer's rights and prerogatives. The object of compensation is to restore the employee to the position he or she would have been in absent the discrimination, but that principle is difficult to apply with precision where there is after-acquired evi-dence of wrongdoing that would have led to termination on legitimate grounds had the employer known about it. Once an employer learns about employee wrongdoing that would lead to a legitimate discharge, we cannot require the employer to ignore the information, even if it is acquired during the course of discovery in a suit against the employer and even if the information might have gone undiscovered absent the suit. The beginning point in the trial court's formulation of a remedy should be calculation of backpay from the date of the unlawful discharge to the date the new information was discovered. In determining the appropriate order for relief, the court can consider taking into further account extraordinary equitable circumstances that affect the legitimate interests of either party. An absolute rule barring any recovery of backpay, however, would undermine the ADEA's objective of forcing employers to consider and examine their motivations, and of penalizing them for employment decisions that spring from age discrimination.

Where an employer seeks to rely upon after-acquired evidence of wrongdoing, it must first establish that the wrongdoing was of such severity that the employee in fact would have been terminated on those grounds alone if the employer had known of it at the time of the discharge. The concern that employers might as a routine matter undertake extensive discovery into an employee's background or performance on the job to resist claims under the Act is not an insubstantial one, but we think the authority of the courts to award attorney's fees, mandated under the statute, and in appropriate cases to invoke the provisions of Rule 11 of the Federal Rules of Civil Procedure will deter most abuses. . . .

NOTES

1. *After-Acquired Evidence Rule.* Under the ADEA, "unpaid wages" in a private suit is a legal, not an equitable, remedy, *Lorillard v. Pons*, 434 U.S. 575 (1978), which makes some of the Court's phrasing somewhat odd. Nevertheless, the general approach of *McKennon* to after-acquired evidence is accepted as a general rule across all the discrimination statutes. *E.g.*, *Zisumbo v. Ogden Reg'l Med. Ctr.*, 801 F.3d 1185 (10th Cir. 2015). The doctrine has also been applied where the employee's wrongdoing occurred before hiring, as in the case of a fraudulent resume or job application. *See Harris v. Chand*, 506 F.3d 1135 (8th Cir. 2007). *McKennon* has also been invoked to limit a front pay award for loss of income after the date of judgment on the ground that her misconduct made the plaintiff unsuitable for re-employment in her former field. *Sellers v. Mineta*, 358 F.3d 1058 (8th Cir. 2004). Can compensatory and punitive damages nevertheless be recovered in an after-acquired evidence case for the defendant's discrimination?

2. *Chilling Effects?* The *McKennon* rule gives the employer every incentive to discover and over-value misconduct once suit is filed, so the courts may well be skeptical that a plaintiff would have been terminated for the misconduct in question. In any event, and regardless of the abstract merits of the after-acquired evidence rule, it creates litigation incentives for employers to turn every discrimination case into an inquiry into the employee's character and past acts. Melissa Hart, *Retaliatory Litigation Tactics: The Chilling Effects of "After-Acquired Evidence,"* 40 Ariz. St. L.J. 401 (2008). *See also* Sachin S. Pandya, *The After-Acquired Evidence Rule Lacks Any Justification. Unpacking the Employee-Misconduct Defense*, 14 U. Pa. J. Bus. L. 867 (2012).

b. The Duty to Mitigate Damages

Ford stressed the duty of mitigation, which has a statutory basis in Title VII. Section 2000e-5(g)(1) (and, by incorporation, the ADA) requires the backpay award to be reduced by amounts that were earned and could have been earned with reasonable diligence. *See Brown v. Smith*, 827 F.3d 609, 616 (7th Cir. 2016) (self-employment, if reasonable, is permissible mitigation, and plaintiff's business "was a legitimate and reasonable attempt to make money"); *Overman v. City of E. Baton Rouge*, 656 F. App'x 664 (5th Cir. 2016) (a plaintiff would have appropriately mitigated her damages even when deciding to attend school full time if she had diligently but unsuccessfully sought other employment and reasonably concluded that further efforts would have been fruitless). The same principle is applied in ADEA and §1981 actions, even without explicit statutory authorization. *E.g.*, *Hansard v. Pepsi-Cola Metro. Bottling Co.*, 865 F.2d 1461 (5th Cir. 1989) (ADEA); *Murphy v. City of Flagler Beach*, 846 F.2d 1306 (11th Cir. 1988) (§1981).

The courts are not entirely consistent in allocating the evidentiary burdens on these issues. While the plaintiff must show the difference between her actual earnings and what she would have been paid earned absent the discrimination, *Kamberos v. GTE Automatic Elec., Inc.*, 603 F.2d 598, 602 (7th Cir. 1979), the defendant has the burden of showing what the plaintiff could have earned with reasonable diligence. This typically requires proof of substantially equivalent jobs that the plaintiff could have obtained. *E.g., Donlin v. Philips Lighting N. Am. Corp.*, 581 F.3d 73, 89 (3d Cir. 2009). Some recent decisions, however, shift this traditional allocation by allowing an employer to carry its burden merely by showing that the plaintiff made no effort to find comparable employment, effectively presuming that a reasonably diligent plaintiff would have obtained equivalent employment. *See Broadnax v. City of New Haven*, 415 F.3d 265, 270 (2d Cir. 2005). The assumption seems to be that a qualified person can always find a suitable job, but the Great Recession has proven that not to be true. And even if the person is objectively qualified, the market might view him as "damaged goods," precisely because he was fired. *See generally* J. Hoult Verkerke, *Legal Regulation of Employment Reference Practices*, 65 U. Chi. L. Rev. 115, 118 (1998). See Note 2, p. 584, dealing with lost earning capacity.

4.   Front Pay

Backpay ends on the date of the court's judgment. Sometimes, however, the plaintiff has yet to receive full make-whole relief. For example, the court may have ordered the defendant to hire or to reinstate the plaintiff, but, at the time of the judgment, no job is open for which the plaintiff is qualified. Therefore, "front pay" continues backpay until that opening occurs; it is equivalent to suing for backpay at that future date and subject to similar constraints. *See Lulaj v. Wackenhut Corp.*, 512 F.3d 760, 767 (6th Cir. 2008) ("front pay is analogous to back pay in that it imagines the situation that gives rise to back pay continuing to some future date").

While it is often stated that the preferred remedy is to order the instatement or reinstatement of the plaintiff, in practice neither the plaintiff nor the defendant may want that relief for a variety of reasons, including the mutual hostility that often develops during litigation and the problems generated by bumping an incumbent. *See Palasota v. Haggar Clothing Co.*, 499 F.3d 474, 486 (5th Cir. 2007) (hostility coupled with changes in the industry and the employer made reinstatement inappropriate). Where no position is currently available, front pay, less mitigation, may be awarded until a position opens up, which is the preferred approach. *Kucia v. Southeast Ark. Cmty. Action Corp.*, 284 F.3d 944, 949 (8th Cir. 2002) ("[r]einstatement should be the norm" unless it proves to be impractical). When the court concludes that reinstatement will never be possible, the discriminatee may be awarded front pay in the form of "damages in lieu of reinstatement" — a lump sum award. In calculating that amount, it is necessary to determine (1) the appropriate time front pay should extend into the future and (2) the amount of pay for, say, each year, (3) taking into account projected future earnings but (4) reduced by projected mitigation; and (5), where a lump sum is awarded, reducing the award by appropriate present-value calculations. The amount of future pay must also include the value of fringe benefits the plaintiff would have received if she were working for the defendant.

Such a lump sum may extend throughout plaintiff's expected working life, *see Padilla v. Metro-North Commuter R.R.*, 92 F.3d 117 (2d Cir. 1996), although courts are reluctant to find that a victim of discrimination will remain permanently unemployable.

Peyton v. DiMario, 287 F.3d 1121, 1030 (D.C. Cir. 2002) (disapproving future lost earnings award as an abuse of discretion when plaintiff was only 34 years old and not incapacitated). When awards stretch out over long periods, the plaintiff's life expectancy is also relevant. *Price v. Marshall Erdman & Assocs., Inc.*, 966 F.2d 320 (7th Cir. 1992), said that each year's projected earnings should be discounted by the probability that he would not have lived that long.

We leave to Remedies courses more granular concerns with calculating future lost earnings, including inflation increases and reducing a lump sum award to current value, the "discount rate." The calculations can be complex, but the concept is simple: the plaintiff should be awarded an amount of money now that would, if prudently invested, produce the amount she is projected to have received in the future. More concretely, if the plaintiff is projected to earn $100,000 in Year 10, the amount awarded now must be reduced to reflect the interest she could earn on the sum for the next 9 years. Only then will the plaintiff have the "correct" amount, rather than a windfall, when Year 10 arrives. Other issues involve the extent to which the plaintiff's testimony will suffice or an expert is required. *See Donlin v. Philips Lighting N. Am. Corp.*, 564 F.3d 207, 216-17 (3d Cir. 2009) (while plaintiff could testify as to facts within her personal knowledge (such as her current and past earnings), she could not testify as to aspects requiring specialized knowledge, such as the probability of annual pay raises and present-value discounting).

Under Title VII (and the ADA), front pay is equitable and therefore determined by the judge, not the jury. That is, in cases that involve claims for both equitable and legal relief, the jury decides the compensatory and punitive damage issues and may also give an advisory opinion on backpay and front pay, which the trial judge may accept or reject in favor of what she considers the appropriate amounts. The same is likely true under the ADEA: although "unpaid wages" award is legal relief subject to the constitutional right to a jury trial, the circuits generally find no right to a jury on the amount of front pay.

However, the ADEA (but not the other statutes) permits successful plaintiffs to recover "liquidated damages," which double the amount of "unpaid wages." See p. 592. Where such damages are awarded, front pay should not be factored into that award. *Farley v. Nationwide Mut. Ins. Co.*, 197 F.3d 1322, 1340 (11th Cir. 1999) (noting that eight federal circuits have concluded that front pay should not be included in liquidated damages awards). However, the question whether a substantial liquidated damage award should affect, or even preclude, front pay is less clear. *See* Justin A. Walters, Note, *Drawing a Line: The Need to Rethink Remedies Under the Age Discrimination in Employment Act*, 2012 U. ILL. L. REV. 255. *See also Trainor v. HEI Hospitality, LLC*, 699 F.3d 19, 31 (1st Cir. 2012) (award of front pay not inconsistent with multiplied damages under state law since the purpose of a front pay award is to help to make a plaintiff whole while multiplication of damages under the relevant state law was punitive in nature).

Finally, where Title VII is concerned, *Pollard v. E.I. Du Pont De Nemours & Co.*, 532 U.S. 843 (2001), held that front pay is not a part of "compensatory damages" under 42 U.S.C. §1981a(b)(3) and therefore not subject to the statutory caps. Defining front pay as "simply money awarded for lost compensation during the period between judgment and reinstatement or in lieu of reinstatement," *id.* at 846, the Court read the statutory language as suggesting that Congress intended to provide victims of employment discrimination with remedies "*in addition to* the relief authorized by §706(g)." Thus, since "front pay was a type of relief authorized under §706(g), it is excluded from the meaning of compensatory damages under §1981a." *Id.* at 852.

C. LEGAL REMEDIES FOR THE VICTIMS OF DISCRIMINATION

Compensatory and punitive damages have been available under §1981 since the cause of action was recognized, *Johnson v. Railroad Express Agency*, 421 U.S. 454 (1975), but were not awardable under Title VII until the Civil Rights Act of 1991 enacted 42 U.S.C. §1981a, which authorizes such damages in certain Title VII and ADA cases and grants the right to a jury trial when such damages are sought. §1981a(c).

Thus, §1981a(1) provides for "compensatory and punitive damages" (in addition to any equitable relief under §706(g)), for "unlawful intentional discrimination," thus excluding disparate impact. However, while describing compensatory damages broadly ("future pecuniary losses, emotional pain, suffering, inconvenience, mental anguish, loss of enjoyment of life, and other nonpecuniary losses"), §1981(a) caps both compensatory and punitive damages at between $50,000 and $300,000, depending on the size of the employer. The caps are not applicable to Title VII equitable relief, such as "backpay, interest on backpay, or any other type of relief authorized under section 706(g)," §1981a(b)(2), nor do they apply to suits under §1981. §1981a(b)(4). The new section explicitly address punitive damages, which apply when defendant acted "with malice or with reckless indifference to the federally protected rights of an aggrieved individual." §1981a(b)(1).

The 1991 Amendments did not alter the remedial scheme of the ADEA, which does not authorize either compensatory or punitive damages for age discrimination, *Vaughan v. Anderson Reg'l Med. Ctr.*, 849 F.3d 588 (5th Cir. 2017), but, as we have seen, does allow the recovery of "liquidated damages" which may serve some of the same purposes. *Collazo v. Nicholson*, 535 F.3d 41 (1st Cir. 2008). See p. 592.

1. Compensatory Damages

TURIC v. HOLLAND HOSPITALITY, INC.
85 F.3d 1211 (6th Cir. 1996)

KRUPANSKY, Circuit Judge.

[Holland Hospitality violated Title VII by discharging Turic, who was pregnant, because she contemplated having an abortion. The district court granted various relief, including $50,000 for emotional distress.]

To be eligible for compensatory damages, Turic was required to prove that Holland Hospitality's unlawful actions caused her emotional distress. A plaintiff's own testimony, along with the circumstances of a particular case, can suffice to sustain the plaintiff's burden in this regard. . . .

The court . . . found that as a young, unwed mother who was walking an "economic tightrope" and who had just discovered she was pregnant for a second time, Turic was in a particularly vulnerable position and was highly dependent upon her job. Vulnerability is relevant in determining damages. See *Williamson v. Handy Button Mach. Co.*, 817 F.2d 1290 (7th Cir. 1987) ("Perhaps [plaintiff] was unusually sensitive, but a tortfeasor takes its victims as it finds them. . . . In some cases unusual sensitivity will enhance the loss; in others unusual hardiness will reduce it; payment of the actual damage in each case will both compensate the victim and lead the injurer to take account of the full consequences of its acts"). Turic's vulnerability is particularly relevant in this case, because her supervisors had direct knowledge of her vulnerability before they discharged her. The trial judge did not err, therefore, in considering the unusual economic and emotional sensitivity of this plaintiff.

[handwritten margin note: π was especially vulnerable]

It is well settled that Title VII plaintiffs can prove emotional injury by testimony without medical support. However, damages for mental and emotional distress will not be presumed, and must be proven by "competent evidence." . . . Witnesses testified that Turic was extremely upset and frightened after being discharged, and that she ran from the meeting in tears. The Supreme Court in *Carey* [*v. Piphus*, 435 U.S. 247 (1978),] instructed that such witness testimony bolsters a finding of emotional distress: "Although essentially subjective, genuine injury in this respect may be evidenced by one's conduct and observed by others." Further, Turic testified that she continued to suffer nightmares, weight loss during her pregnancy (an undesirable occurrence often leading to low birth weight of the baby), and excessive nervousness. This testimony distinguishes the instant case from *Rodgers* [*v. Fisher Body Div., General Motors Corp.*, 739 F.2d 1102 (6th Cir. 1984)], in which the plaintiff failed to testify that he suffered any manifestations of his alleged mental distress, and from *Erebia v. Chrysler Plastic Prods. Corp.*, 772 F.2d 1250 (6th Cir. 1985), wherein the plaintiff testified merely that he was "highly upset" about racial slurs made at his workplace. See also *DeNieva v. Reyes*, 966 F.2d 480 (9th Cir. 1992) (plaintiff testified to suffering emotional distress manifested by insomnia, dizziness and vomiting and received $50,000 compensatory damages); *Secretary of HUD v. Blackwell*, 908 F.2d 864 (11th Cir. 1990) ($40,000 award upheld on basis of testimony regarding humiliation, insomnia and headaches); *Moody v. Pepsi-Cola Metro. Bottling Co.*, 915 F.2d 201 (6th Cir. 1990) ($150,000 award upheld on basis of testimony that plaintiff was shocked and humiliated and forced to live apart from family because of termination). For the above reasons, the amount awarded as compensatory damages is not grossly excessive, and the decision of the court below as to compensatory damages is affirmed. . . .

[handwritten margin note: phys manifestation/symptoms of emotional distress]

NOTES

1. *Proving Mental Distress.* Damages for mental distress can be recovered only when actual injury is proved; such injury cannot be presumed merely from a civil rights violation. *Carey v. Piphus*, 435 U.S. 247 (1978). As in *Turic*, many decisions have upheld awards for distress, humiliation, or anxiety based only on the testimony of the plaintiff and other lay persons. E.g., *Gracia v. Sigmatron Int'l, Inc.*, 842 F.3d 1010, 1022 (7th Cir. 2016) ("award for nonpecuniary loss can be supported, in certain circumstances, solely by a plaintiff's testimony about his or her emotional distress"). However, larger awards predicated solely on such proof may be vulnerable to remittitur. *See Miller v. Raytheon Co.*, 716 F.3d 138 (5th Cir. 2013) (upholding remittitur of mental anguish award from $1 million to $100,000 because the claim was premised solely on the testimony of plaintiff and his wife); *Trainor v. HEI Hospitality, LLC*, 699 F.3d 19, 32 (1st Cir. 2012) ($500,000 award was grossly excessive where there was no evidence of medical treatment or counseling).

Commentators have urged more judicial openness to recovery for emotional distress. *See generally* Scott A. Moss & Peter H. Huang, *How the New Economics Can Improve Employment Discrimination Law, and How Economics Can Survive the Demise of the "Rational Actor,"* 51 WM. & MARY L. REV. 183 (2009); Zachary A.

Kramer, *After Work*, 95 CAL. L. REV. 627, 629 (2007). *See also* Jessica L. Roberts, *Rethinking Employment Discrimination Harms*, 91 IND. L.J. 393 (2016). However, pursuing such recovery requires plaintiff to waive privacy interests in his treatment for mental distress. *Fisher v. Sw. Bell Tel. Co.*, 361 F. App'x 974 (10th Cir. 2010).

2. *Lost Earning Capacity vs. Front Pay*. Compensatory damages can be recovered for injuries other than mental distress. For example, the statute speaks in terms of "future pecuniary losses," which some courts have viewed as embracing lost earning capacity and distinguished from front pay. In *Williams v. Pharmacia, Inc.*, 137 F.3d 944 (7th Cir. 1998), the court held that a Title VII plaintiff can recover both. The jury had awarded the discharged plaintiff $300,000 in compensatory damages, including $250,000 for lost future earnings. The judge then added $180,000 for lost back-pay and, after denying reinstatement, another $115,530 for one year's front pay. The appellate court said that the plaintiff's discriminatory job evaluations and termination justified the damages for lost future earning capacity with other employers. The front pay award compensated a different injury — the loss plaintiff suffered from the failure to regain her old job. Is this correct? Would a different result have been reached if the front pay award had been based on losses to the date of retirement?

3. *Court Review of Compensatory Jury Awards*. Courts may reduce jury compensatory damages awards that are "grossly excessive" or "shock the conscience." *Turley v. ISG Lackawanna, Inc.*, 774 F.3d 140, 162 (2d Cir. 2014). But can a court set aside a damages award under §1981a as "grossly excessive or shocking" even though it is within the statutory limit? *Hennessy v. Penril Datacomm Networks, Inc.*, 69 F.3d 1344 (7th Cir. 1995) (yes). Should courts look to the §1981a caps to determine whether an award is excessive in a §1981 action? Section 1981a(b)(4) provides that §1981a does not "limit" the relief available in §1981 actions. We will shortly encounter constitutional constraints on punitive damages awards. See Note 8, p. 591.

4. *Special ADA Rules*. ADA §12112(d) contains a number of specific prohibitions regarding medical examinations and inquiries, and the maintenance of employee medical records. See p. 516. To date, three circuits have rejected attempts to recover compensatory or punitive damages for violations of these provisions, insisting that no actual injury had been shown. *E.g., Griffin v. Steeltek, Inc.*, 261 F.3d 1026 (10th Cir. 2001).

5. *Federal Employee Suits*. Claims by federal employees against the federal government begin with a formal administrative hearing procedure by the EEOC. The Supreme Court has held that, when the Commission holds in favor of the employee, it has the legal authority to require the employing federal agency to pay compensatory damages. *West v. Gibson*, 527 U.S. 212, 214 (1999).

2. Punitive Damages

KOLSTAD v. AMERICAN DENTAL ASSOCIATION
527 U.S. 526 (1999)

Justice O'CONNOR delivered the opinion of the Court.

Under the terms of the Civil Rights Act of 1991 (1991 Act) punitive damages are available in claims under [Title VII and the ADA]. Punitive damages are limited, however, to cases in which the employer has engaged in intentional discrimination and has done so "with malice or with reckless indifference to the federally protected rights of an aggrieved individual." 42 U.S.C. §1981a(b)(1). . . .

I

In September 1992, Jack O'Donnell announced that he would be retiring as the Director of Legislation and Legislative Policy . . . for respondent, American Dental Association (respondent or Association). Petitioner, Carole Kolstad, was . . . serving as respondent's Director of Federal Agency Relations. When she learned of O'Donnell's retirement, she expressed an interest in filling his position. Also interested in replacing O'Donnell was Tom Spangler, [who] was serving as the Association's Legislative Counsel. . . . Both petitioner and Spangler . . . had received "distinguished" performance ratings by the acting head of the Washington office, Leonard Wheat. . . . Wheat requested that Dr. William Allen, then serving as respondent's Executive Director in the Association's Chicago office, make the ultimate promotion decision. After interviewing both petitioner and Spangler, Wheat recommended that Allen select Spangler for O'Donnell's post. Allen notified petitioner in December 1992 that he had, in fact, selected Spangler. . . .

. . . In petitioner's view, the entire selection process was a sham. Counsel for petitioner urged the jury to conclude that Allen's stated reasons for selecting Spangler were pretext for gender discrimination, and that Spangler had been chosen for the position before the formal selection process began. Among the evidence offered in support of this view, there was testimony to the effect that Allen modified the description of O'Donnell's post to track aspects of the job description used to hire Spangler. In petitioner's view, this "preselection" procedure suggested an intent by the Association to discriminate on the basis of sex. Petitioner also introduced testimony at trial that Wheat told sexually offensive jokes and that he had referred to certain prominent professional women in derogatory terms. . . .

The District Court denied petitioner's request for a jury instruction on punitive damages. The jury concluded that respondent had discriminated against petitioner on the basis of sex and awarded her backpay totaling $52,718. . . .

The Court of Appeals . . . concluded that, "before the question of punitive damages can go to the jury, the evidence of the defendant's culpability must exceed what is needed to show intentional discrimination." [T]he court determined, specifically, that a defendant must be shown to have engaged in some "egregious" misconduct. . . .

II

A

[The 1991 Act added compensatory and punitive damages to the equitable relief that had previously been available but limited the former awards] to cases of "intentional discrimination" — that is, cases that do not rely on the "disparate impact" theory of discrimination. §1981a(a)(1). Section 1981a(b)(1) further qualifies the availability of punitive awards:

> A complaining party may recover punitive damages . . . if the complaining party demonstrates that the respondent engaged in a discriminatory practice or discriminatory practices *with malice or with reckless indifference to the federally protected rights of an aggrieved individual.*

(Emphasis added.) The very structure of §1981a suggests a congressional intent to authorize punitive awards in only a subset of cases involving intentional discrimination. Section 1981a(a)(1) limits compensatory and punitive awards to instances of intentional discrimination, while §1981a(b)(1) requires plaintiffs to make an additional "demonstrat[ion]" of their eligibility for punitive damages. Congress plainly sought to impose two standards of liability — one for establishing a right to compensatory damages and another, higher standard that a plaintiff must satisfy to qualify for a punitive award.

. . . The terms "malice" and "reckless" [in §1981a(b)(1)] ultimately focus on the actor's state of mind. While egregious misconduct is evidence of the requisite mental state, §1981a does not limit plaintiffs to this form of evidence, and the section does not require a showing of egregious or outrageous discrimination independent of the employer's state of mind. Nor does the statute's structure imply an independent role for "egregiousness" in the face of congressional silence. On the contrary, the view that §1981a provides for punitive awards based solely on an employer's state of mind is consistent with the 1991 Act's distinction between equitable and compensatory relief. Intent determines which remedies are open to a plaintiff here as well; compensatory awards are available only where the employer has engaged in "*intentional* discrimination." (Emphasis added.)

Moreover, §1981a's focus on the employer's state of mind gives some effect to Congress' apparent intent to narrow the class of cases for which punitive awards are available to a subset of those involving intentional discrimination. The employer must act with "malice or with reckless indifference (*to* [*the plaintiff's*] *federally protected rights.*") (Emphasis added). The terms "malice" or "reckless indifference" pertain to the employer's knowledge that it may be acting in violation of federal law, not its awareness that it is engaging in discrimination. . . .

We gain an understanding of the meaning of the terms "malice" and "reckless indifference," as used in §1981a, from this Court's decision in *Smith v. Wade*, 461 U.S. 30 (1983). . . . Employing language similar to what later appeared in §1981a, the Court concluded in *Smith* that "a jury may be permitted to assess punitive damages in an action under §1983 when the defendant's conduct is shown to be motivated by evil motive or intent, or when it involves reckless or callous indifference to the federally protected rights of others." While the *Smith* Court determined that it was unnecessary to show actual malice to qualify for a punitive award, its intent standard, at a minimum, required recklessness in its subjective form. The Court referred to a "subjective consciousness" of a risk of injury or illegality and a "'criminal indifference to civil obligations.'" . . . Applying this standard in the context of §1981a, an employer must at least discriminate in the face of a perceived risk that its actions will violate federal law to be liable in punitive damages.

There will be circumstances where intentional discrimination does not give rise to punitive damages liability under this standard. In some instances, the employer may simply be unaware of the relevant federal prohibition. There will be cases, moreover, in which the employer discriminates with the distinct belief that its discrimination is lawful. The underlying theory of discrimination may be novel or otherwise poorly recognized, or an employer may reasonably believe that its discrimination satisfies a bona fide occupational qualification defense or other statutory exception to liability. . . .

To be sure, egregious or outrageous acts may serve as evidence supporting an inference of the requisite "evil motive." "The allowance of exemplary damages depends upon the bad motive of the wrong-doer *as exhibited by his acts*." Sedgwick [Measure of Damages, p. 529 (8th ed. 1891)] (emphasis added). Likewise, under §1981a(b)(1), pointing to evidence of an employer's egregious behavior would provide one means of satisfying the plaintiff's burden to "demonstrat[e]" that the employer acted with the requisite "malice or . . . reckless indifference." Again, however, respondent has not shown that the terms "reckless indifference" and "malice," in the punitive damages context, have taken on a consistent definition including an independent, "egregious-ness" requirement.

B

The inquiry does not end with a showing of the requisite "malice or . . . reckless indifference" on the part of certain individuals, however. The plaintiff must impute liability for punitive damages to respondent. . . . While we decline to engage in any definitive application of the agency standards to the facts of this case, it is important that we address the proper legal standards for imputing liability to an employer in the punitive damages context. . . .

Although jurisdictions disagree over whether and how to limit vicarious liability for punitive damages, our interpretation of Title VII is informed by "the general com-mon law of agency, rather than . . . the law of any particular State." The common law as codified in the Restatement (Second) of Agency (1957), provides a useful starting point for defining this general common law. The Restatement of Agency places strict limits on the extent to which an agent's misconduct may be imputed to the principal for purposes of awarding punitive damages:

> Punitive damages can properly be awarded against a master or other principal because of an act by an agent if, but only if:
>   (a) the principal authorized the doing and the manner of the act, or
>   (b) the agent was unfit and the principal was reckless in employing him, or
>   (c) the agent was employed in a managerial capacity and was acting in the scope of employment, or
>   (d) the principal or a managerial agent of the principal ratified or approved puni-tive damages if it authorizes or ratifies the agent's tortious act, or if it acts recklessly in employing the malfeasing agent.

See also Restatement (Second) of Torts §909 (same).

The Restatement, for example, provides that the principal may be liable for puni-tive damages if it authorizes or ratifies the agent's tortuous act, or if it acts recklessly in employing the malfeasing agent. The Restatement also contemplates liability for punitive awards where an employee serving in a "managerial capacity" committed the wrong while "acting in the scope of employment." "Unfortunately, no good definition of what constitutes a 'managerial capacity' has been found," and determining whether an employee meets this description requires a fact-intensive inquiry. "In making this determination, the court should review the type of authority that the employer has given to the employee, the amount of discretion that the employee has in what is done and how it is accomplished." Suffice it to say here that the examples provided in the Restatement of Torts suggest that an employee must be "important," but perhaps need not be the employer's "top management, officers, or directors," to be acting "in a managerial capacity."

Additional questions arise from the meaning of the "scope of employment" require-ment. The Restatement of Agency provides that even intentional torts are within the scope of an agent's employment if the conduct is "the kind [the employee] is employed to perform," "occurs substantially within the authorized time and space limits," and "is actuated, at least in part, by a purpose to serve the" employer. Accord-ing to the Restatement, so long as these rules are satisfied, an employee may be said to act within the scope of employment even if the employee engages in acts "specifically forbidden" by the employer and uses "forbidden means of accomplishing results." On this view, even an employer who makes every effort to comply with Title VII would be held liable for the discriminatory acts of agents acting in a "managerial capacity."

Holding employers liable for punitive damages when they engage in good faith efforts to comply with Title VII, however, is in some tension with the very principles underlying common law limitations on vicarious liability for punitive damage — that it is "improper ordinarily to award punitive damages against one who himself is personally innocent and therefore liable only vicariously." Where an employer has undertaken such good faith efforts at Title VII compliance, it "demonstrat[es] that it never acted in reckless disregard of federally protected rights."

Applying the Restatement of Agency's "scope of employment" rule in the Title VII punitive damages context, moreover, would reduce the incentive for employers to implement antidiscrimination programs. In fact, such a rule would likely exacerbate concerns among employers that §1981a's "malice" and "reckless indifference" standard penalizes those employers who educate themselves and their employees on Title VII's prohibitions. Dissuading employers from implementing programs or policies to prevent discrimination in the workplace is directly contrary to the purposes underlying Title VII. The statute's "primary objective" is "a prophylactic one"; it aims, chiefly, "not to provide redress but to avoid harm." . . . The purposes underlying Title VII are similarly advanced where employers are encouraged to adopt antidiscrimination policies and to educate their personnel on Title VII's prohibitions.

In light of the perverse incentives that the Restatement's "scope of employment" rules create, we are compelled to modify these principles to avoid undermining the objectives underlying Title VII. Recognizing Title VII as an effort to promote prevention as well as remediation, and observing the very principles underlying the Restatement's strict limits on vicarious liability for punitive damages, we agree that, in the punitive damages context, an employer may not be vicariously liable for the discriminatory employment decisions of managerial agents where these decisions are contrary to the employer's "good-faith efforts to comply with Title VII." As [Judge Tatel] recognized, "[g]iving punitive damages protection to employers who make good-faith efforts to prevent discrimination in the workplace accomplishes" Title VII's objective of "motivat[ing] employers to detect and deter Title VII violations."

. . . We leave for remand the question whether petitioner can identify facts sufficient to support an inference that the requisite mental state can be imputed to respondent. . . .

[Chief Justice Rehnquist, with whom Justice Thomas joined, concurred in Part II-B of the Court's opinion. The partial dissent and partial concurrence of Justice Stevens, with whom Justice Souter, Justice Ginsburg, and Justice Breyer joined, is omitted.]

NOTES

1. *Different Kinds of Incentives.* One purpose of punitive damages is to incentivize compliance with the law by increasing the penalties for violations. But *Kolstad* seems to believe that the correct incentive structure looks to what the corporate employer did (or didn't do) rather than to the conduct of a "rogue" supervisor. The result is to encourage voluntary employer policies prohibiting discrimination. The obvious comparison is the liability structure for sexual harassment. See p. 337. Do you think the Court got the incentives right? In answering this question, recall that only *punitive* damages are at stake; the incentives to avoid compensatory and equitable awards

remain in place. In any event, the *Kolstad* standard seems applicable to §1981 cases. *See Lowery v. Circuit City Stores, Inc.*, 206 F.3d 431 (4th Cir. 2000). And it seems to pose two hurdles to the recovery of §1981a punitive damages — first, the malice or reckless indifference requirement and, second, satisfaction of the agency principles, as the Court adapted them to satisfy statutory goals.

2. *Defendant's State of Mind.* As to the first, it would usually seem easy to establish that the employer knew that it was — or might be — violating the ADA or Title VII. In today's environment, how likely is it that an employer is "unaware of the relevant federal prohibition" or even that it "has the distinct belief that its discrimination is lawful"? *E.g., EEOC v. Autozone, Inc.*, 707 F.3d 824 (7th Cir. 2013) (upholding punitive damages award when the employer did not respond to multiple requests for accommodation despite ADA training of the relevant managers and a company procedure regarding accommodations). Or is that right? *See EEOC v. Boh Bros. Constr. Co., L.L.C.*, 731 F.3d 444, 468 (5th Cir. 2013) (actors' subjective understandings of same-sex harassment, and employer's failure to train its workers regarding it "may have been ill-advised, [but] it was not malicious or recklessly indifferent"); *Smith v. Xerox Corp.*, 602 F.3d 320, 336 (5th Cir. 2010) ("In light of the competing evidence that impugned Smith's performance, we cannot say that the evidence supports a finding that Xerox managers acted with malice or reckless indifference to the possibility that her termination could violate federal law."). And the standard might prove an especially serious obstacle in ADA cases. *See Tobin v. Liberty Mut. Ins. Co.*, 553 F.3d 121, 148-49 (1st Cir. 2009) (evidence insufficient to support punitive damages even though the jury correctly found denials of accommodations that would have enabled plaintiff to perform his job when the employer considered the relevant factors each time). *Cf. Henry v. Corpcar Servs. Hous., Ltd.*, 625 F. App'x 607 (5th Cir. 2015) (punitive damages justified when the employer acted with reckless indifference to plaintiff's rights by twice having a white woman appear in a gorilla suit and using racial remarks to compare black employees to apes).

3. *The Agency Element.* Aside from the hostile work environment cases like *Ellerth*, p. 337, agency principles have not limited backpay or compensatory damages for an ADA or Title VII violation. Why do agency principles have more bite in actions seeking punitive damages? Is it because the Court fears that the low threshold for showing malice would otherwise make punitive damages available in almost all disparate treatment cases? Are you satisfied with the Court's policy reasons for not imputing a lower-level manager's malicious discrimination to the corporate employer? Recall that individuals are not personally liable under Title VII, see p. 594, so a failure to impute liability will leave such conduct unpunished by the law.

4. *The Two-Step Agency Issue.* The agency determination requires two steps. The threshold question is whether liability is appropriate at all — whether the actor was in a managerial capacity and acting within the scope of her employment. Second, there must be a determination of whether the employer used good faith efforts to comply with the law.

(a) *A Manager Acting Within the Scope of Her Employment?* Although the Supreme Court has defined "supervisor" for purposes of discriminatory harassment liability, *see Vance v. Ball State Univ.*, reproduced at p. 345, it has provided no further guidance on the meaning of "manager" for punitive damages purposes. Are the concepts the same, or does "manager" imply wider responsibilities? The lower courts seem confused although some of these cases precede *Vance*. Thus, is the manager of a Wal-Mart store a "manager"? *EEOC v. Wal-Mart Stores, Inc.*, 187 F.3d 1241 (10th Cir. 1999) (yes; even the power to make hiring and firing recommendations is sufficient to render someone a manager); *Dudley v. Wal-Mart Stores, Inc.*, 166 F.3d 1317 (11th Cir. 1999) (no). And what about scope of employment? One case held that a supervisor who created a hostile environment and who had authority over the victim acted within the scope of his employment. *Anderson v. G.D.C., Inc.*, 281 F.3d 452 (4th Cir. 2002).

(b) *Employer's Good Faith Compliance.* Even if a manager acting within the scope of his employment discriminates maliciously, the employer is still not liable for punitive damages if it meets the *Kolstad* standard, which has been held to require the employer to "at least 1) adopt antidiscrimination policies; 2) make a good faith effort to educate its employees about these policies and the statutory prohibitions; and 3) make good faith efforts to *enforce* an antidiscrimination policy." *McInnis v. Fairfield Cmtys., Inc.*, 458 F.3d 1129, 1138 (10th Cir. 2006) (internal quotations omitted). *See also Romano v. U-Haul Int'l*, 233 F.3d 655 (1st Cir. 2000). Thus, a number of cases have found employers liable for punitives when their efforts were viewed as ineffective or half-hearted. *See May v. Chrysler Group, LLC*, 692 F.3d 734, 747 (7th Cir. 2012); *Heaton v. Weitz Co.*, 534 F.3d 882 (8th Cir. 2008) (punitive damages appropriate when, despite initially handling a complaint appropriately, the employer placed a "biased or perceived partial person" in charge of investigations that were cursory and indifferent). Nevertheless, some employers have successfully invoked the defense despite deficiencies in their enforcement efforts. *E.g., Bryant v. Aiken Reg'l Med. Ctrs., Inc.*, 333 F.3d 536, 548-49 (4th Cir. 2003) (equal employment opportunity policy, grievance policy, diversity training program, and voluntary monitoring of departmental demographics were "widespread antidiscrimination efforts" that barred award of punitive damages). *See generally* Joseph Seiner, *The Failure of Punitive Damages in Employment Discrimination Cases: A Call for Change*, 50 Wm. & Mary L. Rev. 735 (2008) (only 24 of more than 600 district court Title VII cases in the sample awarded punitive damages, although 29 percent of juries finding for plaintiffs awarded such punitive damages).

5. *No Affirmative Defense for Direct Liability.* The good faith defense is available only where the employer has derivative liability, as opposed to direct liability, for the discrimination. Accordingly, the defense is unavailable where the discriminator was such a high-level person as to be a proxy for the corporation. *E.g., Townsend v. Benjamin Enters.*, 679 F.3d 41 (2d Cir. 2012). Similarly, the defense is unavailable where the employees charged with enforcing the company's antidiscrimination policies knew or should have known of the discrimination but failed to act. *Deters v. Equifax Credit Info. Servs.*, 202 F.3d 1262 (10th Cir. 2000).

6. *Are Compensatory and Punitive Damages Linked?* Some circuits have added an additional threshold to the grant of punitive damages — that punitive damages require an award of compensatory damages or at least backpay, *e.g., Provencher v. CVS Pharmacy*, 145 F.3d 5 (1st Cir. 1998); *Corti v. Storage Tech. Corp.*, 304 F.3d 336 (4th Cir. 2002), but there is certainly contrary authority. *Abner v. Kan. City S. R.R. Co.*, 513 F.3d 154 (5th Cir. 2008); *Tisdale v. Fed. Express Corp.*, 415 F.3d 516, 535 (6th Cir. 2005).

7. *Jury Discretion.* If the jury finds that the two *Kolstad* requirements have been satisfied, it has discretion to award punitive damages. This discretion is exercised in light of the need for punishment and deterrence. *See Smith v. Wade*, 461 U.S. 30 (1983). The amount of the award should take into account "such factors as the grievousness of the conduct, the solvency of the guilty party, and the potential for deterrence of the verdict." *Rowlett v. Anheuser-Busch, Inc.*, 832 F.2d 194, 207 (1st Cir. 1987). *See also Patterson v. Balsamico*, 440 F.3d 104, 122 (2d Cir. 2006) (reducing $20,000 punitive damages award against individual in §1983 case in light of his personal financial situation).

8. *Substantive Due Process Limits on Punitive Damages.* Over the last decade, the Supreme Court has held that punitive damage awards may violate due process even if they satisfy state law standards. Jury awards are to be reviewed by both trial and appellate courts de novo to assure compliance with due process. As to what due process requires, *BMW of N. Am., Inc. v. Gore*, 517 U.S. 559 (1996), held that a punitive damages award that is "grossly excessive" is impermissible. An award is "grossly excessive" when either the amount of the award exceeds the state's legitimate interests in punishment and deterrence or the controlling legal principles fail to provide fair notice of the conduct subject to punishment and the severity of the punishment. Thereafter, *State Farm Mut. Auto. Ins. Co. v. Campbell*, 538 U.S. 408 (2003), set a presumptive constitutional cap on punitive damages by limiting them to a single-digit ratio to compensatory damages. While not establishing a bright-line ratio, the Court wrote, "in practice, few awards exceeding a single-digit ratio between punitive and compensatory damages, to a significant degree, will satisfy due process." *Id.* at 424. The Court then went further to suggest that a limit of quadruple punitive damages while not binding was "instructive." *Id.* Does *State Farm* link punitive damages to some multiple of compensatory damages? If a plaintiff proves only $100 in compensatory damages, does that limit her punitive damages to a maximum of $1,000? (Note that probably backpay would count as compensatory damages for any such calculation. *Provencher v. CVS Pharmacy*, 145 F.3d 5 (1st Cir. 1998).) Most recently, *Philip Morris USA v. Williams*, 549 U.S. 346, 353 (2007), held that "the Constitution's Due Process Clause forbids a State to use a punitive damages award to punish a defendant for injury that it inflicts upon nonparties or those whom they directly represent, *i.e.*, injury that it inflicts upon those who are, essentially, strangers to the litigation." *See generally* Joseph A. Seiner, *Punitive Damages, Due Process, and Employment Discrimination*, 97 Iowa L. Rev. 473 (2012); Stacy A. Hickox, *Reduction of Punitive Damages for Employment Discrimination: Are Courts Ignoring Our Juries?*, 54 Mercer L. Rev. 1081 (2003); Sandra F. Sperino, *Judicial Preemption of Punitive Damages*, 78 U. Cin. L. Rev. 227 (2009).

These constitutional cases clearly apply in a §1981 action, which has no statutory ceiling on punitive damages awards. *Turley v. ISG Lackawanna, Inc.*, 774 F.3d 140, 165 (2d Cir. 2014) (overturning a $5 million punitive damages award where compensatory damages were set at $1.3 million; the four-to-one ratio of punishment to compensation was especially problematic since the compensatory award was "for intangible — and therefore immeasurable — emotional damages"). But several courts have indicated that statutory damage caps in Title VII and ADA actions obviate any need to apply constitutional analysis in that context. *E.g., EEOC v. Autozone, Inc.*, 707 F.3d 824 (7th Cir. 2013) (upholding a punitive damages award in part because of the statutory cap); *EEOC v. Fed. Express Corp.*, 513 F.3d 360 (4th Cir. 2008). *But see Arizona v. ASARCO, LLC*, 733 F.3d 882, 888-90 (9th Cir. 2013) (an award with a ratio of $300,000 punitive damages to $1 of nominal damages was excessive even though its mirrored the statutory cap). *See generally* Colleen P. Murphy, *Statutory Caps and Judicial Review of Damages*, 39 Akron L. Rev. 1001 (2006).

9. *Compensatory and Punitive Damages in ADA Actions.* Section 1981a(a)(2) authorizes compensatory and punitive damages in ADA actions for disparate treatment discrimination. *But see Kramer v. Banc of Am. Sec., LLC*, 355 F.3d 961 (7th Cir. 2004) (the section does not authorize compensatory or punitive damages for retaliation claims); *Alvarado v. Cajun Operating Co.*, 588 F.3d 1261 (9th Cir. 2009) (same). This relief is in addition to the backpay, front pay, and interest permitted by §706(g). However, compensatory and punitive damage awards are subject to the

same limitations and conditions as in Title VII actions, including the immunity of governmental entities from punitive damage awards. *See Cook County v. U.S. ex rel. Chandler*, 538 U.S. 119, 129 (2003). In addition §1981a(a)(3) provides that damages may not be awarded for the failure to make a reasonable accommodation in an ADA case where the defendant demonstrates good faith efforts to make such an accommodation. *See generally* Mark C. Weber, *Accidentally on Purpose: Intent in Disability Discrimination Law*, 56 BC L. Rev. 1417, 1428 (2015).

NOTE ON LIQUIDATED DAMAGES IN ADEA CASES

The ADEA, unlike the other antidiscrimination laws, allows the recovery of "liquidated damages" (which in effect double the amount of the claim for unpaid wages) where the defendant's statutory violation was "willful." They are authorized by 29 U.S.C. §626(b) (2018), which incorporates the enforcement procedures and remedies of §216 of the Fair Labor Standards Act. In turn, §216 allows recovery both of unpaid wages and of liquidated damages in an amount equal to the unpaid wages (including lost fringe benefits). *E.g., Blim v. Western Elec. Co.*, 731 F.2d 1473 (10th Cir. 1984). However, this award should not include front pay. See p. 581. *See also Greene v. Safeway Stores, Inc.*, 210 F.3d 1237 (10th Cir. 2000) (an award of future lost gains on stock options was properly excluded from the liquidated damages calculation since the speculative nature of the award made it more like front pay than backpay).

However, liquidated damages are not available in federal employee ADEA actions. *See Lehman v. Nakshian*, 453 U.S. 156 (1981). More generally, the ADEA imposes a notable condition on their recovery since they are "payable only in cases of willful violations of this chapter." §626(b). In *Trans World Airlines, Inc. v. Thurston*, 469 U.S. 111 (1985), the Court concluded that a violation of the Act would be "'willful' if the employer knew or showed reckless disregard for the matter of whether its conduct was prohibited by the ADEA." After lower courts failed to apply the *Thurston* standard, the Supreme Court revisited the issue in *Hazen Paper Co. v. Biggins*, 507 U.S. 604 (1993), and made clear that those engaged in "willful" conduct were only a subset of those violating the law:

> It is not true that an employer who knowingly relies on age in reaching its decision invariably commits a knowing or reckless violation of the ADEA. The ADEA is not an unqualified prohibition on the use of age in employment decisions, but affords the employer a "bona fide occupational qualification" defense, and exempts certain subject matters and persons, [such as those for bona fide seniority systems and employee benefit plans and bona fide executives and high policymakers]. If an employer incorrectly but in good faith and nonrecklessly believes that the statute permits a particular age-based decision, then liquidated damages should not be imposed.

It seems unlikely that employers will often plausibly be able to claim "nonreckless" ignorance of the statute's general prohibition on age discrimination, *see Miller v. Raytheon Co.*, 716 F.3d 138, 146 (5th Cir. 2013) (affirming award of liquidated damages despite the employer's use of facially neutral RIF procedures), although they may more often be able to escape liquidated damages by claiming that they believed their actions were sheltered by the BFOQ or an exemption.

Biggins also clarified two other aspects of the liquidated damages award. First, liquidated damages *must* be awarded to a plaintiff who proves a "willful violation." *See also Loveless v. John's Ford, Inc.*, 232 F. App'x 229 (4th Cir. 2007) (award affirmed despite claim that plaintiff would receive a windfall). Second, the liquidated damages award has a punitive purpose. *See also Comm'r v. Schleier*, 515 U.S. 323 (1995) (legislative history suggests Congress intended ADEA liquidated damages to be punitive in nature and not compensatory).

The Supreme Court's interpretation of "willful" in the ADEA closely aligns with its interpretation of "malice or reckless indifference" in §1981a. As for agency questions, *Biggins* did not mention any limitation based on the position of the decisionmaker in the organization or the reasonableness of the employer's antidiscrimination efforts. Do the *Kolstad* agency principles limit liability for the ADEA award? Arguably, the provision reflects Congress's judgment that it is fair to impose double liability (but not more open-ended punitive damages) whenever its conditions are met, regardless of the moral culpability of the employer. *But see Miller v. Raytheon Co.*, 716 F.3d 138 (5th Cir. 2013) (when an ADEA claim warranted liquidated damages and a state claim capped punitive damages, the court should not award both but rather the higher amount). *See generally* Judith J. Johnson, *A Uniform Standard for Exemplary Damages in Employment Discrimination Cases*, 33 U. RICH. L. REV. 41 (1999).

NOTE ON OPERATION OF THE STATUTORY CAPS

As we have seen, the sum of compensatory plus punitive damages available to any one claimant under Title VII and the ADA is capped. You may be surprised to discover that the existence of the caps is not revealed to the jury, which explains why courts so often reduce jury awards to comply with the caps. *See generally* Rebecca Hollander-Blumoff & Matthew T. Bodie, *The Effects of Jury Ignorance About Damage Caps: The Case of the 1991 Civil Rights Act*, 90 IOWA L. REV. 1361 (2005). What does this tell you about the differing perceptions of the wrongfulness of discrimination in the eyes of Congress as compared to juries?

The operation of the caps can be complicated. First, for purposes of which cap applies, the employer's size is computed as of the time of the violation, *e.g.*, *Hernández-Miranda v. Empresas Díaz Masso, Inc.*, 651 F.3d 167 (1st Cir. 2011). The award is capped separately for each plaintiff, *see EEOC v. W&O Inc.*, 213 F.3d 600, 613 (11th Cir. 2000), but the caps apply to the entire amount recoverable by any one claimant on all of her Title VII claims. *See Hudson v. Reno*, 130 F.3d 1193 (6th Cir. 1997); *Baty v. Willamette Indus.*, 172 F.3d 1232, 1246 (10th Cir. 1999).

Despite these limitations, questions have arisen as to how the caps operate when different statutory claims intersect. The most basic issue, the interrelationship of Title VII claims with claims brought under §1981, is addressed in the statute: in Title VII actions under §1981a(a)(1), the plaintiff is eligible for compensatory damages as long as she "cannot recover under 42 U.S.C. 1981." This section, then, seeks to avoid double recovery for the same harm, with the §1981 claim taking priority because it is not capped.

A second interrelationship question arises when a jury finds the same discrimination violates both federal and state employment statutes and awards compensatory damages without apportioning the award between the two claims. When the award exceeds the §1981a(b)(3) cap, the courts have tended to treat the amount in excess of the cap as having been awarded under state law, thus allowing the entire award to stand. *E.g.*, *Rodríguez-Torres v. Caribbean Forms Mfr., Inc.*, 399 F.3d 52, 66 (1st Cir. 2005); *Gagliardo v. Connaught Labs*, 311 F.3d 565 (3d Cir. 2002) (ADA). Suppose the state statute contained the same cap. *See Giles v. GE*, 245 F.3d 474 (5th Cir. 2001) (caps are coextensive, not cumulative); *Bradshaw v. Sch. Bd. of Broward Cnty.*, 486 F.3d 1205 (11th Cir. 2007) (federal cap could not be avoided by attributing some recovery to state claims where state had its own, lower, cap).

NOTE ON PERSONAL LIABILITY OF EMPLOYEES

Another important issue is whether the person who committed the discriminatory act has personal liability or whether liability is limited to the employer. *See generally* Rebecca Hanner White, *Vicarious and Personal Liability for Employment Discrimination*, 30 GA. L. REV. 509 (1996). The seminal case is *Miller v. Maxwell's Int'l, Inc.*, 991 F.2d 583 (9th Cir. 1993), which held that neither Title VII nor the ADEA imposes personal liability. The court reasoned that these statutes are addressed to "employers." While that term is defined to include "agents" of the employer, this inclusion was intended to incorporate the doctrine of respondeat superior, not to impose liability on the agent. Moreover, because both statutes exempt small employers from coverage, the court thought it "inconceivable" that Congress would have intended to impose liability on individual employees. Although a dissenting judge disagreed as to the ADEA, *Miller* has been very influential with other appellate decisions agreeing that employees do not have personal liability under Title VII, *e.g.*, *Fantini v. Salem State Coll.*, 557 F.3d 22 (1st Cir. 2009); the ADEA, *e.g.*, *Stults v. Conoco, Inc.*, 76 F.3d 651 (5th Cir. 1996), or the ADA. *E.g.*, *Albra v. Advan, Inc.*, 490 F.3d 826 (11th Cir. 2007).

In contrast to these statutes, individuals do have personal liability under §1981. *E.g.*, *Patterson v. County of Oneida*, 375 F.3d 206 (2d Cir. 2004); *Jones v. Continental Corp.*, 789 F.2d 308 (6th Cir. 1986). *Contra, Oden v. Oktibbeha County*, 246 F.3d 458 (5th Cir. 2001). While a public official may have qualified immunity from §1981 (and §1983) suits, such immunity can often be overcome in a race discrimination case. *See generally* Alan K. Chen, *The Facts About Qualified Immunity*, 55 EMORY L.J. 229 (2006).

D. ATTORNEYS' FEES

The general "American" rule as to attorneys' fees is that each side pays its own. However, §706(k) of Title VII provides for the grant of attorneys' fees:

> In any action or proceeding under this title the court, in its discretion, may allow the prevailing party, other than the Commission or the United States, a reasonable attorney's fee (including expert fees) as part of the costs, and the Commission and the United States shall be liable for costs the same as a private person.

The fee provisions for §1981 actions, 42 U.S.C. §1988(b), (c), and ADA actions, 42 U.S.C. §12205, generally follow the Title VII pattern although the ADA provision permits the recovery of "litigation expenses," and permits the EEOC, as well as a court, to make a fee award, presumably in federal employee proceedings.

CHRISTIANSBURG GARMENT CO. v. EEOC
434 U.S. 412 (1978)

Justice STEWART delivered the opinion of the Court.

. . . The question in this case is under what circumstances an attorney's fee should be allowed when the defendant is the prevailing party in a Title VII action — a question about which the federal courts have expressed divergent views.

II

It is the general rule in the United States that in the absence of legislation providing otherwise, litigants must pay their own attorney's fees. Congress has provided only limited exceptions to this rule "under selected statutes granting or protecting various federal rights." Some of these statutes make fee awards mandatory for prevailing plaintiffs [citing 29 U.S.C. §216(b), governing awards in ADEA suits]; others make awards permissive but limit them to certain parties, usually prevailing plaintiffs. But many of the statutes are more flexible, authorizing the award of attorney's fees to either plaintiffs or defendants, and entrusting the effectuation of the statutory policy to the discretion of the district courts. Section 706(k) of Title VII of the Civil Rights Act of 1964 falls into this last category, providing as it does that a district court may in its discretion allow an attorney's fee to the prevailing party.

In *Newman v. Piggie Park Enterprises*, 390 U.S. 400 (1968), the Court considered a substantially identical statute authorizing the award of attorney's fees under Title II of the Civil Rights Act of 1964. In that case the plaintiffs had prevailed, and the Court of Appeals had held that they should be awarded their attorney's fees "only to the extent that the respondents' defenses had been advanced 'for purposes of delay and not in good faith.' " We ruled that this "subjective standard" did not properly effectuate the purposes of the counsel-fee provision of Title II. Relying primarily on the intent of Congress to cast a Title II plaintiff in the role of "a 'private attorney general,' vindicating a policy that Congress considered of the highest priority," we held that a prevailing plaintiff under Title II "should ordinarily recover an attorney's fee unless special circumstances would render such an award unjust." We noted in passing that if the objective of Congress had been to permit the award of attorney's fees only against defendants who had acted in bad faith, "no new statutory provision would have been necessary," since even the American common-law rule allows the award of attorney's fees in those exceptional circumstances.

In *Albemarle Paper Co. v. Moody* [reproduced at p. 561], the Court made clear that the *Piggie Park* standard of awarding attorney's fees to a successful plaintiff is equally applicable in an action under Title VII of the Civil Rights Act. It can thus be taken as established, as the parties in this case both acknowledge, that under §706(k) of Title VII a prevailing *plaintiff* ordinarily is to be awarded attorney's fees in all but special circumstances.

III

The question in the case before us is what standard should inform a district court's discretion in deciding whether to award attorney's fees to a successful *defendant* in a Title VII action. . . .

. . . The terms of §706(k) provide no indication whatever of the circumstances under which either a plaintiff or a defendant should be entitled to attorney's fees.

And a moment's reflection reveals that there are at least two strong equitable considerations counseling an attorney's fee award to a prevailing Title VII plaintiff that are wholly absent in the case of a prevailing Title VII defendant.

First, as emphasized so forcefully in *Piggie Park*, the plaintiff is the chosen instrument of Congress to vindicate "a policy that Congress considered of the highest priority." Second, when a district court awards counsel fees to a prevailing plaintiff, it is awarding them against a violator of federal law. As the Court of Appeals clearly perceived, "these policy considerations which support the award of fees to a prevailing plaintiff are not present in the case of a prevailing defendant." A successful defendant seeking counsel fees under §706(k) must rely on quite different equitable considerations. . . .

. . . The first federal appellate court to consider what criteria should govern the award of attorney's fees to a prevailing Title VII defendant was . . . in *United States Steel Corp. v. United States*, 519 F.2d 359 [3d Cir. 1975]. There a District Court had denied a fee award to a defendant that had successfully resisted a Commission demand for documents, the court finding that the Commission's action had not been "'unfounded, meritless, frivolous or vexatiously brought.'" The Court of Appeals concluded that the District Court had not abused its discretion in denying the award. A similar standard was adopted by . . . the Second Circuit in *Carrion v. Yeshiva University*, 535 F.2d 722 [1976]. In upholding an attorney's fee award to a successful defendant, that court stated that such awards should be permitted "not routinely, not simply because he succeeds, but only where the action brought is found to be unreasonable, frivolous, meritless or vexatious."

To the extent that abstract words can deal with concrete cases, we think that the concept embodied in the language adopted by these two Courts of Appeals is correct. We would qualify their words only by pointing out that the term "meritless" is to be understood as meaning groundless or without foundation, rather than simply that the plaintiff has ultimately lost his case, and that the term "vexatious" in no way implies that the plaintiff's subjective bad faith is a necessary prerequisite to a fee award against him. In sum, a district court may in its discretion award attorney's fees to a prevailing defendant in a Title VII case upon a finding that the plaintiff's action was frivolous, unreasonable, or without foundation, even though not brought in subjective bad faith.

In applying these criteria, it is important that a district court resist the understandable temptation to engage in post hoc reasoning by concluding that, because a plaintiff did not ultimately prevail, his action must have been unreasonable or without foundation. This kind of hindsight logic could discourage all but the most airtight claims, for seldom can a prospective plaintiff be sure of ultimate success. No matter how honest one's belief that he has been the victim of discrimination, no matter how meritorious one's claim may appear at the outset, the course of litigation is rarely predictable. Decisive facts may not emerge until discovery or trial. The law may change or clarify in the midst of litigation. Even when the law or the facts appear questionable or unfavorable at the outset, a party may have an entirely reasonable ground for bringing suit. . . . Hence, a plaintiff should not be assessed his opponent's attorney's fees unless a court finds that his claim was frivolous, unreasonable, or groundless, or that the plaintiff continued to litigate after it clearly became so. And, needless to say, if a plaintiff is found to have brought or continued such a claim in *bad faith*, there will be an even stronger basis for charging him with the attorney's fees incurred by the defense. . . .

NOTES

1. *Different Standards for "Prevailing" Parties.* The Court lays out dramatically different standards for prevailing plaintiffs and prevailing defendants, and, for the latter, the standard is not appreciably different from the general rules of federal litigation. *See* Fed. R. Civ. P. 11. Are the Court's policy considerations persuasive in light of the language of §706(k)? Do you agree with the Court that plaintiffs' special role as "private attorneys general" protecting civil rights against violators of federal law justifies differentiating between the standards for attorneys' fees for prevailing plaintiffs versus prevailing defendants?

2. *Prevailing Defendants' Entitlement to Fees.* A number of factors are potentially relevant to whether a prevailing defendant is entitled to a fee award under the Court's standard. One court looked to "(1) whether the plaintiff established a prima facie case; (2) whether the defendant offered to settle; and (3) whether the trial court dismissed the case prior to trial or held a full-blown trial on the merits." *EEOC v. L.B. Foster Co.*, 123 F.3d 746, 751 (3d Cir. 1997). Another found an award of fees merely because of the failure of a plaintiff to prove pretext was an abuse of discretion. *Quintana v. Jenne*, 414 F.3d 1306, 1311 (11th Cir. 2005). *See also Stover v. Hattiesburg Pub. Sch. Dist.*, 549 F.3d 985 (5th Cir. 2008) (no fees award to prevailing defendant despite unanimous verdict for defendant when the trial court had denied employer's motions for summary judgment and judgment as matter of law). But even a case not frivolous when filed can lead to a fee award when plaintiff refuses to dismiss in light of new developments. *See EEOC v. Peoplemark, Inc.*, 732 F.3d 584 (6th Cir. 2013).

Even when a defendant establishes that some of the plaintiff's claims are frivolous and the defendant is therefore entitled to attorneys' fees, it does not follow that the defendant is compensated for all the work entailed in the case. It can recover only for fees related to the frivolous claims, but only "rough justice" is required in sorting out the compensable work from that which would have been entailed in the absence of the frivolous claims. *Fox v. Vice*, 563 U.S. 826, 838 (2011) ("But trial courts need not, and indeed should not, become green-eyeshade accountants. The essential goal in shifting fees (to either party) is to do rough justice, not to achieve auditing perfection.").

3. *When Does a Plaintiff "Prevail"?* Under the statute, only a "prevailing party" is eligible for a fee award. In *Farrar v. Hobby*, 506 U.S. 103 (1992), the issue was whether a plaintiff who had recovered only nominal damages in a §1983 action was the "prevailing party." After reviewing its previous decisions, the Court held that "a plaintiff 'prevails' when actual relief on the merits of his claim materially alters the legal relationship between the parties by modifying the defendant's behavior in a way that directly benefits the plaintiff." *Id.* at 111. That means that the plaintiff must be "entitled to enforce a judgment, consent decree, or settlement against the defendant." *Id.* at 114. Applying that rule, the plaintiff was the "prevailing party" because he could enforce the nominal damages award.

The importance of an actual court judgment was underscored by *Buchannon Board & Care Home, Inc. v. West Virginia Department of Health and Human Resources*, 532 U.S. 598 (2001), where the Court found that plaintiffs were not prevailing parties because the defendants had altered the challenged practices when the suit was filed, thus mooting the case: "A defendant's voluntary change in conduct, although perhaps accomplishing what the plaintiff sought to achieve by the lawsuit, lacks the necessary judicial imprimatur on the change." *Id.* at 605. Further, the Supreme Court has held that a plaintiff who obtains a preliminary injunction but is denied a permanent injunction has not materially altered the legal relationship: it has won the battle but lost the war. *Sole v. Wyner*, 551 U.S. 74 (2007). Note, however, that in *Wyner*, the court ultimately denied a permanent injunction. In many cases, the grant of a preliminary injunction is the functional end of the proceedings, and it seems likely that its award in such cases makes the plaintiff a prevailing party. *See Watson v. Cnty. of Riverside*, 300 F.3d 1092 (9th Cir. 2002).

Even when a plaintiff prevails on one claim, she may not recover fees for unsuccessful claims, although the successful and unsuccessful claims may be so intertwined that it will not be an abuse of discretion for the district court to give full recovery. *See Waldo v. Consumers Energy Co.*, 726 F.3d 802, 823 (6th Cir. 2013) (no abuse of discretion in not reducing a fee award when plaintiff prevailed on only one of seven claims since all the claims were related and focused on a common core of sexual harassment); *Trainor v. HEI Hospitality, LLC*, 699 F.3d 19 (1st Cir. 2012) (no abuse of discretion in not deducting hours pursuing plaintiff's unsuccessful age discrimination claim when it was inextricably intertwined with his successful retaliation claim, which was successful).

Finally, while the plaintiff must receive some relief to be eligible for fees, the degree of plaintiff's success may be taken into account in the amount of the award. The *Farrar* nominal damages award justified a fee award, but not necessarily a substantial one, and subsequent authority conforms that plaintiffs recovering only nominal damages are not likely to receive substantial fees. *See generally* Lawrence D. Rosenthal, *Adding Insult to No Injury: The Denial of Attorney's Fees to "Victorious" Employment Discrimination and Other Civil Rights Plaintiffs*, 37 Fla. St. U. L. Rev. 49 (2009).

4. *When Does a Defendant Prevail?* We saw in *Christiansburg* that a defendant is not entitled to fees unless the plaintiff's claims are frivolous, but *CRST Van Expedited, Inc. v. EEOC*, 136 S. Ct. 1642 (2016), held, consistent with the *Fox v. Vice*, 563 U.S. 826 (2011), rule as to prevailing plaintiffs, see Note 2 above, that defendant could prevail on some claims, even if it did not win on all claims. More importantly, it rejected the argument that, to be prevailing, a defendant must have obtained a ruling "on the merits" of the claim on which it was successful. Since the purpose of the fee-shifting provision is to spare defendants from the costs of frivolous litigation, "Congress must have intended that a defendant could recover fees expended in frivolous, unreasonable, or groundless litigation when the case is resolved in the defendant's favor, whether on the merits or not." *Id.* at 1652. The Court, however, remanded for consideration of whether a defendant must also obtain a preclusive judgment in order to prevail.

5. *The Legal Work That Counts.* A plaintiff's fee award includes the attorney's services for every stage in the enforcement scheme. In a Title VII action, for example, these stages may include arbitration, *Keenan v. City of Phila.*, 983 F.2d 459 (3d Cir. 1992); proceedings before a state agency, *New York Gaslight Club, Inc. v. Carey*, 447 U.S. 54 (1980); taking of a successful appeal, *Morrow v. Dillard*, 580 F.2d 1284 (5th Cir. 1978); post-judgment monitoring of the decree, *Pennsylvania v. Delaware Valley Citizens' Council for Clean Air*, 478 U.S. 546 (1986); *Johnson v. City of Tulsa*, 489 F.3d 1089 (10th Cir. 2007); and even the hearing to establish the propriety and amount of the fee award, *Davis v. City and County of San Francisco*, 976 F.2d 1536 (9th Cir. 1992). *But see Maner v. Linkan LLC*, 602 F. App'x 489 (11th Cir. 2015) (no abuse of discretion to exclude attorney time working on plaintiff's application for state unemployment benefits since these were not "necessary" or "related" to the federal litigation when an adverse result would have had no preclusive effect); *Barrett v. Salt Lake County*, 754 F.3d 854 (10th Cir. 2014) (successful plaintiff not entitled to fees incurred in an internal grievance process).

6. *Calculating the Fee*. Once a court decides that a party is eligible for a fee award pursuant to the principles we have surveyed, it must then calculate that award, a process that has its own complications. The general approach requires first determining the "lodestar," which is the product of hours worked and hourly rate. "There is a 'strong presumption' that the lodestar figure is reasonable, but that presumption may be overcome in those rare circumstances in which the lodestar does not adequately take into account a factor that may properly be considered in determining a reasonable fee." *Perdue v. Kenny A.*, 559 U.S. 542, 554 (2010). The hourly rate should generally be the prevailing rate in the district in which the court sits although a court may increase it to account for a reasonable decision to retain out-of-district counsel. *See Arbor Hill Concerned Citizens Neighborhood Ass'n v. County of Albany*, 484 F.3d 162 (2d Cir. 2007). *Cf. Combs v. City of Huntington*, 829 F.3d 388 (5th Cir. 2016) (while the lodestar bears a "strong presumption" against enhancements, it may be decreased in light of the plaintiff's limited success; however, there is no "proportionality" rule as between the plaintiff's recovery and the fees awarded).

7. *Few "Special Circumstances."* Courts have rejected most arguments that "special circumstances" require the denial of a fee award to a prevailing plaintiff. *E.g., Saski v. Class*, 92 F.3d 232 (4th Cir. 1996) (generous damages recovered); *Love v. Mayor of Cheyenne*, 620 F.2d 235 (10th Cir. 1980) (defendant's good faith); *Int'l Soc'y for Krishna Consciousness, Inc. v. Collins*, 609 F.2d 151 (5th Cir. 1980) (plaintiff's ability to pay). In *New York Gaslight Club, Inc. v. Carey*, 447 U.S. 54 (1980), the Supreme Court found no special circumstances where the plaintiff had been represented by a "public interest group" and was eligible for limited assistance by a state attorney. Where special circumstances have been found, several factors were usually present, such as the defendant's extraordinary good faith, the adverse effect of the award on innocent third persons, and the questionable conduct of the plaintiff. *E.g., Walker v. NationsBank of Fla., N.A.*, 53 F.3d 1548 (11th Cir. 1995). *See also Lewis v. Kendrick*, 944 F.2d 949 (1st Cir. 1991) (fee award denied because plaintiff had greatly exaggerated her injuries and had failed to reduce the amount of her fee request to reflect her very limited recovery ($1,000) at trial).

8. *Balance Billing*. The prospect of the recovery of an attorneys' fee award is often insufficient to attract lawyers to take employment discrimination cases. In *Venegas v. Mitchell*, 495 U.S. 82 (1990), the Supreme Court held that a fee award did not invalidate a contingent-fee contract that entitled the attorney to a larger amount. The Court found nothing in the text or legislative history of §1988 that suggested otherwise. Moreover, "depriving plaintiffs of the option of promising to pay more than the statutory fee if that is necessary to secure counsel of their choice would not further §1988's general purpose of enabling such plaintiffs in civil rights cases to secure competent counsel." *Id.* at 89. *See also Gobert v. Williams*, 323 F.3d 1099, 1100 (5th Cir. 2003) (Title VII does not "regulate what plaintiffs may or may not promise to pay their attorneys if they lose or if they win").

9. *§703(m) Cases*. As we saw in Chapter 1, when a plaintiff demonstrates that race or sex was "a motivating factor" in an employer's action, liability is established. Section 706(g)(2)(B)(i) permits the plaintiff attorneys' fees, even if the defendant is successful in proving it would have made the same decision anyway, so long as the fees are "demonstrated to be directly attributable only to the pursuit of a claim under section 703(m)." A fee award under this provision turns on such factors as whether the plaintiff obtained injunctive or declaratory relief, the public interest in the litigation, and the conduct of the parties. *Canup v. Chipman-Union, Inc.*, 123 F.3d 1440 (11th Cir. 1997); *Sheppard v. Riverview Nursing Ctr., Inc.*, 88 F.3d 1332 (4th Cir. 1996). *But*

see Gudenkauf v. Stauffer Commc'n, Inc., 158 F.3d 1074 (10th Cir. 1998) (attorneys' fees awarded at discretion of court, even when plaintiff did not recover damages). Thus, the standards for making a fee award under §706(k) are inapplicable, although the amount of the award should be calculated in the same way.

10. *Rule 68 and Fees.* Under Fed. R. Civ. P. 68, a defendant may make an offer of judgment. If that offer is not accepted and the plaintiff does not ultimately recover a "more favorable" judgment, the plaintiff is liable for any further costs of the defendant, *Pittari v. Am. Eagle Airlines, Inc.*, 468 F.3d 1056 (8th Cir. 2006), and, of course, cannot recover attorneys' fees or other costs incurred after the offer of judgment. In any event, a defendant who makes an offer of judgment does not become a "prevailing party" for purposes of the award of attorneys' fees merely because the plaintiff ultimately obtains a lower judgment. *See Payne v. Milwaukee County*, 288 F.3d 1021 (7th Cir. 2002).

11. *The Take-Away.* Many believe that the crisis in employment discrimination law is not that plaintiffs' attorneys are getting rich at the expense of more or less innocent defendants. Instead, the crisis is that, even with the right to recover attorneys' fees if a plaintiff prevails, all too many employment discrimination cases are not brought at all or proceed on a *pro se* basis. Even with the prospect of an attorneys' fee award, these cases are still not that attractive to lawyers in comparison to other kinds of legal work. Keep this in mind when you consider whether and when arbitration might be a good alternative to traditional litigation. See Chapter 10. You should also realize that, at least in the class action context, attorneys' fees pose different problems. Most such cases are resolved by settlement, and the argument in that context is that plaintiffs' class attorneys are overcompensated, not undercompensated. *See generally* Myriam Gilles & Gary B. Friedman *Exploding the Class Action Agency Costs Myth: The Social Utility of Entrepreneurial Lawyers*, 155 U. Pa. L. Rev. 103 (2006). See p. 554.

NOTE ON TAXATION, INSURANCE, AND BANKRUPTCY

Three issues not normally considered part of the study of "remedies" can nevertheless have important implications for employment discrimination litigation and settlement. They are the taxation of recoveries, the extent of insurance coverage, and the effect of the bankruptcy of the employer.

Taxation. The Internal Revenue Code, 26 U.S.C §104(a)(2), excludes from gross income only damages received on account of physical injuries or physical sickness. As a result, employment discrimination recoveries for backpay and front pay are taxable as are emotional distress damages, *see Murphy v. IRS*, 493 F.3d 170 (D.C. Cir. 2007), and punitive damages. I.R.C. §104(a)(2) (2006). And, if proceeds of a settlement are taxable, the employer may legally withhold taxes from any payment. *See Rivera v. Baker West, Inc.*, 430 F.3d 1253 (9th Cir. 2005).

For a time, awards of attorneys' fees were also included in gross income. *See Comm'r v. Banks*, 543 U.S. 426 (2005). Although such fees were then deductible as business expenses, some taxpayers were not able to take full advantage of the deduction due to the alternative minimum tax. This problem and other tax rules sometimes resulted in plaintiffs owing more in taxes than they recovered from the defendant! *See generally* Gregg D. Polsky, *The Contingent Attorney's Fee Tax Trap: Ethical, Fiduciary Duty, and Malpractice Implications*, 23 Va. Tax Rev. 615 (2004). Congress addressed this problem by amending §62 of the Internal Revenue Code to allow successful discrimination litigants to deduct from their income taxes attorneys' fees and court

costs associated with monetary awards received by litigation or settlement Pub. L. No.
108-357, 118 Stat. 1418 (2004).

Even after the new statute, the award of a lump sum in backpay may result in
greater tax liability than the plaintiff would have incurred had the compensation been
paid nondiscriminatorily, for example, when the award pushes the employee into a
higher tax bracket. Because of this reality, some courts allow "gross-ups" of monetary
awards to offset tax consequences. *EEOC v. Beverage Distribs. Co., LLC*, 780 F.3d
1018 (10th Cir. 2015); *EEOC v. Northern Star Hospitality, Inc.*, 777 F.3d 898 (7th
Cir. 2015); *but see Fogg v. Gonzales*, 492 F.3d 447 (D.C. Cir. 2007) (no authority for
grossing up backpay). *See generally* Gregg D. Polsky & Stephen F. Befort, *Employment Discrimination Remedies and Tax Gross Ups*, 90 Iowa L. Rev. 67, 69 (2004).

Insurance. Individuals and businesses shift the risk for financial losses they may
incur by paying premiums to insurance carriers. Since a large discrimination claim
could result in a severe financial loss for an employer, several carriers offer coverage
for Title VII violations. Richard A. Bales & Julie McGhghy, in *Insuring Title VII Violations*, 27 S. Ill. U. L.J. 71 (2002), outline various policies. Many insurance carriers
have developed Employment Practices Liability Insurance (EPLI) policies specifically geared to employment-related practices. These policies typically cover liability
arising out of the insured's employment-related offenses against its employees, including court costs. *Id.* However, such policies usually exclude intentional acts from coverage as against public policy. *But see Mo. Pub. Entity Risk Mgmt. Fund v. Investors
Ins. Co. of Am.*, 451 F.3d 925 (8th Cir. 2006) (upholding indemnification for sex
harassment settlement and holding that payment does not violate state public policy).
Under that same rationale, punitive damages are also usually excluded. Other Title
VII forms of relief such as equitable or injunctive relief may be excluded because they
are not deemed to be "damages." The net result can be very limited coverage. Further, EPLI policies are costly, making them not common among employers. Instead
employers hope that if discrimination claims do arise, courts will find coverage under
the traditional general insurance policies they have purchased.

The typical General Liability policy obligates the insurer to pay damages arising
from property damage or personal injury caused by a covered occurrence. *See* Francis
J. Mootz III, *Insurance Coverage of Employment Discrimination Claims*, 52 U. Miami
L. Rev. 1, 10-11 (1997). However, these policies often include specific exclusions of
coverage for employment-related claims. And a policy often obligates the insurer to
pay only for "damages," which might be read to exclude backpay or front pay. Bales
& McGhghy, *supra*, at 80. Other provisions may limit coverage to "bodily injury,"
which may exclude mental distress claims. Finally, most policies contain an exclusion
for any injuries "expected or intended from the standpoint of the insured," which is
aimed at excluding coverage for intentional tort claims. *Id. See Cornett Mgmt. Co.,
LLC v. Fireman's Fund Ins. Co.*, 332 F. App'x 146 (4th Cir. 2009) (no personal injury
coverage for sexual harassment and false-imprisonment claims by female employees
in light of exclusion for "employment-related practices, policies, acts or omissions").

The question of whether insurance policies should cover intentional discrimination is complicated. Holding insurance companies responsible for intentional acts of
their insureds would reduce the incentives for employers not to engage in those acts.
However, to bar insurance carriers from covering these claims might deny compensation to the victims of discrimination when the employer goes bankrupt or is otherwise
unable to pay valid claims. *See* Bales & McGhghy and Mootz for a more in-depth
analysis of these questions.

Bankruptcy. The question of what happens to employment discrimination claims against employers that go into bankruptcy has, surprisingly, not been much litigated. Joanne Gelfand, *The Treatment of Employment Discrimination Claims in Bankruptcy: Priority Status, Stay Relief, Dischargeability, and Exemptions*, 56 U. Miami L. Rev. 601 (2002), lays out the issues that would likely arise. The first question is the priority of employment discrimination claims vis-à-vis other unsecured claims by creditors. Ms. Gelfand argues that claims that arise after the commencement of bankruptcy, as well as claims incurred during the bankruptcy case, should be treated as administrative expenses, which have the highest priority among unsecured claims. In contrast, "[b]ack pay, front pay, and damages stemming from pre-petition acts may be eligible for priority as wages in amounts up to $4,650"; they are entitled to third priority status as long as the claims arose within 90 days of the date that the bankruptcy petition was filed. *Id.* at 621. Claims for earlier periods are paid only after all the priority claims are satisfied. Employees, however, must not sleep on their rights. *See Rederford v. US Airways, Inc.*, 589 F.3d 30 (1st Cir. 2009) (an employment discrimination claim discharged if the employee was notified of the bankruptcy and fails to submit proof of her claim even though she sought reinstatement). *But see Sanchez v. Nw. Airlines, Inc.*, 659 F.3d 671 (8th Cir. 2011) (employee's discrimination claim not discharged despite his failure to file a timely proof because his ADA claim was liability incurred in ordinary course of business exception to filing requirement).

When it is the employee who files for bankruptcy, her failure to disclose a discrimination claim as an asset in her bankruptcy filing may judicially estop her from pursuing it. *Marshall v. Honeywell Tech. Sys.*, 828 F.3d 923 (D.C. Cir. 2016) (applying an abuse of discretion standard, the court upheld the district court's determination that plaintiff was estopped to bring this suit since it was flatly inconsistent with the position she took in the bankruptcy proceedings); *Slater v. U.S. Steel Corp.*, 820 F.3d 193 (11th Cir. 2016); Jones *v. Bob Evans Farms, Inc.*, 811 F.3d 1030 (8th Cir. 2016). *But see Spaine v. Cmty. Contacts, Inc.*, 756 F.3d 542, 548 (7th Cir. 2014) (no judicial estoppel when the failure to disclose in filings was cured by oral disclosure to the trustee and no proof of intentional concealment); *Ah Quin v. Cnty. of Kauai Dep't of Transp.*, 733 F.3d 2676 (9th Cir. 2013) (judicial estoppel inappropriate when plaintiff's omission of her claim in her filings was "inadvertent or mistaken," rather than stemming from an intent to conceal). *See generally* Theresa M. Beiner & Robert B. Chapman, *Take What You Can, Give Nothing Back: Judicial Estoppel, Employment Discrimination, Bankruptcy, and Piracy in the Courts*, 60 U. Miami L. Rev. 1 (2005).

Chapter 10

Managing Risks in Employment Discrimination Disputes

A. INTRODUCTION

The antidiscrimination laws, like other employment regulations, create enormous incentives for employers to manage the risks of liability and the costs of defending lawsuits. Perhaps the most obvious example we have seen is the Supreme Court's effort to structure sexual harassment liability for employers in order to encourage them to take steps to prevent and correct violations. See p. 337. But we also have seen more general efforts by employers to "bullet proof" the workplace in various ways, including diversity training. See Note 4, p. 361.

The antidiscrimination laws confer nonwaivable rights on employees, at least rights that are not waivable prospectively. Thus, discrimination claims provide less room to engage in the kind of "private ordering" that typifies other areas of employment law. Nevertheless, there is some room for maneuver. For example, in Chapter 5 we explored the definition of "employee," distinguishing the employment relationship from other legal relationships such as independent contractor or partner. A firm, therefore, can avoid the antidiscrimination laws by not having employees, or not having enough employees to satisfy the statutory minimums. (Of course, state laws may reach smaller employers.) In addition, firms can sometimes shift the risks of employment by "leasing" workers or by outsourcing, although doctrines such as joint employment limit those strategies. See Note 6, p. 271. One kind of private ordering, then, is the decision not to become a statutory employer at all. Even this approach, however, will not always avoid risks under §1981 because that covers all contractual relationships.

Although it is the employer who has the most control over the employment relationship and thus more room to manage risk in structuring that relationship, employees can play a significant role. In the first instance, the employee decides whether the terms offered are ones he is willing to accept, or to continue working under, and thus the employer's need to attract and retain good workers serves as a practical limit on how the workplace is structured. Additionally, there are some risks an employer cannot avoid. For example, a victim of harassment often can preclude the affirmative defense by promptly invoking internal mechanisms for relief. Further, employee complaints of discrimination create difficult problems for employers because of the statutory proscriptions on retaliation.

But there are some strategies statutory employers can take to avoid or minimize risks. Such techniques include efforts to ensure compliance with the law (such as promulgating harassment policies and undertaking investigations of grievances) to prevent disputes, and to reduce the costs associated with legal disputes when they inevitably arise. Larger employers frequently consult with attorneys and human resource experts in advance of making termination decisions to ensure compliance with the law and to avoid even the appearance of a violation. And where an employee contests a decision, employers frequently seek cost-effective ways of dealing with the dispute short of litigation, such as private resolution or settlement.

Other risk management techniques are explored in more detail in TIMOTHY GLYNN, RACHEL ARNOW-RICHMAN & CHARLES A. SULLIVAN, EMPLOYMENT LAW: PRIVATE ORDERING AND ITS LIMITATIONS (3d ed. Aspen 2015). For example, employers have attempted to reduce risks in litigation by using forum selection and choice-of-law clauses to channel litigation to the employer's benefit. Stipulated damages clauses safeguard employer interests by providing a monetary remedy in the event that an employee breaches its obligations to the employer. And noncompetition clauses can, effectively, bind an employee to an employer and thus discourage suit.

This chapter focuses on two of the more common risk management techniques used by employers and, therefore, ones that must be faced by employees. The first is the use of severance and release agreements in employment terminations to avoid possible litigation. The second is the increasingly common practice of requiring all employees to sign mandatory arbitration agreements.

B.   SETTLEMENTS AND RELEASES

From a litigation perspective, settlement of a plaintiff's claim offers both sides valuable opportunities, although it obviously requires each side to trade off the bird in the bush for the one in the hand. Settlements can occur at any stage during the dispute process. Indeed, Title VII is predicated on the notion that the EEOC will "conciliate" claims before they get to court. *See generally* Michael Z. Green, *Tackling Employment Discrimination with ADR: Does Mediation Offer a Shield for the Haves or Real Opportunity for the Have-Nots?*, 26 BERKELEY J. EMP. & LAB. L. 321 (2005); Michael J. Yelnosky, *Title VII, Mediation, and Collective Action*, 1999 U. ILL. L. REV. 583.

From a risk management perspective, however, it is preferable to avoid a dispute entirely rather than to settle it once it has arisen. Thus, an important risk management technique for employers is obtaining contractual releases of liability from employees as part of the termination process. Such "buyouts" occur frequently in cases of individual discharges. A common technique is for the employer to condition severance pay on the employee's execution of a release. Indeed, buyouts are standard in the context of large-scale reductions in force. As we saw in Chapters 2 and 3, RIFs pose many challenges for employers under the two systematic theories.

Employees cannot *prospectively* waive substantive claims under any of the antidiscrimination statutes: such legislation would be rendered wholly inoperative if employees could be required to waive, or to release, rights as a condition of employment. *See 14 Penn Plaza LLC v. Pyett*, 556 U.S. 247, 265 (2009). *See also Boaz v. FedEx Customer Info. Servs., Inc.*, 725 F.3d 603 (6th Cir. 2013) (agreement that purported to reduce the statute of limitations for claims operated as a waiver of rights and was therefore invalid). However, once a cause of action arises, the employee may release (or waive) any claims she may have. Releases, like all contracts, require consideration, and effective release agreements typically are obtained by providing terminated employees with severance pay contingent upon signing a waiver of rights.

The other requirements for a valid release vary among the antidiscrimination statutes. The 1990 Older Workers Benefit Protection Act, codified at 29 U.S.C. §626(f), authorized waivers of ADEA rights while simultaneously providing some safeguards: "an individual may not waive any right or claim under this Act unless the waiver is knowing and voluntary." The statute then lists specific requirements before a release is "knowing and voluntary."

Although OWBPA borrowed its "voluntary and knowing" standard from the Supreme Court's decision in *Alexander v. Gardner-Denver Co.*, 415 U.S. 36, 52 n.15, *Gardner-Denver* did not elaborate on what is necessary for a waiver to be knowing and voluntary. OWBPA's innovations were to place on the employer the burden of establishing that a waiver qualifies, §626(f)(3), and to specify a laundry list of substantive and procedural requirements. To satisfy the statute, then, an agreement is knowing and voluntary, if it *at least*

(A) is "written in a manner calculated to be understood";
(B) makes specific reference to ADEA claims;
(C) does not waive rights arising after its execution;
(D) is supported by "consideration in addition to anything of value to which the individual already is entitled";
(E) advises the individual in writing to consult an attorney;
(F) provides at least 21 days for the employee to consider her decision; and
(G) provides a seven-day period during which the waiver may be revoked.

[handwritten margin note: OWBPA requirements for a valid release]

§626(f)(1). There are additional requirements when the waiver is sought as part of a program offered to a group of workers, such as an early retirement incentive plan. §626(f)(1)(H). First, the notice period is expanded from 21 days to 45 days. Second, the employer must provide the group being offered the plan with detailed information concerning it, including job titles and ages of those selected for the program. Obviously, this kind of information can help recipients assess the legality of the plan from the perspective of a systemic violation. *See Adams v. Ameritech Servs., Inc.*, 231 F.3d 414 (7th Cir. 2000). The courts have tended to strictly enforce the requirements of OWBPA for a valid release.

OUBRE v. ENTERGY OPERATIONS, INC.
522 U.S. 422 (1998)

Justice KENNEDY delivered the opinion of the Court.

An employee, as part of a termination agreement, signed a release of all claims against her employer. In consideration, she received severance pay in installments. The release, however, did not comply with specific federal statutory requirements for a release of claims under the Age Discrimination in Employment Act of 1967. After receiving the last payment, the employee brought suit under the ADEA. The employer claims the employee ratified and validated the nonconforming release by retaining the monies paid to secure it. The employer also insists the release bars the action unless, as a precondition to filing suit, the employee tenders back the monies received. We disagree and rule that, as the release did not comply with the statute, it cannot bar the ADEA claim. . . .

[Dolores Oubre received a poor performance rating. Her supervisor gave her the option of either improving her performance or accepting a severance package. She had 14 days to consider her options, during which she consulted with attorneys. Oubre decided to accept, and she signed a release], in which she "agree[d] to waive, settle, release, and discharge any and all claims, demands, damages, actions, or causes of action . . . that I may have against Entergy . . . " In exchange, she received six installment payments over the next four months, totaling $6,258.

The Older Workers Benefits Protection Act (OWBPA) imposes specific requirements for releases covering ADEA claims. 29 U.S.C. §§626(f)(1)(B), (F), (G). In procuring the release, Entergy did not comply with the OWBPA in at least three respects: (1) Entergy did not give Oubre enough time to consider her options. (2) Entergy did not give Oubre seven days after she signed the release to change her mind. And (3) the release made no specific reference to claims under the ADEA.

Oubre filed [suit] alleging constructive discharge on the basis of her age in violation of the ADEA and state law. Oubre has not offered or tried to return the $6,258 to Entergy, nor is it clear she has the means to do so. [Entergy was awarded summary judgment on the basis that] Oubre had ratified the defective release by failing to return or offer to return the monies she had received. . . .

II

The employer rests its case upon general principles of state contract jurisprudence. As the employer recites the rule, contracts tainted by mistake, duress, or even fraud are voidable at the option of the innocent party. See 1 Restatement (Second) of Contracts §7, and Comment b (1979). The employer maintains, however, that before the innocent party can elect avoidance, she must first tender back any benefits received under the contract. See, e.g., Dreiling v. Home State Life Ins. Co., 515 P.2d 757, 766-767 (Kan. 1973). If she fails to do so within a reasonable time after learning of her rights, the employer contends, she ratifies the contract and so makes it binding. Restatement (Second) of Contracts, supra, §7, Comments d, e. The employer also invokes the doctrine of equitable estoppel. As a rule, equitable estoppel bars a party from shirking the burdens of a voidable transaction for as long as she retains the benefits received under it. See, e.g., Buffum v. Peter Barceloux Co., 289 U.S. 227, 234 (1933) (citing state case law from Indiana and New York). Applying these principles, the employer claims the employee ratified the ineffective release (or faces estoppel) by retaining all the sums paid in consideration of it. The employer, then, relies not upon the execution of the release but upon a later, distinct ratification of its terms.

[These rules may not be as clear as the employer asserts but in any event common law "tender back" requirements] do not consider the question raised by statutory standards for releases and a statutory declaration making nonconforming releases ineffective. It is the latter question we confront here.

In 1990, Congress amended the ADEA by passing the OWBPA. The OWBPA provides: "An individual may not waive any right or claim under [the ADEA] unless the waiver is knowing and voluntary. . . . [A] waiver may not be considered knowing and voluntary unless at a minimum" it satisfies certain enumerated requirements, including the three listed above. 29 U.S.C. §626(f)(1).

The statutory command is clear: An employee "may not waive" an ADEA claim unless the waiver or release satisfies the OWBPA's requirements. The policy of the Older Workers Benefit Protection Act is likewise clear from its title: It is designed to protect the rights and benefits of older workers. The OWBPA implements Congress' policy via a strict, unqualified statutory stricture on waivers, and we are bound to take Congress at its word. Congress imposed specific duties on employers who seek releases of certain claims created by statute. Congress delineated these duties with precision and without qualification: An employee "may not waive" an ADEA claim unless the employer complies with the statute. Courts cannot with ease presume ratification of that which Congress forbids. . . .

The rule proposed by the employer would frustrate the statute's practical operation as well as its formal command. In many instances a discharged employee likely will have spent the monies received and will lack the means to tender their return. These realities might tempt employers to risk noncompliance with the OWBPA's waiver provisions, knowing it will be difficult to repay the monies and relying on ratification. We ought not to open the door to an evasion of the statute by this device. . . .

In further proceedings in this or other cases, courts may need to inquire whether the employer has claims for restitution, recoupment, or setoff against the employee, and these questions may be complex where a release is effective as to some claims but not as to ADEA claims. We need not decide those issues here, however. It suffices to hold that the release cannot bar the ADEA claim because it does not conform to the statute. Nor did the employee's mere retention of monies amount to a ratification equivalent to a valid release of her ADEA claims, since the retention did not comply with the OWBPA any more than the original release did. The statute governs the effect of the release on ADEA claims, and the employer cannot invoke the employee's failure to tender back as a way of excusing its own failure to comply. . . . ✳

[Justice Breyer, joined by Justice O'Connor, concurred, writing that the statute made the contract voidable, not void, which meant that the employee could continue to enforce it if she so elected. Thus, it is doubtful that an employer could cancel its own obligations, such as providing ongoing health benefits. However, when an employee has elected to void the contract and sue, "nothing in the statute prevents his employer from asking for restitution of his reciprocal payment or relief from any ongoing reciprocal obligation."]

[Justice Thomas, joined by Chief Justice Rehnquist, dissented, as did Justice SCALIA.]

NOTES

1. *Reading OWBPA Strictly.* As *Oubre* makes clear, releases of ADEA claims are subject to a number of strict requirements. *See also Ruehl v. Viacom, Inc.*, 500 F.3d 375 (3d Cir. 2007) (waiver invalid even though it acknowledged employee's receipt of required information when such information was not actually provided the employee); *Syverson v. IBM*, 472 F.3d 1072 (9th Cir. 2006) (direction to consult an attorney did not cure ambiguous waiver language used since waiver was not written in a manner calculated to be understood by the intended participants). But beyond the enumerated conditions for the validity of waivers, the statute's overarching requirement is that

any waiver be "knowing and voluntary." This suggests that even a waiver that satisfies the specific requirements may still not be valid.

2. *Releases Under Other Discrimination Statutes.* OWBPA on its face reaches only ADEA claims, not claims under other antidiscrimination statutes. However, because releases that satisfy OWBPA are the "gold standard," employers structure their forms to ensure that they meet its requirements and use them for the release of all kinds of discrimination and other employment-related claims. However, when employers' releases fall short of OWBPA standards, the principles governing releases under other federal laws is less clear. Some courts have applied the policies underlying OWBPA to other statutes. *See Richardson v. Sugg*, 448 F.3d 1046, 1054 (8th Cir. 2006) (the policy concerns that led *Oubre* to reject the tender-back requirement for the ADEA also apply to Title VII). The dominant approach, however, is more amorphous, with courts looking to the "totality of the circumstances" to determine whether the release was "knowing and voluntary." *E.g.*, *Hampton v. Ford Motor Co.*, 561 F.3d 709 (7th Cir. 2009). *See generally* Daniel P. O'Gorman, *Show Me the Money: The Applicability of Contract Law's Ratification and Tender-Back Doctrines to Title VII Releases*, 84 Tul. L. Rev. 675 (2010); Daniel P. O'Gorman, A *State of Disarray: The "Knowing and Voluntary" Standard for Releasing Claims Under Title VII of the Civil Rights Act of 1964*, 8 U. Pa. J. Lab. & Emp. L. 73 (2005). While this approach allows courts to enforce releases that would not be valid under OWBPA, it is a somewhat more demanding standard than would govern under normal contract law.

3. *Employer Rights After* Oubre. The *Oubre* majority did not wholly deprive employers of remedies for breach of a release that does not satisfy OWBPA since the employer may be able to recover back the money paid by a claim for "restitution, recoupment or setoff." What did the Court mean? Does Justice Breyer's concurrence help? EEOC regulations provide that the employee cannot be liable for more than the lesser of "the amount recovered by the employee, or the consideration the employee received for signing the waiver." 29 C.F.R. §1625.23(c)(1) (2018).

4. *Good or Bad Policy?* Professor Michael C. Harper, in *Age-Based Exit Incentives, Coercion, and the Prospective Waiver of ADEA Rights: The Failure of the Older Workers Benefit Protection Act*, 79 Va. L. Rev. 1271, 1277-79 (1993), argues that the release scheme, in effect, encourages age discrimination because in large-scale reductions in force employers typically offer "retirement incentives," which are more generous than normal severance arrangements. Because employees who do not opt in to such programs may well end up being riffed anyway, there is substantial pressure to accept the offer even if the employee would prefer to continue working. The release she then signs precludes later suit. In short, Professor Harper argues that the statute functionally approves a prospective waiver of ADEA rights, *id.* at 1294, although OWBPA expressly bars such waivers.

Of course, releases pose difficult choices for employees in any setting. They are least problematic for employees settling suits after significant discovery and with the advice of their attorney. At the other extreme, an individual employee faced with an imminent termination and the offer of relatively little severance must decide whether to waive rights (often for a sum that ranges between one week's and one month's pay for every year worked) with little opportunity to assess the worth of any claims he or she may have.

5. *Prospective Waivers.* Waivers of prospective rights are explicitly barred by OWBPA, which requires that a valid release "not waive rights arising after its execution." This rule originated in a Title VII case, *Alexander v. Gardner-Denver Co.*, 415 U.S. 36, 51

many releases seek to conform to OWBPA standard

(1974) ("we think it clear that there can be no prospective waiver of an employee's rights under Title VII"), and it was reiterated more recently in *14 Penn Plaza LLC v. Pyett*, 556 U.S. 247, 265 (2009). The courts, therefore, have generally refused to enforce agreements that purport to waive discrimination claims that may arise in the future. *See Richardson v. Sugg*, 448 F.3d 1046, 1057 (8th Cir. 2006) (former Arkansas Razorbacks basketball coach held not bound by a clause in his employment contract releasing the university from all liability for a discharge before the end of his contract). *But see Nilsson v. City of Mesa*, 503 F.3d 947 (9th Cir. 2007) (upholding waiver of discrimination claims relating to employer's pre-hire background investigation). However, the courts have been unclear about the validity of releases that explicitly absolve the employer of any duty to rehire the releasing employee. *Kellogg Co. v. Sabhlok*, 471 F.3d 629 (6th Cir. 2006).

6. *Gag Clauses.* One advantage of settlement for the employer is the ability to avoid the publicity inherent in any lawsuit. Releases, therefore, typically have "confidentiality" clauses that bar the employee from voluntarily providing information about her claim to others (although they typically allow the former employee to respond to legal process or file with the EEOC). Such releases sometimes go further and have very broad "nondisparagement" clauses, which limit the former employee's ability to "bad mouth" the employer at all. There is a lively debate about the systemic effects of these kinds of clauses. *See generally* Scott A. Moss *Illuminating Secrecy: A New Economic Analysis of Confidential Settlements*, 105 Mich. L. Rev. 867 (2007); Minna J. Kotkin, *Invisible Settlements, Invisible Discrimination*, 84 N.C. L. Rev. 927 (2006). *See also* Jon Bauer, *Buying Witness Silence: Evidence-Suppressing Settlements and Lawyers' Ethics*, 87 Or. L. Rev. 481, 486-87 (2008) (the model rules bar lawyers from requesting that nonclients "refrain from voluntarily providing relevant information to another party. Lawyers who make settlement offers conditioned on noncooperation are doing precisely what the rule prohibits"). Employees often insist that the employer also promise not to disparage them, but such demands are not as often successful.

C. ARBITRATING DISCRIMINATION CLAIMS

Perhaps the most common and important employer risk management technique is arbitration. While parties can agree to arbitrate (or use other alternate dispute resolution techniques) at any point in the dispute resolution process, employers increasingly require their current workers and applicants for employment to agree to arbitrate any employment-related disputes that may arise. Such mandatory arbitration is a continuing subject of fierce dispute.

Arbitration has a long and respectable history in labor relations, and the first Title VII arbitration case arose in that context. *Alexander v. Gardner-Denver Co.*, 415 U.S. 36 (1974), involved a plaintiff who sued his employer after his union had unsuccessfully pursued arbitration on his behalf claiming that the employer had discriminated in violation of the governing collective bargaining agreement. The Court viewed Title VII and collective bargaining agreement remedies as independent, which meant that the failure in arbitration did not prejudice the plaintiff's right to a federal court action to vindicate his Title VII rights.

Gardner-Denver not only held that submission of a dispute to arbitration does not preclude a subsequent Title VII suit but also ruled against judicial deference to prior arbitral awards. The Court noted that enforcing Title VII compliance was entrusted to federal courts, not to arbitrators; that the elaborate statutory suit prerequisites did not refer to arbitration; and that Congress had evinced an intent to provide parallel or overlapping remedies. The Court also stressed the inappropriateness of deference to collective bargaining arbitration because arbitrators are selected for their knowledge of industrial relations, not public law concepts; further, arbitrators are bound to effectuate the intent of the parties as embodied in the contract, even though that intent may conflict with the law. In addition, unions controlled the process under a collective bargaining agreement, which may prejudice individual rights. Finally, the Court thought that limitations in arbitral procedure might affect the quality of the decisions rendered, including limited discovery and "the absence of compulsory process, cross-examination, and testimony under oath." 415 U.S. at 57-58. The Court did state that, while an arbitration award was in no sense preclusive in a later court suit, courts might admit arbitral decisions as evidence. *Id.* at 60 n.21.

Gardner-Denver seemed fatal to pre-dispute agreements to arbitrate employment discrimination claims. However, a number of later Court decisions outside the employment context reinvigorated the use of arbitration as part of the ADR movement, *see* Margaret L. Moses, *Statutory Misconstruction: How the Supreme Court Created a Federal Arbitration Law Never Enacted by Congress*, 34 Fla. St. U. L. Rev. 99 (2006), and the Supreme Court functionally overturned *Gardner-Denver* in a series of employment decisions culminating in the next principal case.

14 PENN PLAZA, LLC v. PYETT
556 U.S. 247 (2009)

Justice THOMAS delivered the opinion of the Court.

The question presented by this case is whether a provision in a collective-bargaining agreement that clearly and unmistakably requires union members to arbitrate claims arising under the Age Discrimination in Employment Act of 1967 is enforceable. The United States Court of Appeals for the Second Circuit held that this Court's decision in *Alexander v. Gardner-Denver Co.* forbids enforcement of such arbitration provisions. We disagree and reverse the judgment of the Court of Appeals.

I

Respondents are members of the Service Employees International Union, Local 32BJ[, which is the exclusive bargaining representative of employees within the building-services industry in New York City. Since the 1930s, the Union has engaged in industry-wide collective bargaining with the Realty Advisory Board on Labor Relations, Inc., a multiemployer bargaining association for the New York City real-estate industry.] The agreement between the Union and the RAB is embodied in their Collective Bargaining Agreement for Contractors and Building Owners (CBA). The CBA requires union members to submit all claims of employment discrimination to binding arbitration under the CBA's grievance and dispute resolution procedures:

30. NO DISCRIMINATION. There shall be no discrimination against any present or future employee by reason of race, creed, color, age, disability, national origin, sex,

union membership, or any characteristic protected by law, including, but not limited to, claims made pursuant to Title VII of the Civil Rights Act, the Americans with Disabilities Act, the Age Discrimination in Employment Act, the New York State Human Rights Law, the New York City Human Rights Code, . . . or any other similar laws, rules, or regulations. All such claims shall be subject to the grievance and arbitration procedure (Articles V and VI) as the sole and exclusive remedy for violations. Arbitrators shall apply appropriate law in rendering decisions based upon claims of discrimination.

1

Petitioner 14 Penn Plaza LLC is a member of the RAB. It owns and operates the New York City office building where, prior to August 2003, respondents worked as night lobby watchmen and in other similar capacities. Respondents were directly employed by petitioner Temco Service Industries, Inc. (Temco), a maintenance service and cleaning contractor. In August 2003, with the Union's consent, 14 Penn Plaza engaged Spartan Security, a unionized security services contractor and affiliate of Temco, to provide licensed security guards to staff the lobby and entrances of its building. Because this rendered respondents' lobby services unnecessary, Temco reassigned them to jobs as night porters and light duty cleaners in other locations in the building. Respondents contend that these reassignments led to a loss in income, caused them emotional distress, and were otherwise less desirable than their former positions.

[At respondents' request, the Union filed grievances on various grounds, including age discrimination in violation of the CBA. When the grievances failed, the Union filed for arbitration on the other grounds but did not prosecute the age discrimination claim: "[b]ecause it had consented to the contract for new security personnel at 14 Penn Plaza, the Union believed that it could not legitimately object to respondents' reassignments as discriminatory." At that point, the plaintiffs filed with the EEOC and later sued in federal court alleging that their reassignment violated the ADEA. The employer moved to compel arbitration under the FAA. The district court denied the motion and the Second Circuit affirmed because *Gardner-Denver* "remains good law."]

II

A

The NLRA governs federal labor-relations law. As permitted by that statute, respondents designated the Union as their "exclusive representativ[e] . . . for the purposes of collective bargaining in respect to rates of pay, wages, hours of employment, or other conditions of employment." As the employees' exclusive bargaining representative, the Union "enjoys broad authority . . . in the negotiation and administration of [the] collective bargaining contract." But this broad authority "is accompanied by a responsibility of equal scope, the responsibility and duty of fair representation." The employer has a corresponding duty under the NLRA to bargain in good faith "with the representatives of his employees" on wages, hours, and conditions of employment.

In this instance, the Union and the RAB, negotiating on behalf of 14 Penn Plaza, collectively bargained in good faith and agreed that employment-related discrimination claims, including claims brought under the ADEA, would be resolved in arbitration. This freely negotiated term between the Union and the RAB easily qualifies as a "conditio[n] of employment" that is subject to mandatory bargaining under §159(a). [The] decision to fashion a collective bargaining agreement to require arbitration of employment-discrimination claims is no different from the many other decisions made by parties in designing grievance machinery.

Respondents, however, contend that the arbitration clause here is outside the permissible scope of the collective-bargaining process because it affects the "employees' individual, non-economic statutory rights." We disagree. Parties generally favor arbitration precisely because of the economics of dispute resolution. *See Circuit City Stores, Inc. v. Adams*, 532 U.S. 105, 123 (2001) ("Arbitration agreements allow parties to avoid the costs of litigation, a benefit that may be of particular importance in employment litigation, which often involves smaller sums of money than disputes concerning commercial contracts"). As in any contractual negotiation, a union may agree to the inclusion of an arbitration provision in a collective-bargaining agreement in return for other concessions from the employer. Courts generally may not interfere in this bargained-for exchange. "Judicial nullification of contractual concessions . . . is contrary to what the Court has recognized as one of the fundamental policies of the National Labor Relations Act — freedom of contract."

As a result, the CBA's arbitration provision must be honored unless the ADEA itself removes this particular class of grievances from the NLRA's broad sweep. *See Mitsubishi Motors Corp. v. Soler Chrysler-Plymouth, Inc.*, 473 U.S. 614, 628 (1985). It does not. This Court has squarely held that the ADEA does not preclude arbitration of claims brought under the statute. *See Gilmer [v. Interstate/Johnson Lane Corp.*, 500 U.S. 20 (1991)].

In *Gilmer,* the Court explained that "[a]lthough all statutory claims may not be appropriate for arbitration, '[h]aving made the bargain to arbitrate, the party should be held to it unless Congress itself has evinced an intention to preclude a waiver of judicial remedies for the statutory rights at issue.'" And "[i]f Congress intended the substantive protection afforded by the ADEA to include protection against waiver of the right to a judicial forum, that intention will be deducible from text or legislative history." The Court determined that "nothing in the text of the ADEA or its legislative history explicitly precludes arbitration." The Court also concluded that arbitrating ADEA disputes would not undermine the statute's "remedial and deterrent function." In the end, the employee's "generalized attacks" on "the adequacy of arbitration procedures" were "insufficient to preclude arbitration of statutory claims" because there was no evidence that "Congress, in enacting the ADEA, intended to preclude arbitration of claims under that Act."

The *Gilmer* Court's interpretation of the ADEA fully applies in the collective-bargaining context. Nothing in the law suggests a distinction between the status of arbitration agreements signed by an individual employee and those agreed to by a union representative. This Court has required only that an agreement to arbitrate statutory antidiscrimination claims be "explicitly stated" in the collective-bargaining agreement. *Wright [v. Universal Maritime Service Corp.*, 525 U.S. 70 (1998)]. The CBA under review here meets that obligation. Respondents incorrectly counter that an individual employee must personally "waive" a "[substantive] right" to proceed in court for a waiver to be "knowing and voluntary" under the [OWBPA amendment to the ADEA]. 29 U.S.C. §626(f)(1). As explained below, however, the agreement to arbitrate ADEA claims is not the waiver of a "substantive right" as that term is employed in the ADEA. Indeed, if the "right" referred to in §626(f)(1) included the prospective waiver of the right to bring an ADEA claim in court, even a waiver signed by an individual employee would be invalid as the statute also prevents individuals from "waiv[ing] rights or claims that may arise after the date the waiver is executed." §626(f)(1)(C).[6]

Examination of the two federal statutes at issue in this case, therefore, yields a straightforward answer to the question presented: The NLRA provided the Union and the RAB with statutory authority to collectively bargain for arbitration of workplace discrimination claims, and Congress did not terminate that authority with respect to federal age-discrimination claims in the ADEA. . . .

B

The CBA's arbitration provision is also fully enforceable under the *Gardner-Denver* line of cases. Respondents interpret *Gardner-Denver* and its progeny to hold that "a union cannot waive an employee's right to a judicial forum under the federal antidiscrimination statutes" because "allowing the union to waive this right would substitute the union's interests for the employee's antidiscrimination rights." The "combination of union control over the process and inherent conflict of interest with respect to discrimination claims," they argue, "provided the foundation for the Court's holding [in *Gardner-Denver*] that arbitration under a collective bargaining agreement could not preclude an individual employee's right to bring a lawsuit in court to vindicate a statutory discrimination claim." We disagree.

1

[The holding of *Gardner-Denver* is not as broad as respondents suggest. The collective-bargaining agreement in that case prohibited discrimination and also guaranteed against discharge "except for just cause." The employee claimed both discrimination and unjust discharge, and the arbitrator found just cause for the termination but did not explicitly address the race discrimination claim. The employee then filed a Title VII suit in federal court only to have it dismissed because the election to pursue arbitration bound the employee to the arbitral decision and precluded suit on any other grounds.]

This Court reversed the judgment on the narrow ground that the arbitration was not preclusive because the collective-bargaining agreement did not cover statutory claims. As a result, the lower courts erred in relying on the "doctrine of election of remedies" to bar the employee's Title VII claim. "That doctrine, which refers to

---

6. Respondents' contention that §118 of the Civil Rights Act of 1991, note following 42 U.S.C. §1981 (2000 ed.), precludes the enforcement of this arbitration agreement also is misplaced. Section 118 expresses Congress' support for alternative dispute resolution: "Where appropriate and to the extent authorized by law, the use of alternative means of dispute resolution, including . . . arbitration, is encouraged to resolve disputes arising under" the ADEA. Respondents argue that the legislative history actually signals Congress' intent to preclude arbitration waivers in the collective-bargaining context. In particular, respondents point to a House Report that, in spite of the statute's plain language, interprets §118 to support their position. See H.R. Rep. No. 102-40, pt. 1, p. 97 (1991) ("[A]ny agreement to submit disputed issues to arbitration . . . in the context of a collective bargaining agreement . . . does not preclude the affected person from seeking relief under the enforcement provisions of Title VII. This view is consistent with the Supreme Court's interpretation of Title VII in *Alexander v. Gardner-Denver Co.*"). But the legislative history mischaracterizes the holding of *Gardner-Denver*, which does not prohibit collective bargaining for arbitration of ADEA claims. Moreover, reading the legislative history in the manner suggested by respondents would create a direct conflict with the statutory text, which encourages the use of arbitration for dispute resolution without imposing any constraints on collective bargaining. In such a contest, the text must prevail.

situations where an individual pursues remedies that are legally or factually inconsistent" with each other, did not apply to the employee's dual pursuit of arbitration and a Title VII discrimination claim in district court. The employee's collective-bargaining agreement did not mandate arbitration of statutory antidiscrimination claims. "As the proctor of the bargain, the arbitrator's task is to effectuate the intent of the parties." Because the collective-bargaining agreement gave the arbitrator "authority to resolve only questions of contractual rights," his decision could not prevent the employee from bringing the Title VII claim in federal court "regardless of whether certain contractual rights are similar to, or duplicative of, the substantive rights secured by Title VII."

The Court also explained that the employee had not waived his right to pursue his Title VII claim in federal court by participating in an arbitration that was premised on the same underlying facts as the Title VII claim. Thus, whether the legal theory of preclusion advanced by the employer rested on "the doctrines of election of remedies" or was recast "as resting instead on the doctrine of equitable estoppel and on themes of res judicata and collateral estoppel," it could not prevail in light of the collective-bargaining agreement's failure to address arbitration of Title VII claims.

["The Court's decisions following *Gardner-Denver* have not broadened its holding to make it applicable to the facts of this case." *Barrentine v. Arkansas-Best Freight System, Inc.*, 450 U.S. 728 (1981), found that arbitration of a collective bargaining agreement wage claim did not bar a later Fair Labor Standards Act suit when the arbitration provision "did not expressly reference the statutory claim at issue." *McDonald v. West Branch*, 466 U.S. 284 (1984), rejected "preclusive effect" for an unappealed arbitration award in a §1983 case when rights under that statute were "left unaddressed by the arbitration agreement." In all three cases, the Court's decision] hinged on the scope of the collective-bargaining agreement and the arbitrator's parallel mandate.

The facts underlying *Gardner-Denver*, *Barrentine*, and *McDonald* reveal the narrow scope of the legal rule arising from that trilogy of decisions. Summarizing those opinions in *Gilmer*, this Court made clear that the *Gardner-Denver* line of cases "did not involve the issue of the enforceability of an agreement to arbitrate statutory claims." Those decisions instead "involved the quite different issue whether arbitration of contract-based claims precluded subsequent judicial resolution of statutory claims. Since the employees there had not agreed to arbitrate their statutory claims, and the labor arbitrators were not authorized to resolve such claims, the arbitration in those cases understandably was held not to preclude subsequent statutory actions." See also *Wright*. *Gardner-Denver* and its progeny thus do not control the outcome where, as is the case here, the collective-bargaining agreement's arbitration provision expressly covers both statutory and contractual discrimination claims.[8]

2

We recognize that apart from their narrow holdings, the *Gardner-Denver* line of cases included broad dicta that were highly critical of the use of arbitration for the

---

8. Because today's decision does not contradict the holding of *Gardner-Denver*, we need not resolve the *stare decisis* concerns raised by the dissenting opinions. But given the development of this Court's arbitration jurisprudence in the intervening years, *Gardner-Denver* would appear to be a strong candidate for overruling if the dissents' broad view of its holding were correct.

vindication of statutory antidiscrimination rights. That skepticism, however, rested on a misconceived view of arbitration that this Court has since abandoned.

[First, *Gardner-Denver* was in error to assume that "an agreement to submit statutory discrimination claims to arbitration was tantamount to a waiver of those rights."] The Court was correct in concluding that federal antidiscrimination rights may not be prospectively waived, see 29 U.S.C. §626(f)(1)(C), but it confused an agreement to arbitrate those statutory claims with a prospective waiver of the substantive right. The decision to resolve ADEA claims by way of arbitration instead of litigation does not waive the statutory right to be free from workplace age discrimination; it waives only the right to seek relief from a court in the first instance. . . . The suggestion in *Gardner-Denver* that the decision to arbitrate statutory discrimination claims was tantamount to a substantive waiver of those rights, therefore, reveals a distorted understanding of the compromise made when an employee agrees to compulsory arbitration.

[The Court viewed *Gardner-Denver* as "a direct descendant" of other decisions that were hostile to arbitration but have since been overruled.] The timeworn "mistrust of the arbitral process" harbored by the Court in *Gardner-Denver* thus weighs against reliance on anything more than its core holding. Indeed, in light of the "radical change, over two decades, in the Court's receptivity to arbitration," *Wright*, reliance on any judicial decision similarly littered with . . . overt hostility to the enforcement of arbitration agreements would be ill advised.[9]

Second, *Gardner-Denver* mistakenly suggested that certain features of arbitration made it a forum "well suited to the resolution of contractual disputes," but "a comparatively inappropriate forum for the final resolution of rights created by Title VII." According to the Court, the "factfinding process in arbitration" is "not equivalent to judicial factfinding" and the "informality of arbitral procedure . . . makes arbitration a less appropriate forum for final resolution of Title VII issues than the federal courts." The Court also questioned the competence of arbitrators to decide federal statutory claims. In the Court's view, "the resolution of statutory or constitutional issues is a primary responsibility of courts, and judicial construction has proved especially necessary with respect to Title VII, whose broad language frequently can be given meaning only by reference to public law concepts." *Gardner-Denver*.

These misconceptions have been corrected. For example, the Court has "recognized that arbitral tribunals are readily capable of handling the factual and legal complexities of antitrust claims, notwithstanding the absence of judicial instruction and supervision" and that "there is no reason to assume at the outset that arbitrators will not follow the law." [*Shearson/American Express Inc. v.*] *McMahon*[, 482 U.S. 220, 232 (1987)]. An arbitrator's capacity to resolve complex questions of fact and law extends with equal force to discrimination claims brought under the ADEA. Moreover, the recognition that arbitration procedures are more streamlined than federal litigation is not a basis for finding the forum somehow inadequate; the relative informality of

---

9. Justice Stevens suggests that the Court is displacing its "earlier determination of the relevant provisions' meaning" based on a "preference for arbitration." But his criticism lacks any basis. . . . [C]ontrary to Justice Stevens' accusation, it is the Court's fidelity to the ADEA's text — not an alleged preference for arbitration — that dictates the answer to the question presented. As *Gilmer* explained, nothing in the text of Title VII or the ADEA precludes contractual arbitration, and Justice Stevens has never suggested otherwise. Rather, he has always contended that permitting the "compulsory arbitration" of employment-discrimination claims conflicts with his perception of "the congressional purpose animating the ADEA." *Gilmer* (Stevens, J., dissenting). The *Gilmer* Court did not adopt Justice Stevens' personal view of the purposes underlying the ADEA, for good reason: That view is not embodied within the statute's text. . . .

arbitration is one of the chief reasons that parties select arbitration. Parties "trad[e] the procedures and opportunity for review of the courtroom for the simplicity, informality, and expedition of arbitration." *Mitsubishi Motors Corp.* In any event, "[i]t is unlikely . . . that age discrimination claims require more extensive discovery than other claims that we have found to be arbitrable, such as Racketeer Influenced and Corrupt Organizations Act and antitrust claims." *Gilmer.* At bottom, objections centered on the nature of arbitration do not offer a credible basis for discrediting the choice of that forum to resolve statutory antidiscrimination claims.

Third, the Court in *Gardner-Denver* raised in a footnote a "further concern" regarding "the union's exclusive control over the manner and extent to which an individual grievance is presented." The Court suggested that in arbitration, as in the collective-bargaining process, a union may subordinate the interests of an individual employee to the collective interests of all employees in the bargaining unit.

We cannot rely on this judicial policy concern as a source of authority for introducing a qualification into the ADEA that is not found in its text. . . . Congress is fully equipped "to identify any category of claims as to which agreements to arbitrate will be held unenforceable." *Mitsubishi Motors Corp.* Until Congress amends the ADEA to meet the conflict-of-interest concern identified in the *Gardner-Denver* dicta, and seized on by respondents here, there is "no reason to color the lens through which the arbitration clause is read" simply because of an alleged conflict of interest between a union and its members. This is a "battl[e] that should be fought among the political branches and the industry. Those parties should not seek to amend the statute by appeal to the Judicial Branch."

The conflict-of-interest argument also proves too much. Labor unions certainly balance the economic interests of some employees against the needs of the larger work force as they negotiate collective-bargaining agreements and implement them on a daily basis. But this attribute of organized labor does not justify singling out an arbitration provision for disfavored treatment. . . . Respondents' argument that they were deprived of the right to pursue their ADEA claims in federal court by a labor union with a conflict of interest is therefore unsustainable; it amounts to a collateral attack on the NLRA.

[The Court noted that "Congress has accounted for this conflict of interest in several ways," including unions' "duty of fair representation," applicable to collective bargaining agreement administration and enforcement as well as negotiation activities.] Thus, a union is subject to liability under the NLRA if it illegally discriminates against older workers in either the formation or governance of the collective-bargaining agreement, such as by deciding not to pursue a grievance on behalf of one of its members for discriminatory reasons. *See Vaca v. Sipes*, 386 U.S. 171, 177 (1967) (describing the duty of fair representation as the "statutory obligation to serve the interests of *all* members without hostility or discrimination toward any, to exercise its discretion with complete good faith and honesty, and to avoid arbitrary conduct" (emphasis added)). Respondents in fact brought a fair representation suit against the Union based on its withdrawal of support for their age-discrimination claims. Given this avenue that Congress has made available to redress a union's violation of its duty to its members, it is particularly inappropriate to ask this Court to impose an artificial limitation on the collective-bargaining process.

In addition, a union is subject to liability under the ADEA if the union itself discriminates against its members on the basis of age. See 29 U.S.C. §623(d); see also 1 B. Lindemann & P. Grossman, Employment Discrimination Law 1575-1581 (4th ed. 2007). . . . In sum, Congress has provided remedies for the situation where a labor union is less than vigorous in defense of its members' claims of discrimination under the ADEA.

III . . .

[The plaintiffs argued that "the CBA operates as a substantive waiver of their ADEA rights because it not only precludes a federal lawsuit, but also allows the Union to block arbitration of these claims,"] but the Court did not feel itself "positioned to resolve in the first instance whether the CBA allows the Union to prevent respondents from 'effectively vindicating' their 'federal statutory rights in the arbitral forum,'" *Green Tree Financial Corp.-Ala. v. Randolph*, 531 U.S. 79, 90 (2000). Resolution of this question at this juncture would be particularly inappropriate in light of our hesitation to invalidate arbitration agreements on the basis of speculation.

IV

We hold that a collective-bargaining agreement that clearly and unmistakably requires union members to arbitrate ADEA claims is enforceable as a matter of federal law. . . .

[Justice Stevens dissented, stressing that the Court ignored *Gardner-Denver's* holding.]

Justice SOUTER, with whom Justice STEVENS, Justice GINSBURG, and Justice BREYER join, dissenting. . . .

I

[Both the ADEA and Title VII provide that a plaintiff may "bring a civil action in any court of competent jurisdiction for legal or equitable relief." In *Gardner-Denver*] we unanimously held that "the rights conferred" by Title VII (with no exception for the right to a judicial forum) cannot be waived as "part of the collective bargaining process." We stressed the contrast between two categories of rights in labor and employment law. There were "statutory rights related to collective activity," which "are conferred on employees collectively to foster the processes of bargaining[, which] properly may be exercised or relinquished by the union as collective-bargaining agent to obtain economic benefits for union members." But "Title VII . . . stands on plainly different [categorical] ground; it concerns not majoritarian processes, but an individual's right to equal employment opportunities." . . .

We supported the judgment with several other lines of complementary reasoning. [First, the antidiscrimination statutes reflect a congressional intent to accord parallel or overlapping remedies against discrimination.] Second, we rejected the District Court's view that simply participating in the arbitration amounted to electing the arbitration remedy and waiving the plaintiff's right to sue. We said that the arbitration agreement at issue covered only a contractual right under the CBA to be free from discrimination, not the "independent statutory rights accorded by Congress" in Title VII. Third, we rebuffed the employer's argument that federal courts should defer to arbitral rulings. We declined to make the "assumption that arbitral processes are commensurate with judicial processes," and described arbitration as "a less appropriate forum for final resolution of Title VII issues than the federal courts."

Finally, we took note that "[i]n arbitration, as in the collective-bargaining process, the interests of the individual employee may be subordinated to the collective interests of all employees in the bargaining unit," a result we deemed unacceptable when it came to Title VII claims. In sum, *Gardner-Denver* held that an individual's statutory right of freedom from discrimination and access to court for enforcement were beyond a union's power to waive. . . .

II

[The dissent argued that *Gardner-Denver* controlled, and rejected the] majority's statement that "[t]he decision to fashion a [CBA] to require arbitration of employment-discrimination claims is no different from the many other decisions made by parties in designing grievance machinery." That is simply impossible to square with our conclusion in that "Title VII . . . stands on plainly different ground" from "statutory rights related to collective activity": "it concerns not majoritarian processes, but an individual's right to equal employment opportunities."

When the majority does speak to *Gardner-Denver*, it misreads the case in claiming that it turned solely "on the narrow ground that the arbitration was not preclusive because the collective-bargaining agreement did not cover statutory claims." That, however, was merely one of several reasons given in support of the decision. . . .

[As for the risk that "a union may subordinate the interests of an individual employee to the collective interests of all employees in the bargaining unit," the] majority tries to diminish this reasoning, and the previously stated holding it supported, by making the remarkable rejoinder that "[w]e cannot rely on this judicial policy concern as a source of authority for introducing a qualification into the ADEA that is not found in its text."[4] It is enough to recall that respondents are not seeking to "introduc[e] a qualification into" the law; they are justifiably relying on statutory-interpretation precedent decades old, never overruled, and serially reaffirmed over the years. With that precedent on the books, it makes no sense for the majority to claim that "judicial policy concern[s]" about unions sacrificing individual antidiscrimination rights should be left to Congress.

For that matter, Congress has unsurprisingly understood *Gardner-Denver* the way we have repeatedly explained it and has operated on the assumption that a CBA cannot waive employees' rights to a judicial forum to enforce antidiscrimination statutes. *See, e.g.*, H.R. Rep. No. 102-40, pt. 1, p. 97 (1991) (stating that, "consistent with the Supreme Court's interpretation of Title VII in [*Gardner-Denver*]," "any agreement to submit disputed issues to arbitration . . . in the context of a collective bargaining agreement . . . does not preclude the affected person from seeking relief under the enforcement provisions of Title VII"). . . .

III

On one level, the majority opinion may have little effect, for it explicitly reserves the question whether a CBA's waiver of a judicial forum is enforceable when the

---

4. [The majority's reliance on a duty of fair representation as a reason to discount the conflict of interest argument] misunderstands the law, for unions may decline for a variety of reasons to pursue potentially meritorious discrimination claims without succumbing to a member's suit for failure of fair representation. More importantly, we have rejected precisely this argument in the past, making this yet another occasion where the majority ignores precedent. See, *e.g.*, *Barrentine*; *Gardner-Denver*. And we were wise to reject it. When the Court construes statutes to allow a union to eliminate a statutory right to sue in favor of arbitration in which the union cannot represent the employee because it agreed to the employer's challenged action, it is not very consoling to add that the employee can sue the union for being unfair.

union controls access to and presentation of employees' claims in arbitration, which "is usually the case," *McDonald*. But as a treatment of precedent in statutory interpretation, the majority's opinion cannot be reconciled with the *Gardner-Denver* Court's own view of its holding, repeated over the years and generally understood, and I respectfully dissent.

NOTES

1. *Arbitration Triumphant*. The *Pyett* decision is a good summary of the arguments for and against mandatory arbitration of claims under the employment discrimination statutes, but in many ways it merely ices the cake that the Court had baked in *Gilmer*, which did not involve a collective bargaining agreement. Although the plaintiff there claimed that the individual agreement he signed agreeing to arbitrate could not waive his right to bring an ADEA claim in court, the Supreme Court disagreed. In essence, it found that the Federal Arbitration Act trumped the ADEA and, presumably, other antidiscrimination laws because those laws did not expressly create exceptions to the FAA's validation of arbitration. *Gilmer* clearly confined *Gardner-Denver* to the collective bargaining context, but most circuit courts had viewed it as still good law there. *Pyett*, of course, rejects that view entirely. Nevertheless, there remains some bite to the requirement that a union cannot waive individual rights unless it does so clearly. *See Ibarra v. UPS*, 695 F.3d 354, 358 (5th Cir. 2012).

In the wake of these decisions, it may take a statute expressly barring mandatory arbitration to trump the FAA, *see* 18 U.S.C. §1514A(e) (2018) (barring predispute arbitration agreements for certain whistleblower claims); *see also* Fair Pay and Safe Workplaces Executive Order, July 31, 2014 (Obama executive order barring predispute arbitration provisions in government contractor employment), which means that most employment laws remain subject to the *Gilmer-Pyett* regime. *See generally* Alan Hyde, *Labor Arbitration of Discrimination Claims After* 14 Penn Plaza v. Pyett: *Letting Discrimination Defendants Decide Whether Plaintiffs May Sue Them*, 25 Ohio St. J. on Disp. Resol. 975, 976 (2010); Margaret L. Moses, *The Pretext of Textualism: Disregarding Stare Decisis in* 14 Penn Plaza v. Pyett, 14 Lewis & Clark L. Rev. 825 (2010); David L. Gregory & Edward McNamara, *Mandatory Labor Arbitration of Statutory Claims, and the Future of Fair Employment:* 14 Penn Plaza v. Pyett, 19 Cornell J.L. & Pub. Pol'y 429 (2010).

2. *The FAA as a "Super Statute."* Some read the Supreme Court's numerous opinions in the area as enshrining the Federal Arbitration Act as a kind of "super statute," one that is of higher status than other statutes and that, therefore, can be avoided only by legislation with some sort of "clear statement." *See* William N. Eskridge, Jr. & John Ferejohn, *Super-Statutes*, 50 Duke L.J. 1215 (2001). *Pyett* denies doing more than applying the texts of the relevant statutes, see footnote 9, but there were at least three textual reasons to question whether an employee could waive her right to bring a court suit under the antidiscrimination laws.

First, although resolved prior to *Pyett*, there was doubt whether the FAA reached agreements between employers and employees since that statute provides that "nothing herein contained shall apply to contracts of employment of seamen, railroad employees, or any other class of workers engaged in foreign or interstate commerce." 9 U.S.C. §1. That issue was decided in favor of broad coverage of the FAA in *Circuit City Stores, Inc. v. Adams*, 532 U.S. 105 (2001).

A second potential limitation on the FAA's reach was OWBPA, which we encountered in Section A and which the *Pyett* Court addresses briefly. Although that statute explicitly prohibits prospective waivers of rights under the ADEA, *Pyett* held that OWBPA barred waivers of *substantive* rights only, not waivers of *procedural* rights such as the right to a jury trial. The *Pyett* majority stresses that its decision is a straight-forward application of the FAA's statutory language. How straightforward is reading the unmodified noun "rights" in OWBPA as modified by the adjective "substantive"? The Court also was concerned that so reading OWBPA would mean that "even a waiver signed by an individual employee would be invalid." That's probably true, but so what? In other words, why is that an argument that OWBPA doesn't bar all prospective waivers of ADEA rights? If you're wondering about precedent, OWBPA was passed after the cause of action arose in *Gilmer*, so that case did not consider its effect on ADEA claims.

Third, prior to *Pyett*, there had been some question as to the effect of §118 of the Civil Rights Act of 1991. That section's approval of arbitration "where appropriate" is admittedly ambiguous, but the Court has traditionally looked to legislative history to resolve statutory ambiguity, and the Court's footnote quotes a House Report as disapproving predispute arbitration agreements. Despite this, *Pyett* found that §118 was no barrier to mandatory arbitration. Why?

Pyett doesn't mention a final question we encountered in Chapter 8: whether an arbitration agreement can, consistent with the Norris LaGuardia Act and the NLRA's prohibitions of agreements limiting employee "concerted action for mutual aid or protection," bar both class actions and class arbitration. See p. 544.

3. *Arbitration as a Viable Alternative to Litigation*. The *Pyett* opinion echoes *Gilmer* in downplaying the concerns *Gardner-Denver* had raised about the inherent limitations of the arbitral forums as compared to court proceedings. *Gilmer* had also rejected several frontal attacks on arbitration as a means of deciding ADEA cases. It first dismissed as speculative the plaintiff's claim that the arbitral process, governed by the New York Stock Exchange rules, would be biased toward the employer. It then noted that there was no showing that discovery would be inadequate for an ADEA claim under those rules. Additionally, awards would be public so that objections to hidden decisions were inapplicable. Finally, the Court stressed that arbitrators have the power to award broad equitable relief, and, to the extent their remedial powers are deficient, the EEOC remains able to sue the employer. Although the arbitration process in *Pyett* is not detailed in the Court's opinion, there's no hint in the opinion that the Court would scrutinize the process skeptically, nor that the arbitration system at issue in *Gilmer* sets some sort of floor. Indeed, it seems pretty clear that the majority would accept pretty substantial limitations as part of the tradeoff "bargain" between the two parties.

4. *Duty of Fair Representation*. You will learn more about a union's duty to those it represents in Labor Law, but note the awkwardness of the procedure that the Court finds adequate: should the union not take the case to arbitration or not prosecute it appropriately there, the employee may sue the union, presumably for what he or she would have won had the arbitration been well conducted. Alternatively, the union can be sued directly under the ADEA, but the claim has similar problems — proof that, if the union didn't discriminate in representing the plaintiff, he would have won in arbitration. Maybe attorney malpractice is the best analogy. Does this seem like an adequate alternative to you? *See generally* Michael Z. Green, *Reading* Ricci *and* Pyett *to Provide Racial Justice Through Union Arbitration*, 87 IND. L.J. 367 (2012).

5. *Reviewing Arbitration Awards*. If the duty of fair representation is designed to keep the unions honest, what safeguards are there for ensuring arbitrator fairness? In

an omitted footnote, the *Pyett* majority stressed that an arbitrator's decision "remains subject to judicial review under the FAA," citing 9 U.S.C. §10(a). It also noted that while "judicial scrutiny of arbitration awards necessarily is limited, such review is sufficient to ensure that arbitrators comply with the requirements of the statute," quoting *Shearson/American Express Inc. v. McMahon*, 482 U.S. 220, 232 (1987). Some would disagree about the adequacy of such review. Students tend to think that these post-arbitration court proceedings are like an appeal, with the court able to correct arbitrator errors in the same way that an appeals court can review a district court's decision. That is *not* true.

That's because a court may not overturn an arbitrator's decision even if it believes that the arbitrator is wrong on the facts and the law. The FAA provides that an award may be vacated only in extreme circumstances: where it was procured by corruption, fraud, or undue means; there was evident partiality or corruption in the arbitrators' decision; the arbitrators were guilty of misconduct; or they exceeded their powers. 9 U.S.C. §10(a). There may or may not also be a broader "manifest disregard for the law" criterion. *Hall St. Assocs. v. Mattel, Inc.*, 552 U.S. 576, 585 (2008), refused to decide whether "manifest disregard" was "a new ground for review" or merely a shorthand for some or all of the listed grounds, and subsequent circuit opinions are divided as to whether the standard continues to be an independent basis for review. *See Bellantuono v. ICAP Secs. USA, LLC*, 557 F. App'x 168, 173 n.3 (3d Cir. 2014) (collecting cases on circuit split). *See generally* Michael H. LeRoy, *Are Arbitrators Above the Law? The "Manifest Disregard of the Law" Standard*, 52 BC L. REV. 137 (2011); Rebecca Hanner White, *Arbitration and the Administrative State*, 38 WAKE FOREST L. REV. 1283, 1303 (2003). Further, the parties to an arbitration agreement cannot agree to give the reviewing court broader authority than does the FAA itself. *Hall St. Assocs. v. Mattel, Inc., supra. See also In re Wal-Mart Wage & Hour Emp't Practices Litig. v. Class Counsel & Party to Arbitration*, 737 F.3d 1262, 1267 (9th Cir. 2013) (the text of the FAA renders the grounds for review unwaivable, thus rendering a non-appealability clause invalid). *See generally* Margaret L. Moses, *Arbitration Law: Who's in Charge*, 40 SETON HALL L. REV. 147, 152 (2010).

6. *EEOC Enforcement.* The effect of agreements to arbitrate on the EEOC's right to bring suit on behalf of individual employees was addressed in *EEOC v. Waffle House, Inc.*, 534 U.S. 279 (2002), where the Court permitted the EEOC to obtain relief on behalf of employees even if these employees had agreed to arbitration with their employers. While duplicate recovery would presumably be barred, the agency cannot be foreclosed from suing by virtue of an arbitration agreement to which it is not a party.

NOTE ON THE POLICY IMPLICATIONS OF ARBITRATION

Both *Pyett* and *Gilmer* are written as straightforward applications of the 1925 Federal Arbitration Act, which provides that a written arbitration clause in any "contract evidencing a transaction involving commerce . . . shall be valid, irrevocable, and enforceable, save upon such grounds as exist at law or in equity for the revocation of any contract." 9 U.S.C.A. §2. Both cases view the ultimate policy decision to favor arbitration as one made by Congress, not the courts. We have seen reasons to doubt that, but even if the courts are not imposing their own policy preferences, perhaps influenced largely by the benefits of arbitration in reducing court dockets, there still remain significant policy concerns. After all, Congress enacted the FAA in 1925 and was mainly focused on what we now call commercial arbitration. The American economy and work force have changed enormously since then. Is arbitration a good idea in such settings? Or, more precisely, is arbitration as a condition of employment a good idea?

There is a consensus that employers and employees ought to be free to agree to arbitration after a dispute has arisen. In this setting, the parties can make an informed tradeoff between the likely lower costs and greater speed of arbitration and the greater procedural protections of traditional court proceedings. The controversy arises, as in *Pyett* and *Gilmer*, when arbitration agreements are required as a condition of employment, and, in cases like Mr. Pyett's, without his consent. In theory, opting for arbitration does not increase the risk of being on the losing end of a dispute but merely reduces the costs of resolving it by substituting a cheaper and speedier alternative mechanism. Such features could make arbitration a more accessible and, hence, more effective form of dispute resolution for employees who lack the time, financial resources, and access to counsel necessary to pursue litigation in court. *See* Samuel Estreicher, *Saturns for Rickshaws: The Stakes in the Debate over Predispute Employment Arbitration Agreements*, 16 OHIO ST. J. ON DISP. RESOL. 559 (2001). *But see* David S. Schwartz, *If You Love Arbitration, Set It Free: How "Mandatory" Undermines "Arbitration,"* 8 NEV. L.J. 400 (2007).

However, arbitration is quicker and less costly precisely because it sacrifices certain procedures associated with court litigation. Further, since employers select the forum and its procedures, it is possible that arbitration will favor employers in both substantive outcomes and generosity of remedies. Even assuming an objectively neutral forum, the EEOC believes that mandatory arbitration has a built-in bias favoring employers who tend to be "repeat players." Policy Statement on Mandatory Binding Arbitration of Employment Disputes as a Condition of Employment, No. 915.002 (July 10, 1997), https://www.eeoc.gov/policy/docs/mandarb.html. *See also* Michael Z. Green, *An Essay Challenging the Racially Biased Selection of Arbitrators for Employment Discrimination Suits*, 4 J. AM. ARB. 1 (2005).

Such concerns are heightened by the common employer practice of requiring employees to sign contracts to arbitrate upon applying for or commencing a job, that is, well before a dispute arises. In contrast to the decision to arbitrate an existing dispute, an employee faced with a predispute arbitration agreement is less likely to appreciate the importance of choice of forum or to have had the opportunity to consult counsel. *See* Matthew T. Bodie, *Questions About the Efficiency of Employment Arbitration Agreements*, 39 GA. L. REV. 1 (2004) (employers have significant informational advantages that they may use "to construct inefficient agreements"); Katherine Van Wezel Stone, *Mandatory Arbitration of Individual Employment Rights: The Yellow Dog Contract of the 1990s*, 73 DENV. U. L. REV. 1017 (1996).

Yet another set of objections to arbitration stems from the fact that, as a private dispute resolution mechanism, arbitration may not serve the wider goals of the antidiscrimination laws, even if it achieves justice in individual cases. The confidentiality of the process arguably inhibits public education about discrimination and limits the development of the law by eliminating a substantial number of potential precedential cases. *See* Geraldine Szott Moohr, *Arbitration and the Goals of Employment Discrimination Law*, 56 WASH. & LEE L. REV. 395, 426-39 (1999).

Intermingled with the policy objections to mandatory arbitration per se are arguments about how arbitration works in practice. This objection has two thrusts. First, the structure of the particular arbitral forum may be problematic. Because it is private, the controlling process varies depending on the particular forum and rules the parties select. In many instances, parties opt for an established arbitration service, such as the American Arbitration Association, which has an extensive set of rules and procedures for resolving employment disputes. *See AAA National Rules for the Resolution of Employment Disputes* (2005), *available at* http://www.adr.org/sp.asp?id=22075. But an employer might choose a less formal venue or develop its own set of procedures. The nonstandard nature of arbitration systems means that arbitrators can vary significantly in terms of their expertise and background and that the rules governing arbitration can vary dramatically from those before the Supreme Court in *Pyett* and *Gilmer*. An ADR Protocol, endorsed by organizations such as the AAA, suggests procedures for arbitrating workplace disputes, and urges arbitrators to refuse cases that do not provide appropriate safeguards. *See* http:www.naarb.org/protocol.html. *See* Richard A. Bales, *The Employment Due Process Protocol at Ten: Twenty Unresolved Issues, and a Focus on Conflicts of Interest*, 21 Ohio St. J. on Disp. Resol. 165 (2005).

In addition, arbitration agreements typically specify who pays the costs of arbitration, and this can itself be an obstacle to the vindication of rights under the antidiscrimination statutes. See Note on the Elephant in the Room, p. 631. Such agreements may go beyond merely substituting an arbitral forum for a court by narrowing the remedial rights of the employee, as by capping damages or excluding punitive damages. Further, while arbitration necessarily changes the procedural rights of employees by eliminating the judicial forum and its concomitant protections, particular arbitration agreements might go further down this road. For example, they might limit the time within which a claim is filed. Again, these issues are not objections to arbitration as such but rather problems with particular arbitration regimes. *See generally* Richard A. Bales, *A Normative Consideration of Employment Arbitration at* Gilmer's *Quinceañera*, 81 Tul. L. Rev. 331 (2006); Kenneth R. Davis, *A Model for Arbitration: Autonomy, Cooperation, and Curtailment of State Power*, 26 Fordham Urb. L.J. 167 (1999). Further, such restrictive provisions would not seem to be within the ambit of the FAA and therefore could be analyzed for consistency with the antidiscrimination statutes.

[handwritten margin note: can limit remedies]

All this theorizing leaves unanswered the underlying question: is arbitration an inferior alternative to litigation for employees? This is essentially an empirical question and one complicated by both the secrecy of arbitral regimes and their variability. Some argue that arbitration is more effective than litigation for lower-level workers who cannot afford legal representation or at least cannot afford the more costly representation that a court suit might require. It is, for them, the only game in town. Others argue that arbitration discourages claims that would be brought if the employee were free to file suit. Finally, many contend that, even if arbitration achieves desirable results, *mandatory* arbitration is not necessary for those benefits. If both sides wish to arbitrate after a dispute arises, there are no legal obstacles. *But see* David Sherwyn, J. Bruce Tracey & Zev J. Eigen, *In Defense of Mandatory Arbitration of Employment Disputes: Saving the Baby, Tossing Out the Bath Water, and Constructing a New Sink in the Process*, 2 U. Pa. J. Lab. & Emp. L. 73 (1999).

Now that you know how arbitration works in the employment setting, the remaining question is when two parties will have been deemed to have agreed to arbitrate. When the FAA was passed, arbitration was a pretty big deal, and the parties frequently, perhaps usually, entered into formal contracts, often after a dispute arose. Things have changed pretty radically, however.

HERGENREDER v. BICKFORD SENIOR LIVING GROUP, LLC
656 F.3d 411 (6th Cir. 2011)

KAREN NELSON MOORE, Circuit Judge. . . .

I.   BACKGROUND INFORMATION . . .

When Hergenreder began her employment, she signed numerous documents, including her employment application, tax and insurance forms, a background-check-consent form, a form agreeing to notify Bickford of any subsequent criminal convictions, and a form acknowledging that she received notice of Bickford's worker's compensation procedure. It is undisputed, however, that none of these documents mentioned anything about arbitration. Hergenreder also signed an acknowledgment that she had read and understood the terms of Bickford's Employee Handbook.

The Employee Handbook — and whether it does or does not inform Hergenreder of Bickford's arbitration policy — plays the central role in this appeal. The Handbook is divided into sixteen different sections, covering a wide variety of topics relevant to Hergenreder's employment. It begins by stating in Section I [that it is intended as a summary only and is not a contract" and ends] by stating, in Section XVI, that:

> This handbook has been provided to you for the purpose of acquainting you with the personnel policies and procedures, responsibilities of Bickford Cottage. It does not constitute a contract of employment in whole or in part. Bickford Cottage may add to, change or delete any of the contents at any time with no notice.

Based on these statements, the parties agree that the terms of the Handbook are not part of a contract.

What the parties do not agree on, however, is the significance of one sentence within Section XII, which is entitled "Employee Actions," and which provides, in full, as follows: "*Dispute Resolution Process* Please refer to the Eby Companies Dispute Resolution Procedure (DRP) for details." Handbook at 19 (emphasis in original). [A review of that DRP] makes clear in both an eleven-page summary of the procedure as well as the nine-page procedure itself that all employees are required to submit all covered claims against Bickford to binding arbitration. [For example, an "Agreement to Dispute Resolution Procedure" form at the end of DRP indicated employee assent to the DRP and included in block letters the statement: "THIS AGREEMENT CONTAINS A BINDING ARBITRATION PROVISION THAT MAY BE ENFORCED BY THE PARTIES."]

In the Frequently Asked Questions portion of the DRP Summary, Bickford answers the question, "Why am I being asked to sign a written agreement to the Dispute Resolution Procedure?" with the following:

> While your employment and/or continued employment is all that is required for you to be bound to resolve your employment disputes with The Eby Group under the DRP, the Company is committed to this new program and is requesting every employee to commit to it in writing on a form prepared by the Company which signed form will be placed in your personnel file.

Although the text of this answer indicates that a "commit[ment]" is made by the parties, this commitment must be purely a symbolic one, given that a *legal* commitment is made only by entering or continuing employment with Bickford. The implicit message in this answer, then, seems to be the important one: Bickford asks employees to sign the agreement so that there will be objective evidence of the employee's agreement to submit all covered claims to binding arbitration, even though the employee's signature is not necessary to enter into the agreement. The wisdom behind an employer's desire to have objective evidence of an employee's assent to arbitration is clear: an acknowledgment form, signed after an employee has been given a copy of an arbitration agreement, can serve as ironclad proof that an employee was reasonably notified of an arbitration agreement. Put another way, the acknowledgment form decreases the possibility that Bickford might have an employee who has never seen or signed any arbitration documents.

Hergenreder swears that she has "never seen or signed any of these documents," referring to the DRP. Moreover, she avers, "I have never, to my knowledge, signed any Agreement with the Defendant that gave up my right to a jury trial and that compelled me to file for Arbitration for any type of wrongful discharge claim. No one ever even raised the issue of Arbitration in all of the forms that I signed as part of the hiring process." Bickford has not provided a copy of the DRP with an acknowledgment form signed by Hergenreder. Instead, it has provided an affidavit from its Vice President of Employee Relations, Jerry Knight, who states that the DRP "is distributed to employees."

[The district court held Hergenreder bound by the DRP and therefore dismissed this suit.]

II. ANALYSIS . . .

Hergenreder makes three arguments against the district court's order, all of which establish, she asserts, that she is not bound by any arbitration agreement with Bickford. First, she argues that she was never advised about any arbitration policy and that she "never saw or signed any arbitration agreement." Second, she argues that nothing in the Handbook constitutes a legally binding contract and that nothing in the Handbook mentions arbitration. Third, she argues that there is nothing else in the record that constitutes an agreement to submit her claims to arbitration. *[π's argument]*

Bickford disputes only some of these contentions. First, it agrees that the Handbook does not constitute a legally binding contract. It also apparently does not dispute that Hergenreder did not sign the DRP, and despite Knight's affidavit stating that the DRP "is distributed to employees," Bickford does not in any way dispute Hergenreder's sworn statement that she has not seen the DRP. Instead, what Bickford *does* *[Δ's argument]* dispute are Hergenreder's claims that she was not advised of the DRP and that nothing else in the record establishes that a legally binding agreement to arbitrate was created between Hergenreder and Bickford.

A. MICHIGAN CONTRACT LAW DETERMINES WHETHER AN ARBITRATION AGREEMENT WAS FORMED HERE

[The FAA provides that a written agreement to arbitrate disputes arising out of a transaction in interstate commerce "shall be valid, irrevocable, and enforceable, save upon such grounds as exist at law or in equity for the revocation of any contract." 9 U.S.C. §2. To that end, the Act provides for a stay of proceedings when an issue is referable to arbitration and for orders compelling arbitration. §§3 and 4. The law *[Michigan's contract law]* governing whether something qualifies as a "contract" is state law, in this case Michigan's, and Michigan law requires offer and acceptance and "(1) parties competent to contract, (2) a proper subject matter, (3) a legal consideration, (4) mutuality of agreement, and (5) mutuality of obligation."]

B.   HERGENREDER DID NOT ASSENT TO AN ARBITRATION AGREEMENT
      WITH BICKFORD. . . .

Bickford agrees that the Handbook did not form a legally binding contract with Hergenreder. Instead, it argues that "the DRP — a document separate and distinct from the Handbook — forms the contract," and it claims that Hergenreder "assented" to the DRP. The key analytical step in Bickford's argument comes from the notion that Bickford needed only to "reasonably notif[y]" Hergenreder of the arbitration agreement, which it did, Bickford argues, by requesting that Hergenreder "Please refer to the Eby Companies Dispute Resolution Procedure (DRP) for details."

We agree with Hergenreder. There was neither an offer nor an acceptance. The objective signs that Bickford made Hergenreder an offer to be part of the arbitration agreement are few in number. The best Bickford can say is that Hergenreder was informed that, for "Employee Actions," she should "refer" to the DRP. In Bickford's view, Hergenreder "was or should have been aware of the DRP and so is bound by it." Yet she was not *required* to refer to the DRP; the "handbook does not constitute any contractual obligation on [Hergenreder's] part nor on the part of Bickford Cottage[.]" Moreover, the simple reference in the Handbook to "the P10 Eby Companies Dispute Resolution Procedure" for "details" is *not* "the manifestation of willingness to enter into a bargain, so made as to justify another person in understanding that his assent to that bargain is invited and will conclude it." This statement says nothing about arbitration, and it says nothing that would indicate to Hergenreder that accepting or continuing her job with Bickford would constitute acceptance. Indeed, it is incorrect to conflate the fact that Hergenreder knew generally of the DRP with the notion that she knew of the arbitration language — and Bickford's desire to create an arbitration agreement — contained within the DRP. Were Hergenreder required to read, or even notified of the importance of reading, the DRP, the analysis here might be different. But this court's inquiry is focused on whether there is an objective manifestation of intent by Bickford to enter into an agreement with (and invite acceptance by) Hergenreder, and we are not convinced that there is any such manifestation made by Bickford in the record in this case.

We are also not persuaded by Bickford's reliance on *Mannix v. Cnty. of Monroe*, 348 F.3d 526 (6th Cir. 2003), which interpreted Michigan law on employment-contract formation. *Mannix* stands for the proposition that "[d]istribution of a new employee handbook constitutes reasonable notice, regardless of whether the affected employee actually reads it." [The company in *Mannix* had posted the policies for at least four months prior to the plaintiff's termination on an internal database available to employees and had held meetings between department heads and employees and put the policies on the County's e-mail system.] "This," the court held, "was reasonable notice." In the present case, however, there is no evidence that the DRP was "posted" in a place — either physical or electronic — available to Hergenreder, that there were meetings at which Hergenreder was notified of the policies, or that Hergenreder was aware of the DRP at all. Despite Knight's vague claim that the DRP "is distributed to employees," Bickford does not argue that it actually distributed or made the DRP available to Hergenreder.

Furthermore, even if Bickford were deemed to have made an offer to Hergenreder, we see no evidence that Hergenreder "manifest[ed] an intent to be bound by the offer, and all legal consequences flowing from the offer, through voluntarily undertaking some unequivocal act sufficient for that purpose." Bickford claims that her acceptance occurred when she elected to accept or continue her employment, but there is no evidence that Hergenreder knew (1) that the DRP contained arbitration information or an arbitration agreement, or, more specifically, (2) that the arbitration provisions in the DRP provided that electing to accept or continue employment with Bickford would constitute acceptance of the DRP's arbitration terms. Indeed, Hergenreder had no reason to believe that electing to work for Bickford would constitute her acceptance of *anything*. She therefore did not "voluntarily undertak[e] some unequivocal act sufficient for th[e] purpose" of accepting the arbitration terms contained in the DRP. . . .

At bottom, Bickford's argument boils down to the following contention: if Hergenreder has no reason to believe that a certain document contains an offer to enter into an agreement, and if she is not contractually obligated to read that document, then she will nonetheless be bound to the agreement contained in that document if she unwittingly takes actions that the document says will constitute acceptance of the offer. There is no support for this proposition in Michigan law.

performance not enough here b/c she did not know of offer and she did not accept

Lastly, we also note that the parties dispute whether, in addition to assenting to the arbitration agreement contained in the DRP, Hergenreder waived her right to a jury trial under the Seventh Amendment. "[T]he question of right to jury trial is governed by federal and not state law"; this court must ask whether that waiver was knowing and voluntary. *K.M.C. Co. v. Irving Trust Co.*, 757 F.2d 752, 755-56 (6th Cir. 1985). This court uses the following factors to determine whether a waiver of the right to a jury trial has been knowing and voluntary:

> (1) plaintiff's experience, background, and education; (2) the amount of time the plaintiff had to consider whether to sign the waiver, including whether the employee had an opportunity to consult with a lawyer; (3) the clarity of the waiver; (4) consideration for the waiver; as well as (5) the totality of the circumstances.

Morrison v. Circuit City Stores, Inc., 317 F.3d 646, 668 (6th Cir. 2003) (en banc). Yet "[i]f the claims are properly before an arbitral forum pursuant to an arbitration agreement, the jury trial right vanishes." *Cooper v. MRM Inv. Co.*, 367 F.3d 493, 506 (6th Cir. 2004).

Bickford argues that these factors have been met by Hergenreder's assent to the arbitration agreement. As explained above, we hold that Hergenreder did not enter into an arbitration agreement, but even if she did, we believe that the *Morrison* factors weigh against a finding of a knowing and voluntary waiver. Her "experience, background, and education" are not provided in the record, but "consideration for the waiver" favors Bickford, because there was consideration — her continued employment by Bickford. The other factors favor Hergenreder, however, because the fact that she was not reasonably notified of the agreement makes it impossible to say that she had time to consider the waiver of her right to a jury trial or that the clarity of the waiver matters. Of greatest importance is the "totality of the circumstances" factor, which best sums up the issue of whether Hergenreder knowingly and voluntarily waived her right to a jury trial: She simply did not know that the DRP contained an arbitration agreement, nor was she obligated to inform herself of what the DRP contained. Therefore, even if an arbitration agreement were formed, on these facts Hergenreder did not knowingly and voluntarily waive her right to a jury trial. . . .

she did not waive her right to a jury trial

NOTES

1. *Who Decides Whether an Agreement Is Valid?* The principal case is standard in one respect: the court is being asked to decide whether an agreement to arbitrate is valid on a motion to stay court proceedings and compel arbitration. But determining the decisionmaker — court or arbitrator — is not always so easy. One would think the decision was for the court since *Granite Rock Co. v. Int'l Brotherhood of Teamsters*, 561 U.S. 287 (2010), viewed it as "well settled that where the dispute at issue concerns contract formation, the dispute is generally for the court to decide." As the majority described the "proper framework" for deciding who decides arbitrability, "a court may order arbitration of a particular dispute only where the court is satisfied that the parties intended to arbitrate *that dispute*." *Id.* at 297 (emphasis in original). Indeed, at one point the Court wrote:

> Arbitration is strictly "a matter of consent," and thus "is a way to resolve those disputes — *but only those disputes* — that the parties have agreed to submit to arbitration." Applying this principle, our precedents hold that courts should order arbitration of a dispute only where the court is satisfied that neither the formation of the parties' arbitration agreement nor (absent a valid provision specifically committing such disputes to an arbitrator) its enforceability or applicability to the dispute is in issue. Where a party contests either or both matters, "the court" must resolve the disagreement.

Id. at 299-300 (citations omitted) (emphasis in original). This would seem to include questions not only of formation, as in *Hergenreder*, but also questions as to enforceability, such as consideration, and perhaps satisfaction of any formalities, such as an adequate writing. *See also Opalinski v. Robert Half Int'l, Inc.*, 761 F.3d 326, 329 (3d Cir. 2014) (since classwide arbitration is a question of arbitrability, it was presumptively a matter for the court; silence in the agreement as to the availability of classwide arbitration left the presumption unrebutted).

However, the same week that *Granite Rock* was decided, the Court handed down *Rent-A-Center West, Inc. v. Jackson*, 561 U.S. 63 (2010), which held that an unconscionability challenge to the arbitration agreement as a whole could be decided by the arbitrator. There is obviously a tension here, but, as rationalized by the *Granite Rock* Court, *Rent-A-Center West* fell within the exception stated by its formulation. Thus, formation questions are for the court, as are issues concerning enforceability and applicability to the dispute in question "absent a valid provision specifically committing such disputes to an arbitrator." 561 U.S. at 299. Because an arbitration clause is severable from the rest of the agreement as a matter of federal law, an attack (say for fraud, illegality, or unconscionability) on the contract in which the clause is embedded is not necessarily an attack on the arbitration clause. In sum, reading the two opinions together, the rule is that courts decide questions of arbitrability that go to whether the contract is formed but the parties can agree that questions of enforceability or applicability can be delegated to the arbitrator.

2. *Finding an Agreement.* As *Hergenreder* reminds us, employers seeking to enforce an arbitration agreement must at least establish offer, acceptance, and consideration. Bickford failed to make sure its workers all signed its form, and thus failed on the formation test. Ironically, the disclaimers in the employee handbook (designed to protect Bickford from other kinds of liability) prevented it from getting the arbitral forum it desired. *See also Campbell v. Gen. Dynamics Gov't Sys. Corp.*, 407 F.3d 546, 556-58 (1st Cir. 2005) (no enforceable arbitration agreement

where policy distributed via hyperlink in e-mail notification and employee did not reply to message). *But see Davis v. Nordstrom, Inc.*, 755 F.3d 1089 (9th Cir. 2014) (modification of employee handbook requiring class action waiver was valid when the employer did not try to enforce it during the 30-day notice period it provided; employer had no duty to specifically inform employees that continued work constituted acceptance of the modification); *Tillman v. Macy's, Inc.*, 735 F.3d 453, 454 (6th Cir. 2013) (employer notice sufficient when it required employee to watch a video about the arbitration program and mailed information to her home; she accepted by continuing her employment and not returning opt-out forms). Should the manner in which the employer establishes and communicates its arbitration policy matter in assessing contract enforceability? If most employees simply sign whatever documents the employer places before them in the application process, why is it any more objectionable to bind them to a handbook or e-mail arbitration policy?

3. *Consideration or a Substitute.* Like all contracts, agreements to arbitrate require consideration or a consideration substitute, and some employers have failed to satisfy that requirement. *See, e.g., Nelson v. Watch House Int'l, L.L.C.*, 815 F.3d 190 (5th Cir. 2016) (employer's reservation of power to unilaterally make changes to an arbitration agreement effective immediately renders the agreement illusory and thus unenforceable under Texas law); *contra Hill v. PeopleSoft USA, Inc.*, 412 F.3d 540, 543-44 (4th Cir. 2005) (arbitration agreement not illusory due to lack of consideration because employer reserved right to change without notice). *See generally* Richard A. Bales, *Contract Formation Issues in Employment Arbitration*, 44 BRANDEIS L.J. 415 (2006).

Some courts have required arbitration agreements to bind both parties in order for there to be consideration, *see Goins v. Ryan's Family Steakhouses, Inc.*, 181 F. App'x 435 (5th Cir. 2006), perhaps to provide incentives to the employer to ensure that the arbitral process is fair. *See* Cynthia Estlund, *Rebuilding the Law of the Workplace in an Era of Self-Regulation*, 105 COLUM. L. REV. 319, 436 (2005). However, this is contrary to normal consideration analysis, and most courts have rejected this theory. *Oblix v. Winiecki*, 374 F.3d 488, 491 (7th Cir. 2004).

4. *Statute of Frauds.* The FAA itself requires the agreement to arbitrate to be in writing in order to be enforceable. 9 U.S.C. §2. However, unlike the usual statutes of frauds, the writing need not be signed by the party to be charged. *Tillman v. Macy's, Inc.*, 735 F.3d 453, 455 (6th Cir. 2013) (employer's written offer was sufficient even though employee never signed anything mentioning arbitration).

5. *Invalidating Doctrines.* If assent, consideration, and a satisfactory writing are established, an employee's only means of defeating an arbitration agreement is to invoke one of the traditional defenses to contract, such as fraud, duress, mistake, or unconscionability. Each of these doctrines has been deployed to resist arbitration, but only unconscionability has gained any traction. You may recall that doctrine from your first-year Contracts class; it is often defined as a lack of meaningful choice coupled with terms unreasonably favorable to one side. *See, e.g., Williams v. Walker-Thomas*, 350 F.2d 445 (D.C. Cir. 1965). Given the limited role unconscionability plays in other areas of contract law, there are a surprising number of cases striking arbitration clauses as unconscionable. Indeed, arbitration may be the only area of American law where unconscionability doctrine has some bite. *Hall v. Treasure Bay V.I. Corp.*, 371 F. App'x 311 (3d Cir. 2010); *Murray v. United Food & Commercial Workers Int'l Union*, 289 F.3d 297, 302-04 (4th Cir. 2002) (arbitration agreement

giving employer discretion in naming possible arbitrators and constraining arbitrators' ability to rule on authority of employer's president was unconscionable and unenforceable), although even here the Supreme Court has limited the scope of the defense. See Note 6 *infra*.

6. *Class Actions and Arbitration.* One potentially critical advantage of arbitration is avoiding class actions. As with all arbitration, class arbitrations are permissible, but only if the parties in fact so agree. *See Stolt-Nielsen S.A. v. AnimalFeeds Int'l Corp.*, 559 U.S. Ct. 662 (2010). *But see Oxford Health Plans LLC v. Sutter*, 133 S. Ct. 2064 (2013) (upholding arbitrator's decision finding parties had agreed to class arbitration even though the contract did not explicitly so provide). As a result, provisions barring arbitral class claims are common in the consumer context, and the Supreme Court has upheld such waivers in arbitration agreements against state law-based unconscionability attacks. *AT&T Mobility LLC v. Concepción*, 563 U.S. 333 (2011), held that the Federal Arbitration Act preempts state laws that impede the accomplishment of the FAA's objectives, and thus it invalidated the California rule barring class action waivers in all circumstances. *Concepción*'s imprimatur is leading to the dramatic decline of class litigation — either in court or before arbitrators — in consumer contracts, and it has accelerated the use of arbitration with class action waivers for employers. As a result, employment discrimination class actions are likely to continue to decline in the future, entirely aside from the results in *Wal-Mart Stores Inc. v. Dukes*. The major remaining legal question is whether federal labor law guarantees of workers' rights to engage in concerted activity for mutual aid or protection will bar such provisions. See p. 544.

7. *Heightened Scrutiny?* Although *Hergenreder* found that plaintiff had not agreed to arbitrate, it went on to consider whether, assuming an agreement, her promise was still not enforceable. The argument is that waiver of the federal right to jury trial must be "knowing and voluntary," which requires something more than contractual assent. *Hergenreder* is not the only such case. This obviously harks back to the "knowing and voluntary" standard for releases under OWBPA for ADEA claims. But does such a rule make sense to you in light of the FAA's approval of arbitration under normal contract analysis? Other courts have applied plain vanilla contracts law and held general language about arbitration to include discrimination claims. *E.g., Seus v. Nuveen*, 146 F.3d 175 (3d Cir. 1998) (rejecting a heightened knowing and voluntary standard).

8. *Fixing Overreaching?* Separate from the question of whether arbitration per se is unconscionable is the issue of whether particular provisions in arbitral contracts are valid. Often these agreements purport to do far more than merely substitute an arbitral tribunal for a judicial forum. They also limit the employees' substantive rights by providing lesser remedies than would be available in a court suit or altering time limitations. Given that we have seen that prospective waivers of substantive rights are generally invalid, see Note 5, p. 608, it would seem that such provisions should not be enforced. Even when the courts agree, however, they typically simply "sever" bad clauses, striking down only the objectionable provisions while still enforcing the agreement to arbitrate. *See Booker v. Robert Half Int'l, Inc.*, 413 F.3d 77 (D.C. Cir. 2005) (severing the punitive damages bar and otherwise enforcing the arbitration clause when the agreement contained a severability clause and only one discrete illegal provision); *Spinetti v. Service Corp. Int'l*, 324 F.3d 212 (3d Cir. 2003) (agreement to arbitrate enforceable after severing attorneys' fees and costs provision). A few courts find that the entire agreement is tainted. *See Ingle v. Circuit City Stores, Inc.*, 328 F.3d 1165 (9th Cir. 2003) (procedurally and substantively unconscionable provisions of pre-employment arbitration agreement not severable because they overwhelmingly

and unconscionably favored employer). *See also Rodríguez v. Raymours Furniture Co., Inc.*, 138 A.3d 528 (N.J. 2016) (finding invalid a contractual provision, not in an arbitration clause, that shortened the time to bring a state fair employment practices claim). *See generally* Cynthia Estlund, *Rebuilding the Law of the Workplace in an Era of Self-Regulation*, 105 COLUM. L. REV. 319 (2005). A final twist is the Supreme Court's decision in *PacifiCare Health Sys. v. Book*, 538 U.S. 401 (2003), which suggests that any ambiguity about the limitations imposed by an agreement is, in the first instance, for the arbitrator to decide.

9. *Not Really Arbitration?* Some agreements to arbitrate may provide a process that is so one-sided that it is not fairly described as arbitration. *Gilmer* left open the possibility that an arbitral system might be so deficient as to not be enforceable, and a few cases have refused to enforce agreements on that ground. *See McMullen v. Meijer Inc.*, 355 F.3d 485 (6th Cir. 2004) (arbitration agreement did not preclude suit because it gave employer unilateral control over the pool of arbitrators); *Hooters of Am., Inc. v. Phillips*, 173 F.3d 933, 938 (4th Cir. 1999) ("The Hooters rules when taken as a whole, however, are so one-sided that their only possible purpose is to undermine the neutrality of the proceeding").

10. *Waiver of Arbitration.* Even where an arbitration agreement is valid and enforceable, the parties may expressly or implicitly waive arbitration; the latter occurs most obviously by not moving to stay court proceedings in a timely manner. *See Cole v. Jersey City Med. Ctr.*, 72 A.3d 224 (N.J. 2013) (waiver found when the defendant litigated for 21 months and only sought arbitration on the eve of trial). *See generally* Thomas J. Lilly, Jr., *Participation in Litigation as a Waiver of the Contractual Right to Arbitrate: Toward a Unified Theory*, 92 NEB. L. Rev. 86, 88-89 (2013).

NOTE ON THE ELEPHANT IN THE ROOM: ALLOCATING THE COSTS OF ARBITRATION

A continuing conundrum of arbitration agreements is who pays. Unlike judges, arbitrators are not civil servants and the parties must pay for their services, which can cost thousands of dollars. In contrast, a party need only pay a one-time filing fee to initiate a suit in federal court, and this may be waived on a demonstration of indigence.

Before you conclude that courts are more financially accessible than arbitration, however, consider the time and money that attorneys invest in preparing cases for trial. Many plaintiffs in employment cases cannot pay out-of-pocket for legal representation. As a consequence, lawyers are extremely cautious about the cases they will pursue on contingency. It has been suggested that lawyers in private practice whose fees are largely, or wholly, contingent will not take on cases without a minimum of $75,000 in provable economic damages. Think about what types of employees are likely to have claims with this much money at stake. Would it surprise you to learn that an estimated 95 percent of employees who seek legal help are turned away? Does this change how you feel about arbitration? *See* Christopher R. Drahozal, *Arbitration Costs and Contingent Fee Contracts*, 59 VAND. L. REV. 729 (2006); David S. Schwartz, *Mandatory Arbitration and Fairness*, 84 NOTRE DAME L. REV. 1247 (2009). But even if mandatory arbitration is beneficial to some, or most, employees, that doesn't answer the question about who pays for it. If shifting part of the cost to the employee is prohibited, that must mean that the employer pays the full freight. Is this a good idea? Won't arbitrators tend to be influenced by who is paying their fees?

In *Green Tree Fin. Corp. v. Randolph*, 531 U.S. 79 (2000), the Court held an arbitration agreement valid even though it "was silent with respect to payment of filing fees, arbitrators' costs, and other arbitration expenses." *Id.* at 84. The Supreme Court found that the "risk [of the plaintiff being] saddled with prohibitive costs is too speculative to justify the invalidation of an arbitration agreement." *Id.* at 91. But *Green Tree* did not address an agreement that specifically allocated costs to the employee, and, after the decision, some circuits held that allocations of costs could invalidate the agreement to arbitrate, but they typically did so in finding the allocation to infringe upon a plaintiff's substantive right to a remedy. For example, in *McCaskill v. SCI Mgmt. Corp.*, 298 F.3d 677 (7th Cir. 2002), the court held that a provision in an arbitration agreement requiring each party to bear its own attorneys' fees, regardless of the outcome, was unenforceable. *Contra Summers v. Dillards, Inc.*, 351 F.3d 1100, 1101 (11th Cir. 2003). *See also Mazera v. Varsity Ford Mgmt. Servs., LLC*, 565 F.3d 997 (6th Cir. 2009) (employee could not avoid arbitration by showing costs made it functionally unavailable unless he was denied a waiver of the fee). While arguments about functional availability seem dubious in the wake of *Am. Express Co. v. Italian Colors Restaurants*, 133 S. Ct. 2304 (2013) (upholding class action waiver even though individual claims were not economically feasible), employers often draft agreements to provide that they will bear the fees.

PROBLEM 10.1

You are in-house employment counsel for My-Tube.Com, an Internet start-up company. Although it has relatively few employees at this point, it expects to expand rapidly and to have employees in a number of different states. You are looking down the road regarding potential liability and know that many employers require all employees to sign arbitration agreements. Is this a good strategy for My-Tube to pursue, and, if so, what kind of arbitration would you recommend? How would you get employees (both existing and prospective) to agree to arbitration?

TABLE OF CASES

TABLE OF SELECTED SECONDARY AUTHORITIES

Bauer, Jon, Buying Witness Silence: Evidence-Suppressing Settlements and Lawyers' Ethics, 87 Or. L. Rev. 481 (2008), 609

Befort, Stephen F., An Empirical Analysis of Case Outcomes under the ADA Amendments Act, 70 Wash. & Lee L. Rev. 2027 (2013), 449

Befort, Stephen F., Let's Try This Again: The ADA Amendments Act of 2008 Attempts to Reinvigorate the "Regarded As" Prong of the Statutory Definition of Disability, 2010 Utah L. Rev. 993, 456

Befort, Stephen F., The Most Difficult Reasonable Accommodation Issues: Reassignment and Leave of Absence, 37 Wake Forest L. Rev. 439 (2002), 488

Befort, Stephen F., Reasonable Accommodation and Reassignment Under the Americans with Disabilities Act: Answers, Questions and Suggested Solutions After *U.S. Airways, Inc. v. Barnett*, 45 Ariz. L. Rev. 931 (2003), 484

Befort, Stephen F. & Michael J. Vargas, Same-Sex Marriage and Title VII, 56 Santa Clara L. Rev. 207 (2016), 299

Beiner, Theresa M., Sex, Science and Social Knowledge: The Implications of Social Science Research on Imputing Liability to Employers for Sexual Harassment, 7 Wm. & Mary J. Women & L. 273 (2001), 363

Beiner, Theresa M., Sexy Dressing Revisited: Does Target Dress Play a Part in Sexual Harassment Cases?, 14 Duke J. Gender L. & Pol'y 125 (2007), 330

Beiner, Theresa M., Using Evidence of Women's Stories in Sexual Harassment Cases, 24 U. Ark. Little Rock L. Rev. 117 (2001), 363

Beiner, Theresa M. & Robert B. Chapman, Take What You Can, Give Nothing Back: Judicial Estoppel, Employment Discrimination, Bankruptcy, and Piracy in the Courts, 60 U. Miami L. Rev. 1 (2005), 602

Beiner, Theresa M. & John M.A. DiPappa, Hostile Environments and the Religious Employee, 19 U. Ark. Little Rock L.J. 577 (1997), 381

Belton, Robert, The Crusade For Equality In The Workplace: The *Griggs v. Duke Power* Story (Stephen L. Wasby ed., 2014), 172

Bent, Jason, Hidden Priors: Toward a Unifying Theory of Systemic Disparate Treatment Law, 91 Denv. U. L. Rev. 807 (2014), 121

Bent, Jason, The Telltale Sign of Discrimination: Probabilities, Information Asymmetries, and the Systemic Disparate Treatment Theory, 44 U. of Mich. J.L. Reform 797 (2011), 113, 233

Bent, Jason, What the Lilly Ledbetter Fair Pay Act Doesn't Do: "Discrete Acts" and the Future of Pattern or Practice Litigation, 33 Rutgers L. Rev. 31 (2009), 535

Berrey, Ellen, Steve G. Hoffman, & Laura Beth Nielsen, Situated Justice: A Contextual Analysis of Fairness and Inequality in Employment Discrimination Litigation, 46 Law & Soc'y Rev. 1 (2012), 92

Bertrand, Marianne & Sendhil Mullainathan, Are Emily and Greg More Employable than Lakisha and Jamal? A Field Experiment on Labor Market Discrimination, 94 Am. Econ. Rev. 991 (2004), 7

Best, Rachel Kahn, Linda Hamilton Krieger, Lauren B. Edelman, and Scott R. Eliason, Multiple Disadvantages: An Empirical Test of Intersectionality Theory in EEO Litigation, 5 Law & Soc'y Rev. 991 (2011), 42

Bierman, Leonard & Rafael Gely, So, You Want to Be a Partner at Sidley & Austin?, 40 Hous. L. Rev. 969 (2003), 270

Bisom-Rapp, Susan, Fixing Watches with Sledgehammers: The Questionable Embrace of Employee Sexual Harassment Training by the Legal Profession, 24 U. Ark. Little Rock L. Rev. 147 (2001), 361

Bisom-Rapp, Susan, An Ounce of Prevention Is a Poor Substitute for a Pound of Cure: Confronting the Developing Jurisprudence of Education and Prevention in Employment Discrimination Law, 22 Berkeley J. Emp. & Lab. L. 1 (2001), 361

Blalock, H., Social Statistics (1972), 109

Blumrosen, Alfred W., Strangers in Paradise: *Griggs v. Duke Power Co.* and the Concept of Employment Discrimination, 71 Mich. L. Rev. 59 (1972), 17

Bodie, Matthew T., Questions About the Efficiency of Employment Arbitration Agreements, 39 Ga. L. Rev. 1 (2004), 622

Bornstein, Stephanie, Rights in Recession: Towards Administrative Antidiscrimination Law, 33 Yale L. & Pol'y Rev. 119 (2014), 556

Boso, Luke A., Real Men, 37 Haw. L. Rev. 107 (2015), 280

Brake, Deborah L., Retaliation in an EEO World, 89 Ind. L.J. 115 (2014), 416, 417

Brake, Deborah L., Retaliation in the EEO Office, 50 Tulsa L. Rev. 1 (2014), 412

Brake, Deborah L., Reviving Paycheck Fairness: Why and How the Factor-Other-Than-Sex Defense Matters, 52 Idaho L. Rev. 889 (2016), 99

Brake, Deborah L., The Shifting Sands of Employment Discrimination: From Unjustified Impact to Disparate Treatment in Pregnancy and Pay, 105 Geo. L. J. 559 (2017), 321

Brake, Deborah L., Tortifying Retaliation: Protected Activity at the Intersection of Fault, Duty, and Causation, 75 Ohio St. L. Rev. 6 (2014), 412

Brake, Deborah L. & Joanna Grossman, The Failure of Title VII as a Rights Claiming System, 86 N.C. L. Rev. 859 (2008), 417

Brennan, Megan I., Need I Prove More: Why an Adverse Employment Action Prong Has No Place in a Failure to Accommodate Disability Claim, 36 Hamline L. Rev. 497 (2013), 493

Brodin, Mark S., *Ricci v. DeStefano*: The New Haven Firefighters Case and the Triumph of White Privilege, 20 S. Cal. Rev. L. & Soc. Justice 161 (2011), 260

Harper, Michael C., Age-Based Exit Incentives, Coercion, and the Prospective Waiver of ADEA Rights: The Failure of the Older Workers Benefit Protection Act, 79 Va. L. Rev. 1271 (1993), 404, 608

Harper, Michael C., The Causation Standard in Federal Employment Law: *Gross v. FBL Financial Services, Inc.*, and the Unfulfilled Promise of the Civil Rights Act of 1991, 58 Buffalo L. Rev. 69 (2010), 87

Harper, Michael C., Class-Based Adjudication of Title VII Claims in the Age of the Roberts Court, 95 B.U. L. Rev. 1099 (2015), 550

Harper, Michael C., Employer Liability for Harassment Under Title VII: A Functional Rationale for *Faragher* and *Ellerth*, 36 San Diego L. Rev. 41 (1999), 345

Harris, Cheryl I. & Kimberly West-Faulcon, Reading *Ricci*: White(ning) Discrimination, Raceing Test Fairness, 58 UCLA L. Rev. 73 (2010), 260

Harris, Seth D., Innocence and *The Sopranos*, 46 N.Y.L. Sch. L. Rev. 577 (2004), 566

Harris, Seth D., Re-thinking the Economics of Discrimination: *US Airways v. Barnett*, the ADA, and the Application of Internal Labor Markets Theory, 89 Iowa L. Rev. 123 (2003), 487

Hart, Melissa, Civil Rights and Systemic Wrongs, 32 Berkeley J. Emp. & Lab. L. 455 (2011), 117, 553, 571

Hart, Melissa, From *Wards Cove* to *Ricci*: Struggling Against the "Built-in-Headwinds" of a Skeptical Court, 46 Wake Forest L. Rev. 261 (2011), 260

Hart, Melissa, Procedural Extremism: The Supreme Court's 2008–2009 Employment and Labor Cases, 13 Emp. Rts. & Emp. Pol'y J. 253 (2010), 439

Hart, Melissa, Retaliatory Litigation Tactics: The Chilling Effect of "After-Acquired Evidence," 40 Ariz. St. L.J. 401 (2008), 579

Hart, Melissa, Skepticism and Expertise: The Supreme Court and the EEOC, 74 Fordham L. Rev. 1937 (2006), 508

Hart, Melissa, Subjective Decisionmaking and Unconscious Discrimination, 56 Ala. L. Rev. 741 (2005), 80

Hart, Melissa & Paul M. Secunda, A Matter of Context: Social Framework Evidence in Employment Discrimination Class Actions, 78 Fordham L. Rev. 37 (2009), 551

Hawkins, Stacy L., The Long Arc of Diversity Bends Towards Equality: Deconstructing the Progressive Critique of Workplace Diversity Efforts, 16 U. Md. L. J. Race, Religion, Gender & Class 2 (2016), 162

Hébert, L. Camille, Disparate Impact and Pregnancy: Title VII's Other Accommodation Requirement, 24 Am. U. J. Gender Soc. Pol'y & L. 107 (2015), 323

Hébert, L. Camille, Transforming Transsexual and Transgender Rights, 15 Wm. & Mary J. Women & L. 535 (2009), 280

Hébert, L. Camille, Why Don't "Reasonable Women" Complain about Sexual Harassment?, 82 Indiana L.J. 711 (2007), 363

Helfand, Michael A., Religion's Footnote Four: Church Autonomy as Arbitration, 97 Minn. L. Rev. 1891 (2013), 393

Herch, Jodi & Jennifer Bennett Shinall, Something to Talk About: Information Exchange Under Employment Law, 165 U. Pa. L. Rev. 49 (2016), 325

Hernández, Tanya Katerí, Latino Inter-Ethnic Employment Discrimination and the "Diversity" Defense, Harv. C.R.-C.L. L. Rev. 259 (2007), 42

Herrnstein, Richard & Charles Murray, The Bell Curve: Intelligence and Class Structure in American Life (1994), 140

Hickox, Stacy A., Reduction of Punitive Damages for Employment Discrimination: Are Courts Ignoring Our Juries?, 54 Mercer L. Rev. 1081 (2003), 591

Hickox, Stacy A., Transfer as an Accommodation: Standards from Discrimination Cases and Theory, 62 Ark. L. Rev. 195 (2009), 484

Hickox, Stacy A. & Joseph M. Guzman, Leave as an Accommodation: When Is Enough, Enough?, 62 Clev. St. L. Rev. 437 (2014), 488

Hollander-Blumoff, Rebecca & Matthew T. Bodie, The Effects of Jury Ignorance About Damage Caps: The Case of the 1991 Civil Rights Act, 90 Iowa L. Rev. 1361 (2005), 593

Holzer, Harry J. & Steven Raphael, Perceived Criminality, Criminal Background Checks, and the Racial Hiring Practices of Employers, 49 J. Law & Econ. 451 (2006), 211

Hubbard, Ann, The ADA, The Workplace, and the Myth of the "Dangerous Mentally Ill," 34 U.C. Davis L. Rev. 849 (2001), 506

Hubbard, Ann, Understanding and Implementing the ADA's Direct Threat Defense, 95 Nw. U. L. Rev. 1279 (2001), 506

Hyde, Alan, Labor Arbitration of Discrimination Claims After *14 Penn Plaza v. Pyett*: Letting Discrimination Defendants Decide Whether Plaintiffs May Sue Them, 25 Ohio St. J. Disp. Resol. 975 (2010), 619

Issacharoff, Samuel & Justin Nelson, Discrimination with a Difference: Can Employment Discrimination Law Accommodate the Americans with Disabilities Act?, 79 N.C. L. Rev. 307 (2001), 487

Jacobi, John V., Genetic Discrimination in a Time of False Hopes, 30 Fla. St. U. L. Rev. 363 (2003), 447

Jaffe, Ina, Older Workers Find Age Discrimination Built Right into Some Job Websites, http://www.npr.org/2017/03/28/521771515/older-workers-find-age-discriminationbuilt-right-into-some-job-sites (Mar. 28, 2017), 14

Jensen, Arthur, How Much Can We Boost IQ and Scholastic Achievement?, 39 Harv. Educ. Rev. 1 (1969), 140

INDEX